WORLD HISTORY

Patterns of Civilization

Huge crowds flocked to London in 1851 to visit the Great Exhibition. It was the first international display of the marvels of the Industrial Revolution, including the sewing machine and McCormick's reaper. The painting, at right and on the cover, shows the opening ceremonies in the Crystal Palace, a magnificent structure built of glass and cast iron. Queen Victoria of England welcomed dignitaries from around the world.

Area Specialists

Early Civilizations	Elizabeth Carney, Clemson University, Clemson, South Carolina
Classical Civilizations	Louis Cohn-Haft, Smith College, Northampton, Massachusetts
Middle Ages	Thomas Glick, Boston University, Boston, Massachusetts
Early Modern Europe	Helen Nader, Indiana University, Bloomington, Indiana
Nineteenth-Century Europe	Charles F. Delzell, Vanderbilt University, Nashville, Tennessee
Twentieth-Century Europe	Marian P. Nelson, University of Nebraska, Omaha, Nebraska
Africa	Marylee Crofts, University of Wisconsin, Madison, Wisconsin
Asia	Burton F. Beers, North Carolina State University, Raleigh, North Carolina
Latin America	Jonathan Brown, University of Texas, Austin, Texas
Middle East	Donald Quataert, State University of New York, Binghamton, New York

Curriculum Advisers

Susan K. Hustleby, Byron-Bergen Central School, Bergen, New York
Sharon L. Pope, Formerly of Westchester Senior High School, Houston, Texas

Teacher Reviewers

Dean Barlow, Kennedy High School, Winston-Salem, North Carolina
Dennis R. Dreher, DeVilbiss High School, Toledo, Ohio
Sara Hamm, Palo Duro High School, Amarillo, Texas
Jocelyn E. Kimm, North High School, Evansville, Indiana
Ronald W. Kruse, Ygnacio Valley High School, Concord, California
Elizabeth S. Mefford, Northwest School District, Cincinnati, Ohio
Louis Pappas, Highline School District, Seattle, Washington
Doris Stratton, Dallas Independent School District, Pittsburg, Texas
Charles A. Thompson, Wichita Public Schools, Wichita, Kansas

WORLD HISTORY
Patterns of Civilization

Burton F. Beers
Professor of History
North Carolina State University

PRENTICE HALL
Englewood Cliffs, New Jersey
Needham, Massachusetts

Burton F. Beers

Burton F. Beers is Professor of History at North Carolina State University. In the course of his career, Dr. Beers has taught European history, Asian history, and American history. He has published numerous articles in historical journals and has written several books on East Asia, including *The Far East: A History of Western Impacts and Eastern Responses* with Paul H. Clyde, and *China in Old Photographs*. As a consultant to the North Carolina Department of Public Instruction for many years, Dr. Beers has developed social studies curriculum in western and nonwestern studies. He has also planned and directed numerous workshops for social studies teachers.

HERITAGE EDITION

SUPPLEMENTARY MATERIALS
Annotated Teacher's Edition
Teacher's Resource Book
Student Study Guide
Computer Test Bank

1991 EDITION

ISBN 0-13-968645-2   10 9 8 7 6 5 4

Photo Consultant: Michal Heron
Photo Research: Julie DeWitt, Carole Frohlich (in London), Kate Lewin (in Paris)
Commissioned Paintings: Art Source
Text Graphs and Charts: Lee Ames & Zak, Ltd.
Text Maps: Mapping Specialists
Reference Maps: R.R. Donnelley & Sons Company

STAFF CREDITS

Editorial: B'Ann Bowman, Anne Falzone, Helene Baum, Maryellen Cancellieri, Frank Tangredi
Design: Sue Walrath, AnnMarie Roselli, Barbara Barrios, Leslie Osher
Production: Charles Ramsay, Cleasta Wilburn, Lisa Meyerhoff
Editorial Systems: Andrew Bommarito, Ralph O'Brien
Marketing: Steve Lewin
Manufacturing: Laura Sanderson, Rhett Conklin, Denise Herckenrath

PRENTICE HALL
A Division of Simon & Schuster
Englewood Cliffs, New Jersey

Illustration Credits

Frequently cited sources are abbreviated as follows: TBM, The British Museum; EPA, Editorial Photocolor Archives (Art Resource); LC, Library of Congress; UPI, United Press International.
Key to position of illustrations: *b,* bottom, *l,* left, *r,* right, *m,* middle, *t,* top.

Cover Victoria and Albert Museum, London **Pages ii–iii** Victoria and Albert Museum, London; **v** *t* David Mazonovicz/Art Resource; *m* Scala/Art Resource; *b* Newsweek Books Picture Collection; **vi** *t* Newsweek Books Picture Collection; *m* Borromeo/Art Resource; *b* Giraudon/Art Resource; **vii** *bl* Giraudon/Art Resource; *tr* The Granger Collection; *m, br* Collection of Laurie Platt Winfrey; **viii** *t* The Granger Collection; *m, bl* Giraudon/Art Resource; *br* Lee Boltin; **ix** EPA/Scala; **x** *t* The Granger Collection; *m* Giraudon/Art Resource; *bl* The Granger Collection; *br* Scala/Art Resource; **xi** *t,m* The Granger Collection; *b* Giraudon/Art Resource; **xii** *t,m* The Granger Collection; *b* Collection of Laurie Platt Winfrey; **xiii** *t* The Bettmann Archive; *bl* Collection of Laurie Platt Winfrey; *br* ORION/Art Resource; **xiv** *t, m* The Granger Collection; *b* Giraudon/Art Resource; **xv** *t* LC; *b* Tannenbaum/Sygma; **xvi** M. Heron; **xxi** Robert A. Flynn.

UNIT ONE **Page xxiv** *tl* © David Mazonovicz/Art Resource; *tr* Lee Boltin; *bl* Giraudon/Art Resource; *br* Collection of Laurie Platt Winfrey; **1** *tl* SEF/Art Resource; *tr* Newsweek Books Picture Collection; *bl, br* Scala/Art Resource; **2** Nelson-Atkins Museum of Art; **4** Art Resource; **8** Gianni Tortoli/Photo Researchers, Inc.; **11** Explorer; **13** EPA/Scala; **14** Art Resource; **15** Giraudon/Art Resource; **18** Lee Boltin; **20** *l* TBM; *r* Diane Shapiro; **22** TBM; **24** Art Resource; **25** The Metropolitan Museum of Art; **28** Oriental Institute; **29** Egyptian Expedition of the Metropolitan Museum of Art, Rogers Fund, 1930; **31** The Louvre; **34** TBM; **37** Scala/Art Resource; **39** TBM; **41** Scala/Art Resource; **43** The Granger Collection; **44** Giraudon/Art Resource; **48** Ronald Sheridan; **52** The Cultural Relics Bureau, Beijing, and the Metropolitan Museum of Art; **56** John Woolen; **58** The Cleveland Museum of Art, Gift of George P. Bickford; **63** Columbia University Library; **64** Michael Holford; **65** Museum of Fine Arts, Boston; **67** Nelson Atkins Museum of Art, Kansas City, Missouri.

UNIT TWO **Page 72** *tl* Giraudon/Art Resource; *tr* Borromeo/Art Resource; *bl* Newsweek Books Picture Collection; *br* Giraudon/Art Resource; **73** *tl tr, bl* Collection of Laurie Platt Winfrey; *br* The Granger Collection; **74** Clyde/Michael Holford; **77** Shostal; **79** EPA/Scala; **80** Nelson-Atkins Museum of Art; **82** Museum of Fine Arts, Boston; **84** TBM; **85** Newsweek Books/Carousel; **88** Michael Holford; **89** Scala/Art Resource; **90** Georgio Picatto/Shostal; **91** Scala; **93** Art Resource; **94** EPA/Scala; **100** Art Resource; **103** EPA/Scala; **104** *t* The Louvre; *b* Art Resource; **105** Art Resource; **106** The Louvre; **109** Art Resource; **111** EPA/Scala; **112** Shostal; **113** Laurie Platt Winfrey, Inc.; **118** Art Resource; **121** EPA/Scala; **122** Art Resource; **124** Art Resource/Scala; **125** Explorer; **128** Jan Lukas/Art Resource; **129** Explorer; **130** The Louvre; **133** EPA; **136** Borromeo/Art Resource; **138** Nelson Atkins Museum of Art; **139** Laurie Platt Winfrey, Inc.; **142** Art Resource/Scala; **145** EPA; **147** Explorer; **148**

(continued on page 903)

CONTENTS

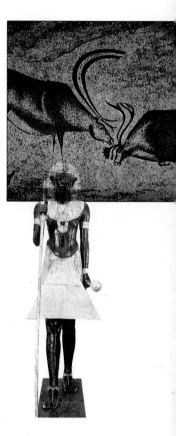

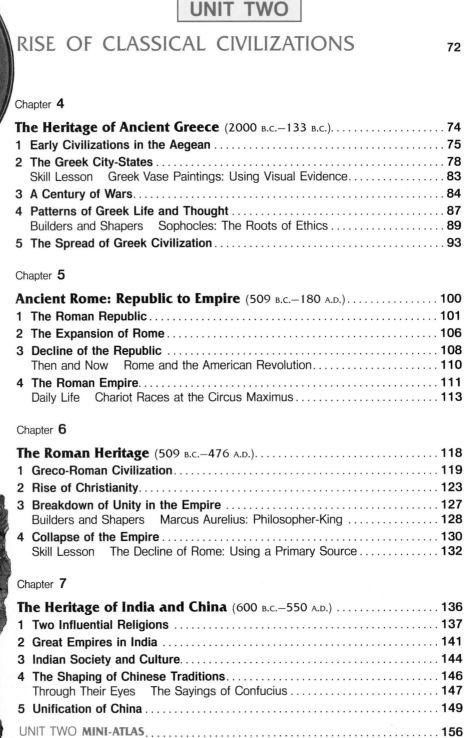

UNIT THREE

MIDDLE AGES IN WESTERN EUROPE 158

GOLDEN AGES OUTSIDE WESTERN EUROPE

220

A Brief Survey of World History
From Prehistoric Times to 1500

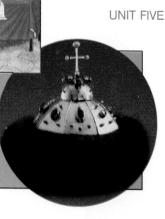

UNIT EIGHT

THE AGE OF IMPERIALISM 556

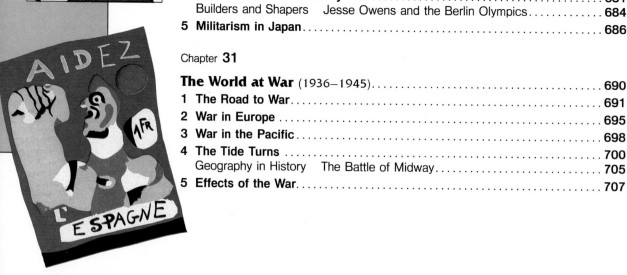

UNIT TEN

THE WORLD TODAY

734

SPECIAL FEATURES

BUILDERS AND SHAPERS

THROUGH THEIR EYES

DAILY LIFE

ECONOMICS AND HISTORY

THEN AND NOW

GEOGRAPHY IN HISTORY

SKILL LESSONS

HISTORICAL RECREATIONS
(Commissioned for This Book)

MAPS

MINI-ATLAS MAPS

REFERENCE SECTION ATLAS

CHARTS AND GRAPHS

A Note From Burton Beers

World history is the story of great human adventures. Some of the characters in this story, like Napoleon Bonaparte, the French general and emperor, were colorful as well as famous. "I am no ordinary man," Napoleon once boasted. Napoleon knew that he could command the attention of friends and enemies throughout Europe and even in the Americas. He was proud of his razor-sharp mind. He thought and spoke so fast that he could dictate letters to four secretaries on four separate topics, all at the same time.

Napoleon made history. So did a Sumerian school boy 5,000 years earlier. The school boy copied on a clay tablet his father's angry lecture. "Why do you idle about? Go to school, stand before your schoolfather [teacher], recite your assignment, open your schoolbag, write your tablet . . . ."

These words certainly reveal that for hundreds of centuries parents and students have held different opinions about assignments. But these words from the distant past tell us even more. The student's tablet shows how much work was needed to master a new invention, a system for writing a spoken language. Sumerians were among the first people to learn how to write. Their discovery marked a major advance in civilization.

World history tells of events that changed the direction of human affairs. For example, you will read how Japan, isolated off the coast of East Asia and guided by ancient traditions, joined the modern world in a surprising way.

The United States took the first steps. Americans wanted a treaty to protect sailors shipwrecked in Japanese waters, to open Japanese ports to ships for supplies of food and water, and to grant the United States the right to trade. In 1853, a small fleet of steam-propelled American warships sailed into Tokyo Bay to back up the request with a show of force.

Japanese peasants watching the ships were frightened. They had never seen ships move without sails or oars. Japan's leaders had much cooler heads, but they realized their nation could not match foreign guns. They decided to grant what the Americans asked, because Japanese "are not the equals of foreigners in the mechanical arts . . . ." Japan's best hope was to open "relations with foreign countries, learn their drills and tactics . . . ," and to grow strong.

These decisions touched off remarkable changes. Within a few years Japan was working hard to build modern schools, banks, factories, and railroads on the foundations of its old society. By the early 1900s, Japan was the leading power in Asia. As the 1900s closed, Japan, a nation about the size of California, was one of the world's most important manufacturing and financial powers.

The Uses of History

Don't be surprised when the people, events, and cultures described in this book appear in other courses on your schedule. World history covers many kinds of human achievements. Marching across the stage of history will come such fascinating personalities as Marie Curie, a discoverer of radium; Nicolaus Copernicus, a pioneering astronomer; William Shakespeare, one of the world's great writers; or Michelangelo, an equally great artist. A sound knowledge of history can enrich your understanding of many subjects.

Themes

World history is more than a collection of stories or biographies. The chapters in this book are designed to show you how our world has grown and changed. American democracy, for example, is built on ancient foundations. Greek ideas on freedom and Roman law, two essential building blocks, are more than 2,000 years old. Other contributions to American democracy come from the struggles of the English over many centuries to limit the authority of their kings. Our nation's founders knew this history and used it to create our government.

Many people and events contributed to the growth of democracy. When you put them together, these individual contributions become a theme, a big idea that you can remember. As you read, other themes will stand out. You will discover how nations developed, how people have interacted with their natural environment, how modern science and technology took shape, how religious values have affected civilization, how different societies were formed and changed, and how the arts—painting, writing, sculpture, and music—have been ever-changing expressions of beauty.

The Patterns of Civilization

Many of the themes of world history describe the emergence of modern western civilization. The United States is part of this civilization. Other themes describe quite different civilizations that developed in Africa, the Middle East, and Asia. The heritage of many of these civilizations is as old, or even older, than western civilization. In today's world, people with widely different heritages often come into contact with one another. Television is just one of the many new technologies that put people around the world in touch with one another. The United States, in fact, has always been the home of people from many different backgrounds. Thus, to truly understand our own history, we need to understand world history and the patterns of civilization.

Good reading to you.

Burt Beers

Burt Beers

About This Book

This book is organized into 10 units including 37 chapters, as well as an introduction and epilogue. The Table of Contents (pages v–xx) lists the titles of the units and chapters. It also lists skill lessons, special features, and the maps, charts, and graphs in the book. Many features have been included in this book to assist you in your course of study:

1. **Unit Time Line** Each unit opens with a colorful, illustrated time line. It provides an overview of the political, economic, social, and cultural developments you will study in the unit.

2. **Chapter Opener** Every chapter opens with an outline of the chapter as well as an illustration and an introductory story about a major theme, person, or event in the chapter.

3. **Aids for Understanding** Several features help you read and understand the chapters. Each section begins with Read to Understand statements that provide a focus for reading. Historical terms and vocabulary words appear in boldface and are defined the first time they are used. These terms are also included in the Glossary in the Reference Section. Section Reviews include questions to test your understanding.

4. **Illustrations** Maps, graphs, charts, paintings, and photographs are much more than decoration. They help you understand major events and also bring history to life. Captions provide additional tidbits of information. They also tie the illustration into what you are reading.

5. **Special Features** These features give you a close look at the people and events of world history. Some are profiles of individuals or extracts from historical sources. Others are about daily life, the relationship of history and geography, the impact of economics on history, and the relationship of the past and the present.

6. **Skill Lessons** These step-by-step skill lessons help you understand and practice important skills such as reading maps and graphs, using visual evidence and statistics, and analyzing conflicting sources.

7. **Chapter Review** The material at the end of each chapter allows you to review and apply what you have learned. They include:

   - Summary to outline the main ideas of each section
   - Recalling Facts to review basic information
   - Chapter Checkup to review important ideas
   - Critical Thinking to apply critical thinking skills in order to deepen your understanding of world history
   - Developing Basic Skills to apply such skills as comparing, classifying, map and graph reading, and using primary sources and illustrations
   - Writing About History to help you develop writing and research skills needed for studying history

8. **Reference Section** At the back of the book, you will find a section of reference material to be used throughout the course. It includes an atlas with both physical and political maps, a chronology, a glossary with pronunciation key, and an index.

BEGINNINGS OF ANCIENT CIVILIZATIONS

Cave paintings, such as this one found in France, provide information about prehistoric peoples.

Items made from gold and precious stones, such as this pair of sandals, were created for the pharaohs of Egypt.

	3000 B.C.	2500 B.C.	2000 B.C.
POLITICS AND GOVERNMENT		**2700 B.C.** Egyptian rulers take title of pharaoh	**2500–1500 B.C.** Indus Valley civilization in India
ECONOMICS AND TECHNOLOGY	**3000 B.C.** City-states develop in Sumer		**2200 B.C.** Bronzemaking develops in China
SOCIETY AND CULTURE		**2650 B.C.** Step Pyramid built in Egypt	**2000 B.C.** Egyptian literature flourishes

In this tomb painting, Egyptians carry offerings of food for their gods.

Bronze bird from ancient China, representing wealth and prestige.

UNIT OUTLINE

In ancient Persia, scenes of heroic events were carved on the sides of mountains.

Phoenician statue of a woman from Baza.

1500 B.C.	1000 B.C.	500 B.C.
1600 B.C. Shang dynasty is first in China	**1000 B.C.** Kingdom of Israel flourishes under King David	**550 B.C.** Cyrus begins creation of Persian Empire
1500 B.C. Hittites among first to use iron spears and battle axes	**800 B.C.** Metal coins become medium of exchange in China and Lydia	
1700 B.C. Hammurabi's Code is first effort to record all laws	**1000 B.C.** Phoenicians develop alphabet	**700 B.C.** Sanskrit emerges as written language in India

1339 B.C. *Figure of an Egyptian official, decorated with gold, found in the tomb of Tutankhamon.*

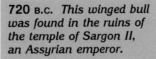

720 B.C. *This winged bull was found in the ruins of the temple of Sargon II, an Assyrian emperor.*

INTRODUCTION

Foundations of Civilization (Prehistory—3000 B.C.)

CHAPTER OUTLINE

Much about Stonehenge in southern England remains a mystery. Some of the huge stones used in the monument are up to 30 feet long and weigh as much as 50 tons.

Before dawn, crowds gather at Stonehenge, an ancient monument in southern England. The sky brightens early on June 21, the longest day of the year. All eyes are fixed on the huge, heel-shaped stone beyond the great circle of stones. At dawn, the sun sweeps above the horizon. Its warm light shines directly above the heel stone and slices through an archway of stones.

The crowd of visitors is filled with awe. Like others before them, they are fascinated by the stone monument. For centuries, people have wondered who designed this massive circle of stones. When was Stonehenge built? How were the enormous blocks raised into position? Most important, what purpose did Stonehenge serve?

Scholars have offered some answers to questions about Stonehenge. They have learned, for example, that early inhabitants of England started to build Stonehenge about 3,800 years ago. Experts have discovered that the 82 enormous stones of Stonehenge were quarried from a mountain in Wales about 240 miles (386 kilometers) away. The stones were probably loaded on barges, shipped by water, and then hauled on sleds over log rollers to Stonehenge.

Yet many questions about the purpose of Stonehenge remain unanswered. Was it a temple, a palace, or a fort defended by warrior kings? Or was it, as one astronomer has suggested, an ancient calendar used to predict eclipses and other heavenly events?

Stonehenge is one of the many puzzles left by early peoples. Tantalizing clues about the past are uncovered all the time in different parts of the world. Some evidence, like that at Stonehenge, is on a grand scale. Other evidence includes only fragments of stone, pottery, or bone.

By studying the evidence, scholars have begun to answer questions about early peoples as well as later civilizations. They are weaving a picture of people interacting with the world around them and with one another, a picture that begins from the earliest prehistoric times and continues to the present. ■

1 Geography and World History

READ TO UNDERSTAND

☐ **What the five major themes of geography are.**

☐ **How those themes help you understand world history.**

☐ **How map projections affect what you see on a map.**

☐ *Vocabulary:* **geography, latitude, longitude, projection.**

Every human activity takes place somewhere. A rock band might perform in a gigantic open-air stadium before thousands of people or in a small recording studio with only a small technical crew. Where the band performs affects how the band plays. You can easily tell the difference between a live recording and one done in a recording studio.

The story of world history takes place on a complex stage of great variety, the earth. Knowing *where* something happened helps you understand *why* it happened. Understanding the connections between places and between groups of people can help you understand the events and developments of world history. For this reason, it is important to study the connections between history and geography. **Geography** is the study of people, their environments, and their resources.

Geographers have developed five major themes to help you understand these connections: location, place, interactions between people and their environment, movement, and regions.

Location

Location means basically where something is. In world history, you sometimes want to know exactly where a place is located. For example, imagine that you were reading about the famous hanging gardens of ancient Babylon (see page 43), but you did not know where Babylon was located. If you found the latitude and longitude of Babylon in an encyclopedia, you could find its exact location on a map.

Latitude lines on a map or globe measure distance north and south of the Equator. **Longitude** lines measure distance east and west of the Prime Meridian, which runs through Greenwich, England. Any place on earth can be located exactly using the grid of latitude and longitude. For example, by using a world map, you can locate Babylon at 32° N latitude and 44° E longitude.

At other times, the relative location is more important to understanding a historical event. Relative location refers to the relationship of one place to another. For example, Rome was the center of a large empire, as you will read. Romans built an extensive road system to help them control distant parts of their empire. Thus, this road system changed the relationship between Rome and its colonies.

Place

The term place refers to the physical and human characteristics of a specific location.

For example, the land along the Nile River in ancient Egypt was fertile because of the river's yearly floods. This physical characteristic meant that Egyptian farmers produced good harvests. If we were to look at a human characteristic of the Nile River valley, we would observe that most people in ancient Egypt lived near the river and that farming was important to them. (See page 19.)

Interactions Between People and Their Environment

In world history, you will study how people have been affected by their environment and how they have modified it. As long as 3,000 years ago, the Maya of Central America built canals to drain swampland. Much later, European settlers in North America cut down acres of trees in order to plant crops. All such interactions influenced the ways people lived.

Movement

Throughout human history, people have been on the move. The earliest people moved from one place to another in search of food or a place to live. In the 1800s, thousands of Irish moved to the United States because of famine in Ireland. Today, people might move in search

In addition to building canals to drain swampland, the Maya cleared dense rain forests to build their cities. These remains are of the Temples of the Warriors and the Thousand Columns in Chichen Itzá.

Your textbook is an important tool as you begin your study of world history. You can get the most from the textbook by learning to use it effectively. Review pages xxi–xxiii to familiarize yourself with the main features of *World History: Patterns of Civilization*. Then follow these steps to use these features.

1 **Scan the Table of Contents.** You can use the Table of Contents to preview what topics will be covered in the book. Turn to page v and answer these questions: (a) How many chapters, including the Introduction, are in Unit One? (b) What information is listed for the Introduction? (c) Turn to pages xvii–xx. On what page can you find the feature, Who Was the Bog Man? (d) On what page is the map called Early Civilizations?

2 **Preview the Unit.** Study pages xxiv–1. (a) What is the main topic of the unit? (b) What categories of information are shown on the time line? (c) How can you tell which categories the illustrations are related to?

3 **Preview the Chapter.** Study pages 2–3 and 16–17. (a) What topics are covered in the Introduction? (b) What time span is included? (c) List the headings in the Review. (d) Which set of questions reviews the main ideas of the chapter?

4 **Preview the Section.** Scan Section 1. (a) What information is included under the title, Read to Understand? (b) What topics are covered by illustrations in the section? (c) What types of questions are included in the Section Review?

of a place to work or in search of political or religious freedom. Some move to another part of their town, from the country to a city, while others move to a different country.

Many types of movement are important to world history. These include the movement of ideas from one people to another, the spread of diseases or air pollution, and the movement of products from one place to another.

Regions

Geographers and historians use the theme of regions to refer to an area with specific characteristics. A region might be defined by its physical characteristics. For example, the Great Plains region of the United States can be defined as the area between the Rocky Mountains and the 98th Meridian, where there is little rain and few trees. Or a region might be defined by human characteristics such as politics, religion, language, or economics. The area of Central and South America is called Latin America because the Europeans who settled in that region spoke Spanish, Portu-

guese, and French, all of which are related to Latin.

Globes and Maps

Geographers and historians use globes and maps to represent the earth. A globe is like a small model of the earth. It shows major geographic features, and it shows the land masses and bodies of water accurately. However, a globe is not always convenient to use. You might study a globe in class, but you wouldn't want to carry a globe home to do your homework.

Maps are a more convenient way to show the earth. A road map of your state can be folded and put in the glove compartment of a car. A map of your town or city can be printed in the phone book. And, of course, many maps can fit in this world history textbook. However, no map can be an exact picture of the earth because all maps are flat and the earth's surface is curved. You can understand the problem of map makers if you try to make an orange skin lie flat.

Map Projections

Interrupted Projection

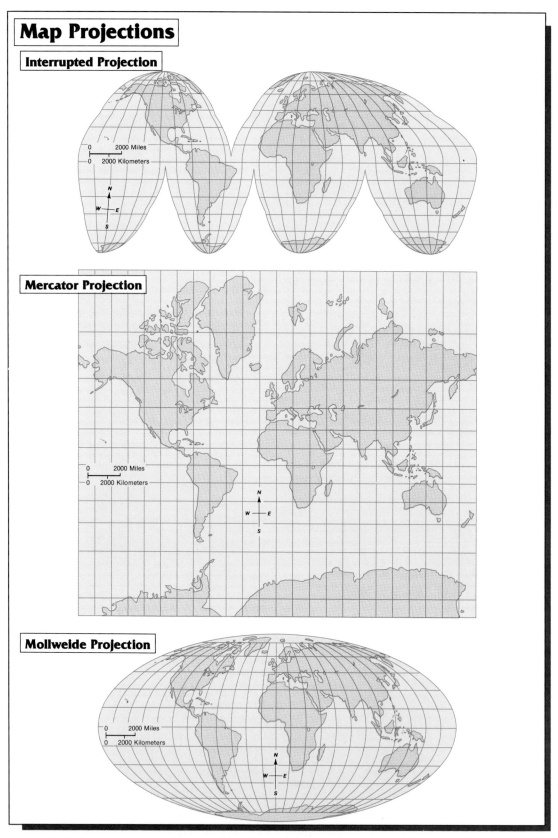

Mercator Projection

Mollweide Projection

MAP STUDY

The interrupted projection, the Mercator projection, and the Mollweide projection are three of many projections that geographers use to show the earth on a flat surface. Which projection would you use to map the sea routes of explorers?

Map projections. Map makers have developed many different ways of showing the curved earth on a flat surface. Each of these ways is called a **projection.** Three of these projections are shown on page 6. Each has its strengths and weaknesses. The interrupted projection shows the correct sizes and shapes of land masses. However, because of the cuts in the oceans, you could not use it to measure distances across water.

The Mercator projection shows accurate directions of north, south, east, and west. For this reason, it was often used by ship captains in the 1500s. The shape and size of land areas close to the Equator are accurate, but the Mercator projection distorts the shape and size of land areas far away from the Equator. Compare the size of Greenland in the different projections. Although Greenland is about one-ninth as large as South America, it looks larger on the Mercator projection.

In the Mollweide (mohl VĪD uh) projection, the shapes of land areas are distorted, but the proportions of the land and water areas are accurate. No single projection is perfect. When a historian wants to use a map to show a particular development, he or she chooses a projection most useful for that purpose.

SECTION 1 REVIEW

1. **Locate:** (a) Babylon, (b) Nile River.

2. **Define:** (a) geography, (b) latitude, (c) longitude, (d) projection.

3. List one physical characteristic and one human characteristic of the Nile River valley.

4. What types of movement are important in world history?

5. (a) What does the interrupted map projection show accurately? (b) What is distorted on a map with a Mercator projection?

6. **Critical Thinking** Explain how you use one of the major themes of geography in your daily life.

2 Discovering Prehistory

READ TO UNDERSTAND

☐ **How scientists study prehistory.**

☐ **How archaeologists search for evidence about early people.**

☐ **Why there are unanswered questions about prehistory.**

☐ *Vocabulary:* **prehistory, archaeologist, artifact, anthropologist, fossil.**

In addition to geography, historians use many other sources to learn about the past. Among the most important of these are written records such as inscriptions, letters, diaries, and newspapers. But written records have existed for only 5,000 or 6,000 years.

Scholars use the term **prehistory** to describe the long period before writing was invented. To learn about prehistory, they use unwritten records such as buildings, pottery, and bones. Historians and scientists work together to unravel the mysteries of the prehistoric period.

The Study of Prehistory

Evidence from prehistory is of special interest to **archaeologists,** scientists who find and analyze objects left by early people. These objects, called **artifacts,** include anything shaped by human beings, such as tools, pottery, and weapons. Archaeology is a branch of anthropology. **Anthropologists** use artifacts and bone fragments to study the ways people organize societies.

Other scientists are also interested in prehistory. For example, geologists often find **fossils,** evidence of plant or animal life preserved in rock. Fossils show the types of plants and animals that existed at a particular time.

Like detectives, archaeologists piece together what they and other scientists discover to form a picture of the past. As new evidence is uncovered, this picture changes.

Archaeologists must take great care to preserve the artifacts they uncover. The man shown here is painstakingly cleaning vases unearthed from a prehistoric city in Greece.

Uncovering Archaeological Evidence

Archaeologists have a three-part task in their search for evidence about early people. First, they find a site, or area, where they think early people lived. Second, they excavate, or dig, at the site to uncover artifacts. Third, they analyze any artifacts and draw conclusions about the people who made them.

Although some important sites have been found by accident, more often archaeologists choose places where they think people would have lived. For example, they might pick a location because it was near water. Once a site is located, archaeologists begin to dig carefully. Even the smallest fragment of a piece of pottery can be important. The exact location of every find is noted. Then the objects are cleaned and marked for identification.

A major step in the analysis of artifacts is estimating their ages, or dating them. Scientists have developed several methods for dating an object. Some are used to date plant or animal remains. Others calculate the age of volcanic rock and thereby the age of any objects preserved in that rock.

Unanswered Questions

Archaeologists have made impressive advances over the past 30 years. New methods of dating artifacts, aerial photography to find likely sites, and computer analysis of bone fragments are just a few of the techniques that are revealing new evidence about prehistory. But new discoveries can raise as many questions as they answer.

Many questions remain unanswered because so few artifacts survive. Over thousands of years, much evidence has been destroyed by natural forces and human settlement. Excavations often produce only tiny bone fragments or a few tools. With such limited evidence, views of prehistoric life can vary.

Yet much remains. Even today, construction workers discover artifacts. For example, ancient ruins were uncovered in Mexico City during the construction of subways. In a race with time, archaeologists have been able to preserve some valuable remains. As you will read later, the discoveries of archaeologists, combined with written records, have helped answer many questions about the first ancient civilizations.

SECTION 2 REVIEW

1. **Define:** (a) prehistory, (b) archaeologist, (c) artifact, (d) anthropologist, (e) fossil.

2. What evidence do anthropologists use to expand knowledge of the past?

3. Describe the three-part task of archaeologists.

4. Why are there so many unanswered questions about prehistory?

5. **Critical Thinking** How might knowing the geography of an area help an archaeologist decide where to dig?

On a hot August day in 1984, Andy Mould was gathering peat moss from a bog in northern England. As he was about to throw a load of peat into a shredder, something strange caught his eye. He dropped the peat and took a closer look—a human foot was sticking out of the wet moss.

Mould reported his discovery, and scientists rushed to the site. They found the head, torso, and arms of a man who had died 2,200 years earlier. Although the bones of the Bog Man had dissolved, the peat had turned his flesh to leather. He was so well preserved that scientists found traces of his last meal in his stomach. And they could even reconstruct the expression on his face!

Many different scientists worked to find out who the Bog Man was and what had happened to him. Archaeologists looked at the first puzzle. The Bog Man had died horribly. His throat had been cut and his skull smashed before he was thrust under the water. Yet, he apparently died with a peaceful expression on his face.

The archaeologists decided that the Bog Man had been sacrificed in a religious ritual. The ancient Druids, who lived in England thousands of years ago, sacrificed humans to their gods. They believed that each god wanted his victims killed in a certain way. Sacrifices to Esus had their throats cut; those offered to Teuttates were drowned. The Druid priests honored Tarainis by bludgeoning his victims to death.

Since the Bog Man had been executed all three ways, the scientists concluded that he had probably been sacrificed to all three gods. Therefore, he was an important man, perhaps even a priest. A priest might also have considered it an honor to be sacrificed, which would explain the peaceful expression on his face. Other investigators noted that the Bog Man had no calluses on his hands. This made it even more likely that he had belonged to the elite group of Druid priests.

Other evidence confirmed that the Bog Man was a priest. The scientists found the remains of a burned barley cake in the Bog Man's stomach. Archaeologists knew that Druid priests had a special use for burned barley cake. They would burn part of the cake, then break the whole cake up and put it in a bag. They passed the bag around and each priest took out a piece. Whoever drew the burned piece would be sacrificed. A chemist tested the electrons in the cake and showed that it had been cooked for eight minutes—exactly what the Druid ritual called for.

The study of the Bog Man shows how scientists must be detectives to shed light on the shadowy past. By recreating how the Bog Man died, they uncovered new evidence about life in ancient Europe.

1. What evidence led scientists to think the Bog Man had been important?

2. **Critical Thinking** How does the case of the Bog Man show that knowledge of both science and culture is needed to unravel the mysteries of the ancient past?

3 Stone Age Peoples

READE TO UNDERSTAND

☐ How people lived in the Old Stone Age.

☐ What effect the last ice age had.

☐ How life changed in the New Stone Age.

☐ *Vocabulary:* nomad, glacier, technology, bronze.

In their search for prehistoric artifacts, archaeologists have uncovered many stone axes and arrow tips. As a result, scholars use the term "Stone Age" to describe the prehistoric period of time when people used simple stone tools. The term also describes a way of life in which people rely on such stone tools.

The Stone Age is often divided into the Old Stone Age, or Paleolithic (PAY lee uh LIHTH ihk) Age, and the New Stone Age, or Neolithic (NEE uh LIHTH ihk) Age. The Paleolithic Age may have begun as early as 500,000 B.C.* It lasted to about 10,000 B.C. The Neolithic Age lasted from about 10,000 B.C. to about 3500 B.C.

The Old Stone Age

Archaeologists have found remains and artifacts of Paleolithic people in many parts of the world, including East Africa, China, Southeast Asia, Europe, the Middle East, and the Americas. Based on their findings, scientists have begun to construct a picture of life in the Old Stone Age.

Paleolithic people lived by fishing, hunting, and gathering plants that grew wild. They were **nomads,** people who moved in search of food. For example, they would follow herds of animals such as the woolly mammoth. Or if wild berries and nuts became scarce in an area, they would migrate to another area where food was plentiful.

---

* Civilizations influenced by Christianity date historical events from the birth of Christ. B.C. stands for dates before the birth of Christ. For B.C. dates, the higher number is always the earlier date. A.D. stands for "anno domini," a Latin phrase meaning "in the year of our Lord." A.D. is used for dates after the birth of Christ.

A simple social structure developed during the Old Stone Age. Groups of related families joined to form small hunting bands numbering about 30 people. They built no permanent shelters. Instead, they camped in caves or slept under lean-tos made of branches and grasses. While some people hunted, others stayed near the camp to gather wild food and care for the young.

There is evidence that during the Old Stone Age people developed spoken languages and learned how to control fire. With spoken language, hunters could organize hunts of large animals. Fire provided light and warmth, protection against wild animals, and heat for cooking food.

Paleolithic people made simple tools such as hand axes and choppers. The earliest tools were pieces of flint, a hard stone, chipped to produce a sharp cutting edge. Later, people made stone and bone tools for more specialized uses. These tools included needles, skin scrapers, harpoons, fishhooks, arrowheads, and spear points.

Some scholars suggest that during the Old Stone Age people accepted basic religious beliefs. For example, they think that cave paintings made by prehistoric hunters had a religious meaning. (See page 11.) Perhaps the hunters believed that drawing the animals would help them in the hunt.

GEOGRAPHIC SETTING
Changes in the Environment

The date often used to indicate the end of the Old Stone Age, about 10,000 B.C., also marks the end of the last ice age. Scientists think the earth has experienced four ice ages over millions of years. During the last ice age, thick sheets of ice, called **glaciers,** spread out from the polar regions. In North America, glaciers stretched as far south as present-day Kentucky. Glaciers also covered much of northern Europe and parts of Asia.

According to scientific theory, much of the world's water was frozen during the last ice age. As a result, ocean levels dropped, and land areas today covered with water were exposed. A land bridge may have connected North America and Asia where the Bering Sea is today. Some scientists think that about

25,000 years ago people from Asia followed herds of wild animals across the land bridge into North America. When the glaciers melted, the level of the ocean rose. The land bridge disappeared, and the people in North America were cut off from Asia.

The end of the last ice age caused dramatic changes in local climates around the world. Deserts appeared where lush plants had grown, and warm weather brought new plants to life in formerly frigid areas. The new climate patterns contributed to a change in the way people lived—a change so profound that scholars often call it a revolution. This revolution marked the beginning of the Neolithic Age. ■

The New Stone Age

Between 10,000 B.C. and 3500 B.C., people in many parts of the world gradually stopped hunting and gathering food and became farmers. They domesticated, or tamed, wild animals such as dogs, sheep, and goats and began to grow grain and vegetables for food. Scholars speculate that women were the farmers in many of these early societies and that men hunted.

In the New Stone Age, agriculture developed in many places. Anthropologists have generally concluded that it began first in the Middle East. People grew crops that were suited to the local soil and climate. In the Middle East and Africa, for example, they grew wheat, barley, and oats. They grew rice and root crops such as yams in Asia. Beans, squash, and maize, or corn, were grown in the Americas.

The agricultural revolution, or the change from hunting and gathering food to growing food, had a far-reaching effect on the way people lived. Since people no longer had to move in search of food, they formed permanent settlements, or villages. They built houses, and property became important. Even so, not everyone abandoned the nomadic way of life. Some people remained hunters and gatherers. Others established a stable way of life as herders of sheep, cattle, or goats.

In farming villages, people had to cooperate in new ways. The heads of each family probably met to make decisions about plant-

In 1940, four boys discovered this cave painting in Lascaux, France. The work of Stone Age artists, this red and black bison is one of 20 painted in the cave. The artists created colors by grinding ores and mixing them with animal fat. They used mortars and pestles for grinding, shells for holding pigment, and scrapers for blending colors.

ing and harvesting. As villages grew, a chieftain and a council of elders assumed the task of making decisions. Increasingly, people relied on these leaders to settle disputes over such issues as land ownership. This issue had not come up among nomadic people, who did not own land.

According to archaeologists, Neolithic farmers believed that spirits, or gods, controlled the forces of nature. Since floods and drought meant starvation or death, farmers took care to keep the spirits happy.

Technology of the New Stone Age

The growth of a farming economy led to the development of new **technology,** that is, tools and skills people use to meet their basic needs. To turn over the soil, people fashioned sturdy hoes from granite, a hard stone that could be sharpened. They also invented weaving. When they learned to make cloth from wool and flax, Neolithic people no longer had to slaughter their animals for the hides. They made baskets for storing grain, nets for fishing, and fire-hardened pottery for cooking.

Toward the end of the New Stone Age, several more developments greatly changed the way some people lived. For example, farmers began to use animals such as the ox to pull plows instead of pulling the plows themselves. As a result, farmers could plow more land and reap larger harvests, which supported a growing population.

Other important developments included the invention of the wheel and the sail and the use of metal. Wheeled carts gradually replaced wooden sleds, making land transportation easier. The invention of the potter's wheel meant that people could make better pots and other vessels. The sail improved transportation on water and made longer voyages possible. In addition, people in the late Neolithic Age began to use metal as well as stone for tools and weapons. They first used copper. Then they discovered that copper combined with tin formed a harder metal, called **bronze.**

By 3000 B.C., each of these inventions was being used in some part of the world. However, they were not invented everywhere at the same time. Most appeared first in the Middle East. Some were not used in other places for thousands of years. The people of Central America, for example, used the wheel on toys but did not use wheels on carts until after the arrival of Europeans in the 1500s A.D. People used the inventions of the late Neolithic Age to build more complex societies called civilizations.

SECTION 3 REVIEW

1. **Identify:** (a) Paleolithic Age, (b) Neolithic Age, (c) agricultural revolution.

2. **Define:** (a) nomad, (b) glacier, (c) technology, (d) bronze.

3. Why was learning to control fire important for Paleolithic people?

4. List two ways in which the agricultural revolution affected the way people lived.

5. What metals did late Neolithic people begin to use?

6. **Critical Thinking** Which technology of the New Stone Age do you think had the most impact on daily life? Explain.

4 Emergence of Civilization

READ TO UNDERSTAND

☐ **What the characteristics of early civilization were.**

☐ **How early cities developed.**

☐ **Why keeping records was important in early civilizations.**

☐ *Vocabulary:* silt, polytheistic, theocracy, artisan, barter economy, scribe, culture.

Early civilizations did not just appear overnight. They gradually developed in different parts of the world. Simple farming settlements grew into large cities by the end of the Neolithic Age, about 3500 B.C. This urban revolution marked the beginning of civilization. In fact, the word "civilization" comes from the Latin root "civitas," meaning city.

The development of cities was only one characteristic of early civilizations. Other characteristics included complex religions and governments, specialized skills and occupations, social classes, and methods of keeping records.

Growth of Cities

The earliest cities appeared in four great river valleys. Cities may have emerged as early as 6000 B.C. in the valley of the Tigris (TĪ grihs) and Euphrates (yoo FRAY teez) rivers in western Asia. Other cities developed in the valleys of the Nile River in North Africa, the Indus River in South Asia, and the Yellow River in East Asia.* (See the map on page 13.)

Conditions in the river valleys favored the development of cities. For example, fertile soil in the valleys made a surplus of food possible. When the rivers flooded, the water left deposits of **silt,** a soil rich in minerals, which made the land especially fertile. Flood waters also brought needed moisture to the land, and people used river water for irrigation during dry

---

* Early cities were not limited to river valleys. As you will read in Chapter 12, cities also grew in the highlands of the Americas.

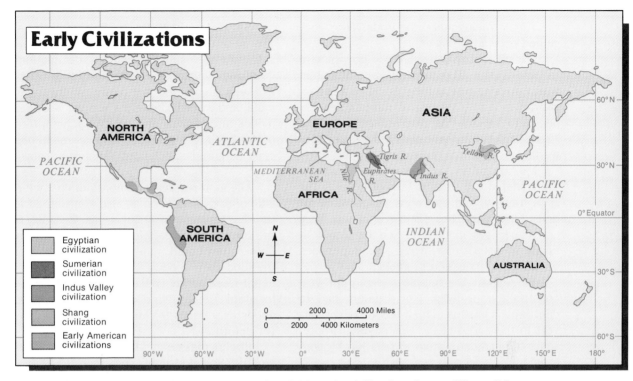

Early Civilizations

NORTH AMERICA

EUROPE

ASIA

PACIFIC OCEAN

ATLANTIC OCEAN

PACIFIC OCEAN

MEDITERRANEAN SEA

Nile R.

Tigris R.

Euphrates R.

Indus R.

Yellow R.

AFRICA

SOUTH AMERICA

INDIAN OCEAN

AUSTRALIA

0° Equator

60° N

30° N

30° S

60° S

90° W   60° W   30° W   0°   30° E   60° E   90° E   120° E   150° E   180°

Egyptian civilization

Sumerian civilization

Indus Valley civilization

Shang civilization

Early American civilizations

N
W — E
S

0   2000   4000 Miles
0   2000   4000 Kilometers

MAP STUDY *Name the four river valleys in which early civilizations began. Where did civilizations develop in the Americas?*

periods. In addition, the rivers contained plentiful fish and attracted animals, two additional sources of food. Finally, the rivers served as transportation arteries, which allowed people to trade for goods.

With food surpluses, the populations of farming settlements increased, and villages grew into cities. Some early cities had as many as half a million residents. City dwellers undertook major projects such as clearing new farmland and building vast irrigation systems as well as constructing temples, palaces, and walls for defense. Because such projects required organization and leadership, they contributed to the development of governments.

Religion and Government

In the early cities, government and religion were closely related. Like the people of the New Stone Age, city dwellers were **polytheistic**—that is, they worshipped many gods. They believed that gods and goddesses controlled the forces of nature. It was, therefore, important to them to win the gods' favor in order to prevent disasters. Only priests knew

In early civilizations, people spent much of their time planting, cultivating, and harvesting grain crops. Once harvested, grains such as wheat and barley had to be ground by hand. This statue shows a slave using a stone board and roller to crush the kernels of grain into flour.

the rituals to influence the gods. Thus they gained enormous power.

Priests probably headed the government as priest-kings. The form of government in which priests serve as kings is called a **theocracy.** Gradually, successful military leaders began to replace the priest-kings as rulers. These leaders may have emerged as a result of warfare over scarce resources.

Military rulers had clear responsibilities. They shared the priests' task of keeping the gods friendly, and they were responsible for defending their cities against enemies. They acted as judges, made laws, and appointed officials to keep order. They also supervised building and irrigation projects.

To support the temple and pay for vast construction projects, city dwellers had to contribute a portion of their labor or their harvest to the government. This payment represents the earliest system of taxation by government.

The Economy and Society

The innovations in technology of the late Neolithic Age were important to city dwellers. Bronze came into such widespread use for vessels, tools, and weapons that historians have often called the period of early civilization the "Bronze Age." Important social and economic changes also occurred during the Bronze Age.

Ancient people used jewelry both for decoration and for religious rituals. As early as 3500 B.C., artisans had learned how to shape metal to create jewelry. This necklace shows the skill of the people of the Indus River valley.

Specialized skills and occupations. The new technology often required special skills. As a result, specialized occupations gradually developed. Skilled workers called **artisans** hammered out plows, scythes, helmets, and swords. Jewelers shaped precious metals into charms and necklaces. Sculptors, potters, painters, priests, and government officials acquired specialized skills and knowledge.

The food surplus, an important characteristic of early civilizations, also contributed to the development of occupations. Because of the surplus, some people did not have to farm. Rather, they could trade products or labor for the food they needed. For example, a potter might trade a clay cooking vessel to a farmer for grain. The system of exchanging one set of goods or services for another is called a **barter economy.**

Social classes. As a city grew, a more complex social structure emerged. The social structure defined a person's place in society. At the top of the structure was the priest-king or king. Below the priest-king or king was a class of priests and nobles. Nobles generally based their power and wealth on owning large amounts of land. Being a noble was hereditary—that is, the children of nobles were also nobles.

In some cities, government officials and wealthy merchants formed the class below the nobility. Artisans and small traders ranked next, followed by the largest class, made up of peasant farmers and workers. At the bottom of the social structure were slaves. Slaves were men, women, and children who had been taken captive in war or who were enslaved to pay their debts.

In early civilizations, people generally could not move from one social class to another. Children usually learned a trade from their parents and so tended to stay in the same occupation.

Keeping Records

Some historians consider keeping records one of the most important characteristics of civilization. The Inca of South America kept detailed records on pieces of knotted string called quipus (KEE pooz). Most ancient peoples, however, developed writing in order to keep accurate records.

Priests were probably the first to start making the marks or drawing the pictures that eventually evolved into systems of writing. They needed precise information about how and when to perform ceremonies.

Temples became the schools of ancient civilizations. Priests taught only a select few the secrets of writing. A young man who mastered the difficult task of learning to read and write was called a **scribe.** Scribes worked in the ruler's service, in the temples, or in the homes of wealthy merchants. Rulers depended on scribes to keep track of taxes, property deeds, treaties, and marriage documents. Merchants needed copies of business contracts and records of debts.

Writing was more than keeping records, however. It became the means of passing the wisdom and learning of one generation on to the next.

Contacts Among Early Civilizations

Although the first river valley civilizations appear to have developed independently, they did have some contact with one another. Trade, warfare, and migration helped spread ideas and products from one city to another and from one civilization to another. For example, city dwellers along the Tigris and Euphrates rivers traded with people in other parts of the Middle East for timber, metal, and stone.

Warfare sometimes destroyed elements of a civilization, but it also helped spread ideas. When a highly civilized people conquered a region, the conquered people often absorbed ideas from the conquerors. In addition, migrating people exchanged skills with people they encountered.

In early civilizations, people absorbed or adapted only those ideas that seemed to suit their own way of life. From this process, distinct patterns of culture developed that were passed on to future generations. **Culture** is the customs, ideas, and ways of life of a group of people.

Ancient civilizations of the Middle East, Asia, and Africa developed traditions that still

Long, tedious training was needed to master the skill of writing. Once a scribe acquired this knowledge, he became indispensable in ancient civilizations.

influence large parts of the world. In addition, the early civilizations of the Americas helped shape later cultures.

SECTION 4 REVIEW

1. **Locate:** (a) Tigris River, (b) Euphrates River, (c) Nile River, (d) Indus River, (e) Yellow River.

2. **Define:** (a) silt, (b) polytheistic, (c) theocracy, (d) artisan, (e) barter economy, (f) scribe, (g) culture.

3. Why were farmers in river valleys able to produce a surplus of food?

4. Why were priests powerful in early cities?

5. Why did the people of early civilizations develop writing?

6. **Critical Thinking** (a) How did early civilization spread? (b) Which method do you think was most effective? Why?

Summary

1. Understanding geography is important for the study of world history. Knowing where something happened is a clue to knowing why it happened. Five themes of geography are useful in the study of history: location, place, interactions between people and their environment, movement, and regions.

2. Scientists and historians work together to explore the mysteries of prehistory. They have uncovered thousands of artifacts at ancient sites all over the world. Archaeologists have developed sophisticated techniques for analyzing and dating their finds. However, many questions about prehistoric peoples remain unanswered.

3. During the Paleolithic Age, people were nomadic, moving in small bands in search of food. But when the last ice age ended, revolutionary changes ushered in the Neolithic Age. The agricultural revolution radically changed the way people lived. As people learned to raise crops, some formed permanent farming communities. In the late Neolithic Age, farmers began producing food surpluses that could support large populations.

4. Early civilizations appeared in many parts of the world. Favorable geographical conditions encouraged the growth of civilizations in the Nile, Tigris-Euphrates, Indus, and Yellow river valleys. Characteristics of these early civilizations included the development of cities, complex religions and governments, specialized skills, social classes, and methods of keeping records.

Recalling Facts

Decide if the following statements are true or false. If a statement is false, rewrite it to make it true.

1. A region may be defined by physical or cultural characteristics.

2. Latitude lines on a map measure distance east and west of the Prime Meridian.

3. Written records have existed for about 5,000 to 6,000 years.

4. Artifacts include weapons and tools.

5. Paleolithic people lived in permanent farming communities.

6. The Old Stone Age emerged after the end of the last ice age.

7. The wheel was invented in the New Stone Age.

8. Food surpluses favored population growth.

9. Early city dwellers believed in one god.

10. People in early cities had no contact with outsiders.

Chapter Checkup

1. (a) Why is it important to study the connections between history and geography? (b) Define the five major themes of geography.

2. (a) What types of evidence provide information about prehistoric peoples? (b) How is such evidence found?

3. What new techniques have enabled archaeologists to make impressive advances?

4. Compare the way Paleolithic and Neolithic people lived, in terms of food and shelter.

5. (a) What evidence suggests that Paleolithic people developed religious beliefs? (b) Why was religion important to Neolithic farmers?

6. (a) List three inventions of the late Neolithic Age. (b) How did each invention affect the way people lived?

7. (a) How were early civilizations different from Neolithic farming communities? (b) How were they similar?

Critical Thinking

1. **Analyzing** (a) Why was writing an important development? (b) How do you think it affected the way people lived?

2. **Relating Past to Present** (a) How did the end of the last ice age affect local climates? (b) What effects might these changes have had on the way people lived? (c) Do you think major climate changes today would alter the way people live? Explain your answer.

3. **Analyzing Geography in History** (a) Describe three ways in which new ideas and products were spread from one area to another. (b) What modern ideas or products have spread from one culture to another? (c) By what means were they spread?

Developing Basic Skills

1. **Studying an Artifact** Study the statue shown on page 13. (a) What is the woman doing? (b) What can you learn about the technology of early peoples from the statue? (c) Do you think grain was important to the people who made the statue? Explain.

2. **Map Reading** Study the map on page 13. Then answer the following questions: (a) On what continents did early civilizations develop? (b) What geographical features made travel between different regions difficult? (c) Which early civilizations were most likely to have had some contact with other peoples? Explain.

Writing About History

Answering Essay Questions

To write an answer to an essay question, you need to understand the instruction word. Below are some common instruction words and the type of answer each requires.

Discuss: tell the significance of a person or event

Describe: write a full account of what happened

Explain: tell how or why an action or event affects something else

Identify: give a person's or event's place in time and the relation to other persons or events

Compare: give similarities and differences

Sometimes an essay question will have a question word. Below are some of the most common question words and the type of answer each requires.

Why: give reasons

How: tell in what way or by what means something was done

What: give specific examples or illustrations

Practice: Read each of the Critical Thinking questions above. Which type of answer does each question require?

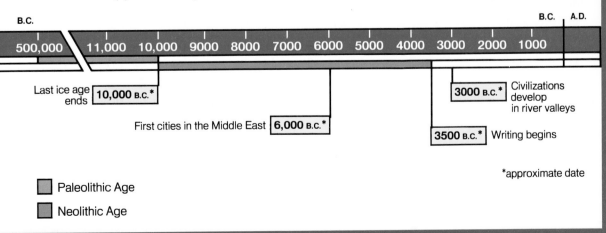

B.C.

| 500,000 | 11,000 | 10,000 | 9000 | 8000 | 7000 | 6000 | 5000 | 4000 | 3000 | 2000 | 1000 | B.C. | A.D. |

Last ice age ends 10,000 B.C.*

First cities in the Middle East 6,000 B.C.*

3000 B.C.* Civilizations develop in river valleys

3500 B.C.* Writing begins

*approximate date

■ Paleolithic Age
■ Neolithic Age

17

Ancient Egypt (7000 B.C.–30 B.C.)

CHAPTER OUTLINE

1. **Early Egyptian Civilization**
2. **Government in Ancient Egypt**
3. **Ancient Egyptian Society**

Among the priceless treasures uncovered in King Tutankhamon's tomb was his gold throne. This detail from the back of the throne shows some of the riches the king enjoyed.

"At first I could see nothing. The hot air escaping from the chamber caused the candle flame to flicker. But presently, as my eyes grew accustomed to the light, details of the room within emerged slowly from the mist, strange figures of animals, statues, and gold—everywhere the glint of gold." With these words, Howard Carter described his first glimpse of the inside of the tomb of King Tutankhamon (TOOT ahngk AH muhn) of Egypt. Carter then shone a light into the room, "the first light that had pierced the darkness of the chamber for three thousand years. The effect was bewildering, overwhelming."

In the burial chamber, Carter found Tutankhamon's coffin. Carved on the lid of the coffin was a golden statue of the king, decorated with precious jewels. On his forehead "were two emblems delicately worked in brilliant inlay—the Cobra and the Vulture—symbols of Upper and Lower Egypt, but perhaps the most touching by its human simplicity was the tiny wreath of flowers around these symbols, the last farewell offering of the widowed queen."

Tutankhamon was one of many Egyptian rulers buried in the Valley of the Kings. This rocky and narrow gorge lies on the west bank of the Nile River near Thebes. Egyptian kings and nobles were buried with many of their possessions to make them comfortable in the afterlife. Their tombs were mazes of corridors and chambers cut out of the rock. The tombs were often hidden from view and tightly sealed to protect their treasures.

In the late 1800s, archaeologists had begun to explore the Valley of the Kings. All the tombs they found had been plundered by grave robbers. Then in 1922, after a long search, English archaeologist Howard Carter finally discovered Tutankhamon's tomb.

Since Carter's discovery, the riches of Tutankhamon's tomb have come to symbolize the achievements of Egyptian civilization. By the time Tutankhamon inherited the throne, in 1361 B.C., Egyptian civilization was already almost 2,000 years old. Between 3500 B.C. and 3000 B.C., people living in the Nile River valley had established the first civilization in Africa. Early Egyptians probably had some contact with Sumer, a civilization in the Tigris-Euphrates Valley of western Asia. But the life-giving Nile had far greater influence on the development of Egyptian civilization. ■

1 Early Egyptian Civilization

READ TO UNDERSTAND

☐ **How the Nile influenced the development of ancient Egypt.**

☐ **What role religion played in ancient Egypt.**

☐ **How Egyptians developed a system of writing.**

☐ *Vocabulary:* **delta, papyrus, cataract, hieroglyphics, pictograms, ideogram.**

A search for food led Stone Age hunters to the lush Nile River valley about 8000 B.C. The climate of northern Africa had gradually become drier and food was scarce. This forced hunters in the region to move. Some migrated to northeastern Africa where they discovered the Nile River valley. There they found plentiful wild game and water.

Archaeologists think that by 7000 B.C. the agricultural revolution had reached the Nile Valley. People living there grew barley, wheat, and vegetables. Early farmers eventually grew enough food to support permanent settlements. By 3500 B.C., many small farming villages clung to the banks of the Nile.

The people called their land Kemet, meaning rich, black soil. As farmers, they valued the fertile soil that produced good harvests. Yet fertile soil was only one geographic advantage enjoyed by the Nile villages as they grew over the next few centuries.

GEOGRAPHIC SETTING
The Nile River: Giver of Life

The Nile River is the longest river in the world. It flows north from its remote headwaters in the highlands of central Africa to the Mediterranean Sea, 4,160 miles (6,660 kilometers) away. In ancient times, as today, the Nile was considered the source of life in Egypt. Without

The language of ancient Egypt reflected the influence of the Nile River. The word for "travel" was either "khed," meaning "to go downstream," or "khent," meaning "to go upstream." In this photograph Egyptians use sailboats to carry goods along the Nile today much as their ancestors did 4,000 years ago. The inset picture shows a tomb model of a sailboat used by ancient Egyptians. The crew is preparing the sail for traveling upstream.

the Nile, which brings valuable moisture to the parched land, Egypt would be an extension of the Libyan Desert.

Until recently, the Nile overflowed its banks every July following the rainy season in central Africa. The Nile floods were predictable. Although the floods occasionally caused destruction or failed to bring enough water, Egyptians usually knew about how high the waters would rise. The flood waters soaked deep into the soil where the next crop of grain would be planted.

In addition to moisture, the flood waters carried silt, which was deposited on the fields as the waters receded. The rich soil replenished the farmland each year.* At the mouth of the Nile, where the river empties into the Med-

iterranean Sea, deposits of silt have formed a **delta,** that is, a triangle-shaped area of marshy flatlands.

Throughout Egyptian history, the Nile has helped to unite the villages along its banks. It served as a major highway, connecting Upper Egypt in the south to Lower Egypt in the north. (See the map on page 21.) Trade along the river was active. The river currents carried barges loaded with grain downstream to the delta. Then with sails raised, the barges caught the prevailing winds and returned upstream.

The Nile touched people's lives in many other ways. It provided river wildlife, which Egyptians hunted for food and sport. Furthermore, Egyptians used a reed called **papyrus** (puh PĪ ruhs) that grew along the Nile's marshy shores for making paper. The ancient Egyptians recognized the importance of the Nile, as the following lines from one of their hymns show: "If the Nile smiles the earth is joyous, every stomach is full of rejoicing."

---

* The yearly floods continued until 1970, when the Aswan High Dam was completed. The dam provides electrical power and a steady supply of water to Egypt, but it also traps silt behind its walls. Today, Egyptian farmers spread artificial fertilizers on their fields.

Natural Barriers

Although the Nile River dominated everyday life, other geographic features also influenced early Egyptian civilization. As you can see on the map below, the Libyan and Nubian deserts, the Mediterranean Sea, and the Red Sea form natural barriers that almost surround Egypt. These barriers protected the early Nile villages from attack by outsiders. To the south, the Nile is interrupted six times by **cataracts** (KAT uh RAKTS), or waterfalls and rapids. The cataracts and a huge swamp, where the Nile was impassable, posed obstacles to invaders from Kush, present-day Ethiopia.

Egyptians were not completely protected by natural barriers, however. Over the centuries, Egyptian rulers faced many invaders. Most reached Egypt across the Sinai Peninsula, the triangle of land that connects Egypt and western Asia. The northern Sinai also served as a path for Egyptian armies when they marched off to conquer people in western Asia.

The natural barriers of Egypt presented obstacles to Egyptians as well as to outsiders. Although the narrow strip of land along the river was fertile, farmers could not grow crops in the surrounding deserts. Thus, most Egyptians lived in crowded Nile villages. As the population grew, Egyptians had to overcome the limits of their local geography. They built extensive irrigation systems to carry Nile water into the desert, and they drained the marshy swamps of the Nile delta. ∎

Religion in Ancient Egypt

Religion was a thread deeply woven into Egyptian life. The Egyptians' religious beliefs reflected the importance of nature in their lives. Egyptians believed that different gods controlled the forces of nature, giving good harvests or causing crops to die. They thought gods had the power of life and death over everyone. Egyptians were polytheistic. People in each village worshipped a village god in addition to other gods. They also identified certain gods with animals such as cats.

Egyptian gods. The sun god Amon-Re (AH muhn RAY) was the most important Egyptian god. The east, where the sun rose, symbolized birth to the Egyptians. The west, where the sun set, represented death. Thus, Egyptians always built tombs and funeral temples on the west bank of the Nile.

Egyptian farmers gave special attention to Osiris (oh SĪ rihs), god of the Nile. According to an Egyptian legend, Osiris was murdered by his brother Set, an evil god who caused harvests to wither and die. Isis (Ī sihs), the wife of Osiris, brought her husband back to life. But Osiris did not return to the world of the living. Instead, he reigned as god of the underworld and judge of the dead. Every year, Egyptians celebrated the death and rebirth of Osiris, which they identified with the rise and fall of the Nile.

Life after death. Belief in life after death was central to Egyptian religion. When a person died, friends said, "You have not gone away dead. You have gone away alive." Egyptians thought that in the afterlife people were happy, well fed, and busy with the same activities they had enjoyed in life.

They believed that the dead did not automatically go to the afterlife. Instead, they went first to the underworld, where they were

MAP STUDY *During a visit to Egypt, the Greek historian Herodotus declared that the land was "wholly the gift of the Nile." Egyptian civilization developed on narrow strips of fertile land (shown in green on the map) along the river. What type of land lay beyond the reach of the annual flood waters?*

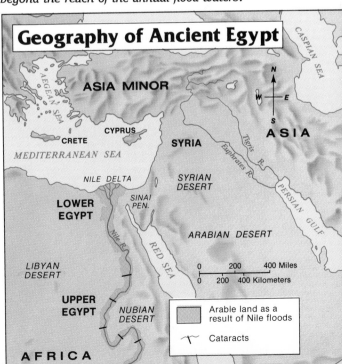

judged by Osiris. Standing before Osiris, the dead declared that they were innocent of sin. To see if they spoke the truth, Osiris weighed each heart against a feather, the symbol of truth. Those who failed the test were eaten by a monster. The reward for those who had lived moral lives was entry into the afterlife, or "the Happy Field of Food."

Egyptians planned carefully for life after death. The wealthy prepared elaborate tombs, or "Houses for Eternity." Early Egyptian rulers built huge stone pyramids as tombs, which they filled with the treasures, furniture, and food they thought they would need in the afterlife. Although the poor made simpler preparations, they, too, believed in the afterlife.

Egyptians believed that they would need their bodies as a home for the soul in the afterlife. For this reason, they practiced mummification, a process that preserved the body of the dead. At first, only rulers and nobles were allowed to have their bodies preserved after death. Eventually, the lower classes gained the same right. The Egyptians developed remarkably effective techniques of mummification. By examining the well-preserved mummies from Egyptian tombs, scientists have even been able to identify many health problems and causes of death among ancient Egyptians.

A System of Writing

The need to keep records of religious rituals and temple property probably led Egyptian priests to develop a system of writing, later known as **hieroglyphics** (HĪ er oh GLIHF ihks). The earliest hieroglyphics, dating from about 3100 B.C., were **pictograms,** or pictures of objects. In a pictogram, a picture of an ox meant an ox. Gradually, Egyptian hieroglyphics became more complex. Because a pictogram could not express an action or an idea, such as truth or honesty, Egyptians added ideograms. An **ideogram** is a picture that symbolizes an idea or action. For example, a picture of a reclining figure meant sleep.

As writing became more important, Egyptians modified their system, adding symbols to represent sounds. An example of this in English would be using a picture of a bee and a leaf to represent the word "belief." Egyptians developed symbols for consonant sounds but not for vowel sounds.

Egyptians first wrote by carving hieroglyphics on stone or wood. Later, they flattened papyrus reeds into strips and wrote on the strips with brushes and ink. In fact, the English word "paper" comes from the word "papyrus."

The meaning of Egyptian hieroglyphics was lost until the early 1800s, when a French scholar, Jean Champollion (shahm poh LYOHN), deciphered the Rosetta Stone. The stone, a slab of black rock, was found in 1799 by French soldiers in Egypt. On it was an inscription in three kinds of writing: Egyptian hieroglyphics, demotic, which was a shorthand version of hieroglyphics, and Greek. Champollion, who read Greek, spent years comparing the Greek words with the hieroglyphics. By 1822, he had translated the entire Egyptian text. After Champollion cracked the code of Egyptian hieroglyphics, scholars began translating thousands of records written on papyrus as well as elaborate inscriptions on temple and tomb walls.

To preserve the bodies of the dead, Egyptians extracted the brain of the dead person through the nostrils and removed most of the internal organs. Then they filled the body cavity with spices and put the corpse in a preserving fluid. After 70 days, they wrapped the body in bandages. A lifelike mask, such as this one decorated with gold and jewels, covered the head and shoulders of the mummy.

1. **Locate:** (a) Nile River, (b) Libyan Desert, (c) Mediterranean Sea, (d) Nubian Desert, (e) Red Sea, (f) Sinai Peninsula.

2. **Identify:** (a) Amon-Re, (b) Osiris, (c) Isis, (d) Champollion, (e) Rosetta Stone.

3. **Define:** (a) delta, (b) papyrus, (c) cataract, (d) hieroglyphics, (e) pictogram, (f) ideogram.

4. List three reasons for the importance of the Nile in Egyptian life.

5. What need probably led to the development of an Egyptian system of writing?

6. **Critical Thinking** Why is the Rosetta Stone important to our understanding of ancient Egypt?

2 Government in Ancient Egypt

READ TO UNDERSTAND

☐ How the rulers of the Old Kingdom created a centralized government.

☐ How the Old and Middle Egyptian Kingdoms differed.

☐ What developments occurred during the New Kingdom.

☐ *Vocabulary:* dynasty, pharaoh, empire, monotheism.

Before Champollion deciphered the Rosetta Stone, most of what we knew about ancient Egypt came from studying unwritten records such as temples, pyramids, tomb paintings, and mummified bodies. Since 1822, written records have revealed a great deal about government in ancient Egypt.

Uniting Upper and Lower Egypt

The villages that grew up along the Nile gradually became part of one of two kingdoms, Upper Egypt in the south or Lower Egypt in the north. About 3100 B.C., Menes (MEE neez), the ruler of Upper Egypt, united the two kingdoms by conquering Lower Egypt, thus greatly increasing his power. He gained both farmland and access to copper mines in the Sinai Peninsula. He also controlled trade from Upper Egypt to the mouth of the Nile. Menes' successors wore a double crown symbolizing the unity of the two kingdoms. They built their capital at Memphis, where Upper and Lower Egypt met. (See the map on page 26.)

Although little is known about Menes, he probably established the first **dynasty,** or ruling family, in Egypt. In a dynasty, the right to rule passes from the ruler to one of the children of the ruler. Occasionally, a ruling family dies out or is overthrown by a powerful challenger who establishes a new dynasty.

According to a history of Egypt written about 250 B.C., there were at least 30 dynasties in Egypt between 2700 B.C. and 1090 B.C. Scholars have used this history to divide ancient Egyptian history into three major periods: the Old Kingdom (2700 B.C.–2200 B.C.), the Middle Kingdom (2050 B.C.–1800 B.C.), and the New Kingdom or Empire Age (1570 B.C.–1090 B.C.).* In the years between the three kingdoms, civil wars and invasions left Egypt without a strong dynasty.

The Old Kingdom

During the Old Kingdom, Egyptian rulers acquired extensive power. They took the title **pharaoh** (FAIR oh), meaning "great house." Egyptians believed that the pharaoh was a god, the son of the sun god, Amon-Re. The pharaoh had absolute control over people's lives. Not only was he the source of all law, but he also owned all land, quarries, mines, and water in Egypt.

With this absolute power, pharaohs could organize a strong centralized government. They divided the kingdom into provinces and appointed officials to supervise tax collection,

---

* Since Egyptians recorded events according to which dynasty was in power, historians have no exact dates to guide them. They make educated guesses based on written and archaeological evidence, but they sometimes differ over the exact dates of the three kingdoms.

building projects, and irrigation systems in each province. At first, officials were responsible to the pharaoh and could be replaced. But gradually their positions became hereditary, and the officials became part of the noble class.

The Old Kingdom was a period of significant achievements. Egyptians improved hieroglyphics and developed the engineering skills needed to construct more elaborate tombs for the pharaohs. The Egyptians believed that, as a god, the pharaoh needed a suitable house for his spirit in the afterlife. When the pharaoh Zoser ordered a tomb prepared, his chief minister, Imhotep (ihm HOH tehp), a brilliant engineer, designed the Step Pyramid at Sakkara (sah KAH rah). This terraced tomb, constructed about 2650 B.C., is the world's oldest surviving stone building.

The Old Kingdom has sometimes been called the Pyramid Age because Zoser's successors, as well as many wealthy nobles, erected pyramid tombs. Three gigantic pyramids built during that period still stand at Giza.

These massive tombs are evidence of the great wealth and power of Egyptian rulers in the Old Kingdom. Thousands of laborers had to be recruited, fed, clothed, and housed during the years it took to build a pyramid. The cost in human lives and suffering was enormous. The common people resented the nobles and pharaoh who made them work in labor gangs and who increased taxes to pay for the tombs.

Despite heavy taxes, the huge expense of building pyramids exhausted the treasury. Gradually, the power of the pharaohs weakened. By 2200 B.C., officials in the provinces seized control of their territories. Peasant revolts and civil wars disrupted trade and farming. A period of disorder lasting about 150 years marked the end of the Old Kingdom.

The Middle Kingdom

Around 2050 B.C., a new dynasty from the south restored order in Egypt and established the Middle Kingdom. Compared to earlier rul-

BUILDING THE PYRAMID AT GIZA Built without the aid of the wheel, the Great Pyramid at Giza was a marvel of the ancient world. This recreation by artist Hal Stone shows how workers used winding ramps of earth and brick to haul sleds loaded with limestone blocks weighing over two tons each. The interior of the pyramid contained the tomb of the pharaoh Khufu (a) as well as chambers filled with fabulous treasures the pharaoh would need in the afterlife.

This tomb painting shows prisoners from nations subject to the Egyptian Empire. Among them are captives from Nubia, Crete, Libya, and Babylonia. A papyrus stem, symbolic of Egypt, binds them together.

ers, pharaohs of the Middle Kingdom seemed more interested in the common people. During this period, lower-class Egyptians gained the right to have their bodies mummified after death. The common people believed that this privilege gave them the same access to the afterlife as nobles and pharaohs.

Pharaohs of the Middle Kingdom undertook some major projects. One project, the draining of swampland in the Nile delta, created thousands of acres of new farmland. Another undertaking, the digging of a canal to connect the Nile to the Red Sea, benefited trade and transportation. At about the same time, two huge temples were built at Luxor and Karnak near the new capital city of Thebes on the east bank of the Nile.

During the Middle Kingdom, Egypt expanded its borders and had greater contact with other civilizations. Pharaohs sent trade expeditions to Kush, Syria, Mesopotamia, and Crete. Contact with outsiders contributed to the flourishing of Egyptian literature and art. One famous story, the *Tale of Sinuhe,* described the adventures of an Egyptian traveling in foreign lands. It became the basis of the Sinbad the Sailor stories.

By 1800 B.C., a succession of weak pharaohs again left Egypt in turmoil, with strong nobles battling for power in the provinces. Divided by civil wars, the Egyptians suddenly faced another threat. The Hyksos (HIHK sohs) of western Asia streamed across the Sinai Pe-

ninsula into northern Egypt. The newcomers used horses and war chariots, both unknown in Egypt. They easily crushed the disorganized Egyptian forces, who fought from donkey carts.

The Hyksos ruled Egypt for about 200 years. During that time, the Egyptians learned important military skills from their conquerors. They learned to ride horses and became expert charioteers. By 1570 B.C., Egyptian nobles united to expel the foreigners. The nobles established another Egyptian dynasty, which began the New Kingdom.

The New Kingdom

During the New Kingdom, Egyptian power reached its peak. Ambitious pharaohs established an empire stretching from Kush to the Euphrates River. An **empire** is group of territories or peoples controlled by one ruler. (See the map on page 26.) Tribute and loot from conquered territories filled the treasury. Taxes on flourishing trade further increased Egyptian wealth. Because of the growth during the New Kingdom, this period is also called the Empire Age.

The first woman ruler known to history, Queen Hatshepsut (haht SHEHP soot), reigned during the Empire Age. For 22 years, she administered an efficient government. Hatshepsut sent a trading expedition south to the area of present-day Somalia. Merchants re-

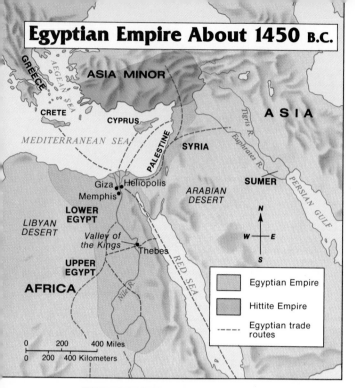

Egyptian Empire About 1450 B.C.

GREECE
AEGEAN SEA
ASIA MINOR
ASIA
CRETE
CYPRUS
MEDITERRANEAN SEA
PALESTINE
SYRIA
Tigris R.
Euphrates R.
PERSIAN GULF
Giza Heliopolis
Memphis
ARABIAN DESERT
SUMER
LOWER EGYPT
LIBYAN DESERT
Valley of the Kings
Thebes
RED SEA
UPPER EGYPT
AFRICA
Nile R.

N
W E
S

Egyptian Empire

Hittite Empire

Egyptian trade routes

0   200   400 Miles
0   200   400 Kilometers

MAP STUDY *The Nile River remained at the heart of Egyptian civilization even at the height of the empire, as you can see on this map. However, trade routes greatly extended Egyptian influence. Into what areas did Egyptian trade routes penetrate?*

turned to Egypt with a rich cargo of ivory, incense, ebony, gold, and monkeys for private zoos. A record of this successful expedition was carved onto the walls of Hatshepsut's funeral temple near Thebes.

Hatshepsut was succeeded by her stepson, Thutmose III (thoot MOH suh). A brilliant military leader, Thutmose expanded the Egyptian Empire to its greatest size. He conquered Palestine and Syria and organized a navy to subdue cities along the eastern Mediterranean coast. Like other rulers, Thutmose raised monuments to his own greatness. On tall, pointed stone pillars, called obelisks (AHB uh lihsks), stonemasons carved hieroglyphic inscriptions describing the pharaoh's military victories.

A controversial pharaoh. The pharaoh Amenhotep IV (ah muhn HOH tehp) was less interested in foreign conquests than in changing some traditional religious practices. He wanted Egyptians to worship only the god Aton, whose symbol was the sun disk. After **26** ordering the priests to stop worshipping other gods and to remove these gods' names from the temples, he changed his own name from Amenhotep to Akenaton (AH kuh NAH tahn), meaning "It goes well with Aton."

During his lifetime, Akenaton's policies created serious divisions in Egypt. The priests of other gods bitterly opposed the pharaoh's reforms. When Akenaton neglected the defense of the empire in order to worship Aton, he lost the support of the military. The common people were afraid to abandon their old gods in favor of Aton.

Today, Akenaton remains a controversial figure. Historians are unsure if he was trying to introduce **monotheism,** the worship of a single god, or if he just wanted to raise Aton to the highest status among the gods.

When Akenaton died in 1361 B.C., his son-in-law, a boy just eight years old, inherited the throne. The young pharaoh soon changed his name from Tutankhaton to Tutankhamon. By dropping Aton's name in favor of Amon's, Tutankhamon showed he had returned to traditional religious practices.

Decline of Egyptian power. The last great ruler of the New Kingdom was Ramses II (RAM seez). He spent most of his 67-year reign reviving the empire and fighting the Hittites (HIHT its) of Asia Minor. In 1280 B.C., the first written treaty in history ended the costly struggle between the Hittites and the Egyptians. Ramses II raised many monuments to commemorate his victories.

Following the reign of Ramses II, Egyptian power steadily declined. By 1090 B.C., civil wars had left Egypt too weak to defeat a stream of invaders. First came raiders known as the Sea Peoples. Scholars think these people came from islands in the Aegean to attack the Nile delta.

After the Sea Peoples, the Assyrians and then the Persians conquered Egypt. In 331 B.C., the Greeks, led by Alexander the Great, occupied the Nile lands. Three hundred years later, Queen Cleopatra (KLEE oh PAT ruh), a descendant of one of Alexander's generals, tried to restore Egyptian greatness. But Cleopatra was the last pharaoh. In 31 B.C., a Roman fleet defeated Egyptian naval forces, and the next year Egypt became a province of the Roman Empire.

Maps are very important to the study of world history because they answer the question "Where did it happen?" Maps help show why certain events or developments took place. They also illustrate how geography has influenced the way people live.

Maps provide many different kinds of information. Most maps include a title, legend, scale, and direction arrow. In addition, some maps in this book also give topographical, political, or economic information.

The following steps will help you read the map on page 26 and draw conclusions about the influence of geography on ancient Egyptian civilization. You can use the steps to study other maps in this book.

1 **Decide what is shown on the map.** The **title** tells what the map is about and, usually, the date or time period covered. The **legend** explains the meaning of colors and symbols used. The **scale** allows you to translate distances on the map into distances in miles and kilometers, while the **direction arrow** shows which way is north. Study the map on page 26: (a) What is the title of the map? (b) What color represents the Egyptian Empire?

(c) What is the approximate distance in miles from Thebes to the mouth of the Nile? (d) In what direction does the Nile River flow?

2 **Practice reading the information on the map.** **Topographical** maps include the physical features of a region, such as mountains, oceans, rivers, and lakes. **Political** maps show the sizes of empires or boundaries of nations. **Economic** maps give information about topics such as population, trade, and natural resources. Many maps in this book give all three kinds of information. (a) Name four physical features shown on the map on page 26. (b) What political information does the map give? (c) What economic information does the map show?

3 **Study the map to draw conclusions about a historical event or development.** (a) What geographic features limited Egyptian expansion? (b) Why did Egypt need a strong navy during the height of its empire? (c) Where was Egypt most open to invasion? Explain.

SECTION 2 REVIEW

1. **Locate:** (a) Memphis, (b) Giza, (c) Thebes.

2. **Identify:** (a) Menes, (b) Hyksos, (c) Hatshepsut, (d) Akenaton, (e) Tutankhamon, (f) Ramses II.

3. **Define:** (a) dynasty, (b) pharaoh, (c) empire, (d) monotheism.

4. List one important development that occurred during the (a) Old Kingdom; (b) Middle Kingdom; (c) New Kingdom.

5. (a) How did Akenaton try to change the religious practices of the Egyptians? (b) Did he succeed? Explain.

6. **Critical Thinking** Compare and contrast the three kingdoms in ancient Egypt.

3 Ancient Egyptian Society

READ TO UNDERSTAND

☐ How Egyptian society was structured.

☐ What the role of education in Egyptian society was.

☐ What scientific contributions Egypt made to civilization.

In the Old Kingdom, a person's social class and occupation were set at birth. Children of peasants farmed the same fields their parents and grandparents had. Artisans, such as weavers, taught their children their trades. This structure of Egyptian society barely changed for thousands of years.

Sunlight glinted on the gold trim of the royal barge as it drew near the harbor at Thebes. Inside, the pharaoh's new bride peered through a veiled window. She had traveled all the way from Mesopotamia to marry Amenhotep III. At last, she arrived in the biggest and richest city in the world—Thebes, capital of Egypt.

Close to the Nile, she could see the sprawling houses of the rich, their yards bursting with flowers. The harbor where the ship docked swarmed with slaves unloading figs, wine, cattle, and other goods. The future queen, who was only 15 years old, stepped from the royal ship and prepared to meet her husband, the pharaoh of Egypt.

The young girl quickly won the hearts of the Egyptian people. They called her Nefertiti, meaning "the beautiful one who has come." But the pharaoh, who was a sick man, died just three years after Nefertiti's arrival. The new pharaoh, Amenhotep IV, then married her.

Amenhotep IV was only 12 when he inherited the throne. Nefertiti, who was now 18, had great influence over him. Since he cared little about politics, he was happy to let his wife make decisions for him.

Nefertiti and her husband were happy, and Egypt was at peace. But the calm did not last. When he was 16, Amenhotep began to favor the god Aton above all other gods. Soon, he became obsessed with making Aton the most important god in Egypt.

Nefertiti supported her husband against the angry outcry of the priests. For a time so did the common people, who attacked the temples of the other gods. But the pharaoh was not content. He proclaimed that a new city would be built to honor Aton. Far up the Nile, in the middle of the desert, rose Aton's city. At the center of the lavish city stood the magnificent temple of Aton, nearly 300 yards wide and half a mile long.

Amenhotep died only a few years after he and Nefertiti moved to the city. Nefertiti died a short time later, friendless and alone. People abandoned the gleaming city of Aton, and it was slowly swallowed by the desert sands.

1. When she arrived at Thebes, how could Nefertiti tell it was a wealthy city?

2. **Critical Thinking** What does Nefertiti's life show about the role of women in ancient Egypt?

Social Classes

Egyptian social structure resembled a pyramid. The pharaoh, living in great splendor, stood at the top of society. Just below the pharaoh was a ruling class of priests and nobles. Next came a small middle class of merchants, artisans, doctors, and other skilled workers. Far below, at the base of the pyramid, were free peasants and, finally, slaves.

The ruling class. Because Egyptian life revolved around religion, priests had the highest status after the pharaoh. Egyptians believed that the gods, who controlled the universe, required constant attention. Only the priests knew how to please the gods. Priests conducted daily sacrifices to the gods, cast spells to make the land fertile, and recited prayers to help souls of the dead reach the afterlife. As guardians of this special religious knowledge, priests enjoyed great power and prestige. To support priests and temples, Egyptians paid taxes in the form of grain, linen, gold, and wine.

This tomb painting illustrates the importance of agriculture in Egyptian life. At top, a man and woman plow and sow a field. Well-stocked orchards and a lush garden along the banks of the Nile show the fertility of the soil.

Nobles made up the second segment of the ruling class. Nobles often held positions as governors of provinces, court officials, or tax collectors. The chief minister, who administered the business of the country, was usually chosen from the noble class. Many nobles owned large estates with gardens and pools surrounding spacious homes.

The middle class. Egypt was mainly a civilization of farming villages, but a small middle class of merchants, traders, and artisans did develop. As the wealth of Egypt increased, the middle class settled in cities, such as Memphis and Thebes, which grew up around temples and palaces.

Merchants provided goods and services to the ruling class. Traders brought dyes, ivory, or other items, which merchants sold to nobles. And nobles paid artisans to produce goods such as pottery and glass, intricate stone and wood carvings, and linen so fine that it looked like silk.

Peasants and slaves. The vast majority of Egyptians were peasant farmers whose way of life changed little over thousands of years. Each year, farmers waited for the Nile floods to renew the land. When the waters receded, they planted crops of wheat and barley. Since the pharaoh owned all the land, peasants paid over half of each harvest to government tax collectors. In addition to farming, peasants were often required to work on palaces and temples, clear irrigation channels, and serve in the army.

The peasants lived very simply. Their homes were low, thick-walled buildings made of sunbaked mud bricks. They furnished their few rooms with a bench, a bed, baskets, pots for cooking, and utensils for grinding grain.

Like peasants, slaves also worked on temples and irrigation projects. Most slaves were descendants of people brought back to Egypt as prisoners of war. Some lived like free peasants, farming plots of land. Those who served in the houses of nobles sometimes enjoyed comfortable lives or gained their freedom. On occasion, pharaohs appointed trusted slaves to high positions in the palace or in government. However, such opportunities were rare, and most slaves endured a hard existence.

The Status of Women

Compared to women in other ancient civilizations you will study, women in Egypt enjoyed a relatively high status. During the New Kingdom, women had the right to buy and sell property and to testify in court. Although divorce was rare, women as well as men had the right to seek divorce. Moreover, in Egyptian

29

society, property was inherited through the female line.

Egyptians especially valued the woman's role as wife and mother. Women gained greater status when they had children. Yet Egyptian writers often referred to wives as property of their husbands and urged men to treat their wives kindly. This advice suggests that women were not always well treated.

In the royal family, the queen occupied a privileged position because she was the wife of a god. At times, queens ruled jointly with their husbands. Although the pharaoh might have more than one wife, his first wife was the most important because her son would become the next pharaoh.

Education

In ancient Egypt, schools were first established to train priests. Students learned reading, writing, and arithmetic, as well as religious ceremonies and rituals. As Egyptian civilization became more complex, temple schools provided a more general education. Most students who attended temple schools were sons of the wealthy, but occasionally a poor child received an education. Girls did not attend temple schools, although they learned the skills they would need at home.

In the temple schools, students learned by dictation, copying the words of the teacher as he spoke. Most students took notes on scraps of broken pottery. Only advanced students wrote on papyrus, which was expensive. Pottery fragments unearthed by archaeologists show that school discipline was strict. One Egyptian student copied this warning: "Do not spend your time in wishing, or you will come to a bad end." After completing their studies, students either learned a trade or were apprenticed as scribes, or clerks, to priests or government officials.

Scribes performed an important function in ancient Egypt. They were essential to an efficient government since they kept records of taxes and expenses. As recordkeepers, they noted the heroic deeds of pharaohs as well as

THROUGH THEIR EYES Instructions of the Vizier Ptah-hotep

The ancient Egyptians produced a large body of written literature. Many texts were prayers, hymns, or charms that people believed would help the souls of the dead reach the happy afterlife. Egyptians also wrote biographies, histories, love songs, and poems.

Still another kind of Egyptian literature included practical advice on how to succeed in life. The following excerpts are from the Instructions of the Vizier Ptah-hotep, *one of the oldest books in the world. Ptah-hotep, who lived about 2450 B.C., was vizier, or chief minister, to the pharaoh. In the* Instructions, *he gives advice to his son.*

From the *Instructions*

Do not let your heart be puffed up because of your knowledge; do not be confident because you are a wise man. Take counsel with the ignorant as well as with the wise.

If you, as a leader, have to decide on the conduct of a great many people, seek the most perfect manner of doing so, that your own conduct may be blameless.

If you are sitting at the table of one greater than you, take what he may give when it is set before you. Let your face be cast down until he addresses you, and you should speak only when he addresses you. Laugh after he laughs, and it will be pleasing to his heart.

Be active while you live, doing more than is commanded. Activity produces riches, but riches do not last when activity slackens.

If you are one to whom petition is made, be calm as you listen to the petitioner's speech. Do not rebuff him before he has said what he came for. A petitioner likes attention to his words better than fulfilling of that for which he came.

If a son accepts what his father says, no project of his miscarries. Train your son to be a teachable man whose wisdom is agreeable to the great.

1. What advice about leadership did the vizier give his son?
2. **Critical Thinking** Would any parts of the vizier's advice be useful today? Explain.

the ordinary events of daily life, such as births, marriages, and deaths. A scribe who served a powerful noble or pharaoh might become rich, acquire great influence, or be appointed to an official position himself. In this way, a man from the lower class might move up in society.

In addition to temple schools, Egyptians established centers for higher education. The center of learning at Heliopolis, for example, was famous for teaching astronomy—the study of the planets and stars.

Scientific Accomplishments

During the Old Kingdom, the Egyptians made many practical advances in mathematics and the sciences. Egyptian farmers devised methods of surveying land out of necessity. When annual floods washed away boundary markers, farmers had to remeasure their fields. The need to survey land led to the development of mathematics, particularly geometry. Egyptians learned to measure the areas of squares and circles and to figure the volumes of cylinders and spheres.

The need to predict regular events such as Nile floods and eclipses led to advances in astronomy. Priests observed the skies and plotted the courses of stars and planets. These priest-astronomers used their knowledge to produce a calendar with a 365-day year. They divided a year into 12 months, with three seasons: the Nile flood season, the planting season, and the harvest season. They calculated that each month had 30 days, and they added five days to the last month to total 365 days. Although the Egyptians made no allowance for leap years, their calendar, as modified by the Greeks and Romans, is the basis for the modern calendar.

The Egyptians also invented techniques to build impressive stone monuments. Stone workers learned how to cut tall obelisks from a single rock, using hot fires and cold water to make the surrounding rocks crack. They then finished the job with hammers and crowbars. Egyptian engineering of temples and pyramids was so precise that each block fit perfectly into the next one.

Egyptians also made important medical discoveries. Although Egyptian doctors relied

Hieroglyphics are clearly visible on this sculpture of an Egyptian scribe. Originally few in number, Egyptian hieroglyphics eventually included over 700 symbols representing words or sounds.

heavily on magic, they made scientific inquiries. By studying the human body, doctors learned to perform surgery. Ancient papyrus texts describe successful operations to set fractured bones and treat spinal injuries. The Greeks and Romans acquired much of their medical knowledge from Egyptian sources.

SECTION 3 REVIEW

1. Why did priests hold such a high position in Egyptian society?

2. What rights did women have in ancient Egypt?

3. Why were scribes necessary to an efficient government?

4. How did the Nile floods contribute to the development of land surveying?

5. **Critical Thinking** Why do you think Egyptians developed advanced building techniques?

Summary

1. The Nile River was the center of development in ancient Egypt. Small farming villages prospered, largely because of the fertile soil and favorable geography of the Nile River valley. The importance of good harvests was reflected in Egyptian religious beliefs.

2. The history of ancient Egypt is divided into three major periods. The Old Kingdom was known as the Pyramid Age. During the Middle Kingdom, Egypt expanded and traded with other peoples. Egyptian power reached its peak during the New Kingdom.

3. Egyptian society barely changed for thousands of years. Sharp differences separated the ruling class from the small middle class and the huge class of peasant farmers. Egyptians made important advances in engineering, trade, literature, and art. Their discoveries not only affected their own civilization but also helped shape later civilizations.

Recalling Facts

Match each name at left with the correct description at right.

1. Osiris
2. Hatshepsut
3. Giza
4. Akenaton
5. Sinai

a. pharaoh who tried to change traditional religious practices
b. queen who ruled Egypt for 22 years during the New Kingdom
c. Egyptian god of the Nile
d. site of three great pyramids
e. peninsula connecting Egypt to western Asia

Chapter Checkup

1. Describe how the Nile River affected each of the following in ancient Egypt: (a) farming; (b) trade; (c) religion.

2. (a) How did Egyptians view life after death? (b) What preparations did Egyptians believe were necessary for the afterlife?

3. Describe how the pharaohs in the Old Kingdom organized the government.

4. (a) What did the pharaohs of the Middle Kingdom do for the people of Egypt? (b) Why was the New Kingdom called the Empire Age?

5. (a) What were the main social classes in ancient Egypt? (b) How did each class contribute to Egyptian civilization?

6. Describe ancient Egyptian accomplishments in: (a) mathematics; (b) astronomy; (c) engineering; (d) medicine.

Critical Thinking

1. **Analyzing Geography in History** (a) Discuss the ways in which the geographic setting of ancient Egypt both helped and hindered the Egyptians. (b) Do you think the effect of geography was mainly positive or negative? Explain.

2. **Relating Past to Present** (a) How did the pyramids demonstrate the wealth and power of Egyptian rulers? (b) How do buildings today indicate power and influence?

3. **Understanding Economic Ideas** (a) How did the Egyptian pharaohs acquire their great wealth? (b) Why do you think the Egyptian people accepted the economic system that allowed this?

4. **Applying Information** Akenaton's religious reforms created controversy in ancient Egypt. (a) What factors do you think

might explain the failure of his reforms? (b) How might his reforms have been successful?

5. **Understanding the Roots of Democracy** (a) How could an Egyptian from a lower class move up in the rigid social structure of Egyptian society? (b) Why is the ability to move up in a social structure an important part of democracy?

Developing Basic Skills

1. **Using Time Lines** A time line enables you to see the order in which events occurred. The earliest date on a horizontal time line is on the left, and the latest date is on the right. Study the time line below. (a) What is the date of the latest event shown on the time line? (b) Which lasted longer, the Old Kingdom or the Middle Kingdom? (c) Did the Hyksos invasions come before or after the New Kingdom was formed?

2. **Map Reading** Review the map reading steps given on page 27. Then study the map on page 21. (a) What information does the map provide? (b) For about how many miles on either side of the Nile were the lands flooded during the flood season? (c) Describe the route an Egyptian army might take to travel from Upper Egypt to the Euphrates River.

Writing About History

Using Question Clues

Before you begin to write the answer to an essay question, study the question for clues. Read the following essay question: *Why was religion important to the ancient Egyptians?* Then apply the following questions.

1. *What does the question word ask you to do?* Look for the word that tells you what you are to do in your answer. In the essay question above, the key word is *why*. In the answer, you must give reasons why religion was important to the Egyptians.

2. *What is the scope of the essay?* Look for limits on what you are to discuss. In this question, the geographic area is Egypt and the time frame is the ancient period. The question also asks only about the topic of religion.

3. *What information do you have that is related to the topic of the question?* In addition to the text section called Religion in Ancient Egypt, you can study the pictures and captions for information.

Practice: Apply these questions to the Critical Thinking questions in this Chapter Review before you begin to write the answers.

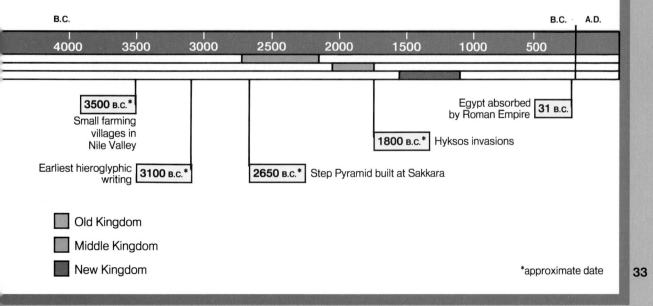

B.C.   B.C.   A.D.

4000   3500   3000   2500   2000   1500   1000   500

3500 B.C.* Small farming villages in Nile Valley

Earliest hieroglyphic writing **3100 B.C.***

2650 B.C.* Step Pyramid built at Sakkara

1800 B.C.* Hyksos invasions

Egypt absorbed by Roman Empire **31 B.C.**

Old Kingdom
Middle Kingdom
New Kingdom

*approximate date

The Ancient Middle East

2

(4500 B.C.—331 B.C.)

Warfare was common among the ancient Sumerians. This scene based on a standard carried into battle shows a victory celebration. At top left, the king of Ur faces his officers, who are being entertained by the musician with the harp.

"Why do you idle about? Go to school, stand before your schoolfather [teacher], recite your assignment, open your schoolbag, write your tablet, let your big brother [assistant teacher] write your new tablet for you. After you have finished your assignment, come to me, and do not wander about in the street. Come now, do you know what I said?"

Nearly 4,000 years ago, a father wrote these words to his son. Then he made his son copy the instructions so he would not forget them. The father was a scribe in ancient Sumer. Sumerian scribes held influential positions in government. The father, who wanted his son to follow his profession, criticized the boy's ungrateful behavior and lack of interest in school.

"I never said to you 'Follow my caravans.' I never sent you to work, to plow my field," continued the scribe. "Others like you support their parents by working. . . . Night and day am I tortured because of you. Night and day you waste in pleasures."

The clay tablet containing these words is one of thousands of written records that give us a picture of Sumerian civilization. The people of Sumer lived in the Tigris-Euphrates Valley in what is today Iraq. The Sumerians may have been the first people to develop a system of writing, sometime after 3500 B.C. This was one of the most important advances in history because it let people record their beliefs and traditions.

The Sumerians were the first of many peoples to contribute to the civilization of the ancient Middle East. Later peoples built on Sumerian achievements. The Sumerians and their successors were establishing their patterns of civilization at the same time the Egyptians were shaping their civilization in the Nile River valley.

Unlike Egypt, the Middle East was a battleground on which wave after wave of invaders fought for power. The result of these invasions was a constant exchange of ideas and mingling of beliefs. The great palaces and temples of the ancient Middle East have long since disappeared. Yet the Middle East was a source of ideas that have influenced the world to the present day. ■

1 Sumerian Civilization

READ TO UNDERSTAND

☐ **How the geography of Mesopotamia differed from that of Egypt.**

☐ **What religious beliefs the Sumerians held.**

☐ **What contributions the Sumerians made to civilization.**

☐ *Vocabulary:* **city-state, ziggurat, cuneiform.**

If you had visited the ancient city of Erech in the lower Euphrates Valley about 3000 B.C., you would have seen farmers using metal sickles to harvest crops in their fields. Ox-drawn wheeled carts are carrying the harvested grain toward the city. Rising out of the center of the city is a huge terraced building, the temple where the people worship their local god. Potters and goldsmiths work busily at their tasks in the city. On the river, merchants and scribes check the goods being loaded and unloaded from high-prowed boats.

How do we know that people lived this way? Archaeologists have found evidence dating back to 4500 B.C. of early settlements on the delta plains of the Tigris and Euphrates rivers. By 4000 B.C., a nomadic people had migrated from the Armenian Plateau and conquered the delta region. The newcomers were the Sumerians, who created the first known civilization in the ancient Middle East.

Sumerian civilization differed in many ways from Egyptian civilization. The Sumerian outlook on life, their government, and their religion were unlike those in Egypt. So, too, was the geography of the area, which affected life there.

GEOGRAPHIC SETTING
The Fertile Crescent: Crossroads of the World

The Tigris-Euphrates Valley lies in the eastern end of the Fertile Crescent, an area that stretches in a large arc from the Persian Gulf to the Mediterranean Sea. (See the map below.) The Fertile Crescent received its name from the rich soil of the region and its crescent shape.

The Fertile Crescent has often been called the "crossroads of the world" because it commands the land routes to three continents: Asia, Africa, and Europe. Unlike Egypt, the Fertile Crescent has few natural barriers. The Arabian and Syrian deserts offered less protection to early civilizations than the Libyan Desert did in Egypt.

MAP STUDY *The fertile soil and the wild game of the Tigris-Euphrates Valley made the area attractive for early settlers. The rivers served as arteries for trade among the cities of Mesopotamia. Why was the Fertile Crescent called the crossroads of the world?*

Geography of the Ancient Middle East

Because of its position, the region was frequently overrun by invaders. Waves of migrating peoples came down from the mountains north and west of the Tigris-Euphrates Valley. Invaders such as the Hittites swept into the Fertile Crescent from Asia Minor.

The diversity of the people living in the Fertile Crescent made it difficult to unite the area under a single ruler. Yet the constant contact among different peoples also led to an exchange of ideas that led to major achievements.

Land Between Two Rivers

The Greeks called the Tigris-Euphrates Valley "Mesopotamia," meaning "land between two rivers." Like the Nile in Egypt, the Tigris and Euphrates rivers dominated the lives of the people in Mesopotamia. The two rivers flow from the rugged highlands of the Armenian Plateau to the Persian Gulf. They run parallel for over 1,000 miles (1,600 kilometers).

In the spring or early summer, melting snows from the mountains sometimes cause the rivers to overflow. However, the floods of the Tigris and Euphrates, unlike those of the Nile, are unpredictable. In some years, the rivers do not rise above their banks. In others, savage floods cause enormous damage.

In ancient times, many floods swept across lower Mesopotamia. About 4000 B.C., a massive flood deposited a bed of clay eight feet (2.4 meters) thick. The flood destroyed farms, villages, and animals and drowned many people. Only a few towns built on high ground survived. In addition to floods, lower Mesopotamia suffered summer droughts and hot winds, which could turn fertile soil to dust, shrivel crops, and cause famine.

Despite the danger of flooding, however, the rivers supported the development of an advanced civilization. Trade along the rivers made Mesopotamian cities wealthy and powerful. Silt left by floods made the soil fertile. Good soil meant that the people living in Mesopotamia could rely on a stable food supply in most years.

Year after year, silt created a delta at the mouths of the Tigris and Euphrates rivers. Like the Nile delta, the delta in lower Mesopotamia was a maze of swamps and marshlands. To drain the swamps and channel the water to farmland, the people of Mesopotamia built an intricate network of dikes and canals. The building and upkeep of such a complex irrigation system required an elaborate, well-run government. ■

City-State Government

By 3000 B.C., the villages of lower Mesopotamia had grown into prosperous cities. Tens of thousands of people lived in the chief Sumerian cities of Ur, Erech, and Kish. Each city was an independent city-state with its own government and ruler. In a **city-state,** a large town or city and the surrounding countryside cooperate for mutual defense. The government of a Sumerian city-state supervised the building and maintenance of dikes and canals in the surrounding farmlands. It also constructed strong defensive walls and stored food in case of invasion. When threatened by attack, farmers took refuge behind the city walls.

Each city-state worshipped its own god or goddess as well as other gods. The people of the city-state believed they were wholly dependent on their city's god for food and protection. The land and everything people produced belonged to the god. In fact, farmers turned over about two thirds of each harvest to the temple.

Because a disaster such as a flood or invasion could strike suddenly, people in Mesopotamia believed that their survival depended on keeping their gods content. Priests alone knew how to please the gods, and they spoke with the gods for the people. As a result, in the early city-states priests ruled in the name of the gods.

As Sumerian city-states grew, they were constantly at war with each other. For example, Ur fought with Erech for control of the lower Euphrates. This frequent warfare may have increased the power of military leaders who could successfully defend their city-states. Military leaders then gradually replaced priests as rulers of the Sumerian city-states.

The Sumerians did not worship their rulers as gods. Instead, they believed their kings

Gudea, governor of a Sumerian city-state, ruled during a period of great prosperity and cultural advancement. He is shown here holding a vessel from which spring two streams of water, representing the Tigris and Euphrates rivers.

were the gods' representatives on earth. But because they spoke directly with the gods and the people, Sumerian kings commanded absolute obedience.

Religion

Towering above each Sumerian city-state was the **ziggurat** (ZIHG u rat), the home or temple of the god of the city. Pyramid-shaped, the ziggurat was often six to seven stories high. The Sumerians believed that gods descended to earth using the ziggurat as a ladder.

Like the Egyptians, the Sumerians were polytheistic. They worshipped other gods in addition to the god of their city-state. Sumerians believed that a council of gods and goddesses ruled the earth, deciding the fate of individuals and cities. Each god had a specific rank or place within this council.

37

A SUMERIAN ZIGGURAT A seven-story ziggurat towers over a Sumerian city in this recreation by artist Hal Stone. Note the exterior stairway that made it possible to reach the temple at the top. Unlike the pyramids, ziggurats contained no interior chambers. Always constructed of brick, they were decorated by carefully landscaped gardens covering the sloping sides and terraces.

Sumerians explained natural events as the results of actions by gods and goddesses. For example, they believed that winter, the season of hunger and hardship, occurred when the god Dumuzi (duh MOO zee) died and descended into the underworld. Only when the goddess Inanna (ihn AH nah) rescued her husband Dumuzi from the underworld did spring arrive, bringing new life. Every year, to ensure the return of the growing season, priests and priestesses reenacted the story of Inanna and Dumuzi.

In Egypt, the favorable climate of the Nile Valley allowed the people to enjoy life and see their gods as kindly forces. By contrast, fear of natural disasters and invasions probably contributed to the Sumerians' gloomy outlook on life. They believed that the gods punished them by sending floods or famine. This gloomy outlook colored their belief about the afterlife. At death, they expected to descend forever into a dark underworld, a huge cave filled with nothing but dust and silence.

A Written Language

The need for accurate records led to the development of writing sometime after 3500 B.C. Sumerian writing began as pictograms and ideograms. Scribes gradually simplified the system, using symbols to represent sounds and syllables.

Sumerians used a stylus, or sharpened reed instrument, to make symbols on tablets of wet clay. They then baked the tablets to harden the clay. Because the symbols were made up of wedge-like shapes, the writing was later called **cuneiform** (kyoo NEE uh form), from the Latin word "cuneus," or wedge. Traders and conquering armies helped spread cuneiform across the Fertile Crescent.

As the Sumerian city-states grew, the need for scribes increased. Scribes wrote down laws, treaties, and religious texts. As trade expanded, merchants hired scribes to record business deals, property holdings, and contracts.

To train scribes, priests set up schools in the temples. Only boys, usually the sons of scribes, attended temple schools. Students endured strict discipline in order to earn a privileged position as a scribe. Although no schools existed for girls, priestesses and the daughters of wealthy Sumerians probably learned to read and write from private tutors.

Legacy for Later Peoples

Sumerians were the first people known to use a wheel. They either invented it or borrowed the idea from earlier settlers in Mesopotamia. Wheeled carts and the sail, another Sumerian invention, enabled merchants to engage in long-distance trade. Sumerians also used wheels on war chariots. The use of wheeled vehicles spread slowly across the ancient world. You will recall that the Hyksos used war chariots when they conquered Egypt.

The Sumerians made many improvements in farming. They built complex irrigation systems to channel water through the sunbaked

The Sumerians, who were skilled artisans, often used plants and animals in their art as symbols of the fertility of nature. A bull's head decorates the sound box of this harp.

THROUGH THEIR EYES The Gilgamesh Epic

In long narrative poems, or epics, the peoples of Mesopotamia preserved ancient legends and passed on religious teachings, accounts of disasters, and stories of heroes. The oldest example is the Gilgamesh Epic from Sumer.

The Gilgamesh Epic is a rich collection of stories and myths. Different characters speak with Gilgamesh, ruler of an early city-state, about matters of life and death. Here Enkidu describes to Gilgamesh a place he was forced to enter in a dream.

A lion-pawed man seized me and led me
   down to the house of darkness, house of
   Irkalla,
the house where one who goes in and never
   comes out again,
the road that, if one takes it, one never comes
   back,
the house that, if one lives there, one never
   sees light,
the place where they live on dust, their food is
   mud;

their clothes are like birds' clothes, a garment
   of wings, and they see no light, living in
   blackness:
on the door and door-bolt, deeply settled
   dust.

In the house of ashes, where I entered,
there lives the funeral priest who brings together gods and men.
There sits the queen of below-earth, Ereshkigal:
Belit-tseri, tablet scribe of the underworld,
   kneels before her.
She holds a tablet and reads aloud to her.
Lifting her head, Ereshkigal looked directly at
   me—*me:*
"Who has brought this one here?"

1. What place is Enkidu describing to Gilgamesh?

2. **Critical Thinking** What does the extract show about the Sumerian view of the afterlife?

39

plains, planted trees to serve as wind breaks, and invented a plow. They also developed an accurate 12-month calendar to keep track of the seasons.

Like the Egyptians, the Sumerians used arithmetic and geometry to survey land and reestablish property lines after floods swept away boundary markers. The Sumerian system of arithmetic was based on the number 60, which led to such present-day measurements as the 60-second minute, the 60-minute hour, and the 360° circle.

Sumerian architecture influenced the civilizations of Mesopotamia for more than a thousand years. The Sumerians were the first to use arches, columns, ramps, and inclined walks. Because stone was scarce, Sumerian builders used bricks made of sunbaked clay. Later peoples built temples that rose in a series of terraces to heights of six or seven stories like the Sumerian ziggurat. The Egyptians may have adopted the idea of pyramids from the Sumerians.

About 2500 B.C., invaders conquered the city-states of Sumer. Sumerian civilization ceased to exist about 1750 B.C., but its traditions and achievements left a lasting mark on the newcomers.

SECTION 1 REVIEW

1. **Locate:** (a) Sumer, (b) Tigris River, (c) Euphrates River, (d) Armenian Plateau, (e) Arabian Desert, (f) Syrian Desert, (g) Ur.

2. **Identify:** (a) Fertile Crescent, (b) Mesopotamia.

3. **Define:** (a) city-state, (b) ziggurat, (c) cuneiform.

4. Describe two results of the movement of peoples across the Fertile Crescent.

5. How did the Sumerian view of an afterlife differ from the Egyptian view?

6. List four contributions the Sumerians made to civilization.

7. **Critical Thinking** Compare the role and training of scribes in Egypt and the Sumerian city-states.

40

2 A Blending of Cultures

READ TO UNDERSTAND

☐ How ideas spread throughout the Fertile Crescent.

☐ Why Hammurabi's Code was a major accomplishment.

☐ What the Assyrians, Chaldeans, and Persians contributed to the civilization of the ancient Middle East.

☐ *Vocabulary:* satrapy.

From tens of thousands of clay tablets found at sites throughout Mesopotamia, scholars have pieced together an extraordinary record of the many peoples who invaded the area between 2500 B.C. and 500 B.C. Though each group of invaders brought with them their own culture, they also adopted some of the achievements of the people they conquered. During this period, the peoples of the Fertile Crescent made many contributions to civilization.

The First Empire

As older Sumerian city-states declined, Akkad, a city to the north, rose to power. About 2350 B.C., Sargon, an Akkadian soldier, founded the first empire in recorded history. With an empire reaching from southern Mesopotamia to the Mediterranean Sea, Sargon proclaimed himself "Lord of the Four Quarters of the World," a title used by many later conquerors. A talented ruler, Sargon repaired and extended the flood control and irrigation systems of Mesopotamia. He also sent his armies to protect trade caravans.

The Akkadians borrowed many things from Sumerian civilization. Although the Akkadian language differed from the Sumerian, the conquerors adopted cuneiform for writing. Scribes translated Sumerian religious, scientific, and literary works into Akkadian. As a result, the Akkadians absorbed Sumerian religious beliefs and ideas about government and society.

Later Akkadian rulers lacked Sargon's abilities, and civil war resumed. For a brief time, Ur-Nammu, ruler of Ur, reunited the city-

Reading a textbook can be a lot different than reading a novel. In the Skill Lesson on page 5, you reviewed many of the features of a textbook and practiced using them as guides to better learning. One technique that will help you learn the most from reading your textbook is the SQ3R Method—survey, question, read, recite, and review. Use the steps below to apply the SQ3R Method to Section 2.

1 **Survey the reading selection.** Before you begin reading, look over the selection. Read the section title, the Read to Understand statements, and the subtitles. Looking at the illustrations and captions can also provide hints about the reading. (a) What is the title of the section? (b) Based on the Read to Understand statements, list two main ideas that will be covered. (c) What clue about the section does the illustration on page 43 provide?

2 **Think of the questions you want to answer from your reading.** Reading is more meaningful if you have questions in mind before you begin. Write a question for each of the subheads in Section 2. Use words such as how, what, why, when, and who to form your questions.

3 **Read to answer your questions.** Read Section 2 to find the answers to each of the questions you posed above.

4 **Recite your answers.** Ask yourself the questions and recite the answers without looking back at what you have read. Then write down the answers so you will have notes to study from.

5 **Review your answers.** Review the answers to your questions without looking at your notes. Then review them again tomorrow and in a week.

---

states. About 2050 B.C., Ur-Nammu compiled the first known code of laws. This code summarized Sumerian ideas of justice, emphasizing the king's duty to protect the people and to correct any existing wrongs.

About 2000 B.C., groups of nomadic peoples invaded Mesopotamia, attacking the rich river valley cities. One group, the Amorites, built the small village of Babylon on the Euphrates River. Slowly, the small village rose from obscurity into a magnificent city-state boasting of a giant ziggurat dedicated to the chief Babylonian god, Marduk. By 1700 B.C., the king of Babylon, Hammurabi (HAH mu RAH bee), had carved out an empire in Mesopotamia. (See the map on page 42.)

The Code of Hammurabi

Hammurabi was one of the great rulers of ancient times. He was an outstanding general, an excellent administrator, and a patron of the arts. In hundreds of surviving letters, he shows concern for details such as clearing blocked river channels, punishing dishonest officials, reforming the calendar, and honoring the

Glorifying the ruler was the aim of the artist who created this majestic bronze head of an Akkadian ruler. The eyes, which are now hollowed out, were once inlaid with precious jewels.

gods. However, he is best known for drawing up a uniform code of laws.

Hammurabi appointed a committee to revise existing laws and to create one set of laws for the whole empire. His purpose, he declared, was "to cause justice to prevail in the land, to destroy the wicked and the evil, to prevent the strong from oppressing the weak, and to further the welfare of the people."

Although the resulting system of laws relied on earlier law codes, the Code of Hammurabi was the first effort by an empire to record all its laws. The code contained 282 laws arranged under headings such as trade, family, labor, real estate, and personal property.

The basic principle behind Hammurabi's Code was "an eye for an eye and a tooth for a tooth." A man who blinded another was punished by losing an eye. If a house collapsed and killed the owner, the builder was put to death.

MAP STUDY *The empire established by Hammurabi included most of the land that had been ruled by the Akkadians. How many miles did Hammurabi's Empire extend along the Tigris River?*

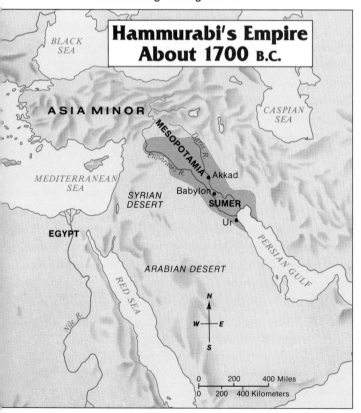

Hammurabi's Empire About 1700 B.C.

Despite the severity of most punishments, Hammurabi's Code was an important contribution to civilization. It distinguished between major and minor offenses, and it established the state as the authority that would enforce the law. It also tried to guarantee social justice. The punishment was supposed to fit the crime.

Hammurabi had the laws carved on a stone column, which was placed for everyone to see. Atop the column sat Shamash, the sun god and god of justice, handing the laws to Hammurabi. The god's image reminded Babylonians that by breaking a law they not only offended the king but also the gods.

Beginning of the Iron Age

After Hammurabi's death, rebellions and invasions weakened the Babylonian Empire. In 1600 B.C., it fell to invaders from the east. About 1550 B.C., another group of invaders, the Hittites, moved into the Fertile Crescent from Asia Minor. The empire established by the Hittites eventually reached as far as the northern Euphrates Valley. Hittite rulers adopted Babylonian cuneiform and ideas about government and religion, which they carried back into Asia Minor.

The Hittites owed their military success to careful strategy, skillful diplomacy, and superior weapons. Expert metalworkers, they were among the first people to use iron for spears and battle axes. Iron weapons gave the Hittites an advantage over enemies armed with softer bronze spears.

The Hittites carefully guarded the secret of ironworking. Even so, the new technology spread to other peoples. By 1200 B.C., iron was being used in place of bronze, ushering in the Iron Age. The Hittites soon lost their military advantage. About the same time, a new onslaught of invaders swept into Asia Minor and the Fertile Crescent, destroying the Hittite Empire and the sophisticated city-state civilizations of Mesopotamia.

The Assyrians

Among the peoples who invaded the Fertile Crescent after 1200 B.C., the most feared and hated were the Assyrians (uh SIHR ee uhnz).

The Assyrians were hardy nomads who settled in the Tigris Valley, where they built a city-state named after their chief god, Assur (AH sur). Beginning about 1100 B.C., the Assyrians conquered people after people until they had an empire that included the entire Fertile Crescent as well as Egypt. (See the map on page 45.)

The mighty Assyrian Empire depended on a highly disciplined army. Iron weapons, an excellent cavalry, and iron-tipped battering rams carried the Assyrians from one victory to the next. Once a city was conquered, the Assyrians showed no mercy. "I cut off their heads and like heaps of grain, I piled them up," boasted one Assyrian ruler. "I skinned alive all the chief men. Their young men and maidens I burned in the fire," wrote another. When the Assyrians captured Babylon, about 700 B.C., they tortured and beheaded prisoners, enslaved women and children, and reduced the city to rubble.

Assyrian government was as harsh and efficient as the Assyrian army. The empire was divided into provinces, each ruled by a governor responsible to the king, who had absolute power. The Assyrians built roads to speed the movement of their army from the capital to the provinces. They deported groups of troublesome people to remote parts of the empire, where they could not organize rebellions. One side effect of these forced migrations was an exchange of ideas among the conquered peoples of the Fertile Crescent.

With war loot and taxes collected from conquered peoples, the Assyrians built a capital at Nineveh (NIHN uh vuh). The Assyrian king Assurbanipal (AH sur BAHN ih pahl) built a great library at Nineveh. In it, he stored a vast collection of over 22,000 clay tablets written in the cuneiform of Sumer and Babylon. Although the Assyrians were despised as brutal conquerors, they made a lasting contribution to civilization by organizing and preserving these invaluable records in the world's first library.

Revival of Babylon

In 612 B.C., oppressed peoples within the Assyrian Empire joined the Medes and Chaldeans (kal DEE uhnz) to capture and destroy Nine-

"I am Assurbanipal, King of the Universe, King of Assyria. I seized a fierce lion of the plain by his ears. I pierced his body with my lance." Thus, the ruthless Assyrian leader celebrated his hunting skill. The lion hunt shown here was one of a series of sculptures that decorated Assurbanipal's palace at Nineveh.

veh. The victors divided up the Assyrian Empire. The Medes occupied the highlands north of Mesopotamia, and the Chaldeans established an empire in Mesopotamia proper. During the reign of Nebuchadnezzar (NEHB uh kuhd NEHZ uhr), the Chaldeans extended their empire over the Fertile Crescent.

Nebuchadnezzar rebuilt Babylon as a symbol of his power. Massive walls surrounded the city and the outlying farmlands, protecting the food supply during a siege. Nebuchadnezzar's immense palace, decorated with blue glazed bricks, was rivaled in splendor by the famous hanging gardens of Babylon. According to legend, Nebuchadnezzar designed the gardens for his wife, who despised the flat plains of Mesopotamia and longed for the mountains of her Median homeland. The many terraces filled with exotic plants and trees amazed travelers, who returned home awed by this wonder of the ancient world.

Like earlier peoples of Mesopotamia, the Chaldeans advanced the study of mathematics and astronomy, largely because of their interest in astrology. They believed that the positions of the stars and planets and the movement of comets determined the fates of

43

Much praised by visitors for the palace of Nebuchadnezzar and its magnificent hanging gardens, ancient Babylon was a truly remarkable city. This lion of glazed tiles once decorated a gate to the city, the great Gate of Ishtar.

individuals and empires. By charting the paths of planets, stars, and comets, Chaldean priests acquired a vast store of knowledge about eclipses and the movement of heavenly bodies. They also accurately calculated the length of a year to within a few minutes. Priests, who used their knowledge of the stars to predict the future, occupied a privileged position in Chaldean society.

After the death of Nebuchadnezzar, the Chaldean Empire, like those before it, suffered civil wars. In 539 B.C., Babylon fell to invading Persians. Unlike the Assyrians, the Persians left the city standing, and it remained a flourishing center of commerce and learning.

The Persians

The Persians rapidly became a powerful force in the ancient Middle East. In 550 B.C., Cyrus (SĪ rehs), king of Persia, led a successful revolt against the Medes. Within 20 years, he had conquered the Fertile Crescent and Asia Minor. His successors added Afghanistan, northern India, and Egypt to the Persian Empire. (See the map on page 45.) Cyrus was a remarkable military leader and a wise ruler. He treated conquered peoples with tolerance, allowed them some self-government, and respected their religions and customs.

Government. Cyrus's son-in-law, Darius (duh RĪ uhs), completed the task of organizing the vast Persian Empire. Copying the Assyrian model, he divided the empire into 20 provinces, or **satrapies** (SAY truh peez). Each satrapy was ruled by a governor, or satrap, who collected taxes and administered uniform laws. As a check on the satrap, Darius sent royal inspectors, called "the Eyes and Ears of the King," into every province.

To ensure rapid communication, the Persians improved the Assyrian road system. The main highway, the Great Royal Road, stretched from Asia Minor to Susa, one of the four capitals of the empire. Relay stations with fresh horses were set up along the Great Royal Road so that royal messengers could cover 1,600 miles (2,560 kilometers) in ten days.

The efficient government and transportation system, as well as trade and the policy of toleration, helped draw the empire together. Yet Persian power did not go unchallenged. As you will read in Chapter 4, Darius and his heirs failed to conquer Greece. In 331 B.C., a weakened Persian Empire fell to the armies of Alexander the Great.

Religion. Although the early Persians believed in many gods, by the time of Darius they had adopted a new religion named after its founder, Zoroaster (ZOH roh AS ter). According to Zoroaster, who lived about 600 B.C., the world was a battleground for the forces of good and evil. Every individual made a choice in his or her lifetime to join Ahura Mazda (AH hu ruh MAZ duh), god of goodness, wisdom, and truth, or to follow Ahriman (AH rih muhn), the evil spirit. Zoroaster predicted that at the end of the world Ahura Mazda would win the final battle. Those who had lived moral lives would be rewarded with eternal life in paradise. Those who had followed Ahriman would be condemned to eternal suffering.

The sacred book of Zoroastrians was the *Zend Avesta* (ZEHND uh VEHS tuh). This collection of hymns and religious poems contained several ideas that influenced later peoples of the Fertile Crescent. For example, Zoroastrians emphasized ethical, or moral, conduct. They also believed in a final day of judgment and in the role of the individual in determining his or her salvation. Later, Hebrews and Christians stressed similar concepts.

SECTION 2 REVIEW

1. **Locate:** (a) Akkad, (b) Babylon, (c) Asia Minor, (d) Nineveh, (e) Susa.

2. **Identify:** (a) Sargon, (b) Hammurabi, (c) Assurbanipal, (d) Nebuchadnezzar, (e) Zoroaster, (f) *Zend Avesta*.

3. **Define:** satrapy.

4. (a) Why did Hammurabi draw up a law code? (b) What aspects of life did it cover?

5. How did the Assyrians organize their empire?

6. According to Zoroaster, what two forces were at war in the world?

7. **Critical Thinking** How do you think the policies Cyrus followed toward the people he conquered benefited the Persian Empire?

MAP STUDY *The Assyrians and the Persians established vast empires in the ancient Middle East. Both depended on good roads to help tie their empires together. Why do you think the Persians created four separate capitals?*

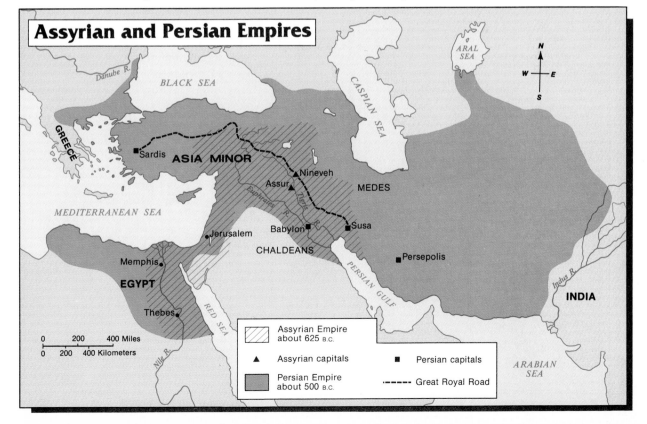

Assyrian and Persian Empires

3 Contributions of Smaller States

READD TO UNDERSTAND

☐ How the Phoenicians helped spread civilization.

☐ How the Lydians influenced economic life in the Middle East.

☐ What religious and ethical beliefs the Hebrews developed.

☐ *Vocabulary:* money economy, covenant.

While the great empires of the ancient Middle East were expanding through conquest, several small, independent states were also making lasting contributions. Between 1200 B.C. and 500 B.C., the Phoenicians (fuh NEESH uhnz), Lydians (LIHD ee uhnz), and Hebrews made advances in the areas of writing, trade, and religion.

Phoenicians: Carriers of Civilization

The Phoenicians built small city-states along the eastern Mediterranean coast, in the area of present-day Lebanon. They thrived on profits from trading. To cities around the Mediterranean, the Phoenicians brought timber from cedar trees and a rare purple dye made from a tiny sea snail. Because Phoenician purple cloth was very expensive and was worn mostly by kings, the color purple came to be associated with royalty.

MAP STUDY *The Phoenicians founded colonies along the shores of the Mediterranean Sea, as this map shows. Daring Phoenician sailors ventured into the Atlantic as far north as Britain and probably rounded southern Africa in search of gold and ivory. How did the locations of Phoenicia and Palestine make them vulnerable to invasion by other peoples?*

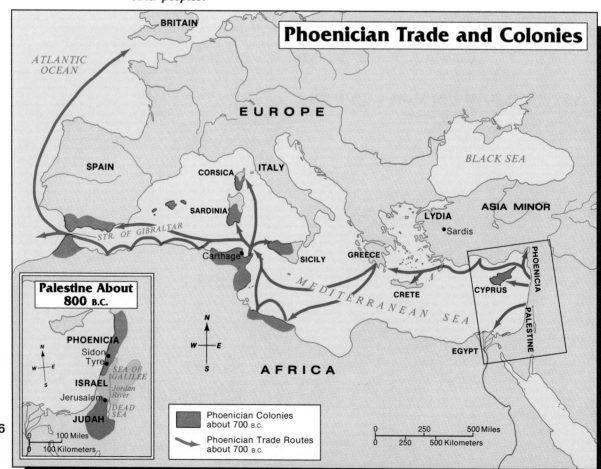

Phoenician Trade and Colonies

Phoenician Colonies about 700 B.C.

Phoenician Trade Routes about 700 B.C.

Palestine About 800 B.C.

PHOENICIA
Sidon
Tyre
SEA OF GALILEE
ISRAEL
Jerusalem
Jordan River
DEAD SEA
JUDAH
100 Miles
100 Kilometers

46

From the bustling port cities of Tyre and Sidon, Phoenician traders crisscrossed the Mediterranean. Beginning about 1200 B.C., they founded a network of colonies from Cyprus to Gibraltar. (See the map at left.) About 814 B.C., they settled Carthage in northern Africa. Carthage dominated trade in the western Mediterranean until 146 B.C., when it was destroyed by the Romans.

The Phoenicians earned the name "carriers of civilization" for their role in spreading the culture of the ancient world. Through trade and colonization, they introduced the achievements of Mesopotamia and Egypt to the less-advanced peoples of the western Mediterranean. They also made their own contribution by improving the alphabet.

The Phoenician alphabet contained 22 symbols, each of which represented a single consonant. Unlike cuneiform and the Egyptian system of writing, the new alphabet was fairly easy to learn.

Phoenician merchants and colonists spread the use of their alphabet. About 800 B.C., the Greeks adopted it and added symbols for vowel sounds. Later, the Romans adapted the Greek alphabet, and they passed the resulting written language on to the western world. The very word "alphabet" comes from "aleph" and "beth," the first two symbols of the Phoenician alphabet.

The Lydians: Influential Traders

Like the Phoenicians, the Lydians left their mark on history through trade rather than conquest. From their capital, Sardis, the Lydians dominated trade in Asia Minor.

The most significant contribution of the Lydians was the introduction of coined money as a medium of exchange in trade. Earlier, people had relied on the barter system, exchanging one set of goods for another. The barter system limited trade because two people could trade with one another only if each had a product the other one wanted. The use of coins eliminated that problem. Furthermore, coins could be stored and saved for later use, and they allowed merchants to establish a system of set prices. An economic system based on money rather than barter is called a **money economy.**

Through trade with the Greeks and Persians, Lydian merchants spread the idea of using coined money. Lydian coins were imprinted with the king's image as a guarantee that they were the correct weight and value. Wherever coinage came into use, a more complex economic system developed.

The Hebrews

South of Phoenicia was Palestine, another crossroads for nomadic herders and conquering armies. (See the map at left.) Among the many peoples who migrated into the Jordan River valley of Palestine after 2000 B.C. were the Hebrews. Although the Hebrews ruled a small state for a relatively brief period, their religious beliefs profoundly affected later civilizations in the western world.

Early history. The Hebrews believed that God was the moving force behind everything that happened to them. To show God's role in history, they preserved their early history in a sacred text, known today as the Old Testament. According to the Old Testament, God gave Canaan, or Palestine, to the Hebrews. About 1800 B.C., drought and famine forced some Hebrews to migrate to Egypt, where the pharaohs eventually enslaved them. The Old Testament book of Exodus records how a courageous man named Moses forced the pharaoh to free the Hebrews.

The Hebrews considered Moses one of their most important leaders and their chief law giver. After leading the Hebrews out of Egypt, Moses gave them the Ten Commandments, a set of religious and moral laws. The Hebrews believed that God had revealed the laws to Moses and had thereby made a **covenant,** or binding agreement, with them. According to that covenant, God would protect the Hebrews as the "Chosen People" if they obeyed the commandments.

Obedience to God's laws bound the Hebrews together as they wandered from Egypt, across the Sinai, into Palestine. Hardened by life in the desert, they fought the Philistines and other peoples for control of the Jordan River valley. About 1025 B.C., the Hebrews organized the kingdom of Israel in Palestine.

The kingdom of Israel. During the reigns of David and Solomon, from about 1000

Two women stood before Solomon, king of Israel, begging him to settle a bitter quarrel. We share a house, explained the first woman. Recently, we both gave birth to sons. Her son died during the night, she went on, but she switched her dead child with my live son and claimed it was hers! That's not true, interrupted the second woman. My child is alive—yours is dead!

Solomon, famous for his wisdom, listened to the women argue. Then he turned to a servant and ordered him to bring a sword. Cut the live child in half, he commanded the servant, and give half to each woman.

The second woman agreed to Solomon's solution. No, cried the first one. Do not hurt the child. Let her have him instead. The king stared at the women, then gave his judgment. Do not touch the child, he said. The first woman was moved by a mother's love, and the child is hers. When the people of Israel heard the story, they praised the wisdom of Solomon.

Most of what we know about Solomon comes from Old Testament accounts such as this one. The Old Testament shows Solomon as a builder and a man of peace. But he was also a ruler who saw the need for military strength. He spent huge sums on horse-drawn chariots—high technology weapons at the time. He fortified Israel's frontier cities, sent squads of charioteers to guard them, and rebuilt the walls of Jerusalem.

Solomon's greatest work was not a fortress, but a temple dedicated to the one God of the Hebrews. The outside of the temple was pure gold. This First Temple of the Hebrews was so famous that 1,500 years later, when the Christian emperor Justinian completed his huge cathedral of Santa Sophia, he exclaimed, "Oh, Solomon, at last I have outdone you!"

During Solomon's reign, art and learning flourished. The king himself led the way. Besides writing 3,000 proverbs, he was an expert on botany and zoology. The mosaic of Solomon below is from the twelfth century A.D.

Despite his wisdom, Solomon created resentment among his people. He not only raised taxes to build his many projects but also forced his subjects to "donate" their labor to get the work done. Solomon's heirs paid the price for his ambitions.

1. How did Solomon's order to cut the child in half settle the dispute between the two women?

2. **Critical Thinking** How did Solomon's policies both strengthen and weaken Israel?

to 930 B.C., the kingdom of Israel flourished. A successful general and skillful diplomat, David decisively defeated the Philistines and forged alliances with other peoples to make the Hebrews supreme in Palestine. David's son Solomon transformed the city of Jerusalem into a magnificent capital. In the center of Jerusalem, he built a massive temple that symbolized the Hebrew faith.

Solomon's lavish spending required heavy taxes, which caused popular discontent. After Solomon died, in 930 B.C., violent disagreements split the kingdom into two separate states: Israel in the north and Judah in the south. Powerful empires soon threatened the Hebrew kingdoms. In 722 B.C., the Assyrians conquered Israel and exiled thousands of Hebrews to distant corners of their empire. In 586 B.C., Nebuchadnezzar seized Judah, destroyed the temple in Jerusalem, and sent the Hebrews as slaves to Babylon.

The Persians later freed the Hebrews from captivity. Some of the Hebrews returned to Jerusalem and rebuilt their temple. However,

Israel no longer existed as an independent state. The Persians, then the Greeks, and later the Romans ruled Palestine. Although they no longer had their own state, the Hebrews preserved their religious ideas and cultural traditions because of the covenant they believed they had with God. Many of these ideas would influence two other religions that later rose in the Middle East—Christianity and Islam.

An Ethical World View

Unlike other peoples of the ancient Middle East, the Hebrews were monotheistic. They believed in one all-powerful God, called Yahweh. But their view of God changed over time. To the early Hebrews, God was a fierce, vengeful figure who inflicted harsh punishments if angered. Later, the Hebrews came to see God as wise and forgiving.

Hebrew law. The Hebrews developed an ethical world view—that is, they believed that people and their rulers should lead moral lives. This view grew out of the moral and religious laws recorded in the first five books of the Old Testament, which are called the Torah. Among the most important laws of the Torah are the Ten Commandments, which forbid lying, cheating, stealing, and murder. The commandments also counsel men and women to be just, love their neighbors, and obey their parents.

According to the Hebrews, no one was above God's law, not even a king. A Hebrew king was not considered a god or the earthly representative of gods as kings were in other cultures of the ancient Middle East.

Hebrew laws, as expressed in the Torah, have been compared to Hammurabi's Code since both law codes contained the principle of "an eye for an eye." However, Hammurabi's laws, which set the death penalty for many minor offenses, were more severe. Hebrew law generally held human life in greater respect, leaving the ultimate judgment and punishment to God. Furthermore, while slavery was an accepted practice in the ancient world, Hebrew law demanded that slaves be treated with kindness.

Women had few rights under Hebrew law, but respect for women was taught in the commandment "honor thy father and thy mother." In addition, the Hebrews honored certain outstanding women, such as the prophet Deborah, who, according to the Old Testament, led the Hebrews to a victory against their enemies in Palestine.

Prophets. Prophets contributed to the Hebrews' ethical world view. The Hebrews believed that the prophets were messengers God sent to reveal His will. Prophets scolded the Hebrews for wickedness, laziness, and worshipping other gods. The prophet Isaiah (ī ZAY uh), for example, called on the king and people of Judah to "cease to do evil, learn to do good, seek justice, relieve the oppressed, judge [look after] the fatherless, plead for the widow." Out of the teachings of the prophets, the Hebrews developed strong traditions that stressed respect for the individual, concern for the poor, and obedience to God's laws.

Some Hebrew beliefs were similar to the beliefs of other peoples in the ancient Middle East. Like the Zoroastrians, for example, they believed that individuals had to make a choice between good and evil. However, the Hebrews were the first people to develop an ethical world view, which included the basic principles of belief in one God and concern for individuals.

SECTION 3 REVIEW

1. **Locate:** (a) Sidon, (b) Tyre, (c) Phoenicia, (d) Carthage, (e) Sardis, (f) Palestine, (g) Jordan River, (h) Jerusalem.

2. **Identify:** (a) Ten Commandments, (b) Moses, (c) David, (d) Solomon, (e) Torah.

3. **Define:** (a) money economy, (b) covenant.

4. Why were the Phoenicians called "carriers of civilization"?

5. How did Hebrew law differ from Hammurabi's code?

6. **Critical Thinking** How did the Ten Commandments contribute to the Hebrew ethical world view?

CHAPTER 2 REVIEW

Summary

1. **Sumer was the first civilization to develop in the ancient Middle East.** It rose in the fertile Tigris-Euphrates Valley. But the Tigris and Euphrates rivers behaved very differently from the Nile, with its predictable floods. Despite destructive floods, the Sumerians built an advanced civilization.

2. **Migrations and invasions spread Sumerian achievements across the ancient Middle East.** Conquerors also left their marks on the civilization of this region. Hammurabi developed a unified code of law. The Hittites introduced ironworking, and the Assyrians imposed an efficient government organization. The Persians' system of government and religion had widespread influence.

3. **Smaller states also made contributions to civilization.** The Phoenicians improved the alphabet, and the Lydians introduced coined money. The Hebrews developed a monotheistic religion that stressed ethical conduct.

Recalling Facts

Decide if the following statements are true or false. If a statement is false, rewrite it to make it true.

1. The Sumerians viewed their gods as friendly and helpful.

2. Many peoples of the ancient Middle East adopted cuneiform writing.

3. Under Hammurabi's Code, the penalty for every crime was death.

4. The Assyrians destroyed the records of earlier civilizations.

5. Zoroaster believed the forces of evil would defeat the forces of good.

6. The Phoenicians improved the alphabet by using symbols to represent sounds.

7. The Hebrews were polytheistic.

Chapter Checkup

1. How did the geography of Mesopotamia probably affect Sumerian religious beliefs?

2. (a) What was the basic principle of the Code of Hammurabi? (b) Why was Hammurabi's Code an important achievement?

3. Describe the contributions the following peoples made to civilization: (a) Hittites; (b) Assyrians; (c) Chaldeans.

4. Based on the map on page 45 and your reading, compare the Assyrian and Persian empires in terms of: (a) size; (b) treatment of conquered peoples; (c) government organization.

5. (a) What were the main religious beliefs of the Zoroastrians? (b) How did the teachings of Zoroaster encourage people to live good lives?

6. (a) How did the teachings of the prophets contribute to the Hebrew world view? (b) How did Hebrew religious beliefs differ from the beliefs of other peoples of the ancient Middle East?

Critical Thinking

1. **Comparing Civilizations** (a) What practical advances did the Sumerians make in writing, mathematics, and architecture? (b) How were these advances similar to Egyptian achievements? (c) How might you explain similar achievements in both civilizations?

2. **Applying Information** Rulers of the great empires of the ancient Middle East had to develop ways to unite many different peoples and control large territories. Describe the methods Sargon, Hammurabi, and Darius used to bind their empires together. Which ruler do you think developed the most effective methods of creating unity? Explain.

3. **Relating Past to Present** Which civilization of the ancient Middle East do you think had the greatest impact on the world today? Give examples to support your answer.

4. **Understanding the Roots of Democracy** (a) What attitude did the Hebrews develop toward the individual in society? (b) What view did the Hebrews and Zoroastrians share about individual responsibility? (c) Compare these attitudes and views with those held by people in a democratic society today.

Developing Basic Skills

1. **Comparing Geographic Settings** Make a chart with four columns. In column one, list the geographical advantages of Egypt. In column two, list the disadvantages. In columns three and four, list the geographical advantages and disadvantages of Sumer. (a) Which civilization had the most geographic advantages? (b) Which had the most geographic disadvantages? (c) How might geography have contributed to the differing outlooks of the Egyptians and Sumerians?

2. **Map Reading** Study the map and the inset map on page 46. (a) What information do the maps provide? (b) Where did the Phoenicians establish colonies? (c) What geographic factors might have encouraged the Phoenicians to turn from agriculture to trade? (d) Why were the Phoenicians in a good position to become "carriers of civilization"?

Writing About History

Rewording a Question as a Topic Sentence

The topic sentence expresses the central idea of a paragraph. It tells the reader what the paragraph is about. In the answer to an essay question, the topic sentence is often the first sentence in the paragraph. It should say what the instruction word is calling for and what ideas will be covered. You can often rewrite the essay question in order to form this type of topic sentence.

Read the following essay question: *Compare the religious beliefs of the Hebrews and the Sumerians.* A topic sentence based on this question might read: *The religious views of the Hebrews differed from those of the Sumerians in many ways.* A clear topic sentence is important because the other sentences in the paragraph develop the idea in the topic sentence.

Practice: Reword the question as a topic sentence for an answer to each of the Critical Thinking questions in this Chapter Review.

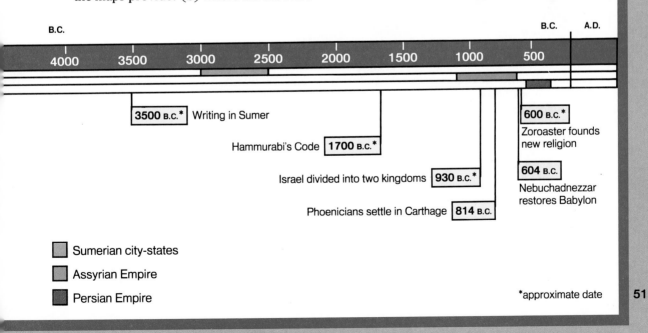

B.C.   B.C.   A.D.

| 4000 | 3500 | 3000 | 2500 | 2000 | 1500 | 1000 | 500 |

3500 B.C.* Writing in Sumer

Hammurabi's Code **1700 B.C.***

Israel divided into two kingdoms **930 B.C.***

Phoenicians settle in Carthage **814 B.C.**

600 B.C.*
Zoroaster founds new religion

604 B.C.
Nebuchadnezzar restores Babylon

◻ Sumerian city-states

◼ Assyrian Empire

◼ Persian Empire

*approximate date

51

Ancient India and China

3

(2500 B.C.—256 B.C.)

This ancient bronze rhinoceros, about 13 inches high, was accidentally discovered by a Chinese farmer plowing his field. It was probably a container for liquids, since there is a hinged lid on its back and its mouth is a spout.

Waiting in his chariot for the great battle to begin, Arjuna was filled with doubts. "My limbs are weakened, my mouth is parching, my body trembles, my hair stands upright," he complained to Krishna, his chariot driver. At that moment, all of India seemed to be caught in a vast civil war. To Arjuna, the thought of fighting friends and relatives was agonizing. Even though he knew his cause was just, Arjuna hesitated. "How could we dare spill the blood that unites us? Where is the joy in the killing of kinsmen?"

But Krishna, a god who had taken mortal form, scolded Arjuna for his weakness. Through the night, Krishna instructed the young warrior about life, death, and the right course of human action. "There is more joy in doing one's own duty badly," said Krishna, "than in doing another man's duty well." It was Arjuna's duty, Krishna explained, to destroy his enemies. "If you do not fight this just battle, you will fail in your own law and in your honor and you will incur sin." The battle raged for 18 days. In the end, Arjuna and his brothers were victorious, and they restored peace to India.

The conversation between Arjuna and Krishna appears in the "Bhagavad-Gita" (BUHG uh vuhd GEE tuh) or "The Song of God," a religious poem of India. The Aryan (AIR ee uhn) civilization that produced "The Song of God" was not the first civilization to develop in India. Around 2500 B.C., the earliest Indian civilization had emerged in the Indus River valley. The great cities of the Indus Valley civilization flourished for about 1,000 years but were destroyed by invading Aryans. As Aryan civilization evolved, it created traditions that have shaped Indian culture up to the present.

Thousands of miles northeast of India, in the Yellow River valley of China, small farming villages formed the basis of the first Chinese civilization. Like the Aryans in India, the Chinese established traditions that endured for centuries. ■

1 The First Civilization in India

READ TO UNDERSTAND

☐ **How geography has influenced the history of India.**

☐ **Why our knowledge of the earliest civilizations in India is limited.**

☐ **What the cities of the Indus Valley civilization were like.**

☐ *Vocabulary:* **monsoon.**

Clouds darken the sky, boiling up in huge banks as they roll in from the sea. Thunder and lightning clash furiously. People wait eagerly for the clouds to give up their promised moisture. The rain pours in torrents, reviving the parched land. Today, as in ancient times, the people of India welcome the rains as a sign of the goodness from heaven.

In India, as in Egypt and Sumer, farming villages in a fertile river valley gave birth to the first civilization. From 2500 B.C. to 1500 B.C., the great cities of Harappa (hah RAP ah) and Mohenjo-Daro (moh HEHN joh DAHR roh) were the center of a prosperous civilization in the Indus River valley. To understand the development of civilization in ancient India, we need to look further at the geography of India.

GEOGRAPHIC SETTING
The Indian Subcontinent

The Indian subcontinent is a large peninsula, surrounded on three sides by water—the Arabian Sea, the Indian Ocean, and the Bay of Bengal. In the north, the Himalaya (HIH muh LAY uh) Mountains separate India from the rest of Asia. The towering Himalayas form a nearly impassable barrier 1,500 miles (2,400 kilometers) long. The rugged Hindu Kush Mountains to the northwest also presented barriers to travel. (See the map on page 54.)

These geographic barriers allowed the first Indian civilization to develop mostly on its own. Yet India was not totally isolated. Determined invaders pushed their way through steep passes, such as the Khyber (KI ber) Pass in the Hindu Kush. Indian traders carried goods through the mountain passes to the Middle East and China. Furthermore, the surrounding seas served as highways for commercial and cultural contact.

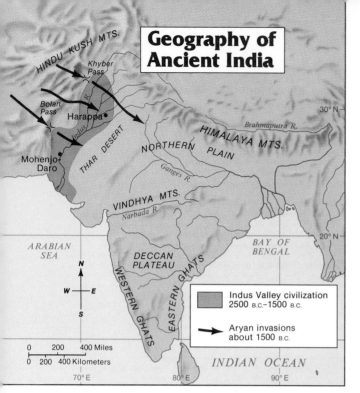

Geography of Ancient India

MAP STUDY *Geography played an important role in the development of civilization in India as it did elsewhere. How did invading Aryans find their way into India?*

Three regions of India. The vast Indian subcontinent has many diverse geographic features. However, the three major regions are: the northern plain, the Deccan (DEHK uhn) Plateau, and the coastal plains.

Three great rivers—the Indus, Ganges (GAN jeez), and Brahmaputra (BRAH muh POO truh)—flow through the northern plain. These broad, slow rivers flow from the snow-covered Himalayas. Together with their tributaries, they supply water for farming and for transportation across the northern plain. The fertile soil of the river valleys supports extensive farming. For these reasons, the northern plain became the home of the first Indian civilization. Later, invaders set up powerful empires in the northern plain. As a result, the area has played a dominant role in Indian history.

The Deccan Plateau is the triangular-shaped heart of the subcontinent. The Vindhya (VIHND yah) Mountains separate the plateau from the northern plain. The Deccan Plateau is bordered on the west and east by long mountain ranges, the Western and Eastern Ghats. Because it lacks the snow-fed rivers found in

the north, the Deccan Plateau suffers from droughts, which makes farming difficult.

Along the eastern and western coasts of India lie narrow coastal plains, which support both agriculture and fishing. Although India has few good natural harbors, many coastal peoples of India were seafarers who traded with peoples in other parts of Asia, Africa, and the Middle East.

The monsoon. The chief feature of the Indian climate is the **monsoon,** a seasonal wind. The monsoon regulates Indian life much as the various seasons affect life in North America. From June until September, the summer monsoon blows from the southwest, picking up moisture over the Indian Ocean and dropping torrential rains on the coast and on the northern plain. From October to May, the winter monsoon blows from lands to the northeast. These hot, dry winds raise temperatures to over 100° F (38° C), shrivel crops, and make outdoor work nearly impossible.

Every year, the people of India wait anxiously for the summer monsoon to bring desperately needed moisture to the parched farmlands. When the rains come, temperatures drop and crops spring to life. If the monsoon is late, crops fail and food shortages result. The heavy rains can cause destructive floods, especially in the lower Ganges Valley. ■

Discovery of the Indus Valley Civilization

In 1921, archaeologists discovered traces of an ancient civilization in the Indus River valley. Since then, excavations have revealed that this civilization developed about the same time as the early Egyptian and Sumerian civilizations. The Indus Valley civilization stretched for 950 miles (1,500 kilometers), covering an area larger than the Old Kingdom in Egypt. Each of its chief cities, Harappa and Mohenjo-Daro, was larger than any Sumerian city-state. Yet we know relatively little about the Indus Valley civilization.

Two factors have left us with many unanswered questions. First, scholars have so far been unable to decipher the written language of the Indus Valley people. Second, Harappa and Mohenjo-Daro can only be partially excavated. Because these cities lie close to rivers, deep trenches cannot be dug without the danger of flooding. Despite these handicaps, archaeologists have uncovered some valuable information about India's first civilization.

Planned Cities

The ruins of Harappa and Mohenjo-Daro reveal that they were the products of the first city planning in history. Wide, straight streets divide residential areas into square city blocks. Archaeologists have excavated houses, granaries, public halls, and shops. Both cities had extensive sewer systems. Walled fortresses with towers provided protection.

To create such well-planned cities, the people needed a knowledge of surveying and geometry. Furthermore, only a strong central government in each city could have supervised the planning and construction.

Government and religion. Scholars are not sure who ruled the Indus Valley cities, but they think that a priest-king probably headed the government of each city. The rulers must have had considerable power because the governments exercised strict control. For ex-

ample, they controlled construction of new buildings and established standards of weights and measures. Because of the tight control, writing, building styles, street plans, and even the size of bricks remained unchanged for nearly 1,000 years.

Like the Egyptians and Sumerians, the Indus Valley people were polytheistic. Statues and masks show that they worshipped a mother-goddess and a three-faced god. They also revered sacred animals such as the bull and certain sacred trees.

Economic life. The Indus Valley civilization had a thriving agricultural economy. On lands surrounding the cities, farmers constructed dams and levees to channel water from the rivers to crops of wheat, barley, melons, and dates. Food surpluses supported the large city populations and prompted a growth of trade. Indus Valley farmers were the first people to grow cotton, and cotton cloth became a major item of trade.

A merchant class prospered from the trade and commerce in the cities. Merchants exported cotton cloth to places as far away as Mesopotamia. In return, they received precious metals. Wealthy citizens could then hire

SKILL LESSON Ancient India and China: Skimming a Chapter

Skimming can be very useful when studying world history. To skim a chapter, you read through it rapidly to get a general idea of what the chapter is about. Having an overview can help you pick out the main ideas as you read the chapter more carefully. Use these steps to skim Chapter 3.

1 **Read the complete title.** (a) Write a sentence describing the topic of the chapter. (b) What years of history are covered in the chapter?

2 **Read the chapter outline and introduction.** (a) How many sections are in the chapter? (b) In which section would you expect to learn about the first Chinese civilization? (c) What clues does the introductory story give you about the history of ancient India?

3 **Read the main headings, the Read to Understand statements, and the introductory paragraphs.** (a) What is the topic of Section 1? (b) List one main idea of the section based on the Read to Understand statements. (c) Based on the section introduction, why should you study the geographic setting of India?

4 **Read the subheadings within the sections.** (a) List the subheadings of Section 1. (b) State one characteristic of the first civilization in India based on the subheadings.

5 **Read the chapter summary.** (a) Based on the summary, who conquered the Indus Valley in 1500 B.C.? (b) Which dynasty ruled during the first civilization in China?

THE CITY OF MOHENJO-DARO *Using the latest information uncovered by archaeologists, artist Robert Casilla has recreated a street in Mohenjo-Daro, one of the chief cities of the ancient Indus Valley. Public baths, shops, and dwellings were built according to strict rules. Even the bricks used were uniform. Streets were laid out in regular patterns, determined by Mohenjo-Daro's rulers.*

artisans to make furniture inlaid with the precious metals. Artisans also crafted fine gold jewelry and made realistic stone carvings of monkeys and birds.

Decline of the Indus Valley civilization. Evidence from the diggings shows that the Indus Valley civilization began to decline many years before it finally ended about 1500 B.C. Builders abandoned the uniform standards of earlier times, and the quality of work declined. The arts showed less creativity, and trade with Mesopotamia dwindled. These signs of decay indicate that the government had lost some of its power.

Most authorities believe that about 1500 B.C. Aryan invaders struck the final blow to the Indus Valley civilization. When the Indus Valley cities fell the people fled to other parts of India. Thus, while the civilizations of Egypt and Sumer affected later peoples, the Indus Valley civilization had little lasting impact. After 1500 B.C., it was virtually forgotten until modern times.

SECTION 1 REVIEW

1. **Locate:** (a) Arabian Sea, (b) Indian Ocean, (c) Bay of Bengal, (d) Himalaya Mountains, (e) Hindu Kush Mountains, (f) Indus River, (g) Ganges River, (h) Deccan Plateau, (i) Harappa, (j) Mohenjo-Daro.

2. **Define:** monsoon.

3. Which geographical region was the home of the first Indian civilization? Why?

4. Why is the summer monsoon important to the people of India?

5. What evidence suggests that the Indus Valley cities were the result of careful planning?

6. **Critical Thinking** Why was farming essential to the prosperous trade of the Indus Valley people?

2 The Aryans

READ TO UNDERSTAND

☐ **What role rajahs came to play in Indian life.**

☐ **How Aryan religious beliefs evolved.**

☐ **How the Aryan social class system changed over time.**

☐ *Vocabulary:* **tribe, rajah, reincarnation, extended family, caste.**

Danger threatened from the west. The people of Harappa strengthened their defensive walls and blocked a main gateway to the city. But to no avail. When the fierce horse-riding Aryans attacked and occupied outlying villages, thousands fled the city. With their superior weapons and terrifying beasts, the newcomers overpowered the few who remained.

Thus did cities of the Indus Valley civilization fall to invaders about 1500 B.C. The Aryans swept into India through the passes of the Hindu Kush Mountains. These fierce nomadic herders had come originally from the region between the Black and Caspian seas north of the Caucasus Mountains.*

Conquest by the Aryans

Like many nomadic people, the Aryans did not move as a single unit. Rather, they were loosely organized into tribes. A **tribe** consists of groups of related families who recognize a common ancestor, speak the same language, and share the same traditions and beliefs. In each Aryan tribe, a **rajah** (RAH juh), or elected chief, served as the leader in war. He governed the tribe with the aid of councils made up of elders and other free men. The rajah was not

---

* The Aryans were one of several groups of people to migrate out of that area between about 2000 B.C. and 1500 B.C. Some, such as the Hittites, invaded the Middle East. Others, such as the ancestors of the Greeks and Romans, moved into Europe. Because of the common origins of these groups, historians have called them Indo-Europeans.

worshipped as a god, nor did he have power to impose taxes. His wealth depended on gifts from the people and loot taken in war.

Under the rajahs, Aryan tribes fought their way into the Indus Valley. Between 1500 B.C. and 1000 B.C., they pushed eastward, bringing the northern plain under their control. Gradually, the Aryans gave up their nomadic way of life and settled into villages.

The chief enemies of the Aryans during the conquest of the northern plain were the Dravidians (druh VIHD ee uhnz), who were probably survivors of the Indus Valley civilization. In time, the Dravidians retreated into southern India, where their kingdoms later rivaled those of the north.

Even after the Aryans conquered the northern plain, warfare continued to dominate their life. Between 1000 B.C. and 700 B.C., local rajahs battled each other for control of the region. Slowly, the more successful rajahs forged strong, independent kingdoms. By 700 B.C., powerful rajahs were building large capital cities and encouraging trade with the Middle East.

Aryan Religious Beliefs

We know about the early Aryans mostly from their religious traditions, which are contained in the Vedas (VAY duhz). The Vedas were composed between 1500 B.C. and 1000 B.C. They include sacred hymns, prayers, and magic spells used by priests in religious ceremonies. Aryan priests memorized the Vedas and carefully handed them on to each new generation. They are one of the world's oldest surviving religious works.

The Vedas show that the early Aryans worshipped gods of nature, the sun, sky, thunder, and fire. But Indra, the warrior god, led the others. Courageous, youthful, and unbeatable, Indra reflected the optimism and confidence of the Aryans. The Aryans made sacrifices to the gods and in return sought long life, prosperity, and healthy sons. They were more interested in day-to-day concerns than in an afterlife.

Over time, Aryan religious beliefs changed. The oldest of the Vedas has over 1,000 hymns addressed to different gods. But

An ancient Hindu epic, the Ramayana, *has inspired artists for centuries. Its hero, Rama, hurtles from one lively adventure to the next. Rama is sent to earth by the gods to overcome the ten-headed Ravanna, the powerful king of demons. Disguised as a monk, the evil Ravanna kidnaps Rama's beautiful wife Sita, shown in this illustration from the 1700s A.D. Aided by the monkey god, Rama eventually rescues his wife and defeats Ravanna.*

later hymns suggest a growing belief in a single unifying force.

Other changes in religious beliefs appear in the Upanishads (oo PAN ih SHADZ), oral teachings composed between 800 B.C. and 600 B.C. In the Upanishads, priests introduced the belief in **reincarnation,** or rebirth of the soul in another bodily form.

As you will read in Chapter 7, both the Vedas and the Upanishads form part of the sacred literature of Hinduism, the religion that developed out of early Aryan beliefs.

Epic literature. The power struggles between rival Aryan kingdoms gave rise to stories about civil wars and great heroes. Such stories formed the basis of two long epic poems: the *Mahabharata* (muh HAH BAH ruh tuh) and the *Ramayana* (rah MAH yuh nuh).

Like most epics, the *Mahabharata* mixes fact and fiction and glorifies the deeds of heroes. The many short stories in the *Ramayana* illustrate the duties and ideals of Aryan warriors. While the epics focus on worldly concerns such as success in battle, they also weave in religious themes. Because of their religious teachings, they became part of the sacred Hindu texts.

Sanskrit. By about 700 B.C., the Aryans had developed a written language called Sanskrit. Knowledge of Sanskrit belonged mostly to priests, who used the language to record sacred texts. However, even with a written language, priests continued to memorize the ancient hymns and epics and to recite them for the people. In this way, the oral traditions were preserved.

Village Life

As the nomadic Aryans settled into villages, they developed patterns of life that have given order to Indian culture down to the present.

Although a rajah ruled all the villages within a region, most villages enjoyed some self-government. A headman, usually a wealthy farmer, was responsible for a village. Appointed by the rajah, the headman worked with a village council to settle disputes. He also made sure that community irrigation ditches and canals were maintained.

People in Aryan villages farmed and herded cattle. Aryans had valued cattle since their nomadic days, when a major goal of Aryan warriors had been to seize cattle from their enemies. In fact, their word for war meant "the desire for cattle." In early Aryan society, people killed cattle for food. Later, the slaughter of cattle was forbidden although the milk could be used. People also used cattle for plowing and transportation. Even the value of land and tools was expressed in heads of cattle.

The extended family. The extended family was at the heart of village life. An **extended family** includes a husband and wife, their unmarried children, their married sons, and the sons' wives and children. The several generations of an extended family generally live under the same roof. Family members looked after each other and provided for the weak, the old, and even the lazy.

As head of the family, the oldest man had many responsibilities. He performed the family's religious rituals and was its spokesman in village affairs. He arranged marriages for his daughters, educated his sons, and managed the family income.

The status of women. In early Aryan society, women enjoyed relatively high status. When the Aryans invaded India, women warriors fought alongside the men. Women composed hymns in the Vedas, and the Upanishads mention one educated woman who asked her teacher so many searching questions that he exclaimed, "You mustn't ask too much, or your head will drop off!"

As Aryan civilization developed, the status of women declined. At first women were active in village life and joined in public debates. Later, they were forbidden to attend public meetings, although they still were free to walk unattended in the village.

Women eventually became subordinate to men. As a child, a girl obeyed her father. In her teens, she married the man chosen by her family and moved into her husband's household. A young wife owed the same obedience to her husband and his family that she once had owed to her own family.

Social Classes

As the nomadic Aryans settled into villages, their social structure changed. The early Aryans were loosely divided into three classes: warriors, priests, and commoners. Because the classes were not strictly defined, a person could rise from a lower class to a higher one. However, by the time powerful rajahs established united kingdoms, a new social organization had emerged.

In the new social structure, the Aryans recognized four classes: Kshatriyas (KSHAT ree uhz), or warriors; Brahmans (BRAH muhnz), or priests; Vaisyas (VĪS yuhz), or landowners, merchants, and herders; and Sudras (SOO druhz), or servants and peasants tied to the land. As religious rituals grew more complex, the Brahmans became more powerful. In time, they replaced the Kshatriyas as the highest class.

Historians think that the social structure became more rigid because the Aryans wanted to maintain a separate racial and cultural identity. During their conquests, some Aryans had intermarried with the Dravidians, and a few Dravidians had found a place in Aryan society. But as the new social system developed, the top three classes were reserved for Aryans, and the lowest class was made up of non-Aryans, such as the Dravidians.

In time, the four main social classes were further divided into **castes,** or social groups based on birth. Children belonged to the same caste as their parents. As the caste system evolved, a strict set of rules emerged that prohibited marriage between members of different castes and stated the jobs that members of each caste could hold.

The caste system grew immensely complex. Over 3,000 subcastes, or groups, eventually developed. There were also many people outside the caste system. Because they were considered to be impure, these people were called "untouchables," and they had the lowest status in society. In Chapter 7, you will read how the developing caste system was closely tied to Hindu religious beliefs.

| SECTION 2 REVIEW |

1. **Identify:** (a) Dravidian, (b) Vedas, (c) Upanishads, (d) Sanskrit.

2. **Define:** (a) tribe, (b) rajah, (c) reincarnation, (d) extended family, (e) caste.

3. Compare the responsibilities of the rajah and the village headmen.

4. What new religious belief did the Upanishads contain?

5. (a) List the four main classes in Aryan society. (b) What occupations were identified with each class?

6. **Critical Thinking** What major changes took place in the beliefs of Aryans after 1500 B.C.? Suggest reasons for those changes.

3 Beginning of Chinese Civilization

READ TO UNDERSTAND

☐ How geography helped shape China's view of the world.

☐ What the major achievements of Shang civilization were.

☐ How the Chinese viewed their gods.

☐ *Vocabulary:* loess, oracle bone.

Farmers plowing their fields in northern China were delighted at their good luck. From the loose soil, they pulled out a rich collection of "dragon bones"—teeth, ribs, and shoulder bones. Without a second thought about the puzzling cracks and notches on the bones, the farmers sold them to local pharmacists. From their medical books, the pharmacists had learned that powdered "dragon bones" could cure diseases. In the late 1800s, scholars realized that the animal bones contained the earliest form of Chinese writing. The farmers had unknowingly been destroying records of China's ancient civilization.

You have read about the civilizations that rose in the river valleys of the Nile, the Tigris and Euphrates, and the Indus. A fourth civilization developed in the Yellow River valley of northern China. By 3000 B.C., Stone Age farmers began building permanent villages in northern China. As they discovered better ways to produce food, they developed a more complex social and economic system, which by 1600 B.C. gave rise to the Shang civilization.

GEOGRAPHIC SETTING
Ancient China

China covers an immense area. (See the map at right.) Today, as in the past, the good farmland of the river valleys and coastal plains of central China support most of the population. Four outlying regions—Manchuria, Mongolia, Sinkiang (sihn kyang), and Tibet—surround the heartland of China.

Imposing geographic barriers encircle China. The Himalayas in Tibet are among the world's highest, coldest mountains. Barren deserts, such as the Gobi, rugged plateaus, and dense subtropical forests stretch along China's frontiers. To the east is the vast Pacific Ocean.

The Middle Kingdom. Geographic barriers and great distances limited contact between China and other centers of civilization. As a result, the Chinese developed a civilization quite different from others. The Chinese considered themselves unique and believed that their land was at the center of the world. They called it Chung Kuo (juhng gwoh), meaning the "Middle Kingdom."

However, China's isolation was far from complete. The early farming villages of China had contact with people as far away as the Fertile Crescent. As civilization advanced in both regions, trade and travel across western China increased. Also, nomadic invaders from Manchuria and Mongolia frequently overran the cities and villages of northern China.

Although the Chinese adopted some ideas of outsiders, foreign influence was limited. The Chinese considered people who did not speak Chinese to be barbarians. Newcomers, even successful conquerors, found it neces-

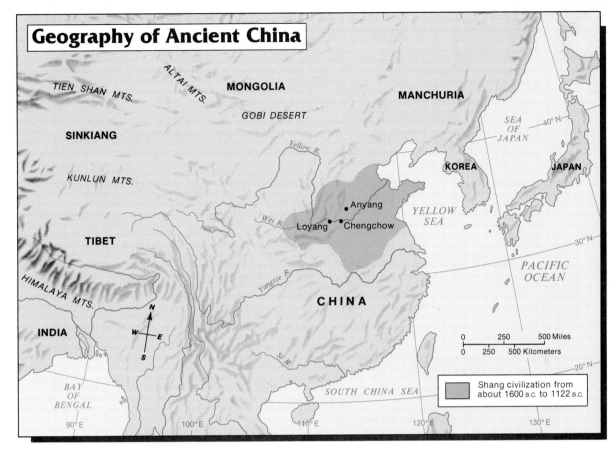

Geography of Ancient China

TIEN SHAN MTS.

ALTAI MTS.

MONGOLIA

MANCHURIA

GOBI DESERT

SINKIANG

KUNLUN MTS.

Yellow R.

SEA OF JAPAN

40° N

KOREA

JAPAN

TIBET

Wei R.

•Anyang

Loyang• •Chengchow

YELLOW SEA

30° N

HIMALAYA MTS.

Yangtze R.

CHINA

PACIFIC OCEAN

N
W   E
S

INDIA

Si R.

0   250   500 Miles
0   250   500 Kilometers

20° N

BAY OF BENGAL

SOUTH CHINA SEA

Shang civilization from about 1600 B.C. to 1122 B.C.

90° E   100° E   110° E   120° E   130° E

MAP STUDY   *Early Chinese traders guided rafts of wood and bamboo up and down the Yellow River. This trade helped transform small farming villages into thriving cities. Cities such as Anyang, Loyang, and Chengchow were centers of Shang civilization. Besides aiding trade, how else did the Yellow River affect life in China?*

sary to adopt Chinese traditions and customs. Thus, the Chinese gained a reputation for absorbing their conquerors.

The Yellow River. In the Yellow River valley, winter winds and river flood waters deposit a fine yellow soil called **loess** (LOH ehs) across the broad, flat plain. The loess is fertile and easily worked.

The Yellow River provides water for irrigation, fishing, and transportation. However, because rainfall is not regular, the area suffers from both droughts and floods. In fact, the Chinese have called the Yellow River the "River of Sorrows" because its floods have caused much death and destruction. (See the feature on page 62.) The early Chinese learned to dredge the river channel and construct dikes to lessen the danger of floods. They also built their villages on high ground. ■

Shang Civilization

As in Egypt and Sumer, busy farming villages in northern China grew into towns and cities. Local rulers fought for power until about 1600 B.C., when powerful kings established control over northern China and founded the Shang dynasty. The Shang dynasty, or ruling family, was the first in China. It survived until 1122 B.C. and gave its name to the earliest Chinese civilization.

A Shang king ruled over his capital city and the surrounding region. Other land was governed by nobles, usually the king's relatives. These nobles paid tribute to the king or performed military service for him. In this way, Shang rulers could raise armies to fight wars against nomads who threatened the frontier.

According to legend, the Great Yu tamed the Yellow River, which regularly flooded the plains of northern China. The floods drowned peasants and ruined crops, often leading to terrible famines. The Chinese were so grateful to Yu for taming the river that they regarded him as a god. He had, they said, separated the land from the water.

Despite the legend of Yu, the Yellow River flooded northern China for thousands of years. The river was not really tamed until this century. Until then, the "River of Sorrows" was a source of both life and death to the Chinese. From its source high in the mountains of Tibet, the Yellow River crashes down toward the plains. The racing waters erode tons of rich soil from the riverbanks. This yellow soil gives the river its color and its name. When the river reaches the flat plains downstream, it becomes wide and calm. There the soil, or silt, settles to the bottom of the river or is heaped up along the banks.

In ancient times, peasants built dikes along the riverbank to keep the river from overflowing. They also dug canals for irrigation. The canals helped control the runoff from floods.

Every year, the Yellow River deposited more silt on the river bottom. Slowly this raised the riverbed, forcing the peasants to build higher dikes. Soon, the river rose far above the surrounding land. A peasant working in his field could look up and see the sail of a boat high above his head. But the raised river beds made floods even deadlier. If the dikes broke, a wall of water poured onto the plains, destroying everything in its path.

The flooding of the Yellow River deeply affected the Chinese. They had to work together to build dikes and canals. And they needed a strong leader to organize the work. By providing this leadership, Shang rulers, as well as later rulers, had an easier time winning the loyalty of their subjects. By working together to control the river, the Chinese created a stable government.

1. How did peasants try to control the flooding of the Yellow River?

2. **Critical Thinking** Study the map on page 61. Why do you think the Yellow River was especially hard to control?

Chinese Writing

During the Shang dynasty, the Chinese developed a system of writing. Like the Egyptians and Sumerians, the early Chinese used pictograms, or drawings of objects. Later, they added ideograms, symbols that expressed ideas such as wisdom or unity. Under the Shang, Chinese writing included over 3,000 symbols, or characters.

Chinese written characters have remained in use for more than 3,500 years. Each character has two parts, one that tells its meaning and one that suggests its pronunciation. As the language developed, the number of characters increased to over 50,000. Until recent reforms simplified the system, every Chinese student had to learn at least 10,000 characters. For centuries, it was so difficult to learn the complicated characters that only the wealthy had the time to learn to read and write.

Shang scribes drew characters with a sharp stick or brush on many types of material, including bronze, pottery, jade, and silk. Scribes usually wrote on strips of bamboo or wood, which were tied together in rolled bundles. Because the strips were narrow, the characters were written in vertical columns rather than horizontally as English is written.

Shang Religious Beliefs

The Shang people believed that many gods and spirits lived in nature. The main god, Shang Ti, presided over heaven and the other gods. The power of the gods was awesome. They could cause floods, drought, and locust plagues.

The people tried to influence the gods by calling on the spirits of their own ancestors to act as go-betweens. The Shang believed that if they made the right sacrifices, their ancestors would bring them good fortune. Bad fortune was considered a sign of an ancestor's displeasure. Therefore, ancestor worship became central to Shang religion. As chief priest, the Shang king made daily sacrifices to make sure that his ancestors acted favorably on behalf of the kingdom.

Shang priests also tried to tell the future. Before taking an important action, a person would ask a priest to consult his or her ancestors. To do this, the priest scratched a question on an ox bone. Then he carved notches in the bone and touched the notches with a heated bronze rod. The heat caused the bone to crack. The priest interpreted the cracks to find an answer to the question. Bones used for telling the future in this way are called **oracle bones.**

As you read earlier, for centuries Chinese farmers had been digging up large oracle bones and calling them "dragon bones." Most oracle bones that archaeologists have found near Shang cities were inscribed with questions that kings asked their ancestors. One king asked if 5,000 soldiers would be enough to defeat an enemy. Another wondered if his ancestors were responsible for his toothache. By reading the oracle bones, scholars have learned much about religious beliefs and daily life in Shang China.

Daily Life

Shang society had a strict division of classes. The king, supported by nobles and priests, performed political and religious duties in the capital. The majority of the people were peasants living in villages. They paid part of each harvest to the king or governor of the region. Sometimes peasants were drafted to serve as foot soldiers or to build royal palaces, tombs, and temples.

In contrast to the luxurious dwellings of the wealthy, Shang farmers lived in tiny houses, built partially underground. The ground helped insulate the house during the hot summers and cold winters on the north China plain.

The extended family was the focus of Shang village life, as it was in Aryan villages in India. Several generations lived in the same household, which was headed by the oldest male. Because the Shang worshipped their ancestors, they had great respect for age and a deep feeling of duty to family.

Little is known about women in Shang China. Queens seem to have been respected. Among the royal family and nobles, men often had more than one wife, but the first wife and her sons were the most important. Among peasant families, men probably married only one woman. Peasant women worked in the fields alongside men. They were also responsible for silkmaking and weaving.

Shang Achievements

Bronzemaking was a special skill of Shang artisans. They invented bronze weapons, such as daggers, spears, and armor. They also made splendid bronze vessels for religious rituals. First, the artisan made a clay or stone mold.

Oracle bones like the one shown here commonly were inscribed with questions such as: "Will the weather be good tomorrow?" and "Are the prospects for hunting good?" The questions usually required only a yes or no answer from a person's ancestors.

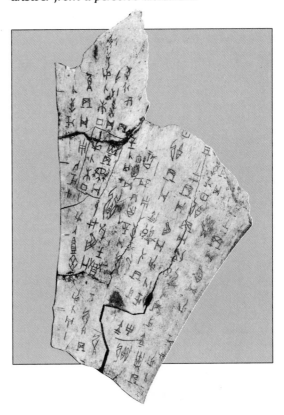

The Chinese have made silk since ancient times. Oracle bones indicate that in Shang times, the Chinese already knew how to extract silk thread from the cocoon of the silkworm caterpillar. Yet how they discovered the process of silkmaking remains a mystery to this day.

In ancient China, as today, silk farmers cultivated mulberry trees because young silkworms fed on mulberry leaves. Silkworms spin cocoons to protect them while they change into moths. Silkworkers placed these cocoons in boiling water to soften them so that the delicate threads could be unwound. The Chinese designed special looms to weave the silk thread into cloth. They then dipped the cloth in brilliant dyes to give it a rich, lustrous look.

The ancient Chinese recognized the value of the silk industry. They made every effort to keep spies from smuggling silkworm eggs or the seeds of the mulberry tree out of China. To do so was punishable by death. In this way, the Chinese managed to keep the process of gathering and weaving silk a secret for almost 3,000 years.

1. Why was the mulberry tree an important part of silkmaking?

2. **Critical Thinking** Why do you think the silk industry was so valuable to the Chinese?

Decorated with animal figures, this bronze offering vessel from the Shang period was used in religious rituals. In return, the Chinese hoped to receive good fortune. An inscription on one offering vessel said that food and wine were being offered "to solicit tranquility of heart, a steady salary and long life."

Around this mold, he fashioned a second mold. Then, he poured heated bronze between the two molds. When the bronze cooled, the artisan removed the molds and polished the surface of the vessel to a smooth finish.

The Shang invented the yoke, harness, and spoked wheel. These led to the development of the two-horse war chariot. With the chariot and bronze weapons, Shang rulers had military superiority over neighboring peoples who did not know about them.

The Shang also made advances in the arts and sciences. Working with a white clay, artisans manufactured fine pottery, which was the forerunner of porcelain. Artisans made stunning silk textiles, jade ornaments, and ivory carvings. In mathematics, the Shang developed a decimal system. Priest-astronomers devised a calendar with 12 months and $365\frac{1}{4}$ days. Such advances became the foundation on which later Chinese built.

From northern China, the Shang civilization spread in many directions. Some people moved eastward along the Yellow River to the Pacific. Many migrated toward the south, spreading Chinese culture into the Yangtze (YANG see) River valley and eventually in the Si (shee) River valley. Others pushed into Manchuria, Mongolia, and central Asia.

1. **Locate:** (a) China, (b) Manchuria, (c) Mongolia, (d) Tibet, (e) Himalaya Mountains, (f) Gobi Desert, (g) Yellow River.

2. **Define:** (a) loess, (b) oracle bone.

3. Describe two factors that limited outside influence on Chinese civilization.

4. Why was the Yellow River called the "River of Sorrows"?

5. Why was Chinese writing difficult to learn?

6. **Critical Thinking** What customs and beliefs contributed to Chinese respect for the elderly?

4 Expansion Under the Chou Dynasty

READ TO UNDERSTAND

☐ **How the idea of the Mandate of Heaven was used by Chinese rulers.**

☐ **Why bureaucratic government developed in Chou China.**

☐ **What social and economic life was like under the Chou.**

☐ *Vocabulary:* **dynastic cycle, bureaucracy.**

In 1122 B.C. the Shang king issued a desperate call. Wu Wang, leader of the barbarian Chou people, was threatening the city of Anyang. The barbarians had settled on the western frontier and learned to use war chariots and bronze weapons from the Shang. Now they dared to rebel against the Shang king.

Wu Wang, the "Martial King," as he was later called, won the day and established a new dynasty. The Chou dynasty lasted from 1122 B.C. to 256 B.C., longer than any other in history. But the new rulers did not wipe out the defeated Shang. They let the Shang settle in their own state, and they kept many Shang laws and customs. They then made their own contributions to Chinese civilization.

The beauty of the bronze art of ancient China was unrivaled. This finely detailed figure from the Chou period shows a young boy holding birds carved of jade. To the Chou, bronze was more than a valuable metal, it was also magical.

The Mandate of Heaven

To justify their seizure of power from the Shang, the Chou developed the idea of the "Mandate of Heaven." According to the Chou, a dynasty enjoyed heaven's blessing only as long as it governed wisely and justly. If a ruler was lazy, cruel, or corrupt, heaven withdrew the mandate, or right to rule.

"It was the case that the last sovereign of your Shang was luxurious to the extreme of luxury," proclaimed the Chou, "while his schemes of government showed neither purity nor progress, so that heaven sent down such ruin on him." Heaven then found "our kings of Chou, who were able to sustain the burden of virtuous government."

A key part of the Mandate of Heaven was a ruler's responsibility to provide good govern-

65

ment and put the well-being of the people above self-interest. The Chinese believed that natural disasters and invasions revealed a ruler's failure to please heaven.

It was not considered a crime to rebel against a ruler who had lost the Mandate of Heaven. The overthrow of the Shang by the Chou was the first of many dynastic changes in China. Historians refer to the rise and fall of Chinese dynasties as the **dynastic cycle.** (See the diagram below.)

Chou Government

During the Chou dynasty, a feudal system* emerged in China. Since the Chou controlled more territory than the Shang had, Chou kings allowed powerful nobles to govern large parts of the kingdom. In exchange, the nobles owed loyalty, military service, and tribute to the king.

For about 250 years, Chou kings controlled the feudal nobles. But as Chou strength declined, powerful lords carved out independent states and expanded north into Manchuria and south into the Yangtze Valley. Between 771 B.C. and 256 B.C., weak Chou rulers could not stop warfare among hundreds of feudal states.

During these centuries of upheaval, nobles protected their power by replacing hereditary office holders with appointed officials. In the larger states, complex government bureaucracies developed. A **bureaucracy** (byoo RAH kruh see) is a system of organizing government by departments or bureaus.

In the feudal states of Chou China, different bureaus controlled finances, the armed forces, law enforcement, and recordkeeping. The state with the most efficient organization had the advantage in the power struggles of the late Chou period. Government bureaucracy has remained an important feature in China since Chou times.

Life in Chou China

Constant warfare in late Chou China weakened the warrior class. As large, well-organized states emerged, a new class of able, ambitious government officials gradually gained power. Eventually, these officials became the new ruling class in China.

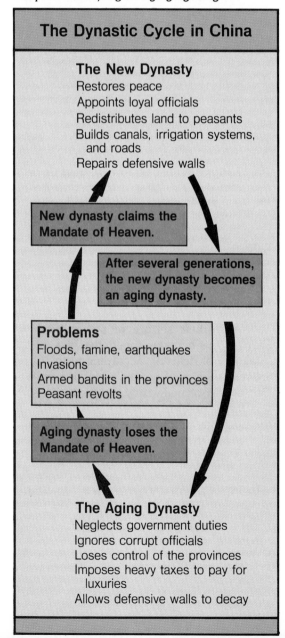

CHART STUDY *The idea of a Mandate of Heaven was an important part of the dynastic cycle in China. To the Chinese, problems like those shown here indicated that a ruler had lost the Mandate of Heaven. How did a new dynasty try to solve the problems left by an aging dynasty?*

The Dynastic Cycle in China

The New Dynasty
Restores peace
Appoints loyal officials
Redistributes land to peasants
Builds canals, irrigation systems, and roads
Repairs defensive walls

New dynasty claims the Mandate of Heaven.

After several generations, the new dynasty becomes an aging dynasty.

Problems
Floods, famine, earthquakes
Invasions
Armed bandits in the provinces
Peasant revolts

Aging dynasty loses the Mandate of Heaven.

The Aging Dynasty
Neglects government duties
Ignores corrupt officials
Loses control of the provinces
Imposes heavy taxes to pay for luxuries
Allows defensive walls to decay

---

* In a feudal system, lords held lands that, in theory, belonged to the king. The local lords governed these lands, protected the people who farmed them, and owed military and other services to the king or other lords. In practice, local lords often became virtually independent.

By the late Chou period, a social system had evolved in China that would remain a stable force through later dynasties. At the head of society were the government officials. They gained greater status by becoming landowners. Below them was the huge peasant class. Some peasants were tenant farmers on estates owned by wealthy landlords. Others farmed land allotted to them by villages. Artisans and merchants ranked below peasants because they did not work the land. Although warfare was a prominent feature of Chou China, soldiers had a low position in society.

Education became increasingly important as the need for government officials grew. In the cities and at feudal courts, tutors trained boys for government service. Educated people wrote books that were later considered classics. The *Book of Odes,* for example, contained myths, legends, and love poems. Students memorized the *Book of Odes,* together with royal histories and books of court etiquette.

Economic Growth

The Chou era was a time of economic growth. Peasants began to use fertilizers and iron tools. With the help of government-sponsored irrigation projects and a new ox-drawn plow, they farmed more land and increased food production. Feudal lords also offered peasants favorable terms to settle in newly conquered territories. These settlers carried Chinese culture well beyond the old borders of the Shang kingdom.

Under the Chou, trade expanded and cities grew. To encourage trade and good communications, feudal lords built many roads and canals. Goods flowed along roads, rivers, and canals from villages to cities and back. By trading with people in western Asia, the Chinese learned about such animals as the mule, donkey, and camel.

When the Chinese began to use metal coins, trade grew even faster. This money economy helped the rich but not the poor. Merchants made huge profits by buying grain and then selling it in times of famine for high prices. But during famines, peasants had to borrow money or grain to survive. If a peasant could not pay back a loan, he and his family lost the right to farm the land. The problem of

This carved jade disc was a symbol of heaven. Jade, valued for both its rarity and its beauty, was thought to serve as a link between the gods and humanity. Since prehistoric times, the Chinese have regarded jade as more precious than gold.

peasants being forced off the land would haunt Chinese rulers for the next 3,000 years.

Warfare among the feudal states marked the end of the Chou dynasty. Yet institutions such as the bureaucracy and traditions such as the Mandate of Heaven would become the cornerstone of a unified Chinese state.

SECTION 4 REVIEW

1. **Define:** (a) dynastic cycle, (b) bureaucracy.

2. How did the idea of the Mandate of Heaven encourage good government?

3. Why did the Chou dynasty decline?

4. What group made up the ruling class in Chou China?

5. What economic problems did Chinese peasants face?

6. **Critical Thinking** Why would rulers prefer a government run by appointed officials rather than hereditary office holders?

CHAPTER 3 REVIEW

Summary

1. **Geography helped shape the patterns of life of ancient India.** The first Indian civilization developed in the fertile Indus River valley. Excavations of its major cities reveal a well-organized society with a thriving agricultural economy and active trade.

2. **Around 1500 B.C., nomadic Aryan tribes conquered the Indus Valley and established a new civilization.** The Aryans preserved their religious beliefs and history in their oral literature. Eventually, powerful rajahs established kingdoms, and a strict class system evolved.

3. **The first civilization in China grew up along the Yellow River.** There the Shang kings established a dynasty about 1600 B.C. During the Shang dynasty, the Chinese developed writing, a calendar, and advanced skills in bronzeworking as well as other artistic and scientific techniques.

4. **Under the Chou, who followed the Shang, a feudal system of government emerged.** The Chou believed that the "Mandate of Heaven" gave them divine right to rule. Despite constant warfare among feudal lords, the Chou period was one of economic growth.

Recalling Facts

Choose the best word or phrase to complete each of the following statements.

1. The chief feature of the Indian climate is the (a) constant heat; (b) inadequate rainfall; (c) monsoon.

2. The first civilization in India developed in the (a) Indus Valley; (b) Deccan Plateau; (c) Eastern Ghats.

3. The sacred hymns and prayers of the early Aryans are called the (a) Sudras; (b) Vedas; (c) Ramayana.

4. In the Aryan economy, the medium of exchange was (a) gold; (b) iron tools; (c) cattle.

5. The ancient Chinese called their land (a) the Middle Kingdom; (b) the Mandate of Heaven; (c) Anyang.

Chapter Checkup

1. (a) Explain how geographic barriers helped isolate both India and China from other parts of the world. (b) What contacts in each land existed despite these barriers?

2. (a) Why is there less evidence of Indus Valley civilization than Egyptian or Sumerian civilization? (b) Why do scholars think Indus Valley rulers were strong?

3. Describe the following aspects of Aryan society: (a) village government; (b) economy; (c) family structure.

4. (a) Describe the class system that developed in Aryan society. (b) Why did such a rigid system develop?

5. (a) Describe the class structure of Chou China. (b) How was it different from the class structure of Shang China?

6. What factors contributed to economic growth in Chou China?

Critical Thinking

1. **Analyzing Geography in History** How do climate conditions affect the economic life of people (a) in India? (b) in the region where you live? (c) Do you think climate has more impact on the economy in India or where you live? Explain.

2. **Comparing** (a) Compare the calendars developed by the various civilizations you have studied in Chapters 1, 2, and 3. (b) Why do you think most early civilizations developed a calendar?

3. **Relating Past to Present** (a) What kinds of questions did Shang priests ask on oracle bones? (b) What do the questions tell you about the concerns of the people? (c) Do you see any similarities between the use of oracle bones in ancient China and the way people use horoscopes today? Explain.

Developing Basic Skills

1. **Making a Review Chart** Information that is organized in a chart can be easily reviewed and compared. Make a large chart with four columns and five rows. Title the columns Egypt, Sumer, Indus, and Shang. Title the rows Location, Government, Religious Beliefs, Social Classes, and Achievements. Fill in the chart with information you learned in Chapters 1, 2, and 3. (a) What similarities do you notice in the locations of all four civilizations? (b) Did Egyptians and Sumerians have the same kind of government? Explain. (c) How did the religious beliefs of Shang China differ from Egyptian religious beliefs? (d) What social classes existed in all four civilizations?

2. **Placing Events in Time** The time line lets you see the relationship between events over time. For B.C. dates, remember that the higher number is always the earlier date. Answer the following questions based on the time lines on pages 33, 51, and 69. (a) Did the New Kingdom in Egypt begin before or after the rise of Indus Valley civilization? (b) Did Sumerian civilization develop before or after the Aryan invasions of India? (c) Which civilizations existed at about the same time?

Writing About History

Writing a Generalization

As you have learned, sometimes you can rewrite an essay question to form a topic sentence for the answer. If that won't work, you can write a generalization about the subject as your topic sentence. A generalization is a broad statement based on facts.

Consider this question: *How did people in ancient India and China make a living?* One generalization you could make based on the information in the text would be, "Many people in ancient India and China were farmers, but other occupations also developed." You could then complete the paragraph with specific examples.

Practice: Write a generalization as a topic sentence for each Critical Thinking question in this Chapter Review.

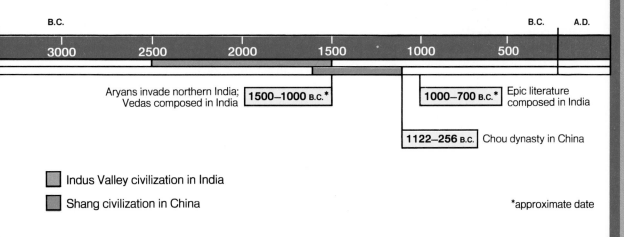

B.C. | 3000 2500 2000 1500 1000 500 | B.C. A.D.

Aryans invade northern India; Vedas composed in India | 1500–1000 B.C.*

1000–700 B.C.* Epic literature composed in India

1122–256 B.C. Chou dynasty in China

Indus Valley civilization in India

Shang civilization in China

*approximate date

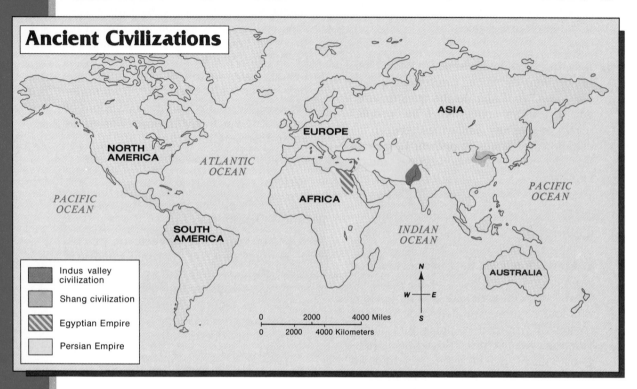

Ancient Civilizations

ASIA
EUROPE
NORTH AMERICA
ATLANTIC OCEAN
PACIFIC OCEAN
PACIFIC OCEAN
AFRICA
SOUTH AMERICA
INDIAN OCEAN
AUSTRALIA

Legend:
- Indus valley civilization
- Shang civilization
- Egyptian Empire
- Persian Empire

0   2000   4000 Miles
0   2000   4000 Kilometers

N / W — E / S

Unit Themes

During the Stone Age, people were nomadic. They moved in small groups searching for food. Eventually, people learned to raise crops, and they began settling in permanent communities. As farmers produced surpluses, they could support larger populations. Eventually, cities emerged.

In these early cities, people in widely scattered parts of the world developed the complex political, social, and economic systems that formed the foundations of civilization.

As you have read, the earliest centers of civilization were in Egypt, Mesopotamia, and the Indus and Yellow river valleys. The civilizations that arose in each of these regions had certain basic features in common, but the patterns of civilization in each region varied enormously. Each civilization left a heritage for those who followed.

1. **Applying Information** (a) On which continents did the first river valley civilizations emerge? (b) Why did cities develop in river valleys?

2. **Synthesizing** (a) How did ideas spread between civilizations in ancient times? (b) How did the spread of ideas affect civilizations discussed in Unit One? (c) Which civilizations shown above were most likely to exchange ideas with one another? Why?

3. **Comparing** (a) Which Chinese dynasty lasted longer, the Shang or the Chou? (b) Which do you think had a greater effect on later Chinese civilization? Why?

4. **Relating Past to Present** (a) What kinds of technology helped transform small farming communities into cities? (b) How is technology changing our society today?

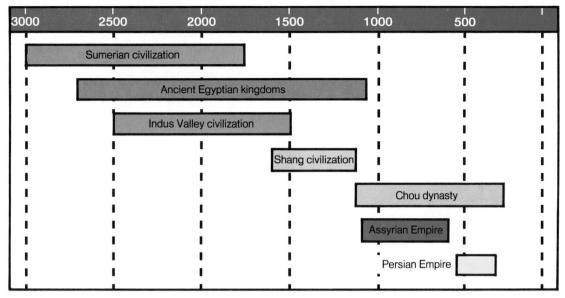

B.C. | B.C. A.D.

3000 — 2500 — 2000 — 1500 — 1000 — 500

Sumerian civilization

Ancient Egyptian kingdoms

Indus Valley civilization

Shang civilization

Chou dynasty

Assyrian Empire

Persian Empire

TIME LINE STUDY — *The time line shows the time span of some of the civilizations discussed in Unit One. About how long did the Indus Valley civilization last? Which ancient civilization lasted the longest?*

MAP STUDY — *The Chou dynasty, the longest dynasty in the history of China, claimed their right to govern through the "Mandate of Heaven." Compare this map with the one on page 61. Did the Chou or Shang rule a larger empire?*

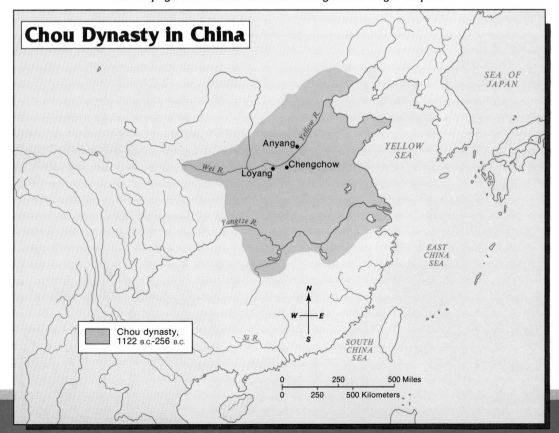

Chou Dynasty in China

SEA OF JAPAN

Anyang
Chengchow
Loyang
Wei R.
Yellow R.

YELLOW SEA

Yangtze R.

EAST CHINA SEA

N
W — E
S

Chou dynasty,
1122 B.C.-256 B.C.

Si R.

SOUTH CHINA SEA

0   250   500 Miles
0   250   500 Kilometers

71

UNIT TWO

RISE OF CLASSICAL CIVILIZATIONS

The Buddha taught in India, but the religion he founded spread throughout Asia.

79 A.D. This glass jug was found in the ruins of Pompeii, a Roman city buried by a volcanic eruption.

	600 B.C.	400 B.C.	200 B.C.	0
POLITICS AND GOVERNMENT	**594 B.C.** Solon reforms government of Athens		**210 B.C.–220 A.D.** Han dynasty rules in China	
ECONOMICS AND TECHNOLOGY	**600s B.C.** Greeks found colonies around the Mediterranean		**221–210 B.C.** Great Wall built in China under the Ch'in	
SOCIETY AND CULTURE		**461–429 B.C.** Golden Age of Athens under Pericles	**70–19 B.C.** Virgil, author of *Aeneid*, lives in Rome	

Greeks used sailing ships to trade throughout the Mediterranean world.

Women in Athens were expected only to manage their homes and raise children.

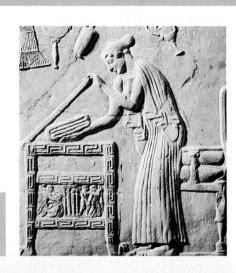

UNIT OUTLINE

The Romans inherited many things from the Greeks, including theater and drama, where masks such as these were used.

64 A.D. *During the reign of Nero, shown on this coin, a fire nearly destroyed the city of Rome.*

0	200 A.D.	400 A.D.	600 A.D.

27 B.C.–180 A.D. Pax Romana

320 A.D. Gupta Empire founded in India   **476 A.D.** Fall of Rome

100s A.D. Chinese develop process for making paper

400s A.D. Ideas of zero and a decimal system developed in India

100s A.D. Buddhism reaches China

312 A.D. Roman emperor Constantine converts to Christianity

During the Han dynasty, the Chinese invented the water mill to grind grain in granaries such as this one.

The fish remained a symbol of early Christians even after Christianity became the official religion of the Roman Empire in 395 A.D.

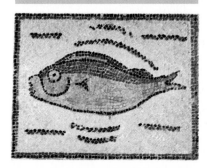

The Heritage of Ancient Greece

4

(2000 B.C.—133 B.C.)

Greek architecture combined grace and beauty with usefulness. These standing maidens are columns that support the roof of a temple on the Acropolis in Athens.

Despite the cool winter wind, the men sweated as they lifted the heavy cypress-wood coffins from the funeral carts. As gently as possible, they placed their burdens in the special burial area reserved for those who had fallen in the war. The wailing of relatives of the dead filled the air. After a time, a man emerged from the crowd and moved toward an elevated platform. He waited solemnly as the mourners hushed one another. Then he began to speak.

The speaker was Pericles (PEHR uh KLEEZ), a respected Athenian general. He had been chosen to address the people of Athens gathered to honor the soldiers killed in the opening battle of the Peloponnesian Wars. The wars pitted

Athens and Sparta, two strong and proud city-states, against each other. In his funeral oration, Pericles praised Athenian greatness.

"Our system of government is called a democracy because power is in the hands not of a minority but of the whole people. When it is a question of settling private disputes, everyone is equal before the law. When it is a question of putting one person before another in positions of public responsibility, what counts is not membership in a particular class but the actual ability which the man possesses."

Pericles reminded Athenians of the importance of public service in a democracy. "Here each individual is interested not only in his own affairs but in the affairs of the state as well. . . . We do not say that a man who takes no interest in politics is a man who minds his own business; we say that he has no business here at all."

Pericles' Funeral Oration symbolizes the Greeks' ideas about the individual's role in society and about democratic government. These ideas form the basis of many of our values today.

The systems of government that evolved in Greece differed from those of the river valley civilizations described in Unit One. The ancient Greeks were not united under a single ruler. They lived in small, independent cities constantly at war with one another. Their struggles to maintain their independence may have led the Greeks to develop a concern for the rights and responsibilities of individual citizens. ■

1 Early Civilizations in the Aegean

READ TO UNDERSTAND

☐ **How geography influenced Aegean civilizations.**

☐ **How Achaean civilization built on Minoan achievements.**

☐ **What the *Iliad* and the *Odyssey* tell about the Trojan War.**

☐ *Vocabulary:* **fresco.**

The salt waters of the Aegean Sea wash the coast of Greece and of Asia Minor. They lap at the shores of many islands that for centuries have offered shelter to storm-tossed ships. One of those islands, Crete, was the home of the first Aegean civilization. From there, it spread to the Greek mainland. Unlike the river valley civilizations of Egypt, the Fertile Crescent, India, and China, neither the Cretans nor the Greeks created a large land empire. Instead, each became a great sea power. To understand why this happened, you need to look at the geography of the Aegean islands and the nearby Greek mainland.

GEOGRAPHIC SETTING
Ancient Greece

Greece is a mountainous peninsula that juts into the eastern Mediterranean Sea. Because of the rugged terrain, only about a quarter of the land can be farmed. The early Greeks were herders and farmers. Olive trees and grapevines thrived in the mild climate. But as the Greek population increased, the limited amount of usable land forced many Greeks to turn to fishing and trading for a living. The Greeks traded olive oil and wine for the wheat and grain needed to feed a growing population.

The mountains limited transportation and communication and made the country difficult to unite. Cut off from each other, Greeks developed small, separate communities. Each community valued its independence and fiercely resisted outside interference. As a result, the Greeks were frequently at war with one another.

As you can see from the map below, hundreds of fingers of land poke out from the Greek coastline, forming good natural harbors. Aided by favorable winds, Greek sailors crossed to North Africa and the eastern Mediterranean. Through trade, the Greeks learned about other civilizations. As a result, the Greeks were open to new ideas. They sifted through the achievements of other peoples, adopting some, such as the Phoenician alphabet, and rejecting others. ■

Minoan Civilization

Between about 2000 B.C. and 1400 B.C., Minoan (mih NOH uhn) civilization* flourished on

---

* Minoan civilization is named after Minos, a legendary Cretan king. Minos was credited with building a huge palace in which he kept the Minotaur, a monster that was half human and half bull.

MAP STUDY *The sea was crucial to the development of early Aegean civilization. For hundreds of years, it protected the Minoan civilization on the island of Crete. The sea also served as a highway for trading ships from Crete and the Greek mainland. Sailors traveled by day in boats equipped with sails and oars. At night, they sought the safety of harbors. What cities on the mainland were trading centers?*

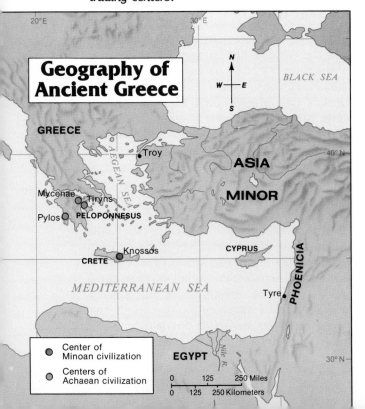

Crete. The Minoans were a great trading power in the eastern Mediterranean. Powered by sails and oars, Minoan vessels carried goods from the Black Sea to the Nile Valley and to Phoenicia. The Minoans exchanged olive oil, honey, and wine for gold, precious stones, grain, and linen.

At the height of Minoan civilization, a king ruled the prosperous cities of Crete from his palace-city at Knossos (NAHS uhs). In 1898 A.D., British archaeologist Sir Arthur Evans excavated the site of the palace. He discovered that the palace contained over 800 rooms, including a magnificent throne room. The rooms were connected by courtyards and corridors. The huge building served as royal residence, temple, storeroom, and government center. It had an elaborate drainage system but no defensive walls. Apparently, the Minoans felt that their ships and the sea itself protected them from invaders.

The colorful **frescoes** (FREHS kohz), or wall paintings, decorating the palace at Knossos illustrate many aspects of Minoan life. Some frescoes show athletic young men and women competing in acrobatic contests. Others picture elegantly dressed women strolling in the royal gardens. Among the Minoans, women probably enjoyed nearly equal status with men.

From frescoes and statues, it appears that Minoan religious beliefs centered on worship of the bull and a mother goddess. The people obviously enjoyed life. Wealthy merchants spent lavishly on their homes and on personal comforts rather than on temples and tombs as the Egyptians and Sumerians had.

The Minoan civilization eventually grew weak, and Crete was invaded by people from the Greek mainland. About 1400 B.C., Knossos itself was destroyed, perhaps by an earthquake, a volcano, or invaders. Like the Indus Valley civilization, this early civilization on Crete remained buried and forgotten for a long time. Yet Crete directly influenced the peoples of mainland Greece.

Achaean Civilization

About 2000 B.C., the Achaeans (uh KEE uhnz), an Indo-European people like the Hittites and Aryans, invaded the Greek peninsula from the

The frescoes uncovered at the palace at Knossos have told us much about life on the island of Crete. This painting shows the lively style and movement that were typical of Minoan art. The dolphins are a reminder of the importance of the sea to the Minoan people.

north. As the Achaeans pushed farther south, they intermarried with the local people. Eventually, the Achaeans extended their conquests over the Peloponnesus (PEHL uh puh NEE suhs), the southern half of Greece.

By about 1400 B.C., the Achaeans controlled the Aegean and probably occupied Knossos. They built strong fortress cities on the mainland, each one ruled by a warrior king. Riches from trade and war allowed Achaean rulers to fill their palaces and tombs with gold treasures. Outside each city, traders, merchants, artisans, and farmers lived in small villages that paid tribute to the king.

The Achaeans built on the achievements of Minoan civilization. Artisans at Mycenae (mī SEE nee) reproduced Minoan designs on jewelry, pottery, and tools. The Achaeans also learned writing from the Minoans.

The Trojan War

Around 1250 B.C., the Achaeans banded together under the leadership of the king of Mycenae to attack Troy, a rival power. From the map on page 76, you can see that Troy controlled trade routes between the Aegean and Black seas. After a long and devastating war, the Achaeans emerged the victors.

Historians first learned about the Trojan War from the *Iliad* (IHL ee uhd) and the *Odyssey* (AHD uh see), two of the best-known epic poems in the world. The poems were probably composed by Homer, a blind Greek poet, about 750 B.C., long after the fall of Troy. Homer based his poems on stories that had been passed on by earlier generations.

According to the *Iliad,* the war occurred because Paris, a Trojan prince, kidnapped Helen, wife of the king of Sparta. The Spartan king and his brother, King Agamemnon (AG uh MEHM nahn) of Mycenae, enlisted the help of other rulers and eventually involved all of Greece in the effort to rescue Helen. After ten years of war, the Achaeans destroyed Troy and drove the Trojans into exile. In the *Odyssey,* Homer described the wandering and adventures of the Achaean warrior Odysseus (oh DIHS ee uhs) after the fall of Troy.

Until the late 1800s, historians considered the *Iliad* and *Odyssey* to be fiction. The poems mixed stories of gods and goddesses with legends of human heroes and seemed to have no real historical value. However, Heinrich Schliemann (SHLEE muhn), an amateur archaeologist, believed otherwise. He thought Troy had really existed, and he set out to prove it.

Schliemann began to excavate a site in northwestern Asia Minor that matched Homer's description of Troy. Digging revealed the ruins of an ancient city, but Schliemann soon discovered that at least nine cities had been built at different times on the same spot. Finally, the charred wood and destruction found on one level suggested that this was actually the city of Troy. His excavations showed that Homer's poems were more than great literature. They also had some basis in fact.

The Dark Age

Shortly after the fall of Troy, Achaean civilization suffered a disastrous blow when Dorian invaders swarmed into Greece. The invaders had a military advantage because they had iron weapons and the Achaeans did not. The Dorians plundered the rich cities of the Peloponnesus and disrupted trade. The Achaeans never recovered from this blow. Between about 1100 B.C. and 750 B.C., Greece entered a troubled period. The glory of Achaean civilization vanished. Artistic skills and writing were largely forgotten. This period of Greek history is called the Dark Age.

During the invasions, some Greeks fled to Asia Minor. There, they thrived from trade and travel to the centers of Middle Eastern and Egyptian civilizations. During this period, the Greeks adopted the Phoenician alphabet.

In addition, a few Greek thinkers began to put traditional ideas to the test of reason and logic. From this would come unique contributions in philosophy and science that you will read about later in this chapter.

SECTION 1 REVIEW

1. **Locate:** (a) Aegean Sea, (b) Crete, (c) Greece, (d) Mediterranean Sea, (e) Knossos, (f) Peloponnesus, (g) Troy, (h) Black Sea.

2. **Identify:** (a) Achaeans, (b) *Iliad,* (c) *Odyssey,* (d) Homer.

3. **Define:** fresco.

4. Describe two ways in which geography affected the early Greeks.

5. What did the Achaeans adopt from Minoan civilization?

6. **Critical Thinking** How might geography have affected the attitudes of Greeks in one area toward Greeks in another?

---

2 The Greek City-States

READ TO UNDERSTAND

☐ **What kinds of government emerged in Greece.**

☐ **How democracy developed in Athens.**

☐ **How Sparta differed from Athens.**

☐ *Vocabulary:* **polis, acropolis, monarchy, aristocracy, phalanx, tyranny, democracy, archon, ostracism, helot, ephor.**

During the Dark Age, some Greek villages prospered. They grew into towns that gradually developed into independent city-states. A city-state, or **polis** (POH lihs), consisted of a fortified hilltop and the surrounding fields. Eventually, Athens and Sparta emerged as the leading Greek city-states, but their governments and outlooks on life differed dramatically.

Early City-States

In the Greek city-state, life revolved around the **acropolis** (uh KRAHP uhl ihs), or hilltop fortress. There, the people assembled to defend the polis, to discuss local affairs, and to honor the gods. During the Dark Age, a **monarchy,** or government headed by a king, ruled each polis. This system of government changed about 800 B.C. when noble families, who advised the king and provided leadership in war, gained power.

Eventually, **aristocracies,** or governments by a privileged minority or upper class, replaced the monarchies. Aristocrats exercised power because they owned most of the land. However, social and economic changes between 750 B.C. and 500 B.C. spurred the development of new forms of government.

Greek colonies. After 750 B.C., thousands of Greeks left the mainland and set up colonies on distant shores. Some colonists were involved in the growing trade of the city-states. Others were farmers who fled Greece to escape their debts. Still others were discontented citizens seeking their fortunes. By 600

B.C., Greek settlements were thriving from the Black Sea coasts to southern Italy, North Africa, and Spain. See the map on page 157.

The Greek colonies put the Greeks in touch with other Mediterranean peoples. Contact with those peoples made Greeks aware of their common heritage. While local rivalries often divided Greek city-states, the Greeks had the same traditions and spoke the same language. To the Greeks, outsiders were "barbaroi," chatterers who spoke unintelligible languages. The modern word "barbarian," which has come to mean an uncivilized person, is derived from this Greek word.

Contact with other peoples also led to the sharing of new ideas. For example, the Greeks gradually adopted coins, which had been introduced by the Lydians. The use of coined money and increased trade gave rise to a strong merchant class. This new class began to challenge the nobles and to demand a greater say in government.

The rise of tyranny. Another challenge to the nobles came from citizen-soldiers. Military service was the duty of every citizen in a Greek city-state. However, a change in the nature of warfare had made foot soldiers even more important than before.

War chariots driven by nobles had been the decisive force on the battlefield. By 650 B.C., war chariots were replaced by the **phalanx** (FAY langks), a massive formation of heavily armed foot soldiers, standing shoulder to shoulder. The phalanx was the most feared fighting technique of its time. However, its success depended on long hours of training. As their role in defending their city-state grew, citizen-soldiers demanded a greater voice in government.

During the sixth century B.C.,* citizen-soldiers supported revolts of the lower class that broke out in many city-states. The lower class had become discontented as a result of the practice of debt slavery. People who could not afford to repay loans had to sell themselves into slavery to pay off their debts. Widespread discontent resulted in the rise of **tyr-**

---
* Since B.C. dates are counted backwards from zero, the span 100 B.C. to 1 B.C. represents the first century B.C. Therefore, the sixth century B.C. is the 500s B.C.

anny, government by an individual, or tyrant, who seizes power by force.

To the ancient Greeks, the words tyranny and tyrant did not have a negative meaning. A tyrant gained power as a champion of the people. He ruled for as long as he could keep their support. In order to stay in power, tyrants increased employment through public works such as building temples and defensive walls. They also supported the arts. As a result, some city-states made great cultural and economic progress under the tyrants.

In some Greek city-states, the rule of tyrants did not last long. A new form of government, **democracy,** or government by the citizens, emerged. Although a number of city-states eventually became democracies, democracy first developed in Athens and it reached its greatest height there.

Greeks founded colonies and traded throughout the ancient Mediterranean world. They exchanged wine, olive oil, and finely decorated pottery for spices and purple dye from the eastern Mediterranean and grain from the Black Sea area. To protect their farflung trade, Greeks built warships like the one painted on this vase.

Early Government of Athens

According to Greek legend, the sea god Poseidon (poh SĪ duhn) competed with the goddess Athena for control of Athens. Although Athena won, giving her name to the city, Athenians still felt close to the sea. Located in Attica, a peninsula with poor, rocky soil, Athenians looked outward to the sea and trade. The sea linked Athens to the outside world and new ideas.

Athens moved slowly toward democratic rule. As in other city-states, the landowning aristocracy in Athens replaced the king as head of government around 800 B.C. The aristocracy governed through a council headed by three **archons** (AHR kahnz), or officials. The nobles often put their own interests above those of the polis. Although an assembly of citizens met to discuss government affairs, citizens who were not nobles were almost powerless.

Tensions ran high in Athens. Merchants, small farmers, and many noncitizens deeply resented the nobles. Merchants demanded more political rights, but the nobles resisted sharing power. At the same time, many small farmers were being forced into debt by poor harvests. Some became tenants on the estates of noble landowners. Others had to sell themselves into slavery to pay their debts.

Many residents who came from other parts of Greece, especially skilled artisans, resented their inability to become citizens.* The discontent of these groups led to violence.

Foundations of Democracy in Athens

In 621 B.C., the archons of Athens appointed Draco (DRAY koh), a noble, to draw up a written code of law. They felt that such a code was necessary to prevent civil war. Like Hammurabi's Code, the first Athenian law code was harsh. It ordered the death penalty for many offenses. But Draco's code made the laws public and required that judges, usually nobles, apply the laws equally to all classes.

Unfortunately, Draco's code failed to satisfy the demands of most Athenians, and violence continued to disrupt the city. In the next century, other leaders would make further changes that became the foundations for democracy in Athens.

Beginnings of reform. In 594 B.C., Athenians turned to Solon (SOH luhn), a wise, well-educated leader, to ease tensions. Solon abolished debt slavery and freed citizens previously forced into slavery. He limited the amount of land one citizen could own and extended citizenship to some skilled artisans from other cities. To increase the food supply and keep prices down, he stopped the sale of grain abroad. But he encouraged the export of olive oil and wine, which helped make Athens a great trade center.

Greek roots of democracy are evident on this ceramic jar, which has the first known illustration of a secret ballot. After the voters wrote their choice on olive leaves, they deposited their ballots in a bowl held by Athena, the Greek goddess of wisdom, reason, and purity.

---

* Like other Greeks, Athenians considered anyone born outside their city a foreigner, and foreigners could not be citizens.

Through Solon's reforms, ordinary citizens gained greater political power. The assembly of citizens obtained the right to approve government decisions. A new law code, milder than Draco's, guaranteed citizens the right to bring charges against other citizens in a law court. To check the power of those who administered the laws, Solon created new law courts in which citizens owning a certain amount of property served as jurors.

Despite Solon's reforms, unrest persisted. Land ownership was still the basis of real political power. Landless citizens could not hold many official positions, and families freed from debt slavery could not afford to buy land. As a result, landowning nobles continued to dominate Athenian government.

This smouldering discontent eventually paved the way for the establishment of a tyranny. In 560 B.C., Pisistratus (pī SIHS truh tuhs) seized power with the support of poor citizens. Pisistratus took some land from the nobles and gave it to the peasants. He also reduced the privileges of the nobles and directed new building projects. Athenian trade and commerce thrived, and Athens gained prestige throughout the Greek world.

Cleisthenes. In 508 B.C., Cleisthenes (KLĪS thuh NEEZ) moved Athens further along the road to democratic government. He made the Athenian Assembly the lawmaking body. All citizens, regardless of whether they owned land, took part in the Assembly. Cleisthenes also granted citizenship to some immigrants and former slaves. He set up a council of 500 citizens over the age of 30 to propose laws and to administer laws that the Assembly approved. Members of the council were chosen by lot.

Cleisthenes tried to extend the power of citizens further by introducing the idea of ostracism. **Ostracism** (AHS trah sihzm) was the temporary exile of a citizen from the city. If citizens thought a person was a threat to Athens, they could vote to ostracize him by writing his name on a piece of pottery. Anyone receiving more than 6,000 such votes was banished from Athens for ten years.

The development of democracy in Athens continued in the fifth century B.C. It reached its height under the great statesman Pericles, as you will read in the next section.

Training for Athenian Citizenship

In general, citizenship in Athens was a privilege and responsibility reserved for free men whose parents were both free, native-born Athenians. At age 18, these men took an oath to defend the city and its gods. After two years of military training, they became citizens and took their places in the Assembly.

Athenian education prepared young men for citizenship. Curiosity and the free discussion of ideas were encouraged. An educated slave served as tutor and companion, supervising a boy's learning between the ages of 8 and 18. Students learned grammar, music, and rhetoric—that is, the art of public speaking. The study of grammar included memorizing literature, such as the *Iliad* and *Odyssey*. From such ancient works, Athenian boys learned Greek religious beliefs and history, as well as the values of the ideal warrior.

Athenians prized a sound mind and a well-trained body. In lively public discussions, young men debated questions on art, politics, and philosophy. Sports and gymnastics occupied an equally important place in a youth's training.

Women in Athenian Society

Women in Athens had no political or legal rights. They could not attend the Assembly, hold office, own property, or conduct any legal business. A woman's nearest male relative acted as her legal guardian.

Athenian women lived in strict seclusion, attending only occasional religious festivals. When they left the house, they were always attended by slaves. Furthermore, husbands and wives lived in separate parts of the house. "The best reputation a woman can have," claimed the Athenian leader Pericles, "is not to be spoken of among men either for good or for evil."

Another Greek wrote that the duty of a wife was "to bear us . . . children and to be faithful guardians of our households." In this role, women managed their homes and slaves and raised children. A mother trained her daughters in domestic skills. Between the ages of 14 and 16, a daughter married a man chosen by her parents.

81

In Athens, women seldom left the home. Men did the shopping, and slaves carried the food home. However, in most Greek towns and villages, getting water from the town fountain was a woman's chore. Going for water was a social occasion, as this painting on a water jug shows.

Sparta

Life in the city-state of Sparta differed greatly from life in Athens. As you can see from the map on page 86, Sparta was located in Laconia (luh KOH nee uh), an isolated region in the Peloponnesus. During the Dark Age, Dorian invaders settled in Sparta and enslaved the local population. The slaves, called **helots** (HEHL uhtz), worked the land for the Spartans. Because the helots outnumbered their rulers 20 to 1, the Spartans created a strong military state to prevent slave uprisings.

The Spartan government was a monarchy headed by two kings. A council of 28 elders advised the kings, and an assembly of Spartan citizens met to approve all government decisions. At such meetings, citizens showed their support by shouting loudly. Each year, the assembly elected five overseers, or **ephors** (EHF orz), to direct the daily affairs. The ephors

supervised the helots and kept a close watch on the private lives of citizens.

The Spartan way of life. In Sparta, the desire for a strong military state dominated all other interests. To achieve such a state, the Spartans developed a strict system that governed every aspect of a citizen's life from birth to death.

State control began when a newborn infant was brought before the ephors. Weak and sickly babies were placed on mountainsides to die of exposure. To prepare brave warriors who displayed absolute loyalty, training began early. At the age of seven, boys left home to live in military barracks. Brutal discipline during training taught Spartan youths to fend for themselves. They had no shoes and few clothes even in winter. They were expected to steal food to supplement a meager diet, but they were beaten if caught.

Like detectives, historians examine many kinds of evidence for clues to the past. One valuable source of information is visual evidence, such as paintings, statues, drawings, and photographs.

The ancient Greeks left many written records that tell us how they lived. They also left a visual record of their lives in their pottery, buildings, and stone carvings.

The Greeks decorated their pottery with scenes from daily life as well as stories of gods and goddesses. Paintings on Greek vases are useful because they show how people saw themselves, how they dressed, what games they played, and what events they thought were important.

When you study visual evidence, however, you must remember that you are seeing only what the artist wanted you to see. In order to make the best use of visual evidence, you need to study each piece carefully. Use the following steps to study the painting on page 82.

1 Identify the subject of the painting. Sometimes when you look at a picture two or three times, you see details you did not notice at first glance. (a) Who is shown in the painting? (b) What do you think the people are doing?

2 Study the visual evidence to learn about a particular people, event, or development. As you look at details in the painting, think about what they tell you about the subject. (a) What does the vase painting tell you about clothing worn by Greek women? (b) What do the carvings on the wall suggest about water fountains in Greek towns?

3 Evaluate the visual evidence to decide if it is a reliable source. One picture or one piece of evidence seldom tells all there is to know about a subject. An artist may have painted it with a specific purpose and left out some details. You have to decide if the evidence is a reliable source. (a) Based on what you know about Greek life, does the vase painting seem accurate? (b) In what way is it limited evidence about Greek life? (c) Using the painting as evidence, draw two conclusions about life in ancient Greece.

Spartans told a story about a boy caught stealing a fox. The boy allowed the animal to claw him to death rather than admit he had it hidden under his coat. To the Spartans, the endurance and courage displayed by the youth were admirable.

In addition to long hours of military drill, boys spent time learning to read and write. Discussion was discouraged. When asked a question, a boy was expected to answer in the fewest words possible. Today, a person who gives very brief answers is called laconic (luh KAHN ihk), from Laconia, the region around Sparta.

At the age of 20, Spartan soldiers married, but they continued to live in barracks for another 40 years. At the age of 30, they became citizens and took their places in the assembly. The state provided each citizen with land and slaves to support his family.

Spartan women also endured strict discipline and learned to defend Sparta. They were expected to show absolute obedience first to their fathers and later to their husbands. Unlike women in other Greek city-states, Spartan women took part in public group exercises and military drills. They participated in gymnastics so they would be strong mothers.

Spartan women were tough-minded, and they expected the same of Spartan men. Once, as Spartan soldiers were leaving for battle, a group of Spartan women called out, "Come back with your shield or on it."

Sparta and the Greek world. Art and literature had little place in Spartan education. The state discouraged new ideas and forbade travel outside Sparta. Sparta increased its isolation from other Greek city-states by prohibiting the use of coined money, which was considered a corrupting influence.

Spartan girls learned to accept the same harsh discipline as boys. They were expected to stay as physically fit as this young Spartan runner. Athenians, who thought women should remain in seclusion, considered the women of Sparta immodest.

Other Greeks respected the Spartans for their discipline and courage. To the historian Herodotus (heh RAHD uh tus), the Spartans were "the best fighters in the world." The secret of their success, he believed, was their discipline and absolute obedience to the law: "never to retreat in battle, however great the odds, but always to stand firm, and to conquer or die."

SECTION 2 REVIEW

1. **Locate:** (a) Attica, (b) Athens, (c) Sparta, (d) Laconia.

2. **Identify:** (a) Draco, (b) Solon, (c) Pisistratus, (d) Cleisthenes.

3. **Define:** (a) polis, (b) acropolis, (c) monarchy, (d) aristocracy, (e) phalanx, (f) tyranny, (g) democracy, (h) archon, (i) ostracism, (j) helot, (k) ephor.

4. Describe the effects of the expansion of trade in the Greek world after 750 B.C.

5. Explain three steps by which Athens became more democratic.

6. Why did the Spartans feel the need for a strong military state?

7. **Critical Thinking** How might ostracism have served as a safety valve in ancient Athens?

3 A Century of Wars

READ TO UNDERSTAND

☐ **How the Persian Wars affected Greece.**

☐ **How Athenians lived during the city's Golden Age.**

☐ **What effect the Peloponnesian Wars had on Athens.**

☐ *Vocabulary:* **direct democracy.**

The Greeks believed that if an individual became too successful, the gods might become jealous and rain hardships, even death, on him or her. To the Greeks, the pride, ambition, and the jealousy of the gods explained the great military struggles of the sixth and fifth centuries B.C. As you read in Chapter 2, the Persian ruler Cyrus and his successors had carved out a vast empire extending from the Indus Valley to the Black Sea. The Persian empire included Greek city-states in Asia Minor.

These Greek city-states remained largely self-governing under Persian rule. But in 499 B.C., the city-state of Miletus (mī LEET uhs) revolted. Soon the Greek world came under attack by Persia.

Beginning of the Persian Wars

Miletus led the Greek cities of Asia Minor against the powerful Persian Empire. Despite aid from Athens, the rebel cities were crushed by the Persians in 493 B.C. Herodotus wrote in his history of the Persian Wars that when the Persian king Darius learned of the Athenian intervention he swore revenge and ordered a servant to repeat every day, "Master, remember the Athenians."

In 490 B.C., Darius launched an attack across the Aegean Sea. When the main Persian force landed near the plain of Marathon, Athens asked for help. But it received little support. Nevertheless, the outnumbered Athenians won a stunning victory over the Persians. According to legend, Pheidippides (fī DIHP uh DEEZ), the best runner in the Athenian army, was chosen to carry news of the victory to Athens. He ran 26 miles (about 42 kilometers) over hilly terrain, gasped, "Rejoice, we conquer," and died. Today, a marathon is a 26-mile foot race.

Athenians regarded the battle of Marathon as their finest hour. They honored their fallen soldiers by setting up a stone in the central marketplace of Athens that read: "The valor of these men will shine as a light imperishable forever."

Even as they celebrated their victory, the Athenians realized the Persians would seek revenge. The Athenian leader Themistocles (thuh MIHS tuh KLEEZ) convinced the Assembly that Athens should build a fleet of ships. With a strong navy, Themistocles reasoned, Athens could not only defend itself against a new Persian attack but could also become dominant in trade.

Victory for the Greeks

Darius died before he could renew his attack. However, his son Xerxes (ZERK seez) prepared a huge invasion force. But first he sent envoys to demand the surrender of the Greek cities. Fearing Persian strength, many cities submitted. The rest formed an alliance and chose Sparta to lead them.

In 480 B.C., the Persians landed in Greece. A small Spartan force marched north to delay them. Led by Leonidas (lee AHN uh duhs), the Spartans and soldiers from Thespia heroically defended the narrow mountain pass of Thermopylae (ther MAHP uh lee).

A generation after the battle Herodotus wrote about the outnumbered Greeks:

They withdrew into the narrow neck of the pass. . . . Here they resisted to the last, with their swords, if they had them, and if not, with their hands and teeth, until the Persians . . . finally overwhelmed them.

The stand at Thermopylae gave the Athenians time to take refuge on the nearby island of Salamis. From there, they watched the Persians burn and loot their homes and temples. At the same time, Themistocles tricked Xerxes into sending his fleet into the narrow straits of Salamis. Xerxes expected an easy Persian victory. He was so confident that he had a throne brought to the cliffs so he could watch the battle. But instead of victory, he saw the new Athenian navy trap and destroy most of the Persian fleet.

The Greek success at the battle of Salamis forced Xerxes to withdraw to Asia Minor. The following year, the Greeks soundly defeated the remaining Persian forces at the battle of Plataea (pluh TEE uh).

The Greek victories marked the end of the Persian Wars and created an upsurge in Greek

The Persian king Darius ruled a huge empire from the Black Sea to the Persian Gulf. An able and ambitious general, Darius dreamed of extending his empire into Europe by conquering Greece. In this council of war, Darius and his advisers plan an expedition against Greece.

confidence. Persian armies never again invaded mainland Greece, although Persian rulers used bribery and intrigue to foster disunity among the city-states. Because of its decisive role in the Persian Wars and its superb navy, Athens emerged as the leader of Greece.

The Athenian Empire

In 477 B.C., more than 160 delegates from Greek cities met on the island of Delos. They formed a defensive alliance to guard against possible future Persian attacks. The alliance was called the Delian League. Athens dominated the alliance from the start. It collected the tribute, commanded the league's fleet, and dictated policy. In 454 B.C., as evidence of its dominance, Athens moved the league treasury from Delos to the Acropolis in Athens.

Through its control of the Delian League, Athens established an empire. Riches from trade and tribute poured into the city. In an

MAP STUDY *During the Dark Age, many Greeks settled in cities along the coast of Asia Minor. In the fifth century B.C., some of these cities became part of the Athenian Empire, as you can see on this map. How did the geography of the Athenian Empire differ from that of other ancient empires you have studied?*

Ancient Greece

Area settled by Greeks

Athenian Empire about 450 B.C.

★ Persian War battles

atmosphere of prosperity, Athenians enjoyed their greatest political freedom ever, and Greek culture bloomed. The period following the Persian Wars has often been called the "Golden Age of Athens."

The chief architect of Athenian policy during this period was Pericles. The son of a noble family, Pericles had received an excellent education and had won fame as a general, statesman, poet, and philosopher. Between 461 B.C. and 429 B.C., Pericles dominated Athenian political life.

Pericles undertook an ambitious building program to beautify Athens. In 480 B.C., the Persians had destroyed the city and its sacred shrines. For years, the ruined temples served as reminders of the Persian menace. But Pericles proposed to rebuild the temples as monuments to the greatness of Athens. Atop the Acropolis, Athenians built the dazzling, white marble Parthenon (PAHR thuh NAHN), a temple to Athena. Phideas (FIHD ee uhs), considered the greatest sculptor of his day, carved a huge statue of Athena that stood inside the temple. Outside, there was another statue of Athena so large that returning sailors could see it far out at sea.

Athenians also strengthened the defensive walls that connected Athens to the busy port of Piraeus (pī REE uhs). The building programs employed thousands of workers and attracted stonemasons and artisans from all over Greece. At the same time, talented artists, philosophers, and poets converged on Athens, making it the center of Greek culture. Pericles called Athens the "school of Greece" for its artistic and intellectual achievements as well as for its political system.

The Height of Athenian Democracy

Democracy, which had been developing in Athens over many years, reached its peak under the leadership of Pericles. He opened all political offices to any citizen. And he paid jurors so that poor citizens as well as the wealthy could serve.

Athens had a **direct democracy**—that is, all citizens had the right to attend the Assembly and cast a vote. Citizens did not elect people to represent them. Since only a minority of people who lived in Athens were citizens, the entire citizen body could meet in open discussion. Pericles believed that Athenian democracy owed its success to shared values, loyalty to the city, and a willingness to do public service.

But Athenian democracy was far from complete. Citizens had time for public service largely because they owned slaves who worked their land and ran their businesses. Most residents of Athens were not citizens and had no say in government. The many Greeks who flocked to Athens from other cities were considered foreigners and were usually denied citizenship. Women, too, had no political rights. Still, with all its flaws, Athenian democracy served as a model for other Greek city-states as well as for democratic governments down through the ages.

The Peloponnesian Wars

As Athens' power grew, so did the resentment of other Greek city-states. Some of them formed an alliance called the Peloponnesian League. The alliance was headed by Sparta. In 431 B.C., a dispute between Athens and Corinth, a member of the Peloponnesian League, flared into an open conflict. War engulfed all of Greece as Athens and its allies battled the Peloponnesian League. At the start, the Athenian navy triumphed on the seas. But a Spartan army marched north into Attica and surrounded Athens. Pericles ordered everyone to move inside the city walls. In the overcrowded city, a plague broke out, killing over a third of the people, including Pericles.

Fighting dragged on for 27 years. Finally, with help from the Persian navy, Sparta blockaded Athens while Spartan armies again surrounded the city. Facing starvation, Athens surrendered in 404 B.C. Sparta's allies called for the destruction of Athens. However, Sparta spared the city out of respect for Athens' role in the Persian Wars.

The Peloponnesian Wars cost Athens its navy, its empire, and for a time its democratic form of government. Although Athens remained the cultural center of Greece, it never regained the power it had enjoyed during its golden age.

SECTION 3 REVIEW

1. **Locate:** (a) Miletus, (b) Marathon, (c) Thermopylae, (d) Delos.

2. **Identify:** (a) Themistocles, (b) Xerxes, (c) Delian League, (d) Pericles, (e) Parthenon.

3. **Define:** direct democracy.

4. (a) What event led to the Persian Wars? (b) List two results of these wars.

5. (a) What were the democratic features of Athenian government? (b) How was Athenian democracy limited?

6. What effect did the Peloponnesian Wars have on Athens?

7. **Critical Thinking** How did Athens' success in the Persian Wars lead ultimately to its downfall?

4 Patterns of Greek Life and Thought

READ TO UNDERSTAND

☐ How religion influenced Greek life.

☐ What views of the world were held by Greek philosophers.

☐ How the Greeks developed new approaches to the study of history.

☐ *Vocabulary:* tragedy, comedy, lyric poem, philosopher, Socratic method.

In the mild climate of Greece, people spent much time outdoors. Men gathered on the street corners or in the marketplace to discuss the news of the day. They talked mostly about worldly concerns since the Greeks were more interested in this life than in an afterlife. But the Greeks did not neglect their gods. They often took part in religious festivals and contributed to the building of the temples that graced every Greek city-state.

Religious Beliefs

The Greeks loved to hear stories about their many Greek gods and goddesses. They believed that the 12 most powerful gods and goddesses met in a council on Mount Olympus, a snow-covered peak in northern Greece. The chief Olympian god was Zeus. He ruled the universe and made his presence known through thunder, lightning, and earthquakes, which often shook the Greek peninsula. Poseidon, lord of the seas, and Hades, ruler of the underworld, were Zeus' brothers. Their sister Hestia was the goddess of the hearth, or home fire.

Each Olympian presided over different aspects of life. For example, Hera, the wife of Zeus, was the goddess of marriage. Athena, the daughter of Zeus and the patron of Athens, embodied wisdom and protected handicrafts and agriculture.

Each Greek city-state held festivals to honor individual gods. Athens, for example, set aside about 60 days each year for religious celebrations. Many religious festivals included

This bronze head of Aphrodite shows the beauty for which the goddess was famous. Her importance to the ancient Greeks is evident in her many roles: Aphrodite was goddess of the sea and seafaring, of war, and of love.

athletic contests dedicated to a particular god. Every four years, athletes assembled at Olympia to honor Zeus. Unlike local religious festivals, the Olympic games were open to all Greeks.

In addition to festivals honoring the Olympian gods, many Greeks participated in festivals connected with mystery religions. These religions emphasized secret rituals and promised immortality, or eternal life, to followers. Because they offered spiritual comfort to the poor, the mystery religions were very popular.

Greek Drama and Literature

In ancient Greece, religion, drama, and poetry were linked. Drama and poetry grew out of the celebrations in Athens honoring Dionysus (DĪ uh NĪ suhs), the god of wine. By the fifth century B.C., Athenian playwrights competed for prizes by presenting their works at the annual festival of Dionysus.

Greek plays were performed in outdoor theaters built into hillsides. The audience sat on sloping tiers of stone seats. There was no scenery or curtain on the stage. Three male actors performed all the parts, while an all-male chorus chanted verses to explain the play's action. Actors wore elaborate costumes and high boots to set them off from the chorus. Only men were allowed to attend the performances.

Tragedies. The earliest Greek plays were **tragedies,** dramas that focused on the suffering of a major character and usually ended in disaster. Inspired by stories from the *Iliad* and *Odyssey* and by ancient myths, Greek playwrights posed profound questions about the behavior of the gods and the causes of human suffering. They were especially concerned with individuals who struggled to achieve excellence but failed because of fate or their own weaknesses.

Among the greatest writers of tragedy were Aeschylus (EHS kuh luhs), Sophocles (SAHF uh KLEEZ), and Euripides (yoo RIHP uh DEEZ). Aeschylus has been called the father of Greek tragedy because his work served as a model for others. His plays were concerned with the relationships between humans and the gods. He treated the themes of murder, revenge, and divine justice in the *Oresteia* (aw

Young Sophocles was proud and excited. What greater honor could there be than to lead the young men of Athens in the celebrations of the victory over the Persians at Salamis? For the 15-year-old Sophocles, being chosen as the symbol of his city's youth was a moment to treasure all his life.

Born in Athens in 496 B.C., Sophocles witnessed the city's years of greatness—as well as the beginning of its decline. While he was growing up, Athens was becoming a democracy. During the Golden Age of Athens, Sophocles became a prize-winning tragic poet. From age 65 until his death at age 90, he watched the bitter struggles of the Peloponnesian Wars that would leave his beloved Athens wrecked physically and morally.

In the moving tragedy *Antigone*, Sophocles examined a fundamental ethical question: What is the proper relation of the individual citizen to the state? Antigone, a courageous young woman, learns that her brother has been killed while attacking the city of Thebes. Creon, the king of Thebes, has ordered that no one may bury the traitor on pain of death. Antigone disobeys Creon's order because it goes against the gods' laws. She sprinkles dust over the body as a symbol of burial. Caught in this illegal act, she is brought before Creon and condemned to death.

At the root of the conflict between Antigone and Creon are the questions: What should a citizen do if his or her duty to obey the government conflicts with other duties? What obligations, if any, are higher than loyalty to the laws of the state? In his tragedy, Sophocles gave this answer: Antigone was right to disobey Creon. The law of the gods was higher than Creon's.

In *Antigone*, Sophocles raised questions that concerned the citizens of Athens. But such questions have echoed through the ages and are still at the root of ethics in our lives.

1. What law had Antigone broken?

2. **Critical Thinking** Describe an incident in recent history that illustrates the ethical question Sophocles described in *Antigone*.

REHS tee ah). This series of three plays told the fate of the Greek hero Agamemnon and his family after the Trojan War.

The poet Sophocles wrote 123 plays, but only 7 have survived. In *Oedipus the King,* he examined how destiny affected the lives of individuals. Warned by the Delphic oracle that he would commit an unforgivable deed, Oedipus (EHD uh puhs) left home to avoid his fate. But in the end, he could not escape it.

Euripides was a controversial playwright because he was critical of traditional ideas. In *Medea* and *The Trojan Women,* for example, he expressed sympathy for women and the oppressed.

Comedies. Like tragedy, Greek comedy originated in celebrations honoring Dionysus. **Comedies** were plays in which poets ridiculed people, ideas, and social customs. In plays such as *The Birds* and *The Clouds,* the playwright Aristophanes (AR uh STAHF uh NEEZ) mocked just about every figure in Greek life, from politicians and philosophers to poets and even his audience. Skilled in poking fun at pretense and self-importance, Aristophanes enjoyed great popularity.

Through trade and conquest, Greek theaters and plays were spread across the Mediterranean world. As a result, drama and the theater became a part of western civilization.

Performances of tragedies and comedies were well attended in ancient Greece. One theater in Athens held about 20,000 people. Because the outdoor theaters were so large, actors wore huge masks that symbolized the characters and emotions they were portraying. A funnel built into the mouth of each mask probably amplified the actor's voice.

Poetry. The Greeks admired epic poetry such as the *Iliad* and *Odyssey.* They also enjoyed **lyric poems,** in which the poet expresses his or her emotions or thoughts. Lyric poems were sung by a musician playing a lyre, a small harplike instrument. Although Greeks seldom admired the accomplishments of women, Sappho (SAF oh) won fame for her lyric poetry.

The Visual Arts

The Greeks excelled in architecture, sculpture, and painting. Their simple, elegant buildings reflected their love of balance and beauty. No buildings were more important to them than their temples. Thus, when Pericles decided to rebuild Athens, he lavished attention on the Parthenon and other temples on the Acropolis.

The Parthenon, which still stands, is a rectangular building supported by stately marble columns. Its graceful carved columns glitter in the sunlight, giving the impression of lightness and height. Today, many public buildings use columns modeled on Greek designs.

Greek sculptors believed that perfect harmony and proportion existed in the natural world. They tried to show this perfection in their work by portraying the ideal rather than the real. When the sculptor Polyclitus (PAHL ee KLĪT uhs) carved statues of athletes, generals, and statesmen, he showed Greek idealism by portraying the human body in its most beautiful and graceful form.

Greek artisans produced fine pottery that was exported all over the Mediterranean. On vases and bowls, artists painted figures of legendary warriors, chariot races, or simple scenes from the marketplace. The elegant designs and beautiful proportions of such common items as water jugs are further evidence of the Greek love of beauty.

The arts of ancient Greece were widely admired and frequently copied. As a result, Greek art influenced first the Romans and later the peoples of Western Europe.

Faith in Human Reason

Greek thinkers were intensely curious about the world and the place of people in it. They believed in the individual's ability to reason and discover important truths. The Greeks called these thinkers **philosophers,** or seekers of wisdom. Greek philosophers searched for order in nature. By studying the world systematically, they made many discoveries.

According to tradition, the first Greek philosopher was Thales (THAY leez), who lived about 600 B.C. Thales observed the physical world to discover the basis of life. He and his followers made an important breakthrough. They claimed that the universe was governed by natural laws that people could understand through reason. By rejecting the belief that gods controlled the universe, they provided the basis for later scientific achievement.

A scientific approach to learning. Greek philosophers studied all areas of human knowledge, from physics and astronomy to music and art. Pythagoras (pih THAG er uhs) was a musician, mathematician, and astronomer. He is well known to students of geometry because he found a relationship between the lengths of the sides of a right triangle.

Curiosity along with reason and observation led to impressive advances in medicine. Greek physicians detailed the symptoms and stages of many diseases. From their observations, they concluded that illnesses have natural causes and are not the result of evil spirits, as most people believed.

Physicians trained on the island of Cos at a medical school associated with a great legendary doctor, Hippocrates (hih PAHK ruh TEEZ). According to tradition, Hippocrates urged physicians to maintain high moral standards. Today, doctors still take a version of the Hippocratic Oath, to act "for the benefit of the sick, to give no deadly medicine to anyone if asked, nor suggest such a course, and to avoid intentional wrong-doing and harm."

The Sophists. Toward the end of the Peloponnesian Wars, a new school of philosophy appeared in Athens. The Sophists, or "men of wisdom," were not interested in the nature of the physical world. Instead, their main concern was how to achieve political and social success.

The Sophists were professional teachers who trained rich, ambitious young men for public life. From the Sophists, Athenian youths learned rhetoric, the art of public speaking. The Sophists prized highly the ability to argue clearly before the Assembly or a jury. However, some Athenians criticized the Sophists for emphasizing success over obedience to laws or respect for tradition. They disapproved of the Sophists' lack of concern for ethical standards.

Socrates: The Questioning Philosopher

One critic of the Sophists was Socrates, a philosopher and teacher who lived in Athens from 469 B.C. to 399 B.C. He was one of the most influential figures in history. Socrates championed the use of reason. He thought that individuals should be guided by reason alone in their search for knowledge and truth. Socrates

left no writings of his teachings. He is known instead through the works of his famous pupil, Plato.

Socrates spent his days in the streets of Athens teaching those who would listen. He attracted many young students, who admired his intelligence and applauded his use of reason to challenge traditional ideas. Socrates was searching for a code of conduct for human behavior. The most important thing, he felt, was: "Know thyself." Through knowledge, Socrates believed, people discover how to act correctly.

Socrates developed a conversational, question-and-answer technique that today is called the **Socratic method.** He asked his students questions and insisted that they answer clearly. The Socratic method was designed to make people examine their beliefs using reason.

Socrates' search for truth using reason alarmed many Athenians. Stung by defeat in

In the fourth century B.C., the sculptor Praxiteles (prak SIHT uh LEEZ) carved this marble statue of the god Hermes holding the infant Dionysus. The elegant, graceful pose of Hermes is an example of the Greek desire to portray the ideal. Even though Praxiteles was portraying two gods, he showed them in human form.

the Peloponnesian Wars, they looked for a scapegoat. They came to see Socrates as a dangerous troublemaker. The authorities accused him of failing to honor the gods and corrupting the youth of Athens. Socrates could have gone into exile, but he chose to stand trial and was condemned to death by an Athenian jury. Socrates accepted the penalty, maintaining that a citizen should obey the laws of the state. "Above all," he told the jury, "I shall be able to continue my search into true and false knowledge; as in this world, so also in that, I shall find out who is wise, and who pretends to be wise and is not."

Plato and Aristotle: The Heirs of Socrates

Plato was 28 years old when Socrates died. Upset by his teacher's death, Plato left Athens for ten years. On his return, he set up a school, the Academy, that survived as a center of learning for nearly 900 years.

At the Academy, Plato taught philosophy, science, and mathematics. Most of his students were men, although a few women were allowed to attend. Like Socrates, Plato examined issues such as the meaning of justice, the nature of truth and beauty, and the rights and responsibilities of citizenship.

Plato's written works are in the form of dialogues, or conversations in which different speakers express their views. In the *Republic,* Plato explained his concept of the ideal state. He believed that it should be based on the ideal of justice—the satisfaction of the common good. It would have three classes: workers to produce basic necessities, soldiers to defend the state, and philosophers to govern in the public interest. Plato's state included such controversial ideas as abolishing the family and private property because they led to selfishness.

The most brilliant student at the Academy was Aristotle (AIR ihs TAHT'L). After the death of Plato, Aristotle left the Academy. Eventually, Philip II, king of Macedonia, invited Aristotle to teach his son, Alexander. When Alexander inherited the Macedonian throne (see page 94), he gave Aristotle a generous gift of money. Aristotle used the money to establish the Lyceum (lī SEE uhm), a school in Athens.

The Lyceum became the world's first scientific institute.

Aristotle explored dozens of subjects, ranging from philosophy to biology to the arts. In each field, his ideas have influenced thinking to the present. Aristotle believed that reason was the highest good. He taught that people should aim for moderation in all things. To Aristotle, virtue, or moral behavior, was a balance between extremes. He praised the virtues of self-control and self-reliance.

Aristotle's ideas on government differed from Plato's. For example, he valued family life and property. During Aristotle's day, Athenian democracy had become corrupt. As a result, Aristotle believed that the best kind of government was a mixture of monarchy, aristocracy, and democracy. An enlightened king should rule with the help of an educated aristocracy and with a popular assembly that respected the rule of law.

The Greek Historians

The Greeks developed a new approach to history that became the basis of the way we study history today. Unlike the Egyptians, who recorded only the deeds of the pharaohs, and the Hebrews, whose history was aimed at showing God's hand in events, the Greeks tried to understand why people acted as they did. To them, history was the study of human behavior.

Herodotus has been called the founder of history because he made the first attempt to gather and analyze historical evidence. To write his *History of the Persian Wars,* Herodotus traveled widely. He questioned many people and recorded the customs of the people he met and the geography of the places he visited. Although he did not always distinguish between fact and legend, he presented much useful information about the ancient world.

Thucydides, who wrote the *History of the Peloponnesian Wars,* improved on Herodotus' methods. He tried to remain impartial and included only facts that he could prove. Although he was an Athenian, he tried to present a balanced account of the war between Sparta and Athens. In the process, Thucydides set an example of unbiased reporting for future historians.

Socrates' teachings had a profound impact on later Greek philosophers, most notably on Plato and Aristotle. This mosaic from a Roman villa shows Plato, seated under the tree, teaching. Aristotle, his most famous pupil, is standing at the far right.

SECTION 4 REVIEW

1. **Identify:** (a) Aeschylus, (b) Sophocles, (c) Euripides, (d) Pythagoras, (e) Hippocratic Oath, (f) Sophists, (g) Socrates, (h) Plato, (i) Aristotle.

2. **Define:** (a) tragedy, (b) comedy, (c) lyric poem, (d) philosopher, (e) Socratic method.

3. Describe two ways that religion was connected to daily life in Greece.

4. (a) What rule did Socrates think people should live by? (b) How did he show himself to be a good citizen?

5. (a) Why is Herodotus called the founder of history? (b) What did Thucydides contribute to the study of history?

6. **Critical Thinking** Compare the views of Plato and Aristotle on the ideal state.

5 The Spread of Greek Civilization

READ TO UNDERSTAND

☐ What role Alexander played in the spread of Greek civilization.

☐ What characteristics marked Hellenistic civilization.

☐ What advances in science were made during the Hellenistic period.

☐ *Vocabulary:* Hellenistic civilization.

From Macedonia, north of Greece, Philip II watched the quarrelsome Greek city-states indulge in their endless wars. He saw, too, how the Persians egged on the bickering. An ambitious man, Philip dreamed of uniting Greece and Macedonia into a grand alliance to fight the Persian Empire. Philip's son, Alexander, fulfilled this dream and spread Greek civilization across a vast empire.

Philip of Macedonia

Philip II became king of Macedonia in 359 B.C. Because he respected Greek military techniques, he hired Greek generals to train his soldiers. He also admired Greek culture and invited Aristotle to supervise the education of his son, Alexander.

Philip did not let his admiration for Greek culture stand in the way of his ambitions. He wanted to expand his power over Greece and sought to divide the Greek city-states by playing on their distrust of one another. He won the support of many through bribery and threats.

The Greeks were divided in their opinions of Philip. Some favored this energetic leader. Others, especially the Athenian orator Demosthenes (dih MAHS thuh NEEZ), warned that Philip posed a serious threat to Greek independence. When Athens and Thebes finally united against Philip in 338 B.C., they were quickly defeated at the battle of Chaeronea (KEHR un NEE uh). Philip made himself master of Greece and began to plan an invasion of Persia. But at his daughter's wedding in 336 B.C., Philip was killed by an assassin.

Alexander the Great

Alexander was only 20 years old when he inherited his father's kingdom—and his ambition. However, he was well prepared to rule. He had commanded a cavalry force at the battle of Chaeronea and had served as an ambassador to Athens. Through his teacher, Aristotle, Alexander had come to respect Greek culture and learning.

By 334 B.C., Alexander felt strong enough in Macedonia and Greece to take on the Persian Empire. He assembled a large, well-organized and well-equipped army and crossed into Asia Minor. He swiftly defeated a Persian army and liberated the Greek cities of Asia Minor.

According to legend, while in Gordium Alexander heard a story about a knot that no one could undo. The man who untied the Gordian knot, people said, would rule the world. The impatient Alexander wasted no time. He drew his sword and slashed the knot in two.

Just as swiftly, Alexander defeated the Persians at Issus and then marched into Egypt. There, he founded the city of Alexandria at the mouth of the Nile. It was ideally located to link

Alexander the Great, shown in this mosaic, was not only a brilliant military leader, but was also an admirer of learning and culture. Shortly after Alexander became king, the Greek city-state of Thebes rebelled against Macedonian rule. Alexander crushed the rebels and leveled their city. But he ordered his soldiers to spare the home of Pindar, a poet whose writing he admired.

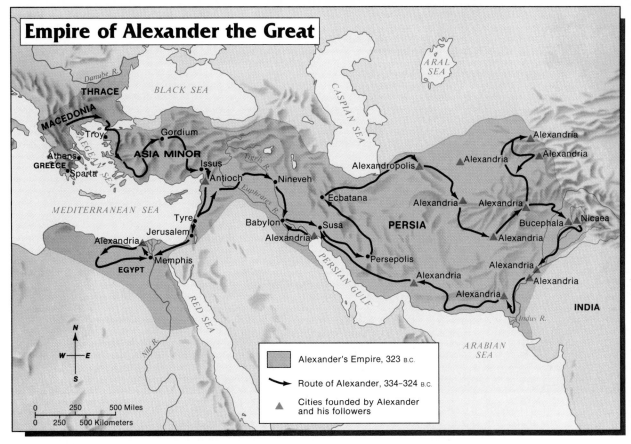

Empire of Alexander the Great

ARAL SEA

BLACK SEA

CASPIAN SEA

Danube R.

THRACE

MACEDONIA

Troy

Gordium

Athens
GREECE
Sparta

ASIA MINOR

Issus

Antioch

Nineveh

Tigris R.

Euphrates R.

Alexandropolis

Alexandria

Alexandria

Alexandria

Alexandria

Ecbatana

Alexandria

MEDITERRANEAN SEA

Tyre

Jerusalem

Babylon

Susa

PERSIA

Bucephala

Nicaea

Alexandria

Alexandria

Memphis

EGYPT

Alexandria

Persepolis

Alexandria

Alexandria

Alexandria

PERSIAN GULF

RED SEA

Nile R.

Alexandria

Alexandria

INDIA

Indus R.

ARABIAN SEA

N
W—E
S

| 0 | 250 | 500 Miles |
| 0 | 250 | 500 Kilometers |

Alexander's Empire, 323 B.C.

Route of Alexander, 334–324 B.C.

Cities founded by Alexander and his followers

MAP STUDY *Alexander the Great's empire stretched from Greece to India. The cities he and his followers founded became centers of Hellenistic civilization. Many of these cities were named after Alexander. One, Bucephala, was named after Alexander's horse, Bucephalus (byoo SEHF uh luhs). Describe the relationship between the route of Alexander's armies and the extent of the empire.*

Egypt, Greece, and the eastern Mediterranean. Alexander and his armies then turned east and conquered the rest of the Persian Empire. At Susa, Alexander found two statues of Athena that had been stolen by Xerxes during the Persian Wars. He sent them back to Greece and later burned the palace at Persepolis to avenge the destruction of Athens 150 years earlier.

Alexander made Babylon his capital, but he did not stay there long. He pushed eastward into India, where he faced the toughest battles of his life. In India, his soldiers mutinied. They had marched for over 11,000 miles (18,000 kilometers) since they had left Macedonia and had fought many battles. They would go no farther. Alexander was forced to return to Babylon, where he began organizing his empire. But within a year he caught a fever, and at the age of 32, he died.

Between 334 B.C. and 323 B.C., Alexander had conquered the largest empire the world had ever seen and had spread Greek civilization as far east as the Indus River. (See the map above.) After his death, however, the empire fell into confusion. For years, Alexander's generals and his family fought for power.

At last, about 305 B.C., three of Alexander's generals divided the empire among themselves. But warfare plagued the three kingdoms until Rome eventually conquered them all.

Blend of East and West

Alexander's most lasting achievement was the spread of Greek culture. As his armies marched across the Persian Empire into northwestern India, thousands of Greek officials, merchants, artisans, and artists fol-

95

LIGHTHOUSE AT ALEXANDRIA *Rising more than 400 feet (122 meters) above the water, the lighthouse at Alexandria, Egypt, was the tallest ever built. The lighthouse, built in 280 B.C., provided a beacon for sailors for more than 1,500 years before it was toppled by an earthquake. This recreation of the lighthouse by artist Larry Bernetti shows why sailors entering the port felt a sense of awe at the sight of it.*

lowed. They settled in these eastern lands, bringing Greek ways with them. In the lands he conquered, Alexander established cities modeled on the Greek polis.

Alexander encouraged the mixing of Greek culture with the cultures of the ancient Middle East. For example, he married a Persian princess and arranged a huge ceremony in which thousands of his soldiers married Persian women. He hoped the children of these marriages would help to unite the empire. Although Alexander thought of himself as Greek, he gained the support of his new subjects by adopting some of their practices. Thus, he worshipped Persian as well as Greek gods and adopted Persian customs and dress.

After Alexander's death, a rich new culture known as **Hellenistic civilization** emerged in Greece and in the other lands he had conquered. Hellenistic civilization was a blend of eastern and western influences, including Persian, Egyptian, Indian, and Greek. Alexandria in Egypt was the center of Hellenistic civilization. Sailors, merchants, and scholars from Greece, Italy, and the Middle East came to Alexandria to exchange products and ideas.

Many scholars came to a museum, or temple dedicated to the Muses, the Greek goddesses of the arts and sciences. The museum boasted of botanical and zoological gardens, used for research. It also had art galleries, an astronomical observatory, and a paid staff of scholars. It housed an enormous library with more than 500,000 papyrus scrolls containing the ancient world's knowledge of science, philosophy, and literature.

Hellenistic Science

During the Hellenistic Age, great progress was made in the sciences. Greek physicians described the human nervous system and discovered how the blood circulates through veins and arteries. Greek physicians living in

Alexandria learned from the Egyptians how to perform surgery using anesthetics. Hellenistic medical advances were not matched in Western Europe for 1,800 years.

Greek astronomers and geographers who worked in Alexandria developed new scientific theories. One astronomer reasoned that the earth was round and accurately computed its diameter. Another concluded that the earth revolved around the sun, but this idea was not widely accepted. Most people believed that the earth was the center of the universe and that the sun and moon revolved around it.

Euclid (YOO klihd) advanced the study of geometry. His work *The Elements* summarized the mathematical learning of the ancient world. Today, nearly 2,300 years later, Euclid's work is still the basis for high school geometry courses.

Another Hellenistic scientist, Archimedes (AHR kuh MEE deez), discovered the principle of the lever. "Give me a lever long enough," Archimedes reportedly boasted, "and I will move the world." He also invented the double pulley and a catapult, a machine for hurling stones at enemy forts. But to Archimedes, such practical inventions were unimportant. He preferred to be remembered for his work as a mathematician.

New Currents of Thought

After the conquests of Alexander, individual Greek city-states declined in importance. However, Athens continued to thrive as a center of learning and culture. Two new schools of philosophy took root in Athens. During the Golden Age of Athens, philosophers had been concerned with the role of the citizen in society. But Hellenistic philosophers were less interested in citizenship and more interested in the individual.

The philosopher Epicurus (EHP uh KYOOR uhs) claimed that the gods took no interest in human affairs and that there was no afterlife. Therefore, he argued, the greatest good was being happy in life. He defined happiness as freedom from fear and pain.

Epicureans believed that they could achieve happiness by living calm, simple, well-regulated lives. However, some Epicureans later emphasized personal enjoyment over moral conduct. As a result, "epicurean" has come to mean a person who is fond of luxury and pleasure.

Another philosopher, Zeno, founded a rival school of thought. Zeno and his followers were called Stoics. Like Epicurus, Zeno believed that happiness was the greatest good. However, he taught that a divine lawgiver had a fixed plan for the universe, in which everything had its place. Stoics believed that happiness resulted from living in harmony with nature and accepting whatever life brought, including misfortune.

The Stoics developed several ideas that later influenced Roman and Christian thinkers. They thought all people were basically alike because they shared the power of reason. The Stoics stressed self-discipline, courage, and moral conduct. Because Stoics urged people not to be upset by events, "stoic" has come to mean a person who remains calm in the face of pain or misfortune.

New currents of thought were reflected in the arts. In architecture, the simple classical style of Athenian temples gave way to grander, more elaborate buildings. In sculpture, huge heroic figures replaced the balanced, idealized portraits of generals, statesmen, and athletes. Hellenistic poets wrote more comedies than tragedies, and they dealt with lighter topics than earlier Greek poets had.

SECTION 5 REVIEW

1. **Locate:** (a) Macedonia, (b) Issus.

2. **Identify:** (a) Demosthenes, (b) Euclid, (c) Archimedes, (d) Epicurus, (e) Stoics.

3. **Define:** Hellenistic civilization.

4. How did Philip II of Macedonia show that he admired Greek culture?

5. How did Alexander encourage the blend of eastern and western cultures?

6. List two medical discoveries of the Hellenistic period.

7. **Critical Thinking** How successful do you think Alexander might have been if he had lived to the age of 60? Explain.

Summary

1. **Between 2000 B.C. and 1400 B.C., the Minoan civilization flourished on the island of Crete.** About 1400 B.C., the Achaeans invaded from the Greek mainland and captured the Minoan capital. Both the Minoans and the Achaeans prospered as a result of trade.

2. **After 750 B.C., independent city-states began to emerge in Greece.** These city-states gradually developed new forms of government in which individual citizens played an increasingly important role. In Athens, reformers laid the foundations of democratic government. In Sparta, the government maintained strict controls over the lives of the people.

3. **Victory in the Persian Wars increased the wealth and power of Athens.** During its golden age, Athens became a center of Greek culture and a model of democracy. Resentment of Athenian power among other Greek city-states led to the Peloponnesian Wars, which ended with the defeat of Athens in 404 B.C.

4. **Greek civilization reached its height during the fifth and fourth centuries B.C.** Greek playwrights and poets produced great works of literature. Sculptors and other artists tried to reproduce the harmony and perfection they saw in nature. Philosophers studied every branch of knowledge, searching for order in nature.

5. **Alexander the Great spread the Greek heritage across a huge empire.** The mixing of Greek culture with eastern cultures helped create Hellenistic civilization. During the Hellenistic period, great advances took place in the sciences and mathematics.

Recalling Facts

Match each name at left with the correct description at right.

1. Homer
2. Pericles
3. Plato
4. Archimedes
5. Thucydides

a. inventor of the double pulley
b. philosopher who set up the Academy
c. historian who wrote *History of the Peloponnesian Wars*
d. Athenian leader during its golden age
e. poet who wrote the *Iliad*

Chapter Checkup

1. Compare and contrast Minoan and Achaean civilizations.

2. Describe the following types of government developed by the Greeks: (a) monarchy; (b) aristocracy; (c) tyranny; (d) democracy.

3. Compare each of the following features of life in Athens and in Sparta: (a) government; (b) education; (c) role of women.

4. (a) How did the Persian Wars affect the Greek city-states? (b) How did the Peloponnesian Wars affect them?

5. (a) What method did Socrates use to try to teach people to act correctly? (b) How did Plato and Aristotle carry on Socrates' work?

6. Describe the conquests of Alexander the Great.

7. Describe the scientific advances made during the Hellenistic period.

1. **Understanding the Roots of Democracy** (a) Why do you think the individual played an important role in Greek life? (b) What relationship was there between the importance of the individual and the development of democracy?

2. **Relating Past to Present** (a) What purpose do you think the Hippocratic Oath served in ancient Greece? (b) Why do you think it is still used today?

Developing Basic Skills

1. **Identifying Immediate and Long-Range Causes** When historians investigate the causes of an event or development, they distinguish between immediate and long-range causes. An immediate cause is the actual incident or change that triggers an event or historical development. Long-range causes are the underlying reasons. (a) Based on your reading in this chapter, what was the immediate cause of the Peloponnesian Wars? (b) What long-range cause or causes can you identify?

2. **Placing Events in Time** Historians use the terms "decade" and "century" to describe specific lengths of time. A decade is 10 years. A century is 100 years. The 100 years from 200 B.C. to 101 B.C. are called the second century B.C. The years from 100 B.C. to 1 B.C. are called the first century B.C. The period from 1 A.D. to 100 A.D. is the first century A.D. There is no year 0. Review the chapter and study the time line below. (a) What years are included in the decade before the Battle of Marathon? (b) In what century was the Delian League formed? (c) Which events shown on the time line took place in the fifth century B.C.?

Writing About History

Supporting a Topic Sentence

Once you have written a good topic sentence, you must support the sentence with specific, related information. There are several kinds of supporting information that are commonly used to develop a main idea. A paragraph may include one kind of support or several kinds. Supporting information can include examples, details, facts, reasons, and incidents.

Examples: specific instances that provide evidence to support a generalization

Details: descriptive pieces of additional information

Facts: verifiable information that could include evidence such as statistics

Reasons: information that provides the causes for the main idea or explains it

Practice: For each of your answers to the Critical Thinking questions in this Chapter Review, underline the topic sentence and identify the type of supporting detail you used.

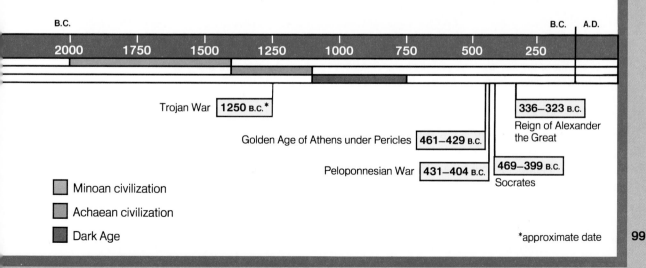

B.C. | B.C. | A.D.

2000 1750 1500 1250 1000 750 500 250

Trojan War **1250 B.C.***

Golden Age of Athens under Pericles **461–429 B.C.**

Peloponnesian War **431–404 B.C.**

336–323 B.C.
Reign of Alexander the Great

469–399 B.C.
Socrates

■ Minoan civilization

■ Achaean civilization

■ Dark Age

*approximate date

Ancient Rome: Republic to Empire

5

(509 B.C.—180 A.D.)

Rome's strong military tradition was reflected both in stories like the Aeneid and in works of art like the one shown here. Soldiers, ready to fight for the glory of Rome, are being carried to battle aboard a ship.

If you could have asked someone in ancient Rome how Rome began, you might have heard the following story of the twin brothers Romulus and Remus. About a year before the twins were born, their great-uncle had seized power from their grandfather. When the new king learned of the twins' birth, he ordered them thrown into the Tiber River, fearing that they would grow up to threaten his rule.

But the gods took pity on the infants and directed the river to place them safely on the shore. A wolf heard the babies crying and protected them. After a shepherd discovered the twins, he took them home and raised them as his own sons. When Romulus and Remus grew up, they took revenge on their great-uncle and restored their grandfather to his throne. Then, on the seven hills overlooking the Tiber River, the two young men founded the city of Rome.

Years later, when Romans encountered the older, more sophisticated cultures of the eastern Mediterranean, the story of Romulus and Remus seemed pale when compared to the heroic Greek tales of the Trojan War. So the Roman poet Virgil created a new legend. In his epic poem the *Aeneid* (ih NEE uhd), he told the story of the valiant Trojan hero Aeneas, who fled from the fiery destruction of Troy, carrying his father on his back. After years of wandering and many adventures, Aeneas founded a colony in Italy, where years later Romulus and Remus were born.

Both of these legends were important to the Romans. The story of Romulus and Remus said that strength, justice, and the favor of the gods were the best protection against danger and greed. The *Aeneid* linked Rome to the older civilizations of Greece and Asia Minor. This assured Romans that they were not mere newcomers to the Mediterranean world.

Rome was only a small town on the west coast of Italy when Athens flourished. By 323 B.C., however, when Alexander the Great had conquered his empire, Rome was emerging as a strong city-state. Between 265 B.C. and 44 B.C., Rome won control of the Mediterranean world, uniting many different peoples and regions under its rule. ■

---

1 The Roman Republic

READ TO UNDERSTAND

☐ How geography influenced early Rome.

☐ How government changed as Rome grew.

☐ What views Romans held about family, education, and religion.

☐ *Vocabulary:* republic, patrician, plebeian, consul, veto, dictator, legion, censor, tribune.

Today, historians speak of "the glories that were Greece and the grandeur that was Rome." Yet Rome like Greece had humble beginnings. About the time the Achaeans migrated into Greece (see page 76), other Indo-European tribes invaded Italy. Among them were the Latins, who followed their grazing herds into the lands just south of the Tiber River. By 750 B.C., they had settled into a farming life and built several small villages, which slowly grew into the city of Rome.

GEOGRAPHIC SETTING
Ancient Rome

As you can see from the map on page 102, the Italian peninsula juts out like a boot into the Mediterranean Sea. Off the toe of the boot lies the island of Sicily. The sea provided some protection for the early peoples of Italy. Later, the Romans used the sea as a highway for conquest and trade.

At the top of the boot are the Alps, which block cold winds and give the region a pleasant climate. However, the Alps give only limited protection from invaders. The Po River, which is fed by melting snows from the Alps, provides water for the rich farming region of the northern plain. Another mountain range, the Apennines (AP uh NINZ), runs down the length of Italy. Unlike the mountains in Greece, which isolated the city-states, the Apennines were a less serious barrier to unity in Italy. Most people lived in the west, where the land was more fertile than in the east. In the west, there were also good harbors and long rivers that could be easily navigated by small boats.

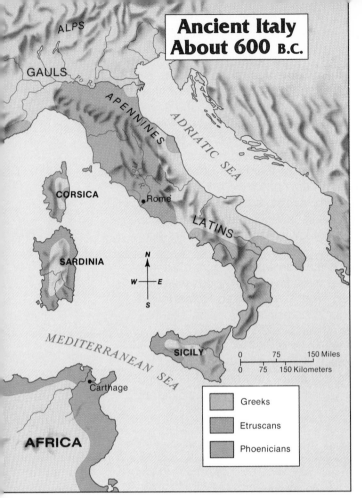

Ancient Italy About 600 B.C.

Greeks

Etruscans

Phoenicians

Many people influenced civilization on the Italian peninsula. The Latin people who settled Rome learned much from Greek and Phoenician traders. Who controlled Rome in 600 B.C.?

The city of Rome enjoyed many natural advantages. It was located on the fertile coastal plain halfway up Italy's west coast. From the seven hills overlooking the Tiber River, Romans could watch for enemy attacks. The Tiber provided food and transportation. Since Rome lay some distance inland, it was not exposed to raids from the sea. Romans built the port of Ostia at the mouth of the Tiber for ships too large to move up the river. ■

The Peoples of Italy

The Latins who founded Rome were farmers and herders. During their early history, they fought with other Latins for control of neighboring areas. Their struggles helped shape a belief in duty, discipline, and patriotism.

At the same time, Romans adopted ideas from the advanced civilizations of the Phoenicians and Greeks, who had set up colonies in Sicily and Italy. For example, from the Greeks, the Romans learned to build fortified cities and to grow grapes and olives.

The Etruscans (ih TRUHS kuhnz), who had migrated into Italy from Asia Minor, seized Rome about 600 B.C. During the next 100 years, the Romans absorbed many ideas from their Etruscan conquerors. They adopted the Etruscan alphabet, which the Etruscans had borrowed from the Greeks. They copied Etruscan styles of art and worshipped Etruscan gods alongside their own. And they learned Etruscan building techniques, including the arch.

Founding the Republic

In 509 B.C., the Romans overthrew the Etruscan king and established a republic. In a **republic,** all citizens with the right to vote choose their leaders. The elected leaders represent the people and rule in their name. The Roman Republic lasted for 500 years, during which time Rome grew from a small city-state into a world power.

In the early Republic, Roman society was dominated by a class of wealthy landowners, or **patricians** (puh TRIHSH uhnz). The common people, including farmers, artisans, small merchants, and traders, were called **plebeians** (plih BEE uhnz). Plebeians were citizens and could own land, but they could not hold public office or marry into patrician families.

Slaves made up the lowest class in Roman society. Most slaves were prisoners of war, but some were plebeians who had been enslaved for debt. Slaves were not citizens and had no legal rights.

In the early Republic, most people were farmers who worked on small plots of land. Later, as Rome expanded, its economy grew to include manufacturing and commerce.

Early government. Patricians controlled the government of the early Republic through the Senate. The Senate was made up of 300 patricians who served for life. It guided foreign and domestic policies. Every year, the Senate chose two **consuls,** or officials, from their own class to administer the laws of

102

Rome. A popular assembly, elected by the plebeians, approved the choice of consuls, but it had little real power.

During their one-year terms, the consuls directed the government and commanded the army. The consuls had equal power. Each had the right to **veto,** or block, an action of the other. In Latin, the word "veto" means "I forbid."

In times of crisis, the Senate would appoint a dictator to replace the consuls. A **dictator** had absolute power but could only hold office for six months.

The Roman army. At first, only patricians served in the Roman army. But the Republic faced many enemies, including the Etruscans, neighboring Latins, and the Gauls who lived north of the Po River. After the Gauls burned Rome in 390 B.C., the Senate turned to the plebeians for help. It required all citizens who owned land—plebeians and patricians—to serve in the army.

Roman soldiers trained in the use of slings, javelins, spears, and swords. Wealthy Romans provided their own equipment and served without pay. Poorer citizens received small salaries. Roman commanders enforced strict discipline. Such training and discipline made the Roman army highly effective.

The Roman army was divided into **legions** of about 6,000 soldiers. Each legion was divided into smaller units that could be moved around swiftly. This freedom of movement gave the Roman army an advantage over the massed ranks of its enemies.

Changes in Government

As you will read, Rome conquered many lands between 509 B.C. and 133 B.C. As Rome grew, plebeians who fought in its wars demanded more rights. The Senate kept its power and prestige, but the government gradually changed.

An Assembly of Centuries and an Assembly of Tribes replaced the popular assembly. The Assembly of Centuries was made up of the entire Roman army, including patricians and plebeians. It passed laws and elected the consuls, who until then had been chosen by the Senate. It also chose other officials, including the **censor,** who registered the population for

The Romans adopted many ideas from the Etruscans, including the art of wall painting. This wall painting once decorated a Roman house. The man, probably a Roman official, grasps a papyrus scroll. The woman holds a stylus and wax tablets, symbols of learning.

tax and voting purposes. The censor also enforced the moral code. Still, all government officials were patricians.

The Assembly of Tribes was made up of plebeians. It elected ten **tribunes** to speak for plebeian interests. At first, the tribunes had no official role in government. But when angry plebeians refused to fight for Rome, the Senate accepted the demand for a law code.

In 451 B.C., Rome's first written law code was carved onto 12 stone tablets that were set up in the Forum, or central marketplace. The Twelve Tables of Law showed the strict separation between patricians and plebeians. Laws prohibited plebeians from serving as consuls, entering the Senate, or marrying patricians. Yet by listing laws and punishments, the Twelve Tables protected all citizens from unfair treatment.

Over the next 200 years, the plebeians won more rights. Marriages between patricians and plebeians were allowed. And tribunes won the power to veto any government action that threatened the rights of plebeians. The Assembly of Tribes gained the right to

103

The education of a Roman child usually began at home. At right in this bas relief, a sculpture in which figures project from the background, a father listens patiently as his son recites his lesson. Children often went on to attend school. Roman schools were open to all who could pay a small fee. Girls as well as boys could attend.

pass laws. Eventually, plebeians won the right to hold any office, including consul. They were even allowed into the Senate.

The reforms did not mean equality, however. During Rome's wars of expansion, a new class of rich plebeians gained control of the government. Their wealth came from the growing trade and industry of Rome. This powerful new class guarded its power closely. Only the tribunes continued to speak for common citizens.

This painting from a Roman villa shows a wealthy woman and her servant. Women, especially those from wealthy families, enjoyed some power and influence in ancient Rome.

The Roman Family

Romans lived in large extended families. The government rewarded parents of many children and penalized bachelors. Large families guaranteed a steady supply of soldiers to fight in wars and of farmers to settle newly conquered lands.

Under Roman law, the father had absolute power over the entire household. Roman law gave him the right to sell his son or daughter into slavery and to abandon an unwanted infant.

In practice, Roman fathers were generally fair-minded. Their discipline was strict, but they were also concerned for the family welfare. Children learned the responsibilities of citizenship early. Parents stressed the virtues of hard work, courage, and loyalty.

Education. By 250 B.C., some wealthy families began importing Greek tutors to educate their children. But most fathers supervised their children's education personally. Some boys and girls from rich families attended private schools. Girls often received as thorough an education as boys.

Schools emphasized history, which students recited aloud. Stories of Roman heroes gave children a sense of pride in their city. Students also learned practical skills such as reading, writing, and public speaking.

Women in Roman society. During the early Republic, Roman women had few legal rights. They were citizens and might be called on to testify in court, but they could not vote or hold public office. Fathers usually arranged marriages for their daughters by the time the girls were 14 years old.

Later, Roman women gained more rights when new laws gave them control over their own property. Women could then make wills leaving their property as they chose.

Roman attitudes toward women differed from Greek attitudes. Romans did not restrict women to a separate part of the house. Women could attend the theater and join in public festivals. Some women had political influence in Rome, especially if their husbands or fathers held public office. Roman women often shared in household decisions and kept the family accounts. In addition, they supervised the children and any slaves owned by the family.

Religion

The Romans worshipped many gods in private and public. Each household had a shrine devoted to spirits that Romans believed protected the home and the fields. Every day, family members gathered to make offerings to Vesta, goddess of the hearth. Such daily rituals taught children to respect and defend the family and its gods.

Romans were fond of public religious festivals and games dedicated to individual gods and goddesses. For example, at the start of each month and year, Romans worshipped Janus, the god of beginnings. His name has survived in the English word "January." Festivals honoring Janus lasted several days and included street carnivals and feasts.

Romans absorbed religious beliefs from other people. They worshipped Jupiter, an Etruscan god, who was also identified with the Greek god Zeus. The Roman goddess Venus was similar to Aphrodite (AF ruh DĪT ee), the Greek goddess of love. As Rome grew stronger, its gods took on new powers. Mars, once simply the god of the fields, became god of war during the centuries of Roman conquests.

Like the Greeks, the Romans believed that different gods and goddesses influenced different aspects of life. This bronze statue portrays a Roman deity. The stalks of grain she is holding identify her as a household goddess. Roman families made daily sacrifices to the goddess of the hearth to protect their homes and fields.

SECTION 1 REVIEW

1. **Locate:** (a) Italy, (b) Sicily, (c) Alps, (d) Po River, (e) Apennines, (f) Rome, (g) Tiber River.

2. **Identify:** (a) Twelve Tables, (b) Jupiter, (c) Mars.

3. **Define:** (a) republic, (b) patrician, (c) plebeian, (d) consul, (e) veto, (f) dictator, (g) legion, (h) censor, (i) tribune.

4. List three natural advantages that helped Rome become a powerful city.

5. What powers did the Senate have in the early Republic?

6. **Critical Thinking** Why were plebeians able to gain more rights as Rome expanded?

2 The Expansion of Rome

READ TO UNDERSTAND

☐ How Rome gained power in the Mediterranean.

☐ Why Rome and Carthage fought.

☐ How winning an empire affected Rome.

☐ *Vocabulary:* tribute, latifundia.

Between 509 B.C. and 133 B.C., Roman legions fought first for control of Italy and then for supremacy in the Mediterranean world. Success in war transformed the small city of Rome into the rich, turbulent capital of a huge empire.

The Conquest of Italy

For 200 years after the founding of the Republic, Romans fought for control of central Italy. Then Rome expanded southward, threatening the Greek cities of southern Italy. The Greeks appealed to Pyrrhus (PIHR uhs), king of Epirus, for aid. Pyrrhus raised a large army and defeated the Romans in two hard-fought battles. But his own casualties were so heavy that he reportedly complained, "Another such victory

Roman legions conquered an empire stretching from the Atlantic Ocean to the Euphrates River. Scenes of Roman victories, such as this one, decorated public buildings and monuments.

and I am lost." Today, the expression "pyrrhic victory" refers to a victory won at great cost. Unable to gain a final victory over Rome, Pyrrhus abandoned the Greek cities and returned home.

By 264 B.C., Rome ruled all of Italy. (See the map at right.) The Romans gave full citizenship to nearby Latins, thereby winning their loyalty. More distant peoples did not receive Roman citizenship, but they were allowed to control their own affairs.

Romans built military roads such as the Appian Way to connect Rome to other Italian cities. The roads not only allowed troops to move rapidly, but also encouraged trade, which helped unify the peoples of Italy. Roman farmers and soldiers who received land in the new territories spread Roman customs and the use of Latin, the Roman language.

Rivalry Between Rome and Carthage

Rome's conquest of Italy set the stage for a deadly rivalry with Carthage, a city-state on the coast of North Africa. Carthage, as you read earlier, had been founded by Phoenician traders about 814 B.C. It had then grown into a huge trading empire stretching across North Africa and into Spain.

When Rome conquered the Greek cities of southern Italy, it inherited the rivalry between those cities and Carthage over trade. Soon, Rome and Carthage became increasingly suspicious of each other. A struggle between them for control of the western Mediterranean seemed unavoidable. Between 264 B.C. and 146 B.C., Rome and Carthage fought three exhausting wars. They are called the Punic Wars, from the Latin word "Punicus," meaning Phoenician.

The early wars. The First Punic War broke out in 264 B.C. It centered on control of Sicily. Although Rome had excellent armies, Carthage controlled the seas. However, the Romans quickly built a fleet and learned to fight at sea. The war raged for 23 years. Finally in 241 B.C., an exhausted Carthage sued for peace. It had to pay Rome a fine and surrender Sicily, Sardinia, and Corsica. The war made Rome an important naval power and gave the Romans their first overseas provinces.

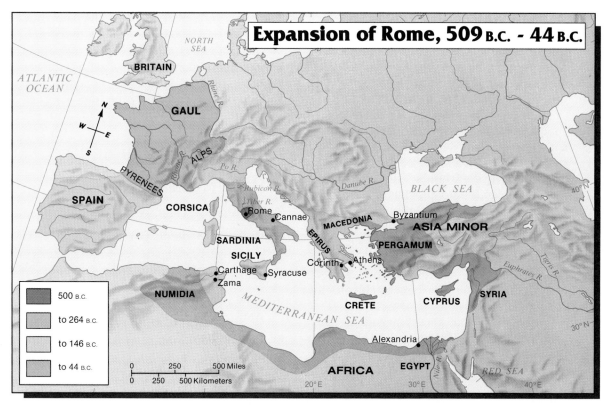

Expansion of Rome, 509 B.C. - 44 B.C.

Map legend:
- 500 B.C.
- to 264 B.C.
- to 146 B.C.
- to 44 B.C.

0   250   500 Miles
0   250   500 Kilometers

MAP STUDY *Rome expanded its empire mostly through war. The Punic Wars, which ended in 146 B.C., brought large amounts of territory into the empire. Rome also acquired territory when the king of Pergamum died, leaving his empire in Asia Minor to Rome. During which period did Rome gain the most territory in Africa?*

The proud Carthaginians did not accept defeat easily. Their general Hamilcar and his son Hannibal sought revenge. According to legend, Hamilcar had made his son swear on a sacred altar to remain Rome's enemy for life. After his father's death, Hannibal took the offensive against Rome.

Hannibal's daring march. In 218 B.C., Hannibal led an army on a hazardous winter march from Spain, across the Alps, into northern Italy. He used African war elephants to carry heavy equipment. But in the icy winter crossing, all but one of the elephants died. Roman legions rushed north, but Hannibal soundly defeated them. Hannibal then marched south, hoping to rally the peoples of Italy against their Roman conquerors. However, since Rome had granted citizenship to the Latins, most remained loyal.

In the Second Punic War, from 218 B.C. to 201 B.C., Hannibal's troops roamed across Italy,

destroying towns. Roman legions harassed him but avoided open battle. Then a Roman army landed in North Africa, and Hannibal had to leave Italy to defend Carthage.

At the battle of Zama, Hannibal was decisively defeated. Carthage was forced to pay a heavy fine and give Spain to Rome. It also promised not to wage any war without Roman consent. The peace terms made Rome supreme in the western Mediterranean.

"Carthage must be destroyed." When Carthage violated the peace terms, the Senate rang with the words of Cato, a veteran of the Second Punic War. "Carthage must be destroyed!" he cried.

The Third Punic War lasted only three years, from 149 B.C. to 146 B.C. A Roman army totally destroyed the ancient city of Carthage. The people were massacred or sold into slavery, and the territory around Carthage became the Roman province of Africa.

107

Winning an Empire

During the Punic Wars, Roman armies won other territory as well. They conquered parts of Spain, southern Gaul, Macedonia, and Greece. (See the map on page 107.) As Rome expanded into the eastern Mediterranean, it subdued many states that Alexander the Great had conquered. By 44 B.C., Rome controlled a vast empire of diverse peoples.

Ruling foreign lands. Rome organized its foreign lands into provinces, headed by governors appointed by the Senate. Each Roman governor supervised tax collection and organized the defense of the province. Rome did not try to change local customs, religion, or governments. This tolerant policy made Roman domination more acceptable to the conquered peoples.

Yet Roman rule was a mixed blessing. Some governors built roads and developed the economy. However, others abused their power. Governors received no pay because the job was considered an honor, but many grew rich by accepting bribes.

Changes at home. Winning an empire brought Romans many gains. They were introduced to the advanced learning of Hellenistic civilization. Also, trade and commerce increased as wealthy Romans demanded expensive luxuries from the conquered territories. But the wars of expansion created problems for Romans at home. Three "prizes" of war had a profound effect on life in the capital: grain, treasure, and slaves.

Tons of grain poured into Rome as **tribute,** or forced payment, from the conquered areas. The resulting surplus drove down the price of grain. The low prices hurt small farmers, many of whom had to sell their land to pay debts.

At the same time, a new class of Romans grew rich from war loot and trade in luxury goods. This new class bought up land from small farmers and created vast estates called **latifundia** (LAT uh FUHN dee uh). They used thousands of slaves brought back as prisoners of war as cheap labor on the latifundia. Small farmers could not compete with the slave labor and lost their land.

Landless farmers drifted to Rome, where they joined unemployed soldiers also at-tracted to the capital. In Rome, the poor complained bitterly about the luxuries of the rich. As their numbers grew, the poor became a huge, restless mob easily swayed to violence by bribes and promises. The economic and social problems created by the wars of expansion were to plague Rome for years.

SECTION 2 REVIEW

1. **Locate:** (a) Carthage, (b) Zama.

2. **Identify:** (a) Punic Wars, (b) Hannibal.

3. **Define:** (a) tribute, (b) latifundia.

4. What factors contributed to rivalry between Rome and Carthage?

5. What was the outcome of the Second Punic War?

6. **Critical Thinking** Do you think that the advantages of winning an empire outweighed the disadvantages? Explain.

---

3 Decline of the Republic

READ TO UNDERSTAND

☐ Why the Roman government needed reform.

☐ How a series of generals gained power in Rome.

☐ What changes Julius Caesar introduced.

"The men who fight their country's battles enjoy nothing but the air and sunlight," declared the tribune Tiberius Gracchus (GRAK uhs) in 133 B.C. "They fight and die to protect the wealth and luxury of others. They are called masters of the world, but they have not a foot of ground to call their own."

As spokesman for the plebeians, Tiberius raised the issue that haunted Rome. Hordes of landless poor roamed the streets. The Senate was the governing body of Rome. But it was full of wealthy men who were more interested in preserving their privileges than in solving the problems of the poor.

Revolts and Upheavals

Popular leaders such as Tiberius Gracchus and his brother Gaius championed the poor. They called for the Senate to limit the size of large estates, redistribute land to the poor, and settle landless farmers in the provinces. The Senate feared the popularity of the Gracchus brothers, and most senators opposed land reform. Therefore, they turned to violence. Mobs of wealthy nobles murdered first Tiberius and later Gaius Gracchus, along with hundreds of their followers.

In time, the Senate was forced to pass some minor land reform. But it did nothing to prevent growing numbers of unemployed soldiers and landless farmers from swelling the mobs in Rome.

Between 133 B.C. and 44 B.C., violent upheavals shook Rome. Abroad, slave revolts erupted, and Rome's allies in Italy and elsewhere rebelled. The Senate relied on Roman legions to suppress the rebellions. But the Roman army itself had changed, and Roman generals began to take a hand in politics.

In the early Republic, you will recall, only landowning citizens served in Roman legions. By 100 B.C., popular generals were recruiting soldiers from among Rome's landless poor. With promises of loot, they attracted many volunteers. They built a strong professional army loyal to them rather than to Rome. They won victories for Rome abroad but then returned home to reap their rewards.

In 88 B.C., a bloody civil war erupted in Rome between the armies of two successful generals. Lucius Cornelius Sulla triumphed and then abolished the law limiting a dictator's length of rule to six months. Although the Senate retained its prestige, Sulla held the real power. For the next 40 years, Rome was ruled by a series of generals.

Rise of Julius Caesar

One general, Gnaeus Pompey (NĪ uhs PAHM pee), led his legions in a series of successful campaigns in Asia Minor, Syria, and Palestine. However, when he returned to Rome, the Senate refused to approve land grants to Pompey's soldiers. Pompey disbanded his army

This bas relief shows a Roman dry goods store. Under the critical eye of their customers, these clerks are displaying the goods that are available. After 133 B.C., civil wars disrupted life in Rome, and scenes such as this became less common.

and looked for allies. He found one in a talented young general, Julius Caesar.

Caesar had won victories in Spain and had attracted a large following in Rome. Like Pompey, Caesar resented the Senate. In 61 B.C., he had hoped to be elected consul, but the Senate, fearing his popularity, blocked his bid for power.

In 60 B.C., Caesar and Pompey formed an alliance with Marcus Lucius Crassus, a wealthy general. They agreed to pool their resources and rule Rome together. Their alliance is known as the First Triumvirate (trī UHM ver iht), or three-man commission.

The First Triumvirate gained control of Rome but was soon split by rivalries. In 53 B.C., Crassus died fighting in the east. But Caesar piled up new conquests in Gaul and Britain. Fearing Caesar's power, Pompey allied himself with the Senate. In 49 B.C., the Senate ordered Caesar to disband his armies and return to Rome.

Caesar refused. With his legions, he crossed the Rubicon River, the boundary between Gaul and Italy. In defying the Senate, Caesar took an irreversible step toward seizing power in Rome. Today, the expression "crossing the Rubicon" means taking a final, decisive step. Caesar then crushed an army led by Pompey.

About 1,800 years after Julius Caesar ruled, and many thousands of miles from Italy, the story of Rome was part of a heated political debate. On the eve of the American Revolution, patriots such as Thomas Jefferson and John Adams looked to the history of Rome for lessons about their own times.

To the Americans, Rome was both a model and a warning. The Romans had built a republic with an admirable system of government. But all too quickly, that republic had dissolved into tyranny and chaos. Even as they fought for independence, Americans debated why the Roman Republic had failed and how their new republic could avoid that fate.

Nearly all educated Americans in the 1700s had studied the story of Rome. They found in the early Romans the virtues they admired most—self-sacrifice, patriotism, and love of liberty.

In the decline of the Roman Republic, however, Americans saw all of their worst fears. After winning independence, they tried to create a government that would avoid the pitfalls that cost Romans their liberty. The root of Rome's decline, said James Otis of Massachusetts, was that the Romans "never had a proper balance between the Senate and the people."

Roman examples came up so often in the discussion that one frustrated New Englander finally exclaimed that the quoting of ancient history was no more to the point "than to tell how our forefathers dug clams at Plymouth." Nonetheless, the fate of Rome was very much on the minds of Americans when the Constitution was written and ratified.

1. Why were Americans interested in the history of Rome?

2. **Critical Thinking** What lessons do you think people today can learn from the decline of the Roman Republic?

Caesar's Reforms

Between 49 B.C. and 44 B.C., Caesar won a string of victories in the Middle East, North Africa, and Spain. On his triumphant return to Rome, he pardoned many senators who had supported Pompey. In 44 B.C., he was appointed dictator for life.

Caesar introduced reforms meant to strengthen Rome and protect his own power. He distributed land to the poor and granted Roman citizenship to people in provinces outside Italy. This action helped unite the empire by giving people in the provinces a stake in Rome. To reduce unemployment, he began many building projects. He increased pay for soldiers and moved to end corruption in the provinces. He also introduced a more accurate calendar based on Hellenistic astronomy. The Julian calendar, as it was called, was used in Europe until 1582 A.D.

Although the Senate and Assembly of Tribes continued to exist, Caesar had absolute power. Opposition to him grew in the Senate. Some senators denounced him as a tyrant who was destroying the Republic. Others were jealous of his popularity. On March 15, 44 B.C., a group of conspirators led by Gaius Cassius and Marcus Brutus stabbed Caesar to death in the Senate. In the civil war that followed, the Republic suffered a fatal blow.

The Second Triumvirate

Before his death, Caesar had adopted his 18-year-old grandnephew Octavian as his son and heir. After Caesar's assassination, Octavian formed the Second Triumvirate with two of Caesar's chief commanders, Mark Antony and Marcus Lepidus.

After crushing Caesar's assassins, the Second Triumvirate dissolved into a power struggle between Antony and Octavian. When Antony married Cleopatra, queen of Egypt, Octavian feared they planned to seize power. So he declared war. In 31 B.C., at the naval battle of Actium off Greece, Octavian defeated them. Antony and Cleopatra fled back to Egypt. They later committed suicide when they learned that Octavian's forces had landed at Alexandria. The next year, Egypt became part of the Roman Empire.

On his return to Rome, Octavian promised to share control of the empire with the Senate. In practice, however, he had absolute authority. In 27 B.C., the Senate, realizing that peace depended on his leadership, gave Octavian the title Augustus, or "Exalted One," a name normally reserved for the gods. After 100 years of civil war, peace was finally restored under Augustus.

SECTION 3 REVIEW

1. **Identify:** (a) Julius Caesar, (b) Julian calendar, (c) Octavian, (d) Antony.

2. **Locate:** (a) Gaul, (b) Rubicon River.

3. Why did leaders such as Tiberius Gracchus demand reform of the Roman government?

4. Why did Pompey, Caesar, and Crassus form the First Triumvirate?

5. List three ways in which Caesar tried to strengthen Rome and protect his own power.

6. **Critical Thinking** Why do you think both the First and Second triumvirates lasted such a short period of time?

4 The Roman Empire

READ TO UNDERSTAND

☐ How Augustus brought peace to Rome.

☐ How people lived under the Pax Romana.

☐ What problems existed alongside the prosperity of the Pax Romana.

☐ *Vocabulary:* imperator, devalue, inflation.

"May I be privileged to build firm and lasting foundations for the government of Rome," Augustus wished in 27 B.C. Augustus achieved his goal. Under him and his successors, Rome entered a period known as the Pax Romana (pahks roh MAH nah), or Roman peace, which lasted from 27 B.C. to 180 A.D.

As the first Roman emperor, Augustus presided over many important reforms in the Roman Empire. An able soldier, he is most noted for bringing Rome a long period of peace.

The Age of Augustus

Under Augustus, Rome ceased to be a republic and became an empire. The Senate gave him the title **imperator** (IHM puh RAHT uhr), or commander-in-chief of the Roman armies. The English word "emperor" is derived from this Latin title. Although the Senate still existed, Augustus ruled as a monarch.

Between 27 B.C. and 14 A.D., Augustus sponsored many reforms to strengthen the empire. He reorganized the army into a highly disciplined, professional body, loyal to the emperor. He encouraged former soldiers to settle in the provinces, where they could bolster local defense. He continued Caesar's policy of granting Roman citizenship to people in the provinces. Such measures ensured the loyalty of these people to Rome and spread Roman ideas.

The reforms helped restore confidence in Rome. To reduce corruption and improve local administration, Augustus created an efficient civil service. High-level jobs were open to men of talent, regardless of their social class. Also, civil servants were given salaries for their service. The emperor ordered a complete census, or population survey, so that taxes could be set fairly.

Remains of the emperor Hadrian's rule, such as this fort and a part of Hadrian's Wall, can still be seen in Britain today. The wall, originally 74 miles (120 kilometers) long, was designed to thwart invaders. Hadrian personally supervised many details of its construction.

The Successors of Augustus

The first four emperors who followed Augustus were members of his family. Tiberius and Claudius were efficient rulers who continued to make reforms. However, Caligula and Nero were notorious for their insane behavior.

In 64 A.D., a great fire destroyed much of Rome. Nero blamed Christians for the fire and killed hundreds of them. His rule then sank into a vicious reign of terror. After his death in 68 A.D., the first of many struggles broke out over who would become emperor. The Roman Empire had no laws for choosing a new ruler. As a result, when an emperor died without naming an heir, civil wars often erupted, with ambitious generals scrambling for power.

In the second century A.D., Rome benefited from the peaceful succession of several outstanding emperors. Under Trajan, a Spaniard, the empire reached its greatest size. (See the map on page 114.) Trajan ensured a peaceful succession by adopting Hadrian as his heir.

Hadrian was an able and tireless ruler. He issued laws protecting women, children, and slaves from mistreatment. Hadrian also reorganized the army so that soldiers were recruited in each province to defend their homelands. He built defensive walls across northern Britain. Long stretches of Hadrian's Wall still stand.

The emperor Marcus Aurelius (aw REE lee uhs) was a student of the Greek Stoic philosophers. He took on the difficult job of ruling the empire with a strong sense of duty. In his *Meditations,* the emperor set out his philosophy:

> Keep yourself simple, good, pure, grave, unaffected, the friend of justice, religious, kind, affectionate, strong for your proper work. Wrestle to continue to be the man Philosophy wished to make you. Reverence the gods, save men.

Although the scholarly Marcus Aurelius preferred his books and studies to war, he spent much of his reign fighting on the frontiers of the Roman Empire. German tribes, which you will read more about in Chapter 6, attacked along the Danube River. To restore peace, the emperor allowed many Germans to settle inside the frontiers. Before his death, Marcus Aurelius appointed his son Commodus (KAHM uh duhs), a vain, violent man, as heir. Although no one realized it at the time, Rome entered a long period of decline after 180 A.D.

Prosperity During the Pax Romana

Between 27 B.C. and 180 A.D., an efficient, stable government ensured peace and allowed the Roman Empire to grow in wealth and power. Most Romans believed the Roman Empire was the entire civilized world. They did not know much about the Persian Empire beyond the Euphrates River or the more distant civilizations of India and China. Most Romans also believed the empire was eternal, that it would last forever. They saw the city of Rome as the symbol of Roman eternity.

DAILY LIFE Chariot Races at the Circus Maximus

Shortly before dawn, crowds of men, women, and children streamed through the streets of Rome toward the Circus Maximus, the vast outdoor arena where chariot races took place. Admission to the races was free, but to get a good seat, Romans set out early. As the crowds surged toward the Circus, bets were shouted back and forth. Sometimes Romans bet on a well-known charioteer. More often, they chose a color because charioteers raced under the colors of four teams: the blues, greens, reds, or whites.

To race, charioteers stood on very frail-looking, two-wheeled chariots pulled by teams of two or four horses. The reins were lashed around their waists. They held a whip in one hand and a knife in the other to slash the reins if the chariots overturned. Charioteers were usually slaves trained by wealthy owners. Only the most skillful drivers survived the hazardous course.

The greatest danger in chariot racing was the tight turn at either end of the track. Slaves and race officials stood near these spots to drag fallen charioteers and horses out of the way before they were trampled to death. Despite the danger, a few successful charioteers won as many as 3,000 races and earned fortunes for themselves and their owners.

Chariot races and other spectacles amused the idle crowds who might otherwise be bored and troublesome. On one occasion, an emperor had a Roman naval victory reenacted. He built an artificial lake and two fleets. He then sent slaves to fight and die as enemies of Rome. Thousands of people died in such events. The poet Juvenal groaned that Romans only cared about free "bread and games in the circus."

1. Why was chariot racing a dangerous sport?

2. **Critical Thinking** Why do you think Juvenal was unhappy about the Roman attitude toward free bread and games?

Rome: The Eternal City. During the Pax Romana, Rome became an international city. Its population grew to nearly one million, as people from the provinces flocked to the capital in search of education, advancement, and entertainment. People from the eastern Mediterranean brought with them the achievements of Hellenistic civilization as well as the ideas of older cultures.

Roman emperors undertook costly projects to beautify the city. "I found Rome built of sun-dried brick; I leave her clothed in marble," boasted Augustus. Indeed, the face of Rome had changed. Its culture was far richer and more sophisticated than it had been during the Republic.

Thanks to trade, most people enjoyed a varied diet, with meat and fish in addition to the traditional Roman menu of porridge and vegetables. A few wealthy people feasted on imported delicacies such as peacocks and ostriches.

Yet Rome was a city of contrasts. On the seven hills and along the Tiber, the rich built spacious townhouses with lavish gardens and exotic fish ponds. But the poor crowded into seven-story tenements that kept narrow back streets in continual gloom.

Trade and commerce. During the Pax Romana, trade and commerce flourished. The Roman navy protected merchants and travelers on the seas, and Roman legions protected them on land. As trade expanded, cities of the empire prospered. Coined money, issued by the emperors, further aided trade and commerce.

MAP STUDY *Products flowed into Rome from far and wide, as you can see on this map. Straight, paved roads radiating from Rome also carried Roman goods and culture across the empire. What products came to Rome from Arabia?*

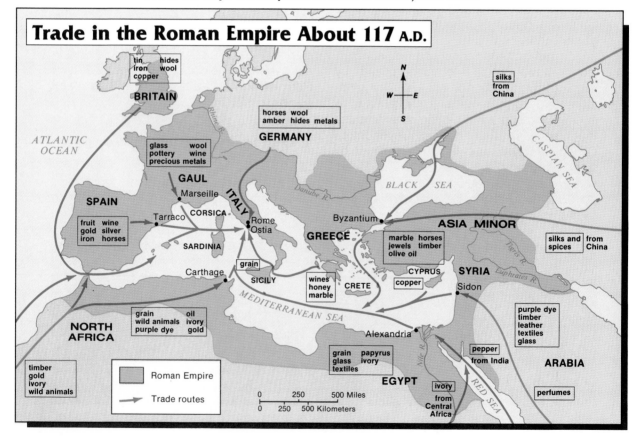

Trade in the Roman Empire About 117 A.D.

A Greek traveler marveled at the "endless flow of goods" that poured into Rome. Cargoes of grain from Sicily and Egypt, copper from Cyprus, and tin from Britain jammed the docks of Ostia at the mouth of the Tiber. (See the map on page 114.) "Anyone who wants to behold all these products," he noted, "must either journey through the whole world to see them or else come to this city. Whatever cannot be seen here belongs to the category of nonexistent things."

Social Conditions

Not everyone prospered during the Pax Romana. Sharp divisions between rich and poor could be found everywhere in the empire. Emperors appointed wealthy men from a small but powerful business class to high offices, confident of their support for a strong, central government to keep order. In Rome, poorer citizens worked in shops and markets or built monuments. Thousands of unemployed depended on the emperor to provide bread. If grain ran short, riots broke out.

Social conditions in provincial cities mirrored those of Rome. Roman officials ruled with the help of local leaders. Merchants and artisans formed an active middle class. The poor were not as numerous as in Rome, but they depended on the government for food, too. Outside the cities, most people were small farmers or tenants who worked on huge estates owned by rich landlords.

During the Pax Romana, slaves did much of the labor. Legally, slaves were considered property, not people. Their treatment varied, however. Romans prized household slaves, especially highly skilled or well-educated Greeks. Some slaves owned property, and a few amassed large fortunes. But most slaves suffered inhumane treatment. They worked until they were too old or weak to be profitable. Then they were abandoned.

The use of slaves undermined the small farmer and destroyed many small businesses because rich people employed slaves rather than free workers. Furthermore, some people came to consider hard work as fit only for slaves.

Troubling Signs

The general prosperity of the Pax Romana hid signs of trouble. Governing the empire was costly, especially paying soldiers along the frontiers. When the wars of conquest ended, the government no longer had war loot to pay expenses, so it increased taxes. Emperors tried to limit costs by reducing the size of the army. But such cutbacks slowly weakened Roman defenses.

The economy suffered because Romans imported more goods than they exported. Money, especially gold, flowed out of Rome to pay for imported luxuries. To increase the supply of money at home, emperors issued new coins, mixing lead with the gold. The addition of lead **devalued** the coins, or lowered their value, because their value was based on their gold content.

Since the devalued coins were worth less than older coins, merchants demanded more new coins for the same product—that is, they raised prices. Higher prices, in turn, meant that more money was needed. An increase in the money supply followed by an increase in prices is called **inflation.** Yet problems such as inflation bothered few Romans during the Pax Romana, as everyone scrambled for a share of the wealth.

SECTION 4 REVIEW

1. **Identify:** (a) Pax Romana, (b) Hadrian, (c) Marcus Aurelius.
2. **Define:** (a) imperator, (b) devalue, (c) inflation.
3. (a) List three reforms introduced by Augustus. (b) How did each strengthen Rome?
4. What conditions helped trade and commerce flourish during the Pax Romana?
5. Describe one economic problem of the Roman Empire during the Pax Romana.
6. **Critical Thinking** Compare Roman life and values during the Pax Romana and during the early Republic.

CHAPTER 5 REVIEW

Summary

1. **When the Roman Republic was founded in 509 B.C., Rome was only a small city-state.** The Romans adapted ideas and beliefs from the Greeks, Etruscans, and others who lived in Italy. Although the early Republic was dominated by patricians, plebeians slowly gained more rights. Romans taught their children to value hard work and loyalty.

2. **Rome grew into a vast empire by 44 B.C.** Rome battled Carthage in three costly wars, eventually destroying its rival. Winning an empire brought Rome riches, but it also created economic and social problems that were to plague Rome for years.

3. **Between 133 B.C. and 31 B.C., the Roman Republic suffered from civil wars and social unrest.** In 49 B.C., Julius Caesar gained absolute power and introduced many reforms to strengthen Rome. After Caesar's assassination, his heir Octavian was given the title Augustus.

4. **The reign of the emperor Augustus marked the end of the Roman Republic and beginning of the Pax Romana.** For almost 200 years, the Roman Empire enjoyed relative peace and prosperity. However, troubling social and economic problems existed throughout the empire.

Recalling Facts

Decide if the following statements are true or false. If a statement is false, rewrite it to make it true.

1. In the early Republic, patricians and plebeians were equal.

2. The Twelve Tables of Law was the first written law code in Rome.

3. The Punic Wars helped establish Rome as a great Mediterranean power.

4. Julius Caesar was popular with the Roman Senate.

5. The Roman Empire began under Nero.

Chapter Checkup

1. Describe each of the following in the early Republic: (a) army; (b) family; (c) religion.

2. (a) Who had political power in Rome during the early Republic? (b) Why were changes in government necessary during the wars of expansion? (c) How did government change?

3. What did Rome gain from each of the three Punic Wars?

4. How did conquering an empire affect the Roman economy?

5. (a) How did Julius Caesar come to power in Rome? (b) What reforms did he introduce?

6. How did Augustus strengthen the empire?

7. (a) Why was the Pax Romana a time of prosperity? (b) What signs of trouble existed even during the Pax Romana?

Critical Thinking

1. **Relating Past to Present** (a) How is the government of the United States similar to that of the early Roman Republic? (b) How is it different?

2. **Understanding the Roots of Democracy** (a) Explain three ways the powers of government officials were limited in the Roman Republic. (b) Why are such limits important in democracies today?

3. **Comparing** (a) Compare the lives of women in Rome with the lives of women in Athens. (b) What differences existed in the legal rights of Greek and Roman women?

4. **Drawing Conclusions** (a) What Roman policies contributed to the unity of the Roman Empire? Explain. (b) Do you think

extending Roman citizenship to conquered peoples was a good idea? Why or why not?

5. **Understanding Economic Ideas** (a) How did Roman emperors increase the supply of money? (b) What effect did this increase have on the Roman economy? (c) What measures do you think the emperors could have taken to prevent inflation?

Developing Basic Skills

1. **Map Reading** Study the map on page 107. (a) During what period did Rome conquer Italy? (b) Describe the areas Rome conquered between 264 B.C. and 146 B.C. (c) During what period did Rome acquire the most territory?

2. **Map Reading** Study the map on page 114. (a) What economic information is given on the map? (b) What political information is given? (c) What trade goods came to Rome from Asia Minor? (d) From which areas did Rome acquire horses? Gold?

3. **Using Time Lines** Roman history covers both B.C. and A.D. dates. Study the time line below. (a) What is the date of the first event shown on the time line? (b) What is the date of the last event shown? (c) How many years does the time line cover?

(d) Was Caesar assassinated before or after Augustus ruled?

Writing About History

Organizing Supporting Detail

Once you have written a topic sentence and gathered supporting information, you must arrange the information in some logical order, or sequence. Several common sequences are listed below. You will learn more about them in upcoming Chapter Reviews.

Chronological order: arranging events in the time order in which they occurred

Order of importance: organizing ideas from the least significant to the most significant, or vice versa

Comparison and contrast: arranging ideas according to similarities or differences

Cause and effect: organizing events based on whether one caused another

Developmental or topical order: presenting information in an order suggested by the topic sentence

Practice: For each of the Critical Thinking questions here, indicate which order of information would be most logical.

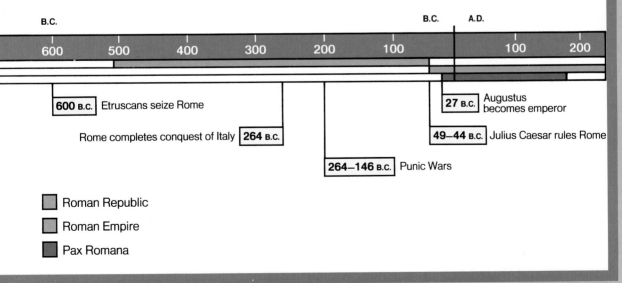

B.C.   B.C.   A.D.

600   500   400   300   200   100   100   200

600 B.C. Etruscans seize Rome

Rome completes conquest of Italy | 264 B.C.

264–146 B.C. | Punic Wars

27 B.C. Augustus becomes emperor

49–44 B.C. | Julius Caesar rules Rome

Roman Republic

Roman Empire

Pax Romana

The Roman Heritage (509 B.C.—476 A.D.)

Christian themes became common subjects of art in the Roman Empire, especially after Christianity was recognized as the official religion. This Christian mosaic shows Saint Apollinare as a shepherd, perhaps a reminder of Christ's command to his disciples to care for his sheep.

As Constantine marched on Rome in 312 A.D., he knew his forces were badly outnumbered. For six years, he had fought many rivals for control of the western part of the Roman Empire. Although he was now master of most of Italy, he had to fight yet another battle for the city of Rome.

About noon on the day before the crucial battle, Constantine looked up into the sky. Suddenly he saw a cross of light above the sun with these words, "Conquer by this." Eusebius (u SEE bee uhs), a Christian bishop and friend of Constantine, later described the scene. "At this sight, [Constantine] was struck with amazement, and his whole army also witnessed this miracle. And while he continued to ponder its meaning, night suddenly came on; then in his sleep the Christ appeared to him with the same sign and commanded him to make a likeness of the sign that he had seen in the heavens and to use it as a safeguard against his enemies."

At dawn, Constantine called in artisans and described the sign in his dream. They shaped "a long spear, overlaid with gold" into a cross. Above the cross was a "wreath of gold and precious stones" around the first two letters of Christ's name. Constantine ordered his soldiers to inscribe the same two letters on their shields.

Carrying the jeweled cross into battle, Constantine's army triumphed, and Constantine became emperor of Rome. A year later, in 313 A.D., he proclaimed freedom of worship for everyone in the Roman Empire, including Christians. Before his death in 337 A.D., he was baptized a Christian, opening the way for Christianity to become the official religion of the empire.

Christianity was only part of the heritage Rome passed on to the peoples of its empire. Through Rome, Western Europe was introduced to the learning of ancient Greece. Rome also made its own contributions, especially in government, law, and engineering. Yet even while Roman civilization flourished, forces were weakening the ties that bound the empire together. ■

1 Greco-Roman Civilization

READ TO UNDERSTAND

☐ **How Greek culture influenced Rome.**

☐ **What contributions Romans made in science, technology, and law.**

☐ *Vocabulary:* mosaic, aqueduct.

"Greece has conquered her rude conqueror," observed the Roman poet Horace early in the Pax Romana. Everywhere Horace looked, he saw evidence of Greek influence. Romans studied Greek art and architecture as well as theories of government. Romans who traveled to Athens or to Alexandria in Egypt absorbed the ideas of Hellenistic civilization.

Romans absorbed much of Greek culture but also kept their own traditions. The result was a blend of Greek and Roman traditions. Through conquest, Romans spread Greco-Roman civilization to every corner of their empire.

Art and Architecture

When the Romans conquered Greece, they shipped home thousands of Greek statues. Roman sculptors did a brisk business copying Greek works, and talented Greek artists found rich patrons in Rome. In time, however, Roman sculptors developed their own style. Greek sculptors, you will recall, idealized the human form, using athletes as models of perfection. Romans created more realistic portraits.

Roman artists produced beautiful paintings to decorate walls of homes. Although few Roman paintings have survived, landscapes and scenes based on the *Iliad* or *Odyssey* were preserved in Pompeii (pahm PAY), a city buried by the eruption of a volcano in 79 A.D. Romans also designed magnificent **mosaics,** which are pictures formed of chips of colored stone.

While Romans borrowed many ideas in architecture, they also made important advances. From the Etruscans and Greeks, they learned to use columns and arches. They improved on the arch by inventing the dome, a roof formed by rounded arches. The Romans also introduced new building materials such as concrete. New building techniques allowed architects to design massive structures. For example, the Colosseum had three stories of arches and columns.

Roman architecture was more ornate than the simple, elegant temples of classical Greece. Emperors erected solid, richly decorated monuments, such as huge stadiums, to symbolize Roman strength.

Technology and Science

The Romans applied their technical knowledge to many practical concerns. They built strong bridges, supported by arches, to span turbulent rivers. Romans designed roads to last forever. They made them of heavy blocks set in layers of crushed stones and pebbles. Roman roads were still in use as recently as 100 years ago, and the stone foundations can be seen in parts of Europe today.

THE ROMAN COLOSSEUM In this recreation of the majestic Colosseum, artist Scott Gladden shows the amphitheater as it existed in ancient Rome. Made of concrete, the Colosseum was built so well that the arena could be flooded for mock naval battles without leaking. Rising rows of marble and wooden benches held up to 50,000 spectators. A 15-foot wall protected spectators during the brutal events. The ruins of the Colosseum, standing today, are shown at left.

Romans built **aqueducts** (AK wuh DUHKTS) to carry water from reservoirs in the country to the cities. Roman aqueducts, some of which still stand today, were canal-like stone structures that tunneled through mountains and spanned valleys.

In science and medicine, Romans collected masses of information in works similar to encyclopedias. Pliny (PLIHN ee) the Elder produced the 37-volume work *Natural History,* a storehouse of information on subjects ranging from astronomy to medicine, geography, and botany. Pliny's curiosity about natural events proved to be his downfall. In 79 A.D., he visited Pompeii to observe the erupting Mount Vesuvius (vuh SOO vee uhs) and was killed by poisonous gases from the volcano.

Scientific works produced during Roman times were studied for centuries. The Greek physician Galen (GAY luhn) wrote a medical encyclopedia that was used in Europe until the 1400s. The ideas of the astronomer Ptolemy were long thought to be true. Ptolemy taught that the earth was at the center of the universe and that the sun and planets revolved around it. Those theories were not disproved until the 1500s.

Roman Literature

Roman writers adapted Greek literary forms such as lyric poetry and drama to the Latin language. Romans also developed new styles of writing that were influenced by Greek oratory, the art of persuading an audience.

Some statesmen, such as Caesar and Cicero, were fine writers. When Caesar was away on military campaigns, he kept his name before the public by writing *Commentaries on the Gallic Wars.* In this work, he skillfully combined a history of the wars with reminders of his own military successes. Cicero perfected a clear, logical style of writing that became a model for other writers. In essays on government, morality, and philosophy, he showed his admiration for the Roman Republic and for the Roman idea of justice.

Poets. Under the emperor Augustus, Roman literature flourished. Augustus supported writers, especially those who praised Roman achievements. The poet Horace was famous for his odes glorifying Rome and the Pax Romana.

Many Roman women were well educated in history and literature. With slaves to do the housework, well-to-do women like the one pictured here had the leisure to take an active part in the intellectual and political life of Rome.

The poet Virgil admired the early Republic. When Augustus commissioned him to write a poem celebrating the rise of Rome, Virgil composed the *Aeneid.* (See page 101.) Although the *Aeneid* imitated the heroic epics of Homer, it emphasized Roman justice, practical wisdom, and power:

> You, O Roman, remember to rule the nations with might. This will be your genius— to impose the way of peace, to spare the conquered and crush the proud.

Historians. Rome produced many historians. Livy, who lived at the same time as Virgil, wrote the lengthy *History of Rome.* Unlike the Greek historian Thucydides, who tried to be impartial, Livy admitted that his goal was to glorify Rome. "I do honestly believe that no country has ever been greater or purer than ours or richer in good citizens and noble deeds," he claimed.

Another well-known historian, Tacitus (TAS uh tuhs), wrote the *Annals,* a history of Rome from the death of Augustus to 70 A.D. Unlike Livy, he was critical of Roman emperors. But he seemed resigned to the present. "I

The tunes of strolling musicians, like the three shown in this mosaic, contributed to the din commonly heard in the streets of Rome. Other sounds rose from the shops of craftsmen, the shouting of peddlers, and the cries of beggars.

may regard with admiration an earlier period," noted Tacitus, "but I accept the present, and while I pray for good emperors, I can endure whomever we may have."

Roman Law

To deal with the practical problems of government, Romans developed a system of law, today considered one of their greatest achievements. Roman law established a common standard of justice for the entire empire. Under Roman law, an accused person was considered innocent until proven guilty. Judges were supposed to base their decisions only on evidence presented in court. They also followed standard procedures to guarantee a fair hearing for both sides in a dispute.

Roman law evolved during the Republic and was suited to the needs of a simple farming society. The Twelve Tables of Law, for example, had applied only to Roman citizens. (See page 103.) As Rome expanded, two systems of law developed: civil law and the law of nations. Civil law dealt with claims of Roman citizens. The law of nations dealt with the claims of foreigners and took local customs into account. Eventually, the two codes were merged into a single law system that applied everywhere in the empire.

During the Pax Romana, punishments were less severe than they had been during the Republic. Furthermore, the law code provided some protection for slaves and women. It set limits on the absolute rights of fathers and husbands. Also, women and slaves were given the right to own property.

Roman law was the foundation for the law codes that developed in Europe and were carried to other parts of the world. Today, in many American courthouses, you can see statues of the Roman goddess of justice. She is blindfolded and holds a scale in each hand as a symbol of balanced judgment.

| SECTION 1 REVIEW |

1. **Identify:** (a) Pliny the Elder, (b) Ptolemy, (c) Virgil, (d) Livy, (e) Tacitus.

2. **Define:** (a) mosaic, (b) aqueduct.

3. How did Roman sculpture differ from Greek sculpture?

4. What contributions did the Romans make to science and medicine?

5. What was Livy's opinion of Rome?

6. What two systems of law developed as Rome expanded?

7. **Critical Thinking** How did the Roman emphasis on practical ideas and inventions help unify and strengthen the empire?

2 Rise of Christianity

READ TO UNDERSTAND

☐ How Rome treated the Jews in Palestine.

☐ What the teachings of early Christianity were.

☐ Why Christianity spread throughout the Roman Empire.

☐ *Vocabulary:* messiah, parable, martyr, hierarchy, pope.

Wherever Jesus went, crowds followed. They brought the sick to him to be healed. And they took comfort in his words, "Blessed are the poor in spirit, for theirs is the kingdom of heaven." All the while, Jewish leaders and Roman officials looked on uneasily.

During the Pax Romana, a new religion, Christianity, spread across the Greco-Roman world. At first, Christianity was just one of the many religions practiced within the Roman Empire. But by 395 A.D., it had become the official religion of the empire. The success of Christianity was due in part to the religious climate of the Roman world.

The Religious Climate

Roman emperors tolerated different religious practices. Officially, Romans were required to offer sacrifices to the emperor, who was thought to have divine power. These ceremonies had little religious meaning, however. They merely showed loyalty to Rome. As long as people performed the ritual, they could worship as they chose.

Many Romans continued to worship the old gods, such as Jupiter and Mars. Others turned to mystery religions like those in ancient Greece. (See page 88.) People who believed in mystery religions used magical signs and secret passwords hoping to win immortality. Mystery religions gave people in the huge impersonal Roman Empire a sense of belonging.

Roman Rule in Palestine

The Hebrews, or Jews, were among the peoples in the Roman Empire whose religions were tolerated. Roman officials in Palestine respected the Hebrew belief in one God, and they excused Jews from worshipping the emperor. For example, the face of the emperor was not imprinted on coins issued in Palestine because Hebrew law forbade Jews to worship images.

Although Rome allowed Jews to follow traditional laws, many Jews resented foreign rule. Some believed that a **messiah**, a savior chosen by God, would lead them to freedom from Roman rule. The Zealots sought political freedom through armed resistance. But Rome responded to criticism and rebellion with severe punishment.

In 66 A.D., the Jews in Palestine rose in revolt. Rome sent an army to destroy Jerusalem. In 70 A.D., Rome abolished the Jewish state, which had existed since ancient times. The Jews were enslaved and dispersed throughout the empire. In their scattered communities, however, Jews preserved their ancient religion and culture.

The Life and Teachings of Jesus

About 70 years before the Jewish uprising against Rome, Jesus, the founder of Christianity, was born in Bethlehem, a town in southern Palestine. Information about the life of Jesus comes from accounts written by his disciples after his death. These accounts, called the Gospels, or good news, make up the first four books of the New Testament of the Bible.

According to the Gospels, Jesus grew up in Nazareth, studied with priests in the synagogue, and learned the trade of a carpenter. As a young man, Jesus began preaching to the poor. The Gospels say that Jesus performed miracles such as healing the sick. Many people who heard Jesus or witnessed the miracles believed he was the Messiah. The Greek word for messiah was Christos. Followers of Jesus eventually became known as Christians.

The large crowds Jesus attracted when he preached worried both Jewish and Roman authorities. Some Jewish officials saw Jesus as a troublemaker bent on challenging traditional Hebrew laws. Others rejected Jesus' claim to be the Son of God. Denounced by his enemies, Jesus was arrested and taken before Pontius Pilate, a Roman official. Pilate saw Jesus as a threat to Rome's authority in Palestine. As a result, Jesus was condemned to die. He was executed according to Roman custom by crucifixion, or being nailed to a cross to die of exposure.

In his teachings, Jesus stressed love for God and compassion for other people. A person's chief duties, he said, were to "love the Lord thy God with all thy heart" and to "love

Jesus and his apostles met together for the Last Supper the night before he was put to death. This mosaic commemorates that event. Jesus is shown at the left. Judas, the disciple who would betray him, is on the right.

thy neighbor as thyself." In **parables,** short stories with simple moral lessons, Jesus taught people how to show kindness to one another. He offered his followers a loving and forgiving God. He taught that earthly riches were unimportant and that people who were humble, merciful, and unselfish would be rewarded with eternal life.

The teachings of Jesus were rooted in Hebrew religious traditions. (See page 49.) For example, Jesus preached obedience to one God, to the Ten Commandments, and to the other laws of the Old Testament. Like the ancient Hebrew prophets, Jesus condemned injustice and criticized false pride. As a result, the Hebrew ethical world view became a fundamental part of Christianity.

The Apostles and Paul

According to the New Testament, Jesus chose 12 disciples as Apostles to carry on his teachings. At first, the Apostles preached to the Jews of Palestine. The Apostle Peter traveled to Rome, where he converted Jews in the capital to Christianity. But Paul, the person most responsible for spreading the message of Jesus, was not one of the original Apostles.

Paul, a Greek-speaking Jew from Asia Minor, helped establish Christian communities in the eastern cities of the Roman Empire. For 30 years, he traveled tirelessly through Palestine and Syria to Asia Minor, Macedonia, Greece, and Rome. Like the Apostles, he sought converts among the Jews. But Paul also took Christianity on a new course when he decided to preach the Gospel to Gentiles, or non-Jews.

Paul played a key role in shaping Christian thought. As part of his missionary work, he wrote hundreds of letters to Christian communities. These letters, in which he explained Christian beliefs, are part of the New Testament. Paul taught that people who believed in Jesus need not fear death because Jesus promised everlasting life.

Persecution and Toleration

Unlike other religions within the Roman Empire, Christianity aroused official persecution because Christians refused to worship the

In the New Testament, the apostle John quotes Jesus as saying, "I am the good shepherd. The good shepherd lays down his life for his sheep." The symbol of the good shepherd was often used in early Christian art.

emperor. Roman authorities had excused Jews from emperor worship out of respect for their ancient traditions. But Roman authorities saw Christians as dangerous troublemakers who were winning converts throughout the empire.

Roman emperors tended to use Christians as scapegoats, especially when political or economic conditions were bad. Both Peter and Paul perished in Rome under the persecution of the emperor Nero.

Persecution strengthened rather than weakened the new religion. During periods of intense persecution, some Christians renounced their faith. But many others became **martyrs,** people who suffer or die for their beliefs. Christians believed that martyrs received God's special favor. "The blood of the martyrs," wrote one Roman, "is the seed of the Church." Many people were impressed by a faith that inspired such devotion in its followers, and they converted in great numbers.

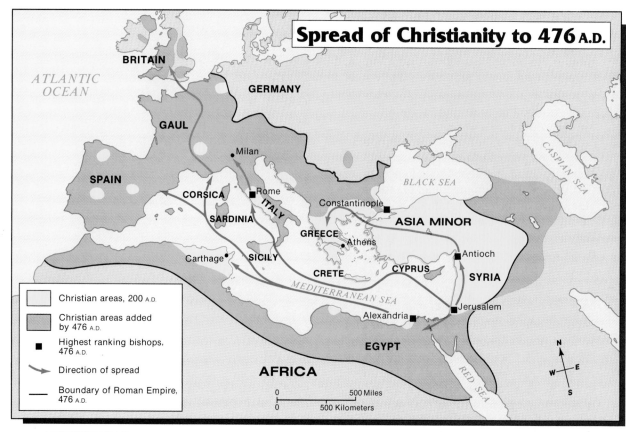

ATLANTIC
OCEAN

BRITAIN

GERMANY

GAUL

SPAIN

•Milan

CORSICA ■Rome

SARDINIA ITALY

GREECE
Athens•

Carthage• SICILY

CRETE CYPRUS

Constantinople

BLACK SEA

CASPIAN SEA

ASIA MINOR

■Antioch

SYRIA

MEDITERRANEAN SEA

Alexandria

Jerusalem

EGYPT

AFRICA

RED SEA

Christian areas, 200 A.D.

Christian areas added
by 476 A.D.

■ Highest ranking bishops,
476 A.D.

Direction of spread

Boundary of Roman Empire,
476 A.D.

0   500 Miles

0   500 Kilometers

N
W   E
S

MAP STUDY   *Christianity gradually spread from Jerusalem throughout the Roman Empire.
What areas were Christian by 200 A.D.? Why do you think these areas were the
first to become Christian?*

As you have read, the emperor Constantine officially recognized Christianity. In 313 A.D., he introduced a policy of official toleration by the Edict of Milan. Later, in 395 A.D., Christianity achieved its greatest triumph when it was made the official religion of the Roman Empire.

The Appeal of Christianity

From humble beginnings in Palestine, Christianity spread to the eastern cities of the Roman Empire and then throughout the entire Roman world. (See the map above.) It spread for several reasons.

The simple, direct message of Christianity appealed to many people. The poor and oppressed, especially, found hope in the God who loved people regardless of their place in society. Equality, human dignity, and, above all, the promise of eternal life were comforting teachings. Many educated people who had rejected the Roman gods and the mystery religions turned to Christianity. To them, the Christian emphasis on a life of moderation and discipline echoed Greek and Roman philosophies.

The work of dedicated missionaries such as Paul was made easier by the unity of the Roman Empire and the ease of travel between cities. In the eastern Mediterranean, Greek was a common language, and many people lived in cities. Thus missionaries could reach many people at one time. Furthermore, many early Christians were women who brought other members of their families into the faith. In some Christian communities, women conducted worship services and enjoyed equality with men.

As Christianity gained in strength, more people turned to it. Eventually, Christians developed an efficient, dynamic church organization. The Christian Church maintained unity among its members and guaranteed the survival of the new faith.

Church Organization

The Christian Church developed gradually during the first few centuries A.D. At first, bishops ranked as the highest officials. Each bishop administered the churches in a territory called a see. Below the bishops were priests, who conducted worship services and taught Christian beliefs. As the Church expanded, archbishops were appointed to oversee the bishops. An archbishop's territory was called a province. The type of organization in which officials are arranged according to rank is called a **hierarchy** (HĪ uh RAHR kee).

As the Church hierarchy emerged, women lost their influence in Church government. They could not become priests or conduct the Mass, the Christian worship service. But women continued to play a prominent role in spreading Christian teachings across the Roman world.

In time, the bishop of Rome acquired a dominant position in the Church by claiming that Peter, the chief Apostle, had made Rome the center of the Christian Church. The bishop of Rome eventually took the title **pope,** or father of the Church. Bishops in the eastern Mediterranean cities such as Constantinople, Alexandria, Jerusalem, and Antioch opposed the pope's claim to be supreme ruler of the Church.

Together, the clergy, which included archbishops, bishops, and priests, helped keep Christianity alive in the early years of persecution. The clergy also maintained order and discipline in the Church. Bishops and archbishops met in councils to decide which ideas or practices the Church would accept. One of the most important of these was in 325 A.D. Church officials met in Nicaea (nī SEE uh) in Asia Minor, where they drew up the Nicene Creed, a statement of basic Christian beliefs.

SECTION 2 REVIEW

1. **Identify:** (a) Gospels, (b) Peter, (c) Paul, (d) Gentiles, (e) Nicene Creed.

2. **Define:** (a) messiah, (b) parable, (c) martyr, (d) hierarchy, (e) pope.

3. How did Rome treat the Jews in Palestine?

4. Why did Roman authorities believe Jesus was dangerous?

5. What did Paul teach Christians?

6. List three reasons for the spread of Christianity.

7. **Critical Thinking** How did the Church hierarchy mirror the structure of the Roman government?

3 Breakdown of Unity in the Empire

READ TO UNDERSTAND

☐ **Why the Pax Romana ended.**

☐ **How Diocletian and Constantine tried to strengthen the empire.**

☐ **Why reforms failed to stop the decline of Rome.**

☐ *Vocabulary:* coloni.

During the centuries that Christianity was struggling to survive, the Roman Empire was declining. After the death of Marcus Aurelius in 180 A.D., Rome plunged into civil wars and chaos. At one point, Roman soldiers auctioned the office of emperor to the highest bidder. But when he did not pay up, they murdered him. A more successful emperor, Septimus Severus, advised his son from his deathbed, "Make the soldiers rich and don't worry about the rest."

End of the Pax Romana

The Romans never set up an effective way for one emperor to succeed another. Often, an emperor would name his son or an adopted

"Nations flourish if philosophers rule, or if rulers are philosophers." No man had more reason to ponder these words of Plato than Marcus Aurelius, emperor of Rome from 161 A.D. to 180 A.D. Aurelius followed the Stoic philosophy and its belief in a disciplined, thoughtful life. In keeping with this philosophy, he accepted the call to become emperor because he felt it was his duty.

As emperor, Marcus Aurelius won the favor of the Roman masses. He lived simply and became known for being just. He made it easier for slaves to win their freedom. Revolted by the bloody combat between gladiators in the arena, he ordered their swords blunted so they would not kill one another.

Marcus Aurelius would have been happy to rule over a peaceful empire, but this was not to be. Soldiers returning home to Rome from war in the east brought back a deadly plague. Thousands died as the disease rampaged through the crowded city. In their panic, Romans blamed Christians for the disease. Thousands of Christians were burned alive or mutilated by lions and bears in the arena. Aurelius was appalled, but he did not stop the slaughter. According to Roman law, being a Christian was punishable by death. And he felt that it was his duty to uphold the law.

The emperor faced other grave problems as well. Egyptians rose up against Roman rule, and to the north, Germanic tribes raided Roman settlements. Although he was in poor health and had little military experience, Marcus Aurelius dutifully led an army against the Germans. Without complaint, he endured the hardships of war. "Let it make no difference to you," he declared, "whether you are shivering or warm, sleepy or well-rested, or even dying, so long as you do your duty."

In 180 A.D., while in the field against the Germans, Marcus Aurelius died. News of the emperor's death saddened the Roman people. The philosopher-king had preserved the empire in the face of exceptional hardships. Those who came after him would not be able to do so.

1. Why did Marcus Aurelius allow the slaughter of the Christians?

2. **Critical Thinking** Do you think his interest in philosophy made Marcus Aurelius a better or worse ruler? Explain.

son as his heir, and the Senate would approve the new ruler. However, after the death of Marcus Aurelius, this system broke down, and the Pax Romana ended. Civil wars plagued Rome as generals competed for the throne. Between 234 A.D. and 284 A.D., at least 26 emperors ruled. Some held power for only a few months. All but one suffered violent deaths.

During the years of turmoil, the authority of Rome weakened. Law and order declined. And civil wars disrupted commerce in the cities. To raise money, emperors continued to devalue the coinage. (See page 115.) By making coins of copper with only a thin coating of gold, they could issue more and more coins. Because the new coins were worth less than the old ones, prices and wages rose sharply. In this unstable atmosphere, businesses and cities declined further.

At the same time, invaders attacked the empire. Many farmers abandoned their land or turned their land over to wealthy nobles. The small farmers, or **coloni** (kuh LOH nī), continued to work the land, but the noble landowner paid the taxes and protected the coloni. In frontier regions, powerful nobles acquired vast holdings, which they governed almost independently of Rome.

Reforms of Diocletian

In 284 A.D., legions in the east made the general Diocletian (DĪ uh KLEE shuhn) emperor. The new ruler introduced harsh new laws meant to strengthen the empire. Diocletian divided the Roman Empire in half and took control of the wealthier eastern provinces himself. He then appointed a co-emperor to rule the western provinces. The co-emperor was responsible to Diocletian.

To restore government efficiency, Diocletian reorganized the civil service and made officials directly responsible to the emperor. He enlarged the army and trained new cavalry units to fight invaders. He also had new forts and roads built to reinforce the frontier defenses. For a time, these measures kept the peace.

Diocletian also tried to solve the economic problems of the empire. To slow the rapid rise in prices, he set limits on prices and wages. To make sure there were enough farm products and manufactured goods, he ordered people to remain in their jobs. A shoemaker or farmer, for example, could not change occupations. Neither could their children or grandchildren.

The Reign of Constantine

When illness forced Diocletian to retire in 305 A.D., a long power struggle resulted. In 312 A.D., Constantine emerged victorious, as you have read. The new emperor reunited the eastern and western territories under his personal rule. But he took a significant step when he built a new capital at Byzantium, a Greek city on the Bosporus. The new Roman capital came to be called Constantinople. Making Constantinople the capital symbolized the declining influence of the city of Rome and the growing importance of the eastern provinces of the Roman Empire.

Constantine had many reasons for building a new capital. He believed that Rome was full of its "pagan," or non-Christian, past. Constantine wanted the new capital to be a Christian city. Also, Constantinople was closer to the great commercial centers of the eastern Mediterranean. The trade and commerce of those cities supplied most of the empire's

A portrait of the reigning emperor was stamped on Roman coins. This coin shows the profile of Diocletian.

riches. Furthermore, the eastern frontiers were more secure from invaders than the western frontiers.

Constantine expanded the reforms of Diocletian. He ordered officials to enforce the harsh laws tying artisans to their trades and farmers to the land. But this had few positive results. Without the hope of getting ahead, people saw little reason to work hard.

The policies of Diocletian and Constantine did not halt the political and economic decay. Corruption and violence resurfaced after Constantine's death in 337 A.D. The empire was again divided. The Eastern Roman Empire flourished, but the Western Roman Empire was collapsing under internal stress and the pressure of invaders.

SECTION 3 REVIEW

1. **Locate:** (a) Constantinople.

2. **Identify:** (a) Diocletian, (b) Constantine.

3. **Define:** coloni.

4. List two problems the Roman Empire faced after the death of Marcus Aurelius.

5. (a) How did Diocletian increase the military strength of the Roman Empire? (b) How did he fight rising prices?

6. **Critical Thinking** Which of the reforms undertaken by Diocletian and Constantine do you think were most effective? Which were least effective? Explain.

The Germanic tribes who attacked the Roman Empire placed a high value on courage and strength. Young warriors, such as the one shown here fighting a helmeted Roman soldier, fought to the death for their chief.

4 Collapse of the Empire

READ TO UNDERSTAND

☐ How Germanic tribes were organized.

☐ Why Germanic tribes invaded the Roman Empire.

☐ What political, economic, and social problems led to the decline of Rome.

Diocletian and Constantine had struggled to restore Roman power. But invaders sweeping across the frontiers shattered forever the unity of the Roman Empire.

The Germanic Tribes

During the Pax Romana, Roman armies had often fought Germanic tribes living north of the Danube River. The Germans included many different groups of seminomadic herd-ers and farmers who had migrated from Scandinavia, the area of present-day Norway, Sweden, and Denmark.

The Roman historian Tacitus left one of the earliest descriptions of the Germanic tribes. Their military strength, courage, and strict morality impressed Tacitus.

An elected king ruled each tribe with the aid of a council of chiefs. Chiefs were chosen for their bravery by assemblies of free men. Each chief led a band of young warriors. In exchange for their services in battle, the chief supplied his warriors with a shield, a javelin, food, and shelter. "The chief fights for victory," Tacitus noted, while his "companions fight for their chief." Each chief administered justice in his region. Under the Germanic system, a person who was guilty of assault had to pay a fine to the injured person.

By the third century A.D., the pressure of a growing population forced the Germans to seek new land. Attracted by the wealth and the warmer climate of southern Europe, some crossed into the Roman Empire. Weakened by civil wars, frontier legions were hard pressed to hold back them back. Then, about 375 A.D., the Huns, a fierce nomadic people from Central Asia, attacked the Germanic tribes of Eastern Europe.

Invasions of the Roman Empire

We do not know why the Huns burst out of Asia into Europe. Huns were superb riders and warriors who easily defeated the Ostrogoths, a Germanic tribe that lived north of the Black Sea.

Fearing a similar fate, a neighboring Germanic tribe, the Visigoths, looked for protection inside the Roman Empire. In 376 A.D., they received permission to cross the Danube River. Two years later, the Romans regretted their decision and sent an army against the Visigoths. But at the Battle of Adrianople, the Visigoths crushed the Roman legions. The Roman defeat signaled to all that Rome was no longer unbeatable.

After Adrianople, Germanic tribes flooded into the empire seeking safety from the Huns. As they came, they looted Roman cities. In 410 A.D., the Visigoth general Alaric (AL uh rihk) invaded Italy and sacked Rome. Roman officials eventually bought peace by granting Alaric much of southern Gaul and Spain.

Meanwhile, the Huns conquered Eastern Europe, including the areas of present-day Romania, Hungary, Poland, and Czechoslovakia. Under their leader Attila, whom Christians called the "Scourge of God," they poured across the Rhine into Gaul. Rome then formed a hasty alliance with some Germanic tribes. At the Battle of Troyes (trwah) in 451 A.D., Rome and its allies stopped the Hun advance. Attila withdrew his forces. When he died soon after, the Hun empire collapsed.

Other invaders continued to threaten Rome. A Germanic tribe, the Vandals, moved through Gaul into Spain before settling in northern Africa. From Carthage, the Vandals

raided Italy. In 455 A.D., they sacked Rome. As Roman legions were withdrawn from the frontiers to defend cities in Italy, the Burgundians, the Franks, and later the Lombards moved into the western empire.

The "Fall of Rome"

In 476 A.D., a minor Germanic chief, Odoacer (OH doh AY suhr), captured Rome and forced the emperor to give up the throne. Odoacer then proclaimed himself king of Italy. Many historians refer to this event as the "fall of Rome." Yet Rome did not collapse suddenly.

As you have read, the Roman Empire had faced severe problems for centuries. Moreover, Roman civilization did not simply disappear after 476 A.D. Although Germanic tribes

MAP STUDY *Diocletian hoped to strengthen the Roman Empire by dividing it into the Western Roman Empire and the Eastern Roman Empire. What was the actual result of his action? Which tribes reached Rome?*

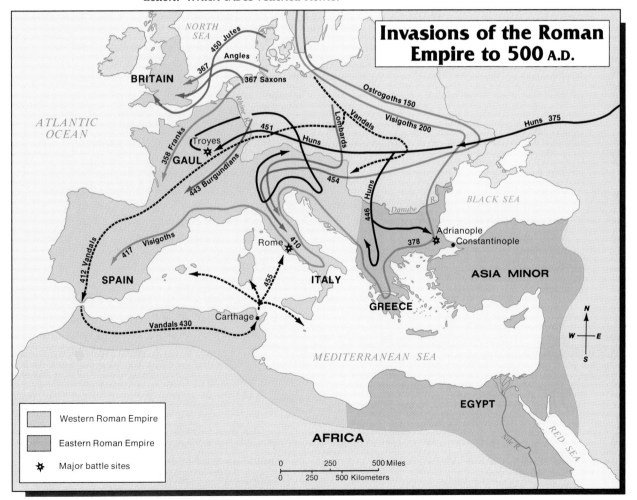

Invasions of the Roman Empire to 500 A.D.

conquered the western empire, the people of Gaul, for example, still considered themselves Romans. People continued to enforce Roman laws, and they spoke Latin, although local dialects developed. However, after 476 A.D., there was no emperor in the west. Without an emperor to serve as a rallying point, the unity of the Western Roman Empire ended.

The Eastern Roman Empire survived for 1,000 years after the "fall" of Rome. From Constantinople, emperors played one Germanic ruler off against another, hoping to control af-

---

SKILL LESSON   The Decline of Rome: Using a Primary Source

Written records provide us with useful information about historical events, everyday life, and the beliefs of different peoples. Historians use two types of written records: primary sources and secondary sources.

Primary sources are first-hand accounts based on the experiences of people who were involved in an event. Eyewitness accounts, government documents, treaties, and letters are primary sources. **Secondary sources** are second-hand accounts based on the writings or evidence of others. Textbooks and encyclopedias are secondary sources.

Some primary sources are written for a particular reason so the writer might not tell a completely objective story. Therefore, they have to be judged carefully.

The following excerpt is from the *Histories of Ammianus Marcellinus,* written about 378 A.D. Ammianus was a soldier who had often visited Rome. Use these steps to evaluate the excerpt as a primary source.

1 **Determine what information is being given.** (a) What aspects of Roman life does the writer describe? (b) What does the writer say about the clothing worn by Romans? (c) How did poor Romans spend their time?

2 **Distinguish between fact and opinion.** A **fact** is something that has actually happened. It can be proven or observed. An **opinion** is a judgment that reflects a person's beliefs. (a) What three facts about life in Rome can you identify in this excerpt? (b) What is the writer's opinion of the amusements of Romans?

3 **Evaluate the reliability of the source.** (a) How could the fact that Ammianus was a visitor to Rome have affected his view of the capital? (b) What aspects of Roman life does Ammianus seem to ignore? (c) Would you consider this a reliable description of life in Rome? Why or why not?

4 **Use the source to draw conclusions about a historical development.** What generalizations about the decline of Rome can be made from this source?

From the *Histories* by Marcellinus

Rome is still looked on as the queen of the earth, and the name of the Roman people is respected. But the magnificence of Rome is defaced by the thoughtless conduct of a few, who fall away into error and vice. Some men think they can become immortal by having statues made of them—as if they could be rewarded after death by being cast as bronze figures that have no sense or feeling rather than by striving to perform upright and honorable actions. And they are even eager to have their statues plated with gold.

Others place greater importance on having a couch higher than usual, or splendid clothing. They toil and sweat under a vast burden of cloaks which are fastened to their necks by many clasps.

The whirlpool of banquets and other luxuries I shall pass over lest I go too far. Many people drive their horses recklessly over the flint-paved city streets. They drag behind them huge numbers of slaves, like bands of robbers. As for the lower and poorer classes, some spend the whole night in the wine shops. Some lie concealed in the shady arcades of the theaters. They play at dice so eagerly as to quarrel over them. Such pursuits as these prevent anything worth mentioning from being done in Rome.

fairs in the west. Thriving commerce and a strong civil service in the eastern empire enabled it to preserve Greco-Roman civilization. In Chapter 11, you will read more about the Byzantine Empire, as the Eastern Roman Empire was later called.

Causes of the Decline

Why did Rome decline? Most historians agree that no single problem caused the decline of Rome. Instead, they point out that a combination of political, economic, and social problems gradually destroyed the strength of the Roman Empire.

Political causes. Roman citizens gradually felt less responsibility toward government. They expected the emperor to look after their needs. The vast size of the empire and widespread corruption made efficient government difficult even under good rulers. And many emperors were weak or evil rulers.

The division of the empire hurt the western empire because the best officials and generals served the eastern emperor. Just when the tide of invasions was strongest, Rome suffered from a lack of capable leaders. Furthermore, as Roman authority weakened, some wealthy landowners withdrew their support from Rome and set up independent states.

Economic causes. Governing the Roman Empire required huge amounts of money. Much of the empire's wealth came from the eastern provinces. Thus, the division of the empire deprived Rome of desperately needed revenues. Moreover, Roman armies were no longer bringing in loot from newly conquered territories. Civil wars and Germanic invasions hurt trade and agriculture, making tax collection difficult, if not impossible. Efforts to increase the money supply by devaluing the currency only increased inflation. The resulting high prices were a burden to most Romans.

In the cities, heavy taxes and high unemployment meant less prosperity. The idleness of the wealthy and the expense of providing free grain to the poor drained Roman resources.

Social causes. As historians at the time noted, the loyalty and civic pride that once unified Rome had gradually decayed. Because citizens evaded military service, soldiers had

Although their art was less sophisticated than Roman art, Germanic artisans produced fine animal figures in metal. The horse and rider shown here may have been part of a pendant.

to be recruited from people who had little loyalty to Rome. These soldiers lacked the discipline and patriotism of the armies of the Roman Republic, which had conquered the Mediterranean world. As a result, they were no match for the well-trained Germans, who were inspired by loyalty to their chiefs.

Many people no longer felt they had a stake in the empire. They did not care whether the ruler was Roman or Germanic. Devastating epidemics swept through the western provinces in the 300s, increasing the sense of hopelessness. Despite these tremendous pressures, the breakup of the Western Roman Empire was a slow process. The remarkable feature of the empire was that it lasted for so long.

SECTION 4 REVIEW

1. **Locate:** (a) Adrianople, (b) Troyes.

2. **Identify:** (a) Huns, (b) Visigoths, (c) Attila, (d) Vandals.

3. What role did the chief play in Germanic tribes?

4. List two reasons why Germanic tribes moved into the Roman Empire.

5. How did the division of the Roman Empire hurt the western provinces?

6. **Critical Thinking** Which of the reasons for Rome's decline do you think was most important?

Summary

1. During the Pax Romana, Greco-Roman civilization flourished. Romans adopted Greek ideas of art, architecture, and literature but made many contributions of their own, especially in practical areas such as engineering and technology. The Romans developed a system of law, based on standards of justice, that influenced later law codes in Europe.

2. Christianity began in Palestine and spread throughout the Roman Empire. Its teachings were rooted in Hebrew traditions and included love of God and compassion for other people. Despite persecution, Christianity survived. By 395 A.D., it had become the official religion of the empire.

3. Civil wars after 180 A.D. ended the Pax Romana. They also disrupted the economy of the empire. Attempts by Diocletian and Constantine to revive Roman authority failed.

4. In the 300s and 400s A.D., Germanic and Hun invaders crippled the Western Roman Empire. The capture of the city of Rome in 476 A.D. marked the end of political unity in the west. Yet the Roman heritage survived in both Western Europe and the Eastern Roman Empire.

Recalling Facts

Arrange the events in each of the following groups in the order in which they occurred.

1. (a) The Pax Romana ends.
   (b) Odoacer captures Rome.
   (c) The Roman Empire is divided into an eastern and a western empire.

2. (a) Diocletian introduces government and economic reforms.
   (b) Constantine builds a new capital in the east.
   (c) Christianity becomes the official religion of the Roman Empire.

3. (a) Roman armies destroy Jerusalem.
   (b) Nicene Creed is adopted.
   (c) Jesus is born in Bethlehem.

4. (a) Huns attack Germanic tribes in Eastern Europe.
   (b) Visigoths defeat Romans at the battle of Adrianople.
   (c) Vandals sack Rome.

Chapter Checkup

1. (a) How did Greek culture influence Roman civilization? (b) In what fields did Rome make its own contributions?

2. (a) What were the main themes emphasized by Roman writers? (b) How did Livy's writing of history differ from that of the Greek historian Thucydides?

3. Describe the system of law that developed under the Roman Empire.

4. (a) In general, what was the Roman attitude toward the many different religions in the empire? (b) Why did Roman authorities persecute Christians?

5. Explain how each of the following contributed to the spread of Christianity: (a) Paul; (b) Roman persecution; (c) the message of Christianity; (d) unity of the Roman Empire.

6. (a) Describe the reforms of Diocletian and Constantine. (b) How were they successful? (c) How were they unsuccessful?

Critical Thinking

1. **Relating Past to Present** (a) In your opinion, why did Rome borrow so much from Greek civilization? (b) What present-day example can you give of one culture strongly influencing another?

2. **Understanding the Roots of Democracy** (a) How is law in the United States today

similar to law in the Roman Empire? (b) How is it different? (c) How might you explain the similarities and differences?

3. **Analyzing** (a) How did the Pax Romana help the spread of Christianity? (b) How do you think the later decline of Rome's political power made Christianity appealing to more people?

4. **Understanding Economic Ideas** (a) Why did emperors who ruled after the end of the Pax Romana devalue the coinage? (b) What effect did that action have on the economy? (c) How did Diocletian and Constantine try to solve economic problems? (d) Why do you think their reforms did not work?

Developing Basic Skills

1. **Using Visual Evidence** Study the mosaic on page 122. (a) How would you describe the mood of the musicians? (b) What might you conclude about life in Rome based on this mosaic? (c) Does the mosaic provide a complete picture? Why or why not?

2. **Map Reading** Use the map on page 131 and your reading in this chapter to answer these questions: (a) Which of the invaders of Rome came from Asia? (b) Describe the route taken by the Vandals through the Roman Empire. (c) Which part of the Roman Empire suffered most from the invasions? Which suffered the least? (d) How do the routes taken by the invaders help explain the fall of the Western Roman Empire?

3. **Classifying** Make a chart with three columns. In column one, list political causes for Rome's decline. In column two, list economic causes. In column three, list social causes. Then answer the following questions: (a) What connections do you see between political and economic causes? (b) How did economic problems contribute to social problems? (c) What do you think was the most important cause of Rome's decline? Explain.

Writing About History

Chronological Order

Events that are arranged in the order in which they happened are said to be in chronological order. You would use chronological order, for example, if you were describing the Germanic invasions of Rome or the development of early Christianity. Some words that may be used to show the way events are related in time are: *first, later, soon, immediately, then, as soon as, while,* and *next.*

Practice: Write a paragraph on one of the topics mentioned above. Organize your facts in chronological order, using some of the time words listed.

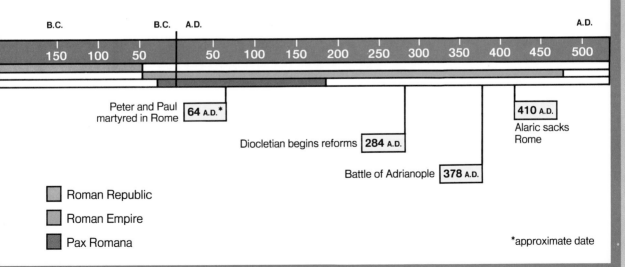

B.C.   B.C.   A.D.   A.D.

150   100   50   50   100   150   200   250   300   350   400   450   500

Peter and Paul martyred in Rome **64 A.D.** *

Diocletian begins reforms **284 A.D.**

Battle of Adrianople **378 A.D.**

410 A.D.
Alaric sacks Rome

☐ Roman Republic
☐ Roman Empire
☐ Pax Romana

*approximate date

135

The Heritage of India and China

7

(600 B.C.–550 A.D.)

Buddhism, founded in India, eventually spread across Asia. In many places, Buddha came to be worshipped as a god. Here, he is shown surrounded by four minor deities.

"The people are numerous and happy. The king governs without beheading or other cruel punishments." A Chinese traveler, Fa-hsien (FAH shee ehn), visited India in the early 400s A.D., and made these observations. Fa-hsien, a Buddhist monk, had set out on foot from China in 399 A.D. He traveled into Afghanistan and then crossed the Hindu Kush Mountains. Six years after he left China, he arrived in India, the land where Buddhism, one of the world's major religions, had been born.

Fa-hsien described many of the customs and practices that he saw in India in a journal of his trip. "Throughout the whole country, the people do not kill any living creatures, nor drink intoxicating liquor, nor eat onions or garlic. The only exception is the untouchable caste who are held to be wicked people and live apart from the others. Only the untouchables are fishermen and hunters and sell flesh meat.

"In the cities and towns of this country, the people are rich and prosperous. Certain families establish houses for dispensing charity and medicines to the poor. Doctors examine their diseases. The poor get the food and medicines which their cases require, and are made to feel at ease."

Fa-hsien visited India at the height of the Gupta (GUP tuh) Empire. At the same time that Greco-Roman civilization flourished in the Mediterranean world, the civilizations of India and China also reached new heights. Between 600 B.C. and 550 A.D., both India and China made impressive advances and spread their cultures to other parts of Asia.

In the sixth and fifth centuries B.C., great philosophers in India and China developed ideas about the goals of life and about the individual's place in society—ideas that have lasted through the centuries. This was the same time that Socrates, the Hebrew prophets, and Zoroaster were developing their ideas in other parts of the world.

Like Rome, both India and China suffered from civil wars and invasions. Yet they did not experience the drastic upheavals that led to the collapse of Rome. As a result, the civilizations in India and China continued to thrive at a time when people in Western Europe were building the foundations for a new civilization. ■

1 Two Influential Religions

READ TO UNDERSTAND

☐ How the basic beliefs of Hinduism developed.

☐ How Hinduism was connected to the caste system.

☐ What beliefs of Buddhism emerged and how they spread.

☐ *Vocabulary:* brahma, atman, karma, nirvana.

Two major religions helped shape the civilization of India. First, ancient Aryan beliefs and practices evolved into Hinduism. In turn, Hindu traditions influenced Buddhism, which emerged in India about 500 B.C. Both religions still have millions of followers.

Hinduism

Hinduism did not grow out of one person's ideas. Instead, it blended ancient Aryan traditions with the religious beliefs of peoples the Aryans conquered. To Hindus, sacred texts such as the Vedas and the Upanishads reveal basic truths about life and the place of the individual in the universe. (See page 57.)

Hindus believe in **brahma,** a single, supreme force that unites everything in the universe. They worship many gods, but each god symbolizes a different aspect of brahma. Thus, the three main gods in Hinduism—Brahma, Vishnu, and Shiva—are part of the same universal spirit. The god Brahma is seen as the creator of the world, Vishnu as the preserver, and Shiva as the destroyer.

The Hindu belief in the unity of all life is reflected in the idea of soul. Hinduism teaches that every individual has a soul, which is part of a larger universal soul, called **atman.** How-

137

Shiva, one of the leading gods in Hinduism, appears in many roles. In this statue, he is shown as lord of the cosmic dance. The dwarf under his foot represents the illusions that Shiva dispels. Shiva holds a drum, symbol of creation, in one hand and a flame, symbol of destruction, in another hand.

ever, most individuals pursue imperfect goals such as material riches and personal pleasures. Hindus believe that trying to reach these goals brings suffering and pain and keeps the soul separate from the universal soul. The goal of life, according to Hinduism, is to free the soul from its individual existence through reunion with atman.

The process of freeing the soul takes more than one lifetime. Thus, Hindus believe that the soul passes through a series of rebirths. When the body dies, the soul is reincarnated, or reborn, in another person or in an animal. According to Hinduism, the cycle of reincarnation continues until the individual soul has reached the highest level of spiritual understanding and is reunited with the universal soul.

Hinduism provides a guide for correct conduct. It encourages virtues such as truth, respect for all life, and detachment from the material world.

Hinduism and the Caste System

Hinduism is woven deeply into Indian culture, and its teachings supported the caste system. In early Aryan society, there were four major classes that were eventually divided into many castes and subcastes. (See page 59.) Hindus believe that the law of karma determines whether a person is born into a high or low caste. **Karma** includes all the actions in a person's life that affect his or her fate in the next life.

At birth, a person has a set of social and religious duties that include obedience to caste rules as well as to moral laws. People acquire good karma by obeying caste rules about diet, work, and social behavior. For example, if a servant, a member of the Sudra caste, was a faithful servant and followed caste rules, his or her soul would be reincarnated in a higher caste in the next life. However, those who ignore their duties could be reborn in a lower caste or as an animal.

By 600 B.C., Brahmans, or priests, had emerged as the highest caste. They alone could perform the rituals that guided the soul to this reunion. Because most people believed that their current positions were due to actions in previous lives, they felt they had no choice but to obey the rules set up by the priests.

However, a few people rejected the idea that only complicated rituals performed by Brahmans could open the way to salvation. One influential reformer was Siddhartha Gautama (GOWT uh muh). His ideas gave rise to a new religion, Buddhism.

Siddhartha Gautama: Founder of Buddhism

Siddhartha Gautama was born into the warrior class about 563 B.C. He apparently grew up in luxury, protected from the world outside his father's palace. He married and had one son. According to legend, one day when Gautama was 29 he saw an old man, then a sick man, and finally a dead body. This was the first time Gautama had encountered human suffering. The experience haunted him, making him see the world as a place full of misery and decay.

Soon after, Gautama exchanged the silks and jewels he wore for beggar's rags and set out to discover the causes of human suffering. First, he studied the sacred Hindu texts. Then he tried self-denial, disciplining his body to near starvation. But neither course satisfied him.

One day, after six years of wandering, Gautama sat meditating under a sacred tree. Suddenly, he felt he had found the knowledge he had been seeking. In that moment, he believed he had attained enlightenment. Thereafter, Gautama was called the Buddha, or "the Enlightened One."

From that day on, the Buddha taught the way to salvation that he had discovered. He attracted many followers, many of whom left their families and possessions for a life devoted to poverty and self-discipline.

According to Buddhist tradition, Gautama died in 483 B.C., while visiting a poor blacksmith. The Buddha had eaten the spoiled food set before him rather than embarrass the poor family. As he lay dying, he advised his disciples: "Decay is inherent [natural] in all things. Work out your own salvation with diligence."

The Teachings of Buddhism

At the heart of Buddhist teachings are the "Four Noble Truths"—the knowledge Buddha discovered while he sat under the sacred tree. The first truth is that suffering and misery are universal. The second truth is that the cause of suffering is desire. Happiness, riches, and other pleasures cause pain because they cannot last.

The third truth is that the way to end suffering is to overcome desire. The ultimate goal of life is escape from desire in nirvana. **Nirvana** is the condition of wanting nothing. The fourth truth is that the way to escape pain and suffering is to follow the Middle Way.

The Middle Way offered practical guidelines that stressed virtuous conduct and compassion for all living things. They also stressed right knowledge, intentions, speech, conduct, livelihood, and meditation.

Buddhism and Hinduism compared. The Buddha had set out to reform Hinduism, not set up a new religion. Therefore, Buddhism reflected many Hindu beliefs. For example, the Buddha believed in karma and a cycle of rebirth. Both religions viewed the world as a place of sadness and suffering from which people wished to escape.

Yet Buddhism also differed from Hinduism. The Buddha denied the existence of any gods. He believed that all people, no matter what their social class, could achieve nirvana through the Middle Way. Furthermore, he rejected the caste system and the Hindu view that priests were more worthy than other people.

The spread of Buddhism. After the Buddha's death, missionaries carried the new religion across India and Asia. (See the map on page 140.) The Buddha's disciples collected Buddhist teachings into sacred texts called the *Three Baskets of Wisdom.*

This Chinese bronze shows a seated Buddha. Sitting in a similar pose under a sacred tree, Siddhartha Guatama believed he had reached enlightenment. His followers believed that they too could find the meaning of existence through meditation.

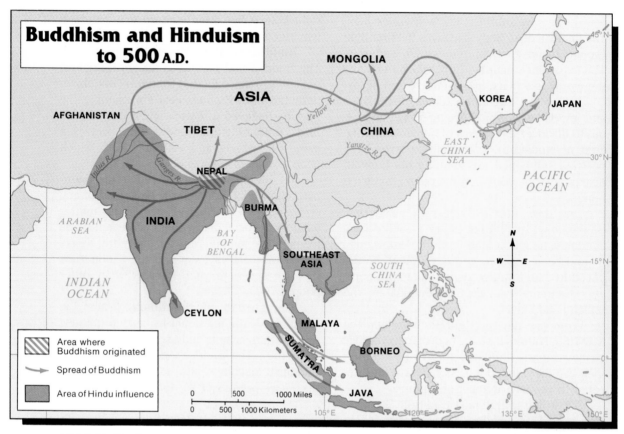

Buddhism and Hinduism to 500 A.D.

MONGOLIA

ASIA

KOREA

JAPAN

AFGHANISTAN

TIBET

CHINA

Yellow R.

EAST CHINA SEA

PACIFIC OCEAN

NEPAL

Yangtze R.

Indus R.

Ganges R.

INDIA

BURMA

ARABIAN SEA

BAY OF BENGAL

SOUTHEAST ASIA

SOUTH CHINA SEA

N

W—E

S

INDIAN OCEAN

CEYLON

MALAYA

BORNEO

SUMATRA

JAVA

Area where Buddhism originated

Spread of Buddhism

Area of Hindu influence

0   500   1000 Miles

0   500   1000 Kilometers

105°E   120°E   135°E   150°E

45°N   30°N   15°N   0°

MAP STUDY *From its birthplace, Buddhism spread to other parts of Asia. Although it was absorbed back into Hinduism in India, Buddhism has remained a vital force in other parts of Asia. In which areas outside India was Hinduism influential? In which major directions did Buddhism spread?*

Gradually, two sects, or schools, developed within Buddhism. The Theravada (THER uh VAH duh) sect spread from India to Sri Lanka and to Southeast Asia. It emphasized the original sayings of the Buddha and taught that people must seek nirvana through ethical conduct.

The Mahayana (MAH huh YAH nuh) sect spread into China, Korea, Tibet, and Japan. Mahayana Buddhists worshiped the Buddha as a god. They taught that other people had reached enlightenment and become buddhas.

In India, Buddhism and Hinduism existed side by side for centuries. Gradually, Hinduism absorbed many Buddhist beliefs, and Buddha was worshiped as a Hindu god. Eventually, Buddhism merged back into Hinduism.

SECTION 1 REVIEW

1. **Identify:** (a) Brahma, (b) Vishnu, (c) Shiva, (d) Four Noble Truths, (e) Middle Way.

2. **Define:** (a) brahma, (b) atman, (c) karma, (d) nirvana.

3. According to Hindu beliefs, what should be the goal of life?

4. What did the Buddha teach about suffering and the way to overcome it?

5. **Critical Thinking** Why do you think Buddha rejected the caste system?

2 Great Empires in India

READI TO UNDERSTAND

☐ How Asoka's conversion to Buddhism influenced his rule.

☐ What the Bactrian kingdom contributed to India.

☐ Why the Gupta Empire is considered a golden age in India.

☐ *Vocabulary:* stupa.

In about 285 B.C., an Indian king, Bindusara, sent a request to Antiochus, the Greek king of Syria. He asked for a sample of figs, Greek wine, and a philosopher. Antiochus sent the first two items but politely replied that Greeks did not export philosophers.

The exchange shows that India at that time was not isolated from the rest of the world. In fact, it was often subject to invasions from outsiders. The Persians had conquered the Indus Valley for a brief period in the 500s B.C. After the Persians were ousted, several Indian states struggled to unite the many Aryan kingdoms and to defeat invaders.

The Maurya Empire

In 321 B.C., Chandragupta Maurya (CHUHN druh GUP tuh MAWR yah) came to power in northern India. He founded the Maurya dynasty that ruled the largest empire yet seen in India. It stretched across northern India from the Bay of Bengal to the Hindu Kush.

To Chandragupta's court at Pataliputra (PAH tah lih POO trah) came ambassadors from all over the world. The entire city was surrounded by a wide moat and wooden walls. The emperor lived in a splendid wooden palace, attended by servants dressed in gold-embroidered robes. Armed women guarded the emperor and hunted with him.

Organizing the empire. Chandragupta and his successors created a well-run empire. They divided it into provinces. Governors sent out from the capital oversaw tax collecting, justice, and defense. Government spies travel-

ing in disguise reported on the honesty of officials. These paid informers used homing pigeons to send messages to the capital. To improve communications, Maurya emperors built roads that local governors had to keep in repair.

Under the Maurya dynasty, trade flourished. Indian merchants exported elephants, silk, cotton, perfumes, and precious stones to China and to the Hellenistic cities of western Asia.

Reign of Asoka. Asoka (uh SOH kuh), the best-known Maurya ruler, ruled from about 269 B.C. to 232 B.C. He expanded the empire to its greatest size. (See the map below.) After a brutal campaign to subdue Kalinga, a state in southern India, Asoka learned that more than 100,000 people had been slaughtered. Stricken with remorse, he renounced

MAP STUDY *Maurya emperors extended their rule over much of India. The Maurya Empire, shown here, reached its greatest extent under the emperor Asoka. Why was Maurya expansion limited to the north?*

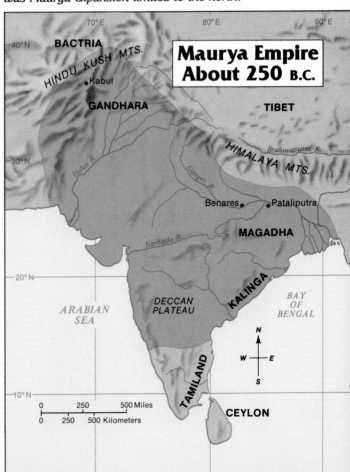

violence and warfare. Soon after, he converted to Buddhism because it rejected hatred and killing.

Asoka then set out to rule by example instead of by force. He relaxed the harsh justice of earlier rulers. He sent officials across the empire to teach the importance of good works, nonviolence, and religious toleration. Asoka himself traveled widely, urging people to live in peace with one another. His edicts were carved onto stone pillars set along the roads for all to see. "It is good to give," proclaimed one edict, "but there is no gift, no service, like the gift of Righteousness."

A convert to Buddhism, Asoka, shown here, applied its teachings in the way he ruled India. He was especially concerned with promoting peace and good works: "All men are my children. As for my own children I desire that they may be provided with all the welfare and happiness of this world and of the next, so do I desire for all men as well."

During Asoka's reign, Buddhism strongly influenced life in India. The emperor built many **stupas** (STOOP uhs), large domelike structures that contained the remains of saintly monks. He encouraged pilgrimages, or journeys to religious shrines. To make travel easier, he repaired roads and built rest houses that provided water, shade, and food for weary pilgrims. By sending Buddhist missionaries to Ceylon, Burma, and Southeast Asia, Asoka helped make Buddhism a major world religion as well as spread Indian civilization to those areas.

An Age of Invasions

Civil war shattered the unity of the Maurya Empire after Asoka's death. From about 180 B.C. to 300 A.D., many small kingdoms rose and fell in northern India. During the same period, numerous invaders crossed the Hindu Kush Mountains into the northern plain.

One group of invaders were the Bactrian Greeks. They were descendants of Alexander the Great's soldiers who had settled in Bactria, a region to the northwest of India. In the second century B.C., the Bactrians pushed deep into northwestern India.

Under the Bactrians, there was a blending of Greek and Indian culture. Indian scholars studied Hellenistic medicine, astronomy, and astrology. Like other invaders, however, the Bactrian Greeks were eventually absorbed into Indian culture. Finally, around 30 B.C., a new wave of invaders swept into India and defeated the Bactrians.

Among the newcomers were the Kushans, who ruled for about 200 years. One Kushan ruler, Kanishka (kuh NIHSH kuh), converted to Buddhism and called a council of 500 monks to regulate Buddhist teachings. Out of these meetings came the Mahayana school of Buddhism. (See page 140.) The Kushans carried Mahayana Buddhism along caravan routes into Central Asia and China.

The Gupta Empire

The third century A.D. was a time of much upheaval in India. Out of the confusion rose a powerful new empire ruled by the Gupta dynasty. At the height of Gupta power, the empire reached to the Narbada (ner BUHD uh) River in the south and to the Hindu Kush and Himalaya Mountains in the north. (See the map at right.)

The Gupta Empire flourished from 320 A.D. to about 535 A.D. at a time when the Western Roman Empire was collapsing. The age of the Guptas is considered a golden age because India enjoyed peace and prosperity and made advances in the arts and sciences. You will read about these in the next section.

Hinduism dominated Indian life under the Guptas. Buddhist influences remained, but by this time Buddhism in India had been gradually absorbed into Hinduism.

In the late 400s A.D., the Gupta Empire weakened. About the same time, Huns invaded from Central Asia and dealt the final blow to the empire. For 1,000 years after the breakup of the Gupta Empire, small, independent kingdoms ruled in India.

Central and Southern India

In central and southern India, fighting among many small kingdoms prevented unity. The Deccan Plateau occasionally came under the control of northern kingdoms, but southern India remained untouched.

The Dravidians, who lived in the south, followed traditions different from those in the Aryan north. Physically different from the northerners, they also spoke different languages. The most widespread was Tamil, from which their culture takes its name. Over time, Hinduism spread into the south and absorbed the gods and religious practices of the region. As a result, Hinduism became a diverse religion with hundreds of gods.

Trade was important to the Tamil kingdoms of the south. Tamil sailors crossed the Indian Ocean with cargoes of silk, spices, and wild animals, which were highly prized in the Roman Empire. During the reign of Augustus, Tamil merchants traveled to Rome—a trip that took four years. Tamil rulers improved harbors to attract the profitable overseas trade. As the Roman Empire declined, the Tamil kingdoms increased their trade with China.

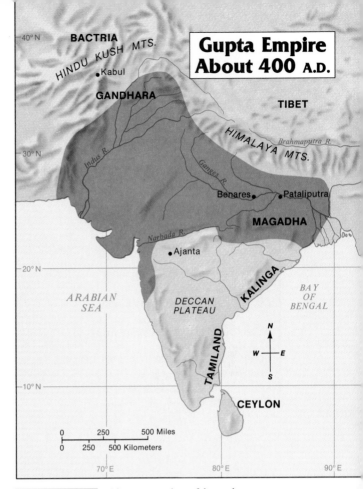

Gupta Empire About 400 A.D.

MAP STUDY *After centuries of invasions, northern India was reunited by the Gupta rulers. What territories included in the Maurya Empire (see page 141) were not included in the Gupta Empire?*

SECTION 2 REVIEW

1. **Locate:** (a) Pataliputra, (b) Bactria.

2. **Identify:** Asoka.

3. **Define:** stupa.

4. How did Maurya rulers govern their empire?

5. What effect did the Bactrian Greeks have on India?

6. What achievement made the Gupta Empire a golden age?

7. **Critical Thinking** Why do you think Asoka is considered one of India's greatest rulers?

500 B.C.*	Magadha rulers unite Aryan kingdoms
326 B.C.	Alexander the Great invades India
321–183 B.C.	Maurya Empire
269–232 B.C.	Asoka rules Maurya Empire
250–150 B.C.*	Bactrian kingdoms flourish
78*–227 A.D.	Kushan Kingdom
320–535 A.D.	Gupta Empire
450 A.D.*	Hun invasions begin

*Approximate dates

3. Indian Society and Culture

READD TO UNDERSTAND

- ☐ How the caste system changed over time.
- ☐ What place women had in Indian society.
- ☐ How Indian art and religion were linked.
- ☐ What contributions Gupta India made to science and technology.

During the Maurya and Gupta empires, Hinduism continued to shape Indian traditions. Religious beliefs influenced not only the caste system but also the arts and literature. In this period, Indians made major advances in science, art, medicine, and astronomy.

Social Changes

Under the Maurya and Gupta dynasties, the caste system became more restrictive. Many new subcastes emerged, and caste rules became more complex. People of different castes were forbidden to speak together or eat at the same table. By the time of the Gupta Empire,

contact with "untouchables," or outcastes, was severely restricted. Untouchables had to strike a piece of wood as they entered a town so that people could hear them and avoid them. Marriage outside a person's caste became almost impossible.

Changes in Indian society also affected the status of women. Under Hindu laws, women could own a certain amount of money, jewelry, and clothing, but they had fewer rights than in earlier Aryan society. More and more, women married in their very early teens. As a wife, a woman's first duty was to obey her husband and his family, with whom she, her husband, and their children lived. If a man died before his wife, she stayed with his family and was expected to devote herself to his memory.

Because a widow was considered unlucky, she was isolated and generally ignored by her husband's family. In some parts of India, widows threw themselves on their husbands' funeral fires rather than endure isolation. This practice was called suttee. A widow of a high caste was more likely to follow the practice of suttee than a widow from a lower class.

Caste also influenced other family practices. For example, high caste women were more secluded than women who had to earn a living outside the home. The practice of having more than one wife was more common in wealthy families than among the lower classes. A first wife dominated the household, especially if she gave birth to sons.

In Indian families, sons were valued more highly than daughters. Only a son could perform the sacrifices at his father's funeral that enabled a man's soul to pass into the next life. Also, a son carried on the family line whereas a daughter on her marriage became part of her husband's family.

Art and Literature

Indian art generally reflected religious themes. Great stupas were built to honor the Buddha. Although the Buddha had forbidden his followers to worship statues or idols, this teaching was later ignored. As a result, sculptors decorated Buddhist stupas with elaborate carvings showing gods and animals as well as scenes from the life of the Buddha.

Sculpture and painting. During the Kushan kingdom, a new style of sculpture flourished. (See page 142.) Gandharan art, as it is called today, showed Greco-Roman influences. The most typical subject of Gandharan sculptors was the Buddha. They portrayed him as a graceful figure. The half-closed eyes and suggestion of a smile were meant to convey the compassion the Buddha had shown toward all living things.

During the Gupta Empire, artists produced some of India's finest paintings and sculptures. The best-preserved examples of Gupta art were found in the cave temples at Ajanta (uh JUHN tuh). Centuries before the Guptas, monks had excavated these caves to use as temples and monasteries. Gupta artists decorated the walls of the Ajanta caves with brilliantly colored murals.

Indian poets. During the same period, many fine writers added to the rich literature of India. Among the finest was Kalidasa (KAH lee DAH sah), a poet and playwright. He drew on ancient legends to write about the gods, nature, and love. In one poem, "The Birth of the War-God," Kalidasa dramatically pictured a battle between an army of demons and a god. Before the demons go into battle, they see a fearful sight foretelling the future:

> The sun put on a ghastly robe
> of great and terrible snakes, curling
>   together,
> as if to mark his joy
> at the death of the enemy demon.

While poets such as Kalidasa were writing in Sanskrit in northern India, the Tamil kingdoms of the south produced their own fine literature. The lives of ordinary people, the grim results of famine, and the fierceness of warfare were featured prominently in Tamil writings. Among the earliest known Tamil poets was a woman named Avvaiyar (AH vay YAHR). In the following excerpt, Avvaiyar praises the conduct of her king:

> My king, when rich, freely gives food away,
>   when poor he eats with his men.
> He is the head of the family of the poor,
>   yet great is he, with his sharp-
>   pointed spear.

Science and Technology

Science and technology flourished during the Gupta Empire. Scholars gathered in cities, where they taught young men from the upper class. Universities and monasteries became important centers of learning.

Indian scholars made a major breakthrough in mathematics. They developed the concept of zero and developed a symbol for it. They also devised a decimal system, with symbols for the numerals 1 through 9. In the 700s A.D., the Arabs adopted these symbols, and today they are known as Hindu-Arabic numerals. At that time, Europeans were using the cumbersome Roman numerals.

Indian physicians advanced the study of medicine. They made new medicines from animal, plant, and mineral sources. They knew the importance of keeping wounds clean, invented the scalpel for use in surgery, and were skilled in setting broken bones. In addition, they developed plastic surgery to a high degree. A thousand years later, Europeans learned this art from the Indians.

At Ajanta in western India, artists painted murals on the walls of cave temples. Most of the Ajanta paintings illustrate the life of Buddha, but this scene, painted during the Gupta Empire, presents various castes and ethnic groups in India.

About 100 A.D., a great Indian doctor, Caraka (kah RAH kah), established a code of ethics to be taught to all medical students. Like the Hippocratic Oath of ancient Greece, this code governed medical behavior.

SECTION 3 REVIEW

1. **Identify:** (a) Ajanta, (b) Kalidasa, (c) Avvaiyar, (d) Caraka.

2. (a) List two ways in which the caste system became more restrictive during the Maurya and Gupta ages. (b) How did the status of women change?

3. Why were sons valued in Indian families?

4. What was the main subject of Indian art?

5. Describe two contributions Indians made to mathematics.

6. **Critical Thinking** Many of India's advances in art and science came during the Gupta Empire. Why do such advances often happen during a period of political unity?

4 The Shaping of Chinese Traditions

READ TO UNDERSTAND

☐ **What values Confucianism stressed.**

☐ **How Taoism shaped Chinese traditions.**

☐ **How Legalism differed from other Chinese philosophies.**

☐ *Vocabulary:* tao.

In China, as in India, thinkers puzzled over perplexing questions of human nature as well as the place of the individual in society and in the universe. Unlike Hindus or Buddhists, who wanted to free the individual soul from its cycle of rebirth, Chinese philosophers were concerned with this world. They sought ways of establishing a stable, orderly society.

Between 500 B.C. and 200 B.C., three schools of thought emerged: Confucianism (kuhn FYOO shuhn izm), Taoism (DOW izm), and Legalism. Each proposed a different route for achieving good government. Each viewed the individual in society in a different way. Yet all three philosophies profoundly influenced China for over 2,000 years.

Confucius: A Great Teacher

Confucius, the most influential Chinese philosopher, was born around 551 B.C. He was a scholar who held a minor government position. Eventually, he became a teacher to the sons of noble families.

Confucius did not record his teachings. However, his students often inscribed his answers to questions. They would write: "K'ung Fu-Tze says." In China, K'ung was a family name; Tze meant master or philosopher. Thus, they wrote: "The Master K'ung says." When European visitors to China first heard of the great philosopher and teacher, K'ung Fu-Tze, they pronounced the name "Confucius."

Confucius lived during the troubled years of the late Chou dynasty. It was a time of constant warfare among rival feudal lords. The violence and moral decay of Chou China dismayed Confucius. To return to the harmony of the past, he suggested a code of conduct based on high moral ideas.

For years, Confucius traveled about China, trying to convert warring rulers to his way of thinking. But he had no success. After his death in 479 B.C., however, his ideas slowly won acceptance. In time, they became the official philosophy of China and had an enormous impact on Chinese civilization.

The Confucian code of conduct. Confucius was interested in ways to organize a good society. To him, a good society was one that preserved peace and order among individuals and between people and their government. As a result, Confucius offered a code of conduct for individuals to follow in their social and political relationships. Confucius did not write books, but his followers collected his teachings into the *Analects.*

The Confucian code of conduct stressed virtues such as loyalty, courtesy, hard work, and kindness. These virtues, Confucius believed, would contribute to social harmony.

Confucius set out five basic relationships that defined everyone's place in society. These were the relationships between ruler and subject, parent and child, husband and wife, older brother and younger brother, and friend and friend.

In each relationship, each individual had responsibilities, or duties, toward the other. Confucius reasoned that if everyone obeyed his or her duty, an orderly, balanced society was possible. For example, a ruler had the responsibility to provide good government. In return, the subject owed loyalty and respect to the ruler. Confucius also felt that a ruler could achieve more by setting a good example than by passing laws.

Confucius emphasized family relationships. He felt that the virtues of loyalty and

THROUGH THEIR EYES The Sayings of Confucius

Confucius learned about government first-hand during the years he traveled to different feudal courts. He gained a reputation for wisdom and acquired a devoted following of students. The following excerpts from the Analects *include answers Confucius gave to people who sought advice on government and the right way to act.*

From the *Analects*

Tzu Chang asked Confucius about humanity. Confucius said: "To be able to practice five virtues everywhere in the world constitutes humanity. These virtues are courtesy, unselfishness, good faith, diligence, and kindness. He who is courteous is not humiliated; he who is unselfish wins the multitude; he who is of good faith is trusted by the people; he who is kind can get service from the people.

"If a ruler himself is upright, all will go well without orders. But if he himself is not upright, even though he gives orders they will not be obeyed.

"Lead the people by laws and regulate them by penalties, and the people will try to keep out of jail, but will have no sense of shame. Lead the people by virtue and restrain them by the rules of good taste, and the people will have a sense of shame, and moreover will become good."

Tzu Kung asked about government. Confucius said: "The essentials are sufficient food, sufficient troops, and the confidence of the people. If you are forced to give up one of these three, you should first let go of the troops. If you are forced to give up one of the two remaining, you should let go of food. For from of old, death has been the lot of all men, but a people without faith cannot survive."

1. According to Confucius, what five virtues make up humanity?

2. **Critical Thinking** Do you agree that the most important essential of government is the confidence of the people? Explain.

respect for authority were essential to the family. Thus, he stressed respect for one's parents and elders. A child was expected to show respect to both parents as well as to other relatives. Although women were considered inferior to men, sons and daughters learned to honor their mothers.

Unlike Hinduism or Buddhism, Confucianism was not a religion. Confucius accepted traditional Chinese religious practices. He believed in the power of heaven, where the gods and the ancestors' spirits lived. But his teachings were mainly concerned with life on earth. The goal of Confucianism was not the soul's salvation but order in society.

The impact of Confucianism. Over the centuries, Confucian ideals shaped Chinese society. Chinese law was based on Confucian principles, and the idea of respect for elders dominated family life. Emperors had temples honoring Confucius built in every province. Confucian scholars became the main force in government. Every candidate for government office had to memorize the Five Classics and the Four Books, which contained the teachings of Confucius and his followers.

Taoism: Following "The Way"

Taoism was another philosophy that shaped Chinese traditions. Little is known about its founder, Lao-tse (low dzoo). However, his teachings have survived in the *Tao Te Ching,* or *The Way and Its Power.* Like Confucius, Lao-tse was concerned with how to achieve a good society. However, he rejected the rules of behavior laid down by Confucius. Taoist philosophy stressed simplicity, meditation, and a closeness with nature.

Lao-tse taught that the goal of life was to become attuned to the tao. The **tao** was a universal force that could not be defined. It could only be felt. The tao also meant the way or the road a person followed to reach that goal. Lao-tse believed a person reached harmony with nature not by using reason but through contemplation.

To the Taoists, the best government was the one that governed the least. "The more laws and edicts are imposed," began one Taoist saying, "the more thieves and bandits there will be."

Taoism was both a philosophy and a religion. Yet it was concerned with ways of improving a person's life in this world rather than with saving souls. The Chinese believed that spirits and ghosts were everywhere and had to be appeased. Taoist priests provided charms and magic to influence the spirits. As a result, Taoism became very popular among the common people.

The Taoist emphasis on nature shaped Chinese science and technology. Taoists recorded the movement of the planets, thereby gaining knowledge of astronomy. They also studied and recorded their observations in chemistry and botany. Taoist priests may have invented gunpowder for use in firecrackers to frighten ghosts. They may also have developed the magnetic compass to determine the most favorable position for graves. Later, the magnetic compass would make long ocean voyages possible.

This bronze incense burner shows Lao-tse riding on a water buffalo. "The Way," taught by Lao-tse, stressed unity with nature, shown here in the harmony between buffalo and rider.

The Strict Code of Legalism

Legalism was the third major Chinese philosophy. Among its chief supporters was Han Fei Tzu (hahn fay dzoo), who died in 233 B.C. Unlike Confucius, Han Fei Tzu was not interested in ethical conduct. He also opposed the Taoist emphasis on meditation. He felt that the way to create a stable society was through efficient government. And he believed that the ruler should have absolute power to make the system work.

Legalism was an authoritarian philosophy—that is, it taught unquestioning obedience to authority. Han Fei Tzu said that people were easily swayed by greed or fear. Only the ruler knew how to look after their best interest. Therefore, the ruler should make laws as needed, enforcing them with rich rewards for obedience and severe punishment for disobedience.

To the Legalists, rule by law was far superior to the Confucian idea of rule by good example. Legalists had such a low opinion of human nature that they did not believe people were capable of loyalty, honesty, or trust. Only the threat of harsh punishment, they argued, would ensure order and stability in society. As you will read in the next section, China's first emperor adopted Legalist ideas as he set about unifying the country.

SECTION 4 REVIEW

1. **Identify:** (a) Confucius, (b) Lao-tse, (c) Han Fei Tzu.

2. **Define:** tao.

3. What were the five basic relationships according to Confucius?

4. What kind of government did the Taoists favor?

5. According to Han Fei Tzu, how could a stable society be created?

6. **Critical Thinking** In what ways do you think Confucianism affected everyday life in China?

---

5 Unification of China

READ TO UNDERSTAND

☐ **How the Ch'in dynasty reorganized China.**

☐ **How the Han built a powerful empire.**

☐ **How the civil service system strengthened Confucianism.**

☐ **What advances the Han made in learning and technology.**

In Chinese writing, the character for king looks like this: 王 . The three horizontal strokes stand for heaven, earth, and humanity. The vertical stroke is the king, the person who connects heaven, earth, and humanity. The kings of the Chou dynasty used this symbol. In 221 B.C., the leader of the feudal state of Ch'in seized power. He took the title Shih Huang Ti (shee hwahng dee), "First Emperor." The character for First Emperor is 皇 . It added the symbol for antiquity to the old symbol for king. In creating this new title, the new ruler showed his respect for China's ancient civilization.

First Emperor of China

When Shih Huang Ti emerged as master of China, he founded the Ch'in dynasty. Some historians think the name China may have come from the Ch'in dynasty.

With iron discipline and constant watchfulness, Shih Huang Ti imposed unity on China. He reorganized the old feudal states into provinces and appointed provincial officials responsible to him. His policies were guided by the ruthless principles of Legalism. The emperor eliminated all opponents, by execution if necessary. Ancient Chinese sources claim that he forced 120,000 noble families to resettle in his capital so he could watch over them. Wearing disguises, he would spy on his own officials.

The emperor also tried to control ideas and prevent the teaching of different points of view. He ordered the burning of almost all books. Only practical works, he said, were worth saving.

BUILDING THE GREAT WALL Under the watchful eye of a well-armed overseer, a worker positions one of the millions of bricks that make up the Great Wall of China. More than 700,000 slaves and unpaid workers endured intense heat and brutal cold as they worked day and night. This recreation by artist Vince Caputo shows how parts of the wall wind through mountains. Workers paved the top of the wall with bricks and mortar, creating a road along which they could carry building materials. The inset photo shows a section of the Great Wall today.

Like other strong rulers, the Chinese emperor issued coins, dug new canals, and built a highway system that reached out from the capital to distant regions. These improvements helped bind the empire together. But they took a terrible toll of human lives. The Ch'in government forced millions of peasants to work on roads and canals. Many of them died of starvation or overwork.

The emperor's most spectacular achievement was the construction of the long defense wall, known today as the Great Wall of China. The Great Wall connected many smaller walls that had been built earlier to prevent nomadic tribes from raiding northern China. It stretched for 1,400 miles (2,200 kilometers), from the Yellow Sea to the interior of China.

Although the Great Wall did not always hold back invading armies, it established a clear boundary between China and "barbarian" foreigners.

Shih Huang Ti set out to create an empire that would last forever. Yet it collapsed a few years after his death in 210 B.C. After eight years of turmoil, a new military leader seized power and established the Han dynasty, which lasted for over 400 years.

Founding the Han Dynasty

During the Han dynasty, China enjoyed one of its most brilliant periods. Han emperors restored the unity achieved by Shih Huang Ti and expanded the borders of China. They adopted Confucianism and spread Chinese culture over much of East Asia.

The best-known Han ruler was the energetic and ambitious Wu Ti (woo dee), the "Warrior Emperor." When Wu Ti came to the throne in 140 B.C., the Huns were threatening China in the north and west. These nomadic people were ancestors of the Huns who would invade Europe in the fourth century A.D. Wu Ti drove the Huns back and extended the Han Empire over Central Asia, southern China, and parts of Southeast Asia.

By the time Wu Ti died in 87 B.C., he had established peace that was to last for almost 200 years. Soldiers patrolled the Han Empire from the Yellow Sea to Central Asia and protected thriving trade along the caravan routes.

An Efficient Civil Service

When Han rulers centralized power, they needed well-trained officials to administer the government. They encouraged the growth of an educational system to provide these officials.

Education for service. The system of education that developed under the Han dynasty influenced Chinese culture for 2,000 years. The Han thought officials should be scholars who were thoroughly familiar with the teachings of Confucius. As a result, students memorized the Confucian classics. They also learned Chinese history and law.

The requirements of Chinese education were rigorous. Learning to read the Chinese

MAP STUDY *Ch'in and Han rulers greatly expanded their empires and spread Chinese civilization over a wide area. Like the Roman Empire to the west, the Han Empire enjoyed two centuries of peace and prosperity. Why do you think Han rulers extended the Great Wall westward?*

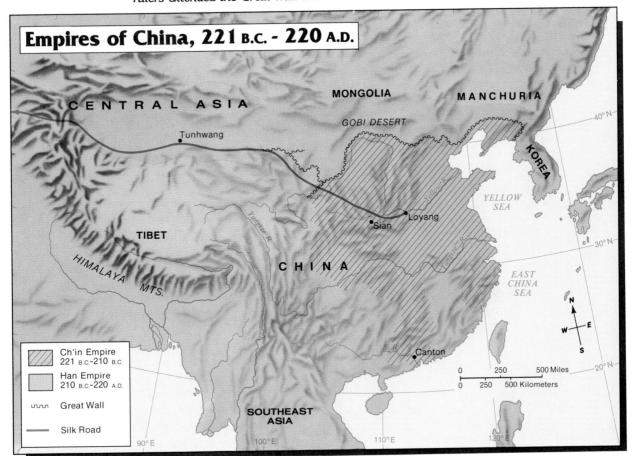

Empires of China, 221 B.C. - 220 A.D.

language was a life-long task. Scholars were expected to perfect their skills in calligraphy, the art of fine writing. And students had to memorize an immense amount of material. The Chinese code of law alone consisted of 960 scrolls. Only science and mathematics were missing from the demanding course of studies. Chinese scholars did not consider these subjects to be essential.

The civil service examination. The Han developed a system of testing candidates for government service. In theory, the civil service examination, as it was called, was open to anyone. But usually only the sons of nobles or government officials could afford the years of study needed to pass the rigorous tests.

The teachings of Confucius influenced education for women as well as for men. At court, women learned the correct behavior for every occasion. This painting on silk shows two students waiting for their imperial governess. The governess will write instructions on proper conduct, which the young women must memorize.

The civil service examination involved a series of tests on the local, provincial, and national levels. The provincial examinations alone lasted for three days. During that time, students were walled up in cells, where they ate, slept, and wrote their examinations. The fortunate few who reached the highest level took their final examinations before the emperor.

To pass the exams, a candidate had to have a thorough knowledge of the Confucian classics. This requirement increased the influence of Confucianism on the government. The examination system regularly provided a group of well-trained officials. This helped maintain social and political stability in China through many dynasties.

Advances in Learning

Under the Han, important advances were made in learning. The Ch'in emperor had introduced a uniform writing system. By 100 A.D., scholars had compiled a dictionary of 10,000 Chinese characters. The Chinese spoke many different dialects and might not have been able to understand one another when speaking. However, they could all read the same written language. About the same time, the Chinese invented paper. Gradually, they began to write on paper instead of bamboo, wood, and silk.

The Chinese made many advances in science. Like the Greeks, they based their ideas on observation and searched for natural laws. "Eclipses happen naturally," wrote the philosopher Wang Ch'ung, "and are not caused by political action." Chinese astronomers observed sunspots, which were not described by Europeans until the 1600s A.D. Timekeepers invented sundials and waterclocks superior to any instruments known elsewhere. And they invented an accurate calendar that remained in use until 1912.

Practical inventions improved the lives of the common people in many ways. The wheelbarrow made it easier for peasants to carry heavy loads. The water mill reduced the time needed to grind grain. The development of the harness made farming more efficient because animals could be used to pull plows.

Trade and Travel

Han rulers encouraged commerce between China and western Asia and Europe. The silk industry in China expanded rapidly. Silk was light and easy to carry, and people in Rome and other foreign markets would pay high prices for it. Besides silk, the Chinese traded jade and bronze for horses, rugs, and Roman glass.

The Silk Road. Camel caravans laden with exports traveled from Chinese cities to Central Asia and the Middle East. So much silk was carried on this route to the west that the route became known as the Silk Road. (See the map on page 151.) Sea routes between Southeast Asia and India also opened up.

Trade brought new products into China. For example, delegates from the emperor Wu Ti who had visited Bactria introduced grapes and alfalfa into China. One of the most important effects of the increased trade and travel, however, was the spread of Buddhism.

Buddhism reaches China. At first, Buddhism won few converts in China. Buddhism seemed very different from Chinese philosophies such as Taoism and Confucianism. Buddhist monks and nuns left their families for a life of poverty and seclusion. But this practice ran against the Chinese devotion to the family. Buddhism was also unlike Chinese philosophies because of its focus on the afterlife.

Nevertheless, Buddhism appealed to many Chinese. Scholars were interested in the ideas contained in Buddhist literature. And peasants found spiritual comfort in the Buddha, who recognized the pain and suffering of this world and offered them hope.

Downfall of the Han. Buddhism attracted many new converts as the Han dynasty declined. Like Rome, the Han Empire was unable to defend its borders against invaders. Weak rulers and economic problems hastened its collapse. The fall of the Han dynasty in 220 A.D. plunged China into civil wars.

After 220 A.D., contact between China and the Mediterranean world ended. However, a steady flow of traders and travelers passed between China and India. Chinese travelers returning from India brought back Indian ideas in such fields as medicine, science, and art.

The Chinese developed a process for making paper about 100 A.D. They used bark from mulberry trees, rags, and fishing nets. The materials were beaten into a pulp, which was then stiffened with starch. Next, papermakers rolled the pulpy mixture into sheets and dyed them to an even color. In this paper shop, paper hangs on racks so that customers can select the sheets they want to buy.

SECTION 5 REVIEW

1. **Locate:** (a) Great Wall, (b) Silk Road.

2. **Identify:** (a) Shih Huang Ti, (b) Wu Ti.

3. Why was the Great Wall built?

4. (a) Why did Han rulers encourage education? (b) What areas of study were considered most important?

5. (a) List two practical inventions of the Chinese during the Han dynasty. (b) How did these make life easier?

6. Why did Buddhism appeal to some Chinese?

7. **Critical Thinking** What steps did strong rulers, whether in India, China, or Rome, take to unify their land?

CHAPTER 7 REVIEW

Summary

1. **Both Hinduism and Buddhism influenced Indian civilization.** Hinduism developed out of Aryan religious beliefs. Hindu beliefs were closely tied to the caste system, which defined everyone's role in society. Buddhism, which began as an attempt to reform Hinduism, spread from India to other parts of Asia.

2. **During the Maurya and Gupta empires, rulers united much of northern and central India.** The Maurya emperor Asoka converted to Buddhism and brought peace to India.

3. **Under the Guptas, India enjoyed a golden age.** The arts and sciences flourished, but the caste system grew more restrictive.

4. **In China, philosophers looked for ways to establish order in society.** Confucius taught that people should follow an ethical code of conduct. Taoists believed in harmony with nature. Legalists emphasized strict laws.

5. **The Ch'in emperor followed Legalist ideas in unifying China.** Later, Han rulers followed Confucian thought. Their powerful empire lasted 400 years.

Recalling Facts

The following statements describe beliefs or practices in Hinduism, Buddhism, Confucianism, Taoism, or Legalism. Identify the religion or philosophy each statement describes.

1. Strict laws and harsh punishment will ensure good government.

2. Both a ruler and the people should follow an ethical code of conduct.

3. The Four Noble Truths explain the cause of suffering.

4. People acquire good karma by obeying caste rules.

5. The best government is the one that governs least.

Chapter Checkup

1. Explain how Hinduism supported the caste system in India.

2. (a) How were Hinduism and Buddhism similar? (b) How were they different?

3. What problems did rulers face in uniting India?

4. Describe Indian achievements in each of the following areas: (a) art; (b) medicine; (c) technology.

5. How did Confucianism affect Chinese (a) family life; (b) education; and (c) government.

6. (a) How did the First Emperor centralize power in China? (b) How did the Han dynasty build on the First Emperor's achievements? (c) What new policies did the Han introduce?

Critical Thinking

1. **Expressing an Opinion** Do you think Confucianism, Taoism, or Legalism was most likely to produce a peaceful, orderly society? Explain.

2. **Comparing Civilizations** (a) In what ways was the Han Empire like the Roman Empire? (b) How was it different?

3. **Relating Past to Present** (a) How did the Chinese civil service examination ensure that qualified people were chosen for government? (b) What subjects or skills do you think civil service exams in the United States today should test? Explain.

4. **Comparing Ideas** (a) What were the main beliefs of Hinduism? (b) What were the main ideas of Confucianism? (c) How might the ideas of Hinduism and Confucianism contribute to different outlooks on life?

1. **Map Reading** Study the map on page 151 and answer these questions: (a) What part of China did the Great Wall protect? (b) In what directions did the Han Empire expand? (c) What relationship do you see between the Han expansion and Chinese trade with other parts of the world?

2. **Analyzing a Primary Source** Use the steps you learned on page 132 to analyze the excerpts from the teachings of Confucius on page 147. (a) What did Confucius say were the essentials of good government? Was this fact or opinion? (b) What five virtues did Confucius think people should practice? (c) According to Confucius, how should a ruler behave? (d) Do you think such behavior would ensure good government? Explain.

Writing About History

Order of Importance

One way to arrange reasons or facts is in order of importance. By doing so, you are able to emphasize the events that had the greatest effect on later events or led to the most important results. When organizing information in order of importance, you have to think about which ideas are essential and should be developed and which ideas are minor and could be given less attention.

Transition words are often used to show the relationship between ideas. They help make the order of ideas clear. Some transition words used to show order of importance are: *first, second, third, even more, even greater, most significant, greatest, more important,* and *most important.*

Practice: Decide which item in each pair was more important to the development of India and China. Then write a sentence explaining why the item you chose was more important than the other.

1. (a) Under the Maurya and Gupta dynasties in India, the caste system became more restrictive.
   (b) A man's first wife dominated the household in India.

2. (a) The Chinese examination system played a role in the long-term stability of China.
   (b) During the time students took the civil service examination, they lived in cells.

3. (a) Taoist priests tried to influence the spirits with magic.
   (b) Confucius described five basic relationships among people in society.

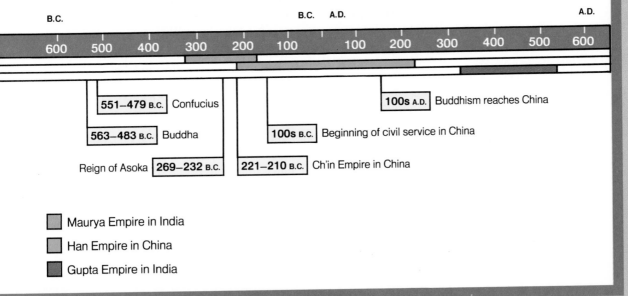

B.C.

| 600 | 500 | 400 | 300 | 200 | 100 |

B.C. A.D.

| 100 | 200 | 300 | 400 | 500 | 600 |

A.D.

551–479 B.C. Confucius

563–483 B.C. Buddha

Reign of Asoka 269–232 B.C.

221–210 B.C. Ch'in Empire in China

100s B.C. Beginning of civil service in China

100s A.D. Buddhism reaches China

Maurya Empire in India
Han Empire in China
Gupta Empire in India

Unit Two — Mini-Atlas

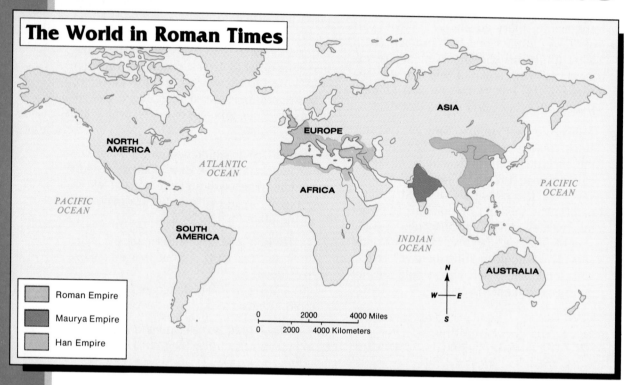

The World in Roman Times

ASIA

EUROPE

NORTH AMERICA

ATLANTIC OCEAN

AFRICA

PACIFIC OCEAN

PACIFIC OCEAN

SOUTH AMERICA

INDIAN OCEAN

AUSTRALIA

N
W—E
S

0   2000   4000 Miles
0   2000   4000 Kilometers

Roman Empire

Maurya Empire

Han Empire

Unit Themes

The civilizations of ancient Greece and Rome made their most impressive achievements long ago. Yet the ideas and inventions of these advanced civilizations still influence the world today. Greece and Rome earned the title "classical civilizations" because their standards of excellence became those by which later civilizations were judged.

While Greece and Rome directly influenced people living from the Fertile Crescent to the Atlantic Ocean, advanced civilizations also developed in two other regions of the world: India and China. Hinduism and Buddhism emerged in India and spread across Asia. The Maurya and Gupta empires brought periods of peace and prosperity to India. These periods were times of important cultural advances. During the same period, the Chinese built on Shang and Chou traditions. They created the Han dynasty that left a lasting heritage for future generations.

1. **Applying Information** Each of the empires on the world map above was subject to invasion. (a) Name the groups who threatened each empire and tell where they were located. (b) What steps did the empires take to protect themselves?

2. **Inferring** (a) Summarize the beliefs of Confucianism, Taoism, and Legalism. (b) Which of these philosophies do you think Roman emperors would have supported? Explain.

3. **Analyzing Maps** Study the maps on these pages. (a) Which empire included the lands that Greeks had once colonized? (b) What was the relationship between that empire and ancient Greece?

4. **Comparing** (a) Which of the three empires shown on the world map lasted the longest? (b) What were the results of their declines?

156

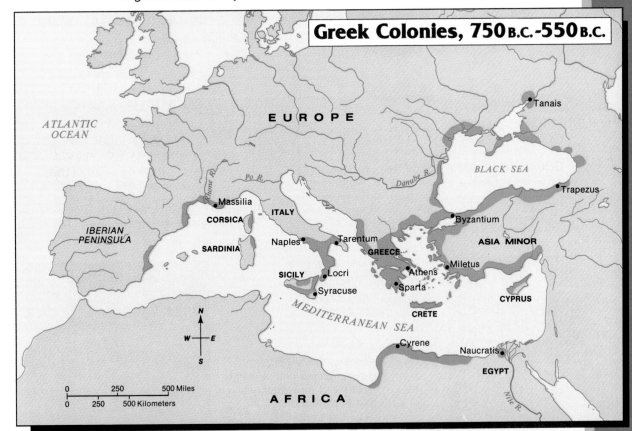

B.C.　　　　　　　　　　　　　　　　　　B.C.　A.D.　　　　　　　　　　　　　A.D.

| 500 | 400 | 300 | 200 | 100 | | 100 | 200 | 300 | 400 | 500 |

Athenian Empire ▮　▯ Empire of Alexander the Great

Roman Republic　　　　　Roman Empire

Maurya Empire

Gupta Empire

Ch'in Empire　Han Empire

TIME LINE STUDY Compare the time span of the Athenian Empire and the Roman Empire. Is there a relationship between how long each lasted and how much each affected later civilizations? Explain.

MAP STUDY Greeks established colonies from the Iberian Peninsula in the west to the Black Sea in the east. On which Mediterranean islands were Greek colonies founded? Why was trade so important to the Greek economy?

UNIT THREE

MIDDLE AGES IN WESTERN EUROPE

800 *Gifts of foreign kings being offered to Emperor Charlemagne.*

900s *Feudal knights had to provide their own armor, weapons, and horses.*

	800	900	1000	1100
POLITICS AND GOVERNMENT	**800** Charlemagne crowned emperor	**900s** Vikings invade Europe	**1096** Crusades to reclaim Holy Land begin	
ECONOMICS AND TECHNOLOGY	**800s** Three-field system of farming develops		**1100s** Trade fairs held at Champagne	
SOCIETY AND CULTURE	**800s** Charlemagne orders monasteries to set up schools	**900s** Feudalism develops in response to invasions and warfare		

800 *This illustration is from the Book of Kells, an early illuminated manuscript.*

Farming in the Middle Ages changed dramatically because of new methods and inventions.

UNIT OUTLINE

1492 *Ferdinand and Isabella of Spain are shown here entering Granada after the defeat of the Muslims.*

Scribes, who were often monks, laboriously made copies of manuscripts by hand.

1200	1300	1400	1500

1215 King John of England signs the Magna Carta

1337 Hundred Years' War begins

1492 Ferdinand and Isabella complete reconquest of Spain

1290 Eyeglasses are invented

1400s Longbow invented during Hundred Years' War

1321 Dante completes *The Divine Comedy*

1386 Chaucer writes *The Canterbury Tales*

1189 *Family and friends gather to bid farewell to knights as they leave on the Third Crusade.*

Many examples of Muslim art remained in Spain after the Reconquista.

159

Foundations of Medieval Europe

8

(500–1050)

On Christmas Day in 800, Charlemagne, king of the Franks, was crowned "Emperor of the Romans" by Pope Leo III. For centuries afterwards, popes claimed that this act gave them supremacy over emperors.

The huge stone blocks oozed cold moisture. Even the rich in their fur-lined cloaks shivered in the damp chill of the great church. But today was Christmas, and the crowds filling St. Peter's Basilica in Rome were more interested in staring at the swarm of Frankish nobles than in the cold.

The Franks and their leader, King Charlemagne (SHAR luh MAYN), had ridden into Rome a month earlier. Rebelling Romans had brutally beaten up Pope Leo III, and he had called on the Franks for help. Rumor had it that Leo was going to reward Charlemagne for coming to his rescue. What would that reward be?

The curious Romans soon found out. "As the king rose from praying before the tomb of the blessed apostle Peter," noted a Frankish writer some years later, "Pope Leo placed a crown on his head." As though they had known all along what was planned, "all the Roman people cried out, 'To Charles Augustus, crowned by God, great and peace-giving emperor of the Romans, life and victory.'"

The coronation of Charlemagne on Christmas Day in 800 was symbolic of changes in Europe after the fall of the Western Roman Empire. In the heart of the old Roman Empire, the head of the Christian Church had crowned a Germanic king as emperor. By his action, the pope kept alive the ideal of a unified empire like that of ancient Rome. Roman traditions were just one of the forces that would shape a new civilization during the Middle Ages. The new civilization, known as medieval civilization, blended Roman, Christian, and Germanic traditions.

Western Europe seemed an unlikely place to build a new civilization. As you read in Chapter 6, Roman political power in Western Europe collapsed in the 400s. Trade slowed, Roman cities dwindled in size, and some fell into ruins. Knowledge of the ancient world as well as practical skills such as road building were largely forgotten. Crude wooden buildings replaced massive Roman structures. Roman roads and aqueducts fell into disrepair.

Despite the disorder and decay, Western Europe was a place of great potential. It had fertile land and other resources, such as timber, furs, and tin. In the early Middle Ages, from about 500 to 1050, a new political system emerged and restored a measure of order. ∎

1 The Germanic Kingdoms

READ TO UNDERSTAND

☐ **How the Germanic kingdoms in Western Europe were governed.**

☐ **What Charlemagne accomplished during his reign.**

☐ **What threats Western Europe faced in the 700s and 800s.**

☐ *Vocabulary:* **heretic, missi dominici, parish, tithe, illumination.**

Clotilde was determined to make her husband, Clovis, listen. As King of the Franks, he was energetic and ambitious, she said, but he was also shortsighted. If only he would convert to Christianity, he could achieve greatness. In answer to her plea, the Frankish king agreed to a bargain. If he defeated his enemies, the Alamanni, he would convert. In 496, Clovis crushed the Alamanni in battle. Then he was baptized a Christian as he had promised and ordered his soldiers to do the same. Clovis then moved aggressively against neighboring Germanic tribes.

During the early Middle Ages, many Germanic tribes, including the Franks, set up small kingdoms in Italy, Gaul, Spain, Britain, and North Africa. They were constantly at war with one another. Gradually, however, the Kingdom of the Franks under Clovis established control over much of the Western Roman Empire.

Roman Influence on Government

The governments of the Germanic tribes were simple compared to the complex system Rome had developed to rule its vast empire. Whereas Roman emperors depended on a highly organized government, Germanic rulers depended on the loyalty of their warriors. Germanic tribes had few government officials and few taxes. Because free men gave unpaid military service to their rulers, taxation was largely unnecessary. The Romans had written law codes to settle disputes among the many peoples they ruled. Germanic laws were based on custom and were designed mainly to prevent feuds between families.

As Germanic kings extended their rule over parts of the Western Roman Empire, some adapted ideas of Roman government. For example, when Theodoric (thee AHD uhr ihk) established the Kingdom of Ostrogoths in Italy, he issued a simplified version of Roman law. In other areas, however, Roman influence was weaker. The Angles, Saxons, and Jutes moved into Britain after Roman legions had withdrawn. These peoples kept their Germanic customs and languages, which eventually evolved into modern English.

The Christian Church helped preserve Roman traditions in the Germanic kingdoms. For example, when the Roman monk Augustine converted the Anglo-Saxons in England, he set up Christian communities based on Roman systems. Also, Germanic kings used the clergy as government officials because the clergy were almost the only educated people in Western Europe. The clergy spoke Latin and preserved many Roman ways.

Kingdom of the Franks

The strongest kingdom to emerge in the early Middle Ages was that of the Franks, who lived originally in the areas of present-day Germany and Belgium. The Franks rose to power in the late fifth century under the brilliant but ruthless leadership of King Clovis. Through cunning and treachery, Clovis conquered lands from the Pyrenees Mountains to central Europe.

Clovis's reign reached a turning point when he became a Christian. Although encouraged by his wife, he may also have had political reasons for converting. Clovis thought that the support of the Church in Rome would make him more powerful than neighboring Germanic kings. These kings were also Christian, but they belonged to the Arian sect, which had developed in the early years of Christianity. The Church in Rome, now calling itself the Roman Catholic Church, regarded the Arians as **heretics,** or untrue Christians. Thus, as the only Roman Catholic king in Gaul, Clovis won the Church's support.

When Clovis died in 511, his lands were divided among his four sons, according to Germanic custom. Although Clovis's family ruled until 751, its power declined by the mid-600s. The chief court official, the Mayor of the Palace, had actually become the real ruler of the Frankish kingdom.

Invasion by the Muslims

In the 700s, the Germanic kingdoms of Western Europe faced invasion by Muslim armies. Muslims believed in the teachings of Islam, the religion founded in the Middle East during the 600s. (You will read about Islam in Chapter 11.) Muslims won many converts around the southern rim of the Mediterranean. Then they pushed into Europe through Spain.

The Germanic kingdoms of Spain fell before the advancing Muslim armies. By 732, Muslim forces were spilling into France. Charles Martel, the Frankish Mayor of the Palace, rallied Christians against the invaders. At a battle near Tours (toor), Christian armies defeated the Muslims. Because this battle stopped the spread of Islam into Western Europe, it was a turning point in history.

Yet during the Middle Ages, Islamic civilization greatly influenced Europeans. For centuries, Muslims ruled Spain, Sicily, and parts of southern Italy. From these areas, much of the learning of the Islamic Empire reached the people of Europe.

The Age of Charlemagne

After the defeat of the Muslims, Charles Martel founded the Carolingian (KAR uh LIHN jee uhn) dynasty in the Frankish kingdom and began to organize a strong central government. His son Pepin was elected king by the Frankish nobles. Pepin then had his election approved by the pope. This action symbolized the strong ties between the king and the Church. Later popes would use this incident to justify their claims of authority over political rulers.

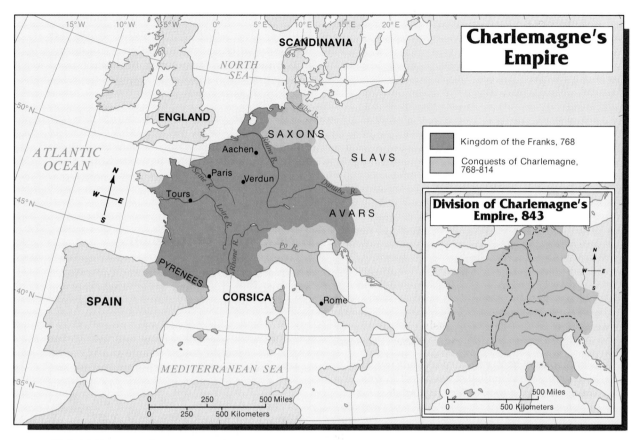

Charlemagne's Empire

Kingdom of the Franks, 768
Conquests of Charlemagne, 768-814

Division of Charlemagne's Empire, 843

MAP STUDY *Charlemagne had a reputation as "the most able and noble-spirited" ruler of his time in part because he was successful in warfare. Notice the areas he added to Frankish lands. After Charlemagne's death, his empire was divided by the Treaty of Verdun. What geographic factors made it difficult for the empire to remain united?*

After Pepin's death, his son Charles moved forcefully to strengthen the central government. During his long reign, from 768 to 814, he so impressed his contemporaries that he was called Charlemagne, or Charles the Great.

An able general, Charlemagne conquered an empire that reunited large areas of the Western Roman Empire. (See the map above.) He defeated the Lombards who had occupied Italy. In a hard-fought campaign, he won land in northern Spain back from the Muslims. In an effort to spread Christianity, he battled the non-Christian Saxons in the north. In the east, he defeated the Avars and occupied their land. In 800, as you read, Pope Leo III crowned Charlemagne "Emperor of the Romans."

Charlemagne was an energetic ruler. From his court at Aachen (AH kuhn), he kept firm control over the empire. He recruited talented officials to carry out policies designed to improve government and unify the empire. Royal officials, called **missi dominici** (MIH see DOHM ih NEE kee), or lord's messengers, checked on local nobles who were responsible for justice and defense in their own lands. Charlemagne helped establish uniform laws and appointed local judges to uphold the laws.

Charlemagne wanted to spread Christianity throughout the empire. He encouraged Christian missionaries who risked their lives trying to convert the Saxons. He also supported the efforts of the Church to organize **parishes**, or rural districts, each with its own priest. To finance the parishes, Charlemagne required all Christians to pay a **tithe** (tīth), 10 percent of their income, to the Church.

163

Charlemagne encouraged education; however, often only the clergy were educated. In this ivory carving, a monk diligently pursues his studies.

A Revival of Learning

To encourage education, Charlemagne invited scholars from all over Europe to his court. Alcuin (AL kwihn), a learned Anglo-Saxon monk, set up a palace school to teach Charlemagne's sons and daughters as well as the children of Frankish nobles. Charlemagne himself could read, but he did not know how to write. In an unsuccessful effort to teach himself to write, he supposedly slept with pen, ink, and paper under his pillow.

Charlemagne issued rules for the education of the clergy. He also ordered monasteries to set up schools and libraries. In monastery schools, students learned Latin, the language of the Church.

Monks made copies of the Bible and of the few surviving ancient Greek and Roman texts. They also developed the art of illumination. **Illumination** involved decorating the first letter of a paragraph and the margins of a page with brilliant designs. In addition, monks invented a clear written script known as the Carolingian minuscule. Romans had written only in capital letters. Carolingian minuscule used both capital and lower-case letters, the form of writing still used today.

By encouraging scholarship throughout the empire, Charlemagne strengthened the foundations of medieval civilization. During his reign, the distinctions between Roman and Germanic traditions blurred, and a new European culture began to emerge.

A New Wave of Invasions

The heirs of Charlemagne lacked his wisdom and forceful character. They weakened the empire by fighting among themselves. In 843, Charlemagne's grandsons drew up the Treaty of Verdun, which divided the empire into three kingdoms. (See the map on page 163.) Despite the Treaty of Verdun, rulers in the western and eastern regions fought for control of the middle region. These struggles would shape events in Europe for over 1,000 years.

The division of Charlemagne's empire happened just when a new wave of invaders battered Europe. In the 800s, the Magyars, or Hungarians, a nomadic people from Asia, drove the Slavs from their lands in Eastern Europe. Soon, both Slavs and Magyars were attacking Western Europe. About the same time, Muslims gained ground in Italy. But the longest-lasting invasions were those of the Vikings.

The Vikings were farmers and traders from Scandinavia, the area of present-day Norway, Sweden, and Denmark. A growing population may have forced these expert sailors to seek land in other parts of Europe. Sailing from northern harbors in long boats, the Vikings burned and looted towns, castles, churches, and monasteries in Western Europe.

In 911, the king of the Franks gave part of northern France to some Viking raiders. This region acquired its name, Normandy, from the French word "Norman," meaning "men from the north." Vikings from Sweden explored, raided, and traded along the rivers of Eastern Europe and Russia, traveling as far as Constan-

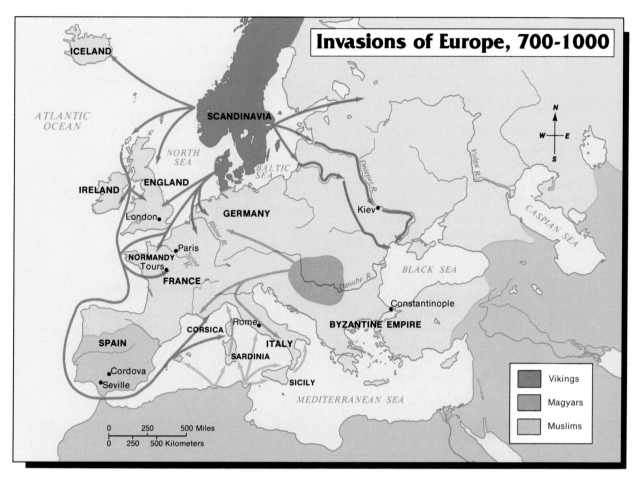

Invasions of Europe, 700-1000

ICELAND

ATLANTIC OCEAN

SCANDINAVIA

NORTH SEA

BALTIC SEA

IRELAND

ENGLAND

GERMANY

Kiev

Volga R.

Dnieper R.

CASPIAN SEA

London

Rhine R.

Paris

Seine R.

NORMANDY

Tours

FRANCE

Danube R.

BLACK SEA

Constantinople

Rome

CORSICA

BYZANTINE EMPIRE

SPAIN

ITALY

Cordova

SARDINIA

Seville

SICILY

MEDITERRANEAN SEA

N W E S

0 250 500 Miles
0 250 500 Kilometers

Vikings
Magyars
Muslims

MAP STUDY *During the 800s and 900s, Western Europe was battered by Viking, Magyar, and Muslim invaders. The Viking raids lasted the longest. Which areas did the Vikings attack? Why might they have been able to cover such distances?*

tinople. Other Vikings settled in Iceland and Greenland. About 1000, the Viking Leif Ericson spent a winter in Newfoundland on the eastern coast of North America.

In the 800s, the Vikings, whom the English called Danes, occupied part of England. The area they took became known as the Danelaw because the Danes lived there under their own laws. Anglo-Saxons resisted the Danish invasions, however, and eventually won back the lost territories.

The Viking invasions seriously disrupted life in Western Europe, but they did not completely destroy the work of Charlemagne. The Church sent missionaries to convert the Vikings. Throughout Western Europe, people turned to strong local leaders to protect them from the invaders.

SECTION 1 REVIEW

1. **Locate:** (a) Pyrenees Mountains, (b) Tours, (c) Aachen.

2. **Identify:** (a) Clovis, (b) Charles Martel, (c) Charlemagne, (d) Treaty of Verdun.

3. **Define:** (a) heretic, (b) missi dominici, (c) parish, (d) tithe, (e) illumination.

4. How did Charlemagne improve education?

5. What groups invaded Western Europe in the 700s and 800s?

6. **Critical Thinking** Compare and contrast Charlemagne's empire with the Roman Empire at its height.

165

2 Feudal Society

READ TO UNDERSTAND

☐ How warfare and feudalism were linked.

☐ What the relationship between lords and vassals was.

☐ What the role of noblewomen was in feudal society.

☐ *Vocabulary:* feudalism, knight, lord, vassal, feudal contract, fief, chivalry, troubadour.

From out of the mists, the terror appeared: fleets of ships with huge, square-rigged sails and prows of grinning dragons. Rough men with reddish hair and fair skins came ashore, ready for battle. On shore, the people prayed in vain, "From the fury of the Northmen, O Lord, protect us." But the Northmen, or Vikings, had come and would not leave without plundering and killing.

From the death of Charlemagne until about 1000, invaders such as the Vikings disrupted life in Western Europe. Most rulers were too weak to resist the invaders. So powerful nobles had to defend their own lands. While remaining loyal to the king, they usually acted independently. The system of rule by local lords who were bound to a king by ties of loyalty is now called **feudalism.** Feudalism brought order out of chaos during the Middle Ages. It also helped to produce a new way of life.

The Beginnings of Feudalism

Feudalism grew out of Germanic customs. In Germanic tribes, warriors swore an oath of loyalty to their chief. They fought for their leader, and in turn he provided for their needs. Nobles in the Germanic kingdoms carried on

ECONOMICS AND HISTORY Viking Traders in the East

On the morning of June 18, in the year 760, the people of Constantinople looked toward the sea in disbelief. Surrounding the city were hundreds of dragon-shaped boats manned by thousands of wild-looking, blond, blue-eyed giants. Constantinople, the seat of the Eastern Roman Empire, was the greatest city in the world. No army had ever captured it. But Constantinople fell to these Viking troops, who swarmed from their ships and charged through the city looting, burning, and murdering.

Although the people of Constantinople did not know who the Vikings were, all Europe soon would. From Scandinavia in the north, Viking raiders crisscrossed the world, from Turkey in the east to North America in the west. To reach Constantinople, they had first crossed the Baltic Sea. Then, in their light vessels they rowed upriver into what is now Russia. Dragging their boats overland for miles, they met other rivers flowing south and pushed deeper into Russia's heartland. The Viking fleets eventually floated downstream on the Dnieper and other rivers to the Black Sea. It was by this roundabout route that they reached the shores of Constantinople.

Although Vikings usually arrived as fierce raiders, they often settled down in the places they had attacked and became traders. A few years after their attack on Constantinople, the Vikings signed a trade agreement with the emperor. He agreed to sell them bread, wine, fish, and other goods. He even promised to let them take baths if they wished. The Vikings in turn swore they would not carry weapons or enter the city in groups of more than 50.

As restless seafarers, the Vikings survived by trading. Everywhere they moved they set up markets, exchanging furs, slaves, and spears for food and other goods. The city of Kiev, in the Ukraine, was founded by Viking traders in the early 800s. It became a major trading center, where merchants from all over the world met and conducted business.

1. How did the Vikings reach Constantinople?

2. **Critical Thinking** Why do you think the Vikings were such successful traders?

this tradition. Lesser nobles would serve as **knights,** or mounted warriors, for a **lord,** or greater noble.

In the 700s, a new invention, the stirrup, reinforced feudalism. The stirrup changed the nature of warfare. By supporting the knight while he was on horseback, the stirrup allowed him to wear heavy protective armor and carry heavier weapons. But armor and horses were costly. And, to be effective, a knight had to be well trained. Most knights did not have the money to buy armor and horses or the time for training.

Charles Martel realized the value of heavily armed knights in his campaigns against the Muslims. Since he had no money to pay his knights, he gave them land. With the land, a knight could support himself and his family while he served the king. In the next few centuries, the practice of granting land in exchange for military service spread across Western Europe.

During the Viking invasions, powerful lords took control of large tracts of land, which they divided among lesser lords called **vassals.** A lesser lord, in turn, might divide his land among his own vassals. The process could continue down to the lowest knight, who had no vassals. He had only enough land for himself and his family. (See the diagram above.) The relationship between lord and vassal was central to feudalism.

An Unwritten Arrangement

Feudalism was based on an exchange of rights and duties between nobles. Many unwritten rules governed the relationship between a lord and his vassal. These rules, which became known as the **feudal contract,** grew out of customs and traditional practices.

Under the feudal contract, a lord provided his vassal with a **fief**, or estate. A fief ranged in size from a few acres to hundreds of square miles, depending on the importance of the vassal. The fief included the peasants who worked the land as well as any houses or villages on the estate. The lord still owned the land, but the vassal had the right to use it and pass it on to his heirs. The lord also protected his vassals. He provided a court of justice to

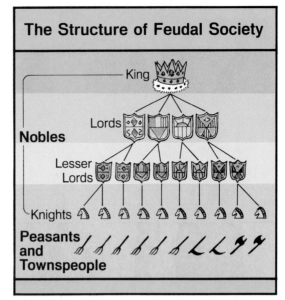

The Structure of Feudal Society

King

Lords

Nobles

Lesser Lords

Knights

Peasants and Townspeople

CHART STUDY *Everyone had a well-defined place in feudal society.* Nobles could be powerful lords or simply knights. The common people, peasants and townspeople, made up 90 percent of the population. What term could be used to describe feudal society?

settle disputes between vassals, and he acted as a guardian for young children if a vassal died.

In exchange for his fief, a vassal gave his lord military service, usually about 40 days a year. In addition, he agreed to serve his lord on certain holidays and special occasions. A vassal took part in the lord's court of justice, giving advice or participating in legal decisions. A vassal also had financial obligations to his lord. These included payment of an annual fee, called a relief; payment of ransom money if his lord was captured in battle; and payment of a fee when the lord's eldest daughter was married or when his eldest son was knighted.

At a public ceremony, the lord and his vassal confirmed the feudal contract. The vassal knelt before his lord. Placing his hands between the hands of his lord, he swore allegiance to the lord and promised to be loyal. The lord then gave the vassal the rights to his fief. Often, the lord gave his vassal a handful of earth or a blade of grass as a symbol of the fief. The ceremony took place whenever a new fief was granted or when a son inherited his father's fief.

Part entertainment and part preparation for battle, jousts were common in the Middle Ages. While onlookers cheered, knights on horseback practiced the skills that they would need in time of war. They used long lances to try to unseat their opponents. These knights are parading before the start of the joust.

A Complex System

In theory, everyone in feudal society had a lord except the king. The king owned all the land and granted fiefs to his chief nobles. As vassals of the king, the chief nobles owed him loyalty and military service. They, in turn, were lords to numerous vassals. Even commoners, such as peasants and townspeople, were part of the social structure because they had obligations to the lord on whose land they lived.

In reality, feudal kings had very limited power. They could not collect taxes or enforce laws outside their own estates. As feudal lords, they could summon their vassals to fight. But their chief vassals also ruled large fiefs. These vassals could challenge the king's authority and call on their own knights to support them.

Despite a king's limited power, people still thought of him as the highest noble in the land.

As feudalism developed, it became more complex because of the practice of subdividing fiefs. With each new generation, fiefs changed hands. Vassals gained land through inheritance, marriage, and war. A powerful lord might inherit a fief that would make him a vassal to a weaker lord. Or a vassal might have several fiefs, each from a different lord. The vassal owed loyalty to each of his lords even if the lords were fighting each other. This practice created a web of conflicting loyalties, which fragmented power.

Feudalism was never a single, unified system. Nor did it emerge everywhere at the same time. It grew up first in northern France during the eighth and ninth centuries. It reached the Netherlands, England, and western Germany in the eleventh century. Feudalism was weaker in frontier areas such as eastern Germany, Poland, Russia, and Spain. In Italy, too, it never fully took hold.

The Importance of Warfare

Feudalism emerged as a result of invasions. But even when the threat of invasions lessened, warfare continued. Powerful lords were constantly competing with one another for power. Nobles fought over boundaries and over inheritance rights. Greed, honor, and family feuds fueled small local wars. When a conflict arose over the rights or obligations of a vassal, the issue was often solved by warfare.

In the Middle Ages, most battles were small, involving only a few hundred or a few thousand knights. Knights were more likely to be captured than killed because as hostages they could be held for ransom. Fighting in medieval battles involved tough hand-to-hand combat. Knights wore cumbersome suits of iron armor. A full suit of armor, which weighed up to 30 pounds, was hot and uncomfortable. A knight's horse also had armor to protect its head and flanks. A knight carried heavy weapons such as lances, axes, and maces.

Among feudal nobles, warfare was a way of life. "It gives me great joy to see, drawn up on the field, knights and horses in battle array," wrote one noble. For the peasants who farmed the land, however, warfare was a disaster. An attacking army could destroy their crops, seize their animals, and burn their homes. Sometimes the army would murder everyone—men, women, and children—with no hesitation.

Feudal lords built strong stone castles or fortified homes for protection. When attacked, the lord, his family, his vassals, and the peasants from his estate took refuge behind the thick stone walls. Castles were built on top of hills or near rivers for added protection. A heavy iron gate as well as a water-filled ditch, or moat, helped people defend the castle.

Although castles provided protection, they were unpleasant places to live in. They were dark, damp, and drafty and had no windows. Narrow openings high in the walls provided the only light. But the openings also let in cold air, rain, and snow. Banquets were held in a large central hall, where a huge fireplace offered a hint of warmth. Only in the late Middle Ages did homes of nobles become relatively luxurious or even comfortable.

Feudal warfare declined gradually in the eleventh and twelfth centuries. This was partly because the Church tried to stop the fighting among nobles. Also, some feudal lords built large, powerful states and were able to control the fighting among their vassals.

Chivalry: A Code of Conduct for Knights

Beginning in the eleventh century, feudal nobles developed a code of conduct called **chivalry.** The code of chivalry combined Christian values and the virtues of being a warrior. A knight was expected to be brave, generous, and loyal. He was supposed to respect and protect noblewomen and to defend his family's honor.

This scene of courtship in a garden presents an idealized view of the life of nobles during the Middle Ages. One young couple talks by the gate while inside a musician entertains a group of noblewomen.

Chivalry also dictated rules of warfare. For example, armor was so hot that knights wore it only during a battle. According to the code of chivalry, it was disgraceful to attack a knight before he had put on his armor. Chivalry promoted ideals of behavior for knights that reduced the brutality of a fighting age. But few knights followed all the rules. Also, the code of chivalry did not govern a knight's behavior toward peasants and other common people.

Noblewomen in Feudal Society

In early feudal society, warfare dominated life. Since noblemen were the warriors, they controlled society, and noblewomen had few rights. A woman could inherit a fief, but she was not allowed to rule it. Her father, husband, or eldest son acted as her legal guardian. Some women did gain influence either because of their husbands' power or when their husbands were off fighting. When a lord was absent, his wife could command his vassals and servants.

Among nobles, a woman's father or guardian arranged her marriage. A married woman's main duty was to raise a large family. She also supervised the household and entertained her husband's guests. Because travel was often difficult and dangerous, guests stayed for long visits. A woman had to see that they were well fed and entertained.

Education for women focused on practical skills. Girls learned to spin, weave, and cook. Women also learned medical remedies, since they usually cared for the sick and wounded. In early feudal society, few men or women could read or write. But later, when women acquired these skills, they would teach their children to read and write.

In the 1100s, the treatment of noblewomen improved. The code of chivalry placed them on a pedestal as objects to be cherished and protected. Wandering poets, or **troubadours** (TROO buh DORZ), who entertained at feudal castles, did much to further this view. In their songs and poems, they glorified women, praising their beauty, wisdom, and kindness.

The lives of most women in the Middle Ages revolved around their homes and families. Christine de Pisan was an exception. Born to a wealthy family in Venice, she received an excellent education and wrote about many subjects. In this illustration, de Pisan shows some of her diverse talents. At left, she instructs a group of women, possibly from her book Cité des Dames, *which told of women famous for heroism and virtue. At right, she puts her learning to practical use.*

The poets' idealistic image of noblewomen was far from reality. Noblewomen, as well as peasant women, worked extremely hard. They gave birth to many children and endured the dangers of disease and warfare.

SECTION 2 REVIEW

1. **Define:** (a) feudalism, (b) knight, (c) lord, (d) vassal, (e) feudal contract, (f) fief, (g) chivalry, (h) troubadour.

2. (a) What duties did a vassal have? (b) What were the responsibilities of a lord?

3. (a) Where did feudalism develop first? (b) Where was feudalism weakest?

4. List three causes of feudal warfare.

5. **Critical Thinking** How did feudalism bring order to medieval society?

3 Life on the Manor

READ TO UNDERSTAND

☐ What life was like on a medieval manor.

☐ How advances in agriculture affected medieval Europe.

☐ How feudal justice worked.

☐ *Vocabulary:* manor, serf, demesne, bailiff.

During the ninth and tenth centuries, a new economic system, closely tied to feudalism, evolved in Western Europe. Because nobles were busy fighting or training for battle, they depended on peasants to farm their lands.

In early feudal society, most peasants barely produced enough crops to support the nobles and themselves. But by about 1050, advances in agriculture resulted in crop surpluses.

Peasants and Lords

At the heart of the medieval economy was the manor, administered by a lord. A **manor** might include a village or several villages and the surrounding lands. Like feudalism, the manorial system grew out of earlier traditions. Under the Roman Empire, coloni, or peasant farmers, had worked the estates of great landowners. (See page 128.) In exchange for their labor, the coloni had received cottages and small plots of land. The coloni were not slaves, but they could not leave the estate without permission. When Germanic nobles replaced Roman landowners, they retained the coloni system.

During the turbulent years of the early Middle Ages, many free peasants gave their land to powerful lords in exchange for protection. Eventually, they, too, became tied to the lord's land. Peasants who were tied to the land were called **serfs.** By the 1100s, most peasants were considered part of the fief that a lord gave to his vassal.

The relationship between a lord and his serfs involved duties on both sides. The arrangement was somewhat similar to the one between a lord and his vassals. A lord divided most of the manor land among his serfs, but he reserved a portion, called the **demesne** (dih MAYN), for his own use. In theory, at least, the lord could not seize peasant land unless the peasants failed to fulfill their duties. The lord was supposed to protect his peasants in time of war and provide justice through the manor court.

Serfs owed their lords certain payments. They had to spend about three days a week working for the lord. They farmed the lord's demesne, repaired his castle, and dug his moat. Each peasant family had to pay rent for the land they farmed themselves. They also had to pay fees to use the mill for grinding grain and the ovens for baking bread. When the head of a peasant family died, his heirs paid a fee for the right to continue farming the land. Because coined money had largely disappeared in the early Middle Ages, peasants often paid their fees with grain, woven cloth, chickens, or eggs.

A Self-Sufficient Community

During most of the Middle Ages, each manor was a small, self-sufficient world. Peasants grew grain for food. They raised sheep for wool, which was spun into cloth. In the village, a blacksmith made tools and weapons. Since towns were small and scattered, there was little traffic or trade between the manor and towns. Only a few items such as salt and iron came from outside the manor. The manor had its own court and usually its own church and priest. If a lord owned several manors, a **bailiff,** or agent, managed his smaller estates.

Manors could be large or small. Although each was different, they usually had certain features in common. (See the painting below.) Set on the highest land was the manor house. Depending on the lord's wealth and power, the manor house could be simply a large, fortified wooden house or a huge, stone castle. Below the manor house were peasant cottages clustered in a small village, the church, the lord's mill, and village workshops. Fields and forest lands surrounded the village and manor house.

The cycle of planting and harvesting controlled peasant life. Occasionally, a local fair brought entertainment, and there were important religious festivals, such as Christmas and Easter, to celebrate. But the hazards of warfare, disease, flood, drought, and other natural disasters overshadowed daily life.

Improvements in Agriculture

In the early Middle Ages, farming methods were primitive and inefficient. At planting time, peasants tossed seeds onto plowed fields, where grateful birds greedily ate their fill. Few plants grew, and yields were low. However, people gradually adopted new methods and technology. As a result, the manor economy of Western Europe developed an efficient farming system.

Improvements in agriculture began in the 700s and 800s and became widespread after 1000. One important advance was the three-field system, a method of crop rotation. On the manor, there were usually several large fields. Each fall, peasants planted one field with a winter crop such as wheat or rye. In the spring, they planted a second field with a summer crop such as oats, peas, beans, and barley.

LIFE ON A MANOR Medieval peasants knew little of the world beyond the manors on which they were born and died. In this recreation, artist Wayne Anthony Stills shows daily life on the manor. Typically, each peasant family had its own cottage, like those shown at left. In the shadow of a palatial manor house, peasants work, tossing handfuls of seed onto a freshly plowed field. The spire of the manor church rises in the background.

What was it like to be a peasant in the early Middle Ages? Historian Eileen Power studied many different sources to find out. She then recreated the life of Bodo and Ermentrude, a typical peasant family.

Bodo and his wife Ermentrude lived during the reign of Charlemagne. Bodo farmed the land on a manor near Paris. Every day, the family rose at dawn. Bodo and his son Wido plowed the fields, tended their small flock of sheep, or worked in their vineyard. Often they joined other peasants to do heavy work such as carting wood and harvesting crops.

Three times a week, Bodo worked on the lord's demesne. Three times a year, Ermentrude walked up to the lord's house to deliver a fine plump chicken and some fresh eggs. In these ways, they paid the dues and other fees they owed their lord.

Like Bodo and Wido, Ermentrude worked from dawn to dusk. She watched her two smallest children, sheared the sheep, spun the wool, and sewed the garments that would keep her family warm. Some days she worked in the vineyard. She also prepared the breads and puddings that the family ate.

The family welcomed Sundays and holy days. At the urging of the Church, Charlemagne had forbidden "tending vines, plowing fields, reaping corn and mowing hay, setting up hedges or fencing woods, cutting trees, or working in quarries or building houses" on holy days. Instead, peasants attended church or celebrated the feast days of saints.

Every year on October 9, Bodo and his family would walk to the great fair of St. Denys held just outside the gates of Paris. Merchants from all over Europe came to display their wares at the month-long fair. Even though Bodo's family had no money to buy the exotic foods, clothes, and jewelry that the merchants offered, they had fun looking.

1. How did Bodo and Ermentrude pay their dues to the lord?

2 **Critical Thinking** What do you think Bodo and Ermentrude liked best about their life? What do you think they liked least?

They left the third field fallow, or uncultivated, to allow the soil to rest. The following year, the crops were rotated, and a different field was left fallow.

The three-field system worked better than earlier farming systems. It spread planting and harvesting over the year, and it did not wear out the soil. New crops, especially peas, helped improve the peasant diet. In addition, by planting different crops, peasants were less likely to face starvation if one crop failed.

By using new inventions, peasants also grew more food. The heavy plow could turn the dense, moist soils of northern Europe. The invention of the horseshoe and a better harness meant that horses could be used for plowing. Because horses plowed faster than oxen, peasants could farm more land and produce more food. The watermill and windmill provided new sources of energy for grinding grain. Moreover, in northern France and England, miners began producing large quantities of iron, which was used for farm implements as well as weapons.

Changes in farming had the most effect in northern Europe. There, peasants produced food surpluses, which supported a growing population. Gradually, as the population increased in the north, the center of western civilization shifted from the Mediterranean world to the north.

From the mid-1000s to the 1200s, agriculture continued to improve. Lords cleared large areas of forest and drained swamps for farm-

173

land. The "Great Clearing" helped some serfs gain their freedom. Clearing the land was not one of the serfs' traditional obligations to the lord. Therefore, lords sometimes offered freedom to serfs who would work clearing land. These free peasants would then live on the new land and pay rent rather than the feudal duties they had owed in the past.

Feudal Justice

During the Middle Ages, lords preserved order on their own land. They were supposed to provide justice for both vassals and peasants. Feudal justice was based largely on custom because there were few written laws. One custom recognized the right of an individual to be tried by his peers, or equals. Another prevented a lord from taking away a vassal's fief unless the vassal's peers agreed that the action was just.

A feudal lord administered two courts: one for his vassals, another for the peasants on his manor. Many disputes between a lord and his vassal were settled by war, but some were decided in the court. On such an occasion, a lord would summon all his vassals to meet as a court and decide the issue. Although all free men and women had the right to be tried by their peers, the feudal lord could override a court's decision. The lord or his bailiff presided over the manor court, which settled disputes between peasants. Peasants were also protected to some extent by customs, which had the weight of law.

Most cases in either court involved minor issues. In cases of serious crime, however, the accused had two choices. He or she could admit guilt and be sentenced or deny any guilt. The accused then faced trial by ordeal or, if he were a knight, trial by combat. In trial by combat, another knight challenged the accused to battle. If the accused won, he was considered innocent. If he lost, he was considered guilty.

Trial by ordeal involved a painful physical test. In one trial by ordeal, the accused had to carry a burning hot iron over a certain distance. If "blood be found on the iron the accused shall be judged guilty. But if, however, he shall go forth uninjured, praise shall be rendered to God." Thus, the people believed God decided guilt or innocence of the accused.

1. **Identify:** (a) three-field system, (b) trial by combat, (c) trial by ordeal.

2. **Define:** (a) manor, (b) serf, (c) demesne, (d) bailiff.

3. (a) List two duties a lord had toward his peasants. (b) List three obligations a peasant owed the lord.

4. How did the three-field system make farming more efficient?

5. **Critical Thinking** How was the manor system suited to conditions in Western Europe during the Middle Ages?

4 The Medieval Church

READ TO UNDERSTAND

☐ **How Christianity spread across medieval Europe.**

☐ **How the Church influenced all aspects of life in the Middle Ages.**

☐ **How the Church was a force for civilization.**

☐ *Vocabulary:* **sacrament, excommunication, simony.**

During the Middle Ages, faith in God was an accepted fact of life. A church with its spire pointed toward heaven was a prominent feature in the medieval village. But the Church was more than a place of worship. It became a powerful institution, with its own government, laws, courts, and system of taxation. Church teachings influenced everyone in feudal society, from king to peasant.

The Church's Growing Influence

In the early Middle Ages, the Church faced two difficult tasks in Europe. One was converting non-Christians. The other was adapting Church organization to new conditions. Missionaries preached the gospel in northern and eastern Europe. Monks, such as Patrick in Ireland and Augustine in England, won many converts. In the 700s, the Anglo-Saxon monk Boniface carried Christian teachings to the Germanic peoples in Saxony. Later, other dedicated men and women converted the Slavs, Magyars, and Vikings.

Under the Roman Empire, Christianity had flourished in the cities. Yet in the early Middle Ages, most Christians lived in scattered rural villages. As you have read, Charlemagne helped the Church develop a system of rural parishes. A priest was appointed in each parish, which was often a single manor.

Several parishes made up a see or diocese, the district ruled by a bishop. In turn, an archbishop administered several dioceses. In the Middle Ages, bishops and archbishops were usually nobles. Parish priests generally were commoners. The pope in Rome was the spiritual leader of Christendom, as Christians in Western Europe called their world. The pope also ruled vast lands in central Italy owned by the Church. These lands became known as the Papal States.

For most Christians, the parish priest was their only contact with the Church. The priest celebrated the Mass in the manor church. He helped care for the sick and poor. He collected the tithe, the tax paid each year to the Church. If he could read and write, he served as the only teacher in the village. Yet many parish priests were poorly educated. Charlemagne had been so shocked at their ignorance that he introduced reforms to make sure that parish priests could read and write Latin.

The Church and Feudal Society

The Church was an essential part of feudal society. During much of the Middle Ages, kings and great feudal lords depended on educated clergy to fill positions in their courts. The clergy thus gained great influence in political affairs. Furthermore, churches and monasteries controlled huge tracts of land in Western Europe. High church officials were feudal lords with their own fiefs and vassals. As nobles, some Church officials were also vassals to a king or other lord. As churchmen, they were not required to fight in battle. But they often had to decide between loyalty to a feudal lord and loyalty to the Church.

The Church influenced every aspect of feudal life. Church officials gave blessings at

Spread of Christianity in Europe, 476-1050

Christian areas, 476

Christian areas added by 1050

Muslim areas, 1050

MAP STUDY The Christian Church helped shape the civilization of Western Europe during the early Middle Ages. In the centuries after the fall of Rome, into which areas did missionaries carry Christianity?

ceremonies for knighthood. Documents such as marriage contracts between two noble families were sworn before a member of the clergy. Knights waged war in the name of Christian ideals. They frequently carried a holy relic, or sacred object, embedded in their sword belts.

In the eleventh century, the Church used its authority to reduce feudal warfare. It tried to enforce periods of peace known as the "Peace of God." The Church also demanded that warring nobles avoid harming noncombatants and clergy "so that those who travel and those who remain at home may enjoy security and peace." When nobles ignored such restrictions, the Church declared that fighting must stop between Friday and Sunday each week and during religious holidays. These efforts may have contributed to the decline of feudal warfare in the 1100s.

175

Importance of Salvation

Faced with the hardships of everyday life, people found comfort in Christian teachings. Christians believed that life on earth was less important than salvation and everlasting life in heaven. The route to salvation was through the **sacraments,** the seven sacred rites, which were administered by the Church through the parish priest.

The Church taught that the alternative to salvation was eternal suffering. Those who wavered in their faith were thought to be doomed to this fate. Since the Church believed that its mission was to save souls, it used harsh measures to enforce discipline.

Christians who disobeyed the Church faced the threat of **excommunication.** People who were excommunicated could not receive the sacraments. They lost their property and were treated as outcasts. A king who defied the Church could also be excommunicated. The pope could then release the king's subjects from their feudal obligations.

In the 1100s, the Church established a special court, the Inquisition, to try people accused of heresy, or holding beliefs that differed from those of the Church. If convicted, the guilty person was usually burned at the stake. If a heretic admitted guilt and asked forgiveness, the Church court then decided whether to show mercy.

Religious Orders

In the early centuries A.D., some Christian men and women believed that the best way to serve God and achieve salvation was to withdraw from the world. This tradition gave rise to religious orders, groups of monks and nuns who dedicated their lives to God. During the Middle Ages, monasteries and convents dotted the European landscape. Some religious orders became rich, powerful landowners. Their land, like other feudal manors, was farmed by serfs and free peasants.

In the sixth century, St. Benedict established a monastery at Monte Cassino in Italy. To ensure strict discipline among the monks, he drew up a set of rules. According to the Rule of St. Benedict, a monk "shall not have anything of his own, neither a book, nor tab-

lets, nor a pen." In addition to poverty, monks took vows of chastity, or purity, and of absolute obedience to the abbot, the head of the monastery. The Rule of St. Benedict served as a guideline for other religious orders.

Although the Church barred women from becoming priests, women were allowed to become nuns. Some nuns, like the Abbess Hilda in England, achieved lasting fame. "So great was her prudence," wrote an Anglo-Saxon monk after Hilda's death, "that not only ordinary folk, but kings and princes used to ask her advice and take it."

Life in a monastery or convent revolved around prayer and hard work. A bell summoned monks or nuns to prayer at dawn and at set hours during the day. Each monk or nun also had regular duties such as working on the land, copying manuscripts, and teaching.

Some religious orders helped improve medieval life. Monastery farms often experimented with new agricultural techniques. Some orders were famous for their herb gardens and medical knowledge. Charitable religious orders cared for the sick, orphans, and the homeless. Since inns were rare, monasteries and convents welcomed travelers. They also set up schools, usually for the children of nobles.

Later in the Middle Ages, two teaching orders became prominent. In the 1200s, a wealthy young man, Francis of Assisi, decided to dedicate his life to poverty and service. He founded the Franciscan order of monks. The Franciscans owned no property or worldly goods. They survived on charity and worked to help the poor. About the same time, a Spanish priest, Dominic, founded a new order of monks. The Dominicans were teachers who set up schools in the new towns that were springing up in the 1200s.

A Force for Civilization

Parish priests, religious orders, and Church officials helped to make Christian values part of everyday life in Western Europe. The medieval Church also helped preserve ancient learning. In the 800s, Charlemagne had ordered monks to copy classical Greek and Latin texts. But at the time, education was in such a poor state that the monks, who were supposed to know Greek and Latin, often wrote in the margins of manuscripts: "Greek, it can't be read." The situation slowly improved as clergy became better educated.

Generally, only a few scholars studied the ancient works, and they rejected any portions that were contrary to Christian faith. However, by carefully copying Greek and Roman works, they preserved the traditions of the ancient world for future generations.

Eventually, great monasteries and convents flowered as centers of learning and the arts. On the island of Iona, for example, Irish monks produced beautiful illuminated manuscripts such as the *Book of Kells*. Like other religious works, this beautifully decorated masterpiece was designed to glorify the Christian faith. Outstanding religious music was also composed in many monasteries.

Challenges to Church Authority

Despite its strength, the Church faced challenges to its authority. One problem it faced was control of the clergy. Influential churchmen often ignored vows of poverty and obedience. They dressed in expensive clothes and lavishly entertained kings and nobles. Corruption and immorality among the clergy led to demands for reform.

By the 900s, some monasteries had grown extremely rich and careless in their standards. A reform movement begun by the monastery of Cluny in France swept across Europe. The abbot of Cluny banned **simony** (SĪ muh nee), the buying and selling of religious offices. He stressed the virtues of hard work and service to God. The Cluny reforms helped restore discipline among the clergy.

The Church also waged a constant campaign against people who disagreed with its teachings. Some heretics denied the value of the sacraments in achieving salvation. Others, like the Albigensians (AL buh JEHN see uhnz) in southern France, condemned the Church for its worldliness. They wanted the Church to return to what they saw as the simple ways of early Christianity. Seeing the Albigensians as a threat, the Church launched a holy war to destroy them in the 1200s.

In this picture, an abbot is teaching a group of monks. During the Middle Ages, religious orders helped preserve the knowledge of earlier times.

The Church also met opposition when it competed with kings and feudal lords for political power. As you will read in Chapter 10, when kings began to centralize their power, they considered the Church an obstacle.

SECTION 4 REVIEW

1. **Identify:** (a) Peace of God, (b) Inquisition, (c) Rule of St. Benedict, (d) Hilda, (e) Francis of Assisi, (f) Dominic.

2. **Define:** (a) sacrament, (b) excommunication, (c) simony.

3. What tasks faced the Church in the early Middle Ages?

4. Describe two ways in which the Church influenced feudal society.

5. How did religious orders improve life?

6. **Critical Thinking** How did the Church's involvement in political affairs open the door to corruption?

Summary

1. **After 500, small Germanic kingdoms competed for power in Western Europe.** The kingdom of the Franks emerged as the strongest. About 800, Charlemagne united a large empire in Western Europe. He encouraged a revival of learning. This revival became the foundation for medieval civilization.

2. **Civil wars and invasions devastated Europe after Charlemagne's death.** During this time, feudalism took firm root. Local lords established order over their own lands. In feudal society, vassals and lords had mutual duties.

3. **The medieval economic system was based on the manor.** Most peasants were serfs tied to their lord's land. Advances in agriculture and new technology eventually improved medieval life. Peasants cleared new lands and produced food surpluses.

4. **In the early Middle Ages, the Church extended its influence across Europe.** It converted people to Christianity and organized rural parishes. The Church also helped shape the values of feudal society and, through the educated clergy, preserved some learning from the ancient world.

Recalling Facts

Choose the word or phrase that best completes each of the following statements.

1. The battle of Tours was important because it (a) stopped the Muslim advance into Europe; (b) ended Roman rule in the west; (c) showed the strength of the Church.

2. Charlemagne sent out missi dominici to (a) collect taxes; (b) teach people to read and write; (c) check on the administration of justice and defense.

3. After Charlemagne's death, his empire was (a) conquered by Muslims; (b) attacked by Vikings; (c) ruled by the Danes.

4. A vassal's chief duty to his lord was (a) military service; (b) paying ransom; (c) giving advice in legal matters.

5. Under the manorial system, a peasant owed his lord (a) a tithe; (b) about three days' work each week; (c) free use of the village mill.

6. One way the Church disciplined its critics was by (a) demesne; (b) excommunication; (c) simony.

Chapter Checkup

1. (a) How did the governments of the Germanic tribes differ from the government of the Roman Empire? (b) What Roman ideas did the Germanic tribes adopt?

2. (a) What steps did Charlemagne take to improve government and unify the empire? (b) What happened to Charlemagne's empire after his death?

3. (a) Why did feudalism develop in Western Europe? (b) How did feudalism become more complex?

4. (a) What rights and duties did noblewomen have in feudal society? (b) How did the lives of noblewomen and peasant women differ? (c) How were they similar?

5. (a) Describe a medieval manor. (b) In what ways was it self-sufficient?

6. (a) How did changes in methods and technology improve agriculture? (b) What effect did the "Great Clearing" have?

7. Describe how each of the following influenced life in the Middle Ages: (a) parish priests; (b) "Peace of God"; (c) religious orders.

Critical Thinking

1. **Relating Past to Present** (a) Why was the code of chivalry important to medieval society? (b) Are there any modern rules of conduct that remind you of a code of chivalry? Explain.

2. **Understanding the Roots of Democracy** (a) What aspects of feudal justice might be considered democratic? (b) What aspects were undemocratic?

3. **Taking a Stand** In the 1400s, some people referred to the early Middle Ages as the "Dark Ages" because they thought civilization had disappeared after the fall of Rome. Do you agree or disagree? Explain.

4. **Applying Information** The medieval Church has often been described as the heir of the Roman Empire. What evidence supports this view?

Developing Basic Skills

1. **Map Reading** Study the map on page 163. (a) Describe the territories Charlemagne added to his empire. (b) What do you think prevented further expansion? (c) How did the Treaty of Verdun affect Charlemagne's empire?

2. **Using Visual Evidence** The illustrations in this chapter portray many aspects of life during the Middle Ages. Study them and answer these questions about each: (a) Who is shown? (b) What are they doing? (c) What social class is represented? (d) How does the illustration help you understand life during the Middle Ages?

3. **Making Generalizations** Reread the feature on page 173 and the discussion of life on the manor on pages 171–174. Then answer the following questions about peasant life: (a) What three facts support the idea that peasants worked very hard? (b) Make a generalization about payments peasants owed their lord. (c) What generalization can you make about peasants' leisure time?

Writing About History

Comparing and Contrasting

When you *compare* events or items, you show how they are the same. When you *contrast* elements, you show how they are different. One way to compare and contrast is to arrange your information in chart form. If you were comparing the relationship between a lord and his vassals and between a lord and his serfs, you might prepare a chart with four rows headed: Lord to Vassal, Lord to Serf, Vassal to Lord, and Serf to Lord. The headings for the columns might be Duties and Benefits. Such a chart would allow you to tell at a glance how the relationships were the same and how they were different.

Practice: Make a chart as described above. Then write a paragraph describing the main similarity and the main difference.

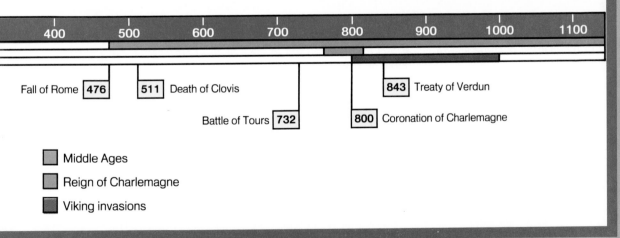

| 400 | 500 | 600 | 700 | 800 | 900 | 1000 | 1100 |

Fall of Rome **476**   **511** Death of Clovis   **843** Treaty of Verdun

Battle of Tours **732**   **800** Coronation of Charlemagne

Middle Ages

Reign of Charlemagne

Viking invasions

The Height of Medieval Civilization 9

(1050–1350)

To the dismay of some spectators at this tournament and to the delight of others, this knight was knocked from his horse by his skillful adversary.

"Sir John Holland and Sir Reginald de Roye armed themselves and rode into the spacious enclosure," noted an eyewitness to a medieval tournament. The two proud knights were eager to begin the contest. The next few minutes would give them a chance to display their strength, skill, and courage.

"There were stands for the ladies, the king, the duke, and the many English lords who came to witness this combat. The two knights were so well armed that they lacked nothing. Each knight was mounted on the best of horses. They placed themselves about a bow-shot distance apart, and at times they pranced about on their horses; for they knew that every eye was upon them.

"They viewed each other through the visors of their helmets, then they spurred their horses, spear in hand. Though they allowed their horses to gallop as they pleased, they advanced on as straight a line as if it had been drawn with a cord; and hit each other in their visors with such force that Sir Reginald's lance was shivered into four pieces."

The knights took up new lances and galloped at each other two more times. Then they fought three rounds with swords, battle-axes, and daggers, without either of them being wounded. Not all tournaments ended so well. Sometimes, groups of mounted knights charged each other on horseback, and the contest became a violent brawl.

Tournaments were held to celebrate religious occasions or simply for entertainment. Only the wealthiest nobles could afford to sponsor them and entertain the throngs of knights and their followers who attended. Even peasants could watch the exciting contests since tournaments were held out of doors. Tournaments not only kept knights in training for war but also channeled their energies into mock battles rather than real ones. Thus, tournaments may have helped reduce the fighting that had plagued Europe in the early Middle Ages.

The knight in armor has become a symbol of the late Middle Ages, from about 1050 to 1350. During these centuries, medieval civilization reached its height. Feudalism, the manor economy, and the Church provided the solid foundations for that society. ■

1 Economic Patterns

READ TO UNDERSTAND

- ☐ **Why trade revived in the later Middle Ages.**
- ☐ **How the growth of towns affected the economy.**
- ☐ **What role guilds played in town life.**
- ☐ *Vocabulary:* **charter, guild, just price, apprentice, journeyman.**

William Marshal, an English knight, needed a new war horse. He set out for one of the large trade fairs being held in northern France, found the horse he needed, and returned home ready to serve his lord.

The trade fair Marshal attended was a sign of a changing economy in the late Middle Ages. In the 1000s and 1100s, warfare declined in much of Western Europe. The manor economy became more productive, and the population expanded. Trade revived and towns grew. Slowly, peasants and nobles became aware of the world outside the isolated manor.

The Revival of Trade

Western Europe had been part of the lively trade of the Roman Empire. Although trade and towns declined after the collapse of the empire, they never completely disappeared. Constant feudal warfare had limited trade, but as warfare declined, trade revived.

Wool was the basis for much of the new trade. Sheep farming was widespread in England and Flanders, a region on the North Sea. Weavers in Antwerp and Bruges (broozh) produced a fine woolen cloth that was prized all over Europe. The Italian towns of Milan and Florence also prospered from the wool trade.

In the 1000s and 1100s, newly built fleets from the coastal cities of northern Italy regained control of the Mediterranean from the Muslims, who had dominated it for centuries.

During the Crusades, as you will read later in this chapter, these cities extended their trade to the eastern Mediterranean.

Gradually, some obstacles to trade were overcome. Crumbling roads of the Roman Empire were slowly repaired, and traffic increased. The gradual reappearance of coined money also simplified trade. Even so, both river traffic and overland travel were expensive because each feudal lord charged tolls to cross his territory.

Trade Fairs and the Hanseatic League

Yearly trade fairs were a sign of an improving economy. The Champagne region of northern France attracted traders from northern and southern Europe. They met in Troyes and other towns to exchange goods. The trading there lasted for weeks or months.

During the 1100s, nobles of Champagne encouraged trade fairs. They also provided protection for people traveling to the fairs. They also hired money changers to evaluate coins from different regions. The nobles in turn profited from fees and a tax imposed on all sales.

The Champagne trade fairs introduced people to the languages, customs, and goods of other places. Italian traders bought raw wool, furs from Russia, and hides. Northern merchants and feudal lords bought luxuries from the eastern Mediterranean as well as weapons, armor, and horses. Peasants, too, gazed at exotic cloaks made of peacock feathers and marveled at monkeys imported from Asia.

MAP STUDY *Italian city-states and cities of the Hanseatic League dominated trade in Western Europe during the late Middle Ages. Merchants from Venice and Genoa brought silks and spices from the eastern Mediterranean to northern markets, where they met merchants who traded in furs, fish, and textiles. What towns and cities of northern Europe were becoming important centers of trade?*

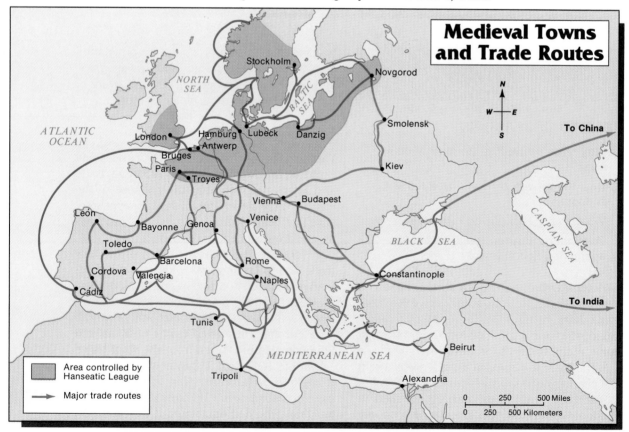

Medieval Towns and Trade Routes

Shops of every kind lined the narrow, crowded streets of medieval towns. In this picture, a tailor and a spice merchant sell their wares. In the background, a barber shaves a customer.

In the late 1200s, the Champagne trade fairs declined, in part because rents and taxes became too high. Competition from the Hanseatic League also hurt the fairs. The Hanseatic League was an association of about 80 large towns and cities in northern Germany that banded together for protection and trade purposes. Most of the cities, such as Hamburg and Bremen, bordered the North or Baltic seas.

Members of the Hanseatic League had large fleets because they had long been involved in fishing. They used their fleets to carry wool between England and Flanders. Eventually, the league dominated the shipping lanes of northern Europe. League fleets cleared the northern seas of pirates so that its ships could safely transport rich cargoes of furs, timber, and fish. The league also gained control of the overland trade through Germany and Italy.

Cities that belonged to the league had immense power. They coined their own money, negotiated treaties, and maintained their own armies and warships. They were even strong enough to wage war on rulers who threatened their interests.

Growth of Towns

As trade increased, merchants set up permanent headquarters in ancient Roman towns along the trade routes and at important river crossings. Some merchants and traders stayed year-round at the sites of popular trade fairs. Gradually, these headquarters grew into towns with inns to shelter travelers. Artisans such as shoemakers, bakers, carpenters, and tailors moved to towns, where they found customers for their goods and services.

The growth of towns stimulated local economies. Peasants sold food grown on the manor to townspeople. With the money they earned, peasants could buy products in town. Local industries, such as the manufacturing of wool cloth in Flanders, expanded. In time, Flanders became a great commercial center. Elsewhere, towns specialized in other industries, such as lacemaking or leatherworking. As townspeople prospered, they demanded imported products. Their demands further stimulated trade.

Chartering a town. Most medieval towns were located on lands owned by feudal lords or monasteries. Townspeople paid fees to the local lord or abbot. But often their obligations were unclear or disputed. As towns grew, townspeople began to ask for **charters,** written documents that guaranteed their rights.

Although charters varied, most gave towns limited control over their own affairs. Town charters usually allowed townspeople to pay the lord a fixed money rent instead of many separate fees. Some charters prevented the lord from seizing the property of townspeople. Others permitted towns to set up special courts for commercial cases. An important provision in many charters granted freedom to serfs who spent a year and a day in a town. "Town air makes a person free" was a common saying.

Many feudal lords came to realize that towns were a valuable source of money. Fees from town courts and taxes on trade helped them pay for the luxuries they wanted. Furthermore, towns trained their own militias, which fought for the lord in wartime.

A middle class. In feudal society, townspeople formed a new, middle class between nobles and peasants. In France, middle-class townspeople were called the bourgeoisie (boor zhwah ZEE); in England, they were called burgesses; and in Germany, burghers. All these terms come from words meaning a walled or fortified place.

Some townspeople were runaway serfs. Others were peasants who had bought their freedom. Still others were merchants or artisans. Like everyone else in medieval society, townspeople developed a social order, or hierarchy. However, in towns, wealth rather than hereditary titles or land ownership usually determined a person's status. A person's status was also related to the guild system that developed in the towns.

Medieval Guilds

Many town charters gave the people the right to form a **guild,** an association of merchants and artisans that governed the town. The first guilds were called merchant guilds. They governed prices and wages in the towns. Merchant guilds maintained standards of quality on goods produced and sold in town. They also controlled the activities of foreign merchants and settled disputes among guild members in their own courts.

Craft guilds. Because merchants dominated the early guilds, artisans set up their own craft guilds. Like merchant guilds, craft guilds protected their members and imposed standards of quality to protect the public. Only members of a guild for a particular trade could practice that trade in a town. Guilds of shoemakers, weavers, wool dyers, and goldsmiths set prices and wages, regulated work hours, and supervised the standards of goods produced. Craft guilds provided money to needy members, sponsored entertainment on feast days, and contributed to the building and repair of the local church.

Craft guilds set what was considered a just price for their goods. According to the Church, it was immoral to make money at the expense of other people. Pricing goods according to what people would pay was considered sinful. Therefore, a **just price** included the cost of materials plus a reasonable profit. Once the guild set a just price for a product, the price was expected to remain unchanged.

Training for membership. By the late 1200s, craft guilds had begun restricting membership, in part to prevent an oversupply of goods. Only a man who completed a long, rigorous training could become a guild member. At the age of seven or eight, a boy could become an apprentice. An **apprentice** learned the trade from a master craftsman who was a guild member. The apprentice earned no wages but was housed, fed, and clothed by the master craftsman.

After an apprenticeship that lasted from 3 to 12 years, the apprentice became a journeyman. A **journeyman** earned wages by working for a master craftsman while he perfected his skills. Eventually, the journeyman submitted a "masterpiece," or sample of his work, to the guild masters. If they decided that his masterpiece met guild standards and that his character was worthy, the journeyman became a master craftsman. Only then could he open his own shop.

Guilds protected their members by preventing competition. Membership in a guild often passed from father to son. Most guilds excluded women, although women worked in many crafts, especially in textiles. However, if a master craftsman died, his wife often kept the business going with his apprentices and journeymen.

Town Life

Most medieval towns had only a few thousand residents. A typical town was surrounded by thick defensive walls. As the town grew, people settled outside the walls, but they retreated inside if the town were attacked. The church, the homes of the wealthiest citizens, and an open square stood in the center of town. Narrow streets radiated out from the central square. Closely packed houses five or six stories high blocked out most of the daylight along the streets.

Towns seldom had any sanitation system. People walked with care along the streets, where pigs and dogs scavenged in the garbage. Waste was flung out a window with a warning cry to passersby. Members of the most powerful guilds enjoyed the privilege of walking close to building walls, where they were better protected from debris.

Each craft had its own district within a town. For example, hatmakers and everyone connected with hatmaking would have their shops along the same street. In this way, those who supplied the material for the hats, merchants who would sell the hats, and people who would buy the hats could all meet in the same place.

A town was a dangerous place. Most buildings were wooden. Once fires started, they raged out of control. Thieves and pickpockets haunted the streets. Some towns had night patrols, but assaults could occur at any hour. The greatest danger, however, was the terrible epidemics of smallpox and typhoid, which were made worse by overcrowding.

Yet towns offered many attractions. There were wrestling contests and visiting jugglers. On feast days, guilds produced elaborate plays based on Bible stories or on the lives of saints. In the late Middle Ages, comedies with clowns became popular. But perhaps the main attraction of town life was the opportunity to make money and to rise in society.

As towns grew, they came to play a greater role in medieval life. The great towns of Flanders and northern Italy were bustling centers

Carefully supervised training was required before a craftsman could become a member of a guild. Under the watchful eye of his master, this apprentice blacksmith is learning how to shoe a horse. By setting and monitoring standards, guilds protected their members and the public.

of commerce and industry. The wealth of these towns contributed to the growth of medieval culture.

SECTION 1 REVIEW

1. **Locate:** (a) Flanders, (b) Antwerp, (c) Bruges, (d) Champagne.

2. **Identify:** Hanseatic League.

3. **Define:** (a) charter, (b) guild, (c) just price, (d) apprentice, (e) journeyman.

4. Describe two changes that contributed to the revival of trade.

5. List three rights that town charters usually gave townspeople.

6. (a) What economic role did the guilds play in the towns? (b) What social role did they play?

7. **Critical Thinking** If you had lived in the late Middle Ages, would you have wanted to live in a town? Why or why not?

2 Medieval Culture

READ TO UNDERSTAND

☐ How medieval art and Christianity were linked.

☐ What new forms of literature developed in the later Middle Ages.

☐ What advances were made in science and technology.

☐ *Vocabulary:* flying buttress, vernacular, scholasticism, alchemist.

No one had seen anything like it, the archbishop reported. Men and women "brought up in honors and in wealth bent their proud and haughty necks to the harness of carts." Like beasts of burden, they dragged stone, timber, and other construction materials to the "abode of Christ," grateful for the chance to join in the building of a great cathedral.

In the 1100s, the largest towns and cities embarked on a frenzy of church building.

This illustration decorated a medieval manuscript. It shows a female artist studying herself in a small hand mirror in order to put the finishing touches on a self-portrait. The subject matter is especially unusual. Most art of the Middle Ages had a religious theme, and women artists were rare.

Towns rang to the sounds of the stonemasons' hammers. Busy towns were centers of cultural activities. Trade and commerce had expanded people's horizons. The reappearance of coined money gave rise to a wealthy class who could afford to educate their children and support the work of artists. Yet, as the dominant force in society, the Church inspired the flowering of medieval culture.

Art and Architecture

Medieval art and architecture reflected the power of the Church. During the 1100s and 1200s, hundreds of churches and monasteries were built. But the greatest efforts were poured into the cathedrals.

The Church, kings, nobles, and townspeople gave money to build new cathedrals. Construction of a single cathedral could take 30 years or more. Architects, stonemasons, carpenters, and sculptors might spend their entire lives working on a cathedral that would be completed by their children or grandchildren.

During the Middle Ages, two distinct styles of church architecture developed: Romanesque and Gothic.* The Romanesque style was popular from 1000 to 1150. Massive churches and monasteries built in this style showed the influence of Roman architecture in the rounded arches and the domed roof. To support the immense weight of the domed roof, the outside walls were made very thick. Since windows would weaken the walls, only a few narrow slits were included to let in light.

In the mid-1100s, French architects overcame great technical difficulties and began to build cathedrals that were tall, light, and airy. The new Gothic architecture depended on inventions such as the flying buttress. The **flying buttress** was a graceful stone arm that leaned against the outside wall to help support the weight of the roof. With this support, architects could make the walls thinner and higher. Gothic cathedrals had tall pointed arches and large windows that lighted the interior. Between 1150 and 1300, townspeople

---

* People in the 1500s made fun of the Middle Ages. They called the great medieval cathedrals the work of "barbarians" or Goths. The word Gothic has remained as the name of one style of medieval architecture.

all over Europe rushed to build cathedrals in the Gothic style.

To decorate the new cathedrals, artists created colorful stained-glass windows with scenes from the Bible. At the entrance, statues of Christ, the Apostles, or saints reminded worshippers of Christian teachings. In an age when few people could read and write, stained glass and stone sculpture were used to illustrate the Bible.

Literature

In the 1100s and 1200s, a new style of literature emerged in Europe. The new literature was written in the **vernacular,** the everyday language of the people. Throughout the Middle Ages, scholars wrote in Latin, the language of the Church. Monks wrote histories in Latin, and documents such as town charters were written in Latin. But most people did not speak or understand it.

The vernacular languages that developed in France, Spain, Italy, and Portugal were strongly influenced by Latin. Today, these languages are called Romance languages—from the language of Rome. In Germany, Scandinavia, and England, the vernacular languages were based on German. Today, these languages are called Germanic languages.

Troubadours wandering from court to court helped spread the use of vernacular languages. They sang love songs and recounted the deeds of legendary warriors in the vernacular. Each region of Europe had its own heroes, although the stories usually focused on the same themes of love and war. Eventually, these tales were written down.

A popular form of vernacular literature was the chanson de geste (SHAN sohn duh JEHST). This long, narrative poem portrayed the ideals of chivalry. One famous chanson de geste, the *Song of Roland,* described the heroic death of Roland, a knight in Charlemagne's army. During Charlemagne's campaign against the Muslims in Spain, Roland displayed the virtues of courage and loyalty expected of a Christian knight. In Germany, Spain, and England, epic poems celebrated heroes such as Siegfried, El Cid, and Beowulf.

The chansons de geste and troubadour poems of love influenced the manners of the

During the Middle Ages, people saw cathedrals as monuments "to the greater glory of God." The soaring heights and pointed arches of Gothic cathedrals, such as the Cathedral of Bourges shown here, were designed to remind worshippers of the power of God.

nobles by encouraging chivalry and courtesy. However, troubadour poetry had little appeal for the new middle class. Townspeople preferred fables. These short, humorous poems mocked nobles, the clergy, and even townspeople themselves. In *Reynard the Fox,* for example, animals behaved like humans with such weaknesses as greed and pride.

Perhaps the most famous medieval poet was Dante (DAHN tay), who lived in Florence from 1265 to 1321. In typical medieval fashion, Dante's *Divine Comedy* combined poetry, theology, and history. In the poem, the Roman poet Virgil guides Dante as he visits souls in hell and purgatory. Dante then journeys to heaven. Dante composed his masterpiece in Italian. The *Divine Comedy* was so widely read and admired that it helped establish the Italian vernacular.

Geoffrey Chaucer's poem The Canterbury Tales *is one of the best-known works in English literature.* The Canterbury Tales *is a collection of stories told by pilgrims on their way to Canterbury, a popular shrine in southern England. To pass the time, they tell each other about their lives. In the following excerpts, Chaucer sketches the character of several pilgrims.*

From *The Canterbury Tales*

There was a *Knight,* a most distinguished
    man,
Who from the day on which he first began
To ride abroad had followed chivalry,
Truth, honour, generousness and courtesy.
He had done nobly in his sovereign's war

And ridden into battle, no man more,
As well in Christian as in heathen places
And ever honoured for his noble graces.

There was a *Merchant* with a forking beard
And motley dress; high on his horse he sat,
Upon his head a Flemish beaver hat
And on his feet daintily buckled boots.
He told of his opinions and pursuits
In solemn tones, he harped on his increase
Of capital; there should be sea-police
(He thought) upon the Harwich-Holland
    ranges;
He was expert at dabbling in exchanges.
This estimable Merchant so had set
His wits to work, none knew he was in debt.

A worthy *woman* from beside Bath city
Was with us, somewhat deaf, which was a
    pity.
In making cloth she showed so great a bent
She bettered those of Ypres and of Ghent.
And she had thrice been to Jerusalem,
Seen many strange rivers and passed over
    them;
She'd been to Rome and also to Boulogne,
St. James of Compostella and Cologne.

1. What values of chivalry does Chaucer's knight express?

2. **Critical Thinking** How do *The Canterbury Tales* reflect the expanding horizons of the Middle Ages?

Like Dante, the English poet Geoffrey Chaucer influenced vernacular literature. Chaucer's work shows the influence of the town life. In *The Canterbury Tales,* Chaucer wrote about the lives of everyday people rather than of legendary heroes. (See the feature above.)

Centers of Learning

In some medieval towns, scholars set up centers of learning that grew into universities. The first universities were associations of students and teachers. Before long, they came under Church control. Universities obtained official charters, just as towns had, which gave them rights to self-government. However, university officials were members of the clergy and therefore answerable to the Church.

Universities were similar to guilds. They protected the interests of students and teachers, established courses of study, and set standards. Like many guilds, universities excluded women.

University students trained for high positions in the Church or in government. They studied the seven liberal arts: grammar, rhetoric, logic, geometry, arithmetic, astronomy, and music. After completing the basic curriculum, a student took an examination to become a bachelor of arts. After further study, he submitted a written masterpiece to become a master of arts. With this degree, a student could join the guild of teachers.

The medieval university offered few comforts. Students sat for hours on hard benches in an unheated room, taking notes while a scholar lectured. Manuscript books were scarce and expensive. The teacher's life was not easy, either. In addition to teaching his students, he also had to find them housing, supervise their behavior outside the classroom, and collect tuition.

Despite the discomforts, universities thrived. Oxford University was founded by English students who had to leave Paris when France and England were at war. Later, some Oxford students formed a new university at Cambridge. Some universities earned reputations for excellence in a particular field. The University of Salerno in Italy was known for medicine. The University of Bologna was famous for teaching Church and Roman law, and the University of Paris specialized in theology and law.

The Challenge of the New Learning

In the 1000s, scholars from Bologna traveled to Constantinople to bring back manuscripts of Roman law. About the same time, new translations of Aristotle's works reached Western Europe from Muslim Spain. When scholars began studying the new translations, debates broke out in the universities. Aristotle's system of knowledge relied on reason. It required people to examine all sides of an issue. Yet medieval thinkers accepted ideas on faith. They believed that Church teachings were the final authority on all questions.

"Why does he speak of the sayings and deeds of the ancients?" complained a student over 600 years ago. "We have inside information; our youth is self-taught." As this picture suggests, the student may have been struggling to stay awake during a three-hour lecture. Although medieval classrooms were cold and uncomfortable, most students were willing to endure these hardships for the sake of an education.

During the late Middle Ages, the most brilliant thinkers tried to resolve apparent differences between faith and reason. Eventually, they developed a school of thought called scholasticism. **Scholasticism** used reason and logic to support Christian beliefs.

The most famous medieval scholastic thinker was Thomas Aquinas (uh KWĪ nuhs). Aquinas taught that there was no conflict between faith and reason. He explained that the ability to reason was the gift of God. Faith, too, came from God. When differences arose between faith and reason, the problem was caused by mistaken reasoning.

In his major work, *Summa Theologica,* Aquinas set out to explain all Christian beliefs in the light of reason. He wrote that rulers should obey the law of God and protect human lives through just laws. He stressed the virtues of wisdom and moderation and the importance of the sacraments for achieving salvation. The teachings of Aquinas have influenced Christian thought to the present.

Science and Technology

The scientific knowledge of the ancient world was largely lost or forgotten in the early Middle Ages. In science, as in all other areas, the Church was the unquestioned authority. Its teachings about the universe were generally based on a few surviving classical works. Yet those works often contained errors. For example, the Church accepted the views of the ancient astronomer Ptolemy, who taught that the sun revolved around the earth.

Despite the lack of scientific observation and experiment in the early Middle Ages, scholars made important advances. In the 800s, Europeans adopted Hindu-Arabic numerals from the Muslims in Spain. The use of Hindu-Arabic numerals opened the way to new developments in mathematics. Although scholars mistakenly believed that the earth was the center of the universe, they did prove mathematically that the earth was round.

Great advances were also made in technology. As you have read, the heavy plow, the waterwheel, and the windmill increased food production. Later inventions included clocks, lenses for glasses, and glass for windows and mirrors. About 1000, an English monk designed and built a glider that flew about 600 feet (180 meters). Three hundred years later, Guido da Vigevano, an Italian physician, sketched plans for an automobile engine and a submarine.

Experiments. In the late Middle Ages, scientists began to draw conclusions from experiments. Experiments had long been used by **alchemists,** who combined philosophy, magical beliefs, and chemistry in an attempt to change worthless metals into gold. Alchemists' workshops resembled some present-day laboratories, with containers of bubbling liquids and smoking furnaces. Although alchemists did not find a way to change other metals into gold, they did set up methods of study that led to the development of laboratory experiments.

In the 1200s, Roger Bacon, an English philosopher and scientist, noted the importance of experiments:

> Experimental science controls all other sciences. It reveals truths which reasoning from general principles would never have discovered. It starts us on the way to marvelous inventions that will change the face of the world.

Bacon conducted many experiments in optics, the branch of physics that studies light and vision. He predicted the invention of cars, flying machines, and fast ships powered by engines. Today, Bacon is known as the founder of experimental science.

Medieval medicine. At the universities of Salerno and Montpellier, physicians received fine training and made some advances in medicine. Most people, however, relied on folk medicine, which combined traditional remedies, superstition, and Christian beliefs.

Cures for minor illnesses were usually herbal medicines. "For toothache, mix vinegar, oil, and sulphur and put it in the mouth of the sufferer," read one prescription. Another suggested: "For headache, take root of peony mixed with oil of roses. Soak linen with the mixture and apply to where the pain is." Although many of these remedies did little good, some worked.

Many people believed that illness was the work of evil spirits or the devil. Surgery was sometimes performed to release evil spirits.

People also prayed to the saints for cures. In cases of serious illnesses, some people made pilgrimages* to holy shrines, where they prayed for a miraculous cure.

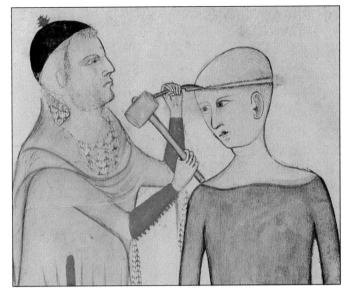

Although medical schools were established at several medieval universities, medical techniques often remained primitive and knowledge was limited. The surgeon shown here appears to be about to open the skull of a patient. Herbs and prayers were usually tried before such drastic measures as surgery.

SECTION 2 REVIEW

1. **Identify:** (a) chanson de geste, (b) Dante, (c) Geoffrey Chaucer, (d) Thomas Aquinas, (e) Roger Bacon.

2. **Define:** (a) flying buttress, (b) vernacular, (c) scholasticism, (d) alchemist.

3. How did art and architecture reflect the power of the Church in the Middle Ages?

4. What two kinds of vernacular literature developed in the late Middle Ages?

5. How were most illnesses treated during the Middle Ages?

6. **Critical Thinking** How did the new translations of Aristotle's works challenge medieval thinkers?

3 Expanding Horizons

READ TO UNDERSTAND

☐ Why the Crusades took place.

☐ How the Crusades helped to change feudal society.

☐ How attitudes toward Jews changed in the late Middle Ages.

☐ *Vocabulary:* crusade, usury, bill of exchange.

During the Middle Ages, Europe was politically divided, but the Church was a powerful unifying force. The Church grew wealthy in the late Middle Ages, and its power increased. In the 1000s, the Church used its enormous influence to send thousands of Christians on holy missions beyond the borders of Europe.

*A pilgrimage is a journey that is taken for a specific purpose, such as visiting a holy place.

The Holy Land

In medieval times, Christians thought of Palestine and the places connected with the life of Jesus as the Holy Land. As early as the 200s, Christians from Western Europe had begun making the long and difficult pilgrimage to Jerusalem. In the 600s, Muslim Arabs conquered Palestine. The new rulers generally tolerated Christian pilgrims. However, in 1071, the Seljuk Turks, a warlike people who had recently converted to Islam, took Palestine. Soon after, returning pilgrims began reporting that the Turks were torturing Christians in Palestine.

Turkish armies also threatened the Byzantine Empire. In 1095, the Byzantine emperor asked Pope Urban II for some knights to help fight the Turks. Relations between Christians in the Byzantine Empire and in Western Europe were far from friendly. In 1054, the Christian Church had split into two churches: the Eastern, or Orthodox, Church in the Byzantine Empire and the Roman Catholic Church in Western Europe. You will read about the causes of this split in Chapter 11. Despite the split, Urban responded quickly to the emperor's plea.

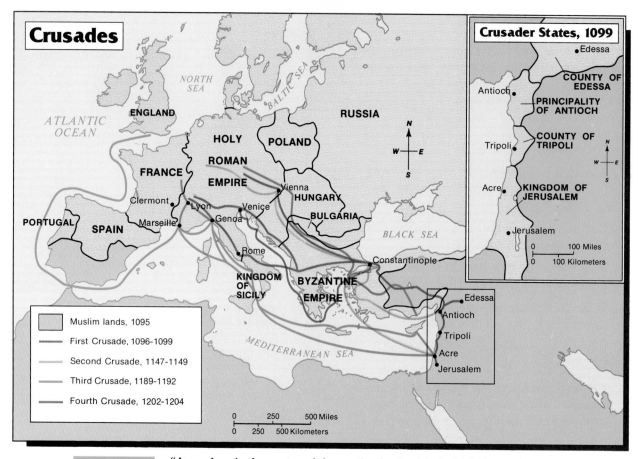

Crusades

Crusader States, 1099

- COUNTY OF EDESSA
- PRINCIPALITY OF ANTIOCH
- COUNTY OF TRIPOLI
- KINGDOM OF JERUSALEM

Muslim lands, 1095
First Crusade, 1096-1099
Second Crusade, 1147-1149
Third Crusade, 1189-1192
Fourth Crusade, 1202-1204

MAP STUDY *"Jerusalem is the center of the earth; the land is fruitful above all others, like another paradise of delights," proclaimed Pope Urban II in 1095. At the pope's urging, many Christians set out on crusades to free Jerusalem from Muslim control. During which crusade did the crusaders travel the longest distance?*

The Crusades Begin

In 1095, at the Council of Clermont in southern France, Urban preached a **crusade,** a military expedition against enemies of the Church. Christian knights, he urged, must rescue the Holy Land from the Muslims. "Undertake this journey for the forgiveness of your sins," the pope declared, "with the assurance of everlasting glory in the kingdom of Heaven." In other words, those who died on a crusade would gain salvation. Moved by the pope's appeal, the assembled nobles and clergy roared, "God wills it."

Urban had several reasons for preaching a great crusade. He hoped a crusade would help reunite the two branches of the Christian Church. Also, a successful crusade would increase the prestige of the Church. Furthermore, the pope saw a crusade as a way to reduce feudal warfare. Instead of fighting in Europe, knights could battle enemies in the Holy Land.

Urban's speech ignited an immediate response. Thousands of peasants and knights sewed crosses to their clothes. They were called crusaders, people who take up the cross. Many crusaders earnestly believed that they were obeying God's command. They wanted only to win salvation. However, some crusaders were more interested in rumors that Palestine was a land of fabulous riches. Others dreamed of carving out kingdoms in the Holy Land. A crusade offered them a chance to fight for the worthiest of all causes—the glory of God. In addition, the pope excused crusaders from certain taxes and debts while they were away fighting.

Before the First Crusade got under way, thousands of poor, unarmed peasants from

France and Germany set off for the Holy Land. Most believed that a barefoot preacher named Peter the Hermit was leading them to heaven. Without food or money, the disorganized peasant bands looted towns in Eastern Europe and attacked non-Christian communities along the way. When they reached Constantinople, the Byzantine emperor rushed them into Asia Minor, where most were killed by the Turks.

In 1096, the first official crusade crossed from Constantinople into Asia Minor. The crusaders fought bravely, winning victories there and in Syria. In 1099, they took Jerusalem. When they entered Jerusalem, the crusading knights slaughtered Muslim and Jewish men, women, and children. "Men rode in blood up to their knees," observed one knight. He justified the massacre because those killed were not Christians.

The crusaders set up four feudal states in Palestine and Syria: Edessa, Antioch, Tripoli, and Jerusalem. (See the map at left.) Although the crusader states lasted for nearly 200 years, they depended for survival on Italian merchants who ferried supplies and knights from Europe. Some crusaders who stayed in Palestine adopted local customs and grew more tolerant of their Muslim and Jewish neighbors.

Later Crusades

Religious enthusiasm prompted many generations of Christians to take up the cross. For 200 years, a steady stream of pilgrims, merchants, and knights traveled back and forth across the Mediterranean. When Edessa fell to the Turks in 1144, a French monk, Bernard of Clairvaux (klehr VOH), called for a second crusade. The armies of the Second Crusade, however, failed to recapture Edessa.

In 1187, Muslim armies commanded by the able general Saladin (SAL uh dihn) captured Jerusalem, prompting the Third Crusade, which lasted from 1189 to 1192. King Richard of England reconquered some land but could not win back Jerusalem. He finally accepted a truce that guaranteed protection for Christians who visited Jerusalem.

The Fourth Crusade assembled in Venice. Venetian merchants convinced the crusaders to attack Constantinople, the Venetians' chief trade rival. In 1204, crusaders captured Constantinople, looted its rich Christian churches, and established a Latin kingdom in Greece.

The Fourth Crusade seriously weakened the Byzantine Empire, which had served as a buffer between the Turks and Western Europe. Also, the attack on Constantinople diverted attention from the Holy Land. In addition, the Fourth Crusade showed that the high ideals of the early crusades had largely given way to greed and political ambition.

Yet religious faith continued to spark new crusades. In 1212, about 20,000 French and German children set out for the Holy Land in what became known as the Children's Crusade. The young crusaders expected the Mediterranean Sea to part miraculously and open a path to Jerusalem. Instead, corrupt merchants at the port of Marseille sold the children into slavery.

Despite several more military crusades, Muslim forces slowly regained lands captured by Europeans. In 1291, they seized Acre, the

In 1099, crusaders besieged the city of Jerusalem in the heart of the Holy Land. Their attacks were fiercely resisted by Muslim defenders, who also saw Jerusalem as a holy city. Finally, Jerusalem fell to the Christians. In this painting, Christian knights surge through gaps in the walls, killing the last Muslim defenders.

About to depart for the Crusades, this ship is being loaded with provisions for the journey. After the Crusades, ships like this one traveled back and forth across the Mediterranean Sea bringing exotic Asian goods to Europe. Italian city-states built large merchant fleets and merchants involved in trade with the East often grew very rich.

last Christian stronghold in the Holy Land. After 200 years of bitter fighting, the Holy Land was again under Muslim rule.

Results of the Crusades

At first, the spirit of the Crusades increased the power and prestige of the Church. As a result, the pope launched crusades against Muslims in Spain and against heretics in other parts of Europe. However, the misguided action of the Fourth Crusade tarnished the image of the Church.

The Crusades began just as Europe was emerging from the isolation of the early Middle Ages. They helped to quicken the pace of changes already under way. Crusaders needed ships to carry them to Palestine, so shipbuilders in the towns of northern Italy built large fleets. Italian merchants increased their trade with the Middle East. In Palestine, they bought Indian and Chinese goods that Arab traders had brought from Asia. They then carried the cotton cloth, silks, and spices to Venice, Genoa, and Pisa. From these cities, the goods were taken to other parts of Europe.

Increased trade and travel influenced the way Europeans saw the world. Pilgrims and merchants discovered that Muslims were not the monsters rumors described. People in Western Europe grew curious about even more distant regions. In the 1270s, Marco Polo, an Italian merchant, traveled overland to China. Few people believed his description of Chinese wealth and splendor. (See page 263.) Yet within a few centuries, adventuresome explorers would use a Chinese invention, the compass, to sail into unknown seas.

New Attitudes Toward Wealth

The increase in trade led to other economic changes. During the 1200s, the use of coined money became more widespread in Europe. As coined money reappeared, people changed their attitudes toward wealth. Making money was no longer seen as cheating the customer. Merchants charged whatever price they could get for a product and were not ashamed to make huge profits.

Some merchants also began to lend money for interest. This practice was called **usury.** The Church had banned usury. But by the 1200s, wealthy merchants found ways to get around the Church ban. Eventually, the Church decided that a reasonable interest charge based on the risk involved was not immoral. Now the term usury is applied to charging excessive or unlawfully high rates of interest.

By the 1300s, wealthy Italian families who made loans to merchants, kings, and popes had become Europe's first bankers. They provided useful banking services such as bills of exchange. **Bills of exchange** allowed merchants to pay for goods in distant cities without actually carrying gold coins. A merchant could deposit money with a banker in Venice, receive a bill of exchange, and travel to London. There, from another Venetian banker, he could receive the cash he needed to buy goods in England. Banks charged fees for such services, but the service helped make foreign trade easier.

Economic Change and Feudal Society

Increased trade and the reappearance of coined money changed life on the manor. Feudal lords now bought imported silks from town merchants and fine steel weapons made in Syria. Peasants also began to buy goods in towns or at trade fairs.

Because feudal lords needed money to buy trade goods, they allowed peasants to pay rents in money rather than in grain or labor. Some lords were willing to grant their serfs freedom in exchange for a large sum of money. The freed serfs could then work as hired laborers, usually on the lord's land. Some free peasants left the manor to try their luck in the towns.

The relationship between feudal lords and townspeople was often strained. Lords looked down on townspeople, who seemed more interested in wealth than warfare and the knightly code of chivalry. They also resented the wealthy merchants and bankers who often lived in greater luxury than nobles.

Yet the most powerful feudal lords benefited from the money economy. They acquired wealth from the towns on their land. Furthermore, they were no longer dependent on their vassals for military or other services because they could hire people to fight for them.

Jewish Communities in Europe

The changes of the late Middle Ages brought hardship to the Jews of Europe. In the early Middle Ages, Christian kings and lords had granted town charters to Jewish communities. The charters gave Jews some self-government

in exchange for tax payments. Jews followed many trades, farmed, and engaged in commerce. In towns and cities, Jewish academies of learning flourished.

During the Crusades, however, fanatical preachers accused Jews of killing Christian children. Christian mobs then attacked Jewish communities. Towns passed laws forbidding Jews to own land. And guilds forced Jewish artisans out of most trades.

Increasingly, the one occupation left for Jews was money-lending. Feudal lords would allow Jews to live on their land and lend money for interest. They would then tax the Jews at a high rate. As Christian lords, they were obeying the Church ban on usury, but they profited from money-lending. Although the Church reluctantly approved the large-scale banking practices of Christian merchants, it loudly condemned the Jews who were generally restricted to lending small sums of money.

In the late Middle Ages, popular resentment led to laws expelling Jews from many parts of Western Europe. Some Jews settled in Eastern Europe and Spain, where local rulers granted them special protection. Despite persecution, Jewish communities maintained their faith and ancient traditions.

SECTION 3 REVIEW

1. **Locate:** (a) Clermont, (b) Edessa, (c) Antioch, (d) Tripoli, (e) Jerusalem, (f) Acre.

2. **Identify:** (a) Seljuk Turks, (b) Urban II, (c) Saladin.

3. **Define:** (a) crusade, (b) usury, (c) bill of exchange.

4. What were two results of the Fourth Crusade?

5. What was the effect of the Crusades on the Holy Land?

6. How did the Crusades affect Jewish communities in Europe?

7. **Critical Thinking** In what ways were the Crusades both a success and a failure? Explain.

CHAPTER 9 REVIEW

Summary

1. **In the late Middle Ages, changing economic conditions transformed Europe.** As warfare declined, trade revived, and towns grew. A new middle class emerged in towns.

2. **The expansion of commerce and growth of towns contributed to the flowering of medieval civilization.** The influence of the Church was reflected in the soaring cathedrals built in many cities of Europe. Literature reflected the concerns of townspeople as well as those of nobles. Scholars studied new translations of Greek and Roman works and tried to prove that Christian beliefs could pass the test of reason.

3. **In the late 1000s, an upsurge in religious feeling led to the Crusades.** Christian knights returned home with a new view of the world beyond Europe. The Crusades quickened the pace of changes already underway in Europe.

Recalling Facts

Decide if the following statements are true or false. If a statement is false, rewrite it to make it true.

1. The Hanseatic League was a group of Italian cities.

2. Medieval towns obtained charters to protect the rights of townspeople.

3. An association of artisans was called a craft guild.

4. In the Middle Ages, a just price meant charging whatever customers would pay.

5. Gothic cathedrals were dark and gloomy.

6. Physicians received advanced medical training at some medieval universities.

7. The Fourth Crusade recaptured the Holy Land.

8. Italian merchants became the first bankers in Europe.

Chapter Checkup

1. Explain how each of the following contributed to the economic revival of the late Middle Ages: (a) decline of warfare; (b) Hanseatic League; (c) growth of towns.

2. (a) Why did townspeople want charters? (b) How did the growth of towns affect the medieval social structure?

3. (a) What was the purpose of merchant and craft guilds? (b) Describe the steps by which a young man became a guild member.

4. (a) How did Aristotle's work influence medieval scholars? (b) How did Thomas Aquinas resolve differences between faith and reason?

5. (a) What contribution did Roger Bacon make to science? (b) What advances in technology were made during the Middle Ages?

6. (a) Why did people go on crusades? (b) Which crusade was most successful for the Christians? Why?

7. (a) What effect did the Crusades have on the Church? (b) How did the Crusades contribute to increased trade and travel?

Critical Thinking

1. **Relating Past to Present** (a) How were medieval towns similar to modern towns and cities? (b) How were they different?

2. **Understanding the Roots of Democracy** (a) Why were documents such as town charters essential to the growth of towns? (b) What people gained a say in government as a result of town charters?

3. **Understanding Economic Ideas** (a) How did the reappearance of coined money contribute to the economic revival of the

late Middle Ages? (b) Why do you think the idea of a just price became less important in the late Middle Ages? (c) Why do you think the Church relaxed its ban on usury in the 1300s?

4. **Analyzing a Quotation** Victor Hugo, a French writer of the 1800s, observed: "In the Middle Ages, men had no great thought which they did not write down in stone." (a) What do you think Hugo meant by this statement? (b) Why do you think people lavished so much time, money, and hard work on stone architecture?

5. **Expressing an Opinion** Some people today consider the Middle Ages an "age of faith." Do you agree? Explain.

Developing Basic Skills

1. **Map Reading** Study the map on page 182. (a) In what region or regions did the Hanseatic League dominate trade? (b) Where did the Italian cities probably dominate trade? (c) How did trade contribute to the expanded horizons of Europeans?

2. **Understanding Literature** Find out more about the hero of one of the epic poems mentioned on page 187. Then answer the following questions: (a) Who was the hero of the poem? (b) What goal or goals did the hero pursue? (c) Did the hero succeed? Explain. (d) How did the hero represent the ideals of chivalry?

3. **Identifying Immediate and Long-Range Causes** Review the discussion of the Crusades on pages 191–194. (a) What was the immediate cause of the First Crusade? (b) What were the long-range causes of the Crusades? (c) How did the Crusades reflect the growing strength of medieval Europe?

Writing About History

Spatial Order

Spatial order is the sensible order to use when you are describing how something looks. Your readers should be able to follow your description easily, as though their eyes were traveling across a scene. Usually, you would organize information in a pattern, such as from left to right, near to far, or top to bottom. Spatial order is useful when you are writing a description of a gathering of people, the strategy of a battle, or the visual results of warfare. Some words used to show spatial order include: *above, near, beside, in front of, in the distance, beyond,* and *overhead.*

Practice: Study the picture of a medieval town on page 183 and write a description of it using spatial order.

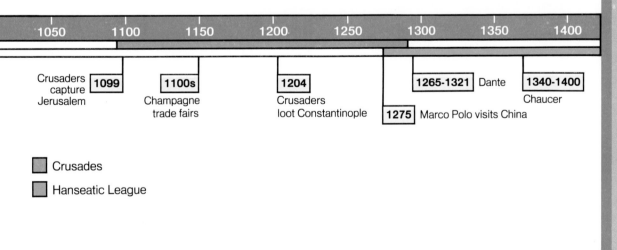

| 1050 | 1100 | 1150 | 1200 | 1250 | 1300 | 1350 | 1400 |

Crusaders capture Jerusalem — 1099

1100s — Champagne trade fairs

1204 — Crusaders loot Constantinople

1265-1321 Dante

1275 Marco Polo visits China

1340-1400 Chaucer

Crusades

Hanseatic League

Building National Monarchies

10

(1000–1500)

CHAPTER OUTLINE

1. Growth of Royal Power in England and France
2. The Struggle Between Popes and Emperors
3. Strong Monarchies in Spain and Scandinavia
4. Decline of Medieval Society

As medieval monarchs tried to build strong nations, they came into conflict with the Church. This painting illustrates the power of both Church and state. The pope and church officials are at left, the emperor and royal officials at right.

In the stifling summer heat of 1137, hundreds of the richest, most respected nobles in France rode out of the gates of Paris. Dressed in the finest silks, they made an impressive escort for Louis, heir to the French throne. It took a month for the expedition to reach Bordeaux in the south. There, they witnessed the marriage of Louis to Eleanor, Duchess of Aquitaine and Countess of Poitou (pwah TOO).

The French considered Eleanor a great prize. When her father had died earlier that year, 15-year-old Eleanor had inherited the rich fiefs of Aquitaine and Poitou. With these lands, she ruled more territory than the king of France.

For almost 70 years, Eleanor played a central role in medieval Europe. She negotiated with popes, kings, and emperors. She traveled across Europe and went on a crusade. When Louis of France divorced her, she married Henry, heir to the English throne. Her vast lands thus passed into English hands. England's possession of Aquitaine fueled a bitter rivalry with France that lasted for 300 years. Two of Eleanor's sons later became kings of England.

In Poitiers, Eleanor presided over the most brilliant court in Western Europe. Troubadours and philosophers flocked to her palace, where learning and culture flourished. Toward the end of her life, an admirer described Queen Eleanor as a "matchless woman, beautiful and chaste, powerful and modest, meek and eloquent, who had two husbands and two sons crowned kings and whose power was the admiration of her age."

Eleanor of Aquitaine was one of many dynamic figures who shaped political life in the late Middle Ages. In the early Middle Ages, feudal monarchs were often pawns of their chief vassals. But by the late Middle Ages, the situation had changed as ambitious rulers extended royal authority.

All medieval monarchs faced similar challenges. They had to establish control over their lands and limit the power of feudal nobles and the Church. Between 1000 and 1500, monarchs formed alliances with the middle class, enriched the royal treasury, and built strong standing armies. They also created new political institutions and established the foundations for the present-day nations of Europe. ■

---

1 Growth of Royal Power in England and France

READ TO UNDERSTAND

☐ **How England developed a strong monarchy.**

☐ **Why the Magna Carta is considered an important document.**

☐ **How kings increased their power in France.**

☐ *Vocabulary:* **exchequer, grand jury, trial jury, common law, limited monarchy.**

In the cool dawn of October 14, 1066, thousands of Norman warriors crowded on a narrow beach near Hastings in England. They waited impatiently for Duke William of Normandy to give the signal to attack. On a ridge opposite, the Saxons led by King Harold faced the attackers, using their shields to form a solid line of defense.

In the Battle of Hastings that followed, both sides fought hard. Hour after hour, the Normans tried to breach the wall of shields. But eventually, the Saxons, armed with battle axes, had to yield to the Norman archers, crossbowmen, and cavalry. By sunset, King Harold was dead, and William was the new king of England.

William was a forceful ruler, who set up a government based on strong central authority. Over the next 500 years in Western Europe, small independent feudal lords lost ground to monarchs who gradually unified their territories. As monarchs grew stronger, especially in England and France, people transferred their loyalty from the local lords to monarchs.

Foundations for Unity

During the Middle Ages, political power was fragmented. Although feudal lords were, in theory, vassals of a king, kings had little real power. Feudal nobles and the Church ruled vast lands, presided over their own courts, and coined their own money. They could also raise armies and make war.

In the early Middle Ages, people had looked to their local lord for protection and order. In the late Middle Ages, however, monarchs took advantage of changing conditions to centralize power. Yet the struggle to assert their authority over the nobles and the Church was not easy.

Monarchs could generally count on the support of townspeople. Townspeople preferred a powerful king who could keep the peace rather than feudal lords whose constant battles disrupted trade. Kings and queens encouraged trade by issuing uniform coins and reducing the number of tolls and taxes along roads. Furthermore, they set up royal courts, which townspeople preferred because these courts administered uniform laws throughout the country.

Monarchs profited from increased trade. A money economy allowed them to tax rich towns and use the income to build armies of paid soldiers. As a result, monarchs became less dependent on the military service of feu-

dal lords. With a strong, professional army, a monarch could suppress rebellious nobles.

Royal power in Western Europe grew slowly over hundreds of years. Monarchs in nations such as England and France faced different conditions, however. As a result, different patterns of government developed.

The Norman Conquest of England

Unlike the rest of Western Europe, England had not become a feudal society as a result of the Viking invasions. Instead, Anglo-Saxon kings kept some authority over the country and united the people against the Danes. As you have read, in 1066, England was conquered by William, Duke of Normandy, later known as William the Conqueror. Although William introduced some elements of feudalism to England, he carefully safeguarded his own power.

William divided Anglo-Saxon lands among the Norman lords, or barons, who had helped in the conquest. To ensure his control over the barons, William made them swear allegiance to him as the sole ruler of England. He declared that everyone, peasant and lord, owed loyalty first to the king, not to another feudal lord. He ordered his barons to build castles as symbols of Norman power. But he forbade them to build any new castles on their fiefs without his permission.

William built the foundation for a strong central government in England. He sent out officials to gather accurate information about all property in the kingdom. These officials asked a group of men in each village to swear under oath to the value of nearby estates. The group was called a jury, from the French word "juré," meaning "sworn under oath." The king's officials then compiled their information into a huge survey called the *Domesday Book*. The king used this survey to decide what taxes people owed. The *Domesday Book* has given historians much useful information about medieval England.

Extending Royal Power in England

William's successors increased royal power. His son Henry I replaced officeholders who inherited their positions with paid royal offi-

Medieval kings increased their power as towns grew and a money economy evolved. Merchants such as the one at right paid high taxes to the king. On the left, townspeople crowd around the king, competing for his favors.

HAROLD: ⱧIC:APPREⱧENDIT:V

The Normans recorded their successful conquest of England on the 200-foot-long Bayeux tapestry. The tapestry, embroidered a few decades after William invaded England, also traces events leading up to the Norman conquest. In this scene, the Saxon leader Harold embarks on a friendly visit to William of Normandy a few years before the invasion. The two men became enemies after Harold was made king of England. William defeated Harold at the Battle of Hastings in 1066.

cials. Because they owed their jobs to the king, these royal officials were more likely to be loyal to him than hereditary officials were. Henry also increased royal income. He allowed vassals to make money payments instead of providing military service. Then he organized a central treasury called the **exchequer.** By keeping accurate tax records, the exchequer added to the king's authority.

In the 1100s, Henry II, grandson of Henry I and husband of Eleanor of Aquitaine, further strengthened royal government. He expanded the power of royal courts by sending circuit judges into the countryside. In each town, a circuit judge ordered juries to report on crimes and disputes.

These early juries also heard cases. No witnesses appeared, and no evidence was presented. The jurors, who were local people, made their decisions based on whatever facts were generally known. In time, two types of juries developed: the **grand jury,** which decided what cases would be brought to trial, and the **trial jury,** which gave verdicts on the cases.

Any free man could bring a case before a royal court. The decisions of royal courts were recorded, and they became the basis for **common law.** Under common law, accepted legal principles were applied to everyone throughout England. People usually preferred royal courts and common law to manor courts and

trial by ordeal. Thus, royal courts increased the king's power. They also helped the royal treasury, which received the fines and fees imposed by the courts.

The Magna Carta

The expansion of royal power in England did not go unopposed. Henry II's efforts to control Church courts resulted in a tragic conflict. Henry had his friend Thomas Becket appointed Archbishop of Canterbury. Once in power, however, Becket opposed the king's policy toward the Church courts, and the two men became enemies. When four of the king's knights murdered the archbishop, Henry was blamed.*

Henry's son John battled unsuccessfully with both the Church and his barons. In 1209, the powerful Pope Innocent III excommunicated John. To regain the pope's favor, John agreed to make England a papal fief and to pay an annual fee to Rome.

Meanwhile, John levied heavy taxes on his barons to support his wars in France. When he

* According to tradition, Henry exclaimed before his knights, "Who will free me of this turbulent priest?" Becket was murdered in 1170 in the cathedral at Canterbury. Two years later, the Church declared him a saint, and Canterbury soon became a popular shrine. As you read in Chapter 9, Chaucer wrote about pilgrims traveling to Canterbury.

The right to petition the king was a privilege eventually extended to all free men in England. The three men shown here, dressed in the garb of commoners, present their petitions to the king. The woman at right, holding the scale, represents justice.

lost land in northern France that England had held since 1066, the barons became angry. They resented the taxes and were outraged at England's loss of prestige. In 1215, they forced John to sign a charter that spelled out their rights. The document became known as the Magna Carta, or Great Charter.

To John's barons, the Magna Carta was simply a written guarantee of their traditional rights and privileges. However, the Magna Carta was of lasting importance for several reasons. First, the rights given to nobles were later extended to all classes. Second, certain clauses were later used to limit the power of the monarch. For example, in one clause, the king agreed to consult the Great Council be-fore imposing any new feudal taxes. The Great Council was made up of high officials, nobles, and bishops. Eventually, that clause was interpreted to mean that a representative body had to approve all taxes. Finally, the Magna Carta established the idea that the king had to respect the law. (See page 203.)

Origins of the English Parliament

Power struggles between the king and his nobles continued in the 1200s. Both sides recognized the growing importance of the towns. Some meetings of the Great Council began to include lesser knights and representatives from the towns. These meetings came to be known as Parliament, from the French word "parler," meaning "to talk."

In 1295, Edward I needed money for wars in France. So he summoned a meeting of Parliament. The meeting was to include the great nobles and bishops, two knights from each county, and two citizens from each town. The Parliament of 1295 is called the Model Parliament because later Parliaments included similar representatives.

When Parliament first met, the great nobles and clergy made the decisions. The lesser knights and commoners from the towns stood at one end of the room and listened. They expressed their opinions only when asked to do so. Later, the two groups met separately. This division eventually resulted in two houses of Parliament. The House of Lords was made up of representatives of great nobles and bishops. And the House of Commons was made up of representatives of lesser knights and towns-people.

Over the centuries, Parliament gradually increased its financial and legislative powers. For example, before voting new taxes needed by the king, Parliament would demand other rights. In this way, Parliament exercised some control over the monarchy. A government where a monarch does not have absolute power is called a **limited monarchy.**

Building the French Monarchy

William the Conqueror had swiftly established royal power in England, but French kings

On June 15, 1215, King John of England made peace with his rebellious barons by putting his seal on the Magna Carta. The document listed the barons' demands for reform. Although many clauses were soon forgotten, the principle that the king had to obey the law of the land was firmly established. The charter eventually became the basis for democratic government in England. Here are some of its provisions.

From the Magna Carta

John, by the grace of God, king of England, lord of Ireland, duke of Normandy and Aquitaine, court of Anjou; to the archbishops, bishops, abbots, earls, barons, justiciars, foresters, sheriffs, reeves, servants, and all bailiffs and his faithful people greeting.

1. In the first place we have granted to God and by this our present charter confirmed that the English church shall be free, and shall hold its rights entire.

We have granted moreover to all free men of our kingdom for us and our heirs forever all the liberties written below, to be held by them and their heirs from us and our heirs. . . .

12. No scutage [a tax paid instead of military service] or aid [tax] shall be imposed in our kingdom except by the common council. . . .

14. And for holding a common council of the kingdom concerning the assessment of an aid, we shall cause to be summoned the archbishops, bishops, abbots, earls, and greater barons. In addition, we shall cause to be summoned by our sheriffs and bailiffs all our other vassals for a certain day and for a certain place. . . .

39. No free man shall be taken, or imprisoned, or dispossessed, or outlawed, or banished, or in any way destroyed, except by the legal judgment of his peers or by the law of the land.

1. Who was to serve on the common council?

2. **Critical Thinking** How do you think the Magna Carta affected the common people of England?

struggled for centuries to unite their kingdom and gain control over feudal lords. In 843, the Treaty of Verdun had divided Charlemagne's empire into three parts. (See page 164.) The western part, which is present-day France, suffered greatly during the Viking invasions. Because French kings were too weak to resist the Vikings, powerful feudal lords set up their own independent states.

The process of building the French monarchy began in 987, when the feudal lords elected Hugh Capet, Count of Paris, as king. Over the next 350 years, the Capetian dynasty slowly increased the power and prestige of French rulers. First, they made the crown hereditary within their family. Then they used diplomacy, marriage, and war to add to royal lands.

The first Capetian kings ruled only a narrow strip of north-central France. The Norman kings of England controlled large parts of northwestern France. Gradually, French kings such as Philip II reduced the English holdings. By defeating King John of England, Philip II added Normandy, Anjou, and Poitou to France. In the 1200s, the Church launched a crusade against the Albigensians, a group of heretics in southern France. The French king then seized the lands of nobles who had sided with the heretics. By 1328, the French king ruled most of central and southern France. (See the map on page 204.)

A Strong Central Government

As they added to their lands, French monarchs set up an efficient royal bureaucracy, a group of officials who govern through departments. The king appointed educated clergy, lesser knights, and townspeople to administer the districts of France. He chose royal officials for their ability and paid them a salary. These officials supported royal policies and added to the power of the French king.

As in England, monarchs in France increased their power through the royal courts. However, the king did not encourage the growth of a common law. Instead, he ordered his officials to respect local customs and traditions if they did not interfere with royal justice. The highest royal court was the Parlement of Paris. Because this court had greater authority than any feudal court, people came to see the king as the source of justice.

Good government ensured the king of his subjects' loyalty. In the late Middle Ages, this loyalty helped French kings in their conflicts with the Church. In 1302, Philip IV clashed with Pope Boniface VIII because the king wanted to tax the clergy and appoint bishops. To show he had the support of the French people, Philip summoned an assembly that represented the three estates, or classes, in France. The first estate was the clergy; the second was the nobility; and the third was the bourgeoisie, or townspeople. This Estates General supported the king against the pope.

The Estates General did not become as powerful as the English Parliament in part because it did not have power over taxation. Instead, the royal bureaucracy grew in strength. Since the king controlled the bureaucracy, he gained great power.

SECTION 1 REVIEW

1. **Identify:** (a) William the Conqueror, (b) Magna Carta, (c) Model Parliament, (d) Hugh Capet, (e) Estates General.

2. **Define:** (a) exchequer, (b) grand jury, (c) trial jury, (d) common law, (e) limited monarchy.

3. How did William keep control over feudal lords in England?

4. What economic power did Parliament acquire in England?

5. What methods did French kings use to increase their landholdings?

6. Why did Philip IV call the Estates General?

7. **Critical Thinking** Compare the methods English and French monarchs used to increase royal power. Which do you think was most effective? Explain.

MAP STUDY *When Hugh Capet was elected king of France in 987, he ruled only the lands around Paris, shown here in purple. During the next 350 years, much of France was brought under royal control. Which regions were held by England in 1328?*

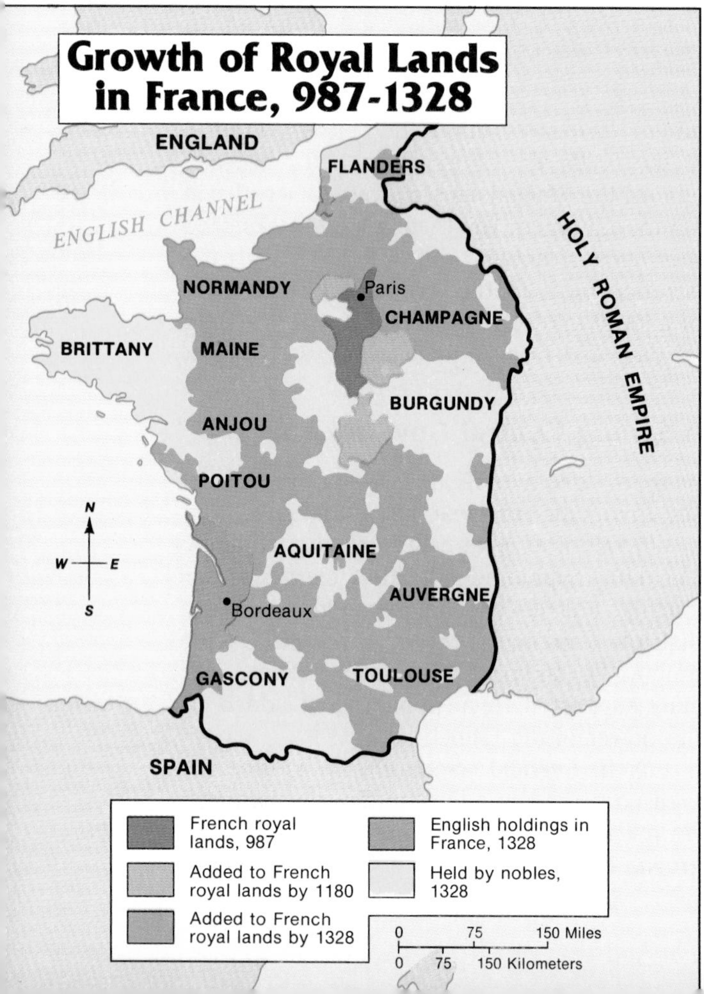

Growth of Royal Lands in France, 987-1328

ENGLAND

FLANDERS

ENGLISH CHANNEL

HOLY ROMAN EMPIRE

NORMANDY   • Paris
                   CHAMPAGNE
BRITTANY   MAINE
                   BURGUNDY
ANJOU

POITOU

N
W — E
S

AQUITAINE

AUVERGNE
• Bordeaux

GASCONY   TOULOUSE

SPAIN

	French royal lands, 987		English holdings in France, 1328
	Added to French royal lands by 1180		Held by nobles, 1328
	Added to French royal lands by 1328		

0   75   150 Miles
0   75   150 Kilometers

2 The Struggle Between Popes and Emperors

READ TO UNDERSTAND

☐ How German emperors became involved in Italy.

☐ How the power struggle between popes and emperors affected Italy and Germany.

☐ How the Church reached its peak of power.

☐ *Vocabulary:* lay investiture.

While French kings were reuniting the western part of Charlemagne's empire, the eastern and central regions fell into turmoil. In the eastern region, which is present-day Germany, Charlemagne's heirs lost power to local lords, called dukes. When the last Carolingian died, the dukes elected one of the dukes as king. The king was able to rule his own lands but could not control the dukes.

In 936, the Duke of Saxony was chosen king. As King Otto I, he soon tried to gain control over the other German dukes. He also extended his power over the central region of Charlemagne's empire in northern Italy.

The Holy Roman Empire

In order to centralize power in Germany, Otto I developed close ties with the Church. He appointed clergy as advisors, and he supported missionary work. In exchange, Otto gained the right to appoint German bishops and archbishops who would support him against the dukes. His ties with the Church led Otto to invade Italy to protect the pope from Roman nobles. In addition, Otto claimed northern Italy through his marriage to Adelaide, widow of an Italian king.

In 962, the pope crowned Otto "Emperor of the Romans." Otto claimed to be the successor of Charlemagne and leader of Christendom. The lands ruled by Otto and his heirs became known as the Holy Roman Empire.

Otto's coronation had long-lasting consequences. In the next 250 years, German emperors became deeply involved in Italian affairs. At first, they supported reforms in the Church, which had fallen under corrupt influences. They often intervened to ensure the election of able popes. But as the power of the Church grew after 1000, popes and emperors clashed in a great power struggle.

Sources of Conflict

As you read in Chapter 8, a religious reform movement that began at the monastery of Cluny swept across Europe in the 1000s. Many of the Cluniac reforms were designed to reduce the influence that political rulers had over the Church. For example, the Holy Roman emperor appointed many high Church officials. In a solemn ceremony, the emperor invested, or gave, a new bishop the symbols of his office—usually a ring and a staff. Because the emperor was a layman, that is, not a member of the clergy, this practice was known as **lay investiture.**

In the winter of 1077, the Holy Roman emperor Henry IV crossed the Alps to find Pope Gregory VII at Canossa. Henry, kneeling in the center, begged the pope to readmit him into the Church. Pope Gregory had gone to Canossa to consult with a powerful ally, Countess Matilda of Tuscany, shown at right. According to tradition, Matilda helped reconcile the pope and the emperor.

The investiture controversy. In 1073, the monk Hildebrand was elected Pope Gregory VII. Hildebrand was an outspoken and able reformer. The new pope worked to end such abuses as the sale of Church offices. He also banned the practice of lay investiture.

Gregory's ban on lay investiture brought an angry response from the Holy Roman emperor Henry IV. Henry wanted to be able to appoint Church officials who would support him against the German dukes. In a bitter letter, addressed to "Hildebrand, now no longer pope, but false monk," the emperor refused to obey the pope's order.

In answer to Henry's challenge, Gregory excommunicated the emperor. He then encouraged the German dukes to elect another emperor. Desperate to save his throne, Henry crossed the Alps into Italy. He found the pope

205

at the castle of Canossa in northern Italy. He is reported to have stood in the snow outside the castle for three days. Barefoot and wearing the rough garments of a repentant sinner, Henry begged the pope's forgiveness. Gregory undoubtedly knew that the emperor only wanted to save his throne, but he obeyed his priestly duty to forgive Henry and readmitted him to the Church.

Concordat of Worms. Henry returned to Germany and continued to appoint bishops. When he was excommunicated a second time, he marched on Rome and drove Gregory into exile. The battle over lay investiture continued until 1122, when a compromise known as the Concordat of Worms (vohrms) was reached. By this agreement, Church officials elected bishops and abbots. The emperor, however, kept the privilege of granting any lands and secular powers that accompanied the Church office.

The Concordat of Worms did not end the struggle between emperors and popes. The investiture controversy had centered on two issues: the Church's spiritual authority, such as its right to choose bishops, and its political authority, such as its power over secular rulers. The Concordat of Worms settled the first issue. The second issue remained a source of conflict, especially in Italy.

The Struggle for Italy

In 1152, Frederick I, who was nicknamed Barbarossa, or "red beard," became Holy Roman emperor. He was determined to rule both Italy and Germany. Frederick spent years fighting to win control of the wealthy towns of northern Italy. By marrying his son to the king of Sicily's daughter, he also secured southern Italy.

The pope saw Frederick's actions as a threat to the Papal States in central Italy. He therefore encouraged the northern Italian towns to unite against the emperor. The struggle for control of Italy involved both pope and emperor in endless wars and intrigue.

The long struggle between popes and emperors had a lasting effect on the Holy Roman Empire. In England and France, rulers were establishing the foundations for unified

nations, but German emperors spent their energies fighting in Italy. As a result, they could not win control over the powerful feudal lords of Germany. German dukes continued to rule their lands as independent kingdoms, largely ignoring the emperor.

Italy, too, suffered from the constant warfare on its soil. Northern towns formed leagues to fight the emperor or the pope, but they were never united under a single ruler. It was not until the 1800s that the many small states of Germany and Italy were finally united into two independent nations.

Church Power at Its Height

Despite the conflict with the Holy Roman emperors, the Church reached its peak of power in the late 1100s. The reforms of the previous century had given it control over the clergy. The success of the early Crusades also added greatly to its prestige. Even kings who challenged the Church in their own lands supported the Crusades. For example, Frederick Barbarossa led his army on a crusade to the Holy Land.

Between 1198 and 1216, Pope Innocent III came close to making the Church supreme in both spiritual and worldly affairs. He kept strict control over the bishops, who in turn watched the lower clergy. He asserted his authority over secular rulers. In 1209, you will recall, Innocent III excommunicated King John. He lifted the ban only when the English king became his vassal. Innocent also deposed one German emperor and intervened to ensure the election of another who promised not to threaten papal power in Italy.

Before his death, Innocent was the unquestioned leader of Christendom. Yet his success hid important problems. The pope had involved the Church in power struggles with many feudal rulers. Critics attacked the Church for being too concerned with political power and for ignoring its spiritual duties. Furthermore, medieval rulers increasingly saw the Church as an obstacle to national unity. In the late Middle Ages, they renewed their efforts to limit Church power.

During most of the Middle Ages, Spain was a center of Islamic civilization. Many examples of Islamic architecture survive. This picture shows the Court of Lions at the Alhambra Palace in Granada, Spain. The elegant, sun-filled buildings of Muslim Spain contrasted sharply with the stern, stone palaces and cathedrals of northern Europe.

SECTION 2 REVIEW

1. **Identify:** (a) Holy Roman Empire, (b) Gregory VII, (c) Concordat of Worms, (d) Innocent III.

2. **Define:** lay investiture.

3. How did German rulers become involved in Italian affairs?

4. Why did Gregory VII excommunicate Emperor Henry IV?

5. What actions by Frederick I threatened the pope?

6. **Critical Thinking** Were the results of the lay investiture controversy a victory for the Church? Explain.

3 Strong Monarchies in Spain and Scandinavia

READ TO UNDERSTAND

☐ How Muslim culture influenced Spain.

☐ How Christian monarchs reconquered Spain.

☐ How Norway, Sweden, and Denmark were united in the late Middle Ages.

☐ *Vocabulary:* reconquista.

"The men of the Cid clutched their shields against their chests. They lowered their lances, from which bright pennants streamed. They did this as one man. They bent their faces over their horses' necks. In stirring tones, the Cid called to them, 'Strike them, knights, for the love of charity. I am Rodrigo Diaz, the Cid of viva.'"

Rodrigo Diaz was a Spanish military leader whose conquests against the Muslims in Spain were immortalized in Spain's epic poem, *El Cid.* Diaz was dubbed the Cid, meaning champion or hero, not by his own knights but by the Muslims whom he defeated. The poem turned Diaz, actually a quarrelsome soldier of fortune, into a national hero whose exploits thrilled Christians all over Europe.

The Cid's conquests were part of the long process by which a strong central government was established in Spain. The process in Spain, as in Scandinavia, involved special challenges. Various cultures had influenced both regions. Muslims had ruled parts of Spain for over 700 years. In Scandinavia, the people had become Christians by 1100, but many Germanic traditions remained.

MAP STUDY *Over hundreds of years, Christian knights slowly pushed Muslim forces farther south in Spain. What area was the last Muslim outpost to fall to the Christian armies?*

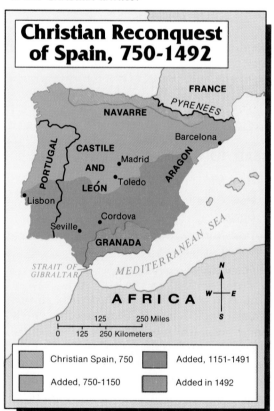

Muslim Spain

In the 700s, Muslim armies conquered most of Spain. Only a few small Christian kingdoms survived in the north. In the early Middle Ages, commerce did not decline in Muslim Spain as it had in other parts of Western Europe. Towns prospered. Jewish communities especially benefited from the tolerant policies of the Muslims.

In large cities such as Cordova and Granada, merchants sold products from all over the world. Markets displayed exotic goods from the eastern Mediterranean and Asia as well as agricultural products such as dates, lemons, and peaches. In the 900s, traders began to carry these goods into the Christian areas of Europe.

Cordova, capital of Spain, was the most prosperous city in Western Europe. Christian visitors marveled at its graceful gardens, splendid mansions, and busy marketplaces. Cordova had police and sanitation services when London was merely a small town.

Spain was also a thriving center of Islamic civilization.* Peaceful contacts took place between Muslim and Christian scholars. Muslim scholars had preserved Greek and Roman texts, many of which were unknown in Western Europe. Christian scholars translated these works and thus rediscovered the learning of the ancient world.

The Reconquest

Despite peaceful exchanges among scholars and traders, Christian kingdoms in the north of Spain had fought to expel the Muslims since the 800s. In the 1100s and 1200s, while crusaders battled in Palestine, Spanish knights launched another crusade in Spain. They called their crusade the **reconquista,** or reconquest, and slowly forced the Muslims to retreat.

By 1250, Muslims held only the kingdom of Granada in southern Spain. Three Christian kingdoms controlled the rest of the peninsula. In the west, Portugal had become an independent state with its own language and a strong interest in overseas trade. The kingdom of

* You will read more about Islamic civilization in Chapter 11.

Castile dominated central Spain. The kingdom of Aragon controlled the northeast. (See the map at left.)

During the reconquest, local Spanish nobles acquired great power. Like the Muslim rulers they replaced, they allowed Muslims and Jews to follow their own beliefs. Towns, where many Muslims and Jews lived, remained prosperous.

Isabella and Ferdinand. In 1469, Queen Isabella of Castile married Ferdinand, heir to the Kingdom of Aragon. Their marriage united most of Spain. The new rulers soon moved to centralize power. They joined forces with the townspeople against the nobles. They limited the power of the Cortes (KOR tehz), an assembly similar to the Estates General in France. Unlike English and French rulers, who had fought bitter battles with the Church, Ferdinand and Isabella made the Church a powerful ally. Isabella worked hard to reform the clergy and won the right to appoint high Church officials in Spain. (See page 210.)

In 1492, a Christian army captured Granada, the last Muslim outpost in Spain. This event ended the centuries of crusades in Spain. It also ignited strong national feeling among Christians in Spain, who united behind Ferdinand and Isabella. While Spain celebrated its victory, an Italian navigator, Christopher Columbus, received permission from Queen Isabella to sail on a voyage of discovery. You will read about the outcome of this voyage in Chapter 15.

Religious policy. Ferdinand and Isabella were determined to bring religious as well as political unity to Spain. Thus, they ended the policy of religious toleration. They ordered Jews and Muslims to convert to Christianity or leave Spain. A few did convert. Many others were expelled. Religious unity came at a high price. Among the Jews and Muslims expelled were many doctors, merchants, scholars, and other leaders of Spanish economic and cultural life.

Spanish rulers used the Inquisition to increase their power and enforce their religious policy. As you will recall, the Inquisition was a special Church court set up to try people accused of heresy. Jews and Muslims who had converted were often accused of practicing their original religions in secret. They were brought before the Inquisition, and their property was seized. If they were condemned as heretics, they were usually burned at the stake.

For centuries, the Inquisition created an atmosphere of suspicion and intolerance in Spain. Later Spanish monarchs followed the example of Ferdinand and Isabella. They allowed no one to challenge their absolute power.

Nations of Scandinavia

As you have read, beginning about 800, Viking raiders from Norway, Sweden, and Denmark terrorized Europe. During the Viking invasions, missionaries worked among the peoples of Scandinavia to convert them to Christianity. Christian missionaries introduced a system of writing as well as other aspects of medieval civilization. By about 1000, the Viking raids ended. However, the Vikings continued to trade with the peoples of Europe.

In Scandinavia, as elsewhere in medieval Europe, great lords competed with kings for power. In Sweden, for example, the leading nobles elected the king, according to Germanic custom. Once they chose a king, however, they prevented him from gaining further power.

Although close ties bound the ruling families of Denmark, Norway, and Sweden, trade rivalries and clashes over boundaries led to frequent warfare. At different times, various strong rulers united the peoples of Scandinavia. In 1017, the Danish king Canute (kuh NOOT) conquered a northern empire that included England, Norway, and parts of Sweden. However, his successors could not hold on to the empire.

In the late Middle Ages, Queen Margrete of Denmark was able to unite Denmark, Norway, and Sweden peacefully. She outlived both her husband and son and in 1387 became Queen of Denmark. The same year, Norway introduced the system of electing a monarch. The nobles chose Margrete. A year later, Swedish nobles deposed their king and asked Margrete to take the throne of Sweden.

While Margrete lived, the union worked well. After her death, however, rivalries resurfaced. In the 1400s, commerce and industry

Thieves and bandits, proclaimed Queen Isabella, are overrunning Spain. On country roads, armed bands attack merchants and farmers, stealing their goods. Spaniards are afraid to send their merchandise to market. Crime is hurting the economy, declared the queen. It must be stopped.

Queen Isabella knew that deeds speak louder than words. She took her campaign against crime to Seville, a rich trading city in southern Spain. Attracted by the wealth of the city, pickpockets, highwaymen, and hordes of other criminals terrorized the people. Isabella set up a special court in Seville, with herself as judge. Every Friday evening, she heard cases and imposed stern punishments—including death. This quickly brought order to the city.

But Isabella's court caught many innocent people as well as guilty ones in its net. The people of Seville were so afraid of the court's harsh methods that thousands fled, abandoning homes and belongings. At last, a group of merchants came before the queen. If she did not show more mercy, they pleaded, Seville would be safe but empty.

Queen Isabella agreed to the demands of the merchants from Seville, but her goal of making Spain a strong nation remained. During her reign, she took many steps toward that goal. One step was to strengthen the monarchy by weakening the nobles. Spanish nobles minted their own coins. Because they minted as many coins as they wanted, the value of Spanish money had dropped. Isabella ordered all of the nobles' mints shut down, leaving only the monarchy's mints to issue coins.

Isabella also forced the nobles to pay new taxes and used the money for projects such as building new universities. The queen believed that learning would help the nation prosper, so she invited scholars from all over Europe to teach and study in Spain.

1. Why did Isabella think that crime had to be stopped?

2. **Critical Thinking** How did Isabella's actions help unify Spain and increase the power of the monarchy?

made Sweden one of the strongest states in Europe. In 1523, it broke away from the union. Denmark and Norway remained united until 1814.

SECTION 3 REVIEW

1. **Locate:** (a) Cordova, (b) Granada, (c) Portugal, (d) Aragon, (e) Castile.

2. **Identify:** (a) Ferdinand, (b) Isabella, (c) Margrete.

3. **Define:** reconquista.

4. In what ways was Muslim Spain a center of Islamic civilization?

5. How did the marriage of Ferdinand and Isabella help unify Spain?

6. (a) What led to frequent warfare among Scandinavian nations? (b) How were they eventually united?

7. **Critical Thinking** Do you think that the religious policy of Ferdinand and Isabella was misguided? Explain.

4 Decline of Medieval Society

READ TO UNDERSTAND

☐ How the Black Death affected Europe.

☐ What challenges the Church faced in the late Middle Ages.

☐ How the Hundred Years' War affected France and England.

☐ Why feudalism declined in Western Europe.

"In one day 812 people died in Avignon," wrote English chronicler Henry Knighton. At least "358 Dominicans died in Provence in Lent; in Montpellier only 7 friars were left of out 149. At Marseille only 1 Franciscan remained of 150." And so the record goes. The "grievous plague" caused death to break out "everywhere the sun goes." Epidemics occurred regularly in the Middle Ages, but none equaled the terrifying outbreak of bubonic plague, often called the Black Death.

The Black Death and Its Aftermath

The late Middle Ages was an unsettled time in Western Europe. Political and economic changes were undermining the very foundations of medieval society. In the early 1300s, poor harvests led to terrible famines. Agriculture, trade, and commerce declined. In 1348, the bubonic plague, a disease carried by fleas on rats, struck Western Europe.* The plague, which broke out first in Asia, spread rapidly along the trade routes. Hundreds of thousands of people died because no one knew how to treat the disease. Panic and fear led to desperate measures. In some towns, the first people to show symptoms of the disease were walled up inside their homes to keep the plague from spreading.

As the disease swept through Europe, it destroyed entire communities. Some towns lost more than half their population. In all, the

---

* The bubonic plague had broken out from time to time in the ancient world. It also caused many deaths in Europe during the 500s and 600s A.D.

Black Death killed about a third of the people of Western Europe.

The huge death toll had a serious effect on the economy. Farms were abandoned. The busy commerce of the 1100s and 1200s, which had spurred the growth of cities, collapsed. Outbreaks of the plague continued into the late 1300s. Western Europe did not fully recover for over 100 years.

Attack on the Church

During the social and economic turmoil of the 1300s and 1400s, the leadership of the Church weakened. At the same time, monarchs and reformers challenged its authority. As you have read, popes had tried to stop kings from increasing their power. In the process, the Church had gained great political power.

Medieval monarchs opposed the Church's political power for several reasons. The Church owned large amounts of land. The clergy and monasteries did not pay royal taxes on their land, but they did pay Church taxes. Thus, money was sent to Rome rather than to the royal treasury. Rulers also resented Church courts, which they felt competed with royal courts. Finally, monarchs became angry when Church officials interfered in political matters. By the early 1300s, monarchs were becoming more successful in their political struggles with the Church.

The Babylonian Captivity. In 1294, King Philip IV of France tried to tax the clergy. The pope ordered the French clergy not to pay the tax. To show that he had the support of the French people in his struggle with the pope, Philip called the first Estates General. (See page 204.) When the dispute continued, Philip kidnapped the pope. Later, he engineered the election of a French pope. The new pope moved the papacy to Avignon (ah vee NYOHN) in southern France. From 1309 to 1378, popes lived in Avignon. During this period, which became known as the Babylonian Captivity, popes were pawns of the French kings. The period was named after the 70-year period the ancient Hebrews had been held captive in Babylon.

In 1378, the Church suffered another humiliation when two competing popes were

Statistics provide factual information in number form. Historians often use statistics to draw conclusions about historical events or developments. Historical statistics can range from population figures to the size of grain harvests or the number of ships built.

Statistics must be used with care. Sometimes statistics are estimates because exact figures are not available. For example, the figures in the following table are estimates of the population in medieval Europe. These estimates are based on the few records that exist for the period. Furthermore, statistics present only a partial picture. The table gives numbers, but it does not give the reasons for population growth or decline. Therefore, statistics must be interpreted using other information.

1 **Identify the type of information given in the table.** The title of the table as well as the titles of the columns and rows show you what information is provided. (a) What is the topic of the chart? (b) What time period is covered? (c) For how many regions are population statistics given?

2 **Practice reading the statistics.** Statistics often involve numbers in the millions. When they do, the zeros are usually left off and the table notes "in millions," which means you add six zeros to the numbers listed. (a) What was the population of Italy

in 500? (b) What was the population of Spain in 1000? (c) When did the total population of Europe reach the highest figure?

3 **Study the table to find relationships among the numbers.** You can use the table to compare the population in different parts of Europe at a specific time period. You can also use the table to study the changes in population in one region during the Middle Ages. (a) How did the population of Spain change between 650 and 1000? (b) In what region did the population grow the most between 1000 and 1340? (c) How does the population of Europe in 1340 compare to the population of Europe in 1450?

4 **Use the statistics to draw conclusions about a historical event or development.** Use your reading in the textbook and the table to draw conclusions about population changes in Western Europe during the Middle Ages. (a) Describe in your own words the population changes in Western Europe between 500 and 1500. (b) What generalization can you make about population changes between 500 and 650 and between 1340 and 1450? (c) What might explain the population change between 1340 and 1450?

Population of Western Europe, 500–1500
(estimated figures, in millions)

Date	500	650	1000	1340	1450	1500
Italy	4.0	2.5	5.0	10.0	7.5	11.0
Spain	4.0	3.5	7.0	9.0	7.0	9.0
France, Belgium, Holland	5.0	3.0	6.0	19.0	12.0	18.0
British Isles	0.5	0.5	2.0	5.0	3.0	5.0
Germany, Scandinavia	3.5	2.0	4.0	11.5	7.5	13.0
Total	17.0	11.5	24.0	54.5	37.0	56.0

Sources: Carlo M. Cipolla, ed., *The Fontana Economic History of Europe: The Middle Ages.*
Carlo M. Cipolla, *Before the Industrial Revolution: European Society and Economy, 1000–1700.*

elected: one in Avignon and the other in Rome. The Great Schism, as the new crisis was called, lasted until 1417. Finally, a Church council ended the crisis. It elected an Italian pope to rule from Rome and persuaded the French king to accept the new pope.

During these scandals, the Church lost much of its political power. In France, kings assumed the right to tax the clergy. In England, Edward I declared that his country was no longer a papal fief. The Great Schism also hurt the religious authority of the Church. Many Christians were outraged at the spectacle of two popes, each claiming supreme spiritual authority.

Demands for reform. In the late 1300s, reformers attacked the Church for its wealth and the worldly concerns of the clergy. They accused the clergy of corruption and failure to perform their religious duties.

One outspoken critic was John Wycliffe, a teacher of theology at Oxford University. Wycliffe questioned the spiritual authority of the Church. He claimed that the sacraments and the priests who administered them were not necessary for salvation. He encouraged his followers to translate the Bible into English so people could read it themselves. Wycliffe's ideas spread across Europe. The Church persecuted Wycliffe's supporters as heretics.

In Bohemia, part of what is today Czechoslovakia, John Huss preached against corruption in the Church. Huss was accused of heresy and burned at the stake. For years afterwards, the Church waged a crusade against the Hussites, as his followers were called. Despite severe punishments, heresies multiplied during the late Middle Ages.

The Hundred Years' War

Medieval monarchs competed with the Church and with one another as they centralized power. The efforts of the English and French kings to build strong central governments involved them in a long struggle. The fighting, known as the Hundred Years' War, lasted from 1337 to 1453.

Outbreak of war. In 1337, the English held many lands in France. As you read at the beginning of this chapter, the marriage of El-

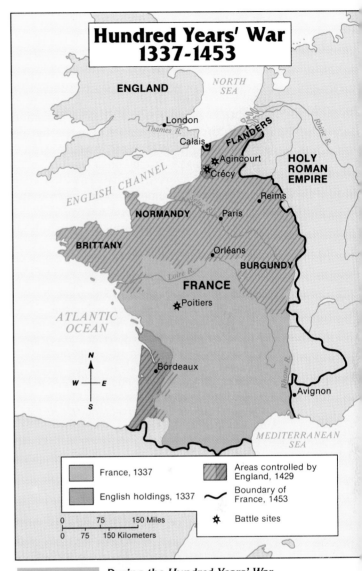

MAP STUDY *During the Hundred Years' War, French and English armies battled for control of France. Joan of Arc helped oust the English from Orléans and Reims, the ancient cathedral city where kings of France were crowned. What was the last French city the English held?*

eanor of Aquitaine and Henry II had brought her vast French lands under English control. Economic rivalries also increased the bitterness between England and France. When Edward III of England claimed the French throne, war broke out.

Early in the Hundred Years' War, England won stunning victories. At the battles of Crécy

213

and Poitiers, English armies easily dispersed the poorly led French knights.

The English victories were due in part to new weapons: the longbow and gunpowder. English archers used the longbow with deadly accuracy against heavily armed, mounted knights. Gunpowder was a Chinese invention that was probably brought to Europe by the Muslims. During the Hundred Years' War, gunpowder was used in cannons. The first cannons were not very effective. But after they were improved, cannons could destroy the walls of fortified castles and towns.

The English victories took a heavy toll on France. The French not only lost territory to the English, but also after each victory, English soldiers plundered the French countryside. To pay for the war, the French king increased taxes. The combination of war, famine, and heavy taxes led French peasants to revolt. Adding to the confusion, bitter quarrels divided the French royal family. Just when England seemed on the point of complete victory, the French rallied behind an uneducated peasant girl named Joan of Arc.

Joan of Arc. In 1429, Joan of Arc made her way to Charles VII, the uncrowned king of France. She claimed that heavenly voices had told her to lead the French forces. Charles reluctantly agreed to give Joan command of his armies. Under her leadership, the French forced the English to retreat from Orléans. Joan's absolute faith and intense patriotism soon inspired the French to new victories.

In 1429, at the cathedral of Reims, Charles was crowned King of France. Joan stood at his side. Shortly afterward, Joan was captured by the Burgundians, allies of the English. The Burgundians sold Joan to the English, who tried her for heresy. In 1431, she was burned at the stake.

Even after her death, Joan continued to inspire the French. Her martyrdom fueled a strong national feeling. Slowly but steadily, the French expelled the English from their lands. In 1453, after almost 120 years of war, the English held only Calais.

Effects of the Hundred Years' War

The people of France emerged from the Hundred Years' War with a growing sense of national pride. The French had also developed strong loyalty to their king. During the war, the king gained the power to raise taxes. Therefore, he could keep a standing army rather than depend on his vassals.

With the English gone, the king ruled most of France. Only Burgundy and Brittany remained outside royal control. The crafty French king Louis XI worked cautiously against the powerful Duke of Burgundy to bring that province under French rule. Brittany came into royal hands when Louis XI's son married the Duchess of Brittany.

Before his death in 1483, Louis XI established the basis for the absolute power of later

According to legend, when a 17-year-old peasant girl, Joan of Arc, appeared at the French court claiming that the saints had told her to save France, the king decided to test her story. He had another man sit on his throne and pretend to be king while he stood among his nobles. Although Joan had never seen the king before, she ignored the impostor on the throne and curtsied to the real king. Thus, the king took her claims seriously and gave her command of his armies.

French kings. He ruled an efficient government bureaucracy that collected taxes and administered justice. He improved the quality of the standing army and restored economic prosperity. Louis also limited the power of feudal lords. At a meeting in 1469, the Estates General asked Louis to rule without consulting it.

Although the English had lost their French lands, both the English king and Parliament emerged from the Hundred Years' War stronger. Because they were no longer distracted by their fiefs in France, English kings could devote their full attention to England. Parliament also benefited from the king's need for money during the war. It bargained for additional rights in exchange for approving new taxes.

Soon after the Hundred Years' War ended, a civil war broke out in England. It was known as the War of the Roses because each side supposedly used a rose as its symbol. During this 30-year struggle, most of England's feudal nobles were killed. When the war ended in 1485, a new king, Henry VII, established the strong Tudor dynasty.

In England, as in France, loyalty to the nation and the monarch replaced old feudal loyalties. But in England, monarchs did not have absolute power. They had to obey the law and learn to deal with Parliament.

Decline of Feudalism

By the late Middle Ages, the world of feudalism had changed. As strong rulers emerged to protect the people and provide good government, the need for a warrior class disappeared. The growth of towns and a money economy hurt feudal nobles. In addition, many nobles had died in battle during the Hundred Years' War.

The changing nature of warfare made mounted, armored knights almost useless. Arrows shot from the longbow knocked knights off their horses. Heavy armor prevented a fallen knight from being an effective fighter on foot. The use of cannons meant that feudal lords could no longer take refuge behind castle walls. With money from taxes, kings hired soldiers for standing armies. The professional soldiers in these armies were often recruited among townspeople or peas-

New weapons used during the Hundred Years' War helped change the nature of warfare. At Crécy, English foot soldiers, at right, used the new longbow to inflict heavy casualties on the French, armed with cumbersome crossbows. With the longbow, foot soldiers could repel charges of mounted knights.

ants. However, nobles did not disappear. Instead, they took their place at the increasingly splendid royal courts.

SECTION 4 REVIEW

1. **Locate:** (a) Avignon, (b) Aquitaine, (c) Crécy, (d) Poitiers, (e) Orléans, (f) Reims, (g) Calais.

2. **Identify:** (a) Black Death, (b) John Wycliffe, (c) John Huss, (d) Joan of Arc.

3. Describe one effect of the Black Death in Western Europe.

4. What led to the Babylonian captivity?

5. Why did the Church lose prestige and power during the late Middle Ages?

6. Describe two reasons feudalism declined in the late Middle Ages.

7. **Critical Thinking** Compare the effects of the Hundred Years' War in France and in England.

215

Summary

1. **During the Middle Ages, rulers in England and France established the foundations for strong central governments.** In England, William the Conqueror and his successors increased royal power. However, the Magna Carta established the principle that the English king was not above the law. In France, kings added to their landholdings and built an efficient royal bureaucracy.

2. **For centuries, popes and Holy Roman emperors struggled for power in Italy and Germany.** When the emperor Henry IV refused to obey the pope's ban on lay investiture, he was excommunicated. While emperors were distracted in Italy, feudal dukes in Germany gained power.

3. **In Spain and Scandinavia, unified nations gradually evolved.** In Spain, Christian crusaders fought to expel the Muslims. In 1492, Ferdinand and Isabella finally won control over the entire country. In close alliance with the Church, they established absolute royal power. In Scandinavia, after the Viking raids subsided, Norway, Sweden, and Denmark took steps to become unified nations.

4. **In the 1300s and 1400s, the foundations of medieval society weakened.** The Black Death had a devastating impact on Western Europe. Both France and England emerged from the Hundred Years' War with strong kings. But the war also contributed to the decline of feudalism.

Recalling Facts

Indicate whether the following events occurred in England, France, the Holy Roman Empire, or Spain.

1. King John signed the Magna Carta.

2. Crusading knights fought to expel Muslims.

3. Philip IV called the first Estates General.

4. The jury system developed.

5. Rulers clashed with the pope over lay investiture.

6. Rulers used the Inquisition to enforce religious unity.

7. Rulers tried to govern both Germany and Italy.

Chapter Checkup

1. Describe how each of the following affected royal power in England: (a) the exchequer; (b) royal courts; (c) common law; (d) the Magna Carta.

2. (a) Why were William the Conqueror's heirs able to unite England more easily than French rulers were able to unite France? (b) How did French rulers increase royal power?

3. (a) What caused the conflict between popes and Holy Roman emperors in the 1000s and 1100s? (b) How did the conflict affect the political developments in Germany and Italy?

4. (a) Describe the Church at the height of its power under Innocent III. (b) What types of attacks were made on the Church in the 1300s and 1400s?

5. (a) Describe the reconquest of Spain. (b) How did the unification of Spain affect Muslim and Jewish residents?

6. (a) How did the Hundred Years' War affect royal power in France? (b) How did it affect royal power in England?

Critical Thinking

1. **Understanding the Roots of Democracy** Which ideas contained in the Magna Carta have been used to support the idea of democratic government?

2. **Expressing an Opinion** (a) Describe the investiture controversy. (b) Do you think Gregory VII should have forgiven Henry IV and readmitted him to the Church? Explain.

3. **Relating Past to Present** New technology often affects the outcome of battles. (a) Explain how this was true in the Hundred Years' War. (b) What new technology had affected warfare in the early Middle Ages? (c) What technological developments today will change how war is fought?

1. **Map Reading** Study the map on page 213. (a) What lands did English kings hold in France in 1429? (b) How did these holdings change between 1429 and 1453? (c) How did these changes probably affect royal power in France?

2. **Making a Review Chart** Make a chart with two columns and four rows. Title the columns Early Middle Ages and Late Middle Ages. Title the rows Government, Law, Economy, and Social Classes. Use what you learned about the Middle Ages in Chapters 8, 9, and 10 to complete the chart. (a) How did government change during the Middle Ages? (b) How did these changes affect law? (c) How did changing economic conditions influence social classes in the late Middle Ages?

Writing About History

Relating Cause and Effect

Events in history do not just happen. Every event or development has at least one *cause*, or reason why it happened. And every event or development has at least one *effect*, or result. In writing about such a chain reaction, you should arrange your information in cause-and-effect order, making clear that a given cause or causes lead to certain effects. Before writing about a series of events, you might find it helpful to prepare a cause-and-effect chart. For example, before writing about the events surrounding the signing of the Magna Carta, you could prepare a chart like this one:

Cause	King John taxes English barons to support his wars in France.
Cause	John loses the war and English territory in France.
Effect	The barons force John to sign the Magna Carta spelling out their rights.

Practice: Prepare a cause-and-effect chart about the conflict between Emperor Henry IV and Pope Gregory VII. Then write a paragraph based on the chart.

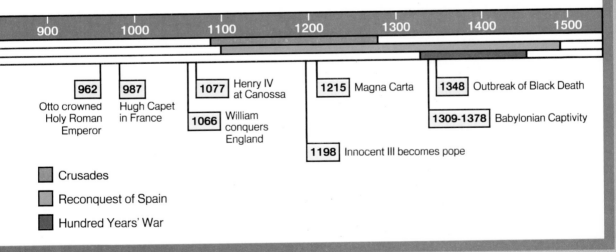

| 900 | 1000 | 1100 | 1200 | 1300 | 1400 | 1500 |

962 Otto crowned Holy Roman Emperor

987 Hugh Capet in France

1077 Henry IV at Canossa

1066 William conquers England

1215 Magna Carta

1198 Innocent III becomes pope

1348 Outbreak of Black Death

1309-1378 Babylonian Captivity

- Crusades
- Reconquest of Spain
- Hundred Years' War

Unit Three   Mini-Atlas

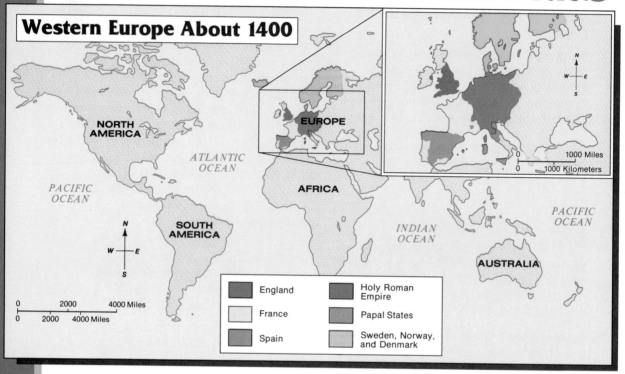

Western Europe About 1400

NORTH
AMERICA

ATLANTIC
OCEAN

PACIFIC
OCEAN

EUROPE

AFRICA

SOUTH
AMERICA

INDIAN
OCEAN

PACIFIC
OCEAN

AUSTRALIA

0   2000   4000 Miles
0   2000   4000 Miles

England
France
Spain
Holy Roman
Empire
Papal States
Sweden, Norway,
and Denmark

0   1000 Miles
0   1000 Kilometers

Unit Themes

In Europe, the centuries after the fall of Rome, from 500 to 1350, are called the Middle Ages. Western Europe had been the least-developed region ruled by Rome. As Roman rule ended, the region became a battleground for many Germanic tribes. The once-flourishing Roman civilization declined. Yet during the early Middle Ages, the foundations were established for a vigorous new civilization.

By the late Middle Ages, a stable society had developed in Western Europe. Warfare declined while trade and agriculture revived. Most people were peasants whose lives were ruled by the cycle of planting and harvesting. But a few wealthy nobles and merchants enjoyed a lifestyle of comfort and elegance.

During the late Middle Ages, some powerful monarchs established strong central governments. Others were caught in a power struggle with the Church. Disease and economic decline marked the end of medieval society.

1. **Analyzing Maps** (a) According to the map at right, which Germanic tribe dominated France during the 500s? (b) Which ruler extended the kingdom to its greatest size? (c) How had the territory of France changed by the 1400s?

2. **Applying Information** (a) Which items on the time line show the influence of the Church? (b) How did the Church affect life in the early Middle Ages?

3. **Understanding Economic Ideas** (a) Which economic system was linked with feudalism? (b) Compare the economies of the early Middle Ages and the late Middle Ages.

4. **Analyzing** (a) Why did townspeople support a strong, centralized government? (b) Which areas in Europe developed strong central governments headed by monarchies? (c) Which did not? Explain.

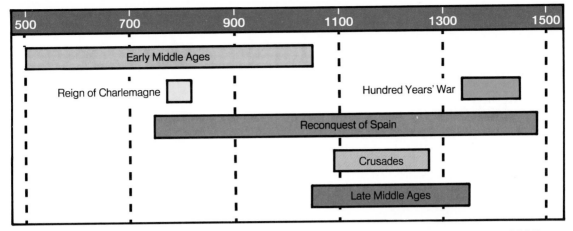

TIME LINE STUDY

Which of the following events on the time line occurred during the early Middle Ages: the crusades, the reign of Charlemagne, the Hundred Years' War? Which event spanned both the early and late Middle Ages?

MAP STUDY

After the fall of the Western Roman Empire, a number of Germanic kingdoms existed in Western Europe. Compare this map with the map at left. Which Germanic kingdoms existed in Spain about 500? In England?

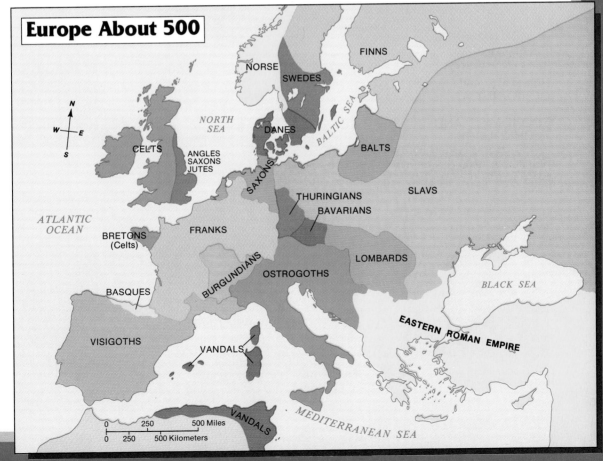

Europe About 500

GOLDEN AGES OUTSIDE WESTERN EUROPE

Porcelain figures manufactured during the T'ang dynasty in China.

Christian themes were important in Byzantine art. This medal from the 1100s shows Saint George.

	500	700	900	1100
POLITICS AND GOVERNMENT	**529** Justinian's Code summarizes Roman law		**800** Ghana rises to power in Africa	**960** Sung restore order in China
ECONOMICS AND TECHNOLOGY			**800s** Gold–salt trade grows in West Africa	**1000s** Avicenna writes medical books
SOCIETY AND CULTURE		**622** Muhammad journeys to Medina	**800s** Cyril and Methodius create Slavic alphabet	**1050** Movable type developed in China

630 When Muhammad returned to Mecca from the hejira, he destroyed idols in the Kaaba.

Golden figures such as this one reveal the skill of African artists and the wealth of early African kingdoms.

UNIT OUTLINE

Muslim mosques such as this one from Persia were decorated with elaborate designs.

Samurai warriors developed a code of chivalry in feudal Japan.

1100	1300	1500	1700
1206 Muslims set up Delhi sultanate in India	**1450** Inca create empire in the Andes	**1603** Tokugawa shogun unites Japan	
	1405 Chinese begin trading expeditions	**1543** Portuguese trading ships first arrive in Japan	
	1325 Aztec build capital of Tenochtitlán	**1632** Muslim ruler of India starts building of Taj Mahal	

Hindu traditions, reflected in this painting, remained strong in India even after the Muslim conquest.

Red grasshopper carved by an Aztec artist.

221

Byzantine and Islamic Civilizations

11

(330–1453)

CHAPTER OUTLINE

1 The Byzantine Empire
2 Eastern Europe: Heir to Byzantine Civilization
3 Emergence of Islam
4 Islamic Civilization

This majestic mosaic reflects the splendor of the Byzantine court of the emperor Justinian and his wife Theodora. Strong-willed and ambitious, Theodora was a powerful force in Byzantine politics.

Benjamin of Tudela was a much-traveled man of the world. But never had he seen anything like Constantinople. Its busy commerce, splendid palaces, and richly dressed nobles dazzled him.

"Great stir and bustle prevails at Constantinople," he noted in his journal, "because of the many merchants who travel there, both by land and by sea, from all parts of the world for purposes of trade." He was amazed at the riches of the emperor's palace. "The pillars and walls are covered with pure gold," he exclaimed. "The throne in this palace is of gold and is decorated with precious stones."

To a visitor like Benjamin of Tudela, who knew only the struggling cities of Western Europe, Constantinople was certainly overwhelming. Its fabulous wealth, he realized, came from "the tribute which is brought here every year from all parts of Greece, consisting of silks, purple cloths, and gold."

In fact, Constantinople was the richest city in Europe in the 1100s, when Benjamin of Tudela visited it. In 330, you will recall, Constantine had moved the capital of the Roman Empire to the Greek town of Byzantium, which was soon renamed Constantinople. When the empire was divided in 395, Constantinople became the capital of the Eastern Roman Empire. Unlike the Western Roman Empire, which was overwhelmed by invaders in the fifth century, the Eastern Roman Empire survived until 1453. It, too, faced constant attacks. However, because it was richer and better governed, it was able to fight off the fiercest challenges.

The Eastern Roman Empire was called the Byzantine Empire from the original name of the Greek town. During the Middle Ages, when Western Europe was divided among many small, weak states, the Byzantine Empire flourished. For centuries, it absorbed the shock waves of invasions from farther east and shielded Western Europe from these invaders. Eventually, Byzantine civilization passed on its heritage to the people of Eastern Europe.

In the 600s, a new religion, Islam, took root in the Middle East. Islam spread rapidly to many parts of the world, and armies of its believers chipped away at the Byzantine Empire. Islam gave birth to a new civilization that built on many ancient traditions. ■

1 The Byzantine Empire

READ TO UNDERSTAND

☐ How the Byzantine Empire survived for more than 1,000 years.

☐ Why a split occurred within the Christian Church.

☐ What achievements Byzantine civilization passed on to other peoples.

☐ *Vocabulary:* patriarch.

If you had sailed into Constantinople in the Middle Ages, you would have seen that the city was shaped like a triangle. Land lies on the western side. On the two other sides are water. To the south is the Bosporus, the strait that separates Europe from Asia Minor. To the north is the Golden Horn, an inlet of the Bosporus.

If you had come overland from Italy, you would have entered the city through the Golden Gate arch in a huge wall built by Constantine to protect the city from attack. You would have been jostled in the crowds entering and leaving the city. Someone might have shown you the building that housed the great milestone, the point from which all distances in the empire were measured. A dozen sights would have greeted you at once—the hippodrome, where horse races were held; the Church of Santa Sophia; statues of emperors; and glistening public baths.

The Byzantine Empire, with its capital at Constantinople, dominated the eastern Mediterranean at a time when medieval civilization was developing in Western Europe. Although both the Byzantine Empire and Western Europe inherited Roman traditions, each developed its own distinct civilization.

THE BYZANTINE SECRET: GREEK FIRE From tubes mounted on the bow of their vessel, Byzantine sailors unleash a deadly weapon against their opponents— Greek fire. To this day, no one knows for sure how the Byzantines made the deadly mixture although it probably contained petroleum, sulfur, and pitch. In this recreation, artist Hal Stone portrays the fury of Greek fire in a sea battle outside the walls of Constantinople.

Building and Defending the Empire

Justinian, who ruled the Byzantine Empire from 527 to 565, came close to restoring a united Roman Empire. He spent most of his reign fighting to recover the western parts of the Roman Empire from Germanic invaders. His armies defeated the Vandals and seized southern Spain. They also won control of parts of northern Africa. In a long and costly war, the Byzantines retook the Italian peninsula from the Ostrogoths. (See the map on page 225.) But these victories were short-lived. Within a few years after Justinian's death, the Lombards drove the Byzantines out of Italy.

Byzantine armies had also been busy closer to Constantinople. Before Justinian's time, they had held off Hun attackers from Asia. Later the armies fought off Slavs, Bulgars, and Magyars, who swept out of Eastern Europe. And for centuries, the Byzantine Empire was locked in a grim struggle with the Persian Empire. Then, in the 600s, the armies of Islam attacked. They reached the walls of Constantinople before being driven back.

To survive, Byzantine emperors became skillful diplomats. A network of spies fed them information. Byzantine rulers acquired a reputation for intrigue because they often played one enemy off against another. Like rulers in Western Europe, they sometimes bought peace by marrying their daughters to possible rivals. When all else failed, they depended on military strength.

Strengths of the Empire

The Byzantine Empire lasted over 1,000 years, from 395 to 1453. During this time, the will of the emperors was law. An efficient civil service administered the daily business of government. A loyal, well-trained army and a strong economy helped the empire survive periods of civil war and invasion.

The emperor had complete control over the economy. He set wages and prices and established a monopoly, or sole control, over manufacturing. For example, in the sixth century, silkworms were smuggled out of China and brought to Constantinople. The emperor made the manufacture of silk a state monopoly. The industry thrived, and its profits helped fill the empire's treasury. The emperor also benefited from taxes on trade.

At a time when trade was at a near standstill in Western Europe, the towns and cities of the Byzantine Empire prospered. Byzantine coins were accepted as the most stable currency in the Mediterranean world. Merchants from the Middle East and Viking traders from the north brought goods to the busy markets of cities such as Constantinople.

Constantinople itself was a center of world commerce. The city, which had about one million people, reflected extremes of rich and poor. The officials and nobles of the court spent huge sums on clothing, jewelry, and entertainment. But the masses of men and women struggled for survival. Riots were common. On occasion, rioters tried to overthrow the emperor.

A Split Between East and West

Religious disputes and economic competition strained relations between the Byzantine Empire and Western Europe. The Byzantine emperor did not recognize the pope as leader of the Christian Church. The emperor was head

MAP STUDY *The Byzantine Empire, which reached its greatest size under Justinian, was constantly threatened by invaders. Parts of the empire fell to the Lombards, the Persians, and other armies. Why did the location of Constantinople help it withstand attacks? What parts of the empire remained by 1000?*

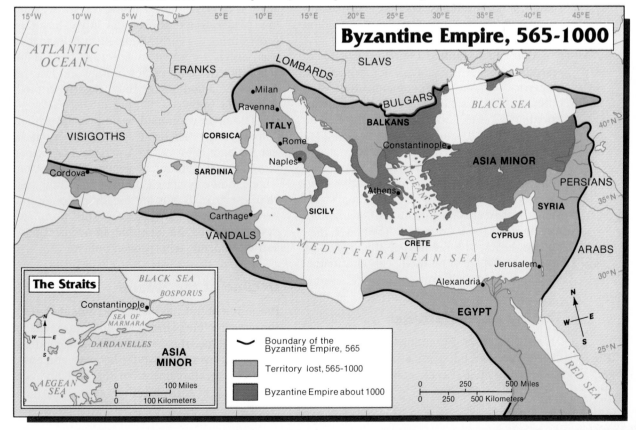

of the church in the empire as well as absolute ruler. Thus, the Church did not become a rival for political power in the Byzantine Empire, as it had in Western Europe.

In the Byzantine Empire, the clergy were considered state officials. As such, they were responsible to the emperor. The emperor appointed **patriarchs,** the bishops of the major cities. He also settled religious disputes and made decisions on matters of faith.

Religion was very important to Christians in both Western Europe and the Byzantine Empire. However, Christian churches in the two areas developed different practices and forms of worship. Greek rather than Latin was the language of the Church in the Byzantine Empire. Unlike clergy in Western Europe, Byzantine priests could marry. Furthermore, the Byzantine Church was tolerant of such non-Christian religions as Islam.

In the 700s, a bitter dispute arose between the emperor and the pope over the use of sacred images called icons. This conflict set the stage for a lasting split in the Christian Church. In an effort to reform the Church, one Byzantine emperor banned the worship of icons. However, the pope thought icons, picturing Christian saints, helped people understand Church teachings. Therefore, he excommunicated the emperor. The dispute raged on for years.

Although Byzantine churches eventually restored the use of icons, later popes and emperors regularly excommunicated each other. In 1054, a schism, or final split, left the Christian Church divided into the Roman Catholic Church and the Eastern Orthodox Church.

As trade revived in Western Europe, economic rivalry further strained relations between the two regions. In 1204, merchants from Venice bribed crusaders to attack Constantinople, their longtime trade rival. (See page 193.) For centuries, the Greeks of the Byzantine Empire kept alive bitter memories of Christian knights looting their city.

The Byzantine Heritage

At the center of Byzantine civilization was Constantinople. Its citizens brought together Roman, Christian, Greek, and Middle Eastern influences. This mixed heritage was evident in Byzantine art and architecture.

The Church of Santa Sophia built by the emperor Justinian reflected a blend of many traditions. It was designed on a grand scale like the monuments of ancient Rome. Beneath the huge domed roof was a magnificent interior. Elaborate mosaics pictured Christian stories. Byzantine artists copied ancient Greek and Roman styles when creating lifelike figures of saints. Middle Eastern styles were seen in the brilliant colors of the mosaics.

Byzantine emperors such as Justinian made significant contributions to civilization because they helped preserve the Greco-Roman heritage. They collected classical works on science, mathematics, and philosophy and stored them in libraries.

Preserving Roman Law

By preserving Roman traditions, the Byzantine Empire had a lasting impact on ideas about law and justice. At the height of his rule, Emperor Justinian ordered scholars to summarize all existing Roman law. They produced a huge work called Justinian's Code.

The code kept Roman legal traditions alive in the Byzantine Empire. It also became the chief source of Roman law in Western Europe. During the early Middle Ages, Roman law was largely forgotten in the west. But when scholars from universities in Italy and France visited Constantinople, they eagerly copied Justinian's Code.

The code contained basic principles that helped shape the legal systems of Western Europe and, later, of the Americas. For example, it listed rules of evidence: "The person who accuses someone must prove that the charge is true. This is not the obligation of the person denying the charge." This principle developed into the idea that an accused person is innocent until proven guilty.

Decline of the Empire

Pressures both from inside and outside led to the slow decline of the Byzantine Empire. As in ancient Rome, the empire was weakened by civil wars over who would become emperor. Outside threats came from the east and the

Byzantine architects created a monument of lasting beauty in the Church of Santa Sophia in Constantinople. Completed in 537, it shows a blend of eastern and western influences. The church is crowned by a huge dome, and its interior walls are decorated with glittering mosaics. Architects in Western Europe later copied Byzantine building techniques.

west. In the late 1000s, the Seljuk Turks conquered the Middle East, including Byzantine lands in Asia Minor. As you have read, Christian crusaders attacked Constantinople in 1204. The empire recovered from both attacks, but it then faced a new threat in Asia Minor when the Ottoman Turks came to power there.

The Ottomans built a strong state with disciplined, able officials and then expanded westward. In the 1400s, they bypassed the city of Constantinople and advanced into the Balkans. The Byzantine emperor appealed to rulers in Western Europe for help but received none. In 1453, the Ottomans took Constantinople. They changed its name to Istanbul and made it the capital of the Ottoman Empire. You will read more about the Ottoman Empire in Chapter 16.

The fall of Constantinople signaled the end of the Byzantine Empire. However, Byzantine traditions continued to influence Western Europe and Eastern Europe.

SECTION 1 REVIEW

1. **Locate:** (a) Constantinople, (b) Bosporus, (c) Balkans.

2. **Identify:** (a) Justinian, (b) Eastern Orthodox Church, (c) Justinian's Code, (d) Ottoman Turks.

3. **Define:** patriarch.

4. List the areas Justinian added to the Byzantine Empire.

5. Describe two factors that strained relations between the Byzantine Empire and Western Europe.

6. How did the Byzantine Empire preserve the Greco-Roman heritage?

7. **Critical Thinking** How did a strong economy help the Byzantine Empire survive?

227

2 Eastern Europe: Heir to Byzantine Civilization

READGTO UNDERSTAND

☐ How Byzantine civilization influenced Eastern Europe.

☐ How Mongol rule affected Russia.

☐ How the princes of Moscow came to dominate Russia.

☐ *Vocabulary:* Cyrillic alphabet, czar, boyar.

"Two Romes have fallen, and the third stands, and a fourth there shall not be." A Russian monk wrote these words in the early 1500s. The first two Romes he referred to were Rome itself and Constantinople. The third Rome was Moscow, which claimed to be the heir of Constantinople after it fell in 1453.

During the centuries of its greatness, the Byzantine Empire influenced the Slavic peoples of Eastern Europe, including the Russians. Much of its influence came through efforts of Byzantine missionaries who converted the Slavs to Christianity.

GEOGRAPHIC SETTING
The Land and Peoples of Eastern Europe

Eastern Europe stretches from the Ural Mountains in the east to the borders of present-day West Germany, Austria, and Italy in the west. It includes the lands lying between the Baltic Sea and the Arctic Ocean in the north and the Mediterranean, Black, and Caspian seas in the south.

Much of this huge area consists of flat plains that offer no protection from the many attackers who have invaded it over the centuries. Through the area flow a number of broad rivers, including the Danube, the Dnieper, and the Don. These rivers have served as major transportation routes. In the southwest of the region lies the Balkan Peninsula, a mountainous region with a long history of fighting among the peoples who have lived there. (See page 867.)

Much of Eastern Europe is populated by Slavic peoples. The Slavs were an Indo-European people who lived in the region around Kiev in the Ukraine in southern Russia. Between 200 A.D. and 400 A.D. some Slavs migrated from Kiev into the Balkans. They settled in what is today Yugoslavia and Bulgaria. Others moved farther west into Poland and Czechoslovakia. ■

The Slavs organized states in Eastern Europe similar to those set up by the Germanic peoples in Western Europe. The Slavs who settled in the Balkans were influenced by the advanced Byzantine civilization. In the ninth century, Cyril and Methodius, two Greek monks, converted many Slavs to Christianity. For their work, they became known as "Apostles to the Slavs."

Cyril and Methodius were successful in part because they spoke the Slavic language. The Slavs had no written language, so the monks devised an alphabet. They used mostly Greek letters, but they also included some Hebrew letters. The Slavic alphabet is called the **Cyrillic alphabet** (suh RIHL ihk) after Cyril. With the new alphabet, people could translate the Bible and other Christian works into Slavic languages.

Kievan Russia

In the 800s and 900s, the city of Kiev emerged as the center of a prosperous Slavic state, known as Kievan Russia. Byzantine civilization had a great impact on the culture of Kievan Russia. Kiev was linked to Constantinople by the Dnieper (NEE puhr) River, which flows into the Black Sea. Kiev became known as the "mother of Russian cities," in part because of its flourishing trade.

Russians first converted to Christianity because of their contacts with the Byzantines. In 988, Prince Vladimir of Kiev ordered the Russians to abandon the old Slavic gods in favor of Byzantine Christianity.

Vladimir actually had several reasons for accepting the Byzantine Church. For one thing, Kiev had extensive contacts with Constantinople. Vladimir was very impressed with reports of the magnificent Byzantine churches. His envoys had exclaimed, "We knew not whether we were in heaven or on earth, for on earth there is no such splendor or beauty." In addition, the Byzantine Church would allow the

Slavs to use their own language in Church services unlike the Roman Church, which insisted on Latin. Finally, in the Byzantine Church, the secular ruler, not the pope, headed the Church. Thus, Vladimir would be spiritual leader as well as political leader.

After they converted to Byzantine Christianity, Russians came into even closer contact with Byzantine culture. The princes who ruled the towns and cities of Kievan Russia imitated Byzantine emperors. The prince of Kiev built his own Church of Saint Sophia, a splendid cathedral that reflected the Byzantine style of architecture. In time, the Kievan Russians also developed their own styles of architecture, including the onion-shaped domes that appear on many churches in Eastern Europe.

The Christian clergy, many of whom came from the Byzantine Empire, became an important class in Kievan society. They set up schools, taught the Cyrillic alphabet, and introduced Byzantine culture.

After about 1050, Kievan Russia declined because of civil wars among the ruling princes. In the 1200s, the Russian cities were too weak to withstand the fierce Mongol armies that burst out of central Asia.

Mongol Invasions

The Mongols were originally nomadic herders. In the 1200s, they conquered an empire extending from China to Eastern Europe. (You will read about Mongol rulers in India and China in Chapter 13.) In 1240, one group of Mongols captured and destroyed Kiev. They killed or enslaved most of its people. The "Golden Horde," as the invaders were called, ruled Russia for nearly 250 years.

The Mongols forced the Russians to pay heavy tribute. As long as the Russians paid their tribute, the Mongols did not interfere in daily life. However, Mongol rule affected Russian life in many ways. Some Russian princes adopted the manners and practices of Mongol rulers. Furthermore, taxes to raise the tribute were a hardship for peasants, who sometimes revolted. Local princes quickly crushed such revolts.

Most important, Mongol rule cut Russia off from contacts with Western Europe. Commerce and industry, which had prospered in early Kievan Russia, largely disappeared. Between 1240 and the 1500s, Russians were scarcely aware of the ideas that were shaping the civilization of Western Europe.

Princes of Moscow

In the 1300s, the princes of Moscow, a city in northern Russia, gained power at the same time as Mongol strength was declining. They grew rich by keeping part of the tribute collected for the Mongols. Before long, a prince of Moscow took the title "Grand Prince of All Russia." He then persuaded the Russian Orthodox Church to move its center from Kiev to Moscow.

During the 1400s, Moscow became the center of a unified Russian state. Ivan III, a

Greek monks carried Christianity to the peoples of Eastern Europe and Russia. When Slavic artists created religious works of art, they often imitated Byzantine styles. This icon from Eastern Europe shows St. Dimiter slaying a dragon. Byzantine influence is evident in the frozen positions of the figures as well as in the domed building and gold background.

prince of Moscow who ruled from 1462 to 1505, has been called the founder of modern Russia. In 1480, Ivan announced that he would no longer pay any tribute to the Mongols. He made alliances with other Russian princes and finally ended Mongol rule. Ivan III also expelled German nobles from the lands they had seized in western Russia.

Ivan established a strong government that reflected Byzantine traditions. He married the niece of the last Byzantine emperor and took the title **czar,** the Russian word for Caesar.

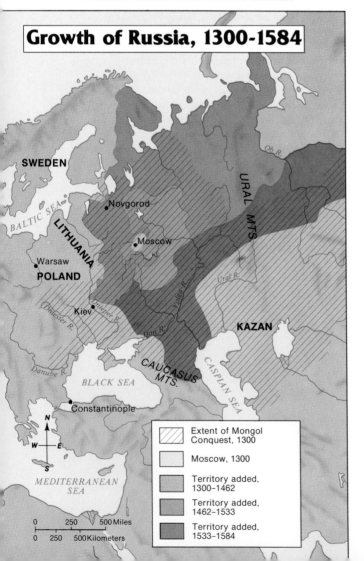

| MAP STUDY | *The princes of Moscow gradually took control of a* |

great deal of territory. By 1584, Ivan IV ruled a large Russian state. However, Russian power and foreign trade were limited by the location of Russia. What geographical factors limited Russian contact with western nations?

Growth of Russia, 1300-1584

SWEDEN

Novgorod

BALTIC SEA

LITHUANIA

Moscow

Warsaw

POLAND

URAL MTS.

Ob. R.

Kiev

Dniester R.

Dnieper R.

Volga R.

Ural R.

Don R.

KAZAN

Danube R.

CAUCASUS MTS.

BLACK SEA

CASPIAN SEA

Constantinople

N W E S

MEDITERRANEAN SEA

	Extent of Mongol Conquest, 1300
	Moscow, 1300
	Territory added, 1300–1462
	Territory added, 1462–1533
	Territory added, 1533–1584

0   250   500 Miles
0   250   500 Kilometers

Ivan looked on Moscow as the "third Rome," heir to ancient Rome and Constantinople. Russian czars adopted the double-headed eagle, symbol of Byzantine emperors, as their own symbol. Like Byzantine rulers, the czars gained absolute power over both the government and the Church.

Ivan IV, who ruled from 1533 to 1584, exercised this absolute power ruthlessly. He claimed his power came directly from God and had hundreds of **boyars,** powerful nobles, killed because they opposed his will. Ivan created a secret police force that brutally enforced his wishes. He was called Ivan the Terrible because of his cruelty and madness.

In the 1500s, Russian rulers renewed their contacts with Western Europe. Yet Russia continued to develop differently from Western European nations. A form of feudalism evolved in Russia just when feudalism was declining in Western Europe. Ivan IV gave fiefs to nobles who agreed to perform military service. But he kept strict control over the nobles. He also issued laws that tied peasants to the land. Thus, many Russian peasants lost their freedom and became serfs at a time when serfs were winning their freedom in Western Europe.

SECTION 2 REVIEW

1. **Locate:** (a) Ural Mountains, (b) Baltic Sea, (c) Kiev, (d) Dnieper River, (e) Moscow.

2. **Identify:** (a) Golden Horde, (b) Ivan III, (c) Ivan IV.

3. **Define:** (a) Cyrillic alphabet, (b) czar, (c) boyar.

4. What factor helped Cyril and Methodius convert the Slavs to Christianity?

5. What was the major effect of the Mongol invasion of Russia?

6. Explain how the princes of Moscow made Moscow the center of a unified Russia.

7. **Critical Thinking** Why did the move of the center of the Russian Orthodox Church from Kiev to Moscow increase the power of the princes of Moscow?

3 Emergence of Islam

READ TO UNDERSTAND

☐ **How Muhammad founded the religion of Islam.**

☐ **What the beliefs of Muslims are.**

☐ **Why Islam spread so rapidly.**

☐ *Vocabulary:* **hejira, mosque, caliph.**

The 4,000 riders raised clouds of dust for miles around. The Arab army followed the much-worn path of Alexander the Great and other conquerors southward along the coast of Palestine into Egypt. Outside of Cairo, they halted. Inside the city walls, the Byzantines had a garrison of 50,000 soldiers.

The Arab general Amr-ibn-al-As had no siege machines, no ships, and no source of new recruits. But he was confident of victory. Within a year, Amr could send the news: "Allahua akbar" ("God is most great"). Cairo, one of the greatest cities of the Byzantine Empire, had fallen.

Cairo was just one of many cities to fall to the armies of Islam during the 600s. The new religion of Islam had united the peoples of Arabia. Like Judaism and Christianity, Islam had a profound impact on history. Within 100 years after it was founded, its followers, known as Muslims, had built an empire that was larger than the Roman Empire at its height.

GEOGRAPHIC SETTING
Arabia

Arabia, the birthplace of Islam, is the largest peninsula in the world. It is a hilly, arid land dotted with occasional oases—fertile areas with enough water to support trees and plants. As great civilizations rose and fell in the Fertile Crescent to the north, the Arabs developed a way of life well adapted to the desert conditions of their homeland.

Most Arabs were nomads who herded goats and camels. They were loosely organized into tribes with strong codes of honor. Their poets praised the fierce independence of their warriors. Yet this independence led to frequent feuds that prevented unity among the different Arab tribes.

Arabia was a vital link that connected the Mediterranean world, Asia, and the east coast of Africa. Some Arabs, who lived in towns along the Red Sea, traded with the Greco-Roman world as well as with India, China, and Africa.

Mecca, a town near the Red Sea, prospered as a trading and religious center. Pilgrims traveled to Mecca to worship at the Kaaba, a sacred shrine that housed images of all the Arab gods. The Kaaba also housed a black stone—probably a meteorite—that the Arabs believed was sent from heaven. ■

Muhammad: Founder of Islam

Muhammad was born in Mecca about 570. His parents died when he was still a child, and he was raised by relatives who belonged to a poor but prominent Arab family. Little else is known about Muhammad's early life.

At age 25, Muhammad married Khadija (kah DEE jah), a wealthy widow who ran her late husband's business. With Khadija's help, Muhammad became a successful merchant. Yet he was troubled by the violence and treachery he saw in the world. He often went into the desert to pray. When he prayed, Muhammad believed that the angel Gabriel spoke to him, saying that God had chosen Muhammad as his prophet. Muhammad's duty, said the angel, was to proclaim that Allah, or God, was the one and only God.

At first, only Khadija and a few friends believed Muhammad. The merchants and inn-keepers of Mecca opposed him. They thought that his teaching about one God would destroy their income from Arab pilgrims. Threatened with death, Muhammad and his followers fled Mecca in 622. They were welcomed at Yathrib, a rival commercial town on the Red Sea. Yathrib, later renamed Medina, became known as the City of the Prophet.

Muslims call Muhammad's journey from Mecca to Medina the **hejira** (hih JĪ ruh), or departure. The year 622 was made the first year of the Muslim calendar. The hejira marked a turning point in Muhammad's life. In Medina, he gained power as both a religious and political leader.

In 630, Muhammad returned to Mecca at the head of an army and captured the city. He went directly to the Kaaba, where he proclaimed, "There is but one God, and Allah is his name." He then destroyed the hundreds of idols inside the Kaaba. Muhammad left the Black Stone untouched because he believed it had come from God. Thus Arabs continued to make pilgrimages to Mecca, which remained the holy city it had been in the past. Before Muhammad died in 632, he worked to unite the Arabs. After his death, his followers carried the message of Islam in many directions.

Teachings of Islam

The word Islam means "submission." Muslims believe that they must submit their will to God. The Five Pillars of Islam refer to the essential duties of every faithful Muslim. First, and most important, is the belief in one God. The Muslim call to prayer repeats this basic belief: "There is no God but Allah, and Muhammad is the prophet of God." Muslims do not worship Muhammad as a god. To them, he is a human who was the messenger of God.

The second duty is prayer. Five times a day, faithful Muslims turn to face the holy city of Mecca and pray. Islam teaches concern for the poor, so giving alms, an act of charity, is the third duty. The fourth duty is fasting during the holy month of Ramadan (RAM uh DAHN). Finally, all Muslims are supposed to make a pilgrimage to Mecca at least once in their lives. The act of worshipping together at the Kaaba has helped to unify Muslims from all over the world.

Islam has no formal church or clergy. All worshippers are considered equal. They may pray alone or assemble at a **mosque,** the Muslim meeting place. At the mosque, an imam (ih MAHM) leads the worshippers in prayer.

The Koran. Muslims rely on the Koran, their holy book, for guidance in all matters. They believe the Koran contains the word of God as it was revealed to his prophet Muhammad. "Let the Koran always be your guide," said Muhammad. "Do what it commands, shun what it forbids." The Koran became the basis for government and law throughout the Islamic world.

The Koran was written in Arabic. As a result, Arabic became the universal language of Muslims from many different cultures. It continues to be used for religious purposes even among Muslims who are not Arabs.

People of the Book. Muhammad accepted the Old and New Testaments as God's word. He called Jews and Christians "People of the Book" because they believed in God's revelations in the Bible. Muslims recognized a close relationship with the People of the Book and protected Jews and Christians—in theory if not always in practice.

Some teachings of Islam are similar to those of Judaism and Christianity. Muslims share the belief in one God. Like Jews and Christians, Muslims believe in a last judgment day, when people will be rewarded or punished, depending on how they conducted their lives. They also believe that Abraham, Moses, and Jesus were great prophets. But Muhammad, as God's final messenger, has the highest authority.

Like other influential teachers and philosophers, Muhammad established rules for ethical behavior. Individuals, he said, are responsible for their own actions. They should behave with charity, humility, and mercy.

The Status of Women Under Islam

The Koran gave women a legal and economic status they had not previously enjoyed in Arabia. Before Muhammad, Arab women had no property rights. They were entirely at the mercy of their fathers or husbands. Islamic law gave women the right to inherit and control property. Although the Koran permitted a man to divorce his wife, he was required to return her dowry, that is, the property she had brought to their marriage. In addition, the Koran strictly forbade the killing of unwanted baby girls, a common practice in many ancient societies.

In early Islamic society, women enjoyed considerable freedom. Women artists, physicians, and religious scholars had influence in society and government. However, gradually, restrictions were placed on them. Women were excluded from public places and were secluded within the home. Yet a woman was always protected. If she was divorced, her family took care of her. If her husband died, her sons looked after her. An unmarried woman could rely on her father or brothers to protect her.

A woman's duties were to obey her husband, care for the children, and manage the household. As head of the household, the man enjoyed complete authority. But within her home, a woman could, and often did, exercise considerable influence.

Expansion of Islam

Between 622 and 732, Islam spread with amazing speed. The Arabs carried their religion to the peoples of Palestine and Syria and across North Africa into Spain. By 732, Muslim forces had crossed the Pyrenees Mountains and advanced into France, until they were stopped by Charles Martel at the Battle of Tours. (See page 162.) Just as swiftly, Islam won converts from the Fertile Crescent east to the Indus Valley. (See the map below.)

There were many reasons for the rapid spread of Islam. Its message was clear and simple. Muslims believed in one God and the equality of all believers. They did not need a church or clergy in order to practice their faith. Furthermore, Muhammad and his successors united the Arabs for the first time and gave them a strong sense of purpose—to spread the message of Islam. Inspired by loyalty to Islam, Arab soldiers believed that if they died fighting for the faith they would immediately enter paradise.

The weakness of the neighboring Byzantine and Persian empires also contributed to the success of Islam. Centuries of warfare had exhausted these empires. Many people were dissatisfied with Byzantine or Persian rule, and they did not fight the Arabs forcefully. Some people welcomed the armies of Islam as liberators. Islam brought stable, orderly gov-

MAP STUDY *Islam spread rapidly in the century after the death of Muhammad. By 750, Muslims controlled much of the trade of the Mediterranean world. Under which caliphs did Islam reach the limits of its expansion? In what years?*

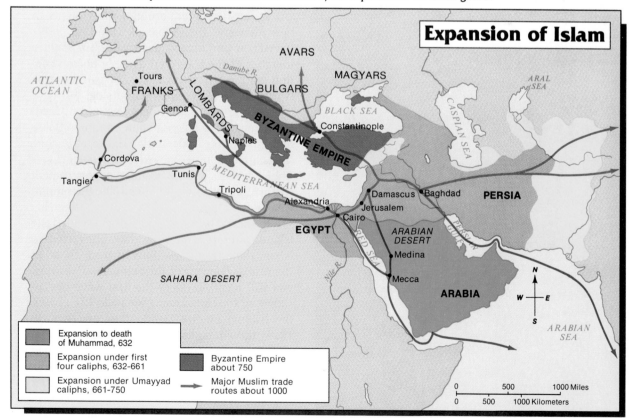

ernment in place of the corruption that existed in many places.

When Muslim armies conquered parts of the Byzantine Empire, some Christians, Jews, and Zoroastrians were ready to accept the teachings of Islam. Yet Muslims did not force people to convert. They required non-Muslims to pay a special tax, but otherwise non-Muslims could worship as they chose. In fact, Muslim conquerors often were not anxious to convert people because this would lower tax revenues.

Ruling an Empire

When Muhammad died, he left no heir to lead Islam. A close friend, Abu Bakr, was elected **caliph** (KAY lihf), or successor to the prophet.

Hard at work in an arms workshop, these skilled artisans are engaged in various stages of producing swords. Swords made in Damascus were famous for their strength and beauty. To produce Damascus swords, artisans braided strands of steel, creating patterned designs.

The caliph acted as both religious and political leader. He used the law of the Koran as the basis for ruling the empire.

Power struggles surrounded the elections of the first four caliphs. Then, in 661, a leading family of Mecca established the Umayyad (oo MĪ ad) dynasty. For a century, the Umayyads presided over the expansion of Islam. The Umayyad dynasty made Damascus in Syria the capital of the Islamic Empire. But Mecca remained the spiritual center of Islam. Under the Umayyads, the Arabs absorbed ideas from Hellenistic and Byzantine civilizations.

Despite the successes of the Umayyad armies, problems appeared within the Islamic Empire. Some of the people who had been absorbed into the empire began to assert their independence. In addition, two competing branches developed within Islam, the Sunnite (SOON īt) and Shiite (SHEE īt).

The two branches differed over who was the rightful successor to Muhammad. The more numerous Sunnites supported the Umayyad caliph. The Shiites were loyal to a religious leader who traced his family back to Ali, Muhammad's son-in-law. Shiite groups often rallied support among people who were discontented with the rulers in power.

In 750, discontent erupted into violence. A new dynasty, the Abbasids (uh BAS ihds), overthrew the Umayyads. However, in Spain, a member of the Umayyad dynasty became caliph and ruled outside of Abbasid control. North Africa also remained outside.

The early Abbasid rulers were strong leaders. They built a splendid new capital in Baghdad. In the late 700s, under Harun al-Rashid, the Islamic Empire enjoyed a golden age. Later Abbasid rulers left the business of government to corrupt officials, and after 1000, the empire weakened.

In the 1000s, the Seljuk Turks invaded the Islamic Empire. Although they converted to Islam, their traditions differed from those of the Arabs. The rule of the Seljuks in Palestine, you will recall, brought the first wave of crusaders to the Holy Land. (See page 191.) Later, the Islamic Empire faced other invaders. In 1258, the Mongols destroyed Baghdad and ended Abbasid rule. Eventually, the Ottoman Turks reunited Egypt, Syria, Iraq, and Arabia into an Islamic state that lasted until 1918.

1. **Locate:** (a) Arabia, (b) Mecca, (c) Medina, (d) Damascus, (e) Baghdad.

2. **Identify:** (a) Kaaba, (b) Muhammad, (c) Koran, (d) People of the Book, (e) Sunnite, (f) Shiite.

3. **Define:** (a) hejira, (b) mosque, (c) caliph.

4. Describe the Five Pillars of Islam.

5. List two reasons for the rapid spread of Islam.

6. **Critical Thinking** Compare and contrast the Islamic Empire's treatment of people it conquered with the Roman Empire's treatment of conquered peoples.

4 Islamic Civilization

READ TO UNDERSTAND

☐ **Why the Islamic world prospered in the Middle Ages.**

☐ **What Muslims contributed to science.**

☐ **What achievements the Muslims made in the arts and literature.**

☐ *Vocabulary:* minaret.

The people of Baghdad were used to seeing great riches and magnificent ceremonies. But nothing they had ever seen could rival the wedding of the caliph al-Mamun to Buran, daughter of his chief minister. A thousand matched pearls were showered on the couple as they stood on a gold mat encrusted with pearls and sapphires. Princes and other special guests received scented balls, each of which contained the name of an estate, a slave, or some other gift. The record of this wedding has lived on in Arabic literature.

Islamic civilization was more than fabulous wealth, however. It drew on the rich heritages of Greek, Roman, Byzantine, Persian, and Indian cultures. Muslims blended these traditions to create their own distinct civilization.

Muslims also played a role in shaping civilization in Western Europe because they passed along many ideas to the peoples of Europe.

A Prosperous Economy

From its center in the Middle East, the Islamic Empire commanded the trade routes of the world. Muslim merchants traded products from three continents—Africa, Asia, and Europe. During much of the Middle Ages, Muslim fleets patrolled the Mediterranean.

Cities and commerce thrived in the Islamic world at a time when most people in Western Europe lived on small, isolated manors. The spectacular wealth and luxury of cities such as Baghdad were unknown in Western Europe. The Abbasid capital boasted hospitals, libraries, palaces, public gardens, and even street lighting.

The Arabs developed commercial practices that made trade easier. They introduced the use of letters of credit in place of cash. They also issued receipts for payment and bills of lading that listed all goods in a shipment. Merchants in Western Europe later adopted these practices from the Arabs.

Within the Islamic Empire, manufacturing flourished. Steel used in swords and textiles such as cotton and satin were the most important products. In addition, improvements in farming helped farmers produce more food to feed large city populations.

Traditions of Learning

Islam brought new life to many fields of learning. Muhammad taught that "the ink of the scholar is holier than the blood of the martyr." Encouraged by this idea, scholars flocked to the centers of learning that grew up in the cities of the Islamic Empire.

The Koran was the focus of much Muslim scholarship. Legal experts wrote many texts in which they interpreted the Koran. Their writings became part of the Islamic law code. Islamic law, along with common religious beliefs and the use of Arabic, helped unite Muslims on three continents.

Yet Muslim scholars did not limit their studies to the Koran. They translated ancient Greek works on philosophy and science. At

235

A 16-year-old boy seems an unlikely physician, but Ibn Sina, later known to Europeans as Avicenna (AV ih SEHN uh), was a talented Persian doctor by that age. He treated Persian nobles and later served as chief minister and personal physician to rulers of Persia.

Avicenna was born in 980 near Bukkara, a center of Islamic culture in Persia. As a boy, he quickly learned the Koran and mastered geometry, law, and Arabic literature. Soon, he knew more than his teachers. When the Muslim ruler of Persia heard of young Avicenna's genius, he invited the boy to study in his library. There, Avicenna taught himself physics, theology, mathematics, astronomy, philosophy, and medicine.

His life at the Persian court was full of adventure. From time to time, he fell into official disfavor and was thrown into prison. Once, he escaped from prison disguised as a religious beggar. During his lifetime, he traveled widely in Persia practicing medicine. It was said that he studied wherever he was, even while on horseback or in prison.

Avicenna wrote over 100 books on subjects ranging from astronomy, music, and philosophy to medicine and poetry. His books on philosophy, which reflected the teachings of Aristotle and Plato, influenced Christian scholars in the late Middle Ages. His major work was the *Canon of Medicine,* a summary of what the Greeks, the Arabs, and Avicenna knew about the diagnosis and treatment of disease. The *Canon* was translated into Latin in the 1100s. It remained the leading medical textbook among Muslims and Christians for about 600 years.

Avicenna was also a dedicated medical researcher and pharmacist. He explained how disease could be spread by water from a polluted well or river. He studied over 750 medical remedies and published the first handbook that told physicians which remedies to use for different diseases.

1. What did Avicenna contribute to medical knowledge?

2. **Critical Thinking** How did Avicenna become an expert in so many different fields? Do you think someone today could do the same? Explain.

centers of learning such as the House of Wisdom in Baghdad, scholars studied Roman, Jewish, Persian, and Indian texts. In this way, the Arabs preserved much ancient learning.

Achievements in Medicine, Mathematics, and the Sciences

Muslim scholars made original contributions in medicine, mathematics, and other sciences. Guided by ancient Greek texts, Muslim doctors perfected techniques for diagnosing and treating diseases. In the 800s, Muhammad al-Razi (RAY zee), known to Europeans as Rhazes, published a huge medical encyclopedia that was used for many years in Western Europe. He was one of the first to describe the symptoms of such contagious diseases as smallpox and measles.

Muslims also set up an advanced system of medical training, which included a qualifying examination for doctors and pharmacists. Medical schools in Europe later drew on Muslim medical research and practices.

Muslim mathematicians studied the works of ancient scholars such as Euclid. As you have read, they also adopted the decimal system and the system of numerals from India. With the decimal system, Muslims made important advances in algebra and trigonometry.

In fact, the word "algebra" is based on an Arabic term.

Like the Greeks, Muslim scientists were interested in all aspects of the natural world. Geographers described their travels from China to Spain. In their search for ways to create precious metals, Muslims advanced the science of chemistry. They invented equipment such as beakers and crystallizing dishes still used in laboratories today.

Other Muslim scientists made significant discoveries. One scholar proposed that the earth was round and accurately estimated its circumference. He also suggested that the earth rotated on its axis. Muslims used the magnetic needle, invented by the Chinese, to produce the mariner's compass. The mariner's compass and the astrolabe, another Muslim invention, enabled sailors to find their position at sea. These inventions would have a great impact on European explorers, as you will read in Chapter 15.

The Arts and Literature

Muslims adapted ideas in architecture from the many peoples within the Islamic Empire. Mosques reflected a blend of Roman, Byzantine, and Persian styles. Graceful Roman arches were decorated with Persian designs. Columns supported domed roofs similar to those of Byzantine churches. Outside the mosque, architects designed slender towers called **minarets,** from which the people were called to prayer.

To Muslims, the Koran was the greatest written work in Arabic because they believed it was the revealed word of God. Muslim philosophers frequently wrote about religious questions. For example, the philosopher Averröes (uh VEHR oh EEZ), a Spanish Muslim, tried to reconcile the teachings of Aristotle with Islam. Through careful logic, he tried to prove that there was no conflict between faith and reason. His writings later influenced Christian thinkers such as Thomas Aquinas. (See page 190.)

Poets held an honored place in the Islamic world. Romantic themes often inspired poetry. In his long poem *The Rubaiyat,* the Persian poet Omar Khayyam wrote about nature and love. In another well-known work, *A Thousand*

Muslim astronomers studied the theories of Ptolemy and discovered that his theories did not fit their own findings. Through careful observation and new methods of calculation, they made important discoveries that influenced scientific thinking everywhere. The astronomers shown here are at work in the Istanbul Observatory.

and One Nights, Muslims collected stories from all over the world. These stories, which include "Aladdin and His Magic Lamp," have been translated into many languages.

SECTION 4 REVIEW

1. **Identify:** (a) Muhammad al-Razi, (b) Averröes, (c) Omar Khayyam.

2. **Define:** minaret.

3. (a) What commercial practices did the Arabs develop? (b) How did these practices improve trade?

4. How did the Arabs preserve much ancient learning?

5. Describe one contribution Muslims made to medicine.

6. **Critical Thinking** Why do you think Islamic civilization reflects a blend of traditions?

CHAPTER 11 REVIEW

Summary

1. During the Middle Ages, the Eastern Roman Empire continued to exist as the Byzantine Empire. The Byzantine Empire, which reached its greatest size under Justinian, preserved Greek learning and Roman law. A strong economy helped it withstand many enemies until it fell to the Ottoman Turks in 1453.

2. The Slavic peoples of Eastern Europe were heirs of the Byzantine Empire. Many Slavs, including those in Russia, converted to the Eastern Orthodox Church. In the 1200s, the Mongol invasions cut Russia off from Western Europe. Later, the princes of Moscow fought to expel the Mongols.

3. In 622, Muhammad founded the religion of Islam in Arabia. Muslims believe that there is only one God and that Muhammad is God's messenger. Islam spread rapidly. For centuries, caliphs presided over the rich and powerful Islamic Empire.

4. Muslims made important contributions in medicine, mathematics, science, and philosophy. Much of this knowledge slowly made its way into Western Europe.

Recalling Facts

Choose the word or phrase that best completes each of the following statements.

1. Constantinople was the capital of the (a) Holy Land; (b) Byzantine Empire; (c) Persian Empire.

2. The head of the Eastern Orthodox Church was the (a) pope; (b) emperor; (c) patriarch.

3. Cyril and Methodius converted many Slavs to Christianity because they (a) spoke the Slavic language; (b) ruled the Balkan peninsula; (c) were successful merchants.

4. The most important pillar of Islam is (a) giving alms; (b) prayer; (c) belief in one God.

5. Islamic law was based on (a) the Koran; (b) Justinian's Code; (c) the work of al-Razi.

Chapter Checkup

1. (a) Why was the Byzantine Empire able to survive for over 1,000 years? (b) Why did it eventually decline?

2. (a) Describe Justinian's law code. (b) How did it influence the people of Western Europe?

3. (a) How did Byzantine civilization influence Kievan Russia? (b) How did it influence the princes of Moscow such as Ivan III?

4. (a) Why did Muhammad become a prophet? (b) What ideas did Islam share with Judaism and Christianity?

5. (a) What effect did Islam have on the status of Arab women at first? (b) How did the status of women change?

6. (a) Why did many people welcome Muslim armies? (b) How did Muslims treat non-Muslims within the Islamic Empire?

7. How did Islamic civilization influence the peoples of Western Europe?

Critical Thinking

1. **Understanding the Roots of Democracy** (a) What important rule of evidence did Justinian's Code include? (b) How does this principle protect the rights of an individual? (c) What does American law say about the guilt or innocence of the accused?

2. **Analyzing** The Byzantine Empire and Western Europe shared the heritage of Rome. Yet during the Middle Ages, they drifted further apart. (a) What aspects of

the Roman heritage did they share? (b) What do you think was the main reason they drifted apart? Explain.

3. **Relating Past to Present** Islam has remained a powerful force in many parts of the world since the time of Muhammad. Describe how each of the following contributed to the unity of Islam: (a) Arabic language; (b) Koran; (c) Islamic law.

Developing Basic Skills

1. **Map Reading** One map can give you useful information about a specific place and historical period. By comparing maps, however, you can make generalizations about changes that took place in a particular region of the world. Compare the maps on pages 225 and 233. (a) What territories in Europe did Islam win from the Byzantine Empire? (b) What other lands did Islam win from the Byzantine Empire? (c) After 661, where would the armies of Islam and the Byzantine Empire be most likely to clash? (d) What areas of the Islamic Empire were probably influenced by Byzantine civilization?

2. **Making a Review Chart** Draw a large chart with five columns and five rows. Title the columns Hinduism, Buddhism, Judaism, Christianity, and Islam. Title the rows Founder, Original Location, Areas of Influence, Main Teachings, and Sacred Book. Use what you have learned about the five world religions discussed in Chapters 2, 6, 7, and 11 to complete the chart. Then answer these questions: (a) Which religion or religions were founded by a single leader? (b) Which religions began in the same area? (c) Which were monotheistic? (d) Which have teachings in common? Can you suggest reasons for this?

Writing About History

Writing a Summary

A summary is a short review of information you read in a source such as an article, a speech, or a book. A summary contains only the main ideas of your source. Finding the topic sentences of paragraphs is one way to pinpoint the main ideas. Another is to ask yourself these questions: *Who? What? When? Where? Why?* and *How?* Be careful to distinguish between main ideas and supporting details. After writing your summary, review the original source to make sure you have not left out anything important.

Practice: Choose a subsection of this chapter such as "Muhammad: Founder of Islam" and write a summary of it.

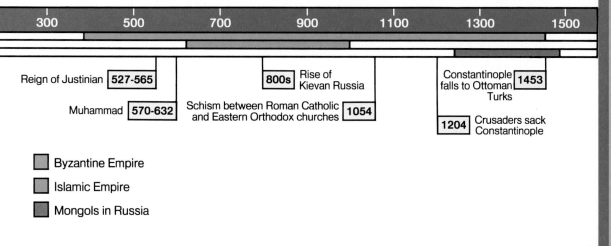

300   500   700   900   1100   1300   1500

Reign of Justinian 527-565

Muhammad 570-632

800s Rise of Kievan Russia

Schism between Roman Catholic and Eastern Orthodox churches 1054

Constantinople falls to Ottoman Turks 1453

1204 Crusaders sack Constantinople

Byzantine Empire
Islamic Empire
Mongols in Russia

239

Africa and the Americas

12

(3000 B.C.—1532 A.D.)

CHAPTER OUTLINE

1. Africa: The Land and Early Peoples
2. African Empires and Trading States
3. Patterns of Daily Life in Africa
4. The First Americans
5. Early Civilizations in the Americas

The intricate bronze work of Benin artisans reveals much about Benin civilization, which flourished in what is today southwestern Nigeria. This bronze plaque shows a king of Benin flanked by his attendants.

The stranger sat near the fire listening intently. The old men of the village had been talking for hours. Suddenly, the stranger leaped to his feet and jumped about as though he had been stung by a scorpion.

The stranger was Emil Torday, a European with a fascination for African history. In the early 1900s, he was visiting a Bushongo village in the forest lands of West Africa. He wanted to learn as much as possible about the Bushongo. Like many other African peoples, the Bushongo preserved their past through careful oral records. That evening, Torday heard the Bushongo leaders describe the 121 kings who had ruled their people. But when did any of these kings rule? That's what Torday had to find out if the history of the Bushongo was to be truly meaningful to his fellow Europeans. Torday kept hoping the elders would mention a date, any date.

"As the elders were talking of the great events of various reigns," Torday later recalled, "and we came to the 98th king, Bo Kama Bomanchala, they said that nothing remarkable had happened during his reign except that one day at noon the sun went out, and there was absolute darkness for a short time."

It was at this point that Torday jumped up, so excited that the elders thought he had gone mad. He was thrilled to have found a clue. Torday realized that the Bushongo were referring to an eclipse of the sun during the chief's reign. Later, he learned that there had been a total eclipse of the sun on March 13, 1680. Now Torday had the time frame he needed.

In many West African societies, specially trained men and women called griots preserved the oral traditions of their people. Griots memorized important events, as well as the names and deeds of rulers, going back for hundreds of years. Oral traditions were one way in which the peoples of Africa kept records of their achievements.

Advanced civilizations developed in both Africa and the Americas. The many different societies that emerged in Africa and the Americas were largely isolated from the European and Asian civilizations you have studied. Yet within each continent, societies often had contact with one another. Through these contacts, people learned about important advances in farming, science, and technology. ■

1 Africa: The Land and Early Peoples

READ TO UNDERSTAND

☐ **What climates and landforms are found in Africa.**

☐ **How geography has influenced cultures in different parts of Africa.**

☐ **How the agricultural revolution affected people in parts of Africa.**

☐ *Vocabulary:* **savanna.**

If you went to Africa today and tried to talk to people from all the different groups living there, you would have to learn more than 800 languages. Why? Africa is a huge continent, more than three times the size of the continental United States. Within Africa, different peoples have developed their own distinct patterns of civilization. The variety of African cultures is reflected in the 800 to 1,000 African languages identified by scholars.

As in other parts of the world, geography has helped shape the civilizations of Africa. The varied climates and landforms of Africa have contributed to the growth of many different traditions and civilizations.

GEOGRAPHIC SETTING
Africa

Most of Africa lies in the tropics, that is, the area between the Tropic of Cancer in the north and the Tropic of Capricorn in the south. As a result, much of the continent has warm temperatures. However, the amount of rainfall varies greatly. Four main climate zones stretch in belts across Africa: rain forest, savanna, desert, and Mediterranean. (See the map on page 242.)

Climate zones. The rain forest zone is located along the Equator, where the heaviest rainfall occurs. The ample moisture and warm

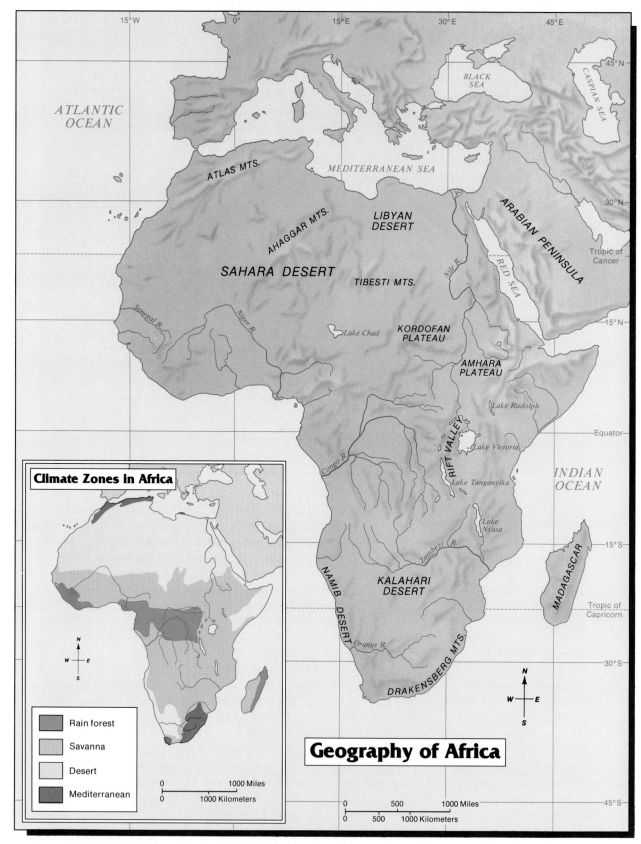

Geography of Africa

Climate Zones in Africa

- Rain forest
- Savanna
- Desert
- Mediterranean

0 — 1000 Miles
0 — 1000 Kilometers

0 — 500 — 1000 Miles
0 — 500 — 1000 Kilometers

MAP STUDY *Africa is a vast continent with varied climates and terrains, as these maps show. Which type of terrain occupies the largest territory? Where might most people live?*

temperatures of the zone support rich plant growth, including dense forests. About eight percent of Africa is covered by rain forests. Some farming is possible in the rain forest zone, but the heavy rains wash out soil nutrients and leave the land infertile.

The damp climate provides favorable conditions for disease-carrying insects. For example, certain mosquitoes are carriers of malaria and yellow fever. The tsetse fly carries sleeping sickness, which can infect both people and animals. Therefore, people living in the rain forest zone do not raise cattle or use animals for plowing or transportation. Today, sleeping sickness has been brought under control in many areas.

The second climate zone, the savanna, stretches across Africa north and south of the rain forests. **Savannas,** or grasslands dotted with trees, cover about half the continent. Rainfall can be unreliable in the savanna climate zone. On the average, enough rain falls to support farming and herding. But the amount of rainfall varies widely from one year to the next. As a result, severe floods or drought can destroy crops and herds.

Deserts make up a third climate zone, which covers 40 percent of Africa. Hardy grasses and shrubs grow in many African deserts. Some people who live in desert regions dig wells at oases and grow a few vegetable crops. Others are herders.

In the north is the giant Sahara Desert. Travel across the Sahara has always been difficult. However, even in ancient times, traders made their way across it. After 400 A.D., when the camel was introduced from Arabia, camel caravans carried goods on the long, dangerous journey across the Sahara. The Kalahari and Namib deserts in southern Africa are much drier than the Sahara. Only a few skilled hunters and food gatherers have been able to adjust to the harsh life there.

A mild Mediterranean climate zone lies at the northern and southern tips of Africa. In northern Africa, farmers grow crops similar to those in southern Europe. The people of northern Africa had frequent contact with other parts of the Mediterranean world. As you have read, Romans, and later Muslims, extended their empires across North Africa. But the southern tip of Africa was sparsely populated, and people there had almost no contact with outsiders until the 1500s.

Physical features. Much of Africa is a high plateau that drops sharply into narrow coastal plains. Rivers that begin in the interior drop steeply from the plateau through a series of cataracts, waterfalls, and rapids. These obstacles protected the interior from outsiders. However, the same rivers provided excellent transportation in the interior. The Nile, Niger, Congo, and Zambezi rivers have carved out wide valleys. Silt from seasonal floods renews the soil and makes the river valleys fertile farming regions.

Another distinctive feature of the African terrain is the Rift Valley in East Africa. The valley was formed by movements in the earth's crust in prehistoric times. The shifting earth pushed up highlands and mountains that tower above deep canyons. As a result, the region has a variety of climates. The peak of Mount Kilimanjaro is ice-capped, while the lowlands around its base are warm. ■

Early Peoples of Africa

In recent years, archaeologists have begun to excavate prehistoric sites in Africa. They have found what they believe is evidence of the earliest human life in East Africa. Yet archaeologists are still searching for evidence that might show a direct connection between the earliest humans and the Stone Age cultures that emerged thousands of years later.

During the Stone Age in Africa, as elsewhere, hunters and food gatherers followed herds of wild game and collected edible roots and berries. Between 8000 B.C. and 2000 B.C., Stone Age people in the Sahara left a painted record of their lives. They drew pictures of their cattle, sheep, and goat herds on rock cliffs. Some paintings showed scenes of women tending children. Others showed hunters stalking wild game.

The Sahara was covered with grasses and trees when these pictures were drawn. It had rivers and lakes filled with fish. However, the climate of the Sahara later grew drier, and Stone Age hunters migrated. Some probably settled in the Nile River valley, and others moved south into the river valleys of West Africa.

The Sahara was not always a desert, as it is today. When a Stone Age artist painted this scene on a cave wall, the region was a grassland, inhabited by herders who depended on grain and cattle for their livelihood. Since cattle were so important to their way of life, the artist took great care in drawing them.

When the agricultural revolution* began in Africa, some hunters and food gatherers gave up their nomadic way of life. Early farmers tamed animals and developed crops suited to the local climate. In the Nile Valley, for example, they grew wheat and barley. In West Africa, farmers planted sorghum and rice, which grew better in the savanna climate.

With the agricultural revolution, populations expanded, and people spread out across many regions of Africa. By 3000 B.C., the first African civilizations were taking shape in Egypt and in Nubia and Kush to the south.

---

* You will recall that an agricultural revolution occurred in parts of the world when Stone Age people changed from hunting and gathering to growing their own food. (See page 11.)

SECTION 1 REVIEW

1. **Locate:** (a) Sahara Desert, (b) Kalahari Desert, (c) Namib Desert, (d) Niger River, (e) Congo River, (f) Rift Valley.

2. **Define:** savanna.

3. Describe the four main climate zones of Africa.

4. What features of many African rivers protected the interior from outsiders?

5. **Critical Thinking** In which climate zones of Africa was the change from hunting and gathering to farming likely to be most successful? In which was it likely to be least successful? Explain.

2 African Empires and Trading States

READ TO UNDERSTAND

☐ How the kingdoms of Kush and Axum developed.

☐ How the gold-salt trade led to the growth of strong states in West Africa.

☐ Why city-states emerged in East Africa.

☐ What role Islam played in early Africa.

Between 3000 B.C. and 1600 A.D., powerful empires and trading states flourished in widely separated areas of Africa. These were very different societies, reflecting the diversity of African geography, peoples, and cultures.

The Kingdoms of Kush and Axum

At a bend in the upper Nile, the Kingdom of Kush developed at the same time as ancient Egypt. An active trade grew up between the two kingdoms. The merchants of Kush traded ivory, gold, ebony wood, and perfumes for products of Egypt and the Mediterranean world. They also traded extensively with people across the Indian Ocean. Kings and queens of Kush used riches from trade to build large walled palaces, a huge temple to the sun, and burial pyramids.

In 750 B.C., King Kasha of Kush led his armies north and conquered Egypt. For about 80 years, Kasha's successors ruled an empire stretching from the Mediterranean to what is today Ethiopia. They retreated back to the south when the Assyrians, who were armed with weapons made of iron, invaded Egypt. The value of iron was not lost on the people of Kush, and they soon learned how to make it. The plentiful supply of iron ore in Kush supported a large iron industry in the capital of Meröe (MEHR oh EE). Huge mounds of black slag, the waste product of iron making, still lie in the ruins of Meröe.

The use of iron began to spread across Africa about 500 B.C. Iron plows enabled farmers to increase food production. And people who had iron weapons had a military advantage over those who did not.

Kush declined by about 200 A.D. At the same time, its southern neighbor, Axum, grew in power. Like Kush, Axum carried on a thriving trade with the Mediterranean world and with Asia. Traders brought gold, ivory, and animal hides from the interior of Africa to ports on the Red Sea. Arabs who took part in this trade settled alongside farmers and merchants of Axum. As a result, the civilization of Axum blended Arab and African cultures.

In 324 A.D., King Ezana of Axum converted to Christianity, as did many of his people. In the 600s, the spread of Islam across North Africa broke the connection between the Christian world and Axum. But Christianity survived in Axum. Today, the people of Ethiopia trace their belief in Christianity back to the civilization of Axum.

Growth of Trade in West Africa

At about the time of the Middle Ages in Europe, from about 500 to 1350, a complex system of trade was carried on in West Africa. The key to this trade was the exchange of gold and salt.

Parts of West Africa had large supplies of gold but little salt. But people living in the warm climate of this region needed salt in their diet. Several hundred miles to the north, in the Sahara, there were large natural salt deposits. At Taghaza, salt was so plentiful that people built their houses out of it. Camel caravans loaded up with salt at Taghaza and made the long desert trip to the West African savanna, where salt was said to be worth its weight in gold.

Trading in salt and gold was central to West African states. Traders placed counterweights, such as the bronze figurine at left, on scales to determine the weight of gold. African artisans created the gold pendant at right.

The chief gold-producing area was Wangara near the Senegal River. Some scholars think that gold and salt were exchanged there in a silent trade. The gold miners of Wangara may have avoided meeting openly with outsiders who could seize their gold fields. So traders left salt and other goods and then withdrew to a safe distance. The miners examined the offerings and set out payment in gold. When the traders returned, they either accepted the price or withdrew to wait for a larger payment.

As the gold-salt trade grew, powerful rulers emerged in West Africa. They sought to control the caravan routes and established strong states to protect trade markets.

The Kingdom of Ghana

Ghana was the first major trading state of West Africa. The gold-salt trade route passed through Ghana, which was located in the Niger Valley.* (See the map on page 248.) About 400

---

* Present-day Ghana is about 500 miles (800 kilometers) to the southeast of the ancient kingdom of Ghana.

A.D., the rulers of Ghana began to build a large empire. They extended their power over neighboring peoples and demanded tribute from them.

Although most people were farmers, the power and prosperity of Ghana depended on gold. In fact, the word "ghana" came to mean gold. The king of Ghana controlled all the gold in his empire. The Arab writer al-Bakri (ahl bahk REE) reported that if the king did not control the amount of gold mined, gold would become so plentiful that it would lose its value.

In the 600s, Muslim merchants from North Africa traveled south along the caravan routes. The king of Ghana did not convert to Islam, but he hired Muslims as interpreters and advisors. Soon, Arab geographers and scholars learned of the wealthy West African kingdom.

Ghana reached the height of its power in the 900s. Tribute and taxes from trade filled the royal treasury. Whenever the king appeared in public, he wore splendid clothes and a rich gold headdress. His pages carried gold-mounted swords. The royal court was guarded by dogs with gold and silver collars.

In the eleventh century, the kingdom of Ghana suffered a severe blow. The Almoravids (ahl MOH rah vihdz), devout Muslims from North Africa, launched a holy war against the non-Muslims of Ghana. When the Almoravids occupied Ghana, states that had been paying tribute broke away. Eventually, Ghana expelled the invaders, but it never recovered its former strength. Ghana ceased to exist as a separate kingdom in the early 1200s.

The Empire of Mali

After Ghana's decline, the Mandingo people to the southeast formed the powerful empire of Mali. A resourceful young leader named Sundiata Keita (suhn dee AH tuh KĪ tuh) defeated his rivals and absorbed the remains of the kingdom of Ghana. By 1240, Mali had won control of the profitable gold-salt trade. During the next century, Mali controlled both the gold mining regions of West Africa and the salt deposits of Taghaza. (See the map on page 248.) Although Mali thrived on commerce, most Mandingo were cattle herders and farmers.

The rulers of Mali converted to Islam in the 1000s. In 1324, Mali's ruler, Mansa Musa,

News of the wealth of Mali reached Europe after Mansa Musa's pilgrimage to Mecca. This detail is from a Spanish map of West Africa that was drawn about 1375. It shows Mansa Musa at right, holding a scepter and a gold nugget. The mapmaker noted: "So abundant is the gold which is found in his country that he is the richest and most noble king in all the land."

"Salt comes from the north, gold from the south, and silver from the country of the white men, but the word of God and the treasures of wisdom are to be found only in Timbuktu." This ancient African proverb shows the special place that the city of Timbuktu held for centuries as a center of learning.

As early as 1100, the city was a busy center of trade. The merchants of Timbuktu grew rich selling gold, salt, cotton cloth, and other goods. In the 1400s and 1500s, however, the city was famous for another product: knowledge. Throughout West Africa, Egypt, and the Middle East, Timbuktu was known as "a city of scholars."

Timbuktu did not have a formal university. Instead, individual scholars gave private lessons in their homes or at one of the city's mosques. Each scholar had a specialty, such as religion, grammar, law, poetry, astronomy, or medicine.

Students came to Timbuktu from all across Africa. Most were sons of wealthy merchants or princes. But there were some poorer students, too, who worked while going to school, often in the city's many tailor shops. So many, in fact, that tailors became well known as learned men.

Although the scholars of Timbuktu were experts in many fields, they frowned on physical education. In fact, students were forbidden to exercise or even to play games. As a result, neither scholars nor students were in good physical condition. One visitor, who was in the city when Sonni Ali (see below) attacked, watched students and teachers trying to escape. "They did not know how to mount a camel," he reported, "and fell miserably to the ground."

1. Describe the system of higher education in Timbuktu.

2. **Critical Thinking** What connection do you think there was between Timbuktu's wealth and its position as a learning center?

left his capital at Timbuktu to make a pilgrimage to Mecca. He passed through Cairo with hundreds of servants and camels loaded with gold. His wealth created a vivid impression in the busy Egyptian city. "This man," observed one Egyptian, "spread upon Cairo the flood of his generosity. There was no person or holder of any office who did not receive a sum of gold from him."

Mansa Musa and his successors respected local traditions within the empire and established a peaceful, orderly government. Ibn Battuta (IHB uhn bah TOO tah), an Arab visitor to Mali, noted the peace and safety of Mali. Battuta described the Mandingo as faithful Muslims, careful in prayer and in their study of the Koran. Yet he observed how the Mandingo blended Islam with their own traditions. For example, women enjoyed greater freedom there than in other Muslim countries. They were not secluded at home, and they could talk to whomever they chose.

In the late 1300s, civil war weakened Mali. Over the next century, the kingdom of Songhai (SAWNG hī) replaced Mali as the most powerful state in West Africa.

The Rise of Songhai

From their capital at Gao, the rulers of Songhai controlled the gold-salt trade. About 1464, Sonni Ali, an able but ruthless leader, came to the throne. Before his death in 1492, Sonni Ali had conquered the largest empire yet seen in West Africa. (See the map on page 248.)

Ali created an efficient government. He divided the empire into provinces and appointed trusted officials to regulate commerce, agriculture, and justice. Inspectors toured local markets to see that merchants used only official weights and measures.

Under Askia Muhammad, Ali's successor, Timbuktu became a great center of learning. Askia Muhammad welcomed Muslim scholars, doctors, and judges to Songhai. The university

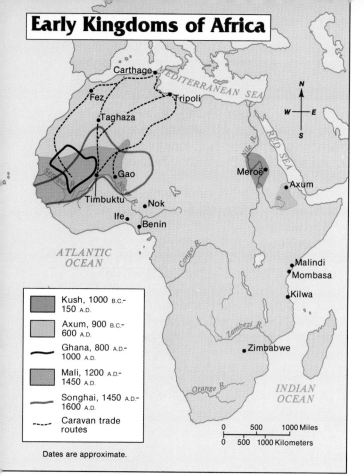

Early Kingdoms of Africa

Carthage
Fez
Tripoli
Taghaza
MEDITERRANEAN SEA
Gao
Meroë
Axum
Timbuktu
Nok
Ife
Benin
ATLANTIC OCEAN
Congo R.
Nile R.
RED SEA
Malindi
Mombasa
Kilwa
Zambezi R.
Zimbabwe
Orange R.
INDIAN OCEAN

N
W E
S

Kush, 1000 B.C.–150 A.D.
Axum, 900 B.C.–600 A.D.
Ghana, 800 A.D.–1000 A.D.
Mali, 1200 A.D.–1450 A.D.
Songhai, 1450 A.D.–1600 A.D.
Caravan trade routes

0   500   1000 Miles
0   500   1000 Kilometers

Dates are approximate.

MAP STUDY *Advanced civilizations emerged in several regions of Africa, as this map shows. Where did the earliest African civilizations develop?*

at Timbuktu produced many scholars, including Ahmad Baba, who gained fame throughout the Muslim world for his knowledge of Islamic law.

In 1590, the ruler of Morocco in northern Africa sent an army across the Sahara to seize the gold mining regions of Songhai. Only about 2,000 soldiers survived the long desert march. But armed with cannon and muskets, which were unknown in Songhai, the invaders defeated the Songhai forces. The Songhai Empire then broke up into small, independent states. Trade continued, but the political unity of the West African trading empires had ended.

City-States of East Africa

Along the coast of East Africa, scattered farming villages grew into independent city-states in the period from 700 to the 1300s. Trade became as important in East Africa as it was in

West Africa. However, East African commerce centered on the sea, not on desert caravans.

The coastal cities made large profits by taxing all goods passing through their markets. Traders brought gold, ivory, and iron from inland states to such cities as Mombasa and Malindi. The goods were then shipped across the Indian Ocean to India and China, where they were sold at high prices. Merchants brought back Indian and Chinese goods to exchange for more products from the interior.

As in Axum to the northeast, many Arab traders settled in the East African coastal cities. The newcomers brought their own culture, including Islam, which blended with African traditions.

As trade across the Indian Ocean increased, Indian civilization also influenced the cities of East Africa. Swahili (swah HEE lee), the language of the coastal people, included Arab and Indian words. Today, Swahili is the most important language of East Africa.

In the 1100s and 1200s, the growth of a money economy in medieval Europe increased the demand for gold there. Arab merchants bought gold in Africa and sold it in Europe for use in coins. The cities of East Africa flourished until the early 1500s. By that time, Portuguese ships had reached East Africa. Not long after their arrival, the Portuguese destroyed the coastal cities.

Zimbabwe: A Powerful Inland State

Zimbabwe (zihm BAH bweh) was the most powerful inland state to export gold to the coastal cities of East Africa. (See the map above.) Around 1000 A.D., migrating farmers and herders settled in the lands between the Zambezi and Limpopo rivers. These pioneers discovered gold in their new homeland. With the wealth from gold, they set up a large trading empire. In the ruins of Zimbabwe, archaeologists have found Chinese and Indian goods, which the rulers of Zimbabwe had bought with profits from the gold trade.

About the time that Europeans set out on the Crusades, the rulers of Zimbabwe built a large walled capital. Skilled masons constructed a huge complex of palaces, stone houses, and temples.

Zimbabwe reached its height in the 1400s. When the Portuguese destroyed the coastal cities, Zimbabwe declined because trade was cut off. About the same time, weak rulers, shortages of salt, and poor crops left the land open to invaders.

SECTION 2 REVIEW

1. **Locate:** (a) Kush, (b) Axum, (c) Ghana, (d) Mali, (e) Timbuktu, (f) Songhai, (g) Zimbabwe.

2. **Identify:** (a) Kasha, (b) Ezana, (c) Mansa Musa, (d) Sonni Ali.

3. Why was iron important to the kingdom of Kush?

4. Describe the effect of the gold-salt trade on Mali.

5. What factors helped make the East African city-states prosperous?

6. What role did Zimbabwe play in African trade?

7. **Critical Thinking** How did Islam influence both West and East Africa?

3 Patterns of Daily Life in Africa

READ TO UNDERSTAND

☐ How family life varied in different African societies.

☐ How villages and small communities regulated their affairs.

☐ What role religion and the arts played in African life.

☐ *Vocabulary:* nuclear family, age grade, matrilineal, patrilineal.

The many peoples of Africa organized their lives in a variety of ways. Their systems of government and social organization differed from place to place. However, respect for the family, law, and religion helped make each society stable.

In some African societies, when boys reached a certain age they underwent training to become hunters and warriors. Not every boy completed this rigorous training successfully. This bronze plaque portrays a warrior dressed for battle. He wears an elaborately decorated helmet and breastplate and carries a shield.

One way in which Africans passed on their values to their children was through proverbs and riddles. Proverbs such as these tell us something about what people thought was important.

> A stone from the hand of a friend is an apple.
> If the music changes, so does the dance.
> We must move with the times.
> Even the mightiest things do not have their own way.

Importance of Family

Family organization in Africa varied according to the needs of individual cultures. People in hunting and food-gathering societies lived in small nuclear families. A **nuclear family** consists of parents, children, and occasionally grandparents. Several nuclear families made up a hunting band.

In farming and herding societies, the extended family was the basic unit of society. As you have read, an extended family includes husband and wife, their unmarried children, and their married sons and their sons' wives

249

and children. In farming areas, the family used the land that its ancestors had cleared and settled. Generally, each family member farmed a different part of the land. But they worked together on projects such as building houses and clearing new land. In herding societies, family members shared the duties of tending the family's cattle.

Members of extended families lived in separate houses built around a common living area. In some African societies, men had more than one wife. Each wife had her own house, where she lived with her children.

In addition to the family, an individual's place in society depended on a system of age grades. An **age grade** included all boys or girls born in the same year. Children of each age grade had privileges and responsibilities particular to that age grade. Children in older age grades took part in certain village activities, which created ties beyond the family.

The Status of Women

The status of women varied in different African societies. Women were respected because marriage and children were basic to family life. However, as in many other cultures, a girl's marriage was arranged by her family when she was in her early teens. If a woman had a child, she won a place in her husband's family. If she had no children, she might be sent back to her family.

In some societies, women had legal rights such as the right to own property. Some women also had religious and political duties. In the Wolof kingdom of West Africa, for example, a woman could become head of state.

In farming cultures, men and women had well-defined roles. Men cleared and plowed the land. In West Africa, women often controlled the granary, the food storage area. Women also sold surplus crops they had harvested in local and regional markets.

In some parts of Africa, families were **matrilineal**—that is, children traced their ancestors through their mother. In these societies, a boy inherited wealth or land from his mother's brother. Many other African societies, however, were **patrilineal**—that is, children traced their family line through their father.

Government and Law

In the large trading states of West Africa, the king was often considered divine, and he had a great deal of power. Kings depended on local officials to maintain order, so they usually did not interfere with local village government. Villages were normally governed by a council of elders. The elders were men who had gained influence because of their age and experience.

In much of Africa, people lived in self-sufficient villages and regulated their affairs by mutual agreement or compromise. The Tiv, a people who lived in what is today Nigeria, numbered nearly one million people. They had no central government, yet Tiv farming villages enjoyed peace and stability. The Tiv depended on kinship—or family ties—which bound people to respect the decisions reached by the community.

Compromise was a central feature of village government. When the community faced an important decision, the elders gathered to discuss all sides of the issue. Discussions would last for days if necessary, until each side gave in a little and an agreement was reached.

Legal questions were settled in a similar way. Courts were more like community meetings than formal hearings. Both parties in a dispute would explain their positions. Then, the judges would help the two sides reach a compromise acceptable to both.

Religious Beliefs

Religion was part of everyday life in Africa, just as it was elsewhere in the world. Although religious rituals varied, many African societies had similar beliefs.

Most African religions were monotheistic. People believed in a Supreme Spirit who had created the universe and everything in it. But people saw the Supreme Spirit as a remote power. They thought that the creator of the universe was too great to be concerned with the details of individual human beings. Therefore, they turned for help to intermediaries, or go-betweens, such as their ancestors and "spirit helpers," who would make their prayers known to the Supreme Spirit.

In many societies, people thought of their ancestors as part of their family. Death only changed the position of the family member. People believed ancestors were closer to the Supreme Spirit and could help the family. They, therefore, showed respect for their ancestors by performing special ceremonies and offering sacrifices.

Many African peoples believed that spirits resided in natural objects such as water and soil. They respected nature because they believed the Supreme Spirit had created all things. For example, a woodcarver in East Africa once explained that he prayed when he cut down a tree because he was changing the Supreme Spirit's creation. He did not believe the wood was a spirit, but he saw it as a part of the natural world that the Supreme Spirit had created.

In some African religions, diviners played a central role. If disasters such as illness or a crop failure struck, people consulted diviners to discover whether a neglected ancestor or spirit had caused the trouble. The diviner revealed the cause and then prescribed a course of action to solve the problem. Diviners had years of training and knew a great deal about the use of herbs as medicines.

The Arts

In African societies, the arts were part of daily life. Musicians and dancers performed at funerals and weddings, or just for entertainment. Musicians also accompanied villagers when they began major projects such as building a wall or clearing forest land. Africans developed a wide range of musical instruments. They played horns, xylophones, bells, drums, and stringed instruments.

Africans passed on their history through oral literature. Storytellers taught their audiences songs and responses so that people could participate in the dramatic tales. Many tales ended with a moral that taught correct behavior.

A variety of art styles developed among the many peoples of Africa. Some of the earliest West African sculpture has been discovered in present-day Nigeria. Between about 900 B.C. and 200 A.D., the Nok culture flourished in this forest region. Working with terra cotta clay, Nok artists fashioned human figures that were nearly life-sized. The work of Nok artists probably influenced later sculptors of Ife and Benin.

About 1000 A.D., the Ife made splendid glazed pottery figures. They also produced bronze portraits that rank among the world's finest sculptures. In the 1300s, bronze workers in Benin created decorative plaques showing scenes of court life. The royal family and wealthy citizens hung the plaques on their palace walls. The art of early Africa has influenced some of today's artists.

Benin sculptors created striking bronze sculptures, such as this one, by a process known as the "lost wax" technique. The artist molded a clay figure and then coated it—first with wax and then with clay. Next, the figure was baked so the wax melted and was "lost" through an opening left in the base. Melted bronze was then poured into the opening. After the bronze cooled and hardened, the clay shell was removed, revealing the bronze figure.

251

1. **Identify:** (a) Tiv, (b) Nok.

2. **Define:** (a) nuclear family, (b) age grade, (c) matrilineal, (d) patrilineal.

3. How did family members in farming societies divide their work?

4. What legal rights did women have in some African societies?

5. How did the village council of elders make decisions?

6. How did many people in Africa pass on their history?

7. **Critical Thinking** Compare the monotheism of African religions with that of Islam or Christianity. Why might Muslims or Christians think that African religions were polytheistic?

4 The First Americans

READ TO UNDERSTAND

☐ What climates and landforms are found in the Americas.

☐ How the first Americans probably reached this continent.

☐ How geography influenced the cultures of the early Americans.

☐ *Vocabulary:* potlatch, adobe, pueblo, sachem.

Like Africa, North and South America are vast continents with varied climates and physical features. Early Americans developed diverse cultures. Scholars have identified over 30 distinct Native American language groups and more than 2,000 dialects.

GEOGRAPHIC SETTING
The Americas

North and South America are lands of great contrast. In the far north, the land is covered permanently with ice and snow. Hot deserts can be found in the southwestern part of North America and along the western coast of South America. Southern Mexico, Central America, and the vast Amazon Basin contain thick rain forests.

The high, rugged Rocky Mountains begin in Alaska and continue into Mexico, where they become the Sierra Madres. In South America, the Andes Mountains stretch from the north to the southern tip of the continent. (See the map on page 869.)

The center of North America is a relatively flat, open plain, where the summers are hot and the winters cold. Thick forests and fertile soils are features of the eastern part of North America. The highlands of the Mexican Plateau also offer rich land for farming. So, too, do the pampas, or grasslands, of Argentina.

Differing environments helped shape a variety of cultures in the Americas. Early people adapted their way of life to local climates and sources of food. Some people hunted or gathered food. Others combined hunting with farming. Still others developed advanced farming civilizations. ■

Path to the Americas

According to scientists, there were no people in the Americas until the last ice age, when much ocean water was frozen into glaciers. Sea levels dropped, exposing new land areas. Between 100,000 and 10,000 years ago, a land bridge connected Asia and the Americas where the Bering Strait is today. Mammoth, bison, and camels wandered across the bridge. Stone Age hunters from Asia followed the animals into North America.

When the climate gradually grew warm again, the melting ice raised sea levels. The sea flooded the land bridge, leaving hunters and their prey cut off in the Americas. The warming climate brought great changes to local environments. However, Stone Age hunters adjusted to the changes and slowly populated the two continents.

As scholars uncover more evidence, they revise their theories about prehistoric life in the Americas. Many scholars suggest that hunters crossed the land bridge in successive waves, but they are uncertain exactly when the first Americans arrived. Recent discoveries indicate that people were living in southern California as early as 70,000 years ago. Most scholars agree that by 7000 B.C. migrating people had reached Cape Horn at the southern tip of South America.

Peoples of North America

The first Americans were organized into many tribes. Each tribe developed its own religious beliefs, technology, and government. In the Americas, as elsewhere, geography affected the way people lived.

Anthropologists have identified many cultural regions, as you can see on the map at right. Within each region, people often had similar traditions. Among the major cultural regions in North America are the far north, the Pacific coast, the southwest, the Great Plains, and the eastern woodlands.

The far north. Some experts suggest that after the land bridge was flooded, a few more people crossed the narrow Bering Strait from Asia by boat. According to this theory, the newcomers were the Eskimos. Like other peoples of the far north, the Eskimos lived by hunting and fishing. But since they lived in the arctic region, the Eskimos had to adjust to one of the harshest environments on earth.

The Eskimos made the most of their limited local resources. They carved harpoons and knives from bone. Using bone needles, they sewed animal skins into clothing, kayaks, and snowshoes. They built temporary shelters out of ice and made permanent homes from driftwood, sod, or stone. As in hunting bands elsewhere, family members cooperated to ensure the group's survival. Among the Eskimos, hospitality and the sharing of food were unwritten laws. Their religion reflected the belief that people should work with nature and not fight against it.

Pacific coast. The peoples of the Pacific coast lived in a much milder climate. They developed a fishing economy. Some fished for salmon along rivers such as the Columbia. Others fished the ocean in huge canoes built from cedar and redwood trees. They extended their fish diet by gathering acorns and seeds or by hunting deer.

Communities on the Pacific coast ranged in size from a few families to over 1,000 people. Some families acquired great wealth, which increased their status. To show their high social position, wealthy families gave feasts called **potlatches** (PAHT latch ehz). The family giving a potlatch served its guests lavishly and gave away valuable possessions.

The southwest. In what is today the southwestern United States and northern Mexico, people developed advanced farming civilizations. In the dry, semidesert climate, the Pueblo grew beans, squash, and maize, or corn. They built houses several stories high out of **adobe,** sundried brick. Each **pueblo,** or

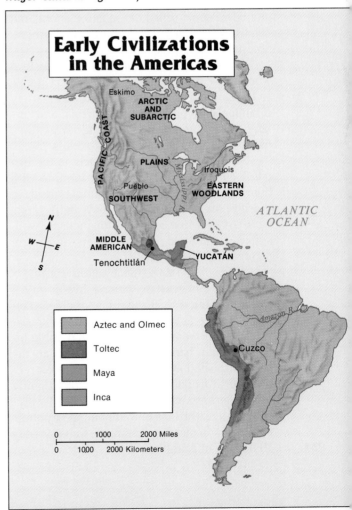

MAP STUDY *After Stone Age hunters crossed into North America, they slowly fanned out across two continents. A rich variety of Native American cultures developed in the Americas. What were the major cultural regions of North America?*

Early Civilizations in the Americas

Eskimo
ARCTIC AND SUBARCTIC
PACIFIC COAST
PLAINS
Iroquois
Pueblo
SOUTHWEST
EASTERN WOODLANDS
ATLANTIC OCEAN
MIDDLE AMERICAN
Tenochtitlán
YUCATÁN
Cuzco
Amazon R.

N
W — E
S

Aztec and Olmec
Toltec
Maya
Inca

0   1000   2000 Miles
0   1000   2000 Kilometers

group of dwellings, was self-contained. It had its own government, elected officials, and council of elders who acted as advisers.

The Pueblo were a peaceful people. Whenever possible, they avoided war. Returning warriors went through purifying rituals to cure them of the "madness of war."

Although men performed the main religious and political duties, Pueblo society was matrilineal. After marriage, a husband moved in with his wife's family.

Great Plains. A wide stretch of grasslands, known as the Great Plains, stretches from the Rocky Mountains to the Mississippi River. People on the Great Plains combined farming and hunting. They lived in villages, usually near rivers to ensure a steady water supply. Women did most of the farming. They raised maize, beans, and squash.

During the summer, men left the villages to hunt buffalo. They planned their hunts carefully. They would stampede the buffalo into a narrow space, where they could then kill many animals. People relied on buffalo for food and used buffalo skins for clothing and for movable tents called teepees.

Eastern woodlands. In the eastern woodlands, a region stretching from Quebec to the Gulf of Mexico, people hunted a variety of animals, including deer, squirrels, and turkeys. Along the coast and inland rivers, they fished or gathered mussels and snails.

Some woodlands people, such as the Iroquois (IHR uh KWOI), combined farming with hunting and fishing. The Iroquois lived in loosely organized bands. They built large, bark-covered homes called longhouses, well-suited to the cold, snowy winters and warm summers of the northeast.

In the late 1400s, the Iroquois formed a league to end warfare among five Iroquois tribes. A council of 50 **sachems,** or chiefs, settled disputes among league members.

Iroquois women enjoyed considerable influence and had a voice in selecting the sachems. The importance of women was recognized in Iroquois law. Anyone found guilty of murdering a woman owed the dead woman's family 20 strings of wampum, the Iroquois money. For a murdered man, the fine was only 10 strings of wampum.

SECTION 4 REVIEW

1. **Define:** (a) potlatch, (b) adobe, (c) pueblo, (d) sachem.

2. Describe three geographic features of North America.

3. How did the end of the last ice age affect people living in the Americas?

4. How did the Eskimos make use of natural resources?

5. What political influence did Iroquois women have?

6. **Critical Thinking** Compare the ways the early peoples of North America adjusted to their varied physical environments.

---

5 Early Civilizations in the Americas

READ TO UNDERSTAND

☐ Why maize was important to the rise of civilization in the Americas.

☐ What advances the Olmec, Maya, Aztec, and Inca made.

☐ How the major civilizations of the Americas differed from one another.

☐ *Vocabulary:* quipu.

When Christopher Columbus reached the Americas in the late 1400s, he saw cornfields 18 miles (29 kilometers) long. Native Americans grew a dozen or more varieties of maize, as corn was called. But the story of corn cultivation had ancient roots.

About 6,000 B.C., early Americans began to harvest the wild corn that grew in the dry valleys of southern Mexico. The first ears of corn were only about an inch long. Slowly, over the centuries, people learned to grow new kinds of corn with larger ears.

The planting and harvesting of corn provided a steady source of food and even produced food surpluses that could be traded. As in the river valleys of Africa, the Middle East, and Asia, some farming villages in the Americas grew into cities at the heart of great civilizations. These civilizations—the Olmec, Maya, Aztec, and Inca—had many features in common, but each developed its own pattern of life.

Legacy of the Olmec

In the swampy lowlands of southern Mexico, the Olmec built one of the earliest civilizations in the Americas. By 1200 B.C., the Olmec had large planned cities. Olmec cities were mainly religious centers. A huge, pyramid-shaped stone temple towered above each city. There, priests performed religious ceremonies. Near the temple, Olmec sculptors carved enormous grim-faced stone heads that may have represented rain gods.

Archaeologists have only recently learned about the Olmec. They have concluded that a highly organized government was needed to supervise the building projects. Thousands of people had to drag huge stone blocks from distant mountains to the building sites.

The Olmec made several important advances. They invented hieroglyphic writing and a counting system that led to practical discoveries in mathematics. They also developed a calendar. The Olmec spread their influence over a wide area through trade.

Sometime around 400 B.C., the Olmec suddenly abandoned their cities. They smashed or buried the giant stone heads. Archaeologists do not know exactly when or even why the Olmec did this. However, the Olmec may have migrated into other parts of Mexico and Central America, taking their advanced knowledge with them.

Maya Civilization

The Olmec may have influenced the Maya, another farming people who lived in the tropical lowlands of the Yucatán Peninsula in what is today Mexico. While Rome was winning control of the Mediterranean world, the Maya cleared dense rain forests, built elaborate irrigation systems, and organized independent city-states. Maya civilization slowly expanded into much of Central America and southern Mexico. (See the map on page 253.) Between 300 A.D. and 900 A.D., during the early Middle

Battles often figured prominently in murals drawn in Maya temples. This scene shows victorious Maya warriors wearing headdresses decorated with features of fierce animals. The warriors hope that they will be as strong and ferocious as the animals. Prisoners from the battle beg for mercy as they wait to learn their fates.

Ages in Europe, the Maya created the most advanced civilization yet seen in the Americas.

Cities. Maya cities were linked to one another by trade and a common language. Like the Olmec cities, Maya cities were chiefly religious centers. An immense pyramid temple stood at the heart of each city. On the edge of the city were cleared fields, and just beyond was the dense tropical forest. (See page 4.)

Priests and warrior nobles made up a powerful ruling class. Priests supervised religious ceremonies, but they may also have influenced government decisions.

The majority of Maya were artisans, peasants, and slaves. Artisans produced fine jewelry and jade ornaments. Sculptors carved huge stone figures and pillars that still stand.

Peasants lived in thatched wooden houses in the maize fields. In addition to farming, peasants worked on temple buildings and constructed long, rectangular courts where ball games related to the Maya religion were played. Slaves did the heaviest and most dangerous work. The Maya had no draft animals, such as oxen and horses, so they used slaves to carry trade goods long distances from the highlands to the coast.

THEN AND NOW   Pok-a-tok: An Ancient Game of the Americas

Amid the jungle ruins of every great Maya city stands a large, rectangular stone court. The Maya used the court when playing a ball game known as pok-a-tok. People started playing pok-a-tok about 500 B.C. The game was popular in many parts of the Americas for more than 2,000 years.

The pok-a-tok court was usually larger than a modern-day football field. Tall stone walls bordered the two long sides of the court. High in the middle of each wall was a stone ring. Unlike the basketball hoops of today, which are mounted horizontally, the stone rings were mounted vertically.

The goal of the game was to hit a ball through the vertical stone ring. The ball, made of solid rubber, was about six inches in diameter. It is a wonder that players ever scored a point, except by luck, because the rings were often mounted as high as 30 feet above the stone floor. Moreover, players could not touch the ball with their hands or feet. They had to hit the ball with their elbows, wrists, or hips. To protect themselves against the hard rubber ball, they wore gloves and hip pads made of wood and leather.

Spectators sat on stone benches above the walls and bet wildly on who would win. Whenever a player scored a point, he could demand the spectators' clothing and jewelry. So, the moment a ball shot through the ring, spectators raced for the gates. The scoring

player's friends dashed to catch them. Luckily for the spectators, few points were scored.

Pok-a-tok was probably more than a game to early Americans. Among the Maya, for example, it was also a religious and patriotic event. Rulers and priests attended the games before important battles. Each game ended with religious and magical ceremonies.

1. Why did spectators race for the gates after a player scored a point?

2. Critical Thinking What sporting events today might you consider patriotic events?

Influence of religion. Religion was central to Maya life. The Maya were polytheistic. They worshipped many gods, but they had special respect for the storm god because without rain their crops would die.

Maya priests were fascinated by time, in part because they had to decide which days were best for hunting, planting, and offering sacrifices to the gods. They used hieroglyphic writing to keep historical records. Priest-astronomers developed a precise calendar, which was more accurate than any used in Western Europe until the 1700s.

Maya priests also made advances in mathematics. They invented a numbering system that included zero. Using this system, they made accurate measurements of days and years.

About 900 A.D., the Maya stopped building cities, and their civilization began to decline. No one knows why. Some historians suggest that overpopulation, disease, or drought disrupted Maya life. Others think that peasants revolted against the priests and nobles. Despite the decline, the Maya continued to live in the Yucatan Peninsula.

The Aztec Empire

As Maya civilization weakened, other people such as the Zapotec and Toltec fought for control of southern Mexico. Like the Maya, they were farmers whose chief crop was maize. They also built large cities and pyramid temples. Then in the 1200s A.D., the Aztec pushed their way into the Valley of Mexico.

The Aztec were a warlike people. In 1325, they established a capital, Tenochtitlán (tay NOHCH tee TLAHN), on an island in the middle of Lake Texcoco. They then conquered neighboring towns and cities. The Aztec forced the conquered peoples to pay tribute in the form of food, feathers of tropical birds, gold, cotton, or slaves. The Aztec Empire reached its height under Montezuma II (MAHN tuh ZOO muh). During his reign, from 1502 to 1521, the Aztec collected tribute from 371 states.

Government and society. The Aztec emperor had supreme power in his own lands. He appointed officials to administer justice and regulate trade. Although the emperor allowed the conquered peoples to govern themselves, he could demand more tribute from them or take prisoners.

Like the Romans, the Aztec built military roads to link distant outposts to the capital. Soldiers were stationed at strategic spots along the roads to protect travelers such as merchants, who carried on a brisk trade.

In the 1500s, Tenochtitlán was a bustling city with about 100,000 inhabitants, including priests, nobles, peasants, and slaves. As the population of the city grew, the Aztec enlarged their island capital. Engineers built causeways, roads made of packed earth, to connect the island to the mainland. Farmers filled in parts of the lake and dug drainage canals to create more farmland. They anchored reed baskets filled with earth in the shallow lake. They then planted crops in the baskets, which became gardens.

A huge pyramid temple and the emperor's palace dominated Tenochtitlán. The palace served as a storehouse for tribute. It also housed the royal family, thousands of servants and officials, a zoo, and a library of history books and accounting records. Like the Romans, the Aztec adapted ideas from the peoples they conquered. Aztec priests used the knowledge of astronomy and mathematics they acquired from other cultures to develop a calendar and counting system.

Religion. The Aztec worshipped many gods, including gods of corn, rain, sun, and war. The Aztec calendar was like a religious text. It told the people which month was sacred to each god and goddess. A large class of priests performed the complicated ceremonies that were meant to ensure the good will of the gods.

Aztec religious practices included human sacrifices. The people believed that the sun god, Huitzilopochtli (WEE tsee loh POHCH tlee), required human sacrifices. The victims in these sacrifices were prisoners of war.

Early in the 1500s, priests predicted that dreadful events were about to happen. They said the gods needed even more sacrifices. When the conquered people fought demands for more tribute, the Aztec put down the revolts and took new captives.

Tlaloc, the rain god, was one of the most feared and respected Aztec gods. The Aztec offered prayers and sacrifices to him so he would send rain for their crops. Tlaloc, whose name means He Who Makes Things Sprout, is shown here grasping a stalk of corn, the main Aztec crop.

The Inca Empire

On the Pacific coast of South America, people began farming about 2000 B.C. In the high Andes Mountains, they grew potatoes. Along the coastal lowlands, they planted maize. Early empires expanded along the coast and fought with one another for control of vital food resources. About 1450 A.D., the Inca founded the last great empire in the Andes region.

The Inca Empire stretched for about 2,500 miles (about 4,000 kilometers) from what is today Ecuador through Peru, Bolivia, Chile, and Argentina. (See the map on page 253.) The Inca ruled as many as 12 million people who lived in coastal villages, in the rugged Andes, and in the rain forests along the Amazon River.

Government and religion. The Inca developed an efficient system to govern their huge empire. The emperor was an absolute ruler. He divided the empire into provinces and appointed nobles to govern them. Governors were responsible for taking a census so people could be taxed.

The government regulated the activities of everyone in the empire. People were divided into groups of ten. Each group was responsible to a local official, who collected a share of their harvest as tax and assigned them to work on public building projects. The government also cared for the aged, sick, and poor.

Like many other peoples, the Inca worshipped many gods and looked to their priests to tell them the will of the gods. The chief god was Inti, the sun god. The Inca believed the emperor was Inti's son, and they called themselves "children of the sun." In the capital of Cuzco, priests and priestesses performed outdoor ceremonies in the Great Sun Temple.

Achievements. The Inca developed advanced technology in many areas. They diverted rivers and streams to mine for gold, which artisans then made into fine ornaments. They learned to use a crowbar to move heavy objects, and they invented a system of measurement. Inca priests had enough medical knowledge to perform successful brain surgery. They also learned to treat victims of malaria with quinine. Europeans did not understand the value of quinine until the 1800s.

As builders, the Inca outshone even the Romans. Early peoples in the Americas did not use the wheel. But even without the wheel, the Inca were able to haul huge stone blocks to build magnificent temples and palaces. They shaped the stones to fit perfectly without cement. During the violent earthquakes that occasionally rock the Andes, Inca stone walls sway, but they do not crumble as do many modern buildings.

The Inca built a road system that linked distant provinces to Cuzco. Roads snaked across the Andes Mountains, and bridges spanned deep gorges. The Inca also used their building skills in farming. Farmers built terraces, or flat areas, on steep mountainsides to create land that could be planted.

The Inca had no system of writing. However, they kept detailed records. As in African societies, certain people memorized their history and taught it to the next generation. In addition, the government recorded census data, the size of harvests, and historical events on the **quipu,** a cord with many knotted strings.

In the early 1500s, the Inca Empire reached its greatest size. When the emperor

MACHU PICCHU Between the peaks of two tall mountains in the Andes, the Inca created the city of Machu Picchu. This recreation by artist Robert Casilla brings the city to life. Terraced gardens surround a stone temple and a fortress. Built on many levels, the city is a good example of how the Inca learned to use their environment. So skilled were they as builders, that many of these buildings, made without mortar between the stones, withstood centuries of earthquakes and other disasters.

died in 1526, two of his sons fought for control of the empire. Finally, in 1532 the younger son, Atahualpa (AH tah WAHL pah), defeated his brother and ended the bloody and bitter conflict. That same year, Spanish soldiers arrived on the coast of Peru.

SECTION 5 REVIEW

1. **Locate:** (a) Yucatán Peninsula, (b) Tenochtitlán, (c) Cuzco.

2. **Identify:** (a) Montezuma, (b) Huitzilopochtli, (c) Inti.

3. **Define:** quipu.

4. List two achievements of the Olmec.

5. (a) What was the main purpose of Maya cities? (b) How were the cities linked to one another?

6. How did the Aztec enlarge their capital?

7. List two ways in which the Inca government was involved in peoples' lives.

8. **Critical Thinking** What aspects of early American civilizations show that the people realized how important maize was to their lives?

CHAPTER 12 REVIEW

Summary

1. **In Africa, people adapted to a wide variety of climates and landforms.** Archaeologists have found evidence of what may be the earliest human life in East Africa. During the agricultural revolution in Africa, some people tamed animals and began to grow a variety of crops.

2. **Over thousands of years, powerful empires and trading states flourished in Africa.** Strong empires rose in Kush and Axum along the Nile River. West African states profited from the trade in gold and salt. In East Africa, city-states traded goods from Central Africa for products from Asia and the Middle East.

3. **African peoples organized their societies in a variety of ways.** Family life and religion were important. Specific religious beliefs varied from one society to another.

4. **The first Americans learned to live in many kinds of environments.** In North America, people developed diverse cultures in environments ranging from the arctic cold of Alaska to the semidesert of the southwest.

5. **The Olmec, Maya, Aztec, and Inca each built strong civilizations.** The Maya developed an accurate calendar. Aztec and Inca civilizations reached their heights about the time Europe was emerging from the Middle Ages.

Recalling Facts

Match each name at left with the correct description at right.

1. Zimbabwe
2. Kush
3. Aztec
4. Timbuktu
5. Maya

a. important center of learning in West Africa

b. Central African kingdom that exported gold to the cities of East Africa

c. early American civilization that flourished between 300 A.D. and 900 A.D.

d. warlike people who conquered much of Mexico in the 1300s

e. ancient African kingdom on the Nile that traded with Egypt

Chapter Checkup

1. (a) Why did powerful trading empires emerge in West Africa? (b) How did Islam influence these kingdoms?

2. (a) How did the city-states of East Africa differ from the West African trading kingdoms? (b) How did events in Europe affect the African gold trade?

3. (a) What types of family organization were found in early African societies? (b) Describe the age-grade system.

4. Describe how early Americans in these regions adapted to their environments: (a) Pacific coast; (b) southwest; (c) Great Plains; (d) eastern woodlands.

5. (a) What advances did the Maya make? (b) What ideas did the Aztec adapt from the peoples they conquered? (c) Describe the main achievements of the Inca.

Critical Thinking

1. **Analyzing Geography in History** (a) Which geographic features in Africa do

you think had the greatest impact on peoples' lives? Explain. (b) Which geographic features in the Americas do you think had the greatest impact on peoples' lives? Explain.

2. **Relating Past to Present** (a) Describe how self-sufficient African villages ruled themselves. (b) How is this system similar to local government in the United States today? (c) How is it different?

3. **Analyzing Geography in History** Compare the ways Maya, Aztec, and Inca civilizations made use of their local geography. Which do you think was most successful? Explain.

Developing Basic Skills

1. **Map Reading** Study the map on page 248. (a) Which West African kingdom controlled the largest territory? (b) Why do you think strong kingdoms rose in West Africa?

2. **Placing Events in Time** Draw a vertical time line on a blank sheet of paper. Make one end of the line 400 A.D. and the other 1500 A.D. Mark off 100-year intervals. Label the right side of the time line Africa and the left side Europe. Use the time line below and the text to identify the major events in Africa. Write them on the right side of the time line. Review Unit Three. Then list on the left side of the line the major events that took place in Europe. (a) What was the first West African trading kingdom?

(b) What was happening in Europe when Mali reached its height? (c) When did the city-states of East Africa flourish? (d) What was happening in Europe then? (e) Why do you think Europeans and Africans were generally unaware of events taking place on each other's continent?

Writing About History

Choosing a Research Topic

When you write a research paper, choose a topic that interests you and about which you can find information. It is a good idea to select several possible topics and then check to see what resources your library has about those topics. If there is very little information on a topic, you should drop it from your list. If there is a geat deal of information on a topic, the topic may be too broad. For example, the topic *The Early Peoples of Africa* would probably be the topic of a book, not a research paper. A more suitable research paper topic would be *The Art of Ancient Ghana.*

Practice: Choose two of the following topics and write a sentence describing what aspect of each subject you would like to research.
1. The gold-salt trade in Africa
2. Askia Muhammad
3. Potlatches of the Pacific coast Indians
4. The religion of the Maya
5. Montezuma

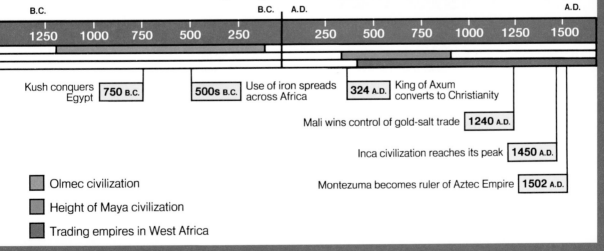

B.C.   B.C.   A.D.   A.D.

| 1250 | 1000 | 750 | 500 | 250 | | 250 | 500 | 750 | 1000 | 1250 | 1500 |

Kush conquers Egypt **750 B.C.**

500s B.C. Use of iron spreads across Africa

324 A.D. King of Axum converts to Christianity

Mali wins control of gold-salt trade **1240 A.D.**

Inca civilization reaches its peak **1450 A.D.**

Montezuma becomes ruler of Aztec Empire **1502 A.D.**

Olmec civilization

Height of Maya civilization

Trading empires in West Africa

261

India, China, and Japan (550–1650)

13

Territory conquered by Genghis Khan was the basis for the Mongol Empire his grandson Kublai Khan founded in China. Genghis Khan is shown here dividing his land among his sons and grandsons. Although he urged his heirs to remain united, they ignored his warning and fought with one another for power.

The new prisoner talked nonstop. For hours, his fellow prisoner, a man named Rustichello, listened. After all, Rustichello had been captured ten years before, and he was eager to hear what the newcomer had to say. Besides, Marco Polo was no ordinary chatterbox. He had traveled to places Rustichello could not even imagine. After a time, Rustichello, a writer of romances, persuaded Polo to let him write an account of those amazing travels. The result was Marco Polo's *Description of the World,* which was read throughout Western Europe.

Polo's account told of how he had left Venice, Italy, in 1271 and traveled across half the world to Peking, China. The trip took four years and involved many risks. For nearly 20 years after his arrival in China, Polo worked for Kublai Khan, the Mongol emperor who had recently conquered China.

"To this city of Peking are brought more precious and costly goods than to any other city in the world," Marco Polo recalled. "People of every description and from every region bring things including precious stones, pearls, and spices from India. Every day, over 1,000 carloads of silk enter the city from which quantities of silk and gold cloth are woven."

Polo told how the Chinese used "a sort of black stone which is dug out of veins in the hillsides and burns like logs." The black stones were used to heat thousands of bathhouses "since there is no one who does not go to a bathhouse at least three times a week."

To Europeans in the late Middle Ages, the splendors of China were unimaginable. The black stones Polo described were coal, which was unknown in Europe. Furthermore, people in Europe seldom bathed. Because Polo's stories seemed so unbelievable, people called him the "prince of liars."

Compared to the tiny warring kingdoms of Western Europe during the Middle Ages, China was a wealthy, unified nation. Indian civilization, too, had advanced. Despite invasions, weak rulers, and regional differences, strong Hindu traditions preserved the underlying unity of Indian culture. Between 550 and 1650, the Japanese on their island nation were shaping their own civilization. Thus, when European sailors began venturing into Asian waters in the 1500s, they discovered advanced civilizations in India, China, and Japan. ∎

1 A Meeting of Cultures in India

READ TO UNDERSTAND

☐ **How invaders conquered northern India between 1200 and 1550.**

☐ **Why Hindus and Muslims clashed in India.**

☐ **How the Mogul Empire was organized.**

☐ *Vocabulary:* **sultan, purdah.**

Along the banks of the Jumna River, the white marble of the Taj Mahal glistens against an intensely blue sky. Its stunning beauty does not hide the fact that the building is a tomb—the last resting place of a greatly loved wife.

In 1631, Mumtaz Mahal, the wife of the Mogul emperor Shah Jahan, died in childbirth. Grief-stricken, the emperor called on architects from India, Persia, and beyond to design a fitting monument to his wife. The Taj Mahal still stands today as a symbol of one man's devotion and of India's cultural achievements.

By the 1600s, India had undergone major upheavals. The Gupta Empire, as you read in Chapter 7, collapsed during the Hun invasions of the fifth century. For hundreds of years afterwards, the northern plain of India was a battleground for rival Indian princes and for invaders drawn to the fertile land. But just as Christianity helped shape medieval Europe, a common cultural tradition based on Hinduism helped support Indian society.

Hindu Traditions

During the Gupta Empire, Hindu traditions had spread throughout India, in part because Hinduism tolerated a wide range of beliefs and practices. As you read in Chapter 7, Hinduism had slowly absorbed Buddhism. In addition, many Hindu sects developed in different parts of India, shaping patterns of daily life.

The caste system and the power of the Brahmans helped ensure a stable society. Caste rules determined what occupations people could follow, whom they could marry, and where they could live. In farming villages, a council of elders made the decisions, but the local Brahman priest often influenced the council. Brahmans also enjoyed great prestige in the palaces of Hindu princes because Brahmans were the educated class who preserved ancient traditions.

Despite these strong social and religious traditions, India had no single ruler. Between the 400s and 900s, warring Hindu princes fought for control of the northern plain. The frequent warfare had relatively little effect on most people. They paid tribute to whichever ruler was in power. Yet because India lacked a strong, unified government, it was unable to resist invaders, who brought with them powerful traditions of their own.

Muslim Expansion into India

As you have read, Islam expanded westward across North Africa and eastward across the Fertile Crescent. In the 900s, Muslim Turks and Afghans from Central Asia conquered the Indus Valley. They then moved farther east. By 1206, Muslim rulers, known as **sultans,** had founded a capital at Delhi. Eventually, they controlled an empire called the Delhi sultanate that included most of India.

The Muslim invaders had several advantages over the Hindu defenders. Muslim armies were highly mobile. Their archers rode horses while the Hindu cavalry rode slow-moving war elephants. Muslim troops were extremely well disciplined. They believed that they were fighting a holy war against "pagan" Hindus. They were also motivated by a desire for loot. The Hindu princes fought bravely, but personal rivalries kept them from organizing a truly united defense.

The Delhi sultans. The Delhi sultans organized a government similar to those of the Maurya and Gupta empires. They divided the empire into provinces, each with a governor responsible for collecting taxes and maintaining order. The sultans also appointed a council of ministers to oversee government departments.

The Delhi sultans had a lavish court, paid for by heavy taxes on non-Muslims. Persian styles were popular at the Delhi court. Under the sultan Firuz Shah Tughlak (fee ROOZ SHAH tuhg LAK), India enjoyed a period of peace and economic prosperity. Between 1351 and 1388, he built new irrigation systems, colleges, towns, and dozens of hospitals. A devout Muslim, he persuaded many Hindus to convert to Islam.

Tamerlane. After the death of Firuz Shah Tughlak, civil war weakened the Delhi sultanate. In 1398, Mongols from Central Asia overran northern India. Their leader, Tamerlane, was an ambitious general who was determined to conquer the world.

Mongol armies looted and destroyed Indian cities in their path. When they reached Delhi, they killed or enslaved the entire population and reduced the buildings to rubble. One witness reported that not a bird on the wing moved for two months. Only artisans were spared. They were sent to build Tamerlane's new capital at Samarkand in what is now the Soviet Union. Intent on further conquests, the Mongols left India. The Muslim Delhi sultanate was restored, but it had been weakened by the conquest.

Impact of Islam

Unlike earlier conquerors of northern India, Muslims were not absorbed into Hindu society. They remained a separate and powerful force, one that was hostile to Hindu traditions. The Muslims who founded the Delhi sultanate were determined to convert nonbelievers. Hindus who did not accept Islam had to pay a heavy tax. Some sultans also persecuted Hindus.

Differing beliefs caused hostility between Hindus and Muslims. Since the first pillar of Islam was the belief in the one God, Muslims were horrified by Hindu temples filled with images of many gods and goddesses. As a result, Muslim armies often destroyed Hindu places of worship. Muslims preached the equality of all believers before God, while Hindus believed in a caste system based on inequality. In addition, Islam required strict obedience to the laws of the Koran, while Hinduism tolerated many different beliefs.

Conflicts between Islamic and Hindu beliefs affected daily life. To Hindus, the cow was a sacred animal that could not be killed. Muslims regarded cattle as a source of food. Also, music was an important part of Hindu festivals, but Muslims considered music an offense to God.

In parts of northern India where the Delhi sultans were strongest, many Hindus converted to Islam. Some converted to avoid paying the nonbeliever tax. Others were glad to escape from the Hindu caste system. Still others converted in order to obtain government jobs or to marry Muslims. In the Deccan Plateau, far from Delhi, few Hindus converted, and Hindu traditions remained strong.

Tensions between Muslims and Hindus sometimes flared into violence, but the two cultures also borrowed ideas from each other. For example, a new language, Urdu, emerged. Urdu was a combination of Persian and Hindi and was written in Arabic script. Muslim mosques were often designed and built by Hindu architects, and Hindu artists painted works that illustrated Persian stories. **Purdah,** the practice of secluding women and making them wear veils in public, probably started in northern India. After the Muslim conquest of northern India, purdah was introduced in other Islamic lands.

The Mogul Empire

The Mongols swept into India again in 1526, and the Delhi sultanate collapsed. The invaders were led by Babur, who claimed to be descended from Tamerlane and Genghis Khan (GEHNG gihs KAHN), another Mongol conqueror. Babur set up the Mogul* Empire in India. (See the map above.)

The Mogul Empire lasted for over 300 years. It reached its golden age during the reign of Akbar, Babur's grandson. Akbar, who ruled from 1556 to 1605, provided efficient,

---

* Mogul was the Persian word for Mongol.

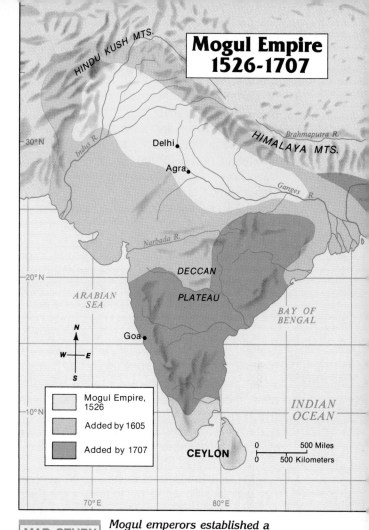

Mogul Empire 1526-1707

MAP STUDY *Mogul emperors established a strong government that ruled most of the Indian subcontinent. The emperor Akbar conquered part of the Deccan Plateau. His successors completed the conquest, but their reigns were often marred by revolts. During which period was the largest amount of territory added to the Mogul Empire?*

honest government. In order to set up a fair tax system, he ordered a land survey to learn about crop yields in each region.

Akbar hoped to unify the empire by following a policy of religious toleration. Although a Muslim himself, he appointed qualified Hindus to high office. He forbade the destruction of Hindu temples, and he lifted the nonbeliever tax. He also married a Hindu princess. Toward the end of his reign, Akbar encouraged a religion that blended Hindu and Muslim beliefs.

The blending of Islamic and Hindu cultures reached its peak under the early Mogul

265

At a time when most people never journeyed more than a few miles from their villages, the Arab adventurer Ibn Battuta traveled the world. He covered more than 75,000 miles in his lifetime and recorded his experiences in a travel book. You read about his impressions of Mali in Africa on page 247.

In 1333, Ibn Battuta reached India. One of the first things that impressed him about India was the efficient mail service. Mail was carried in two ways—by horse and by runners on foot. For mail delivery by horse, horses were stationed every four miles. For foot delivery, runners were posted every third of a mile.

"Each runner has a baton with two bells on top," Ibn Battuta reported. "When a runner starts, he carries a letter in one hand and the baton in the other. He runs as fast as he can. When the men at the next station hear the bells, they get ready. As soon as the runner reaches them, one of them takes the letter and runs at top speed, shaking the bells all the way, to the next station. In this way, foot-delivery is faster than horse-delivery."

In Delhi, Ibn Battuta marveled at the great city with its high walls and towers and its rich mosque. Unusual for that time was a reservoir two miles long and one mile wide that supplied the people of Delhi with fresh drinking water.

Ibn Battuta witnessed how difficult it was to rule a country with deep cultural differences. The ruling elite of India was Muslim, but most of the common people were Hindu. The sultan wanted capable Muslims to work as his officials and even offered Ibn Battuta a job.

The conflict between Muslims and Hindus nearly cost Ibn Battuta his life. On his journey out of India, he was captured by bandits. He managed to escape but then wandered without food for days. Finally, he wrote, "On the seventh day, I arrived in a village of Hindus. I begged of them something to eat, but they refused to give me anything." Luckily, Ibn Battuta found his way to a Muslim village and survived to continue his world travels.

1. What features of India impressed Ibn Battuta?

2. **Critical Thinking** What does Ibn Battuta's experience show about the conflict between Muslims and Hindus in India?

---

emperors. Wealthy Moguls built splendid palaces and mosques with elaborate landscaped gardens. The Taj Mahal in Agra is probably the most famous example of Mogul architecture. (See page 314.)

Although Akbar's successors continued to support the arts, they ended his policy of religious toleration. They closed Hindu schools, destroyed temples, and reimposed the nonbeliever tax. Such actions sparked fierce resistance among Hindus, who struggled to overthrow the Moguls. At the same time, civil wars among Muslim princes weakened Mogul power.

Trade with Western Europeans

The Portuguese navigator Vasco da Gama* reached India in 1498, a few years before the Mogul Empire was established. His voyage led to direct contacts between Western Europe and India. Previously, Arab merchants had carried spices and other goods from India to Mediterranean ports. As a result of da Gama's voyage, the Portuguese were the first Europeans to gain trading privileges in India. They arranged treaties with local rulers on the west coast and made Goa their headquarters.

Goa soon became a center for Christian missionaries who followed Portuguese merchants to India. In the 1500s, the efforts of Christian missionaries to convert Hindus and Muslims angered the Mogul emperor. He sent his armies to end their activities. However, on the whole, the Moguls did not feel threatened by the Europeans. They regarded Europeans as somewhat backward because they did not have the silks, spices, or wealth of India.

---

* You will read about Vasco da Gama and the Portuguese voyages of exploration in Chapter 15.

The Portuguese soon had to compete with merchants from other Western European nations. In 1600, English merchants founded the East India Company to finance trading ventures. As you will read in Chapter 26, the East India Company would play a central role in Indian affairs as Mogul power declined.

As you will read in Chapter 26

SECTION 1 REVIEW

1. **Identify:** (a) Delhi sultanate, (b) Tamerlane, (c) Urdu, (d) Babur, (e) Akbar.

2. **Define:** (a) sultan, (b) purdah.

3. What advantages did Muslim invaders have over Hindu forces?

4. List three differences between Hinduism and Islam.

5. How did Mogul emperors respond to the arrival of Europeans?

6. **Critical Thinking** Why do you think Akbar is today considered one of India's greatest rulers?

Shah Jahan, shown here, was a ruler of the Mogul Empire who has been called the ideal Muslim ruler. His reign was remarkable for wealth and splendor and for the emperor's many successes in battle. The most lasting memorial of Shah Jahan's rule is the Taj Mahal, the magnificent marble tomb he had built for his wife.

2 Flowering of Chinese Civilization

READ TO UNDERSTAND

☐ How Confucian ideas influenced China.

☐ What achievements the Chinese made in the arts during their golden age.

☐ How Chinese inventions affected life.

☐ How contact with foreigners affected China.

Prime Minister Wang Tan was in mourning. His eldest son had just died of smallpox. His great fear was that his other children would develop the deadly disease. The prime minister called on the wise men and physicians of China to find a remedy. Answering his call, a Taoist monk arrived in the capital. He brought with him a technique of inoculating, or vaccinating, people against smallpox.

Wang Tan was lucky to have lived in China in the 900s. It would be over 800 years before the practice of vaccination reached Europe. Between 500 and 1500, the Chinese made important advances in science and the arts. They also invented many practical things, including paper money, mechanical clocks, matches, umbrellas, and a seismograph for measuring earthquakes.

During the period of the Middle Ages in Europe, Chinese civilization reached great heights. Although the Han Empire, like the Roman Empire in the West, had collapsed, other rulers appeared to restore unity to China.

Two Golden Ages

After the Han Empire collapsed in 220, several dynasties rose and fell. (See page 153.) Some lasted for hundreds of years. During the T'ang and Sung dynasties, China enjoyed two long golden ages. The economy expanded, the population grew, and the arts flourished.

The T'ang dynasty lasted from 618 to 907. T'ang rulers united an empire that reached from the Pacific Ocean to the borders of India and Persia. Under the T'ang, Chinese influence spread into Korea, Japan, and parts of Southeast Asia.

Peasant revolts ended T'ang rule, but the Sung dynasty eventually restored order. The Sung ruled China for about 300 years, from 960 to 1279. Under the Sung, China became a truly unified state, a goal not reached by Western European nations until the 1400s.

Chinese Government

During the T'ang and Sung dynasties, an efficient civil service system provided good government. As you read in Chapter 7, Han emperors had begun recruiting Confucian scholars to serve in the government. T'ang and Sung rulers expanded the civil service system.

Scholars who served as government officials had the highest status in Chinese society. In theory, a man from any class could qualify for the civil service. In practice, however, few peasants could afford the expensive education needed to pass the tests. Generally, only the sons of officials and wealthy merchants attended the private schools that were set up across China.

At its best, the civil service attracted educated, loyal officials. Because they had been trained as Confucian scholars, government

BUILDERS AND SHAPERS Wu Chao: China's Woman Emperor

T'ang astrologers watched the skies in amazement. For several days now, the planet Venus had been visible. This was a sign that the throne would soon be occupied by a woman. Such a prediction was astounding because in China women were considered inferior to men. However, the prediction came true less than 50 years later when Wu Chao (woo chow) became emperor of China.

As 13-year-old Wu Chao left home to work at the T'ang court, her mother wept. The position was a low-ranking one, and her daughter seemed doomed to unhappiness. But Wu Chao scolded her tearful mother, saying: "To be admitted to the presence of the Son of Heaven—how can you tell that means unhappiness? Why are you crying like a little girl?"

Wu Chao's confidence and optimism were apparently well placed. She used her wit, intelligence, and beauty to gain power and influence at court. Eventually, she married the emperor, Kao Tsung. When Kao Tsung suffered a serious stroke, Wu took over control of the government. After her husband's death, she took the title of emperor and ruled on her own.

Wu Chao was a brilliant administrator. She reorganized the army and ordered the conquest of Korea. By reducing taxes and encouraging silk production and farming, she stopped the peasant uprisings that had plagued other Chinese rulers.

A strong-willed ruler, Wu Chao ruthlessly killed those who threatened her power. But she was generous toward people in the lower classes. She promoted talented men regardless of their social class. And she used the civil service examination to recruit loyal new officials.

Wu Chao encouraged the growth of Buddhism in China and asked scholars to translate important Buddhist texts. During her reign, Buddhism reached its height.

In 705, the 83-year-old ruler was too ill to prevent a group of generals from seizing the palace and forcing her to give up the throne to her son. Wu Chao died soon after. Yet her successful administrative and social policies had paved the way for one of the most glorious periods of Chinese history.

1. Name three of Wu Chao's accomplishments as emperor.

2. **Critical Thinking** Do you think Wu Chao's rule in China was affected by how she came to be emperor? Explain.

officials helped spread Confucian values and Chinese culture across the huge empire.

Important Inventions

Chinese inventions during the T'ang and Sung dynasties had far-reaching effects. In the 700s, the Chinese invented printing. Earlier Chinese inventions such as paper and the use of seals to stamp documents had paved the way for printing.

Buddhist monks probably developed block printing to make copies of sacred texts and prayers. They carved characters onto wooden blocks that were inked and pressed onto paper. The earliest known printed work is a Buddhist text called the *Diamond Sutra,* produced in 868. It was printed on six large sheets that were then attached to form a 16-foot-long (5-meter) scroll.

About 1050, the Chinese began to use movable type—pieces of metal containing Chinese characters that could be combined to form sentences. The metal pieces could be used again and again. The use of movable type enabled the Chinese to produce many more books.

The people of Korea and Japan soon learned about printing from the Chinese. However, Chinese inventions such as paper and printing did not reach Western Europe until much later. The Arabs brought Chinese paper-making techniques to Europe, but paper was not widely used in Europe until the 1400s.

During the T'ang and Sung dynasties, the Chinese made other practical advances. They used the waterwheel to power forges and blast furnaces. T'ang mapmakers drew the most advanced maps of the day. The Chinese also developed a magnetic compass and built large ships equipped with several masts. By 1000, the Chinese had begun to use gunpowder in weapons such as mines, hand grenades, and explosive rockets.

The Arts

During the centuries of peace and prosperity under the T'ang and Sung, the arts flourished in China. Wealthy people flocked to the cities, especially the T'ang capital of Chang-an. They

T'ang potters captured the rich variety of Chinese life in brightly glazed ceramics. Fine details are shown in this figure of a woman from the T'ang court. Her elaborate headpiece and her flowing gown reflect the fashion of the time.

bought books, paintings, and other fine works of art to decorate their homes and tombs.

T'ang artisans perfected the making of porcelain, a hard, shiny pottery. They created lively porcelain figures of musicians and dancers who entertained at court. They also made porcelain horses, camels, and even bearded foreigners, all of which showed the importance of foreign trade in China.

In T'ang China, educated people enjoyed reading literature, especially poetry. Poets wrote about human emotions, nature, and the individual's place in the universe. One of China's greatest poets was Li Po (lee boh). A Taoist, Li Po wrote about his feelings for nature in the following lines:

> My friend is lodging in the Eastern Range,
> Dearly loving the beauty of valleys and hills.
> A pine-tree wind dusts his sleeves and coat;
> A pebbly stream cleans his heart and ears.
> I envy you who far from strife and talk
> Are high-propped on a pillow of gray mist.

269

Time seems to stand still in Chinese landscape paintings. This painted scroll from the Sung dynasty shows a man gazing at a flock of geese. By emphasizing the trees, rocks, and river, the artist conveyed the idea that people are less important than nature.

Landscape painting reached a high point in China during the Sung dynasty. Sung painters were influenced by Taoist respect for nature and the natural scenery of China. Artists would meditate for days on a landscape, trying to capture the mood of the scene. Then they would paint the scene without looking at it again. Most paintings were done with brushes and ink on silk. Artists captured the sense of rugged mountains and rushing rivers with simple lines in black and shades of gray. Sung styles of painting influenced Chinese artists for hundreds of years.

Patterns of Life

Between about 600 and 1000, the Chinese economy expanded dramatically. Improved seeds and better farming methods helped increase food production. The resulting food surpluses enabled some Chinese to leave the farms and move to the cities, where they worked as artisans, shopkeepers, servants, or actors. However, most Chinese were still farmers.

Trade and commerce also increased in this period. Cities bustled with activity as camel caravans, loaded with porcelains, silks, and other luxuries, left for the Silk Road and the Middle East.

Contacts with the world. The Chinese were open to outside ideas during T'ang and Sung times. The T'ang government officially tolerated Buddhism, which thrived. Many Chinese, both rich and poor, became Buddhist monks or nuns. Chinese Buddhists traveled to India and Southeast Asia and returned home with new knowledge of history, geography, and the sciences.

Trade and travel introduced the Chinese to many new products. They learned about new foods such as peppers and dates. Furthermore, they learned about new seeds and farming methods from their contacts with the foreigners.

Enduring traditions. Under the Sung, China became one of the largest and wealthiest empires in the world. At the same time, Chinese society remained firmly rooted in Confucian ideas.

Confucius had emphasized the importance of harmony in human relationships. The Chinese believed that harmony would result from a well-ordered society where individuals accepted their roles. They did not accept the idea that all people were equal. Instead, they thought that educated people were superior to uneducated people. They also believed that farmers, who produced food, were superior to merchants, who merely exchanged goods.

Confucian ideals led the Chinese to stress a person's duties rather than his or her rights. For example, the people had a duty to obey the emperor. The emperor, in turn, had a duty to provide good government.

Women in China. China was a society of unequals in which women were thought to be inferior to men. As in many other societies, when a girl married, she joined her husband's family. As a wife, she was expected to obey her husband.

During the Sung dynasty, the custom of footbinding was introduced at court. This custom involved binding a girl's feet at birth so they would remain small and delicate. Court dancers were the first to have their feet bound. But soon almost all Chinese women were affected by the custom.

Footbinding severely limited a woman's freedom of movement. She had to take tiny steps, which were considered beautiful and feminine. A woman with unbound feet was considered ugly and was unlikely to marry. Rather than risk such a fate for their daughters, peasants as well as upper-class parents adopted the custom of footbinding. For centuries, Chinese women suffered from this painful and often crippling custom.

SECTION 2 REVIEW

1. **Identify:** (a) *Diamond Sutra*, (b) Li Po.

2. (a) Who usually entered the civil service? (b) How did the civil service spread Confucian ideas?

3. Why was movable type an important advance?

4. (a) What subjects interested T'ang and Sung poets and artists? (b) How did Taoism influence the arts in China?

5. How did footbinding affect Chinese women?

6. **Critical Thinking** Which of the Chinese inventions from this period do you think proved most important for later people? Explain.

Throughout much of China's long history, the silk trade linked China to other parts of the world. The manufacturing of silk, a major industry in China, was largely the work of peasant women. This scroll shows noblewomen ironing a completed bolt of silk cloth.

3 Mongol and Ming Empires

READ TO UNDERSTAND

☐ How the Mongols ruled China.

☐ How the Ming dynasty restored Chinese rule.

☐ Why Ming rulers isolated China from outsiders.

Flames leaped above the walls of the city of Peking, consuming palaces and slum dwellings alike. Masses of defenders lay dead, their bodies piled wherever they had fallen. The victors rode through the streets looting and killing anyone who had survived the initial attack.

Many of them agreed with their merciless leader Genghis Khan, who had exclaimed, "The greatest joy is to conquer one's enemies, to pursue them, to seize their property, to see their families in tears."

In 1215, the Mongol armies of Genghis Khan swept across northern China, crushing the Chinese defenders of Peking. The Sung emperor fled south. After taking Peking, Genghis Khan turned west away from China, winning other victories across Asia and founding the huge Mongol Empire.

A Foreign Dynasty

Under Genghis Khan's sons and grandsons, the Mongol Empire extended from the Pacific Ocean to the Danube River in Europe. The

MAP STUDY *Genghis Khan led nomadic peoples of Central Asia on a ruthless course of world conquest. Mongol armies swept westward into Russia and eastward into China. At one time, the Mongols dominated almost all of Asia. What parts of the Mongol Empire did Marco Polo visit?*

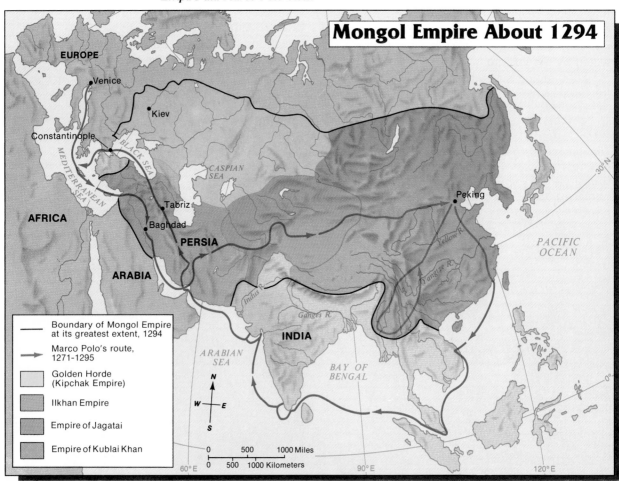

Mongol Empire About 1294

EUROPE
Venice
Kiev
Constantinople
BLACK SEA
MEDITERRANEAN SEA
CASPIAN SEA
30°N
Peking
AFRICA
Tabriz
Baghdad
PERSIA
PACIFIC OCEAN
ARABIA
Yellow R.
Indus R.
Yangtze R.
Ganges R.
INDIA
ARABIAN SEA
BAY OF BENGAL
0°

Boundary of Mongol Empire at its greatest extent, 1294

Marco Polo's route, 1271-1295

Golden Horde (Kipchak Empire)

Ilkhan Empire

Empire of Jagatai

Empire of Kublai Khan

N
W E
S

0   500   1000 Miles
0   500   1000 Kilometers

60°E   90°E   120°E

empire was later divided among several rulers. (See the map on page 272.) In 1279, Kublai Khan, a grandson of Genghis Khan, completed the conquest of China and set up the first foreign dynasty in China.

Aware of China's reputation for absorbing its conquerors, Kublai Khan tried to limit Chinese influence on the Mongols. He had a separate law code for Mongols and allowed only Mongol nobles and foreigners to serve in high positions at court. However, the Mongols used Chinese officials at the local level. And even Kublai Khan himself was influenced by Chinese culture. He rebuilt Peking, making it his capital. He also adopted a Chinese name for his dynasty, the Yuan (yoo AHN).

The Mongols built great highways across their empire. As a result, trade and travel increased, and China was in constant contact with other lands. Arabs, Italians, Russians, and many others went to China. They helped spread knowledge of Chinese inventions across Europe and Asia. As you read earlier, Marco Polo was one of the foreigners who visited China, and he had stayed to serve Kublai Khan.

The Yuan dynasty declined under Kublai Khan's successors. To pay for the expenses of their courts, Yuan emperors printed more and more paper money, which led to inflation. Inflation, combined with Chinese resentment against the foreign dynasty, resulted in revolt. A Chinese Buddhist monk named Hung Wu organized rebel armies and drove out the Mongols. He then founded the Ming dynasty, which ruled China from 1368 to 1644.

Restoring Chinese Rule

Ming emperors wanted to erase all traces of foreign rule. They modeled their government on the T'ang and Sung empires. They revived the civil service system, and Confucian scholars regained influence at court. Under the Ming, the Chinese again felt confident that their culture was second to none.

Between 1405 and 1433, the Ming outfitted several huge fleets, which sailed on voyages of exploration. For the first voyage, the Chinese admiral Cheng Ho assembled 63 ships, which carried over 27,000 sailors, soldiers, and civilians. Some Chinese ships weighed up to 1,500 tons each. In contrast, 60 years later, the largest of the first European vessels that sailed to India weighed only about 300 tons. Ming fleets visited Southeast Asia, India, Arabia, and East Africa. They traded, collected tribute, and gathered information about sea routes.

In 1433, the voyages suddenly stopped. No one knows why. Perhaps court officials were jealous of the fleet admirals, and they may have convinced the emperor that the voyages were too costly. Or maybe the Chinese decided that they did not need to look beyond their borders because they believed they had everything the people needed.

China probably had the most advanced technology in the world when the Ming emperor ended the voyages of exploration. However, the Chinese cut themselves off from the world just as people in Western Europe were beginning to expand their horizons. While Europeans were experimenting with new ideas, the Chinese were content with the institutions and values that had served them so well in the past.

Restrictions on Trade and Travel

Besides ending the voyages of exploration, the Ming emperor brought foreign travel and trade under close regulation. In 1514, when Portuguese trading ships sailed up the coast of China, Ming officials refused to let them land. Instead, the Portuguese had to sell their cargoes to Chinese traders who came out to their ships. As soon as their goods were unloaded, the foreigners had to leave. Later on, the Portuguese won the right to settle in the port of Macao, but the Chinese kept them under close supervision.

In the 1600s, other Europeans tried to win trading rights from the Ming emperor. He agreed, but he limited all foreign merchants to one city, Canton. Every summer, foreigners went to Canton to do their trading. They were not allowed to bring their families, carry firearms, or learn Chinese. All business had to be done through Chinese agents.

For 250 years, Chinese officials enforced the laws limiting the activities of foreigners. As you will read in Chapter 26, it was only during the decline of a later dynasty that foreigners successfully challenged Chinese power.

DEPARTURE OF THE MING FLEET The departure of the Ming fleet, recreated here by artist Larry Bernetti, signaled the start of several Chinese voyages of exploration. Some of the ships in the fleet weighed as much as 1,500 tons. In contrast, 60 years later, the largest of the first European vessels that sailed to India weighed only about 300 tons. The Ming fleets, which sailed as far away as Africa, greatly increased Chinese knowledge of the outside world.

SECTION 3 REVIEW

1. **Identify:** (a) Kublai Khan, (b) Marco Polo, (c) Hung Wu, (d) Cheng Ho.

2. How did Kublai Khan try to keep the Mongols from being absorbed by Chinese culture?

3. What effect did the Mongol system of roads have on China?

4. What did the Ming do to erase traces of Mongol rule?

5. What restrictions did the Ming put on European traders?

6. **Critical Thinking** Why do you think Ming emperors decided to restrict Chinese contacts with the outside world?

4 Foundations of Japanese Civilization

READ TO UNDERSTAND

☐ How geography affected Japanese life.

☐ How early Japanese society was organized.

☐ What the Japanese borrowed from China.

☐ *Vocabulary:* archipelago, clan, kami.

"Zipangu is an island in the eastern ocean located about 1,500 miles from the mainland of Asia," wrote Marco Polo in his *Description of the World.* Polo was describing Japan, but much of what he recorded was inaccurate. Japan lies only 100 miles (160 kilometers) off the coast of Asia, not 1,500 miles. And the Japanese occupy not one island but a chain of islands stretching thousands of miles along the rim of Asia.

In prehistoric times, groups of hunting and fishing people, called the Ainu, crossed to Japan from the Asian mainland. Later, other immigrants from the mainland brought a knowledge of rice farming and metalworking. By the third century A.D., the Japanese had developed their own culture. Although they adopted many ideas from the mainland, they were never overwhelmed by outside influences, in part because of their location.

GEOGRAPHIC SETTING
Japan

Japan is an **archipelago** (AHR kuh PEHL uh GOH), a chain of islands, off the northeast coast of Asia. (See the map at right.) The four main islands of Japan are Hokkaido (hoh KĪ doh), Honshu (hahn shoo), Shikoku (SHEE koh KOO), and Kyushu (kyoo shoo).

Japan has a mild climate, plenty of rainfall, and fertile soil. Farmers grow crops such as rice, barley, and soybeans. However, because Japan is mountainous, only about 20 percent of the land is suitable for farming. Early on, the Japanese learned to create more farmland by making terraces, cutting a series of flat surfaces on hillsides.

The sea strongly influenced early Japanese life. The Japanese fished in the waters surrounding their islands. The Sea of Japan to the west was a barrier to invaders from the Asian mainland and thereby allowed the Japanese to develop largely on their own. Yet the sea also served as a highway for the Japanese, linking the islands to one another and to the mainland. ■

Early Japanese Society

The early Japanese were organized into **clans,** family groups who traced their origins to a common ancestor. A clan was headed by a hereditary chief who was both a military and religious leader. Within the clan, people lived in extended families. Each family's position in society was inherited. A family inherited the right to be farmers, weavers, potters, or warriors—the highest group in society.

Japanese religious beliefs centered on respect for nature. People did not fear nature. Rather, they were in awe of its unseen forces. They worshipped **kami,** or spirits, which they believed controlled the forces of nature.

Ancient Japanese religious traditions were later called Shinto, the way of the gods. Shinto is a religion of festivals and rituals. At shrines dotting the land, people offered gifts to the kami to ensure good harvests. Unlike Judaism, Christianity, Islam, and Buddhism, Shinto has no sacred writings.

About 400 A.D., the Yamato (YAH mah toh) emerged as the strongest clan in Japan. They established the first and only Japanese dy-

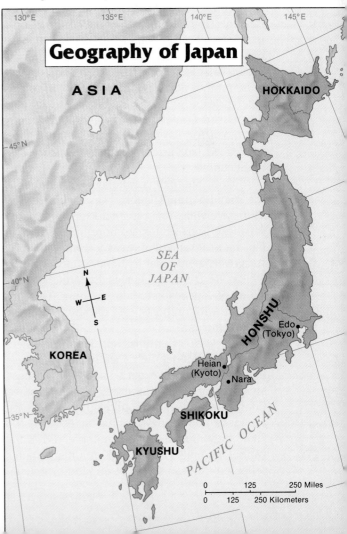

MAP STUDY *The four main islands of Japan, shown here, are the highest peaks of a large underwater mountain chain. Hundreds of other islands, south of Kyushu, are also part of Japan. About how far does Japan extend from north to south?*

nasty. The present Japanese emperor traces his origins to the Yamato clan. According to legend, the sun goddess Amaterasu (ah mah ter AH soo) created Japan, and one of her descendants became the first emperor. The Yamato traced their ancestors back to that first emperor. By claiming to be descended from a god, Japanese emperors gained the respect and support of the people.

Selective Borrowing

Between the fifth and ninth centuries, the Japanese borrowed many ideas from China. They adapted Chinese writing to their own language, which opened the way for further borrowing. However, the Japanese kept only the ideas that fit their own social, political, and religious traditions.

In 552, the Yamato ruler welcomed Chinese Buddhist missionaries who came to Japan by way of Korea. In doing so, he set Japan on a new path. Just as Christianity carried the Greco-Roman heritage to the people of Western Europe, Buddhism became the vehicle for spreading Chinese culture to Japan. Japanese rulers accepted many Buddhist beliefs. Yet they also kept their traditional role as chief priests in Shinto. Buddhist monks also introduced Confucian ideas about the family and ancestor worship. Because these ideas reinforced Japanese traditions, they were easily accepted.

Prince Shotoku, a scholar and member of the Yamato ruling family, was fascinated by Chinese civilization. Under his leadership, the Japanese borrowed even more from China. In 607, he sent representatives to China to study its government, history, and philosophy as well as its arts and sciences. Eventually, thousands of Japanese studied in China. They returned with reports of dazzling Chinese achievements.

In a wave of enthusiasm, Japanese rulers set out to remodel their society along Chinese lines. The court eagerly adopted Chinese styles in art and literature. Nobles studied Confucian and Taoist philosophy. When the Japanese built a new capital at Nara in the 700s, they modeled it on the splendid T'ang capital in China. Palaces and Buddhist temples reflected Chinese styles of architecture. Even Japanese clothing and furniture showed the influence of Chinese culture.

Yet the Japanese rejected some Chinese ideas. At one point, Japanese rulers tried to reform the government based on Chinese ideas. They set up a government bureaucracy and introduced the civil service system. However, the civil service system never took hold in Japan because it did not fit in with the tradition that a person's position in society was inherited. For the same reason, the Japanese could not accept the Confucian idea of opening offices to all social classes. As a result, hereditary nobles rather than scholars held government offices in Japan.

The Court at Heian

In 794, the emperor moved his capital to Heian (hay ahn), present-day Kyoto. At Heian, Chinese ideas were blended with Japanese traditions. But as the T'ang dynasty declined in China during the 800s, Japanese fascination with China decreased. Japanese visitors no longer flocked to the mainland. Trade and travel continued, but on a reduced scale.

The role of the emperor changed during the 800s. In theory, the emperor remained supreme. In practice, he became a figurehead whose chief duties were religious. Noble families at court ran the government.

One family, the Fujiwara (foo jee WAH rah), won power in the government through marriage. The Fujiwara arranged for their daughters to marry the heirs to the Japanese throne. In this way, the Fujiwara could influence the emperor. Outwardly, the Fujiwara showed respect for the emperor. But in practice, they held the real power.

The Fujiwara appointed their followers to government positions. With few government responsibilities, other nobles at court turned to the arts, literature, and music. Noblewomen helped develop a distinctly Japanese literature. Unlike Japanese men, who wrote in Chinese, Japanese women wrote in their own language. Many court women kept diaries and composed poetry. *The Tale of Genji,* written by Lady Murasaki, is a great masterpiece of Japanese literature. The work is considered one of the world's first novels. (See the Skill Lesson on page 278.)

Poets were highly regarded in the court at Heian since their craft was an important part of culture and education. The court honored one group of 36 poets by having their portraits painted. This portrait is of Ono-No-Komaki, a woman poet.

SECTION 4 REVIEW

1. **Locate:** (a) Hokkaido, (b) Honshu, (c) Shikoku, (d) Kyushu, (e) Sea of Japan, (f) Heian.

2. **Identify:** (a) Shinto, (b) Yamato, (c) Lady Murasaki.

3. **Define:** (a) archipelago, (b) clan, (c) kami.

4. Describe one advantage and one disadvantage of the geography of Japan.

5. Why did the Yamato rulers have the respect of the people?

6. (a) List three aspects of Chinese culture the Japanese borrowed. (b) Why did they reject some ideas?

7. How did women contribute to the development of Japanese literature?

8. **Critical Thinking** Why do you think Chinese culture during the T'ang and Sung dynasties was attractive to the Japanese?

5 From Feudalism to Unified Nation

READ TO UNDERSTAND

- How feudal society developed in Japan.
- How the Tokugawa shoguns unified Japan.
- Why the shoguns isolated Japan.
- *Vocabulary:* samurai, shogun, daimyo, bushido, seppuku, haiku.

The court at Heian was the center of an elegant world. However, by the 1100s, the noble court families had lost power to strong rural lords. The system of government then emerging in Japan resembled the feudalism of Western Europe.

Japanese Feudalism

Feudalism in Japan developed during several centuries of warfare. In the early feudal period, warrior knights called **samurai** battled for

277

Fictional works of literature, such as novels, short stories, and plays, can be valuable historical evidence. They sometimes provide useful information about the ideas and customs of people from another culture or from another time. You need to analyze a fictional work carefully before using it as historical evidence. The work might present only a limited picture of a historical period or event.

The excerpt that follows is taken from *The Tale of Genji,* a novel by Lady Murasaki. (See page 276.) As lady-in-waiting to the empress, she took part in the elegant court rituals and ceremonies. The novel, written about 1004, describes the many adventures of a legendary Prince Genji, the young son of a Japanese emperor.

Read the excerpt. Then use the following steps to analyze it as historical evidence.

1. **Identify the nature of the document.** Ask yourself: (a) What type of document is it? (b) Who wrote it? When? (c) What connection, if any, did the author have with the events described?

2. **Study the content of the document.** (a) What preparations for Genji's initiation does the author describe? (b) What does the author say about Genji's appearance? (c) What does the author say about the emperor's role in the preparations?

3. **Analyze the document as a historical source.** (a) What can you learn about Japanese court life from this excerpt? (b) Would you use this document to learn how all Japanese lived in the 1000s? Why or why not?

From *The Tale of Genji*

Though it seemed a shame to put so lovely a child into man's dress, he was now twelve years old and the time for his Initiation was come. The Emperor directed the preparations with tireless zeal and insisted upon a magnificence beyond what was prescribed. The ceremony took place in the eastern wing of the Emperor's own apartments, and the Throne was placed facing toward the east, with the seats of the Initiate-to-be and his Sponsor in front.

Genji arrived at the hour of the Monkey [3 p.m.]. He looked very handsome with his long childish locks, and the Sponsor, whose duty it had just been to bind them with purple ribbon, was sorry to think that all this would soon be changed, and even the Clerk of the Treasury seemed reluctant to sever those lovely tresses with the ritual knife.

Duly crowned, Genji went to his chamber and changed into man's dress. He then went down into the courtyard and performed the Dance of Homage, which he did with such grace that tears stood in every eye. It had been feared that his delicate features would show to less advantage when he had put aside his childish dress; but on the contrary, he looked handsomer than ever.

---

control of the land. Samurai were nobles descended from early clan chiefs.

In 1192, a powerful samurai leader, Yoritomo Minamoto, gained the title of **shogun,** or chief general, from the emperor. Feudal society took shape under Yoritomo and his successors. The emperor remained at the head of society, but he had no political power and performed only religious duties. The shogun, the most powerful samurai, became the key political leader. Like feudal lords in Western Europe, he gave some of his land to lesser nobles—other samurai—in exchange for military service and personal loyalty.

Below the shogun were the **daimyo** (DĪ myoh), other powerful samurai. Sometimes they supported shoguns like Yoritomo. At other times, using their own samurai armies, they fought among themselves or even against the shogun. (See the diagram on page 279.)

Far below the samurai were peasants, artisans, and merchants. Peasants were the backbone of feudal society in Japan. Peasant families farmed the estates of samurai. Some peasants also became foot soldiers. On rare occasions, an able peasant soldier would rise into the ranks of the samurai. Merchants ranked below the peasants.

The way of the warrior. The samurai developed a code of conduct that resembled the European code of chivalry. (See pages 169–170.) The samurai code was called **bushido** (BOO shee DOH), meaning the way of the warrior. Bushido stressed loyalty and unquestioning obedience to one's lord. It also emphasized simplicity, courage, and honor. A samurai who violated the code was thought to have disgraced himself and his family. To remove this disgrace, he was expected to commit **seppuku,** a ritual suicide.

Under feudalism, Japanese women had less freedom than they had enjoyed in the past. In Western Europe, the code of chivalry put noblewomen on a pedestal. In contrast, samurai wives were expected to endure hardships without complaint.

Signs of change. In the 1400s and 1500s, the number of daimyo decreased as stronger lords took over the estates of weaker ones. Furthermore, lower-ranking samurai became so numerous that they lost prestige. Many samurai who had no lord to serve were considered outcasts. Bands of homeless samurai roamed the country, attacking travelers and raiding peasant villages.

Despite the constant feudal warfare, the Japanese economy grew. Foreign trade stimulated economic growth. Merchants developed a busy trade with China and other parts of East Asia. Japanese artisans improved the methods of papermaking, metalworking, and weaving that had been introduced from China. By the 1500s, Japanese swords, folding fans, and screens were in great demand in China. Shipbuilding and manufacturing industries expanded to keep pace with demand.

Creating a Unified Nation

In the late 1500s, a powerful general, Hideyoshi (HEE day YOH shee), laid the foundations of a unified nation. He defeated the warring daimyo and brought all of Japan under his control. Upon Hideyoshi's death, Tokugawa (toh kuh GAH wah) seized power. In 1603, he established the Tokugawa shogunate, which lasted until 1868.

Under the Tokugawa shoguns, the Japanese enjoyed peace and stability. Like European monarchs in the late Middle Ages, the Tokugawa shoguns created a strong central government. They put an end to feudal warfare and organized a government bureaucracy to oversee tax collection, finance, and justice. Although in Europe the rise of strong monarchs led to the decline of feudalism, this did not happen in Japan. The Tokugawa shoguns preserved the traditional feudal order.

To stay in power, the Tokugawa shoguns imposed a new system of government known

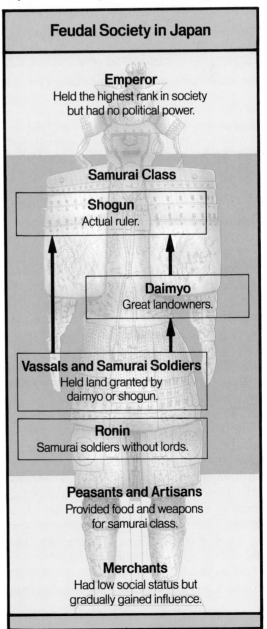

DIAGRAM STUDY *Samurai dominated feudal society in Japan, as this diagram shows. Why do you think the emperor had less power than the shogun?*

Feudal Society in Japan

Emperor
Held the highest rank in society but had no political power.

Samurai Class

Shogun
Actual ruler.

Daimyo
Great landowners.

Vassals and Samurai Soldiers
Held land granted by daimyo or shogun.

Ronin
Samurai soldiers without lords.

Peasants and Artisans
Provided food and weapons for samurai class.

Merchants
Had low social status but gradually gained influence.

279

Buddhist thought had a strong influence on Japan. Through meditation, Buddhists hoped to free themselves from attachments to worldly things and to achieve a state of peace. Total relaxation, as seen in this figure of a priest, was necessary for meditation.

as centralized feudalism. The daimyo were allowed to keep their lands, but the shogun limited their power. The daimyo had to spend every other year in the Tokugawa capital of Edo, present-day Tokyo. Their wives and families had to stay in Edo all year-round to discourage the daimyo from organizing revolts. Furthermore, a daimyo needed official approval before he could repair his castle, arrange his daughter's marriage, or sign a contract. The emperor continued to live in Kyoto, as Heian was now called, and to conduct court ceremonies.

The Japanese economy improved because of the peace and unity of centralized feudalism. The shogun abolished local feudal fees in many cities. Merchants then expanded their activities and developed trade on a national scale. Money replaced rice and grain as the means of exchange, and the merchant class thrived.

Cities, especially Edo, grew rapidly. The daimyo built splendid homes for their families in the capital. They spent lavishly on their trips back and forth to Edo. They traveled with hundreds of servants and wagons loaded with household goods. Innkeepers and shopowners set up businesses along the way, and new roads were built. As a result, travel became easier and safer.

Cultural Traditions

During the long feudal period, samurai values influenced Japanese culture. Paintings and short stories glorified warfare and the samurai code of honor.

Buddhism also shaped Japanese culture. As you read in Chapter 7, Buddhism spread from India to China, where it underwent many changes. In Japan, Buddhism developed in still other directions.

Zen, a Buddhist sect that began in China, strongly influenced Japanese traditions. Zen monks taught the unity of nature, which fit in well with the Shinto idea of respect for the forces of nature. Because Zen Buddhism emphasized physical and mental discipline, it appealed to the samurai. Zen also influenced Japanese drama. The first Japanese dramas included dances and poetry that taught Zen ideas.

Buddhist monasteries were centers of learning and the arts. For example, Zen monks created fine landscape paintings. Monks also taught upper-class men and women to express the Zen devotion to nature in such activities as flower arranging and landscape gardening. Both men and women learned the tea ceremony, which was meant to reflect peace, simplicity, and love of beauty.

Under the Tokugawa shoguns, merchants actively supported the arts. They enjoyed lively entertainments such as Kabuki theater. Kabuki dramas were violent and emotional. In towns, people flocked to see puppet plays and sumo wrestling.

A new kind of poetry, haiku (HĪ koo), also became popular. A **haiku** is a short poem with only 17 syllables. In a few words, a haiku poet sketches a mood or scene that suggests many meanings. In the following haiku, the poet shows his regard for nature:

> All night the ragged
>   clouds and wind
>   had only one
>   companion . . . the moon

When Europeans first set up trading posts, the Japanese greeted them with interest and curiosity. Yet the Japanese considered their European visitors less civilized than they. The Japanese, who bathed frequently, were shocked that Europeans seldom bathed. They referred to Europeans as the "southern barbarians" and "garlic eaters."

Japan and the World

During the feudal period, Japan traded with China, Korea, and Southeast Asia. In 1543, the first Portuguese ships arrived in Japanese waters. Christian missionaries followed the traders. Led by the Jesuit priest Francis Xavier, the missionaries won many converts. By the early 1600s, there were about 300,000 Japanese Christians.

However, the shoguns became suspicious of the missionaries. They disliked the fact that Japanese Christians pledged obedience to the pope, whom they saw as a foreign ruler. The fierce competition that developed among European traders further increased their concern. When Spain conquered the Philippines, the Japanese feared the Europeans might try to seize Japan. Eventually, the shogun outlawed Christian missionaries and persecuted Japanese Christians.

In 1639, the shogun expelled all Europeans and forbade contacts between Japanese and foreigners. He banned foreign trade and travel and stopped the building of ocean-going ships. Only the port of Nagasaki remained open to the world. At Nagasaki, Chinese and a few Dutch merchants were allowed to trade under close supervision. Like the Ming emperors in China, the Tokugawa shoguns strictly enforced their decision. For over 200 years, Japan shut itself off from the world.

SECTION 5 REVIEW

1. **Identify:** (a) Hideyoshi, (b) Tokugawa, (c) Zen, (d) Kabuki.

2. **Define:** (a) samurai, (b) shogun, (c) daimyo, (d) bushido, (e) seppuku, (f) haiku.

3. Describe the class system of feudal Japan.

4. What values did the samurai code emphasize?

5. Why did the shoguns become suspicious of foreigners?

6. **Critical Thinking** How was feudalism in Japan similar to feudalism in Europe? How was it different?

Summary

1. Hindu and Muslim traditions met in India. In the 1200s, Muslims invaded India and set up the Delhi sultanate. Despite the influence of Islam, Hindu traditions survived. In the 1500s, most of India was united under the Mogul Empire.

2. Under the T'ang and Sung dynasties, the Chinese experienced two golden ages. They expanded the civil service system and expanded economically. The Chinese also made practical advances and produced outstanding works of art.

3. In the 1200s, the Mongols conquered China, but they were eventually ousted by the Ming. The Ming dynasty financed voyages of exploration, but in the 1500s, it limited contacts with outsiders.

4. The early Japanese developed their own culture. Later, they borrowed selectively from the advanced Chinese civilization. Besides adapting Chinese writing and artistic styles, the Japanese adapted Buddhist and Confucian teachings to their own needs.

5. Japan developed a feudal society in the 1100s. For centuries warfare was a way of life. But by 1600, the Tokugawa shoguns had successfully transformed Japan into a strong, unified nation.

Recalling Facts

Decide which of the events in each of the following pairs happened first.

1. (a) The Delhi sultanate is established.
   (b) The Mogul Empire enjoys a golden age under Akbar.

2. (a) Genghis Khan invades China.
   (b) The Ming fleet makes voyages of exploration.

3. (a) China restricts all foreign traders to Canton.
   (b) China enjoys a golden age under the T'ang dynasty.

4. (a) Tokugawa shoguns expel all foreigners.
   (b) Yamato clan wins control of Japan.

Chapter Checkup

1. (a) How did Hinduism influence daily life in India? (b) What effect did Muslim rule have on India?

2. (a) How did Akbar try to unify the Mogul Empire? (b) What happened when his successors changed his policies?

3. Describe Chinese achievements in each of the following areas: (a) government; (b) technology; (c) art.

4. (a) How did foreign trade affect China during the T'ang and Sung empires? (b) Why did trade become even more extensive under the Mongols? (c) What attitude did the Chinese take toward foreign trade by the 1500s?

5. (a) What type of government did the Tokugawa shoguns establish in Japan? (b) How did they limit the power of the daimyo?

6. (a) How were Buddhist teachings brought to Japan? (b) How did Buddhism affect Japanese society?

Critical Thinking

1. **Analyzing** (a) How did differences in religious beliefs contribute to clashes between Hindus and Muslims in India? (b) In what ways was there a peaceful blending of the two cultures?

2. **Relating Past to Present** Chinese art flourished during the T'ang and Sung dy-

nasties. (a) Why was this so? (b) What conditions would encourage a "golden age" in art to develop today?

3. **Understanding the Roots of Democracy** (a) Did the Chinese think an individual's duty to society was more important or less important than his or her rights as a citizen? Explain. (b) Which do you think is more important in a democratic society? Why?

4. **Applying Information** (a) How did Chinese and Japanese attitudes toward foreigners change in the 1500s and 1600s? (b) Why do you think their views of foreigners changed?

5. **Analyzing a Quotation** A Japanese saying states: "The rice that Hideyoshi cooked was eaten by Tokugawa." Do you think this saying accurately described what happened in Japan after the late 1500s? Explain.

Developing Basic Skills

1. **Using Visual Evidence** Study the painting on page 270. Does the painting express the same feelings about nature as Li Po's poem on page 269? Explain.

2. **Map Reading** Study the map on page 272 and the maps on pages 858–859. (a) What was the extent of the Mongol Empire? (b) What countries today are located in the

lands once ruled by the Mongols? (c) Why do you think Genghis Khan divided his empire among his sons and grandsons?

3. **Using Diagrams** Study the diagram of feudal society in Japan on page 279. (a) Who held the highest status in Japanese society? (b) Who had the lowest status? (c) Why do you think the daimyo had so much power and influence? (d) What does the diagram tell you about the structure of Japanese society?

Writing About History

Defining Your Purpose

Before you decide on the exact topic of a research paper, you should consider why you are writing the paper. The most common purpose of a history research paper is to inform or to persuade your readers. Topics meant to inform readers might include *Akbar's Contributions to Indian Society* or *The Chinese Influence on Japan*. Topics designed to persuade readers should indicate a position in their titles, for example, *How Japanese Feudalism Encouraged National Unity*.

Practice: Describe two possible topics for a research paper meant to inform readers and two possible topics for a research paper meant to persuade readers.

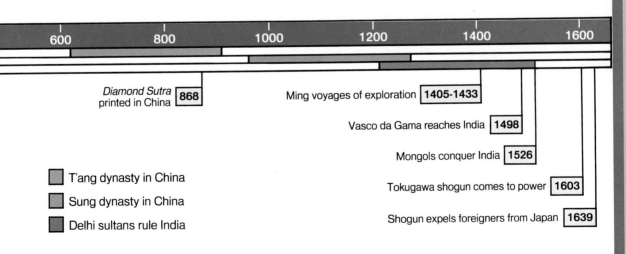

| 600 | 800 | 1000 | 1200 | 1400 | 1600 |

Diamond Sutra printed in China 868

Ming voyages of exploration 1405-1433

Vasco da Gama reaches India 1498

Mongols conquer India 1526

Tokugawa shogun comes to power 1603

Shogun expels foreigners from Japan 1639

T'ang dynasty in China
Sung dynasty in China
Delhi sultans rule India

Unit Four

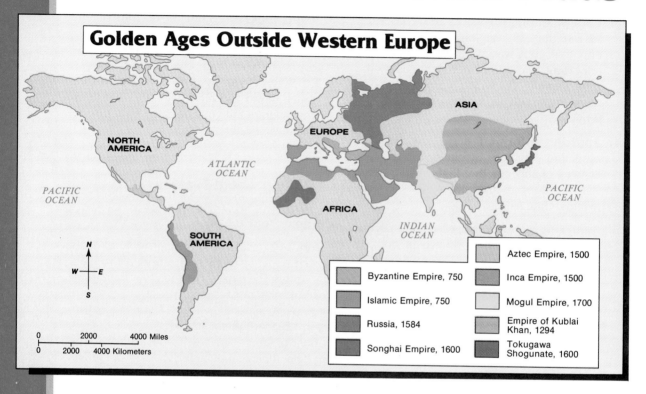

Golden Ages Outside Western Europe

ASIA

EUROPE

NORTH AMERICA

ATLANTIC OCEAN

AFRICA

INDIAN OCEAN

PACIFIC OCEAN

SOUTH AMERICA

PACIFIC OCEAN

N
W E
S

0	2000	4000 Miles
0	2000	4000 Kilometers

- Byzantine Empire, 750
- Islamic Empire, 750
- Russia, 1584
- Songhai Empire, 1600
- Aztec Empire, 1500
- Inca Empire, 1500
- Mogul Empire, 1700
- Empire of Kublai Khan, 1294
- Tokugawa Shogunate, 1600

Unit Themes

After the Roman Empire collapsed in the fifth century, the Mediterranean world split into three parts. One part was Western Europe. A second part was the Byzantine Empire, heir to the Eastern Roman Empire. It passed much of its culture on to the peoples of Eastern Europe. A third part included the lands which became part of the Islamic Empire in the 700s.

The Roman Empire did not influence all civilizations outside Western Europe. In Africa, many different peoples established distinctive patterns of life. Diverse civilizations also emerged in the Americas. The peoples of Africa and the Americas made remarkable achievements during the period of the Middle Ages in Europe.

The civilizations of India and China enjoyed golden ages marked by long periods of peace and prosperity. In Japan, after many years of warfare, the Tokugawa shoguns built a strong central government.

1. **Applying Geography** (a) Which empire on the world map above spanned three continents? (b) Compare the extent of the Delhi Sultanate shown at right and the extent of the Mogul Empire on page 265. (c) Choose one civilization from two different continents. How did geography affect their development?

2. **Analyzing Information** (a) With which outside civilizations did West African kingdoms come into contact? Why? (b) With which did East African city-states trade? Why? (c) How did European and African civilizations affect each other?

3. **Comparing** Compare and contrast the time span and the governments of the following: (a) Byzantine, (b) Inca, (c) Mongol, and (d) Tokugawa.

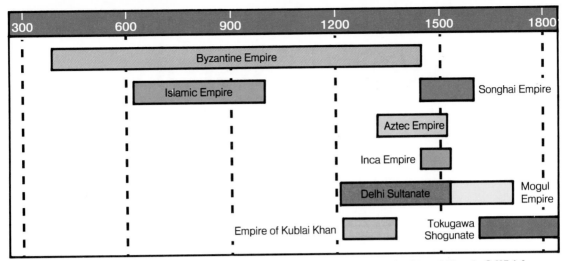

300	600	900	1200	1500	1800

Byzantine Empire

Islamic Empire

Songhai Empire

Aztec Empire

Inca Empire

Delhi Sultanate

Mogul Empire

Empire of Kublai Khan

Tokugawa Shogunate

TIME LINE STUDY *Did the Empire of Kublai Khan exist before or after the Mogul Empire? Which event on the time line indicates that Islam continued to influence the world after the decline of the Islamic Empire?*

MAP STUDY *Muslim invaders established the Delhi sultanate that ruled in India in 1206. Who led an invasion into India in 1398? Through which geographical barrier did the invaders pass?*

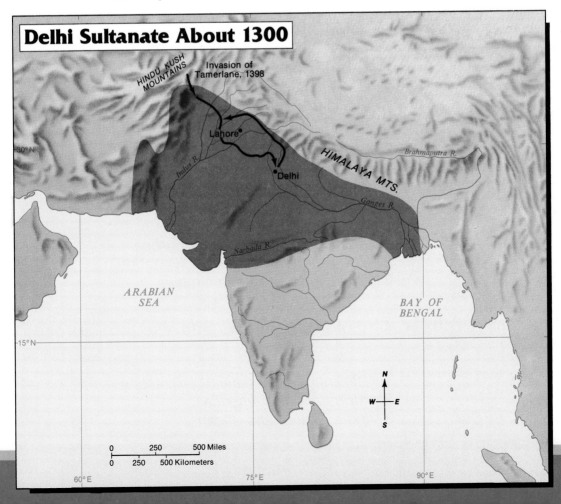

Delhi Sultanate About 1300

A Brief Survey of
World History
From Prehistoric Times
to 1500

Ancient civilizations come to life in the art that has survived throughout the ages. This wheeled cart made of iron symbolizes the creative spirit that spurred early civilizations to new achievements.

Overview 1

Beginnings of Ancient Civilizations

(Prehistory—256 B.C.)

OVERVIEW OUTLINE

1. Foundations of Civilization
2. Ancient Egypt
3. The Ancient Middle East
4. Ancient India and China

About noon on a spring day, Ramses II was encamped with his army near the city of Kadesh in Syria. The Egyptian ruler was planning a surprise attack on the Hittites. Like the Egyptians, the Hittites had conquered a vast empire and were eager to expand their power.

While Ramses waited for his army to assemble, Hittite chariots suddenly appeared out of nowhere. The Egyptian forces fled, leaving Ramses to face the enemy alone. Miraculously, Ramses escaped with his life. He later had scenes of the battle carved on temple walls all over Egypt.

According to these carvings, Ramses had called on Amon, the chief Egyptian god, to save him. "My soldiers and charioteers have forsaken me," Ramses prayed, "but I call and find that Amon is worth more to me than millions of foot soldiers and hundreds of thousands of chariots."

The temple carvings show that Ramses then rallied his forces and defeated the Hittites. However, Hittite texts recently discovered tell us that the Egyptians suffered a setback at the Battle of Kadesh. Eventually, in 1284 B.C., Ramses and the Hittites signed a treaty that set the borders of the two empires. This treaty, in Egyptian and Hittite writing, is the oldest complete treaty in existence.

At the time of the Battle of Kadesh, over 3,000 years ago, powerful civilizations had emerged in several parts of the world. In the fertile river valleys of Egypt, the Middle East, India, and China, people had learned to farm, producing enough food to support large cities and strong governments. These early civilizations had certain similar features, but each also had its own ideas about religion, government, and society. ■

1 Foundations of Civilization

READ TO UNDERSTAND

☐ **What five themes geographers study.**

☐ **How we know about prehistoric people.**

☐ **What features are common to all civilizations.**

☐ *Vocabulary:* **geography, projection, prehistory, artifact, nomad, technology, polytheistic, scribe.**

From written records, art, architecture, and other remains, scholars have pieced together the evidence about how early civilizations emerged. They have learned that the first civilizations were built on the achievements of still earlier people. Finding evidence about these people, however, has often proved difficult.

Geography and World History

Every event and development in world history takes place somewhere. When historians study the past, one of the first things they look at is where something happened. As you will see, the **geography** of a place—its people, environments, and resources—often help shape events and developments.

Historians work closely with geographers, who organize information into five major themes. The first theme is location—where a place is. Location also involves noting where a place is in relationship to other places. For example, was Kadesh, Syria, where Ramses II fought, near Egypt, his home base?

A second concern of geographers is place —the physical and human characteristics of a location. Is the land fertile? Is water available? Are most of the people farmers?

Third, geographers study how people have interacted with their environment. If water is scarce, how do people conserve and use it?

Fourth, geographers look at the movements of people from one place to another. What, for example, brought thousands of Irish people to the United States in the mid-1800s?

Finally, geographers study regions—areas with similar characteristics. Similar physical characteristics are what make the Great Plains a region, while similar political and cultural features are what make Latin America a region.

To study the earth and its people, geographers and historians use globes and maps. Mapmakers use various **projections**—ways of showing the curved earth on a flat surface. Although all map projections have some distortions, geographers and historians choose the projection that best suits the area they are studying.

Stone Age People

Historians use the term **prehistory** to refer to the long period of time before the invention of writing. By analyzing **artifacts,** objects such as tools and weapons left behind by early people, historians have learned about the lives of these ancient people.

Because the earliest tools and weapons were made of stone, scholars have called the long period from about 500,000 B.C. to 3500 B.C. the Stone Age. During the Old Stone Age, from about 500,000 B.C. to about 10,000 B.C., people were **nomads,** living in small bands. They were always on the move, hunting and gathering food. They invented simple tools and learned to control fire. Old Stone Age peoples probably also developed spoken languages.

About 10,000 B.C., people in different parts of the world learned to grow grain and plant vegetables. The development of agriculture ushered in the New Stone Age. The change from hunting and food gathering to farming changed the way people lived. They began to build permanent settlements and to develop new ways to cooperate with one another. In villages, a form of government emerged with a chief and a council of elders who made decisions about planting and harvesting. Religion, too, developed formal rituals as farming people prayed to spirits for good harvests.

In the New Stone Age, people made important advances in **technology,** that is, the tools and skills that people use to meet their basic needs. They made farm tools, learned to use animals to pull plows, and invented the wheel, the sail, and weaving.

Emergence of Civilization

In some places, simple farming communities slowly grew into cities. As the cities grew, civilizations developed. A civilization has seven major features—cities, complex religions, well-organized government, specialized skills, specialized occupations, social classes, and a system of keeping records.

The first cities developed in river valleys in North Africa, the Middle East, and Asia. (See the map on page 13.) Fertile soils and water from the rivers allowed farmers to produce surplus food that supported large populations.

In 1940, four boys discovered this cave painting in Lascaux, France. The work of Stone Age artists, this red and black bison is one of 20 painted in the cave. The artists created colors by grinding ores and mixing them with animal fat.

In the early cities, government and religion were closely related. People were **polytheistic,** that is, they worshipped many gods. Powerful priest-kings combined the tasks of keeping the gods friendly by performing the proper rituals and defending the cities against enemies. These early rulers also organized the people to clear the land and build the irrigation systems that were essential to farming.

With the growth of cities, other patterns emerged. As people learned skills such as weaving or bronze making, different occupations appeared. Most people remained farmers, but some became merchants, traders, or artisans. In the social classes that developed, a person's place in society became well defined and was usually determined by birth.

A major achievement of early civilizations was the development of keeping records. **Scribes,** or people who could read and write, were trained in the temples. Their records of harvests and taxes preserved important information for future generations.

1. **Identify:** Stone Age.

2. **Define:** (a) geography, (b) projection, (c) prehistory, (d) artifact, (e) nomad, (f) technology, (g) polytheistic, (h) scribe.

3. What are the five themes studied by geographers?

4. List two advances made in the Old Stone Age and two in the New Stone Age.

5. How were religion and government related in the early cities?

6. **Critical Thinking** How might geography influence the ways in which different civilizations develop?

2 Ancient Egypt

READ TO UNDERSTAND

☐ **How the Nile influenced ancient Egypt.**

☐ **How the Egyptian government and society were organized.**

☐ **What contributions Egyptians made to civilization.**

☐ *Vocabulary:* **hieroglyphics, dynasty.**

By 7000 B.C., people had begun to farm in the Nile River valley. In time, the farmers of the Nile Valley produced enough food to support a thriving civilization.

Geographic Setting

Geography favored the growth of Egyptian civilization. In ancient times, the Nile River was seen as the "giver of life." Once a year, the Nile flooded, bringing rich soil to the farmlands along its banks. The river also served as a highway that helped to unite Upper Egypt in the south and Lower Egypt in the north. During Egypt's early history, the surrounding natural barriers of seas and deserts protected it from invasion.

Religion

The religious beliefs of the ancient Egyptians reflected the importance of the Nile and other forces of nature. Like other ancient peoples, the Egyptians were polytheistic. Through prayer and religious rituals, they called on the gods to give good harvests. Among their most important gods were Amon-Re, the sun god, and Osiris, god of the Nile.

The Egyptians believed in a life after death. This concern with the afterlife affected their daily lives. They believed, for example, that only those people who lived moral lives would enjoy a happy afterlife. To prepare for the afterlife, Egyptian rulers had elaborate tombs built and had their bodies mummified to preserve them after death. **Hieroglyphics,** the Egyptian system of writing, was also connected to religion. Priests probably developed hieroglyphics to keep records of religious rituals and temple property.

Growth of Unified Government

In its long history, Egypt was ruled by at least 30 **dynasties,** or ruling families. Historians have divided the dynasties into three periods: the Old Kingdom (2700 B.C.–2200 B.C.), the Middle Kingdom (2050 B.C.–1800 B.C.), and the New Kingdom (1570 B.C.–1090 B.C.). At the beginning of each period, strong rulers united the land. Toward the end of each, civil wars, peasant revolts, and invasions occurred.

During the Old Kingdom, Egyptian rulers took the title pharaoh, meaning "great house." To the Egyptians, the pharaoh was a god who ruled with absolute power. The pharaohs set up a strong central government. They appointed officials to oversee the collection of taxes and the building of irrigation systems. The power of the Old Kingdom pharaohs was shown in the building of their vast pyramid tombs. Pyramids required the efforts of thousands of workers and cost huge amounts of money.

During the Middle and New Kingdoms, Egypt expanded its borders. Through trade and conquest, it increased contacts with other lands. The first woman ruler known to history, Hatshepsut, reigned for 22 years during the New Kingdom. Another noted pharaoh of the

To preserve the bodies of the dead, the Egyptians used the process of mummification. First, they extracted the brain of the dead person through the nostrils and removed most of the internal organs. Then they filled the body cavity with spices and put the corpse in a preserving fluid. After 70 days, they wrapped the body in bandages. A lifelike mask, such as this one decorated with gold and jewels, covered the head and shoulders of the mummy.

New Kingdom was Akenaton. He tried to change the traditional religious practices, replacing the worship of Amon-Re with the worship of Aton. But Tutankhamon, his successor, returned to the old ways.

Egyptian Society

During the Old Kingdom, Egypt developed a social order that remained relatively unchanged for thousands of years. At the top was the pharaoh, who lived in luxury and splendor. Below him was the ruling class of priests and nobles. Priests enjoyed great power because only they knew the correct ceremonies to please the gods. Nobles served as government officials.

A small middle class came next. It included artisans, merchants, physicians, and skilled workers who provided services to the ruling class. At the bottom were the majority of people—peasants and slaves. They worked the land, built the irrigation systems, and constructed the palaces, temples, and tombs of the pharaohs.

Achievements of Egyptian Civilization

The Egyptians made remarkable advances in engineering, science, mathematics, the arts, and literature. Many achievements grew out of practical needs. To the Egyptians, building and decorating temples and pyramids were necessary to ensure the goodwill of the gods and to protect individuals in the afterlife.

Egyptians also developed methods of surveying and measuring the land to divide up their fields and set boundaries. Priests studied the skies to know the change of seasons and predict eclipses. Their observations led to the development of a 365-day calendar that became the basis for the calendar used today.

SECTION 2 REVIEW

1. **Identify:** (a) Amon-Re, (b) Osiris, (c) Hatshepsut, (d) Akenaton.

2. **Define:** (a) hieroglyphics, (b) dynasty.

3. List three ways in which geography helped the ancient Egyptians.

4. How did religion affect different aspects of life in Egypt?

5. **Critical Thinking** Why do you think the structure of Egyptian society changed so little over thousands of years?

3 The Ancient Middle East

READ TO UNDERSTAND

☐ Why so much blending of cultures occurred in the ancient Middle East.

☐ What contributions to civilization were made by small Middle Eastern states.

☐ *Vocabulary:* city-state, cuneiform, monotheism.

While the Egyptians were shaping their civilization in the Nile River valley, other people were building the foundations of civilizations in the ancient Middle East.

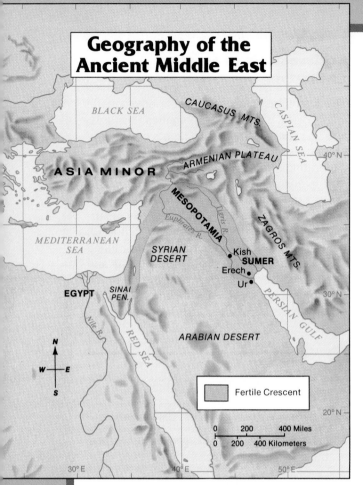

Geography of the Ancient Middle East

MAP STUDY *The fertile soil and the wild game of the Tigris-Euphrates Valley attracted settlers. Why was the Fertile Crescent called the crossroads of the world?*

Geographic Setting

The civilizations of the ancient Middle East developed in the Fertile Crescent, an area of fertile farmland that stretched in an arc from the Persian Gulf to the Mediterranean Sea. The Fertile Crescent has no natural barriers. Thus, it became the "crossroads of the world" as many different people migrated, invaded, or settled in the area. The diversity of people made the region difficult to unite, but it also encouraged a vital exchange of ideas.

The earliest civilization developed in the valley of the Tigris and Euphrates rivers. The area was called Mesopotamia, which means the land between two rivers. Like the Nile, the Tigris and Euphrates were central to the lives of the people. The rivers provided water, brought fertile soil, and served as a means of transportation. However, unlike the Nile, whose annual flood was predictable, the Tigris and Euphrates sometimes overflowed their banks with sudden ferocity, causing much destruction and suffering.

Sumerian Civilization

The need to control the flooding and to clear land for farming led to the development of Sumerian civilization in lower Mesopotamia. As villages expanded, they grew into independent **city-states.** In each city-state, a town and the surrounding countryside cooperated for mutual defense. Rival city-states often competed for power. Still, trade among them helped bring wealth to the region.

As in Egypt, religion played an important role in the lives of the Sumerians. However, the Sumerians had a gloomy outlook on life and did not believe in a happy afterlife. They believed that natural disasters such as floods and famine were punishments sent by the gods. Priests held great power because they were believed to be the only people who knew how to keep the gods happy.

The Sumerians had many achievements to their credit on which later people built. They developed a system of writing, called **cuneiform.** They were among the first people to use the wheel. Like the Egyptians, they developed mathematics to survey land and set boundaries. The Sumerian system of counting, based on the number 60, led to such measurements as the 60-second minute and the 60-minute hour.

Blending of Cultures

As the Sumerian city-states declined, other peoples conquered Mesopotamia. Some built strong empires that lasted for centuries. Among the most powerful rulers of Mesopotamia was Hammurabi. To achieve unity in his empire, Hammurabi had a code drawn up of all existing laws. The Code of Hammurabi was a landmark achievement because it set up a unified system of justice. It distinguished between major and minor crimes and spelled out the punishment for each crime.

As conquerors swept across Mesopotamia, they helped blend many cultures. When the Hittites invaded from Asia Minor, they introduced their knowledge of ironmaking. Later, the Assyrians conquered the Fertile Crescent, destroying their enemies with ruthless brutality. One Assyrian ruler, however, collected a huge library of cuneiform tablets that preserved much of the knowledge of ancient Mesopotamia. By 500 B.C., the Persians had conquered a large empire stretching from the Indus River in the east to the Mediterranean Sea. They set up an efficient system of government that became a model for many later peoples.

Contributions of Smaller States

Several small states also contributed to the civilizations of the ancient Middle East. The Phoenicians were merchants and traders who lived in port cities along the eastern Mediterranean coast. They earned the name "carriers of civilization" because they spread the learning and culture of ancient Mesopotamia to the colonies they had set up throughout the Mediterranean world.

The Hebrews made a lasting impact on the world through their **monotheism,** the worship of one all-powerful God. They also developed the belief that all people should lead moral lives. Hebrew prophets taught their people to do good, respect other individuals, look after the poor, and obey God's laws. Many of these ideas of Judaism would later become a part of two other world religions.

SECTION 3 REVIEW

1. **Identify:** (a) Fertile Crescent, (b) Mesopotamia, (c) Code of Hammurabi.

2. **Define:** (a) city-state, (b) cuneiform, (c) monotheism.

3. List two ways in which the geography of the Fertile Crescent differed from that of the Nile River valley.

4. Describe one contribution of the: (a) Persians, (b) Phoenicians, (c) Hebrews.

5. **Critical Thinking** How did frequent invasions affect the civilizations of the ancient Middle East?

---

4 Ancient India and China

READ TO UNDERSTAND

☐ How geography influenced early civilizations in India and China.

☐ How the Aryan conquest affected Indian civilization.

☐ What beliefs the Chinese developed under the Shang and Chou dynasties.

☐ *Vocabulary:* reincarnation, caste, loess, bureaucracy.

Both India and China have fertile river valleys where early peoples laid the foundation of lasting civilizations. In each region, however, the people developed their own distinct ways of life.

Indus Valley Civilization

In India, as elsewhere, geography influenced early civilizations. Natural barriers such as the towering Hindu Kush and Himalaya mountains limited contact between the Indian subcontinent and the rest of Asia. However, the mountains did not completely protect India. On many occasions, invaders forced their way through steep passes in the Hindu Kush to descend onto the farmers of the fertile plains of northern India.

The first Indian civilization rose about 2500 B.C. in the Indus River valley. Little is known about the Indus Valley civilization, in part because scholars have not yet deciphered its writing. However, the remains of two well-planned cities—Harappa and Mohenjo-Daro—have revealed that a powerful government ruled the Indus Valley for more than 1,000 years.

Aryan Conquest

About 1500 B.C., the Aryans, who were nomadic herders, crossed the Hindu Kush and conquered the Indus Valley civilization. The Aryans brought their own traditions and beliefs to India. They gradually created a new culture whose patterns have shaped India to the present day.

The early Aryans worshipped many gods, but in time they came to believe in a single unifying force. They also developed a belief in **reincarnation,** the rebirth of the soul in another bodily form. These beliefs formed the foundations of Hinduism, the major religion of India today.

The Aryans developed a written language, called Sanskrit, but maintained a rich oral literature. After their conquest of India, the Aryan social structure gradually evolved into a rigid caste system. The four main **castes,** or social groups, were the warriors, priests, landowners and merchants, and peasants. A person's caste was determined by birth alone.

The beauty of the bronze art of ancient China was unrivaled. This finely detailed figure from the Chou period shows a young boy holding birds carved of jade. To the Chou, bronze was more than a valuable metal, it was also magical.

Early Chinese Civilization

Like India, China was surrounded by imposing geographic barriers that limited contact with outsiders. High mountain ranges, rugged plateaus, deserts, and the Pacific Ocean protected China. As a result, the Chinese came to see their land as the center of the universe.

The first Chinese civilization developed in the Yellow River valley. There, fertile soil, called **loess,** was easily worked. However, this region of China suffers from droughts and floods, and the Yellow River earned the title "River of Sorrows" for the death and destruction brought by its flooding.

The Shang dynasty. As in Egypt and Sumer, powerful rulers extended their control over the farming villages of the river valley. The Shang dynasty was the first of many families to rule China. The traditions and beliefs that emerged in Shang times shaped Chinese civilization for thousands of years.

The Chinese believed that the gods controlled the forces of nature. They also believed that their ancestors could influence the gods. Shang kings acted as priests, performing daily ceremonies to ask their ancestors for the favor of the gods.

The Shang invented a system of writing that used pictograms, or pictures of objects, and ideograms as symbols that expressed ideas or actions. In time, the Chinese writing system became so complicated that a person had to study for years in order to learn to read and write well. The Shang also developed skills in bronze working and silk weaving and invented an accurate calendar.

The Chou dynasty. The Chou dynasty, which overthrew the Shang, built on these early achievements. The Chou claimed to have won the "Mandate of Heaven." According to this belief, Heaven supported a just ruler who provided his people with good government. A ruler lost the "Mandate of Heaven" if his people suffered from floods, famines, or invasions.

The Chou ruler divided the land among powerful nobles, who then owed loyalty, military service, and tribute to the king. These feudal lords expanded the borders of China, often setting up their own independent states. As their states expanded, they developed complex bureaucracies. A **bureaucracy** is a system of organizing government with appointed officials. In Chou China, government officials gained an important place in society. Despite frequent warfare among rival feudal states, the Chou era was a time of economic growth.

SECTION 4 REVIEW

1. **Identify:** (a) Harappa, (b) Aryans, (c) Mandate of Heaven.

2. **Define:** (a) reincarnation, (b) caste, (c) loess, (d) bureaucracy.

3. What religious beliefs did the Aryans have?

4. How did Chou rulers govern China?

5. **Critical Thinking** How could the idea of the Mandate of Heaven be used to justify a rebellion?

Review

Checkup

1. What do geographers study?

2. Describe the major differences between the Old Stone Age and the New Stone Age.

3. Explain the basic characteristics of a civilization.

4. Why were scribes important?

5. How were the religious beliefs of ancient Egypt tied to natural forces?

6. What were the major achievements of the ancient Egyptians?

7. Why has the Fertile Crescent been called the "crossroads of the world"?

8. (a) What was the first civilization in India? (b) Why do scholars know little about it?

9. What religious and social ideas shaped early Aryan civilization?

10. Describe two achievements of the Shang dynasty that shaped later Chinese civilization.

Critical Thinking

1. **Applying Information** (a) How do scholars learn about ancient civilizations? (b) What problems do they face in studying these civilizations?

2. **Analyzing Geography in History** (a) Why was the Nile River known as the "giver of life"? (b) Why was the Yellow River known as the "River of Sorrows"? (c) Why did rivers play such an important part in the development of early civilizations?

3. **Comparing Civilizations** Why do you think early civilizations developed different forms of government and different religious beliefs?

4. **Understanding the Roots of Democracy** (a) What moral view of the world did the Hebrews believe in? (b) Why are moral values such as these necessary in a democratic society?

Developing Basic Skills

1. **Using Visual Evidence** Study the picture on page 291. (a) What does the picture show? (b) About when was it created? (c) What does it tell you about Egyptian life?

2. **Map Reading** Study the map on page 292. (a) What does this map show? (b) What geographic features does it include? (c) In which direction would an Egyptian travel to reach the Fertile Crescent?

The Romans adopted many ideas from the ancient Greeks, including drama. In this Roman mosaic, the actor at right dons his costume, which includes the mask on the table.

Overview 2

Rise of Classical Civilizations

(2000 B.C.—550 A.D.)

OVERVIEW OUTLINE

1. The Heritage of Ancient Greece
2. Ancient Rome: Republic to Empire
3. The Roman Heritage
4. The Heritage of India and China

In 399 B.C., the great philosopher Socrates sat in a prison cell under a death sentence. A jury of Athenian citizens had convicted him of failing to honor the gods and corrupting the youth of the city. According to Plato, one of Socrates' students who became a great philosopher, Socrates could have avoided a trial and escaped the death sentence.

Plato reported that a young Athenian named Crito tried to persuade Socrates to escape. Socrates listened to the plan but then carefully reasoned with Crito to show him why escape would be wrong.

Socrates: Are we to say that we are never intentionally to do wrong and that injustice is always an evil, and dishonor comes to him who acts unjustly?
Crito: Yes.
Socrates: Ought a man to do what he admits to be right, or ought he to betray the right?

Crito: He ought to do what he thinks right.

Socrates: But if this is true, what is the application? In leaving the prison against the will of the Athenians, do I not wrong those whom I ought least to wrong? Do I not desert the principles which we acknowledge to be just?

About 2,400 years ago, Socrates was one of many thinkers who was concerned with moral issues. He carefully distinguished between a person's ideas about right and wrong and an individual's duty to obey the laws of the state.

Socrates lived at the height of ancient Greek civilization. Later, Rome built on Greek achievements in the arts, literature, and learning. The civilizations of Greece and Rome became known as "classical civilizations" because they established standards of excellence against which later civilizations were judged.

In India and China, too, strong religious and philosophical traditions arose that had a lasting impact. The civilizations of India and China became highly developed and created strong empires that preserved the unique heritage of each. ■

1 The Heritage of Ancient Greece

READ TO UNDERSTAND

☐ **How geography influenced Greek civilization.**

☐ **How Athens and Sparta differed.**

☐ **What contributions the Greeks made to civilization.**

☐ *Vocabulary:* **monarchy, aristocracy, democracy, direct democracy, tragedy, Socratic method.**

Unlike the river valley civilizations of Egypt, Mesopotamia, India, and China, the civilization that emerged in ancient Greece was built on small, independent cities that were often at war with each other. Although the Greeks did not conquer a vast empire, their civilization has had a lasting impact on the Western world.

Geographic Setting

The Greek mainland is a mountainous peninsula. The rugged terrain made transportation and communication difficult and led the Greeks to develop small, separate communities. Each community valued its freedom and fiercely resisted any outside interference.

The Greek coastline has excellent harbors, and the nearby Aegean Sea is dotted with islands. As a result, the early Greeks turned to the sea. They built a thriving trade, setting up colonies and carrying goods across the Mediterranean. Because of their frequent contact with other civilizations, they developed a practical attitude toward new ideas and adopted any that suited their needs.

Government in the Greek City-States

The Greek city-states developed various forms of government. At first, a **monarchy,** or government headed by a king, ruled each city-state. Gradually, **aristocracies,** or governments by a small, privileged upper class, replaced the monarchies. As city-states grew and prospered, other classes demanded the right to participate in government.

Growth of democracy in Athens. Like other Greek city-states, Athens was ruled first by a monarch and then by a landowning aristocracy. Gradually, however, Athenian leaders

Greek roots of democracy are evident on this ceramic jar, which has the first known illustration of a secret ballot. After the voters write their choice on olive leaves, they deposit their ballots in a bowl held by Athena, the Greek goddess of wisdom, reason, and purity.

Military government in Sparta. Athens' rival for power was the landlocked city-state of Sparta. Spartan life differed greatly from that of Athens. The Spartans created a strong military government headed by a monarch. The government kept a close watch on the lives of its citizens and the thousands of slaves who worked the land. The Spartans valued strict discipline, obedience, and endurance, qualities that made them the most respected fighters in the Greek world.

Rivalry among Athens, Sparta, and other city-states led to frequent warfare. For a brief time in the 400s B.C., the Greeks united to defeat the expanding power of the Persian Empire. However, fighting among the city-states was resumed after the Persian Wars. Athens had emerged as the dominant Greek city-state, and the other city-states resented its success and power. They fought Athens in the Peloponnesian Wars, which lasted from 431 B.C. to 404 B.C. and ended with Sparta's defeat of Athens.

Greek Art and Thought

In the arts and philosophy, the Greeks created works and developed ideas that have enriched the world to the present time. The Greeks built temples and held festivals to honor their gods. Out of the festivals honoring Dionysus, the god of wine, came the first Greek dramas. The early Greek dramas were **tragedies,** plays that focused on the suffering of a major character and usually ended in disaster. Later, in comedies, Greek writers poked fun at human weaknesses.

In art and architecture, the Greeks expressed their love of beauty and harmony. The graceful columns of the Parthenon, the temple of Athena in Athens, show the Greek respect for simple elegance. Greek sculptors always emphasized the ideal, or perfect form, whether they were carving statues of humans or their gods.

The Greeks developed ways of looking at the world that differed from those of earlier people. They questioned the traditional view that the gods were the cause of all natural events. Greek philosophers believed that through observation and the use of reason

introduced a series of reforms that became the basis for Athenian **democracy,** or government by the citizens.

Athens reached the peak of its power under one of its great leaders, Pericles, in the 400s B.C. The government was a **direct democracy,** in which all citizens had the right to vote in the Assembly. Not all Athenians were citizens, however. Resident aliens, slaves, and women had no political rights. But the example of Athenian public service and free exchange of ideas encouraged the growth of democracy in other Greek city-states.

they could discover natural laws to explain the universe. Curiosity and logical reasoning led the Greeks to make important advances in science and medicine.

In pursuit of truth, the philosopher Socrates developed a question-and-answer technique, called the **Socratic method.** By persistent questioning, he tried to make people examine their beliefs using reason. Like Socrates, the philosopher Plato raised many questions about the meaning of justice and the nature of beauty and truth.

Hellenistic Civilization

In the 300s B.C., Alexander the Great of Macedonia emerged as a world conqueror. In just a few years, he won an empire stretching from Greece to the Indus River. Alexander's greatest achievement was not his short-lived empire but his creation of a new culture, known as Hellenistic civilization. The new civilization represented a blend of Greek, Roman, and other ancient civilizations.

Alexandria, a city in Egypt, came to symbolize the vitality of Hellenistic civilization. There, thinkers from Greece, Egypt, and Persia exchanged ideas and produced outstanding works in science, mathematics, medicine, astronomy, and philosophy.

SECTION 1 REVIEW

1. **Identify:** (a) Pericles, (b) Peloponnesian Wars, (c) Parthenon, (d) Socrates, (e) Alexander the Great.

2. **Define:** (a) monarchy, (b) aristocracy, (c) democracy, (d) direct democracy, (e) tragedy, (f) Socratic method.

3. Describe two ways in which geography affected the ancient Greeks.

4. How did Sparta differ from Athens?

5. **Critical Thinking** Which characteristics of government in ancient Athens would be considered democratic today? Which would not?

---

2 Ancient Rome: Republic to Empire

READD TO UNDERSTAND

☐ How the Roman Republic changed as it expanded.

☐ Why the republic declined.

☐ What the successes and failures of the Roman Empire were.

☐ *Vocabulary:* republic, patrician, plebeian, devalue.

While Greek civilization was flourishing, the small city-state of Rome was building the foundations for a strong government. From small beginnings on the Italian peninsula, Rome grew to become a powerful empire that brought many lands and people under its control.

The Roman Republic

In 509 B.C., the Romans overthrew their Etruscan rulers and set up their own form of government. They established a **republic,** a government in which citizens have the right to vote for their leaders. In the early Roman Republic, **patricians,** or wealthy landowners, controlled the government. **Plebeians,** the common people, were citizens, but they had to struggle for 200 years before they gained a voice in government.

The early Romans had to battle to survive against powerful neighbors. These early struggles shaped their belief in the values of duty, discipline, and patriotism. Yet the Romans also benefited from the more advanced civilizations with which they came in contact. From the Greeks, Phoenicians, and Etruscans, they acquired the alphabet, learned skills in building and engineering, and adapted religious ideas.

Expansion of Rome. Between 509 B.C. and 133 B.C., well-trained Roman armies fought many wars of expansion. First, they won control of the Italian peninsula. In the three Punic Wars, Rome defeated Carthage, its North African rival for power in the western Mediterranean, and gained new territories. Roman armies also won lands in the eastern Mediterranean.

As the wars of expansion changed Rome from a small republic into a large empire, they brought social and economic changes. Cheap grain, paid as tribute by the people of the conquered lands, caused hardships for Roman farmers. Many were forced to leave their farms. They swelled the population of landless poor in the city. At the same time, treasure taken from the conquered peoples made other Romans rich.

Decline of the Republic. When attempts at reform failed, Romans turned to military leaders. For years, civil war raged as rival generals battled for power. Then, in 49 B.C., Julius Caesar seized control of Rome and restored order. He made reforms, extended Roman citizenship to many people, and redistributed land to the poor. With Caesar's assassination in 44 B.C., however, the Roman Republic ended.

The Roman Empire

The rule of Caesar's heir, Augustus, marked the beginning of the Roman Empire. Augustus set up a strong, stable government that united the vast Roman Empire. For nearly 200 years, Rome enjoyed the Pax Romana, a period of peace and prosperity. Rome divided its empire into provinces, connected by excellent roads. It administered its government with an efficient civil service.

Despite the prosperity, Rome faced serious social and economic problems. The cost of maintaining the empire was enormous.

MAP STUDY *Rome expanded its empire mostly through war. The Punic Wars, which ended in 146 B.C., brought large amounts of territory into the empire. Rome also acquired territory when the king of Pergamum died, leaving his empire in Asia Minor to Rome. During which period did Rome gain the most territory in Africa?*

Expansion of Rome, 509 B.C. - 44 B.C.

This painting from a Roman villa shows a wealthy woman and her servant. Women, especially those from wealthy families, enjoyed some power and influence in ancient Rome.

Prices rose, and Rome was forced to **devalue,** or lower the value of, its coins. Also, many Romans came to look down on hard work as fit only for slaves. This attitude slowly undermined the strength of the Roman Empire.

SECTION 2 REVIEW

1. **Identify:** (a) Punic Wars, (b) Julius Caesar, (c) Augustus, (d) Pax Romana.

2. **Define:** (a) republic, (b) patrician, (c) plebeian, (d) devalue.

3. What qualities did the early Romans emphasize?

4. What benefits did Roman government bring to the Empire?

5. **Critical Thinking** Do you think the expansion of Rome was positive or negative for the people of Rome? Explain.

3 The Roman Heritage

READ TO UNDERSTAND

☐ **What the Romans contributed to the world.**

☐ **How Christianity arose and spread.**

☐ **Why the Roman Empire declined.**

Roman settlers, soldiers, and officials spread Roman ideas from Spain to Mesopotamia. Through Rome, the knowledge and achievements of the ancient world were gathered, preserved, and handed on to the peoples of Western Europe.

Greco-Roman Civilization

The Romans respected the civilizations they conquered and blended them with their own. "Greece has conquered her rude conquerors," observed the Roman poet Horace, who saw evidence of Greek influence everywhere in Rome. This blend of traditions is known as Greco-Roman civilization.

The Romans emphasized practical matters, developing technical skills and knowledge in building and engineering. They invented the dome, learned to mix concrete, and built strong roads, bridges, and aqueducts.

To solve the practical problems of government, the Romans developed a system of law and justice that was one of their major achievements. They introduced the principle that the accused is innocent until proven guilty. They also allowed the use of evidence in the courtroom and set up procedures to ensure a fair trial. Roman law became the basis for later law systems in Western Europe.

Rise of Christianity

During the Pax Romana, Christianity was founded in Palestine. The new religion was based on the teachings of Jesus, whose message was rooted in Hebrew traditions. He stressed love for God, compassion for other people, and the hope of eternal life. Despite persecution, the followers of Jesus spread this message across the Greco-Roman world. In

Christian themes became common subjects of art in the Roman Empire, especially after Christianity was recognized as the official religion. This Christian mosaic shows Saint Apollinare as a shepherd, perhaps a reminder of Christ's command to his disciples to care for his sheep.

395 A.D., Christianity was made the official religion of the Roman Empire.

In time, Christians developed a strong church organization. At the head of the Church was the pope in Rome. Below him were other members of the clergy, including archbishops, bishops, and priests. The clergy maintained order and discipline in the Church.

Decline of Rome

Christianity was growing stronger at a time when the Roman Empire was growing weaker. Struggles for power over who would succeed each emperor led to frequent civil wars. The fighting disrupted trade, and the economy of the empire declined. Occasionally, a strong ruler rose to stem the tide of decay. Diocletian, for example, introduced reforms to restore order and solve basic economic problems. To govern better, he divided the empire into an eastern and western part. Constantine continued Diocletian's policies and moved the capital to Constantinople, closer to the rich cities of the Eastern Roman Empire. But these attempts at reform failed.

In addition to internal problems, the empire faced threats from invaders. Roman legions were withdrawn from the frontiers to protect towns and cities. As Roman government crumbled, the economy fell into disorder. Under constant pressure from invaders, the Western Roman Empire fell in the fifth century. Yet the Roman heritage survived in Western Europe and in the Eastern Roman Empire.

SECTION 3 REVIEW

1. **Identify:** (a) Greco-Roman civilization, (b) Jesus, (c) Diocletian, (d) Constantine.

2. Describe two practical achievements of the Romans.

3. What ideas did Jesus teach?

4. What external problems did the Roman Empire face?

5. **Critical Thinking** How is the Roman contribution to law connected with the Roman interest in practical matters?

4 The Heritage of India and China

READ TO UNDERSTAND

☐ How Hinduism and Buddhism influenced Indian life.

☐ What philosophies shaped Chinese traditions.

☐ What strong rulers in both India and China achieved.

☐ *Vocabulary:* brahma, nirvana.

While Greco-Roman civilization flourished in the Mediterranean world, the civilizations of India and China were developing their own lasting traditions in Asia. Rulers in both India and China created strong empires. Important advances were made in government, learning, and the arts.

Two Religions of India

India was the birthplace of two major world religions—Hinduism and Buddhism. Hinduism grew out of early Aryan beliefs. Although Hindus worship many gods, they believe that the gods are part of **brahma,** the supreme force that unites everything in the universe. To Hindus, the ultimate goal of life is to free the soul from its individual existence and achieve reunion with a larger universal soul. Hindus believe this takes more than one lifetime.

Hinduism supported the caste system. People were taught to obey caste rules so that they might be reincarnated, or reborn, into a higher caste in the next lifetime. By the 500s B.C., some Hindus were criticizing the power of priests, the highest caste. One critic was Siddhartha Gautama. He set out to reform Hinduism, but his teachings became the basis for a new religion, Buddhism.

After a long search for the meaning of life, Gautama discovered certain basic truths. He taught that the only way to salvation was to overcome desire. Desire was the cause of pain and suffering. Buddhism offered guidelines to achieve **nirvana,** the condition of wanting nothing. From India, Buddhism spread to China, Korea, Japan, and Southeast Asia.

Great Empires

Throughout India's long history, the northern plain was a battleground for rival rulers. Some built strong empires. Among these, the Maurya Empire (321 B.C.–183 B.C.) and the Gupta Empire (320 A.D.–467 A.D.) left their mark on India. Asoka, the best-known Maurya ruler, extended his rule over much of India. After he converted to Buddhism, he set out to establish a government based on nonviolence and religious toleration.

By the time of the Gupta Empire, Buddhism had been reabsorbed into Hinduism. However, its influence remained strong in other parts of Asia. The caste system in India

MAP STUDY *Maurya emperors extended their rule over much of India. The Maurya Empire reached its greatest extent under the emperor Asoka. Why was Maurya expansion probably limited to the north?*

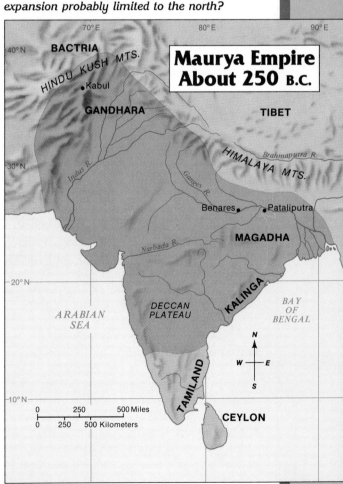

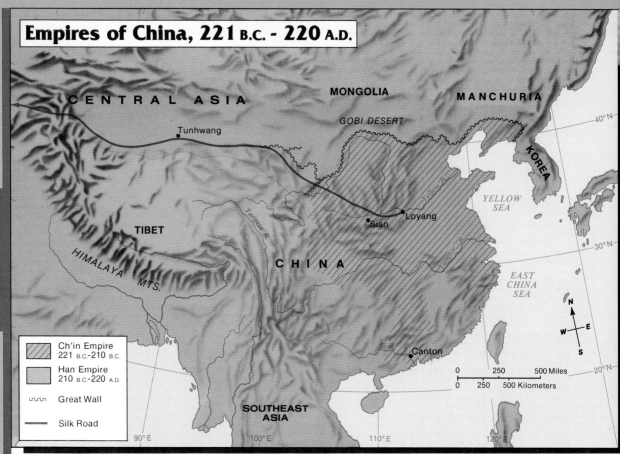

Empires of China, 221 B.C. - 220 A.D.

Ch'in and Han rulers greatly expanded their empires and spread Chinese civilization over a wide area. Like the Roman Empire to the west, the Han Empire enjoyed two centuries of peace and prosperity. Why do you think Han rulers extended the Great Wall westward?

became more restrictive, and many new sub-castes emerged. Strict rules forbade people of different castes from speaking to one another.

During the Gupta period, artists and writers produced some of India's finest works. In science and technology, Indians made important advances. They devised a decimal system and developed the concept of zero, ideas that would later be carried to Western Europe.

Chinese Traditions

While Buddhism was emerging in India, three schools of thought were shaping Chinese traditions: Confucianism, Taoism, and Legalism. Confucius, who was born about 551 B.C., was China's most influential philosopher. He was concerned with how to establish a stable, orderly society. Confucius taught that each per-

son had a place in society, and each individual had responsibilities and duties toward others. He urged the ruler to set a good example. Confucius emphasized respect for one's parents and elders, along with loyalty, courtesy, and hard work.

Taoism was both a religion and a philosophy. Taoists were more concerned with contemplation and achieving harmony with nature than with a proper code of conduct. The third school of thought, Legalism, claimed that the only way to achieve a stable society was through strict government control and rigid obedience to authority.

Unification of China

Legalist principles dominated the government of Shih Huang Ti, a powerful leader of the feudal state of Ch'in, who united China in 221 B.C.

Shih Huang Ti was determined to build a strong central government. He appointed officials loyal to him and improved the transportation system to ensure his control of the empire. His most spectacular achievement was the building of the Great Wall to protect northern China from invaders.

Although the Ch'in Empire was short-lived, its successor, the Han Empire (210 B.C.–220 A.D.), was one of the most brilliant periods in Chinese history. Han rulers extended the borders of China and organized an efficient government based on a civil service open to men of talent. During Han rule, the arts, sciences, and learning advanced. As trade increased, new ideas, including Buddhism, entered China.

SECTION 4 REVIEW

1. **Identify:** (a) Siddhartha Gautama, (b) Asoka, (c) Confucius, (d) Shih Huang Ti.

2. **Define:** (a) brahma, (b) nirvana.

3. How did Hinduism support the caste system?

4. What was the major concern of: (a) Confucianism, (b) Taoism, and (c) Legalism?

5. **Critical Thinking** Why do you think the arts and sciences flourished when India and China had strong governments?

Review

Checkup

1. How did Athenians participate in their government?

2. (a) What was Hellenistic civilization? (b) Why was it important?

3. What social classes existed in the Roman Republic?

4. What legal concepts did the Romans develop?

5. Explain the main teachings of (a) Hinduism and (b) Buddhism.

6. How did Confucianism differ from Taoism?

Critical Thinking

1. **Understanding the Roots of Democracy** The great Athenian statesman Pericles once said: "We do not say that a man who takes no interest in politics is a man who minds his own business; we say that he has no business here at all." (a) What do you think Pericles meant by this statement? (b) How are his ideas important for democratic government?

2. **Drawing Conclusions** (a) What did Confucius believe was the way to establish a stable, orderly society? (b) Why do you think Chinese rulers after Confucius adopted his ideas?

3. **Comparing** (a) In what ways were the Roman Empire and the Han Empire similar? (b) In what ways were they different?

Developing Basic Skills

1. **Map Reading** Study the map on page 300. (a) What political information is given on the map? (b) During which period did Rome conquer Spain? (c) During which period did Rome make the most conquests?

2. **Using Time Lines** Make a time line for this overview. At the far left, write the earliest date B.C. mentioned in this overview. At the far right, put the latest date A.D. in this overview. Remember that historians use the term century to describe a 100-year time period. The 100 years from 500 B.C. to 401 B.C. are called the fifth century B.C.; the 100 years from 400 A.D. to 499 A.D. are called the fifth century A.D. (a) What is the earliest date on your time line? (b) What is the latest date? (c) What event or events occurred in the sixth century B.C.?

Most people in medieval Europe were peasants whose lives were ruled by the cycle of planting and harvesting. By the late Middle Ages, however, a few wealthy nobles and merchants enjoyed the comfort and elegance shown in the scene above.

Overview 3

3 Middle Ages in Western Europe

(500–1500)

OVERVIEW OUTLINE

1 Foundations of Medieval Europe

2 The Height of Medieval Civilization

3 Building National Monarchies

Nowhere could people travel safely as rival lords battled each other. The clergy meeting that early summer of 1083 in Cologne were all in agreement. The fighting must stop. To secure the peace, they issued a declaration called the Truce of God.

"Peace shall be observed on certain days," the truce declared. "Let no one, however irritated by wrong, presume to carry arms, shield, sword, or lance, or any kind of armor, from the Advent of our Lord to the eighth day after Epiphany, and from Septuagesima to the eighth day after Pentecost. On the remaining days, namely on Sundays, Fridays, apostles' days and on every day set aside for fasts or feasts, arms may be carried, but on this condition, that no injury shall be done in any way to anyone."

Like the clergy of Cologne, churchmen elsewhere in Europe were trying to stop the endless battling. To enforce their decree, the clergy of Cologne declared that "if anyone attempts to oppose this pious institution and is unwilling to promise peace to God, no priest in our diocese shall presume to say a mass for him or shall take any care for his salvation."

The Church's attempts to impose order were partly successful. With the collapse of the Roman Empire in the West, Europe had entered a period known as the Middle Ages. During the early Middle Ages, from about 500 to 1050, the remains of Greco-Roman civilization decayed as Europe suffered from repeated invasions. Despite the disorder, Europeans slowly built the foundations for a civilization dominated by the Christian Church.

During the late Middle Ages, from about 1050 to 1350, a stable, orderly society emerged. Farming methods improved, trade revived, and towns grew. Strong monarchs centralized royal power. As conditions grew better, Europeans began to take a broader view of the world. ■

1 Foundations of Medieval Europe

READ TO UNDERSTAND

- ☐ **Why feudalism developed.**
- ☐ **What the manor system was.**
- ☐ **How the Church influenced medieval life.**
- ☐ *Vocabulary:* **feudalism, fief, vassal, knight, chivalry, manor, serf, sacraments.**

As the Western Roman Empire collapsed, Western Europe became a battleground for many Germanic tribes. At the same time, trade and travel became difficult. Learning declined, and much of the knowledge of the ancient world was lost.

The Kingdom of the Franks

During the early Middle Ages, the kingdom of the Franks became the strongest power in Western Europe. Under Charlemagne, who ruled from 768 to 814, the Frankish kingdom enjoyed a golden age. Charlemagne extended the borders of his kingdom. He fought the Muslims in Spain, the Saxons in northern Europe, and the Avars in the east. He set up an efficient government and encouraged learning in his vast empire. The revival of learning helped set the stage for the civilization of the later Middle Ages.

Emergence of Feudalism

For two hundred years after the death of Charlemagne, Western Europe was battered by invaders. The Muslims attacked southern France and Italy. The Magyars and Slavs poured in from the east, and the Vikings raided towns and villages, from England to Russia.

During this time, feudalism emerged in Western Europe. **Feudalism** was a system of rule by local lords who were bound to a king by ties of loyalty. Feudalism produced a way of life that governed the political, social, and economic order.

In the feudal society, everyone had his or her place. In theory, the king ruled the land as a **fief,** or estate, which he divided among his great nobles. In fact, these powerful lords often acted independently of the king. They divided their vast lands among **vassals,** or lesser lords, who in turn subdivided their fiefs among **knights,** or mounted warriors. Each knight or vassal owed loyalty and service to his lord.

During the early Middle Ages, warfare was constant as lords battled for power. To protect their lands, they built fortified castles where

Advances in agriculture helped peasants produce food surpluses. In this scene, a plowman directs a team of horses that are probably shod with iron horseshoes. The speed of horses made them much more efficient for plowing than oxen.

lords and peasants took refuge from attacks. In the later Middle Ages, feudal warfare declined, and **chivalry,** a code of conduct for knights, emerged. Chivalry emphasized Christian virtues, loyalty, and respect for noblewomen.

Life on the Manor

The economic system that supported feudal society was based on the **manor.** The manor included a village and the surrounding land that was administered by a lord. During the invasions of the 800s and 900s, each manor was a self-sufficient unit. Its people produced almost everything they needed to survive.

At this time, almost all the people were peasants who worked on the manor. Most peasants were **serfs,** who were tied to the lord's land. Serfs owed their lords certain services, such as farming their lord's land and giving him a portion of their own harvests. In turn, the lord was supposed to protect his peasants and provide justice.

During the early Middle Ages, peasants barely produced enough to survive. By about 1000, however, peasants were using new tech-

nologies such as crop rotation, the heavy plow, and windmills to increase output. As a result, they began to produce food surpluses to support a growing population.

The Medieval Church

The Church played a powerful role in shaping and unifying medieval Europe. It had its own government, laws, courts, and system of taxation. During the early Middle Ages, the Church increased its influence by converting people in Eastern Europe to Christianity.

The Church was closely tied to feudalism. It controlled huge amounts of land, and high church officials were often also feudal lords. Further, kings and feudal lords used the educated clergy to serve as officials at their courts.

To peasants and nobles alike, the Church offered the only hope of salvation. The Church controlled the **sacraments,** the seven sacred rites that offered the only route to eternal life. Only the clergy could administer the sacraments and save the souls of the faithful from eternal suffering.

The Church served as a force for civilization. In the local parish churches, priests taught Christian virtues that helped shape medieval Europe. In monasteries, monks carefully copied and studied ancient manuscripts. Although much knowledge was lost during this period, the foundations were built for a new civilization.

SECTION 1 REVIEW

1. **Identify:** (a) Kingdom of the Franks, (b) Charlemagne.

2. **Define:** (a) feudalism, (b) fief, (c) vassal, (d) knight, (e) chivalry, (f) manor, (g) serf, (h) sacraments.

3. How did Charlemagne establish order in his kingdom?

4. Describe the relationship between a lord and his vassal.

5. **Critical Thinking** Why was the Church such a powerful unifying influence?

2 The Height of Medieval Civilization

READ TO UNDERSTAND

☐ Why economic and other changes took place in the late Middle Ages.

☐ What ideas shaped medieval culture.

☐ What the causes and effects of the Crusades were.

☐ *Vocabulary:* charter, guild, vernacular, scholasticism, crusade.

In the late Middle Ages, medieval civilization flowered. By the eleventh and twelfth centuries, feudal warfare had declined, and the manor economy was producing surpluses. The narrow world of the manor slowly expanded.

Economic Patterns

The decline in warfare encouraged the growth of trade and travel. Some feudal lords and kings tried to repair roads and bridges. Also, coined money slowly reappeared. At annual trade fairs, merchants and traders from all over Europe gathered to exchange goods.

The increase of trade led to the growth of towns. Merchants set up permanent headquarters in old Roman towns. New towns grew up at important crossroads. Towns negotiated with local feudal lords for **charters,** written documents that guaranteed their rights. In medieval society, a new class of townspeople emerged.

Economic activities within the towns was regulated by **guilds,** associations of merchants or artisans that governed the town. Guilds governed prices, wages, and the quality of goods. They prevented competition and regulated who might become a master craftsman.

Medieval Culture

Towns served as centers not only of new economic activity but also of medieval culture. The middle-class townspeople had money to educate their children and to support the work of artists. The Church still dominated medieval life. Nowhere was the influence of the Church more evident than in the towering Gothic cathedrals built by wealthy towns in the 1100s and 1200s. The new churches had tall pointed arches. Their paintings, sculptures, and large stained-glass windows pictured stories from the Bible.

Medieval culture was a blend of spiritual and worldly concerns. The literature of the late Middle Ages was written in the **vernacular,** the everyday language of the people. In Florence, the poet Dante wrote in the Italian vernacular. In the *Divine Comedy,* Dante combined poetry, theology, and history. The English poet Chaucer used the vernacular in *The Canterbury Tales,* in which ordinary people on a pilgrimage tell stories about their lives.

During the late Middle Ages, associations of students and teachers evolved into the first universities. In these new centers of learning, scholars pored over the works of ancient writers. The writings of Aristotle and others whose works emphasized reason and logic caused medieval thinkers to reexamine ideas that they had taken on faith. A new school of thought, **scholasticism,** flourished. Scholastics, such as Thomas Aquinas, believed that reason and logic could be used to support Christian faith.

Expanding Horizons

In 1095, the pope called for a **crusade,** a military expedition against the enemies of the Church. Rallying to the cry "God wills it," Christians from all over Europe embarked for Palestine to take the Holy Land from the Muslims. Christians went on the Crusades for a variety of reasons. Many believed that they were obeying God's will and wanted to achieve salvation. Others wanted to carve out kingdoms of their own in Palestine. Still others saw the Crusades as a way to avoid taxes and debts at home.

Effects of the Crusades. During the early Crusades, Christian forces seized lands in Syria and Palestine. They divided the conquered territory into four crusader states. In time, however, all four states were retaken by Muslim armies. Yet the Crusades helped to

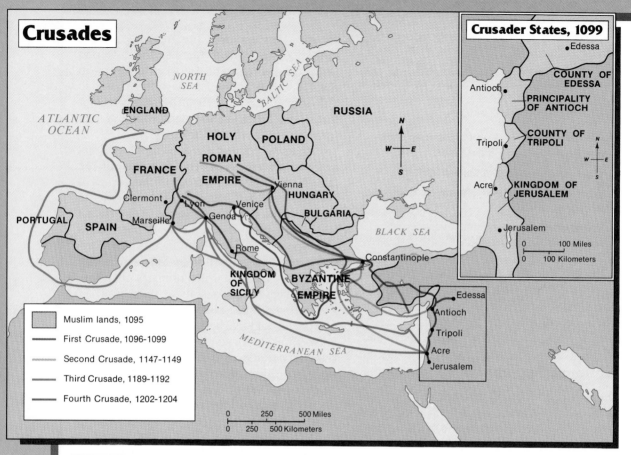

Crusades

Crusader States, 1099

- Edessa
- **COUNTY OF EDESSA**
- Antioch
- **PRINCIPALITY OF ANTIOCH**
- Tripoli
- **COUNTY OF TRIPOLI**
- Acre
- **KINGDOM OF JERUSALEM**
- Jerusalem

100 Miles
100 Kilometers

NORTH SEA

BALTIC SEA

ENGLAND

ATLANTIC OCEAN

RUSSIA

HOLY ROMAN EMPIRE

POLAND

FRANCE

Vienna

HUNGARY

Clermont
Lyon
Venice
Genoa

PORTUGAL

SPAIN

Marseille

BULGARIA

Rome

BLACK SEA

KINGDOM OF SICILY

BYZANTINE EMPIRE

Constantinople

MEDITERRANEAN SEA

Edessa
Antioch
Tripoli
Acre
Jerusalem

Legend:
- Muslim lands, 1095
- First Crusade, 1096-1099
- Second Crusade, 1147-1149
- Third Crusade, 1189-1192
- Fourth Crusade, 1202-1204

0   250   500 Miles
0   250   500 Kilometers

MAP STUDY *"Jerusalem is the center of the earth; the land is fruitful above all others, like another paradise of delights,"* proclaimed Pope Urban II in 1095. At the pope's urging, many Christians set out on crusades to free Jerusalem from Muslim control. During which crusade did the crusaders travel the longest distance?

quicken the pace of changes that were already underway in Europe.

For 200 years during the Crusades, Christian knights, pilgrims, and merchants made their way to the eastern Mediterranean. On their return home, they brought with them new ideas as well as tastes for the goods of Asia and the Middle East. Merchants in the cities of northern Italy who built large fleets to carry the crusaders benefited from the growth in trade with the eastern Mediterranean. Also, the increased trade and travel introduced the people of Western Europe to other civilizations.

Other changes. Other social and economic changes occurred in the late Middle Ages. As a money economy slowly replaced the barter system, a few wealthy families set up banks, making loans to kings, nobles, and popes. With the growth in trade and travel, the manor became less isolated. Peasants and feudal lords bought goods from merchants and no longer had to make everything they needed.

Feudal lords were at a disadvantage in the new money economy. Because their wealth was in land, they lacked money to buy the luxury goods they wanted. As a result, they allowed peasants to pay rents in money. Some lords even permitted serfs to buy their freedom.

Despite the changes, however, the basic structure of medieval society remained the same. The Church dominated the medieval world, and the majority of people worked the land on feudal estates.

1. **Identify:** (a) Dante, (b) Chaucer, (c) Thomas Aquinas.

2. **Define:** (a) charter, (b) guild, (c) vernacular, (d) scholasticism, (e) crusade.

3. Describe two economic changes that took place in the late Middle Ages.

4. Why did Christians go on the Crusades?

5. **Critical Thinking** How did the approach to learning of the ancient philosophers differ from that of medieval thinkers?

3 Building National Monarchies

READ TO UNDERSTAND

■ How English, French, and Spanish monarchs centralized their power.

■ What problems the Church faced in the late Middle Ages.

■ Why medieval society declined.

■ *Vocabulary:* exchequer, common law, reconquista.

In the early Middle Ages, Western Europe was divided into many small states ruled by feudal lords. During the late Middle Ages, the situation changed as monarchs centralized power. As royal power grew, people transferred their loyalty from local lords to national monarchs.

Growth of Royal Power in England

In 1066, William of Normandy conquered England and set up the foundations for royal power. He made all feudal lords swear allegiance to him. He limited the number of fortified castles built in England and had a survey, known as the *Domesday Book,* made of all property that could be taxed.

William's successors further strengthened royal power. They established a royal bureaucracy made up of officials loyal to the king. They set up the **exchequer,** or central treasury, and improved justice in the royal courts. The decisions of royal courts became part of the **common law,** the accepted legal principles that applied to everyone throughout the land.

Challenges to royal power came from the Church and feudal lords. King John I, for example, battled both unsuccessfully. In 1215, John's barons forced him to sign the Magna Carta, or Great Charter, a written guarantee of their rights. In time, the Magna Carta came to be seen as a significant document because the rights given to nobles were gradually extended to other people. Also, it established the principle that the king must obey the law.

In the late 1200s, the power of the king was further limited by a Parliament, or great council made up of officials, nobles, and bishops. Parliament grew into an assembly of two houses. The House of Lords was made up of great nobles and bishops. The House of Commons was made up of representatives of lesser knights and townspeople. Eventually, it helped establish a limited monarchy.

Growth of the French Monarchy

In France, rulers faced a difficult task. By 1000, French kings ruled only a small strip of north-central France. Over the next 300 years, they gradually extended their control over most of France. They set up effective royal government, employing educated clergy and townspeople in the royal bureaucracy. They established royal courts that had more power than local feudal courts. As a result, people gradually turned to the king for justice.

As French kings increased their power, they came into conflict with the Church. To show that they had the support of the people, they summoned the Estates General, a representative assembly. It was made up of representatives from three estates, or classes: the clergy, nobles, and bourgeoisie, as the townspeople were called.

The Holy Roman Empire

In the eastern and central parts of what had once been Charlemagne's empire, a number of powerful dukes ruled over separate states. In

New weapons used during the Hundred Years' War helped change the nature of warfare in the late Middle Ages. At Crécy, English foot soldiers, at the right in this picture, used the new longbow to inflict heavy casualties on the French, armed with cumbersome crossbows.

3

962, Otto, the duke of Saxony, gained the title of Holy Roman emperor and began extending his power over neighboring German lands and northern Italy. This involved the German emperors deeply in Italian affairs. During this period, the Church also increased its political power. The result was a great struggle between the German emperor and the Church.

In the 1100s and 1200s, German emperors were determined to extend their rule over both Italy and Germany. In fact, they neglected their German lands to wage an endless series of wars in Italy. During these struggles, feudal lords in Germany continued to rule their lands as independent kingdoms. Italy, too, remained divided. Thus, unlike England and France, where national monarchs were building a basis for royal power, neither Germany nor Italy were united under a strong ruler.

Emergence of Christian Spain

During the late Middle Ages, Spain emerged as a strong, unified state. In the 700s, Muslims had conquered Spain. For centuries, it was a prosperous center of Islamic civilization. During the 1100s and 1200s, however, Christians in northern Spain launched a series of crusades, known as the **reconquista,** to free Spain from Muslim control. Christian knights slowly pushed the Muslims back to the southern tip of Spain. Several Christian kingdoms emerged, including Portugal in the west, Castile in the center, and Aragon in the northeast.

In 1469, Queen Isabella of Castile and Ferdinand, heir to Aragon, married, thereby uniting their kingdoms. The two rulers then began to build royal power. They made the Church an ally in this battle. Ousting the Muslims from their last stronghold in Granada, they imposed religious unity on Spain. They forced Muslims and Jews to convert to Christianity or leave the country. Although Isabella and Ferdinand established religious and national unity, they paid a high price by losing many productive citizens to exile.

Decline of Medieval Society

In the late Middle Ages, the foundations of medieval society weakened. The 1300s and 1400s were a difficult time for the people of Western Europe. In 1348, bubonic plague, known as the Black Death, struck with terrifying results. The Black Death killed about a third of the population of Western Europe. In the resulting chaos, land was abandoned, commerce declined, and cities shrank in size.

During this time, the Church was under frequent attack. Medieval monarchs increasingly challenged Church power. They tried to tax the clergy and limit the influence of Church courts. In 1305, King Philip IV of France managed to have the papacy moved from Rome to Avignon in France. For the next 70 years, the French controlled the papacy. Another crisis further weakened the Church when it split into two groups, each electing its own pope. Even after unity was restored, the Church came under attack from reformers who criticized its wealth and worldliness.

As monarchs in England and France increased their power, they became involved in a struggle known as the Hundred Years' War, which lasted from 1337 to 1453. For centuries,

English kings had ruled lands in France. However, during the Hundred Years' War, the French ousted the English from France. The war gave the French a strong feeling of national pride and increased their loyalty to their king. In England, the war gave Parliament the opportunity to increase its power, in exchange for approving the king's taxes.

By the mid-1400s, feudalism was declining. Many feudal nobles were killed in the Hundred Years' War. The nature of warfare, too, was changing. With the invention of the longbow and the use of cannons, armored knights and fortified castles were becoming outdated. Nobles remained powerful, however. But instead of fighting frequent battles as in the past, they gathered in the splendid royal courts that were set up by strong monarchs.

SECTION 3 REVIEW

1. **Identify:** (a) *Domesday Book,* (b) Parliament, (c) Estates General, (d) Otto, (e) Black Death, (f) Hundred Years' War.

2. **Define:** (a) exchequer, (b) common law, (c) reconquista.

3. Which groups challenged the growth of royal power?

4. Describe two results of the Hundred Years' War.

5. **Critical Thinking** Describe the forces that were undermining medieval society by the 1400s.

Review

Checkup

1. Describe the structure of medieval society.

2. How did changes in technology influence the lives of peasants around the year 1000?

3. Why did economic conditions change in the later Middle Ages?

4. How did towns influence medieval culture?

5. (a) What was the purpose of the Crusades? (b) Did they succeed or fail? Explain.

6. Explain the importance of each of the following: (a) *Domesday Book;* (b) Magna Carta.

7. Why did Germany remain divided at a time when England and France were becoming united?

8. Describe three developments that contributed to the decline of medieval society.

Critical Thinking

1. **Understanding the Roots of Democracy** (a) How did the Magna Carta and the growth of Parliament affect royal power in England? (b) Why do Americans consider these developments important in our own lives?

2. **Comparing** Compare life in the early Middle Ages with that in the late Middle Ages.

Developing Basic Skills

1. **Map Reading** Study the map on page 310. (a) Which crusade included armies from England, France, and the Holy Roman Empire? (b) Which crusade went only as far as Constantinople? (c) During which crusade were Edessa, Antioch, and Jerusalem taken? (d) Why do you think the Crusades expanded the horizons of Europeans?

2. **Using Statistics** Study the table on page 212. (a) What happened to the population in much of Europe between 500 and 650? Between 650 and 1000? Between 1000 and 1340? (b) Which part of Europe lost the most people in the 100 years after the Black Death? (c) Which part lost almost half its population? (d) About how long did it take for the population of Europe to reach the size it had been before 1348?

313

The Taj Mahal was built by a Muslim ruler of India, the Shah Jahan, in the 1600s. The gleaming white marble walls are decorated with carved quotations from the Koran, the sacred book of Islam.

Overview 4

Golden Ages Outside Western Europe

(330–1650)

OVERVIEW OUTLINE

1. Byzantine and Islamic Civilizations
2. Africa and the Americas
3. India, China, and Japan

4

When Ibn Battuta left Morocco at the age of 22, he had no idea it would be 30 years before he would see his home again. He headed first for the holy city of Mecca in Arabia. From there, his travels took him to Egypt, Syria, Persia, Asia Minor, Afghanistan, India, and China. In 1355, he struck out across the great Sahara Desert to visit the kingdom of Mali in West Africa. By then a veteran world traveler, Ibn Battuta had a wealth of experience by which to judge what he saw.

He noted particularly the peacefulness of the West African kingdom. "The people possess some admirable qualities," he wrote in his travel book. "They have a greater dislike of injustice than any other people. Their ruler shows no mercy to anyone guilty of the least act of injustice. There is complete security in their country. Neither traveler nor inhabitant has anything to fear from robbers or men of violence."

314

Ibn Battuta's narrative of his travels gives us a picture of some of the civilizations that flourished outside Europe during the Middle Ages. His visit to the thriving kingdom of Mali highlighted several key developments. In the mid-600s, the Arabs had erupted out of their desert homeland and started to carry a new religion, Islam, across much of the world from Spain to India and to Africa.

Islam created a dynamic new civilization that blended traditions of the ancient Greeks and Romans with those of the peoples it conquered. As Islam swept into India, it made a lasting impact on the subcontinent. Other important changes also took place around the world. Although the Western Roman Empire collapsed in the 400s, the Eastern Roman Empire, known as the Byzantine Empire, flourished for 1,000 years.

Between 500 and 1500, China enjoyed several golden ages under strong dynasties. Farther east, Japan drew on Chinese achievements to develop its own distinct civilization. In the Americas, too, advanced civilizations were making remarkable achievements at a time when Europeans were struggling to build the foundations of medieval society. ■

1 Byzantine and Islamic Civilizations

READ TO UNDERSTAND

☐ **How the Byzantine and Islamic empires contributed to civilization.**

☐ **What the teachings of Islam are.**

☐ **Why Islam spread so rapidly.**

☐ *Vocabulary:* **caliph.**

In the lands once ruled by Rome, three civilizations arose. The Roman Empire in the West became the seedbed for Western European civilization. After the fall of Rome, the Eastern Roman Empire, known as the Byzantine Empire, flourished. In time, Byzantine civilization was passed on to the people of Eastern Europe. In the easternmost lands of the Roman Empire, a new civilization, based on the religion of Islam, emerged in the 600s and 700s.

The Byzantine Empire

The emperor Constantine, you will recall, made the city of Constantinople the capital of the Eastern Roman Empire. While the Roman empire in the West collapsed under the pressure of invasions, the Eastern Roman Empire managed to survive. For centuries, the Byzantine Empire served as a buffer. It absorbed the attacks of many invading people from the east who might have otherwise overrun Western Europe.

Absolute rulers. Byzantine rulers exercised absolute power over their empire. They created an efficient civil service, kept a strong army, and controlled all parts of the economy. Their capital, Constantinople, was the wealthy center of a flourishing world trade.

Byzantine emperors acted as head of the Christian Church. When they refused to recognize the authority of the pope in Rome, a schism, or split, within Christianity took place. The pope continued to rule the Roman Catholic Church in the west, while the Eastern Orthodox Church was ruled by the Byzantine emperor.

In the 1200s and 1300s, the Byzantine Empire declined. By the 1400s, it was unable to stop the invasions of the Ottoman Turks. In 1453, the Ottomans captured Constantinople, signaling the end of the Byzantine Empire.

The Byzantine heritage. Arts and learning had flourished in the rich cities of the Byzantine Empire. At a time when education was

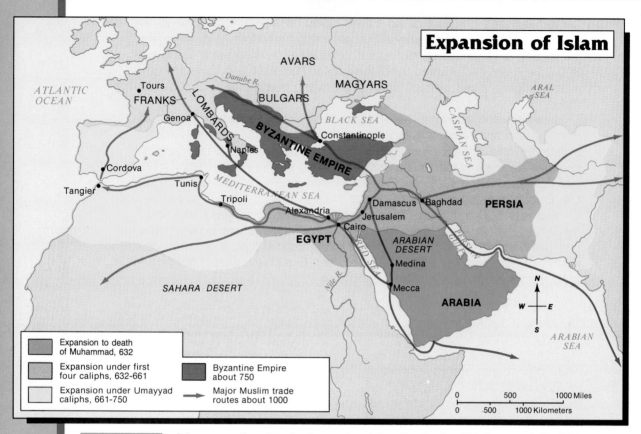

Expansion of Islam

AVARS
MAGYARS
Danube R.
ATLANTIC OCEAN
Tours
FRANKS
BULGARS
Genoa
LOMBARDS
BYZANTINE EMPIRE
BLACK SEA
Constantinople
ARAL SEA
CASPIAN SEA
Naples
Cordova
Tunis
MEDITERRANEAN SEA
Tangier
Tripoli
Alexandria
Damascus
Baghdad
PERSIA
Jerusalem
Cairo
EGYPT
ARABIAN DESERT
SAHARA DESERT
Nile R.
RED SEA
Medina
Mecca
ARABIA
N
W E
S
ARABIAN SEA

Expansion to death of Muhammad, 632
Expansion under first four caliphs, 632–661
Expansion under Umayyad caliphs, 661–750
Byzantine Empire about 750
Major Muslim trade routes about 1000

0   500   1000 Miles
0   500   1000 Kilometers

MAP STUDY *Islam spread rapidly in the century after the death of Muhammad. By 750, Muslims controlled much of the trade of the Mediterranean world. Under which caliphs did Islam reach the limits of its expansion? In what years?*

4

barely kept alive in the monasteries of Western Europe, Byzantine scholars studied and preserved manuscripts from ancient Greece and Rome. Under the emperor Justinian, scholars summarized existing Roman law into a vast work known as Justinian's Code. This code contained many principles of justice that later helped shape legal systems in Western Europe and the Americas.

The Slavs of Eastern Europe had been converted to Christianity by Byzantine missionaries, and they carried on the Byzantine heritage. Vladimir, the prince of Kiev, chose Byzantine Christianity over the Roman Catholic Church. He then encouraged all Russians to convert. That step ensured close ties between Russia and the Byzantine Empire.

After Constantinople fell in 1453, Russian rulers claimed to be the heirs of the Roman and Byzantine emperors. Ivan III, for example,

took the title "czar," the Russian word for Caesar. Russian czars then modeled their government on the absolute rule of the Byzantine emperors.

Rise of Islam

In 622, Muhammad founded the religion of Islam in Arabia. The Five Pillars of Islam taught the basic duties of all Muslims. They included the belief in one God, Allah; prayer five times a day; almsgiving to the poor; fasting during the month of Ramadan; and a pilgrimage to Mecca at least once in a lifetime. The Koran, the holy book of Islam, contains the word of God as revealed to the prophet Muhammad.

The teachings of Islam were rooted in traditional Arab beliefs as well as those of Judaism and Christianity. Muhammad recognized his debt to these two religions. He called Jews and Christians the People of the Book because they believed in God's revelations in the Bible. In theory, if not always in practice, Muslims were tolerant of the People of the Book.

Spread of Islam. Between 622 and 732, Islam spread rapidly from Arabia to Spain in the west and to India in the east. Many people accepted Islam because its teachings were simple and clear. Islam did not require a clergy or a church. Also, Muslims were inspired to fight for Islam. They believed that by dying in its cause they would enter paradise.

As Islam expanded, a government was set up to rule the vast empire. The government was headed by a **caliph,** as the successor to Muhammad was called. The caliph was both the religious and political leader of Islam. The Koran served as the source of law for the Islamic Empire.

In the years after Muhammad's death, a division developed within Islam between the Sunnites and Shiites over who was the rightful heir to Muhammad. Islam also faced other problems over the next centuries. It was attacked by invaders such as the Seljuk and Ottoman Turks and the Mongols. Although the invaders converted to Islam, their traditions differed from those of the Arabs.

Islamic civilization. During the expansion of Islam, a new civilization emerged. It blended Arab, Greek, Roman, Byzantine, Persian, and Indian traditions. The new Islamic civilization benefited from the thriving trade and agriculture within the empire.

Islamic teachings encouraged learning. Throughout the empire, scholars studied the Koran as well as Roman, Jewish, Persian, and Indian texts. By examining ancient Greek texts, Muslim doctors improved the diagnosis and treatment of diseases. In mathematics, Muslims adopted the decimal system from India and made advances in algebra and trigonometry.

In philosophy, Muslim thinkers were influenced by Aristotle. Even before the development of scholasticism in Western Europe, philosophers like Averröes sought to prove that there was no conflict between Islamic faith and reason. Later, these and other ideas made their way into Western Europe.

SECTION 1 REVIEW

1. **Identify:** (a) Eastern Orthodox Church, (b) Justinian's Code, (c) Ivan III, (d) Muhammad, (e) Five Pillars of Islam, (f) Koran, (g) Averröes.

2. **Define:** caliph.

3. How did the Byzantine Empire differ from Western Europe in the early Middle Ages?

4. What are the main teachings of Islam?

5. **Critical Thinking** In what way were both the Byzantine and Islamic empires the heirs of ancient Rome?

2 Africa and the Americas

READ TO UNDERSTAND

☐ **Why strong trading kingdoms arose in West Africa.**

☐ **Why patterns of life varied across Africa.**

☐ **What the early civilizations of the Americas achieved.**

☐ *Vocabulary:* **extended family.**

While advanced civilizations flourished in Europe and Asia, people in different parts of Africa and the Americas produced their own civilizations. As elsewhere, each civilization included cities, well-organized governments, specialized skills and occupations, and a system of keeping records.

The Kingdoms of Kush and Axum

Africa is a vast continent with a variety of climates and terrains. As people adapted to these varied conditions, they developed many distinct cultural patterns. The powerful kingdom of Kush flourished at the same time as ancient Egypt and engaged in a thriving trade with its northern neighbor along the Nile.

After Kush declined about 200 A.D., the neighboring state of Axum carried on a lively trade with the Mediterranean world and Asia.

317

In the 300s, the ruler of Axum converted to Christianity. Today, the Christians of Ethiopia trace their roots to the civilization of Axum.

Rise of Trading States

At the time of the Middle Ages in Europe, several strong trading kingdoms rose in West Africa. Camel caravans from North Africa made the long desert crossing to exchange salt and other goods for gold mined in West Africa. About 400 A.D., the kingdom of Ghana began to extend its control over the gold-producing regions of West Africa. In the 600s, traders from North Africa brought Islam to West Africa. Although the king of Ghana did not convert, the new religion had a lasting impact on West Africa.

After the decline of Ghana, two other trading states—Mali and, later, Songhai—gained control of the profitable gold–salt trade. The rulers of Mali converted to Islam. In 1324, Mansa Musa of Mali made a pilgrimage to Mecca. The wealth displayed by this West African king made a great impression on the people he met in the Middle East.

Trade also contributed to the rise of independent city-states in East Africa. There, goods were brought by sea rather than by desert caravans. The coastal cities taxed all goods that passed through their markets, gaining great wealth. Many Arab traders settled in East African cities. They helped create a culture blending African and Islamic traditions.

Patterns of Daily Life

People in different parts of Africa organized their lives in a variety of ways. As elsewhere, people built their societies around respect for family, law, and religion. Family organization varied according to the needs of individual cultures. In farming and herding societies, the basic unit was the **extended family,** where several generations lived and worked together.

Religion was part of everyday life in Africa. Although religious practices varied, many African people had similar beliefs. Most Africans believed in a single Supreme Spirit, the creator of the universe. They saw everything in nature as part of this Supreme Spirit and called on ancestors and "spirit helpers" to make their prayers known to the Supreme Spirit.

Peoples of the Americas

Like Africa, the Americas are vast continents where many different peoples have developed their own distinct cultures. The first Americans are thought to have crossed a land bridge that connected Siberia and Alaska more than 10,000 years ago. Bands of Stone Age hunters slowly migrated south, adapting to a variety of climates and landforms.

Because the people within each geographic region tended to have similar traditions and ways of life, historians have divided the peoples of North America into culture regions. Among these regions are the far north, Pacific coast, southwest, Great Plains, and eastern woodlands. In the harsh far north, the people lived by hunting and fishing. They used local resources such as bone for harpoons and knives. Farther south, warmer climates allowed people to develop agriculture. The people of the southwest grew crops such as beans, squash, and maize.

Civilizations of the Americas

Farming began in the Americas about 6000 B.C. As elsewhere, agriculture led to the growth of early civilizations, such as that of the Olmec in southern Mexico. By 1200 B.C., the Olmec had built large cities around huge, pyramid-shaped, stone temples. The Olmec developed a form of hieroglyphic writing, a system of counting, and a calendar.

Historians think that the Olmec probably influenced the Maya civilization that grew up later in Central America and southern Mexico. Like the Olmec, the Maya built cities that were largely religious centers. Priests and warriors made up a powerful ruling class. Maya priests were fascinated by time and developed a precise calendar. They also made advances in mathematics and invented a numbering system that included the concept of zero.

Two other civilizations flourished in the Americas. In the 1300s and 1400s, the Aztec conquered a large empire in Mexico. From the Aztec capital at Tenochtitlán, a bustling city of

4

Tlaloc, the rain god, was one of the most feared and respected Aztec gods. The Aztec offered prayers and sacrifices to him so he would send rain for their crops. Tlaloc, whose name means He Who Makes Things Sprout, is shown here grasping a stalk of corn, the main Aztec crop.

about 100,000 people, the Aztec emperor ruled over many conquered peoples.

The Inca built an even larger empire in the Andes region of South America. They developed an efficient system of government and built an excellent road system so that news could be relayed across their vast empire. The Inca built huge stone temples and palaces that withstood centuries of earthquakes.

SECTION 2 REVIEW

1. **Identify:** (a) Kush, (b) Axum, (c) Ghana, (d) Mansa Musa, (e) Olmec, (f) Maya, (g) Aztec, (h) Inca.

2. **Define:** extended family.

3. Why did Ghana, Mali, and Songhai flourish?

4. What were some achievements of the Olmec?

5. **Critical Thinking** How did geographic factors influence the way the peoples of North America lived?

3 India, China, and Japan

READ TO UNDERSTAND

☐ Why Hindus and Muslims clashed in India.

☐ How changes in dynasties affected China.

☐ What influences shaped Japanese life.

☐ *Vocabulary:* sultan, archipelago, samurai, shogun, daimyo, bushido.

At the time of the Middle Ages in Europe, three major civilizations in Asia were making important advances. In India, Hindu traditions helped preserve unity during centuries of invasion. China was a unified nation that enjoyed several golden ages between the 600s and 1500s. Farther east, Japan shaped its own distinct civilization.

A Meeting of Cultures in India

By the 500s A.D., Hindu traditions were deeply rooted in Indian society. The caste system and the power of the Brahmans, or priestly caste, helped ensure a stable social order at a time when warfare among Hindu princes prevented political unity.

Expansion of Islam. In the 900s, Islamic invaders advanced into northern India. During the next 300 years, Muslim rulers, known as **sultans,** extended their control over much of the subcontinent. From their capital at Delhi, sultans set up a strong government.

Unlike earlier conquerors of India, the Muslims were not absorbed into Hindu society. They remained a powerful, separate force that was strongly hostile to Hindu beliefs. To Muslims, who believed in one God, Allah, the Hindu worship of many gods was evil.

Among the other points of conflict was the Muslim belief in the equality of all believers that clashed with the Hindu belief in the caste system. Also, Muslims insisted upon strict obedience to the Koran, while Hindus were tolerant of many religious beliefs. Despite frequent clashes, some blending occurred between Hindu and Muslim cultures, especially in the arts and learning.

319

Buddhist thought had a strong influence on Japan. Through meditation, Buddhists hoped to free themselves from attachments to worldly things and to achieve a state of peace. Total relaxation, as seen in this figure of a priest, is necessary for meditation.

The Mogul Empire. In the 1500s, Mogul invaders swept into India, creating the Mogul Empire, which lasted for over 300 years. The greatest Mogul ruler was Akbar. Although he was a Muslim, he followed a policy of religious toleration. Akbar's successors, however, did not continue this policy. As a result, they faced the constant threat of rebellion from Hindu princes. In the 1500s and 1600s, Europeans began to set up trading posts to profit from the silks, spices, and wealth of Mogul India.

Flowering of Chinese Civilization

During the Middle Ages in Europe, China benefited from two long periods of peace and good government. Under the T'ang dynasty (618–917) and the Sung dynasty (960–1279), Chinese civilization spread. Its influence was seen from Korea and Japan in the east to Southeast Asia and the borders of India.

The Chinese produced remarkable works of art and made important advances in technology. They invented paper and a process for printing, developed the magnetic compass,

and began to use gunpowder. As their economy expanded, the Chinese came in contact with ideas and new products from other parts of the world.

Despite these advances, Chinese society remained largely unchanged. Confucian ideals remained the basis of government and family life. The Chinese accepted the idea that each person had his or her place in society and that an inferior owed loyalty and respect to a superior.

In the 1200s, the Mongols overran China and set up their own government. During the rule of the Mongol emperor Kublai Khan, the Venetian traveler Marco Polo visited China. When he returned home, he published a book describing the advanced civilization he had seen. But Europeans refused to believe his reports.

In the 1300s, the Chinese drove out the foreign rulers and established the Ming dynasty. The early Ming rulers launched several voyages of exploration. Chinese fleets sailed to Southeast Asia, India, and East Africa. Then, suddenly, in 1433, the voyages stopped, and the Ming restricted trade and foreign travel. In the 1400s, China was probably the most technologically advanced civilization in the world. But it slowly fell behind at a time when Western Europeans were beginning to expand their horizons.

Emergence of Japan

To the east of China lies the Japanese **archipelago,** a chain of islands. The sea strongly influenced Japan, providing a source of food and a barrier to invaders. By 400 A.D., the Yamato family had established the first and only Japanese dynasty.

Between the fifth and ninth centuries, the Japanese borrowed many ideas from China. They adapted Chinese writing to their own language and welcomed Buddhist missionaries. They studied Taoist texts and adopted Confucian ideas about family and ancestor worship. At the same time, they kept their traditional religious beliefs, called Shinto.

By the 1100s, strong lords had gained power in the countryside. As **samurai,** or warrior knights, battled for power, feudalism emerged in Japan. As in Western Europe, everyone had a place in feudal society. Although the emperor held the highest rank, he had no political power. The **shogun,** or chief general, was the actual ruler. Below him were the **daimyo,** powerful samurai lords who owned large estates, and the lesser samurai. Peasants worked the land and sometimes fought alongside their lords.

In the 1600s, the Tokugawa shoguns imposed a form of centralized feudalism on Japan. They limited the power of the daimyo and ended the constant warfare. As a result, trade and commerce improved. To stop the growing influence of Christian missionaries and traders who had reached Japan in the 1500s, the Tokugawa shoguns banned all foreign trade and travel. This self-imposed isolation lasted for 200 years.

During the feudal period, the Japanese developed strong traditions. **Bushido,** the samurai code of honor, emphasized simplicity, courage, and honor. Zen, a form of Buddhism, became deeply rooted. Zen emphasized physi-

cal and mental discipline. It also taught the unity of nature that complemented the Shinto idea of respect for the forces of nature.

SECTION 3 REVIEW

1. **Identify:** (a) Mogul Empire, (b) Akbar, (c) Kublai Khan, (d) Shinto, (e) Tokugawa shoguns, (f) Zen.

2. **Define:** (a) sultan, (b) archipelago, (c) samurai, (d) shogun, (e) daimyo, (f) bushido.

3. Explain two differences between Hinduism and Islam.

4. Describe three ideas that shaped Japanese life.

5. **Critical Thinking** Why do you think Chinese civilization had such a strong influence on other civilizations of Asia?

Review

Checkup

1. Why did a division develop within Christianity?

2. Why did many people accept the teachings of Islam?

3. How did the gold–salt trade influence West Africa?

4. (a) Describe the Aztec Empire. (b) How did the Inca control their huge empire?

5. How did Islam affect India?

6. What practical inventions did the Chinese make during the T'ang and Sung dynasties?

7. How did centralized feudalism of the Tokugawa shoguns affect Japan?

Critical Thinking

1. **Understanding the Roots of Democracy** Justinian's law code is regarded as a major

achievement. Yet, Justinian was an absolute ruler. How might his laws differ from those of a democratic society?

2. **Comparing Civilizations** Compare and contrast the early civilizations of the Americas with those of ancient Egypt, Sumer, India, and China that you have read about.

Developing Basic Skills

1. **Map Reading** Study the map on page 316. (a) What political information is shown on the map? (b) With what parts of the world did Muslim merchants trade? (c) What do you think were the results of this vast trading network?

2. **Comparing Diagrams** Study the diagrams "The Structure of Feudal Society" on page 167 and "Feudal Society in Japan" on page 279. (a) How was feudal society similar in both Japan and Western Europe? (b) How was it different?

EUROPE IN TRANSITION

Renaissance artists such as Botticelli emphasized realism in their paintings.

1534 *Henry VIII broke with Rome and became head of the Church of England.*

	1300	1400	1500
POLITICS AND GOVERNMENT	**1300s** Italian city-states grow wealthy and powerful	**1453** Constantinople falls to Turks	**1513** Machiavelli writes *The Prince*
ECONOMICS AND TECHNOLOGY		**1397** Medici bank founded in Florence	**1455** Gutenberg Bible printed with movable type
SOCIETY AND CULTURE		**1348** *Decameron* is first prose written in Italian language	**1508** Michelangelo begins painting in Sistine Chapel

1534 *Ignatius Loyola founded the Society of Jesus to strengthen the Catholic Church.*

By the late Middle Ages, trade and commerce revived. Entrepreneurs opened new businesses such as this tailor's shop.

UNIT OUTLINE

1588 *The defeat of the Spanish Armada marked the end of Spain's dominance in Europe.*

1682 *This hat of sable, gold, and jewels symbolizes the wealth and power of Peter the Great of Russia.*

1600	1700	1800

1588 British sink Spanish Armada

1643 Louis XIV rules France

1762 Catherine the Great becomes ruler of Russia

1577 Sir Francis Drake begins trip around the world

1682 La Salle reaches mouth of the Mississippi River

1605 *Don Quixote* is published

1698 Peter the Great begins modernizing Russia

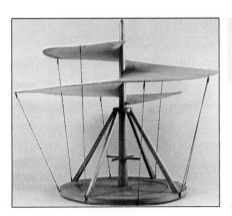

Leonardo da Vinci conducted many scientific experiments. This helicopter model is based on one of his drawings.

New tools of navigation increased trade and exploration, as this Chinese watercolor of a Jesuit missionary shows.

The Renaissance and Reformation

14

(1350–1600)

The Medici of Florence, like many powerful families in Italian city-states, supported the ideas of the Renaissance. The procession of the Medici court, shown here, illustrates its wealth and splendor.

I n Florence, Italy, the Guasconti family was sitting down to dinner when a young man burst into the room. He drew a knife and threw himself at one of the startled diners, crying, "Traitors, this is the day on which I mean to murder you all!" When none of the terror-stricken family dared resist, the man changed his mind. He ran down the stairs, only to find a dozen other members of the Guasconti household, armed with shovels, iron pipes, and clubs.

Later, the young man recalled, "When I got among them, raging like a mad bull, I flung four or five to the earth, and fell down with them myself, continually aiming my dagger now at one and now at another." Incredibly, when the dust settled, no one was hurt, and the man ran off down the street.

The young fighter was Benvenuto Cellini (chehl LEE nee), a talented goldsmith and sculptor who lived from 1500 to 1571. Cellini led an amazingly turbulent and full life, which he described in his *Autobiography*. He explained in the book that he had fought with the Guascontis because they had questioned his skill as a goldsmith.

Cellini was proud of his many talents. He played the flute, wrote elegant poetry, and was a clever diplomat. His drive and determination knew no bounds. When Rome was besieged by a neighboring city-state, Cellini stood at a crucial castle post, firing a cannon at the advancing enemy. In his *Autobiography,* he boasted, "It was I who saved the castle."

Cellini was just one of many gifted people whose bold achievements proclaimed a new age. These individuals left a lasting mark on the European scene during the period from 1350 to 1600, known as the Renaissance. Renaissance is a French word meaning rebirth. During the Renaissance, scholars reacted against what they saw as the "dark ages" of medieval Europe and revived the learning of ancient Greece and Rome. They thought they were bringing about the rebirth of civilization.

The Renaissance was both a worldly and a religious age. It was a time of great achievements in the arts and sciences as well as a period when people were deeply concerned with religious issues. During the Renaissance, fierce debates over questions of faith and salvation sparked the Reformation, a movement that divided Christians in Europe into many different groups. By 1600, Europeans had left behind the world of the Middle Ages and had laid the foundations for modern Europe and the entire western world. ∎

1 Spirit of the Renaissance

READ TO UNDERSTAND

☐ Why the Renaissance began in Italy.

☐ What ideas and attitudes Renaissance thinkers stressed.

☐ How the Renaissance in northern Europe differed from that in Italy.

☐ *Vocabulary:* humanities.

Lorenzo de' Medici, the ruler of Florence, was well pleased with his agent. The man had arrived in Florence with a treasure worth more than gold. From Constantinople, he had brought the manuscripts of 200 ancient Greek works, 80 of which had never been seen before in western Europe. Delighted, Lorenzo added the manuscripts to his already overflowing library.

Even before the fall of Constantinople in 1453, many Greek scholars had fled to the cities of northern Italy, bringing ancient texts with them. So many ideas of the ancient world were resurfacing that some claimed, "Athens has migrated to Florence." During the 1300s, a new creative spirit emerged. This spirit, combined with the "new" learning of the ancient world, heralded the Renaissance. The Renaissance began first in the city-states of northern Italy and later spread to northern Europe.

The Italian City-States

Political and economic conditions in northern Italy provided fertile ground for the Renaissance. During the Middle Ages, many Italian towns had expanded into city-states. Each city-state governed itself and the surrounding countryside. Independent and self-confident, the rulers of the city-states encouraged the exploration of the larger world of ideas.

By the late Middle Ages, Italian city-states had grown wealthy from trade and industry. Merchants from Venice, Genoa, and Pisa controlled trade in the eastern Mediterranean. Other cities, such as Florence, thrived on the sale of manufactured goods, especially wool cloth. In addition, Italian bankers made large profits by financing commercial ventures and making loans to princes and popes. The wealth of the city-states supported the Renaissance.

Merchants and bankers made up a powerful middle class in the Italian city-states. Political and economic leadership was in the hands of this class rather than with landowning nobles because feudalism had never fully developed in northern Italy.

In Italian city-states, rulers lived in great luxury. At the courts of Renaissance rulers like the duke of Mantua, shown here, loyalty, wit, and piety were essential. Their wealth allowed these rulers to pursue risky economic ventures and to become patrons of the arts.

The attitudes and interest of the wealthy middle class helped shape the Renaissance in Italy. Their concern for education and individual achievement was reflected in the Renaissance. Furthermore, they had the time and money to become patrons, or supporters, of the arts, which flourished during the Renaissance.

Florence was typical of the Italian city-states in some ways. During the 1400s, a single powerful family, the Medici (MEHD ih chee), ruled Florence. Giovanni de' Medici had organized a bank in Florence in 1397. Over the next 30 years, the bank flourished, and the family opened offices as far away as London. Giovanni's son, Cosimo, and later his great-grandson, Lorenzo, controlled the government of Florence. The Medici and their supporters frequently clashed with other leading families in an atmosphere of intrigue and treachery. Yet under the Medici, Florence came to symbolize the creative spirit of the Renaissance.

Like many Renaissance rulers, the Medici were well-educated and had many interests. For example, Lorenzo de' Medici, known as "the Magnificent," was a skilled architect. The Medici were proud of Florence and wanted all citizens to share their pride. They used part of the Medici fortune to hire local painters, sculptors, architects, and silversmiths to create works of art to beautify Florence. Many artists felt that as true artists they should be actively involved in the life of their city, not withdrawn from the everyday world.

Study of the Humanities

People in the Italian city-states took a new interest in education, especially in the learning of ancient Greece and Rome. At the universities, theology, law, and medicine were traditionally the most highly respected subjects. However, during the Renaissance, scholars also stressed the studia humanitatis, the study of the humanities. The **humanities** included the subjects taught in ancient Greek and Roman schools—grammar, rhetoric, poetry, and history. Renaissance scholars who studied those subjects were called humanists.

Renaissance humanists were practical people. They wanted to learn more about the world. By reading ancient texts, they rediscovered knowledge that had been lost or forgotten during the Middle Ages. Many were involved in politics and commerce, and they applied the new learning to daily matters. Most Renaissance humanists were also devout Christians. They felt that the study of the humanities enriched their lives as Christians because it went beyond the dry, abstract works of medieval scholars.

Renaissance scholars thought that education was the way to become a well-rounded individual. Only with a proper education, they argued, could a person enjoy a full, rewarding life. One scholar advised a student:

> I beg you, take care. Add a little every day and gather things in. Remember that these studies promise you enormous prizes both in the conduct of your life and the fame and glory of your name. Acquaint yourself with what pertains to life and manners—those things that are called humane studies because they perfect and adorn man.

Such a philosophy expressed a basic feature of the Renaissance—belief in the importance of individual achievement, a much different attitude than that of the Middle Ages.

Recovering the Classics

One of the early Renaissance humanists was Francesco Petrarch (PEE trahrk), a Florentine who lived from 1304 to 1374. Petrarch traveled about Europe in search of old manuscripts. He especially prized the works of the Roman statesman Cicero and the early Christian writer St. Augustine. Medieval scholars had studied the writings of both men, but Petrarch uncovered new evidence about the times when they had lived. During his research, Petrarch began to realize how much of the classical heritage had been lost.

Petrarch's work encouraged others to try to recover writings of the classical world. They searched for ancient manuscripts in monastery libraries. Often, the conditions they found shocked them. In one monastery library, a thick layer of dust covered everything, and grass grew on the window sills. The manuscripts lay in disorganized piles.

While searching for classical texts, humanists rescued many hidden treasures. They

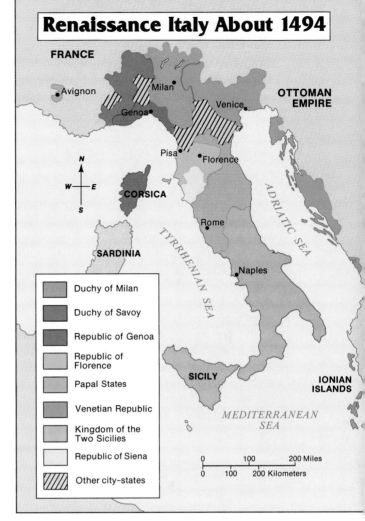

Renaissance Italy About 1494

Legend:
- Duchy of Milan
- Duchy of Savoy
- Republic of Genoa
- Republic of Florence
- Papal States
- Venetian Republic
- Kingdom of the Two Sicilies
- Republic of Siena
- Other city-states

MAP STUDY *The Renaissance spirit flourished in the northern Italian city-states. The major city-states are shown on this map, but there were dozens of smaller ones. Which states were most likely to have used the sea in building their economies? Why?*

wanted to restore the classics they found to their original form. Therefore, they compared copies of the same work to see where mistakes had been made when it was recopied.

Scholars also tried to learn when ancient manuscripts were written. To do so, they developed special techniques for analyzing historical documents. One scholar, Lorenzo Valla, examined the "Donation of Constantine," a document in which the emperor Constantine supposedly gave the pope control over Rome and the Western Roman Empire. By careful analysis, Valla exposed the document as a forgery. He pointed out that it contained the term

327

"fief," which was unknown in Constantine's time. The search for knowledge carried Renaissance thinkers such as Valla into dangerous areas because their work led people to question the accuracy of some ancient writings.

Handbooks for Proper Behavior

Renaissance writers often prepared manuals, or handbooks, that told people how to behave. One well-known manual was *The Prince* by Niccolò Machiavelli (MAHK ee uh VEHL ee). Machiavelli wrote *The Prince* as a handbook for rulers of the Italian city-states, who often faced unstable political conditions. Within a city, different factions, or groups, constantly struggled for power. In addition, city-states were often at war with one another.

In *The Prince,* Machiavelli recommended that a ruler adopt a realistic course of action in order to stay in power. If a ruler could afford to be generous and kind, that was fine. But, Machiavelli warned, "It is much safer to be feared than to be loved, if one must choose."

Niccolò Machiavelli dedicated The Prince *to Lorenzo de' Medici. The advice Machiavelli gave on how a ruler can stay in power is often considered ruthless and cynical. A typical piece of advice was: "If all men were good, this advice would not be good, but since men are wicked and do not keep their promises to you, you likewise do not have to keep yours to them."*

He taught that "the end justifies the means"— that is, a ruler should use any methods to achieve his goal. He advised rulers to use a mixture of cunning, diplomacy, and ruthlessness.

Another influential manual was *The Book of the Courtier* by Baldassare Castiglione (KAHS tee LYOH neh). Castiglione described the qualities that a courtier, or educated aristocrat, should have. He praised the study of the humanities and urged courtiers to nurture their talents. They should learn to appreciate music and play a variety of instruments. They should be able to speak gracefully and provide rulers with witty, pleasant company. In short, Castiglione drew a picture of what he considered an ideal Renaissance person, someone who had a broad education in many different areas. Castiglione's ideas were widely accepted and copied.

The Renaissance in Northern Europe

The Renaissance blossomed first in the Italian city-states, where commerce and a wealthy middle class supported learning and the arts. Then slowly, Renaissance ideas spread northward.

In northern Europe and Spain, the Renaissance took a different form. For one thing, feudalism, with its traditions of knighthood and chivalry, was stronger in northern Europe than in Italy. Therefore, kings, queens, and nobles, rather than merchants and bankers, were the chief patrons of the arts.

Furthermore, Renaissance scholars in northern Europe and Spain took a more traditional approach to religion than some Italian humanists. They studied classical works, but they were more likely to study the writings of early Christians than those of Greeks and Romans. Humanists in northern Europe devoted their time to uncovering what they believed was the purer faith of the early Christians.

Despite differences between the Renaissance in Italy and the Renaissance in the rest of Europe, artists, writers, and scholars pursued similar goals. They stressed individual achievement and classical learning. Furthermore, they stimulated a vigorous creative spirit that revolutionized thinking in Western

Europe. Compared to people in the Middle Ages, people during the Renaissance were more concerned with achieving worldly success. Yet they maintained a strong faith in Christianity.

SECTION 1 REVIEW

1. **Identify:** (a) Lorenzo de' Medici, (b) Francesco Petrarch, (c) Niccolò Machiavelli, (d) Baldassare Castiglione.

2. **Define:** humanities.

3. How did the wealth of the Italian city-states encourage the Renaissance spirit?

4. (a) What subjects made up the humanities? (b) According to Renaissance scholars, what was the purpose of education?

5. What advice did Machiavelli give to rulers?

6. According to Castiglione, what was the ideal Renaissance person?

7. **Critical Thinking** Compare and contrast the Renaissance in northern Europe with the Renaissance in Italy.

2 Art and Literature of the Renaissance

READ TO UNDERSTAND

☐ **What new ideas Renaissance artists contributed.**

☐ **Who were the best-known artists and writers of the Renaissance.**

☐ **What issues concerned Christian humanists of northern Europe.**

The artist was working on a commission to paint the portrait of the third wife of the merchant Giocondo. Patiently, the woman sat as the artist shaped her features on the canvas and applied warm flesh tones to her face. She had little thought that 500 years later people would try to fathom the meaning behind her teasing, half-mocking smile in the portrait. Today, Leonardo da Vinci's portrait of La Gioconda, better known as *Mona Lisa,* is perhaps the most famous painting in the world.

Da Vinci was one of the many great artists and writers who symbolized the spirit of the Renaissance. Dozens of Renaissance artists are world-famous today, unlike the painters and sculptors of the Middle Ages, who received little attention. Popes, rulers, merchants, and bankers competed for the services of Renaissance artists, who proudly accepted the fame that their creative genius brought.

Classical Influence

During the Renaissance, artists returned to the classical principles of Greek and Roman art. The Greeks, you will recall, stressed harmony and balance in nature, and the Romans emphasized realism.

Renaissance artists traveled around Italy, finding inspiration in the remains of ancient Roman buildings and statues. In the early 1400s, the sculptor Donatello (DAHN uh TEHL oh) and the architect Filippo Brunelleschi (BROO nehl LEHS kee) traveled from Florence to Rome. There, they sketched the ruins of ancient buildings as well as ancient marble and bronze statues.

When Donatello returned to Florence, he created a statue of David, a king of the ancient Hebrews. The statue was unlike medieval sculptures, in which individuals were shown only as part of a larger work on tombs or cathedral walls. Instead, like the statues of the ancient Greeks and Romans, Donatello's David stood alone. It could be studied and admired from all sides. Furthermore, it portrayed David with grace and realism.

Brunelleschi and other Renaissance architects rejected medieval Gothic architecture and revived classical styles. They designed elegant buildings, using columns and domes. Brunelleschi created a sensation when he proposed to top the unfinished cathedral of Florence with a huge dome. Many people thought the building would collapse. But Brunelleschi had studied ancient Roman buildings, and he learned how to solve the technical problems involved in raising the dome.

Years later, when the artist and architect Michelangelo Buonarroti (MĪ k'l AHN juh LOH BWOH nahr ROH tee) designed St. Peter's Cathe-

Some new techniques used by Renaissance painters are evident in this scene of the Last Supper by Giotto. Giotto made careful use of light and shadow to add depth to the picture. Jesus and his disciples are more solid and lifelike than figures in earlier paintings. Compare this Last Supper with the one on page 124.

dral in Rome, he designed the dome using the engineering principles developed by Brunelleschi.

New Techniques in Art

Many Renaissance artists tried to show the world realistically, as it actually existed. Early in the Renaissance, the Florentine artist Giotto (JAHT oh) used shadings of dark and light to add a feeling of space to his paintings. Later, the painter Tommaso Masaccio (mah SAHT choh) and Brunelleschi developed rules of perspective. Artists used the rules of perspective to paint scenes that appeared to be three-dimensional. To give a sense of depth or distance in a scene, figures closer to the viewer were drawn larger. Those farther off were drawn smaller.

Artists in Flanders* made significant contributions to Renaissance art by improving paints. Medieval artists had worked with tempera paints. In tempera paints, the pigments, or colors, were mixed with watered-down egg yolk. Tempera paints dried quickly, so artists

could not make changes once they had applied the color. Furthermore, tempera paints did not blend easily.

Flemish artists experimented with paints that had an oil base. The new oil paints dried more slowly and were easier to blend. Therefore, artists could create subtle new shades.

Great Italian Artists

During the late 1400s and early 1500s, three artists dominated the world of Italian art: Leonardo da Vinci, Michelangelo, and Raphael Santi. Together with many other Renaissance artists, these artists have influenced painting and sculpture until the present.

Leonardo da Vinci. Leonardo da Vinci achieved the Renaissance goal of doing many things and excelling in all. He was curious about everything. He continually observed the world around him and recorded his findings in dozens of notebooks. Because he was fascinated by flight, he observed birds on the wing. In his notebooks, he showed how he thought humans might use wings to fly. To understand the anatomy of the human body, he dissected corpses. He then used his knowledge to paint human figures more realistically.

---

* Flanders included parts of what is today Belgium and the Netherlands. People from Flanders were called Flemish.

Sadly, much of Leonardo's work has been lost. Only 15 of his paintings survive, including such masterpieces as *The Last Supper* and the *Mona Lisa*.

Michelangelo. Like Leonardo, Michelangelo had many talents. He thought of himself first and foremost as a sculptor. But he was also a skilled musician, poet, painter, and architect. Like other Renaissance sculptors, Michelangelo carefully studied the human figure. Yet Michelangelo's figures do not exhibit the relaxed poses of other sculptures, such as Donatello's *David*. Instead, Michelangelo's statues suggest a sense of tension.

In 1508, Pope Julius II asked Michelangelo to paint the ceiling of the Sistine Chapel in the Vatican. Michelangelo devoted four years to the task. For hours each day, he lay on his back atop a high scaffold and painted scenes from the Bible, such as God creating the world and Noah and the flood. The work was exhausting, but the final product has been admired for almost 500 years.

Raphael. Raphael Santi was a skillful painter whose work was influenced by both Leonardo and Michelangelo. Born in Umbria, Raphael favored the bright colors traditionally used by painters from that region of Italy. He often painted the Madonna, the mother of Jesus, and the infant Jesus.

Artists of Northern Europe

In the 1400s and 1500s, northern European painters also created splendid masterpieces. Because ancient Roman ruins lay beyond the Alps, northern artists were less influenced by classical styles than their contemporaries in Italy were. However, using the rules of perspective and the new oil-based paints, they produced paintings that marked a break with the works of medieval painters.

Flanders was the artistic center of northern Europe. Flemish artists such as Jan van Eyck (van ĪK) wanted to paint the world realistically. To do this, van Eyck paid careful attention to detail. When he painted a satin robe, he showed every fold in the cloth exactly. Similarly, every jewel in a royal crown sparkled. Van Eyck's paintings often had a religious message. For example, in one work he painted the

This painting by Leonardo da Vinci reflects his theory that "a light figure must be painted against a dark background to give a particular force and brilliancy of effect." The figure of the woman, holding the ferret, is especially striking against the background of darkness and shadow.

Michelangelo's Pietà *demonstrates his mastery of the human form. Every detail of the body of Christ testifies to the sculptor's knowledge of anatomy. This concern with accuracy was common among Renaissance artists.*

Virgin Mary very large compared to her surroundings, in this way making clear her importance to Christianity.

Another Flemish painter, Pieter Bruegel (BROI guhl), was inspired by everyday scenes of country landscapes and of peasants working in the fields. Although Bruegel showed the lives of common people in his paintings, he sometimes used painted figures, as van Eyck had, to express deeper meanings. Bruegel influenced later Flemish and Dutch painters, who painted scenes of daily life rather than religious or classical themes. (See the painting on page 336.)

Northern Renaissance artists often painted realistic scenes of everyday life. This painting by Jan van Eyck shows the artist's friend Giovanni Arnolfini with his wife Jeanne Cenami. Many details of home life can be seen. Certain details have a symbolic meaning. The little dog is a symbol of faithfulness. The single lighted candle in the chandelier represents the presence of Christ.

Many German artists painted realistic portraits. For example, Hans Holbein the Younger painted portraits of nobles and rulers, as well as of philosophers and commoners. Another German artist, Albrecht Dürer (DYOO ruhr), traveled to Italy to study the techniques of the Italian masters. Dürer then brought these techniques to northern Europe.

Renaissance Writers

Like painting and sculpture, literature expressed the attitudes of the Renaissance. In towns and cities, the middle class formed a demanding new audience. The middle class particularly enjoyed dramatic tales and comedies.

Popular literature was often written in the vernacular, although many Renaissance writers continued to use Latin. (See page 187.) The Italian writer Petrarch felt comfortable writing in either Latin or Italian. In his writings, Petrarch celebrated the joys of living. Inspired by his love for a woman named Laura, he perfected a form of poetry known as the sonnet. His sonnets and use of the vernacular greatly influenced other writers of his time.

Another Italian writer, Giovanni Boccaccio (boh KAH chee OH), also influenced Renaissance literature. Boccaccio's best-known work is the *Decameron*. It consists of 100 stories told by seven women and three men who have fled from the plague in Florence. To pass the time, they tell colorful tales that make fun of knights and other medieval figures. The clear narrative style of the *Decameron* served as a model for later writers.

The French writer François Rabelais (RAB uh LAY) fits the ideal of a Renaissance person. He began his career as a monk. Later, he studied the classics and practiced medicine. Rabelais was immensely curious about the world. He summed up his view in these words: "Abandon yourself to Nature's truths, and let nothing in this world be unknown to you."

Rabelais created two famous characters: the giant Gargantua (gahr GAN choo wuh) and his son Pantagruel (pan TAG roo WEHL). Through these humorous characters, he gave his views on many subjects including the need for reform in education and the Church. He also poked fun at the narrow-mindedness of monks and scholars.

Miguel de Cervantes (suhr VAN teez) was a leading Renaissance writer in Spain. As a soldier in the Spanish army, Cervantes had many adventures. He was captured by pirates and held as a slave in North Africa for five years. Later, he turned to writing.

In his novel *Don Quixote* (dahn ke HOHT ee), Cervantes gently mocked the medieval ideals of chivalry. The hero, a knight named Don Quixote, believed that he was still living in the days of chivalry and imagined himself involved in one dangerous adventure after another. Sancho Panza, Don Quixote's servant, tried without success to convince the knight that the "castles" he saw were only lowly inns and the "jousting knights" were simply windmills. Don Quixote was unable to understand the new world, which required the skills of practical men such as Sancho Panza rather than those of battle-ready knights.

Poet and playwright William Shakespeare, one of the finest writers in the English language, brought vital new ideas to literature. He invented hundreds of new words that enriched the English language. In his tragedies, comedies, and historical dramas, Shakespeare explored personal themes such as jealousy, ambition, love, and greed. Most of his plays were performed at the Globe Theater in London. In London, as in other European cities, both well-to-do and poorer people attended the theater. There, they found entertainment, but they also learned about the ideas of their times.

In sixteenth-century Europe, Sofonisba Anguissola was considered a "marvel" since people at that time did not think women could paint. Early in her career, she was advised by Michelangelo. And at one time she served as a court painter to Philip II of Spain. Her most striking works are portraits, such as this one above, of members of her family.

A Call for Reform

Renaissance writers emphasized religious as well as worldly themes. In the early 1500s, some Christian scholars who had made a study of the Bible and early Christian writings urged the Church to reform itself. They wanted the Church to return to its early traditions based on the teachings of Jesus.

In northern Europe, the Dutch scholar and priest Desiderius Erasmus (ee RAZ muhs) led the Christian humanists. Erasmus knew Greek, so he could study the earliest-known versions of the New Testament, which were written in Greek. In his most famous work, *In Praise of Folly,* Erasmus used witty dialogues to point out the ignorance of some clergy. He also criti-

cized the Church for emphasizing pomp and ritual rather than the teachings of Jesus.

Despite his criticism of Church practices, Erasmus accepted its teachings. He remained in the Church even when other reformers rejected its authority and set up their own churches.

A friend of Erasmus who shared his concerns was the English scholar and statesman Sir Thomas More. More thought that literature should serve Christian goals. In his book *Utopia,* More described an ideal society in

333

which people lived at peace with one another.* He created an imaginary kingdom to show how such a society should be organized. People in this kingdom worked hard, were well educated, and had no use for money. They especially valued cleanliness and equality. Later writers used More's method to express their own ideas about society.

SECTION 2 REVIEW

1. **Identify:** (a) Brunelleschi, (b) Leonardo da Vinci, (c) Michelangelo, (d) Raphael, (e) Jan van Eyck, (f) Boccaccio, (g) Rabelais, (h) Cervantes, (i) Shakespeare, (j) Sir Thomas More.

2. How was Donatello's *David* different from medieval sculpture?

3. Describe two new techniques that affected Renaissance art.

4. (a) Why did Erasmus criticize the Church? (b) What did he think the Church should emphasize?

5. **Critical Thinking** Explain how one of the writers you have read about was clearly a product of the Renaissance and could not have written during the Middle Ages.

3 Changing Patterns of Life

READ TO UNDERSTAND

☐ How printing affected people's lives.

☐ What economic and social changes took place during the Renaissance.

☐ What roles women played in the Renaissance.

"Only men of noble birth can obtain perfection," claimed Lorenzo de' Medici. "The poor, who work with their hands and have not time to cultivate their minds, are incapable of it."

That statement expressed the contempt the upper classes felt for the lower classes in Renaissance Europe.

The wealthy filled their palaces with elegant works of art. They had the leisure to read and expand their knowledge of the world. The poor labored to put bread on the table. In time, however, advances in technology, such as the introduction of printing, gradually spread to more and more people. As a result, ordinary people began to come in contact with the new ideas of the Renaissance.

The Introduction of Printing

The invention of printing in the 1400s greatly increased the number of books available. Before this time, few books were reproduced because each one had to be copied by hand. A good copier could complete only about two books a year. Furthermore, books were costly because they were written on parchment made from the skin of a sheep or a goat.

Both problems were gradually overcome. In the 1300s, Europeans learned from the Arabs how to make paper from rags and wood pulp. The Arabs had learned about papermaking from the Chinese.

The technique of printing also grew out of earlier developments. In the 1300s, engravers experimented with printing books from wood blocks. They carved a page on the block, which was then inked and pressed on paper. By the 1400s, German engravers had developed movable type. Movable type consisted of small pieces of metal, each of which was engraved with a letter. The pieces of metal could then be combined to form words and sentences. Also, the pieces of metal could be used again and again.

The final step in the development of printing was probably taken by Johann Gutenberg in Mainz, Germany. Gutenberg developed a type of metal that could be used to make movable type. He used this metal to build a printing press, and in 1455 he printed a complete edition of the Bible on the press. With the Gutenberg Bible, as it was called, the era of printed books began.

Printing spread rapidly. By 1500, there were over 250 presses in Europe turning out

---

* Today, the word utopia is used to mean a perfect place or situation.

books. As printing methods improved, the cost of producing books fell. Because prices were reasonable, people who could never have afforded hand-copied books now bought printed books.

The use of paper and the development of printing had a revolutionary effect on the world of learning. Ideas spread rapidly through the printed word. Many of the newly printed books, pamphlets, and other short works were on religious topics. Others dealt with subjects ranging from mining and medicine to philosophy and politics. More and more people in Europe studied books on the

DAILY LIFE All London's a Stage

In 1576, James Burbage staked his fortune on a risky business venture. On a plot of land just outside London, he began to build a theater—the first public theater in England. Putting up the circular wooden building cost much more than Burbage expected, but the gamble paid off. Londoners packed the new theater, and Burbage soon made his money back. Other stages quickly opened around London, and English drama entered a golden age. William Shakespeare's first play was performed at Burbage's theater in 1591.

For the people of London, going to the theater was an exciting experience. In the streets of London at the time, one person reported, "Walking elbow to elbow you see the knight, the gentleman, the clown, the lawyer, the scholar, the beggar, the doctor, the idiot, the ruffian, the cheater, and the cut-throat." These same people showed up at the theater to see the latest plays.

Inside the theater, however, it was easy to tell a person's social class. Standing room in front of the raised stage cost only a penny. Here stood the groundlings, usually poor members of the working class. At times, groundlings annoyed the actors by noisily cracking open nuts, a favorite snack. If they didn't like the play, the groundlings hissed and pelted the stage with shells.

Middle-class people, such as merchants and artisans, paid an extra penny to sit in real seats. And wealthy theater-goers could pay even more to sit in chairs right on the stage. Since everyone else in the theater could see them, the rich could show off their stylish clothes and hairstyles. One playwright complained that the rich would "laugh aloud in the saddest scene" just to draw attention to themselves.

Authorities in London worried that this new form of entertainment might be dangerous. They shut down plays that criticized the crown or the Church. Once, a group of actors performed Shakespeare's *Richard II,* which tells about the overthrow and murder of the English king. The next day, a rebellion against Queen Elizabeth broke out. Summoned before the queen, the actors pleaded for their lives, swearing that the play had nothing to do with the rebellion. Elizabeth showed mercy. She forgave the actors but ordered them to perform *Richard II* for her at court—the day before the rebellion's leader was to be beheaded.

1. How did seating inside the theater reflect class differences?

2. **Critical Thinking** Why do you think the English authorities worried about the theater causing disorder?

The Flemish painter Pieter Bruegel was nicknamed "peasant Bruegel" because of paintings such as this harvesting scene, which offers a realistic view of everyday life. Bending and stooping, lifting and carrying, peasants gather grain. One man quenches his thirst with a drink from the water jug. The woman at right is carrying fruits and vegetables, only recently added to the European diet.

sciences and technology. The knowledge they gained would greatly affect the Scientific Revolution, as you will read in Chapter 17.

Everyday Life

For most people in Renaissance Europe, life was much as it had been for their parents and grandparents. However, social and economic changes were slowly taking place.

In medieval Europe, most people lived in extended families. On the manor, the extended family was important because many people were needed to work the land. During the Renaissance, the nuclear family gradually began to emerge, especially in the towns and cities. In a nuclear family, only parents and their children live in a household.

Another change affected the way businesses were run. Most businesses in the Middle Ages were small and were managed by a single family. During the Renaissance, some people formed business partnerships with people outside the family. Two or more families might pool their resources in order to expand business activities.

Some changes in agriculture and industry were the result of the continuing effects of the Black Death. As you have read, the Black Death had greatly reduced the population of Europe. (See page 211.) Thus, the demand for wheat and other grains fell. Farmers began producing new types of food, which they hoped would be more profitable. The new foods included meat, fruit, and dairy products such as cheese and butter. As these products gradually became more plentiful, people's diets changed.

As a result of the Black Death, the demand for manufactured goods such as wool cloth also fell. In Florence, for example, half the population had died of the plague, and wool production dropped drastically. When the population throughout Europe began to grow again, the demand for wool cloth increased. Wool workers then found their skills in much demand, and they asked for higher wages. When employers tried to keep wages low, the work-

BUILDERS AND SHAPERS

Isabella d'Este: Renaissance Person

"Keep a tranquil mind, and give all your attention to military matters, for I intend to govern Mantua in such a way that you will not suffer any wrong. Everything possible will be done for the good of her subjects." Isabella d'Este's letter reassured her husband, Francesco, as he led his army against the French. Francesco was confident that his wife could rule in his absence. Isabella's knowledge, wit, and political skill had led one poet to call her "la prima donna del mondo," the first lady of the world.

Isabella d'Este started life with many advantages. Her family ruled Ferrara, a wealthy city-state on the Po River. As a daughter in a noble family, Isabella received a good education. She developed a special love of poetry and, as a child, she delighted visitors by reciting verses from Virgil's *Aeneid* and Dante's *Divine Comedy.* She also learned the skills that women were expected to know—playing the lute, singing, dancing, and embroidering.

Isabella married Francesco Gonzaga, who became ruler of Mantua, a wealthy city in northern Italy. While she was raising her nine children, she threw herself into making Mantua a center of Renaissance culture. Isabella attracted talented artists and poets to Mantua. She was a generous, but demanding, patron of the arts. "You can paint whatever you like," she told one artist at work in her palace, "as long as it is not anything ugly, because if it is ugly, you will have to paint it all over again at your own expense."

When the Venetians captured her husband, Isabella kept the people of Mantua calm and helped win his release. Her clever negotiating prevented other princes from invading the city. The thousands of letters she wrote in her lifetime show the range of her wisdom. Isabella d'Este understood art and politics, war and child raising. She was indeed a Renaissance person.

1. What advantages did Isabella enjoy as a child?

2. **Critical Thinking** In what ways was Isabella a Renaissance person?

---

ers revolted. Although worker revolts were brutally suppressed, the wages of city workers did rise during the Renaissance.

Women in the Renaissance

Women's occupations changed little during the Renaissance. Their main responsibilities were in the home, where they raised the children and took care of the family. At sowing and harvesting time, farm women and children worked in the fields alongside the men.

However, women also worked outside the home. Some worked as servants in households of wealthy farmers, merchants, or nobles. Many women earned money as spinners and weavers, although most workers in the cloth industry were men. Women in the merchant class helped manage family businesses. In addition, many farm and city women ran their own small businesses, selling handwork or garden produce at local markets.

A few women played central roles in governing city-states or nations. Queen Isabella of Spain, for example, was a forceful and effective ruler. (See page 209.) At different times during the Renaissance, queens ruled Naples, Scotland, and England. In France, Catherine de'

Medici, the widow of King Henry II, acted as regent* for her young sons until they were old enough to rule.

Some Renaissance scholars argued that women as well as men would benefit from studying the classics. As the number of schools increased, more women learned to read and write. For example, Isabella d'Este received an excellent education that enabled her to translate Greek and Latin writings and take part in the learned discussions of her day.

SECTION 3 REVIEW

1. **Identify:** Johann Gutenberg.

2. How did the introduction of printing affect the spread of ideas?

3. Describe one way in which the Black Death affected farming.

4. Give three examples of work some Renaissance women did outside the home.

5. **Critical Thinking** Why do you think the changes taking place during the Renaissance did not affect the lives of ordinary people for a long time?

---

4 Beginnings of the Reformation

READ TO UNDERSTAND

☐ **Why demands for Church reform grew.**

☐ **Why and how Martin Luther challenged the Church.**

☐ **Why many people in Germany supported Luther.**

☐ *Vocabulary:* **indulgence.**

"They cheat and steal and when they are at the end of their resources, they set up as saints and work miracles." So went the angry accusa-

---

* A regent governs in place of a monarch who is too young or is otherwise unable to rule.

tions against friars and monks. In church courtyards and at holy places, they hawked goods they said were feathers from the wings of the archangel Gabriel and vials containing the tears of the Madonna. Many people and members of the clergy were truly devout, and they were shocked by such practices.

During the Middle Ages, reform movements had swept the Church and had restored its vigor. Now, during the Renaissance, calls for reform again echoed across Europe. Unlike earlier reform efforts, the new move to cleanse the Church shattered forever the medieval idea of the unity of Christendom.

Need for Reform

In the 1300s and 1400s, many Christians lost confidence in the Church's religious leadership. The Babylonian Captivity and the Great Schism had seriously hurt the power and prestige of the Church. (See page 211.) To many, the Church seemed too concerned with worldly affairs. The pope and clergy struggled to keep Church privileges as powerful monarchs chipped away at its power. Rulers of France, Spain, and Germany often interfered in Italian affairs, forcing the pope into long, costly wars to protect the Papal States.

The worldliness of the Church was evident in the splendor of the papal court. For example, in 1506, Pope Julius II decided to rebuild St. Peter's Cathedral in Rome. He hired architects and artists such as Michelangelo to design and decorate the new church.

To finance such projects and pay for their wars, Renaissance popes increased the fees that Christians paid for baptism, marriage, and funerals. Popes also permitted the sale of indulgences. An **indulgence** was the reduction of the punishment a sinner would suffer in purgatory after death.

Indulgences were first granted during the Crusades, when the pope agreed to cancel penalties for any sins that a crusader committed. Eventually, popes granted indulgences not only in exchange for a specific service, but also for money contributions to the Church. By the 1500s, people could buy indulgences to cancel the punishments dead relatives might be suffering in purgatory.

Many faithful Christians protested such practices. They also objected to the worldliness of the Church. As you read in Chapter 10, reformers such as Wycliffe and Huss had won many followers for their teachings, which emphasized the Bible and the simple lives led by early Christians.

In the 1490s, an outspoken monk, Girolamo Savonarola (SAV oh nuh ROH luh), preached reform in Florence. He attacked the Church and condemned immorality. He urged his listeners to reject worldly possessions. Eventually, Savonarola was executed for heresy. But his death did not silence the voices of protest. Christian scholars such as Erasmus also urged reform. Their suggestions for reform were soon taken up by others who introduced revolutionary changes.

Luther's Challenge

In 1517, the written protests of a German monk, Martin Luther, sparked a reform movement that split the Roman Catholic Church. The son of a wealthy peasant, Martin Luther studied law. In 1505, during a summer storm, Luther was knocked to the ground by a bolt of lightning. "St. Anne, help me!" he cried out in terror. "I will become a monk."

True to his word, Luther entered a monastery and later taught Bible studies at the University of Wittenberg in Saxony. He tried to lead a holy life. However, he became convinced that good works such as fasting and prayer did not ensure salvation because a person could not buy God's favor. He believed that God would grant salvation whether or not a person did good works.

The 95 theses. Luther's beliefs led him to denounce the practice of granting indulgences. In 1517, the monk Johann Tetzel was actively selling indulgences near Luther's home at the University of Wittenberg. Tetzel was quoted as saying, "As soon as the coin in the coffer rings, the soul from purgatory springs." Tetzel was collecting huge sums of money to be sent to Rome.

Luther was outraged at Tetzel's activities. He posted 95 theses, or questions for debate, on the door of the Wittenberg castle church. In the 95 theses, he condemned the selling of in-

Reformers criticized the Catholic Church for its extravagant wealth. In this detail from an altarpiece, gold and jewels decorate the elaborate vestments of the priests.

dulgences. He argued that indulgences could neither release a soul from purgatory nor cancel a person's sins.

Within weeks after Luther's attack, his message had been printed and spread across Europe. Forced to defend his statements, Luther expanded his criticism of the Church. Soon he was denying Church authority in other matters. He claimed that the authority of the Bible and a person's own conscience outweighed the pope's authority.

Pope Leo X became alarmed at the activities of the "wild boar," as he called Luther. In 1520, he excommunicated Luther. The next year, the Holy Roman emperor Charles V ques-

In 1521, Martin Luther was called before Charles V, the Holy Roman emperor, at the Diet of Worms. Luther expected to be allowed to explain his views. Instead, the emperor asked him to renounce his heresy. When Luther refused, Charles V declared him an outlaw. Luther found refuge in Saxony, where he translated the New Testament into German in just 11 weeks.

tioned Luther before the Imperial Diet, or assembly, then meeting at Worms. Luther stood firm and refused to withdraw his criticisms of the Church. Instead, he declared: "I cannot go against my conscience. Here I stand. I cannot do otherwise. God help me." Luther's stand made him the leader of reform-minded churches in the Holy Roman Empire.

Luther's teachings. Three ideas were at the core of Luther's reforms. First, he taught that individuals could not achieve salvation by their own efforts, such as by performing good works. A person's only hope of salvation was faith in God's mercy. The watchwords of Luther's teaching were "faith alone."

Second, Luther maintained that the Bible was the only guide for Christians. He rejected many Church ceremonies as well as the authority of the pope because he said the Bible made no mention of them.

Finally, Luther emphasized the role of the individual. "The pope is no judge of matters pertaining to God's word and faith," he said. "But the Christian man must examine and judge for himself." He claimed that the individual did not need a priest to interpret the Bible. Like Wycliffe and Huss, he urged Christians to study the Bible themselves. Luther translated the Bible into the German vernacular and conducted services in German, instead of Latin, so that people could understand what was being said.

Luther also made other changes. He simplified religious services and rituals. And he said that priests should be allowed to marry because the Bible had not forbidden it. Such changes were adopted by the Lutheran churches set up by Luther's followers.

Impact of Luther's Reforms

Luther's ideas won widespread support in Germany. Among the clergy, many sympathized with his criticism of Church abuses. In the towns, some people applauded Luther's reforms because they resented paying Church taxes, which were sent to Rome. Some townspeople echoed Luther's warning that any messenger from Rome seeking money "should receive a strict command either to keep his distance, or else to jump into the Rhine or the nearest river, and take a cold bath." Many town governments eagerly took over Church property and set up independent churches.

Some German princes supported Luther and his followers. They wanted to assert their independence of the Holy Roman emperor. Like townspeople, these princes seized Church lands and stopped the flow of Church taxes to Rome. When the emperor tried to force the German princes to remain loyal to the pope, they protested. They became known as Protestants. Later, the movement to reform the Church was called the Protestant Reformation.

Luther's reforms also appealed to the peasants, who bore a heavy burden of Church taxes. In 1524, peasants in southern Germany began an armed rebellion against the nobility and the Church. They protested against efforts to increase their feudal dues. And they demanded the right to choose their own priests and the right to cut wood and take game from the lords' forests.

At first, Luther supported the Peasants' Revolt, as it was called. But he drew back in horror when he heard reports of peasants burning, looting, and killing. He bitterly criticized their actions and sided with the nobles, who stamped out the revolt, killing about 100,000 peasants. Many peasants felt betrayed by Luther and returned to the Catholic Church. From this time on, Luther and his followers rejected political revolution.

By Luther's death in 1546, about half the princes within the Holy Roman Empire had adopted the new Protestant faith. In response, the Holy Roman emperor Charles V launched a military campaign in 1547 to force the Lutheran princes back into the Catholic Church. When neither side could win the war, Charles accepted a compromise. In 1555, at the Diet of Augsburg, he agreed that each prince could choose whether his lands would be Catholic or Lutheran. By allowing individual rulers to determine the religion of a territory, the Peace of Augsburg officially recognized the newest split within Christendom.

By 1555, most princes in northern Germany were Lutheran, while most princes in southern Germany were Catholic. Lutheran ideas had also spread to Scandinavia. However, the dispute between Catholics and Protestants did not end. As other reformers won followers, the conflict spread.

SECTION 4 REVIEW

1. **Identify:** (a) Martin Luther, (b) Protestant Reformation, (c) Peasants' Revolt, (d) Peace of Augsburg.

2. **Define:** indulgence.

3. How did the actions of powerful European monarchs affect the Church?

4. (a) What Church practice did Luther attack in his 95 theses? (b) Describe two major teachings of Luther.

5. Give one reason why German princes supported Luther.

6. **Critical Thinking** Why did Luther's challenge cause a split in the Church when earlier reform movements had not?

5 Further Challenges to the Catholic Church

READ TO UNDERSTAND

☐ How the ideas of John Calvin differed from those of Martin Luther.

☐ Why Henry VIII of England broke away form the Catholic Church.

☐ How the Catholic Church met the challenge of the Protestant Reformation.

☐ *Vocabulary:* predestination.

The young Spanish knight, wounded in combat, gritted his teeth and endured the ordeal as the bone protruding from his broken leg was sawed off. Despite the agony, he asked only for a book of knightly romances to read. Instead, someone brought him a book of the lives of the saints and the life of Christ.

His reading inspired the young knight to put himself at the service of the Church. So began the spiritual journey of Ignatius Loyola, who would take a vigorous role in the efforts of the Catholic Church to check the spread of Protestantism.

While Luther's ideas were taking root in Germany, reformers throughout Europe were challenging the authority of the pope. As Protestant movements sprang to life, the Catholic Church took steps to stop them and to revive its spiritual leadership of the Christian world.

The Spread of Protestant Ideas

Switzerland emerged as a center of the Protestant Reformation. Ulrich Zwingli, a priest and admirer of Erasmus, taught in the Swiss city of Zurich during the same years that Luther was launching the Protestant Reformation in Germany. Like Luther, Zwingli had no use for elaborate rituals. In his church, he abolished the Catholic Mass, confessions, and indulgences. He also allowed priests to marry.

Zwingli believed that a good pastor, or minister, and a strong sense of discipline among church members would help Christians lead a spiritual life. He held services in undecorated buildings and read sermons based on the Bible. By 1529, Zwingli's ideas had spread to many parts of Switzerland.

Calvinists. In the Swiss cities of Basel and Geneva, John Calvin led one of the best-organized Protestant movements. Born in France, Calvin studied law at the University of Paris before he decided to devote his life to religion. As part of his studies, Calvin read the works of Erasmus and Luther. In 1536, he published the *Institutes of the Christian Religion,* in which he outlined his beliefs in a clear, orderly way.

Like Luther, Calvin rejected the idea that good works would ensure salvation. However, Lutheran and Calvinist teachings differed in emphasis. Luther taught that people could work toward their own salvation through faith in God. Calvin stressed the all-powerfulness of God. God alone, Calvin said, decided whether an individual received eternal life.

Calvin believed in **predestination,** the idea that God had chosen who would be saved. Calvin's critics warned that predestination would lead people to act irresponsibly. Why should individuals lead a good life, they asked, if God had already determined their fate? But Calvin answered that people should lead good lives in order to show that God had chosen them for salvation.

Calvin set up a church with strong, disciplined leadership. Calvinists practiced the strict morality taught in the Old Testament. With the *Institutes* as a guide, the new faith spread rapidly.

Calvinists won many converts in commercial centers such as the Netherlands. There, as elsewhere, middle-class townspeople were attracted to Calvinism because it reflected their belief that people should live simply and work hard. Moreover, Calvinism answered many people's criticisms of the Catholic Church. French Calvinists, called Huguenots (HYOO guh NAHTS), were powerful in southern France. During the 1550s, John Knox took the new faith to Scotland. Followers also established churches in England, where they later became known as Puritans.

Other Protestant groups. A number of Protestant sects sprang up all across Europe. Some clashed violently with each other and with Catholics. Each group saw itself as God's agent and viewed all others as the devil's workers. Many years would pass before Europeans accepted the idea that two or more religions could coexist.

Protestant sects developed their own beliefs based on reading and interpreting the Bible. For example, the Anabaptists—later called Baptists—argued that infants could not be baptized as members of a church because they were too young to understand the Christian faith. They restricted baptism and church membership to adults. Anabaptists in Germany were vigorously persecuted by other Protestants and by Catholics alike. Yet their ideas continued to influence Protestant thinking in many countries.

Henry VIII's Quarrel with Rome

Throughout his life, Henry VIII of England considered himself a faithful Catholic. In 1521, Henry published a stinging attack on the teachings of Martin Luther. The attack delighted the pope, who awarded Henry the title "Defender of the Faith." However, a few years later, the English king quarreled with the pope over the issue of marriage.

After 18 years of marriage to Catherine of Aragon, Henry had no son to inherit the English throne. Catherine had given birth to many children, including several boys, but only one child, Mary Tudor, survived infancy. When Henry asked Pope Clement VII to grant him an annulment* so he could remarry, the pope refused. A strong-willed man, Henry would not accept defeat. Instead, he built up English resentment against the pope.

Between 1529 and 1536, Henry took the English church from under the pope's control and placed it under his own rule. In 1533, the Archbishop of Canterbury, Thomas Cranmer, annulled Henry's marriage to Catherine of Aragon. Henry then married Anne Boleyn. Parliament recognized the king as the supreme head of the Church of England by the Act of Supremacy of 1534.

---

* An annulment is an official statement declaring a marriage invalid.

English Protestants applauded the steps taken by the king and Parliament to break away from Rome. However, other English reformers, such as Sir Thomas More, wanted change to come from within the Catholic Church. Henry feared his opponents would disrupt the peace, so he ordered the execution of More and others who would not accept the Act of Supremacy.

Before long, Henry took further steps against the Catholic Church. When he heard reports that many monasteries were corrupt, the king promptly closed them. About 10,000 English monks and nuns were forced to seek other homes. Because he needed money, the king then seized monastery lands, which he sold to nobles, wealthy farmers, and merchants. In the years ahead, those who had bought monastery lands would resist any effort to restore land or power to the Catholic Church.

Despite the break with Rome, Henry did not want to change Catholic beliefs. In fact, Henry proclaimed that the Anglican Church, as the Church of England was called, would preserve traditional Catholic practices. However, he did allow priests to use an English translation of the Bible, and he permitted them to marry.

A Protestant Nation

Henry VIII died in 1547 after a turbulent life that included six marriages. After his death, the official religion of England swung back and forth between Protestant and Catholic. Henry's son, Edward VI, inherited the throne at age ten. During Edward's reign, Protestant bishops issued the *Book of Common Prayer,* which outlined the official rituals and prayers for the Anglican services. The *Book of Common Prayer* combined both Protestant and Catholic ideas.

When Edward died in 1553, Henry VIII's daughter, Mary Tudor, inherited the throne. Raised as a Catholic, Mary was determined to make England truly Catholic again. She persecuted Anglican bishops who would not accept the authority of the pope. Mary angered many subjects when she married Philip II, the Catho-

Elizabeth I, Protestant queen of England, did not have strong personal feelings about religion. But she wanted to restore unity to a nation divided over religious questions. Therefore, she reaffirmed the role of the monarch as head of the Anglican church and completed the seizure of church lands that her father, Henry VIII, had begun.

lic king of Spain. When Mary died in 1558, her Protestant half-sister, Elizabeth I, became queen.

Queen Elizabeth adopted a skillful policy of religious compromise. She moved cautiously at first but gradually enforced reforms that she felt moderate Catholics and Protestants could accept. However, Elizabeth persecuted both Catholics and Protestants who opposed her policies. Elizabeth firmly established England as a Protestant nation. Yet she took England along a middle road and preserved many traditional Catholic beliefs.

343

The Catholic Reformation

During the Protestant Reformation, many loyal Catholics worked to revive the spiritual leadership of the Catholic Church. In addition, they fought against Protestants, whom they regarded as heretics. The movement to reform the Catholic Church and fight Protestants became known as the Catholic Reformation. Some historians have also called it the "Counter Reformation."

Paul III, who was pope from 1534 to 1549, led the reform of the Catholic Church. Paul appointed able scholars and reformers to high church offices. He also summoned many officials to a church council at Trent to discuss reforms.

The Council of Trent met from 1545 to 1563. In response to Protestant attacks, the council reaffirmed traditional Catholic doctrines. However, the council also called for better training of priests and for reformed church finances and administration. As a result of the Council of Trent, the Catholic Church ended many abuses that Luther and other Protestant reformers had criticized. Catholic rulers in Spain, France, and Italy strongly supported the reforms.

New religious orders also helped to strengthen the Catholic Church. In Spain, Ignatius Loyola formed the Society of Jesus, a group of dedicated missionaries. As you have read, while he was recovering from an injury, he spent hours reading about the saints and

MAP STUDY The Protestant Reformation shattered the unity of Christendom, as you can see on this map. Anglicans, Lutherans, and Calvinists, as well as other Protestant groups such as the Anabaptists, established separate churches. Which parts of Europe were most affected by the Protestant Reformation?

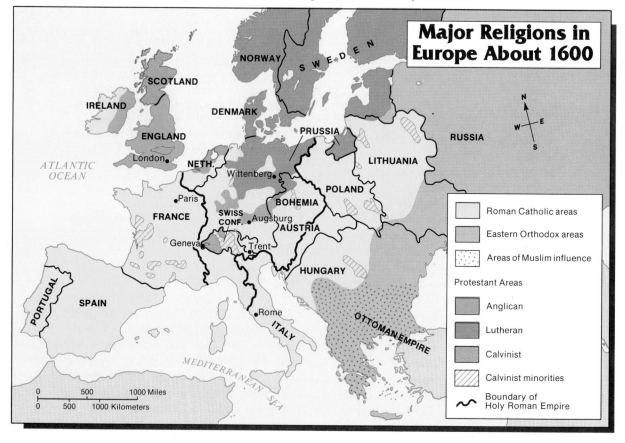

Major Religions in Europe About 1600

Legend:
- Roman Catholic areas
- Eastern Orthodox areas
- Areas of Muslim influence

Protestant Areas
- Anglican
- Lutheran
- Calvinist
- Calvinist minorities
- Boundary of Holy Roman Empire

thinking about religious questions. Loyola then wrote *Spiritual Exercises,* a manual that taught strict religious discipline.

In 1540, Pope Paul III officially recognized the Society of Jesus. The Jesuits, as Loyola's followers were called, swore absolute obedience to the pope. They traveled to the new lands that Europeans were exploring and won many converts. In addition, they brought many Protestants in Germany and Eastern Europe back into the Catholic Church.

The Catholic Church also took other steps to stop the spread of Protestant ideas. For example, it revived the Inquisition. As you read earlier, the Inquisition was the Church court that had tried to root out heresies during the Middle Ages. The Inquisition was most active in Spain, Portugal, and Italy. In addition, the Catholic Church published the Index, a list of forbidden books. By limiting what books Catholics could read, the Church hoped to prevent the spread of the Protestant ideas.

After the Catholic Reformation, Protestants made few new gains. By 1600, the lines between Catholic and Protestant areas in Europe were sharply drawn. They have remained largely unchanged to the present. Lutherans, Calvinists, and other Protestant sects flourished in England, Scotland, Scandinavia, and northern Germany. Catholics remained strong in Italy, France, Spain, Ireland, and southern Germany. (See the map at left.) These religious divisions contributed to bitter wars, as you will read in Chapter 16.

Officials of the Inquisition tried to stamp out heresy by preventing the spread of Protestant ideas. In this scene done at the court of Spain, books are set on fire to determine which contain heresy. Holy books rise from the flames and books with heretical ideas burn.

SECTION 5 REVIEW

1. **Identify:** (a) Ulrich Zwingli, (b) John Calvin, (c) Huguenot, (d) John Knox, (e) Anabaptist, (f) Ignatius Loyola, (g) Jesuits, (h) Index.

2. **Define:** predestination.

3. (a) Why did Calvin believe people should lead good lives? (b) To what parts of Europe did Calvinism spread?

4. (a) Why did Henry VIII of England quarrel with the pope? (b) What religious policy did Elizabeth I follow?

5. Describe two actions of the Council of Trent.

6. (a) By 1600, what parts of Europe were mainly Protestant? (b) What areas remained mainly Catholic?

7. **Critical Thinking** If the Council of Trent had met 30 years earlier, do you think the Protestant Reformation would have occurred? Explain.

Summary

1. **The Renaissance began in northern Italy and spread slowly to other parts of Europe.** Renaissance scholars studied the classics in order to expand their knowledge of the world. In northern Europe, Renaissance scholars studied the writings of early Christians.

2. **During the Renaissance, the arts flourished.** Leonardo da Vinci and Michelangelo added new dimensions to painting and sculpture. Renaissance writers such as Rabelais, Cervantes, and Shakespeare produced many outstanding works.

3. **The invention of the printing press in 1455 helped spread new ideas.** Social and economic changes slowly affected the lives of ordinary people. The nuclear family emerged, people's diets improved, and wages rose.

4. **Many people called on the pope and clergy to reform the Church.** In the early 1500s, Martin Luther rejected the authority of the pope and set up the Lutheran church. In Germany, many townspeople, princes, and peasants supported Luther's reforms.

5. **As the Protestant Reformation spread across Europe, the Catholic Church launched its own reformation.** John Calvin and other reformers set up their own churches. After Henry VIII quarreled with the pope, England became a Protestant nation. At the Council of Trent, the Catholic Church set about reforming itself. However, Europe remained divided between Protestants and Catholics.

Recalling Facts

Match each name at left with the correct description at right.

1. Niccolò Machiavelli
2. William Shakespeare
3. Ignatius Loyola
4. John Calvin
5. Johann Gutenberg
6. Michelangelo

a. founder of the Society of Jesus
b. European inventor of a movable type
c. English poet and playwright
d. Protestant reformer who believed in predestination
e. author of *The Prince,* a handbook for rulers
f. artist who painted the Sistine Chapel ceiling

Chapter Checkup

1. (a) Why did the Renaissance begin in Italy? (b) How did the Medici influence the Renaissance in Florence?

2. (a) What were the main interests of Renaissance scholars? (b) How did the work of Petrarch influence Renaissance scholars?

3. Describe the contributions Renaissance artists made in each of the following areas: (a) sculpture; (b) architecture; (c) painting.

4. What changes were taking place in business and agriculture during the Renaissance?

5. (a) What were Luther's main teachings? (b) How did Calvinist beliefs differ from Lutheran beliefs? (c) How was the Protestant Reformation in England accomplished?

6. (a) What methods did the Catholic Church use to fight the Protestants? (b) What evidence indicates that the Catholic Reformation succeeded?

Critical Thinking

1. **Synthesizing** After a visit to Italy in the early 1500s, a scholar from northern Europe exclaimed: "Immortal God, what a day I see dawning!" What do you think the scholar might have seen or heard that could have led to this remark?

2. **Relating Past to Present** Today, someone who is knowledgeable in many areas is called a "Renaissance person." (a) What ideas might a "Renaissance person" today have in common with a Renaissance figure such as Leonardo da Vinci? (b) How might their ideas differ?

3. **Analyzing** The Renaissance is often considered a time when people were mostly concerned with worldly matters. Yet the Reformation occurred during the Renaissance. How do you think the Renaissance spirit encouraged the Reformation?

4. **Understanding the Roots of Democracy** (a) How did the ideas and attitudes of the Renaissance encourage democratic values? (b) Which teachings of Luther and Calvin supported democratic values?

Developing Basic Skills

1. **Using Visual Evidence** Study the painting on page 332. (a) What is shown in the painting? (b) How does the painting reflect Renaissance ideas?

2. **Researching** Choose one of the men or women who wrote, painted, or ruled during the Renaissance. Research the person's background in order to answer the following questions: (a) Where was the person born and raised? (b) What were the person's main contributions to the Renaissance? (c) Do you think he or she fit Castiglione's ideal of a Renaissance person? Explain.

3. **Ranking** Review the causes of the Protestant Reformation. Then rank them according to their importance in causing a split within the Christian world. Explain your ranking.

Writing About History

Considering Topics for Research

In choosing a topic for a research paper, you must be sure that enough information is available on that topic. As a first step, you should consult the catalogue in your library. Often you will be able to find information on a topic under more than one subject heading. For example, if you are thinking of doing a paper on French painters of the Renaissance, you can look for sources under such headings as French painting, Renaissance painting, or history of art. You can also look up your topic in an encyclopedia. Often, encyclopedia articles provide bibliographies as well as lists of other entries in the encyclopedia on related topics.

Practice: List two topics for research from this chapter and check your library to see whether there is enough information on them.

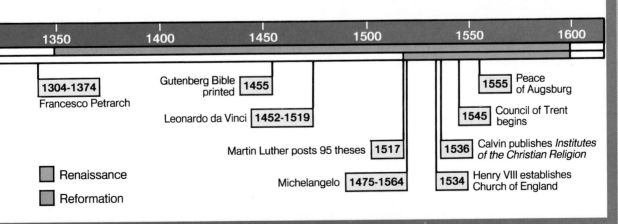

Timeline:

1350 — 1400 — 1450 — 1500 — 1550 — 1600

- 1304–1374 Francesco Petrarch
- Gutenberg Bible printed 1455
- Leonardo da Vinci 1452–1519
- Martin Luther posts 95 theses 1517
- Michelangelo 1475–1564
- 1555 Peace of Augsburg
- 1545 Council of Trent begins
- 1536 Calvin publishes *Institutes of the Christian Religion*
- 1534 Henry VIII establishes Church of England

■ Renaissance
■ Reformation

Exploration and Expansion

15

(1450–1750)

During the Age of Exploration, courageous sailors set out from European ports to journey into the unknown. In this painting, Christopher Columbus supervises as his ships are loaded with supplies for the voyage that led him to America.

The guns thundered a salute, making the earth tremble. But the crowds gathered on the shore scarcely flinched. Like the noisy guns, they, too, were bidding farewell to the five vessels in the harbor. Soon these vessels would be setting out from Seville in Spain for parts unknown. What fate awaited the 268 sailors on board the ships, no one knew. That August of 1519, the Portuguese commander of the small fleet, Ferdinand Magellan, had great hopes for the expedition. He planned to find a sea route around South America, leading to the East Indies and the rich spice trade.

Among Magellan's crew was a Venetian noble, Antonio Pigafetta. In his journal, he recorded both the successes and the terrible hardships of the voyage. By November 1520, the ships had battled through the stormy straits at the southern tip of South America. Magellan and his crew thus became the first Europeans to sail into the Pacific Ocean from the Atlantic.

The voyage across the Pacific was agony. "We remained 3 months and 20 days without taking on any food or other refreshments," wrote Pigafetta. "We ate only old biscuits reduced to powder and full of grubs, and we drank water that was yellow and stinking." In desperation, the starving sailors ate pieces of leather that had to be "soaked four or five days in the sea. After this, we boiled them to eat."

Many sailors died from disease. After 80 days in the Pacific, the fleet finally reached land, the island of Guam. But Magellan did not live to complete the voyage. In the Philippine Islands, he quarreled with local people and was killed in a battle. However, in 1522, Pigafetta and 17 surviving sailors returned to Spain. They were the first Europeans to sail around the world.

Magellan's voyage was but one of many daring exploits of sailors during the Renaissance. While scholars were rediscovering the classics and artists were experimenting with new techniques, other people were exploring lands beyond the world then known to Europeans.

The period from about 1450 to 1750 has been called the "Age of Exploration." In the 1400s, Portuguese and Spanish sailors led the way across the oceans of the world. Soon, other nations followed. Through the voyages of exploration, Europeans learned of two vast continents in the Western Hemisphere. The discovery of new ocean routes and new lands led to a race for trading empires in Asia and the Americas. This increased trade changed the economic life of Europe. ■

---

1 Voyages of Exploration

READ TO UNDERSTAND

☐ **What new technologies helped European sailors explore the oceans of the world.**

☐ **Why Portugal and Spain led the way in exploration.**

☐ **What other nations explored the coast of North America.**

☐ *Vocabulary:* **astrolabe.**

Gil Eanes had certainly heard about the terrors of the southern ocean. Like other Portuguese sea captains, he knew the popular verse:

When old Cape Nun heaves into sight
Turn back, my lad, or else—good night!

Rumor held that if you sailed south of Cape Nun at the bulge of West Africa, you could never get back to Europe because of the strong winds that blew from the north. Also, you would sail into boiling hot seas at the Equator. But Eanes ignored the rumors. He boldly sailed into the South Atlantic and returned safely home. His voyage in 1434 set the stage for even bolder ventures.

By the 1400s, Portugal and Spain wanted to break the trade monopoly of the Italian city-states in the Mediterranean. To find new trade routes, they sponsored many voyages of discovery.

Expanding Horizons in Europe

Advances in technology helped make the European voyages of exploration possible. Using travelers' reports such as those of Marco Polo and information from Arab geographers, mapmakers drew more accurate land and sea maps. On charts of the oceans, they began to include lines of latitude, which showed distance north and south of the Equator.

Navigators developed better ways to chart their ships' courses at sea. Sailors could calculate the ship's latitude using the **astrolabe,** an instrument that measured the positions of stars. They had no instruments to measure longitude, the distance east or west of a certain point, but they could estimate longitude. Europeans improved the magnetic compass, a Chinese invention that the Arabs had brought to Europe. With it, sailors could determine their location at sea even when they were out of sight of land.

Shipbuilders designed sailing vessels that were suited to ocean voyages. For example, the Portuguese developed the three-masted caravel. The caravel could carry more sail than earlier ships, and it had more space for cargo and food supplies. Europeans also used the lateen, or triangular sail, borrowed from the Arabs. The lateen sail and another improvement, the stern rudder, allowed ships to sail closely into the wind.

Building and outfitting ocean-going ships was expensive. Although Italian city-states such as Venice and Genoa organized some early voyages, individual city-states did not have the resources for large undertakings. Instead, it was the rulers of emerging nations who sponsored the great expeditions of the 1400s and 1500s. Through exploration, monarchs hoped to increase trade and build profitable empires.

Portuguese Explorations

Portugal led the way in the voyages of exploration. The Portuguese had been at a disadvantage in trade with Asia because Portugal faced the Atlantic Ocean rather than the Mediterranean Sea. Most spices and other goods from India and China were brought overland by Arab merchants to ports in the eastern Mediterranean. Italian ships then carried goods across the Mediterranean to Europe.

During the 1400s, Portugal was ruled by several practical and ambitious monarchs who wanted to increase their nation's wealth.

They supported voyages in search of gold. They also saw that the only way to get a share of the rich spice trade was to bypass the Italian and Muslim traders who controlled the Mediterranean markets.

Early voyages. Prince Henry, known as Prince Henry the Navigator, encouraged the early Portuguese explorations. Henry, who lived from 1394 to 1460, founded a school for sailors at Sagres on the southern tip of Portugal. There, he brought together astronomers, geographers, and mathematicians to share their learning with Portuguese sea captains and pilots.

At first, the Portuguese tried to open new trade routes by conquering coastal cities in North Africa. But the Sahara caravans that had brought gold to North Africa from the West African kingdoms no longer operated. With the African gold trade dried up, the Portuguese decided to go directly to the source of the gold themselves. They began to explore the west coast of Africa.

The sea route along the West African coast was dangerous because ocean currents and winds off Cape Bojador (boh huh DOHR) and Cape Nun often drove ships onto the rocky coast and wrecked them. To avoid this danger, the Portuguese charted a new route. They sailed west from Portugal and discovered two groups of islands in the Atlantic—Madeira and the Azores. From these islands, they picked up favorable winds and currents that carried them safely south of Cape Bojador to the West African coast.

The Portuguese set up trading stations along the African coast. Portuguese traders bought gold and ivory from people living nearby. In fact, the area became known to Europeans as the "Gold Coast." In 1441, traders also began buying slaves. As you will read in Chapter 25, the slave trade expanded over the next 300 years and ruined many African kingdoms.

Rounding the Cape of Good Hope. After Prince Henry's death in 1460, exploration slowed down. But in 1481, King John II launched new efforts. John dreamed of a rich trading empire in Asia. He knew he had to find an all-water route around Africa that would allow Portugal to trade directly with India and

SAILING SHIPS OF WESTERN EUROPE Voyages of discovery were made possible by improved sailing vessels. Here, artist Paul Birling pictures two ships from the Age of Exploration, the carrack and the caravel. The ship at left is a Portuguese caravel. A small, light vessel with triangular sails, its principal advantage was that it was easy to maneuver. At right is a Flemish carrack—a larger, heavier vessel, ideal for ocean voyages.

China. The king urged Portuguese sea captains to explore farther and farther south along the African coast.

In 1488, Bartholomeu Dias rounded the southern tip of Africa. Dias named it the Cape of Storms because his ship had been buffeted so violently there. But John II renamed it the Cape of Good Hope because he realized Dias had found a passage to India.

King John then decided to send an expedition to India. In July 1497, after much preparation, Vasco da Gama set out from Portugal with four ships. Da Gama quickly rounded the Cape of Good Hope and visited the cities along the East African coast. He reached the Indian port of Calicut in May 1498. His voyage took Portugal a step closer to realizing King John's vision of a trading empire in Asia.

A Westward Voyage

Spain watched the success of neighboring Portugal with envy. In the 1400s, you will recall, Christian monarchs in Spain devoted their energies to conquering the last Muslim stronghold of Granada. When Ferdinand and Isabella

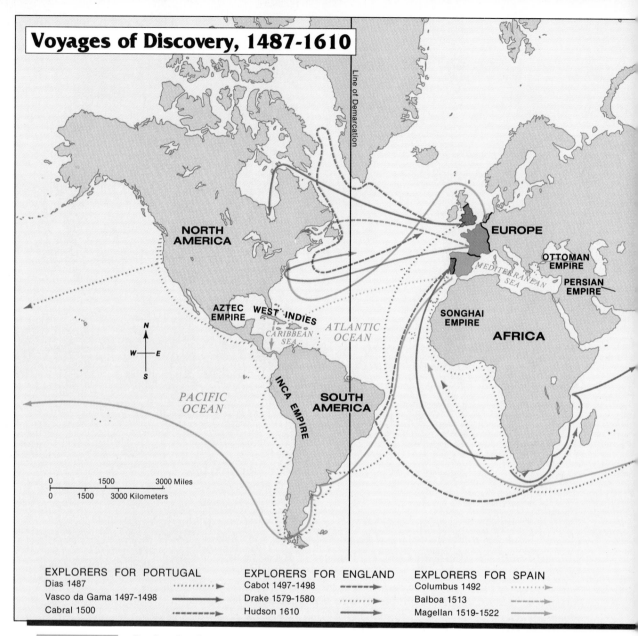

Voyages of Discovery, 1487-1610

Line of Demarcation

NORTH AMERICA

EUROPE

OTTOMAN EMPIRE

PERSIAN EMPIRE

MEDITERRANEAN SEA

AZTEC EMPIRE

WEST INDIES

CARIBBEAN SEA

ATLANTIC OCEAN

SONGHAI EMPIRE

AFRICA

N
W — E
S

PACIFIC OCEAN

INCA EMPIRE

SOUTH AMERICA

0   1500   3000 Miles
0   1500   3000 Kilometers

EXPLORERS FOR PORTUGAL
Dias 1487
Vasco da Gama 1497-1498
Cabral 1500

EXPLORERS FOR ENGLAND
Cabot 1497-1498
Drake 1579-1580
Hudson 1610

EXPLORERS FOR SPAIN
Columbus 1492
Balboa 1513
Magellan 1519-1522

MAP STUDY *During the Age of Exploration, a few daring sailors charted the oceans of the world. Which European nations were chiefly involved in exploration? Why were monarchs willing to support such risky ventures?*

completed this task in 1492, they were ready to pursue other goals.

Like Portugal, Spain wanted to share in the profitable spice trade of Asia. Equally important to the pious Queen Isabella was the opportunity to spread Christianity. She believed Christopher Columbus, a sea captain from Genoa, might help Spain achieve those goals.

For years, Columbus had tried to convince first Portugal, and then Spain, to sponsor a voyage to Asia westward across the Atlantic. Columbus believed that by sailing westward, a ship could reach Asia within two months.

In the 1400s, people held conflicting views about the size of the earth. Some people, such as Columbus, based their estimates on the work of the ancient geographer Ptolemy. However, Ptolemy had underestimated the size of the earth. Scholars at the University of Salamanca in Spain had calculated correctly that

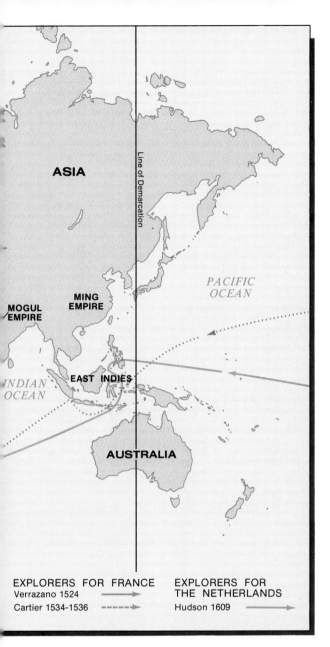

ASIA

Line of Demarcation

MOGUL EMPIRE

MING EMPIRE

PACIFIC OCEAN

INDIAN OCEAN

EAST INDIES

AUSTRALIA

EXPLORERS FOR FRANCE
Verrazano 1524
Cartier 1534-1536

EXPLORERS FOR THE NETHERLANDS
Hudson 1609

warded with their first sight of land. Convinced that he had reached the East Indies, Columbus called the local people "Indians" and happily accepted the gold objects they gave him. In fact, Columbus had reached the islands later called the West Indies.

In three more voyages, Columbus explored the Caribbean islands of Cuba and Hispaniola, present-day Haiti and the Dominican Republic. He claimed the new lands for Spain and founded settlements there. Columbus never realized that he had not reached the East Indies, but his explorations opened the way for Spain to colonize two huge continents.

The Treaty of Tordesillas

Columbus' voyages fueled the rivalry between Spain and Portugal. John II of Portugal rejected Spanish claims to the Caribbean islands. Each country disputed the right of the other to explore the new lands. To keep peace, the pope arranged a settlement.

After long negotiations, Spain and Portugal signed the Treaty of Tordesillas (tor day SEE yahs) in 1494. The treaty drew a Line of Demarcation that ran north and south about 1,100 miles (1,770 kilometers) west of the Azores Islands in the Atlantic. The treaty gave all newly discovered lands west of the line to Spain. Portugal received the right to colonize and trade with any lands that lay east of the line.*

The treaty gave Spain the right to claim most of North and South America, although no one at the time realized the extent of these lands. In 1500, the Portuguese explorer Pedro Cabral was blown off course during a storm. He landed in Brazil. Because Brazil lay east of the Line of Demarcation, Cabral claimed this part of South America for Portugal.

A Continent in the Path to India

Further voyages showed that Columbus had not reached the East Indies but had found a

the earth was much larger. They argued that it would take four months to reach Asia, and ships could not store enough food and fresh water for the trip. What neither the scholars nor Columbus knew was that a continent lay just where a two-month supply of food would run out.

Queen Isabella accepted Columbus' argument and agreed to sponsor his voyage. On August 3, 1492, three small ships carrying 90 sailors left Palos, Spain. Despite good sailing westward, the crews grew anxious as provisions ran low and they had still not sighted land. Finally, on October 12, they were re-

---

* The Line of Demarcation was eventually extended around the globe. (See the map above.) Thus, the Portuguese claimed trading rights in India, China, and the East Indies.

With the development of better instruments, maps became more accurate, and navigators could confidently chart courses across thousands of miles of ocean. In this painting, explorers study the maps, charts, and globe that clutter the desk. Notice the astrolabe next to the globe. Navigators used astrolabes to find their latitude at sea. However, in rough seas, errors of hundreds of miles were common.

vast continent. Amerigo Vespucci (ah may REE goh veh SPOO chee), an Italian who represented the Medici bank in Spain, undertook several voyages for Spain. He charted the coastline of Central America and described the continent as the "Mundus Novus," a Latin phrase meaning "New World." In 1507, a German mapmaker labeled the continent America in recognition of Amerigo Vespucci.

Spanish explorers soon fanned out across the Caribbean Sea. Their discoveries became the basis for a Spanish empire in the Americas. In 1513, Juan Ponce de León set out to find the legendary fountain of youth, whose waters supposedly made people young. Ponce de León never found the fountain, but he set foot on a land that he named Florida.

That same year, Vasco de Balboa pushed through the steaming jungles of Central America and came upon a vast body of water. Balboa named it the South Sea, thinking it lay to the south of Asia. In fact, the body of water was the Pacific Ocean.

Six years later, a Spanish sailing expedition led by Ferdinand Magellan entered the vast Pacific Ocean. As you read at the beginning of the chapter, Magellan set out in 1519 to find a western sea route to Asia. He sailed south along the coast of South America and into the Pacific through the narrow straits that still bear his name.

In 1578, the English sea captain Sir Francis Drake rounded the tip of South America. He raided Spanish settlements on the west coast. Then he continued around the world, returning to England in 1580.

Seeking a Northwest Passage

Spain and Portugal were the first nations to sail across the Atlantic, but other nations soon followed. The Treaty of Tordesillas excluded the claims of these nations to new lands, but England, the Dutch Netherlands, and France ignored the treaty. During the 1500s and early 1600s, these countries sent explorers to chart the coast of North America. Because the southern passage around Cape Horn was so dangerous, they hoped to find a northwest passage to India.

In 1497, John Cabot, an Italian sea captain, agreed to sail for England. In two voyages, he explored the coast of North America from present-day Delaware to Newfoundland. English exploration then lagged until 1576, when Martin Frobisher reached the Hudson Strait, returning home with what he claimed was gold ore. The ore proved to be worthless, however, and the English temporarily gave up the search for a northern sea route to Asia.

In 1524, France financed a voyage by the Italian explorer Giovanni da Verrazano (VEHR rah TSAH noh). He explored the coast of North America from what is today the Carolinas to Nova Scotia. A few years later, Jacques Cartier (kahr tee YAY) sailed up the broad St. Lawrence River, hoping it would lead to the Pacific. Although he heard many tales of gold, Cartier found neither gold nor a sea route to India.

Like the Portuguese, the Dutch were sailing around Africa to reach Asia. But they also hired an English sailor, Henry Hudson, to look for a passage through the Americas. In 1609, Hudson explored the river that bears his name. He sailed as far north as Albany, New York, but realized the river was not a route to India.

Although these explorers did not find a northern passage to Asia, they added greatly to European knowledge of the New World. Furthermore, their voyages brought settlers to the new lands.

SECTION 1 REVIEW

1. **Locate:** (a) East Indies, (b) West Indies, (c) Line of Demarcation.

2. **Identify:** (a) Prince Henry, (b) Bartholomeu Dias, (c) Christopher Columbus, (d) Amerigo Vespucci.

3. **Define:** astrolabe.

4. List three technical advances that helped make the voyages of exploration possible.

5. (a) Why were the discoveries of Ponce de León and Balboa important to Spain? (b) What did Magellan set out to find?

6. (a) What countries sent explorers to seek a northwest passage to Asia? (b) What areas were explored as a result?

7. **Critical Thinking** How did the voyages of exploration fuel rivalry among the European nations?

2 Profitable Trade With the East

READ TO UNDERSTAND

☐ How Portugal built a trading empire in the east.

☐ How European nations competed in the spice trade.

☐ Why relations between European traders and Asian rulers changed.

"May the devil take you! What brought you here?" an Indian official asked one of Vasco da Gama's crew in 1498. "We came in search of Christians and spices," the Portuguese sailor replied. The Portuguese moved quickly to build their spice trade with India and other parts of Asia. By avoiding the Arab and Italian merchants who had controlled the spice trade, they could now buy spices cheaply in Asia and sell them in Europe for a great profit.

Soon other European countries were complaining that the Portuguese were charging as much as the Venetians had. In time, the Dutch, British, French, and Spanish competed for a share in the spice trade of the east.

The Portuguese Trading Empire

Within six months of Vasco da Gama's return to Portugal, a new fleet set sail for India. More soon followed. Christian missionaries accompanied Portuguese traders wherever they established trading posts. But the traders were mainly interested in spices, which Europeans used to preserve meat. Portuguese ships carried cargoes of pepper from India, cinnamon from Ceylon, and cloves and nutmeg from the East Indies.

Arab merchants, who had traded in India for centuries, resisted the Portuguese efforts to win trading privileges from local Hindu and Muslim princes. Because the Arab traders were Muslims, the Portuguese saw the competition for control of the spice trade as a Christian crusade. They burned Arab ships and wharfs, ransacked the Muslim cities of East Africa, and tortured prisoners.

In 1509, the Portuguese appointed Afonso de Albuquerque (AHL boo KEHR kuh) governor of their trading posts. Over the next six years, Albuquerque ruthlessly built a Portuguese trading empire. From his headquarters at Goa on the west coast of India, he seized key points along the trade routes, including Hormuz at the entrance of the Persian Gulf. This gave Portugal control of the Indian Ocean.

Most important, Albuquerque seized the narrow Strait of Malacca, the gateway to the Moluccas, which Europeans called the Spice Islands. By controlling the Strait of Malacca, Portugal hoped to prevent other Europeans from gaining a foothold in the East Indies.

Fierce Competition

By the late 1500s, Portugal faced stiff competition for the spice trade from France, England,

and the Netherlands. The northern European countries knew that by conquering or bypassing a few key ports, they could break Portuguese control of the spice trade.

The Dutch acted first. In 1595, they sent a fleet to explore the East Indies. Seven years later, they formed the Dutch East India Company to finance further trading expeditions. The Dutch were as ruthless as the Portuguese in gaining their ends. They attacked Portuguese ships and raided Portuguese trading stations. During the 1600s, the Dutch replaced the Portuguese as the dominant power in the spice trade. (See the map below.)

England and France also equipped trading expeditions to Asia. Because the Dutch position was so strong in the East Indies, English and French merchants concentrated on India. Both nations set up small trading posts along the southern coasts of India. They were able to win trading privileges in these areas in part because the Mogul Empire in India was weak in the south. In addition, some Hindu princes made alliances with Europeans against their Muslim rulers.

Trade with China and Japan

The early Portuguese traders met Chinese merchants at Malacca. Tempted by Chinese silks, satins, and porcelain, the Portuguese sailed east into Chinese waters. As you read in Chapter 13, the Ming Chinese permitted only limited trade. By 1535, the Portuguese had to confine their trading in China to Macao. Other Europeans were restricted to Canton.

In 1542, a storm blew a Portuguese ship off course. The battered vessel found refuge in

MAP STUDY *European nations competed for control of the rich spice trade of Asia. Although the Portuguese were first to reach India, the Dutch, English, and Spanish soon followed, as this map shows. Which nation held the Strait of Malacca? Why was this strait important?*

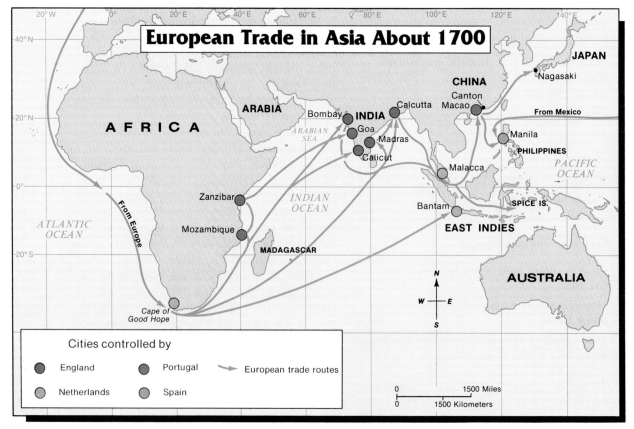

the Japanese islands, and a new source of trade was opened. At first, the Japanese welcomed trade with Portugal. Soon, Spanish ships from the Americas, loaded with potatoes, watermelons, and pumpkins, were also trading with Japan.

Despite the growing trade, both the Chinese and Japanese looked on the Europeans as barbarians. Aside from guns, Europeans had few goods they wanted. Furthermore, the Chinese and Japanese distrusted Europeans. They had heard stories about the Portuguese and Dutch seizing land in the East Indies.

The activities of Jesuit missionaries also strained relations. At first, the Chinese and Japanese tolerated Christians. Later, however, Chinese and Japanese rulers suspected that the Christian missionaries were allies of the foreign traders who were taking land at gunpoint.

In Japan, Protestant merchants from England and the Netherlands encouraged the shogun's suspicion of Portuguese and Spanish Catholics. However, their interference did them little good. As you read in Chapter 13, by 1639, the Japanese had decided to expel all foreigners. Only the Dutch were allowed to send one ship a year to trade at the port of Nagasaki.

This painted screen shows how the Japanese viewed Portuguese merchants. Greed seems to distort the faces of the Portuguese as they think of the fortunes they will make.

SECTION 2 REVIEW

1. **Locate:** (a) Goa, (b) Malacca, (c) Spice Islands, (d) Macao, (e) Canton, (f) Nagasaki.

2. **Identify:** Afonso de Albuquerque.

3. (a) What were the main products Europeans wanted from Asia? (b) What nations competed for trading rights in Asia?

4. (a) What attitude did the rulers of China and Japan have toward European traders? (b) What policy did China and Japan eventually follow toward foreigners?

5. **Critical Thinking** (a) Why do you think the Chinese and Japanese considered Europeans barbarians? (b) How do you think Europeans looked on the Chinese and Japanese?

3 First Colonies in the Americas

READ TO UNDERSTAND

☐ How Spain acquired and ruled its empire in the Americas.

☐ What efforts the Spanish made to protect Native Americans.

☐ How the plantation system and slave trade were connected.

☐ *Vocabulary:* conquistador, cabildo, encomienda, plantation, donatario.

Montezuma, the Aztec ruler, was disturbed by the reports of strange white men appearing along the east coast of his empire. He knew that the powerful god Quetzalcoatl had vowed to return—from the east. The stories made the Aztec feel insecure. The priests called for more human sacrifices. Thousands of prisoners from conquered villages were sacrificed to the gods as the priests sought answers about the odd creatures landing on their shores. The increase in sacrifices aroused anger among the conquered peoples.

According to the Aztec calendar, Quetzalcoatl could only appear in the year that was 1519 by the Christian calendar. And it was in that year that the Spanish, who were the "strange creatures," landed on the shores of the Aztec Empire. And as you will read, under Hernando Cortés, they soon conquered the Aztec Empire.

In the 1500s and 1600s, Europeans set up scattered trading outposts in Asia. But Asian rulers often dictated the terms of trade and limited the movements of Europeans. In the Americas, however, Europeans established colonies—settlements that they ruled. The Spanish and Portuguese were the first Europeans to carve out colonial empires in the Americas.

Conquests in the Americas

By the Treaty of Tordesillas, Spain claimed the right to most of the New World. Hearing of wealthy kingdoms in the Americas, Spanish explorers set out to find them.

Instead of financing expeditions directly, Spanish rulers granted **conquistadores** (kohn KEES tah DOH rehs), or conquerors, the right to establish outposts in the Americas. In exchange, conquistadores agreed to give the crown one fifth of any treasure they discovered. Thus, the Spanish rulers launched expeditions at little risk or cost to themselves. If a conquistador failed, he lost his own fortune. If he succeeded, both he and Spain won fame and riches. One conquistador summed up his reasons for going to the Americas in these words: "We came here to serve God and the king, and also to get rich."

Cortés. In 1519, Hernando Cortés landed on the coast of Mexico. Cortés, a shrewd conquistador and skillful diplomat, came in search of gold. He soon heard about the powerful Aztec Empire, which demanded heavy tribute from the peoples it had conquered. Cortés made alliances with various Indian tribes who hated their Aztec rulers. He then marched his small army of 400 soldiers and 16 horses into the crowded Aztec capital of Te-nochtitlán. There, he began to negotiate with the Aztec ruler, Montezuma.

After a tense game of diplomacy that lasted for months, Montezuma finally agreed to become a subject of the Spanish king. But in 1520, the Aztecs revolted against the Spanish. Cortés and his army barely escaped with their lives. The next year, with the help of his Indian allies, Cortés destroyed Tenochtitlán. Within a few years, the Aztec Empire crumbled, and the Spanish were in control.

Pizarro. Nine years later, the conquistador Francisco Pizarro and 180 Spanish soldiers landed on the Pacific coast of South America. Pizarro learned that a civil war was raging in the Inca Empire. Taking advantage of the civil war, Pizarro captured their ruler Atahualpa and executed many Inca officials. The Inca were accustomed to obeying commands from their rulers. Without this leadership, they were unable to fight effectively. By 1535, Pizarro controlled most of the huge Inca Empire, including the rich capital of Cuzco.

Within 15 years, the two most powerful empires in the Americas had fallen to the conquistadores. Historians have suggested a number of reasons why Cortés and Pizarro, with a handful of Spanish soldiers, were able to conquer the Aztec and Inca. First, the Spanish had better weapons. They used guns and cannons, which were unknown in the Americas. Second, the Aztec and Inca had never seen horses before they saw Spanish soldiers riding them. Some were terrified by the animals. Others believed that the conquistadores riding the horses were gods.

Third, disease played an important role in the Spanish victories. Native Americans had no immunity to many diseases carried by Europeans. Epidemics of smallpox, chicken pox, and measles destroyed entire villages. The death of so many people did much to weaken Aztec and Inca resistance. Finally, many Indian nations hated their Aztec and Inca rulers, and these people helped the Spanish conquistadores.

Organizing the Spanish Empire

Once the conquistadores had overthrown the Native American empires, Spain stepped in to

This picture drawn by a Spanish artist records Aztec priests welcoming Cortés. Heavily armed Spanish troops stand behind him. Cortés was aided by Doña Marina, a Native American who acted as translator. Doña Marina knew several Indian languages as well as Spanish. She helped Cortés negotiate alliances with peoples who opposed Aztec rule, and she kept track of Aztec spies.

rule the new lands. Spanish rulers set up a strong, centralized government in the Americas just as they had done at home. Their empire in the Americas would last for nearly 300 years.

The new lands were divided into five provinces. The wealthiest and most important provinces were New Spain, or Mexico, and Peru. The Spanish king appointed a viceroy as his representative in each province. The viceroy enforced royal policy in the New World. The king also established the Council of the Indies. The council met in Spain and made laws for the colonies.

In theory, the viceroys and the Council of the Indies worked together to rule the empire. In practice, they were often at odds. Because the viceroy lived in his province, he was often in a better position to make decisions. But the Council of the Indies wanted to preserve the king's power in the New World, and it regulated even the most minor matters. It made laws, for instance, about how long a city block must be and in which direction village streets should run. Between 1524 and 1630, the council issued over 400,000 orders.

Spain also supervised local governments in the Americas. In each town or city, the king appointed members of the **cabildo** (cah BEEL doh), or city council. The cabildo had extensive powers, which it used to preserve order and spread Spanish civilization. Local governments supervised the building of towns and cities. By the 1500s, Mexico City, the capital of New Spain, had a public water system, paved and lighted streets, printing presses, and its own university.

Spanish Policy Toward Native Americans

In the early 1500s, conquistadores, settlers, and Christian missionaries flocked to the Spanish colonies. The Spanish government granted settlers **encomiendas** (ehn koh mee EHN dahs), the rights to demand taxes or labor from Indians living on the land. In theory, the encomienda protected the Indians' rights to the land. In practice, it developed into a system of forced labor, which bound Indians to the land.

The discovery of rich silver deposits in Peru and Mexico led to further mistreatment of Indians. The Spanish forced Indians to work the mines. Mining involved exhausting, dangerous work in deep shafts. Cave-ins killed many Indian miners. Others died from malnutrition, overwork, and disease.

359

As you learned in Chapter 10, statistics can provide valuable information about a historical event or development. (See page 212.) Historians often use graphs to present statistics visually. Graphs can be used to show data about such things as population, trade, and government expenses.

Three types of graphs are frequently used: line graphs, bar graphs, and circle graphs. Line graphs and bar graphs can illustrate changes that take place over a period of time. They are often used to show large numbers in the thousands or millions. In a circle graph, a circle is divided into parts. The graph shows how each part relates to the whole circle.

The following steps will help you read the graphs in this book. Use the steps to answer the questions about the line graph at right.

1 **Identify the type of information shown on the graph.** The title of the graph and the labels on the vertical axis and horizontal axis will tell you the subject of the graph. (a) What is the subject of the graph? (b) What do the numbers on the vertical axis show? (c) What do the numbers on the horizontal axis show?

2 **Practice reading the data shown on the graph.** (a) What was the approximate Native American population of central Mexico in 1520? In 1540? (b) About how much did the population decline between 1520 and 1600? (c) During what period did the population decline the most?

3 **Use the information shown on the graph to draw conclusions about an**

event or development. To draw conclusions, you use information from the line graph and your reading. (a) In your own words, describe what happened to the Native American population of central Mexico between 1520 and 1600. (b) What factors help explain the population change? (c) Why do you think so many Indians died at the beginning of this period? (d) What effect do you think the population decline might have had on the Indian cultures of the Americas?

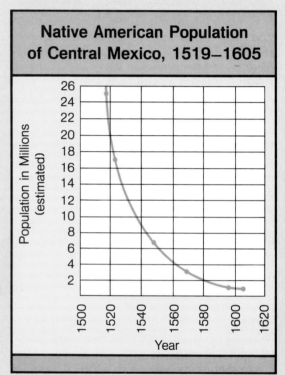

Native American Population of Central Mexico, 1519–1605

Source: Nicolas Sanchez-Albornoz, *The Population of Latin America.*

Spanish missionaries condemned the cruel treatment of the Indians. One outspoken critic was the Dominican priest Bartolomé de Las Casas (lahs KAH sahs). He described the abuses he saw in the New World to the authorities in Madrid and pleaded for strict laws to protect the Indians.

The Spanish government took its responsibility toward the Indians seriously. It be-

lieved the Spanish had a duty to convert the Indians to Christianity. Furthermore, it looked on Indians as loyal subjects. In answer to Las Casas' plea, the government passed the New Laws of 1542. The New Laws forbade making Indians slaves and gave Indians the right to own cattle and raise crops. Although the laws were not always enforced, the Spanish government did try to correct the worst abuses.

The Plantation System

Some settlers in the Americas made fortunes by exporting crops and raw materials to Spain. From Central and South America, they sent gold and silver, as well as cacao, coffee, and lumber. In the West Indies, tobacco and sugar cane were the main exports. Sugar cane became enormously profitable because it could be refined into sugar, molasses, and rum.

To profit from sugar, settlers in the West Indies developed the plantation system. A **plantation** was a large estate operated by the owner or an overseer and farmed by workers living on it. Many workers were needed to grow and harvest a sugar crop. At first, the Spanish used Indians to work their plantations. But in the West Indies, as elsewhere in the Americas, cruel labor practices and European diseases killed off the local people.

In his effort to help the Indians, Bartolomé de Las Casas had suggested that the Spanish replace Indian workers with slaves from Africa. He thought that Africans were better able to withstand hard labor in the hot climate. Although Las Casas later regretted his misguided advice, Spain began importing thousands of Africans to the West Indies.

The Slave Trade

As you have read, Portuguese sailors explored the west coast of Africa in the 1400s. Along with gold, they took a few black slaves back to Europe. In the 1500s, Spain and Portugal took more and more African slaves to their colonies in the Americas.

The newly enslaved Africans suffered brutal hardships on the Middle Passage, as the voyage across the Atlantic was called. Chained together and packed below the ship's deck, they had no room to move. Some captains took so many slaves on board that their ships could carry very little food and fresh water. When the decks above were sealed, the heat below caused many captives to die of suffocation. During the two-month voyage, many more died from disease or in attempted revolts.

Those who survived the Middle Passage were sold to plantation owners. On sugar plantations in the West Indies, African slaves worked long hours. To harvest the sugar crops, they had to work through the night.

As profits from sugar, molasses, and rum grew, so too did the slave trade. By the late 1500s, the plantation system and slavery were

Slave ships brought millions of Africans to the Americas in chains. Captains packed as many men, women, and children as they could carry into the holds of their ships. This painting by a British naval officer is the only existing picture painted from life of the inhuman conditions aboard slave ships.

essential to the economy of Spanish and Portuguese colonies. The products of the plantations of the West Indies along with the gold and silver of the New World made Spain the richest, most powerful nation in Europe.

Portugal's Empire in Brazil

The Portuguese established their own system of government in Brazil. The king appointed a captain general to oversee the entire colony. He then gave loyal subjects large parcels of land. The **donatario,** or landowner, governed the territory he received. He enlisted settlers to farm or trade on his land.

By 1580, Brazil was a thriving colony. Like the Spanish in the West Indies, the Portuguese in Brazil imported thousands of slaves to work on their sugar plantations. In the late 1600s, the Portuguese discovered diamonds and emeralds. Thousands of new settlers streamed to the colony.

In the 1500s, both Spain and Portugal built colonial empires in the Americas. In the 1600s, other European nations would rush to establish colonies, hoping to win a share of the riches.

SECTION 3 REVIEW

1. **Identify:** (a) Hernando Cortés, (b) Francisco Pizarro, (c) Council of the Indies, (d) Bartolomé de Las Casas, (e) Middle Passage.

2. **Define:** (a) conquistador, (b) cabildo, (c) encomienda, (d) plantation, (e) donatario.

3. What three motives brought the conquistadores to the Americas?

4. Why were the Spanish able to defeat the Aztec and Inca empires with so few soldiers?

5. Why did Spain begin bringing slaves to the Americas?

6. **Critical Thinking** Why do you think Spanish efforts to protect the Indians were generally unsuccessful?

---

4 Dividing Up North America

READ TO UNDERSTAND

☐ What European nations competed for power in North America.

☐ How the Dutch, French, and English colonies were organized.

☐ Why English settlers came to North America.

☐ *Vocabulary:* patroon, proprietary colony.

King Henry VII of England had turned down Columbus. But in 1497, when another sailor from Genoa, John Cabot, presented the English king with a plan of his own, Henry agreed to finance it.

Cabot's plan was to sail to the Indies by a shorter route across the North Atlantic. He set off with just one ship. In 11 weeks, he crossed the Atlantic, explored the coast of Newfoundland, and returned to England. Like Columbus, Cabot did not realize the value of his discovery. Nor did the king of England.

For almost 100 years, England took little interest in Cabot's voyage. Spain and Portugal were the only European powers with colonies in the Americas. Political troubles and religious wars in Europe distracted other nations. However, during the 1500s, Dutch, French, and English sea captains often raided Spanish treasure ships sailing from the Caribbean to Spain. They also seized Spanish islands in the West Indies.

Not until the 1600s, however, did the Netherlands, France, and England begin to explore north of present-day Mexico, where neither Spain nor Portugal had a strong foothold.

The First European Settlements

Spanish conquistadores were the first Europeans to explore the area north of Mexico. From the 1520s on, they led expeditions northward, searching for gold. But explorers hunted in vain for the seven cities of gold described by Indian legend.

During the same period, Spanish sea captains explored as far north as present-day Cal-

La Salle, who claimed the Mississippi Valley for France, built one of his ships near Niagara Falls. The falls form the background of this painting of French and Native American fur traders. Fur trading was at the heart of the French empire in the Americas.

ifornia. Wherever the Spanish explored, they claimed the lands for Spain. A few Christian missionaries set up churches in the region north of Mexico, and some settlers built homes in the new territories, but Spain paid more attention to its colonies farther south. The West Indies, Mexico, and South America provided the silver, gold, and sugar that made Spain wealthy.

In the late 1500s, the Netherlands grew into a powerful commercial nation. The Dutch had won a long war for independence from Spain. (See page 375.) They then sponsored trading expeditions to challenge Portugal in the East Indies. They also organized the Dutch West India Company to look into trade opportunities in the New World.

By the early 1600s, the Dutch were building settlements along the Hudson River as far north as present-day Albany, New York. Peter Minuit (MIHN yoo wiht) became the first governor of New Netherland, as the Dutch colony was called. In 1626, Minuit bought Manhattan Island from local Indians for cloth and beads. About 200 Dutch settlers built a village on the island, which they named New Amsterdam.

In order to attract more people to New Netherland, Minuit granted large estates to **patroons,** or wealthy landowners. The patroons then brought over Dutch farmers and other laborers to work as tenants on their estates. Patroons ruled their land like feudal lords. They had their own law courts and settled all local disputes.

When the Dutch West India Company criticized Minuit for giving the patroons too much power, Minuit left New Netherland. At the request of the Swedish government, he then helped Swedish settlers organize a colony on the Delaware River, near what is today Wilmington, Delaware. The Dutch resented the nearby Swedish settlement. During the 1640s and 1650s, Dutch and Swedish colonists raided each other's villages. Finally, in 1655 the Dutch seized the Swedish colony, adding it to New Netherland.

French Fishing and Fur Trading

To the north of the Dutch and Swedish colonies, the French explored along the St. Lawrence River and built settlements in what is today Canada. Since the early 1500s, French fishing vessels had sailed regularly to the waters off Newfoundland to catch cod. After Jacques Cartier explored the St. Lawrence

363

European Claims in the Americas About 1700

UNEXPLORED

HUDSON BAY

NEW FRANCE

NEWFOUNDLAND

NOVA SCOTIA

LOUISIANA

Mississippi

ENGLISH COLONIES

ATLANTIC OCEAN

MEXICO

FLORIDA

GULF OF MEXICO

BAHAMAS (Eng.)

WEST INDIES

CUBA

PUERTO RICO

JAMAICA

HAITI

CARIBBEAN SEA

PACIFIC OCEAN

GUIANA

Amazon R.

BRAZIL

UNEXPLORED

PERU

N
W — E
S

CHILE

UNEXPLORED

Dutch
English
French
Portuguese
Spanish

0   1000   2000 Miles
0 1000 2000 Kilometers

MAP STUDY *In the 1500s and 1600s, Europeans planted settlements in America. By 1700, the English colonies were well established on the eastern seaboard of North America. Which areas were claimed by Spain?*

River in 1535, the French discovered that furs bought from the Indians could be sold in Europe for big profits.

Distracted by political and religious conflicts at home, French rulers did little to encourage settlement in New France, as French territory was called. For example, many Huguenots, French Protestants, wanted to move to Canada to escape persecution at home. But the French government forbade them to settle in New France. As a result, the population of New France remained small.

However, a group of traders obtained exclusive rights to the fur trade. In 1608, the group sent Samuel de Champlain (sham PLAYN) to set up a permanent settlement in Quebec. From Quebec, the French moved into other parts of Canada, where they built trading posts to collect furs gathered by Indian and French trappers. By 1665, French traders had reached Lake Superior. They set up a string of forts across the Great Lakes and along the St. Lawrence to protect the fur trade. Missionaries joined the fur traders on the long, difficult journeys by canoe and on foot. They hoped to win converts to Catholicism among the Indian peoples of North America.

In the late 1600s, King Louis XIV took more interest in North America. Louis limited the privileges of the fur trading companies and appointed his own governor, the Comte de Frontenac (FRAHN tuh nak), to rule New France.

Frontenac encouraged new explorations that spread French influence across North America. In 1673, Louis Joliet, a fur trader, and Jacques Marquette, a Jesuit priest, mapped a route from Lake Michigan down the Wisconsin River into the Mississippi River. Like other explorers, Marquette and Joliet were looking for precious metals as well as a water passage to the Pacific Ocean. When they realized that the Mississippi flowed into the Gulf of Mexico and not into the Pacific Ocean, they returned north.

In 1682, another French explorer, Robert Cavelier, Sieur de la Salle, reached the mouth of the Mississippi. He claimed the lands for France and named the region Louisiana after Louis XIV. (See the map at left.)

The English Colonies

During the 1600s, the English settled in North America from Newfoundland and Nova Scotia south to what is today Georgia. The English eventually founded 13 colonies. Some colonies, such as Massachusetts and Virginia, were set up by trading companies that received charters from the English government. Others were **proprietary colonies**—that is, they

364

were owned by individuals, usually friends of the king.

Each English colony had an elected assembly that passed local laws. In most colonies, the governor was appointed by the king, and he carried out royal policies. Although a governor was responsible to Parliament, he also needed the cooperation of the colonial assembly. The assembly had to approve the governor's salary and consent to laws he issued. Thus, the colonists had some control over their own affairs.

Unlike the French government, the English government encouraged people to settle in its New World colonies. Between 1630 and 1700, the population of the English colonies grew from 900 to 200,000. Eventually, the English colonies would have greater influence on events in North America than the Spanish, Dutch, or French.

People crossed the Atlantic to the English colonies for many reasons. Some sought religious freedom. The Puritans, who were persecuted in England for their strict Calvinist beliefs, founded the colonies of Massachusetts, Rhode Island, and Connecticut. The Quakers, another group seeking religious freedom, settled in Pennsylvania. English Catholics led by Lord Baltimore emigrated to Maryland. In addition to religious freedom, many settlers were looking for a better life. In the colonies, they had the chance to become free farmers, merchants, fur traders, and artisans.

Small farms dominated the northern and middle colonies as well as parts of the south. However, in Virginia, the Carolinas, and Georgia, a plantation system grew up. Like Spanish settlers in the West Indies, large landowners in the southern colonies imported African slaves to work on their tobacco and rice plantations.

French traders had lived in relative peace with the Indians. In the English colonies, however, the large numbers of settlers soon dislodged the Indian population. Settlers sometimes signed treaties with the Indians to purchase land. Just as often, however, they moved onto Indian lands without a treaty. Determined to protect their way of life, Indians attacked and destroyed many English frontier settlements. The English fought back with equal determination. The fierce competition for land would continue until the 1800s.

European Rivalries

During the 1600s, Spain, France, the Netherlands, and England competed for land in North America. As the colonies of each nation grew, they clashed over rival land claims. In the 1700s, wars fought in Europe affected relations among the colonies.

During these struggles, some European powers looked for help from Native Americans. Because the French were interested in the fur trade, they formed an alliance with the Algonquin, their chief trading partner. At the same time, the Dutch formed an alliance with the Iroquois. Fighting between the French and Dutch led to clashes between the two Indian nations.

In 1664, England ousted the Dutch from New Netherland and renamed the colony New York. During the next 100 years, the chief rivals in eastern North America were England and France. England and France battled for control of Canada and the lands west of the Appalachian Mountains. As you will read in Chapter 16, this conflict was part of a larger struggle fought on battlefields in Europe and India.

SECTION 4 REVIEW

1. **Locate:** (a) New France, (b) Louisiana, (c) English colonies.

2. **Identify:** (a) Peter Minuit, (b) Jacques Cartier (c) Samuel de Champlain, (d) Louis Joliet, (e) Jacques Marquette.

3. **Define:** (a) patroon, (b) proprietary colony.

4. Why did Spain show relatively little interest in its northern territory?

5. What were the main economic activities of New France?

6. What motives led people to move to the English colonies?

7. **Critical Thinking** Compare the settlement and government of New France with those of the 13 English colonies.

5 The Commercial Revolution

READ TO UNDERSTAND

☐ **What role entrepreneurs and capitalists played in the commercial revolution.**

☐ **Why mercantilism developed in the 1500s.**

☐ **How the commercial revolution changed daily life in Europe.**

☐ *Vocabulary:* entrepreneur, capital, joint-stock company, mercantilism, domestic system, capitalist.

Behind the bold captains who sailed to the Indies and the Americas stood the merchants who supplied money for the voyages. Investors stood to make a fortune on a successful voyage. With an investment of $25,000 (in today's money) to outfit and supply a ship for a two-year voyage to the Spice Islands, backers could expect a return of $700,000 if it succeeded.

In the 1500s and 1600s, explorers and traders opened up vast new worlds. Expansion overseas helped bring about a commercial revolution that greatly changed the economy of Europe.

Economic Recovery

As you learned in Chapter 10, the economic growth of the late Middle Ages ended when the Black Death wiped out almost one third of the population of Western Europe. As the population grew in the 1400s, however, the economy began to revive.

The demand for clothing and food increased. More workers were needed to produce cloth, and many people moved from the countryside to the cities to work in the textile industries. Growing city populations needed food, so farm workers became highly valued. To keep them from moving to the cities, landowners had to pay farm workers more and allow them to rent land at lower rates.

As the economy recovered, merchants again shipped manufactured goods between cities, both by land and sea. Some merchants sold goods in the countryside, where they bought grain to sell in the cities. Other merchants operated on an international scale. They bought raw wool in Spain and England and sold it to cloth manufacturers in the Netherlands and Italy. Then, they purchased the cloth to sell to the Spanish and English.

During the Renaissance, the growing trade made merchants more important. Some became so wealthy that they lived like princes. Powerful merchants such as the Medici of Florence dominated the politics of their cities.

The Entrepreneur

The hope of high profits lured many merchants into overseas ventures. They imported spices, sugar, silks, and other valuable cargoes. However, overseas trade was both risky and expensive. A merchant had to outfit a ship and hire a crew for a long, dangerous voyage. The merchants also had to buy large quantities of goods before knowing what prices their customers in Europe would pay.

Merchants who were willing to take such risks in the hope of high profits were known as **entrepreneurs.** They expanded commerce by looking for trade opportunities around the world. In doing so, they slowly turned the economy of Europe from a local system into a complex international system.

Entrepreneurs developed new ways of doing business to reduce financial risks. Commerce by both land and sea was dangerous. Merchants faced highway robbers, pirates, floods, and shipwreck. The loss of a single shipment could bankrupt a merchant. To protect against losses, entrepreneurs developed a system of insurance. For a small payment, a merchant would insure his shipment. If the goods arrived safely, the merchant lost only the small insurance payment and still made a good profit. If the shipment was destroyed or lost, the merchant collected most of its value from the insurers.

Another way to reduce business risks was to spread the risk among more people. Italian entrepreneurs often formed partnerships with two or three others so that if the shipment was lost, they would share the loss.

Entrepreneurs further reduced risks by investing in several types of business. A wool manufacturer might also trade grain or buy buildings in the city. If one type of investment suffered because of bad weather, or a poor market, the others still provided income.

Financing New Ventures

Merchants needed **capital,** or large sums of money, to invest in businesses and trading ventures. Monarchs in Spain, Portugal, and France also needed capital to pay for wars and overseas exploration. Increasingly, both merchants and monarchs turned to a few extremely wealthy merchant families who became the bankers of Europe. The Medici bank in Florence, for example, made loans to entrepreneurs and monarchs in Spain, England, and Germany.

In the late 1300s, Johann Fugger (FOO ger) founded a bank in Germany that became one of the most important in Europe. Like the Medici, Fugger was a merchant before he became a banker. In the 1370s, Fugger began importing cotton from Egypt to make fustian, a cloth that was better than the linens and wools most Europeans wore. Soon Fugger branched out into other activities, such as importing spices and silks. With the fortune he made in trade, Fugger became a banker and lent money for interest to merchants and monarchs. By the 1500s, the Fugger family was one of the richest in Europe.

Merchants also developed the joint-stock company to finance new ventures. A **joint-stock company** was a private trading company that sold shares to investors. A group of merchants would pool their resources to form a trading company. They then sold shares of stock in the company to other investors. Once a joint-stock company raised enough capital, it outfitted a voyage. If the ship returned with a good cargo, each investor received a share of the profits. Investors also shared any loss if the ship went down.

European rulers sometimes granted charters to trading companies. A charter gave a company the exclusive right to trade in a particular area. The Dutch East India Company was formed in this way. In the late 1500s, sev-

Gold and silver brought from the Americas enabled Europeans to make and use more coins. Nations, cities, nobles, and bishops minted their own coins. Money changers like the couple shown here charged a fee for exchanging coins. They assessed the metal content of the different coins to determine their values. Some money changers became bankers, making loans for interest.

eral Dutch joint-stock companies sent fleets to the East Indies. The competition among them was so fierce that it threatened to disrupt the spice trade. As a result, in 1602 the Dutch government gave the Dutch East India Company exclusive trading rights in the East Indies.

The Dutch East India Company had wide powers. It could negotiate treaties, enlist soldiers, and wage war on enemies of the Netherlands. Princes, nobles, and merchants eagerly invested in the company. Stockholders could hope to recover as much as 30 times their investment on a single successful voyage.

The Search for Gold and Silver

Increased trade created a need for a larger money supply. The more people bought and sold, the more money they needed to carry on their business. Europeans did not use paper money. They used gold, silver, and copper coins. But Europe had limited supplies of gold and silver. As a result, when business increased, there was a shortage of money.

367

During their voyages of exploration, Europeans encountered foods they had never eaten before. With cinnamon and black pepper from the East Indies, they could add zesty flavors to their foods. From the Americas, explorers brought home new plants such as corn, potatoes, tomatoes, and several kinds of beans. New foods from the Americas, including chocolate, made from cacao beans, changed European customs and eating habits.

In 1502, Columbus carried the first cacao beans to Spain from the Caribbean. But it was not until 1519 that the conquistadores tasted a drink that the Aztec made from cacao beans. The Aztec called this drink xocolatl (CHOH koh lahtl), meaning "bitter water." Europeans called it chocolate.

From the Aztec, the Spanish learned to make chocolate. The Aztec dried, shelled, and roasted cacao beans. They then ground the beans into a paste, which they cooked over a fire. After adding vanilla and spices to the paste, they divided it into small cakes. To make the chocolate drink, they combined the paste with water and shook the mixture vigorously. The chocolate drink delighted the Spaniards, although they preferred to sweeten the bitter taste by adding sugar.

For nearly 100 years, Spain controlled the production and consumption of chocolate. It tried to protect its monopoly over this new food. However, by the early 1600s, the recipe for chocolate had reached Italy and Flanders.

Chocolate became immensely popular wherever it was introduced. People claimed great health benefits from it. As one observer noted, people downed the drink "in one swallow with admirable pleasure and satisfaction." He added that "it gave strength, nourishment, and vigor."

1. How did the voyages of discovery affect the diet of Europeans?

2. **Critical Thinking** Do you think Americans' love for chocolate originated in Europe or in the Americas? Explain.

The situation became worse when Europeans began buying costly spices and silks from Asian merchants, who demanded payment in gold and silver. These metals then became increasingly scarce in Europe. The search for gold had led the Portuguese to explore the coast of Africa. The need for gold had also driven the Spanish, Dutch, French, and English to explore new lands.

The Spanish were the most successful. They found valuable gold and silver deposits in Mexico and Peru. The Spanish minted coins and used their new wealth to become the most powerful country in Europe in the 1500s.

Mercantilism

European monarchs knew that their power depended on a strong economy. During the 1500s, they believed that the key to economic strength was precious metals. They reasoned that a nation should collect and keep as much gold and silver as possible. However, a nation could not merely store gold.

In Spain, for example, gold from the New World was used to buy goods such as cannons, guns, timber, and silk. Because Spain imported more goods than it exported, its gold rapidly disappeared into the hands of other nations. Thus, European rulers came to see that trade was as important as gold.

In the 1600s, a new economic theory called **mercantilism** developed. According to mercantilist ideas, a nation's economic strength depended on keeping and increasing its gold supplies by exporting more goods than it imported.

Mercantilists saw that selling manufactured goods was more profitable than selling raw materials. The person who sold shirts made from woven wool cloth made more profit than the sheep farmer who produced the wool in the first place. So mercantilists encouraged nations to manufacture finished goods for export.

Furthermore, mercantilists thought that rulers should regulate trade and commerce to make a nation self-sufficient. They also said rulers should support industries such as ship-building because new ships were needed to carry increased trade.

Colonies fit into the mercantilist theory because colonies could supply raw materials to the industries of the parent country. The colonies could in turn serve as markets for manufactured goods from the parent country.

Changing Patterns

The expansion of trade and mercantilist practices helped bring about a commercial revolution that affected the way people did business. Guilds declined in part because they regulated production too tightly. They could not meet the needs of a growing population.

Instead of relying on guilds, entrepreneurs developed a system of having work done in the countryside. The arrangement, known as the **domestic system,** bypassed guild regulations. Entrepreneurs sent raw wool to farm women and men who earned money by spinning the wool or weaving the cloth in their own cottages.

Some new industries needed large amounts of money from the start. For example, the printing industry expanded rapidly in the 1500s and 1600s. But to set up shop, a printer had to buy an expensive printing press, paper, and movable type. A printer would, therefore, turn to **capitalists,** or individuals with money to invest in business to make a profit. Capitalists financed many new industries, especially mining and shipbuilding, which were popular with mercantilists.

Another development was the great wealth acquired by the upper classes during this period. Nobles, merchants, and bankers made fortunes from investments in joint-stock companies and other ventures. They built huge palaces and decorated them with the finest works of art. And they dressed in silks from China and furs from Canada.

The Age of Exploration and the growth of commerce changed the way Europeans saw the world. Most Europeans thought their way of life was superior to that of the civilizations they were encountering in Asia, Africa, and the Americas. Yet they sometimes adopted ideas and customs of other civilizations.

As a result of the expansion of trade, members of an emerging class of capitalists amassed great fortunes. The wealth of the two men in this painting is obvious in their fur-trimmed robes and the luxury of the tapestries.

Two centuries of expansion made Europeans confident and optimistic. They believed the world was meant to be explored, conquered, and civilized by them. For better or worse, Europe had outgrown the narrow boundaries of the Middle Ages.

SECTION 5 REVIEW

1. **Define:** (a) entrepreneur, (b) capital, (c) joint-stock company, (d) mercantilism, (e) domestic system, (f) capitalist.

2. What led to economic recovery in the 1400s?

3. (a) What risks did entrepreneurs face? (b) Describe one way in which they reduced these risks.

4. How did growing trade with Asia lead to a shortage of gold and silver in Europe?

5. What economic role did mercantilists think colonies should play?

6. **Critical Thinking** Why were both entrepreneurs and capitalists important in the commercial revolution?

Summary

1. In the 1400s and 1500s, Europeans explored many parts of the world. The Portuguese led the way by sailing around Africa to India. Later, Columbus sailed west, hoping to find another route to India. Instead, his voyages led to exploration of the Americas.

2. In the 1500s, the Portuguese built a profitable trading empire in the East. Other European nations soon competed with Portugal for a share of the trade with India, China, and Japan. By the 1600s, however, the Chinese and Japanese had severely limited foreign trade.

3. The Spanish and Portuguese were the first Europeans to found empires in the Americas. Spain ruled its colonies through viceroys and the Council of the Indies.

To make their plantations profitable, both Spain and Portugal brought African slaves to the Americas.

4. Spain, the Netherlands, Sweden, France, and England planted colonies in North America. France and England became the chief rivals for North America. French fur traders explored much of the middle of North America, while the English set up 13 colonies along the eastern seaboard.

5. The expansion of overseas trade contributed to a commercial revolution in Europe. Entrepreneurs developed new ways of doing business, and mercantilism became the economic policy followed by European rulers.

Recalling Facts

Decide if the following statements are true or false. If a statement is false, rewrite it to make it true.

1. The astrolabe was a three-masted ship that could sail on long voyages.

2. The first European nation to explore the coast of West Africa was Portugal.

3. Columbus believed he had reached the East Indies when he landed in the Americas.

4. The Council of the Indies was the Aztec ruling assembly.

5. Each English colony had its own elected assembly.

6. The commercial revolution benefited the merchant class.

Chapter Checkup

1. (a) Why did Portugal take the lead in exploring a sea route to Asia? (b) Why did Spain want to find a route to Asia? (c) Why did other countries seek a northwest passage?

2. (a) How did the Portuguese build a trading empire in Asia? (b) Why were the Portuguese unable to hold on to their empire?

3. (a) How did Spain organize its empire in the Americas? (b) What was the Spanish government's policy with respect to the Indians?

4. (a) Why did the Spanish and Portuguese develop the plantation system? (b) How did they supply plantations with workers?

5. (a) Why did the French explore North America? (b) What did they achieve?

6. (a) Describe government in the English colonies. (b) How were economic activities in the English colonies different from economic activities in New France?

7. Explain how each of the following contributed to the development of overseas trade and expansion: (a) bankers; (b) insurance; (c) joint-stock companies.

8. (a) What were the chief goals of mercantilists? (b) How did mercantilists think governments should make a nation self-sufficient?

Critical Thinking

1. **Analyzing** Bartolomé de Las Casas later referred to his suggestion to replace Indian workers with African slaves as a "misguided proposal." In your opinion, what did he mean by this statement?

2. **Understanding the Roots of Democracy** Why do you think the English colonists were in a better position to gain more self-government than colonists in New Spain or New France?

3. **Understanding Economic Ideas** (a) What impact did the commercial revolution have on Europeans? (b) Which people in Europe do you think benefited most from the economic changes? Why?

4. **Relating Past to Present** (a) In your opinion, why were entrepreneurs important to economic expansion during the Age of Exploration? (b) What kinds of businesses might be started by entrepreneurs today?

Developing Basic Skills

1. **Making a Review Chart** Make a chart with three columns and five rows. Title the columns Explorer, Purpose of Exploration, and Result. Title the rows Portugal, Spain, Netherlands, France, and England. Use what you have learned in this chapter to fill in the chart. (a) What similarities do you see in the purposes of exploration? (b) What differences do you see? (c) What were the main results of the voyages of exploration?

2. **Map Reading** Study the map on page 364 and review your reading. (a) What nations claimed lands in North America? (b) What areas did each claim? (c) In your opinion, where were conflicts between rival European powers most likely to occur?

Writing About History

Sources of Information

You need to consult a variety of sources of information when preparing a research paper. Some of the most commonly used research aids are the library catalogue, the *Readers' Guide to Periodical Literature,* newspaper indexes, and specialized reference books. The library catalogue is an alphabetical list of books in the library arranged by subject, titles, and author. The *Readers' Guide to Periodical Literature* is an index to articles in almost 200 magazines. A newspaper index lists articles according to subject. Specialized reference books include information on particular topics that are indicated by their titles.

Practice: List one possible source of information for each of the following: Prince Henry the Navigator, Spain's colonies in the Americas, the slave trade. Explain each choice.

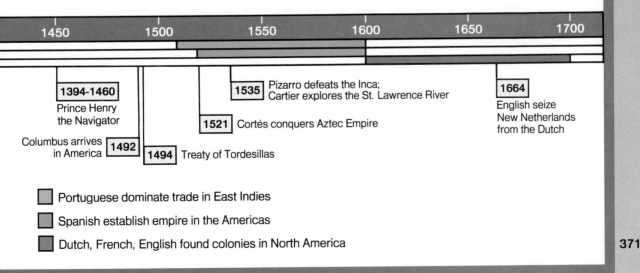

1450   1500   1550   1600   1650   1700

1394-1460 Prince Henry the Navigator

Columbus arrives in America **1492**

1494 Treaty of Tordesillas

1535 Pizarro defeats the Inca; Cartier explores the St. Lawrence River

1521 Cortés conquers Aztec Empire

1664 English seize New Netherlands from the Dutch

Portuguese dominate trade in East Indies

Spanish establish empire in the Americas

Dutch, French, English found colonies in North America

371

The Age of Absolute Monarchs

16

(1500–1795)

Louis XIV of France, shown in the center of this painting, embodied the qualities of an absolute monarch. During his long reign, Louis wielded almost complete control over French government, religion, foreign policy, and economics.

The valet approached the curtained four-poster bed with its canopy of rich red velvet embroidered with gold. "Sire, it is time," he said to the king, who was already awake. Despite the early hour—it was 8 A.M.—the king knew that just beyond his bedchamber at least 200 courtiers were assembled. They had risen even earlier to dress in their finest silks, adorn themselves with their sparkling jewels, and have their wigs arranged to perfection. Each hoped, of course, to have a word with the king, or perhaps receive a nod of recognition.

By 1682, the king, Louis XIV, had ruled France for almost 40 years. In this year, Louis moved his court from Paris to his new palace at Versailles (ver SĪ). The king surrounded himself with splendor at Versailles. He created a daily routine in which the most ordinary aspects of life were transformed into impressive rituals.

Members of the royal family were the first to enter the king's chamber after the king awoke. A few minutes later, court officials were admitted. A doctor and surgeon tended the king, changed his shirt, and washed his hands with wine. The king's priest then led a short prayer service. Afterward, the royal barber gave the king his morning wig.

The ceremonies continued with practiced ease. A few privileged nobles helped the king shave and dress. It was considered a high honor to hand the king an article of clothing, whether it was his silk stockings or diamond-buckled shoes. Once the king was dressed, he led a procession from the royal apartments to the chapel for Mass. As the day unfolded, the king moved from one ceremony to the next. These daily rituals symbolized the absolute power of Louis XIV.

From the 1500s to the 1700s, European monarchs such as Louis XIV gained enormous power. They built strong armies to replace the private armies of the nobles. They took new lands. With their greater resources, they expanded royal government and exercised strict control over the lives of their people.

During this period, powerful monarchs built the foundations for the nations of present-day Europe. As strong monarchies emerged, sharp rivalries developed. Older powers such as Spain, France, England, and the Holy Roman Empire were joined by newer states, including the Dutch Netherlands, Prussia, and Russia. ■

1 Golden Age of Spain

READ TO UNDERSTAND

☐ **How Philip II ruled the most powerful nation in Europe.**

☐ **What problems lay behind Spain's greatness.**

☐ **How Spanish culture bloomed during the Century of Gold.**

☐ *Vocabulary:* **absolute monarch.**

Imagine the most powerful man in Europe sitting in a tiny cell-like room in his huge, gloomy palace. For hours on end, he pores over piles of official papers. They come from all corners of his empire—from Spain, Portugal, Naples, and Sicily; from Mexico and Peru; and from the coastal ports in East Africa, Goa in India, and the Philippines.

In his spidery handwriting, King Philip II of Spain scrawls comments in the margins of the papers and even corrects spelling errors. As a member of the Hapsburg dynasty, he is caught up in the web of European politics. He must ensure the vigor of Spain's colonial empire and its spectacular wealth, the fruits of 30 years of struggle by the conquistadores. Philip takes his responsibilities seriously.

The Hapsburg Empire

The first Hapsburgs were dukes of Austria. Through carefully arranged marriages, they gradually acquired an empire larger than any since the days of ancient Rome. A favorite Hapsburg saying took note of their policy: "Others shall wage war; you O happy Austria, shall marry!"

The Hapsburg Empire reached its greatest size under Charles V, who ruled from 1516 to 1556. Charles inherited Spain and its empire in the Americas through his grandparents, Ferdinand and Isabella. From his other grandparents, he inherited Austria and the Netherlands. In 1519, the German princes elected Charles Holy Roman emperor. The title added to his prestige.

Ruling the many Hapsburg lands was difficult. Early in the reign of Charles V, the Protestant Reformation began in Germany. A devout Catholic, Charles tried to force the German princes to respect the pope's authority. But

"His smile and his dagger were very close," wrote a biographer of Philip II of Spain. Devoted to his family and his religion, the king could be harsh or even cruel to those he considered a threat. He was suspicious of his advisers and intolerant of heretics.

the princes and independent cities resisted his effort to restore religious unity. As you read in Chapter 14, Charles V eventually accepted the Peace of Augsburg in 1555. It allowed each German prince to determine the official religion within his territory.

In Spain, Charles V gained the respect of his subjects through diplomacy and a shrewd use of power. Yet he had to spend the riches of Spain to finance endless wars. Charles battled the French for control of Italy, Burgundy, and Flanders. He also had to defend his Austrian lands against the Ottoman Turks.

The Ottoman Turks, who had captured Constantinople in 1453, expanded into Eastern Europe in the 1500s. Led by Suleiman (soo lay MAHN), the Turks invaded Hungary and advanced up the Danube River to Vienna, in the heart of Austria. Charles V and his brother, King Ferdinand of Hungary, finally arranged a truce that left the Turks in control of most of Hungary.

By 1556, Charles was an exhausted man. He gave up his throne and divided his empire between his brother and son. Then he retired to a monastery. Charles divided the empire because he believed it was too big for any one person to rule. He left Austria to his brother Ferdinand, who was then elected Holy Roman emperor. Charles gave Spain, the Spanish empire in the Americas, the Netherlands, Naples, and Milan to his son, Philip.

A Hardworking Monarch

Philip II ruled Spain from 1556 to 1598. During his reign, Spain was the most powerful nation in Europe. Spanish fleets brought treasure from the New World to Seville. Spanish armies, navies, diplomats, priests, and missionaries fanned out across Europe and the Americas. Behind these Spanish forces stood Philip.

Philip governed as an absolute monarch. An **absolute monarch** is a ruler who has complete authority over the government and over the lives of the people. Philip trusted no one, so he watched over everything.

An intensely religious man, Philip believed that his right to rule came from God. As a result, he governed with a high sense of duty, and he worked hard to ensure justice. In a

The Battle of Lepanto, fought off the Greek coast, pitted the fleets of Spain, Venice, and the Papal States against those of the Muslim Turks. This painting depicts the savage nature of the fighting, which involved fierce hand-to-hand combat. Flags helped identify the hundreds of ships that were involved in the battle. The Turks fought under crescent flags.

legal case in which he stood to lose much, Philip once instructed an official to "inform the Council that, in cases of doubt, the verdict must always be given against me."

Nowhere was Philip's character more evident than in the Escorial (ehs KOHR ee uhl), the somber palace he built outside Madrid. The Escorial served as royal residence, office, monastery, and burial vault. In the palace, Philip kept the coffins of his dead father, brother, wives, and children to remind him of his own mortality. From his bedroom window, he could see the main altar of the monastery. Behind the high palace walls, Philip devoted himself day and night to governing his huge empire.

Philip believed that his mission in life was to fight heretics and restore the unity of the Catholic Church. He led the Catholic Reformation in Spain. He also sent Jesuit priests to convert Protestants all across Europe. In the end, his efforts helped bring parts of Germany, Eastern Europe, and the Netherlands back under the pope's authority.

Like his father, Philip was drawn into many wars. He battled France for control of Italy. As part of his crusade to revive Christendom, Philip attacked Turkish strongholds in the Mediterranean. In 1571, at the Battle of Lepanto, off the coast of Greece, his fleet decisively defeated the Turkish navy. However, the Turks soon rebuilt their navy, and Philip was not able to drive them from the Mediterranean.

Revolt in the Netherlands

Philip's effort to centralize royal power led to a long, bitter struggle with his subjects in the Netherlands. Since the Middle Ages, the Netherlands had flourished as a center of trade and commerce. The wool industry made the cities of Bruges and Ghent prosperous. Antwerp and Amsterdam were busy trading ports. Many people in the Netherlands resented the fact that Philip put the interests of Spain above those of their land.

Religious differences added to Dutch discontent. By the mid-1500s, Calvinist preachers had won many converts among the Dutch. In 1566, when Philip ordered officials to enforce laws against Protestants, the Dutch revolted.

375

Diego Velázquez served as a court painter to Philip IV during the Spanish Century of Gold. Here, Velázquez shows himself painting a portrait of the children of the royal family. Gazing out from the center is the Infanta, the young daughter of the king.

Many Dutch Catholics joined the Protestants because they resented Spanish rule.

The struggle was bitter. Protestants went on a rampage, breaking stained-glass windows and destroying statues of saints in Catholic churches. Philip sent 20,000 Spanish troops to pacify the region. The Spanish commander boasted that in a six-year period his troops killed almost 18,000 people. The Spanish seized Dutch property and imposed harsh taxes that hurt trade.

In 1581, the seven northern provinces of the Netherlands, which were mostly Protestant, declared their independence from Spain. They then became known as the Dutch Netherlands. The ten southern provinces, with their largely Catholic populations, remained the Spanish Netherlands.* The war dragged on into the 1600s, but Spain did not regain its lost provinces in the north.

The Dutch Netherlands emerged from the war with Spain as a leading commercial power. With more ships than any other nation,

---

*In 1830, the ten southern provinces became the nation of Belgium.

376

the Dutch dominated seaborne trade in Europe and overseas. As you have read, they successfully competed with the Portuguese in the East Indies. They also seized islands in the Spanish West Indies and sent settlers to North America.

The Mighty Armada

During the Dutch rebellion, the English watched Philip's activities with concern. Queen Elizabeth, a Protestant, feared that if Philip crushed the Dutch he would then invade England. Therefore, she cautiously supported the Dutch. She also allowed English captains known as sea dogs—a polite name for pirates—to wage an undeclared war on Spain.

The English sea dogs attacked Spanish ports in the Americas and captured Spanish ships. The most famous sea dog, Sir Francis Drake, made several voyages to the West Indies to seize Spanish treasure. Philip wanted Queen Elizabeth to punish Drake as a pirate. Instead, she made Drake a knight, which infuriated the Spanish king.

In 1588, Philip finally moved against the English. He assembled an armada, or armed fleet, of 68 vessels to carry an army of 60,000 soldiers to invade England. As the mighty Spanish Armada sailed up the English Channel, it engaged the English fleet in a great naval battle. The smaller, quicker English ships badly mauled the heavy Spanish ships and forced them to sail into the North Sea. Violent storms in the North Sea destroyed many Spanish ships. The English later nicknamed the storms the "Protestant Wind."

The victory over the Spanish gave the English a feeling of confidence. With the help of the Protestant Wind, they had ended the threat of the Spanish Armada. Yet the defeat did not seriously weaken Spain's power.

A Century of Spanish Genius

Under Philip II, Spanish culture blossomed. His reign was part of what is called the "Century of Gold." From about 1550 to 1650, Spanish writers, philosophers, and artists created great masterpieces that marked a high point in Spanish culture.

As you have read, Cervantes wrote *Don Quixote* during this period. (See page 333.) Another writer, Lope de Vega, a contemporary of Shakespeare, wrote at least 700 plays and greatly influenced drama. His works, which included religious dramas, histories, and comedies, focused on God, the king, and romance. Jesuit writers such as Francisco Suárez wrote about the relationship between faith and reason. Their works influenced both religion and philosophy.

During the Century of Gold, art also flourished in Spain. The painter El Greco expressed intense religious feelings in his portraits of saints. Born in Crete, El Greco received his nickname "The Greek" when he moved to Spain. El Greco drew long, distorted faces and bodies that produced a dramatic effect. Another Spanish artist, Diego Velázquez (vuh LAHS kehs), gained fame as a court painter at Madrid. (See the painting at left.)

A Troubled Economy

Before the Century of Gold ended, Spain had lost its position as the leading nation in Europe. Although Spain still ruled its huge empire in the Americas, it suffered from severe economic problems. In fact, the New World empire contributed to Spain's economic woes.

The Spanish government depended almost entirely on gold and silver from the Americas. Every year, the treasure fleet sailed to Spain with gold and silver from mines in Mexico and Peru. In the 1500s, the value of these shipments rose dramatically. (See the graph at left.) However, Spanish rulers soon drained the treasury to pay for wars. They even had to borrow money from German and Italian bankers.

Thus, Spanish treasure fell into the hands of arms suppliers and foreign bankers. This increased the number of gold and silver coins in circulation and contributed to inflation. As the money supply increased, people tended to charge more for their goods and services. Prices rose all over Europe. However, the steepest rise in prices was in Spain.

Inflation hurt Spanish industries because higher prices meant that it cost more to produce goods in Spain than elsewhere. Even in Spain, foreign goods were cheaper than locally produced goods. As a result, Spanish businesses failed.

The religious policies of Philip II and his successors also contributed to the economic decline. Like Ferdinand and Isabella, later Spanish rulers allowed the Inquisition to persecute the Moriscoes (muh RIHS kohs), Spanish Muslims who had converted to Christianity. Moriscoes were accused of secretly practicing their old religion. In the early 1600s, hundreds of thousands of Moriscoes were driven from Spain.

By 1660, the amount of treasure being brought from the Americas had dwindled.

GRAPH STUDY *Gold and silver treasure from the Americas flowed into Spain, as you can see on this bar graph. The treasure was a mixed blessing because it contributed to steep inflation in Spain. During which period did Spanish income from the colonies begin to decline? Why?*

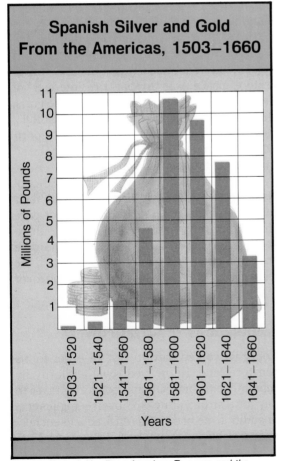

Spanish Silver and Gold From the Americas, 1503–1660

Millions of Pounds

Years: 1503–1520, 1521–1540, 1541–1560, 1561–1580, 1581–1600, 1601–1620, 1621–1640, 1641–1660

Source: Earle J. Hamilton, *American Treasure and the Price Revolution in Spain, 1501–1650.*

Spanish industry and agriculture had also declined. Old rivalries between different regions of Spain resurfaced, and weak rulers were unable to impose unity as Philip II had done. Although the Hapsburgs in Austria continued to play a leading role in European affairs, the Spanish Hapsburgs no longer dominated events on the continent.

SECTION 1 REVIEW

1. **Identify:** (a) Battle of Lepanto, (b) Spanish Armada, (c) Lope de Vega, (d) El Greco, (e) Diego Velázquez, (f) Moriscoes.

2. **Define:** absolute monarch.

3. What lands did Charles V govern?

4. What role did Philip II play in the Catholic Reformation?

5. (a) Why did the Dutch rebel against Spain? (b) How did Queen Elizabeth react to the Dutch rebellion?

6. Describe the Spanish Century of Gold.

7. **Critical Thinking** Describe the events or developments that undermined Spain even at the height of its power. Which do you think was most harmful?

2 The French Monarchy

READ TO UNDERSTAND

☐ How the wars of religion affected France.

☐ How French rulers became absolute monarchs.

☐ What policies Louis XIV and Colbert followed.

☐ *Vocabulary:* intendant.

Catherine de' Medici was queen mother of France. She had her hands full trying to keep one after another of her three incompetent sons on the throne. Ruthless in her tactics, she played off Catholics against the Huguenots, French Protestants.

In August 1572, thousands of Huguenots filled Paris to celebrate the marriage of Catherine's daughter Marguerite to Henry of Navarre, a Huguenot. In the early morning of St. Bartholomew's Day, August 24, the church bells began to ring. On that day 10,000 Huguenots were slaughtered in Paris. Would Catherine, as crafty as she was, have used the occasion of her daughter's wedding to order the massacre? Even 400 years after the event the question cannot be answered with certainty. Nevertheless, the Huguenots blamed her as they fought the civil war that followed.

Wars of Religion

Wars of religion raged on and off in France between 1562 and 1598. The fighting between Protestant and Catholic nobles plunged France into chaos, and royal power melted away. Huguenots sought help from English, Dutch, and German Protestants. The Catholics found an ally in Philip II of Spain.

In 1589, Henry of Navarre inherited the French throne as Henry IV. Henry was a Huguenot, but he saw clearly that the only way to restore peace was to put the interests of France above those of religion. Because Paris, the French capital, was strongly Catholic, Henry IV converted to Catholicism. He reportedly remarked, "Paris is well worth a Mass." Still, the fighting continued.

Finally, in 1598, Henry issued the Edict of Nantes to reassure the Huguenots that their interests would be protected. The edict gave Huguenots freedom of worship and the right to set up churches in certain places. It also gave them the same civil rights as Catholics and the right to have Protestant troops defend over 100 fortified towns in Huguenot areas.

Foundations of Royal Power

Henry IV worked hard to restore order to his war-torn land. He revived royal authority by rebuilding the bureaucracy, collecting taxes to pay for a strong army, and overseeing justice. In addition, he had roads repaired and encouraged new business ventures. However, in 1610,

Henry IV was assassinated, and his ten-year-old son inherited the throne and ruled as Louis XIII.

Early in Louis XIII's reign, French nobles tried to reassert their influence. In 1614, they forced the king to call the Estates General. (See page 204.) But when the Estates met, the nobles could not agree among themselves and the assembly was dismissed in 1615. The Estates General did not meet again for 175 years. During this time, the French kings gained absolute power over the government.

Louis XIII's adviser, Cardinal Richelieu (RIHSH uh LOO), was chiefly responsible for increasing the power and prestige of the French monarchy. Richelieu wanted to prevent the Huguenots from challenging royal power. He realized that he could not destroy the Huguenots without starting another civil war. Therefore, he allowed them religious freedom but forced them to give up the right to fortify their towns.

To further reduce challenges to royal power, Richelieu ordered the destruction of all fortified castles belonging to provincial nobles. He also outlawed dueling because feuding among nobles often led to civil war.

Richelieu was a mercantilist. He believed that trade would strengthen the monarchy. To promote commerce, he encouraged nobles to support overseas trading companies. He rewarded successful merchants, sometimes by allowing them to buy titles of nobility. Since these new nobles were strongly loyal to the king, Richelieu often appointed them to government positions.

The Sun King

When Louis XIII died in 1643, his son, Louis XIV, was a child of four. As a result, his mother, Anne of Austria, and Cardinal Mazarin, Richelieu's successor, ruled in the boy's name. They continued the policy of centralizing power. When Cardinal Mazarin died in 1661, Louis XIV was 23 years old. The king immediately summoned his advisers and announced that he would rule on his own.

This portrait of Richelieu suggests the many-sided nature of the man—French duke, cardinal of the Catholic Church, and virtual ruler of France during the reign of Louis XIII. Richelieu was a skillful diplomat and tough-minded politician. He put the interests of France above those of the Catholic Church and crushed opponents of royal power.

For the next 54 years, Louis XIV ruled France with a skill and power unmatched by any other ruler in Europe. During his long reign, France dominated Europe as Spain had in the late 1500s. Louis XIV's motto was "none his equal." His symbol was the sun, which suggested that just as the earth depended on the sun for its existence so the people of France depended on the Sun King.

"I am the state." Louis XIV believed that as king he had a divine right to rule. He had absolute power because kings were representatives of God's power on earth. Louis XIV summed up his idea of absolute monarchy when he said: "L'état, c'est moi." ("I am the state.")

Louis XIV continued to increase royal authority. For example, until Louis XIV's reign, French armies were similar to feudal armies. Nobles recruited, trained, and paid soldiers, and each noble commanded his own troops.

Under Louis XIV, the French army was reorganized. All French soldiers were to fight for the king. For the first time, they were given uniforms and assigned ranks. Furthermore, Louis XIV increased the standing army from 100,000 to 400,000 soldiers. With a strong, loyal army, the king could put down local uprisings as well as assert French power in Europe.

Louis XIV also closely directed government administration. He appointed **intendants,** or royal agents, to rule the provinces. Intendants collected taxes, recruited soldiers, and administered royal policy. Local parlements were supposed to approve the laws. However, if they tried to resist the king's edicts, Louis would make a grand appearance and leave them speechless.

Louis was a staunch Catholic who was determined to make France a unified Catholic country again. In 1685, he cancelled the Edict of Nantes, which had guaranteed freedom of worship to the Huguenots. During the persecution that resulted, many Huguenots fled to England, the Dutch Netherlands, and the Americas.

The palace of Versailles. Louis XIV built a spectacular new palace at Versailles, 12 miles (19 kilometers) west of Paris. The palace of Versailles, which took more than 27 years to complete, symbolized the splendor and power of the Sun King. The palace faced 20,000 acres of formal gardens and woods. Inside the palace were the royal apartments as well as rooms for hundreds of nobles and servants. On formal occasions, the Hall of Mirrors, a long gallery, was lit with 4,000 candles, mounted in silver and crystal chandeliers.

Versailles served many purposes. Louis made it the center of government, in part because it was a safe distance from Paris, where disturbances had occurred in the past. He encouraged nobles to live there so he could keep close watch on their activities.

Versailles became a center of French culture. The king invited playwrights, poets, and artists to the palace. From Versailles, French influence spread throughout Europe. Other rulers modeled their governments on the absolute monarchy of Louis XIV. People adopted French manners and fashions in clothing and art, and French became the language of European diplomats.

Colbert: Architect of French Economic Policies

Louis XIV needed money to maintain the pomp and splendor of court life. The palace itself cost a fortune to build. Louis XIV's programs for government and the army were also expensive. During much of Louis's reign, Jean Baptiste Colbert (kohl BEHR) successfully managed the royal finances.

Colbert was a mercantilist who was determined to increase royal power by strengthening the economy. He developed a two-part strategy for increasing royal revenues. First, he reformed the system of collecting taxes to reduce corruption among local tax collectors. Second, Colbert introduced higher taxes. This was difficult to do because nobles and even some bourgeoisie, or middle class, did not have to pay taxes. Colbert, therefore, followed the mercantilist policy of promoting trade and commerce. Increased trade would make the country more prosperous, he reasoned. Therefore, the lower classes would earn more and be able to pay higher taxes.

Under Colbert's direction, the French economy prospered. He encouraged new in-

The palace of Versailles and its magnificent gardens were commissioned by Louis XIV. The royal family lived in the palace along with many nobles, who felt privileged to have even a small, damp room there. Construction of the palace required 35,000 workers and took 27 years. Louis XIV destroyed the bills so no one would know how much it had cost to build. Maintaining the court at Versailles cost more than half the taxes collected in France.

dustry and commerce by excusing investors from taxes for a few years. Once new businesses were thriving, they would be taxed. Colbert also encouraged the building of ships, roads, and canals to improve transportation and trade. To promote trade within France, Colbert eliminated some local tariffs that provinces charged for goods coming from other French provinces. However, he imposed high tariffs on foreign imports to protect French industries. In addition, he supported the growth of colonies such as New France.

The Wars of Louis XIV

Louis XIV spent much of the money Colbert raised on foreign wars. He dreamed of extending France to what he called its "natural frontiers." In the south, France had already reached the Pyrenees, a natural frontier. But Louis believed that the frontier in the east should stretch from the Alps, north along the Rhine River, to the North Sea or English Channel.

French ambitions threatened nearly every other European power. For 30 years of Louis XIV's 54-year reign, France was at war. At one time or another, the French fought the Dutch Netherlands, Sweden, England, Spain, and the Holy Roman Empire.

The bitterest struggle was Louis's last war, the War of the Spanish Succession. It began in 1701, when his grandson inherited Spain and all its possessions. Other European powers then formed an alliance to prevent Louis from uniting Spain and France. Years of fighting followed between the allies on one side and France and Spain on the other.

The allies finally got their way. At the Peace of Utrecht in 1713, Louis XIV agreed that

During the 1600s, Paris had to cope with a problem that is haunting many American cities today—homeless people. The number of poor people in Paris had grown throughout the 1500s. In 1596, the city government ordered all homeless people to leave the city within 24 hours "under penalty of being hanged and strangled without a trial."

Despite the threat, however, the problem got worse in the 1600s. During the reign of Louis XIV, many peasants lost their homes because of warfare in the countryside, and they joined the beggars on the streets of Paris. High taxes also led to an increase in the number of poor people on the streets.

In the 1650s, the Paris government tried an ambitious plan to rid the city of the homeless. The king donated six buildings to be used as workshops. Then on the morning of Monday, May 14, 1657, the Paris police began a sweep of the streets, hauling away every beggar they found. They raided the city's worst neighborhoods. One witness described the "flimsy, teetering, dark, deformed houses made of earth and mud, filled with the poorest of the poor." The police locked the

poor up in the workshops, where they were forced to earn their keep. One rich Parisian noted joyfully, "The days of salvation for the poor have arrived."

Not all citizens of Paris supported the lockup of the homeless. The police complained that their job was harder "because of the protection given the beggars by servants, merchants, artisans, and workers." Sometimes, crowds pulled homeless people away from the police and spirited them away. Such dramatic rescues saved many poor people from the workshops.

The workshops took many homeless people off the streets for a time, but soon new beggars took the place of the old. On a visit to Paris in 1700, Louis XIV was shocked "that after all the measures that have been taken to chase the beggars out of Paris, so many still remain."

1. Who opposed locking up the poor in workshops?

2. **Critical Thinking** How did the foreign and domestic policies of Louis XIV make the problem of homelessness worse?

the French and Spanish crowns would never be united. Louis's grandson was recognized by the allies as Philip V of Spain, but it was agreed that Philip could never become king of France. Spain kept its American colonies, but its Italian lands, including Milan, Naples, and Sicily, went to the Austrian Hapsburgs. For its part in the war, England received Newfoundland and Nova Scotia in North America from France as well as Gibraltar and Minorca in the Mediterranean from Spain.

Louis's wars left France deeply in debt, a problem his successors would never solve. Louis himself lost popularity in his last years. But Louis XIV had demonstrated what an absolute monarch at the head of a strong, centralized state could do. During the 1700s, Louis XIV's heirs would try to live up to the brilliant traditions of the Sun King.

SECTION 2 REVIEW

1. **Identify:** (a) Edict of Nantes, (b) Jean Baptiste Colbert, (c) War of the Spanish Succession, (d) Peace of Utrecht.

2. **Define:** intendant.

3. Why did Henry IV become a Catholic?

4. Give two examples of how Cardinal Richelieu increased royal power.

5. What was Louis XIV's main goal in his foreign wars?

6. **Critical Thinking** How did Colbert's economic policies strengthen Louis XIV's power?

3 Struggles Among the German States

READ TO UNDERSTAND

☐ What the causes and results of the Thirty Years' War were.

☐ How Prussia emerged as a powerful state.

☐ How wars in Europe affected other parts of the world.

Tension filled the air of Prague, capital of Bohemia and a Protestant stronghold. The people had no patience for the Catholic emperor, Ferdinand II, or for his officials who had just taken up residence in the city castle. The newcomers had announced that the emperor would no longer tolerate Protestant worship as his predecessors had.

A few hot-headed Czech nobles marched into the castle, seized the officials, and dumped them out an open window. The officials fell 50 feet (15 meters) but landed unharmed. Catholics claimed that this was a miracle. Czech Protestants scornfully replied that the officials had in fact fallen on a soft dunghill. This incident, however, helped spark a general conflict, known as the Thirty Years' War, as the Hapsburgs tried without success to exert their authority over the Holy Roman Empire.

The Thirty Years' War

As you have read, Germany was made up of hundreds of small, independent states. In theory, these states were under the authority of the Holy Roman emperor. In practice, the emperor had little power over them, and the

CHANGES IN WARFARE During the Thirty Years' War, soldiers had pillaged villages for food and supplies, leaving a terrible path of destruction across Europe. In 1650, the French war minister proposed a solution to this problem—in the future, armies would travel with provisions. This recreation by artist Hal Stone shows the French commissariat service with wagon trains of supplies, which became a model for other armies.

princes who ruled each state were often bitter rivals.

Whenever a Holy Roman emperor died, seven leading German princes, called electors, met to choose a new emperor. From the 1400s on, the electors always chose a Hapsburg. As rulers of Austria, Bohemia, and Hungary, the Hapsburgs were the most powerful dynasty in Germany. Although other princes accepted a Hapsburg as emperor, they did not recognize the right of Hapsburgs to rule them. As a result, there was constant friction between the German princes and the emperor.

Political divisions within the empire deepened during the Reformation. Under the Peace of Augsburg, each German prince had the power to decide whether his lands would be Catholic or Lutheran. German Catholics, however, became increasingly upset when one prince after another became Protestant. In their eyes, the problem grew even more serious when some princes converted to Calvinism, which had not even been recognized by the Peace of Augsburg.

Protestants, in turn, became concerned when the Catholic Reformation, under the forceful leadership of the Hapsburgs, began to bring many Protestant princes back into the Catholic Church.

As you read, the Hapsburg emperor Ferdinand II tried to restore the Catholic Church in Bohemia, where many nobles were Protestant. When the Protestants resisted, the emperor decided to crush them. The crisis in Bohemia exploded into the Thirty Years' War.

The war began in 1618 and, with some short periods of peace, lasted until 1648. In the early years of the war, religious issues fueled the fighting. Protestant princes sought help from Denmark, Sweden, and the Dutch Netherlands. Ferdinand was aided by the strongly Catholic Spanish Hapsburgs. However, as the war dragged on, political and territorial issues became more important than religion. Ferdinand tried to establish Hapsburg control over all the German states. To prevent the Hapsburgs from becoming too powerful, the Catholic Cardinal Richelieu of France supported the German Protestants.

During the Thirty Years' War, invading armies devastated the German states. They burned and looted towns and cities. Peasants suffered terribly. In some regions, entire villages were wiped out. Farming became difficult or impossible. Famine and plague broke out, causing even greater misery. Some historians estimate that the population of the Holy Roman Empire dropped from 21 million people in 1618 to about 13.5 million in 1648.

Peace of Westphalia

Neither side could gain a lasting victory in the war. Finally, in 1648, the warring nations of Europe sent representatives to Westphalia, where they negotiated a peace settlement.

The Peace of Westphalia ended the Hapsburg dream of creating a strong central government to rule the Holy Roman Empire. The Hapsburgs still held their family lands in Austria, Bohemia, and Hungary, and they remained the most powerful of the German rulers. But they had little power over the other princes.

The peace settlement guaranteed the independence of about 300 small German states. Each prince had the right to declare war and negotiate treaties. The princes would continue to meet in the Imperial Diet, or assembly, and they had to approve any request from the emperor for taxes. Each prince could choose the religious faith of his territory. The settlement recognized Calvinists along with Lutherans and Catholics, but other Protestant groups still suffered persecution.*

The Peace of Westphalia also acknowledged territorial and political changes that had taken place in the preceding 50 years. European rulers recognized the Dutch Netherlands and the Swiss Confederation as independent states. During the war, King Gustavus Adolphus of Sweden had conquered and then lost large parts of German territory. The treaty left Sweden in control of some German lands along the Baltic and North seas. In addition, France gained parts of Alsace and Lorraine.

---

* To escape persecution, many German Protestants emigrated to the Americas, where quite a few of them settled in the English colony of Pennsylvania.

The boundaries established by the peace remained almost unchanged for 150 years.

Rise of Prussia

One German prince gained more than most from the Peace of Westphalia. He was Frederick William, Elector of Brandenburg. His family, the Hohenzollerns (HOH uhn TSAHL ernz), had ruled Brandenburg since the 1400s. During the Reformation, they became Lutherans. In 1618, the Hohenzollerns inherited Prussia in eastern Germany. Through the Peace of West-

phalia, they acquired other scattered German lands.

Brandenburg was invaded several times during the Thirty Years' War. Invaders devastated the main town of Berlin as well as the countryside. After the war, Frederick William, later called the Great Elector, established strong rule over his lands. To do this, he built a strong army. As he told his son, "A ruler is treated with no consideration if he does not have troops and means of his own."

However, an army cost money. When the Great Elector tried to raise money through

MAP STUDY *The Holy Roman Empire was more fragmented after the Peace of Westphalia than before. Brandenburg-Prussia gained lands that became the basis for a strong Prussian state in the 1700s. Who controlled the largest empire in Central Europe?*

taxes, noble landlords, known as Junkers (YOON kerz), refused to grant him the right to impose taxes. Eventually, by force and compromise, he won the right to collect taxes for the army, but the Junkers themselves did not have to pay any. With a strong army at their command, the Hohenzollerns used every opportunity to expand their power.

Building a Strong Prussian State

During the 1700s, the Hohenzollerns established an absolute monarchy and transformed Prussia from a small kingdom into a major European power. The Great Elector's grandson, King Frederick William I, dedicated his life to strengthening the Prussian army. Between 1713 and 1740, he doubled its size to 80,000 soldiers. He recruited officers from the Junker class and set up universities where they would be trained. In addition, peasants were drafted to serve as soldiers. The army helped unify Prussia because soldiers and officers shared a loyalty to the king.

Frederick William I was a tireless worker who believed in obedience and discipline. In public, he always wore a military uniform. He cared nothing for luxury. On occasion, he would patrol the streets of Berlin lecturing citizens for wearing frivolous clothes or living in too much luxury. His tight-fisted financial policies were necessary to support his large standing army. But he cleverly avoided going to war because that would have put an even greater strain on the economy.

Frederick William I also strengthened the Prussian economy. Because the Prussian population was small, he encouraged Protestants from France and other Catholic areas to settle in his lands. The newcomers included farmers, artisans, and merchants, who contributed to the country's prosperity. When a famine, flood, or war occurred elsewhere in Europe, the king would send agents to recruit new settlers. The agents promised land to peasants and offered loans to merchants so they could reopen their businesses in Prussia.

To Frederick William I, his son Frederick seemed an unlikely successor because the boy loved to read books and play the flute. The king thought such pastimes were useless, and he harshly disciplined his son. Yet when Frederick became King Frederick II in 1740, he proved to be an even more vigorous leader than his father. Frederick still enjoyed reading literature and philosophy, but he ruled Prussia with a firm hand. He eventually became known as Frederick the Great.

Forceful Rulers in Austria

While Prussia was emerging as a new power in Germany, the Austrian Hapsburgs tried to establish tighter control over their empire, which included Austria, Bohemia, and Hungary. However, each region had its own heritage and language. Austria was for the most part German-speaking. Bohemians were descended from the Slavs, and Hungary was the homeland of the Magyars.

Between 1648 and 1740, the Hapsburgs tried to reduce the power of local nobles and make the Austrian Empire a Catholic stronghold. For example, in Bohemia, they took land from Protestant nobles and gave it to Catholic nobles who would be loyal to the emperor. Despite such efforts, the unity of Hapsburg lands remained fragile. This was especially apparent to Charles VI, emperor from 1711 to 1740.

The Pragmatic Sanction. Charles VI had no son to inherit his throne. He feared that the German princes and nobles in the Hapsburg lands might not recognize his daughter Maria Theresa as ruler of Austria. Therefore, he persuaded them to sign the Pragmatic Sanction.

The Pragmatic Sanction guaranteed that the Hapsburg lands would not be divided, and it recognized Maria Theresa's right to inherit the Austrian throne. Charles convinced other European nations to accept the agreement. However, when the emperor died in 1740, Frederick the Great of Prussia ignored the agreement and seized the Austrian province of Silesia. Silesia was a valuable prize because of its iron ore and strong textile industry. Maria Theresa had to move quickly.

War of the Austrian Succession. Maria Theresa was only 23 years old when she became queen of Austria, but she proved to be a capable and decisive leader. Shortly after she gave birth to her first son, Maria Theresa traveled to Hungary to seek help against Prussia. The Hungarian nobles were usually hostile toward Austria, but Maria Theresa made a dramatic appeal to them. She promised to safeguard their traditional rights and showed them her infant son, the future ruler of Austria. The Hungarian nobles responded by sending 100,000 troops to fight the Prussians.

While Maria Theresa mustered her forces, the fighting quickly widened into a general European war, known as the War of the Austrian Succession. France, a longtime rival of the Hapsburgs, and Spain joined Prussia. Great Britain* and the Dutch Netherlands sided with Austria, but they sent only money and few troops.

The war in Europe grew into a worldwide conflict that pitted France against Britain. The French won victories in Europe, but the British attacked French possessions in Canada and the West Indies. Finally, in 1748, the European nations signed a peace treaty at Aix-la-Chapelle. Only Frederick the Great benefited from the war because he was allowed to keep Silesia. Otherwise, the treaty provided that all territories should be returned to the nations that held them before the war.

The European Balance of Power

By the mid-1700s, two German states—Austria and Prussia—were among the major powers in Europe. Like France, they had strong central governments led by absolute monarchs, and they had well-trained standing armies. Two other strong nations, Russia, which you will read about later in this chapter, and Britain, also played important roles in European affairs. Diplomats scurried about Europe negotiating alliances to maintain a balance of power. To them, the balance of power meant that no single nation was strong enough to dominate Europe.

---

* In 1707, the crowns of England and Scotland were joined into the United Kingdom of Great Britain. After 1707, the country became known as Great Britain or Britain.

Soon after Maria Theresa, shown here, inherited the Hapsburg throne, Austria was attacked. When enemy forces approached Vienna, Maria Theresa fled with her infant son to seek help from the Hungarian nobles. According to one story, the nobles rose, drew their swords, and shouted: "Our lives and blood for your Majesty! We will die for our king, Maria Theresa!"

Competition between the major European powers was keen. For example, Britain and France competed for trade and territory in India and North America. These rivalries made them enemies in any European conflict. In Europe, Austria was determined to recover Silesia and take revenge on Prussia. Meanwhile, both Prussia and Russia were eager to expand their territories.

Conflicting interests soon led to the Seven Years' War, which was fought on three continents: Europe, Asia, and North America. In North America, the war was called the French and Indian War.

In 1756, Frederick the Great invaded Saxony, a German state west of Silesia. Prussia was a strong military power, but it soon faced the combined forces of France, Austria, and Russia. Only the withdrawal of Russia from the alliance saved the outnumbered Prussians from disaster.

The French and British fought each other in North America and India. The fighting began in North America in 1754. During the war, British troops and soldiers from the colonies captured Quebec, which in effect gave them control of New France. In India, the British drove the French from their trading outposts.

At the Peace of Paris in 1763, Britain received Canada and all French lands east of the Mississippi River. Spain acquired the French territory of Louisiana. France, however, recovered its trading stations in India. It also kept two profitable sugar-producing islands in the West Indies.

The rivalry between Britain and France would continue for decades. Also, the Seven Years' War left both nations deeply in debt. The policies each nation followed to reduce its debts would undermine British power in North America and the absolute monarchy in France.

SECTION 3 REVIEW

1. **Locate:** (a) Austria, (b) Bohemia, (c) Hungary, (d) Brandenburg, (e) Prussia, (f) Silesia, (g) Saxony.

2. **Identify:** (a) Hohenzollerns, (b) Junker, (c) Maria Theresa, (d) Pragmatic Sanction.

3. (a) Describe two causes of the Thirty Years' War. (b) How did the Peace of Westphalia affect the Hapsburgs?

4. (a) Why did the Great Elector build up the Prussian army? (b) Give two examples of how King Frederick William I tried to strengthen Prussia.

5. Why was the Austrian Empire hard to unite?

6. **Critical Thinking** By the 1700s, why were European wars fought outside of Europe as well as in Europe itself?

---

4 Developments in Eastern Europe

READE TO UNDERSTAND

☐ What the Ottoman Empire was like at its height.

☐ How Peter the Great strengthened Russia.

☐ What foreign policy Catherine the Great followed.

☐ Why and how Poland was divided.

In 1521, when Martin Luther was defending himself at the Diet of Worms, at the other end of Europe, Suleiman had just become head of the Ottoman Empire. Suleiman, named after the Hebrew king Solomon, was a wise ruler within his own lands as well as a successful conqueror. To Christian Europeans, however, he appeared as an agent of the devil.

In Eastern Europe, the Ottoman Empire, Russia, and Poland ruled over large territories. Each state had customs and traditions that differed from those of Western Europe. However, between 1500 and 1795, all three became more involved in developments in Western Europe.

The Ottoman Empire

In the 1500s, the Ottoman Empire extended from Eastern Europe across Asia Minor into the Middle East and Egypt. (See the map at right.) As you read, Constantinople fell to the Ottomans in 1453. They renamed the city Istanbul, converted churches into mosques, and restored the city's earlier splendor.

The Ottoman Empire included peoples who practiced many different religions. The Turks were far more tolerant of religious differences than Europeans were at that time. Islamic law recognized Christians and Jews living in the empire as People of the Book. (See page 232.) As a result, they were allowed to follow their own faiths.

The Ottoman Empire reached its height under Suleiman, who ruled from 1520 to 1566. Suleiman had absolute control over the government and the army.

Suleiman sponsored the building of mosques, schools, hospitals, bridges, and public baths. A strong police force made Istanbul safer than any other European city at that time.

Suleiman also led his armies on successful military campaigns. He captured Belgrade in what is today Yugoslavia. He then moved up the Danube, taking Hungary. In 1529, Suleiman advanced on Vienna with 100,000 troops and almost broke through the city walls before he was beaten back.

After Suleiman's death, the Ottoman Empire began a long, slow decline. Weak sultans ignored their duties and failed to control corrupt officials. Local governors, called pashas, ruled Ottoman provinces in Europe and Africa. As long as they paid tribute to the sultan, they were free to rule as they pleased. Despite the decline, the Ottoman Empire survived until

1918. Although largely isolated from cultural developments in Europe, the empire continued to influence events in Eastern Europe.

The Romanov Dynasty in Russia

During the 1400s and 1500s, Russia emerged as a powerful state in Eastern Europe. As you read in Chapter 11, Ivan III and Ivan IV brought lands around Moscow under their control. As czars, they claimed absolute power. However, for many years after the death of Ivan IV in 1584, Russia had no strong leader.

During the Time of Troubles, from 1604 to 1613, nobles schemed to put their own candidates on the throne. As soon as a new czar was installed, a rival would murder him. Finally, in 1613, the nobles elected 17-year-old Michael Romanov as czar. Once established, the Romanov dynasty ruled Russia until 1917.

MAP STUDY *Under Suleiman the Magnificent, the Ottoman Turks advanced deep into Europe, as you can see on this map. In what other areas did the Ottoman Empire gain substantial territory during his rule?*

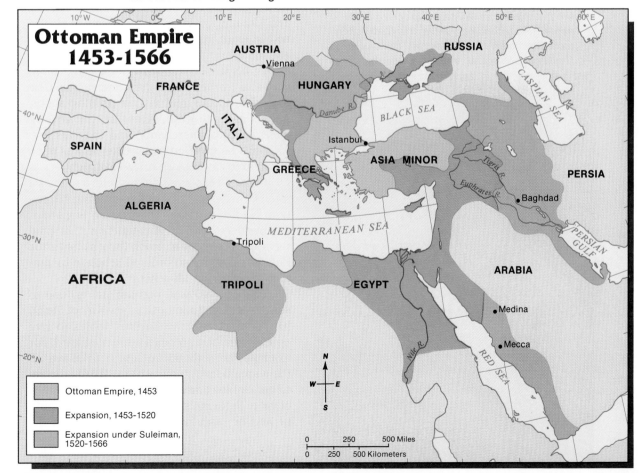

Michael Romanov realized that being an elected monarch would limit his power. Therefore, he and his heirs worked to end the practice of electing monarchs and tried to bring the nobles under their control. To win the support of the nobles, the Romanovs gave them absolute control over their peasants and enacted strict laws to prevent peasants from running away.

Russian peasants were increasingly reduced to serfdom during the 1600s. Unlike serfs elsewhere, Russian serfs were treated like slaves. They were not only forced to give unpaid labor but could also be bought and sold. Harsh treatment of serfs led to many peasant uprisings. But such uprisings were quickly suppressed.

During the 1600s, the Romanovs expanded their territory eastward. Russian traders and trappers had crossed the Ural Mountains during the 1500s and discovered that Siberia had valuable iron, timber, and fur resources. Russian explorers pushed as far east as the Bering Straits. In 1689, Russia signed a treaty with China that recognized Russian claims to lands north of Manchuria. By the end of the century, Russia had acquired an empire stretching to the Pacific Ocean.

Peter the Great

Under the Romanovs, Russia also expanded to the west. As you have read, Russia had been isolated from the west for centuries. During this time, the nations of Western Europe had developed military and technical skills that the Russians lacked. Peter I, who became czar in 1682, was determined to make Russia a powerful nation by introducing western technology and customs. Between 1689 and 1725, his reforms transformed Russia and earned him the title of Peter the Great.

Peter was a towering figure—almost seven feet tall. He had a sharp, inquiring mind. As a boy, he spent much time talking to German and Dutch merchants who lived in Moscow. From them, he learned about developments in the rest of Europe.

In 1696, Peter visited Western Europe. As he traveled through the Netherlands, England, and Germany, he realized how much Russia had to learn from the West. Peter acted more like an apprentice than an absolute monarch during his travels. He worked in a Dutch shipyard and learned about guns and cannons. He toured hospitals and visited printing shops. Always eager to learn, Peter met with government officials, merchants, and sea captains. Although he traveled in disguise, he was often recognized because of his great height.

Peter's reforms. On his return to Russia in 1698, Peter set about westernizing his nation. He hired over 700 European engineers, shipbuilders, and mathematicians. He paid them high salaries to teach their skills to the Russians. Peter also ordered scholars to simplify the Russian alphabet.

The czar allowed nothing and no one to stop his efforts to impose a new way of life on his people. He forced Russian nobles to give up customs that he considered backward. For example, he ordered noblemen to shave off their long beards, and he fined those who refused. Noblewomen in Russia had lived in seclusion. Peter insisted that they appear in public and dress in French fashions.

While traveling in Western Europe to learn about new technology, Peter the Great often wore disguises. In this portrait, the czar of Russia is dressed as a ship's carpenter.

Peter modeled his government after the government of Louis XIV. He replaced the Duma, a council of nobles, with a Senate that would follow his will in all matters. He set up a government bureaucracy and promoted talented commoners to office. Peter required nobles to serve either in the army or as government officials, and he sent sons of nobles abroad to study.

Foreign policy. Like earlier czars, Peter expanded Russia's borders. His main goal was to gain a warm-water port that would allow Russia to trade directly with Western Europe all year round. He hoped to win such a "window on the west" on the Baltic and Black seas.

In 1700, he fought Sweden, which controlled the Baltic coastline. The brilliant Swedish king Charles XII defeated a Russian force of 40,000 with only 8,000 Swedish troops. Undaunted, Peter rebuilt his army on the western model. In 1709, he overwhelmed the Swedes at the Battle of Poltava. The war dragged on, but Peter won his window on the west. Russia did not reach the Black Sea, however, until later in the century.

A new capital. Even before his victory over the Swedes, Peter decided to build a new capital on the icy, swampy shores of the Baltic. The city, named St. Petersburg, was built by thousands of peasant laborers, who were forced to work under terrible conditions. Often they dug only with sticks and carried the dirt away in their coats.

Just as Versailles symbolized the reign of Louis XIV, St. Petersburg stood as a monument to Peter the Great's power. Unlike Moscow, St. Petersburg was a seaport. Through it, the Russians could keep in touch with developments in Western Europe.

Before his death in 1725, Peter had achieved his dream of making Russia a more modern and more powerful nation. From the 1700s on, Russia would be increasingly involved in European affairs.

Catherine the Great

Peter had demanded the right to choose his successor, but on his deathbed he scribbled only the phrase, "I leave all. . . ." No one knew whom he meant to choose as his heir. Power

Peter the Great saw the long beards worn by Russian men as an example of his country's backwardness and ordered nobles to shave their beards. Many men objected because they believed that God had a beard and that man was made in God's image. Eventually, Peter allowed men to keep their beards if they paid a tax. This cartoon shows Peter the Great, at right, clipping the beard of a protesting noble.

struggles among various Romanovs left Russia without a strong czar until 1762. In that year, Czar Peter III died and his wife Catherine became czarina, or empress, of Russia.

For 34 years, Catherine directed the Russian government with a firm hand. Although she was a German princess by birth, Catherine had learned Russian and converted to the Eastern Orthodox faith when she married. She won the support of the Russian nobles by giving them a charter of their rights. It exempted them from taxes and excused them from the service to the state that Peter the Great had required.

After Catherine gave the nobles their charter, peasants expected their own charter of rights from noble landlords. When it did not

One day in 1702, Peter the Great spotted an island at the mouth of the Neva River on the Baltic Sea. The river, flowing around the island, was deep and calm. The island itself was the perfect place for a fortress. And no one lived there except a few fishermen. Yes, Peter decided, here was where St. Petersburg, the new capital of Russia, would be built. At last, Russia would have a port on the Baltic.

Even though Russia was still at war with Sweden, Peter began to issue orders. He commanded that nobles all across Russia send serfs to the site of the city to do the drudge work. But Peter also needed carpenters and stonemasons, more than Russia could supply. He advertised in the great cities of Europe for skilled workers. Peter commanded Russian nobles to come and build mansions in the new city. In fact, he forbade Russians to build a house anywhere in the country until St. Petersburg was finished.

Through the spring and summer of 1703, hundreds of thousands of Russians made their way to the mouth of the Neva. But difficulties soon became obvious. No roads led to the "city," so supplies had to arrive by sea. Tools were in short supply, and so was food. Disease spread rapidly among the hungry and overworked Russians.

The geography of the area created still other problems. The ground around the river was marshy and soft. Before permanent buildings could be put up, rock and wood pilings had to be sunk. Workers spent months shoring up the earth. Meanwhile, there were not enough shelters for the workers, and many had to sleep on the wet ground. In the course of a year, as many as 100,000 workers died. "This is the bottomless pit in which countless Russians perish and are destroyed," one witness despaired.

But Peter did not despair. He planned the city's parks and boulevards himself. His counselors invented new taxes to pay for the city. Nothing seemed to escaped being taxed—hats and shoes, melons and cucumbers, coffins, baths, mustaches and beards.

At terrible cost, the new capital was created. As St. Petersburg became a center of western culture, the city gradually forgot its tragic beginnings.

1. Why did Peter choose the site he did for Russia's new capital?
2. **Critical Thinking** Did Peter's goal of creating a new capital justify the means he used to reach it?

---

come, they rebelled. The peasant rebellion was the largest in Russian history, but it failed. Furthermore, it led Catherine to take stiff measures against the peasants. During Catherine's reign, conditions for peasants grew worse, and more were forced into serfdom.

Catherine earned the title "the Great" for her aggressive foreign policy. Like Peter the Great, she fought to expand Russia's borders. She won a warm-water port on the Black Sea by defeating the Ottoman Empire. Russia might have carved up the declining Ottoman Empire, but Austria and Prussia rushed to prevent Russia from becoming too powerful in Eastern Europe. Frederick the Great of Prussia persuaded Catherine to give up her ambitions in the south in return for a slice of Poland in the west.

The Partitions of Poland

In 1772, the first of three partitions of Poland took place. Catherine took part of eastern Poland, where many Russians and Ukrainians lived. Frederick eagerly took West Prussia, which finally united the scattered lands of Brandenburg and Prussia. Maria Theresa of Austria took Galicia, although she protested the idea of dividing up Poland. Prussia, Russia, and Austria knew that Poland was too weak to resist.

During the 1400s and 1500s, Poland had been a large and powerful nation. It stretched across Eastern Europe from the Oder River to the Dnieper River. However, during the 1600s and 1700s, Polish nobles became increasingly independent of the king. They ruled their own

Growth of Russia, 1689-1796

Legend:
- European Russia, 1689
- Territory added by 1725
- Territory added by 1796
- Boundary of Poland before 1772
- Austria, 1796
- Prussia, 1796

MAP STUDY *Russia acquired new lands in Europe during the 1600s and 1700s. Which nations benefited from the partitions of Poland?*

lands with a free hand, acting like feudal lords. Government in Poland was chaotic.

Nobles met in the Diet, or legislature, to pass laws, but the Diet was ineffective. All laws had to be approved by all nobles. Each noble had a right known as the "liberum veto," or free veto. By saying he was totally opposed to a proposed law, a noble could force the Diet to disband and wipe out all laws the Diet had already passed. Such an action was known as "exploding" the Diet. Between 1652 and 1754, nobles "exploded" 48 of the 55 Diets that met. Poland's weakness left it at the mercy of its neighbors.

After the first partition, the Poles united behind their king, but it was too late. In 1793, Russia and Prussia each took another slice of Poland. Then, in 1795, Russia, Prussia, and Austria carried out the third and final partition. Poland ceased to exist as an independent nation until 1919.

SECTION 4 REVIEW

1. **Locate:** (a) Istanbul, (b) St. Petersburg, (c) Poland.

2. **Identify:** (a) Suleiman, (b) Time of Troubles, (c) Michael Romanov, (d) Peter the Great, (e) Catherine the Great.

3. What was the Ottomans' attitude toward non-Muslims in their empire?

4. (a) How did Peter the Great try to strengthen Russia? (b) How did Catherine gain a warm-water port for Russia?

5. What nations participated in the partition of Poland?

6. **Critical Thinking** Both Peter and Catherine were strong autocratic rulers. Do you think they could have accomplished what they did without this? Explain.

Summary

l. **Under the rule of Philip II, Spain enjoyed a golden age.** Philip was a hard-working, absolute ruler. Treasure from the Americas helped make Spain strong and financed its many wars. However, Spanish power declined in the late 1600s.

2. **In the 1600s, France, under the leadership of Louis XIV, replaced Spain as the most powerful nation in Europe.** For 54 years, Louis XIV ruled with absolute power, keeping the nobles occupied at his glittering court and fighting many wars of expansion.

3. **In the Holy Roman Empire, conflicts between Protestants and Catholics led to the Thirty Years' War.** The years of fighting left Germany physically devastated, and the Peace of Westphalia recognized the independence of hundreds of small German states. However, in the 1700s, Prussia and Austria emerged as the two leading German states.

4. **The Ottoman Empire and Poland were powerful nations in Eastern Europe in the 1500s, but by the 1700s Russia had become a major power.** Peter the Great strengthened Russia by introducing western ideas and technology. Both Peter and Catherine expanded Russia's borders and made Russia a major force in European affairs.

Recalling Facts

Choose the letter of the correct time period for each of the following events.

A	B	C	D	E
1550	1600	1650	1700	1750	1800

1. Suleiman rules the Ottoman Empire.

2. Peter the Great wins a "window on the west."

3. Spain launches the Armada against England.

4. Maria Theresa inherits the Austrian throne.

5. Final partition of Poland occurs.

6. The Thirty Years' War devastates Germany.

Chapter Checkup

1. (a) How did Philip II help make Spain the most powerful nation in Europe? (b) Why did Spanish power decline during the 1600s?

2. Explain how each of the following individuals helped make France an absolute monarchy: (a) Henry IV; (b) Cardinal Richelieu; (c) Louis XIV.

3. (a) How did Colbert's policies strengthen the French economy? (b) Why were his policies important for Louis XIV's foreign policy?

4. What events and developments prevented the creation of a centralized German state in the 1600s?

5. Explain how each of the following rulers helped make Prussia a more powerful nation: (a) the Great Elector; (b) Frederick William I; (c) Frederick the Great.

6. (a) Describe the Ottoman Empire under Suleiman. (b) Why did the empire decline after his death?

7. (a) How did Peter the Great bring Russia into closer contact with Western Europe? (b) What actions by Catherine the Great showed that Russia was a major European power?

Critical Thinking

1. **Understanding Economic Ideas** (a) What effect did the increase in gold and silver from the Americas have on Spain? (b) In the long run, did Spain benefit from the wealth of the New World? Explain.

2. **Analyzing a Quotation** Bishop Bossuet, tutor to Louis XIV's son, defended the idea of absolute monarchy with these words: "The royal throne is not the throne of a man, but the throne of God himself." (a) Explain the meaning of the quotation in your own words. (b) What monarchs discussed in this chapter do you think would have agreed with Bossuet? Explain.

3. **Relating Past to Present** (a) What did Europeans mean by the balance of power? (b) What country or countries might have upset the balance of power in Europe in the 1700s? (c) Are nations still concerned about the balance of power today? Explain.

Developing Basic Skills

1. **Classifying** Make a chart with two columns. In column one, write Philip II, Louis XIV, and Peter I. In column two, list the ways each monarch increased royal power in his own country. (a) What similarities do you see? (b) What differences do you see? (c) What do you think was the most important achievement of each monarch?

2. **Map Reading** Study the map on page 389. (a) What areas did Suleiman add to the Ottoman Empire? (b) What European nations were most directly affected by the expansion of the Ottoman Empire?

Writing About History

Using a Cataloging System

A library card catalog tells you which books are in the library. A card catalog has subject, title, and author cards. Each card in the catalog also contains a call number. The call number classifies a book according to the Dewey Decimal System or the Library of Congress System. Under the more commonly used Dewey Decimal System, history books fall in the 900s.

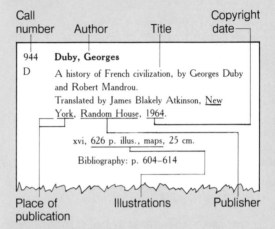

Practice: Study the catalog card below and answer the following questions:

1. What is the title of the book?
2. When was the book published?
3. Does the book include a bibliography?
4. What is the call number of the book?
5. When did the author live?

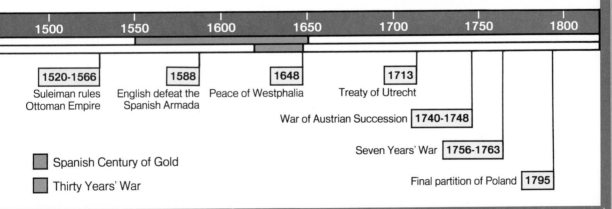

Unit Five — Mini-Atlas

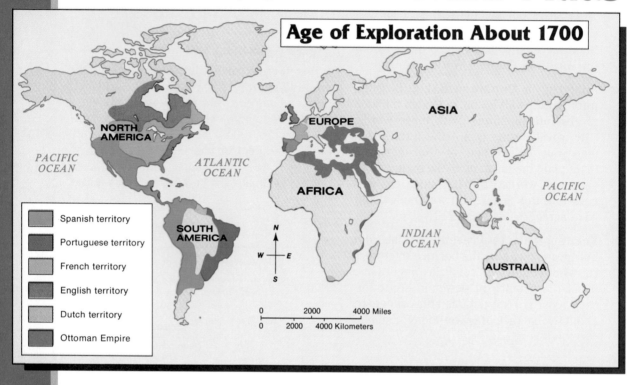

Age of Exploration About 1700

NORTH AMERICA

EUROPE

ASIA

PACIFIC OCEAN

ATLANTIC OCEAN

AFRICA

SOUTH AMERICA

PACIFIC OCEAN

INDIAN OCEAN

AUSTRALIA

N
W — E
S

Spanish territory

Portuguese territory

French territory

English territory

Dutch territory

Ottoman Empire

0   2000   4000 Miles
0   2000   4000 Kilometers

Unit Themes

By the 1400s, the city-states of northern Italy were centers of European trade. Their wealth contributed to the revival of art, literature, and learning known as the Renaissance. A thirst for knowledge and a new interest in classical Greece and Rome helped set the stage for many discoveries.

During the Renaissance, European sailors ventured out into the Atlantic Ocean. Between 1450 and 1550, they sailed around the world and discovered continents and cultures previously unknown to Europeans.

The expansion of trade and voyages of exploration were made possible by developments in shipbuilding and map making. In addition, powerful monarchs, eager for riches and empire, encouraged exploration.

Strong monarchs guided their nations through a period of transition. Out of the traditions of medieval and classical civilization, they forged the foundations of the nations of Europe.

1. **Analyzing Ideas** (a) Summarize Machiavelli's ideas about politics and power. (b) Which European monarchs could be described as Machiavellian? Explain.

2. **Synthesizing** (a) Where did the Protestant Reformation begin? (b) How did it affect politics in Europe? (c) How did it affect the population of overseas colonies?

3. **Applying Information** Study the world map above. (a) On which continents did Europeans claim territory? (b) Which nation claimed the most territory? (c) How did overseas trade and colonization affect Europe politically and economically?

4. **Comparing** Compare the map at right with the one on page 385. (a) When did the Holy Roman emperor rule the most land? (b) Why did Charles V divide his empire? (c) Why do you think no absolute monarch ruled in the Holy Roman Empire?

396

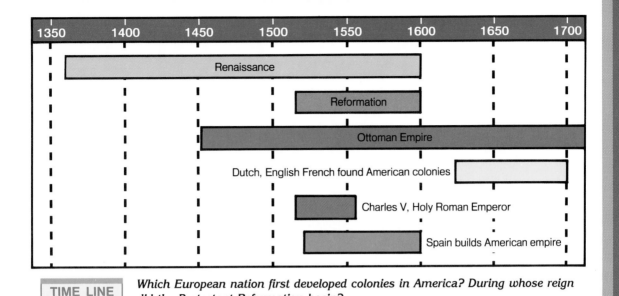

TIME LINE STUDY

Which European nation first developed colonies in America? During whose reign did the Protestant Reformation begin?

MAP STUDY

Charles V inherited Hapsburg lands from both sets of grandparents. Which of his lands were outside of the Holy Roman Empire?

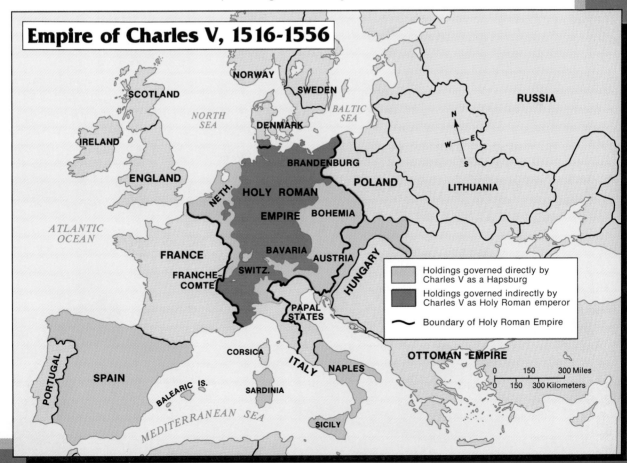

Empire of Charles V, 1516-1556

Holdings governed directly by Charles V as a Hapsburg

Holdings governed indirectly by Charles V as Holy Roman emperor

— Boundary of Holy Roman Empire

UNIT SIX

AN AGE OF REVOLUTION

1649 *Oliver Cromwell was head of the English republic, which lasted until 1660.*

Mozart, at the piano, began composing music before the age of five.

	1600	1650	1700
POLITICS AND GOVERNMENT		**1642** English civil war begins	**1660** Charles II restored to throne	**1715** Louis XIV of France dies
ECONOMICS AND TECHNOLOGY	**1609** Kepler notes elliptical orbit of planets		**1687** Newton publishes book of mathematical proofs
SOCIETY AND CULTURE		**1645** Levellers demand abolition of noble titles in England	**1690** Locke publishes *Two Treatises on Government*

This painted fan shows the opulence of the nobles in France under the Old Regime.

1671 *Model of a telescope developed by Sir Isaac Newton.*

UNIT OUTLINE

1804 *Napoleon, who had become First Consul in 1799, proclaimed himself emperor in 1804.*

During the French Revolution, many French people demanded "liberty," symbolized here by a statue.

1750	1800	1850
1776 American colonies declare independence	**1789** French Revolution begins	**1848** Nationalist revolutions break out in Europe
Mid-1700s Wedgwood develops new methods of pottery making	**1770s** Economic crisis grows in France	**1848** National workshops set up for the unemployed in France
1748 Montesquieu publishes *The Spirit of Laws*	**1819** Carlsbad Decrees suppress freedom of speech	

Jean Jacques Rousseau believed in equality and the will of the majority.

George Washington led the Americans during their fight for independence from Britain.

The Scientific Revolution and the Enlightenment

17

(1500–1800)

The alchemists of the Middle Ages, such as the ones shown here, experimented with ways of turning worthless metals into gold. By the 1500s, however, thinkers were paving the way for the Scientific Revolution by observing facts and applying them to practical problems.

The man peered through his simple microscope. He fixed his gaze on the drop of water on the specimen holder. Could he be seeing things? The tiny droplet of water was alive with little "wretched beasties." They moved about "very nimbly," he wrote later, "because they had incredibly thin feet!"

The "thin-footed" creatures that Anton van Leeuwenhoek (LAY vuhn HOOK) saw were in fact organisms like bacteria. Today, we know a good deal about such microscopic organisms, but in 1671 no one had any idea they existed until Leeuwenhoek invented his primitive microscope.

Leeuwenhoek was a Dutch cloth merchant who was fascinated with lenses. One day he mounted a magnifying lens between two metal plates. He then made a specimen holder, which he attached to his lens. With this primitive microscope, Leeuwenhoek began to study such everyday objects as bits of pepper and plant seeds as well as his own skin. Eventually, he looked at that drop of water.

Leeuwenhoek's startling discovery created a stir among scholars because it opened a whole new world of study. When Leeuwenhoek and others used the microscope in their studies, they discovered hundreds of previously unknown organisms. As they learned more about these tiny organisms, they had to discard long-held ideas about living things.

During the 1500s and 1600s, inventions such as the microscope and many new discoveries greatly changed the natural sciences and medicine. New technology and improved methods of research led to an explosion of knowledge that became known as the Scientific Revolution.

Discoveries about the physical world influenced philosophers, who applied scientific principles to the study of government and society. During the first half of the 1700s, philosophers emphasized the use of reason. They thought that people should use reason to free themselves from ignorance and superstition and thereby become enlightened. They were convinced that enlightened people could perfect themselves and society. Thus, the eighteenth century is known as the Enlightenment.

Together, the Scientific Revolution and the Enlightenment changed the way people saw the world. These two movements helped shape the attitudes that made the scientific advances of the modern world possible. ■

1 New Directions in Science

READ TO UNDERSTAND

☐ **Why mathematics was important to the Scientific Revolution.**

☐ **How scientists developed new views about the universe.**

☐ **What advances were made in medicine.**

☐ *Vocabulary:* **scientific method, law of gravity.**

Leonardo da Vinci, like many people during the Renaissance, was intensely curious about the natural world. Da Vinci kept detailed notebooks in which he recorded his scientific observations. He studied human anatomy, plants, and the structure of the eye. He drew plans for fantastic inventions such as a flying machine and a bicycle. Through observation and experimentation, such inquiring minds expanded people's knowledge of the world.

The Scientific Method

The ancient Greek philosopher Aristotle created a system of thought based on observation and a process of reasoning called logic. During the Middle Ages, scholars relied completely on the teachings of Aristotle and other ancient writers. By the end of the Middle Ages, scholars began to question some of the ancient ideas about nature and the world. They made observations about the movement of the stars and planets, for example, that contradicted the accepted theories.

At the same time, the increased use of Hindu-Arabic numerals made it easier for scientists to make mathematical calculations. Another important advance that aided scientists was the invention of a new kind of mathematics, called analytic geometry, by the French philosopher René Descartes (day KAHRT). Descartes emphasized the importance of reasoning in arriving at the truth. He summarized this idea in the statement, "I think, therefore I am."

Slowly, a new approach to scientific study developed that became known as the **scientific method.** A combination of observation and reason, the scientific method is a three-step approach. First, careful experiments and observations are made. Second, reason is used to interpret the results of the experiments and observations. Third, mathematics rather than logic, or reasoning from principles, is used to prove scientific theories.

Copernicus

Nicolaus Copernicus (koh PUR nih kuhs), a Polish mathematician and astronomer, played a major role in developing the scientific method. In 1543, he published *On the Revolutions of the Heavenly Bodies.* His work challenged Ptolemy's view of the universe. As you read in Chapter 6, Ptolemy taught that the earth was the center of the universe.

Copernicus used mathematical calculations to show that Ptolemy was wrong on two crucial points. First, Copernicus said that the earth was not stationary, but turned on its axis once a day. Second, he declared that the earth was not the center of the universe. Instead, the earth and other planets revolved around the sun. But Copernicus could not provide enough convincing evidence to prove that Ptolemy was wrong. As a result, many educated people rejected his views.

Many scholars argued that Ptolemy and the other ancient philosophers could not have been wrong. In Western Europe, all scientific knowledge and many religious teachings were based on the logical arguments developed by the ancient philosophers. Thus, scholars thought, if their reasoning about the planets was wrong, then the whole of human knowledge would become uncertain.

Although few people accepted Copernicus' ideas, his work had far-reaching consequences because of his method of testing ideas. After Copernicus, more and more scientists backed up their observations of nature with mathematical calculations.

Further Discoveries

In the late 1500s, the Danish astronomer Tycho Brahe built an observatory to study the planets and stars. He carefully recorded what he saw. Brahe's observations, made with the naked eye, were the most detailed of any made to that time. After Brahe's death, the German

Tycho Brahe is sometimes called the first true astronomer because he based his ideas on direct observation. For more than 20 years, Brahe studied the skies and accurately recorded his findings. Here, he and his assistants are at work in Brahe's observatory, called Uraniborg, "the castle of the heavens."

astronomer and mathematician Johannes Kepler used this information to prove Copernicus' theories.

Like Copernicus, Kepler thought that the earth and other planets traveled around the sun. To prove this, Kepler performed thousands of hours of calculations based on Brahe's observations. His calculations supported the idea that the planets revolve around the sun but not that they revolve in perfect circles, as Copernicus had thought. In 1609, Kepler announced that the planets move in another kind of orbit, called an ellipse.

In Italy, the astronomer Galileo Galilei used a new magnifying instrument, the telescope, to observe the planets and stars. With the telescope, Galileo was able to prove by observation what Kepler had proved mathematically—that the planets do move around the sun.

Galileo's observations also led to other discoveries about the universe. Since ancient times, astronomers had believed that the moon, planets, and stars were all perfectly smooth, unchanging bodies. Through the telescope, Galileo saw that the moon had a rough surface broken by jagged mountains. The sun was also imperfect because it had dark, changeable spots on its surface. He discovered that the planet Jupiter had four moons, which no one had seen before. Galileo's discoveries showed that the universe was very different from what ancient philosophers had taught.

Galileo on Trial

When Galileo announced his discoveries in the early 1600s, the conflict between traditional thinking and the new science broke into the open. Galileo offended many scientists by declaring that the heavenly bodies were imperfect and changing. An outspoken man, he did not hesitate to defend his views at the expense of others. He made powerful enemies when he humiliated his critics in public.

These enemies persuaded the Catholic Church to condemn the teachings of Copernicus and to forbid Galileo from defending the new ideas. When Galileo refused to obey, church officials called him before the Inquisition. They demanded that he publicly admit his errors. In order to avoid being put to death

as a heretic, Galileo declared at the trial that the earth stood motionless at the center of the universe. But as he left the court after the trial, Galileo whispered softly under his breath, "And yet it moves."

Newton and Natural Laws

The English mathematician Sir Isaac Newton built on the work of many earlier scientists. In 1687, Newton published *The Mathematical Principles of Natural Philosophy.* In this book, he provided mathematical proofs of what people such as Galileo had observed. Newton invented calculus, a method of calculation, which he used to prove his theories.

Among Newton's most important contributions to science was the law of gravity, which he wrote as a mathematical formula. Newton's **law of gravity** states that there is a force of attraction between objects that is related to their mass and that the force increases as objects move closer together. Newton's law explains mathematically how the moon's gravity causes tides on the earth and how the sun's gravity keeps the planets within their orbits.

According to legend, Newton developed the law of gravity after he saw an apple fall. He wondered why it fell to the ground and did not fly into space. His law explains that an apple falls to the ground because it is pulled by the earth's gravity.

Newton's work helped to develop a new view of the universe. Newton saw the universe as a huge, well-regulated machine that worked according to definite laws of nature, such as the law of gravity. Other thinkers soon took up the search for laws of nature.

Newton's work had many practical applications. Navigators and mapmakers used his mathematics to make more precise charts. Using calculus, engineers improved weapons such as guns and cannons. Later, inventors improved on Newton's ideas and developed such practical devices as the steam engine.

Improvements in Medicine

During the 1500s and 1600s, scientists made important advances in medicine. Some challenged the theories of Galen, a Greek physician whose work had dominated medicine in the Middle Ages. Like Copernicus and Galileo, they faced strong opposition because most scholars accepted the ancient theories over modern views. A story is told about a professor of medicine who found that the body he was dissecting did not look like the one shown in Galen's text. Rather than question Galen, the professor decided there was something wrong with the corpse.

In the early 1500s, a Swiss physician known as Paracelsus (PAR uh SEHL suhs) experimented with chemistry. He disproved Galen's idea that chemical changes, such as transforming one substance into another, were impossible. Paracelsus was hounded out of one university after another because he ridiculed ancient authorities. Although he failed to win the respect of other scholars, he did gain fame for healing the sick. "I pleased no one except the sick whom I healed," he once bitterly remarked.

At the University of Padua in Italy, scholars studied the human body. In 1543, Andreas Vesalius (vih SAY lee uhs), a professor of anatomy, wrote *On the Structure of the Human*

THEN AND NOW The Slow Progress of Medicine

Despite the scientific breakthroughs of the Enlightenment, the day-to-day practice of medicine improved very slowly. Doctors could do very little to stop the epidemics of smallpox, measles, influenza, and yellow fever that regularly swept through cities and towns, killing thousands.

Many obstacles slowed the advance of medicine. For one, it was difficult for doctors to learn about the human body. Religious leaders felt it was a sin to dissect, or cut open, the bodies of the dead, and most people agreed with them. As late as 1788, a mob of angry New Yorkers attacked a hospital where doctors dissected bodies. The surgeons had to take refuge in the city jail, and the local militia killed seven people before the riot ended.

In the face of such strong opposition, many doctors had to learn about human anatomy by working with living people. One French doctor, who was a surgeon in the French army, studied anatomy as he patched up wounded soldiers. And even when a discovery was made, the doctors themselves often clung to old ideas. When Vesalius showed that the hip bone was not shaped the way Galen, the ancient Greek physician, said, many doctors refused to believe him. They insisted that Galen had been right and that human beings had changed shape over the centuries from wearing tight pants.

Some "cures" endangered patients. One Englishwoman could hardly believe the treatment her aristocratic friend suffered through.

"The Duchess has been in great danger of losing her sight by catching cold," she wrote. "They have saved her eyes by almost strangling her with a handkerchief, and forcing all the blood up into her head, and then bleeding her with leeches."

1. Why did doctors have difficulty learning about human anatomy?

2. **Critical Thinking** Why do you think breakthroughs in medicine are so much more common today than in the 1600s and 1700s?

Body. He made accurate drawings of the human anatomy that corrected some of Galen's errors.

A French physician, Ambroise Paré (pah RAY), studied Vesalius' textbook and soon made his own contributions to medicine. Traditionally, doctors had tried to prevent infection in wounds by pouring boiling oil into the wound, an extremely painful remedy. Paré developed an ointment that could be applied instead. Later, Paré also developed a technique for closing wounds with stitches.

In the early 1600s, an Englishman, William Harvey, studied the circulation of the blood through the body. He showed that the heart acted as a pump to circulate blood through the arteries and veins. Traditionally, doctors had thought that blood did not move through the body.

The work of these physicians and others led to further medical breakthroughs. In the 1700s, for example, doctors in Europe learned how to produce a vaccine that could be used to prevent smallpox. As medical and scientific knowledge increased, scholars formed scientific societies to exchange information.

SECTION 1 REVIEW

1. **Identify:** (a) René Descartes, (b) Nicolaus Copernicus, (c) Tycho Brahe, (d) Johannes Kepler, (e) Galileo Galilei.

2. **Define:** (a) scientific method, (b) law of gravity.

3. Why did scholars challenge the ideas of Copernicus?

4. What did Galileo's observations through the telescope reveal?

5. How did Newton think the universe worked?

6. Describe one way each of the following contributed to medical knowledge: (a) Andreas Vesalius, (b) Ambroise Paré, (c) William Harvey.

7. **Critical Thinking** Explain why mathematics was so important to the scientific method.

2 Enlightenment Thinkers

READ TO UNDERSTAND

☐ How the views of Hobbes and Locke differed.

☐ What reforms philosophes and physiocrats wanted.

☐ What democratic principles Montesquieu, Voltaire, and Rousseau supported.

☐ *Vocabulary:* philosophe, physiocrat, free market.

If Newton could discover natural laws to explain the workings of the universe, why not use the scientific method to uncover laws about humankind? So thinkers reasoned in the late 1600s and 1700s. "I believe that morals should be treated like other sciences," wrote the thinker Adam Smith. "One should arrive at a moral principle as one proceeds with an experiment in physics."

During the Enlightenment, philosophers felt sure that they could use reason to discover the natural laws that governed human behavior. As a result, this period is also called the Age of Reason.

Hobbes and Locke

The ideas of two English philosophers, Thomas Hobbes and John Locke, changed the way people viewed the individual's role in society. During the 1640s, Hobbes witnessed the upheaval of a civil war in England.* As a result, he became convinced that if people were left alone without government they would constantly fight among themselves. In 1651, he published his ideas in *Leviathan*. Hobbes described life in a state of nature in which people had no government. Such a life, he claimed, would be "nasty, brutish, and short."

According to Hobbes, to escape the chaos of their natural state, people entered into a contract in which they agreed to give up their freedom to a ruler who guaranteed peace and order. The best government, Hobbes said, was one in which the ruler had absolute power.

---

* You will read about the civil war in England in Chapter 18.

Hobbes insisted once people entered into such a contract, they could not rebel, even if they thought the ruler was a tyrant. Hobbes' ideas, therefore, supported the rule of absolute monarchs.

In 1690, John Locke published *Two Treatises on Government.* Locke agreed with Hobbes that the purpose of government was to create order in society. He also saw government as a contract between the ruler and the ruled. However, Locke's other ideas about government differed greatly from those of Hobbes.

Locke had a more optimistic view of human nature than Hobbes did. He thought people were basically reasonable and would cooperate with one another. Moreover, Locke argued that rulers could stay in power only as long as they had the consent of those they governed. If a ruler were a tyrant, he or she had broken the contract. The people then had the right to rebel.

Locke also presented other ideas that were important in the development of democracy. He believed people had natural rights, including the right to life, liberty, and property. Government was responsible for protecting these rights, he said, but its power should be limited. After Locke's death, his ideas became popular in France and in North America, as you will read in later chapters.

Social and Economic Ideas

In the 1700s, many writers and thinkers, especially in France, expanded on Locke's idea of natural rights. They became known as **philosophes,** a French word meaning philosophers. The philosophes were confident that the use of science and reason would lead to continued human progress.

Many philosophes gathered in Paris, where they helped to make Enlightenment ideas popular. Often, they were middle-class, well-educated men who valued clear thinking as well as wit and humor.

The philosophes were concerned about many social issues. They urged religious toleration and condemned wars of religion. They claimed that people had the right to believe as they wished. The philosophes demanded freedom of speech and the press, and they criti-

cized the strict censorship that most governments exercised. They believed censorship was harmful because it kept people from learning about new ideas. They encouraged education as the way to end ignorance, prejudice, and superstition.

The philosophes called for an end to slavery because it took away a person's most basic rights. They spoke out against torture and cruel punishments for crimes. Some campaigned for more humane treatment of the mentally ill.

One group of philosophes, known as **physiocrats,** searched for natural laws to explain economics. As you have read, mercantilism influenced the economic policies of most European governments at the time. Physiocrats opposed mercantilism. They argued that land was the true source of national wealth, not hoards of gold and silver. They urged rulers to encourage farming.

Physiocrats believed that restrictions on trade should be removed so farmers could sell their products wherever there was a market. They favored a **free market,** that is, a market in which all goods can be bought and sold without controls. They argued that in a free market trade would increase. With more trade, they said, more wealth would become available for everyone.

Three Influential Views on Government

Among the most influential Enlightenment thinkers were Montesquieu (MAHN tuhs KYOO), Voltaire, and Rousseau (roo SOH). Each formed his own ideas about the best way to organize governments. Yet all three shared the basic beliefs of the philosophes.

Montesquieu. Born to a noble family, the Baron de Montesquieu was a keen student of government. He read the works of Newton and Locke. In *The Spirit of Laws,* he discussed various forms of government.

Montesquieu was especially impressed with the system of government that had developed in England by the mid-1700s. He believed that English government protected the liberty of the people by the separation of power among three branches of government: the legislature, executive, and judiciary. Montesquieu thought that in England Parliament, as the legislature, made the laws; the king, as the executive, enforced the laws; and the courts, as the judiciary, interpreted the laws if disputes arose. The English system did not in fact work that way, but Montesquieu's ideas were still widely discussed.

Montesquieu also thought that the power of each branch of government should be carefully defined to provide a system of checks and balances. That way no branch of government could dominate another. Montesquieu's ideas on checks and balances and the separation of powers would later influence the authors of the Constitution of the United States.

Voltaire. Probably the best-known philosophe was François Marie Arouet, who used the pen name Voltaire. Voltaire came from a French middle-class family. He traveled

---

BUILDERS AND SHAPERS
Josiah Wedgwood: A Practical Man of the Enlightenment

In 1775, Josiah Wedgwood heard from friends in America that a rebellion against England was brewing. When war broke out between America and England, most of the English upper class lined up behind their government. But not Josiah Wedgwood. "I am glad that America is free," he wrote, "and rejoice most sincerely that it is so." In the face of hostility from his countrymen, Wedgwood championed the cause of American liberty. He sharply denounced "the absurdity, folly, and wickedness" of England's war against "our brothers and best friends" in America.

As his stand for American freedom shows, Wedgwood was an unusual man. He had risen from humble roots to become a wealthy pottery maker. Even today, Wedgwood pottery is still sold around the world. Like other figures of the Enlightenment, Wedgwood applied the scientific method to his work. He taught himself chemistry so he could understand the chemical changes that take place when clay is heated. When he figured out a way to improve the ovens at his pottery factory, he tore down the old ovens and built new ones.

Wedgwood used his pottery to spread "enlightened" ideas. Late in life, he became active in the movement to end slavery. Wedgwood designed the antislavery medallion shown here, which pictures a chained slave asking, "Am I not a man and a brother?"

At his own expense Wedgwood produced and distributed thousands of the medallions. Fashionable men had the emblem made into rings and coat buttons. And women wore them as hairpins. When he sent a shipment of medallions to his friend Benjamin Franklin in Philadelphia, Wedgwood wrote, "It gives me great pleasure to be embraced in the same great and good cause with yourself, and I ardently hope for the final completion of our wishes."

1. How did Wedgwood apply the scientific method to his work?

2. **Critical Thinking** What Enlightenment ideas help explain why Wedgwood would support freeing the slaves?

widely and became popular for his witty plays and novels as well as for his pamphlets attacking evils in society.

Voltaire spent much of his life arguing for common sense, religious toleration, and freedom of thought. He is credited with saying, "I do not agree with a word you say but I will defend to the death your right to say it."

Voltaire praised English liberties and the works of Newton and Locke. He favored the idea of a strong monarch and thought the best ruler was an "enlightened monarch." By that, he meant a monarch who studied the science of government and protected the basic rights of the people.

Rousseau. The Swiss philosophe Jean Jacques Rousseau came from a poor and unhappy family. When he went to Paris, he always felt out of place among the sophisticated intellectuals who gathered there. A complainer and constant critic of others, Rousseau quarreled with many philosophes. Yet his political and social ideas were an important part of Enlightenment thought.

Rousseau believed that human nature was basically good. In his opinion, society corrupted people. He argued that all people were equal and that all titles of rank and nobility should be abolished. "Man is born free," he wrote, "and everywhere is in chains."

Rousseau admired what he called the "noble savage," who lived in a natural state, free from the influences of civilization. However, Rousseau realized that people could not return to the natural state.

In *The Social Contract,* Rousseau described an ideal society. In this society, people would form a community and make a contract with one another, not with a ruler. People would give up some of their freedom in favor of the "general will," or the decisions of the majority. The community would vote on all decisions, and everyone would accept the community decision.

Rousseau's beliefs in equality and in the will of the majority made him a spokesman for the common people. Revolutionaries in many countries would later adopt his ideas.

At home and in public, the philosophes discussed their ideas for reforming society. Here, Voltaire, with his arm raised, entertains other philosophes at a dinner party. As a boy, Voltaire had told his father that he wanted to become a writer. His father warned that he would starve. Voltaire proved his father wrong by becoming a rich and successful writer.

1. **Identify:** (a) Thomas Hobbes, (b) John Locke, (c) Montesquieu, (d) Voltaire, (e) Jean Jacques Rousseau.

2. **Define:** (a) philosophe, (b) physiocrat, (c) free market.

3. (a) What kind of government did Hobbes support? (b) According to Locke, when did people have a right to rebel?

4. Describe three concerns of the philosophes.

5. Why did Montesquieu support a government system with checks and balances?

6. (a) Who did Voltaire think should govern? (b) What did Rousseau mean by the "general will"?

7. **Critical Thinking** How did the views of the physiocrats differ from the views of the mercantilists you read about in Chapter 15?

3 Impact of the Enlightenment

READ TO UNDERSTAND

☐ How Enlightenment ideas spread.

☐ How women helped shape the Enlightenment.

☐ How the Enlightenment affected government and the arts.

☐ *Vocabulary:* salon.

In beautifully furnished rooms, glittering with candlelight, people gossiped, debated, and discussed philosophical ideas. In this way, the educated elite of Paris spent many a delightful evening. Through their talk, they helped to refine and spread the ideas of the Enlightenment.

At the same time, printing presses did their work, churning out the works of the philosophes. Among the most successful and influential spokespersons of the Enlighten-

ment was Denis Diderot (DEE duh ROH), a French philosophe who supervised the publication of a huge encyclopedia that summarized human knowledge of that time.

Spread of New Ideas

Like many philosophes, Diderot moved to Paris as a young man, where he met the best thinkers of the day. A daring man, Diderot convinced a French bookseller to publish the *Encyclopedia, or Classified Dictionary of the Sciences, Arts, and Occupations.* Between 1751 and 1772, Diderot put together the 35-volume *Encyclopedia.*

Diderot hoped the *Encyclopedia* would bring about "a revolution in the minds of men to free them from prejudice." Voltaire, Montesquieu, Rousseau, and many others contributed articles on philosophy, religion, the arts, literature, and government. Other people wrote about lands in Africa and Asia, where Europeans had begun to explore. But the *Encyclopedia* devoted the most space to articles on science and technology. Diderot included diagrams that showed the latest advances in printing, medicine, and other fields.

In France, the Catholic Church and government censors banned the *Encyclopedia.* They considered it antireligious because some articles criticized religious persecution. However, censorship could not prevent it from becoming a popular work read by educated people all over Europe.

Enlightenment ideas also spread in other ways. As the number of people who could read and write increased in the 1700s, more newspapers and journals were published. Learned societies published reports and held public lectures to let people know about new ideas. In addition, middle-class men met in coffee houses to discuss the latest discoveries in science or recent political news. In working-class neighborhoods, popular songs and political pamphlets spread new ideas.

Women's Contributions to the Enlightenment

Women played an important role in spreading Enlightenment ideas. In Paris, and elsewhere in France, wealthy women held **salons,** or informal gatherings, at which writers, musicians, painters, and philosophes presented their works and exchanged ideas. The salon originated in the 1600s, when a group of noble-women in Paris began inviting a few friends to poetry readings. Only people who were considered witty, intelligent, and well-read were invited to the salons.

During the 1700s, middle-class women such as Madame de Geoffrin (zhahf RAN) began holding salons. Voltaire and leading philosophes gathered at Madame de Geoffrin's salon at least once a week. Through their salons, women helped shape the tastes and manners of the Enlightenment.

Some women also acted as patrons for artists and writers. For example, Louise de Warens supported Rousseau and his family so he could spend his full time writing. In addition, many women produced their own poetry and novels, which they circulated among their friends in the salons. A few women managed to get an education in the sciences. For example,

Emilie du Châtelet became a noted physicist and mathematician and translated Newton's work from Latin into French.

Enlightened Monarchs

Many European rulers were impressed by the ideas of the Enlightenment. Some adopted policies that they hoped would improve social and economic conditions in their countries. They considered themselves "enlightened monarchs." However, they also used the new ideas to centralize their power by reducing the privileges of nobles.

In Austria, the empress Maria Theresa and her son, Joseph II, tried to put Enlightenment principles into practice. Maria Theresa passed laws to limit serfdom by controlling the amount of unpaid work required. Joseph took her policies a step further and abolished serfdom. He also allowed freedom of the press, banned the use of torture, and ended religious persecution. He gave equal rights to Jews and

In salons, men and women enjoyed intelligent, informed conversation on many subjects. "We polish one another, and rub off our corners and rough sides by a sort of amicable [friendly] collision," wrote one man who visited salons in Paris and London. The Paris salon of Madame de Geoffrin, which is shown here, influenced art, literature, and politics in the mid-1700s.

limited the power of the Catholic Church. However, after his death in 1790, his successors reversed his reforms.

Other enlightened monarchs studied the new ideas but made few major changes. Catherine the Great of Russia invited Diderot to visit Russia, and she corresponded with Voltaire. She made some effort to limit torture and introduce religious toleration, but she did nothing to end serfdom.

Frederick the Great of Prussia was so impressed with the French philosophes that he invited Voltaire to his court. Frederick introduced reforms by allowing religious freedom and by encouraging elementary education for children. However, like most enlightened monarchs, he did not change the social structure, which was based on inequality and serfdom.

The Arts During the Enlightenment

During the Enlightenment, artists tried to find laws that would give order to their work. Painters thought their subjects should look natural but at the same time beautiful. They were strongly influenced by classical Greek art, which had represented figures in their most ideal and graceful forms.

Classical styles also influenced European architecture. In the 1600s, buildings had become ornate and elaborate. But in the 1700s, architects returned to the simple elegance of ancient Greece.

Many talented individuals made lasting contributions to music. In the late 1600s and early 1700s, musicians, like architects, favored an ornate style in their work. Two German composers, Johann Sebastian Bach and George Frederick Handel, are among the most important composers of this period. Bach wrote many types of music, but he is perhaps best known for his religious music. Handel eventually settled in England, where his operas became very popular.

In the mid-1700s, music began to reflect the simplicity and elegance expressed by artists and architects of the time. In the late 1700s, this style of music was brought to its height by Franz Joseph Haydn and Wolfgang Amadeus Mozart. Haydn is best known for his symphonies.

At music parties, which became popular in the 1700s, amateur musicians showed off their skills. Often, they would insist that composers such as Mozart and Haydn write new pieces for them to perform. The four musicians in this painting are the son and daughters of King George II of England.

Mozart is especially remembered as a child genius who began composing before he was five years old. At age six, Mozart played for the empress Maria Theresa. Later, his father took him and his talented sister to perform in the salons of Paris. Although he was only 35 when he died, Mozart had already written more than 600 musical works, including symphonies, operas, and church music.

SECTION 3 REVIEW

1. **Identify:** (a) Denis Diderot, (b) Joseph II, (c) Johann Sebastian Bach, (d) Wolfgang Amadeus Mozart.

2. **Define:** salon.

3. How were Enlightenment ideas spread?

4. Describe three reforms introduced by enlightened monarchs.

5. **Critical Thinking** How could Diderot's *Encyclopedia* free "the minds of men from prejudice"?

411

Summary

1. During the 1500s and 1600s, the Scientific Revolution changed the way Europeans viewed the world. Scholars developed a new method to study the natural world. Mathematics played a central role in the scientific method, as did experiments and observation. Although the new theories aroused fierce opposition, they were gradually accepted.

2. Philosophers tried to discover natural laws to explain human behavior. Hobbes and Locke had differing views of human nature, but both influenced the French philosophes such as Montesquieu, Voltaire, and Rousseau. These philosophes put forward ideas about government and society that have influenced us to the present day.

3. Enlightenment ideas spread from philosophers to ordinary people and to monarchs. Enlightenment thinkers were confident that science and reason could solve the major problems facing society. Some absolute monarchs tried to use Enlightenment ideas to govern their nations, although they did so with limited results.

Recalling Facts

Match each name at left with the correct description at right.

1. John Locke

2. William Harvey

3. Sir Isaac Newton

4. Wolfgang Amadeus Mozart

5. Jean Jacques Rousseau

a. English mathematician who developed the law of gravity

b. English philosopher who believed people had natural rights to life, liberty, and property

c. physician who studied the circulation of the blood

d. composer who began writing music before age five

e. philosopher who thought society corrupted people

Chapter Checkup

1. (a) What was the basis of scientific thought during the Middle Ages? (b) Why did scholars begin to question traditional scientific views after 1200? (c) How did Copernicus help develop the scientific method?

2. (a) How did Galileo make so many enemies? (b) How did they get their revenge? (c) Why did Galileo give in to the Inquisition?

3. (a) How did Newton's work help change people's view of the universe? (b) What other effects did his work have?

4. (a) How were the ideas of Hobbes and Locke similar? (b) How were they different?

5. (a) What social and economic changes did the philosophes want? (b) Did they achieve any of their goals during the 1700s? Explain.

6. Describe how the following helped spread Enlightenment ideas: (a) the *Encyclopedia;* (b) learned societies; (c) salons.

Critical Thinking

1. Relating Past to Present List three developments of the Scientific Revolution. What have been the long-term consequences of each?

2. Understanding the Roots of Democracy The writings of Locke, Montesquieu, Voltaire, and Rousseau helped shape our ideas about democracy. Choose two of these philosophers and explain how their ideas supported basic democratic beliefs.

3. **Expressing an Opinion** The philosophes were confident of human progress. They believed that life could be improved. (a) What events and developments of the time do you think contributed to this attitude? (b) Do you think people today still believe in progress? Explain.

4. **Analyzing Economic Ideas** (a) According to the physiocrats, why was a free market a good idea? (b) Do you agree with their views? Why or why not?

Developing Basic Skills

1. **Classifying** Make a chart with three columns. In the first column, list Hobbes, Locke, Montesquieu, Voltaire, and Rousseau. In the second column, describe the kind of government each philosopher thought was best. In the third column, explain why each thought his system was the best. (a) Which philosopher's ideas were most democratic? Why? (b) Who was concerned with individual rights? (c) Which system do you think is most like the government of the United States today? Explain.

2. **Researching** Choose one individual who made a contribution to the Scientific Revolution or the Enlightenment. Research his or her background in order to answer the following questions: (a) To what social class did the person belong? (b) What training or education did the person receive? (c) Why was the individual's contribution to the Scientific Revolution or the Enlightenment important?

Writing About History

Using the *Readers' Guide*

To find information in magazines and journals, you need an index to periodicals. The *Readers' Guide to Periodical Literature* lists articles by subject and author. To help you use the *Readers' Guide,* study the sample entry below.

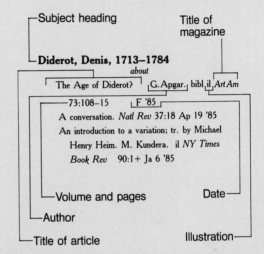

Practice: Use the sample entry from the *Readers' Guide* to answer the following questions:

1. What is the title of the article by G. Apgar?
2. Under what subject heading does it appear?
3. In which issue of the *National Review* would you find an article on Diderot?

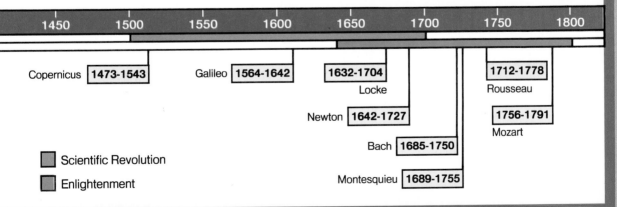

Scientific Revolution

Enlightenment

Copernicus 1473-1543
Galileo 1564-1642
Locke 1632-1704
Newton 1642-1727
Bach 1685-1750
Montesquieu 1689-1755
Rousseau 1712-1778
Mozart 1756-1791

Revolution in England and North America 18

(1509–1791)

Early in July 1776, the leaders of the American colonies, shown here, voted for independence from England. They pledged "our lives, our fortunes, and our sacred honor" in support of the cause.

Blasts of winter wind rattled the windows of Robert Bell's printing house on Third Street in Philadelphia. Inside, Bell reached into the press for the first copies of Thomas Paine's latest pamphlet. The title, *Common Sense,* greeted him from the front page. Did Bell know that Paine's words would stir the colonies as no other pamphlet had? If not, he would soon find out. Between January and July of 1776, more than 500,000 copies of *Common Sense* were circulated throughout the 13 American colonies.

Thomas Paine was in fact a newcomer to the colonies. He had arrived in Pennsylvania from England just two years earlier. Yet he fully understood the

414

colonists' anger with Britain. During the mid-1700s, the British government had introduced new taxes that many colonists felt were unjust. Paine urged the colonists to declare their independence.

Many colonists took a more cautious approach. But Paine had no patience with those who wanted to compromise. He challenged them "to show a single advantage that this continent can reap, by being connected with Great Britain." This connection, Paine declared, only brought disadvantages to the colonies. In addition, he held, for Britain to rule America was contrary to the laws of nature.

"There is something very absurd in supposing a continent to be perpetually governed by an island. In no instance has nature made the satellite larger than its primary planet; and as England and America reverse the common order of nature, it is evident that they belong to different systems—England to Europe, America to itself."

After winning their independence, the colonists had to decide who should govern them and how. Ironically, 100 years earlier the people of England had debated the same questions.

Like the European nations that you read about in Chapter 16, England had developed a strong, centralized government during the 1600s and 1700s. But England had gradually evolved into a limited monarchy rather than an absolute monarchy. The English accepted many of John Locke's ideas. They believed that government should protect certain basic liberties. They also felt that the power to govern came from the consent of the governed. The ideas and institutions that emerged in England paved the way for more democratic forms of government in both England and North America. ■

1 Clashes Between King and Parliament

READ TO UNDERSTAND

☐ **How the Tudors and Stuarts dealt with Parliament.**

☐ **What the causes of the English civil war were.**

☐ **How Oliver Cromwell tried to rule England.**

The crowd waited nervously in the icy January cold. At about 2 P.M., they saw the king emerge from the palace. He spoke briefly to the people who stood near him on the platform. Calmly, he removed his cloak, prayed, then placed his head on the block. A great silence fell on the crowd. The king gave the signal that he was ready, and the executioner swung his ax. Charles I of England was no more. "There was such a groan by the thousands then present as I never heard before and desire I may never hear again," recalled one eyewitness.

The events surrounding the trial and execution of King Charles in 1649 horrified people throughout Europe. Never before had a ruler been tried and condemned by his own people. But, unlike other European monarchs, English kings and queens had limits on their power. They had to respect the tradition dating back to the Magna Carta that rulers could not simply do as they wished. They also had to deal with Parliament. Charles I had tried to ignore these limitations and paid for his efforts with his life.

A Balance With Parliament

By the 1500s, the English Parliament had won several important rights. Parliament approved new taxes, passed laws proposed by the monarch, and advised monarchs. However, monarchs had more power than Parliament. They named officials and judges, summoned and dismissed Parliament, and conducted foreign policy. After 1534, when Henry VIII broke with the Catholic Church, monarchs also headed the Church of England.

The Tudor rulers, Henry VIII and his daughter Elizabeth I, were forceful personalities. However, both recognized the value of good relations with Parliament. Henry, you will recall, had sought and won Parliament's approval to establish the Church of England.

Elizabeth followed a cautious policy in her dealings with Parliament. She lived simply so she would not have to ask for money too often. But she also exercised her rights as monarch. Sometimes she scolded Parliament for interfering in matters that she felt were not its business. However, she also knew when to keep quiet and how not to offend Parliament. During most of her reign, Elizabeth was a popular queen. She managed to keep a balance between exercising her power and giving in to Parliament. In this way, she kept the country united and stable.

In 1603, Elizabeth died, leaving no direct heir. The English throne passed to the Stuarts, the ruling family of Scotland. When James VI of Scotland traveled south to London to be crowned James I of England, he knew little about English politics.

James I and the Divine Right of Kings

James I was a well-meaning ruler and a scholar. He supervised a new translation of the Bible, known as the King James version. He also wrote a book called *The True Law of Free Monarchies.* In it, he presented his belief that kings ruled by divine right. "Kings are called gods," he declared, "because they sit upon God's throne on earth." Furthermore, he argued, the king should have no restraints on his power so that he could rule for the good of all his people. James's belief in his divine right to rule led to conflict with Parliament.

Parliament was made up of two houses: the House of Lords, in which nobles served for life, and the House of Commons, whose members were elected.* Most representatives in the House of Commons were wealthy landowners, called gentry. Many of the gentry had bought monastery lands that Henry VIII had seized from the Catholic Church and sold. The gentry raised sheep for wool, which helped build a prosperous textile industry. The growing merchant class in England also had representatives in the House of Commons.

James I and Parliament quarreled over three main issues: religion, money, and foreign policy. A major religious issue involved the demands of the Puritans. Puritans wanted to

Everyone, "from the Prince to the lowest person in England," is represented there "and the consent of the Parliament is taken to be every man's consent."

"The most high and absolute power in the realm consists in the Parliament," wrote Sir Thomas Smith in the 1560s. Everyone, "from the Prince to the lowest person in England," is represented there "and the consent of the Parliament is taken to be every man's consent." Under the Tudors, Parliament gained confidence and prestige. Elizabeth I is shown here presiding over her last Parliament in 1601.

---

* Only a small number of property owners had the right to vote for members of the House of Commons.

see the Anglican Church "purified" of Catholic rituals and ceremonies. They also demanded that local congregations be allowed to rule themselves rather than be ruled by bishops and archbishops appointed by the king. Among the Puritans were many powerful merchants, some of whom served as members of Parliament.

The House of Commons sympathized with the Puritans' demands. However, the king refused to make any changes in church organization. Elizabeth had tolerated most Puritans, but James vowed to "harry them out of the land." His persecution of Puritans forced some of them to leave England.

James constantly needed money. He spent lavishly on his court and gave generous gifts to his friends. In addition, England owed many debts to bankers for its wars against Catholic Spain. When the king summoned Parliament to approve new taxes, Parliament often refused unless he would accept its wishes on religious matters. James would angrily lecture Parliament on the divine right of kings and send the representatives home.

James then had to find other sources of money. He revived feudal fines and increased customs duties, which went directly to the crown. Although such moves were technically legal, they angered Parliament.

Parliament also criticized the king's foreign policy, especially when James made peace with Spain and tried to arrange a marriage between his son Charles and a Spanish princess. Furthermore, many people in England felt that James did not give enough help to Protestants in Europe during the wars of religion there.

Charles I and Parliament

James's son Charles I inherited the throne in 1625. Like his father, Charles believed in the divine right of kings. When Parliament refused to give him enough money, Charles dismissed it and demanded loans from individual people. He imprisoned anyone who refused to pay the forced loans.

In 1628, Charles had to summon Parliament because he needed funds desperately. Parliament refused to act on his demands for money until he signed the Petition of Right. In

James I was a well-educated monarch. He published articles on such subjects as witchcraft, the dangers of smoking tobacco, and rules for writing Scottish poetry. Unfortunately, he had little skill as a statesman. James was once described as "the most learned fool in Christendom."

the petition, Charles promised not to collect forced loans or levy taxes without the consent of Parliament. He also agreed not to imprison a person without cause or to house soldiers in private homes without the owner's consent. Through the Petition of Right, Parliament hoped to end the king's arbitrary actions.

However, once Parliament approved the funds he needed, Charles dissolved it. For the next 11 years, he ruled without calling another Parliament. He ignored the Petition of Right and returned to the policies of James I.

During the 1630s, Charles made many enemies because of his arbitrary rule. He appointed unpopular officials such as William Laud to be Archbishop of Canterbury. Laud persecuted Puritans and other dissenters, as Protestants who would not accept Anglican practices were called. Charles and his advisors also used special courts such as the Court

417

of High Commission and the Court of Star Chamber to silence opposition. These courts did not have to follow common law or use juries.

The gulf between the king and the country grew wider. A revolt in Scotland finally brought matters to a head. In 1638, Charles tried to impose the Anglican Church on Scotland, where the official religion was Presbyterian. The Scots resisted and invaded England. Because Charles needed money to equip and pay an army, he summoned Parliament in 1640.

The Long Parliament

The Parliament that was called in 1640 would meet in one form or another until 1660. Known as the Long Parliament, it would eventually lead a revolution against the monarchy. But in 1640, Parliament was chiefly concerned with limiting the king's power and removing unpopular officials.

Before granting Charles's request for money, Parliament demanded the trial of Charles's chief ministers, Archbishop Laud and the Earl of Strafford, for abusing power. Both men were found guilty and executed.

Parliament abolished the Court of High Commission and the Court of Star Chamber. It also passed a bill stating that the king had to call a parliament at least once every three years. As the Long Parliament continued to meet, critics of the king grew more outspoken. Eventually they pushed through a bill condemning Charles as a tyrant.

Charles struck back by leading a band of armed supporters into Parliament in an unsuccessful attempt to arrest five outspoken members. The king's use of force made compromise impossible. In 1642, the king and Parliament raised their own armies, and civil war began.

The English Civil War

The civil war lasted from 1642 to 1649. People of all classes fought on both sides. In general, nobles and people in rural areas, especially in northwestern England, rallied to the king's

STYLES OF DRESS DURING THE ENGLISH CIVIL WAR Wide differences help explain the styles of dress of the two men in this painting by artist Larry Bernetti. At left is a flamboyant Cavalier, a supporter of King Charles I. Cavaliers were wealthy aristocrats who usually belonged to the Anglican Church. The man at right is a Roundhead, a Puritan who opposed the king. His close-cut hair and his plain, dark clothes reflect his rejection of the style of the Cavaliers.

side. The king's supporters were called Cavaliers because the aristocratic leaders were mounted horsemen, or cavalry.

Parliament recruited its troops mostly from the middle class, especially from towns in southeastern England. Many Puritans fought for Parliament. Supporters of Parliament were called Roundheads because they cut their hair close to their heads to show that they rejected the aristocratic style of long hair.

In 1645, Oliver Cromwell, a strong-minded Puritan officer, reorganized Parliament's army as the New Model Army. Under his energetic leadership, the New Model Army became a well-disciplined force. In several battles, it defeated the Cavaliers and in 1646 captured Charles I.

The Long Parliament, which had continued to meet during the civil war, decided the king should be put on trial. In January 1649, a court ordered the execution of Charles I, which you read about at the beginning of this section. The House of Commons then abolished the monarchy and the House of Lords and proclaimed England a republic. Thus, the civil war led to a revolution in English government.

The Commonwealth

Oliver Cromwell was chosen to lead the English republic, which became known as the Commonwealth. Cromwell was a man with high moral principles. He supported religious toleration for all Protestants but not for Catholics. He hoped that he could restore peace with the help of Parliament.

Yet the civil war had left England bitterly divided. Presbyterians, Anglicans, and Puritans had differing views about the kind of government England should have. In addition, some extreme reformers wanted to push the revolution further. One group, the Levellers, led by John Lilburne, demanded that titles of nobility be abolished. They also thought all English men should have the right to vote, a startling idea at a time when only a small number of property owners could vote.

Parliament itself was so seriously divided that Cromwell dissolved it in 1654. He then took the title Lord Protector and ruled England as a dictator until his death in 1658. As Lord Protector, Cromwell depended on the army to govern the country. Army officials imposed strict Puritan rule. They closed thea-

DAILY LIFE Life Under the Puritans

From around England, torn by civil war, the reports poured into London. Puritan soldiers were storming Anglican churches, chopping the heads off statues, smashing stained-glass windows, melting down church bells, and burning hymnals and songbooks. To Puritans, it was sinful to mix the worship of God with "worldly" pleasures like art and music. "The more ceremonies," one Puritan said tersely, "the less truth."

Under the Puritan-led Parliament and later under Oliver Cromwell, English men and women had to obey the strict and solemn rule of the "children of God." The Puritans outlawed horse races, gambling, public dancing, newspapers, and wearing fancy clothes. The Puritans also closed the theaters since to them plays were "spectacles of pleasure too commonly expressing mirth and levity."

Such rigid practices were only one side of Puritan belief. Puritans earnestly believed that all men and women were equal in the sight of God. That idea tended to put rich and poor, aristocrat and commoner, on the same footing. "The most despised person in the realm ought to be treated as if he were the king's brother," insisted one Puritan. Because it leveled the differences between social classes, Puritanism contributed to the growth of democratic ideas in England and America.

1. Why did English Puritans attack Anglican churches?

2. **Critical Thinking** What relationship do you see between the Puritans' ideas about equality and their attitude toward the pleasures of daily life? Explain.

ters, banned newspapers and dancing, and enforced laws that forbade dueling, swearing, and such "vain and profane" activities as taking a walk on the Sabbath.

Cromwell tried to bring Scotland and Ireland under tighter English control. When he met strong resistance, he crushed the Scots and brutally suppressed Catholic rebels in Ireland. He then encouraged Protestants to settle in Ireland, replacing Catholic landlords.*

Cromwell's rule became increasingly unpopular, and people began to long for the restoration of the monarchy. After Cromwell's death, the Long Parliament met again. In 1660, it asked the son of Charles I, who was living in France, to return to England and be crowned Charles II.

The monarchy was thus restored, but the civil war and the Commonwealth were to have lasting effects. The new king would be careful in his dealings with Parliament. And Parliament would take steps to prevent Charles II and future rulers from exercising power arbitrarily.

---

* Both Henry VIII and Elizabeth I had given Protestants lands taken from Catholics in Ireland. Cromwell and later English rulers continued this policy.

SECTION 1 REVIEW

1. **Identify:** (a) William Laud, (b) Long Parliament, (c) Cavalier, (d) Roundhead, (e) Oliver Cromwell, (f) Commonwealth.

2. How did Elizabeth I deal with Parliament?

3. Describe one of the issues that created conflict between James I and Parliament.

4. What limits did the Petition of Right put on the king's power?

5. Describe two actions taken by the Long Parliament that limited the power of the monarch.

6. What problems did Cromwell face in trying to rule England?

7. **Critical Thinking** Explain how the attitudes and actions of the James I and Charles I caused the break with Parliament.

2 Establishing a Limited Monarchy

READ TO UNDERSTAND

☐ **How Parliament became supreme in England.**

☐ **How the Glorious Revolution came about.**

☐ **How constitutional government developed in the 1700s.**

☐ *Vocabulary:* **prime minister.**

"In sixteen hundred and sixty-six," began a popular English rhyme, "London burned like rotten sticks." For four days, the Great Fire raged, consuming thousands of homes and 87 churches. The fire came hard on the heels of another disaster. In the worst outbreak of the bubonic plague since the Black Death of the 1300s, at least 68,000 people died in London alone.

Despite the disasters, the court of Charles II lost little of its brilliance and gaiety. With the restoration of the monarchy came an end to the harsh laws of Cromwell's time. The king reopened theaters and presided over a court in which wit and the pursuit of pleasure were more important than moral standards.

The Restoration Under Charles II

Charles II had spent his years in exile at the French court. Although he admired the absolute power enjoyed by Louis XIV, he knew he must accept limits on his own power. Before taking the throne, Charles agreed to respect the Magna Carta and the Petition of Right. He dealt cautiously with Parliament and generally had its support.

Meanwhile, members of Parliament protected their own interests. Most were landowners, and they passed laws abolishing the feudal dues that landowners paid to the king. In place of the feudal dues, Parliament granted the king income from taxes.*

---

* In England, unlike other parts of Europe, nobles as well as commoners paid taxes.

Charles II secretly preferred the Catholic Church to the Anglican Church, but he knew Parliament would not accept a return to Catholicism. Thus, he urged toleration of all religions. However, the English were not ready to accept such religious toleration. In 1673, Parliament passed the Test Act, which required any person holding public office to belong to the Anglican Church. The Test Act also excluded Catholics and Protestant dissenters from the army, the navy, and universities.

In foreign policy, Charles cooperated with France. He made a secret treaty with Louis XIV, in part because he needed money. In return for Louis's financial support, Charles pledged to restore Catholicism in England as soon as it was practical. He also agreed to join France in a war against the Dutch. Under Charles, the English seized the Dutch colony of New Netherland in North America.

Emergence of Political Parties

During Charles's reign, two political parties emerged in England: the Tories and the Whigs. The Tories generally supported the king and the Anglican Church, while the Whigs wanted to strengthen Parliament.

The Whigs tended to favor toleration of Protestants, but they were fiercely anti-Catholic. As a result, they worried that when Charles, who had no heirs, died, his brother James would inherit the throne. Unlike Charles, who hid his religious opinions, James openly admitted to being Catholic. The Whigs tried to pass the Exclusion Act, which would have barred James from becoming king.

In 1679, the Tories were able to defeat the Exclusion Act, but only by accepting another piece of legislation, the Habeas Corpus Act. The Habeas Corpus Act is still considered one of the most basic guarantees of individual rights because it protects a person from arbitrary arrest. The act provided that if a person were arrested, a judge would issue a "writ of habeas corpus." The "writ" was an order to bring the prisoner before a judge and to state the charges against the person. The judge would then decide whether or not the person should be held for trial.

The Habeas Corpus Act made it illegal for an individual to be held in prison without a trial. It also decreed that a person could not be imprisoned twice for the same crime. Later, the Constitution of the United States would include the rights granted in the Habeas Corpus Act.

James II and the Glorious Revolution

In 1685, James II inherited the throne. James was determined to make Parliament grant toleration for Catholics. Ignoring the Test Act, James placed Catholics in high government posts and in the army. Parliament protested, but it did not move against the king because it believed James eventually would be succeeded by one of his Protestant daughters. Then in 1688, James's second wife, a Catholic, gave birth to a son who became heir to the throne.

Major Events in England 1603–1701	
1603	James I inherits the throne
1628	Charles I signs the Petition of Right
1642	English civil war begins
1649	Parliament declares England a republic; Charles I executed
1660	Restoration of the monarchy; Charles II agrees to respect the Magna Carta and the Petition of Right
1679	Habeas Corpus Act passed
1688–1689	Glorious Revolution; William and Mary sign the Bill of Rights
1701	Act of Settlement passed

Parliament feared that the boy would be raised a Catholic so it acted swiftly. It invited Mary, James's oldest daughter, and her husband, Prince William of Orange, who was ruler of the Dutch Netherlands, to take the English throne. When James realized he had no support in England, he fled the country.

William and Mary agreed to become joint rulers of England. In 1689, Parliament had the new monarchs sign a Bill of Rights to ensure its power and protect English liberties. The signing of the Bill of Rights marked the end of the bloodless revolution that the English call the Glorious Revolution.

This illustration of William and Mary appeared in a children's history book. English children at the time learned history by memorizing rhymes. The rhyming verse at bottom lists the rulers' deeds. Why do you think William is shown holding the English Bill of Rights?

XXVIII. WILLIAM *the* THIRD *and* MARY *the* SECOND, *from* 1688 *to* 1702.

WILLIAM the hero, with MARIA mild,
(He James's nephew, she his eldeſt child)
Fix'd freedom and the church, reform'd the coin;
Oppos'd the French, and ſettled Brunſwick's line.

The English Bill of Rights

The Bill of Rights included several provisions that made Parliament stronger than the monarchy. It stated that the king and queen could not suspend any laws without the consent of Parliament. The monarchs also needed the approval of Parliament to raise taxes and maintain an army. Furthermore, they had to summon Parliament frequently and could not interfere in its elections.

In addition to making Parliament supreme, the Bill of Rights protected the rights of individuals. It guaranteed the right of trial by jury for anyone accused of a crime. It also outlawed cruel and unusual punishments and limited the amount of bail that could be imposed on a person being held for trial.

Despite the limits Parliament placed on the power of the monarchy, English government and society were not democratic. Few people had the right to vote. Members of Parliament were not paid, so only the wealthy could afford to run for office. Religious toleration also remained limited. In 1689, Parliament passed the Act of Toleration. It assured all Protestants freedom of worship, but it did not give the same right to Catholics and followers of other religions.

Ireland and Scotland

Even after the Glorious Revolution, Parliament worried that James II or his heirs might reclaim the throne. This concern influenced relations between England and Ireland.

In 1689, James II led a rebellion in Ireland, hoping to regain the English throne. But he was defeated at the Battle of the Boyne. In an effort to prevent James or any other Catholic from claiming the throne, Parliament passed the Act of Settlement in 1701. It stated that only an Anglican could inherit the English throne.

To prevent any future rebellion, the English Parliament imposed harsh penalties on Catholics in Ireland. Even though the Catholics were a majority in Ireland, they could not buy or inherit land from Protestants. Furthermore, Catholics could not be elected to the Irish Parliament, making it easy for the Protestant minority to rule. English policies in Ireland bred a deep-seated resentment among the Catholic Irish.

Since James II had been king of Scotland, Parliament worried that he or his heirs might reclaim the Scottish throne. To prevent this, Parliament negotiated the Act of Union, which the Scots reluctantly accepted in 1707. The Act of Union joined the kingdoms of England and Scotland into the United Kingdom of Great Britain. (See the map on page 424.)

Although James and his heirs hatched plots to seize the throne, their efforts failed. After the deaths of William and Mary, Anne, James's other Protestant daughter, ruled Britain. The Act of Settlement provided that on Queen Anne's death the throne should pass to the nearest Protestant relative. Thus, in 1714, George, the German elector of Hanover, became King George I of Britain. The peaceful transition from the Stuart to the Hanover dynasty was evidence that the Glorious Revolution had created stable government in Britain.

Growth of Constitutional Government

The English civil war and the Glorious Revolution made Britain into a limited constitutional monarchy—that is, a monarchy whose power was limited by laws and traditions. The British did not have a formal written constitution. Instead, the British constitution was composed of all acts of Parliament and documents such as the Magna Carta, the Petition of Right, and the Bill of Rights. It also included traditions and customs. The relationship between the monarch and Parliament, for example, was based largely on tradition.

In the late 1600s and throughout the 1700s, three developments affected constitutional government in England. First, political parties gained a more well-defined role in Parliament. Second, a cabinet system evolved. Third, the office of prime minister came into existence.

Political parties. As you have read, the Whigs and Tories emerged as political parties after the restoration of Charles II. By the late 1600s, the differences between the two parties had become more distinct.

During the Glorious Revolution, the Whigs supported laws that limited royal power. Most Whigs were wealthy landowners who thought their power would increase as the monarch's power declined. Some Whigs were successful merchants. They favored policies, such as a strong navy, to promote and protect British trade.

The Tories usually defended royal power against challenges by Parliament. Although most Tories were landowners, they usually owned less land than Whigs.

The cabinet. During the late 1600s, King William chose his chief ministers, or advisers, from both political parties in Parliament. But he soon realized that Whig and Tory ministers did not get along. As a result, he began to appoint ministers from the party that held the majority of seats in Parliament. The practice of appointing ministers from the majority party eventually led to the cabinet system of government.

The cabinet was made up of the ministers appointed by the king. Each cabinet member was responsible for a department of government, such as the navy or finance. Cabinet members remained members of Parliament. Therefore, they could both vote for their own policies and try to convince others to do the same.

Eventually, a cabinet would stay in power as long as Parliament approved its policies. If Parliament rejected government policies, the king would call for new elections to Parliament. The new majority party would then form the next cabinet.

The prime minister. The cabinet gained much of its power during the reign of George I in the early 1700s. Born and raised in Hanover, the king spoke only German and did not understand English politics. Therefore, he relied heavily on his English advisers. Sir Robert Walpole, an able and powerful Whig member of Parliament, became the king's chief adviser. Although Walpole did not use the title, he is usually considered the first **prime minister,** or head of the cabinet.

Between 1721 and 1742, Walpole skillfully steered laws through Parliament. He gradually took over from the king the job of appointing many government officials, including other cabinet members. He managed finances well, avoided costly wars, and supported laws that encouraged trade and industry. He allowed the

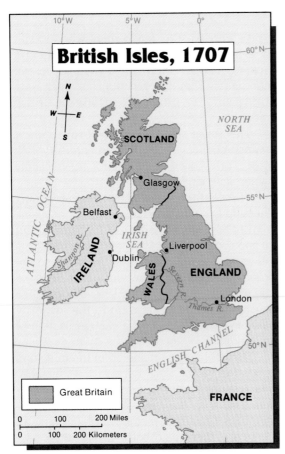

British Isles, 1707

0	100	200 Miles
0	100	200 Kilometers

MAP STUDY *The Act of Union joined Scotland and England in 1707. Ireland remained a separate nation but was ruled by England. What other nation had united with England earlier?*

English colonies in North America to develop on their own and avoided taking a stand on controversial issues. In fact, Walpole's motto was "Let sleeping dogs lie."

Personal Rule of George III

When George III came to the throne in 1760, he felt that the cabinet and Parliament under the Whigs had taken too much power away from the king. Many small landowners agreed with the king, and they supported his efforts to regain control of the government.

From 1770 to 1782, George III supervised the government and appointed ministers. Lord North, George's prime minister, rallied a group in Parliament known as "the king's friends" to support the king's policies. As you will read,

some of those policies angered the American colonists, who declared their independence in 1776.

During the American Revolution, George lost support at home, and Parliament reclaimed its power. It eventually forced the king to accept a new cabinet that would make peace with the United States. Parliament also passed a reform bill that limited the king's right to appoint officials.

SECTION 2 REVIEW

1. **Identify:** (a) Tories, (b) Whigs, (c) Habeas Corpus Act, (d) Glorious Revolution.

2. **Define:** prime minister.

3. Describe the major provision of each of the following acts of Parliament: (a) Test Act; (b) Act of Toleration; (c) Act of Settlement; (d) Act of Union.

4. What limits did the Bill of Rights place on royal power?

5. (a) What policy did Parliament follow in Ireland? (b) What was the result of that policy?

6. **Critical Thinking** How does the system of government that evolved in England during this period differ from the American system of government today?

3 Revolution in Colonial America

READ TO UNDERSTAND

☐ Why English policies angered the American colonists.

☐ How the colonies fought to win independence.

☐ How Enlightenment ideas influenced the writers of the Constitution of the United States.

Young Patrick Henry stood before the Virginia House of Burgesses. He spoke eloquently against Britain's outrageous attempts to tax the colonies. Only the colonial legislatures had the power to raise taxes, he argued. He grew more impassioned as he warned, "Caesar had his Brutus, Charles the First his Cromwell, and George III . . ."

"Treason, treason!" interrupted members of the House. Henry smoothly passed over the interruption, ". . . may profit by their example. If this be treason, make the most of it."

Events in England and Enlightenment ideas greatly influenced people in the 13 American colonies. The colonists believed they should have the same rights that people in England had won during the Glorious Revolution. When the British government appeared to violate these rights, colonial leaders such as Patrick Henry raised a storm of protest.

Governing the Colonies

Between 1700 and 1763, the American colonies expanded rapidly along the eastern seaboard. Busy with wars in Europe, Britain allowed the colonies to develop largely on their own. In most colonies, royal governors appointed by the king controlled trade and appointed judges and other officials. Each colony also had its own elected assembly.* Colonial assemblies had the right to approve laws related to local affairs. They also approved salaries for officials, including the governor, and levied taxes to meet the expenses of local governments.

Although colonists controlled local affairs, Britain regulated colonial trade. During the 1600s, Parliament had passed the Navigation Acts, which reflected mercantilist ideas. One act required colonial merchants to ship goods only on colonial or English vessels. Other acts forbade the colonies to import goods from Europe unless these goods first went to England, where a customs duty was paid to the crown. In addition, certain colonial products,

such as sugar, cotton, and tobacco, could be shipped only to England.

In general, the Navigation Acts benefited the colonies as well as England. The colonies developed their own shipbuilding industries to carry goods to England. In addition, freedom from foreign competition helped colonial merchants build their businesses.

Some New England merchants, however, did not like the Navigation Acts. These merchants relied heavily on sugar and molasses imported from the West Indies. According to the acts, they could buy sugar and molasses only from the British West Indies. In practice, they ignored the law and smuggled sugar and molasses from the French West Indies.

The Road to Revolution

When the Seven Years' War ended in 1763 (see page 388), British policy toward the American colonies changed. The war had been expensive and left Britain deeply in debt. Furthermore, the British had to keep troops in North America to defend the vast territories it won from France. George III and his ministers felt that the American colonies should help pay the costs of their own defense. Therefore, the king urged Parliament to pass a series of laws to raise revenue from the colonies. One of these was the Stamp Act, passed in 1765.

The Stamp Act. The Stamp Act taxed a variety of items, from newspapers, deeds, and wills, to dice and playing cards. People in Britain and in other parts of Europe had been paying such taxes for centuries. But in the American colonies, the Stamp Act caused an angry reaction.

Delegates from 9 colonies met in New York to protest the Stamp Act. They claimed that the colonists had the same rights as other British subjects, including the right to consent to any taxes. They argued that Parliament did not have the right to tax them because they did not send representatives to Parliament. Only colonial assemblies had the right to impose taxes on the colonies.

When the British government tried to enforce the Stamp Act, riots erupted in the major colonial cities. For months, the colonists boycotted British goods, finally forcing Parliament

---

* As in European countries, voting in the colonies was usually limited to men who owned property or paid taxes. However, land was more plentiful in North America, so more people were landowners. Therefore, a much larger percentage of the male population in the colonies could vote than in any European nation.

to repeal the unpopular act. However, Parliament still insisted that it had the right to tax the colonies.

Worsening relations. Between 1765 and 1775, relations between Britain and its American colonies worsened as Parliament imposed new taxes and tried to assert British control over the colonies. In 1773, a group of Bostonians openly showed their contempt for British policies. Disguised as Indians, they dumped a shipment of tea into Boston harbor. Many colonists cheered when they heard of the "Boston Tea Party," as the event was called. The British government was outraged by what it saw as an act of rebellion.

In 1774, to punish the colonists, Parliament passed a series of laws that the colonists called the "Intolerable Acts." Parliament closed the port of Boston, forbade the Massachusetts assembly from holding regular sessions, and placed the colony under military rule. Parliament also passed the Quebec Act, which provided a government for the territories Britain had acquired from France. The act extended the boundaries of Quebec south to the Ohio River. The colonists saw the Quebec Act as an effort to prevent them from moving westward.

In response to these acts, delegates from all the colonies except Georgia met at a Continental Congress in Philadelphia in September 1774. They urged residents of Boston to ignore the Intolerable Acts, and they voted to boycott all British goods. The delegates agreed to meet in a second Continental Congress in the spring of 1775. However, by that time, fighting had broken out between the colonists and British soldiers.

In April 1775, some British troops from Boston were sent to Concord to search for illegal weapons said to be stored there. At Lexington, they met armed colonists, and the first shots of the American Revolution were fired.

The Declaration of Independence

A month later, in May 1775, the Second Continental Congress met in Philadelphia. Some delegates still hoped to reach a compromise with Britain. The more radical delegates ar-

On March 5, 1770, a crowd of angry Bostonians gathered at the Boston customs house. The crowd jeered and threw snowballs at the British soldiers guarding the building. A shot was heard, causing the British to open fire on the crowd. Five colonists were killed in the "Boston Massacre." This engraving of the scene was made by Boston silversmith and patriot Paul Revere. It was widely circulated in the colonies and stirred resentment against the British.

"I thank thee, O Lord, for sparing me to fight this day," prayed an elderly
Massachusetts farmer waiting for the British attack on June 17, 1775. During
the Battle of Bunker Hill, the poorly armed Americans beat back several
British assaults. The battle, fought early in the struggle for freedom, showed
the Americans that they could stand up to well-trained British troops.

gued for independence. Finally, on July 4,
1776, the delegates agreed on a Declaration of
Independence that explained the reasons for
their separation from Britain.

The Declaration of Independence was
drafted largely by Thomas Jefferson from Virginia. A scholar as well as a landowner, Jefferson was familiar with the ideas of Newton,
Locke, and the French philosophes.

Echoing Locke, Jefferson wrote that people had certain natural rights, including "life,
liberty, and the pursuit of happiness." Jefferson also argued that government arose from
an agreement between the ruler and the ruled.
A ruler had power only as long as he or she
had the consent of the governed. Although
people could not overthrow their rulers for
minor reasons, the Declaration of Independence stated that Britain had consistently and
deliberately oppressed the colonists. Therefore, the colonists had the right to rebel.

An American Victory

The American Revolution lasted from 1775 to
1783. At first, the British appeared to have the
military advantage. They had well-trained
troops, and their armies occupied the major
American cities. The Americans had few
trained officers and little military equipment
when the war began. Also, individual colonies
did not always cooperate with one another,
and some colonists did not support the revolution.

Yet the Americans enjoyed several important advantages. They were patriots, fighting
on their own territory for their families and
homes. The British, in contrast, were thousands of miles from home, and it took weeks
or even months for supplies to arrive from
England. Furthermore, although the British
held the cities, the colonists could retreat into
the countryside and then reappear to ambush
the British.

427

Finally, the Americans found a brilliant military leader in George Washington, a Virginia landowner. Washington was able to unite the colonies in their common cause. At first, Washington suffered defeats, but he learned quickly. He successfully reorganized the colonial forces, which won important victories at Trenton in late December 1776 and at Princeton a few days later.

The winter of 1777–1778 marked a turning point in the war. Armed with weapons secretly supplied by France, an American army defeated the British at Saratoga in October 1777. This victory convinced France to give the colonies its official support. In February 1778, France recognized the colonies' independence and signed an alliance with them. France then declared war on its old enemy, Britain, and sent money and troops to the Americans.

In 1781, with the help of the French navy, Washington captured a British army at Yorktown, Virginia. Although George III wanted to continue the war, Parliament forced him to negotiate a peace treaty that recognized the independence of the United States.

Framing a Constitution

The newly independent nation faced many challenges. It had to form a government that

MAP STUDY *In November 1782, the British and the Americans signed the Treaty of Paris, which ended the American Revolutionary War. The American Congress ratified the treaty in April 1783. According to the treaty, the British recognized the independence of the United States. What areas were disputed between the United States and other nations? Which nations claimed Alaska?*

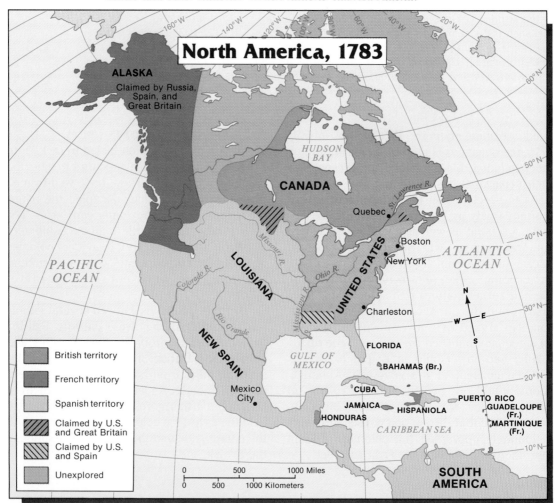

North America, 1783

ALASKA
Claimed by Russia, Spain, and Great Britain

HUDSON BAY

CANADA

Quebec

Boston

New York

UNITED STATES

ATLANTIC OCEAN

PACIFIC OCEAN

LOUISIANA

Missouri R.

Ohio R.

Mississippi R.

Colorado R.

Charleston

Rio Grande

NEW SPAIN

FLORIDA

GULF OF MEXICO

BAHAMAS (Br.)

Mexico City

CUBA

JAMAICA   HISPANIOLA

HONDURAS

PUERTO RICO
GUADELOUPE (Fr.)
MARTINIQUE (Fr.)

CARIBBEAN SEA

SOUTH AMERICA

British territory

French territory

Spanish territory

Claimed by U.S. and Great Britain

Claimed by U.S. and Spain

Unexplored

0   500   1000 Miles

0   500   1000 Kilometers

would bind the 13 states together and at the same time preserve the liberties the people had just won. Between 1781 and 1789, the United States operated under a constitution called the Articles of Confederation. The Articles created a congress that had limited powers. It could not even collect taxes. Most of the political power remained with the individual states.

Washington and other leaders warned that the nation faced great dangers if the states did not cooperate. After all, Britain was still a threat because it had refused to withdraw its troops from several frontier military posts. In 1787, leaders met in Philadelphia to revise the Articles of Confederation. They soon decided to draft a new constitution instead. In 1788, after much debate and compromise, the individual states ratified the Constitution of the United States.

The men who wrote the Constitution were inspired by the works of Locke and Montesquieu. Both philosophers had suggested that the separation of powers would prevent tyranny in government. The Constitution therefore established three separate branches of government: a legislature—the Congress made up of the House of Representatives and the Senate; an executive—the President; and a judiciary—the system of national courts.

In *The Spirit of Laws,* Montesquieu had proposed that none of the branches of government should have too much power. Therefore, the framers of the Constitution set up a system of checks and balances. For example, the President was given the power to appoint officials and negotiate treaties, but the Senate had to approve these actions. Before a bill could become law, it had to be passed by both houses of Congress and signed by the President. The Supreme Court had the power to decide if a law was constitutional.

When the Constitution was sent to the states for approval, several states asked for a bill of rights to guarantee the personal liberties of citizens. In 1791, the Bill of Rights was added as the first ten amendments to the Constitution. The Bill of Rights protected such basic rights as freedom of speech, press, and religion; the rights of persons accused of crimes; and protection against unreasonable searches of people's homes. Many of these rights were the same ones that the English Bill of Rights provided for. (See page 422.)

Impact of the American Revolution

When the states ratified the Constitution, the revolutionary era in America ended. The United States had established itself as an independent, democratic republic that protected the liberties of its citizens. But the American Revolution would have consequences far beyond the United States.

To many people in Europe and other parts of the world, the events in North America symbolized a dramatic struggle for freedom. The colonists had broken away from their powerful British rulers and had created a government that put the ideas of the Enlightenment into practice.

In the years ahead, the Declaration of Independence and the Constitution of the United States would be used as models by other peoples of the world.

SECTION 3 REVIEW

1. **Identify:** (a) Stamp Act, (b) Boston Tea Party, (c) Intolerable Acts, (d) Thomas Jefferson, (e) George Washington, (f) Articles of Confederation, (g) Bill of Rights.

2. (a) How did the Navigation Acts help the colonies? (b) What effect did they have on New England merchants who imported molasses from the West Indies?

3. Why did the colonists object to paying taxes to Britain?

4. List three factors that helped the Americans defeat the British.

5. Why did the framers of the Constitution establish a system of checks and balances?

6. **Critical Thinking** How did the ideas of Enlightenment thinkers affect the American colonies?

CHAPTER 18 REVIEW

Summary

1. **In the early 1600s, the Stuart kings of England and Parliament clashed.** By 1642, the dispute resulted in the English civil war. Under Oliver Cromwell, Parliamentary forces captured, tried, and executed Charles I. Cromwell governed England during the Commonwealth.

2. **After Cromwell's death, the English restored the monarchy, but its power was limited.** By 1688, King James II and Parliament were at odds over religion. When James fled England, Parliament invited William and Mary to take the throne. Parliament protected the rights of individuals through the Bill of Rights.

3. **In 1776, the American colonies declared their independence.** Parliament had tried taxing its American colonies to help pay for their own defense, but the colonists rejected Parliament's authority to tax them. After winning the war against Britain, the United States adopted a constitution that guaranteed a stable, democratic government. That constitution became a model for other peoples.

Recalling Facts

Choose the word or phrase that best completes each of the following statements.

1. Elizabeth I was a popular queen in part because she (a) restored the Catholic Church; (b) kept on good terms with Parliament; (c) reconquered English lands in France.

2. In 1628, Parliament granted money to Charles I only after he signed the (a) Petition of Right; (b) Exclusion Act; (c) Test Act.

3. During the Commonwealth, England was a (a) monarchy; (b) republic; (c) democracy.

4. The Habeas Corpus Act protected individual rights by granting freedom (a) of speech; (b) of religion; (c) from unjust arrest.

5. The English Bill of Rights limited the power of (a) Parliament; (b) the monarchy; (c) the prime minister.

6. The Stamp Act angered many American colonists because it (a) limited their trade with other countries; (b) taxed them without their consent; (c) prevented them from moving westward.

7. The framers of the United States Constitution adopted the ideas of checks and balances that had been proposed by (a) Montesquieu; (b) Hobbes; (c) Locke.

Chapter Checkup

1. (a) Describe James I's views on the power of kings. (b) How did his views contribute to conflict with Parliament?

2. (a) What policies of Charles I angered Parliament? (b) What steps did Parliament take to limit the king's power? (c) How did Charles I respond to the actions of Parliament?

3. (a) What was the outcome of the English civil war? (b) Describe English government during the Commonwealth.

4. (a) Describe the political parties that emerged in Parliament during the Restoration. (b) Which party wanted to prevent James II from becoming king? (c) Did it succeed? Explain.

5. (a) What events led to the Glorious Revolution in England? (b) What was the outcome of the Glorious Revolution?

6. Describe the role of each of the following in British government during the 1700s: (a) political parties; (b) the cabinet; (c) prime minister.

7. (a) In what ways were the American colonies relatively free from British control before 1763? (b) Why did British policy toward the colonies change after 1763?

(c) How did the colonists react to the change?

8. Describe the Enlightenment ideas included in the Constitution of the United States.

Critical Thinking

1. **Evaluating** (a) Which English monarchs that you read about in this chapter dealt most successfully with Parliament? Why? (b) What characteristics do you think would have helped a ruler get along with Parliament?

2. **Understanding the Roots of Democracy** (a) What ideas about government do you think English settlers brought with them to America in the 1600s and 1700s? (b) How might those ideas have contributed to the American Revolution?

3. **Relating Past to Present** How do you think the success of the American Revolution still affects people today?

Developing Basic Skills

1. **Ranking** List the events and acts of Parliament that led to the establishment of a limited constitutional monarchy in England. Then rank them according to which you think was most important in limiting the power of the monarch. Explain why you ranked them in that order.

2. **Comparing** Make a chart with three columns and three rows. Label the columns English Civil War, Glorious Revolution, and American Revolution. Label the rows Date, Causes, Results. Use what you read in this chapter to complete the chart. (a) How were the causes of each struggle similar? (b) How were they different? (c) How were the results of the Glorious Revolution and the American Revolution similar? (d) How were they different?

Writing About History

Using Specialized Reference Books

Specialized reference books provide detailed information about a particular subject area. Several kinds of specialized reference books are listed below. Most of these books can be found in the reference section of your library and may not be taken out of the library.

Encyclopedia of World History—a digest of the whole range of world history, chronologically arranged.

The New Cambridge Modern History—a 14-volume history that begins in 1493.

The Times Atlas of World History—maps of the world throughout history.

Webster's Biographical Dictionary—brief entries on leading men and women in all periods of history.

Webster's Geographical Dictionary—a source book about places in the world.

Practice: Use one of the specialized reference books mentioned above to find additional information about a topic discussed in this chapter. Identify the source and write a brief paragraph explaining what you have learned.

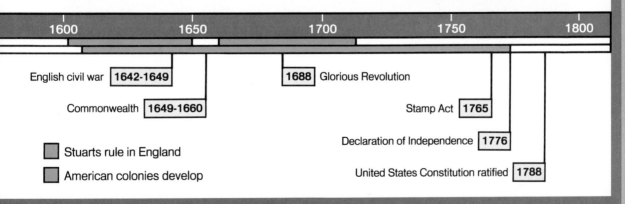

| 1600 | 1650 | 1700 | 1750 | 1800 |

English civil war 1642-1649

1688 Glorious Revolution

Commonwealth 1649-1660

Stamp Act 1765

Declaration of Independence 1776

United States Constitution ratified 1788

☐ Stuarts rule in England

☐ American colonies develop

431

The French Revolution
and Napoleon

19

(1789–1815)

When the Duke de Liancourt told King Louis XVI about the storming of the Bastille, the king angrily exclaimed, "This is a revolt!" "No, Sire," replied the duke, "it is a revolution."

Bread and other foods were scarce all over Paris. Talk of revolution filled the air. From Versailles came reports that the king was refusing to consider reforms demanded by popular leaders. Poor people in Paris were angry with the government, which seemed to be ignoring their problems. They turned that anger into action.

On July 14, 1789, Louis de Flue was expecting trouble. De Flue was an officer in the Swiss guards who protected the Bastille, a huge prison fortress in Paris. Many people believed that hundreds of French citizens were unjustly imprisoned in the Bastille. By 3 P.M. that day, a large mob had surrounded the fortress, demanding its surrender.

Still, Louis de Flue was not worried. He knew that the Bastille could be defended until reinforcements arrived. But to his surprise, as the mob grew, the commander of the Bastille, the Marquis de Launay, did not defend the outer drawbridge. Instead, de Launay offered to surrender the fortress if his troops were allowed to leave peacefully. But the crowd replied, "No surrender! Lower the bridge!"

De Flue watched helplessly as the second drawbridge was lowered, and the mob swarmed into the courtyard. Armed with axes, the crowd ran to the prison cells and freed the astonished inmates. The mob found only seven prisoners in the entire fortress.

De Flue was led roughly along the streets of Paris while angry citizens called for his death. "Swords, bayonets, and pistols were being continually pressed against me," he recalled later. "I felt that my last moment had come." Fortunately for de Flue, the guards held back the crowd. But de Launay and many others died that night.

To the common people in Paris, the Bastille stood for the tyranny of the absolute monarchy in France. The fall of the Bastille showed that the people of Paris would be ready to take the lead in the French Revolution. The French Revolution went through many stages and had far-reaching effects, not only in France but in all of Europe. ■

1 The French Monarchy in Crisis

READ TO UNDERSTAND

☐ **What classes existed in France under the Old Regime.**

☐ **How ancient traditions held back progress in France.**

☐ **Why France needed political and economic reform.**

"After us, the deluge [flood]," went an old French saying. Many people believed King Louis XV spoke these words as he presided over a lavish court, enjoying life to the fullest and not caring about the future. As heir to the Sun King, Louis XIV, he ruled the richest nation in Europe.

France under Louis XV led Europe in culture and manners. French philosophers led the Enlightenment, and Europeans slavishly copied French fashions in clothes, art, and even cooking. Yet, by the mid-1700s, France faced a growing crisis. The French economy was in serious trouble. Before long the French monarchy would be destroyed. Attempts to solve the problems of the country would be hampered by the traditional political and social system of France, which historians call the Old Regime.

Structure of the Old Regime

Under the Old Regime, the king was an absolute monarch. Louis XIV had centralized power in the royal bureaucracy—the departments that carried out his policies. Louis's successors lacked his abilities to govern. Still, they protected royal power and the rigid social structure of the Old Regime.

As you have read, the people of France were divided by law into three estates: clergy, nobility, and commoners. (See page 204.) The first two estates—the clergy and the nobility—enjoyed many privileges. In general, they opposed any reforms that would threaten their privileges. However, the Third Estate—the commoners—had many grievances against the Old Regime.

The First and Second Estates. The First Estate consisted of the higher clergy, who were nobles, and the parish priests, who were commoners. Some of the higher clergy lived in luxury. Parish priests usually lived a simple, hardworking life. Many of them criticized social injustices and resented the privileges of the higher clergy.

The clergy managed church affairs, ran schools, kept birth and death records, and cared for the poor. To support these activities, the clergy collected the tithe, a tax on income. The church owned vast amounts of property on which it paid no taxes.

The Second Estate, or nobility, made up less than 2 percent of the French population. (See the graphs on page 435.) Many nobles enjoyed great wealth and privileges. Only nobles could become officers in the army or fill high offices of the church. In addition, nobles were exempt from most taxes.

Not all French nobles were wealthy. Some lived in near poverty in the country. However, they firmly defended their traditional privileges. When rising prices reduced their income, they made peasants on their estates pay long-forgotten feudal dues.

After Louis XIV's death in 1715, French nobles tried to regain the political power they had lost during his reign. Leading the effort were the wealthy and influential "nobles of the robe," who had received noble status for their services to the royal government. Many were judges in the parlements, or high courts. The parlements had to register, or approve, the king's orders before they became laws. Nobles of the robe sometimes exercised this power and refused to approve the king's orders if the orders limited their power.

The Third Estate. The vast majority of French people were commoners belonging to the Third Estate. The Third Estate included the bourgeoisie, or middle class, as well as peasants, and city workers.

Although small in numbers, the bourgeoisie was the wealthiest, most outspoken group within the Third Estate. The bourgeoisie included successful merchants and manufacturers, lawyers and doctors, as well as small storekeepers and artisans. They resented the privileges of nobles. Many criticized the Old Regime because they believed in the Enlightenment ideas of equality and social justice. The bourgeoisie called for reform of the tax system because the Third Estate had to pay most of the taxes.

Peasants made up the largest group within the Third Estate. In general, French peasants were better off than peasants in other parts of Europe. Serfdom had largely disappeared in France, although French peasants still paid many feudal dues dating back to the Middle Ages. French peasants also had to perform unpaid services for their landlords and the king. For example, if peasants lived near a royal road, they had to spend as much as a month every year repairing the road.

Peasants were burdened by heavy taxes, the tithe to the church, and rents to their landlords. The privileges of nobles added to the peasants' troubles. For example, only nobles could hunt. Peasants were forbidden to kill rabbits and birds that ate their crops. Nobles also damaged crops by galloping across fields during hunts.

Another group within the Third Estate was city workers. In the towns and cities of France, thousands of men and women worked as servants, apprentices, and day laborers. Workers suffered when inflation hit because food prices rose faster than their wages. Like the bourgeoisie and peasants, city workers resented the privileges enjoyed by the First and Second Estates.

The Growing Economic Crisis

During much of the 1700s, the French economy prospered. The population grew from about 18 million people in 1715 to about 25 million in 1789. Farmers produced food surpluses that fed the growing population and supported economic expansion. Mercantilist policies helped manufacturers in the textile and mining industries.

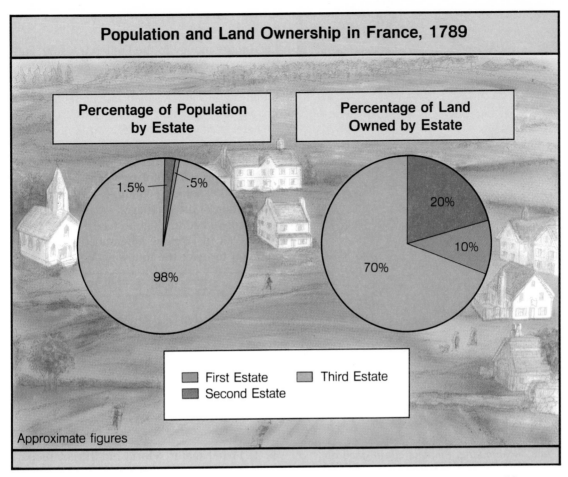

Population and Land Ownership in France, 1789

Percentage of Population by Estate

1.5% .5%

98%

Percentage of Land Owned by Estate

20%

10%

70%

First Estate   Third Estate
Second Estate

Approximate figures

GRAPH STUDY *These graphs clearly show the unequal distribution of land in France. Moreover, within the Third Estate, a small number of bourgeoisie owned much of the land. Thus, peasants ended up with only 45 percent of the land. Which estate owned the largest percentage of land per member?*

In the 1770s, however, economic activity slowed. Poor harvests hurt the economy. In addition, regulations surviving from the Middle Ages limited expansion of trade and manufacturing. A merchant who shipped a wagonload of wine from the upper Loire Valley to Paris had to pay 11 separate customs duties and 12 different tolls. Furthermore, guilds still had monopolies over the production of certain goods. As a result, entrepreneurs could not set up their own businesses.

However, the most serious economic problem facing the French government during the 1770s and 1780s was the huge debt it owed to bankers. The government had borrowed large amounts of money to pay for the wars of Louis XIV. Louis XV and Louis XVI continued to borrow money to support the court at Ver-

sailles and to fight wars to maintain French power in Europe and overseas. French support of the American Revolution alone nearly doubled the government's debt.

Attempts at Reform

When Louis XVI came to the throne in 1774, he saw the need for economic reform. But Louis was not a very determined or able ruler. He preferred to spend his days hunting or tinkering with puzzles rather than coping with economic problems. Moreover, Louis lacked the strength of will to back his ministers when they pressed for reforms.

Louis's first finance minister, Robert Turgot (ter GOH), eased the financial crisis for a time by controlling government spending and

435

At 15 years of age, Marie Antoinette of Austria married Louis, heir to the French throne. When Louis became king, the new queen gave no thought to the welfare of the people. Instead, she spent lavishly on dresses and jewelry. As economic conditions in France worsened, many people blamed the queen.

reducing expenses at Versailles. He also removed some internal customs duties on food and tried to limit the power of the guilds. But he had little success when he proposed a major reform—taxing the nobles.

The king could not tax the nobles unless the parlements approved new tax laws. But these law courts were controlled by the nobles of the robe, and they stubbornly rejected Turgot's suggestion that they should be taxed. As one noble said, "All public financial burdens should be borne by the lower classes."

When Turgot came under attack, the king dismissed him. As he left office in 1776, Turgot ominously warned the king, "Remember, sire, that it was weakness that brought the head of Charles I to the block."

For a time, the government limped along on new bank loans. Then, in 1786, as the government debts mounted, bankers refused to lend more money to the French treasury. Further, in 1787 and 1788 poor harvests caused bread shortages all over France. The economic situation worsened, and Louis XVI went before the Parlement of Paris to try to make it register a new tax law. "Sire, this is illegal!" one member exclaimed. "It is legal," countered Louis XVI, "because I wish it!" But even royal wishes could not prevail.

The desperate economic crisis and the opposition of the privileged classes to any reform convinced the king to take a bold action. In the fall of 1788, he summoned the Estates General to meet the following May.

SECTION 1 REVIEW

1. **Identify:** (a) Old Regime, (b) Robert Turgot.

2. (a) What groups made up each of the three estates in France? (b) What privileges did the First and Second Estates enjoy?

3. List three factors that contributed to the economic crisis in France.

4. (a) What major reform did Turgot recommend? (b) Was he able to make the reform? Why or why not?

5. **Critical Thinking** Explain how traditions and customs from medieval times caused problems for France in the 1700s.

---

2 A Moderate Start to the Revolution

READ TO UNDERSTAND

☐ **What reforms the National Assembly passed.**

☐ **How the Constitution of 1791 changed France.**

☐ **What role the people of Paris and the peasants played in the French Revolution.**

☐ *Vocabulary:* **émigré.**

"We have the baker and the baker's wife and the little cook-boy. Now we shall have bread," shouted the mob in October 1789, referring to the king and his family. They had marched from Paris to Versailles and forced Louis XVI, his wife, Marie Antoinette, and their son to return to Paris with them. There the mob could be sure that the king provided them with bread.

When Louis XVI summoned the Estates General the previous year, he could not have imagined bowing to the demands of a Paris mob. Instead, he had hoped to win support for reforms that would help the economy. The Estates General had not met since 1614. No one could predict what would happen when the representatives of the three estates met at Versailles.

From Estates General to National Assembly

Each estate elected its own delegates, or deputies, to the Estates General. Within the Third Estate, almost all adult men had the right to vote for representatives to local assemblies. These assemblies, in turn, elected their deputies to the Estates General.

When the Estates General met in May 1789, deputies from the Third Estate demanded that the three estates meet together. They also wanted each deputy to have an equal vote. In the past, the three estates had met separately. Each estate voted as a group and had one vote. That way the First and Second Estates could outvote the Third Estate two to one. The Third Estate now hoped that if the estates met together and deputies voted individually, sympathizers among the clergy and nobles would give the Third Estate a majority.

The king rejected the plan, insisting that the estates meet separately. Deputies from the Third Estate then declared themselves the National Assembly. They claimed the right to write a constitution for France. Louis XVI promptly banished them from their meeting hall.

Joined by many of the lower clergy and some reform-minded nobles, deputies of the Third Estate gathered at a nearby tennis court. There, they swore an oath, known as the Tennis Court Oath, promising not to disband until they had written a constitution. Louis XVI hesitated but then ordered the other two estates to join the Third Estate in the National Assembly. The Third Estate had taken a peaceful first step in a revolution that would eventually transform France.

In the National Assembly, there were deep divisions among the estates and even within each one. Most nobles and clergy wanted to protect their privileges. However, some nobles and lower clergy, along with many commoners, wanted to set up a limited, constitutional monarchy like the one in Great Britain. A few radical reformers demanded equality for all classes before the law. They wanted to abolish titles of nobility and all feudal obligations. They distrusted the king and opposed any constitution that would leave him with significant powers.

Popular Uprisings

The National Assembly had scarcely begun work on a constitution in July 1789 when the people of Paris and peasants in the countryside took the French Revolution along a new, more radical course. Peasants and workers

Jacques Louis David, an artist of the French Revolution, painted this work, **The Tennis Court Oath.** *The actual scene was even more chaotic. Members of the Third Estate along with some clergy and nobles pledged "never to separate but to meet in any place that circumstances may require, until the constitution of the kingdom is established on firm foundations."*

had expected quick relief from taxes and poverty when the Estates General met. But little had happened. Instead, they still faced inflation, unemployment, and food shortages. Reports that the king was concentrating troops around Paris added to the unrest.

When Louis brought troops to Versailles, many people feared that he planned to dissolve the National Assembly and crush the revolution. In reaction, on July 14, 1789, a Paris crowd stormed the Bastille, as you read at the beginning of the chapter. They saw the attack on the Bastille as an attack on the injustice and inequality of the Old Regime.

Disturbances soon spread to the countryside. During the summer of 1789, peasants were caught up in what was called the "Great Fear." Rumors flew from village to village that bandits were destroying crops and homes all over France. Peasants took up arms to defend themselves.

When no bandits appeared, the frightened peasants turned on their landlords. They raided grain storehouses, destroyed tax records, and swore never again to pay feudal dues. Like the people of Paris, the peasants were launching their own revolution against the Old Regime.

Reforms of the National Assembly

The events in Paris and the countryside forced the National Assembly into action. During a long session on the night of August 4, 1789, many deputies rose to make impassioned speeches in support of reform. One noble urged that nobles be taxed. Another proposed that nobles give up their hunting rights. The clergy promised to end its tithes.

By the end of the evening, the Assembly had abolished most feudal customs. It ended serfdom and the tax-exempt privileges of the nobles. It also made all male citizens eligible for government and church positions. "Just like our Frenchmen," commented the Comte de Mirabeau, a moderate leader. "They spend an entire month wrangling over syllables, and in a night overturn the whole of the ancient order of the kingdom!"

Before the end of August, the National Assembly adopted the Declaration of the Rights of Man. The Declaration stated the democratic principles that would be the basis for French government. It called for equality for all citizens under the law and protection of personal property. However, the task of turning these ideals into a constitution remained.

While lawyers debated the wording of a constitution, angry Paris crowds rioted, forcing the National Assembly to take note of their demands. Many rioters were middle-class shopkeepers and artisans.

The march on Versailles. In October 1789, a Paris crowd led by thousands of women marched in the rain to Versailles. The women were angry about high food prices. They also suspected that the king and the queen were plotting against the National Assembly. As you read earlier, they demanded that Louis XVI and his family return with them to Paris, where they could watch over the king's activities. To prevent violence, the king agreed.

The return to Paris presented a striking scene. The king rode on horseback, escorted by a cheering crowd. He wore the tricolor, the red, white, and blue ribbon that the revolutionaries had adopted as their symbol. By forcing the king to wear the tricolor, the people showed that they were directing events in France. A few days later, the National Assembly also moved to Paris and continued its work under the watchful eye of revolutionaries in the capital.

Religious reforms. All over France, the revolution swept away ancient customs and privileges. The National Assembly declared freedom of worship and abolished the special privileges of the Catholic Church. In 1790, it passed the Civil Constitution of the Clergy, which gave the French government control of the church and allowed citizens to elect bishops and priests. To raise badly needed money, the government began selling church lands. This action caused many Catholics who had supported the revolution up to this point to condemn it.

The Constitution of 1791. In 1791, the National Assembly finally gave France its first constitution. The Constitution of 1791 made France a limited monarchy and set up a system of separation of powers. At the head of the

Women played a major role in the French Revolution. This picture shows the women's march on Versailles. On October 5, 1789, a rumor that the king had worn the white symbol of the Bourbons rather than the revolutionary tricolor sent Parisian women hurrying to Versailles. Faced with the crowd of angry women, Louis XVI agreed to accompany them back to Paris.

executive branch was the king. A legislature made the laws. The king could veto laws, but the legislature could override his veto. A new system of courts was set up as the judicial branch.

The constitution guaranteed equal rights under the law to all citizens. It erased the old distinctions between clergy, nobles, and commoners. "The feudal system is forever abolished in France," it declared.

Responses to the First Stage of the Revolution

Few people were satisfied with the new constitutional monarchy. Radical revolutionaries wanted a republic rather than a monarchy. For many nobles, the Constitution of 1791 went too far. Frightened by angry crowds, a growing number of nobles fled France. These **émigrés,** or political exiles, urged European rulers to oppose the revolutionaries in France.

Louis XVI grew increasingly alarmed at the actions of the National Assembly. He sought outside help, and Marie Antoinette appealed to her brother, the emperor of Austria, for support. In June 1791, the royal family decided to flee the country. As they fled toward the border, however, the king was recognized. The National Assembly sent officers to arrest the royal family and bring them back to the capital. A virtual prisoner of the Assembly, the king reluctantly accepted the new constitution in September.

In October 1791, the Legislative Assembly, elected under the new constitution, met for the first time. The seating arrangements in the Assembly reflected divisions among the revolutionaries. Moderate revolutionaries sat on the right side of the meeting hall, and radical revolutionaries sat on the left side.*

The king's attempt to flee the country had deepened the divisions among the revolutionaries. Moderates were embarrassed but still wanted a constitutional monarchy. Radicals distrusted the king and demanded a republic.

However, the radicals themselves were split. The most radical group, the Jacobins, demanded a democracy in which all male citizens had the right to vote. As the French Revolution unfolded, the Jacobins and their leader, Maximilien Robespierre (ROHBS pyehr), would gain the upper hand.

---

* The seating arrangement in the Assembly led to the use of "right" and "left" to describe political views. The right came to refer to people who wanted to preserve tradition. The left came to refer to people who supported far-reaching changes. People with views between the right and left were called the center.

1. **Identify:** (a) National Assembly, (b) Tennis Court Oath, (c) Declaration of the Rights of Man, (d) Civil Constitution of the Clergy.

2. **Define:** émigré.

3. Why did the Third Estate want the Estates General to meet as a single body?

4. (a) What conditions led to unrest among workers and peasants in the summer of 1789? (b) How did the National Assembly react to that unrest?

5. What two groups were dissatisfied with the Constitution of 1791? Why?

6. **Critical Thinking** Which of the changes introduced in France between 1789 and 1791 do you think were the most radical? Why?

3 The Revolution Deepens

READ TO UNDERSTAND

☐ How other European nations responded to the French Revolution.

☐ How the National Convention met threats to the revolution.

☐ Why the Reign of Terror occurred.

☐ How the revolution affected the daily life of the French people.

Called to defend the revolution, soldiers from Marseille hurried to Paris. On the way north, they sang a patriotic marching song, called the *Marseillaise*, that later became the national anthem of France:

> Let's go, children of the homeland,
> Our day of glory has arrived.
> Against us stands tyranny,
> The bloody flag is raised.
> To arms, citizens!
> Join the battalions.
> Let us march, let us march!

This stirring call to arms became necessary as the revolution unfolded. Its message and ideas spread across Europe. But the unrest disturbed European rulers, who began to take steps to turn back the tide of the revolution. French émigrés urged Austria and Prussia to invade France and restore Louis XVI to full power. At the same time, many revolutionary leaders in France wanted war because they thought it would unite the people in defense of their homeland.

France at War

France declared war on Austria in April 1792. Prussia then joined Austria. At first, the war went badly for France. French armies were disorganized and poorly led. Many army officers, who were nobles, had left France. Revolutionary ideas also caused problems. For example, in the heat of battle, one democratically minded regiment demanded to vote on whether or not to attack the enemy.

By August 1792, Austrian and Prussian armies were advancing on Paris. The Prussian commander, the Duke of Brunswick, issued a declaration, known as the Brunswick Manifesto. He warned that if Paris did not surrender peacefully Austrian and Prussian troops would burn the city and put its leaders to the "tortures which they have deserved."

Far from being frightened by the duke's message, the people of Paris angrily declared that no émigrés or foreign troops would crush the revolution. All over France, people rallied to defend the revolution and chanted the slogan: "Liberty, Equality, and Fraternity." A hastily assembled army marched out to meet the Prussians. In September, the French defeated the Duke of Brunswick at Valmy. In the months that followed, revolutionary armies forced the invaders to retreat from France.

Despite these victories, the war against Austria and Prussia caused high prices and desperate food shortages in France. Even while foreign troops threatened Paris, angry Parisians and sympathetic troops from the provinces joined in an uprising that has been called the second French Revolution.

Early in the morning of August 10, 1792, radical revolutionaries took over the Paris city government and set up a new administration, the Commune. Revolutionary troops attacked the palace where the king and his family lived and killed many of the king's guards.

The king and queen fled to the Legislative Assembly, hoping for protection. But the radicals had also seized control of the Assembly. They removed the king from office and voted to imprison the royal family. They then called for a national convention to write a new constitution.

The National Convention

The elections for delegates to the National Convention took place in a tense atmosphere. Austrian and Prussian troops were not far from Paris. In early September, mobs of poor people roamed the streets of the capital, killing anyone they suspected of being an enemy of France. The Convention delegates who were elected in such an atmosphere were far more radical than the people in general.

The National Convention met in late September. As its first act, it voted to abolish the monarchy and make France a republic. The Convention then had to decide what to do with the king. The radical Jacobins demanded that Louis be tried for treason. More moderate revolutionaries thought he should be imprisoned until the war ended.

In November, the Convention announced that a trunk had been discovered containing letters written by the king. The letters showed that Louis was plotting with émigrés to crush the revolution. The damaging evidence sealed the king's fate. The Convention tried and convicted Louis XVI of treason. By a majority of one vote, the delegates sentenced him to death. On January 21, 1793, Louis mounted the steps of the guillotine. "People, I die innocent!" were the king's last words to the watching crowd. (See page 442.)

Attacks on the Revolution

News of Louis XVI's execution sent shock waves through the capitals of Europe. Other monarchs now had every reason to fear the spread of the revolution. By 1793, French armies seemed to be fighting well. They had captured the Austrian Netherlands and were

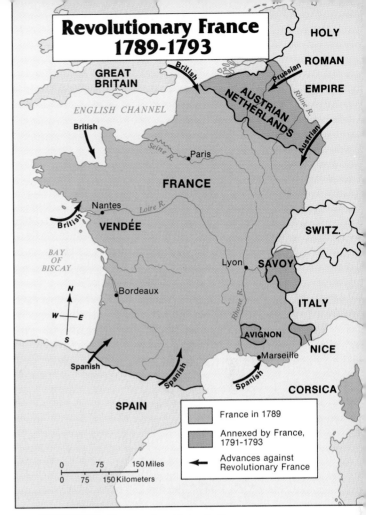

MAP STUDY *The armies of revolutionary France had expanded French territory by 1793, as you can see on this map. At the same time, the government had to contend with uprisings in the province of Vendée and in several cities, including Marseille. Which countries sent armies to fight the French?*

threatening the Dutch Netherlands and Prussia. Moreover, the National Convention issued a proclamation promising to aid "all peoples wishing to recover their liberty."

In March 1793, Great Britain, the Dutch Netherlands, and Spain joined Prussia and Austria in the war against France. With five nations fighting them, the French were hard-pressed. The Prussians and Dutch pushed the French back across the Rhine. Spain sent troops into southern France, and British forces captured the port of Toulon.

Trouble at home also threatened the revolution. The war caused starvation and economic hardships. In many parts of France,

441

As you read earlier, primary sources provide useful information about historical events. However, primary sources can give conflicting views of an event or development. Two statements about the execution of Louis XVI follow. The first is an official announcement published by the National Convention on January 23, 1793. The second is a letter written on January 23 by a noble living in Paris to a friend in England.

1 **Read the sources to find out what information is given.** (a) What does each source say about the attitude of the French people toward the king's execution? (b) What does each source say about conditions in France in 1793? (c) According to each source, what was the outcome of the king's execution?

2 **Compare the two sources.** (a) Do the sources agree on any points about the execution of Louis XVI? Explain. (b) On what points do the sources disagree?

3 **Evaluate the reliability of each source.** (a) How might the fact that the National Convention voted for Louis XVI's execution affect its proclamation? (b) How might the noble's background affect his view of the king's execution? (c) Which source do you think is more reliable? Why?

4 **Use the sources to draw conclusions.** (a) Based on the sources and what you read in this chapter, what conclusions would you draw about reaction to the execution of Louis XVI? (b) How do the differences between the sources reflect divisions in France during the revolution?

The National Convention

Citizens, the tyrant is no more. For a long time, the cries of the victims, whom war and domestic discord have spread over France and Europe, loudly protested his existence. He has paid his penalty, and only approval for the Republic and for liberty have been heard from the people.

We have had to combat deep-seated prejudices and the superstition of centuries concerning monarchy. Uncertainties and disturbances always accompany great changes and revolutions as profound as ours. But respect for liberty of opinion must cause these disturbances to be forgotten; only the good which they have produced through the death of the tyrant and of tyranny now remains. The National Convention and the French people are now to have only one mind, only one sentiment, that of liberty and fraternity.

Now above all we need peace in the Republic, and the most active surveillance of the domestic enemies of liberty. Let us unite to avert the shame that domestic discord [civil war] would bring upon our newborn republic.

A Noble's Report on the Death of the King

The frightful event of the 21st has spread dismay everywhere, and it is worth noting that even the most zealous supporters of the revolution found this measure both excessive and dangerous. It will not save us from the untold ills which threaten us, the reality and length of which are now all the more sure. We must make up our minds to sacrifice peace, security, and fortune. I very much fear that civil war will come as a finishing touch to the horrible crimes and all the misfortunes which now assail us. I doubt, moreover, whether this crime, added to so many others, has the universal approval of France. Even if we thought that the king were guilty, we would not wish for his death, especially after he has endured such a long and sorrowful captivity. Meanwhile, prudence must silence criticism because under the empire of secret accusations, of inquisition, or even more, of tyranny, it is dangerous to speak one's thoughts.

people felt the revolution had gone too far. Uprisings against the revolution occurred in the Vendée region of western France and in the cities of Marseille, Bordeaux, and Lyon.

The Reign of Terror

In the face of domestic and foreign threats, the National Convention took drastic action. It set aside the constitution that had been approved in 1793 and created a Committee of Public Safety. The Committee of Public Safety had almost dictatorial powers. It waged a brutal campaign against people it considered enemies of France. This campaign, known as the Reign of Terror, lasted from July 1793 to July 1794.

Maximilien Robespierre led the Committee of Public Safety during the Reign of Terror. He was determined to create a "Republic of Virtue," in which "our country assures the welfare of each individual and where each individual enjoys with pride the prosperity and the glory of our country."

Robespierre was utterly honest and dedicated to his ideals, but he was also violent, inflexible, and narrow-minded. He believed the state must be ruthless against its enemies.

The Committee of Public Safety sent agents across France to help local revolutionary committees uncover traitors. A Law of Suspects declared that people suspected of working against the revolution could be arrested for "their conduct, their relations, their remarks, or their writings." Such a vague law allowed revolutionary courts to imprison and condemn citizens on very little evidence.

During the Reign of Terror, trials were held almost daily throughout France. Between 20,000 and 40,000 men, women, and children were condemned to the guillotine. The former queen, Marie Antoinette, was one victim. Many nobles and clergy also went to the guillotine. But most victims were commoners, including peasants, laborers, shopkeepers, and merchants. The ruthlessness of the Terror had its effect, and the revolts subsided.

The Committee of Public Safety dealt with the threat of foreign invasion by organizing the nation for war. New French armies were raised, drilled, and equipped. A national draft law made every French man, whatever his age

or occupation, eligible to be drafted into the army.

The committee set strict limits on prices and wages, rationed food, and outlawed the use of scarce white flour. Citizens were asked to use whole-wheat flour to make "equality bread."

By the spring of 1794, the total national effort had paid off. French forces were again victorious on the battlefield. However, even supporters of the revolution were beginning to question the need for constant executions at home. In July 1794, the National Convention ordered Robespierre's arrest. He was quickly tried and executed. With his death, the Reign of Terror ended.

Impact of the Revolution on Daily Life

Between 1789 and 1794, French life had been transformed. The monarchy was gone, and the king was dead. French society had become more democratic. In place of the privileged

This sketch shows a dignified Marie Antoinette on her way to the guillotine. During the Reign of Terror, the queen was accused of plotting with Austria against France. She was executed in October 1793.

estates of the Old Regime, the revolution had declared the equality of all people. The old forms of address, "Monsieur" and "Madame," were replaced by "Citizen" and "Citizeness." The National Convention had abolished all remaining feudal customs and ended slavery in the French colonies. In addition, it had confiscated the land of émigrés.

Styles in fashion and art changed. Among the wealthy, simple dresses and long trousers replaced the elaborate gowns and knee breeches of the Old Regime. Playwrights and painters produced patriotic works that supported the revolution.

Revolutionary leaders established a uniform system of weights and measures, known as the metric system. They also called for free public schools so all citizens could receive an education. However, the schools were never set up.

After Robespierre's death in July 1794, a tide of reaction swept across France. The radical phase of the revolution had ended, and to many the revolution itself seemed to have failed.

SECTION 3 REVIEW

1. **Locate:** (a) Vendée, (b) Marseille, (c) Bordeaux, (d) Lyon.

2. **Identify:** (a) Brunswick Manifesto, (b) Committee of Public Safety, (c) Robespierre, (d) Republic of Virtue.

3. (a) Which nations invaded France in 1792? (b) Why did other nations join the war early in 1793?

4. On what grounds did the National Convention convict Louis XVI of treason?

5. Why did the Reign of Terror begin?

6. Describe three ways the French Revolution affected daily life.

7. **Critical Thinking** Explain why the French Revolution became more and more radical between 1789 and 1794.

---

4 The Rise of Napoleon Bonaparte

READ TO UNDERSTAND

☐ Why the Directory was unpopular.

☐ How and why Napoleon rose to power.

☐ What reforms Napoleon introduced.

☐ *Vocabulary:* lycée.

When Napoleon Bonaparte was 10 years old, his father took him from his home in Corsica and enrolled him in a military school in France. For the next eight years, the boy was on his own. He felt lonely and isolated from his beloved Corsica. When he was 16, he wrote, "I come to my room to dream by myself, to abandon myself to my melancholy in all its sharpness. In which direction does it lead?" Napoleon found his direction in action.

In the summer of 1794, soon after Napoleon had left military school, the people of France reacted against the excesses of the Reign of Terror. They hunted down and executed many leaders of the Terror. In 1795, the National Convention wrote yet another constitution that reflected the more conservative mood of the country. Yet the new government would not last long. It would fall to the young Napoleon.

The Directory

The Constitution of 1795 established a new government, the Directory. It consisted of an elected legislature and an executive branch with five directors. Only men who could read and who owned a certain amount of property could vote. As a result, the middle class and wealthy landowners strongly influenced the new government.

The Directory, which lasted from 1795 to 1799, faced many problems. The five-man executive did not work efficiently. Corrupt deputies in the legislature bargained for political favors. Furthermore, when the government removed the controls on prices imposed during the Reign of Terror, prices rose sharply. As bread prices rose, poor workers rioted in the streets of Paris.

The French Revolution, 1789–1815

Government	Dates	Events
Estates General	1789	Tennis Court Oath Storming of Bastille
National Assembly	1789–1791	Declaration of the Rights of Man Civil Constitution of the Clergy Constitution of 1791
Legislative Assembly	1791–1792	Constitutional monarchy War with Austria and Prussia Brunswick Manifesto issued Royal family imprisoned
National Convention	1792–1795	First French Republic Louis XVI executed Great Britain, the Netherlands, and Spain join war against France
Committee of Public Safety	*(1793–1794)*	*Reign of Terror* 20,000–40,000 people executed National draft begun
Directory	1795–1799	War continued Inefficient, corrupt government Riots among the poor
Napoleon *Consulate* *Empire*	1799–1804 1804–1815	Napoleonic Code Concordat of 1801 Built French Empire Invasion of Russia Defeat at Waterloo

CHART STUDY *The French Revolution passed through several stages, as you can see from this chart. During what period was France most democratic?*

Despite economic problems and discontent, the Directory followed an aggressive foreign policy. During the revolution, France had built the largest army in Europe. This army continued to fight for "liberty, equality, and fraternity." The military successes of one young officer, Napoleon Bonaparte, won the admiration of the French people.

"I am no ordinary man."

Born on the island of Corsica in 1769, Napoleon was the son of a minor noble. After his training at the French military academy, he rose quickly in the army during the revolution because so many officers had fled France.

In 1793, Napoleon commanded the French troops that ousted the British from Toulon. Two years later, he broke up a Paris mob by ordering his troops to fire a "whiff of grapeshot," small pellets shot from cannons. This action brought Napoleon to the attention of the Directory. His marriage to Josephine de Beauharnais (boh ahr NEH) also helped him because his wife had friends among the directors. By age 27, Napoleon was a general.

The young general soon received command of a French army for an invasion of Italy. He won several victories over the Austrians. Napoleon's successes forced Austria to withdraw from the war in 1797. This left Britain as the only country still fighting France.

In 1798, Napoleon invaded Egypt to threaten Britain's route to its outposts in India. Napoleon quickly took Alexandria and his troops overran the entire Nile delta region.* However, he suffered a disastrous setback at sea. The British fleet, under Admiral Horatio Nelson, destroyed the French fleet at the Battle of the Nile. The loss of their fleet meant the French could not supply their troops in Egypt, nor could they take them home.

Leaving the army in Egypt, Napoleon returned to Paris. The French people were not fully aware of the losses in Egypt, so they welcomed him as a hero.

In Paris, Napoleon found that many people were dissatisfied with the Directory. With the help of troops loyal to him, he and two directors overthrew the government in 1799. They drew up another constitution, the fourth since the revolution had begun. Under the new government, Napoleon was named First Consul.

"I am no ordinary man," Napoleon once boasted. He certainly was a person who could command the attention of friends as well as enemies, and he was admired by soldiers all over Europe. Napoleon had a sharp mind. He quickly sized up a situation and decided on a course of action. He thought and spoke so fast that he could dictate letters to four secretaries on four separate topics, all at the same time. Personal qualities and military talent helped Napoleon win widespread popular support. At age 30, Napoleon was the virtual dictator of France.

Napoleon's Domestic Policy

Between 1799 and 1804, Napoleon centralized power in his own hands. In 1802, he had himself made First Consul for life. A plebiscite, or popular vote, overwhelmingly approved this move. Two years later, Napoleon Bonaparte proclaimed himself "Emperor of the French." Once again, the majority of French voters endorsed his actions.

---

* While in Egypt, Napoleon asked French archaeologists and scientists to study the ancient monuments there. Among their discoveries was the Rosetta Stone, which held the clue to Egyptian hieroglyphics. (See page 22.)

In 1810, Napoleon divorced his wife Josephine, a commoner, in order to marry Marie Louise, an Austrian Hapsburg princess. Their children, he believed, would give the Bonaparte dynasty a true claim to royalty. Napoleon and Marie Louise are shown here riding through Paris in a golden carriage on their wedding day.

By 1804, Napoleon had gained almost absolute power. But he knew the French would never stand for a return to the Old Regime. Therefore, he continued many reforms of the revolution. At the same time, however, Napoleon kept firm personal control of the government. He appointed local officials to replace the elected councils that had ruled during the revolution. And while he allowed many émigrés to return home, they had to agree to give up the privileges they had enjoyed before the revolution.

The Napoleonic Code. One of Napoleon's greatest achievements in government was the Napoleonic Code, which has influenced French law to the present. This law code brought together many reforms of the revolution into a unified legal system. It recognized that all men were equal before the law. It guaranteed freedom of religion as well as a person's right to work in any occupation.

The code did not always preserve the ideals of the revolution, however. It put the interests of the state above those of individual citizens. In addition, it dropped laws passed during the revolution that had protected the rights of women and children. In family matters, the Napoleonic code reflected ancient Roman law and made the man absolute head of the household with control over all family property.

Other reforms. To strengthen the economy, Napoleon enforced a law requiring all citizens to pay taxes. He also created the national Bank of France, in which all tax money was deposited. The bank issued paper money and made loans to businesses.

To fill the need for educated, loyal government officials, Napoleon set up **lycées** (lee SAYZ), government-run schools. The lycées encouraged extreme patriotism, and the same courses were taught at each school. Usually, only the children of wealthy parents attended the lycées because tuition was high. However, some students received scholarships. Thus, the lycées were a first step toward a system of public education—a long-standing goal of Enlightenment thinkers and the French revolutionary leaders.

In the area of religion, Napoleon shrewdly combined reform and tradition. He realized that most French people were strongly Roman Catholic and despised the Civil Constitution of the Clergy. (See page 438.) In the Concordat of 1801, an agreement between the French government and the pope, Napoleon ended the election of bishops. Under this agreement, the French government appointed Catholic bishops and paid the clergy, but the pope had authority over them. The Concordat also stated that the Catholic Church would not demand the return of church property seized during the revolution. Thus, Napoleon did not lose the support of people who had acquired church lands.

SECTION 4 REVIEW

1. **Identify:** (a) Directory, (b) Horatio Nelson, (c) Napoleonic Code.

2. **Define:** lycée.

3. What problems did the Directory face?

4. Describe the results of each of the following: (a) Napoleon's invasion of Italy; (b) Napoleon's invasion of Egypt.

5. Give an example of how the Napoleonic Code reflected (a) the ideas of the French Revolution; (b) older traditions.

6. **Critical Thinking** Why do you think the French people turned to Napoleon, allowing him almost absolute power?

---

5 Napoleon in Triumph and Defeat

READ TO UNDERSTAND

☐ How Napoleon created an empire in Europe.

☐ How Napoleon was finally defeated.

☐ How the French Revolution and Napoleon reshaped Europe.

☐ *Vocabulary:* nationalism, guerrilla warfare.

Queen Louise of Prussia hated Napoleon Bonaparte with a passion. The conqueror of Europe had humbled her country and insulted her personally. Napoleon now held the fate of Prussia in his hands. Louise put pride aside and asked for a private meeting with Napoleon. On entering the room, she threw herself at his feet, begging him to leave her country undivided. The queen's efforts to touch Napoleon's heart came to nothing. Her people, however, would take their revenge on the French emperor, but not until after many years of fighting.

Between 1792 and 1815, France was almost constantly at war. At first, French armies fought to defend the revolution. Then, under Napoleon, France won an empire that spanned the continent of Europe.

The Empire of Napoleon

In the early 1800s, France fought all the major European powers, including Austria, Prussia, Britain, and Russia. A skilled military leader, Napoleon moved his troops in unexpected ways. In 1805, he massed his troops against the Austrian army at Ulm in southern Germany. The Austrians expected Napoleon to attack head-on. Instead, he attacked the Austrians from the rear, cutting off any retreat. A few months later, Napoleon defeated Austria and Russia at Austerlitz, a town in present-day Czechoslovakia. Both countries then made peace on Napoleon's terms.

Through shrewd diplomacy, Napoleon usually kept the European powers divided so they could not unite against him. Thus, he managed to keep Prussia neutral during his war with Austria and Russia. But Napoleon's victories made the Prussians fearful of French power. They became even more anxious when Napoleon dissolved the Holy Roman Empire and reorganized the German states into the Confederation of the Rhine. Finally, in 1806, Prussia declared war on France. Napoleon defeated the poorly led Prussian army and occupied Berlin. It was this victory that forced Queen Louise to meet with Napoleon, as you read earlier.

Europe under French rule. From 1807 to 1812, Napoleon was at the height of his power. His empire stretched from France to the borders of Russia. (See the map on page 449.) He governed France and the Netherlands directly as emperor. Other nations, such as Spain and Italy, and the Confederation of the Rhine, were satellite states—that is, their rulers followed Napoleon's policies. In Spain, Napoleon made his brother, Joseph, king. In addition, he tied Austria and Prussia to France as allies.

While ruling this vast empire, Napoleon helped spread the ideas of the French Revolution. Throughout the empire, Napoleon introduced religious toleration, abolished serfdom, and reduced the power of the Catholic Church. He also made the Napoleonic Code the basis of law in many countries.

At first, many people welcomed the French emperor as a liberator. However, he came to be looked upon as an unwelcome tyrant when he drafted thousands of men into his armies and imposed high taxes to pay for his wars.

The Continental System. Napoleon defeated the major powers on the continent. However, he was unable to bring Britain to its knees. In 1805, he readied a fleet to invade Britain. But Admiral Nelson dashed Napoleon's plans by sinking or capturing most of the French fleet at Cape Trafalgar, near Spain. Napoleon then decided to blockade British ports and thereby cut off its vital trade.

Under the blockade, which was called the Continental System, Napoleon ordered all European nations to stop trading with Britain. The British responded swiftly. They declared that any ship bound for France had to stop first at a British port and pay a tax. Napoleon countered with a threat to seize any ship paying the British tax.

Unfortunately for France, the Continental System backfired. Britain did lose trade, but France suffered more. The powerful British navy was able to cut off overseas imports to France and the rest of the continent.* This weakened the French economy. The Continental System also increased opposition to Napoleon among neutral nations, which blamed him for their loss of trade.

---

* During the war with Napoleon, the British interfered with American shipping to Europe and seized American sailors, forcing them to serve on British warships. These disputes were partly responsible for the War of 1812 between the United States and Britain.

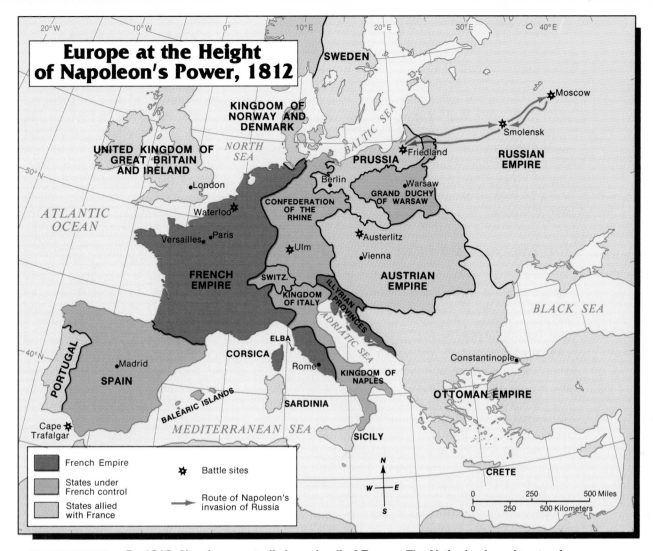

Europe at the Height of Napoleon's Power, 1812

French Empire

States under French control

States allied with France

★ Battle sites

→ Route of Napoleon's invasion of Russia

MAP STUDY By 1812, Napoleon controlled nearly all of Europe. The Netherlands and parts of Italy had been annexed by France. Some areas, shown in light purple on this map, were satellites of France; other areas were allies. What nations were beyond Napoleon's influence in 1812?

Stirrings of Nationalism

Opposition to Napoleon also grew among the conquered and allied peoples of Europe because they were developing a sense of **nationalism,** or pride and devotion to one's own country. They resented paying taxes to France and sending soldiers to serve in Napoleon's armies. They wanted to restore their own governments, customs, and traditions. As nationalist feelings grew, revolts broke out all over Europe.

Trouble came first in Spain with an uprising against Napoleon's brother. Spaniards were loyal to their former king and to the Catholic Church. They despised the French, whom they considered atheists and invaders. Bands of patriotic Spaniards ambushed French troops in hit-and-run attacks that became known as **guerrilla warfare.** (Guerrilla is a Spanish word meaning "little war.")

In 1808, Britain sent troops to help the Spanish and the Portuguese, who were also fighting against French rule. By 1812, Spanish and Portuguese nationalists had ousted the French from their nations. Each nation then set up a limited monarchy with a written constitution.

In Prussia, nationalist leaders reorganized the government to make it more efficient.

449

They urged the Prussian king to create greater loyalty among the middle and lower classes by giving them more political freedom. Prussia also quietly rebuilt its army. The new army rewarded talent and hard work. By 1811, Prussia had an army capable of renewing the struggle against France. It only needed an opportunity to strike. The opportunity came in 1812 when Napoleon undertook an ill-fated invasion of Russia.

The Emperor's Downfall

Although Czar Alexander I of Russia had agreed to abide by the Continental System in 1807, the trade blockade hurt the Russian economy. When Alexander resumed trade with Britain in 1812, Napoleon decided to invade Russia. Napoleon assembled an army of over 500,000 soldiers, and in June 1812, he led this Grand Army into Russia.

Napoleon planned to defeat the Russians in a quick, decisive battle. To his surprise, the Russians refused to stand and fight. Instead, they retreated before his army, burning their crops and homes as they went. They drew Napoleon and his army deeper and deeper into Russia, extending the French supply lines to the danger point. The Russians finally stood and fought the French near Moscow, 500 miles (800 kilometers) inside Russia. The French won the battle, but when Napoleon entered the city he found it deserted and in flames. Napoleon soon realized he could not feed and house his army in the burnt-out city. Thus, in October 1812, with winter approaching, the disappointed emperor ordered a retreat.

The bitterly cold Russian winter turned the French retreat into a disaster. Thousands of Napoleon's soldiers starved or froze to death. The Russian army attacked the stragglers. Fewer than 100,000 soldiers of the Grand Army escaped from Russia.

A powerful alliance made up of Britain, Austria, Russia, and Prussia then pounced on the crippled French army as it limped out of Russia. Napoleon rushed home to raise a new army, but his efforts failed. In March 1814, the allies captured Paris. Napoleon abdicated and went into exile on the island of Elba, off the coast of Italy. The allies installed the brother of the executed Louis XVI as Louis XVIII.*

Although the monarchy was restored, the new king did not revive the Old Regime. In 1814, Louis XVIII issued a constitution that provided for equality under the law for all citizens, an elected legislature, and religious freedom. He also kept the Napoleonic Code.

When Louis XVIII became king, many émigrés returned to France, demanding revenge on supporters of the French Revolution. Napoleon took advantage of the resulting disturbances to return to Paris. In March 1815, he again proclaimed himself emperor. Former soldiers rallied to his side. For 100 days, he worked to rebuild the French army. But the European allies acted swiftly. In June 1815, a joint British and Prussian army led by the Duke of Wellington defeated the French at Waterloo, a town near Brussels, Belgium. Napoleon was exiled to the lonely island of St. Helena in the South Atlantic, where he died in 1821.

Legacy of the French Revolution and Napoleon

The era of the French Revolution and Napoleon had many lasting effects on France and the rest of Europe. In France, the revolution ended feudalism, with its special privileges for clergy and nobles. Although the monarchy was eventually restored in France, a written constitution limited the king's power. In the years ahead, French citizens would continue to struggle for the ideals of "liberty, equality, and fraternity."

Under Napoleon, the revolutionary ideals of political and social justice spread throughout Europe. Through his wars and alliances, Napoleon altered the political boundaries of many European countries. Both the French Revolution and Napoleon contributed to the growing spirit of nationalism in Europe.

Finally, 23 years of warfare had drained French resources. By 1815, France was no

---

* Louis XVI's young son, who died in prison after his father's execution, was considered Louis XVII by supporters of the monarchy.

The retreat of Napoleon's army from Russia ranks among the greatest military disasters of all time. Behind the defeat was the failure of Napoleon to fully understand the forces of geography. The wide plain that stretches 500 miles from Moscow back to the Russian border and the early onset of bitter winter weather turned the retreat into catastrophe. (See the map on page 469.)

The memoirs of François Bourgogne, a sergeant in the French guard, give a startling glimpse of what Napoleon's troops suffered.

"For the last few days," wrote Bourgogne, "we had nothing but horseflesh to eat. The few provisions we had brought from Moscow were all gone, and now, with the cold weather, our real miseries began."

The first snow fell on November 7. With the ground covered, the horses could no longer graze. When they died, soldiers paused to cut strips of flesh from the horses' bodies. Soon the bitter cold eliminated this source of food. "The horses that died during the night were frozen so hard it was impossible to cut their flesh," he wrote.

At Krasnoe, Russian sharpshooters ambushed Bourgogne's regiment, which lost a third of its men. "When our poor wounded saw that they were being abandoned, many of them dragged themselves painfully on their knees after us, raising their hands to heaven, imploring us to help them. But what could we do? The same fate was in store for us, for at every moment men fell, and were abandoned in turn."

1. What aspects of Russian geography helped defeat the French?

2. **Critical Thinking** Napoleon defended his invasion of Russia as "a war of good sense." Do you think his soldiers would have agreed? Explain.

longer the strongest and richest nation in Europe. Great Britain had forged ahead in commerce and industry, as you will read in Chapter 21.

SECTION 5 REVIEW

1. **Locate:** (a) Ulm, (b) Austerlitz, (c) Berlin, (d) Cape Trafalgar, (e) Moscow, (f) Elba, (g) Waterloo.

2. **Identify:** (a) Confederation of the Rhine, (b) Continental System.

3. **Define:** (a) nationalism, (b) guerrilla warfare.

4. What reforms did Napoleon introduce in Europe?

5. What effect did the Continental System have on France?

6. **Critical Thinking** How did Napoleon's invasion of Russia help lead to his downfall?

Summary

1. In the late 1780s, the French monarchy faced a severe economic crisis. Efforts at reform failed in part because of the class system of the Old Regime and in part because of King Louis XVI's weakness. Finally, the king summoned the Estates General.

2. The French Revolution began in 1789. The three estates declared themselves the National Assembly. That body abolished feudalism, introduced sweeping religious reforms, and prepared the Constitution of 1791.

3. The Revolution became more radical after 1792. France was attacked from the outside by other European nations and from the inside by people who opposed the revolution. To defend the revolution, radical revolutionaries launched the Reign of Terror, executing thousands of French people.

4. In 1795, reaction to the Reign of Terror led to creation of the Directory. However, Napoleon Bonaparte overthrew the Directory in 1799 and eventually crowned himself emperor. He reaffirmed many ideas of the revolution in the Napoleonic Code and other reforms.

5. Napoleon built an empire across Europe. Controlling his empire proved difficult, however. Nationalist movements and the ongoing struggle with Britain drained French resources. In 1814, Napoleon's enemies invaded France, forcing the emperor to abdicate. Although the revolutionary era ended, both France and Europe had been greatly changed.

Recalling Facts

Arrange the events in each of the following groups in the order in which they occurred.

1. (a) Paris mob attacks the Bastille.
    (b) Louis XVI is executed.
    (c) The Estates General meets.

2. (a) The National Assembly issues the Declaration of the Rights of Man.
    (b) Foreign invaders issue the Brunswick Manifesto.
    (c) Deputies at the Estates General take the Tennis Court Oath.

3. (a) France is ruled by the Directory.
    (b) National Assembly writes the first French constitution.
    (c) Reign of Terror begins.

4. (a) Allied armies defeat Napoleon at the Battle of Waterloo.
    (b) Napoleon invades Russia.
    (c) Napoleon overthrows the Directory.

Chapter Checkup

1. (a) Describe the economic crisis in France in the 1780s. (b) How did Louis XVI and his ministers try to solve the crisis? (c) How did the Old Regime hamper their efforts?

2. Describe the major reforms introduced by the National Assembly.

3. (a) How did war in 1792 help unite the French people? (b) Why did the war lead to an uprising in Paris? (c) What was the result of the uprising?

4. (a) What actions by the National Convention show that it was more radical than the National Assembly? (b) How did other European monarchs react to the Convention's actions?

5. (a) How did the Committee of Public Safety treat people who opposed the revolution? (b) How did it defend France against foreign invaders?

6. (a) How did Napoleon gain popularity? (b) Why was he able to overthrow the Directory so easily?

7. (a) Describe Napoleon's reforms in France. (b) Which reforms reflected the ideals of the revolution? (c) How did the ideals of the revolution spread to other parts of Europe?

Critical Thinking

1. **Analyzing** Describe how each of the following developments led the French Revolution on a more radical course: (a) the fall of the Bastille; (b) Louis XVI's attempted flight from France; (c) the threat of foreign invasion.

2. **Understanding the Roots of Democracy** (a) During which phase of the revolution was France the most democratic? The least democratic? (b) Do you think a democracy must curtail liberties to survive in an emergency? Explain.

3. **Analyzing a Quotation** Robespierre said: "To establish and consolidate democracy, to achieve the peaceful rule of constitutional laws, we must first finish the war of liberty against tyranny. We must annihilate the enemies of the republic at home and abroad, or else we shall perish." How does Robespierre justify the Reign of Terror in this statement?

4. **Expressing an Opinion** Which of the changes that occurred during the French Revolution do you think had the most effect on the lives of ordinary French citizens? Why?

5. **Relating Past to Present** (a) How did the French Revolution contribute to the growth of nationalism in Europe? (b) Do you think nationalism is a major force in the world today? Explain.

Developing Basic Skills

1. **Graph Reading** Study the graphs on page 435. (a) What percentage of the population made up each of the three estates? (b) What percentage of the land did each estate own? (c) How did the distribution of land contribute to the problems of the Old Regime?

2. **Map Reading** Study the map on page 449. (a) What lands did Napoleon rule directly? (b) What lands did he control by other means? (c) What problems do you think Napoleon faced in ruling his empire?

Writing About History

Evaluating a Source of Information

The quality of your research will depend in part on how well you evaluate your sources. Not all your sources will be impartial. How do you know they are accurate? To help you evaluate a book, check the author's educational background and area of interest. This information is often contained on the title page or on the dust jacket. Look at the date of publication. Recent books may have the benefit of more up-to-date research. Note whether the book cites the sources its information is based on. If you are still in doubt, you might consult your librarian or your teacher for their evaluation of the source.

Practice: Using the suggestions above, evaluate a book that you might use to write a research paper on a topic related to this chapter.

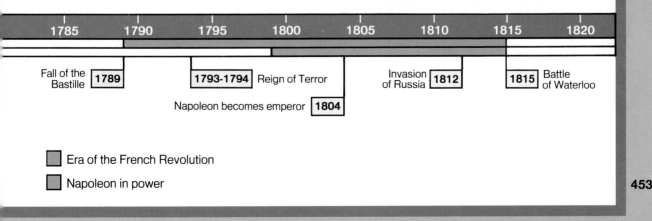

| 1785 | 1790 | 1795 | 1800 | 1805 | 1810 | 1815 | 1820 |

Fall of the Bastille **1789**

1793-1794 Reign of Terror

Napoleon becomes emperor **1804**

Invasion of Russia **1812**

1815 Battle of Waterloo

☐ Era of the French Revolution

☐ Napoleon in power

Revolutions and Reaction

20

(1815–1848)

At the Congress of Vienna, those who had defeated Napoleon restored order in Europe. However, cracks in the new order soon appeared. In 1830, Parisians revolted, waving the tricolor flag, which had not been seen since 1815.

"There is literally a royal mob here," wrote one visitor to Vienna. "I have worn my hat out in taking it off to sovereigns whom I meet at the corner of every street." The visitor was scarcely exaggerating, for in the fall of 1814 nine kings, dozens of princes, and hundreds of diplomats converged on Vienna, the capital of the Austrian Empire. For ten months, these imposing figures attended the Congress of Vienna, an international peace conference. After more than 20 years of war, Europe was enjoying peace. Napoleon was in exile on Elba, and Louis XVIII was on the throne of France.

Suddenly, in March 1815, the peace was shattered. Vienna was in an uproar when news came of Napoleon's return to Paris from Elba. But by June, people sighed with relief. Word reached Vienna that Napoleon had been totally defeated at Waterloo.

During the Congress of Vienna, the Austrian emperor bore the burden of entertaining his prominent guests. He organized elaborate banquets, hunting parties, and firework displays. In the evenings, the dignitaries dressed for fancy balls that continued far into the night. "The Congress dances," one observer noted, "but accomplishes nothing."

However, the festivities served a purpose. They distracted the less powerful diplomats while the leaders of the great powers negotiated important issues. Those leaders wanted to turn the clock back to 1789 and rebuild the balance of power in Europe.

Representatives of Austria, Britain, Russia, and Prussia finally hammered out a treaty. However, the Congress of Vienna could not uproot the ideas of political and social justice that the Enlightenment and the French Revolution had planted throughout Europe. Those ideas, along with the actions of the Congress of Vienna, set the stage for unrest and revolt in many countries during the first half of the 1800s. ■

1 Restoring Peace

READp TO UNDERSTAND

- ☐ **What forces helped shape Europe after 1815.**
- ☐ **What principles guided the decisions of the Congress of Vienna.**
- ☐ **How the Metternich System tried to preserve the status quo.**
- ☐ *Vocabulary:* **liberalism, conservatism, legitimacy, status quo.**

Baron Franz Hager, the chief of police, had an important job to do during the Congress of Vienna. His secret agents infested the residences of the leaders attending the Congress to gather information on their goings and comings. Night after night, Hager's watchdogs sent him reports or scraps of paper rescued from wastebaskets. Imagine the disappointment of these hardworking assistants who painstakingly pieced together pieces of paper

only to find the king of Denmark's laundry list or the prince of Hesse-Homburg's expense account. Hager's task was complicated by the more than 100,000 people, including kings, queens, and hundreds of princes, who had crowded into Vienna for the Congress.

Napoleon's wars had left Europe in chaos. Monarchs had been overthrown, and many nations had been invaded by France. The leaders of the Congress of Vienna were determined to restore the traditions that had existed before the French Revolution. But as they tried to turn the clock back, they faced new forces unleashed by the events of the past 20 years.

Old and New Forces

During the 1800s, the philosophies of liberalism and conservatism influenced the way many people thought about government and society. To people at the time, **liberalism** was a philosophy that supported guarantees for individual freedom, political changes, and social reform. **Conservatism** supported the traditional political and social order and resisted changes that threatened that way of life.

455

Liberals and conservatives. Liberals accepted the ideas of the Enlightenment and the French Revolution. They supported freedom of speech, press, and religion. To safeguard these rights, they called for written constitutions. As heirs to the Enlightenment, liberals stressed reason, progress, and education. They believed that governments should be reformed so that educated, responsible citizens, like themselves, could participate. Few liberals thought that poor and uneducated people should take part in government.

Edmund Burke, an English statesman, was a spokesman for conservative ideas. He condemned the French Revolution because it brought radical changes that destroyed traditional institutions such as the monarchy and the nobility. While most conservatives accepted the idea of gradual change, they emphasized respect for custom and tradition. They believed that only the wisest, most talented people should rule. To many conservative nobles, this meant that they alone should hold positions of power.

After Napoleon's defeat, conservatives were in firm control of governments through-out Europe. However, support for liberalism was growing, especially among the educated middle class.

Nationalism. Another powerful force shaping Europe in the 1800s was nationalism. As it spread, it came to mean not only love of one's country but also pride in a common cultural heritage regardless of political boundaries. Nationalism was both a positive and a negative force. It could unite people behind a common cause, such as political independence. But it could also lead people to persecute those with different cultural traditions.

Liberals and conservatives of the time reacted differently to nationalism. Liberals often supported nationalist leaders who wanted to free their countries from foreign control. Conservatives feared nationalism, in part because it threatened to upset the traditional political order.

The Congress of Vienna

Conservatives dominated the Congress of Vienna. The most influential leaders were Czar Alexander I of Russia; King Frederick William III

Delegates to the Congress of Vienna redrew the map of Europe after Napoleon's downfall. Seated at the far left is the Duke of Wellington, who defeated Napoleon at the Battle of Waterloo. The Austrian statesman, Metternich, standing at left, is introducing Wellington to the other delegates. At right, with his arm resting on the table, is the chief French delegate, Talleyrand.

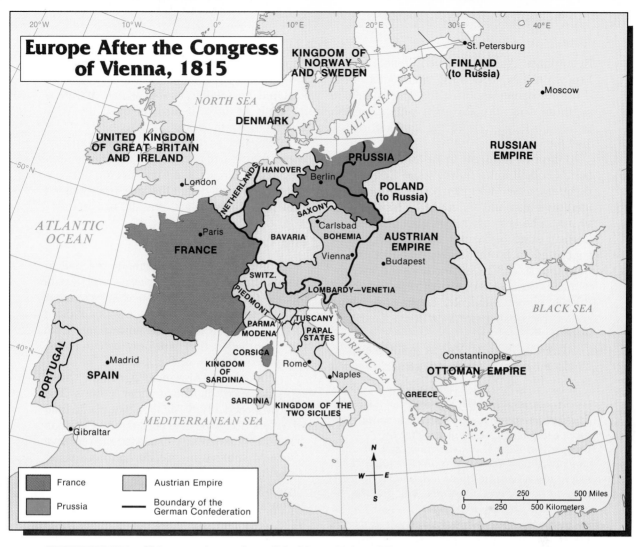

Europe After the Congress of Vienna, 1815

MAP STUDY *This map shows the political boundaries of Europe after the Congress of Vienna. Nations that had fought against Napoleon won new territory, while France lost lands it had conquered. Compare this map with the map on page 449. Which nations gained land from France?*

of Prussia; Lord Castlereagh, the British foreign minister; and Prince Klemens von Metternich, the Austrian foreign minister. The French delegate, Charles Maurice de Talleyrand, also played a major role at the Congress.

Metternich presided over the Congress. He was guided by two general principles: legitimacy and balance of power. By **legitimacy,** he meant restoring to power the royal families that had lost their thrones when Napoleon conquered Europe. The Congress of Vienna recognized Louis XVIII as the legitimate king of France. It also restored royal families in Spain, Portugal, and Sardinia.

Restoring the balance of power. To rebuild the balance of power in Europe and prevent future French aggression, the Congress reduced France to its 1790 frontiers. It then strengthened the countries on the borders of France. To the north of France, the Dutch and Austrian Netherlands were united into a single country, called the Netherlands, which was ruled by the Dutch king. To the east, 39 German states were loosely joined into the German Confederation, headed by Austria. The Congress recognized Switzerland as an independent nation. In addition, it strengthened the kingdom of Sardinia in northern Italy by giving it Piedmont and Genoa. (See the map above.)

The Congress also made other territorial changes. In return for giving up the Austrian

457

Netherlands, Austria received Lombardy and Venetia in Italy. With these lands, Austria became the strongest power in northern Italy. In southern Italy, the Congress put a Spanish prince on the throne of the kingdom of the Two Sicilies.

Other decisions. In Eastern Europe, the fate of Poland was a thorny issue. Early in the Congress, Czar Alexander had pointed to Poland on a map and announced, "This belongs to me." The king of Prussia then claimed the German state of Saxony. Russia and Prussia supported each other's demands. Metternich, Castlereagh, and Talleyrand objected to these demands because they feared the expansion of Russian power. Eventually, Russia and Prussia settled for smaller portions of the land they wanted.

The Congress of Vienna granted Britain handsome rewards for its long struggle against Napoleon. Great Britain acquired Malta, Ceylon (present-day Sri Lanka), and islands in the East and West Indies, as well as part of Guiana in South America. It also received the Cape Colony in South Africa.

Delegates to the Congress generally ignored the aims of nationalists when they rearranged boundaries. The Congress did not consult the people living in the areas they handed over to Austria, Russia, Prussia, or Britain.

The Concert of Europe

To protect the peace settlement reached at Vienna, Britain, Austria, Prussia, and Russia formed the Quadruple Alliance in November 1815. Three years later, France was admitted to the alliance. These great powers met from time to time to deal with any threat to the peace and stability of Europe.

Although Czar Alexander signed the Quadruple Alliance, he had grander visions. The Czar proposed a Holy Alliance that would bind all rulers to govern according to Christian principles. Castlereagh dismissed the idea as a "piece of sublime mysticism and nonsense." Nevertheless, many European rulers eventually joined the Holy Alliance. The two alliances encouraged nations to act together to preserve the peace.

The system of meeting to settle international problems became known as the Concert of Europe.* During most of the 1800s, the Concert of Europe enforced the settlement arranged at Vienna. It preserved the balance of power and prevented local conflicts from flaring into a major European conflict.

The Metternich System

For more than 30 years, Prince Metternich dominated European politics. His main goal was to defend the work of the Congress of Vienna. Metternich opposed both liberalism and nationalism. Instead, he worked hard to defend the **status quo,** that is, the existing state of affairs. His policies were known as the Metternich System.

---

* Concert in this context means a mutual agreement.

Austrian foreign minister Metternich dominated European politics for 30 years after the Congress of Vienna. His enormous self-confidence was expressed in these words: "I say to myself twenty times a day, how right I am and how wrong others are. And yet," he added, "it is so easy to be right."

Despite Metternich's efforts, many challenges to the status quo arose. Students in German universities, for example, demanded liberal reforms and pressed for the unification of all German peoples. Metternich responded by persuading representatives from the German states to pass the Carlsbad Decrees in 1819. These laws imposed press censorship and suppressed freedom of speech.

The Carlsbad Decrees ended student agitation in Germany for nearly a generation. But challenges to the status quo arose elsewhere. In 1820, liberal reformers forced the kings of Naples and Spain to grant constitutions. Metternich then pressured members of the Quadruple Alliance to step in to prevent the spread of liberalism in these countries. Britain opposed intervention and broke away from the alliance. In 1821, an Austrian army marched into Naples and restored the king to power. In 1823, a French army helped the king of Spain suppress Spanish liberals.

Although royal power was restored in Spain, its colonies in Latin America successfully revolted against Spanish rule during the 1820s. You will read about the wars of independence in Latin America in Chapter 27.

The Greeks also fought a successful war for independence. Greece had been part of the Ottoman Empire for nearly 400 years. In 1821, Greek nationalists revolted against Turkish rule. Metternich tried to prevent other European countries from aiding the rebellion. But the British and the French admired ancient Greek civilization and eventually rallied to the Greek cause. In 1829, the Ottoman Empire was forced to recognize Greek independence.

SECTION 1 REVIEW

1. **Identify:** (a) Edmund Burke, (b) German Confederation, (c) Concert of Europe, (d) Carlsbad Decrees.

2. **Define:** (a) liberalism, (b) conservatism, (c) legitimacy, (d) status quo.

3. (a) What political ideas did liberals support? (b) What political ideas did conservatives support?

4. (a) Who were the most influential leaders of the Congress of Vienna? (b) What principles guided them?

5. How did the Congress of Vienna try to prevent future French aggression?

6. **Critical Thinking** Do you think the Metternich System would be successful in the long run? Explain.

2 A New Era of Revolution in France

READ TO UNDERSTAND

☐ What the causes and results of the July Revolution were.

☐ Why Louis Philippe was overthrown in the revolution of 1848.

☐ Why the Second Republic was short-lived.

☐ *Vocabulary:* socialism, universal male suffrage.

When Napoleon gave up power in 1814, a noble announced to Louis XVI's brother and heir, "Sire, you are king of France." The man who had spent the last 23 years in exile replied, "Have I ever ceased to be?" When the Congress of Vienna recognized him as the actual king of France, Louis XVIII still believed in the divine right of kings. But circumstances would soon force him to realize that the time had passed when a king could rule as an absolute monarch. The ideals of the French Revolution continued to inspire demands for reform. And middle-class liberals and workers in France were to join forces in 1830 and 1848 to upset the status quo created at the Congress of Vienna.

The July Revolution

During his reign, Louis XVIII sought a compromise between conservatives and liberals. He realized that he would have to share power with representatives of the people. Thus, he accepted the Constitution of 1814, which provided for an elected legislature and guaranteed individual rights.

Louis's efforts at compromise satisfied few people, however. Liberals criticized the 1814 constitution because it allowed only the wealthiest people of France to vote. Extreme conservatives, led by the king's brother Charles, wanted a return to the Old Regime. On Louis's death in 1824, his brother inherited the throne as Charles X.

A tactless, stubborn man, Charles set about increasing royal power. He warned that the constitution "cannot possibly prevent me from having my way." Supported by the clergy and the nobles, Charles pressured the legislature to pass a law to pay nobles for the lands

Women took part in the July Revolution, as they had in the French Revolution 40 years earlier. Here, a working-class woman takes her place on the barricades.

they had lost during the French Revolution. However, when the legislature refused to approve laws that restricted individual freedom, Charles dissolved it and called for a new election.

The elections of July 1830 surprised the king because voters chose liberal lawmakers who opposed his policies. Unable to control the newly elected legislature, Charles issued the July Ordinances. These laws dissolved the legislature, ended freedom of the press, and put new restrictions on the right to vote.

French newspapers urged citizens to resist the king's arbitrary rule. On July 28, riots broke out in Paris. Workers, university students, and middle-class liberals set up barricades in the streets. Soldiers refused to fire on the rebels and began to join them. Realizing he had lost support, Charles X abdicated and fled to England.

The July Revolution, as it was called, ended quickly. Many people had hoped to create a republic. But the middle-class leaders of the revolution feared that if France became a republic, foreign powers might intervene. Therefore, they established a constitutional monarchy. They chose Louis Philippe, a cousin of Charles X, as king.

The Bourgeois Monarchy

Under Louis Philippe, the 1814 constitution was amended to give more members of the middle class the right to vote. Because the middle class, or bourgeoisie, controlled the legislature and supported the king, Louis Philippe was called the "bourgeois monarch." In keeping with this image, Louis Philippe was the first European monarch to adopt middle-class dress. Wearing a top hat, frock coat, and trousers, he often walked through the streets of Paris, greeting citizens.

Although France prospered during most of Louis Philippe's reign, many French people were discontented with his government. The king's policies favored the wealthy, and many citizens felt betrayed by the July Revolution because they had not won the right to vote. Republicans and some liberals organized secret societies to work for an end to the monarchy.

Socialist demands. Changing social and economic conditions added to tensions in France. In the early 1800s, new factories in the cities attracted workers looking for jobs. Because of poor conditions in the factories and low pay, many workers listened eagerly to reformers who promised improvements.

One reformer was Louis Blanc. He believed in an economic and political theory called **socialism.** Under socialism, society as a whole rather than private individuals would own all property and operate all businesses. Blanc argued that a socialist government would protect the interests of the working class and guarantee all the workers jobs.

Louis Philippe rejected the demands for reform from socialists as well as those from liberals and republicans. "There will be no reform," he said in 1847, "I do not wish it."

The revolution of 1848. On February 22, 1848, François Guizot (gee ZOH), the king's chief minister, cancelled a huge public banquet in Paris because he feared it would lead to demonstrations and disorder. Hearing that the banquet was cancelled, thousands of workers poured into the streets shouting: "Down with Guizot." To restore order, Louis Philippe dismissed his chief minister, but demonstrations continued over the next few days. When troops opened fire and killed some demonstrators, the people of Paris erected barricades as they had in 1830.

The revolution of 1848 ended quickly. When crowds marched on the palace, Louis Philippe abdicated and fled in disguise to England. The mob swarmed into the palace. Finding the table set for lunch, they sat down to eat the royal meal. Meanwhile, leaders of the revolution proclaimed the Second Republic.*

The Second Republic

While Paris was in turmoil, the revolutionaries quickly set up a provisional, or temporary, government, which included the socialist leader Louis Blanc. In response to socialist demands, the government created national workshops that would provide jobs for the unemployed. Nearly 120,000 workers flocked

In 1848, workers and middle-class liberals in Paris tore up paving stones, iron railings, trees, and lampposts to set up barricades. Waving the red flag of revolution, they built more than 1,500 barricades, blocking both streets and intersections. The barricades made it difficult for government troops to move through the streets and put down the uprising.

to Paris to register at the national workshops. Because jobs could not be found for all of them, many received government aid in the form of relief payments.

To pay for the national workshops, the government imposed a heavy tax on property. The increased taxes angered the middle class as well as peasants who owned land. They blamed the socialists. Consequently, when elections were held for a National Assembly, moderate delegates who represented middle-class interests won a majority.

In June 1848, the National Assembly abolished the national workshops. Paris workers immediately revolted. During the days that followed, clashes between workers and troops left more than 10,000 people killed or

---

* The first republic had been created by the National Convention in 1792. See page 441.

wounded. After the revolt was crushed, the National Assembly issued a new constitution. It guaranteed liberty and established an elected legislature and president. In addition, it provided for **universal male suffrage**— that is, all adult men were given the right to vote. However, the fighting left bitter memories and sharp divisions between the middle class and workers.

The first elections under the new constitution were held in December 1848. By a huge majority, voters chose Louis Napoleon, nephew of Napoleon Bonaparte, to be president of the Second Republic. Few people knew much about Louis Napoleon, but they associated his name with order, security, and the glorious victories of French armies.

As president, Louis Napoleon tried to please everyone. He promised jobs to workers, encouraged trade, defended property rights, and supported the Roman Catholic Church. Thus, he met little resistance when he set up a virtual dictatorship in December 1851. A year later, he assumed the title Napoleon III, Emperor of the French. Like his uncle, he won approval for this move in a popular vote. Thus, the short-lived Second Republic ended with the creation of the Second Empire.

SECTION 2 REVIEW

1. **Identify:** (a) July Ordinances, (b) Louis Blanc, (c) Second Republic.

2. **Define:** (a) socialism, (b) universal male suffrage.

3. Why did the French revolt against Charles X in 1830?

4. What problems led to the overthrow of Louis Philippe?

5. What was the purpose of the national workshops?

6. Why did the French support Louis Napoleon?

7. **Critical Thinking** Do you think the revolutions of 1830 and 1848 were successful? Why or why not?

3 Revolts in Other Parts of Europe

READ TO UNDERSTAND

☐ **What role nationalism played in the revolutions of 1830 and 1848.**

☐ **How Austria gained control of its empire after the revolutions of 1848.**

☐ **Why most of the revolutions of 1830 and 1848 failed.**

"When France sneezes, Europe catches cold," Metternich noted dryly in 1830. Indeed, a wave of revolutions, inspired by France, did sweep across Europe in 1830 and 1848. Liberals and nationalists in many parts of Europe renewed their struggles against the old order restored by the Congress of Vienna.

The Revolutions of 1830

As you have read, at the Congress of Vienna, the Dutch and Austrian Netherlands had been united under the Dutch king. However, the Belgians, who lived in the south of the new country, despised the arrangement. They spoke a different language from the Dutch. Also, they were largely Roman Catholic, while most of the Dutch were Protestant.

These cultural and religious differences sparked a nationalist movement among the Belgians. In August 1830, riots broke out in Brussels. The Belgians defeated a Dutch army and won the support of Britain and France for their cause. At first, Austria, Prussia, and Russia opposed any change. In time, however, they signed a treaty recognizing Belgium as an independent nation.

The July Revolution in France and the nationalist revolt in Belgium succeeded in part because each had the support of a strong middle class. Elsewhere, however, revolutions that broke out in 1830 failed.

Polish nationalists tried to win their independence from Russia in 1830. But the Poles were divided among themselves. Moreover, Britain and France did not provide the help the Poles had hoped for. A Russian army crushed the rebels, executed many leaders, and imposed harsh rule in Poland.

Revolts also flared in Italy and Germany. Austria quickly sent troops to suppress nationalists in Italy, and Metternich persuaded the German states to renew the Carlsbad Decrees, which silenced the unrest in Germany. "The dam has broken in Europe," wrote Metternich in 1830. However, he managed to hold back the flood of liberalism and nationalism until 1848.

Revolts in the Austrian Empire

In March 1848, news of the overthrow of Louis Philippe in France led to an uprising in Vienna. University students joined by workers and middle-class liberals poured into the streets. They demanded a constitution, an end to feudalism, and the removal of Metternich. Frightened by the demonstrations, the Austrian emperor promised reform. To show his good faith, he dismissed Metternich.

During the uprising in Vienna, revolts erupted among various nationalities in other parts of the Austrian Empire. In Hungary, the Magyars, led by the fiery nationalist Louis Kossuth (KAH sooth), demanded a constitution and a separate Hungarian government. In Bohemia, the Czechs issued similar demands. In northern Italy, nationalists in Lombardy and Venetia also revolted against Austria. They were supported by the kingdom of Sardinia and other Italian states.

Overwhelmed by these events, the Austrian government granted the demands of the Magyars and the Czechs and withdrew its armies from northern Italy. Within three months, however, the tide of revolution turned. Germans who lived in Bohemia resented being

DAILY LIFE The Brothers Grimm and German Nationalism

"Near a great forest lived a poor woodcutter with his wife and two children. The boy was called Hansel and the girl Gretel." So begins one of the most famous of the fairy tales collected by Jacob and Wilhelm Grimm. In the early 1800s, the Grimm brothers visited German villages and wrote down the stories that peasants told as they sat around the evening fire. The tales—of witches and princesses, talking cats and werewolves, enchanted forests and demons in disguise—had never before been set down in writing. The Grimm brothers published the first collection of these folk tales in 1812 and were astonished when the book became a bestseller, adored by children around the world.

For the rest of their lives, Jacob and Wilhelm continued their work with the "poetry of the common people," as they called the folk stories. Besides Hansel and Gretel, the Grimms popularized the tales of Rapunzel, Cinderella, Little Red Riding Hood, Rumpelstiltskin, and Snow White.

The Grimms never doubted the importance of their work. They were inspired by the spirit of nationalism that was growing among the Germans. At the time, Germany was split into dozens of small states. The Grimms believed that gathering the stories of the German-speaking people would help weld them together into one nation. "These tales deserve attention not only because of their poetry," wrote Jacob, "but also because they belong to our national literature. What else do we have in common but our language and literature?" The poet Heinrich Heine compared each Grimm collection to a cathedral in which Germans from different states blended their voices in a single chorus.

1. Where did the Grimm brothers get the stories for their collections of folk tales?

2. **Critical Thinking** How do you think the folk tales expressed German nationalism?

under Czech control, and they helped an Austrian army occupy Prague. By June 1848, Austria had regained control of Bohemia. In October, government troops bombarded Vienna and crushed the revolution there.

The reconquest of Hungary took longer. To weaken the Magyar cause, the Austrian government took advantage of the cultural differences between the Magyars and the Croatians, a Slavic people who lived in Hungary. The Austrians supplied arms to a Croatian army, which stormed Budapest in September 1848. The Magyars successfully repelled the attack under the leadership of Kossuth. In the spring of 1849, Kossuth proclaimed Hungary a republic.

The Russian czar was anxious to see order restored in Eastern Europe, however, so he offered to help Austria. In August 1849, a Russian army invaded Hungary and suppressed the Magyar revolt.

Uprisings in Italy

The revolts in Lombardy and Venetia against the Austrians were among several uprisings in Italy in 1848. In January, revolutionaries in Sicily had overthrown their king. In other Italian states, people forced their rulers to grant liberal constitutions.

Italian nationalists in Rome tried to win the pope's support for a united Italy. However, the pope refused because he did not want to offend Austria, the strongest Catholic power in Europe. Rebels then took over Rome, and the pope fled into exile. Led by Giuseppe Mazzini, nationalists established the Roman Republic in February 1849.

By this time, however, the Austrians had restored order in Vienna and had begun to reestablish control in northern Italy. Furthermore, Louis Napoleon, who wanted to win favor with the pope, sent French troops to Rome. The French occupied the city and restored the pope to power.

Although the uprisings in Italy were crushed, liberals and nationalists preserved their dreams of a unified Italy. In the years ahead, they looked to the kingdom of Sardinia for leadership because only Sardinia had kept the liberal constitution won in 1848.

The German States

The revolution of 1848 in France inspired German liberals to demand reform. In many German states, rulers promised constitutions and other reforms. However, events took a different course in Prussia.

Prussia. In March 1848, a demonstration in Berlin turned into a riot when police opened fire on the crowd. Workers and middle-class liberals then set up barricades. When told of the revolt, the Prussian king Frederick William IV was amazed. "It cannot be," he said, "my people love me." To avoid further bloodshed, he withdrew his troops from the city and promised reform.

The Prussians elected a National Assembly to draft a constitution, but a split soon developed between middle-class moderates and radical workers. Also, the king was encouraged by the Austrian success in suppressing revolts. In November, Frederick William dissolved the National Assembly and sent troops back to Berlin. Once he was in full control, the king issued his own constitution for Prussia. The constitution provided for universal male suffrage and an elected legislature.

Attempt to unify Germany. One of the goals of the 1848 revolution in Germany was national unification. In May 1848, delegates from the German states met in Frankfurt as a national parliament. They agreed to work peacefully for German unity.

In April 1849, the parliament issued a constitution for Germany. Under the constitution, individual German states would give up many of their own powers to a central government. The delegates then offered the crown of a united Germany to Frederick William IV. To their dismay, the Prussian king rejected the crown because it was offered not by the German princes but by the people—"from the gutter," as he described it. He then sent an army to disband the Frankfurt Parliament, thereby ending this early attempt at unification.

Impact of the Revolutions of 1830 and 1848

The revolutions of 1830 and 1848 had a few successes. Belgium did win its independence.

"One morning toward the end of February 1848," recalled Carl Schurz, "I sat quietly in my attic room, working hard at the tragedy of *Ulrich von Hutten,* when suddenly a friend rushed breathlessly into the room, exclaiming, 'What, you're sitting here! Don't you know what has happened? The French have driven away Louis Philippe and proclaimed the Republic.'"

Schurz was a 19-year-old student at the University of Bonn when the revolutions of 1848 erupted, changing his life. Until the day his friend burst in with news from France, Schurz had planned to be a professor of history. Instead, swept up in the spirit of his time, he became a student leader.

Schurz continued his story of that fateful day. "I threw down my pen—and that was the end of *Ulrich von Hutten.* I never touched the manuscript again. We tore down the stairs, into the street, to the market square, the meeting place for all the student societies. Although it was still morning, the market was already crowded with young men talking excitedly. Now had arrived in Germany the day for the establishment of 'German Unity,' and the founding of a great, powerful national German Empire."

Schurz joined the revolutionary army and fought bravely. He defended one fortress until the moment of surrender, barely escaping a firing squad by clambering through an unused sewer. Although he found a safe refuge in Switzerland, Schurz returned to Germany when he learned that a cherished old professor had been imprisoned for life. Schurz became a hero of the revolution of 1848 when he spirited the professor safely out of Germany.

Even as an exile, Schurz did not give up his political ideals. He championed the cause of German unity in France and England. Then, like many other exiles from the political upheavals of 1848, he set sail for the United States. There he dedicated himself to reform movements, including the abolition of slavery, and eventually won a seat in the United States Senate from Wisconsin.

1. How did the events of 1848 change Carl Schurz's plans?

2. **Critical Thinking** Why do you think the overthrow of Louis Philippe in France was so important to students in Germany?

And in France and Prussia, all adult men were given the right to vote.

For the most part, however, the revolutions of 1830 and 1848 failed. Many revolutionary movements suffered from a lack of unity and clear goals. By 1848, deep divisions had emerged between middle-class liberals, who wanted moderate reforms, and workers, who demanded radical changes. In addition, conservatives were strong enough in most of Europe to defeat the revolutionaries.

During the 1850s, conservative governments tried to suppress revolutionary ideas. Faced with political persecution, some liberals fled their homelands and found refuge in the United States. But as you will read in the next unit, liberalism, nationalism, and socialism would continue to shape events in Europe in the late 1800s.

SECTION 3 REVIEW

1. **Locate:** (a) Poland, (b) Vienna, (c) Budapest, (d) Lombardy, (e) Venetia.

2. **Identify:** (a) Louis Kossuth, (b) Giuseppe Mazzini.

3. (a) Where did revolutions occur in 1830? (b) How was nationalism important in these revolutions?

4. How did Frederick William IV react to the offer of the crown of a united Germany?

5. Why did most of the revolutions of 1848 fail?

6. **Critical Thinking** Why was Austria able to suppress the revolts in its empire?

CHAPTER 20 REVIEW

Summary

1. **In 1814, the Congress of Vienna met to restore peace and stability to Europe.** The victorious powers redrew political boundaries and restored monarchs to the thrones lost during the Napoleonic wars.

2. **The ideals of the French Revolution continued to inspire demands for reform in France.** In 1830, Parisians revolted, forcing King Charles X to flee. In 1848, another uprising in Paris caused Louis Philippe to flee and resulted in the Second Republic. Louis Napoleon was chosen president but soon made himself emperor.

3. **The revolutions of 1830 and 1848 in France ignited forces of liberalism and nationalism in other parts of Europe.** In 1830, the Belgians won independence, but efforts by Poles and others to gain freedom failed. The revolutions of 1848 were at first successful in Bohemia, Hungary, and northern Italy. However, conservative forces soon reasserted power.

Recalling Facts

Decide if the following statements are true or false. If a statement is false, rewrite it to make it true.

1. During the 1800s, liberals wanted written constitutions.

2. The Congress of Vienna was dominated by conservatives.

3. Metternich encouraged nationalist revolts.

4. The Carlsbad Decrees gave German students the right to vote.

5. Greece won independence from Austria in 1829.

6. French liberals supported the July Ordinances.

7. Louis Philippe was a constitutional monarch.

8. Louis Kossuth led the nationalist movement in Hungary.

Chapter Checkup

1. Describe the main concerns of each of the following groups in the early 1800s: (a) liberals; (b) conservatives; (c) nationalists.

2. (a) What steps did the Congress of Vienna take to restore stability in Europe? (b) How did the great powers propose to keep the peace after the Congress?

3. (a) Describe the early challenges to the Metternich System. (b) How did Metternich respond to each challenge?

4. (a) What groups supported the July Revolution in France? (b) Why did revolutionary leaders decide to establish a constitutional monarchy instead of a republic?

5. (a) Describe the revolution of 1848 in France. (b) What was the outcome of that revolution? (c) What effect did the revolution in France have on the rest of Europe?

6. (a) How were the revolutions of 1830 in Belgium and Poland similar? (b) How were they different?

7. (a) What factors contributed to the revolutions of 1848 in the Austrian Empire? (b) What actions did the Austrian government eventually take in response to the revolutionaries?

Critical Thinking

1. **Synthesizing** (a) Why did diplomats at the Congress of Vienna want to restore the old order in Europe? (b) Why did they find it so difficult to turn the clock back?

2. **Analyzing** Louis Philippe's title was "king of the French by the will of the people." Earlier French kings had been called "king

by the grace of God." (a) Do you think Louis Philippe's title was accurate? Why or why not? (b) How does the change in title reflect developments in France since 1789?

3. **Understanding the Roots of Democracy** Demands for universal male suffrage were heard more and more often in the 1800s. (a) Why was this such a revolutionary idea at the time? (b) Why do you think many liberals and conservatives opposed it?

4. **Relating Past to Present** In 1830 and 1848, revolts by liberals and nationalists took place throughout Europe. (a) What revolutionary movements have taken place within the last few years? (b) Compare the reactions of governments today with the response of those in the 1800s.

Developing Basic Skills

1. **Map Reading** Compare the maps on pages 449 and 457. (a) How did the borders of France change between 1812 and 1815? (b) How does the map on page 457 show that the great powers wanted to limit French power? (c) What nation or nations gained new territory in Europe in 1815?

2. **Researching** Choose one of the leaders at the Congress of Vienna. Research his background in order to answer the following questions: (a) What was the person's official title ? (b) How did he gain power in his own country? (c) What were his ideas about government? (d) In your opinion, how did his background and position influence these ideas?

3. **Comparing** Make a chart with two rows and two columns. Title the rows Italy and Germany and the two columns Attempts at Unification and Result. Use what you read about the revolutions of 1848 in Italy and Germany to complete the chart. Then answer the following questions: (a) How were the attempts at unification similar in Italy and Germany? (b) How were they different? (c) Based on your reading in this chapter and earlier chapters, explain what factors made unification in each area difficult.

Writing About History

Bibliography Cards for Books

To prepare a working bibliography, make out a separate card for each book you use in your research. Write the full name of the author, last name first. Underline the title of the work. Include the city of publication, publisher's name, and publication date. Include the library call number of the book.

> 940.2
> L
>
> Langer, William L.
>
> <u>Political and Social Upheaval, 1832–1852.</u>
>
> New York.
>
> Harper & Row, 1969.

Practice: Write a bibliography card for this textbook. Use the call number 909.

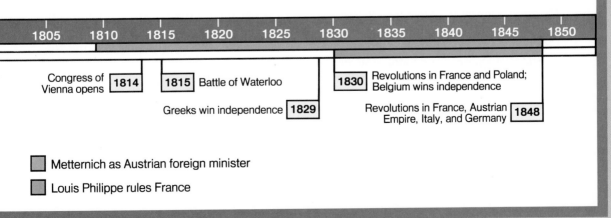

| 1805 | 1810 | 1815 | 1820 | 1825 | 1830 | 1835 | 1840 | 1845 | 1850 |

Congress of Vienna opens **1814**

1815 Battle of Waterloo

Greeks win independence **1829**

1830 Revolutions in France and Poland; Belgium wins independence

Revolutions in France, Austrian Empire, Italy, and Germany **1848**

▓ Metternich as Austrian foreign minister

▓ Louis Philippe rules France

Unit Six

Mini-Atlas

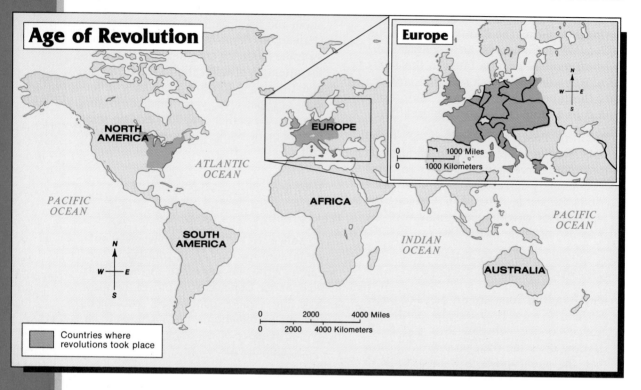

Age of Revolution

NORTH AMERICA

ATLANTIC OCEAN

PACIFIC OCEAN

SOUTH AMERICA

EUROPE

AFRICA

INDIAN OCEAN

PACIFIC OCEAN

AUSTRALIA

N W E S

0   2000   4000 Miles
0   2000   4000 Kilometers

Countries where revolutions took place

Europe

N W E S

0   1000 Miles
0   1000 Kilometers

Unit Themes

In the 1600s and 1700s, revolutionary forces shaped events in Western Europe as well as in the New World. The Scientific Revolution changed the way people saw the world. Many people began to think that once they understood the laws governing natural events they could master the world. During the Enlightenment, people used science and reason to try to solve the world's problems.

The revolution in thinking contributed to political revolutions. Revolutions strengthened Parliament in Britain, helped create the United States of America, and toppled an absolute monarch in France. In all three nations, citizens demanded a larger role in government.

After the fall of Napoleon, the Metternich System restored conservative government to Europe. However, the forces of nationalism, liberalism, and socialism resulted in a wave of revolutions that swept across Europe.

1. **Analyzing** (a) According to the time line, which revolutions occurred during the Enlightenment? (b) How did most Enlightenment thinkers view the results of the English civil war? (c) What effect did Enlightenment ideas have on the American and French revolutions?

2. **Applying Geography** (a) According to the map at right, through which countries did Napoleon pass on his retreat? (b) Why did he invade Russia? (c) How did the Russians use geography to defeat Napoleon?

3. **Expressing an Opinion** (a) Which countries on the world map above experienced revolution? (b) Explain why you agree or disagree with the following statement: "Thanks to Napoleon the ideals of the French Revolution were preserved and spread throughout Europe."

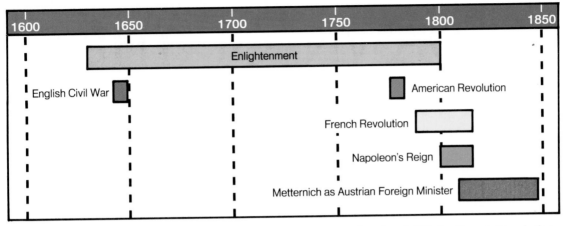

In which century did the English civil war take place? Did the French Revolution take place before or after the American Revolution? Who ruled France through most of the French Revolution?

MAP STUDY

Napoleon marched with over 500,000 soldiers into Russia. Fewer than 100,000 returned. From which direction did Napoleon's troops march into Russia? Which towns did he pass through on the way into Russia?

Napoleon's Invasion of Russia

Napoleon's invasion and retreat from Russia

States under French control

States allied with France

0   250   500 Miles
0   250   500 Kilometers

DAWN OF THE INDUSTRIAL AGE

1825 *Nicholas I gave the Russian secret police almost unlimited power. He is shown here leading a parade.*

During the reign of Queen Victoria, 1837–1901, government in Britain became more democratic.

	1800	1820	1840	1860
POLITICS AND GOVERNMENT		**1815** Corn Laws raise the price of bread in Britain	**1831** Mazzini founds Young Italy to work for unification	
ECONOMICS AND TECHNOLOGY	**1800** Volta builds first electric battery		**1850s** Bessemer improves method of steel production	
SOCIETY AND CULTURE	**1800** Robert Owen sets up a "utopian" community in Scotland		**1834** Victor Hugo publishes *The Hunchback of Notre Dame*	

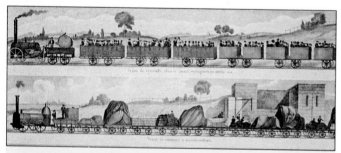

The earliest steam-powered trains carried passengers and freight.

1851 *Crowds flocked to the Crystal Palace in London to see the first international industrial exhibition.*

UNIT OUTLINE

By the late 1800s, reform had become a major theme in American political campaigns.

Peter Carl Fabergé designed exquisite decorative items of gold, enamel, and jewels. This box was made for Czar Nicholas II and his wife, Alexandra.

1860	1880	1900	1920
	1871 German Empire founded after defeat of France		**1905** Revolution breaks out in Russia after Bloody Sunday
	1876 Alexander Graham Bell invents telephone	**1903** Wright brothers make first flight at Kitty Hawk	
	1871 Verdi writes the opera *Aida*	**1890s** European cities adopt the electric streetcar	**1918** Women over 30 win right to vote in Britain

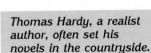

Thomas Hardy, a realist author, often set his novels in the countryside.

This painting shows the luxurious life at the court of the Hapsburgs. Emperor Francis Joseph is the center of attention.

The Industrial Revolution

21

(1750–1914)

During the early years of the Industrial Revolution, the transition from hand to machine labor was very slow. As the machines roar in this factory, workers— men, women, and children—perform much tedious work by hand.

Imagine the place—"a town of machinery and tall chimneys, out of which interminable [endless] serpents of smoke trailed themselves for ever and ever, and never got uncoiled." With these words, British author Charles Dickens described a typical English factory town in the 1800s. His description fit dozens of towns scattered over the landscape. Published in 1854, Dickens's novel, *Hard Times,* told about the miseries faced by people living and working in such towns.

An outsider would be struck by the ugliness of the town. "It had a black canal in it, and a river that ran purple with ill-smelling dye, and vast piles of buildings full of windows where there was a rattling and trembling all day long, and where the piston of the steam engine worked monotonously up and down, like the head of an elephant in a state of melancholy madness."

To Dickens, the people of the town shared the same "melancholy madness." They were "equally like one another. All went in and out at the same hours, with the same sound upon the same pavement, to do the same work and to whom every day was the same as yesterday and tomorrow, and every year the counterpart of last and the next."

The conditions Dickens described were the result of the Industrial Revolution. The Industrial Revolution was neither sudden nor swift. It was a long, slow process in which production shifted from hand tools to machines and in which new sources of power such as steam and electricity replaced human and animal power.

The Industrial Revolution had two distinct stages. During the first stage, from about 1750 to 1850, Great Britain took the lead in shifting to new methods of production. During the second stage, from the mid-1800s to about 1914, the nations of Western Europe and the United States became modern industrial powers. The Industrial Revolution was to transform completely the patterns of life in these nations. ■

1 Beginnings of the Industrial Revolution

READ TO UNDERSTAND

☐ How the Agricultural Revolution contributed to the Industrial Revolution.

☐ How inventions and new methods of production brought changes to industry.

☐ Why Britain led the way in the Industrial Revolution.

☐ *Vocabulary:* enclosure movement, factory system, Bessemer process.

By noon, fashionable ladies, sailors, workers, and bankers filled London's Hyde Park. Suddenly, trumpets blared, the crowds cheered, and Queen Victoria of England stepped down from her carriage.

The occasion was the opening of the Great Exhibition of 1851, which claimed to display "the works of industry of all nations." Its theme was progress. Inside the Crystal Palace, the huge building in which the exhibition was held, visitors marveled at the more than 6,000 exhibits from around the world. But what particularly pleased them was the clear evidence that Britain was truly the "workshop of the world."

As visitors gawked at locomotives, power looms, steam engines, and other mechanical marvels, they could see how far the world had come in the past 100 years. In the mid-1700s, Great Britain and France were developing new methods of production. Inventors applied scientific principles to practical problems—how to make an engine that pulled heavy loads or how to spin cloth more quickly. After 1789, however, France was distracted by its revolution. At this point, Britain forged ahead as the leader of the Industrial Revolution.

The Agricultural Revolution

One reason why the Industrial Revolution got under way first in Britain was a revolution in agriculture. Changes in farming greatly increased the amount and variety of food produced. During the 1700s, farmers began growing new crops, such as potatoes and corn, that had been introduced from the Americas. They also developed new ways of using the land that made it more productive.

Crop rotation. Since the Middle Ages, farmers had planted the same crop in a given field year after year. Every third year, they left the field fallow to prevent the soil from wearing out. In the 1730s, Charles Townshend discovered that fields did not have to be left fallow if farmers would rotate the crops they planted in a field. He suggested that farmers grow wheat or barley in a field for one or two years and then plant clover or turnips in the field for one or two years.

Townshend's ideas helped revolutionize agriculture. Crops such as clover and turnips replenished the soil with the nutrients that wheat and barley used. Also, clover and turnips provided excellent feed for animals. Thus, farmers could raise cattle and sheep. As meat became available at lower cost, people could add more protein to their diet.

New farm machines. The invention of new farm machines also increased food production. Jethro Tull developed a seed drill that planted seeds in straight rows. This was a big improvement over the old method of scattering seeds at random, which made fields a tangle of crops and weeds. The seed drill also reduced the amount of seed used in planting, and it let farmers weed around the straight rows of growing crops.

During the 1700s, farmers began to use new iron plows in place of less efficient wooden plows. In the 1800s, wealthy landowners bought mechanical reapers and threshers, which made harvesting crops easier. This further increased farm production.

The enclosure movement. Changing patterns of land ownership in Britain also contributed to the Agricultural Revolution. Since the Middle Ages, farmers had worked small strips of land in scattered fields. They grazed their animals and gathered timber on common, or public, lands. In the 1500s, wealthy landowners began claiming the right to these common lands. The **enclosure movement,** the fencing off of public lands by landowners, spread rapidly in the 1700s.

The enclosure movement made agriculture more efficient because wealthy landowners farmed larger amounts of land and experimented with new crops. However, it forced many small farmers off land they had worked for years. Some became tenant farmers on land owned by others. Others drifted to towns in search of work.

The Agricultural Revolution helped set the stage for the Industrial Revolution. With more food available, people's diet and health improved. These changes contributed to the rapid growth of population. As the population increased, the demand for manufactured goods, such as clothing, grew. Furthermore, more efficient methods of farming meant that fewer people were needed to work the land. Unemployed farmers, including those forced off the land by the enclosure movement, formed a large new labor force.

Changes in the Textile Industry

While changes in agriculture put many farmers out of work, inventions—especially in the British textile industry—created new demands for laborers. During the 1500s and 1600s, entrepreneurs had developed the domestic system for manufacturing wool cloth. (See page 369.) They supplied rural families with raw wool and cotton. In their own cottages, family members cleaned and spun the wool or cotton into thread. They then used hand looms to weave the thread into cloth.

The domestic system could not keep up with a rising demand for cloth, especially cotton cloth. In the 1700s, practical-minded individuals developed ways to improve the manufacture of cloth. Each invention triggered others, revolutionizing the whole textile industry.

Mechanical inventions. In 1733, John Kay, a clockmaker, invented the flying shuttle, which replaced the hand-held shuttle used in weaving. The introduction of the flying shuttle greatly speeded up the weaving process. Weavers were soon using thread faster than spinners could produce it.

In 1764, James Hargreaves, a carpenter, developed a way to speed up spinning. He attached several spindles to a single spinning wheel. Using this spinning jenny, as it was called, a person could spin several threads at once.

Inventions such as the cotton gin, flying shuttle, spinning jenny, and power loom revolutionized the textile industry. At left, raw cotton is being spun into thread that will be woven into cloth on the loom at right.

In 1769, Richard Arkwright built a machine that could hold up to 100 spindles. Arkwright's invention was too heavy to be operated by hand, so he used water power to turn it. Thus, the machine was called the water frame. Ten years later, Samuel Crompton developed the spinning mule, which used features of Hargreaves's spinning jenny and Arkwright's water frame. Once again, the production of cotton thread was increased.

With more thread now available, inventors tried to make faster looms with which to weave the thread. In 1785, Edward Cartwright built a loom in which the weaving action was powered by water. Using this power loom, a worker could produce 200 times more cloth in a day than had been possible earlier.

In 1793, an American, Eli Whitney, invented a machine that increased the supply of raw cotton and thus gave the British cotton industry a further boost. Before cotton fibers could be spun into thread, workers had to remove sticky seeds by hand, an extremely slow process. Whitney's cotton gin, a machine that tore the fibers from the seeds, sped up the process of cleaning cotton fibers. Whitney's cotton gin made it possible for a single slave on an American cotton plantation to turn out as much raw cotton as 50 slaves had been able to do by hand. Cotton production soared, and the price of cotton fell. By the 1830s, Britain was importing 280 million pounds of raw cotton every year, mostly from the United States. It had become the cotton manufacturing center of the world.

The factory system. The new spinning and weaving machines were expensive. In addition, they had to be set up near rivers, where the running water turned a water wheel to power the machines. Inventors such as Arkwright built spinning mills and started hiring hundreds of workers to run the new machines.

These early textile mills operated under the factory system, which gradually replaced the domestic system of production. Under the

factory system workers and machines were brought together in one place to manufacture goods. Everyone had to work a set number of hours each day, and workers were paid daily or weekly wages.

Development of the Steam Engine

Although many early inventions in the textile industry were powered by running water, steam soon became the major source of energy. The idea of a steam-powered engine had existed for a long time. As early as 1698, Thomas Savery had built a steam-driven pump to remove water from flooded coal mines. Unfortunately, Savery's pump frequently exploded because of the intense pressure of the steam.

In the early 1700s, Thomas Newcomen developed a safer steam-powered pump. But Newcomen's engine broke down frequently and required a lot of coal to fuel it. Finally, in the 1760s, James Watt, who had repaired several Newcomen engines, developed ways of improving the engine. Watt's steam engine got four times more power than Newcomen's engine from the same amount of coal.

Steam powered the Industrial Revolution. Steam engines were used in the growing textile industry. They also brought great changes in the mining of iron and coal, and they revolutionized transportation.

Development of the Iron and Coal Industries

Producing and operating the steam engine and the other new machines required huge quantities of iron and coal. Fortunately, Britain had large deposits of both. During the Industrial Revolution, better methods of production boosted the output of iron and coal and improved the quality of the iron.

To produce iron, ore has to be heated to high temperatures to burn off impurities. At first, charcoal, a fuel made by burning hard wood, was used to heat the ore. But hard woods were becoming scarce in Britain. In the early 1700s, Abraham Darby developed a way to use coke, a form of coal, in place of charcoal.

Iron making was further improved in the 1780s, when Henry Cort devised a puddling process that made iron stronger and less likely to crack under pressure. Cort also developed a technique for producing sheets of iron.

Using the new methods, Britain quadrupled its iron production between 1788 and 1806. At the same time, the demand for coal, both for making iron and for powering steam engines, sparked a boom in coal mining.

In the 1850s, the iron industry received another boost when Henry Bessemer developed a procedure that made the production of steel, an alloy of iron and other materials, cheaper and easier. In the **Bessemer process,** blasts of cold air were blown through heated iron to remove impurities. The result was stronger, more workable steel. As steel became readily available, it triggered the growth of other industries.

Coal fueled the early Industrial Revolution. In this 1814 print, a coal miner stands in front of a steam engine that is pulling a load of coal. The print is the first English picture of a steam-powered vehicle. Despite the use of steam engines, work in the coal mines remained largely dependent on the backbreaking labor of men, women, and children.

Smoke puffs from the engine pulling this early passenger train in France. Carriages on early trains had been adapted from horse-drawn carriages. The first French railway line, which began service in 1832, connected Lyon with Saint Étienne, about 30 miles (50 kilometers) away.

Advances in Transportation and Communication

Industry depends on a good transportation system to bring raw materials to factories and to distribute finished goods. In the 1700s, the need for rapid, inexpensive transportation led to a boom in canal building in Britain. In 1759, the Duke of Bridgewater built a canal to connect his coal mines and factories. Soon, canals were being built all over the country.

The 1700s were also a time of road building in Britain. Scottish engineer John McAdam invented a road surface made of crushed stone. This surface made roads usable in all weather. By the 1800s, road travel in England had become almost as fast as it had been in Roman times.

The need for good transportation also led to the development of the railroad industry. For years, mine carts had been pulled along iron rails by workers or donkeys. In 1829, George Stephenson, a mining engineer, developed the *Rocket,* the first steam-powered locomotive. The *Rocket* could barrel along iron rails at 36 miles (58 kilometers) an hour, an astounding speed at the time.

Between 1840 and 1850, the British built over 5,000 miles (8,000 kilometers) of railroad tracks. As steel rails replaced iron rails, trains reached speeds of 60 miles (96 kilometers) an hour. Railroads brought raw materials, factories, and markets closer together than ever before.

In the 1800s, Britain led the way in railroad building and shipbuilding. However, it was an American engineer, Robert Fulton, who developed a way to use steam power for ships. In 1807, Fulton successfully tested the *Clermont,* a paddle-wheeled steamship, on the Hudson River. By 1850, steamships regularly crossed the oceans.

The railroad and the steamship improved communications within nations and across the world. Britain introduced an inexpensive postal system, which further improved communication. In 1837, American Samuel F. B. Morse invented the telegraph, which sent messages by electrical impulses. Messages that once would have taken days to arrive now took minutes or seconds. In 1851, the first underwater telegraph cable was installed under the English Channel. It made rapid communication between Britain and the continent possible.

Why Britain Led the Industrial Revolution

Britain enjoyed many advantages that helped it take an early lead in the Industrial Revolution. As you have read, the Agricultural Revolution increased food production, which freed many laborers to work in industry. Moreover, Britain had plentiful iron and coal resources, and it developed an excellent transportation system to speed the flow of goods.

Britain was the leading trading nation in Europe. Since the 1500s and 1600s, British merchants had made huge profits from the international trade in tobacco, sugar, tea, and slaves. As a result, British entrepreneurs had the capital to invest in industries such as textiles, mines, railroads, and shipbuilding. Britain also had a large colonial empire that supplied raw materials to its factories. In addition, people in the colonies bought finished goods produced by British industry.

SKILL LESSON The Industrial Revolution: Reading Thematic Maps

Maps provide much useful information about how geography can influence historical events and developments. Many of the maps you have studied in this text have shown topographical features, such as rivers and mountains, as well as political boundaries. Some have also given information about trade routes.

However, there are other kinds of maps that give valuable information about population, natural resources, rainfall, and crop production. Maps that provide this kind of specialized information are called thematic maps. Practice reading thematic maps by using these steps to study the map at right.

1 **Decide what is shown on the map.** On a thematic map, the key tells you what the symbols mean. (a) What do the areas shaded purple represent? (b) What do the red squares represent? (c) What other information is given on the map?

2 **Practice reading the information on the map.** (a) Name two cities on the map with populations of 300,000 or over. (b) Name two cities with populations of 100,000 to 300,000. (c) Which cities with populations over 300,000 were located near iron and coal resources? (d) Which large cities were probably ports?

3 **Draw conclusions about a historical event or development.** (a) What relationship does the map show between areas with coal and iron resources and those with large cities? (b) What areas of Britain were probably the most industrialized? Explain.

Industrial Revolution in Great Britain About 1830

SCOTLAND

Glasgow · Edinburgh

NORTH SEA

· Newcastle

Leeds

Manchester · Liverpool · · Sheffield

IRELAND

WALES

· Birmingham

ENGLAND

Cardiff · · Bristol · London

· Portsmouth

· Plymouth

ENGLISH CHANNEL

0 50 100 Miles
0 50 100 Kilometers

FRANCE

· Cities of 100,000 to 300,000 people

· Cities over 300,000 people

■ Iron ore deposits

Coal fields

The British government encouraged industrial growth. It lifted restrictions on trade. It encouraged road- and canal-building, and it maintained a strong navy to protect British merchant ships all over the world.

The intellectual and social climate in Britain also encouraged industrialization. Although a strong class structure existed in Britain, the British accepted the idea that poor people did not have to stay poor forever but could better themselves.

SECTION 1 REVIEW

1. **Identify:** (a) Charles Townshend, (b) John Kay, (c) James Hargreaves, (d) Richard Arkwright, (e) Edward Cartwright, (f) James Watt, (g) George Stephenson.

2. **Define:** (a) enclosure movement, (b) factory system, (c) Bessemer process.

3. List two factors that led to the Agricultural Revolution in Britain.

4. How did the factory system differ from the domestic system?

5. Why was the invention of the steam engine important to the Industrial Revolution?

6. **Critical Thinking** Explain how improvements or inventions in one area of industry triggered changes in other areas.

2 The Rise of Modern Industry

READ TO UNDERSTAND

☐ How industrialization spread.

☐ How advances in science and technology affected industry.

☐ Where the capital for expanding industry came from.

☐ *Vocabulary:* productivity, interchangeable parts, assembly line, mass production, corporation, monopoly.

"The last rail is laid! The last spike driven! The Pacific railroad is completed!" The words clattered over the telegraph wires. At Promontory

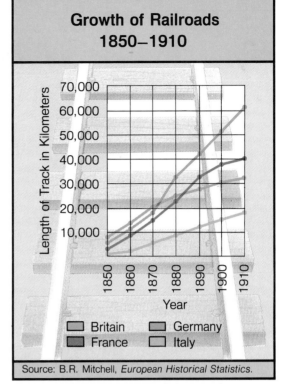

Growth of Railroads 1850–1910

Length of Track in Kilometers

70,000
60,000
50,000
40,000
30,000
20,000
10,000

1850 1860 1870 1880 1890 1900 1910

Year

☐ Britain ☐ Germany
☐ France ☐ Italy

Source: B.R. Mitchell, *European Historical Statistics.*

GRAPH STUDY *The building of railroads stimulated industrial growth in many countries. Because large amounts of iron and coal were needed to build railroads, these industries grew. Where were railroads growing most rapidly between 1850 and 1910?*

Point, Utah, on May 10, 1869, two locomotives, one facing east, the other west, touched. A railroad now spanned the United States from coast to coast.

By the 1850s, the pace of industrialization had quickened, and the Industrial Revolution had entered its second stage. Between 1850 and 1914, industry grew rapidly in the nations of Western Europe, including Belgium, France, and Germany. At the same time, the United States, too, industrialized and soon rivaled Britain in many fields. In Asia, Japan also joined the ranks of industrialized nations.

The Spread of Industrialization

During the second half of the 1800s, other nations began to challenge British leadership in the Industrial Revolution. Belgium was one of the first nations on the European continent to industrialize. Like Britain, Belgium had large deposits of coal and iron. Belgium also had a long manufacturing tradition, especially in textiles. Thus, it had a skilled labor force willing to work in industry. Moreover, Belgian en-

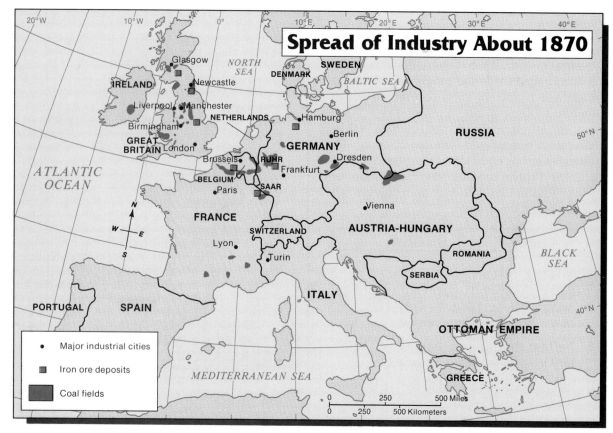

Spread of Industry About 1870

MAP STUDY *During the second half of the 1800s, the Industrial Revolution spread beyond Britain to other European countries. Iron and coal were essential to the growth of industry on the continent, as they had been in Britain. Some of the major iron deposits and coal fields are shown on this map. Which industrial cities in Germany, Belgium, and France were located near these resources?*

trepreneurs had the capital needed to invest in factories and machinery.

France, too, built a strong textile industry with a number of inventions. In the early 1800s, Joseph Marie Jacquard developed the first power loom that could be used to weave complex patterns. The Jacquard loom had a punched card system that controlled the intricate patterns.* Textiles produced on Jacquard looms sold for high prices among the fashion-conscious upper classes in Europe.

The French government encouraged the textile industry at home by imposing high tariffs on cloth imported from other nations. By making imported cloth more expensive, the government pushed people to buy French textiles. The government also backed projects to

improve transportation, especially the building of railroads.

Across the Atlantic, the United States had vast natural resources. Europeans helped Americans exploit these resources by investing capital in the young nation. Railroad building brought rapid economic growth in the United States. As you have read, by 1869 the first railroad spanned the continent. By the 1870s, American iron and steel production was well on the way to outstripping that of Britain. In the next decade, the United States moved ahead of Britain as the leading industrial nation.

Until 1870, German industry suffered because of divisions among many small states. After Germany achieved national unity in 1871, it rivaled the United States and Britain as a leading industrial power, as you will read in Chapter 24.

---

* The punched cards used in early computers were based on Jacquard's idea.

The nations of southern and eastern Europe remained largely agricultural during the 1800s. In Spain, Italy, Austria, and Russia, governments did little to encourage industrial growth.

Advances in Science and Technology

During the early Industrial Revolution, most inventors were people looking for ways to repair tools or improve machinery. After 1850, however, people turned to science not only to solve problems of manufacturing but also to discover new products to manufacture. Scientific research led to many inventions as well as remarkable advances in technology. Knowledge of new technology spread quickly from one nation to another.

The results of scientific research brought sweeping changes to industry. For example, the English chemist William Perkins discov-

---

THEN AND NOW The Invention of Photography

On a summer afternoon in 1839, people crowded into an auditorium in Paris. They had gathered to learn about a new way to make pictures of people and things. Unlike paintings, the new method showed their subjects exactly as they were in real life. The method had just been perfected by a French painter named Louis Daguerre (duh GEHR), shown here. His pictures, called "daguerreotypes," were the first photographs.

The audience listened intently as Daguerre's method was explained. He had placed a metal plate coated with silver iodide, a light-sensitive material, inside a camera. The plate was then exposed to light through a small hole in the camera. When the plate was removed and treated with mercury fumes, an image appeared on the surface. The plate was then washed and coated with table salt to keep the image from fading.

Many people in the audience were excited by Daguerre's discovery. "I ran straight off to buy silver iodide," one of them said. "I hated to see the sun go down, for it forced me to put off my experiments until the next day. The technique was so novel and seemed so marvelous that even the poorest result gave indescribable joy."

One of the drawbacks to this early form of photography was that it was hard to make more than one print of a daguerreotype. But a British inventor, William Fox Talbot, discovered a way to produce paper "negatives" from which photographers could make as many prints as they wished. Talbot's method, which was also announced in 1839, became the basis of modern photography.

The use of photography spread rapidly during the last half of the 1800s. During the American Civil War, Mathew Brady photographed soldiers and battlegrounds. But since his subjects had to hold still for the camera, Brady could not take pictures of actual battles. Soon newspapers and magazines realized the appeal of photographs. When they printed photographs, they boosted their circulation and also made a record of the past for future generations.

1. How did Parisians react to Daguerre's discovery?

2. **Critical Thinking** Why do you think photographs and photography have proven to be so popular?

ered a brilliant dye that could be made cheaply from coal. German chemists also discovered ways to make dyes cheaply. The textile industry quickly adopted the new dyes to replace more costly natural dyes such as indigo. Other discoveries led to the development of chemical fertilizers, which greatly increased food production.

In 1800, Alessandro Volta, an Italian physicist, used his knowledge of electricity to build one of the first electric batteries. The work of Michael Faraday, an English scientist, led to the construction of electric generators, which eventually replaced steam engines in many factories.

Discoveries in the field of electricity improved communications. In 1866, workers completed the first underwater telegraph cable across the Atlantic Ocean. Ten years later, Alexander Graham Bell invented the telephone. By the end of the century, Italian physicist Guglielmo Marconi had developed a way to send electric signals without wire or cable. His invention was called the wireless in England and the radio in America.

During this period, Thomas Alva Edison produced a remarkable number of inventions in his New Jersey workshop. Among Edison's inventions were the phonograph and the incandescent light bulb. He also designed an electric generating plant that provided power to light the streets of New York City.

A Revolution in Transportation

Inventors made dramatic advances in transportation in the late 1800s. Perhaps the most significant one was the development of the internal combustion engine. The internal combustion engine had a number of advantages over the steam engine. For example, it could be started and stopped more easily.

In 1886, the German scientist Gottlieb Daimler built an internal combustion engine, fueled by gasoline, that could power a small vehicle. Daimler used his engine to build one of the first automobiles. A few years later, another German engineer, Rudolf Diesel, developed an internal combustion engine that could power larger vehicles such as trucks, ships, and locomotives. The diesel engine used petroleum oil for fuel.

The internal combustion engine would revolutionize the transportation industry. By the 1920s, automobiles were a familiar sight in the United States and Europe. The growth of this new industry triggered booms in other industries, such as petroleum, steel, and rubber, which supplied materials for making automobiles.

New Methods of Production

New machines and technology greatly improved worker productivity. **Productivity** refers to the amount of goods a worker can turn out in a specific time. Early in the Industrial Revolution, Eli Whitney introduced the idea of **interchangeable parts,** identical components that can be used in place of one another in manufacturing.

Whitney owned a gun-making factory. Before Whitney, parts for guns were handmade, and each similar part was slightly different. Whitney manufactured large numbers of identical parts. When guns were made of these parts, a broken part could be easily replaced. The use of interchangeable parts spread to other industries, where it improved efficiency and made goods less expensive to make.

Thomas Edison called his research laboratory in Menlo Park, New Jersey, the "invention factory." Among his inventions were the incandescent light, storage battery, mimeograph machine, and ore separator. This photograph of Edison was taken after he had just worked 72 hours straight improving the wax cylinder phonograph on the table.

In 1913, Henry Ford, who owned an automobile factory in Highland Park, Michigan, introduced the assembly line to speed up production. On an **assembly line,** the complex job of assembling many parts into a finished product was broken down into a series of small tasks. Each worker performed only one or two tasks along a conveyor belt. As the auto body moved past the workers, each one added parts to it.

Because the assembly line was efficient, goods were produced more cheaply and could be sold at lower prices. As more people were able to afford goods such as automobiles, the demand for these products rose. To meet the demand, manufacturers introduced **mass production,** turning out large quantities of identical goods.

Financing Industrial Growth

As machinery grew more complex and more expensive, new ways of financing industry developed. To provide the large amounts of

---

THROUGH THEIR EYES The Flight at Kitty Hawk

For as long as people have watched the birds, they have dreamed of finding a way to fly. Orville and Wilbur Wright, two bicycle repairmen from Dayton, Ohio, were interested in flying experiments. They built and flew a glider in 1900, developing a way to guide its flight. Then they began work on the next step: attaching a motor to the craft.

Because existing gasoline engines were too heavy for flight, they built one of their own. They attached the engine to a pair of 8-foot wooden propellers and mounted it on their craft, which they christened Flyer. *The Wright brothers took the* Flyer *to Kitty Hawk, North Carolina, for a test flight. Ten years later, Orville Wright recalled the event:*

Orville Wright

During the night of December 16, 1903, a strong cold wind blew from the north. When we arose on the morning of the 17th, the puddles of water which had been standing about camp since the recent rains were covered with ice. We thought that by facing the *Flyer* into a strong wind there ought to be no trouble in launching it from the level ground about camp. We realized the difficulties of flying in so high a wind but estimated that the added dangers in flight would be partly compensated for by the slower speed in landing.

After running the motor a few minutes to heat it up, I released the wire that held the machine to the track, and the machine started forward into the wind. Wilbur ran at the side of the machine, holding the wing to balance it on the track. Wilbur was able to stay with it till it lifted from the track after a 40-foot run.

The course of the flight up and down was exceedingly erratic, partly due to the irregularity of the air and partly to lack of experience in handling this machine. A sudden dart when a little over 100 feet from the end of the track, or a little over 120 feet from the point at which it rose into the air, ended the flight. This flight lasted only 12 seconds, but it was nevertheless the first in the history of the world in which a machine carrying a man had raised itself by its own power into the air in full flight, had sailed forward without reduction of speed, and had finally landed at a point as high as that from which it started.

1. What effect did weather have on the flight of the *Flyer*?

2. **Critical Thinking** How might the Wright brothers' experience as bicycle repairmen have contributed to their success?

capital needed, the corporation developed. A **corporation** is a business owned by many investors. Each investor buys one or more shares in the corporation. Investors have limited liability for the debts of the corporation. That is, they risk only the amount of their investment. They share in the profits of the corporation in proportion to the number of shares they own.

After 1870, giant corporations bought up many small companies. Often, a corporation would establish a **monopoly,** or total control over the market for a particular product. In the United States, the Standard Oil Company, organized by John D. Rockefeller, acquired a virtual monopoly in the oil industry.

Banks played a major role in financing industry. People deposited money in banks and received interest from the bank for the use of their money. Banks invested this money in businesses, which grew as a result. The House of Rothschild in Paris was one of the world's leading investment banks. During the 1840s, it loaned money to pay for the building of the French railway system.

By the late 1800s, industrial growth had helped to create a complex international economy. Trade expanded to meet the demands for raw materials and manufactured products. Goods, services, and money flowed across the world. Distant regions became dependent on one another as suppliers or consumers of goods. Investors in one country organized companies in other countries. Many corporations and banks in Europe and the United States found new opportunities in overseas business ventures such as building railroads in Asia and Africa. As a result, governments became involved in protecting the international markets and investments of their citizens.

SECTION 2 REVIEW

1. **Identify:** (a) Alessandro Volta, (b) Michael Faraday, (c) Alexander Graham Bell, (d) Thomas Edison, (e) Gottlieb Daimler.

2. **Define:** (a) productivity, (b) interchangeable parts, (c) assembly line, (d) mass production, (e) corporation, (f) monopoly.

3. (a) Which European nations industrialized rapidly after 1850? (b) Which European nations remained largely agricultural?

4. Give one example of how scientific research affected industry.

5. Why were corporations and banks necessary to industrialization?

6. **Critical Thinking** Which of the inventions described do you think had the most far-reaching effects? Explain.

3 Effects of Industrialization

READ TO UNDERSTAND

☐ **What caused the population explosion.**

☐ **How the Industrial Revolution changed the lives of workers.**

☐ **How the class system changed as a result of the Industrial Revolution.**

☐ **How the new industrial society affected the lives of women.**

In the 1840s, for workers in English factories, a weekly wage of as little as 62 cents was not unusual. With this, they could barely feed a family of two adults and three children. Their diet consisted mostly of bread, potatoes, turnips, or cabbage. Even a tiny piece of meat was a luxury. As a result, millions of workers were underfed, and many children died from disease and malnutrition. Life for factory workers was grim and filled with hazards.

Before 1800, most people in Europe and North America had farmed the land. They lived and worked in the country or in small towns, owned their tools, and were generally self-employed. The Industrial Revolution radically changed these patterns of life. Millions of people crowded into cities to take jobs as wage earners in industry. By 1900, between a third and a half of the people in the industrialized countries of Western Europe and the United States lived in cities.

The Population Explosion

The Industrial Revolution began just as the population of Europe began to grow rapidly. That population explosion would have far-reaching effects. Between 1750 and 1914, the population of Europe grew from 140 million to 463 million people.

The Agricultural Revolution improved the diets of many people, so people were healthier. The Industrial Revolution also contributed to the population growth. Medical discoveries and public sanitation reduced the numbers of deaths caused by disease. And, from 1815 to 1914, European nations fought few large-scale wars. Industry provided jobs as well as goods for the growing population.

Problems of Growing Cities

Until the 1800s, cities, often located along land or water trade routes, served mainly as marketplaces. The Industrial Revolution changed the nature of cities. Cities seemed to spring up almost overnight as people flocked to mill and factory towns. When people poured into these fast-growing towns in search of jobs, living conditions grew worse.

Manchester, England, provides an example of what often happened. In 1750, Manchester was a fairly quiet market town with 16,000 residents. However, because there were iron and coal deposits nearby, soon textile manufacturers built factories there. By 1855, Manchester was the center of the British cotton industry, and its population had grown to 455,000.

The rapid growth of Manchester brought severe problems. Thousands of factory workers crowded into poorly built houses. A family of six or ten might live in a single dark, airless room. The city's water system was inadequate, and it had almost no sanitation system. Sewage was simply flung into open trenches along the streets. In many cities, pigs roaming the streets were the only "garbage collectors." In the crowded slums, diseases spread rapidly. Manchester was not even chartered as a city, so it could not tax citizens to raise money for improving living conditions. Nor could it pass laws to ensure that housing met minimum standards of safety or sanitation.

Living conditions in rural areas had often been difficult. Many people earned low wages as tenant farmers or day laborers. Farmers

Poverty, hunger, and disease contributed to the misery of life in early industrial cities. Despite the heroic efforts of doctors like the one in this painting, the poor often succumbed to the ravages of infectious disease. Many of those who died were children.

485

INDUSTRIAL MANCHESTER *Artist Wayne Anthony Still captures the overpowering monotony of a working-class neighborhood in Manchester, England. Row upon row of factories and tenements were the workplaces and homes of the city's nearly 500,000 people. In the smoke-filled industrial cities of Europe, most working-class families lived in just one room. Crowded conditions, open sewers, polluted rivers, and filthy streets bred crime and disease.*

seemed to be at the mercy of nature. When crops failed, hunger was an ever-present threat. And housing was often primitive. Still, in the country people usually could count on help from their neighbors.

For newcomers to the city, the lack of person-to-person contact came as a shock. During the early Industrial Revolution, one writer described the plight of city people who sat "in their little cells; divided by partitions of brick and board, they sit as strangers. They do not work together, but scramble against each other." In one house in a London slum, 63 people lived in nine rooms.

Working in a Factory

Most of the new city residents had jobs in factories, where working conditions were as miserable as living conditions at home. The supply of unskilled workers was large, so wages were very low. Often a whole family worked to survive. Women and children—some of whom started to work at age five—were in great demand because they could be paid less than men.

Workdays lasted from 12 to 16 hours, or from sunrise to sunset. Men, women, and children worked six days a week. There were no paid holidays, vacations, or sick leaves. Factories were often unhealthy, dangerous places to work in. Fumes from machines, combined with poor ventilation, made the air foul. The loud, monotonous noise of machines assaulted the ear. Lighting was poor, and machines were not equipped with safety devices, so accidents happened frequently. A worker injured on the job received no compensation. If an injured worker could no longer do the job, he or she was thrown out of work.

A New Social Structure

The Industrial Revolution reshaped the social structure of Europe. Before industrialization, the wealthy, landowning aristocracy held the highest position in society. Below the aristocracy was a relatively small middle class, which included merchants, lawyers, and the clergy. Next came skilled workers such as shoemakers, potters, and silversmiths. Finally, the vast majority of the people were small farmers or farm workers.

During the 1800s, the middle class expanded and challenged the landowning aristocracy in wealth and power. The wealthiest and most powerful members of the new middle class were factory and mine owners, bankers, and merchants. The middle class also included managers and owners of small businesses. They were joined by professional people such as doctors and lawyers. Lower down in the ranks of the new middle class were artisans and business clerks.

Wealthy members of the middle class often tried to adopt the customs of aristocrats. They bought magnificent country estates, which they decorated luxuriously. They took up aristocratic sports such as horseracing and sailing. Other members of the middle class lived comfortably but on a less lavish scale. Most middle-class families were very con-scious of their social position. They were constantly striving to live what they considered to be polite, respectable lives.

The Industrial Revolution produced a new social class of factory workers. Largely unskilled, they occupied the lowest rank in society. Industrial workers were very much aware that they belonged to a separate social class. They saw themselves as people with little political or economic power. By mid-century, workers began banding together to change their working and living conditions.

Changing Roles for Women

Traditionally, most women had either helped farm the land or worked in the home earning money through the domestic system. Some women worked as servants in the homes of the wealthy. The Agricultural Revolution and new farm machinery reduced the need for both men and women workers on farms. Then, as the Industrial Revolution got under way, the factory system replaced the domestic system.

To help support their families in the new industrial economy, many women went to work in the factories or the mines. Often, the entire family worked in the same place. In mines, for example, men dug the coal, women dragged coal trucks through low tunnels, and children sorted coal.

Working in a factory added greatly to a woman's responsibilities. She worked outside her home for 12 to 16 hours a day. Yet, she still had to cook, clean, and sew for her family. A woman's role was made even more difficult by the terrible living conditions in factory towns and cities.

By the late 1800s, other developments affected the role of women in industrialized nations. As you will read in the next section, the standard of living and wages of workers slowly improved. Thus, it became possible for many working-class families to live on the income of only one person. As a result, a new pattern of family life emerged. Husbands tended to be the sole wage earners, and women remained at home.

At the same time, the demand for household servants in the cities was growing. Middle-class families could afford to hire do-

During the Industrial Revolution, many women had to seek jobs outside the home to help support their families. Employers often exploited them by paying them lower wages than men. In this illustration, women shoemakers from Lynn, Massachusetts, carry a banner proclaiming, "American ladies will not be slaves. Give us a fair compensation, and we labor cheerfully."

mestic servants to work as cooks, maids, and nurses for children. Many women, especially single women, left their homes to take these jobs. In Britain in the late 1800s, about a third of all women working outside the home were employed as household servants.

Few middle-class women worked outside their homes. The social attitudes of the time encouraged middle-class women to marry and stay at home to raise their children. During the 1800s, a comfortable home became the ideal of many families. Popular songs about "home, sweet home" and mottoes such as "east, west, home's best" illustrated the belief in the joys of home life.

SECTION 3 REVIEW

1. Give two reasons why the population of Europe increased in the 1800s.

2. What problems did factory workers face in industrial cities such as Manchester?

3. Why were factories often dangerous places in which to work?

4. How did the makeup of the middle class change during the Industrial Revolution?

5. **Critical Thinking** How did the lives of middle-class women differ from those of working-class women? Are those differences still evident today? Explain.

4 Responses to the Industrial Revolution

READY TO UNDERSTAND

☐ Why labor unions were formed.

☐ What reforms led to improvements in the lives of workers.

☐ How living conditions in cities improved.

Deep in dangerous mine tunnels or amid the deafening roar of machines and the foul, polluted air of factories, millions of children labored alongside adults. The inhumane conditions of these workplaces shocked even a West Indian slaveholder visiting Britain. He remarked, "I have always thought myself disgraced by being the owner of slaves, but we never in the West Indies thought it possible for any human being to be so cruel as to require a child of nine years to work twelve and a half hours a day."

The brutal treatment of children was just one of the abuses of the early Industrial Revolution. By and large, factory owners had little sympathy for workers. They had invested their entire capital in risky undertakings, and they wanted to make sure their businesses succeeded. As industrialization continued, however, calls for reform grew.

Demands for Change in Britain

Because the Industrial Revolution began in Britain, workers there were the first to feel its effects. As their suffering grew, they protested, demanding higher wages, better working conditions, and protection against unemployment. Sometimes their protests were violent in Britain as well as on the continent.*

Between 1811 and 1816, workers in many parts of Britain smashed the machines that seemed to be the cause of their suffering. In 1819, a demonstration in Manchester drew an orderly crowd of about 80,000 workers. Demonstrators demanded economic and political reforms. Nervous soldiers fired on the crowd, killing 11 men and women and wounding about 400. At first, the British Parliament had little sympathy for the workers, and it applauded the actions of the soldiers.

Parliament investigates. Eventually, in 1831, Parliament began to investigate factory and mine conditions. Middle-class liberals opposed reforms because they believed the government should not interfere in business. However, conservatives sometimes criticized working conditions in factories and mines. As aristocratic landowners, they despised the way industrialization was changing life. But the findings of the investigators shocked even those opposed to reform.

One cotton-mill worker told lawmakers how the workday of his entire family lasted "from six in the morning till half-past eight at night." His children were worn out at the end of the long day. He and his wife "cried often

---

* As you read in Chapter 20, workers in Paris helped overthrow the French monarchy in the revolutions of 1830 and 1848.

when we have given them the little food we had to give them; we had to shake them, or they would have fallen asleep with the food in their mouths many a time."

A 17-year-old girl described her work in a coal mine. She spent her days on her hands and knees hauling carts loaded with coal through narrow mine shafts. She dragged the carts "a mile or more underground and back. I never went to day school," reported the girl. "I go to Sunday school, but I cannot read or write; I go to the pit at five o'clock in the morning and come out at five in the evening."

While Parliament conducted its official investigations, the cause of reform received a boost from a few reform-minded journalists and writers. They described in vivid detail the terrible conditions they saw in the factories and mines. Journalists awakened thousands of middle-class readers to the appalling poverty among workers. Novelists also helped create a

Child labor was one of the worst abuses of the early Industrial Revolution. Many parents needed what little money their children could earn. As a result, they put their sons and daughters to work as soon as they could walk. These children worked long hours under dangerous conditions and were often subjected to physical punishment.

public climate for reform. Charles Dickens, for example, attacked the evils of child labor in his novels *Oliver Twist* and *David Copperfield.*

Reforms begin. Prodded by its own findings and the growing public concern, Parliament took action. It passed the Factory Act of 1833, which limited the working day for children. Between the ages of 9 and 13, boys and girls could work no more than 8 hours a day. For children aged 14 to 18, the limit was 12 hours a day.

In 1842, Parliament passed the Mines Act. This law barred employers from hiring women or girls to work in mines and made 13 the minimum age for hiring boys. A few years later, the Ten Hours Act limited the workday for women and children under 18 years of age to 10 hours. Finally, in 1874, the 10-hour day was extended to all workers.

Rise of Labor Unions

Early in the Industrial Revolution, factory workers began forming associations to gain better wages, hours, and working conditions. These worker associations developed into labor unions.

Labor unions grew up first in Britain. From the start, they met strong opposition. The government saw labor unions as dangerous organizations. Employers argued that the shorter hours and higher wages demanded by unions would add to the cost of goods, reduce profits, and hurt business. As a result, Parliament passed the Combination Acts in 1799 and 1800 to outlaw labor unions.

On the continent, similar laws were passed. A French banker summed up the attitude many employers and government officials had toward worker demands for better treatment: "The workers must realize that their only salvation lies in patient resignation to their lot."

Yet workers refused to accept "their lot." In Britain, they struggled to have the Combination Acts repealed. They won this battle in the 1820s, although workers were still barred from striking or picketing. In the following decades, skilled workers in Britain formed trade unions based on a craft or trade such as cabinetmak-

ing and hatmaking. Because the workers had skills that were valuable to employers, these trade unions were able to bargain with employers.

Slowly, local trade unions formed larger associations to support both political and economic goals. They demanded the right to vote, the 10-hour workday, and the right to strike. By 1868, over 100,000 workers belonged to trade unions. In the 1870s, British unions won the right to strike and picket peacefully.

The success of the trade unions encouraged unskilled workers to form their own unions in the 1880s. They organized on the basis of their industries, forming unions of coal miners or dock workers. By 1889, London dock workers were organized well enough to strike in support of higher wages. The London dock strike shut down one of the world's busiest ports. From this point on, the strike was a common tool of labor unions. By the end of the century, union membership was growing rapidly in Britain, the rest of Western Europe, and the United States.

Gains for Workers

Between 1870 and 1914, the lot of industrial workers improved greatly. In Britain and France, wages nearly doubled in the last half of the 1800s, so workers could buy more than they had before. In addition, thanks to more efficient methods of production, goods such as clothing were often cheaper than before.

Gradually, employers came to realize that workers were more productive in a safer, healthier environment. They installed proper ventilation in factories, equipped machines with safety devices, and switched to new electric lighting. When some employers refused to make improvements, governments passed laws to ensure better conditions. Britain, Germany, and France led the way in drawing up factory codes that set minimum standards for safety and sanitary conditions.

Governments took other steps to satisfy the demands of workers. In the new industrial society, workers frequently faced financial disaster because of unemployment, accidents, sickness, or old age. To protect workers from such disasters, many governments passed laws creating insurance funds. These funds helped workers who could not earn a living because of sickness or accident. Some governments also set up old-age pension funds as well as systems of unemployment insurance for workers who lost their jobs because of business failure or economic slowdown.

By 1914, workers enjoyed a much better standard of living than workers had 100 years earlier. They could also look forward to a better future for their children. By then, free public schools had been set up in all the industrial nations. Moreover, living conditions in cities had improved.

Improving City Life

As you have read, living conditions in early industrial cities were horrible. As cities continued to grow, the need for action became urgent. In Britain and France, city governments built water and sewage systems. City governments also passed building codes that set minimum standards for housing.

Between 1850 and 1870, large parts of the city of Paris were almost completely rebuilt. Narrow, crooked streets were replaced by straight, wide boulevards. New and better houses were constructed, and large parks were opened for people to spend their leisure time. In London, a reform-minded member of Parliament, Sir Robert Peel, helped establish the first police force in that city. Londoners referred to members of the new police force as Bobbies or Peelers.

Cities became safer when gas and later electricity were used to light the streets at night. Electric power helped improve transportation when many European cities adopted an American invention, the electric streetcar. Electric streetcars were much cheaper and cleaner than the horse-drawn cars. As new streetcars came into use, people could live on the outskirts of the city and travel to work. Cities such as London, New York, and Berlin also built subway systems.

By the 1900s, cities had become more attractive places to live. Poverty and slums still existed, but in general even the poor had money to spend on the products of industry.

Fire posed a hazard to city dwellers. Some cities had voluntary bucket brigades. But steam-powered water pumps introduced in the late 1800s proved to be far more efficient. Fire hydrants were set up along city streets. Professional firefighters gradually replaced volunteers. This 1866 print shows a horse-drawn wagon with a steam pump rushing to a New York fire.

SECTION 4 REVIEW

1. **Identify:** (a) Factory Act of 1833, (b) Mines Act, (c) Combination Acts.

2. (a) What was the attitude of the British government toward labor unions in the early 1800s? (b) How did this attitude change by the late 1800s?

3. (a) What type of labor union developed first in England? (b) Why were these unions able to bargain successfully?

4. List three ways in which the lives of workers had improved by the late 1800s.

5. How did city governments improve living conditions?

6. **Critical Thinking** What do you think was the most significant difference between the early Industrial Revolution and the late 1800s? Explain.

CHAPTER 21 REVIEW

Summary

1. The Industrial Revolution began in Great Britain in the mid-1700s. The coming of the revolution was aided by a revolution in agriculture. Inventions improved the textile industry. Machines and workers were brought together in the factory system. As the Industrial Revolution unfolded, new sources of power such as the steam engine were developed.

2. Between 1850 and 1914, industrialization spread in Western Europe and the United States. Scientific research led to the development of technologies such as electricity and the internal combustion engine. Powerful corporations and banks provided the money to finance new industries.

3. Industrialization contributed to population growth, the rise of large cities, and the development of a new social structure. The early cities that grew up in the Industrial Revolution were overcrowded and filthy. Workers lived under terrible conditions, working long hours for low pay. The middle class expanded and enjoyed a comfortable way of life.

4. During the late 1800s, conditions improved for workers. In Britain, Parliament passed laws to limit the workday and to protect workers. Labor unions slowly won the right to organize workers and to strike in support of their demands. Conditions in the cities improved as well.

Recalling Facts

Match each inventor at left with the appropriate invention at right.

1. Henry Bessemer
2. Jethro Tull
3. Thomas Edison
4. Eli Whitney
5. Robert Fulton
6. Guglielmo Marconi
7. Samuel Morse

a. paddle-wheeled steamship
b. radio
c. phonograph
d. telegraph
e. new process of making steel
f. cotton gin
g. seed drill

Chapter Checkup

1. (a) Describe the Agricultural Revolution in Britain. (b) How did it help make the Industrial Revolution possible?

2. (a) How did inventions revolutionize the textile industry? (b) How did new technology trigger the rise of new industries?

3. (a) Why did the Industrial Revolution start in Britain? (b) Why did Belgium industrialize so early?

4. (a) What improvements were made in communications and transportation? (b) How did these improvements contribute to a further growth in industry?

5. Describe how the Industrial Revolution affected: (a) population; (b) cities; (c) the way people worked; (d) the social structure in European countries.

6. (a) What types of reforms did the British government institute? (b) What other factors contributed to improved conditions for workers?

1. **Understanding the Roots of Democracy** (a) Why did the British Parliament try to eliminate some of the worst abuses of the Industrial Revolution? (b) Why is public information important in a democracy?

2. **Understanding Economic Ideas** (a) What role did corporations play in the Industrial Revolution? (b) Why do you think corporations were so important?

3. **Synthesizing** One historian has suggested that the Industrial Revolution was "the greatest transformation in human history since the remote times when men invented agriculture, writing, the city, and the state." What evidence can you use to support this idea?

4. **Relating Past to Present** Compare the way of life that developed in industrial nations during the 1800s to life in the United States today.

Developing Basic Skills

1. **Graph Reading** Study the graph on page 479. (a) How many kilometers of railroad track did Britain have in 1850? (b) How many kilometers of track did Germany have in 1900? (c) Which nation had the most track in 1910? (d) Why did Italy have the smallest amount of track in 1910?

2. **Researching** Read about the life of one of the inventors discussed in this chapter. Then write a report in which you explain why you think he became an inventor.

Writing About History

Bibliography Cards for Other Sources

You should prepare bibliography cards for encyclopedia, magazine, and newspaper articles as you go along. On each card, write the full name of the author, last name first. For unsigned articles, start with the title of the article. Write the title of the article in quotation marks, followed by the name of the publication. For magazine and newspaper articles, include the date of publication and the page numbers of the article.

"Charles Dickens."
Encyclopaedia Britannica, 1988 ed.
Volume 17, page 267.

Hofstadter, Dan. "A Romantic and Turbulent Life."
Smithsonian, April 1987, page 74.

Practice: Prepare a bibliography card for the following item:

Joseph Gustaitis's article "Locomotive No. 999," published in the October 1986 issue of *American History Illustrated*, Volume XXI, Number 6, page 44.

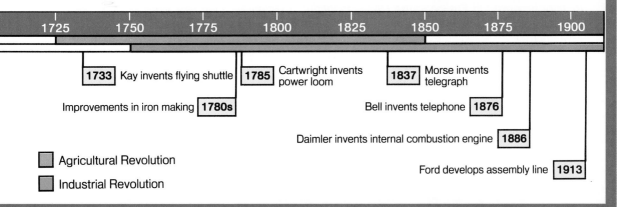

| 1725 | 1750 | 1775 | 1800 | 1825 | 1850 | 1875 | 1900 |

1733 Kay invents flying shuttle

1785 Cartwright invents power loom

1837 Morse invents telegraph

Improvements in iron making 1780s

Bell invents telephone 1876

Daimler invents internal combustion engine 1886

Ford develops assembly line 1913

- Agricultural Revolution
- Industrial Revolution

Currents of Thought

(1800–1914)

Romanticism in art and literature reflected the dramatic changes in life and thought occurring in Europe in the 1800s. Powerful, imaginative paintings, like the one from which this detail is taken, convey a spirit of turmoil, change, and excitement.

"I started from my sleep with horror; a cold dew covered my forehead, my teeth chattered, and every limb became convulsed; when, by the dim and yellow light of the moon, as it forced its way through the window shutters, I beheld the wretch—the miserable monster whom I had created. He held up the curtain of the bed; and his opened eyes, if eyes they may be called, were fixed on me. His jaws opened, and he muttered some inarticulated sounds while a grin wrinkled his cheeks. He might have spoken, but I did not hear; one hand stretched out, seemingly to detain me."

This scene is from the novel *Frankenstein*, written by Mary Shelley in 1818. It describes a nightmarish encounter between a young scientist, Frankenstein, and the grotesque monster he created. *Frankenstein* weaves together two major influences on thought during the 1800s: a growing interest in science and the belief that imagination and emotion were as important as reason. In the newly industrialized societies of Europe and the United States, many people had great faith in science. Scientific research, they thought, could solve the problems facing society.

The Industrial Revolution and the great changes it caused influenced the work of many philosophers and artists during the 1800s. Philosophers tried to explain the changes, and they often suggested solutions to the problems created by industrialization. Early in the century, some artists rejected industrial society. They looked back longingly at the simple, rural way of life. By mid-century, however, many writers and painters had come to accept industrialized society, and they portrayed it realistically. The feelings of nationalism unleashed by the French Revolution and Napoleon's conquests also influenced currents of thought in Europe during the 1800s. ■

1 New Ideas About Organizing Society

READ TO UNDERSTAND

☐ How laissez-faire thinkers explained the economic world.

☐ What changes utopian socialists called for.

☐ What predictions Karl Marx made about capitalism and communism.

☐ *Vocabulary:* laissez faire, communism, proletariat.

"Working men of all countries, unite!" declared Karl Marx and Friedrich Engels in 1848. In their *Communist Manifesto,* Marx and Engels urged workers to rise up against the system that oppressed them. "You have a world to win and nothing to lose but your chains," they proclaimed.

As the Industrial Revolution spread, thinkers debated how the problems of industrial society could be solved. Marx and Engels' idea of communism was one of many solutions proposed. Others argued against any interference because natural laws governed the economy, and one should not try to change them.

Laissez-Faire Economics

During the Enlightenment, the physiocrats held that natural laws controlled the economy. (See page 406.) They argued that these natural laws should be allowed to operate without interference. Consequently, the physiocrats opposed any attempt by government to interfere with the natural laws of economics. The economic system the physiocrats described is called **laissez faire** (LEHS ay FEHR), a French term meaning let people do as they choose.

The laissez-faire idea of the physiocrats was echoed in the late 1700s by Adam Smith, a Scottish philosopher and economist, in his book *The Wealth of Nations.* Smith contended that even though people acted in their own self-interest, society as a whole benefited. For example, industrialists use some of their profits to pay the salaries of workers and thus contribute to the wealth of the nation. Therefore, the government should not try to restrict the actions of industrialists.

Another supporter of laissez-faire economics in England was the economist Thomas Malthus. In his *Essay on Population,* Malthus stated that the human population grew faster than food production. Only forces such as disease and famine kept the population from out-

The Industrial Revolution brought both misery and plenty. While many workers suffered from low wages and poor working conditions, the middle class was becoming more prosperous. This painting by Edgar Degas shows women working in a millinery, where middle-class women could buy fashionable hats.

distancing food supplies. Malthus believed that interfering with the process would make conditions worse. He argued that if the government tried to correct social problems, the population would increase more rapidly. This would put greater strains on the food supply and increase the number of workers competing for jobs. Wages would then go down, and workers would be more miserable.

David Ricardo, an English stockbroker and economist, agreed with Malthus. His ideas gave rise to what his followers called the Iron Law of Wages. According to this law, population and wages go through cycles. When wages are high, workers have more children. The result is a surplus of workers and lower wages. When wages are low, workers have fewer children. Thus, there is a shortage of workers, and employers have to pay higher wages. When wages rise, the cycle begins again.

Malthus and Ricardo presented a gloomy picture of economics. In their view, workers were condemned to repeated periods of low wages and misery. Thus, economics as they described it came to be called the "dismal science."

Laissez-faire theories influenced people throughout the 1800s. Industrialists supported these theories because they wanted to run their businesses as they saw fit. They warned that attempts to interfere by labor unions or governments would violate the natural laws of economics and create even more misery.

Calls for Reform

Not all thinkers agreed that poverty was natural or inevitable. Some, such as English philosophers Jeremy Bentham and John Stuart Mill, thought efforts should be made to improve living and working conditions.

Like the laissez-faire economists, Jeremy Bentham believed that it would be best if the government did not become involved in the way people ran their businesses. However, he argued that the government should intervene if the actions of a few individuals brought misery to many.

John Stuart Mill called for reform to correct the problems created by industrialization. He thought workers should act through labor unions or other organizations to improve working conditions. He believed that the government should take action, when necessary, to protect workers. Mill also thought both men and women should have the right to vote and to have a good education.

Both Bentham and Mill supported the capitalist system, in which private investors own and control the means of production. (The means of production include land, machines, and factories, which are used to produce food and manufactured goods.) They thought industry should remain in private hands, and they approved of government action only as a way of correcting abuses of the system.

Another group of reformers, the socialists, challenged the whole idea of capitalism. Socialists argued that the capitalist system rewarded only the industrialists and not the workers whose labor supported it. Many socialists thought that the capitalist system should be replaced by a system in which the workers or the government owned and controlled the means of production. They wanted the means of production to be operated for the benefit of all the people.

Utopian Socialists

A group of early socialists, called utopian socialists, dreamed of reorganizing industry so that a new kind of society could grow out of it. In this utopia, or ideal society, there would be no poverty, and all people would be treated fairly.

One utopian socialist was Robert Owen. As a child, he had worked in the textile mills of Manchester, England. But, by age 23, Owen had become a successful cotton manufacturer. He believed that he could set up a system where he could make a profit and treat his workers well at the same time.

In 1800, Owen founded an industrial community in New Lanark, Scotland, to test his ideas. He paid high wages, built comfortable housing, provided schools, and set up stores where goods were sold at low prices. Owen's experiment worked. The textile mill was profitable, and the workers prospered.

In France, Charles Fourier (foo ree AY), like Owen, believed that poverty would end if workers were given the chance to work together in their own best interests. Fourier drew up plans for small model communities of 500 to 2,000 people. In each community, people would do the jobs for which they were best suited and would share the profits. Several such communities were set up in France, and two were founded in the United States. All the experiments failed, but many ideas of the utopian socialists lived on.

In the mid-1800s, Louis Blanc, a French journalist, called for the government to organize cooperative workshops run by workers. As you have read, national workshops were set up briefly in France during the revolution of 1848. Blanc's guiding principle—"from each according to ability, to each according to need"—was taken up by two German thinkers, Karl Marx and Friedrich Engels.

This cartoon was inspired by a report about working conditions in British coal mines. Deep in the mine, pitiful men, women, and children live a life of poverty and despair. On the surface, the wealthy industrialist lives a life of great luxury.

Karl Marx and Scientific Socialism

Karl Marx was a journalist who was exiled from Germany for his political and religious views. Marx moved to Paris where he met Friedrich Engels, whose father owned a textile mill in England. That meeting began a lifelong working partnership.

Both men blamed the system of industrial capitalism for the terrible conditions in factories. In 1848, Marx and Engels explained their theories in the *Communist Manifesto.* In it, they described a form of socialism in which there would be public ownership of all land and all other means of production. Today, such a system is called **communism.**

Marx's theories. Marx thought utopian socialists were impractical dreamers whose ideas would never work. He claimed that his theories of socialism were based on a scientific study of history, and he called his theories "scientific socialism."

This print illustrates the bleak lives of workers, wearily trudging to labor in the mines. The miserable conditions of the early Industrial Revolution led to worker protests and demands that governments correct abuses. Socialists such as Karl Marx blamed the entire capitalist system for the abuses. Marx believed that workers would overthrow capitalism in an international revolution.

Marx believed that history followed scientific laws just as nature did. He claimed that history was determined by economics, that is, the way goods are produced shapes the social and political structure of a society. According to Marx, throughout history societies have been divided into two classes—the "haves" and the "have nots." The "haves"—the people who control the means of production—have all the power and wealth and thus control society. As examples, Marx pointed out the masters and slaves of ancient Greece, the patricians and plebeians of ancient Rome, and the lords and serfs of the Middle Ages. He argued that the "haves" and "have nots" have always struggled with each other.

In industrialized societies, Marx theorized, the bourgeoisie, the middle class, were the "haves" and the **proletariat,** or working class, were the "have nots." Just as earlier ruling classes had been replaced, Marx argued, the bourgeoisie led by industrial capitalists would be replaced. He predicted that the proletariat would revolt, take control of the means of production, and destroy the capitalist ruling class. A classless society would then emerge in which everyone shared wealth and power.

Weaknesses of Marxism. Marx believed that capitalism would drag more and more people into poverty until, in desperation, they rebelled. But this did not happen. As you have read, the standard of living rose in industrialized countries.

Many abuses that were common early in the Industrial Revolution disappeared. Governments introduced reforms that improved working conditions, public health, and public education. Labor unions gradually won higher wages and shorter working hours. Health and accident insurance, unemployment insurance, and paid vacations also improved the lives of workers. As workers made gains under the capitalist system, they were not eager to overthrow it.

Also, Marx failed to understand the power of nationalism. He believed that workers, regardless of nationality, would unite against their common enemy, the capitalists. However, most workers had strong feelings of nationalism. They did not see themselves as part of an international community of workers, striving to build a socialist state.

Still, Marx's ideas of a classless society in which all would share equally appealed to many people. During the late 1800s and early 1900s, socialist parties were formed in many countries. These parties have had a significant impact on history, as you will read in later chapters.

SECTION 1 REVIEW

1. **Identify:** (a) Adam Smith, (b) Iron Law of Wages, (c) utopian socialists.

2. **Define:** (a) laissez faire, (b) communism, (c) proletariat.

3. Why was economics, as described by Malthus and Ricardo, called the "dismal science"?

4. Under what conditions did Bentham and Mill think the government should interfere in the way people ran their businesses?

5. (a) According to Karl Marx, what two classes were struggling against one another during the 1800s? (b) What did he think the outcome of the struggle would be?

6. **Critical Thinking** Explain in what way history has not followed the course Marx predicted.

2 An Age of Science

READ TO UNDERSTAND

☐ What Darwin's theory of evolution was and why it was so controversial.

☐ What advances were made in medicine, chemistry, and physics.

☐ What new social sciences developed.

☐ *Vocabulary:* survival of the fittest, sociology, psychology.

From small towns on the American frontier to big cities in Europe, there was hardly a person whose daily life was not affected by the scientific discoveries of the 1800s. Important developments took place in biology, chemistry, physics, medicine, and the new social sciences of sociology and psychology. Many of these developments improved people's lives. Some created great controversy.

Charles Darwin

In 1859, the British biologist Charles Darwin published a book that revolutionized the science of biology and sparked controversies that have lasted until the present. In that book, *On the Origin of Species,* Darwin presented a theory of evolution. According to Darwin's theory, all forms of life evolve, or change, over a long period of time. Simpler forms of life evolve into more complex forms, and new forms evolve out of older ones.

Darwin based his theory on the work of earlier scientists and on observations he made of plant and animal life during a five-year expedition to South America and the Pacific islands. During that trip, he made a detailed study of the many and varied forms of life he saw. Upon his return to England, he began working out a theory of how and why forms of life change over time.

Darwin accepted Malthus's theory that living things tended to multiply faster than the food supply. Darwin concluded that living things competed with one another for scarce food. Those living things with some type of advantage survived to reproduce. Their offspring inherited the biological traits that had helped them survive. Over time, the living things with these advantages became more numerous than those that lacked them. Darwin called this process natural selection. Others called it **survival of the fittest,** meaning that nature weeded out weak characteristics.

A bitter controversy. When Darwin first published his ideas in 1859, he was greeted with a storm of protest. Darwin proposed that all life had evolved from one original organism. Some scientists accused Darwin of saying that human beings were descended from apes.

Religious leaders such as Samuel Wilberforce, a bishop in the Church of England, said Darwin's theory of evolution contradicted the Bible, ignored the human soul, and failed to explain why humans were supreme on earth.

At age 22, Charles Darwin signed on as a member of a British scientific expedition to South America. Its mission was to chart the coastline of South America and study the plant and animal life. The expedition sailed on H.M.S. Beagle, shown here off Rio de Janeiro, Brazil. During the voyage, Darwin observed many species of plants and animals he had never seen before. In Brazil, for example, he counted over 60 different varieties of beetles.

Wilberforce claimed that Darwin's theory denied God's role in creation. Many Roman Catholics and fundamentalist Protestants, who believed that the words of the Bible had to be interpreted literally, also condemned Darwin's theory.

In time, many religious people concluded that the theory of evolution did not deny God's role in creation. They believed that God was still the creator of life, but that the biblical account of creation was a symbolic rather than a literal one. Others continued to believe that Darwin's theory was in error. Scientific study of Darwin's theory of evolution has continued to the present.

Social Darwinism. Some people applied Darwin's ideas to the social, economic, and political issues of the 1800s. The English philosopher Herbert Spencer turned Darwin's biological theory into a social theory. All human life, Spencer argued, is a struggle for existence. In this struggle, only the fittest survive. The theories of people like Spencer are called "Social Darwinism."

Many industrialists adopted Social Darwinism. They saw economic competition as a struggle for survival in which the strong drove out the weak. They believed their success in business proved they were fit to survive. Extreme nationalists also borrowed Darwin's ideas. Nations struggle for existence, they argued. Strong nations that defeated weaker nations were superior and therefore fit to survive.

Rudyard Kipling summed up this idea: "They should take who have the power. And they should keep who can."

Advances in Biology and Medicine

During the late 1800s, scientists showed how living things passed their biological characteristics on to their offspring. German biologist August Weismann based his work on the theory that all living things are made up of tiny cells. He identified two kinds of cells: reproductive cells that transmit biological characteristics to the next generation and body cells that die when the living thing dies.

At about the same time, Gregor Mendel, an Austrian monk, was also investigating how living things pass on biological characteristics. By crossing different strains of garden peas, he was able to change their characteristics over several generations. He then developed a series of laws to explain how heredity worked. Mendel's work became the basis for the scientific breeding of plants and animals.

The work of other scientists led to significant advances in medicine. The French chemist Louis Pasteur proved that tiny organisms called bacteria caused beer and wine to turn sour. He also found that bacteria could be killed by heat. Pasteur then applied this knowledge to the problem of milk spoiling. He developed a process called pasteurization, in which milk was heated enough to kill most bacteria and then cooled to slow the growth of remaining bacteria.

The German scientist Robert Koch showed that bacteria cause many diseases. He also found the specific bacteria that cause anthrax, a disease of sheep and cattle, as well as tuberculosis and cholera. Pasteur then developed a way to protect animals and humans from diseases caused by bacteria. When he

injected a weakened strain of anthrax bacteria into sheep, the sheep developed resistance to the disease. Later, he used the same method, called vaccination, to protect people from rabies, which is caused by viruses. After Pasteur, scientists found ways to immunize people against many other diseases.

The English surgeon Joseph Lister applied the findings of Koch and Pasteur to the problem of infection after surgery. Lister developed ways to kill bacteria on surgeons' hands and surgical instruments so bacteria would not be introduced into a patient's body during surgery. As Lister's methods were adopted, deaths due to post-operative infection declined dramatically. Such advances in medicine helped increase life expectancy. (See the graph on page 503.)

Discoveries in Chemistry and Physics

The study of chemistry was revolutionized in the early 1800s by the work of John Dalton, an English schoolteacher. Earlier scientists had suggested that everything is made up of tiny, indivisible particles called atoms. Dalton proposed that all the atoms of a particular element are identical and unlike the atoms of any other element. This theory is the foundation of modern chemistry.

Years later, the Russian scientist Dmitri Mendeleev (MEHN duh LAY uhf) found that the properties of elements are based on their atomic makeup. He then drew up what is called a periodic table in which he listed elements according to their atomic structures. Chemists used Mendeleev's discoveries to predict what will happen when elements are combined. With this knowledge, scientists developed many of the new substances, such as alloys and synthetics, used in industry.

The revolution in chemistry was accompanied by a revolution in physics. The Scottish physicist James Clerk Maxwell predicted that electric and magnetic energy moves in waves. In 1895, Wilhelm Röentgen, a German physicist, discovered energy waves that could penetrate solid matter. He called these waves X-rays. X-rays were soon put to work in the field of medicine.

French scientist Louis Pasteur made important breakthroughs in the study of bacteria and immunity. He won great fame when he successfully prevented a nine-year-old boy who had been bitten by a rabid dog from contracting rabies.

At about the same time, in France, Henri Becquerel discovered that the element uranium has unusual properties. Marie and Pierre Curie determined that these properties were due to uranium's atomic structure. They found two new elements—radium and polonium—that had similar properties.

In the early 1900s, the German-born scientist Albert Einstein built on the work of other physicists to develop new laws of physics. He

BUILDERS AND SHAPERS
Marie Curie: A Pioneer in the Study of Radioactivity

The abandoned shack did not look like a research laboratory. Tucked behind the School of Physics in Paris, the decaying wooden shed had no floor. The roof leaked, and a few discarded kitchen tables were the only furniture. Yet in this unlikely place, Marie Curie and her husband, Pierre, began their pioneering work in radioactivity.

Marie Sklodowska had left her native Poland in 1891 to study at the University of Paris. There she led the life of a poor student, skimping on coal for her stove and often having nothing to eat but bread and tea. Totally devoted to science, Marie had no time to take part in the social life of Paris. It was not surprising, then, that she met and married another scientist, Pierre Curie. They settled into a lifestyle of rigorous work. "Our life is always the same," wrote Marie. "We see nobody but my husband's parents. We hardly ever go to the theater and we give ourselves no diversions."

The Curies were inspired by the work of another Parisian, Henri Becquerel. In 1896, Becquerel found that uranium could darken a photographic plate from across a room. Fascinated by this discovery, Marie and Pierre Curie began to work with pitchblende, the rock in which uranium is found. Marie discovered that pitchblende was more radioactive than uranium alone. She concluded that there were other radioactive substances, as yet unknown, in the pitchblende.

The Curies had tons of pitchblende carted to their laboratory. During the four years of their research, they boiled over eight tons of pitchblende on their castiron stove.

The work was heavy and difficult. Marie wrote, "I came to treat as many as 20 kilograms [44 pounds] of matter at a time, which had the effect of filling the shed with great jars. It was killing work to carry the receivers, to pour off the liquids, and to stir, for hours at a stretch, the boiling matter in a smelting basin."

The breakthrough came in 1898. The Curies identified two new elements in the pitchblende. They named one polonium, for Marie's native Poland. The other, called radium, was a hundred times more radioactive than uranium. In 1903, the Curies and Henri Becquerel received the Nobel Prize in physics for their work on radioactivity. In 1911, Marie Curie won a second Nobel prize, this time in chemistry, for her study of the chemical properties of radium.

1. What led Marie Curie to begin her work with pitchblende?

2. **Critical Thinking** Why do you think the Curies were willing to spend four years of drudgery working with pitchblende?

rejected the idea that matter and energy are separate things. Instead, he proposed that matter and energy are interchangeable. Einstein also stated that there is no fixed point from which to measure motion. The motion of one object can be measured only by comparing it to the motion of another object. All measurements are therefore relative. This theory is called the theory of relativity. It represented a major departure from the physics of Isaac Newton and helped usher in the era of modern physics.

New Fields of Study

During the 1800s, thinkers once again tried to use the scientific method to study human behavior. This led to the development of two new social sciences—**sociology,** the study of society, and **psychology,** the study of behavior. Sociologists study how people act in groups. Psychologists study the behavior of individuals.

The French philosopher Auguste Comte was one of the founders of sociology. Comte argued that society, like nature, operated according to certain laws. He thought that once these laws were discovered, there would be a scientific basis for social organization and action.

The Russian psychologist Ivan Pavlov studied the behavior of dogs. Pavlov set up an experiment in which he always rang a bell before he gave food to a dog. Food caused the dog to salivate. Eventually, the dog would salivate as soon as it heard the bell. Pavlov concluded that the dog had been "conditioned" to respond even when the original stimulus, the food, was no longer there. Pavlov thought that people also were conditioned to respond automatically to a given stimulus. Therefore, some human behavior is based on unconscious responses rather than on conscious thought.

The Austrian physician Sigmund Freud based his work in psychology on the idea that an unconscious part of the mind governs much human behavior. A person's motives in taking certain action, he said, are sometimes hidden in the unconscious. Freud developed psychoanalysis, a method of trying to discover those motives.

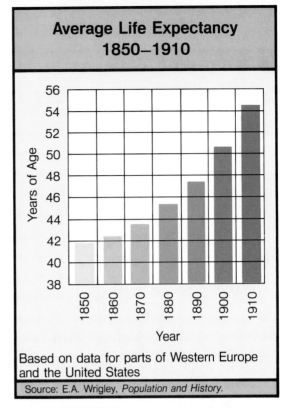

Average Life Expectancy 1850–1910

Based on data for parts of Western Europe and the United States

Source: E.A. Wrigley, *Population and History.*

GRAPH STUDY *An increase in the average life expectancy contributed to population growth during the 1800s and early 1900s. The average life expectancy is the average number of years people born in a given year could be expected to live. What was the average life expectancy of people born in 1860? Between which years did it increase the most?*

SECTION 2 REVIEW

1. **Identify:** (a) Social Darwinism, (b) Gregor Mendel, (c) Louis Pasteur, (d) Wilhelm Röentgen, (e) Marie and Pierre Curie, (f) Ivan Pavlov, (g) Sigmund Freud.

2. **Define:** (a) survival of the fittest, (b) sociology, (c) psychology.

3. (a) Explain Darwin's theory of evolution. (b) Why did some religious leaders object to it?

4. List one advance in each of the following sciences: (a) biology, (b) chemistry, (c) physics.

5. **Critical Thinking** How did the practical applications of scientific discoveries change people's lives?

3 Changing Patterns in the Arts

READ TO UNDERSTAND

☐ How romanticism influenced literature, art, and music.

☐ How romanticism and realism differed.

☐ What the goals of the impressionist painters were.

☐ How new ideas and technologies affected architecture.

The work of artists during the 1800s reflected the social and economic conditions of the time. Nationalism, advances in science, industrialization, and the growth of cities all affected artists' views of the world. As a result, new forms, styles, and themes emerged.

At the same time, a growing middle class provided a new audience for the arts. More people than ever had the education and leisure time to appreciate the arts. They also had money to buy books and paintings and to attend concerts. Artists no longer had to depend on wealthy patrons as they had since the Middle Ages, so they had greater freedom to express their ideas.

The Rise of Romanticism in Literature

Late in the 1700s, many writers began to reject the Enlightenment faith in reason. They thought people should be ruled by their hearts, not their heads. Emotion, imagination, and intuition, they felt, outweighed intellect and reason. This school of thought is called romanticism.

Romantics glorified the individual. They thought people should be free from confining rules so they could develop individually. Many romantics supported the emerging nationalist movements. The English poet Lord Byron combined the romantic ideal of nationalism and the yearning for individual liberty. In the 1820s, Byron rushed off to Greece to help the Greeks fight for independence from the Turks. He became a hero to many romantics when he died at the age of 36 while fighting there.

Rebelling against the ugliness of industrialization, romantics glorified beauty, especially the beauty of nature. Poets such as William Wordsworth, Percy Bysshe Shelley, and John Keats celebrated the simple life, close to nature. Wordsworth expressed this idea in his poem *The Tables Turned.* In this poem, he proclaimed that nature

> May teach you more of man,
> Of moral evil and of good,
> Than all the sages can.

The romantics looked longingly back to the past. They considered the Middle Ages a time of adventure and romance. The French romantic writer Victor Hugo set his novel *The Hunchback of Notre Dame* in the Middle Ages. Many romantic writers also reflected the upsurge in nationalism. The Russian poet Alexander Pushkin, for example, based many works on traditional Russian folk tales.

The Turn Toward Realism in Literature

By the mid-1800s, many writers began to rebel against romanticism. They thought that writers should present a realistic view of life, including the ugly parts. This turn toward realism reshaped literature, especially fiction. In his massive work of 90 volumes, which he called *The Human Comedy,* Honoré de Balzac realistically portrayed many aspects of French life. With great clarity, he described the crudeness and greed of the middle class. In contrast to the romantics, Balzac found beauty in cities and factories.

Other novelists who presented realistic views of life include the Russians Feodor Dostoevski, author of *Crime and Punishment,* and Leo Tolstoy, author of *War and Peace.* The English novelist Charles Dickens drew highly realistic portraits of life in British cities. (See page 472.) Thomas Hardy, another English author, frequently used rural settings for his novels, but he too presented a realistic picture of life. Hardy portrayed nature as an impersonal force against which people had to struggle. His view of nature stood in sharp contrast to that of the romantics.

French artist Jean François Millet painted the everyday lives of peasants and workers. In his work The Gleaners, *he shows poor peasants gathering the few remaining stalks of grain from the fields after reaping is finished.*

Painting

In the early 1800s, romanticism appealed to many painters. They wanted to throw off the rules of the formal and rather cold classical paintings of the 1700s. Romantic painters developed dramatic and emotional styles of art in which they explored new themes, such as imagination, nature, and the past.

Eugène Delacroix (duh lah KWAH), an early French romantic painter, believed that the purpose of art was "not to imitate nature but to strike the imagination." Delacroix portrayed actual events, but he painted them with brighter colors and more sweeping strokes than earlier painters had used.

In England, the romantics' love for nature sent John Constable and J.M.W. Turner out of doors for the subjects of their paintings. They revolutionized landscape painting with their new use of color and their attempt to express their own emotions.

By the mid-1800s, realism began creeping into painting, just as it had into literature. French painters such as Gustave Courbet and Honoré Daumier wanted to show everyday life as it really was. They made no attempt to beautify life but instead reported it objectively.

In the late 1800s, other trends in painting emerged. One group of artists turned away from both romantic and realistic ideas. They concentrated on capturing fleeting impressions of what they saw. Thus, their school of painting is called impressionism.

Impressionists such as Pierre Auguste Renoir, Edgar Degas, and Claude Monet were intrigued with placing colors side by side on the canvas rather than blending them to achieve a sense of brilliance. Monet painted the cathedral at Rouen, France, dozens of times to show it at different times of day. He wanted to capture his impression of how the cathedral looked in different lights.

Several artists, including Paul Cézanne and Paul Gauguin (goh GAN) from France and Vincent van Gogh from the Netherlands, thought that impressionist paintings lacked solidity. They experimented with new ways to show form. Their school of art is called post-impressionism. Cézanne concentrated on the shapes of objects. By the way he arranged shapes in a painting, he tried to capture a mood or express an emotion.

Architecture

The romantic spirit and new technology changed the face of architecture during the 1800s. In the early 1800s, architecture was still dominated by the classical style of the 1700s. Buildings reflected the balanced style of Greek and Roman architecture.

As the century wore on, however, many architects were swept up by the romantics' fascination with the past, especially the Middle Ages. They began using medieval Gothic cathedrals as their models. (See page 186.) The Gothic style became so popular that when the British Houses of Parliament burned down in 1834 they were replaced with Gothic buildings.

During the late 1800s, steel became an important building material. Steel was both

Claude Monet is among the best known impressionist painters. In Water Lilies, *he created shimmering effects by placing bands of different colors next to each other. Thus, the viewer's eye rather than the artist mixes the colors.*

strong and lightweight. Therefore, architects could design taller buildings of steel than they could of stone. The results were the first skyscrapers.

An early architect of skyscrapers was the American Louis Sullivan. He departed from classical and Gothic styles to design steel buildings with simple, clean lines. Sullivan's pupil Frank Lloyd Wright shared his enthusiasm for new materials and clean design. Wright's buildings, which include skyscrapers, homes, and museums, reflect his belief that "form follows function." By this, he meant that the design of a building should be determined by how it is to be used.

Music of the 1800s

The romantic spirit also influenced music. Romantic composers reacted against what they saw as the cold formal music of the 1700s. They sought a freer expression of emotion.

Ludwig van Beethoven wrote music that often anticipated the romantic style and themes. His Third Symphony, the *Eroica,* was written as an expression of freedom and liberty. The beauty of nature was the theme of his Sixth Symphony, the *Pastoral.*

Early romantic composers expressed emotion by creating beautiful melodies. Composers such as Franz Schubert and Robert Schumann wrote warmly melodic symphonies, songs, and other works. Later romantic composers, such as Hector Berlioz and Franz Liszt, expressed even more powerful emotions. Feelings of nationalism are apparent in the works of many romantic composers.

The 1800s saw the flowering of opera. Giuseppe Verdi brought the art of Italian opera to a peak in such operas as *Rigoletto, Aida,* and *Otello.* The German composer Richard Wagner wrote powerful nationalistic operas that he called music dramas. His *Ring of the Nibelungen,* a cycle of four operas, was based on a heroic German epic from the Middle Ages.

Toward the end of the century, some composers rebelled against the emotionalism of the romantics. French composer Claude Debussy created the same effect in his music that impressionist painters created in their works. He concentrated on creating a subtle mood rather than on stirring emotions.

The post-impressionist painter Vincent van Gogh used short, heavy brush strokes and startlingly bright colors to convey intense energy. Van Gogh was pleased with this work, **Road With Cypress and Stars.** He described it in a letter to a friend, painter Paul Gauguin: "I still have a last attempt—a night sky with a moon without brilliance . . . a star with exaggerated radiance . . . a very tall cypress, very straight, very somber."

SECTION 3 REVIEW

1. **Identify:** (a) Lord Byron, (b) Thomas Hardy, (c) Claude Monet, (d) Louis Sullivan, (e) Ludwig van Beethoven, (f) Richard Wagner, (g) Claude Debussy.

2. Describe three ideas shared by most romantic writers and artists.

3. How did realism differ from romanticism?

4. What did impressionist painters want to show in their works?

5. How did architecture change during the late 1800s?

6. **Critical Thinking** In what way were both romanticism and realism reactions to the industrial age?

Summary

1. Philosophers, economists, and other thinkers proposed different ways to deal with problems created by the Industrial Revolution. Laissez-faire economists thought that governments should not interfere in the economy because it was ruled by natural laws. Other economists thought reforms were needed. Utopian socialists and Marxist socialists argued that the capitalist economic system needed to be replaced.

2. During the 1800s, scientists in many fields made discoveries that had long-lasting effects. Charles Darwin's theory of evolution sparked a continuing controversy among scientists and religious leaders. Research about the causes of disease helped improve the lives of people. Discoveries in chemistry and physics laid the groundwork for major developments in the 1900s. The fields of sociology and psychology were born when scientists began to study society and human behavior.

3. Writers, artists, architects, and composers developed styles in the 1800s that showed their reaction to the Industrial Revolution. Romantics often rejected life in industrial society while realists tried to portray what that life was really like. Much painting and music of the period reflected feelings of nationalism. Advances in science and technology were reflected in skyscrapers that appeared on urban skylines.

Recalling Facts

Decide if the following statements are true or false. If a statement is false, rewrite it to make it true.

1. Adam Smith thought governments should correct problems created by industrialists.

2. Industrialists opposed the ideas of laissez-faire economics.

3. Gregor Mendel discovered that bacteria caused disease.

4. Pierre and Marie Curie discovered the X-ray.

5. Psychology is the study of behavior.

6. Romantic painters most often painted scenes of factory life.

7. *The Human Comedy* is an example of realism in literature.

Chapter Checkup

1. Explain how the ideas of each of the following people contributed to the laissez-faire theory of economics: (a) Adam Smith; (b) Thomas Malthus; (c) David Ricardo.

2. (a) What was the goal of the utopian socialists? (b) What were the weaknesses of Marx's socialist theories?

3. How were Darwin's ideas applied to social, political, and economic issues?

4. Describe how the work of each of the following scientists helped improve human health: (a) Louis Pasteur; (b) Robert Koch; (c) Joseph Lister.

5. (a) How was romanticism related to the nationalism of the 1800s? (b) What developments in literature and architecture reflected the impact of industrialization?

6. What did the composers Franz Schubert and Robert Schumann have in common?

Critical Thinking

1. **Expressing an Opinion** Adam Smith thought that government had only three duties: (1) "the duty of protecting the society from invasion"; (2) "the duty of establishing an exact administration of justice"; (3) "the duty of erecting and maintaining certain public institutions." Do you agree that these are the only duties a government should have? Why or why not?

2. **Understanding the Roots of Democracy** Each of the thinkers you read about in the first section of this chapter has influenced the way people think about democracy. Choose one of these thinkers and explain how his ideas have had an effect on Americans' attitude toward democracy.

3. **Synthesizing** Review what you learned in Chapter 21 about the development of labor unions in Great Britain. Which of the following people do you think would have approved of this development: Karl Marx, Adam Smith, John Stuart Mill, David Ricardo? Explain.

4. **Relating Past to Present** Which of the scientific discoveries discussed in this chapter do you think has had the most direct effect on your life? Why?

Developing Basic Skills

1. **Graph Reading** Study the graph on page 503. (a) What was the average life expectancy in 1850? (b) What was the average life expectancy in 1880? (c) How did the average life expectancy change between 1850 and 1910? (d) What developments help explain this change?

2. **Using Visual Evidence** Study the painting on page 506. (a) What characteristics of this work indicate that it was done by an impressionist painter? (b) How do the paintings in this chapter help you understand the history of the 1800s?

Writing About History

Preparing the Final Bibliography

The final bibliography is an alphabetical list of the sources you used to prepare your research paper. Alphabetize unsigned articles according to the first word of the title of the source. When you have more than one source by the same author, arrange them alphabetically by title. Write the author's name only once, replacing the name by three short dashes from the second entry on. Study the sample entries for style and punctuation.

```
Dubos, Rene.  Pasteur and Modern Science.
    New York,  Doubleday,  1960.
"Renoir:  a Symposium."   Art in America,
    March  1986, pp. 102-125.
"Victor Hugo:  Hundredth Anniversary of Death."
    New York Times,  May 22, 1985,  Section 3, p. 25.
```

Practice: Arrange, capitalize, and punctuate the following bibliography entries.

1. An article entitled Marie Sklodowska Curie by Romualdas Sviedrys published in The World Book Encyclopedia, 1988 edition.

2. A book by Patrick J. Rooke entitled The Age of Dickens, published in 1970 by G.P. Putnam in New York.

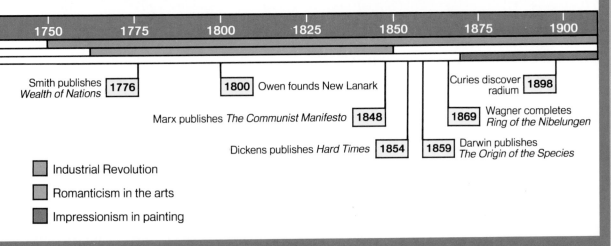

| 1750 | 1775 | 1800 | 1825 | 1850 | 1875 | 1900 |

Smith publishes *Wealth of Nations* **1776**

1800 Owen founds New Lanark

Marx publishes *The Communist Manifesto* **1848**

Dickens publishes *Hard Times* **1854**

1859 Darwin publishes *The Origin of the Species*

1869 Wagner completes *Ring of the Nibelungen*

Curies discover radium **1898**

■ Industrial Revolution
□ Romanticism in the arts
■ Impressionism in painting

Growth of Democracy

23

(1815–1914)

CHAPTER OUTLINE

1. **Reforms in Great Britain**
2. **Moving Away From British Rule**
3. **From Empire to Republic in France**
4. **Expansion of the United States**
5. **Reform in the United States**

Life in Britain was transformed during the long reign of Queen Victoria. Among the many changes was a revolution in transportation. In this painting, well-dressed Londoners board trains at Charing Cross Station.

Diary entry for June 21, 1887: "The morning was beautiful and bright with a fresh air. Troops began passing early with bands playing, and one heard constant cheering." The diary belonged to Queen Victoria of Great Britain. The day she described was a joyful occasion—the queen's Diamond Jubilee, her 50th year on the British throne.

"At half-past eleven we left the palace," the queen wrote, "I driving in a handsomely gilt landau [carriage] drawn by six of the Creams, with dear Vicky and Alix [two of her daughters]. Just in front of my carriage rode my three sons, five sons-in-law, nine grandsons, and grandsons-in-law. Then came the carriage containing my three other daughters, three daughters-in-law, grand-daughters, one granddaughter-in-law, and some of the suite. The crowds from the palace gates up to the Abbey were enormous, and there was such an extraordinary outburst of enthusiasm as I had hardly seen in London before.

"Dinner was again in the Supper-room. I wore a dress with the rose, thistle, and shamrock embroidered in silver on it. The noise of the crowd, which began yesterday, went on till late. This never-to-be forgotten day will always leave the most gratifying and heart-stirring memories behind."

The celebration of Queen Victoria's Diamond Jubilee did not just show the respect and admiration the British people felt for their queen. It also symbolized British pride in the nation and its achievements. During the 1800s, Great Britain was the leading industrial and commercial power in the world. Victoria's reign of 63 years became the symbol of the nineteenth century and has often been called the Victorian Age. Although a monarch symbolized the age, this was also a time of growing democracy in Britain, France, and the United States. ■

1 Reforms in Great Britain

READ TO UNDERSTAND

☐ **How the British Parliament became more democratic.**

☐ **How more British men won the right to vote.**

☐ **What social reforms were passed in the late 1800s.**

☐ *Vocabulary:* **suffrage.**

On a bright summer's day in 1819, a crowd of about 60,000 workers milled about St. Peter's Field in Manchester. They had come to a rally there to hear a leading reformer speak. Suddenly, hordes of mounted soldiers charged the crowd, killing 11 people and injuring 400. Local officials, nervous about the gathering, had ordered the troops to charge in and arrest the speaker.

The government expressed no regrets at this "Peterloo Massacre." Instead, it responded with harsh measures, designed both to stop such public meetings and silence those who demanded reform. The cause of reform seemed doomed.

There were "two great divisions of society," pointed out one British newspaper a few days after the massacre, "the masters, who have reduced the rate of wages, and the workmen, who complain of their masters for having done so." The "masters" controlled Parliament and had little desire for change. However, workers and middle-class reformers applied pressure, and in time they pushed Parliament to make Britain more democratic.

Early Attempts at Reform

Unlike other European nations, Great Britain had had a parliamentary system of government for hundreds of years. However, in the early 1800s, a small number of people dominated the British Parliament. Members of the House of Lords inherited their positions. Only 6 percent of British men could vote for members of the House of Commons. Few middle-class men or workers had voting rights. No British women had the right to vote.

Also, election districts, set up originally in 1688, did not reflect population changes. Rural districts with small populations, called "rotten boroughs," were well represented in the House of Commons. But growing industrial centers, such as Birmingham and Manchester, had little representation.

Reform Bill of 1832. As it grew in numbers and economic power, the middle class demanded the vote and greater representation in Parliament. Workers supported these demands. They hoped in time to win the vote themselves. In 1832, a major political reform bill was passed by Parliament.

The Reform Bill of 1832 gave industrial areas more representation in Parliament, and it extended **suffrage,** or the right to vote, to virtually all middle-class men. Under the new law, 20 percent of adult men were qualified to vote. However, since voters were still required to own a certain amount of property, neither urban nor rural workers qualified.

The Chartist movement. Reformers were disappointed with the Reform Bill of 1832 and continued to demand the vote for workers. In 1838, one group drew up a document called the People's Charter. The Chartists, as these reformers were called, demanded the secret ballot and universal male suffrage, or the vote for all adult men. They also wanted members of Parliament to be paid a salary so that poor people could afford to serve. None of the demands of the Chartist movement were met before it died out in the 1850s, but most of them eventually did become law.

The Corn Laws. Another reform that city workers wanted was repeal of the Corn Laws. In 1815, Parliament had passed the Corn Laws, which put a tariff, or tax, on imported grain. Landlords and farmers favored the Corn Laws because the tariff kept the price of grain high. However, city dwellers hated these laws because high prices for grain meant high prices for bread, the major food of the working class.

The battle to repeal the Corn Laws finally met with success in 1846. Because of crop failures in the early 1840s, the British had to import grain. Therefore, Parliament repealed the unpopular Corn Laws. Cheap grain flowed in from outside Britain, and the price of bread went down.

Extending Democracy

In the 1700s, both British political parties, the Whigs and the Tories, had represented wealthy landowners. (See page 421.) As more middle-class men won the right to vote in the 1800s, both the Whig party, which became known as the Liberal party, and the Tory party, which became known as the Conservative party, tried to win the support of the new voters. They also responded to continuing demands to extend suffrage. Two capable politicians led the parties in this direction—the Conservative Benjamin Disraeli (dihz RAY lee) and the Liberal William Gladstone.

Benjamin Disraeli thought that the Conservative party should support reforms that would improve the country. He considered himself "a conservative to preserve all that is good in our constitution and a radical to remove all that is bad." William Gladstone began his career as a Conservative, but he became a strong Liberal. These two men served alternately as prime minister from the mid-1860s to the early 1880s. Both played key roles in pushing through political and social reform.

In 1866, Gladstone introduced a bill to extend the vote to working men in cities. The bill did not pass, but Disraeli introduced a similar bill the next year. In his opinion, the reform was bound to come, so he wanted the Conservatives to get credit for it and thereby win the votes of urban workers. The Reform Bill of 1867 passed with both Liberal and Conservative support. It nearly doubled the number of men with the right to vote.

Five years later, Parliament passed a bill introducing the secret ballot. In 1884 and 1885, other reform bills gave the vote to rural working men. Thus, by 1885, most adult men in Britain had the right to vote. By the late 1800s, women were demanding the right to vote. Their struggle did not succeed completely until 1928. (See the feature at right.)

In 1911, the House of Commons passed a bill to reduce the power of the House of Lords by ending its right to veto measures. Although the House of Lords resisted, it gave in when the king threatened to appoint new lords who would vote for the bill.

Throughout the late 1800s, the Conservatives and Liberals competed for support from the new working-class voters. Social reforms were passed, but many workers felt that the existing political parties did not do enough for them. In 1900, they founded the Labour party, headed by Ramsay MacDonald. ("Labour" is the British spelling of "labor.")

In 1908, Londoners were fascinated by the trial of Emmeline Pankhurst and her daughter Christabel. The Pankhursts were well-known leaders of the movement to win the vote for women. That October, they had distributed leaflets urging women to "rush the House of Commons" on the day Parliament opened. They were arrested for encouraging violence.

Both mother and daughter were convicted. Before she was sentenced, Emmeline Pankhurst told the court, "If you had the power to send us to prison, not for six months, but for six years, or for our lives, the Government must not think they could stop this agitation. It would go on!"

In 1903, the Pankhursts organized the Women's Social and Political Union (WSPU), which demanded that Parliament extend the vote to women. When the government failed to act, the WSPU began holding rallies and marches.

The suffragettes, as women who demanded the right to vote were called, often faced violence. Mounted police charged suffragette marches and broke them up. Emmeline Pankhurst's younger daughter, Sylvia, described suffragettes returning from one rally: "They came in bruised, hatless, faces scratched, eyes swollen, noses bleeding."

The WSPU responded with still more militant action. WSPU supporters broke into cabinet meetings. Women chained themselves to the visitors' gallery in the House of Commons. They broke the windows of government buildings, stoned the cars of officials, and painted the slogan "Votes for Women" on walls and sidewalks. Imprisoned for these offenses, the suffragettes went on hunger strikes. On one occasion, a prison doctor tried to persuade Emmeline Pankhurst to break her hunger strike. "What are you going to have for dinner?" he asked with concern. "My determination," shot back Pankhurst.

Finally, in 1918, during World War I, British women over 30 years of age won the right to vote. Weakened by hunger strikes and many prison terms, Emmeline Pankhurst died in 1928, one week before Parliament passed a bill at last giving all women over 21 years of age the right to vote.

1. Why did the WSPU use rallies, marches, and disturbances to achieve their goals?

2. **Critical Thinking** Do you think the activities of the WSPU were the reason British women finally won the vote? Explain.

Other Reforms

Throughout most of the 1800s, social reform accompanied political reform in Britain. During the 1820s, Parliament lifted restrictions on the political rights of Catholics and of Protestants who did not belong to the Church of England. Parliament also repealed the law forbidding workers to organize, and it reformed the criminal code, reducing the number of crimes that were punishable by death. The slave trade had been outlawed in 1807. And in 1833, slavery itself was abolished throughout the British Empire.

The Factory Acts of the mid-1800s were followed by additional laws to protect workers. (See page 490.) By the end of the century, Parliament had passed laws that limited the number of hours a person could work and protected working women and children. David Lloyd George, a leader of the Liberal party, summed up the need for such laws. "Four spectres haunt the poor," he said, "old age, accident, sickness, and unemployment." He vowed to rid the country of them.

In 1909, Parliament passed an old-age pension bill that offered benefits to every British subject "of good character." Labor exchanges were set up to help find jobs for the unemployed. In 1911, the National Insurance Act provided health and unemployment insurance. A year later, Parliament passed a law setting minimum wages. It also extended workers' compensation to cover more workers in case of sickness or accidents on the job.

By the late 1800s, both Liberals and Conservatives recognized the need for better educated voters. In the 1860s, education was not compulsory, and students usually left school by age 11. The Education Act passed in 1870 allowed local school boards to require attendance. It also extended government aid to more schools. Later acts made education free and compulsory.

SECTION 1 REVIEW

1. **Locate:** (a) Birmingham, (b) Manchester.

2. **Identify:** (a) People's Charter, (b) Benjamin Disraeli, (c) William Gladstone.

3. **Define:** suffrage.

4. (a) Who won the right to vote by the Reform Bill of 1832? (b) Who won the right to vote between 1832 and 1885?

5. (a) Why did city dwellers oppose the Corn Laws? (b) What effect did the repeal of the Corn Laws have on urban workers?

6. Describe three social reforms passed by Parliament in the 1800s.

7. **Critical Thinking** What did Parliament do to try to rid Great Britain of the "four spectres that haunted the poor"?

2 Moving Away From British Rule

READ TO UNDERSTAND

☐ Why the Irish resented British rule.

☐ Why the Dominion of Canada was created.

☐ How democracy grew in Australia and New Zealand.

The O'Donnells raised potatoes on their tiny plot of Irish soil, growing enough to feed their family of eight. In 1845, disaster struck. A potato blight destroyed their entire crop. The O'Donnells faced starvation and death, along with millions of other Irish people.

Over a million Irish died of starvation and disease in the potato famine. Millions more left Ireland, many for the United States. The Irish blamed the British for doing too little too late to help them. Their bitterness against British rule increased, and their demand for the right to rule themselves, or home rule, grew stronger. In the same period, three other countries in the British Empire—Canada, Australia, and New Zealand—also pushed for self-government.

The Question of Ireland

Since the time of Henry VIII, English rulers had encouraged Protestants from England and Scotland to settle in Ireland, a Catholic stronghold. Many Protestants moved into the northern Irish province of Ulster. Others took over large estates throughout Ireland. During the 1600s and 1700s, the Protestant minority gained political and economic control over Ireland. The Protestants passed harsh laws limiting the rights of the majority of Irish, who were Catholic.

Irish Catholics constantly protested their lack of political and economic freedom. In 1801, the British tried to ease tensions in Ireland by formally joining Ireland and Great Britain and giving Ireland representation in the British Parliament. Parliament also repealed the law that forbade Catholics from being elected to office in Ireland. Many British political reforms, such as the Reform Bill of 1832, also applied to Ireland.

Anger toward Britain. These moves did not satisfy Irish Catholics. Their anger had deep religious and economic roots. They resented the taxes they had to pay to the Anglican Church and the high rents that Irish Catholic peasants had to pay to Protestant landlords. They were especially bitter because the land had originally belonged to the Irish.

Irish hatred of Britain increased as a result of the disastrous famine that struck in 1845. The potato was the mainstay of the Irish diet. As you have read, when the potato crops failed, there was a terrible famine. At first, the British government did little to help, although the repeal of the Corn Laws brought down the price of grain.

Struggle for home rule. The famine fanned a revolutionary movement in Ireland, which grew stronger during the late 1800s and early 1900s. The revolutionaries demanded home rule for Ireland. For years, Parliament resisted this idea. It wanted to protect the Protestants in Ulster. If Ireland had home rule, Protestants would lose their political power, since Catholics were a majority.

Under Gladstone's leadership, Parliament did grant some concessions to the Irish, however. In 1869, an act was passed to free Catholics from paying taxes to support the Anglican Church. Two land acts passed in 1870 and 1881 protected Irish peasants from sudden eviction from their land, made rents fairer, and made it possible for them to buy land.

Gladstone also introduced a home rule bill for Ireland, but it was defeated each time he proposed it. Finally, in 1912, Parliament passed a home rule bill, but it never went into effect. The Protestant minority in Ulster was determined to prevent home rule, and they organized an army of 100,000 volunteers to resist it. In 1914, Parliament passed another home rule bill that did not apply to Ulster. But the outbreak of World War I in August of that year postponed any attempt to give southern Ireland home rule.

Demands for Self-Rule in Canada

Canada was originally settled by the French, but the English gained the territory in 1763

Irish peasants suffered great hardships in the 1800s. Extremely poor, they depended on potatoes as their principal food. When the potato crop failed between 1845 and 1847, over one million died of starvation or disease. To escape the famine, hundreds of thousands more left Ireland and came to America, seeking a better way of life.

after their victory in the Seven Years' War. To win the loyalty of its French subjects, who lived mainly in Quebec, Britain passed the Quebec Act in 1774. This act gave French Canadians who were Catholic the right to practice their religion. It also allowed them to continue living under traditional French laws and customs.

As early as the 1600s, some English-speaking settlers had begun moving to Canada. Among them were Scottish settlers who came to Nova Scotia, or New Scotland. English settlers also arrived to fish the waters off Newfoundland and to set up fur-trading posts around Hudson Bay. During the American Revolution and afterward, many English-speaking settlers arrived in Canada from the United States. They settled mainly in the Maritime Provinces—Nova Scotia, New Brunswick, and Prince Edward Island—and in the area north of the Great Lakes in what is today Ontario.

This British family is enjoying a summer day in London's Hyde Park. But this comfortable life was a far cry from that of pioneers in Australia and New Zealand. These pioneers passed democratic reforms earlier than the British.

From the start, there were disagreements between French Canadians and English Canadians. In an effort to govern the two groups separately, the British Parliament passed the Canada Act of 1791. This act divided Canada into three provinces—Upper Canada (present-day Ontario), Lower Canada (present-day Quebec), and the Maritime Provinces. Each province had a governor appointed by Britain, a royal council, and an elected assembly.

Neither the English Canadians nor the French Canadians were satisfied with this arrangement, and discontent with British rule grew. After an uprising in 1837, the British sent a special commissioner, Lord Durham, to be governor of Canada. In a report to Parliament in 1839, Durham recommended that Upper and Lower Canada be united and that the Ca-nadians be given control of their domestic affairs. He proposed that the British government involve itself only in Canada's foreign affairs. The Durham Report was well received by the British government, and it became the basis for Canadian self-rule.

The Dominion of Canada

The Union Act of 1840 united Upper and Lower Canada. In 1849, Canada was granted the right to self-government, and in 1867 Nova Scotia and New Brunswick were joined with Ontario and Quebec to create the Dominion of Canada. In the next few decades, Prince Edward Island, Manitoba, Alberta, Saskatchewan, and British Columbia would join the Dominion.

The government of the Dominion of Canada was modeled on the British government. A governor general represented the British monarch, but his role was mainly ceremonial. The Canadian parliament had two houses, one appointed and one elected, and the government was led by a prime minister.

Britain retained some power over Canadian foreign affairs until 1931, when the Statute of Westminster was passed. This statute created the British Commonwealth of Nations, which made Canada, as well as other former British colonies, equal partners with Britain. It declared all members of the Commonwealth "equal in status, in no way subordinate to each other," but it still bound members of the British crown.

After Canada became a dominion in 1867, it set out to build a united nation. A transcontinental railroad helped unite the sprawling country. The nation's rich natural resources attracted industries. The Canadian government encouraged immigrants to come to work in these industries and farm the vast western prairies. In the 20 years before 1914, more than three million immigrants went to Canada. They brought the population to over 7 million—three times what it had been in 1850.

Self-Government for Australia and New Zealand

During the second half of the 1800s, Australia and New Zealand also moved toward self-government. The first European settlers in

Australia were convicted criminals who had been exiled from Great Britain. Some of these exiles later fled Australia and settled in New Zealand.

Both Australia and New Zealand were rich in mineral deposits and in land suitable for raising wheat and grazing sheep. As a result, both attracted new settlers in the 1700s and 1800s. As the populations grew, people demanded that Britain stop exiling convicted criminals to Australia. In 1840, the British government stopped this practice.

Independent and proud of their progress, the people of Australia and New Zealand did not want to be governed by faraway Britain. They called for self-government. Australia won self-government in 1850, and New Zealand won it in 1852. Like Canada, Australia and New Zealand became "equal partners" in the British Commonwealth of Nations in 1931.

Democratic reforms made early headway in Australia and New Zealand. Australia introduced the secret ballot nearly 20 years before Great Britain did. In fact, the secret ballot is sometimes called the Australian ballot. In 1893, women won the right to vote in New Zealand. Australian women won the same right nine years later. Women in Britain had to wait many years for this right.

SECTION 2 REVIEW

1. **Locate:** (a) Canada, (b) Australia, (c) New Zealand.

2. How did the potato famine contribute to Irish hatred of Britain?

3. Describe two concessions Parliament made to the Irish after 1869.

4. Who resisted home rule in Ireland? Why?

5. What did Lord Durham recommend should be done about Canadian discontent with British rule?

6. **Critical Thinking** Why do you think democratic reforms were enacted in Australia and New Zealand before they were in Britain?

---

3 From Empire to Republic in France

READ TO UNDERSTAND

☐ **How Napoleon III was both a success and a failure.**

☐ **What problems the Third Republic faced.**

☐ **How the Dreyfus affair reflected divisions within France.**

☐ *Vocabulary:* **coalition.**

Paris was under siege, surrounded by a Prussian army. Parisians suffered severe food shortages, but they also complained about another hardship: the lack of outside news. The Prussians did allow the American minister to France to receive a copy of the *London Times* each week on the condition that he keep the news to himself. Parisians begged him to share his treasure. "We gave you Lafayette," wrote one Paris journalist. "In return, we ask only for one copy of an English paper."

Paris had come under siege as a result of the policies of Napoleon III. As you read in Chapter 20, Louis Napoleon proclaimed himself Napoleon III in 1852. Napoleon's action was approved by popular vote, but many French citizens wanted a democratic republic. Others supported a return to a monarchy.

Napoleon III

When Napoleon III came to power, many French people looked to him to restore order after the chaos of 1848. He responded by cracking down on dissent. He enforced strict censorship and maintained a powerful secret police. The empire had a constitution and an elected assembly, but the assembly could only discuss issues brought to it by the emperor. Power was actually in the hands of Napoleon and his ministers.

Despite the harsh measures he took to suppress dissent, Napoleon III considered himself a great reformer. He promised to use strong government to improve the life of the people and to bring peace to France. "The empire is peace," he proclaimed.

Production of Iron 1865–1910

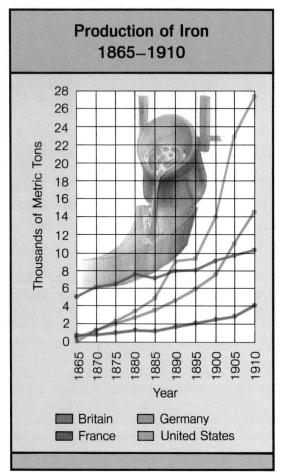

Source: Witt Bowden, *et al. An Economic History of Europe Since 1750.*

Britain **Germany**
France **United States**

GRAPH STUDY *In 1870, iron production in France was about the same as iron production in Germany and the United States. In what year did German iron production surpass that of Britain? When did the United States outdistance the other nations?*

Napoleon III sponsored laws to improve working conditions and to provide public housing. He also supported public works, both to beautify French cities and towns and to provide employment. The broad boulevards of present-day Paris, for example, were built during the Second Empire, as his reign was called. The wide new streets also served a political purpose. It would be much more difficult for revolutionaries to build barricades across the new streets than it was to build them across the narrow winding streets they replaced. Furthermore, the wide streets allowed government troops to move in quickly if an uprising began.

Napoleon's government promoted the growth of industry in France. It improved roads and harbors and encouraged companies to build railroads. It also sponsored credit agencies to increase business investment. By 1870, France was a major industrial power. Later, it was surpassed by Germany and other nations in part because the French preferred traditional ways of doing business. Nevertheless, the growth of industry during the Second Empire led to general prosperity.

Despite economic prosperity, many people, including both the republicans and the monarchists, opposed Napoleon's rule. Also, many French were unhappy with Napoleon's foreign policy, as you will read.

In an attempt to revive his popularity, Napoleon began to ease his repressive laws and make his government more democratic. He ended press censorship and allowed the elected assembly a greater role in government. By 1869, the assembly had the right to vote on the budget and propose laws.

The effort to create a "Liberal Empire" only increased discontent. Once opponents of the regime could openly criticize it, more of them were elected to the assembly. Strikes also increased dramatically when the ban on unions and strikes was lifted. However, it was a setback in foreign policy that brought the Second Empire down.

Adventures in Foreign Policy

French foreign policy during the 1850s seemed successful. France had begun to create a colonial empire in parts of Africa and Asia. The French people supported their country's role in the Crimean War and were proud when France hosted the peace conference ending the war. However, French Catholics bitterly resented the government's support for Italian nationalists at the expense of the papacy during Italy's struggle for unification. (You will read more about the unification of Italy in Chapter 24.)

Another damaging foreign policy adventure was Napoleon III's attempt to gain influence in Mexico. In 1862, Napoleon sent 40,000 French troops to Mexico. He justified this action on the grounds that the Mexican government had refused to pay debts owed to

European countries. The French declared Mexico "the Empire of Mexico." And they installed as emperor Maximilian, the brother of Francis Joseph, who was the Austrian emperor.

Maximilian's reign was a disaster from the start. Only the presence of French troops kept him on the throne. The United States considered Napoleon's actions a threat to the Western Hemisphere, but the Civil War, which began in 1861, prevented it from taking any action. After the Civil War ended in 1865, the United States pressured Napoleon to withdraw his troops. Napoleon, who needed his troops in Europe, gradually withdrew them. Without French troops, Maximilian could not rule. In 1867, he was captured by Mexican soldiers and executed. The disaster in Mexico dealt a severe blow to Napoleon III's prestige and popularity.

A Bitter Defeat

The crowning blow for Napoleon was his defeat and capture in the Franco-Prussian War. As you will read in Chapter 24, the war broke out in 1870 over the question of who would become king of Spain. The Prussians surrounded the French army at Sedan and captured the emperor. Napoleon's surrender came as a shock to the French people. Within a few days, a group of republicans in Paris proclaimed the end of the Second Empire and the beginning of the Third Republic.

A National Assembly was elected. Its first duty was to negotiate a peace treaty with Germany. Under the treaty, France was forced to give Germany the province of Alsace and part of the province of Lorraine. It also had to pay Germany $1 billion for damages. The Germans would occupy France until this sum was paid. The harshness of the treaty angered the French. For many years, they harbored a deep hatred of Germany and a desire for revenge for the loss of Alsace and Lorraine.

Radicals in Paris were furious when the National Assembly accepted the peace treaty. They also feared that the monarchy in France would be restored because a majority of the assembly members were monarchists. In March 1871, they rose in revolt and set up a government called the Paris Commune.

His aim was prosperity at home and glory abroad, yet most of the foreign policy ventures of Napoleon III met with failure. He did, however, extend French influence in Southeast Asia. Here, King Mongkut of Siam is receiving the French ambassador. Although Siam remained independent, the French as well as other Europeans had the right to be protected by their own laws while in Siam.

French artist Honoré Daumier painted scenes of social protest. In The Uprising, *shown here, he expresses sympathy for poor city workers. Workers like these supported the Paris Commune in 1871.*

Leaders of the Paris Commune demanded reforms such as lower prices, higher wages, and better working conditions. Their demands were fairly moderate, and there were only a few socialists among the leaders of the Commune. However, many French feared a new revolution. The National Assembly viewed the leaders of the Commune as dangerous radicals and sent troops that crushed the Commune. In a week-long battle that was incredibly harsh and violent, over 20,000 supporters of the Commune were killed by French troops.

Government troops were burying bodies so fast that they buried some people who were still alive. People who lived near one mass grave reportedly heard groans in the night and in the morning saw a clenched fist sticking out of the soil.

The uprising and its suppression left bitter divisions between monarchists and republicans—divisions that threatened the stability of the Third Republic.

The Third Republic

Monarchists dominated the National Assembly, but they themselves were divided between supporters of the House of Bourbon and supporters of the House of Orléans. This division gave the republicans a chance to gain strength. In 1875, by a margin of one vote, the Assembly adopted a constitution.

According to the Constitution of 1875, the National Assembly, which was composed of a Chamber of Deputies and a Senate, passed the laws. All adult males could vote, and they elected representatives to the Chamber of Deputies. Local government officials elected members of the Senate. The National Assembly then chose the president of France. Real power rested in a cabinet of ministries that was responsible to the National Assembly.

The Third Republic got off to a shaky start. It had enemies among the many monarchists and among many Catholics, who were afraid the republicans would weaken the Catholic Church in France. As many as 12 political parties were represented in the National Assembly, so governments had to be based on broad **coalitions,** or temporary alliances of parties. These coalitions often broke down. The Third Republic was also beset by political scandals and official corruption.

One serious crisis revolved around General Georges Boulanger (boo lahn ZHAY), who crushed the Paris Commune in 1871. In 1886, Boulanger became minister of war. A firm believer in monarchy, he won the support of many French citizens by playing on their desire for revenge against Germany. In 1889, it appeared that Boulanger might overthrow the Third Republic. The government ordered Boulanger's arrest for treason, but he fled to Belgium.

A financial scandal concerning the building of the Panama Canal also shook the Third Republic. The French company formed to build a canal across Panama was in danger of bankruptcy. In the early 1890s, the public learned that several Assembly members and government ministers had accepted bribes from the faltering company. A storm of public protest followed. The Third Republic weathered the storm, but it soon faced an even more serious crisis.

The Dreyfus Affair

In 1894, Captain Alfred Dreyfus, the first Jewish officer to be named to the general staff of the French army, was accused of giving military secrets to the Germans. Although Dreyfus claimed he was innocent, he was convicted of treason and sent to the French penal colony on Devil's Island, off the coast of South America. The trial touched off a wave of anti-Semitism, or hostility toward Jews, in France.

It soon came to light that Major Ferdinand Esterhazy, a Catholic monarchist, was the real traitor. But top officials in the French army refused to reopen the case. Their action reflected a deep-seated anti-Semitism, shared by many French army officers, as well as a desire to protect the reputation of the army. The case was kept before the public, however. The French author Émile Zola helped rouse sympathy for Dreyfus when he published a letter accusing the army command of persecuting an innocent man.

The Dreyfus case deepened the divisions in France. On one side were Catholics, monarchists, and the military. They saw the demand to reopen the case as an effort to undermine authority, especially that of the army. On the other side were the republicans and leftists, including the socialists. They thought the injustice suffered by Dreyfus threatened democratic government and individual rights.

During the Third Republic, Paris was a magnet for artists. French impressionist painters such as Auguste Renoir recorded scenes of Paris life. In this painting, Renoir captures the carefree mood of young couples dancing at a famous cafe, Le Moulin de la Galette—The Pancake Mill.

521

In 1899, five years after his conviction, Captain Dreyfus was finally pardoned by the president of France. The republicans considered this a victory, and they moved to further strengthen the republic.

Reform in the Third Republic

Partly as a result of the Dreyfus affair, republicans in the National Assembly passed a series of laws that weakened the power of the Catholic Church in France. The government stopped paying the salaries of clergy. Catholic teaching orders were broken up, and thousands of Catholic schools were forced to close. These laws effectively separated church and state in France.

Like other European governments, the government of the Third Republic passed laws to deal with problems brought on by industrialization. It approved a 12-hour workday and forbade hiring children under 13 years of age. However, France was slower to introduce social reforms than Britain and Germany. Furthermore, it did not set up unemployment or health insurance programs. Such reforms seemed less important in France since it remained largely a nation of small farms and small family-run businesses.

SECTION 3 REVIEW

1. **Identify:** (a) Napoleon III, (b) Paris Commune, (c) Georges Boulanger, (d) Alfred Dreyfus.

2. **Define:** coalition.

3. (a) How did Napoleon III try to create a "Liberal Empire" in the 1860s? (b) Did he succeed? Why or why not?

4. How did Napoleon III interfere in Mexico?

5. How did the National Assembly react to the Paris Commune?

6. Describe one of the crises that threatened the Third Republic during the late 1800s.

7. **Critical Thinking** Why do you think the Dreyfus affair became such a bitter issue in France?

---

4 Expansion of the United States

READ TO UNDERSTAND

☐ How the United States expanded in the 1800s.

☐ What the causes and results of the Civil War were.

☐ How the United States changed in the years after the Civil War.

"Go west, young man, and grow up with the country," urged newspaper editor Horace Greeley in the mid-1800s. Millions of Americans—many of them newcomers—obeyed. They moved into the sparsely settled land that the United States had recently acquired and helped push the frontier to the Pacific Ocean. In the United States, as in Britain and France, the 1800s were a period of growth—in population, agriculture, industry, and democracy.

New Territories

The United States grew dramatically in size in the 1800s. President Thomas Jefferson doubled the size of the country when he purchased Louisiana from France in 1803. Napoleon Bonaparte, in desperate need of money to fight wars in Europe, sold the vast Louisiana Territory to the United States for $15 million. In 1804, Meriwether Lewis and William Clark led an expedition to explore the Louisiana Purchase. Settlers soon followed.

Since they had won their independence, Americans had been moving westward across the Appalachian Mountains toward the Mississippi River. As a result of the Louisiana Purchase, the American frontier was moved west to the Rocky Mountains. Gradually, Americans came to believe that it was their destiny to extend the United States across the entire continent. In 1845, a newspaper editor labeled this idea "Manifest Destiny," and Americans quickly took up the phrase.

Even before Manifest Destiny became popular, the United States expanded further. In 1819, Spain ceded Florida to it. In 1845, the United States annexed the Republic of Texas. Texas had originally been part of Mexico. But

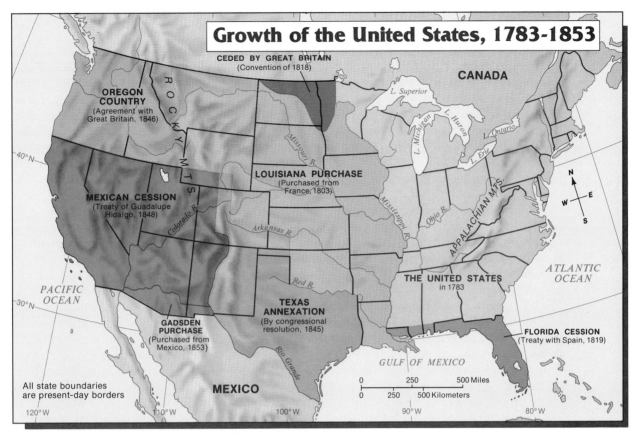

Growth of the United States, 1783-1853

CEDED BY GREAT BRITAIN
(Convention of 1818)

CANADA

OREGON COUNTRY
(Agreement with Great Britain, 1846)

ROCKY MTS.

L. Superior

L. Michigan

L. Huron

L. Ontario

L. Erie

40°N

MEXICAN CESSION
(Treaty of Guadalupe Hidalgo, 1848)

Missouri R.

LOUISIANA PURCHASE
(Purchased from France, 1803)

Mississippi R.

Ohio R.

APPALACHIAN MTS.

ATLANTIC OCEAN

Colorado R.

Arkansas R.

THE UNITED STATES
in 1783

PACIFIC OCEAN

30°N

Red R.

TEXAS ANNEXATION
(By congressional resolution, 1845)

GADSDEN PURCHASE
(Purchased from Mexico, 1853)

Rio Grande

FLORIDA CESSION
(Treaty with Spain, 1819)

N
W E
S

GULF OF MEXICO

0   250   500 Miles
0 250   500 Kilometers

All state boundaries are present-day borders

MEXICO

120°W   110°W   100°W   90°W   80°W

MAP STUDY *Between 1803 and 1853, the United States expanded from the Mississippi River to the Pacific Ocean. Present-day state boundaries are shown on this map. Which areas became part of the United States after 1840?*

in 1836, settlers from the United States had proclaimed Texas an independent republic and won a war for independence against Mexico.

In 1846, a dispute over the Texas border sparked a war between Mexico and the United States. The United States won the Mexican War and thereby gained California and the New Mexico territory in 1848. Two years earlier, the American government had gained title to the Oregon Country as a result of a treaty with Great Britain. It arranged the Gadsden Purchase from Mexico in 1853 and bought Alaska from Russia in 1867, thereby extending the nation to its current continental borders. (See the map above.)

The Right to Vote

As the nation expanded westward, democracy also expanded. In most of the 13 colonies, only white men with property could vote. In some colonies, voters also had to meet religious requirements. After independence, many states kept property qualifications for voters, and some required voters to pay a poll tax. However, by 1850, most states had dropped these restrictions and had adopted white male suffrage, voting by all white men.

As in Europe, women in the United States had no political rights. Nor did most black Americans. A few states had allowed blacks to vote after the colonies won independence, but the right was withdrawn in some of these states during the early 1800s.

A Split Between North and South

Slavery became a major issue between northern and southern states after 1820. As new territories in the west were added to the country, people debated bitterly whether slavery should be allowed in territories that wanted to join the union as states.

Most people who favored the extension of slavery were southerners. In the South, slavery

523

supported the plantation economy. Also, many southerners hoped that if the new states allowed slavery, they would support the South in Congress. Many northerners resisted the admission of new slave states because they were afraid of losing power in Congress. Other people opposed the extension of slavery in the west because they believed that slavery was evil and should be abolished throughout the country.

For a while, Congress maintained a balance between slave states and free states. For each state that was admitted as a slave state, another was admitted as a free state. But the tension between the North and the South continued to grow.

Differences over economic issues added to the tension. The North was becoming industrialized. So northerners favored high tariffs on imported goods to protect new industries from foreign competition. But the South remained mostly agricultural, with cotton as the major crop. Southerners objected to high tariffs on imported goods. They had to buy many products from foreign countries, and the tariffs hurt them by raising prices on the goods they imported.

Civil War and Reconstruction

By 1860, tensions between the North and the South had reached the breaking point. Many southerners felt that the southern states should secede, or withdraw, from the Union. The election of Abraham Lincoln as President in 1860 finally pushed the South into secession. Lincoln strongly opposed extending slavery to new territories. First, South Carolina and then ten other southern states seceded from the Union. They proclaimed themselves an independent nation—the Confederate States of America.

President Lincoln wanted to preserve the Union, and he hoped it could be done without war. In his inaugural address in March 1861, he addressed the Confederate States: "The issue of war is in your hands, my dissatisfied countrymen, not mine. The government will not attack you. You can have no conflict unless you begin it." The next month, Confederate troops attacked federally held Fort Sumter in the har-

bor of Charleston, South Carolina. The Civil War had begun.

The war raged for four years. The North had a larger population than the South, more factories to arm and supply its soldiers, and more railroads to transport soldiers and supplies. Even though southern generals were better military leaders, they could not withstand the North's advantages. On April 9, 1865, General Robert E. Lee, the southern commander, surrendered to General Ulysses S. Grant, the northern commander.

During the war, President Lincoln had issued the Emancipation Proclamation, freeing slaves in states controlled by the Confederacy. The Thirteenth Amendment to the Constitution abolishing slavery throughout the country was ratified in 1865.

Most of the fighting in the war had taken place on southern soil, leaving the South in a desperate economic condition. Its agriculture was destroyed. Major cities, such as Atlanta and Richmond, lay in ruins. Many white southerners were now impoverished, as were the newly freed slaves.

For 12 years after the war, federal troops were stationed in much of the South, a reminder to southerners of bitter defeat. During this period, known as the Reconstruction, the occupying forces tried to enforce laws guaranteeing equality for blacks. But many southerners were determined not to allow blacks to vote or to enjoy the same rights as white people. Also, northerners, who had once wanted to punish the South for the war, gradually seemed to lose interest. By 1877, all federal troops had been removed from the South.

Slowly, the South recovered from the war. Cities were rebuilt, and new industries were started. By the early 1900s, a "New South" was emerging. The New South was more economically diverse than the Old South, which had relied on agriculture.

Economic Expansion

The years following the Civil War were a time of great economic growth for the entire nation. The United States industrialized rapidly. By 1914, it had outpaced Great Britain, the early industrial leader. In that year, the value of goods manufactured by factories in the Northeast and Middle West was 12 times greater than it had been in 1860.

In the west, mining boomed. Huge deposits of gold, silver, and copper were discovered in Nevada, Colorado, and the Dakotas. Cattle-ranching became big business, especially in Texas. When a metal plow was developed that could cut through the tough sod of Kansas and Nebraska, farmers flocked to these states. In time, the Great Plains became one of the greatest grain-producing areas of the world.

The building of railroads sparked economic expansion in the United States, as it did in Europe. The first transcontinental railroad was completed in 1869. By 1900, the number of miles of railroad tracks crisscrossing the country had increased by seven times. Manufactured goods flowed westward from eastern factories. Texas cattle were shipped to meat-packing plants in Chicago and St. Louis. The grain harvested on the Great Plains was sent by railroad to eastern markets and to seaports,

from which it was shipped overseas. (See the map below.)

Money from European investors financed much early industry in the United States. However, American profits and investments grew rapidly. By the early 1900s, Americans were investing millions of dollars in Europe.

During the last years of the 1800s, business in the United States truly became "big business." Giant corporations such as United States Steel and Standard Oil established near monopolies over the production and sale of certain products. Some corporations also joined together to form trusts that controlled entire industries. Because trusts could produce goods at low cost, they could reduce prices and drive competitors out of business.

American Workers

The ever-expanding economy needed large numbers of workers. One source of workers was immigrants. Between 1860 and 1910,

MAP STUDY *Railroads helped tie distant parts of the United States together. Which part of the country had the most north–south branches? Why was this so?*

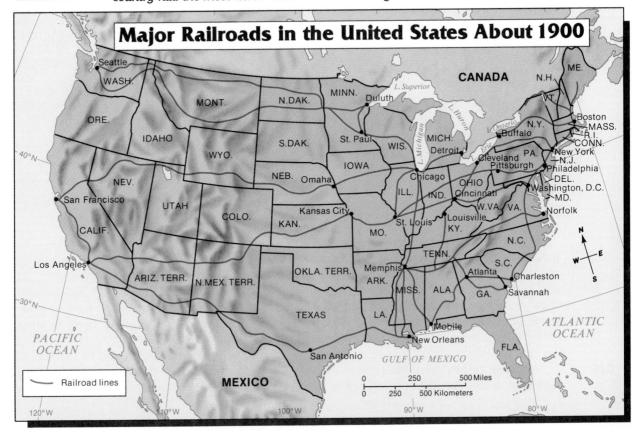

Shortly after he had arrived in the United States from Ireland, an immigrant worker showed his boss a letter he was writing to his family back home. "But why," asked his employer, "do you say that you have meat three times a week, when you have it three times a day?" The immigrant replied, "It is because they wouldn't believe me if I told them so."

In the 1840s, famine had struck Ireland. (See page 514.) To avoid starvation, millions of Irish set off across the Atlantic for the promised land of the United States. Thus began a stream of immigrants from Europe that was to change the face of the nation. Almost all the new arrivals, like the Irish letter writer, found a way of life that their relatives back home would find hard to believe.

Europeans left their native lands for different reasons. Some, like the Irish, fled their country to avoid starvation. Italy, for example, was overcrowded, and Italian farmers could barely eke out a living. In Eastern Europe, too, peasants lived lives of grinding poverty. "We'd have meat about once a year," recalled one Czech. "Once in a while, Mother would buy one of those short bolognas, cut it up, and put it in the soup, and everybody would get a little piece. Well, when we came to America, for a few cents we ate like kings compared with what we had over there."

People living in Germany, Russia, Austria-Hungary, and the Ottoman Empire also hungered for American religious and political freedom. For example, Poles living under Russian and German rule were forbidden to speak their own language. They were often excluded from schools and jobs because their names identified them as Poles.

Some who came to America were fleeing for their very lives. In Russia, thousands of Jews died in pogroms, organized attacks on Jewish communities. Armenians, who were Christians living in Muslim-ruled areas, also faced periodic attacks. To all these persecuted people, the United States was an oasis of freedom.

Some immigrants were disappointed to find that American streets were not paved with gold. Still, many found decent jobs. Though their letters might complain about life in America, they also sent money home. To those still in Europe, there was no better proof that life was better in the United States.

1. What reasons did people in Eastern Europe have for coming to the United States?

2. **Critical Thinking** Do people still come to the United States to find a better life? Explain.

about 23 million immigrants from Europe, Asia, and other parts of the world poured into the United States. Many came in search of political or religious freedom. All hoped to find a better life. The native-born population of the United States also increased rapidly during the late 1800s.

As a result, American cities grew at a rapid rate. Boston and Philadelphia doubled in size; New York and Pittsburgh tripled. The population of Cleveland and Detroit grew by six times, and the population of Chicago grew by seven times. In 1914, for the first time, as many Americans lived in cities as lived in rural areas.

Rapid industrialization and the growth of cities in the United States led to many of the same problems found in Europe. Factory workers faced long hours, low wages, dangerous working conditions, and deplorable living conditions. Workers organized labor unions to help them improve their lives.

The path to labor organization in the United States was a rocky one. Opposition to labor unions came from several sides. Employers objected to unions because they felt that unions limited the freedom to run their businesses as they saw fit. Some Americans thought that organized workers' groups denied traditional American values such as "rugged individualism." Many Americans were suspicious of labor unions because of the large numbers of immigrants who joined them. As a result, unions were often considered un-American.

Still, efforts to organize labor continued, although they were often marked by violent conflict between employers and workers. In 1881, the American Federation of Labor (AFL) was founded. The AFL was a "union of unions" made up of hundreds of smaller, self-governing unions that joined together to gain greater strength. By 1914, AFL membership had grown to over 2 million workers.

SECTION 4 REVIEW

1. **Locate:** (a) Louisiana Purchase, (b) Mississippi River, (c) Rocky Mountains, (d) Oregon Country, (e) Gadsden Purchase.

2. **Identify:** (a) Manifest Destiny, (b) Abraham Lincoln, (c) Emancipation Proclamation, (d) AFL.

3. From which nations did the United States acquire territory between 1819 and 1867?

4. In the early 1800s, what groups did not have the right to vote in the United States?

5. What two issues caused tension between the North and South after 1820?

6. (a) How were the slaves freed in the Confederate states? (b) How were they freed in the rest of the nation?

7. **Critical Thinking** Why do you think democracy was extended in the United States as the nation grew?

---

5 Reform in the United States

READ TO UNDERSTAND

☐ **What reforms the progressives wanted.**

☐ **What gains women and black Americans made.**

☐ **How the United States became a world power.**

☐ *Vocabulary:* direct primary, recall.

"The old nations of the world creep on at a snail's pace; the Republic thunders past with the rush of an express," declared steel magnate Andrew Carnegie in 1886. If the first part of Carnegie's statement is an exaggeration, the second part is not. In the late 1800s, the United States thundered ahead in industry and commerce. Yet, as the economy roared forward, many Americans called on the country to make reforms in government, in living conditions in cities, and in the way businesses operated.

An Age of Reform

Among the leaders of the reform movement in the early 1900s were the progressives. Progressives were reformers who believed that progress was possible, and they intended to work for it. They uncovered widespread corruption in government and accused city officials of stealing city funds and accepting bribes. They also criticized the efforts by big business to eliminate competition. Trusts were a special target of the progressives.

Between 1900 and 1914, progressives met with much success in their efforts to reform state and local governments. Several notoriously corrupt mayors lost elections to reform-minded candidates. A number of states adopted measures, including the direct primary and recall, that gave voters more control of government. In a **direct primary,** voters select candidates for office. Previously, candidates for office had been chosen by a few party bosses. A **recall** is a vote that allows voters to remove elected officials from office if they are considered incompetent or otherwise unfit to serve.

The progressives also campaigned to limit the power of big business. President Theodore Roosevelt, who took office in 1901, was a leader in this effort. Under Roosevelt, the government prosecuted several large trusts accused of wrongdoing. He also supported laws allowing the government to regulate businesses in order to protect the public. For example, the Pure Food and Drug Act, passed in 1906, forbade the use of harmful additives in food.

Improving the Quality of Life

The progressives worked to improve the terrible conditions under which many families in industrial cities lived. They encouraged city governments to write building codes that set minimum standards for space, light, sanitation, and fire safety. Reformers such as Jane Addams and Lillian Wald organized settlement houses in city slums to improve the life of the poor. Addams' Hull House in Chicago offered English lessons to immigrants and set up nursery schools for children of working mothers.

Tenements teeming with immigrants could be found in many American cities. In Cliff Dwellers, *artist George Bellows depicted crowds of people on stoops and fire escapes and spilling over onto sidewalks and streets. Reformers such as the progressives struggled to improve life in these overcrowded urban areas.*

Education helped many people rise out of poverty. The number of American school children more than doubled between 1870 and 1910. By the early 1900s, most Americans believed that children had a right to a free public education.

Reformers fought for improvements in the lives of factory workers. Some states passed labor legislation such as accident insurance. The federal government set limits on working hours for some jobs. However, the type of wide-ranging labor laws found in Britain and Germany were not passed in the United States.

Some labor laws that did pass were aimed at protecting women who worked outside the home. Women had long worked in American factories and mills. Inventions such as the telephone and the typewriter opened up new jobs for them. As a result, the number of women in business grew dramatically. As women became more economically independent, they demanded equal political rights, especially the right to vote. By 1915, most states allowed women to vote, but a federal constitutional amendment guaranteeing the right to vote to all women in the country was not approved until 1920.

Black Americans also sought political equality. The Fourteenth Amendment to the Constitution, passed in 1868, had guaranteed blacks all the rights of citizenship, and the Fifteenth Amendment, passed two years later, had guaranteed black men the right to vote. However, in the late 1800s, southern states passed laws that made it difficult or impossible for blacks to vote. One such law stated that a man could vote only if his father or grandfather had been eligible to vote in 1867, three years before the Fifteenth Amendment was ratified.

In many parts of the nation, blacks faced economic and social discrimination. Some people violently opposed the demands of black Americans for equality. Anti-black riots broke out in a number of communities. In 1909, after a riot in Springfield, Illinois, a group of black and white reformers formed the National Association for the Advancement of Colored People (NAACP). The NAACP set out to end discrimination against black Americans. It fought for laws to protect the rights of blacks, and it defended these rights in the courts.

Higher education was crucial to black Americans in their struggle to overcome discrimination. This photograph shows the chemistry laboratory at Tuskegee Institute in Alabama. George Washington Carver, a noted inventor and teacher at Tuskegee, works with the student at left.

A New World Role

For most of the 1800s, the United States had followed George Washington's advice and had avoided close involvement in European affairs. As the United States became a large industrial nation, however, its contacts with other parts of the world increased. American industries needed raw materials from around the world. They also needed foreign markets in which to sell their goods.

In 1898, Albert J. Beveridge, a senator from Indiana, described the American position: "American factories are making more than the American people can use. American soil is producing more than they can eat. The trade of the world must and shall be ours."

In part to protect the nation's growing international trade, the government began to build up the navy. By the early 1900s, the United States had become the third-greatest naval power in the world. At the time, the size of a nation's navy was widely recognized as a sign of its overall power.

In addition to trade, Americans began taking a more active interest in political developments throughout the world. Some Americans believed that the United States had a mission to carry democracy to other peoples and to enforce peace, especially in the Western Hemisphere. These attitudes made the United States more willing than before to take a direct hand in the affairs of other nations. The United States would also acquire overseas territories in the late 1800s, as you will read in Chapters 26 and 27.

SECTION 5 REVIEW

1. **Identify:** (a) progressives, (b) Jane Addams, (c) NAACP.

2. **Define:** (a) direct primary, (b) recall.

3. (a) What were the goals of the progressives? (b) Did they achieve their goals? Explain.

4. What types of services did settlement houses such as Hull House provide?

5. (a) Which constitutional amendment granted black men the right to vote? (b) Why were many blacks unable to vote?

6. How did industrialization increase American involvement in world affairs?

7. **Critical Thinking** Many Americans believed in "rugged individualism." How do you think that attitude helps explain why the United States passed fewer laws to help workers than Great Britain?

CHAPTER 23 REVIEW

Summary

1. **During the 1800s, Great Britain became more democratic.** First middle-class men and then working-class men won the right to vote. In the late 1800s and early 1900s, Parliament passed laws to protect workers from some of the hardships of industrialization.

2. **Parts of the British Empire demanded greater self-rule and political freedom.** The Irish struggled to win the right to rule themselves. Canadians gained control over their own domestic affairs, becoming a self-ruling dominion in 1867. Australia and New Zealand won self-government and pioneered in several democratic advances.

3. **France had to struggle to achieve a more democratic government in the 1800s.** The Second Empire under Napoleon III began as a repressive regime, although Napoleon eventually allowed an elected assembly to exercise some power. After France was defeated in the Franco-Prussian War, the Second Empire collapsed, and the Third Republic was set up.

4. **Territorial expansion, civil war, and industrial growth marked the 1800s in the United States.** The nation spread across the continent from the Atlantic to the Pacific. In mid-century, divisions between the North and the South over the expansion of slavery led to the Civil War. After the war, industries grew, and the United States became an industrial leader.

5. **Late in the century, progressives campaigned for reforms to improve life in the United States.** They wanted to end corruption in government, limit the power of trusts, and improve life for workers. Women and blacks struggled to win equality, especially the right to vote. As the United States became a leading industrial nation, it took a more active role in world affairs.

Recalling Facts

Choose the word or phrase that best completes each of the following statements.

1. The Reform Bill of 1867 extended the vote to (a) urban working men; (b) middle-class men; (c) rural working men.

2. Home rule for Ireland was a demand of (a) Protestants in Ulster; (b) Scottish landlords; (c) Irish Catholics.

3. Real political power in the French Third Republic was in the hands of the (a) cabinet of ministries; (b) Catholic Church; (c) president.

4. In 1845, the United States annexed (a) Florida; (b) California; (c) Texas.

5. Progressives supported (a) the direct primary; (b) trusts; (c) monopolies.

6. An amendment giving American women the right to vote in national elections was passed in (a) 1877; (b) 1914; (c) 1920.

Chapter Checkup

1. (a) How did the selection of members of the British Parliament become more democratic during the 1800s? (b) Which political parties supported the growth of democracy? Why?

2. (a) How did Irish Catholics react to Protestant political and economic control of Ireland during the 1800s? (b) What was the response of the British government to Irish demands?

3. How did Napoleon III's foreign policy lead to his downfall?

4. (a) How was the Third Republic created in France? (b) Why did the circumstances in which it was set up threaten its existence?

5. (a) Describe the expansion of the United States between 1803 and 1853. (b) How did this expansion contribute to tensions between the North and the South?

6. (a) How did rapid industrialization affect American workers? **(b)** Why did labor unions run into such strong opposition in the United States?

7. What steps did reformers take to improve the quality of life in American cities?

Critical Thinking

1. Relating Past to Present **(a)** What rights and benefits did workers in Great Britain win in the late 1800s and early 1900s? **(b)** Which of those rights and benefits do American workers have today?

2. Analyzing **(a)** Describe how Canada gained its independence from Great Britain. **(b)** How does it compare with the way the United States gained its independence? **(c)** How might you explain the difference?

3. Understanding the Roots of Democracy Review the growth of democracy in Great Britain and France. Why do you think bringing about democratic reforms was more difficult in France than in Britain?

Developing Basic Skills

1. Map Reading Study the map on page 523. **(a)** What territory did the United States acquire in 1819? In 1848? **(b)** By what methods did the United States acquire territory between 1819 and 1853? **(c)** By which method did the United States acquire the most territory?

2. Graph Reading Study the graph on page 518. **(a)** About how much iron did France produce in 1895? **(b)** About how much iron did the United States produce in 1900? **(c)** Which country was the largest producer of iron in 1885? In 1910? **(d)** What conclusions about industrial development in these four countries can you draw from this graph?

Writing About History

Writing a Preliminary Thesis Statement

The thesis statement is the main idea of a paper stated in a declarative sentence. Writing this statement helps you limit your topic and guide your research. It is called a preliminary statement because you may have to revise it if you find that there is not enough information to support it or if you find that it is incorrect.

A possible thesis statement for a paper on French democracy in the 1800s is: *The Dreyfus affair was a serious blow to the Third Republic.*

Practice: Write a possible thesis statement for each of the topics below:

1. The Irish attitude toward Great Britain.

2. Jane Addams and her settlement house.

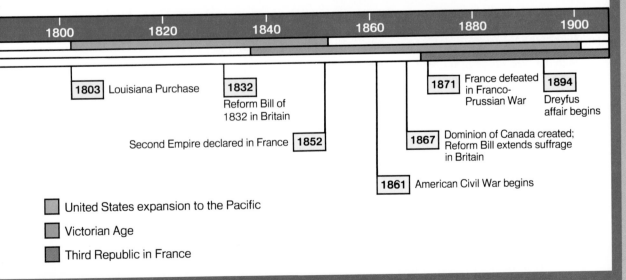

United States expansion to the Pacific

Victorian Age

Third Republic in France

531

Triumph of Nationalism (1848–1914)

24

Crowds line the shore at the Italian seaport of Livorno waiting for the festivities to begin. Resounding cries of "Viva Victor Emmanuel" greet the new king as crowds celebrate the unification of Italy.

Cigars—Austrian cigars—caused the trouble. On January 3, 1848, the soldiers received their orders. Their officers had given out the cigars and told the soldiers to smoke them. The soldiers obeyed. As they patrolled the streets of Milan, the capital of Lombardy in northern Italy, they puffed on their cigars. As the smoke rose into the crisp January air, the people of Milan grew furious. They attacked the cigar-smoking soldiers with angry words, flying fists, and rocks. The Austrian troops answered with drawn swords. By the end of the day, Milan's hospitals were filled with injured and dying Italian patriots. The tense city edged toward rebellion.

How did cigars spark a rebellion? Cigars were a major source of revenue for the Austrians, who ruled Lombardy. To protest foreign control of their province, the residents of Milan refused to smoke cigars. Almost overnight, the cigar became a symbol of Italian nationalism.

In February, news of uprisings in France reached Milan, making the mood of Italian patriots even uglier. The moment had come, they declared, to throw off the yoke of Austrian rule and create a democratic Italy. On March 17, a large crowd gathered outside the Austrian government headquarters. The crowd made the Austrian soldiers nervous, and they fired a blank volley to scatter it. Shouting "Viva l'Italia" (Long live Italy), a 16-year-old boy fired his pistol at the troops. The mob rushed forward, quickly overpowering the guards.

The Austrians were able to crush the uprising in Milan, but their victory was short-lived. The citizens of Milan were inspired by nationalism, one of the most powerful forces during the 1800s. Between 1848 and 1914, nationalism played a key role in events in Central and Eastern Europe. In some areas, it helped create unified nations. In other areas, nationalism threatened to break up large, diverse empires. ■

1 The Unification of Italy

READ TO UNDERSTAND

☐ How the movement to unite Italy got under way.

☐ What role Mazzini, Cavour, and Garibaldi played in winning Italian unity.

☐ What problems Italy faced after unification.

Italy, said Prince Metternich of Austria, is "a geographic expression." By that he meant that Italy was a place, not a nation. To millions of people living on the Italian peninsula, Italy was much more than a place. They looked back to the glorious days of the Roman Empire and to the time when Italian city-states had given birth to the Renaissance. As one Italian patriot declared, they wanted a "new Italy, a united Italy, the Italy of all Italians."

Nationalism in Italy

Italian nationalism had roots in the French Revolution, with its ideals of liberty, equality, and fraternity. Furthermore, Napoleon Bona-

parte had combined small Italian states into larger kingdoms. (See the map on page 449.) This gave Italians a taste of unity.

After the Congress of Vienna, however, most of Italy was under foreign rule. Austria ruled Venetia and Lombardy directly, and Austrian princes ruled in Parma, Lucca, Modena, and Tuscany. The Congress of Vienna had set up the Spanish Bourbon family as rulers of the kingdom of the Two Sicilies.

Italian nationalists struggled for independence and unity throughout the 1830s and 1840s. In 1831, the nationalist leader Giuseppe Mazzini (maht TZEE nee) organized a secret society called Young Italy. Its goal was to work for the unification of Italy. In addition, Mazzini wanted Italy to be a republic. "I give my name to Young Italy," he proclaimed, "and swear to dedicate myself to making Italy one free republican nation."

Other nationalists favored a unified Italy led by the kingdom of Sardinia.* Count Camillo Cavour led this group. He edited a newspaper called *Il Risorgimento* (ree SOHR jee MEHN toh), meaning the resurgence or revival. Eventually,

---

* As you can see from the map on page 534, the kingdom of Sardinia included the island of Sardinia plus Piedmont, Nice, and Savoy on the mainland. The capital, Turin, was located in Piedmont.

the entire movement for Italian unity was called the Risorgimento.

Nationalists tried to rid Italy of foreign rule in 1848 but failed. (See Chapter 20.) Sardinia emerged from the revolutions of 1848 as the leader of the struggle for unification. Furthermore, Victor Emmanuel II, who became king of Sardinia in 1849, was a strong supporter of the Risorgimento.

The First Steps

Victor Emmanuel gave the cause of Italian unification an enormous boost when he named Count Cavour his prime minister in 1852. Cavour was a skillful politician. He wanted Sardinia to be a model for Italian unification.

MAP STUDY *Italy was united between 1858 and 1870. By 1860, most Italian states had united with Sardinia. In 1861, they declared themselves the kingdom of Italy. What area was added to Italy in 1866? In 1870?*

Unification of Italy, 1858-1870

Legend:
- Kingdom of Sardinia, 1858
- Added to Sardinia, 1859 and 1860
- Added to Italy, 1866
- Added to Italy, 1870

Therefore, he introduced road- and canal-building projects, land reforms, and new tariff policies. His policies brought rapid economic growth. Sardinia was soon recognized as an emerging power.

The Crimean War. Cavour believed that tough, practical international diplomacy was essential to unification. He saw the Crimean War, which broke out in 1854, as a chance to win the allies he needed to drive Austria out of Italy.

France and Great Britain had declared war on Russia to prevent Russia from gaining too much influence over the weak Ottoman Empire. Sardinia entered the war on the side of France and Britain, which won it in 1856. Sardinia's participation in the war had two important results. First, Sardinia took part in the peace conference. Cavour used the conference as a stage from which to publicize the demand for Italian unification. Second, Cavour won the support of Napoleon III of France in his struggle to end Austrian rule in Italy.

War with Austria. In 1858, Cavour met secretly with Napoleon III to plan a strategy against Austria. They decided to trick Austria into declaring war on Sardinia. Then France would send troops to help the Sardinians. In return, Sardinia agreed to give Savoy and Nice to France.

The following year Sardinia put the plan into action. By encouraging nationalist revolts in the Austrian provinces of Lombardy and Venetia, Cavour provoked Austria into declaring war. As promised, France sent troops. Following bloody battles at Magenta and Solferino, the French and Sardinians drove Austria from Lombardy.

At this point, Napoleon III suddenly withdrew his support because he realized that a unified Italy might be a threat to France. Therefore, he negotiated a separate peace treaty with Austria. According to this treaty, Sardinia won Lombardy, but Venetia remained under Austrian control. The status of other states in northern Italy remained unchanged. Soon, however, the people of these states took action themselves. Several states held plebiscites, or popular votes, demanding unification with Sardinia. In this way, Tuscany, Modena, Parma, and the papal province of Romagna joined Sardinia.

Garibaldi and his Red Shirts helped free Sicily and all of southern Italy from foreign control. On May 11, 1860, Garibaldi and his forces landed in western Sicily. As they marched inland, recruits flocked to the cause. Four days after landing, Garibaldi's Red Shirts won the battle at Calatafimi, pictured here. Within two weeks, Garibaldi had taken the city of Palermo and set up a provisional government in Sicily.

Unification Completed

Meanwhile, in southern Italy, the nationalist movement was growing under the leadership of Giuseppe Garibaldi, a dashing military commander. Garibaldi, who had belonged to Young Italy, wanted nothing less than a completely unified Italy with a republican form of government.

In 1860, with the unofficial approval and secret support of Sardinia, Garibaldi formed a volunteer army of over 1,000 "Red Shirts," so-named for the color of their uniforms. Their aim was to attack the kingdom of the Two Sicilies and drive out the Bourbon rulers. "To arms," Garibaldi urged Italian patriots. "Let me put an end, once and for all, to the miseries of so many centuries. Prove to the world that it is no lie that Roman generations inhabited this land."

Garibaldi and his Red Shirts landed on the island of Sicily and conquered it in a brief but daring military campaign. They then sailed to the mainland, where once again they were victorious. The Bourbon forces fled, and Garibaldi entered Naples in triumph.

Next, Garibaldi turned his attention to Rome and the Papal States, which were under French protection. At this point, Cavour stepped in. He was afraid an attack on Rome would offend Italians as well as the French government. Cavour sent a Sardinian army to Naples to block Garibaldi. Cavour convinced Garibaldi to turn over Sicily and Naples to Victor Emmanuel. By the end of 1860, Sardinia had annexed Sicily, Naples, and two outlying papal provinces.

In March 1861, a parliament representing all of Italy except Venetia and Rome with its surrounding lands met in Turin. The parlia-

This cartoon illustrates Garibaldi's contribution to Italian unification. Garibaldi is fitting the boot of Italy onto the foot of Victor Emmanuel, advising him: "If it won't go on, Sire, try a little more powder."

ment proclaimed the kingdom of Italy with Victor Emmanuel as king. Three months later, just as the unification of Italy neared completion, Cavour died.

In 1866, Italy joined Prussia in a brief war against Austria. When Prussia won, Italy acquired Venetia from Austria. Four years later, when the Franco-Prussian War broke out, France was forced to withdraw its troops from Rome. Italian troops entered the city in September 1870, and the people of Rome voted to join the kingdom of Italy. Nine years after the death of Cavour, his dream of unifying the entire Italian peninsula at last came true.

Problems of a Unified Italy

The unification of Italy created problems of its own. Pope Pius IX was angry at losing control of Rome and the Papal States. He withdrew into the Vatican and urged Italian Catholics not to cooperate with their new government. This action strained relations between the

Catholic Church and the Italian state. It also put pressure on those people who wanted to be loyal both to Italy and the Catholic Church.

Unification increased the antagonism between people living in the north and in the south. Southern Italians resented the fact that Sardinians dominated the government. Economic differences contributed to the gap between north and south. While the north began to industrialize, the south remained rural and poor.

Many republicans such as Garibaldi were disappointed that the government of the new nation was not more democratic. Although Italy had a constitution that limited the power of the king and provided for an elected parliament, only a few men had the right to vote. Of 20 million people, only about 600,000—fewer than 1 in 30—could vote.

Some Italian nationalists were unhappy with unification because they thought it was not complete. They pushed to add Trentino, Trieste, and Dalmatia, still controlled by Austria, as well as Savoy and Nice, which France ruled. Nationalists called these areas "Italia irredenta," which means Italy unredeemed. The "Italia irredenta," like the other problems of unified Italy, would contribute to unrest and instability in the future.

SECTION 1 REVIEW

1. **Locate:** (a) Venetia, (b) Lombardy, (c) kingdom of the Two Sicilies, (d) kingdom of Sardinia, (e) Nice, (f) Savoy.

2. **Identify:** (a) Giuseppe Mazzini, (b) Camillo Cavour, (c) Risorgimento, (d) Victor Emmanuel, (e) Giuseppe Garibaldi, (f) Italia irredenta.

3. How did the French Revolution affect Italian nationalism?

4. Why did Sardinia become involved in the Crimean War?

5. (a) How did Sardinia gain Lombardy? (b) How did it gain other states in northern Italy?

6. **Critical Thinking** How was unification a "mixed blessing" for Italy?

2 The Unification of Germany

READ TO UNDERSTAND

☐ **What obstacles to German unity existed in 1850.**

☐ **Why Prussia took the lead in uniting Germany.**

☐ **How Bismarck used Realpolitik to promote German unity.**

☐ *Vocabulary:* **militarism.**

The Nibelungs were an evil family who owned a hoard of magic gold. The dragon Fafnir got possession of the gold, but the hero Siegfried killed Fafnir, thus gaining the gold for himself. Later, Siegfried rescued, but then betrayed, the warrior maiden Brünhilde. The stories of Siegfried and of other heroes were told in German poems of the Middle Ages. As the flames of German nationalism rose in the 1800s, poets and composers glorified the heroes of these ballads of long ago.

Like the Italians, the Germans were divided into many separate states in 1815. The Congress of Vienna created the German Confederation, a loose organization of 39 separate states. But many Germans wanted a unified nation. As you have read, nationalists and liberals tried but failed to unite Germany in 1848. Over the next two decades, the obstacles to German unity were overcome.

Obstacles to Unity

The presence of Austria in the German Confederation was one of the most serious obstacles to German unity. Austria opposed attempts to unify Germany, worrying that it would lose influence among the German states. In addition, Austria feared competition if a powerful German nation were created in Central Europe. For the same reason, other countries, especially France and Russia, did not want to see the German states united.

Many smaller German states also opposed unification. They were afraid that Prussia would control a united Germany. Catholic states in southern Germany were especially concerned about domination by Protestant Prussia. Also, smaller German states wanted to protect their own customs and traditions. They did not want to be absorbed into a large nation.

Prussian Leadership

During the 1850s, Prussia led the effort to unify Germany. Prussia had many advantages over other German states. Since the early 1700s, absolute rulers had made Prussia a strong and powerful state with a large, well-disciplined army.

In the 1800s, the king and the Junkers, who were aristocratic landowners, controlled the Prussian government. Most government officials and army officers were Junkers. The constitution approved by the king in 1850 called for a parliament. But wealthy Junkers dominated the parliament, along with a newly emerging class of industrial capitalists.

The Industrial Revolution added to Prussian economic strength. The Ruhr Valley in western Germany, which was controlled by Prussia, had the largest coal deposits in Europe. During the 1850s, these coal fields fueled the growing Prussian iron and steel industry. Iron and steel production stimulated the economy and allowed the government to build an efficient network of railroads. In planning the railroads, the government worked closely with the military.

Government reforms in the first half of the 1800s further strengthened the Prussian state. Although the constitution left power in the hands of the king and the Junkers, its very existence gave the Prussians a reputation for being forward looking. When Prussia abolished serfdom and created a system of public education, this reputation grew. However, these reforms did not mean that Prussia was either liberal or democratic. In fact, it was an authoritarian state that rigorously supported **militarism,** the glorification of the military and a readiness for war.

King William I, who came to the throne in 1861, wanted to make sure Prussia would remain both authoritarian and militaristic. To help him meet this goal, the king appointed Count Otto von Bismarck as prime minister and minister of foreign affairs.

Bismarck's "Blood and Iron"

Bismarck came from a conservative Junker family. A former military officer, he believed in royal power. Although Bismarck had served in the Prussian parliament, he had no respect for representative government or for liberals. "Germany does not look to Prussia's liberalism," he said, "but to her power."

Bismarck and William I shared the goal of uniting Germany under Prussian control. They wanted to make a unified Germany that would be the most powerful nation in Europe. These goals, Bismarck insisted, would be achieved "not with speeches and majority decisions . . . but with blood and iron."

By "blood and iron," Bismarck meant warfare and the military. Once in office, he began to carry out the king's plan to expand the army. However, to get the money, he needed the approval of the lower house of parliament. It refused to pass the military budget. Bismarck did not let parliament stand in his way. He simply claimed that the government did not need parliament's approval. According to the constitution, Bismarck was wrong. But he ignored the constitution and collected taxes to pay military expenses anyway.

In this matter as in all others, Bismarck followed a policy of "Realpolitik," a German word meaning realism. He took whatever political action he thought necessary, whether or not it was legal or ethical. He freely applied the policy of Realpolitik in the process of creating a united Germany.

First Steps

Bismarck's first step toward unification was to weaken Austria. Ironically, he began his campaign against Austria by forming a military alliance with it.

War over Schleswig-Holstein. In 1864, Prussia and Austria joined forces to seize the provinces of Schleswig and Holstein, which were ruled by the king of Denmark. (See the map at right.) Although the Danish army fiercely resisted, the Austrians and Prussians quickly overran the provinces. According to the treaty that ended the war, Austria would administer Holstein, while Prussia would administer Schleswig.

Bismarck was pleased with the outcome of the war. First, it expanded Prussian influence. Second, the division of the spoils of war soon created trouble between Prussia and Austria. This gave Bismarck an excuse to go to war with Austria.

War with Austria. Before going to war with Austria, Bismarck wanted to make certain that other nations would not support Austria. He made vague promises of ceding territory to France to make sure the French stayed out of any conflict. The Russians also promised to remain neutral after Bismarck reminded them that Prussia had helped suppress an anti-Russian uprising in Poland in 1863. By promising Venetia to Italy if Austria were defeated, he won Italian support.

In 1866, Bismarck used a dispute over Holstein to provoke Austria into war. Prussian troops marched into Holstein, and Austria declared war. Austrian forces were no match for the highly disciplined Prussian army and its brilliant military leadership. The Prussians moved troops rapidly by railroad. They used new rapid-firing weapons such as a needle gun that fired five rounds per minute. In just seven weeks, the war was over. Observers were stunned at the speed with which the Prussians defeated the Austrians in the Seven Weeks' War.

Bismarck did nothing to humiliate Austria after the Seven Weeks' War. "We had to avoid leaving behind in her any desire for revenge," he wrote later. He followed a fairly lenient policy. Austria had to give Venetia to Italy and was forced out of the German Confederation, which was then disbanded. Several states, including Schleswig and Holstein, were annexed by Prussia. One year later, the 21 German states north of the Main River formed the North German Confederation led by Prussia. (See the map at right.)

The Franco-Prussian War

After the war with Austria, only the Catholic states of southern Germany remained outside Prussian control. These states were deeply suspicious of Prussia. They valued their independence and did not want to be dominated by a Protestant nation. But people in the southern states also feared control by France.

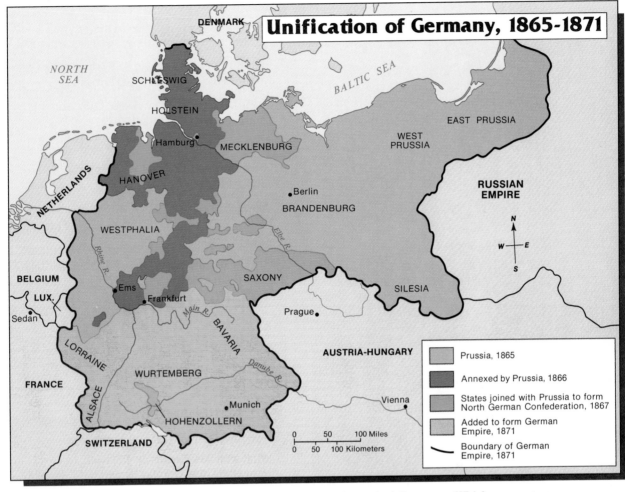

Unification of Germany, 1865-1871

NORTH SEA

BALTIC SEA

DENMARK

SCHLESWIG

HOLSTEIN

• Hamburg

MECKLENBURG

EAST PRUSSIA

WEST PRUSSIA

HANOVER

NETHERLANDS

WESTPHALIA

• Berlin

BRANDENBURG

RUSSIAN EMPIRE

Elbe R.

BELGIUM

LUX.

Ems •

• Frankfurt

SAXONY

Sedan

Rhine R.

Main R.

BAVARIA

SILESIA

Prague •

AUSTRIA-HUNGARY

LORRAINE

FRANCE

WURTEMBERG

Danube R.

ALSACE

HOHENZOLLERN

• Munich

Vienna •

SWITZERLAND

N W E S

0   50   100 Miles
0 50 100 Kilometers

Prussia, 1865

Annexed by Prussia, 1866

States joined with Prussia to form North German Confederation, 1867

Added to form German Empire, 1871

Boundary of German Empire, 1871

MAP STUDY *Over a six-year period, Bismarck created a united Germany. Which areas were added to Germany in 1871? What long-time enemy was made as a result?*

Bismarck decided to play on these fears. He convinced the southern German states to form a military alliance with Prussia for protection against France. Such a military alliance, he hoped, would eventually lead to political unity. Moreover, he believed that war with France would guarantee this result.

France also seemed to want war. France had suffered several disastrous foreign adventures, and Napoleon III faced growing domestic problems. (See page 518.) Also, Napoleon was alarmed at the growing power of Prussia and hoped that a successful war would save his failing regime.

A minor dispute over who would assume the throne of Spain led to the Franco-Prussian War. In 1868, the Spanish government had offered the throne to a cousin of William I. This

angered the French. A French ambassador visited William I and demanded that the Prussian king promise that his relative would not accept the Spanish throne. William refused and sent a telegram to Bismarck describing the meeting.

The crafty Bismarck saw his chance. He edited the telegram so that it seemed that the king and ambassador had been rude to one another. Then Bismarck released the telegram to the press. People in both France and Prussia felt their nations had been insulted, and they clamored for war. On July 15, 1870, France declared war.

Once again, the Prussian army could not be stopped. In September, the Prussians defeated the French army and took Napoleon III prisoner. By January 1871, all French resist-

539

William I was proclaimed emperor in the Hall of Mirrors at the palace of Versailles after Prussia defeated France in the Franco-Prussian War. The event was momentous for German nationalists, whose goal of unification had finally been achieved. The French, however, considered the ceremony at Versailles an insult, which they hoped to avenge.

ance was crushed. As you have read, the French had to sign a treaty giving up Alsace and part of Lorraine.

On January 18, 1871, at the palace of Versailles, William I was proclaimed kaiser, or emperor, of Germany. The new German Empire included all the members of the North German Confederation, the southern German states, and Alsace-Lorraine. German unification was complete, but the Germans had created a lasting enemy in France.

1. **Locate:** (a) Schleswig, (b) Holstein, (c) Main River, (d) Alsace, (e) Lorraine.

2. **Identify:** (a) William I, (b) Otto von Bismarck, (c) Realpolitik.

3 **Define:** militarism.

4. Describe two reasons why Prussia led the effort to unify Germany.

5. What did Bismarck gain by going to war with (a) Denmark, (b) Austria, (c) France?

6. **Critical Thinking** Compare and contrast the goals and methods of Cavour in Italy and Bismarck in Germany.

3 Consolidating the German Empire

READ TO UNDERSTAND

☐ How the German Empire was ruled.

☐ What policies Bismarck followed to strengthen the German Reich.

☐ What William II's goals for Germany were.

Following the Prussian victory over France, Bismarck needed to bind the German Empire together. Prussian Junkers were afraid of losing their traditional privileges. Many Catholics distrusted the Protestant Prussians. Liberals and socialists disliked Bismarck's conservatism. Indeed, the forces of disunity were so great that some observers predicted a quick break-up of the German Empire. But they underestimated the skills of Bismarck.

The New German Empire

The new German Empire was called the Second Reich.* The constitution of the Second Reich established a federation, a union of 25

---

*Reich is the German word for empire. This empire was named the Second Reich because Germany considered the Holy Roman Empire the first Reich.

540

In 1826, the Krupp Steel Works in Germany faced a crisis. Its founder, Friedrich Krupp, had built a small steel mill in the Ruhr Valley in 1812. As orders for tools and gun barrels rolled in, Friedrich expanded ambitiously. But business did not keep up with his dreams, and soon Friedrich was deep in debt. When Friedrich died in 1826, his business was on the verge of bankruptcy.

Left to handle the crisis, Krupp's widow, Theresa, and his 14-year-old son Alfred moved quickly. Theresa and Alfred assured the mill's customers that they could fill their orders.

The long workdays of the widow and her son paid off, and the Krupp Works prospered. Alfred found a way to manufacture huge rolls of steel from which spoons and forks could be cheaply cut. As railroads expanded throughout Europe, the Krupp Works began turning out high-quality steel rails and wheels.

In the 1840s, the Krupps decided to produce rifles and cannons. At first, their largest potential customer—the Prussian army—had little interest in their wares. Alfred showed the Prussian generals how the new Krupp cannon was loaded through an opening in the side of the barrel and could be fired faster and more safely than traditional cannons. But the Prussian generals believed that the old-fashioned brass cannons were better than Krupp's gleaming steel models.

Alfred was disappointed but not ready to give up. He wrote a letter to the new king of Prussia, William I. Alfred told the king that for patriotic reasons, he had not sold his cannons to other countries, but that he could no longer

afford to turn down their orders. William got the point, and Prussia soon became one of Krupp's best customers. Krupp's cannons proved their value when Prussia fought Austria in 1866 and again during the Franco-Prussian War of 1870. In the end, though, Prussia was not Alfred's only customer. By the time he died in 1887, he had armed over 40 countries. He had become one of the richest men in Europe, and his steel works employed over 20,000 workers.

1. How did Alfred Krupp get the Prussian army to buy his cannons?

2. **Critical Thinking** As a German, was Alfred Krupp justified in supplying arms to other nations? Why or why not?

---

states, with each governed by its own king, prince, archduke, or duke. Each ruler appointed representatives to the upper house of a parliament, called the Bundesrat (BOON duhs RAHT). Members of the lower house, called the Reichstag (RĪKS tahg), were elected by male citizens over the age of 25.

The constitution appeared to create a representative government, but the appearance was deceiving. The Bundesrat could veto any decision made by the Reichstag. The emperor and his chancellor, or chief minister, controlled enough votes in the Bundesrat to determine its decisions. Thus, political power rested firmly in the hands of the emperor and the chancellor.

From the start, Prussia dominated the Second Reich. William I was king of Prussia as well as emperor, and he appointed Bismarck chancellor. Prussians were appointed to most top positions in the government of the empire. The Prussian tradition of compulsory military service was extended throughout the empire, with Prussian officers in charge of the army. These developments won the support of Prussian Junkers for the Second Reich.

During the early years of the empire, Bismarck created a smooth-running government. He set up a uniform legal system for all the states in the empire. He brought the coining of money under the control of the imperial bank. In addition, he saw to it that the railroad, mail, and telegraph systems of the individual states were coordinated throughout the empire. Bismarck administered the Second Reich with a firm hand, earning the title of the Iron Chancellor.

Conflict Over Religion

Bismarck's efforts to create a strong central government soon led to conflict with the Catholics in Germany. Bismarck considered the Catholic Church a threat to government power. Catholics were a large minority in Germany, and their political party, the Center party, was the second strongest party in the Reichstag. In 1872, Bismarck launched an all-out attack on the Catholic Church. He called his policy the "Kulturkampf," meaning struggle for civilization. The government passed laws expelling the Jesuit order from Germany. Members of the clergy were forbidden to criticize the government, and schools run by Catholic orders were closed.

But rather than weakening the Catholic Church, the Kulturkampf unified Catholics and strengthened the Center party. Bismarck realized that his attack on the Catholic Church had backfired, and in 1880 he began to have most of the anti-Catholic laws repealed. Bismarck needed the support of the Catholics because he faced a serious challenge from socialists.

Demands for Political and Social Reform

German liberals had at first been unhappy with the government of the Second Reich. They wanted a more democratic government with a truly representative parliament. Many

admired the British constitutional monarchy. However, gradually, many German liberals came to support Bismarck. A major reason for this change was economic prosperity. Once Germany was unified, it increased the pace of its industrialization. This economic growth benefited the middle class and industrial capitalists. Liberal feelings were strongest among these groups, and many liberals were willing to support Bismarck's government in return for economic well-being.

German workers, however, were less enthusiastic about Bismarck and his programs. As in other nations, rapid industrialization in Germany created poor living and working conditions for workers. In the 1870s, many workers supported the German Social Democratic

GRAPH STUDY *Rising steel production was evidence of rapid economic growth in the German Empire. How does German steel production shown in this graph compare with German railroad construction and iron production shown in the graphs on page 479 and 518?*

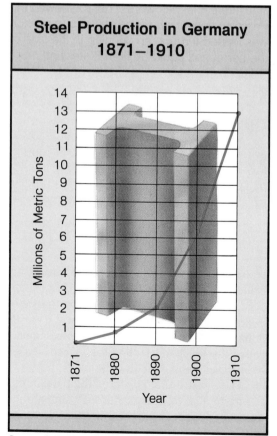

Steel Production in Germany 1871–1910

Source: B.R. Mitchell, *European Historical Statistics.*

party. This party, founded in 1869, promoted the ideas of Marxist socialism. (See page 498.) But many German Social Democrats were more interested in social and economic reform than in the violent revolution that Marx had predicted.

Bismarck hated and feared socialism, and he was determined to destroy it in Germany. In 1878, he pressured the Reichstag to pass laws restricting the Social Democrats. The laws forbade publication of socialist books and pamphlets. It also gave the police the right to break up socialist meetings and imprison socialist leaders. However, this crackdown only strengthened the socialists.

Bismarck then changed his tactics. He decided to defeat the Social Democratic party by introducing reforms to win worker support for the government. During the late 1800s, the government introduced accident, health, and old-age insurance. German workers thus won a basic social security program from one of Europe's most conservative regimes. Despite Bismarck's plan, however, the Social Democrats continued to win seats in the Reichstag.

A New Emperor

In 1888, the 29-year-old grandson of William I inherited the German throne as William II. (William II's father had died after a brief reign.) The new emperor believed in the divine right of his family to rule Germany. Like Bismarck, he believed that a strong Germany rested on a powerful monarchy as well as on a powerful army. At first, he kept the Iron Chancellor as his chief minister. But William II was an impulsive, self-centered man, and he resented Bismarck's domination. In 1890, the young emperor decided to be his own chief minister and forced Bismarck to resign.

William II tried hard to win the support of all Germans, including the working class. He allowed the anti-socialist laws to lapse and extended the social insurance programs. No longer repressed, the Social Democratic party won widespread support and became the single largest party in the Reichstag. While it continued to demand more democracy, it became less revolutionary in outlook.

Under William II's personal, and often erratic, leadership, Germany set a new course in

As a young man, William II admired Bismarck. But after he became kaiser, he often clashed with the Iron Chancellor. This cartoon compares William II's dismissal of Bismarck to a ship's captain putting the pilot ashore after a difficult voyage.

foreign policy. The ambitious ruler wanted to win for Germany "a place in the sun" among great world powers such as Britain, France, and Russia. He was determined to make Germany a major commercial, colonial, and military power. He joined other European powers in competing for colonies in Asia, Africa, and the Pacific.

Between 1892 and 1913, William II almost doubled the size of the army. He also devoted much attention to building a large navy that would rival the British navy. Both the army and navy benefited from increased German steel production. By 1900, Germany produced more steel than Britain. Only the United States produced more.

A National Spirit

During the late 1800s, Germans developed a strong sense of national pride. German military victories and economic progress contributed to this pride. By the turn of the century, Germany was the leading industrial nation in Europe.

Germans were also proud of their cultural heritage. They took special pride in the achievements of composers such as Ludwig van Beethoven and Richard Wagner. Another source of national pride was the German educational system, which was considered the best in Europe by 1900. Students from all over the world flocked to German universities, which had a reputation for offering the most advanced scientific education.

In many ways, Prussia still dominated German national life. Prussian admiration for the military was just one example of this dominance. As Germany became a major world power, the spirit of militarism increased. One writer summed up German attitudes toward the military in these words:

> After God the Father comes the cavalry officer, then his horse, then nothing, nothing, still nothing, then the infantry officer. Very far behind come the civilians: first the reserve officers and at last the remainder.

SECTION 3 REVIEW

1. **Identify:** (a) Second Reich, (b) Bundesrat, (c) Reichstag, (d) William II.

2. Describe three ways in which Prussia dominated the Second Reich.

3. Was Bismarck's Kulturkampf successful? Why or why not?

4. What two tactics did Bismarck use in his effort to destroy socialism in Germany?

5. What were William II's foreign policy goals?

6. **Critical Thinking** Do you think Bismarck successfully built and strengthened the Second Reich? Why or why not?

4 Repression and Reform in Russia

READ TO UNDERSTAND

☐ What problems Russia faced in the 1800s.

☐ How various czars tried to solve these problems.

☐ What the causes and results of the revolution of 1905 were.

☐ *Vocabulary:* autocracy, mir, zemstvo, pogrom.

"Placed between the two great divisions of the world, between East and West, our head on Germany and our feet in China, we ought to have combined within ourselves the two great principles of human life—imagination and reason," wrote a Russian thinker in the mid-1800s. "Destiny has given us no such role," he concluded sadly.

By the mid-1800s, the Russian Empire sprawled from Europe to the Pacific Ocean. The economic and political system had changed little since the days of Peter the Great. Those who spoke out for freedom or reform faced harsh punishments, exile, or death. The Russian czars and most aristocrats wanted to preserve the traditional order, but forces of change were at work in Russia as they were in other parts of Europe.

Russia in the Early 1800s

The backbone of the Russian economy was farming, and the farming was done by serfs, as it had been for hundreds of years. Serfdom had been abolished in most of Europe by the mid-1800s, but in Russia 40 million serfs lived much as they had during the Middle Ages. They were permanently attached to the land and could be sold along with the land or used as servants. Owners could force them to work in factories and take their wages. Runaway serfs risked brutal punishment.

The system of serfdom was inefficient. Poor, ignorant serfs made reluctant workers. At the same time, many landowners were poor managers. As long as they had serfs to do the work, they did not feel the need to introduce better farming methods. As a result, Russian agriculture suffered.

The Russian Empire was an **autocracy,** that is, a government in which the ruler has unlimited power. To rule their vast empire, the czars relied on a bureaucracy of thousands of officials. These officials often enforced the laws harshly.

Strengthening the Autocracy

Alexander I became czar in 1801. As a young man, he was influenced by Enlightenment thinkers. But when he realized that reform would weaken his power, he abandoned Enlightenment ideas. At the Congress of Vienna in 1815, Alexander was a strong defender of the traditional order.

Yet the ideas that Napoleon had spread across Europe took root in Russia. Many Russian officers who had fought against Napoleon in Western Europe were impressed with what they saw there. When they returned to Russia, some formed secret societies to discuss and spread ideas for reform. When Alexander I died in 1825, a group of army officers staged an uprising called the Decembrist Revolt because it took place on December 26. The Decembrists demanded a constitutional monarchy. The revolt was quickly crushed, but it made a strong impression on Alexander I's successor, Nicholas I.

GEOGRAPHY IN HISTORY
The Decembrist Exiles: Aristocrats In Siberia

Czar Nicholas I responded quickly to the Decembrist Revolt of 1825. Although the rebels were from Russia's wealthiest and most noble families, Nicholas had the leaders executed. He sentenced many others to hard labor in Siberia, followed by permanent exile there. In the summer of 1826, the "state criminals" began the 4,000-mile (6,400-kilometer) trek into the forbidding wilds of Siberia.

Russia's leaders used the vast, almost uninhabited area to isolate criminals. Both political prisoners, like the Decembrists, and ordinary criminals were sent to Siberia. There they mined the rich resources of the area, including salt, silver, and gold. They repaired roads and labored in grain mills. Banishing prisoners to Siberia was cheaper than building prisons in Moscow or St. Petersburg. Besides, it also kept revolutionaries at a safe distance from the cities, where, even from prison, they might stir up trouble.

As the Decembrists were shipped to Siberia, their wives faced a painful choice. Should they stay with their families in western Russia or follow their husbands into exile? The decision was made harder by the czar's decree that wives, but not children, could go with the prisoners to Siberia. Even so, few of the wives hesitated. When a friend asked the Princess Volkonskaya how she could leave her infant son and go to Siberia, she replied, "My son is fortunate, my husband is unfortunate, so my place is with my husband."

1. How did geography influence the government's decision to send prisoners to Siberia?

2. **Critical Thinking** Do you think exile to Siberia was an effective way for the czars to deal with political prisoners?

Before 1861, Russian nobles owned huge estates on which serfs lived and worked in virtual slavery. Nobles often led idle lives. They wasted time and money gambling and attending lavish parties. In this cartoon by French artist Gustave Doré, Russian nobles use bundles of serfs as bets in a card game.

Nicholas I, determined to strengthen the autocracy, unleashed the forces of reaction. He did everything he could to stamp out opposition to the government. He gave his secret police almost unlimited power over Russian life. People suspected of treason could be arrested, imprisoned, and deported without trial. The police censored newspapers and other written material to suppress dangerous ideas.

Universities were a special target because Nicholas was afraid students would adopt revolutionary ideas from Western Europe. When the revolutions of 1848 broke out in other parts of Europe, the czar was convinced that strict control was necessary to prevent such uprisings in Russia.

A Period of Reform

Despite the efforts of Nicholas I to prevent change in Russia, demands for reform grew. Many Russians came to realize that serfdom was holding back progress. As Russia began to slowly industrialize, factory owners could not find enough free workers because so many people were serfs. In addition, the number of serf revolts had increased.

When Russia was defeated in the Crimean War, many Russians blamed the defeat on their backward economic and political system. Nicholas I died during the Crimean War and was succeeded by his son Alexander II. Like his father, the new czar believed in autocracy, but he thought that some reforms were needed to prevent revolution.

In 1861, Alexander II issued the Emancipation Edict freeing the serfs. The czar declared: "It is better to abolish serfdom from above than to wait until it is abolished from below." Serfs were given personal freedom, but they received no free land, as many had hoped. Instead, the government paid landowners handsomely for part of their land. Then it parceled the land out to village communities, called **mirs.** The peasants who lived in the mirs had to pay the government for the land over a period of 49 years.

Peasants were hardly better off after emancipation than they were before. They were heavily in debt and seldom had enough land to farm efficiently. As a result, Russian agriculture improved little.

Alexander introduced other reforms. He relaxed press censorship and eased restrictions on universities. The jury system was introduced. The government also created local elected assemblies called **zemstvos.** Many zemstvos established schools and improved health care. In addition, through the zemstvos, some Russians gained experience in government.

The reforms of Alexander II encouraged revolutionaries to spread their ideas. During the 1870s, thousands of educated young Russian people left the cities and went into the countryside to convince peasants to support revolutionary goals. These populists, as they were called, had little success organizing the peasants. A few populists eventually formed political parties to work for revolution. The most radical populists formed a group called the People's Will. Its goal was to assassinate the czar. After several attempts, they finally succeeded, killing Alexander II in 1881.

A Return to Repression

Alexander III, who succeeded his father, returned to the reactionary policies of Nicholas I. He moved quickly to crush revolutionaries and end reform. He reduced the powers of the zemstvos, restored strict censorship, and ordered the secret police to arrest critics.

Because of its vast size, the Russian Empire contained many ethnic minorities, including Ukrainians, Finns, Poles, and Jews. Many of these people opposed Russian rule. Alexander III decided to strengthen his rule through a policy called Russification. He tried to force all people in the empire to use the Russian language and to adopt the Russian Orthodox religion.

The Jews were a special target. They were forbidden to own land and were forced to live in certain areas of the country. Government troops took part in **pogroms,** murderous raids on Jewish communities. This persecution drove hundreds of thousands of Jews out of Russia. Many immigrated to the United States.

In 1894, Nicholas II succeeded his father. A weak and uncertain ruler, he continued his father's repressive policies. Nicholas II faced increased unrest as Russia began to industri-

alize more rapidly. By 1900, Russia was the fourth largest iron producer in the world, and the number of industrial workers had reached 2 million. Like workers in other countries, Russian workers labored long hours for little pay. Labor unions were illegal in Russia, but labor unrest led to numerous strikes, many of them violent.

The Revolution of 1905

As the new century dawned, Nicholas II sat uneasily on the throne. Besides labor unrest, the government faced opposition from landless peasants, national minorities, and middle-class liberals, who demanded a constitutional government. Revolutionaries made their views known in even more violent ways—by assassinating government officials.

In 1904, war broke out between Russia and a rapidly industrializing Japan. The two nations had been competing for influence in Manchuria and Korea. Nicholas II hoped that a Russian victory would ease discontent at home. But the Russians were soundly defeated by Japan. For the first time, an Asian nation had defeated a European power. Such a humiliating defeat further increased tensions at home.

On January 22, 1905, a crowd of workers peacefully paraded toward the czar's palace in St. Petersburg. The workers carried a petition for the czar asking him for better working conditions, greater personal liberties, and an elected national legislature. Some carried large pictures of the czar as a sign of their respect and loyalty. Only the czar, their "little father," they believed, could help improve their lot. But Nicholas saw the parade as a threat to his power. As he hurriedly left the palace, he ordered the soldiers to open fire on the crowd. About 1,000 workers were killed on that day, which became known as Bloody Sunday.

After Bloody Sunday, the discontent that had been building for years exploded. Russia was quickly engulfed in revolution. Riots and strikes swept the cities. Bands of peasants roamed the countryside, looting and burning the homes of nobles.

By October 1905, the clamor for more freedom and a democratic government was so loud that the czar reluctantly promised "freedom of person, conscience, assembly, and union." He agreed to set up a national assembly called the Duma. By making concessions, he hoped to end the violence. For a time, it did. The Revolution of 1905 came to an end. However, Nicholas never gave the Duma any real power. In 1906, he simply dismissed the first Duma when it would not cooperate with him.

The czar emerged from the Revolution of 1905 with his power largely intact. New Dumas were elected, but they were dominated by supporters of the autocracy. Nevertheless, between 1906 and 1911, the government introduced some reform. The czar's chief minister, Peter Stolypin (stoh LEE puhn), began a program to help peasants buy their own land. But when Stolypin was assassinated in 1911, the government again became repressive. The Revolution of 1905 left Russia's problems unsolved, and those problems remained as the seeds for a future revolution.

SECTION 4 REVIEW

1. **Identify:** (a) Decembrist Revolt, (b) Nicholas I, (c) Alexander II, (d) Alexander III, (e) Russification, (f) Nicholas II.

2. **Define:** (a) autocracy, (b) mir, (c) zemstvo, (d) pogrom.

3. Why did Nicholas I think he had to strengthen the autocracy?

4. What helped convince Alexander II to free the serfs?

5. (a) What were the causes of the Revolution of 1905? (b) How did Nicholas II respond to it?

6. **Critical Thinking** Why do you think the Russian czars in the 1800s moved back and forth between harsh and more liberal policies?

The Russian people's faith in the czar was badly shaken by the events of Bloody Sunday. The massacre of unarmed demonstrators led to further protests and bloodshed in the Revolution of 1905. This painting shows mounted Russian soldiers charging a crowd and scattering them by using whips.

548

5 Nationalism in Eastern Europe

READ TO UNDERSTAND

☐ How nationalism affected both the Austrian and the Ottoman empires.

☐ Why the Dual Monarchy was created.

☐ Why the Ottoman Empire was called the "sick man of Europe."

☐ *Vocabulary:* autonomy.

"My people are strangers to one another," the emperor of Austria once said. "And yet it is for the best. They never have the same ills at the same time." Each is suspicious of the other, he explained, and because they cannot understand one another, it is easier to keep the peace.

The Austrian emperor ruled a collection of peoples in Eastern Europe. To the southeast of the Austrian Empire lay the Ottoman Empire, itself made up of dozens of ethnic and religious groups. Nationalism, which helped create unity in Italy and Germany, threatened to destroy both the Austrian and Ottoman empires. Between 1848 and 1914, national groups in Eastern Europe pushed for self-rule or independence from the Austrians and the Ottomans. The struggles of these peoples added to the tensions within each empire and throughout Europe.

The Austrian Empire

The Austrian Empire included more than 12 different nationalities. The Germans of Austria and the Magyars of Hungary were the two largest groups, but neither was a majority in the empire. Other major nationalities included Poles, Czechs, Croatians, Slovaks, and Romanians. (See the map on page 550.)

Each national group within the Austrian Empire had a strong sense of pride in its own language and customs. Most resented domination by the Austrians. As you read earlier, the Hapsburg rulers of Austria had successfully crushed the nationalist revolts of 1848. (See page 463.) But those defeats did not end the struggle by nationalist groups for greater control of their own affairs.

Francis Joseph became emperor of Austria in 1848 at the age of 18. Throughout his long reign, which lasted until 1916, he sought ways to keep his diverse empire together. During the 1850s, he cracked down hard on nationalist leaders. However, setbacks in foreign policy forced him to consider a new policy.

In 1859, Austria lost Lombardy to Italy. Then, in 1866, it was defeated by Prussia and lost its influence among the German states. (See page 538.) Although Francis Joseph continued to oppose nationalism, he realized that he had to strengthen his empire at home. So he decided to compromise with the Magyars.

Creation of the Dual Monarchy

The Magyars had long demanded greater **autonomy,** or self-government, within the Austrian Empire. Even though the Austrians had ignored Hungarian demands, the Magyars fought loyally with them in the war with Prussia. After the war, the Hungarian leader Francis Deák (DEH ahk) thought the time was right to win concessions from the emperor. Deák wanted Hungary to be recognized as a separate kingdom with its own territory and its own constitution.

In 1867, Francis Joseph agreed, and a dual monarchy was created. The Austrian Empire was divided into two parts: the empire of Austria and the kingdom of Hungary.

The Dual Monarchy of Austria-Hungary was united under a single ruler, the Hapsburg emperor, who would be the emperor of Austria and king of Hungary. Austria and Hungary shared ministries of war, finance, and foreign affairs, but in other areas they were independent of each other. Each had its own constitution and its own parliament.

The Dual Monarchy satisfied the Magyars but did nothing to please other nationalities in Austria-Hungary. Austrians were a minority in Austria, and Magyars were a minority in Hungary. The Austrian government made a few concessions to other nationalities. But the Magyars tried to force other groups in Hungary to give up their own ethnic identity and become Magyars. The Romanians and the

Slavs in Hungary felt especially oppressed by Magyar rule. Unrest among the various nationalities in Austria-Hungary undermined the unity of the empire and the peace in Europe.

Life in Austria-Hungary

In both Austria and Hungary, a small noble class dominated the political, economic, and social life. Nobles owned huge estates, while peasants had only small plots of land. In 1895, fewer than 200 noble families owned over half the farmland in Austria-Hungary. At the same time, over 1 million peasants subsisted on seven acres or less per person.

Democracy made little headway in Austria-Hungary. For the most part, the govern-ment remained in the hands of wealthy nobles. Universal male suffrage was introduced in Austria in 1907. However, when the parliament was elected, the various national groups could not agree on anything. At times, deputies ended up throwing inkwells at one another instead of debating proposed laws. In Hungary, only 6 percent of the population had the right to vote. This prevented any effective challenge to the Magyar ruling class.

The economy of Austria-Hungary remained mainly agricultural during the 1800s. Late in the century, Austria began to industrialize slowly, and Hungary followed behind.

The Ottoman Empire and the Balkans

Like Austria-Hungary, the Ottoman Empire was torn by ethnic conflict. The Ottoman Empire reached the height of its power in the 1500s, as you read in Chapter 16. But since that time it had steadily declined. Many nationalities sought freedom from Ottoman rule. Gradually, portions of the empire had broken away. By 1850, Egypt and Arabia had gained autonomy within the empire, and Algeria was controlled by France. In the Balkans, Greece won independence in 1830, and Serbia and Montenegro gained autonomy.

In 1844, Czar Nicholas I called the Ottoman Empire "the sick man of Europe." Throughout the 1800s, many diplomats expected it to collapse, as one national group after another fought for independence. However, Britain and France worked to prevent a collapse. They saw the Ottoman Empire as a block against the expansion of Russia or Austria-Hungary into the Balkans. This was the reason why, in 1854, Britain and France entered the Crimean War on the side of the Ottoman Empire. They wanted to prevent Russia from gaining control of Constantinople and the Dardanelles.

Although Russia was defeated in the Crimean War, the Ottoman Empire continued to decline. Romania gained autonomy in 1859. In 1875, various groups in the Balkans revolted against the Turks. The Turks put down the revolts, but the Russians came to the aid of the Slavic peoples in the Balkans. In 1877, the Rus-

MAP STUDY *Many different nationalities lived in Austria-Hungary, the Russian Empire, and the Ottoman Empire. Some major nationalities are shown on this map. Which nationalities lived in more than one country?*

Nationalities in Eastern Europe About 1870

sians defeated the Turks and forced them to sign the Treaty of San Stefano. It gave the Russians the right to occupy a large, independent Bulgarian state.

Other European powers objected to the treaty, fearing increased Russian influence in the Balkans. They pressured the Russians to attend an international congress at Berlin in 1878. The Congress of Berlin created a much smaller Bulgarian state, which was to be autonomous within the Ottoman Empire. The Balkan peoples of Serbia, Romania, and Montenegro gained complete independence. Britain received Cyprus from the Ottoman Empire, and Austria-Hungary won the right to administer the areas of Bosnia and Herzegovina. (See the map at right.)

The Congress of Berlin recognized new states in the Balkans, which pleased nationalists. However, it also caused much bitterness and left unfulfilled hopes. The Russians felt cheated. Furthermore, the new states did not include all members of a nationality. For example, many Serbs lived in Hungary, while fellow Serbs had an independent nation across the border. In the years ahead, the Balkans continued to be a source of conflict.

A New International Order

The Congress of Berlin showed that a new international order had developed in Europe by the late 1800s. New nations such as Germany and Italy had arrived on the scene, while the decline of old empires was upsetting the balance of power so carefully worked out at the Congress of Vienna in 1815. During the early 1800s, the Austrian Empire under Metternich had been the dominant force in Europe. During the second half, Germany under Bismarck took the lead.

The international order was further affected by the Industrial Revolution, which had fueled economic growth in all parts of Europe, especially in Britain and Germany. As scientists developed new technologies, they also helped invent new, more powerful military weapons, which increased the capacity for war. By the early 1900s, disputes over territory in Europe and the scramble for empires would cause conflict and war, as you will read.

In the 1800s, independent states were created in the Balkans. Compare this map to the one on page 389. Which states had been part of the Ottoman Empire?

SECTION 5 REVIEW

1. **Locate:** (a) Greece, (b) Bulgaria, (c) Serbia, (d) Montenegro, (e) Bosnia, (f) Herzegovina.

2. **Identify:** (a) Francis Joseph, (b) Francis Deák.

3. **Define:** autonomy.

4. What two events led the Austrians to agree to the creation of the Dual Monarchy?

5. Why did Britain and France want to preserve the Ottoman Empire?

6. **Critical Thinking** How did nationalism create instability in Eastern Europe in the 1800s?

Summary

1. Nationalism helped unify Italy. Cavour and Garibaldi led the struggle to forge a united country. Once united, however, Italy still faced major problems.

2. Prussia took the lead in unifying Germany. Under the firm hand of William I and Bismarck, Prussia fought Denmark, Austria, and France until it created a large and powerful empire.

3. Bismarck used his political skills to unite the Second Empire. He moved against the Catholic Church and socialists because he considered them threats to the empire. When William II became emperor, he directed German affairs himself.

4. During the 1800s, Russian czars maintained their autocratic rule. Alexander II freed the serfs in 1861 and eased some of his predecessors' harsh laws. When he was assassinated, however, his successors renewed repression. Russia's defeat in a war against Japan helped trigger the revolution of 1905.

5. Nationalism created problems for the Austrian and Ottoman empires. The Austrians created the Dual Monarchy to satisfy the Magyars. But the other nationalities continued to demand greater autonomy. Ethnic groups within the Ottoman Empire broke away, further weakening that once powerful state.

Recalling Facts

Review the time line on page 553 and your reading in this chapter. Then choose the letter of the correct time period for each of the following events.

A	B	C	D	E	F
1850	1860	1870	1880	1890	1900	1910

1. Serfs freed in Russia.

2. Bloody Sunday takes place.

3. Austria-Hungary created.

4. Kingdom of Italy declared.

5. Cavour becomes prime minister of Sardinia.

6. Franco-Prussian War begins.

Chapter Checkup

1. (a) How did the goals of Young Italy and Cavour differ? (b) Which goal was achieved by 1870? (c) What groups were unhappy with the unification that was achieved? Why?

2. (a) What obstacles stood in the way of German unification? (b) How did Bismarck overcome these obstacles?

3. (a) Was the government of the German Empire representative? Explain.

4. (a) How did Bismarck try to strengthen the German Empire? (b) How did William II try to win public support?

5. (a) How did serfdom affect Russian agriculture? (b) What effect did emancipation have on the serfs?

6. How did each of the following try to strengthen the autocracy in Russia: (a) Nicholas I; (b) Alexander III; (c) Nicholas II?

7. (a) How did nationalism threaten the existence of the Austrian Empire? (b) How were national minorities dealt with?

8. What evidence convinced many diplomats that the Ottoman Empire was going to collapse during the 1800s?

Critical Thinking

1. **Comparing** Compare the ways in which Italy and Germany were unified. (a) What role did warfare play in the unification of each nation? (b) What role did international diplomacy play? (c) In which nation do you think a strong national leader was more important? Why?

2. **Analyzing** Otto von Bismarck believed that the key to German unity and power was "blood and iron." Which national leaders discussed in this chapter do you think would have agreed with Bismarck's philosophy? Explain.

3. **Relating Past to Present** (a) Do any nations today have problems with national minorities? (b) How do these problems compare with those faced by the Austrians? (c) How are they different?

4. **Understanding the Roots of Democracy** Millions of people fled from Central and Eastern Europe to the United States in the late 1800s. How do you think the experiences of these people affected the way they regarded American democracy?

Developing Basic Skills

1. **Analyzing Political Cartoons** By analyzing political cartoons, you can learn how people at the time viewed public issues. Study the cartoon on page 536. (a) What political figures are shown? (b) What does the boot represent? (c) Do you think the cartoonist approved of the events taking place in Italy? Explain.

2. **Map Reading** Study the map on page 539. (a) Describe the area of Prussia in 1865. (b) What territory was added to Prussia in 1866? (c) Why do you think Austrian influence was greater among the southern German states than among the northern?

3. **Graph Reading** Study the graph on page 542. (a) How much steel did Germany produce in 1880? (b) How did German steel production change between 1871 and 1910? (c) How do you think steel production reflected economic development?

Writing About History

Preparing a Preliminary Outline

A preliminary outline helps you focus on specific areas for research. The first steps in preparing a preliminary outline are to write down the title and thesis statement of your paper. Then formulate questions about the topic, and draw up a simple outline of your paper. Study the following example.

Title: Three Leaders of Italian Unity

Thesis statement: Mazzini, Cavour, and Garibaldi held different views about how to unite Italy, but each contributed to bringing about an Italian nation.

1. Mazzini laid the groundwork with his Young Italy movement.

2. Cavour made the kingdom of Sardinia the focal point in the drive against Austria.

3. Though Garibaldi was an impulsive leader, he helped rouse Italians' passion for liberty.

Practice: Choose a topic from this chapter and prepare a preliminary outline for it.

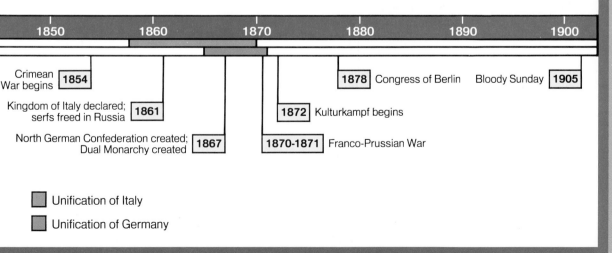

| 1850 | 1860 | 1870 | 1880 | 1890 | 1900 |

Crimean War begins **1854**

Kingdom of Italy declared; serfs freed in Russia **1861**

North German Confederation created; Dual Monarchy created **1867**

1878 Congress of Berlin   Bloody Sunday **1905**

1872 Kulturkampf begins

1870-1871 Franco-Prussian War

■ Unification of Italy

■ Unification of Germany

Unit Seven   Mini-Atlas

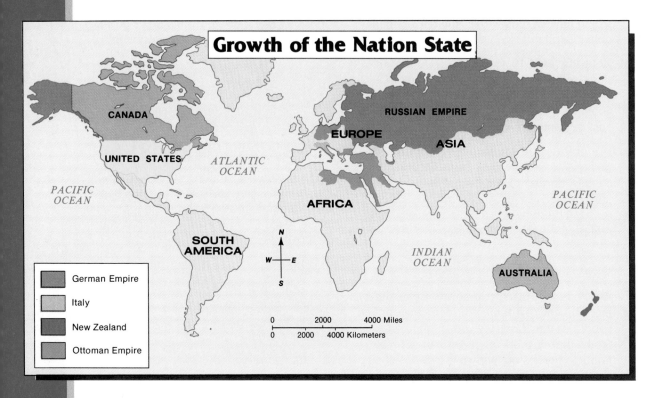

Growth of the Nation State

CANADA

RUSSIAN EMPIRE

EUROPE

ASIA

UNITED STATES

ATLANTIC
OCEAN

PACIFIC
OCEAN

AFRICA

PACIFIC
OCEAN

SOUTH
AMERICA

INDIAN
OCEAN

AUSTRALIA

N
W — E
S

Legend:
- German Empire
- Italy
- New Zealand
- Ottoman Empire

```
0        2000        4000 Miles
0    2000    4000 Kilometers
```

Unit Themes

The Industrial Revolution began in Great Britain in the mid-1700s and spread to the nations of Western Europe and the United States. With the dawn of the Industrial Age, goods began to be mass-produced in factories by machines. Within the brief span of 200 years, the Industrial Revolution changed the world more than any development in the previous 5,000 years.

The effects of the Industrial Revolution provoked significant political, social, and intellectual changes. Democratic traditions flourished in some Western European nations and in the United States. The forces of nationalism unleashed by the French Revolution inspired peoples around the globe. Parts of the British Empire achieved self-government, Germany and Italy achieved unity, Russians struggled for reform, and the peoples of Eastern Europe fought to break away from the Austrian and Ottoman empires.

1. **Synthesizing** (a) Which began first, the Agricultural or the Industrial revolution? (b) How did industrialization affect social and political conditions in Britain, the United States, and France?

2. **Analyzing** (a) Which nations on the map at right had railroad lines by 1850? (b) By 1900? (c) How did the growth of railroads affect nationalism?

3. **Evaluating** Arrange the following countries from most to least democratic during the mid-1800s: Russia, United States, Germany, Britain. Explain your ranking.

4. **Understanding Economic Ideas** (a) What economic theories developed because of the Industrial Revolution? (b) Did industrialization make countries more or less economically dependent on each other? Explain.

554

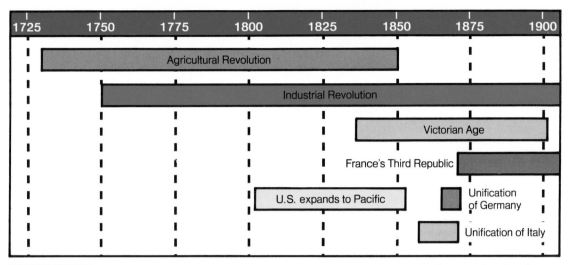

TIME LINE STUDY

In which century did United States expansion to the Pacific Ocean take place? Which events show the effects of nationalism?

MAP STUDY

Between 1830 and 1850, 6,600 miles of railroad track were laid in Great Britain. Which European cities appear to be major centers of railroad activity by 1900?

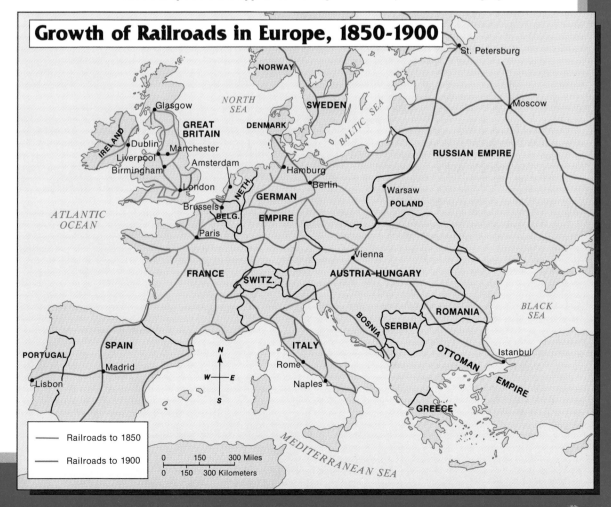

Growth of Railroads in Europe, 1850-1900

THE AGE OF IMPERIALISM

The slave trade continued even after most European nations abolished it. In 1839, Cinque, the son of a Mendi chief from Sierra Leone, and a group of fellow captives seized control of a slave ship off the coast of Cuba.

During the Meiji period, Japanese art became known all over the world.

	1800	1825	1850
POLITICS AND GOVERNMENT		**1821** Mexico wins independence from Spain	**1850** In Taiping Rebellion, Chinese peasants demand land
ECONOMICS AND TECHNOLOGY		**1840** Opium War begins	**1853** Japanese trade isolation ends
SOCIETY AND CULTURE	**Early 1800s** Islam revives in West Africa		**1857** Hindu and Muslim soldiers revolt against British

1816 Officers like this one led the fight for Argentina's independence.

Before Japan was opened to trade, only one foreign ship a year could dock in Nagasaki harbor.

Mexico and other Latin American nations inherited a rigid social structure from their days as Spanish colonies.

The French expected people in their African colonies to give up their traditions and become French. Here they are recruiting people from Madagascar for the French army.

1875	1900	1925
1868 Last shogun in Japan resigns	**1896** Ethiopians defeat Italians at Adowa	**1911** Manchu dynasty in China is overthrown
1869 Suez Canal completed	**1880s** Rinderpest leads to famine in East Africa	**1914** Panama Canal completed
1872 Japan introduces universal military service	**1898** Manchu emperor tries to reform schools	

557

Fine silk made by Chinese artisans, like those shown here, was in demand all over the world.

Africa in the Age of Imperialism

25

(1700–1914)

CHAPTER OUTLINE

1. A New Age of European Expansion
2. North Africa
3. West and Central Africa
4. Southern and Eastern Africa
5. European Rule in Africa

For centuries, Europeans traded with Africans, establishing outposts in villages like this one at the mouth of the Congo River. Then in the late 1800s, European nations carved up Africa and uprooted traditional ways of life.

An African villager and his friend are talking: "What has happened to that piece of land in dispute?" asked Okonkwo.

"The white man's court has decided that it should belong to Nnama's family, who had given much money to the white man's interpreter and messenger."

"Does the white man understand our customs about land?"

"How can he when he does not even speak our tongue? But he says that our customs are bad; and our brothers who have taken up his religion also say that our customs are bad. How do you think we can fight when our brothers have turned against us? The white man is very clever. He came quietly and peaceably with his religion. We were amused at his foolishness and allowed him to stay. Now he has put a knife on things that held us together and we have fallen apart."

In this excerpt from the novel *Things Fall Apart,* by Nigerian writer Chinua Achebe (ah CHEE bee), an African villager named Okonkwo and his friend reveal what they thought about the Europeans who had come to Africa. In the late 1800s, Europeans once again expanded overseas, as they had in the 1600s and 1700s. They explored and rapidly colonized much of the world. In Africa, as elsewhere, Europeans changed the way local peoples lived, thus upsetting traditional patterns of life.

During the Age of Exploration, Europeans had built a few trading posts on the coasts of Africa, but for centuries they had little direct influence on the lives of most Africans. In the 1800s, a dramatic change took place. The Industrial Revolution and the growth of nationalism strengthened European nations. By the 1870s, they were competing with one another for new resources and markets. They found these resources and outlets in many parts of the world, including Africa. Within a few decades, they extended their control over large parts of the world. ■

---

1 A New Age of European Expansion

READ TO UNDERSTAND

☐ Why European nations competed in the "scramble for Africa."

☐ What forms of imperialism European nations developed.

☐ How technology helped Europeans in Africa.

☐ *Vocabulary:* imperialism, colony, sphere of influence, protectorate.

"I am sorry to say that of 45 Europeans who left the Gambia in perfect health, five only at present are alive, namely three soldiers, Lieutenant Martyn, and myself," wrote the Scottish doctor and explorer Mungo Park in 1805. Park was determined to find the source of the Niger River in West Africa. "Though all the Europe-ans who are with me should die, I would at least die on the Niger."

And die on the Niger he did. Other Europe-ans followed in Park's footsteps, plunging through Africa, mapping rivers and lakes, and enduring incredible hardships. In Europe, people applauded the success of explorers such as David Livingstone, who "discovered" Victoria Falls in East Africa. But no one asked how Livingstone could "discover" these spectacular waterfalls that Africans had known for centuries as Mosi Oa Tunya, the "smoke that thunders."

Scramble for Africa

Explorers prepared the way for conquerors. As the nations of Europe industrialized, they started looking overseas for new markets and resources. Africa, which had been largely unknown to Europeans, now became the focus of their attention.

Until the 1870s, Europeans had little interest in Africa. In the 1600s and 1700s, the Portuguese and Dutch had established forts and trading posts along the African coast. The British and French had also acquired outposts. However, they used these posts only for trade, not as bases for conquest.

Between 1870 and 1914, a dramatic development occurred. The entire African continent came under European rule, with the exception of Liberia and Ethiopia. First, King Leopold II of Belgium acquired the Congo, today called Zaire (zah EER). Then the French moved into West Africa, while the British took control of much of the rest of the continent. Germany, Spain, Portugal, and Italy also entered the race for African territory.

This "scramble for Africa" brought European powers to the brink of war. To settle their disagreements, they held a conference in Berlin in 1884–1885. Without consulting the African people, the European nations drew boundary lines on a map of Africa, dividing the continent among themselves. (See the map at right.) They then proceeded to establish control over these regions.

The Age of Imperialism

The partitioning of Africa is just one example of European expansion in the late 1800s. As you will read in Chapters 26 and 27, the nations of Western Europe and the United States gained influence or won control of land in Asia and Latin America as well. The period from about 1870 to 1914 is often called the Age of Imperialism. **Imperialism** is the domination by one country of the political, economic, or cultural life of another country or region.

European nations controlled other parts of the world in many ways. The most common forms of imperial rule were colonies, spheres of influence, and protectorates. A **colony** is a possession that the imperial power controls directly. A **sphere of influence** is a region in which the imperial power claims exclusive investment or trading privileges. The local government usually controls all other matters. A **protectorate** is a country that has its own government but whose policies are directed by the imperial power.

A number of forces set off European expansion in the Age of Imperialism. Nationalism played a major role in sending Europeans overseas. A nation increased its prestige and power by winning an overseas empire. Political rivalries and military strategy also contributed to imperialism. One nation might seize a territory to prevent a rival from expanding into that region.

The desire to expand economically was also a strong motive. Industrialists urged their governments to acquire new markets for their products. In addition, they wanted to control the supply of raw materials. Individuals, too, sought personal wealth or glory in the new lands.

Humanitarian and religious concerns often motivated individuals and their governments. Some Europeans wanted to end the slave trade in Africa. Christian missionaries were convinced that the peoples of Africa and Asia would become "civilized" only if they became Christians and adopted European ways. Many Europeans believed in the superiority of the white race. They spoke of the "white man's burden" to carry the benefits of western civilization to other parts of the world.

Many Europeans used the philosophy of Social Darwinism to justify imperialism. As you read in Chapter 22, Social Darwinists argued that in nature only the strongest creatures survive. They applied this idea to world affairs, arguing that it was natural for strong nations to conquer weaker peoples.

Exploring the Interior

Until the 1800s, Europeans knew little about the interior of Africa. African and Arab merchants on the coasts knew the best routes into the interior, but few Europeans bothered to ask them for such information. Instead, Europeans and Americans financed dozens of expeditions to explore what they called the "unknown" continent.

Perhaps the best-known explorer was David Livingstone, a British doctor and missionary. Livingstone spent many years setting up Christian missions in Central Africa. He wrote detailed reports that made the British

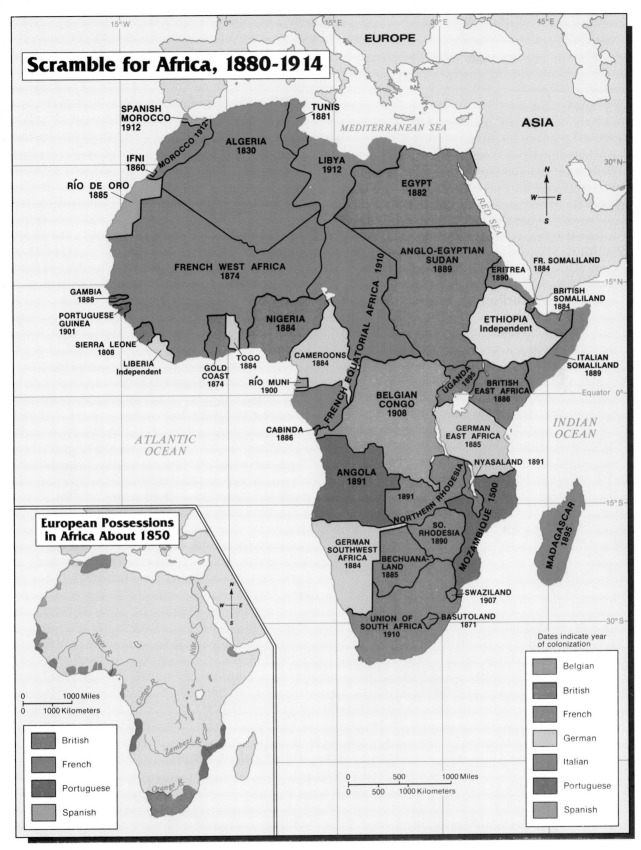

Scramble for Africa, 1880-1914

EUROPE

ASIA

MEDITERRANEAN SEA

SPANISH
MOROCCO
1912

TUNIS
1881

ALGERIA
1830

MOROCCO 1912

IFNI
1860

LIBYA
1912

EGYPT
1882

RÍO DE ORO
1885

RED SEA

FRENCH WEST AFRICA
1874

FRENCH EQUATORIAL AFRICA 1910

ANGLO-EGYPTIAN
SUDAN
1889

ERITREA
1890

FR. SOMALILAND
1884

GAMBIA
1888

BRITISH
SOMALILAND
1884

PORTUGUESE
GUINEA
1901

NIGERIA
1884

ETHIOPIA
Independent

SIERRA LEONE
1808

ITALIAN
SOMALILAND
1889

LIBERIA
Independent

TOGO
1884

CAMEROONS
1884

UGANDA
1895

GOLD
COAST
1874

RÍO MUNI
1900

BRITISH
EAST AFRICA
1886

Equator 0°

BELGIAN
CONGO
1908

INDIAN
OCEAN

ATLANTIC
OCEAN

CABINDA
1886

GERMAN
EAST AFRICA
1885

NYASALAND 1891

ANGOLA
1891

NORTHERN RHODESIA

MOZAMBIQUE 1500

MADAGASCAR
1895

1891

15°S

GERMAN
SOUTHWEST
AFRICA
1884

SO.
RHODESIA
1890

BECHUANA-
LAND
1885

SWAZILAND
1907

UNION OF
SOUTH AFRICA
1910

BASUTOLAND
1871

30°S

Dates indicate year
of colonization

Belgian

British

French

German

Italian

Portuguese

Spanish

European Possessions in Africa About 1850

N

0   1000 Miles
0   1000 Kilometers

Niger R.

Nile R.

Congo R.

Zambezi R.

Orange R.

British

French

Portuguese

Spanish

0   500   1000 Miles
0   500   1000 Kilometers

MAP STUDY   *In the late 1800s, European nations scrambled to claim territory in Africa. By 1914, almost the entire continent had been partitioned, as you can see above. Which nations remained independent?*

public aware of opportunities in Africa for businesspeople as well as for missionaries.

As a first step toward opening the continent to expansion, Europeans explored along African rivers. In the 1830s, Sir George Goldie completed the task Mungo Park had begun by charting the Niger River. Dozens of other Europeans explored the various regions of Africa. In the 1870s, Henry Stanley trekked inland from the East African coast. He found the source of the Congo River and sailed down it to the Atlantic Ocean. (See the map on page 619.)

New Technology

Although a few hardy explorers visited the African interior, disease and resistance by Africans prevented much European expansion beyond the coastal areas before 1870.

As European interest in Africa grew, doctors searched for the causes and treatment of diseases such as malaria and yellow fever, which claimed many European lives in Africa. By the 1880s, they had learned that mosquitoes carry malaria and yellow fever. They also found that quinine, made from the bark of the cinchona tree, is effective in treating malaria. Such medical discoveries made it easier for Europeans to move into the interior of Africa.

Europeans developed new weapons that gave them a military advantage over Africans. These weapons included rifles and the Maxim gun, the earliest machine gun. Africans fought with weapons such as muskets but had little success against Europeans using the new weapons.

SECTION 1 REVIEW

1. **Locate:** (a) Liberia, (b) Ethiopia, (c) Niger River, (d) Congo River.

2. **Identify:** (a) Berlin Conference, (b) David Livingstone, (c) George Goldie, (d) Henry Stanley.

3. **Define:** (a) imperialism, (b) colony, (c) sphere of influence, (d) protectorate.

4. Describe three motives behind European imperialism.

5. What advantages did Europeans have over the people they conquered?

6. **Critical Thinking** Why do you think a European power would choose to set up one type of imperial rule over another?

2 North Africa

READ TO UNDERSTAND

☐ **How and why Britain gained control over Egypt.**

☐ **How rivalries among European nations in North Africa brought them close to war.**

☐ **How North African rulers resisted foreign control.**

☐ *Vocabulary:* **cash crop.**

The ceremonies began as planned on November 17, 1869. At exactly 8 A.M., a cannon boomed. Dozens of warships, merchant ships, and yachts carrying monarchs and diplomats weighed anchor and sailed into the waterway. On shore, the sounds of sirens, military bands, and steam whistles filled the air. Huge crowds of workers, soldiers, and officials cheered. The Suez Canal was now officially open.

Ferdinand de Lesseps, the entrepreneur who had organized the canal project, and his workers revolutionized world transportation by digging the canal. The Suez Canal, which joined the Mediterranean Sea with the Red Sea, cut the distance between Europe and the East by thousands of miles and placed Egypt at the center of world trade routes.

The Egyptian Empire

Egypt, like the rest of North Africa, had been part of the Islamic Empire during the Middle Ages, and Islamic culture had shaped its political and cultural life. In the 1500s, the Ottomans had conquered North Africa. But as

Ferdinand de Lesseps, the successful promoter and engineer of the Suez Canal, predicted that the canal "will open the world to all people." Here, Egyptians on shore celebrate the opening of the canal in 1869, while European ships sail past in the background. The canal greatly increased European interest in Egypt.

the Ottoman Empire weakened in the late 1700s, Egypt, along with other North African states, became virtually independent.

When Napoleon invaded Egypt in 1798, the Egyptians broke free of Ottoman rule. Although the French invasion was brief, it sparked a long civil war in Egypt. Muhammad Ali, who led Egyptians against the French, seized control of the country in 1805.

Ali ruthlessly suppressed his opponents and began an ambitious program of reform to make Egypt a strong modern power. He introduced more efficient farming methods and he had dykes and irrigation canals built so that dry lands could be farmed. Ali then sent peasant farmers to grow cash crops on the new lands. **Cash crops** are crops such as cotton, sugar, and tobacco that can be sold for money on the world market. Egypt soon became a major exporter of cotton to industrial nations such as Great Britain.

Income from cash crops helped pay for Ali's other projects. He set up schools and sent thousands of Egyptians to study in Europe. He brought European experts to Egypt to help set up textile mills, iron works, and shipyards. He also invited French military officers to train and equip the army. With a strong modern army to support him, Ali built an empire. During the 1820s and 1830s, Egyptian armies seized territory along the Red Sea coast and moved up the Nile River into the Sudan.

Growing European Interest in Egypt

Ali's programs were expensive. To finance them, he borrowed money from European banks. Under Ali's successors, Egyptian debts increased. As a result, Europeans gained political and economic influence in Egypt. They pressured Egyptian leaders to follow policies that favored their financial interests.

The Suez Canal. European interest in Egypt sharpened after 1859, when the French began building the Suez Canal. Ali had opposed the canal because he feared that it would draw Europe's attention to Egypt. He was afraid that, with this vital waterway passing through his country, the European powers would want to make sure Egypt would not interfere with the free passage of their ships through the canal. However, Ali's successors approved the project.

Between 1859 and 1869, a French company headed by Ferdinand de Lesseps built the Suez Canal. At first, Egyptians controlled the canal. But, as the British increased their trade with India, they became the major users of the waterway and soon began to regard the Suez Canal as the "lifeline of the British Empire." They also began to see the need to have a voice in the control of the canal.

British occupation of Egypt. During the 1870s, Britain acquired partial control over the Suez Canal by buying shares of stock from the Egyptian ruler Ismail. Ismail sold the stock because Egyptian finances were in chaos. This eventually gave the British an excuse to intervene in Egypt. Claiming that it wanted to protect European loans and investments and reorganize the Egyptian treasury, Britain sent an army to occupy Egypt in 1882. The British then made Egypt a protectorate.

Under British control, Egypt paid off its foreign debts and built a dam at Aswan on the upper Nile. The dam improved farm output by supplying water for irrigation. However, Egyptian nationalists resented foreign control. They especially criticized the British for not encouraging education or helping Egyptian industries.

The Fashoda incident. British occupation of Egypt led to an explosive confrontation with France. The British felt they had to control the headwaters of the Nile River in the Sudan to protect Egypt and the Suez Canal. For 16 years, Sudanese nationalists resisted attempts to occupy their land. Finally, in 1898, a combined force of British and Egyptian soldiers conquered the Sudan. Meanwhile, French troops had reached the Sudan from bases in West Africa. The rival British and French forces faced each other at Fashoda, a town on the upper Nile. For weeks, the two European powers seemed on the brink of war.

In the end, the domestic crisis over the Dreyfus affair forced the French to withdraw. (See page 521.) Britain and Egypt then agreed to control the Sudan jointly. The Fashoda incident made Europeans aware of the very real possibility that overseas rivalries could drag them into war.

French and Italian Expansion

While Britain was establishing control over Egypt and the Sudan, France was extending its rule over other parts of North Africa. Between 1830 and 1912, France conquered Algiers, Tunis, and Morocco. (Algiers and Tunis are called Algeria and Tunisia today.) By 1861, Italy had begun to challenge the French in North Africa.

Algeria. In 1830, King Charles X of France launched an expedition against the ruler of Algeria, in part to avenge an insult to a French diplomat. Charles was also in serious political trouble at home. He hoped that a victory in Algeria would divert the attention of the French people. However, although Charles gained a foothold in Algeria, he was toppled by the Revolution of 1830. (See page 460.)

During the following decades, the French government encouraged its citizens to settle in Algeria. Colonists took over the fertile lands along the Mediterranean coast and elsewhere and established successful farming and business communities.

For 40 years, the Algerians fiercely resisted French expansion into their land. So many Algerians were killed in the fighting that France became even more eager to attract European settlers to Algeria. In all, almost 1 million Europeans settled in Algeria during the 1800s.

France took little interest in other North African lands until the 1880s. Then, as Britain moved into Egypt, the French rapidly occupied Tunisia. French expansion along the Mediterranean worried the Italians, whose interest in North Africa was growing.

Ethiopia and Libya. Both France and Italy sought to control the horn of Africa, present-day Somalia and Ethiopia. The Ethio-

During the Age of Imperialism, Ethiopians remained independent largely because of the enlightened policies of the Ethiopian emperor, Menelik II. Menelik was a member of a dynasty that had ruled Ethiopia since the 1200s. When he came to the throne in 1889, he faced many problems. Ethiopia was only loosely united, and local rulers showed little loyalty to the emperor. Most threatening of all, both Italy and France were building colonies on its borders.

Menelik moved quickly to strengthen the nation. He skillfully brought local rulers under his control and built a new capital city at Addis Ababa. Menelik knew that Ethiopia would have to modernize through improving education. "Our young men must be educated," he said. "We have much to do." Menelik asked Europeans to help him upgrade the schools of Ethiopia. Gradually, Ethiopians developed a stronger sense of national unity and pride.

In his dealings with Europeans, Menelik proved to be a shrewd diplomat. He played off one European power against another. Thus, he managed to acquire arms from both Italy and France, each of which was eager to stay on friendly terms with him.

Menelik used his new armed strength in a showdown with Italy. In 1893, Menelik renounced a treaty he had signed with Italy. Two years later, Italian troops seized several Ethiopian towns. To stall the Italian advance, Menelik called for negotiations. In the meantime, he arranged for inaccurate maps of his country to fall into Italian hands, and he had spies pass misleading information to the enemy. He also carefully concealed the size of the army he was massing.

On March 1, 1896, Ethiopian and Italian troops fought a decisive battle at Adowa. Menelik's army routed the outnumbered Italians. The painting here shows the Ethiopian triumph over their European foes. The victory at Adowa ensured the independence of Ethiopia and guaranteed the success of Menelik's program of strengthening his nation.

1. What problems did Ethiopia face at the time Menelik II became emperor?

2. **Critical Thinking** How do you think other African peoples felt about Ethiopia's victory at Adowa?

pian emperor Menelik II realized that Europeans posed a threat, so he bought rifles and other modern weapons and trained his army to use them. Thus, when the Italians invaded Ethiopia in 1896, they were defeated by strong, well-armed Ethiopian forces.

Italy had to be content with setting up protectorates over Eritrea and part of Somaliland. In 1912, the Italians occupied Tripoli, which they set up as the colony of Libya. By controlling Libya, the Italians prevented the French from expanding farther across North Africa.

Crisis Over Morocco

Morocco, at the northwestern tip of Africa, remained largely outside European control until the 1880s. Learning from the Egyptian example, the Moroccan ruler avoided borrowing large amounts of money from Europeans. Despite his efforts, European nations used Morocco as a pawn in their political maneuverings.

For years, Britain and France had quarreled over Egypt. In 1904, they finally reached an agreement. France would recognize British interests in Egypt, and Britain would let France establish a sphere of influence in Morocco. Moreover, Britain agreed not to protest if France took over Morocco directly.

The agreement between Britain and France alarmed the German emperor William II. He considered it a threat to German power. Thus, in 1905, he visited Morocco and boldly announced that Germany would support an independent Morocco. William II's actions, however, only brought France and Britain closer together. In 1906, an international conference of European powers recognized French influence in Morocco.

SECTION 2 REVIEW

1. **Locate:** (a) Sudan, (b) Algeria, (c) Tunisia, (d) Morocco, (e) Ethiopia, (f) Somaliland, (g) Libya.

2. **Identify:** (a) Muhammad Ali, (b) Ferdinand de Lesseps, (c) Menelik II.

3. **Define:** cash crop.

4. Describe three reforms Muhammad Ali introduced in Egypt.

5. How did Britain gain control of Egypt?

6. (a) What parts of North Africa did France claim? (b) What was the reaction of the people living in those areas to French claims?

7. **Critical Thinking** How do you think the African people regarded the rivalries of the colonial powers? Explain your answer.

3 West and Central Africa

READ TO UNDERSTAND

☐ How the transatlantic slave trade affected West Africa before 1800.

☐ What internal changes reshaped West African society in the early 1800s.

☐ How Africans responded to European expansion into West and Central Africa.

The ruler of Futa Toro in northern Senegal was angry. No more slaves, he declared, were to be taken through Futa Toro for sale abroad. He followed up his words with action. He returned the gifts of the French slave dealers who were waiting in their ships on the Senegal River to carry slaves to the coast. All the riches in the world, the ruler said, would not make him change his mind.

But the ruler "was up against a powerful trading system which yielded great profits," noted a Swedish traveler in Futa Toro. "And this system defeated his good intentions." The French slave dealers simply found another route by which to take slaves to the coast.

By the 1600s, Portugal and other European nations had set up trading posts on the west coast of Africa that became the center of a profitable slave trade with the Americas. Until the 1800s, most European interest in West Africa centered around this transatlantic slave trade.

The Transatlantic Slave Trade

Slavery had existed in Africa since ancient times, as it had in many other parts of the world. In Africa, slaves were often people captured in war. Others were people who sold themselves into slavery for food and shelter during drought or famine. Sometimes a society took slaves in order to increase its population. In time, many slaves were absorbed into their new societies.

The transatlantic slave trade was very different from African slavery. Africans were forced to leave their own societies and were shipped thousands of miles across the Atlantic. In the Americas, they faced a completely unfamiliar culture. White slave owners looked down on black Africans. They saw Africans as inferior beings whose only value was their labor.

Millions of Africans were sold into slavery in the New World. Experts estimate that by 1870 about 9.5 million Africans had been sent to the Americas. As you read in Chapter 15, thousands died during the brutal Middle Passage. And uncounted thousands more were killed in slave raids in Africa and during forced marches from inland regions to the coast.

Europeans relied on African rulers and merchants to bring slaves to trading posts on the coast. The Africans traded slaves for guns, ammunition, and manufactured goods. They used the guns to raid villages and capture more slaves. This exchange between Africans and Europeans has often been called the slave-gun cycle.

The demand for slaves brought major changes to West African societies. New states rose whose wealth and power were based on the slave-gun cycle. For example, in the 1700s and early 1800s, the rulers of the Dahomey and Ashanti kingdoms used muskets acquired through the slave trade to conquer large areas. Raids to capture slaves created tensions among West African societies. Some rulers, as you read, tried to stop the slave trade in their lands. But the pressure and profits were too great, and their efforts failed.

A Century of Change

In the century before 1870, two developments changed conditions in West Africa. First, European nations abolished the slave trade. Second, there was a revival of Islam in several West African states.

Abolition of the slave trade. During the Enlightenment, some Europeans called for an end to the slave trade and slavery. By the early 1800s, this appeal was having an effect. Britain outlawed the slave trade in 1807. Britain also convinced other nations at the Congress of Vienna to condemn the slave trade. But Portugal, Spain, and France did not end their slave trade until 1820.*

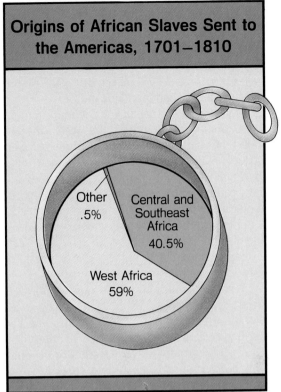

Origins of African Slaves Sent to the Americas, 1701–1810

Other .5%

Central and Southeast Africa 40.5%

West Africa 59%

Source: Philip D. Curtin, *The Atlantic Slave Trade.*

GRAPH STUDY *Over a period of 300 years, more than 9 million Africans were sent to the Americas as slaves. Why do you think the majority of these Africans came from West Africa?*

Soon after Britain abolished the slave trade, it created the West African Patrol, a naval force with orders to prevent slave ships from leaving West African ports. When the patrol captured ships with slaves on board, it carried the Africans to Freetown in the British colony of Sierra Leone. The British had established Freetown for slaves they had freed during the American Revolution. In the 1800s, Sierra Leone became a haven for other freed slaves. Christian missionaries worked among the African settlers there, encouraging them to adopt European ways.

In 1822, a refuge for former American slaves, called Liberia, was founded in West Africa. Most free American blacks thought of the

---

* Although these European nations officially abolished the slave trade, many people still participated in it illegally. Moreover, European nations did not abolish slavery itself until later. Britain abolished slavery in all its territories in the 1830s. Other European nations ended slavery by the 1860s.

United States, not Africa, as their home, but in the 1830s and 1840s, hundreds of former slaves did emigrate to Liberia. By 1850, Liberia had become an independent nation.

The decline in the slave trade undermined the economic strength of the West African states that had supplied slaves to the Europeans. As the demand for slaves fell, West African societies shifted to growing farm products they could trade for European manufactured goods. They began to plant cash crops, including cotton and cacao beans, which were introduced from the Americas. As a result, West African economies remained closely tied to European demand for these products.

Revival of Islam. The most important development in West Africa during this period was the revival of Islam. Arab traders had introduced Islam into West Africa in the 800s. However, generally only rulers and their officials converted to Islam. Most people in West Africa either continued to believe in their traditional religions or mixed Muslim beliefs with their own faiths.

Devout Muslims detested mixing Islam with other faiths. Therefore, in the early 1800s, religious leaders called for a jihad, or holy war, to restore the purity of Islam. Muslims believe that a Muslim killed in a jihad is assured a place in heaven. With armies inspired by this belief, several Islamic states in West Africa conquered large empires.

Among the best known of these Islamic empires was the Hausa-Fulani Empire, located in present-day Nigeria. In 1804, Usuman dan Fodio, a Muslim scholar, united the nomadic Fulani people. The next year, he led them in a jihad against the Hausa people because he thought the Hausa had corrupted Muslim practices. Usuman's forces seized control of the Hausa cities. Usuman then organized the new lands into a strong Islamic state.

European Conquests

The scramble for colonies in West and Central Africa began in the 1870s. In that period, the king of Belgium, with the help of Henry Stanley, carved out an empire along the Congo River. Stanley, you will recall, had explored the Congo River basin. He hoped that Britain would send settlers to the Congo, but Britain

was not interested. So Stanley turned to King Leopold II of Belgium, who was eager to set up Belgian settlements there. At the king's request, Stanley negotiated treaties with local rulers for the right to exploit the mineral wealth of the region. The king thereby gained control of the enormous area, which became known as the Congo Free State.

The brutal treatment of the local people in the Congo Free State has come to symbolize the worst aspects of European imperialism. Leopold II ruled the Congo Free State as his own private possession. The area was rich in ivory as well as rubber, copper, and other minerals. Leopold granted monopolies to European companies to exploit these resources and earned huge profits for himself.

The European companies ruthlessly exploited both the land and the people in the Congo Free State. To ensure maximum profits, company managers forced Africans to work long hours. If workers failed to produce enough rubber or copper, labor bosses felt free to cut off their hands or ears. They also imprisoned African women to make their husbands work harder. The brutal system took a huge toll in human lives. Between 1885 and 1908, the population of the Congo fell from about 20 million to about 10 million.

When Christian missionaries in the Congo revealed these atrocities, the Belgian government investigated. Eventually, in 1908, the government took over the administration of the Congo Free State, which then became known as the Belgian Congo.

France, too, expanded into West Africa in the 1870s. In 1879, the French built a railroad from Dakar, on the coast, into the interior. Britain felt threatened by French expansion into West Africa and took control of Nigeria and the Gold Coast, present-day Ghana. Germany, Portugal, and Spain also took over territory. However, France acquired the largest part of West Africa.

African Resistance

Europeans used persuasion, force, and bribery to make individual African rulers sign agreements giving them economic and political rights. Once they had a foothold, Europeans often ignored the agreements and simply took

The French pushed into West Africa, hoping to link the region with Algeria, their colony in North Africa. Along with traders and soldiers came Christian missionaries. Some Africans adopted Christian teachings and spread Christianity into villages such as this one.

what they wanted. If African rulers resisted, well-armed troops were sent to crush them. Still, many African rulers vigorously opposed European expansion.

Samori Touré, ruler of an empire in what is today Senegal, signed an agreement with the French in the 1890s. When the French broke the agreement and tried to seize control of his land, Touré fought back. For seven years, he led his army against the French. Finally, in 1898, the French captured Touré.

In Dahomey, King Behanzin battled the French until 1894, when he was captured and exiled to Algeria. The Ashanti, who had established a powerful state in what is today Ghana, stubbornly resisted the British. However, not all West and Central African people fought the Europeans. Some accepted agreements that gave them minimum levels of self-rule. Others did not fight because they had no hope of defeating the well-armed Europeans.

SECTION 3 REVIEW

1. **Locate:** (a) Sierra Leone, (b) Liberia, (c) Nigeria, (d) Belgian Congo.

2. **Identify:** (a) West African Patrol, (b) Usuman dan Fodio, (c) Leopold II, (d) Samori Touré.

3. (a) Why did the British found the colony of Sierra Leone? (b) Why was Liberia established?

4. Why did Muslim leaders call for holy wars in West Africa?

5. (a) Why was Leopold II of Belgium interested in the Congo? (b) Why did the Belgian government take direct control of the area in 1908?

6. **Critical Thinking** Why do you think the ending of the slave trade was not welcomed throughout West Africa?

4 Southern and Eastern Africa

READ TO UNDERSTAND

☐ **What groups of people fought for control of southern Africa in the 1800s.**

☐ **What East Africa was like when Europeans began to take colonies there.**

☐ **Why East African resistance to European conquest failed.**

Henry Fynn, an English trader, watched in amazement as about 80,000 Zulu formed into regiments at the command of Shaka, the great Zulu king. "It was a most exciting scene," wrote Fynn, "surprising to us, who could not have imagined that a nation termed 'savages' could be so disciplined."

During his stay with the Zulu in 1824, Fynn recorded other examples of how Europeans and Africans differed in the way they viewed each other. When Shaka asked what use Europeans made of cowhides, Fynn replied they were used for leather shoes. The Zulu did not need such protection for their feet, Shaka explained, for their ancestors had shown them better uses for cowhides, such as for making shields.

Settlers in Southern Africa

Fynn traveled through southern Africa almost 200 years after the first whites had settled there. In 1652, the Dutch founded Cape Town at the southern tip of Africa. The settlers supplied water, fresh meat, and vegetables to Dutch ships traveling to the East Indies. In the Cape area, the Dutch came in contact with local African herders. The Dutch gradually enslaved some of these people and forced others into the desert region to the north. However, by the early 1800s, the migration of other African peoples into southern Africa radically changed conditions there.

For almost 1,000 years before 1800, groups of Africans had been migrating into eastern and southern Africa. These peoples spoke related Bantu languages. However, the cultures of the groups differed.

Zulu expansion. The Zulu were one of the Bantu-speaking peoples who had migrated into southern Africa. By the early 1800s, the Zulu king Shaka had conquered a huge empire northeast of the Orange River. Shaka intro-

The movement of peoples into South Africa led to conflict after 1830. The Zulu, who had created a large empire, clashed with the Boers. Where did the Boers migrate after the British gained control of Cape Colony?

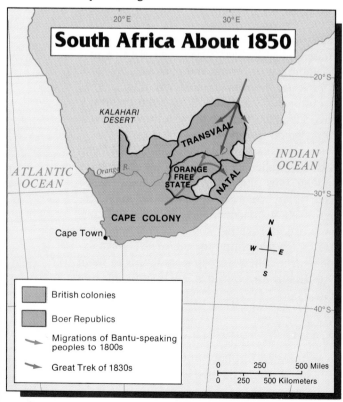

duced new fighting methods among the Zulu. He replaced the long throwing spears they had been using with short, stabbing swords. Shaka also reorganized the Zulu army into a powerful fighting force that expanded the empire.

As the Zulu expanded, they created turmoil in southern Africa. The people defeated by the Zulu fled their homelands and retreated across southern and central Africa. They displaced other African peoples, who then migrated northward.

The Boer republics. At about the same time as the Zulu were expanding their empire, the Boers, descendants of the Dutch who had founded Cape Town, were migrating north from the Cape Colony. The Boers were on the move because the British had gained control of the Cape Colony in 1806.

The Boers resented British rule because they felt that the British threatened their way of life. The British made English the official language of the colony and abolished slavery, which the Boers believed God had ordained. In the 1830s, about 10,000 Boers left the Cape Colony. They headed north in a vast migration of covered wagons, called the Great Trek. In the interior of southern Africa, the Boers set up two independent republics, the Transvaal and the Orange Free State. (See the map at left.)

The Boers soon came into conflict with the Zulu. For years the two groups fought for control of the land. Neither side was able to win a decisive victory. Finally, in 1879, the British became involved in these wars with the Zulu. The Zulu defeated the British in several battles, but with superior weapons and numbers, the British eventually destroyed the Zulu empire.

The Boer War

The British officially recognized the independence of the Boer republics in 1852. However, in the 1880s, gold and diamonds were discovered in the Transvaal and the Orange Free State. Thousands of British adventurers flocked north from the Cape Colony to seek their fortunes in the mines.

By the end of the 1800s, the British had decided that they must control all of South

The discovery of diamonds at Kimberley in 1871 sent thousands of fortune hunters to South Africa, including Cecil Rhodes, the son of an English minister. Kimberley soon grew into a sprawling mining town of 50,000 people. In time, Rhodes gained control of all the diamond mines of southern Africa. This print shows open-shaft mining at Kimberley. African mine workers were harshly treated, as you can see in this picture.

Africa because it was on the sea route to India. Moreover, Cecil Rhodes, the prime minister of the Cape Colony, had a grand plan to build a "Cape to Cairo" railroad, linking these British outposts in Africa.

In 1899, tension between the British and the Boers exploded into war. The Boer War lasted for nearly three years before the Boers surrendered. The war left the Boers with bitter memories because the British placed thousands of Boers in concentration camps, where many died. After the war, the Boers had to accept British rule, but the British promised them self-government as soon as possible. In 1910, the British united their South African colonies into the Union of South Africa.

Under the constitution of the new nation, only white men had the right to vote. The British felt that in time the Africans might be given the right to vote. The Boers opposed any such move because they believed black Africans were inferior to whites. The Boers were a majority of the white population of South Africa. As a result, they won control of the government.

Powerful States in East Africa

In East Africa, a profitable slave trade had developed by the 1700s. Arab traders who lived in the cities along the east coast used slaves to carry ivory and gold from Central Africa to the coast. As the slave trade expanded, the Arabs extended their control to include the inland trade routes.

In the 1800s, several African rulers challenged Arab authority over these trade routes and the growing slave trade. Mirambo, leader of the Nyamwezi people, carved out an empire in part of what is today Tanzania. Because he controlled a vital trade route, Mirambo demanded large sums of money from traders to assure safe passage. He used this wealth to buy weapons and further increase his power. However, Mirambo's empire was based on his personal leadership, and it collapsed soon after his death.

Another African leader, Tippu Tib, created a strong state in what is today eastern Zaire. Like Mirambo, Tippu Tib controlled a vital trade route from the interior to the east coast.

He built a strong army and conquered new lands. But Tippu Tib's empire, too, was based on personal leadership, and it was crushed by the Belgians after he retired to Zanzibar.

The rise of empires such as Mirambo's and Tippu Tib's disrupted the traditional way of life in East Africa and in some ways made European expansion in the late 1800s easier. The slave trade weakened many African societies and made African peoples suspicious of one another. When Europeans arrived in East Africa, they often gained support of Africans who wanted protection from the slave-trading states.

Many Europeans dreamed of empire in Africa. Cecil Rhodes's vision was probably the most ambitious, as this cartoon suggests. He spoke often of seeing Africa "all British from Cape to Cairo." Britain came close to achieving that goal, blocked only by German territory in East Africa.

THE RHODES COLOSSUS

European Rivalries in East Africa

European trade along the East African coast increased in the early 1800s. After the American Revolution, ships from Boston and Salem carried cotton cloth to East African ports. The word for cotton cloth in East Africa is still "merikani" because of that trade. German, French, and British merchants also sought trading rights from local rulers.

By the 1870s, Britain and Germany were the chief rivals in East Africa. Germany, a latecomer to the scramble for colonies, wanted what it called "a place in the sun." It sought colonies in East Africa because that was the only part of the continent that had not yet been claimed by other European powers. At the same time, British imperialists felt that control of East Africa was vital if Britain were to extend its empire from South Africa to Egypt. Also, both Portugal and Belgium claimed parts of East Africa in an effort to extend their colonial empires across the continent from the Atlantic Ocean to the Indian Ocean.

At the Berlin Conference of 1884–1885, the European nations settled their rival claims in East Africa. They recognized British and German rule over large parts of East Africa. Mozambique became a Portuguese colony, and Belgium took two small states in the interior. (See the map on page 561.) As with the arrangement about other parts of Africa, no Africans were consulted.

Fighting Colonial Rule

In East Africa, as elsewhere, Africans resisted European colonization. The Shana and the Matabele peoples in what is today Zimbabwe fought two major wars against the British. The Germans put down rebellions in their colony, but at great cost. The Hehe (HEE hee), for example, successfully fought the Germans for seven years. In the end, however, like so many other African peoples, the Hehe were defeated by European cannons and machine guns.

Two other factors also limited African resistance in East Africa. First, as you have read, the slave states had disrupted many African societies and made some Africans sympathetic to European expansion. Second, the outbreak of rinderpest, a cattle disease, caused a disastrous famine that kept people from fighting the invaders.

Rinderpest was brought into Africa by accident in the late 1800s. The Italians imported cattle infected with the disease from southern Europe to feed their troops in Somaliland. Because East African cattle had never been exposed to rinderpest before, they had no resistance to the disease. In some areas, 95 percent of all cattle died.

The epidemic spread south with terrible consequences because most East African people were cattle herders. Almost overnight their wealth and way of life were destroyed. Many people died of starvation. Others suffered severe malnutrition. Malnutrition made people vulnerable to diseases such as smallpox and malaria. Crushed by this disaster, many people lacked the resources and the will to fight the foreigners who took their lands.

SECTION 4 REVIEW

1. **Locate:** (a) Cape Town, (b) Transvaal, (c) Orange Free State, (d) Mozambique.

2. **Identify:** (a) Zulu, (b) Shaka, (c) Boers, (d) Great Trek, (e) Cecil Rhodes, (f) Union of South Africa, (g) Tippu Tib.

3. (a) Why did the Boers move inland from the Cape Colony? (b) Whom did they fight for control of the land?

4. Describe two reasons why the British took a greater interest in South Africa in the late 1800s.

5. (a) What European countries claimed land in East Africa? (b) Why were they interested in the area?

6. **Critical Thinking** Explain why Europeans were able to conquer the peoples of East Africa.

5 European Rule in Africa

READ TO UNDERSTAND

- ☐ How Europeans nations ruled their African colonies.

- ☐ How colonial rule had both negative and positive effects on the peoples of Africa.

- ☐ How western-educated Africans viewed colonial rule.

- ☐ *Vocabulary:* paternalism, assimilation.

In mid-1917, a British colonial official traveled to East Africa to set up local governments. When he arrived, the official summoned the local chiefs. "I explained that I was the government," he wrote, "and would they please provide me with 20 men to be policemen? Would they also please note that from now on people must not kill their wives or children whose teeth appeared in ill-omened order? Nor must the chiefs make war on their neighbors without consulting me. In fact, a whole lot of customary and often agreeable things must be given up." As the official discovered, ruling colonies involved a clash of cultures.

European imperialism in Africa lasted about 100 years, from the 1870s to the 1970s. Compared to Africa's long history, this period was short. However, the impact of colonial rule on Africa was immense.

Colonial Governments

Once European nations had carved up Africa, they faced the question of how to rule their new colonies. They developed two types of colonial government: direct rule, practiced by France, Germany, Belgium, and Portugal; and indirect rule, used by Great Britain.

Direct rule. Through direct rule, a European nation controlled government at all levels in its colony. It appointed its own officials to replace African leaders and cast aside traditional African ways of governing.

The European nations that chose direct rule believed that Africans were incapable of

573

As you have read, eyewitness accounts are not always completely objective or accurate. They can be affected by **cultural bias,** or the way the writer's culture shapes his or her attitude toward an event.

During the Age of Imperialism, Europeans who visited Africa judged the diverse peoples and cultures they saw in terms of European civilization. The following excerpt is from the journal British explorer Sir Richard Burton kept as he traveled through East Africa in 1858. Use the following steps to identify the writer's cultural bias.

1 **Identify the nature of the document.** (a) What type of document is it? (b) Who wrote it? (c) When was the document written? (d) Under what circumstances was it written?

2 **Review the contents of the document.** (a) What does the writer say about the early morning activities of the people in the African village? (b) What does he say about the way the people spend the rest of the day? (c) What does the writer say about the activities of women and girls?

3 **Study the source to discover the writer's cultural bias.** Look at the words the writer uses and the tone of the excerpt. (a) What word does the writer use to describe the dwellings in which the people live? (b) What word is used to describe the chief occupation of the people? (c) What seems to be the writer's attitude toward the people he is describing?

4 **Evaluate the document as a historical source.** (a) What parts of the description are most likely to be accurate? (b) What parts of the description reflect the writer's cultural bias? (c) Would you use this document as evidence about life in East Africa? Why or why not?

From Richard Burton's Travel Journal
The African rises with the dawn from his couch of cowhide. The hut is cool and comfortable during the day, but the barred door impeding ventilation at night causes it to be close and disagreeable. The hour before sunrise being the coldest time, he usually kindles a fire and addresses himself to his constant companion, the pipe. When the sun becomes sufficiently powerful, he removes the reed screen from the entrance and issues forth to bask in the morning beams. The villages are populous, and the houses touching one another enable the occupants, when squatting outside . . . to chat and chatter without moving.

About 7 A.M., when the dew has partially disappeared from the grass, the elder boys drive the flocks and herds to pasture with loud shouts. . . . At 8 A.M., those who have provisions at home enter the hut to eat porridge; those who have not, join a friend.

After breaking his fast, the African repairs, pipe in hand, to the iwanza [the village inn], where he will spend the greater part of the day talking and laughing, smoking, or torpid [sluggish] with sleep. . . .

After eating, the East African invariably indulges in a long fit of torpidity [sluggishness], from which he awakes to pass the afternoon as he did the forenoon. Toward sunset, all issue forth to enjoy the coolness: the men sit outside the iwanza, whilst the women and the girls, after fetching water from the well, collect in a group upon their little stools and indulge in the pleasures of gossip. . . . As the hours of darkness draw nigh, the village doors are carefully closed, and after milking his cows each peasant retires to his hut or passes his time with his friends in the iwanza.

ruling themselves. They used this belief to justify **paternalism,** the system of governing colonies as parents would guide their children. Europeans thought they had to teach their African subjects the "proper" way to live, by which they meant the European way.

Direct rule varied among the different European colonies. France practiced a policy of

assimilation, under which the parent nation tried to absorb its colonies politically and culturally. Africans in the French colonies were expected to exchange their own heritage for French culture. Then, when the colonies became truly French, they would be made provinces of France proper, not just overseas territories.

To achieve assimilation, French colonial officials set up schools, businesses, and law courts just like those in France. Some Africans were sent to school in France and eventually gained minor government positions in the French colonies.

Portugal also followed a policy of assimilation, but it exercised rigid control over its colonies. It wanted the Africans in its colonies to become Portuguese Christians. Although some Africans converted to Christianity, very few were allowed to become Portuguese citizens.

Paternalism was the main characteristic of direct rule by Germany and Belgium. Germany looked on its African colonies as a source of wealth and labor. It exercised strict control over its colonial subjects, claiming that Africans could never learn to rule themselves. Belgium wanted to make Europeans forget the atrocities committed in the Congo during Leopold's rule. Therefore, it tried to make the Congo a model colony. The Belgians claimed to protect the interests of their African subjects by making all decisions for them.

Indirect rule. Britain was the only colonial power to rely on indirect rule. Under the system of indirect rule, a British governor and council of advisors made laws for each colony. But local African rulers loyal to the governor kept some of their traditional authority. Thus, indirect rule differed from direct rule because it did not replace local rulers with European officials. Yet local rulers had only limited power.

The British had practical reasons for using indirect rule. Even before the European scramble for Africa, Britain had more colonies than any other European nation. During the late 1800s, it took over one third of the African continent, with 64 million people to rule. A small nation, Britain did not have enough officials or soldiers to control its huge empire without the help of local leaders.

Making Colonies Profitable

Although the European nations had different methods of governing their colonies, their policies had a common goal. They all believed their colonies should be self-sufficient. That is, each colony should pay all its own expenses. This included the salaries for government officials and the military as well as the costs of building and maintaining roads, railroads, and schools.

These expenses were immense, but the European powers found ways to make their colonies pay for them. In the process, they made the colonies both self-sufficient and profitable. Europeans tapped the mineral and agricultural resources of their colonies and built trade by exporting these resources. They also developed internal systems of transportation.

In some colonies, Europeans found valuable mineral resources, such as copper in the Belgian Congo and gold in South Africa. Where mineral resources were lacking, Europeans developed cash crops such as rubber, palm oil, and peanuts.

Colonial governments also imposed taxes on Africans, which they had to pay in cash. The only way Africans could earn cash was to work for individual Europeans or for the colonial government. Thus, many Africans had to work on large plantations or in factories and mines owned by Europeans.

Europeans made their colonies more profitable by encouraging individuals to invest in enterprises such as railroads and mines. Europeans built railroads for both political and economic reasons. Politically, the railroads helped colonial governments maintain their authority by providing a reliable transportation system.

Economically, railroads gave Europeans a relatively cheap way of moving cash crops and other products to ports for shipment overseas. In Uganda, for example, many British farmers established cotton plantations in the interior. They needed the railroad to send the cotton to the coast so it could be shipped to factories in Britain. Because investors were interested in high profits, they built railroads only in those areas where Europeans had settled or had businesses.

The Impact of Colonial Rule

Colonial rule greatly affected the political, economic, and social structure of African societies. Europeans believed Africans were primitive people. They generally refused to recognize the customs and traditions that had shaped African societies for centuries.

The breakdown of traditional culture. During the Age of Imperialism, many African economic and social traditions were destroyed. As colonial cities grew, some families moved to the cities, hoping to improve their positions. Others were forced to take jobs in European-owned factories or businesses in order to pay taxes. Still others became migrant workers, leaving their villages for long periods to work in distant mines and plantations. As a result, the close-knit village, once the center of African life, declined. People no longer had the same concern for helping one another as they had in the past.

Christian missionaries actively tried to convert Africans to Christianity. As some Africans became Christians, however, conflicts broke out within communities. Christian converts rejected the religious practices and beliefs of their families and neighbors.

Education further helped to break down traditional ways of life. Colonial schools were run by Europeans, and they presented a negative view of African cultures. African children were taught that their parents' beliefs and traditions were backward. In school, children studied European, not African, history.

Educated Africans who worked for the colonial governments were affected by European paternalism. Africans found they had to conform to European ways to succeed. For example, if they wore their traditional flowing robes to work, they would lose their jobs. Only European clothes were considered correct.

The benefits. Although colonial governments helped destroy traditional patterns of life in Africa, some people argued that colonial rule brought important benefits. Europeans used the wealth from mining diamonds, gold, copper, and iron ore to develop their colonies

Europeans were fascinated by African wildlife, as this painting by artist Thomas Baines shows. Baines accompanied David Livingstone on his expedition up the Zambezi River. Paintings such as this one and written accounts of Europeans who traveled in Africa often emphasized the aspects of African life that differed the most from life in Europe.

economically. They built roads, railroads, and harbors. This economic development created jobs in which Africans acquired new skills.

Europeans increased literacy, the ability to read and write, among Africans, although there were literate societies in Africa before the Age of Imperialism. Christian missionaries were particularly active in setting up schools and developing written alphabets for some African languages.

Colonial governments and missionaries also introduced improved medical care and better methods of sanitation. New crops, tools, and farming methods helped increase food production. In addition, colonial rulers ended the local warfare among Africans, which had grown out of the slave trade.

A New Generation of African Leaders

By 1914, many Africans had graduated from colonial schools. Some had completed their education at European universities. At first, many educated Africans imitated everything European and denied their African traditions. After a time, however, a new generation of educated Africans emerged. They accepted some of the benefits of European civilization. However, they also recognized the importance of their own heritage.

These Africans came to appreciate their own culture, in part because of their experiences in Europe. There, they discovered more about their colonial rulers. In Africa, they had been taught that Europeans were superior and did not work with their hands. As a result, many of the Africans who went to Paris, London, and Berlin were shocked to see Europeans employed as street cleaners and factory workers. In addition, in European universities, Africans studied the ideas of self-government discussed by thinkers such as John Locke and Thomas Jefferson.

On their return to Africa, these western-educated Africans experienced a sense of frustration. Colonial governments continued to treat them as inferiors. They realized that Europeans would never view them as equals no matter how westernized they became. In the early 1900s, this new generation of African

By the early 1900s, Europeans had founded schools and colleges in their African colonies. This photograph shows a medical school in Uganda, a British colony.

leaders began to organize nationalist movements aimed at ending colonial rule.

SECTION 5 REVIEW

1. **Define:** (a) paternalism, (b) assimilation.

2. (a) Describe two features of direct rule. (b) What European nations used direct rule in Africa?

3. (a) How did indirect rule differ from direct rule? (b) Why did Britain govern through indirect rule?

4. How did colonial governments try to make their colonies self-sufficient?

5. How did colonial rule affect traditional African culture?

6. **Critical Thinking** Why did Africans educated at European universities organize nationalist movements?

577

CHAPTER 25 REVIEW

Summary

1. **Between 1870 and 1914, European nations carved up most of Africa.** A variety of motives, including nationalism, economic rivalries, and humanitarian concerns, sent Europeans to Africa in ever-increasing numbers.

2. **Bitter rivalries among European nations in North Africa marked the late 1800s.** Britain's control of Egypt was challenged by France and led to the Fashoda incident. France took Algeria as a colony, while Italy gained control of Libya.

3. **The end of the slave trade and the revival of Islam affected life in West and Central Africa.** After King Leopold of Belgium gained control of the Congo Free State, other European nations, especially France and Great Britain, carved up West Africa. People in many parts of Africa resisted European expansion, but their resistance failed.

4. **Southern and eastern Africa were also colonized by European powers.** In the 1800s, the Zulu and the Boers fought for power in South Africa. Eventually, the British won control of South Africa. Britain, Germany, Portugal, and Belgium took over East Africa.

5. **European rule in Africa affected African societies deeply.** Most European nations governed their colonies through direct control, but Britain used indirect control, giving local leaders limited power. European rule helped to break down traditional African cultures but brought benefits such as more schools and better medical care.

Recalling Facts

Decide if the following statements are true or false. If it is false, rewrite it to make it true.

1. Christian missionaries wanted to preserve traditional African culture.

2. David Livingstone helped open up Central Africa to Europeans.

3. Under Muhammad Ali, Egypt increased its exports of cotton.

4. The Congo Free State was owned by the king of France.

5. The Boers set out on the Great Trek to escape British control.

Chapter Checkup

1. (a) Describe the major causes of European imperialism in the 1800s. (b) How did explorers increase interest in Africa?

2. (a) How did Muhammad Ali strengthen Egypt? (b) Why did his policies eventually result in greater European influence in Egypt?

3. (a) How did the demand for slaves affect West Africa? (b) What effect did the abolition of the slave trade have on West Africa?

4. Explain how the expansion of each of the following groups in South Africa led to conflict: (a) Zulu; (b) Boers; (c) British.

5. (a) What powerful leaders ruled in East Africa in the 1800s? (b) Why were their empires short-lived?

6. (a) What attitude did most Europeans have toward the African peoples they ruled? (b) How did this view affect the kinds of government Europeans established in their colonies?

7. Explain how colonial rule affected African (a) government; (b) farming; (c) village life; (d) religion.

Critical Thinking

1. **Analyzing a Quotation** A British poet, Rudyard Kipling, wrote the following lines in 1899:

   Take up the white man's burden—
   Send out the best ye breed—
   Go bind your sons to exile,

To serve your captives' need;
To wait in heavy harness,
On fluttered folk and wild—
Your new-caught sullen peoples,
Half-devil and half-child.

How do these lines express European paternalism in the Age of Imperialism?

2. **Relating Past to Present** (a) Why did the British want to control the Suez Canal? (b) Do you think the Suez Canal is as important today as it was in the late 1800s? Explain.

3. **Understanding the Roots of Democracy** During the Age of Imperialism, Western European nations extended voting rights to more citizens and promoted other democratic goals. At the same time, they were colonizing Africa and other parts of the world. (a) How did European nations justify these apparently contradictory developments? (b) How would democratic nations today view the taking of colonies?

Developing Basic Skills

1. **Map Reading** Study the map on page 561. (a) Which European countries claimed land in North Africa? (b) What areas of Africa did Germany claim? (c) How do you think the scramble for Africa affected relationships among European nations?

2. **Classifying** Make a chart with two columns. In the first column, describe the benefits of European imperialism for African societies. In the second column, describe the disadvantages of European imperialism for African societies. After completing the chart, answer the following questions: (a) What economic benefits resulted from imperialism? (b) What economic problems were caused by imperialism? (c) How did imperialism affect African cultures? (d) In your opinion, which were greater—the benefits or the disadvantages of imperialism? Explain.

Writing About History

Taking Notes

If you have followed the suggestions in the previous lessons, you are now ready to begin taking notes for your research paper. Use index cards for your notes rather than a notebook. Use a separate card for each source and for different subjects from the same source. Write the subject in the upper right-hand corner so that you will be able to arrange the cards according to your outline. In the upper left-hand corner, write the title, author, and publishing information of your source to use in your footnotes and bibliography. Record the page numbers from which you have obtained each fact, idea, or quotation. Write your notes on the front of the card only.

Practice: Write a sample note card on the topic "Imperialism in Egypt." Use your textbook as the source.

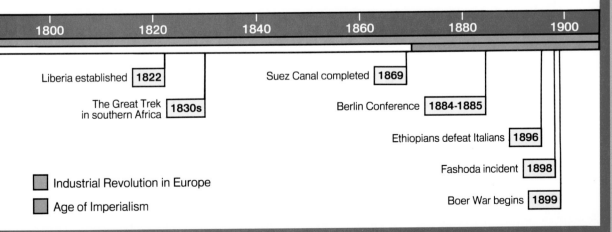

| 1800 | 1820 | 1840 | 1860 | 1880 | 1900 |

Liberia established 1822

The Great Trek in southern Africa 1830s

Suez Canal completed 1869

Berlin Conference 1884-1885

Ethiopians defeat Italians 1896

Fashoda incident 1898

Boer War begins 1899

☐ Industrial Revolution in Europe

☐ Age of Imperialism

Asia and the West

(1650–1920)

26

In the 1700s, Chinese emperors ruled over a vast and prosperous empire. Lord Macartney might have visited a Chinese city such as this one during his unsuccessful mission to the emperor Ch'ien-lung.

Lord George Macartney, an ambassador of King George III of Britain, entered the emperor's splendid tent. Macartney watched the hundreds of Chinese officials there throw themselves to the ground before Ch'ien-lung, the emperor of China, but he refused to kowtow like the others. He did, however, bow on one knee, as he would have before his own ruler.

Even though Macartney had not been allowed into the Forbidden City, the emperor's palace in Peking, he was at least going to get an answer from

Ch'ien-lung. He had brought a request from George III asking for expanded trade and better conditions for British merchants.

However, Ch'ien-lung's reply was disappointing. Although Macartney knew that Britain was one of the most powerful nations in Europe, Ch'ien-lung considered it weak and uncivilized. "You, O King," Ch'ien-lung wrote in his reply to George III, "have yearned from afar for our civilizing influence and have sent an embassy across the sea bearing a diplomatic request. I have taken note of your respectful spirit of submission and have treated your mission with extreme favor and loaded it with gifts.

"Yesterday, your Ambassador petitioned my Ministers regarding your trade with China, but his proposal is contrary to the custom of our dynasty and cannot be considered. Hitherto, all European nations, including your own country's barbarian merchants, have carried on trade with our Celestial Empire at Canton. Such has been the practice for many centuries, although our Celestial Empire possesses all things in great abundance and lacks no product within its own borders. There is, therefore, no need to import any product manufactured by outside barbarians in exchange for our own goods."

The emperor's refusal to treat Britain as an equal was due in part to the Chinese belief that no nation could match China's achievements. In 1793, Emperor Ch'ien-lung did not foresee that Britain and other western nations would soon challenge China. In the late 1700s, European powers were already advancing into Asia. During the Age of Imperialism, India, China, Japan, and Southeast Asia would all feel the effects of foreign expansion. ■

1 India Under British Rule

READ TO UNDERSTAND

☐ How the East India Company gained control of India.

☐ How British rule affected the lives of the people of India.

☐ How Indian nationalism grew stronger in the late 1800s.

☐ *Vocabulary:* commercial colonialism, sepoy.

The Mogul rulers of India looked down on the European traders. All that the Europeans were interested in, they knew, was expanding their commercial power, and their gifts were barely worth acknowledging. Besides, the riches of the Mogul court, with its glittering jewels and elephants laden with gold, surely had no need of even the most expensive and elaborate offerings of the Europeans. The Moguls' contempt for the foreign traders lasted for 200 years. By the mid-1700s, however, the Mogul Empire was collapsing, and one group of the detested foreigners, the British, took full advantage of the power vacuum to gain control of India.

An Empire in Decline

From 1526 to about 1712, able Mogul emperors ruled a powerful empire in India. But during the 1700s, the empire suffered from a lack of strong rulers. The government became inefficient, and provincial governors grew increasingly independent.

In the early days of the Mogul Empire, both Hindus and Muslims had supported the emperor. As the emperor's prestige faded, however, war broke out between Hindus and Muslims. In addition, a growing number of people criticized the Mogul government as extravagant and oppressive. In the mid-1700s, rival Indian princes were competing for power. Europeans took advantage of these internal struggles to advance into India.

By the early 1800s, the British East India Company was master of much of India. Although the company was mainly interested in profits, it had its own armed forces and governing officials. This Indian ceramic sculpture shows an officer of the company, at right, presiding over an Indian court in Hyderabad.

The British East India Company

As the Mogul Empire weakened, French and British trading companies battled for control of trade with India. During the 1700s, the British East India Company increased its influence on the subcontinent. The East India Company had been founded in 1600 to sell Indian products such as cotton cloth, silk, sugar, and jute in world markets. However, as rivalry with France and the turmoil in the Mogul Empire threatened its profits, the East India Company became increasingly involved in India's political and military affairs.

In 1756, at the outbreak of the Seven Years' War in Europe, Robert Clive, an administrator of the East India Company, raised an army and ousted the French from their trading posts in India. He then used his army to support governments favorable to the East India Company in the Indian state of Bengal. Clive and his successors continued to interfere in local Indian affairs until the East India Company became the most powerful authority in India.

The East India Company practiced **commercial colonialism**—that is, it controlled India's foreign trade and used its soldiers to keep friendly local rulers in power. To protect its interests, the company built forts and maintained its own army of Indian soldiers, known as **sepoys.** During the late 1700s and

early 1800s, the East India Company gained direct political control over parts of India.

Extending British Rule

Although the British government regulated the East India Company, the company's officials in India had a fairly free hand until the mid-1800s. By that time, many members of Parliament felt that the British government itself should assume responsibility for India. In 1857, an uprising known as the Sepoy Rebellion gave Parliament the excuse it needed to end the rule of the East India Company in India.

The Sepoy Rebellion. The immediate cause of the Sepoy Rebellion was rumors that bullet cartridges used by the sepoys were greased with beef or pork fat. These rumors angered both Hindu and Muslim soldiers. Hindus were forbidden to touch beef, and Muslims were forbidden to touch pork. The sepoys also resented British efforts to make them adopt Christianity and follow European customs. The rebellion among the sepoys spread across India.

Hindu and Muslim princes supported the Sepoy Rebellion because they saw the British as a threat to their power. Peasants joined the uprising to protest the hardships of their lives. British troops suppressed the rebellion, and in

1858 the British Parliament took over control of India from the East India Company.

Colonial government. After 1858, the British government set up a system of colonial rule in India. A cabinet minister in London was responsible for Indian affairs. A British viceroy in India carried out government policies. British governors ruled about two-thirds of India, including the parts that the East India Company had controlled directly. Local Indian princes stayed on as rulers in the rest of the country. But British officials called residents closely supervised these Indian rulers. In 1877, British Prime Minister Benjamin Disraeli had Queen Victoria recognized as Empress of India.

By 1890, about 1,000 British officials were running a colonial government that ruled some 280 million Indians. During the Age of Imperialism, the British had a clear idea of what they thought India should become. Unlike the East India Company, which had encouraged its officials to learn Indian languages and observe local customs, the British colonial government tried to impose British culture on India.

Thomas Babington Macauley, a prominent government administrator in India, called for Britain to educate a class of Indians who could interpret British culture to the mass of the people. Such a class, he said, would be "Indian in blood and color, but English in taste, opinions, in morals, and in intellect." Colonial officials believed that by adopting European ways, Indians would improve their lives.

Impact of British Rule

British rule affected Indian life in various ways. In countless Indian villages, the coming of the British had little direct impact. Farmers tilled their fields as they had for centuries. The caste system dominated village life, and the people observed traditional religious practices. However, British policies opened the door to major economic and social changes.

Economic changes. The Industrial Revolution in Britain influenced British economic policies toward India. The East India Company had sold Indian-made luxury items abroad, but the British government saw India as a source of cheap raw materials for British factories. It also felt that India, which had a large population, would serve as a market for British manufactured goods. Britain, therefore, tied the Indian economy closely to its own.

The British discouraged local Indian industries. Instead, they encouraged Indian farmers to shift from growing food crops to raising cotton. Factories in Britain then used the Indian cotton to make finished goods, some of which were sent back to India to be sold. Although this policy benefited British manufacturers, it hurt local industries in India. Village artisans could not compete with the cheaper, mass-produced British imports.

British efforts to encourage the production of export crops, such as cotton, reduced the amount of food grown. As a result, famines killed millions of Indians during the 1800s.

MAP STUDY *Britain controlled all of India after 1858. In the light and dark purple areas below, British officials ruled directly. In the pink areas, they governed through local Indian rulers. Why do you think Bengal was ruled directly?*

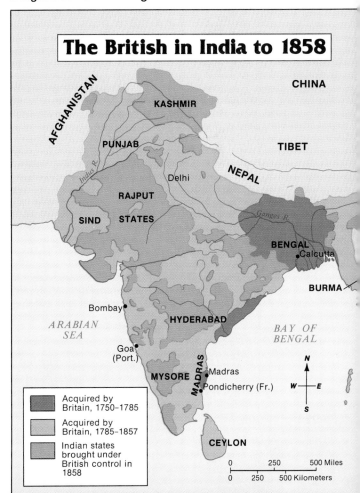

The British in India to 1858

AFGHANISTAN
CHINA
KASHMIR
PUNJAB
TIBET
Indus R.
Delhi
NEPAL
RAJPUT
SIND STATES
Ganges R.
BENGAL
Calcutta
BURMA
Bombay
HYDERABAD
ARABIAN SEA
BAY OF BENGAL
Goa (Port.)
MYSORE
MADRAS
Madras
Pondicherry (Fr.)

Acquired by Britain, 1750–1785

Acquired by Britain, 1785–1857

Indian states brought under British control in 1858

CEYLON

0   250   500 Miles
0   250   500 Kilometers

N
W   E
S

British rule in India led to better communication and increased trade. By building new canals, roads, and railways, the British opened up India's vast interior to trade. The opening of the Suez Canal in 1869 made trade faster and easier between Europe and India as well as between Europe and the rest of Asia. Telegraph lines also made communications easier between Britain and India. These developments dramatically increased exports from India.

Social changes. The British sponsored programs to improve health care and control epidemics, which occurred frequently. They also built hospitals and trained doctors to work in the countryside. Improved medical care contributed to a rapid growth of the Indian population. In some regions, population growth combined with inadequate food supplies resulted in terrible famines. Yet at the same time, the new railroads helped reduce the effect of famine because food could be shipped quickly from one region to another.

India's growing population made its cities among the largest in the world. In the cities, the influence of British culture was especially strong. There, British-educated Indian professionals and businesspeople worked alongside British officials.

Young Indians, mainly from higher-caste families, attended British-run schools and colleges. They studied the same courses in science, mathematics, history, literature, and philosophy as students in Britain. These young students became doctors, lawyers, professors, civil servants, and businesspeople and formed a new upper class in India. British officials depended on them to carry out colonial policies. However, by the late 1800s, some members of the new upper class began voicing discontent with British rule.

Indian Nationalism

Opposition to British rule was not new in India. Economic hardships in the countryside had touched off periodic uprisings. On occasion, British troops faced thousands of enraged peasants. However, these revolts did not threaten British control. The peasants were too poorly armed and organized to defeat the British.

In 1885, a group of well-educated, middle-class Indians formed a political party called the Indian National Congress. Known as the Congress, this party led the nationalist movement in India. At first, the Congress did not seek independence from Britain. It campaigned for reforms such as free compulsory education for boys and girls and a greater role for Indians in local government.

By the early 1900s, however, Indian nationalists were calling for an end to British rule. They urged Indians to boycott, or stop buying, British goods. At the same time, Indian writers published books about the country's past that restored people's pride in their ancient heritage.

The best-known nationalist leader was Mohandas Gandhi. Gandhi's greatest success was turning what had been a middle-class movement for independence into a struggle that the masses of Indian people supported. India should be free, Gandhi urged, so that Indians could restore their village life and live according to their ancient traditions. As you

This Indian woodcut shows one of the effects of British rule—the building of thousands of miles of railroads. Notice that the last car, known as the "purdah carriage," was reserved for women and children.

will read in Chapter 29, Gandhi eventually united the Hindu population behind the call for Indian independence.

At first, the British did not take the independence movement seriously. They expected the Indians to be able to rule themselves some day, but they felt that time was far off. They knew that Hindus and Muslims were so deeply divided that they would not cooperate against the British. Therefore, Britain refused to give in to the demands of Indian nationalists.

The Balance Sheet of British Rule

As with colonial rule in Africa, people have long debated the pluses and minuses of British rule of India. A supporter of the British argued, "Englishmen can look back on their work in India with legitimate pride. They have conferred on the people of India what is the greatest human blessing—peace."

From the other side came this view: "In India, every European is automatically a member of the ruling race. Railway carriages, station waiting rooms, benches in parks are marked 'For Europeans Only.' To have to put up with this in one's own country is a humiliating reminder of our enslaved condition."

SECTION 1 REVIEW

1. **Identify:** (a) Robert Clive, (b) Sepoy Rebellion, (c) Indian National Congress, (d) Mohandas Gandhi.

2. **Define:** (a) commercial colonialism, (b) sepoy.

3. (a) Why did the Mogul Empire decline in the 1700s? (b) How did the East India Company gain control of India?

4. Describe one cause and one effect of the Sepoy Rebellion.

5. (a) What reforms did the early Indian nationalists want? (b) How did their demands change by the early 1900s?

6. **Critical Thinking** Describe British rule in India from the point of view of either a British official or an Indian nationalist.

---

2 Conflict Between China and the West

READ TO UNDERSTAND

☐ Why Europeans were able to gain spheres of influence in China.

☐ What the causes and results of the Opium War and the Taiping Rebellion were.

☐ What the revolutionaries who overthrew the Manchu dynasty wanted.

☐ *Vocabulary:* extraterritoriality.

In 1793, when the emperor Ch'ien-lung wrote the letter you read at the beginning of this chapter, China was probably the wealthiest, most powerful country in the world. A strong central government was successfully administering a vast empire. Yet its strength hid some basic weaknesses. In the 1800s, this prosperous empire would be torn apart by internal rebellion and the growing influence of western nations in Asia.

The Manchu Dynasty

In the early 1600s, invaders from Manchuria swept into China. They toppled the Ming dynasty, which had ruled China since the 1300s. (See page 273.) The victorious Manchu, as the invaders were called, established their capital at Peking. They adopted the customs and traditions of the Chinese and won the support of the Confucian official class. Claiming they had received the Mandate of Heaven, the Manchu founded a new dynasty. The Manchu dynasty ruled China from 1644 to 1911.

The Manchu ruled over a powerful and prosperous empire. Western merchants who reached China in the 1600s and 1700s were amazed at the splendor of Chinese civilization. They began arriving in ever-greater numbers to buy Chinese tea, silk, and porcelain.

As you have read, the Chinese restricted foreigners to trading at Canton. Europeans had to pay for Chinese products with gold and silver because the Chinese had no interest in the goods that the Europeans offered in exchange.

585

Chinese porcelain was highly prized by westerners who went to China to trade. Gradually, all glazed pottery—no matter where it came from—was called chinaware or simply china. In this Chinese print, skilled artisans are making pottery in a shed. Finished pots are set outside to dry on long tables.

If foreign merchants did not observe Chinese customs, the Chinese expelled them. Although the restrictions irritated foreign merchants, they accepted them because they could make huge profits selling Chinese goods in Europe and the United States.

In the 1800s, however, conditions changed as revolts disrupted life in Manchu China. This turmoil had several sources. Under the Manchu, the Chinese population had grown to about 300 million people. Such large numbers strained the country's food resources. A flood or drought could cause mass starvation. During times of famine, peasants in many parts of China rebelled against the government.

Furthermore, like earlier dynasties, the Manchu eventually became corrupt. Even during the reign of the powerful emperor Ch'ien-lung, official corruption was weakening China. For 30 years, a court official and friend of the emperor, Ho-shen, ran wild with government money. Ho-shen skimmed a personal fortune estimated at $1 billion from taxes. Throughout the empire, officials enriched themselves from public funds. To offset the loss of these revenues, officials raised the taxes peasants had to

pay. Burdened with heavy taxes, peasants rebelled.

Beginning of European Imperialism

While the Manchu government struggled to put down the peasant uprisings, Europeans were pressuring China to end its trade restrictions. European governments also demanded that China receive their diplomats and treat them as equals. However, the Chinese saw their land as the center of civilization, and they thought China should receive only "tribute bearers" from states they considered inferior.

The Opium War. Tensions between China and European powers increased until they flared into violence over the opium trade. In the early 1800s, British merchants discovered that they could make huge profits trading opium from India and Turkey for Chinese goods. The opium trade enriched many foreign and Chinese merchants, but the Chinese government was outraged as opium smoking spread throughout China. Not only was opium harmful to the Chinese people, but the opium trade also drained China of silver, which was used to pay foreign merchants who imported the drug.

The Chinese decided to end the opium trade. In 1839, the government destroyed $6 million worth of opium that the British had brought to Canton. To China's surprise, the British responded with military force. In 1840, the British seized Canton and attacked Chinese forces along the coast. In this conflict, known as the Opium War, the British used their navy and superior weapons to defeat the Chinese.

The unequal treaties. In 1842, the Chinese were forced to sign the humiliating Treaty of Nanking. Under the treaty, China agreed to receive foreign diplomats and to open more ports to foreign trade. Britain acquired the island of Hong Kong and was paid for the opium destroyed by the Chinese.

Other terms of the treaty limited China's ability to govern itself even more seriously. For example, China agreed to let Britain determine its tariffs, or taxes on imports. The Chinese also had to give the British the right of **extraterritoriality**—that is, the British in

China would be protected by the laws of their own nation, not the laws of China. Extraterritoriality meant that China would have little authority over foreigners.

The Treaty of Nanking was the first of a series of "unequal treaties" that China was forced to make with foreign powers. Other nations soon demanded most of the rights that the British had won in the Treaty of Nanking. In later struggles with western powers and Japan, China gave up still more rights.

China had to yield to these demands in part because its military technology had fallen behind that of the foreign powers. By the 1800s, European advances in science and technology had, for the first time, made European nations more powerful than China.

The Taiping Rebellion

Internal unrest continued to weaken the Manchu dynasty. In 1850, discontent with Manchu rule led to a widespread peasant uprising known as the Taiping Rebellion. The rebels were inspired by a mixture of ancient Chinese traditions and ideas learned from Christian missionaries. Their leaders demanded reforms such as the redistribution of land to poor peasants, an end to high taxes, and equality for men and women.

The rebels seized the central region of China and nearly toppled the government. They sought the aid of European nations by claiming to be Christians. But in the end, the Europeans helped the Manchu emperor since they had already signed favorable treaties with him. The fighting lasted for 14 years before the government finally defeated the Taiping rebels. The long rebellion further weakened the Manchu dynasty and created a strong wish for reform within China.

During the Taiping Rebellion, European powers forced China to grant them more concessions. The Chinese government had to open more ports to foreign trade and to make the opium trade legal. It also had to allow foreign diplomats to live in Peking.

Spheres of Influence

In 1860, the Russians seized a large stretch of land on China's northern border and built the port of Vladivostok on the Pacific coast. Japan,

too, took advantage of Chinese weakness to increase its influence in Korea, a country that China had dominated. In 1894, China tried to stop the Japanese advance in Korea, and war broke out. Japan quickly defeated China. China was forced to recognize Korean independence, and Japan won several islands from China, including Formosa, present-day Taiwan.

Toward the end of the century, China lost still more power. Russia, Germany, France, and Britain each acquired a sphere of influence in China. (See the map below.) Each nation won special economic privileges in its sphere of influence, including the right to invest in mines, railways, and factories. These four European powers also forced China to lease them land so they could build naval bases to protect their spheres of influence.

The United States did not acquire a sphere of influence in China, but the American government insisted that it receive the same com-

MAP STUDY *By the early 1900s, several European nations and Japan had acquired spheres of influence in China. Within its sphere of influence, each nation claimed exclusive trading rights. What relationship do you see between the spheres of influence and the rivers in China?*

mercial rights as other foreign powers. It demanded equal access to trade in China for all nations. This Open Door Policy, as it was called, was meant to prevent foreign powers from carving China up into colonies. The United States called on foreign powers to allow free trade in their spheres of influence and to maintain Chinese political unity. The American policy did help preserve an open door to trade in China, but it did little to keep China free from foreign domination.

Chinese Efforts at Reform

Many Chinese leaders were outraged at the sad condition of their country. As early as the 1860s, after the defeat of the Taiping rebels, the government had adopted a policy known as "self-strengthening." It hoped to restore government control over both the Chinese and the foreigners living in China.

This "self-strengthening" policy involved finding ways to modernize China while keeping Confucian traditions. The government tried to introduce modern weapons and began building telegraph and railroad lines. Chinese students were sent abroad to study. The government also tried to weed out corrupt officials. Many officials opposed these reforms, however, so the policy had little success.

Sun Yat-sen despised the corrupt Manchu dynasty that ruled China. In the early 1900s, he wrote: "Today we are the poorest and weakest nation in the world and occupy the lowest position in international affairs. Other men are the carving knife and serving dish; we are the fish and the meat."

Hundred days of reform. In 1898, as foreign interference increased, Kuang-hsu (kwahng shee), a young and idealistic Manchu emperor, made another attempt to save China. On the advice of reformers at court, he sent diplomats and other officials abroad to study. He issued decrees to reform schools, to add practical subjects to the curriculum, and to translate foreign books into Chinese.

Kuang's program was known as the "hundred days of reform." Because many of the changes in this program challenged the traditional Confucian order, conservatives at the imperial court opposed his reforms. They turned for help to the dowager empress Tz'u-hsi (tsoo shee), who also opposed the reforms. In 1898, she ousted the reformers from power and had the emperor imprisoned. For the next ten years, Tz'u-hsi ruled China and prevented any major reforms from being enacted.

The Boxer Rebellion. Tz'u-hsi faced two serious problems: foreign imperialism and a growing Chinese belief that the Manchu dynasty had lost the Mandate of Heaven. In 1899, a group of Chinese founded a secret society called the "Fists of Righteous Harmony" or "Boxers." The Boxers wanted to expel the Manchu and all foreigners from China. But Tz'u-hsi negotiated with the Boxers and agreed to aid them secretly against foreigners.

In 1900, the Boxers moved through northeastern China, attacking foreigners and killing more than 200 missionaries and thousands of Chinese Christians. They then besieged diplomats in their embassies in Peking. The foreign powers responded by organizing an international army to march on Peking and rescue the diplomats. The army defeated the Boxers and forced Tz'u-hsi to grant them new concessions. China agreed to allow foreign troops to be stationed on Chinese soil and to allow foreign naval vessels to patrol Chinese rivers and coastal waters.

The Revolution of 1911

In 1908, the empress Tz'u-hsi died. She had named a two-year-old prince, P'u-yi, to succeed her. P'u-yi would be the last emperor of China. In 1911, revolutionaries overthrew the government and proclaimed a republic.

The leading figure in the Revolution of 1911 was Dr. Sun Yat-sen. Sun had led revolutionaries in earlier uprisings against the Manchu. However, he was living in the United States when the revolution broke out in 1911. Sun returned to China at once and was named the first president of the Chinese Republic. He also helped found the Kuomintang (KWOH mihn TANG), or Nationalist party.

The new republic faced civil war in the provinces. Military leaders known as warlords fought one another and looted the countryside. Amid this confusion, Sun worked to build a united, powerful, and independent China. He set out a revolutionary program called "Three Principles of the People." The principles were political unity, democracy, and a basic living for all Chinese.

Sun was influenced by his travels in the United States and Western Europe. He wanted China to have the same high standard of living he saw in these nations. Sun believed that China had to be completely reorganized to achieve this goal. In the years ahead, Sun and the Kuomintang would struggle to make China a powerful modern nation.

SECTION 2 REVIEW

1. **Locate:** (a) Manchuria, (b) Canton, (c) Vladivostok, (d) Formosa.

2. **Identify:** (a) Manchu, (b) Treaty of Nanking, (c) Taiping Rebellion, (d) Open Door Policy, (e) Tz'u-hsi, (f) Boxer Rebellion, (g) Sun Yat-sen, (h) Kuomintang.

3. **Define:** extraterritoriality.

4. (a) What caused the Opium War? (b) What was the outcome of the war?

5. (a) Which nations gained spheres of influence in China? (b) What privileges did they have in their spheres of influence?

6. What were the Three Principles of the People proposed by Sun Yat-sen?

7. **Critical Thinking** Why do you think Chinese reformers met with such strong resistance?

3 Modernizing Japan

READ TO UNDERSTAND

☐ How Japanese ports were opened to foreigners.

☐ What the purpose and results of the Meiji reforms were.

☐ Why Japan expanded in Asia in the late 1800s.

☐ *Vocabulary:* zaibatsu.

The Japanese have long used slogans as a way of stating in few words what their goals as a people ought to be. From about 500 to 700, when the Japanese were borrowing heavily from Chinese culture, their slogan was "Japanese spirit, Chinese knowledge." In the 1800s, when Japan was faced with the menacing power of western nations, their slogan was "Expel the barbarians." But when the "barbarians" turned their guns on Japanese forts, the Japanese took up a new slogan, "Eastern morale, Western arts." With this slogan to guide them, the Japanese quickly set about making their country a rich industrial nation with a strong modern military.

Tokugawa Japan

In the 1600s, you will recall, Japanese rulers expelled Europeans from their land and forbade Japanese to leave the country. Only one Dutch ship was allowed to visit Nagasaki each year. For 200 years, the Tokugawa shoguns were strong enough to enforce this policy of isolation.

The shoguns created a strong unified government in Japan. They established a system of centralized feudalism that rested on a rigidly controlled economic and social order. The samurai were the highest class. Below them were the peasants. The lowest social class were merchants. (See page 278.)

During 200 years of peace under the Tokugawa shoguns, commerce and trade within Japan expanded. As a result, Japanese

Although the Tokugawa shoguns had isolated Japan, the Japanese kept up some contacts with the outside world. This painting shows a Red Seal Ship, one of a few Japanese ships allowed to trade in foreign ports.

merchants often were wealthier than the samurai. Increasingly, these wealthy merchants resented their low social status.

At the same time, discontented samurai were organizing revolts against the Tokugawa shogun. They were encouraged by scholars who argued that the shogun had seized power unlawfully from the true ruler, the emperor. By the 1800s, these opposition forces posed a serious threat to the Tokugawa government. Criticism of the government grew in the 1850s when foreigners reappeared in Japan.

An End to Isolation

In 1853, the United States sent a naval force to Japan under the command of Commodore Matthew C. Perry to open diplomatic negotiations with the Japanese government. Perry carried a letter from the American President that presented three demands to the Japanese: (1) that the Japanese grant the United States the right to trade with their country, (2) that they guarantee the safety of American sailors shipwrecked in Japanese waters, and (3) that they allow American ships to take on food,

fuel, and water at Japanese ports. Perry told the Japanese that he would return the next year for their answer. He made it clear that the alternative to a treaty granting these rights would be war.

Some Japanese leaders opposed yielding to the Americans, but other, more realistic voices, were aware of America's growing military power. They argued:

> If we try to drive them away, they will immediately commence hostilities, and then we shall be obliged to fight. In time, the country would be put to an immense expense, and the people [would] be plunged into misery. Rather than allow this, as we are not the equals of foreigners in the mechanical arts, let us have relations with foreign countries, learn their drills and tactics, and it will not be too late then to declare war.

This point of view carried the day, and, when Perry returned in 1854, Japan signed the Treaty of Kanagawa with the United States. The treaty opened up two Japanese ports to foreign trade and met the other American demands.

This treaty marked the end of Japanese isolation. Japan, like China, soon had to grant further concessions to foreign powers. In the late 1850s and in the 1860s, the Tokugawa government signed "unequal treaties" with the United States and the major European powers. The treaties gave these foreign countries control over Japanese tariffs, extensive trading rights in Japan, and the right of extraterritoriality.

The Meiji Period

The treaties granting privileges to foreigners aroused fierce opposition to the shogun among the Japanese. In southern Japan, samurai leaders bitterly denounced the foreigners, who were arriving in growing numbers. The samurai rallied around the emperor and proclaimed a restoration of imperial rule.

In 1868, the last Tokugawa shogun resigned, and the emperor, who was only 15 years old, moved his capital from Kyoto to Tokyo. He took the name Meiji (may jee), meaning "enlightened government." During the Meiji period, from 1868 to 1912, the Japanese government embarked on a course that transformed the country from a feudal state into a modern industrial nation.

An end to feudalism. Leaders of the Meiji government were determined to save Japan from foreign control by building up its political, military, and economic strength. They therefore decided to abandon the centralized feudalism of the Tokugawa period. By ending feudalism, they reshaped the political and social structure of Japan. Large landowners were persuaded to turn their fiefs, or vast estates, over to the emperor. They were paid for their lands and were given high positions in government.

Other reforms introduced at this time affected all classes in Japan. The samurai class lost power and prestige because the Meiji government made all classes equal before the law. Moreover, in 1872, Japan introduced a system of universal military service. This meant peasants and merchants as well as samurai would serve in the armed forces. The samurai were no longer the only class with the right to bear arms, a privilege that had been a major source of their power and prestige.

Constitutional government. In 1884, the emperor asked Ito Hirobumi, a Japanese official, to draft a constitution for Japan. Ito visited the United States and several European nations to study their constitutional governments. He met with Bismarck and was especially impressed with the constitutional system of government in Germany. On his return to Japan, Ito drafted a constitution based in part on the German model.

In 1889, the emperor presented the constitution to the Japanese people. The Meiji constitution established a two-house diet, or parliament. But the Diet had limited power because the emperor had the greatest authority. He could issue laws, veto laws passed by the Diet, and declare war. In practice, however, ministers appointed by the emperor did the actual governing.

Economic and Social Changes

During the Meiji period, Japan moved rapidly to strengthen its economy. The government led the effort to modernize Japan by sponsoring new industries. Once again, the Meiji leaders borrowed ideas from abroad. Japanese visited factories in Europe and the United States. The government hired thousands of foreign engineers to teach their skills in Japan.

The government built defense industries such as shipyards and munitions plants. It also encouraged the mining of coal and iron and developed a modern communication system by building railroads and stringing telegraph lines. Finally, it supported consumer industries such as textile manufacturing.

In the 1880s, the Meiji government decided to sell some of its factories and mills to private businesspeople. A few wealthy families, known as **zaibatsu** (ZĪ baht soo), bought the chief industries and came to dominate the Japanese economy. Families such as the Mitsubishi and Mitsui owned many large companies and controlled whole industries.

In Japan, cooperation among companies was more important than competition, so companies were often merged to make them more efficient. By 1914, the combination of government support and private initiative had made Japan a powerful industrial nation.

Yukichi Fukuzawa, a Japanese scholar, made many trips to Europe and the United States during the late 1800s. Fukuzawa enthusiastically supported modernization in Japan. In these excerpts from his autobiography, he expresses his interest in western ideas.

From Fukuzawa's Autobiography

During this mission in Europe, I tried to learn some of the most commonplace details of foreign culture. I did not care to study scientific or technical subjects while on the journey, because I could study them as well from books after I had returned home. But I felt that I had to learn the more common matters of daily life directly from the people because the Europeans would not describe them in books as being too obvious. Yet to us those common matters were the most difficult to comprehend.

For instance, when I saw a hospital, I wanted to know how it was run—who paid the running expenses; when I visited a bank, I wished to learn how the money was deposited and paid out. By similar firsthand queries [questions], I learned something of the postal system and the military conscription [draft] then in force in France but not in England. A perplexing institution was representative government.

When I asked a gentleman what the "election law" was and what kind of an institution the Parliament really was, he simply replied with a smile, meaning, I suppose, that no intelligent person was expected to ask such a question. But these were the things most difficult of all for me to understand. In this connection, I learned that there were different political parties . . . who were always "fighting" against each other in the government.

For some time it was beyond my comprehension to understand what they were "fighting" for, and what was meant, anyway, by "fighting" in peace time. "This man and that man are 'enemies' in the House," they would tell me. But these "enemies" were to be seen at the same table, eating and drinking with each other. I felt as if I could not make much out of this. It took me a long time, with some tedious thinking, before I could gather a general notion of these . . . mysterious facts.

1. What type of things did Fukuzawa want to learn during his trip?

2. **Critical Thinking** Why do you think representative government was so puzzling to Fukuzawa?

Industrialization transformed Japanese society. Millions of people gave up farming and moved to the cities to work in factories. Because the samurai no longer enjoyed their old privileges, many of them became officers in the Japanese army and navy. Others went into business or government.

As part of its program of modernization, the government created a new educational system. By 1900, almost all Japanese children were enrolled in elementary schools. Some students continued their education in middle schools and high schools. The government also set up commercial and technical schools. At the top of the system were prestigious imperial universities, which admitted only a small number of outstanding students.

Japanese Expansion in the Pacific

By 1900, Japan was reaping the benefits of modernization. It negotiated new treaties with western nations. It withdrew privileges such as extraterritoriality and regained full control over its own tariffs.

As Japan gained strength, it undertook imperialist ventures. As you have read, Japanese expansion in Korea led to war with China in 1894. After defeating China, Japan acquired Taiwan and the same trading privileges enjoyed by western powers in China.

Ten years later, Japan surprised people in the West by winning a stunning victory over Russia. The Russo-Japanese War broke out in 1904 over rival Russian and Japanese claims in

Under Meiji rulers, Japan modernized rapidly. It financed the building of modern factories and imported textile machinery and other western inventions. This 1883 print shows people stopping to watch the first electric street lamps being lighted in Tokyo.

Manchuria. The Japanese army forced the Russians to retreat from Manchuria, and the Japanese navy defeated two Russian fleets.

In 1905, President Theodore Roosevelt invited Japanese and Russian diplomats to meet in Portsmouth, New Hampshire. There they worked out a treaty ending the war. Japan acquired Port Arthur and concessions in southern Manchuria from Russia. Japan thus gained a foothold for an empire on the Asian mainland. Furthermore, the Russo-Japanese War showed the world that an Asian power could defeat a major European nation.

SECTION 3 REVIEW

1. **Identify:** (a) Matthew C. Perry, (b) Treaty of Kanagawa, (c) Ito Hirobumi, (d) Russo-Japanese War.

2. **Define:** zaibatsu.

3. Which groups in Japanese society opposed the Tokugawa shogun in the 1800s? Why?

4. Why did the United States want a treaty with Japan in 1853?

5. (a) What led to the Russo-Japanese War? (b) List two results of the war.

6. **Critical Thinking** Why do you think Japan was able to modernize in the late 1800s while China was not?

4 Southeast Asia and the Pacific

READ TO UNDERSTAND

☐ What civilizations influenced the peoples of Southeast Asia.

☐ Why European powers scrambled for colonies in Southeast Asia.

☐ How the United States acquired colonies in the Pacific.

☐ How imperialism affected the peoples of Southeast Asia.

Southeast Asia was another area of interest to western powers during the Age of Imperialism. As you read in Chapter 15, during the 1500s, several European nations competed for control of the spice trade in the East Indies. Later, European nations extended their influence over most of Southeast Asia.

Peoples of Southeast Asia

Southeast Asia includes the area of the Asian mainland south of China. This area stretches from present-day Bangladesh in the west to present-day Vietnam in the east. Southeast Asia also includes the Philippine Islands, the East Indies, and Indonesia. (See the map on page 596.)

Southeast Asia is home to peoples with many different languages, customs, and political systems. Geography has influenced the peoples of Southeast Asia. The language and customs of people in many of the mountainous regions of Southeast Asia often differ from those of nearby people in the lowland areas. In addition, the cultures of the peoples who live on the islands of Southeast Asia are different from those of the mainland peoples. ■

The early civilizations of India and China also influenced the peoples of Southeast Asia. Traders and Buddhist missionaries from India helped spread both Hindu and Buddhist beliefs. Indian culture had its greatest impact on the area that today includes Burma, Thailand, Laos, Cambodia, and the southern part of Vietnam. During the T'ang dynasty, China extended its influence into northern Vietnam. In the 1200s, Arab and Indian Muslims carried Islam to Indonesia.

When Europeans first arrived in Southeast Asia, they found a region with many kingdoms and forms of government. In some areas, powerful rulers united the people. Today, the ruins of Angkor Wat, an enormous temple built in the 1100s, recall the splendor of the Khmer Empire in Cambodia. In other parts of Southeast Asia, there was no strong central authority. For example, when the Spanish reached the Philippines in the 1500s, they found only minor local rulers.

In the 1500s, when Europeans entered the spice trade, there were many separate states with their own cultural, social, and political traditions in Southeast Asia. Geography, trade rivalries, and religious differences further divided the peoples of the region, so they did not respond in a united fashion to the coming of the Europeans.

The Spice Trade

The early spice trade had little direct effect on the peoples of Southeast Asia. Portuguese, Spanish, and Dutch traders tried to drive Arab, Indian, and Chinese merchants out of the spice trade. They also competed fiercely with one another. They built trading posts along the coasts but did not extend their influence inland.

Only in the Philippines did Europeans have an immediate impact. In 1571, the Spanish conquered the Philippine Islands and sent a Spanish governor-general to rule the colony. For the first time, the Philippines were united under a single government. Catholic missionaries entered the islands with Spanish officials and converted many of the people to Christianity.

The Spanish seized the Philippines because they wanted to establish a direct trade route between Asia and their empire in the Americas. Spanish ships carried silver from the New World to the Philippines. They then sailed to China to buy porcelains and silk or to the Spice Islands to buy spices.

Scramble for Colonies in Southeast Asia

In the 1700s, Europeans developed new interests in Southeast Asia as they shifted from buying spices to developing cash crops such as sugar, coffee, and rice. To ensure a supply of these crops, Europeans took over large parts of the region and set up huge plantations. Later, as European nations industrialized, they also looked to Southeast Asia as a source of raw materials such as tin, rubber, and oil.

During the 1800s, the Dutch expanded their trading posts in Southeast Asia into a colony called the Dutch East Indies. By this time, however, Britain and France had become

"The eruption began on Sunday afternoon. We did not take much notice at first, until the sounds grew very loud. Then we noticed that Krakatoa was completely enveloped in smoke. Afterwards came on the thick darkness, so intense that I could not see my hand before my eyes.

"About 6 A.M. I was walking along the beach. Some of the darkness had cleared off. Looking out to sea, I noticed a dark black object through the gloom, traveling toward the shore. A second glance convinced me that it was a lofty ridge of water many feet high. I turned and ran for my life. In a few minutes, I heard the water with a loud roar break upon the shore.

"A few yards more brought me to some rising ground, and here the torrent of water overtook me. I gave up all for lost, as I saw with dismay how high the wave still was. I remember nothing more until I found myself clinging to a palm tree."

As the diary of this survivor shows, the violent eruption of the volcano Krakatoa in 1883 had devastating effects. The volcano, located in the Strait of Sudra between Java and Sumatra, lay in one of the busiest sea routes of Asia. (See the map on page 596.) Krakatoa's eruption sent tsunamis, or tidal waves, over 100 feet high crashing against the coast of Java and Sumatra. The waves wiped out busy seaport towns, killing over 36,000 people.

The eruption of Krakatoa had global as well as local effects. When Krakatoa exploded, people in India and Australia, thousands of miles away, and even as far distant as Madagascar, off the coast of Africa, heard the sound. The tidal waves were also felt at a great distance. In New Zealand, huge tides swept the harbor and threw docked ships onto dry land.

Krakatoa had striking effects on the atmosphere. Three months after the eruption, spectacular sunsets caused by volcanic dust were seen in the eastern United States. "Soon after 5 o'clock," reported a New York newspaper, "the western horizon suddenly flamed into a brilliant scarlet. Many thought a great fire was in progress." The dust cut down on the sunlight reaching the earth, causing several years of unusually cold weather.

The eruption of Krakatoa focused worldwide attention on Asia. It also helped foster a new sense of global interconnection. Many people realized that the most distant corners of the planet were really not as far away as they had thought.

1. What effects did Krakatoa have on faraway places?

2. **Critical Thinking** (a) Why might the eruption of Krakatoa have fostered a new sense of global interconnection? (b) Can you think of other natural disasters that have achieved the same result?

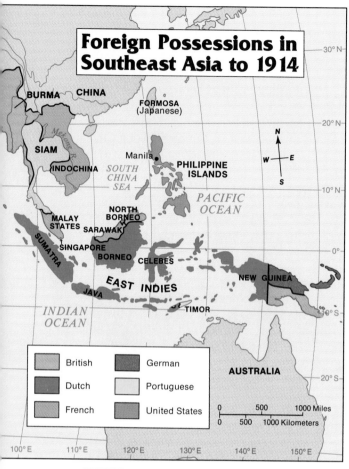

Foreign Possessions in Southeast Asia to 1914

Legend:
- British
- Dutch
- French
- German
- Portuguese
- United States

MAP STUDY The spice trade originally attracted Europeans to Southeast Asia in the 1500s. In the 1800s, Europeans were more interested in cash crops such as sugar and rice and in natural resources such as oil and rubber. Which European nations claimed territory on the mainland?

the chief European rivals in the region. It was the fierce competition between these two nations that led to a scramble for colonies on the mainland of Southeast Asia.

To protect the eastern frontier of India, Britain took over Burma piece by piece between 1820 and 1890. Britain also established control over Malaya and the island of Singapore, which commands an important sea route to China. While Britain extended its influence over these regions, France established the colony of French Indochina. Both the British and the French planned to use their colonies as stepping stones to southern China.

During the scramble for colonies, only Siam, today called Thailand, escaped European control. During the 1800s, Siamese rulers introduced western technology to modernize their country. They also encouraged trade with western nations. Furthermore, the Siamese skillfully exploited the rivalry between Britain and France. By establishing their kingdom as a neutral buffer between the British in Burma and the French in Indochina, the Siamese kept themselves free from foreign control.

Western Expansion in the Pacific

Even before the Age of Imperialism, several western powers had taken over various Pacific islands. As you have read, Spain conquered the Philippines, and Britain set up colonies in Australia and New Zealand. In the late 1800s, Britain, Germany, and the United States seized other islands.

The United States, too, expanded in the Pacific region after the American Civil War. As more and more American merchant ships began trading with China and Japan, they needed friendly ports where they could take on fuel. In addition, the United States wanted naval bases to protect American trade. Thus, the United States began to take control of islands scattered across the Pacific. American interest in Southeast Asia and the Pacific also grew as a result of a war the United States fought to free Cuba from Spain.*

The Spanish-American War took place in 1898. One American target in the war was a Spanish fleet in Manila Bay, the chief harbor in the Philippines. An American fleet commanded by Commodore George Dewey destroyed the Spanish ships and paved the way for American victory in the war. As part of the peace settlement, the United States acquired the Philippine Islands and Guam. However, the Americans first had to fight Filipino revolutionaries who wanted independence. In 1898, the United States annexed Hawaii, where

---

* You will read more about the causes of the Spanish-American War in Chapter 27.

American merchants and sugar growers had extensive interests.

Many Americans were strongly opposed to American expansion in the Pacific. One New York newspaper published this response to Rudyard Kipling's call to "take up the white man's burden" (see page 578):

> We've taken up the white man's burden
> Of ebony and brown;
> Now will you kindly tell us, Rudyard,
> How we may put it down?

Southeast Asia Under Colonial Rule

Western imperialism greatly affected Southeast Asia. Almost everywhere, local leaders were replaced by foreign officials. The economies of the region also changed. The European powers wanted their colonies to produce cash crops and raw materials for export. As a result, the peoples of Southeast Asia became dependent on international markets, where prices could rise and fall sharply.

A few independence movements developed in Southeast Asia. The first nationalist revolution began in the 1880s in the Philippines. In fact, Filipinos who were rebelling against Spanish rule helped American forces in the Spanish-American War, thinking an American victory would bring independence. After the war, Filipino nationalists were bitterly disappointed when the United States refused to grant them independence at once. They then turned their struggle against the United States. Other colonial powers also faced rebellions in Southeast Asia. However, western powers were confident that they could continue to rule their colonies indefinitely.

Many westerners had a romantic view of life on the islands of the South Pacific. They believed the people of these islands led simple lives, unspoiled by the Industrial Revolution. In 1891, Paul Gauguin, a French painter, went to live in Tahiti. Once there, he was horrified to find that missionaries had introduced western ways. He then painted the Tahitian people as he thought they had lived.

SECTION 4 REVIEW

1. **Locate:** (a) Philippine Islands, (b) Burma, (c) Malaya, (d) Indochina, (e) Siam.

2. What different civilizations influenced the peoples of Southeast Asia?

3. Why did Spain seize the Philippine Islands in the late 1500s?

4. (a) What products did Europeans want from Southeast Asia during the Age of Imperialism? (b) What countries established colonies in Southeast Asia?

5. How did the United States acquire the Philippine Islands?

6. Describe two effects of colonial rule in Southeast Asia.

7. **Critical Thinking** Why do you think the Filipino nationalists expected the United States to grant the Philippines immediate independence?

Summary

1. **As the Mogul Empire collapsed, the British gained a larger role in India.** In 1858, the British government took control of India. The British tied the Indian economy to their own but also improved transportation and medical care. By the late 1800s, nationalists were calling for independence.

2. **In the 1800s, the Manchu dynasty declined, and western powers gained influence in China.** After the Opium War showed China's weakness, western nations acquired spheres of influence. Chinese efforts at reform failed. Then in 1911, revolutionaries overthrew the Manchu dynasty and set up a republic.

3. **In the late 1800s, Japan started on the road to modernization.** Its long period of isolation ended when the United States forced Japan to sign a treaty opening its ports to foreign trade. During the Meiji period, Japan was transformed from a feudal state into a modern industrial power. It defeated China and Russia and expanded into Asia.

4. **In the 1800s, most of Southeast Asia was colonized by western imperial powers.** Britain and France divided much of the mainland. Only Siam escaped European control. The United States acquired the Philippines and other islands in the Pacific.

Recalling Facts

Indicate whether each of the following statements refers to India, China, Japan, or Southeast Asia.

1. Meiji leaders introduced a program for modernization.

2. Grievances against the British touched off the Sepoy Rebellion.

3. The Opium War resulted in the first of the "unequal treaties."

4. A strong army and navy were used to defeat Russia in 1905.

5. Sun Yat-sen worked to build a unified country.

6. Britain encouraged farmers to grow cotton for its factories.

7. Europeans sought tin, rubber, and oil.

Chapter Checkup

1. (a) Why did the British government end the East India Company's control of India? (b) How did the policies of the British government differ from those of the East India Company?

2. Describe the impact of British rule in each of the following aspects of Indian life: (a) political; (b) economic; (c) social.

3. (a) What attitude did the Manchu dynasty take toward European merchants in the 1600s and 1700s? (b) How did the Opium War affect relations between China and western powers?

4. Describe how each of the following affected the Manchu dynasty: (a) Taiping Rebellion; (b) Open Door Policy; (c) Revolution of 1911.

5. How did the Chinese try to end western imperialism?

6. (a) Why did Commodore Perry visit Japan? (b) What effect did his visit have on Japan?

7. What steps did the Japanese take to modernize their nation?

8. Why did European nations want to control Southeast Asia during the 1800s?

Critical Thinking

1. **Analyzing** Benjamin Disraeli called India "the brightest jewel in the British Crown." (a) What do you think he meant by this

statement? (b) Why do you think he felt that India was important to Britain?

2. **Synthesizing** In the 1700s, China was the richest, most powerful nation in the world. Yet within less than 100 years it was carved into spheres of influence. How did this happen? Give specific reasons to explain your answer.

3. **Relating Past to Present** (a) Why do you think Japan was able to industrialize so quickly in the 1800s? (b) How do you think the Japanese policy of selective borrowing from other nations affected its rapid industrialization? (c) What present-day examples of Japanese success in industry can you cite?

Developing Basic Skills

1. **Analyzing a Primary Source** Reread the special feature on page 592. (a) What kind of document is included in the feature? (b) What type of information did the author want to learn on his trip to Europe? (c) What did he find most confusing during his trip? Why? (d) Do you think the document is a good source of information about Japanese attitudes toward Europe in the late 1800s? Why or why not?

2. **Map Reading** Compare the maps on pages 587 and 596. (a) What nation's sphere of influence included Korea? (b) What three nations possessed New Guinea? (c) What nations had spheres of influence in China? (d) Which of these nations had possessions in Southeast Asia? (e) Based on both maps, which nation do you think was most powerful in eastern Asia? Explain.

Writing About History

Using Quotations

Some of the notes you will take while researching your paper will probably include direct quotations from an authority or a primary source. You may not want to use the entire quotation. If you use only a part, you indicate the omitted words with ellipses (. . .). Examine this quotation from "A Japanese View of Europe," on page 592 and compare it with the original document to see how ellipses are used.

> ". . . I tried to learn some of the most commonplace details of foreign culture. . . . For instance, when I saw a hospital, I wanted to know how it was run . . . when I visited a bank, I wished to learn how the money was deposited and paid out. . . ."

Note that there are four dots in an ellipsis at the end of a sentence because one dot represents the period.

Practice: Quote a passage from your textbook using ellipses to indicate the words you have omitted.

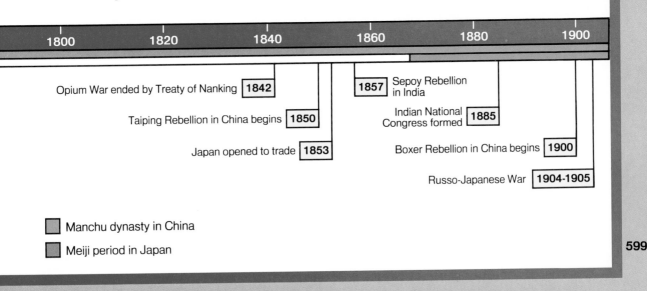

1800	1820	1840	1860	1880	1900

Opium War ended by Treaty of Nanking 1842

Taiping Rebellion in China begins 1850

Japan opened to trade 1853

1857 Sepoy Rebellion in India

Indian National Congress formed 1885

Boxer Rebellion in China begins 1900

Russo-Japanese War 1904-1905

Manchu dynasty in China

Meiji period in Japan

Revolution and Independence in Latin America

27

(1750–1917)

By 1825, the nations of Latin America had won independence from Spain.
Freedom, however remained an unfulfilled dream for many people. In the early
1900s, Mexican peasants, most of them Indians like the ones in this painting by
José Orozco, struggled to repossess their land.

James Biggs managed to write with a steady hand despite the swelling sea
that tossed the sloop *Leander* through deepening troughs. "Generally, I can
say," he wrote, "that we are engaged in an expedition to some part of the
Spanish dominions, probably South America, with a view of assisting the inhabitants in throwing off the oppressive yoke of the parent country and establishing a government for themselves."

Biggs was an American adventurer. In February 1806, he had thrown in his lot with Francisco Miranda, the son of an aristocratic family from Venezuela. Miranda had recruited 200 men, including Biggs, and hurried them on board the *Leander* and two smaller ships.

"We may be plucking a thousand daggers on our heads," Biggs wrote ominously, "but we presume our Conductor [Miranda] knows what he is doing and will lead us to great exploits and splendid fortunes." Although Biggs and most of the others on this daring expedition were interested only in "splendid fortunes," Miranda had another goal. For 30 years, Miranda had been scheming to free the Spanish colonies in South America. This expedition, he hoped, would spark a revolt against Spain.

Miranda had badly miscalculated, however. When he arrived off the coast of Venezuela, he found that the Spanish had been forewarned of his attack. No general uprising occurred, and Miranda and his forces barely escaped with their lives. Nevertheless, Miranda was not discouraged. Four years later, he returned to Venezuela, as you will read in this chapter.

Miranda has often been called "the Morning Star of Independence" for his work in the cause of freedom for South America. In Latin America, as in Europe, nationalism and liberalism were threatening the old order during the 1800s. The success of the American Revolution made a great impression on the people of Latin America. It gave them hope that they, too, might win freedom from colonial rule. ■

1 The Wars of Independence

READ TO UNDERSTAND

☐ **What the sources of discontent with Spanish rule in Latin America were.**

☐ **How Haiti won independence from France.**

☐ **How revolutionary leaders helped the people of Mexico and Central and South America win independence.**

☐ *Vocabulary:* **peninsular, creole, mestizo.**

In the small Mexican village of Dolores, the parish priest, Father Miguel Hidalgo (hih DAL goh), rang the church bell to call his people together. He had a stirring message for them.

"My children," Father Hidalgo proclaimed, "will you not be free? Will you make the effort to recover from the hated Spaniards the land stolen from your forefathers 300 years ago?"

That day, September 16, 1810, Father Hidalgo raised a battle cry for independence from Spain—the "grito de Dolores"—that would echo through Mexico for 100 years. September 16 is celebrated today as Mexico's Independence Day.

Like the 13 British colonies in North America, other colonies in the Americas had many grievances against their European rulers. In the late 1700s, dissatisfaction increased. Leaders like Father Hidalgo had read Enlightenment writers such as Locke, Voltaire, and Rousseau. The success of the American and French revolutions encouraged the peoples of Latin America* in their struggles for independence. In Mexico, Central and South America, and the West Indies, colonists began trying to gain control over their own affairs.

---

* Latin America is the term used to describe the part of the Western Hemisphere south of the United States where the Latin languages Spanish, French, and Portuguese are spoken.

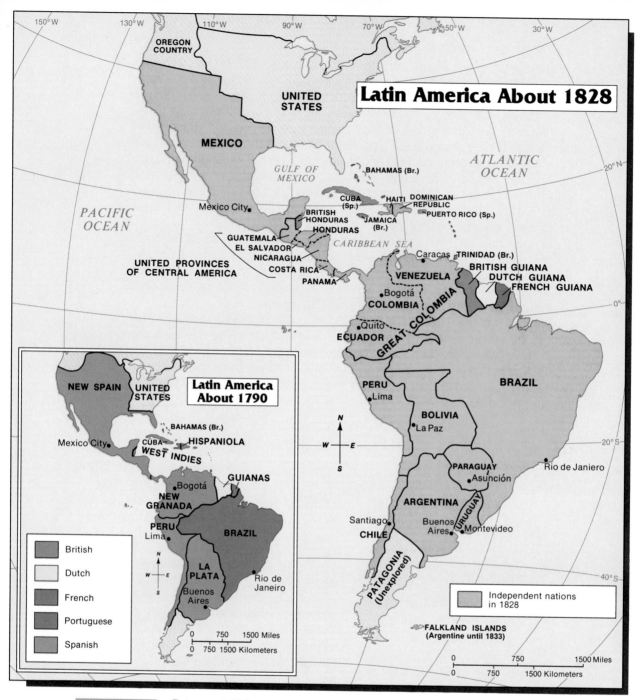

Latin America About 1828

OREGON COUNTRY

UNITED STATES

MEXICO

PACIFIC OCEAN

GULF OF MEXICO

Mexico City

BAHAMAS (Br.)

ATLANTIC OCEAN

CUBA (Sp.) HAITI DOMINICAN REPUBLIC

PUERTO RICO (Sp.)

BRITISH HONDURAS

JAMAICA (Br.)

GUATEMALA-
EL SALVADOR
NICARAGUA

HONDURAS

CARIBBEAN SEA

UNITED PROVINCES
OF CENTRAL AMERICA

COSTA RICA

PANAMA

Caracas TRINIDAD (Br.)

VENEZUELA

BRITISH GUIANA
DUTCH GUIANA
FRENCH GUIANA

Bogotá

COLOMBIA

GREAT COLOMBIA

Quito

ECUADOR

PERU

Lima

BRAZIL

BOLIVIA

La Paz

Rio de Janiero

PARAGUAY

Asunción

ARGENTINA

URUGUAY

Santiago

Buenos
Aires

Montevideo

CHILE

N W E S

PATAGONIA
(Unexplored)

Independent nations
in 1828

FALKLAND ISLANDS
(Argentine until 1833)

0   750   1500 Miles
0   750 1500 Kilometers

Latin America About 1790

NEW SPAIN UNITED STATES

Mexico City

BAHAMAS (Br.)

CUBA

HISPANIOLA

WEST INDIES

GUIANAS

Bogotá

NEW GRANADA

PERU

Lima

BRAZIL

N W E S

LA PLATA

Buenos
Aires

Rio de
Janeiro

British
Dutch
French
Portuguese
Spanish

0   750   1500 Miles
0   750 1500 Kilometers

MAP STUDY   *Between 1804 and 1828, most of Latin America won independence from European rule. Which of the nations that won independence in this period were part of the Spanish territory of La Plata in 1790?*

Sources of Discontent

As you have read, Spain built a colonial empire in the Americas during the 1500s. Over the next 300 years, the rigid social structure that emerged caused much discontent. At the top of colonial society was a small, privileged class of peninsulares. A **peninsular** was an official sent from Spain to rule the colonies. (The term peninsular referred to the Iberian Peninsula on which Spain and Portugal were located.) Only peninsulares could hold high offices in colonial governments or in the Catholic Church, a powerful force in the colonies. The Spanish king often granted peninsulares huge estates in the colonies, so they became extremely wealthy.

Below the peninsulares were the **creoles** (KREE ohls), descendants of Spanish settlers who were born in the Americas. In theory, creoles were equal to the peninsulares, but in practice they were barred from the highest official positions. Nevertheless, many creoles became businessmen and wealthy land and mine owners.

After the creoles came the **mestizos** (mehs TEE zohs), people of mixed European and Indian heritage. Mestizos held many different jobs in the colonial economy. During the 1600s and 1700s, the mestizo population grew rapidly. At the lowest level of colonial society were Indians and African slaves. African slaves were brought to the Americas to work on the plantations and in the mines.

Except for the peninsulares, each group had reason to resent colonial rule. Creoles objected to colonial rule because it gave the European-born peninsulares superior social, political, and economic positions. Furthermore, many creoles had been educated in Europe, where they had absorbed Enlightenment ideas about liberty and equality. On their return home, they helped spread these ideas. Eventually, Spain banned the writings of Rousseau and Voltaire in its colonies because they were considered a threat to Spanish rule.

Mestizos disliked colonial rule because they were treated as third-class citizens by both the Spanish and the creoles. In theory, Indians were free, but many were forced to work for Europeans. Both Indians and African slaves were ready to fight for freedom.

Early Revolts

During the late 1700s and early 1800s, uprisings occurred in several parts of Latin America. In 1781, the Indian leader Tupac Amaru II led a revolt against Spanish rule in Peru. The Indian army was poorly armed, and it was soon defeated by Spanish troops. In the 1780s, nearly 20,000 mestizos and Indians marched on Bogotá, in what is today Colombia, to protest high taxes imposed by Spain. The Spanish eventually crushed this revolt and executed the rebel leaders.

As you read at the beginning of the chapter, Francisco Miranda, a creole leader, tried unsuccessfully to organize an uprising against Spanish rule in 1806. Miranda returned to Venezuela in 1810. This time, he had the support of the people of Caracas. With other rebel leaders, he ousted the Spanish and set up the first Venezuelan Republic. However, jealousies among the revolutionary leaders allowed Spain to regain control of the colony. Miranda was captured and sent to Spain, where he died in 1816. Although the revolution led by Miranda failed, the Spanish colonies would soon wage successful wars for independence.

Independence for Haiti

While Spanish subjects in the Americas were plotting against their colonial rulers, a successful uprising took place in the French West Indies. The French ruled Haiti, the western part of the island of Hispaniola. In the 1700s, a few French families owned huge sugar plantations worked by a half-million African slaves who were brutally mistreated.

When the French Revolution broke out in 1789, the people of Haiti quickly adopted the ideals of "liberty, equality, and fraternity" proclaimed by the revolutionaries in Paris. When their hopes for freedom were disappointed, thousands of slaves revolted in 1791. They murdered their masters and destroyed many plantations. For the next 13 years, Haiti was the scene of violent struggles as slaves fought the French for freedom.

The leading figure in this struggle was Toussaint L'Ouverture (too SAN loo vehr TYOOR), a former slave. By 1801, L'Ouverture had driven the French from Haiti and conquered the Spanish-held eastern part of Hispaniola. He declared the entire island free from foreign control. In France, Napoleon was outraged by the loss of Haiti, which had been the source of huge profits from the sugar trade. He decided to restore French rule in Haiti. He sent his brother-in-law, General Charles Leclerc, and 20,000 soldiers to carry out his plan.

Toussaint L'Ouverture led the people of Haiti in a successful revolution against French rule. Although Toussaint was taken prisoner by the French, he warned before his death: "In overthrowing me, the French have only felled the tree of black liberty in Saint Domingue [Haiti]. It will shoot up again for it is deeply rooted and its roots are many."

The French soldiers suffered heavy casualties at the hands of the Haitians. Moreover, an unanticipated enemy—yellow fever—killed hundreds of French troops each week. Leclerc finally tricked Toussaint by agreeing to peace. He then lured him to a dinner party at which the Haitian leader was taken prisoner. Later, L'Ouverture was sent to France, where he died in prison in 1803.

Two other Haitian leaders, Jean Jacques Dessalines and Henri Christophe, took up the struggle. The fighting took a terrible toll. Finally, on January 1, 1804, Dessalines declared Haiti independent, making it the first independent nation in Latin America.

Elsewhere in Latin America, people watched events in Haiti with mixed feelings. Creole landowners, for example, were horrified by the slave revolt. But they were also encouraged to see that local revolutionaries could defeat a strong European power.

The Revolutionary Spirit Spreads

Spanish colonists were inspired by the revolutionary ideals spreading across Europe. During the early 1800s, events in Europe set off a series of successful revolts in Latin America.

In 1808, Napoleon conquered Spain and ousted the Spanish king Ferdinand VII. He then put his brother, Joseph Bonaparte, on the Spanish throne. The Spanish colonies in Latin America refused to recognize Joseph Bonaparte as king and began setting up their own governments.

After Napoleon's defeat in 1815, the European powers restored Ferdinand VII to his throne. Ferdinand tried to regain control of the Spanish colonies in Latin America. However, strong revolutionary leaders had emerged there who resisted the return of Spanish rule.

Simón Bolívar. Perhaps the best-known revolutionary leader was Simón Bolívar. He is often called "the Liberator" for his role in the Latin American wars of independence. Bolívar was born to a wealthy creole family in Caracas, Venezuela. He was educated in Spain and traveled in Europe during the French Revolution. Deeply moved by revolutionary ideals, Bolívar became a firm believer in Latin American independence. He once vowed: "I will never allow my hands to be idle nor my soul to rest until I have broken the shackles which chain us to Spain."

Bolívar also visited the United States and studied the republican form of government there. In 1810, he returned to Venezuela and fought alongside Miranda. Over the next nine years, Bolívar led rebel armies in a series of battles against Spain, but he did not shake Spain's hold on its colonies.

Finally, in August 1819, Bolívar led an army on a daring march from Venezuela, over the icecapped Andes, into Colombia. There he won a stunning victory over the Spanish. In December, he was named president of the Republic of Great Colombia, which included what is today Venezuela, Colombia, Ecuador, and Panama. (See the map on page 602.)

José de San Martín. While Bolívar was leading revolutionary forces in Colombia, another creole, José de San Martín, helped organize a rebel army in Argentina. In 1812, San Martín returned from Europe, where he had been educated, to join Argentina's struggle for independence. Argentina won its freedom in 1816.

A year later, San Martín joined forces with General Bernardo O'Higgins of Chile, and the two led their armies from Argentina across the southern Andes into Chile. Scaling heights as high as 15,000 feet (4,500 meters), the armies endured terrible hardships before advancing into Chile. There, the Spanish, who had never dreamed such a march was possible, were caught off guard and were forced to withdraw from Chile. By 1818, Chile had declared its independence. In the early 1820s, San Martín joined forces with Bolívar to help free Peru and Ecuador from Spanish rule.

Independence for Mexico and Central America

During the early 1800s, the people of Mexico also fought for independence from Spain. In 1810, Father Miguel Hidalgo, the creole priest you read about earlier, organized a large army of Indians who were dissatisfied with Spanish rule. Hidalgo captured several Mexican provinces. He then founded a government that reflected the ideals of the French Revolution. For example, he abolished slavery and returned land to the Indians. However, in 1811 Hidalgo was captured by troops who were loyal to Spain and was executed.

Another creole priest, José Morelos, took up the cause of Mexican independence. Like Hidalgo, Morelos was successful at first. He announced his goal of liberal reforms, including equal rights for all races and redistribution of land to poor peasants. Morelos's program angered the peninsulares and creoles, who helped Spanish troops suppress the revolt. In 1815, Morelos was captured and shot.

The Mexican war for independence dragged on. Eventually, both liberal and conservative groups united against Spain. In 1821, Agustín de Iturbide, a conservative who had once fought for Spain, declared Mexico an independent state. Because Spain had few remaining supporters, it was forced to recognize Mexican independence.

Iturbide proclaimed himself emperor of Mexico, but his unpopular rule was shortlived. In 1823, he was forced to abdicate, and a convention met to draw up a constitution. The constitution established Mexico as a republic with a president and a two-house congress.

Inspired by Mexico's example, creoles in Central America declared their independence from Spain in 1821. Two years later, they created the United Provinces of Central America, including what is today Nicaragua, Costa Rica, El Salvador, Honduras, and Guatemala. (See the map on page 602.)

Simón Bolívar led the fight for freedom from Spanish rule in much of South America. Like other revolutionary leaders, he was inspired by the ideas of the Enlightenment. True to these ideas, Bolívar freed his slaves and spent his personal fortune to finance wars for independence.

This painting uses symbols to tell the story of the Mexican struggle for independence. Father Miguel Hidalgo, at left, places a crown of laurel—the symbol of victory—on the head of a woman representing Mexico. The feathers in the crown worn by Mexico symbolize the nation's Indian heritage.

Brazil Gains Independence

Creoles in Brazil, who were descended from the Portuguese, also led the struggle for independence. However, Brazil won its independence more easily than its neighbors in Spanish America had. In 1808, when Napoleon invaded Portugal, the Portuguese royal family fled to safety in Brazil. In 1821, after the defeat of Napoleon, the Portuguese king returned home. But he left his son, Prince Pedro, in charge of Brazil. The creoles asked Prince Pedro to declare Brazil independent. They offered to make him ruler of the new nation.

In 1822, Pedro, who had lived in Brazil since he was ten, was proclaimed Emperor Pedro I. He agreed to accept a constitution that provided for freedom of the press and religion as well as an elected legislature.

By 1825, most colonies in Latin America had thrown off European rule. Ahead, the newly independent nations faced the difficult task of building stable governments.

SECTION 1 REVIEW

1. **Locate:** (a) Peru, (b) Bogotá, (c) Colombia, (d) Haiti, (e) Venezuela, (f) Chile.

2. **Identify:** (a) Francisco Miranda, (b) Toussaint L'Ouverture, (c) Simón Bolívar, (d) José de San Martín, (e) Miguel Hidalgo, (f) José Morelos.

3. **Define:** (a) peninsular, (b) creole, (c) mestizo.

4. (a) What European country ruled Haiti? (b) How did Haiti win independence?

5. How did Napoleon's conquest of Spain affect the Spanish colonies in America?

6. What reforms did Morelos want to introduce in Mexico?

7. **Critical Thinking** Compare the way Mexico and Brazil achieved independence.

606

2 Strengthening the New Nations

READO TO UNDERSTAND

☐ Why Latin America became divided into many nations.

☐ What problems the nations of Latin America faced.

☐ How the struggle between conservatives and liberals shaped Mexico in the 1800s.

☐ *Vocabulary:* regionalism, caudillo.

Simón Bolívar traveled endlessly, trying desperately to keep the lands he had liberated from breaking into smaller nations. During the wars of independence, Bolívar and other nationalists had dreamed of uniting the Spanish colonies into a single nation. They hoped that a common political and religious heritage would help unite the peoples of Latin America. But in the years after independence, the dream of unity faded as bitter rivalries surfaced. Discouraged at this turn of events, Bolívar headed into exile, sadly convinced that "America is ungovernable. He who serves a revolution plows the sea."

Barriers to Unity

The new nations of Latin America faced many problems that prevented unity. During the wars of independence, various political and social groups had joined in the struggle against Spain. After independence, however, these groups disagreed over what kind of government should be organized. Power struggles broke out among rival leaders, triggering violent civil wars.

Another barrier to unity was the diverse geography of Central and South America. Rugged mountains, high plateaus, the arid Atacama Desert, and the rain forests of the Amazon region limited contact between people. Rough terrain made trade and transporta-

---

THEN AND NOW The Gauchos of Argentina

Gauchos were the cowboys of Argentina. They lived on the pampas, open grassy plains, and made a living selling the hides of wild cattle and horses. Gauchos were daring and skillful horsemen. They rode in swift pursuit of cattle and horses using a boleadora—three stones or iron balls lashed together with a long leather thong—to entangle the legs of the animals.

Life on the pampas was scarcely glamorous. Gauchos lived in one-room mud huts that were shingled with grass mats. They slept on heaps of hides. Their traditional costume was a pair of wide-legged trousers, high boots, and a long woolen poncho that protected them from the cold and rain.

The introduction of barbed-wire fencing and refrigerated ships in the late 1800s marked the end of the gauchos' way of life. Refrigerated ships allowed people to raise cattle for meat instead of hides. Soon, cattle were fed in stalls rather than on the pampas. Farmers fenced in the open spaces on the pampas to grow wheat and alfalfa.

As the gauchos gave way to the farmers, their way of life passed into folklore. Payadors, guitar-playing cowboys, wrote songs praising the brave deeds of the gauchos. These songs became an important part of Argentine culture. One of the most popular figures in Argentine literature is the fictional gaucho hero Martín Fierro. His life was summed up in these lines:

A son am I of the rolling plain.
A gaucho born and bred;
For me the whole great world is small,
Believe me, my heart can hold it all,
The snake strikes not at my passing foot,
The sun burns not my head.

1. What developments made the gauchos obsolete?

2. **Critical Thinking** How does the celebration of gauchos in Argentine literature compare with the view of cowboys in the United States?

tion difficult and encouraged **regionalism,** loyalty to a small geographic area.

Because of their differing interests, 18 separate nations were established in Latin America. The Republic of Great Colombia, which Bolívar had organized, splintered into three separate countries: Colombia, Venezuela, and Ecuador. South America was further divided when Peru, Bolivia, Argentina, Chile, Paraguay, Uruguay, and Brazil set up their own governments. After gaining independence, the United Provinces of Central America broke up into five separate nations. On the island of Hispaniola, the Dominican Republic declared its independence from Haiti. (See the map on page 614.)

The Colonial Heritage

The newly independent nations of Latin America became republics. And most wrote constitutions modeled on the Constitution of the United States. Putting these constitutions into effect, however, proved to be difficult.

Unlike the 13 British colonies in North America, the Spanish colonies had no experience with representative government. During the colonial period, they had been under the absolute rule of the Spanish viceroy. In many of the new nations, ambitious leaders won the backing of the army and installed themselves as military dictators. These dictators, known as **caudillos** (kaw DEE yohs), stayed in power by force. They simply ignored constitutions that called for elections.

Social structure. The nations of Latin America inherited other problems from their colonial past. Rigid social and racial divisions created a stumbling block to representative government. Many creoles who had led the struggle for independence did not want to share political power with other classes once they had ousted the Spanish.

Mestizos, Indians, and blacks were angry at still being excluded from political power. Slavery was abolished, but neither blacks nor Indians had many rights. The majority of mestizos, Indians, and blacks worked on plantations and in mines owned by wealthy creoles. They deeply resented the social and political system that kept them in poverty.

Role of the Catholic Church. The Catholic Church had been a powerful political and economic force in Latin America during the colonial period. It remained so after independence. The church owned huge tracts of land and controlled education. You have seen that during the wars of independence, some members of the clergy, such as Father Miguel Hidalgo and José Morelos, fought for liberal ideas. However, high church officials often favored the interests of creole landowners over other classes. After independence, the church generally continued to be a conservative force, opposing far-reaching reform.

Economic problems. Economic conditions remained largely unchanged after independence. Although Latin America was rich in natural resources, the wealth was controlled by a handful of people. The church and a few powerful families owned much of the land. The majority of the people were landless and poor.

The economies of most Latin American nations were closely tied to Europe. They supplied raw materials to Europe and were a market for European manufactured goods.

Many nations became dependent on the export of one or two products. Haiti, for example, relied mainly on the export of sugar. Chile exported silver and copper. When these products sold for high prices on world markets, the nations benefited. But when world demand dropped and prices sank, as often happened, they suffered. Thus, Latin American nations had little control over their own economies.

Changing Economic and Social Conditions

Despite many ongoing problems, some nations, including Argentina, Brazil, Chile, Uruguay, and Costa Rica, moved toward stable government in the 1800s. In these nations, governments worked to improve economic conditions. Chile, for example, varied its economy by growing a variety of agricultural products, developing new exports such as nitrates, and building its industries. Brazil increased its foreign trade by establishing coffee and rubber plantations. Argentina attracted many European immigrants, who raised cattle and wheat, mostly for export to Europe.

Sugar was the chief export of many Caribbean nations. Single-crop economies left these countries at the mercy of the world demand for sugar. Workers labored long hours for low pay in cane fields or in boiling houses such as this one. After the sugar cane is cut, it is pressed to extract the juice. Workers then concentrate the liquid into sugar by boiling and evaporation.

As the economies of the Latin American countries expanded, the cities of the nations grew, and some social change took place. Rio de Janeiro, Buenos Aires, and Santiago became major cities. Although the class system remained fairly rigid, new economic opportunities favored the growth of a middle class. In Argentina, Brazil, Chile, and Mexico, the middle class made up about 10 percent of the population. In other Latin American countries, it remained smaller.

A Century of Change in Mexico

Mexico, you will recall, won its independence in 1821. During the next hundred years, it struggled to achieve political, economic, and social stability. These struggles were similar in some ways to those that took place in many other Latin American countries during the 1800s.

Clashes between conservatives and liberals shaped political developments in Mexico. Conservatives wanted to maintain the traditional social and economic order. Liberals favored reforms and greater democracy. They supported reducing the size of large estates and redistributing land to small farmers. Liberals also wanted to limit the power of the army and the church.

During the power struggles between conservatives and liberals, several strong leaders emerged. In the 1830s and 1840s, General Antonio Santa Anna was in and out of power many times. At first, he supported liberal reforms. Later, he won the backing of conservatives and ruled as a military dictator.

War with the United States. During this troubled time, Mexico became involved in a war with the United States. Many people from the United States had settled in Texas, an area that belonged to Mexico. In 1836, these settlers defeated Santa Anna's forces and declared Texas an independent republic. In 1845, Texas became part of the United States. Soon after, disputes along the Texas-Mexico border led to war between the United States and Mexico. The war lasted from 1846 to 1848 and ended in defeat for Mexico. As a result, Mexico lost almost half its territory to the United States, including what is today California, Nevada, and Utah as well as parts of Arizona, New Mexico, and Colorado.

An age of reform. In the following decades, Mexico introduced liberal reforms under the leadership of Benito Juárez. Born to a poor Indian family, Juárez earned a reputation as a brilliant lawyer and was elected president. He extended political power to more people, thereby reducing the influence of the creoles.

In 1910, Mexico was plunged into an era of revolution and social change that uprooted the old class structure and improved living conditions for the vast majority of Mexicans. Women took an active part in the revolution, although it was unusual for women to be involved in politics at all.

Women in Mexico, as elsewhere in Latin America, were expected to remain at home and raise large families. They were taught to be subordinate to men and to obey their fathers or husbands in all matters. By the early 1900s, however, some Mexican women were working in factories. And some upper-class women had become teachers and journalists. Women journalists were often outspoken in their opposition to the dictator Porfirio Díaz.

Juana Belen Gutiérrez de Mendoza began her career as a teacher. She became increasingly concerned with educating poor Indian children and gaining rights for farm and factory workers. Gutiérrez sold a few goats she owned in order to buy a printing press and founded the newspaper *Vesper*. Eventually, she was jailed for criticizing Díaz in her newspaper. In prison, Gutiérrez met other women who shared her hopes for reform. She even managed to direct the publication of another newspaper while in prison. Later, Gutiérrez joined the rebel forces of Emiliano Zapata during the Mexican Revolution and earned the rank of colonel.

Other women also gained distinction in the Mexican Revolution. Carmen Alanis commanded 300 troops who helped capture the city of Juárez. Ramona Flores, a wealthy widow, used her inheritance to buy arms for rebel troops and later became chief of staff to a rebel general. Many women served as soldiers. In addition to fighting, women served as train dispatchers, telegraph operators, nurses, and spies.

By the time the Mexican Revolution was over, women's place in Mexican life had changed permanently. The Constitution of 1917 guaranteed women basic legal rights, free education, and access to all professions. However, the constitution did not grant women suffrage. Although some Mexican states gave women the vote in the 1920s, women did not win that right nationally until 1953.

1. What roles did women take in the Mexican Revolution?

2. **Critical Thinking** Why do you think women journalists opposed the government of Díaz?

During the 1860s, he reduced the power of the Catholic Church by selling its lands. He also established a system of public education and made the state, not the church, responsible for marriage laws.

Soon after the death of Juárez, Porfirio Díaz was elected president. Although Díaz promised to continue the reforms of Juárez, he gradually became more conservative. He rigged elections so that he remained in power for 35 years. During this time, Mexico made important economic progress. Landowners and businesspeople reaped huge profits from mining and the building of railroads. But the poor gained little, and large landowners took control of many Indian lands.

The Constitution of 1917. In 1910, a revolution broke out against Díaz. The Mexican Revolution plunged the nation into years of chaos and swept away most of the traditional order. Finally, in 1917, a new constitution was adopted. It passed into law many reforms that people had been demanding for decades.

Under the Constitution of 1917, large estates were broken up, and the land was sold to peasants. Over half the farmland in Mexico changed hands in this way. The new constitution reduced the creoles' power and enabled the mestizos and Indians to participate fully in government. It provided for the separation of church and state and set up a labor code dealing with hours and wages. Although many provisions of the constitution were not carried out right away, the constitution gave Mexico a stable government. As peace was restored, the Mexican economy began to grow.

SECTION 2 REVIEW

1. **Locate:** (a) Ecuador, (b) Bolivia, (c) Argentina, (d) Paraguay, (e) Uruguay.

2. **Identify:** (a) Santa Anna, (b) Benito Juárez, (c) Porfirio Díaz.

3. **Define:** (a) regionalism, (b) caudillo.

4. How did geography contribute to disunity in Latin America?

5. (a) What group or groups had the most political power in Latin American nations after independence? (b) What group or groups had little political power?

6. How did stable governments in some countries improve economic conditions?

7. **Critical Thinking** Did the Mexican Constitution of 1917 reflect conservative or liberal goals? Explain.

---

3 Imperialism in Latin America

READ TO UNDERSTAND

☐ Why the United States announced the Monroe Doctrine and how it was used.

☐ How foreign investments led to economic imperialism in Latin America.

☐ How the United States increased its influence in the region.

In November 1906, President Theodore Roosevelt sailed to Panama to see how work was progressing on the canal, which he had backed so strongly. On shipboard, he wrote to his sons, "Americans are changing the face of the continent, are doing the greatest engineering feat of the ages, and the effect of their work will be felt while our civilization lasts."

Roosevelt's enthusiasm was shared by most people in the United States. There was no doubt in their minds that the United States had a right to shape the destiny of the Western Hemisphere. The people of Latin America, on the other hand, were less enthusiastic. They wanted to be able to shape their own destinies.

The Monroe Doctrine and the British Navy

After winning independence, the nations of Latin America faced many internal problems as well as external threats. In the 1820s, Spain asked its allies in Europe to help it reconquer its former colonies. Although Prince Metternich of Austria was willing to support Spain, Britain and the United States opposed any intervention in Latin America.

Both Britain and the United States had reasons for opposing intervention. Britain wanted to increase its trade with the new nations. A return of Spanish rule would prevent new commercial ties. The United States wanted to keep European countries from regaining influence in the hemisphere.

In 1823, the British asked the United States to make a joint declaration against European intervention in Latin America. Instead, President James Monroe decided to make a statement of his own. In his annual message to Congress in December 1823, Monroe announced United States policy toward Latin America.

"The American continents," Monroe declared, "are henceforth not to be considered as subjects for future colonization by any European powers." His policy, which became known as the Monroe Doctrine, further stated, "With the governments who have declared their independence and maintained it, we would consider any European intervention the manifestation of an unfriendly disposition [attitude] toward the United States."

The United States did not have the military power to enforce this policy. But Britain let other European powers know that it was prepared to use its strong navy to prevent foreign intervention in Latin America. Thus, the Monroe Doctrine, backed up by British seapower, freed the nations of Latin America from the threat of reconquest.

Foreign Interests in Latin America

Although the United States and Britain were determined to keep other powers out of Latin America, they did not oppose foreign investment. During the 1800s, the United States and the industrial nations of Europe turned to Latin America as a source of raw materials and a market for their manufactured goods. Moreover, they invested heavily in building mines, railroads, bridges, and ports there.

By the early 1900s, Britain alone had invested $5 billion in Latin America. The United States and France each had investments of over $1 billion, and Germany was close behind. Thus, although the nations of Latin America remained technically independent, these large foreign investments gave European nations and the United States a stake in their economic well-being and political stability. This type of interest in other countries is known as economic imperialism.

In 1863, while the United States was distracted by its civil war, Napoleon III of France placed a young Austrian archduke, Maximilian, on the throne of Mexico. Napoleon was angry because Mexican president Benito Juárez had stopped payments on foreign debts. However, the Mexicans resisted foreign rule and helped Juárez regain power. As this painting by Edouard Manet shows, the unfortunate Maximilian was captured and executed by troops loyal to Juárez.

Some foreign investments were made in the form of loans to governments for building railroads and ports. Sometimes, a corrupt dictator would use the money to make himself rich instead of applying it to the building project. Also, if the dictator were overthrown, the new government might default or refuse to repay the loan. In 1863, France used the excuse that Mexico had defaulted on foreign loans to send its army to collect the debts and to install Maximilian as emperor of Mexico. (See page 519.)

Similar situations arose frequently in the 1800s. When investors thought their loans were in danger of not being repaid, they appealed to their governments to protect their investments. Foreign warships would then arrive and foreign governments would force their demands on the Latin American government.

Nevertheless, foreign investments did lead to economic growth in some Latin American nations. In politically stable nations, many loans were used to develop new industries. For example, in Argentina, the number of industrial businesses grew from 41 in 1869 to nearly 50,000 in 1914.

In addition, many Europeans settled in parts of Latin America. In the 1800s, about 3 million immigrants poured into Argentina, Brazil, and Chile. These immigrants played an important role in stimulating Latin American commerce and industry.

The United States and Latin America

In 1783, a Spanish official made the following prediction about the United States:

> We have just recognized a new power in a great region where there exists no other to challenge its growth. The day will come when it grows and becomes a giant and even a colossus [a gigantic power] in those regions. Within a few years we will regard the existence of this colossus with real sorrow.

A century later, many people in Latin America were sure that this prediction had come true. They called the United States "the Colossus of the North."

Relations between the United States and the nations of Latin America began on a friendly note with the Monroe Doctrine. But Latin American governments came to distrust the Monroe Doctrine. They believed the United States was using it to dominate them.

In 1895, during a boundary dispute between Venezuela and Britain, the United States forced Great Britain to accept its proposal to settle the dispute. At the same time, the United States made clear to Britain that it "was sovereign on this continent." These words disturbed many people in Latin America, for they implied that the United States was free to do as it wished in the Western Hemisphere.

The Spanish-American War

Three years later, the United States fought a war with Spain that involved it even more deeply in Latin America. In 1898, Cuba and Puerto Rico were still Spanish colonies. However, Cuban rebels were fighting for independence. American journalists whipped up public sympathy for the Cuban cause. The United States sent the battleship *Maine* to Havana to protect American citizens and property in Cuba. When the *Maine* was blown up in a mysterious explosion, newspapers in the United States clamored for war.

In April 1898, the United States recognized Cuban independence, and Spain declared war. During the Spanish-American War, the United States won quick victories in the Caribbean and the Pacific. (See page 596.) In December, Spain agreed to a peace treaty, giving the United States control of Puerto Rico as well as the Philippines and Guam in the Pacific. The United States ruled Puerto Rico directly through an American governor and an American-appointed executive council.

Cuba became an independent nation. When Cubans drafted a constitution in 1900, however, the United States forced them to add a document known as the Platt Amendment. The Platt Amendment gave the United States the right to intervene in Cuban affairs to protect American lives and property. It put limits on Cuba's right to borrow from foreign powers, and it allowed the United States to establish two naval stations in Cuba.

Many Latin American nations looked on the expansion of the United States into the Caribbean with alarm. They feared that the United States had imperialist ambitions that would threaten their own independence.

Roosevelt Corollary to the Monroe Doctrine

In the early 1900s, Venezuela and the Dominican Republic defaulted on loans from Britain, Germany, and Italy. Once again, European warships menaced Latin American nations. President Theodore Roosevelt invoked the Monroe Doctrine and sent American battleships to force the Europeans to withdraw their ships. The European nations protested. They insisted that if they could not send warships to make nations pay their debts the United States must take that responsibility.

To satisfy this demand, Roosevelt announced the Roosevelt Corollary to the Monroe Doctrine in 1904. Roosevelt declared that the United States would exercise "international police power" to get Latin American nations to honor their financial commitments.

Over the next 20 years, several American presidents used this police power. President William Howard Taft sent troops to Nicaragua and Honduras in order to guarantee repayment of foreign debts. On other occasions, United States troops occupied parts of Latin American nations to protect American and European investments.

The Panama Canal

During the Age of Imperialism, the United States competed with the industrial nations of Europe for international markets. As the

MAP STUDY *In the early 1900s, some Caribbean areas were still under foreign rule, as this map shows. In addition, foreign governments often intervened when Caribbean nations were unable to pay their debts. Why would Cuba have been geographically important to the United States?*

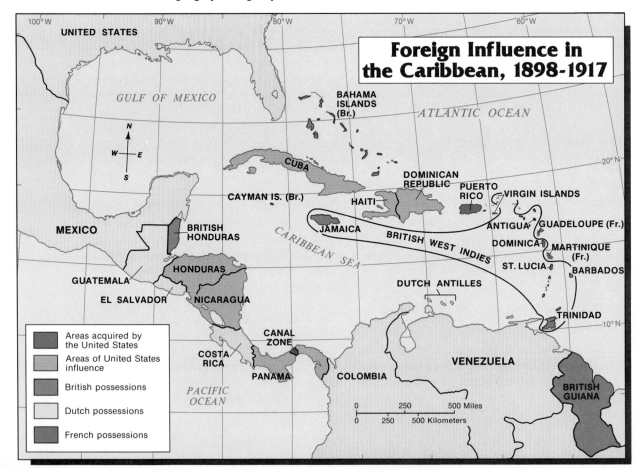

President Theodore Roosevelt was fond of quoting a West African proverb: "Speak softly and carry a big stick; you will go far." Roosevelt used a "big stick" in the form of American economic and military strength in his dealings with Latin America. In this cartoon, Roosevelt, once police commissioner of New York City, is portrayed as the world's policeman.

United States expanded its interest in the Pacific, it wanted to be able to move its fleet easily between the Atlantic and Pacific oceans without making the long voyage around South America. President Theodore Roosevelt proposed building a canal across the narrow Isthmus of Panama, which belonged to Colombia.

Colombia was reluctant to grant the United States the right to build such a canal, fearing it would lose control of the region. In 1903, however, the United States encouraged Panama to revolt against Colombia. The rebels quickly won independence for Panama. Then, they signed an agreement allowing the United States to build the canal.

The United States began work on the Panama Canal in 1904. First, workers drained swamps and marshes, the breeding grounds of mosquitoes that carried yellow fever. Next, they moved millions of tons of earth to create the "big ditch." Finally, in August 1914, the first ship traveled through the Panama Canal.

The United States benefited most from the Panama Canal, although the new sea route also helped many other nations. Still, in Latin America, many people regarded it only as more proof of United States imperialism in the region.

SECTION 3 REVIEW

1. **Locate:** (a) Cuba, (b) Puerto Rico, (c) Panama.

2. **Identify:** (a) Monroe Doctrine, (b) Spanish-American War, (c) *Maine*, (d) Platt Amendment, (e) Roosevelt Corollary.

3. (a) Why did the United States announce the Monroe Doctrine? (b) Why were Latin American nations suspicious of it?

4. In what ways did foreign investments help the nations of Latin America?

5. **Critical Thinking** What role did economic imperialism play in the dealings of foreign countries with Latin America?

Summary

1. Discontent, Enlightenment ideas, and the example of the American Revolution paved the way for independence movements in Latin America. Many people resented foreign rule and the rigid social structure that had developed in the Spanish colonies. The first successful revolt took place in Haiti. By 1825, most of Latin America had thrown off the colonial yoke.

2. The newly independent nations of Latin America faced many problems. They had little experience in self-government, and their economies were undeveloped. Strong rulers often seized power and set themselves up as military dictators. In Mexico, as elsewhere, struggles between conservatives and liberals shaped politics.

3. Latin American nations frequently experienced foreign intervention during the Age of Imperialism. The United States and the industrial nations of Europe invested in Latin America. They felt they had the right to use force, if necessary, to protect their investments. The United States gained influence as a result of the Spanish-American War. Later, it built the Panama Canal. These developments increased Latin American suspicion of United States power in the region.

Recalling Facts

Choose the word or phrase that best completes each of the following statements.

1. The highest class in Spanish colonial society was the (a) creoles; (b) peninsulares; (c) mestizos.

2. Haiti won its independence from (a) Britain; (b) France; (c) Spain.

3. Spanish colonists were encouraged to fight for independence by the ideas of (a) the French Revolution; (b) Metternich; (c) Ferdinand VII.

4. One problem facing the new nations of Latin America was (a) lack of natural resources; (b) unequal land ownership; (c) revival of slavery.

5. As a result of war with the United States in the 1840s, Mexico (a) became a united country; (b) introduced liberal reforms; (c) lost half of its territory.

Chapter Checkup

1. Describe why each of the following groups was dissatisfied with Spanish rule: (a) creoles; (b) mestizos; (c) Indians; (d) slaves.

2. Describe the role of each of the following leaders played in the Latin American wars of independence: (a) Simón Bolívar; (b) José de San Martín; (c) Miguel Hidalgo.

3. Which group of people led the fight for independence in most Latin American countries? Why?

4. (a) Why were the Spanish colonies poorly prepared for self-government? (b) What social problems did they face?

5. (a) What kind of economic growth occurred in Argentina, Brazil, and Chile? (b) How did economic growth affect society in these nations?

6. (a) Why did Britain and the United States oppose foreign intervention in Latin America in the 1800s? (b) What steps did they take to prevent it?

7. (a) Why did industrial nations invest in Latin America? (b) How did foreign loans lead to economic imperialism in Latin America?

Critical Thinking

1. Comparing (a) How was the experience of the United States during its war of independence and after independence similar to that of the nations of Latin America? (b) How was it different?

2. **Understanding Economic Ideas** (a) Describe the economic ties between Latin America and Europe after the nations of Latin America won independence. (b) Why did most Latin American nations have little control over their own economies?

3. **Relating Past to Present** Many people in Latin America still refer to the United States as the Colossus of the North. (a) What actions of the United States in the 1800s contributed to this view? (b) Why do you think this image of the United States still exists?

4. **Understanding the Roots of Democracy** Many of the newly independent nations of Latin America modeled their constitutions on that of the United States. Yet few of them were able to build stable democratic governments. What conditions in Latin America made it difficult for these nations to achieve democracy?

Developing Basic Skills

1. **Ranking** Review the problems that the newly independent nations of Latin America faced. Then rank them according to their influence on developments in Latin America. Explain your ranking.

2. **Researching** Choose one of the leaders of Mexico in the 1800s. Research his background in order to answer the following questions: (a) How did he become involved in Mexican politics? (b) What political ideas did he support? (c) How might his background have influenced his political ideas?

Writing About History

Deciding When to Document
There are certain times when you must document, or identify, the sources of the information you include in a research paper. These include: (a) any direct quotation, (b) the summary of an author's ideas, (c) statistical facts, (d) a fact that is not common knowledge or a fact that is in dispute.

Documenting your sources serves many purposes. You give credit to a person for the work he or she has done, and you show that your information is reliable. You also give your reader a way of checking your information. And you provide a way for readers to do further research on the topic themselves.

You do not have to identify the source of any fact that is generally known. Biographical information about a public figure, such as birthplace, education, and accomplishments, is usually considered general knowledge.

Practice: Which items below would require documentation in a research paper?

1. Simón Bolívar's birthplace.
2. The wording of the Roosevelt Corollary to the Monroe Doctrine.
3. The fact that the battleship *Maine* was in Havana harbor in 1898.
4. An account by a participant of her part in the Mexican Revolution.

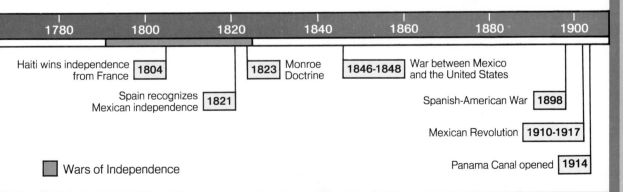

| 1780 | 1800 | 1820 | 1840 | 1860 | 1880 | 1900 |

Haiti wins independence from France **1804**

Spain recognizes Mexican independence **1821**

1823 Monroe Doctrine

1846-1848 War between Mexico and the United States

Spanish-American War **1898**

Mexican Revolution **1910-1917**

Panama Canal opened **1914**

Wars of Independence

Unit Eight   Mini-Atlas

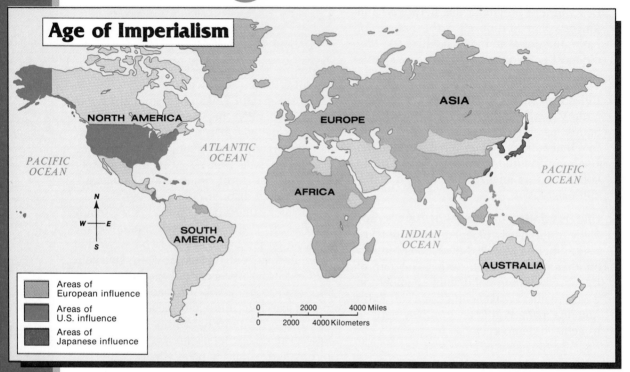

Age of Imperialism

NORTH AMERICA

PACIFIC OCEAN

ATLANTIC OCEAN

EUROPE

ASIA

AFRICA

PACIFIC OCEAN

N
W — E
S

SOUTH AMERICA

INDIAN OCEAN

AUSTRALIA

0   2000   4000 Miles
0   2000   4000 Kilometers

Areas of European influence
Areas of U.S. influence
Areas of Japanese influence

Unit Themes

Until the 1800s, there was limited contact among the civilizations of Africa, Asia, and Western Europe. When Europeans expanded overseas in the 1500s and 1600s, they conquered the New World but established only a few trading outposts in Africa and Asia.

In the 1800s, the effects of the scientific, political, and industrial revolutions greatly strengthened Western European nations and the United States. The Industrial Revolution enabled Europeans to dominate the world for a time.

During the Age of Imperialism, the civilizations of different parts of the world were brought into closer contact than ever before. Europeans extended their control over parts of Asia and Africa. Japan began to expand in the Pacific. In Latin America, European colonies gained political independence. But in the 1800s, Europe and the United States exercised influence over the new nations.

1. **Analyzing Information** (a) Study the world map above. Where were European areas of influence? Where were American and Japanese areas of influence? (b) What did these nations hope to gain by claiming areas of influence? (c) Do you think the Age of Imperialism was a natural result of the Industrial Revolution? Explain.

2. **Comparing** (a) According to the map at right, who explored the Niger River? (b) Compare European imperialism in Africa and in China? (c) How did Ethiopia and Siam maintain their independence?

3. **Evaluating** (a) Approximately how many years did the Latin American Wars of Independence last? (b) How did the United States justify its intervention in Latin America? (c) Do you think Latin Americans thought differently about this? Explain.

618

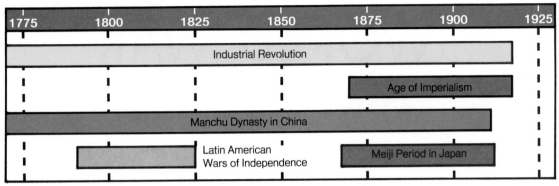

1775	1800	1825	1850	1875	1900	1925

Industrial Revolution

Age of Imperialism

Manchu Dynasty in China

Latin American Wars of Independence

Meiji Period in Japan

TIME LINE STUDY

How many years are covered on the time line? Which dynasty was ruling China during the Meiji era in Japan? Which came first, independence for Latin American countries or the Age of Imperialism?

MAP STUDY

European exploration of Africa in the 1700s and 1800s opened up the continent to imperialism. Which explorer crossed the continent from east to west? Which river did James Bruce explore?

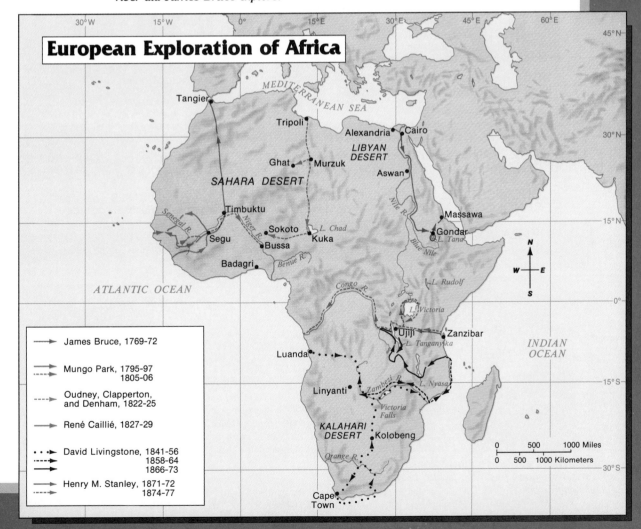

European Exploration of Africa

James Bruce, 1769-72

Mungo Park, 1795-97
           1805-06

Oudney, Clapperton,
and Denham, 1822-25

René Caillié, 1827-29

David Livingstone, 1841-56
                 1858-64
                 1866-73

Henry M. Stanley, 1871-72
                 1874-77

WORLD WAR AND PEACE

1918 *The signing of the armistice ending World War I was greeted with great celebration.*

Soviet art of the 1920s reflected the struggle to establish a socialist state.

	1914	1920	1926	1932
POLITICS AND GOVERNMENT	**1914** World War I breaks out in Europe	**1922** Mussolini marches on Rome and takes power		**1931** Japanese invade Manchuria
ECONOMICS AND TECHNOLOGY	**1916** Tank developed for use in World War I		**1929** U.S. stock crash leads to worldwide depression	
SOCIETY AND CULTURE		**1924** Danish woman elected to national post	**1929** *All Quiet on the Western Front* is best seller	

In World War I, airplane gunners armed with machine guns had "dog fights" in the skies over Europe.

Some political parties used the fear of communist revolution to win support, as shown in this German poster from the 1920s.

UNIT OUTLINE

1936 *This poster appeals for support for the republicans in the Spanish Civil War.*

During World War II, the Allies tried to build support among their people with posters such as this.

1932	1938	1944	1950

1933 Hitler comes to power in Germany

1939 World War II begins when Germany invades Poland

1947 Marshall Plan proposed to help rebuild Western Europe

1930s Passenger airlines become common

1940 Radar used in Battle of Britain

1945 Atomic bombs dropped on two Japanese cities

1935 Nuremberg Laws deprive Jews of citizenship

1942 Japanese slogan "Asia for the Asians" builds on anticolonial feelings

After World War II, the Soviets set up satellite governments in much of Eastern Europe. Stalin is shown here with his "puppets."

The Nazi Party in Germany encouraged young people to join the Hitler Youth.

621

World War I

(1914–1919)

28

Weary survivors trudge through a barren and desolate World War I battlefield in this painting by French artist Luc Albert Moreau. The field is littered with the bodies of their fallen comrades.

"We wake up in the middle of the night. The earth booms. Heavy fire is falling on us. We crouch into corners. We distinguish shells of every caliber. The dug-out heaves, the night roars and flashes."

The words are those of a young German soldier as told in the novel *All Quiet on the Western Front* by Erich Maria Remarque. Remarque was a German soldier in the war that broke out in Europe in August 1914. He knew only too well the horrors of battle.

Night after night, the young soldier and tens of thousands of others on both sides wake up to the terrifying sounds of a bombardment. After the awful bombardment ends, they leave the shelter of their trenches to meet the enemy.

"We seize the hand grenades, pitch them out in front of the dug-out, and jump after them. No one would believe that in this howling waste there could still be men; but steel helmets now appear on all sides of the trench."

"We recognize the distorted faces, the smooth helmets: They are French," notes Remarque's young soldier. "Under one of the helmets a dark pointed beard and two eyes are fastened on me. I raise my hand but I cannot throw into those strange eyes; for one mad moment the whole slaughter whirls like a circus around me, and these two eyes that are alone motionless; then the head rises up, a hand, a movement, and my hand grenade flies through the air and into him."

The scene of this "howling waste" is northern France. There, as elsewhere in Europe, tens of thousands of nameless, faceless soldiers battled almost daily. The war, which was called the Great War at the time, lasted from 1914 to 1918. After 1939, when a second global conflict broke out, the earlier war was called World War I.

Few would have predicted the outbreak of a worldwide war at the beginning of the century. In the early 1900s, many people in Western Europe and the United States had great confidence in western civilization. They had seen much progress in industry and technology, and they had carried their ideas to every corner of the globe. Many believed that treaties and law would allow nations to keep the peace. But in 1914, the peace was shattered. Europeans suffered through the most devastating war they had ever known. The war profoundly changed both Europe and the rest of the world. ■

1 Sources of Tension

READ TO UNDERSTAND

☐ How nationalism and imperialism increased tension among European powers.

☐ What role militarism played in starting the war.

☐ Why the alliance system added to tensions in Europe.

"The situation is extraordinary. It is militarism run stark mad," wrote an American official visiting Europe early in 1914. "There is too much hatred, too many jealousies." All that was needed, he said, was "a spark to set the whole thing off."

By 1914, Europeans had known peace for almost 100 years, since the Congress of Vi-

enna. They had seen brief, localized conflicts, such as the Crimean and Franco-Prussian wars, but no long, large-scale war. As a result, many Europeans had come to believe that another general war simply could not happen. However, since the late 1800s, war clouds had been gathering. Intense rivalries among nations fed mistrust and even outright hatred. The spark that the American visitor noted was soon to be ignited.

Nationalism

At the root of much of the rivalry was the growth of nationalism. As you have read, nationalism flourished in Europe during the 1800s. It brought unity to some nations and disunity to others. Peoples such as the British and the French, who had been politically united for centuries, felt great pride in their countries. Others, such as the ethnic groups in Austria-Hungary and the Ottoman Empire, were still struggling to win political independence. As they did, they threatened the very existence of those states.

Nationalism created tensions between France and Germany. The French bitterly resented their defeat in the Franco-Prussian War and were eager for revenge. Moreover, they were determined to regain Alsace-Lorraine. Germany was equally determined to keep its conquests.

Nationalist feelings were also strong in Italy. Although Italy had become a united country in 1870, a million Italians still lived in territories controlled by Austria-Hungary. And in other parts of Austria-Hungary, ethnic minorities looked for every opportunity to free themselves from the empire.

Rising feelings of nationalism came from many sides. In the late 1870s, an English music hall singer wrote these lines:

> We don't want to fight, but by jingo, if we
> do,
> We've got the ships, we've got the men,
> and got the money too!

His song added the word "jingoism," meaning extreme patriotism, to the English language.

Colonial Rivalries

Events outside Europe contributed to growing tensions in the early 1900s. During the scramble for colonies in Africa and Asia, European nations reached the brink of war more than once.

In North Africa, France and Germany narrowly avoided war over Morocco in 1905. (See page 566.) A second Moroccan crisis developed in 1911 when the French used riots in Morocco as an excuse to send in troops to protect Europeans. In response to the French move, the German emperor sent a warship to the Moroccan port of Agadir. Germany then demanded the French Congo in exchange for German recognition of French claims in Morocco. Many Europeans expected that the crisis would lead to war. Only swift efforts by British diplomats to ease the crisis prevented the outbreak of a war. But in France and Britain, anti-German feeling ran high.

There were many other trouble spots. Tensions were growing in Persia, present-day Iran. There, Britain and Russia each wanted control of Mesopotamia. And, as you have read, Europeans' competing spheres of influence in China were a continuing source of irritation, while Russia and Japan fought a war over Manchuria.

Military Buildup

In this tense climate, the nations of Europe took steps to prepare for war. Military spending across the continent jumped 300 percent between 1870 and 1914. Some nations embraced militarism, giving military officers a strong hand in government.

The military buildup was especially evident in the naval rivalry between Britain and Germany. For most of the 1800s, the British had maintained a "two-power standard." This meant that their navy was always to be more powerful than the navies of any other two countries combined. Then, in 1898, Germany began an ambitious program to increase the size of its navy. Between 1900 and 1914, Germany tripled its spending on warships and became the second strongest naval power. Britain saw this as a clear threat to its naval supremacy. It responded by increasing its own naval spending. This naval race contributed to the growing tensions between these two countries.

European nations also competed for power and prestige by enlarging their armies. In 1913, France increased the size of its army by extending required military service from two to three years. Russia almost doubled spending on its army between 1900 and 1914.

The Triple Alliance

In the late 1800s, the major European powers not only built up their military power but also looked for allies who would support them in case a war broke out. The German chancellor Otto von Bismarck arranged several alliances with other great powers. His chief goal was to isolate France so it could not take revenge on Germany.

In 1879, Bismarck negotiated a military alliance between Germany and Austria-Hungary. Two years later, he arranged the "Three Emperors' League," a secret agree-

Colonial wars were commonplace in the early 1900s. This painting shows French troops fighting in Morocco in 1907. In the scramble for colonies in Asia and Africa, colonial powers often came into conflict. Their differences were usually resolved without war. But frequent colonial crises increased tension in Europe.

ment among the emperors of Germany, Austria-Hungary, and Russia. In 1882, Bismarck masterminded the Triple Alliance, which brought Italy into the alliance between Germany and Austria-Hungary. Because the Italians had not been able to block French influence in Tunisia, they willingly joined Germany and Austria-Hungary.

Bismarck's alliance system almost collapsed when rivalry between Russia and Austria-Hungary in the Balkans caused the Three Emperors' League to break up. But the Iron Chancellor quickly reached out for Russian friendship in an agreement called the Reinsurance Treaty of 1887. Bismarck thereby succeeded in his aim of isolating France.

The Triple Entente

The diplomatic isolation of France, however, did not last. When William II became kaiser, or German emperor, he wanted to make his own foreign policy. As you have read, William forced Bismarck to resign in 1890. Soon after, William allowed the Reinsurance Treaty with Russia to lapse.

France seized this opportunity to ally itself with Russia. Russia accepted the French offer of friendship because it was at odds with Austria-Hungary and worried about German power. France and Russia signed a military agreement in 1894. Under this pact, if either France or Russia were attacked by any member of the Triple Alliance, the other nation would come to its aid.

Britain remained outside the alliance system that was dividing Europe into rival camps. Britain had long prided itself on its "splendid isolation," its independence from alliances. But the growing power of Germany, especially its expanding navy, worried the British. In addition, the British were furious with Germany because it had denounced British imperialism in Africa during the Boer War.

Thus, Britain began looking for allies. In 1904, Britain and France signed an entente cordiale (ahn TAHNT kor DYAHL), or "friendly understanding." The agreement only settled some colonial issues between the two nations and did not contain any promises of mutual protection. But France hailed it as a major triumph because it now had agreements with both Russia and Britain. In 1907, Britain and Russia signed an agreement that completed the Triple Entente, a loose coalition of Britain, Russia, and France.

Thus, between 1879 and 1907, the major powers became caught up in a dangerous system of alliances. The alliances increased international tensions because now any crisis involving one of the great powers would also affect that nation's allies. The alliance system also raised the possibility that a minor incident could lead to a general war.

SECTION 1 REVIEW

1. **Identify:** (a) Three Emperors' League, (b) Triple Alliance, (c) Triple Entente.

2. Give two examples of how nationalism added to tensions in Europe.

3. (a) What European nations were involved in the second Moroccan crisis? (b) How did the crisis increase tension in Europe?

4. Describe evidence of increasing militarism in Europe during the late 1800s and early 1900s.

MAP STUDY *Between 1879 and 1907, the major European powers formed two rival alliances. Other European nations remained outside the alliance system but looked to one of the major powers for protection. What geographical advantage did the Triple Entente have?*

European Alliance System, 1907

Triple Entente
Triple Alliance

0   250   500 Miles
0   250   500 Kilometers

5. **Critical Thinking** Based on what you have read, describe how a minor crisis between two nations could end in European war.

2 On the Brink

READ TO UNDERSTAND

☐ Why the Balkans were known as the "powder keg of Europe."

☐ How the assassination of Francis Ferdinand led to the outbreak of war.

☐ What role the alliance system played in the outbreak of war.

☐ *Vocabulary:* ultimatum, mobilization.

"Peace remains at the mercy of an accident," observed the German ambassador in Paris early in 1914. The "accident" came all too soon—just months after he spoke these words.

As you learned in Chapter 24, nationalism was contributing to the breakup of the Ottoman Empire and the weakening of Austria-Hungary in the early 1900s. The Balkan Peninsula was the focus of these nationalist movements. Increasingly, turmoil in the Balkans brought Europe closer to war.

The Balkan Powder Keg

In the early 1900s, the Ottoman Empire ruled only a small part of the Balkans. The Greeks had won independence in 1829. And the Slavs had established the independent nations of Serbia and Montenegro in the late 1800s. However, at the Congress of Berlin in 1878, Austria-Hungary had been given the right to administer the government of Bosnia and Herzegovina on the western border of Serbia. Thousands of Slavs lived in Bosnia and Herzegovina. In 1908, Austria-Hungary annexed these areas outright.

This action infuriated the Serbs, who had hoped to absorb all the southern Slavs into their nation. Russia also denounced the Austro-Hungarian move. The Russians, who wanted to increase their own influence in the Balkans, were motivated both by feelings of kinship with fellow Slavs and by their desire for warm-water ports. But Russia was too weak to risk a war. Reluctantly, it pressured Serbia into accepting the situation. Although the crisis passed, both Serbia and Russia remained bitter toward Austria-Hungary.

Three years later, in 1912, trouble again broke out in the Balkans. This time, Serbia, along with Bulgaria and Greece, attacked the Ottoman Empire and took most of its remaining European possessions. One result of this First Balkan War was the creation of the independent nation of Albania. However, the three victors soon quarreled over the spoils of war. The Second Balkan War erupted in 1913. Bulgaria attacked its former allies, Serbia and Greece, but was defeated.

An uneasy peace followed these two wars. To many people, the Balkans were "the powder keg of Europe." Serbia, especially, was not satisfied with the peace settlements. As the Serbian prime minister remarked in 1913, "The first round is won; now we must prepare the second against Austria."

Assassination in Sarajevo

The second round began in June 1914, when Archduke Francis Ferdinand, heir to the throne of Austria-Hungary, paid a state visit to Sarajevo (sar uh YAY voh), capital of Bosnia. The neighboring Serbs were furious about the visit. In their minds, the Austrians were sending the archduke into the province that Austria had annexed illegally. "Death to the Hapsburg dynasty!" cried Serbian extremists.

On Sunday morning, June 28, the archduke and his wife were driven through the streets in an open car. A bomb had exploded before the car appeared, so the route of the motorcade had to be changed. The archduke's chauffeur could not turn the car in the narrow street, so he began to back up. Just as he did, a 19-year-old Bosnian revolutionary, Gavrilo Princip, stepped from the curb and fatally shot the archduke and his wife.

Princip belonged to the Black Hand, a Serbian nationalist organization that wanted to unite Bosnia and Herzegovina with Serbia. The

Archduke Francis Ferdinand and his wife, Sophie, are shown here on a visit to Sarajevo, Bosnia, on June 28, 1914. Five minutes after this photograph was taken, they were assassinated.

Black Hand was not a tool of the Serbian government, though some Serbian officials were sympathetic to it and even knew of the assassination plot. However, Austria-Hungary believed that Serbian officials were deeply involved in the murder plot.

Francis Joseph, the emperor of Austria-Hungary, wrote to Kaiser William II of Germany that "the Sarajevo affair was the result of a well-organized conspiracy, the threads of which can be traced to Belgrade [the capital of Serbia]." In reply, William promised to "faithfully stand by Austria-Hungary, as is required by the obligations of his alliance." Austria-Hungary took the kaiser's response as a "blank check" from Germany. That is, it believed the Germans would back any action it took against Serbia. And many Austrians were eager to crush Serbia.

Diplomatic Crisis

Tensions mounted in the month after the assassination. On July 23, Austria-Hungary issued Serbia an **ultimatum,** a final set of demands. The ultimatum required Serbia to suppress all anti-Austrian activities and to dismiss all officials hostile to Austria-Hungary. The ultimatum also demanded that Austria-Hungary have the right to send its own officials to Serbia to investigate the archduke's murder. The Austrians insisted on an answer within 48 hours.

Serbia faced a difficult choice. Refusal to meet the Austrian demands would undoubtedly mean war. But allowing Austrian officials to investigate the assassination would violate Serbian independence. In the end, Serbia accepted all the Austrian demands except this last one.

The Serbian response did not satisfy Austria-Hungary. It was determined to punish Serbia in order to discourage nationalist movements within its empire. The German kaiser now advised moderation. But Austria-Hungary ignored his caution and began to mobilize its armed forces. **Mobilization** is a process that involves calling troops into active service. It does not necessarily mean war, but it is generally viewed as a step toward war.

The other European powers condemned the murder of the archduke but expected the crisis between Austria-Hungary and Serbia to pass. However, the threatening moves on the part of Austria-Hungary alarmed Russia and France. Russia was prepared to aid Serbia if Austria-Hungary declared war, so it ordered a partial mobilization of its armed forces. As the crisis deepened, France assured Russia of its support.

Diplomats scurried across Europe desperately trying to find a solution to the crisis. Britain proposed a great-power conference to settle the dispute between Austria-Hungary and Serbia. Germany and Austria-Hungary rejected the British proposal, however. They claimed that the national honor of Austria-Hungary was at stake and that such an issue should not become the subject of international debate.

The Outbreak of War

On July 28, 1914, Austria-Hungary declared war on Serbia. Over the next few days, the alliance system began to operate. On July 29, the Russian czar Nicholas II ordered a general mobilization of his armed forces. Germany asked Russia to cancel the mobilization order. If it did not, the Germans warned, war would begin. When Russia did not reply, Germany declared war on Russia on August 1. Convinced that France would sooner or later come to the aid of its Russian ally, Germany declared war on France on August 3.

Germany had long foreseen the possibility of having to fight on two fronts at the same time: in the east against Russia and in the west against France. To avoid this, Germany had adopted the Schlieffen Plan. It called for German troops to crush France quickly before the Russians could gear up their war machine to full readiness.

The Schlieffen Plan called for German troops to bypass the heavily defended eastern border of France and to invade northern France through Belgium. (See the map on page 629.) Thus, on August 3, German troops marched into the neutral nation of Belgium. This German move brought Britain into the war because in 1830 Britain had pledged to defend Belgian neutrality. On August 4, Britain declared war on Germany.

What had begun on June 28 as a local incident had now mushroomed into a major war involving the five great powers of Europe. Today, people still debate the question of war guilt—which nation or nations were responsible for the outbreak of war. Most people agree that no one nation was responsible. Years of tensions in Europe and overseas had contributed to the climate of war. When war came, many people welcomed it. Others, however, feared what war might bring.

SECTION 2 REVIEW

1. **Locate:** (a) Serbia, (b) Bosnia, (c) Sarajevo.

2. **Identify:** (a) Francis Ferdinand, (b) Gavrilo Princip, (c) Black Hand, (d) Schlieffen Plan.

3. **Define:** (a) ultimatum, (b) mobilization.

4. Why did Serbia resent Austria-Hungary?

5. (a) Why did Austria-Hungary take a strong stand against Serbia after the assassination of Archduke Ferdinand? (b) How did Serbia respond to the Austro-Hungarian ultimatum?

6. **Critical Thinking** Do you think war could have been avoided in the summer of 1914? Why or why not?

3 The War Years

READ TO UNDERSTAND

☐ What were the results of the fighting on the western and eastern fronts.

☐ Why the war resulted in such huge casualties.

☐ How new technologies affected the fighting.

☐ Why Russia withdrew from the war.

"The boys will be home by Christmas," Europeans on both sides declared confidently in August 1914. Few people expected the war to drag on for four years with appalling losses on both sides.

On one side were the Central Powers: Germany, Austria-Hungary, and the Ottoman Empire. On the other side were the Allied Powers: Britain, France, and Russia. Italy declared its neutrality. Eventually, 20 other nations, including Japan and the United States, joined the Allies. The war was fought on a larger scale than any previous war in history.

Stalemate on the Western Front

During the early months of World War I, much attention was focused on the western front—southern Belgium and northern France. Within three weeks after invading Belgium, the Germans had overrun that small country. Soon German soldiers were fighting their way toward Paris. However, the German offensive stalled in early September 1914, when French and British troops took a stand along the Marne River and pushed the Germans back.

Western Front 1914–1918

Farthest German advance, 1914

Armistice line, 1918

✦ Major battle sites

MAP STUDY *Fighting on the western front was limited to a relatively small area. But the number of dead and wounded was huge. In the Battle of the Somme in the summer of 1916, the Allies gained 125 square miles of land at the cost of 600,000 dead and wounded. What battles were fought at the farthest points of German advance?*

The Battle of the Marne ended the German hope for a quick victory in the west.

During the autumn of 1914, the British and French fought the Germans in a series of battles known as the "race to the sea." At Ypres (EE preh), the British stopped a German attack. The western front then stabilized along an arc from the North Sea to the Swiss border.

By November 1914, it was clear that neither side could deal a final blow to the other. The opposing armies then settled down to a strategy of trench warfare. Soldiers dug long series of trenches protected by mines and barbed wire. For the next three years, fighting on the western front only preserved the stalemate. There was heavy fighting with terrible losses, but almost no change in the position of either side.

629

A British sentry keeps watch in the trenches. His companions have fallen asleep from exhaustion. One huddles against the earth embankment, while others sleep wherever they can find a bit of space.

In the maze of trenches on the western front, a new way of life emerged. Thousands of soldiers spent weeks at a time in the muddy, rat-infested trenches. Some trenches were simple shelters. Others were elaborate tunnels that served as headquarters and first-aid stations. Between the front-line trenches of the opposing sides lay "no-man's land," a wasteland of barbed wire and land mines.

Trench warfare consisted of days of shelling the enemy's defenses. Then front-line troops would be ordered "over the top." Soldiers would scramble out of their trenches to race across no-man's land and attack the enemy lines. Most offensives resulted in huge casualties and little gain of territory. During the 11-month battle of Verdun in 1916, the Germans lost 330,000 men trying to overrun the French lines. "They shall not pass," was the rallying cry of the French defenders. The French lost at least as many soldiers as the Germans. In 1916 alone, at least 2 million soldiers were killed in Europe.

New Weapons

The staggering toll of dead and wounded was due in part to the use of deadly new weapons. During World War I, the machine gun was used with tragic results. Its rapid fire mowed down waves of soldiers as they raced across no-man's land.

Early in 1915, the Germans began using poison gas that blinded and choked its victims. Later that year, the Allies also began using poison gas. Although poison gas could be fatal, it was an uncertain weapon. Shifting winds could blow the gas back on the side that had launched it. In time, soldiers were given gas masks and so could survive the gas attacks.

In 1916, the British introduced a new weapon, the armored tank. Tanks, mounted with machine guns, were designed to move across broken ground and through barbed wire. The first tanks moved slowly and broke down often, but they terrified the German sol-

When historians study primary sources, they often develop different interpretations of the meaning of those sources. Their interpretations may be shaped by the mood of the times or the place in which they live. Thus, a historian's environment influences his or her **frame of reference,** the way one views an event or development.

Historians have debated the causes of World War I since 1914. The following excerpts give the views of two historians. The first one was written by Emil Ludwig in 1929. The second was written by Raymond Aron in 1954. Use the following steps to analyze their interpretations of the causes of World War I.

1 **Identify the interpretations.** (a) What does Ludwig suggest was the main cause of World War I? (b) What does Aron suggest was the main cause of World War I?

2 **Decide how a historian's frame of reference affects his or her interpretation.** To do this, you need to know about the mood of the times in which the historian lived. In the 1920s, many European historians rejected the view of the Allies that Germany alone was responsible for the war. They hoped to learn a lesson from the war that would prevent another world conflict. In the 1950s, the world seemed to be divided into two parts: the "free world," led by the United States, and the "communist world," led by the Soviet Union. Both sides built up large arsenals of weapons. Use this background information to answer the following questions: (a) How does Ludwig think World War I might have been avoided? (b) How does this view show the influence of the 1920s on Ludwig's interpretation? (c) How might the tensions in the 1950s have affected Aron's interpretation?

3 **Evaluate the reliability of the interpretation.** (a) Do you think individual government leaders could have prevented the outbreak of war? Why or why not? (b) In your opinion, how important was the division of Europe into two armed camps in causing World War I? (c) What other factors do you think contributed to the outbreak of World War I?

Emil Ludwig

The war-guilt belongs to all Europe . . . Germany's exclusive guilt or Germany's innocence are fairy-tales for children on both sides of the Rhine. . . . This book is a study of the stupidity of the men who in 1914 were all-powerful. . . . Economic crises, questions of competition, and colonies had, indeed, complicated the European situation; yet war had been averted time and again, and three capable statesmen could once more have achieved what the great majority desired. . . . The picture of July 1914 shows a continent in which the nations trusted and obeyed their leaders, while those leaders in their turn were responsible to no central authority. The absence of any control over the individual governments had brought about European anarchy. . . . Hurry, carelessness, surprise, and, above all, mutual fear . . . finally brought about a war which a sound League of Nations could have prevented.

Raymond Aron

Before the assassination of the Archduke Francis Ferdinand, Europe was living in a state of preparedness, but no one expected an outbreak from one day to the next. Following the assassination . . . , chancelleries [governments] and populations alike felt the dread of approaching disaster. . . . The rise of Germany, whose hegemony [supremacy] France dreaded and whose navy menaced England, had created an opposition that claimed to be defensive but was denounced by German propaganda as an attempt at encirclement. The two camps alarmed each other, and each tried to soothe its own fears by piling up defensive armaments. The atmosphere grew heavy with multiplied incidents, which spread the conviction of approaching disaster.

diers. By the end of the war, however, both sides were using tanks.

Both sides also used aircraft. At first, planes simply observed enemy troop movements. In 1915, Germany used zeppelins, gas-filled balloons, to bomb the English coast. Later, the Germans and Allies equipped their planes with machine guns, and pilots battled in the skies. Although these "dogfights" were spectacular, they had little effect on the course of the war.

Another weapon, the submarine, was used on a large scale for the first time. Germany used its submarine fleet with deadly effect. When the war began, the British navy block-aded the North Sea coast of Germany. The German surface navy was no match for the large British navy, which patrolled the North Sea and seized the cargoes of neutral ships bound for Germany. However, German submarines roamed the Atlantic at will and inflicted enormous damage by sinking merchant ships that carried vital supplies to the British Isles. To counteract submarine warfare, the Allies organized convoys, or groups of merchant ships protected by warships.

The Eastern Front

While British, French, and German forces were fighting on the western front, huge armies fought a seesaw battle on the eastern front. This front was much larger than the western front. It extended from the Baltic Sea to the Black Sea. (See the map on page 637.) The Russians and Serbs battled Germans, Austrians, and Turks. Although Russia had the largest reserves of manpower in Europe, its armies often suffered from an appalling lack of supplies and poor leadership. In some battles, a quarter of the Russian soldiers had no weapons. Soldiers in the rear were told to arm themselves by picking up the weapons of the dead and wounded.

In August 1914, at Tannenburg in East Prussia, the Germans destroyed two Russian armies. The Russians never again threatened Germany. The Russians were at first more successful against Austrian troops in Galicia. But in 1915, a combined German-Austrian offensive drove the Russians back. In the fall of 1915, Bulgaria joined the Central Powers. With German aid, Bulgaria then overran Serbia.

As in the west, fighting in the east killed and wounded millions but produced few decisive results. In mid-1916, the Russians launched a massive assault in the Ukraine and captured over half a million Austrian prisoners. But the Russians lost a million of their own men trying to hold their line and failed to advance farther.

Revolution in Russia. Many Russians had welcomed the war in 1914, but before long they saw the terrible toll it was taking. News from the front was full of losses. Soldiers returned home with stories of disasters and poor

At the Battle of the Argonne, French soldiers perched in trees take aim at the enemy with machine guns. Faster and more accurate than earlier weapons, the machine gun was one of the deadly new weapons used in World War I.

leadership. Closer to home, the government was unable to cope with food and other shortages. Finally, in March 1917, bread riots in Petrograd led to a revolution in Russia and the downfall of the czar.*

A provisional, or temporary, government was set up. Its leaders promised to continue the war. Leaders of the other Allied nations hoped that the new government would strengthen the Russian will to fight because it was important to keep Germans tied down on the eastern front. But morale among Russian forces remained low. Many soldiers left the front and returned to their villages. An official report in October 1917 described the Russian army as "an immense, desperate, and weary crowd of men united by their common desire for peace."

The Treaty of Brest-Litovsk. As the war dragged on, many Russians stopped supporting the Provisional Government. Radical revolutionaries led by Vladimir Lenin promised peace if they won power. In November 1917, Lenin and his supporters overthrew the Provisional Government in a second revolution. They seized the reins of government and negotiated a peace treaty with Germany. The Treaty of Brest-Litovsk, signed in March 1918, was harsh. Russia lost about 25 percent of its land and population. But the new Russian government was willing to pay this heavy price for peace.

Russia's withdrawal from the war caused grave concern among the Allies. With the collapse of the eastern front, Germany could now shift its resources to the west.

---

* St. Petersburg had been renamed Petrograd early in the war. You will read more about the Russian Revolution in Chapter 30.

Piercing cold, inadequate provisions, and enormous casualties lowered the morale of Russian troops, and many soldiers were unwilling to continue fighting. Scenes of Russian soldiers surrendering, such as this one, became common.

SECTION 3 REVIEW

1. **Locate:** (a) Marne River, (b) Ypres, (c) Verdun, (d) Tannenburg, (e) Galicia.

2. **Identify:** (a) Central Powers, (b) Allied Powers, (c) no-man's land, (d) Vladimir Lenin, (e) Treaty of Brest-Litovsk.

3. What nations were fighting (a) on the western front?; (b) on the eastern front?

4. Describe three new weapons and how they affected the fighting in World War I.

5. What problems did the Russian army face?

6. (a) What promise did Lenin make to the Russians? (b) Did he keep his promise? Explain.

7. **Critical Thinking** How do you think trench warfare contributed to the terrible loss of life in World War I?

4 An End to the Stalemate

READD TO UNDERSTAND

☐ How governments mobilized the home fronts during the war.

☐ Why the United States entered the war.

☐ How the Central Powers were defeated.

☐ *Vocabulary:* propaganda, armistice.

Early in World War I, the English poet Rupert Brooke wrote these lines:

> If I should die, think only this of me:
> That there's some corner in a foreign field
> That is for ever England.

Brooke did die tragically in the war. His poems expressed the romantic patriotism of the early years of the war. As the war dragged on and the slaughter continued, governments had to use every means in their power to convince their people to believe in the justice of their cause.

Both sides threw all their resources into the drive for victory. The Allies hoped to win by attacking the Central Powers on several fronts in Europe. The war was also fought in lands overseas.

Fighting on Other Fronts

During World War I, the Allied and Central Powers fought to a standstill on several fronts other than those in France and Russia. A new front was opened in May 1915 when Italy joined the Allies and declared war on Austria-Hungary and later on Germany. Italy had signed a secret treaty with the Allies. The treaty promised Italy Austrian lands in which many Italians lived.

Italian forces pinned down 200,000 Austrian troops along the border between Italy and Austria. In October 1917, the Austrians, reinforced by German troops, launched a major offensive against the Italian position at Caporetto. The Italians retreated in confusion. A month later, British and French forces helped Italy stop the Austro-German advance about 20 miles north of Venice.

In 1915, the British devised a plan to capture the Dardanelles, the vital straits connecting the Black Sea and the Mediterranean Sea. The Dardanelles were controlled by the Ottoman Empire. The British believed that by seizing the Dardanelles, they could then take Istanbul. Such a victory would improve links with Russia and free the Balkans, which were occupied by the Central Powers. British troops landed on the Gallipoli (guh LIHP uh lee) Peninsula, where they met stiff Turkish resistance. After almost a year of fighting, with huge casualties, the British had to withdraw from Gallipoli.

The Allies were more successful in Africa, the Middle East, and Asia. Britain and France seized most of German East Africa. In the Middle East, the British colonel T.E. Lawrence—later known as Lawrence of Arabia—organized Arab nationalists who had revolted against Ottoman rule. He led guerrilla raids against the Turks. Eventually, the Turks lost a great deal of territory to the Arabs, including the key city of Baghdad. In Asia, Japan seized Germany's sphere of influence in China as well as German islands in the Pacific.

On the Home Front

World War I was a total war. It involved civilian populations more directly than any previous conflict. In other wars, cities, villages, and farms had been damaged or destroyed by the fighting. But this time the damage and destruction were on a much larger scale.

During World War I, the power of governments increased everywhere as fighting nations struggled to meet the demands for more soldiers and more weapons. Governments drafted millions of men into the armed forces. Germany set up a system of forced civilian labor as well.

Governments tightly controlled their economies to further the war effort. They set up central planning boards that ordered factories what and how much to produce. The boards set limits on wages and prices and monitored foreign trade. As one German leader put it, victory was possible only "if all the treasures of our soil that agriculture and industry can produce are used exclusively for the combat of the war." Naval blockades and

At the height of the Battle of the Marne, in September 1914, German troops seemed about to break through French defenses and capture Paris. Desperate to get reinforcements to the front lines, the French government ordered the taxicabs of Paris to drive reserve troops north to the battle. The line held, and Paris was saved.

The incident shows how everyone—civilian as well as soldier—was drawn into the ordeal of total war. Paris became a very different city during the war. Once filled with the sound of music halls and cabarets, wartime Paris echoed with the pounding of cannon factories and the screech of troop trains. From time to time, the "city of light" was shelled by distant German artillery.

Across Europe, men of all ages were expected to join the war effort. In Germany, a law required all men from ages 17 to 60 to work in whichever industry needed them. In Britain, women gave white feathers to young, healthy men who were not in uniform. The white feather was a symbol of cowardice.

Not only men took part in wartime mobilization. Millions of women worked as bus drivers, bank tellers, steel workers, and miners—jobs once thought suitable only for men. On farms, women often planted and harvested crops alone, since their husbands, sons, and brothers were away at the front. Others worked at more traditional jobs, nursing wounded men at field hospitals behind the trenches.

In many countries, children joined the effort to use every resource to win the war. They collected coffee grounds, fruit seeds, and pine cones to be recycled into foods and other products. They took care of "victory gardens," small lots planted with vegetables to combat food shortages. Victory in a total war, people realized, meant a total war effort.

1. How did children contribute to the war effort?

2. **Critical Thinking** It has been said that total wars are won not by soldiers on the battlefield but by civilians at home. Do you agree or disagree? Explain.

the need to supply huge armies led to shortages at home. As a result, most countries rationed food and other necessities.

On the home front, war transformed the lives of many women. Thousands went to work outside the home for the first time. They took jobs in weapons factories, in offices, and as bus drivers.

Governments encouraged people to support the war through propaganda campaigns. **Propaganda** is the spreading of ideas or beliefs that further a particular cause or damage an opposing cause. As the war dragged on and the terrible casualties sapped civilian morale, each side tried to build confidence in victory and increase hatred of the enemy. Allied propagandists created the view of Germans as barbarian "Huns." Germans learned to sing the patriotic "Hymn of Hate":

> Hate by water and hate by land;
> Hate of the heart and hate of the hand;
> We love as one; we hate as one;
> We have but one foe alone—England.

Journalists on both sides even invented reports of atrocities to make the enemy seem inhuman. Governments also manipulated public opinion by controlling the news. The British government, for example, censored newspapers and imprisoned critics of the war. German reporters were barred from the front. They were often given misleading and optimistic "news" stories of the fighting.

The United States Enters the War

Both sides aimed a strong propaganda campaign at the United States. When war broke out in August 1914, President Woodrow Wilson proclaimed American neutrality and urged Americans to be "impartial in thought as well as in action." Most Americans believed that the war in Europe did not directly affect them. But as the war progressed, they were drawn into the conflict on the Allied side.

Americans were swayed in part by British propaganda, which portrayed German soldiers as barbarians torturing the people of occupied Belgium. However, German submarine warfare played a more important part in bringing the United States into the war. In May 1915, the Germans torpedoed an American tanker. Then the next week, they sank the British passenger liner *Lusitania*. Over 1,000 people on the *Lusitania* died, including 128 Americans. President Wilson protested angrily. Germany feared that new submarine attacks might bring the United States into the war. Therefore, it limited submarine warfare for a time.

In December 1916, however, Germany decided to break the stalemate in the war by isolating Britain and starving it into submission. The Germans announced a policy of unrestricted submarine warfare. They declared that their submarines would sink any ship in waters near enemy coasts. German leaders knew that unrestricted submarine warfare might bring the United States into the conflict.

Both the Allies and the Central Powers used propaganda posters to win support for the war effort from people on the home front. The American poster, at left, called on women to "knit a bit," to supply clothing for sailors. At right, Germans are asked to "sign the sixth war loan" to help pay for the war.

KNIT A BIT
FOR OUR FIRST LINE OF DEFENSE
WOOL, NEEDLES AND DIRECTIONS
Comforts Committee of the Navy League
OF THE UNITED STATES
509 FIFTH AVENUE, NEW YORK CITY

Zeichnet die
6. Kriegsanleihe!
Centralbank der deutschen Sparkaſſen

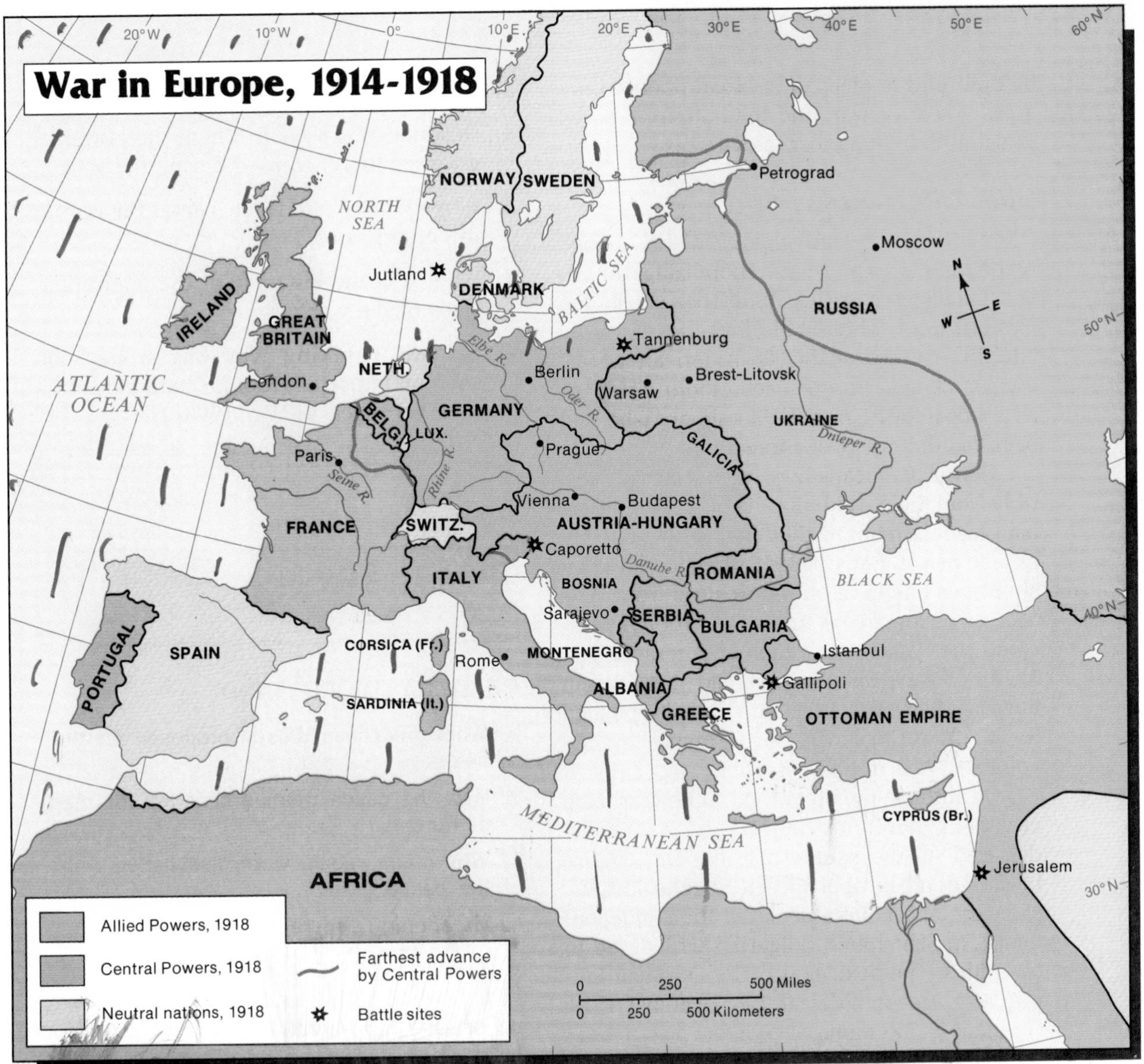

MAP STUDY *World War I was fought on many fronts. What special problems did the Russian front present to the Central Powers?*

But they took this risk. They hoped to defeat Britain before the United States could ready its forces for war.

Early in 1917, German submarines attacked American merchant ships. President Wilson broke off diplomatic relations with Germany. He hoped that Germany would abandon unrestricted submarine warfare as it had in 1915. Wilson soon learned, however, that Germany would not back down.

Then Americans became incensed when they read newspaper accounts about the Zimmermann telegram, a secret message from the German foreign minister, Arthur Zimmermann. The British had intercepted the telegram and passed it on to the American government. In it, Zimmermann suggested that if Mexico became a German ally, it could regain territory in New Mexico, Texas, and Arizona that it had lost to the United States in 1848.

On April 2, 1917, President Wilson asked Congress to declare war on Germany. "The world must be made safe for democracy," Wilson declared. To him the war had been caused by undemocratic governments acting in their own interests. The peace, when it came, must

be built on the ideas of political liberty. Congress voted for war, and the nation prepared to send its fighting forces overseas.

Final Offensives

During the spring and summer of 1917, while American forces were still mobilizing, the Allies launched a series of offensives on the western front. They made little headway. By late 1917, however, 50,000 American troops were landing in Europe each month. Their arrival boosted the morale of soldiers who had been fighting for over three years.

Germany, meanwhile, was suffering terribly from the naval blockade of its ports. German leaders realized they had to win quickly or face defeat. Early in 1918, they mounted an ambitious offensive on the western front. The Allies, reinforced by American troops, withstood the assaults and then counterattacked. An Allied tank offensive pierced the German lines on August 8, 1918, and steadily pushed the German army back. In Germany, morale collapsed and troops deserted.

By autumn, the other Central Powers were crumbling, too. Austria-Hungary was badly defeated on the southern front. The empire began to break apart when Czechoslovakia, Hungary, and Poland declared their independence. In September, Bulgaria surrendered to the Allies. The next month, the Ottoman Empire also accepted defeat. By November 1918, Germany stood alone.

While German leaders tried to negotiate an **armistice,** an end to the fighting, a revolt broke out against the government. On November 9, a German republic was proclaimed. The same day, William II abdicated and fled to the Netherlands. At 11 A.M. on November 11, the Allies and Germany signed an armistice agreement. The Great War had ended. The Allies now faced the difficult task of establishing peace in a world torn apart by war.

SECTION 4 REVIEW

1. **Locate:** (a) Caporetto, (b) Gallipoli.

2. **Identify:** (a) *Lusitania,* (b) unrestricted submarine warfare, (c) Zimmermann telegram.

3. **Define:** (a) propaganda, (b) armistice.

4. Describe two ways in which the power of governments increased during the war.

5. Why did the United States enter the war on the Allied side?

6. What was the outcome of the final offensives of the war?

7. **Critical Thinking** Why was propaganda such an important tool for both sides in a total war such as World War I?

5 The Peace Settlements

READ TO UNDERSTAND

☐ **What guidelines Wilson proposed for the peace.**

☐ **How the peace treaties changed the map of Europe.**

☐ **Why many people were dissatisfied with the peace.**

☐ *Vocabulary:* reparation, mandate.

"We have no selfish ends to serve. We desire no conquest, no dominion," President Wilson had declared when he asked Congress to declare war in 1917. "We are but one of the champions of the rights of mankind. We shall be satisfied when those rights have been made as secure as the faith and the freedom of the nations can make them."

Wilson's words caused many people in Europe and the United States to hope that the peace would bring justice. People needed hope after the death and destruction of the past four years. World War I was the costliest war fought up to that time. Almost 10 million soldiers had been killed in battle, and 20 million more had been wounded. About 1 million civilians had died in the fighting, and the toll grew as a terrible flu epidemic swept across the world. The war had also cost the fighting powers over $350 billion.

By the summer of 1918, the world had staggered through four years of brutal war. Just as people began to hope for peace, a new and deadly foe appeared. It killed soldier and civilian alike, and there was no defense against it. The enemy was a new type of influenza, or flu.

On October 17, 1918, an American doctor treating troops in France wrote in his diary: "Everything is overflowing with patients. The wards are full of machine gun wounds. There is rain, mud, flu, and pneumonia. Every sort of infectious case is there, packed in as close as sardines with no protection. Rain, rain; mud, blood; blood, death!"

The flu epidemic of 1918 began in East Asia and traveled west with amazing speed. In July, the disease broke out in China. By early August, it had reached Persia and the Middle East. France reported its first cases in mid-August. And by late August the disease hit the East Coast of the United States. The disease spread like wildfire as infected soldiers were shipped from eastern army camps to camps in the Midwest, South, and West.

Influenza had been a common but mild disease before 1918. This new variety, called Spanish flu by Americans, was different. It often developed into pneumonia. In 1918, little could be done to save the lives of pneumonia patients as their lungs filled with fluid.

Wartime conditions fed the raging epidemic. Young soldiers from farms and small towns went for training to crowded army camps where they were exposed. In the war zones, soldiers and civilians had been weakened by poor diets and overwork. "Exhausted, driven, anxious men are easy prey to infec-

tion," warned one group of doctors. Although doctors called for a halt to the draft and to troop movements, the war went on.

In just two months, Spanish flu struck in every country on every continent. It killed about 22 million people worldwide—twice the total number who died during World War I. Over 500,000 people died from it in the United States alone.

1. (a) Where did the flu originate? (b) In what direction did it spread?

2. **Critical Thinking** Why do you think doctors urged a halt to the draft and troop movements?

Wilson's Fourteen Points

Early in 1919, the victorious Allies gathered at the Palace of Versailles near Paris to hammer out a peace settlement. Woodrow Wilson traveled to Paris for the peace conference, the first American President to visit Europe while in office. He was greeted everywhere by enthusiastic crowds. Ordinary people saw him, more

than any other Allied leader, as offering hope for the future. People admired Wilson partly because he represented the United States, which had helped end the war, and partly because of his Fourteen Points, his goal for a postwar settlement.

Wilson had issued his Fourteen Points in January 1918, almost a year before the war ended. The Fourteen Points offered a framework for a just peace. Wilson hoped his plan would prevent future international tensions such as those that had led to war in 1914.

The first point called for "open covenants [treaties] of peace, openly arrived at," because Wilson believed secret diplomacy had led to the war. Points two through five called for freedom of the seas, free trade, limits on armaments, and the peaceful adjustment of all colonial claims. Points six through thirteen involved making territorial settlements in Europe "along clearly recognizable lines of nationality." This meant determining borders on the basis of ethnic groups living in an area. Wilson also supported self-determination by which the people would choose their own governments.

The fourteenth point called for the creation of a "general association of nations" to guarantee the "political independence" and territorial integrity of great and small nations alike. Wilson firmly believed that such a league of nations could prevent war by settling disputes peacefully.

In 1918, the European Allies accepted Wilson's Fourteen Points as the basis for the peace talks. However, once the peace conference began, the European Allies became impatient with Wilson's idealism.

Crosscurrents of the Peace Conference

During the war, President Wilson had spoken of a "peace without victory"—a "just peace" that would not involve seeking revenge on the defeated powers. Many Allied leaders did not share this goal for the peace. Moreover, only the victors met in Paris. The Central Powers were not allowed to attend the peace conference.

All Allied nations sent representatives except Russia, which was torn apart by revolution. The chief architects of the peace were the "Big Four": Woodrow Wilson of the United States, David Lloyd George of Britain, Georges Clemenceau (KLEH muhn SOH) of France, and Vittorio Orlando of Italy. Each leader had his own aims for the peace settlement.

Wilson believed that planning for peace was more important than settling boundaries or arranging for **reparations,** payment for war damages. Therefore, he insisted on the creation of a league of nations. The European Allies were determined to punish Germany and demanded reparations. Lloyd George had recently campaigned for reelection to Parliament, declaring: "We shall squeeze the orange [Germany] until the pips squeak." Although he was later to soften his stand, the British people were fiercely anti-German in 1919. Also, he wanted to be sure Britain got control of the former German colonies in Africa.

During the war, fighting on the western front had taken place mostly on French soil. Much of northern France was a wasteland, and many French people had died. At the peace conference, Clemenceau wanted revenge as well as security against any future German attack. He demanded the return of Alsace-Lorraine. And he called for an independent state, the Rhineland, to be set up as a buffer between France and Germany. Clemenceau also sought huge reparations and wanted to annex the coal-rich Saar Basin.

Italy was determined to claim the Austrian territories that it had been promised by its secret treaty with the Allies in 1915. It also demanded the city of Fiume, which it had seized during the war.

The conflicting interests of the Allies almost brought the peace conference to a standstill. Wilson once packed his bags to leave when the French refused to soften their demands. After months of bargaining, however, the Allies finally reached a compromise.

The Peace Treaties

The victors drafted five separate peace treaties: for Germany; for Austria and Hungary, which had become separate nations; and for Turkey and Bulgaria. The most controversial treaty was the Versailles Treaty with Germany.

The Versailles Treaty. The peace treaty with Germany included several compromises among the Big Four. France, for example, achieved only some of its aims. It received Alsace-Lorraine but had to give up its demands for the Saar Basin and an independent Rhineland. To calm French fears, however, Germany was forbidden to maintain any military forces in the Rhineland, and the Allies were to occupy the region for 15 years.

The question of reparations proved to be a difficult issue. In the end, the Versailles Treaty required Germany to admit responsibility for the war. On the basis of this "war guilt" clause, the Allies required Germany to pay reparations for the total cost of the war. The "war guilt" clause and reparations would fuel much German bitterness toward the Versailles Treaty in the years ahead.

The Versailles Treaty deprived Germany of its overseas colonies, which were turned over to the newly created League of Nations. The league established these former German colonies as **mandates,** territories that were administered but not owned by league members.

Britain and France received German colonies in Africa as mandates. German colonies in Asia and the Pacific were given as mandates to Japan, Australia, and New Zealand.

The treaty also limited the size of the German army and required Germany to turn its fleet over to the Allies. Areas of eastern Germany, inhabited mainly by Poles, were added to a newly created Polish state.

In May 1919, the Allies summoned a German delegation to Versailles and told it to sign the treaty. At first, the Germans refused to sign such a severe treaty. However, when the Allies threatened to renew the war, the Germans signed. The day was June 28, 1919, exactly five

In 1919, the peace treaty ending World War I was signed in the Hall of Mirrors at the palace of Versailles. Nearly 50 years earlier, Bismarck had proclaimed the German Empire in this same room after the Franco–Prussian War. (See page 540.) The Versailles Treaty humiliated Germany, which was not allowed to participate in the negotiations. This painting shows two German officials on one side of the table. Facing them, in the center, is Georges Clemenceau. David Lloyd George sits on the right. Woodrow Wilson, on the left, holds a copy of the treaty.

Europe After World War I

NORTH SEA

IRELAND

GREAT BRITAIN

NORWAY   SWEDEN   FINLAND

DENMARK   ESTONIA

LATVIA

BALTIC SEA   LITHUANIA

DANZIG GER.

NETH.   GERMANY   POLAND   RUSSIA

BELG.   RHINELAND

LUX.   SAAR BASIN   CZECHOSLOVAKIA

ALSACE-LORRAINE

FRANCE   SWITZ.   AUSTRIA   HUNGARY

Fiume   ROMANIA

YUGOSLAVIA

SPAIN   ITALY   BULGARIA

ALBANIA

N   W   E   S   GREECE   TURKEY

MEDITERRANEAN SEA

Territories lost by:

Austria-Hungary

Germany

Bulgaria

Russia

0   200 Miles

0   200 Kilometers

MAP STUDY *The peace treaties that ended World War I redrew the map of Europe. The defeated Central Powers lost land to newly created nations in Eastern Europe. Which of the Central Powers lost the most territory? Which of the Allies also lost much territory?*

years after Francis Ferdinand was assassinated at Sarajevo.

The Germans were not the only ones to criticize the treaty. President Wilson described the Versailles Treaty as "severe." But he agreed to the harsh demands of Britain and France in order to gain their backing for the League of Nations. The league covenant, or constitution, was included as part of the Versailles Treaty.

The other settlements. The other Central Powers had to sign peace treaties that changed many boundaries in Europe. (See the map above.) The Austro-Hungarian Empire had already ceased to exist. Its place was taken by the independent nations of Austria and Hungary. In addition, two new nations, Czechoslovakia and Yugoslavia, were created in Eastern Europe.

Romania gained territory from the former Austro-Hungarian Empire, as did Italy. However, Italy was unhappy with the peace settlement because it did not receive Fiume. Bulgaria lost its Aegean coastline to Greece. Like Germany, Austria, Hungary, and Bulgaria had to pay reparations. In addition, Austria, a German-speaking nation, was barred forever from uniting with its neighbor Germany.

In his Fourteen Points, Wilson had supported the idea of national self-determination. The peace treaties, therefore, set up several new nations in Eastern Europe. Poland was recreated as a nation for the first time since 1795. (See page 393.) The lands Germany had acquired from Russia by the Treaty of Brest-Litovsk became the independent Baltic nations of Lithuania, Latvia, and Estonia.

The Ottoman Empire was broken up. Turkey kept Asia Minor and the area around Istanbul. The Dardanelles were placed under international control, and Greece was given control of many Aegean islands. In the Middle East, former Ottoman lands became mandates of the League of Nations. Britain acquired mandates in Iraq, Transjordan, and Palestine, while France took Lebanon and Syria.

Problems of the Peace

The peace settlements dealt with issues that involved the lives of millions of people. Sometimes, haste and the need for compromise led to solutions that were unsatisfactory to all parties. As a result, many people felt angry and bitter about the peace settlements. These feelings were especially strong among the defeated powers.

Germans resented the loss of territory in Europe and of their colonies overseas. They were burdened with billions of dollars in reparations payments. They also felt the Versailles Treaty was unjust in holding Germany alone responsible for the war.

Another cause for discontent grew out of the fact that the principle of national self-determination had not always been followed. Many Germans, for example, lived in western Poland. Several million German-speaking people lived within the new nation of Czechoslovakia. These people and others felt betrayed by the peace settlements.

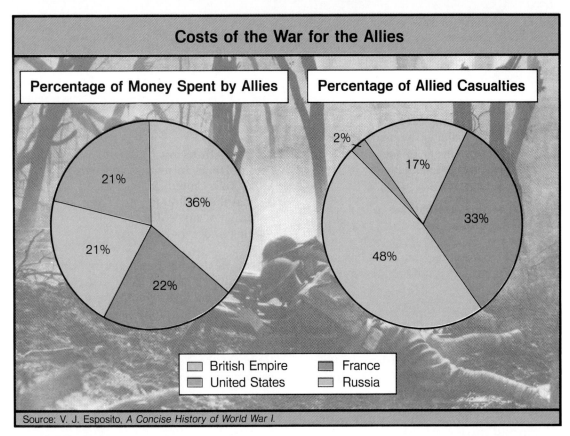

Costs of the War for the Allies

Percentage of Money Spent by Allies

36%
21%
21%
22%

Percentage of Allied Casualties

2%
17%
33%
48%

British Empire
United States
France
Russia

Source: V. J. Esposito, *A Concise History of World War I.*

GRAPH STUDY *The costs of the war were staggering. The Allies spent over $100 billion and suffered more than 18 million casualties. According to this graph, which nation had the largest number of casualties?*

The peace settlement reduced Austria to a small landlocked nation that lacked self-sufficiency in agriculture and industry. The newly created nations of Eastern Europe tried to establish democratic governments, but they faced many problems, as you will read.

Even some of the victors were dissatisfied with the peace settlements. France feared that Germany might rebuild its military power. Both Italy and Japan felt they had been denied rewards due to them. Although Russia had fought with the Allies until 1917, it had been excluded from the peace conference and in fact had lost more territory than Germany. (See the map on page 642.)

Finally, Wilson's great hope for maintaining peace in the postwar world, the League of Nations, was launched without American support. When Wilson returned home after the Paris Peace Conference, he found that the American people and Congress preferred isolationism to further involvement in world affairs. The Senate refused to ratify the Versailles Treaty because many senators objected to the League of Nations.

SECTION 5 REVIEW

1. **Locate:** (a) Rhineland, (b) Saar Basin.

2. **Identify:** (a) Fourteen Points, (b) League of Nations, (c) Versailles Treaty.

3. **Define:** (a) reparation, (b) mandate.

4. Describe two of Wilson's main goals for the peace settlements.

5. How did the Versailles Treaty punish Germany?

6. What new nations were created in Eastern Europe by the peace settlements?

7. **Critical Thinking** Do you think Wilson's Fourteen Points were too idealistic? Why or why not?

Summary

1. By the early 1900s, dangerous tensions existed among European nations. Increasingly, the major powers sought allies to help them in the event of war. However, the alliance system that emerged only heightened tensions.

2. The assassination of Archduke Francis Ferdinand in June 1914 led to the outbreak of World War I. Austria-Hungary blamed Serbia for the murder. Efforts to resolve the crisis failed and Europe was plunged into war.

3. World War I lasted from 1914 to 1918. It involved almost all European nations, the United States, and Japan. Hopes for quick victory faded as trench warfare tied down armies. New weapons such as poison gas, tanks, and submarines were used with deadly effect.

4. Nations on both sides devoted all their efforts to achieving victory. In April 1917, the United States joined the Allies against the Central Powers. Later in 1918, the Central Powers collapsed one by one. The fighting ended in November.

5. Restoring peace in a world torn apart by war proved to be difficult. Each of the Allies had its own goals for the peace settlement. Wilson's Fourteen Points had been accepted as the basis for the talks, but these guidelines were often ignored. The harsh terms of the Versailles Treaty created deep resentment among Germans.

Recalling Facts

Identify each of the following as a cause or an effect of World War I.

1. The Balkans become the "powder keg" of Europe.

2. Germany is required to pay reparations to other European nations.

3. Britain receives German colonies in Africa.

4. President Wilson issues his Fourteen Points.

5. Francis Ferdinand is assassinated at Sarajevo.

6. European nations compete for overseas colonies.

7. The League of Nations is created.

8. Rival alliance systems are formed in Europe.

Chapter Checkup

1. (a) Describe the rivalries among European powers in the early 1900s. (b) How did each help set the stage for war?

2. (a) Which major European powers were interested in the Balkans? (b) Why were they interested? (c) How did rivalries among Balkan nations create further problems in the region?

3. Why were other European powers drawn into the crisis over Archduke Ferdinand's assassination?

4. (a) How did trench warfare develop on the western front? (b) What was the result of trench warfare there?

5. (a) Why did Russia withdraw from the war? (b) How did the Russian move affect Germany?

6. (a) What position did the United States take at the beginning of World War I? (b) Why did American public opinion change during the war?

7. (a) Why did Wilson issue the Fourteen Points? (b) How did other European leaders view Wilson's Fourteen Points?

Critical Thinking

1. **Relating Past to Present** (a) Why were the Balkans known as "the powder keg of Europe"? (b) Do you think there is any re-

gion of the world today that might be called a "powder keg"? Explain.

2. **Understanding the Roots of Democracy** During the war, even democratic nations such as Britain and the United States took steps to silence critics and censor the press. What arguments can be made for and against a democratic government taking such steps in wartime?

3. **Synthesizing** "Sad peace! Laughable interlude between the massacres of peoples," wrote one European author in June 1919 after learning about the Versailles Treaty. How did the peace settlements contain the seeds of new conflicts?

Developing Basic Skills

1. **Map Reading** Study the map on page 642.
(a) Which European nations gained territory after the war? (b) Which nations lost territory? (c) How did the peace settlements affect the territory once ruled by Austria-Hungary? (d) Which nation or nations were most likely to resent the territorial changes? Why?

2. **Making a Review Chart** Make a chart with four rows titled United States, Britain, France, and Italy and two columns titled Goals for the Peace and Actual Results. Use what you have learned about the peace settlements to complete the chart. (a) How were British and French goals for the peace similar? (b) How were they different? (c) What did Italy receive in the peace settlements? (d) In your opinion, which of the Big Four was most likely to be dissatisfied with the peace?

Writing About History

Avoiding Plagiarism

Plagiarism is copying information or closely paraphrasing information without giving credit to the original source. To avoid plagiarism, you can give credit to your source or use information from your source but restate it in your own words.

Practice: Compare the paragraphs below with the second paragraph under "Nationalism" on page 624. Which paragraph is an example of plagiarism?

1. One of the reasons for hard feelings between France and Germany was nationalism. France's defeat by Germany in the Franco-Prussian War was a bitter memory to all French people. Nothing would please them more than to have a chance to take revenge on their neighbor to the east and to regain Alsace-Lorraine. For its part, Germany was in no mood to give up what it had gained.

2. Nationalism created tensions between Germany and France. The French felt bitter about their defeat in the Franco-Prussian War, so they were anxious for revenge. They were also determined to regain Alsace-Lorraine. Germany was just as determined to keep its conquests.

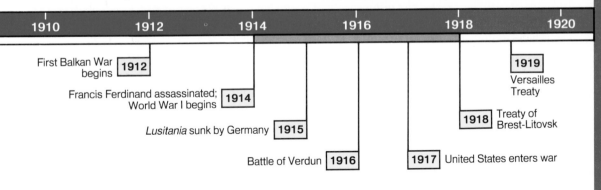

| 1910 | 1912 | 1914 | 1916 | 1918 | 1920 |

First Balkan War begins **1912**

Francis Ferdinand assassinated; World War I begins **1914**

Lusitania sunk by Germany **1915**

Battle of Verdun **1916**

1917 United States enters war

1918 Treaty of Brest-Litovsk

1919 Versailles Treaty

World War I

The Aftermath of War (1919–1939)

29

CHAPTER OUTLINE

1 Western Europe in the 1920s
2 Changing Patterns of Life
3 The United States in the 1920s and 1930s
4 Crises of the 1930s in Europe
5 Nationalist Struggles Outside Europe

Artists in the 1920s reflected the turbulence and confusion of the postwar world in their paintings. With his use of vibrant colors and light, Robert Delaunay was able to capture the era's excitement in his murals.

Hour after hour, the young pilot peered through drifting fog and clouds. After 33 hours alone, guiding the plane through light and darkness, the pilot was exhausted. Now, at last, he was over land. As he looked out of the cockpit of his small plane, he saw that he had reached his destination.

"I flew over the field once, then circled around into the wind and landed," the pilot, a 25-year-old American named Charles A. Lindbergh, later recalled. "After the plane stopped rolling, I turned it around and started to taxi back to the lights. The entire field, however, was covered with thousands of people all running towards my ship."

Lindbergh's "ship" was the *Spirit of St. Louis.* On the night of May 21, 1927, after flying more than 3,600 miles (5,760 kilometers), Lindbergh landed outside Paris. The crowds had gathered to greet the first man to fly across the Atlantic alone. Lindbergh won worldwide fame for his achievement. He was showered with awards, including the French Legion of Honor, the English Royal Air Cross, and the Belgian Order of Leopold. American President Calvin Coolidge sent a cruiser to bring the young flyer and his plane back to the United States. On his return, Lindbergh received the Distinguished Flying Cross from the President.

A modest and appealing young man, Lindbergh seemed to represent values that all the world could admire: self-reliance, dedication, and bravery. Said one speaker in praising Lindbergh: "We are all better men and women because of this flight of our young friend. Our boys and girls have before them a stirring, inspiring vision of real manhood. What a wonderful thing it is to live in a time when science and character join hands to lift up humanity with a vision of its own dignity."

Lindbergh's flight was not only a daring individual achievement, but it also announced a new age—the age of air travel. Soon it would no longer take days or weeks of sea travel to journey between continents. Regular air travel between the United States and Europe would bring these two continents into close contact.

In the spring of 1927, people gladly celebrated Lindbergh's feat. The world was recovering from the terrible destruction of the Great War. Yet the war had left a feeling of uncertainty and anxiety. It had shattered the lives of so many people. These people felt adrift in the postwar world. In the 1920s and 1930s, they searched for a new sense of security in an uncertain world. ■

1 Western Europe in the 1920s

READ TO UNDERSTAND

☐ **What economic problems Britain and France faced after World War I.**

☐ **Why Germany suffered a severe inflation that caused great hardship.**

☐ **How European nations tried to create a stable peace.**

☐ *Vocabulary:* **general strike, passive resistance, collective security.**

"Europe has lost its role as banker to the world," complained a French statesman after the war. "The financial power of the United States is increasing. The power of Japan is growing. Our North American friends have seized domination of the great routes which lead from the Atlantic to the Pacific."

For four years, European nations had devoted their energies to war. Their economies had been mobilized to supply the men at the front. While soldiers celebrated their homecoming, European leaders faced the challenge of returning to a peacetime economy. But they found themselves at a disadvantage in the postwar competition.

Economic Problems in Britain

Britain welcomed returning veterans with the slogan that they deserved "homes fit for heroes." Certainly, the British wanted to honor their fighting men. But when the parades ended, many soldiers found there were no jobs for them. In the early 1920s, Britain faced severe economic problems.

A small island kingdom, Britain depended on trade for prosperity. In the postwar years, however, British commerce was suffering from a number of severe blows to its export industries—cotton textiles, steel, and coal. First,

"LANDLESS"

The 1920s were difficult years for many people in Britain, as 1 million found themselves unemployed. In this poster from the election of 1920, the Labour party tries to show its sympathy for those who were suffering.

German submarines had destroyed about 40 percent of the British merchant fleet during the war. Second, other trading nations, especially the United States and Japan, were competing against Britain in many overseas markets. Third, many nations imposed high tariffs on imports after the war. Although these tariffs were aimed at protecting domestic industries from foreign competition, they cut deeply into British exports.

Finally, the decline in trade was due in part to Britain's outdated technology. As you have read, Britain was the first nation to industrialize. Even before the war, many of its factories were old, with machines and other equipment needing replacement. Coal mines lacked modern machinery. Outdated equipment also hurt British steel and shipbuilding industries, which faced stiff competition from newer industrial nations.

As trade declined, British manufacturers had to cut back production and lay off workers. Unemployment, which stood at 700,000 in 1920, jumped to over 2 million—almost a quarter of the work force—in 1921. Although unemployment fell in 1922, about 1 million people were jobless for the rest of the decade.

High unemployment fueled unrest among workers. In 1926, as coal exports fell, mine owners announced wage cuts. In protest, coal miners went on strike and called for a **general strike,** a mass walkout by unionized workers in all industries. The General Strike of 1926 lasted for nine days. Troops and nonunion workers supplied vital services, and the strike failed. The government then passed anti-labor legislation which caused widespread bitterness among workers.

Britain faced still another economic problem. During the war, it had borrowed billions of dollars from the United States. Because of the loss of trade, Britain was having a hard time repaying this debt. At the same time, Germany was unable to make the reparations payments owed to the British under the Versailles Treaty. Despite these economic problems, however, Britain remained a stable democratic nation.

An Independent Ireland

During the war and afterward, Britain faced a crisis in Ireland. As you have read, the Irish had for centuries fought for freedom from British rule. The British Parliament had passed a home rule bill in 1914, but it delayed taking action when the war broke out. In 1916, nationalist leaders in Ireland organized the Easter Rebellion against British rule. British troops put down this uprising, and many rebel leaders were executed.

The executions turned many Irish even more strongly against the British. Many supported the Irish Republican Army, an underground force that waged guerrilla war against the British.

In 1921, Britain tried to end the fighting by dividing Ireland into two parts. The southern counties, which were Catholic, became the Irish Free State, a dominion in the British Commonwealth. The northern section of Ulster, which was largely Protestant, remained part of Great Britain. The Protestants in Northern Ireland did not want to become part of the Irish Free State. But many Catholics in Northern Ireland demanded a united Ireland. As you will read in Chapter 37, this issue has remained a source of conflict to the present.

Postwar Recovery in France

France had suffered terrible damage from the fighting on the western front. Ten million acres of farmland had been turned into wasteland. About 20,000 factories and 6,000 public buildings had been destroyed. When the war ended, the French embarked on an ambitious program to rebuild their battered land and economy. This effort helped keep French unemployment relatively low in the 1920s.

France, like Britain, had borrowed heavily during the war. The French government borrowed more money to pay for the reconstruction. The combined debts placed a great burden on the French economy. The result was inflation and a loss of confidence in the French currency. In 1926, a government headed by Raymond Poincaré (pwahn kay RAY) reduced government expenses, raised taxes, and stabilized the currency. These reforms helped bring about a strong economic recovery.

France also invested in military preparedness. Two times within recent memory, Germany had invaded France. In the 1920s, the French were determined to prevent this from happening again. Therefore, they built the Maginot Line, an elaborate system of fortifications, along the French borders with Germany and Luxembourg.

German Inflation

The Versailles Treaty required Germany to pay stiff reparations, eventually totaling $33 billion. The German government tried to pay these debts by borrowing and by printing more paper money. The result was disastrous inflation. As more money was printed, its value kept dropping.

In 1923, the worst year of German inflation, a person had to fill a wheelbarrow with money simply to buy a loaf of bread. A newspaper cost 100 billion marks. Millions of Germans found that their savings had become worthless. The hardships caused by the inflation of the 1920s contributed to political unrest, as you will read in Chapter 30.

When Germany tried to ease the economic crisis by calling a temporary halt to reparations payments, France took matters into its own hands. Early in 1923, French troops occupied the Ruhr, the industrial heartland of Germany. France intended to collect reparations from German steel mills and coal mines. However, German workers in the Ruhr responded with **passive resistance,** nonviolent opposition. They simply refused to work.

German inflation worsened as people in other parts of the country supported the Ruhr workers. Eventually, an international committee headed by American banker Charles G. Dawes resolved the crisis. Under the Dawes Plan of 1924, Germany agreed to resume reparations payments to the Allies, but on a reduced scale. The United States promised to provide loans to help Germany rebuild its economy. France withdrew its troops from the Ruhr in 1925. As the German economy recovered, Germany increased its reparations payments. This allowed France and Britain to repay some of their debts to the United States.

The Diplomacy of Peace

During the 1920s, leaders in Western Europe were hopeful that a new era in international relations would dawn. They rejected balance-

Postwar inflation ruined many middle-class people in Germany. Families often sold treasured family possessions to buy food. A loaf of bread, if available, cost billions of marks. This photograph shows workers picking up money for one week's payroll from a Berlin bank.

Heavy reparations payments made Germans increasingly bitter about the Versailles Treaty. The bitterness remained even after the Dawes Plan reduced the reparations payments. This cartoon shows a German worker laboring under the burdens of the Versailles Treaty while the United States turns away.

guarantee existing borders and to seek peaceful solutions to any dispute. In addition, Germany agreed to seek a peaceful settlement of border disputes with its neighbors in Eastern Europe—Poland and Czechoslovakia. Thus, the Locarno Pact improved relations in Western Europe.

In the mid-1920s, Europeans were optimistic about the "spirit of Locarno," which seemed to offer the hope of a stable and lasting peace. In 1926, Germany was allowed to join the League of Nations, regaining its place in the world community.

Throughout the 1920s, the great powers talked about disarmament, mainly naval disarmament. The United States as well as Japan joined in disarmament conferences held in Washington, D.C., and Geneva, Switzerland.

In 1928, efforts to maintain peace resulted in the Kellogg-Briand Pact. American Secretary of State Frank B. Kellogg and French Foreign Minister Aristide Briand were the architects of this agreement. Sixty-two nations, including the United States, signed the pact and agreed to "renounce war as an instrument of national policy." The Kellogg-Briand Pact symbolized the optimism of the period. However, although nations gallantly banished war, they established no machinery to enforce peace.

SECTION 1 REVIEW

1. **Identify:** (a) Irish Free State, (b) Maginot Line, (c) Dawes Plan, (d) Locarno Pact, (e) Kellogg-Briand Pact.

2. **Define:** (a) general strike, (b) passive resistance, (c) collective security.

3. Describe the economic problems faced by each of the following countries in the postwar period: (a) Britain; (b) France; (c) Germany.

4. What role did the League of Nations play in the 1920s?

5. **Critical Thinking** What reasons did Europeans have to be optimistic about world peace in the 1920s?

of-power politics and the alliance system, which many people believed had contributed to the Great War. They looked instead to the League of Nations to keep the peace.

The league was based on the idea of **collective security,** that is, an organized community of nations acting together to preserve peace. In the 1920s, the league helped settle a number of disputes between small powers. It was less successful in resolving crises that involved major powers. Moreover, three major powers—the United States, Germany, and Russia—were not members of the league.

German unhappiness with the Versailles Treaty continued to haunt Europe. In 1925, the Allies met with Germany at the Swiss town of Locarno. France, Britain, and Germany signed a series of agreements known as the Locarno Pact. Western European nations agreed to

2 Changing Patterns of Life

READ TO UNDERSTAND

☐ **How the war changed women's lives.**

☐ **How new technology changed daily life in western nations.**

☐ **How the war affected writers and painters.**

> This is the way the world ends
> This is the way the world ends
> This is the way the world ends
> Not with a bang but a whimper.

These lines appear at the end of T.S. Eliot's poem *The Hollow Men.* Like many writers of the 1920s, Eliot wrote of the emptiness and decay of modern life. The war had swept away many accepted ideas of the past, including the belief in progress. Many thoughtful men and women mourned their friends who had been killed in the war and expressed disgust with the leaders who had sent them to die.

During the 1920s, many features of today's world took shape. Most changes were quite slow, but gradually new patterns of life emerged in Europe and the United States.

Expanded Horizons for Women

Before the war, women had won suffrage in only a few countries. After the war, women gained the vote in most of Western Europe, the United States, Russia, and India. In 1924, the Danes elected the first woman to a national cabinet post.

Changes in styles were only one indication of women's changing role in the postwar world. As shorter skirts, bobbed hair, and makeup became more widely accepted, so did the notion that women could contribute to society. In Britain, women over 21 won the vote in 1928, but in France they had to wait until 1944.

The war had helped to expand horizons for women. Many women had joined the war effort by working in factories and offices. But when the war ended, many employers replaced them with men. Other women voluntarily left their jobs after the armistice. However, the number of women in the work force remained higher than it had been in 1914, and it continued to increase during the 1920s.

During the war, some single women had moved into their own apartments instead of living with relatives. Women worked outside the home, earning their own money and feeling a sense of independence. During the 1920s, they gained more political and economic rights. Also, European and American families became smaller in the postwar period. With fewer children to raise than in the past, some women had more time to work outside the home or to take active roles in their communities.

Women's fashions in the 1920s reflected the new freedom. Short skirts and short hair replaced the styles of the prewar period. Women also wore make-up, a practice that had been unacceptable in 1914.

The Impact of New Technology

Many jobs traditionally done by women at home were made easier by new technology. Stores sold a variety of canned and packaged foods, so women no longer had to spend so much time preparing family meals. Labor-saving devices such as electric irons and vacuum cleaners simplified housekeeping.

New technology was not limited to household appliances. As Lindbergh's flight across the Atlantic showed, the air age was beginning. The first international airmail was carried between London and Paris in 1919. Big cities built airports as passenger travel by air became more common. In 1930, the first transcontinental airline service was started in the United States. In 1939, regular transatlantic passenger service by air was begun. At the same time, more people bought automobiles. France, which had only 125,000 registered motor vehicles in 1913, had over 2 million in 1938.

Some postwar technology made people's lives more fun as well as easier. The radio came into wide use, and thousands of movie theaters opened. People danced to tunes coming from hand-cranked phonographs, and the record business boomed.

Postwar Currents of Thought

A revolution in ideas had begun even before 1914. After the terrible slaughter of the war, many thinkers rejected the Enlightenment faith in progress and reason. They no longer celebrated the success of science and industry as they had in prewar Europe. In the 1920s, European writers expressed a sense of helplessness and pessimism. French writer Paul Valéry summed up the postwar mood:

> The storm has died away, and still we are restless, uneasy, as if the storm were about to break. Almost all the affairs of men remain in a terrible uncertainty. We think of what has disappeared, and we are almost destroyed by what has been destroyed; we do not know what will be born, and we fear the future, not without reason.

Some writers expressed the horror and waste of the war, as German novelist Erich Maria Remarque did in *All Quiet on the Western Front.* (See page 622.) In his long poem *The Waste Land,* T.S. Eliot expressed anguish and disillusionment with an increasingly desolate world. German playwright Bertolt Brecht attacked capitalism in *The Three-Penny Opera* and other plays.

Many writers were strongly influenced by the work of Sigmund Freud. As you read in Chapter 22, this Viennese physician taught that irrational, unconscious forces shaped human behavior. At first, Freud's ideas were ridiculed. By the 1920s, however, his theories about human psychology were becoming more accepted.

Many writers used techniques such as stream of consciousness to probe the unconscious minds of their characters. In his novel *Ulysses,* Irish author James Joyce used stream of consciousness to depict a day in the life of a middle-class Dubliner. Joyce ignored standard grammar and used bits of thought, foreign words, and unconventional language to suggest the confusion of the unconscious mind. English writer Virginia Woolf gained fame for her novel *To the Lighthouse,* in which characters come to life through complex internal monologues.

Modern Painting

European artists used unconventional means to explore the inner worlds of human emotions. Many artists of the early 1900s had rejected realism and impressionism. Their works were increasingly abstract—that is, they did not represent objects as most people saw them.

Cubists used geometric forms in complex patterns to represent human forms and objects such as a guitar, a newspaper headline, or a pipe. After painting many masterpieces in the cubist style, one of the founders of cubism, Pablo Picasso, went on to paint other equally famous paintings in a variety of modern styles.

Other painters abandoned realism altogether and stressed color, line, and form. In *Composition with Red, Yellow, and Blue,* Dutch artist Piet Mondrian presented a series of brightly colored, boxlike shapes that had no conventional meaning.

An unusual artistic movement that flourished briefly in the 1920s was dada. The word dada, meaning "hobby horse" in French, was chosen because it implied nonsense. Dada painters and writers scorned traditional artistic forms. Such forms, they felt, were meaningless in a world turned upside down by the senseless slaughter of the war.

Marcel Duchamp, a leading dada artist, ridiculed traditional art by exhibiting shovels as works of art. Followers of dada glorified outrageous behavior. One produced a copy of Leonardo da Vinci's *Mona Lisa* with a mustache and ridiculous graffiti. Dada writers wrote poems by picking words out of a hat.

SECTION 2 REVIEW

1. **Identify:** (a) T.S. Eliot, (b) Bertolt Brecht, (c) James Joyce, (d) Virginia Woolf, (e) Pablo Picasso, (f) dada.

2. How did women's lives change after the war?

3. Describe three postwar developments in technology that affected the way people lived.

4. How was the mood of postwar Europe different from the mood of the 1800s?

5. **Critical Thinking** Why do you think there was a general feeling of unease in Europe after the war?

Pablo Picasso's painting, The Harlequin, *shows cubist ideas. Cubist painters translated natural shapes into geometrical forms. They often portrayed different sides of a subject, such as front and side, in the same picture.*

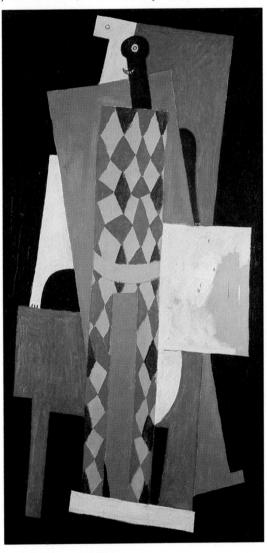

653

3 The United States in the 1920s and 1930s

READ TO UNDERSTAND

☐ Why isolationist feeling was strong in the United States after World War I.

☐ Why the 1920s seemed so prosperous in the United States.

☐ What the causes and results of the Great Depression were.

☐ How the United States government coped with the depression.

"The business of America is business," declared President Calvin Coolidge in the mid-l920s. During much of his term in office, the nation's businesses boomed. Factories poured out new products. The labor force was almost fully employed. Millions of people invested in the stock market, gambling on the hope of making even more money.

The United States had been reluctantly drawn into World War I. After the war, many Americans wanted nothing more to do with world affairs. Instead, they wanted to concentrate on business and other matters at home.

Postwar Isolationism

After World War I, isolationist feeling swept across the United States. President Wilson campaigned hard to win approval for the Versailles Treaty, which would have made the United States a member of the League of Nations. But the Senate rejected the treaty in November 1919. Senator William E. Borah expressed the fear of many Americans when he predicted that the United States would become "a part of European turmoils and conflicts from the time we enter this league."

Events in Europe strengthened isolationist feelings in the United States. During the Russian Revolution, the radical Bolshevik party under Lenin had seized power and made Russia a communist state. (See page 633.) When bombs exploded in several American cities in 1919 and 1920, many Americans feared that foreign-born radicals were plotting a Bolshevik uprising in the United States. In 1919, Attorney General A. Mitchell Palmer launched a series of raids to round up suspected "Reds." The government arrested and imprisoned thousands of people during this so-called Red Scare.

Isolationism and the Red Scare led many Americans to demand a change in the nation's immigration policy. The United States had restricted the number of immigrants allowed from China and Japan but had never limited immigration from Europe. After World War I, some people worried that immigrants were changing the character of American society for the worse. As a result, in 1921 and again in 1924, Congress passed acts placing quotas on European immigration.

Yet the United States did not withdraw entirely from world affairs. As you have read, it participated in naval disarmament negotiations and sponsored the Dawes Plan to ease German problems with reparation payments. And, by its role in drawing up the Kellogg-Briand Pact, the United States showed the world it wanted to preserve world peace.

Prosperity—On the Surface

During the 1920s, Americans were preoccupied with domestic affairs. When Warren G. Harding succeeded Woodrow Wilson as President in 1921, he promised a return to "normalcy." The word was a new one, but his audience had no difficulty understanding it. Normalcy meant withdrawing from foreign involvement and building a healthy peacetime economy. Indeed, many Americans prospered during the 1920s.

Unemployment, which stood at 11.7 percent in 1921, dropped to 2.4 percent in 1923. For the rest of the decade, the jobless rate never rose above 5 percent. Steady employment and good wages turned many American families into eager consumers. Sales of passenger cars more than tripled between 1921 and 1929. Thousands of new homes were built, creating a soaring demand for appliances and other home furnishings.

The patterns of daily life changed more noticeably in the United States than in Europe. Newspapers and magazines featured stories about free-spirited "flappers." These young women shocked their elders with their flashy clothes and use of slang. The average family owned a radio. About 60 million Americans went to the movies every week to see such stars as Charlie Chaplin and Rudolph Valentino. Jazz swept the country, along with such daring dances as the fox trot and the Charleston. During the Roaring Twenties, many Americans seemed to spend their time pursuing wealth and pleasure.

Beneath the surface of the Roaring Twenties, however, all was not well. As a group, farmers did not share in the general prosperity. During the war, farmers had found a ready market for their crops at home and in Europe and had increased production. After the war, however, demand fell off because European farms were back in operation. Crop surpluses drove prices down. The price of wheat fell from a wartime high of $2.26 a bushel to less than $1.00 a bushel in 1922. Other groups, such as coal miners and textile workers, were also doing poorly.

The Stock Market Crash and the Great Depression

Americans who had money to invest bought stocks and celebrated their good fortune as stock prices soared in the late 1920s. But stock prices were artificially high. In 1929, the stock market bubble burst. In October, stock prices tumbled, causing panicked investors to sell at a loss. By November, the total market value of stocks traded on the New York Stock Exchange had fallen by about $30 billion. Investors

Wall Street investors told success stories that made it seem impossible to lose money on the stock market. Millions of Americans invested their savings in stocks in the 1920s. This cover of a popular magazine from 1928 shows people of all ages and classes watching the ticker tape that recorded the market's rise and fall.

whose stocks had been worth millions suddenly found that they were worthless.

The stock market crash undermined confidence in the economy. It led to the Great Depression, a period of slow business activity, high unemployment, and falling prices and wages. The Great Depression was the worst business slump in American history. It soon triggered a worldwide economic crisis, as you will read.

By 1932, about 85,000 American businesses had failed. Unemployment rocketed from 3.2 percent in 1929 to 23.6 percent in 1932. In the United States, panic-stricken citizens rushed to withdraw their money from banks. But banks had loaned money to European and American businesses and did not have enough cash to honor their customers' deposits. As a result, thousands of banks closed.

The Great Depression caused enormous hardships. Many unemployed roamed the country vainly searching for jobs. Families broke up under the pressure of despair. People could not pay their rent and were evicted from their homes. Some moved into tarpaper shacks built in vacant lots and lived as best they could.

The United States had weathered depressions in the past, and the economy had eventually recovered on its own. Herbert Hoover, who had been elected President in 1928, and most other government leaders expected the same thing to happen this time. Hoover did, however, ask Congress to vote money for public works projects so that the government could hire workers for building jobs. He also favored creating the Reconstruction Finance Corporation, a government agency that lent money to banks and businesses.

These measures did little to ease the severe economic crisis. Hoover publicly predicted an early end to the depression, stating: "Prosperity is just around the corner." He

During the Great Depression, many small farmers were forced off their farms because they could not pay their debts. In addition, in the 1930s a severe drought drove many farmers off their land. Families such as this one piled their possessions into old cars and headed west. Known as "Okies" or "Arkies" because so many of them were from Oklahoma or Arkansas, these people hoped to find work in California, Washington, and Oregon.

hoped that his optimism would help restore confidence in the economy and encourage business leaders to invest in new ventures, thereby creating more jobs. But the depression dragged on.

The New Deal

In 1932, Americans voted overwhelmingly for the candidate of the Democratic party, Franklin D. Roosevelt. During the presidential campaign, Roosevelt had promised a "new deal for the American people," although he did not say just what this would involve. During Roosevelt's first three months in office, the New Deal took shape. It was a bold program to combat the Great Depression. It committed the government to becoming involved in the economy in many new ways.

The New Deal called for both economic and social programs. Among the first measures passed by Congress were laws to restore confidence in banks. The Emergency Banking Relief Act, for example, allowed some banks to reopen under federal supervision. Under the Glass-Steagall Act, the government guaranteed bank deposits of up to $5,000 for each depositor.

To reduce unemployment, the Works Progress Administration (WPA) was established. The WPA put millions of people to work building bridges, highways, dams, schools, and parks. In addition, the WPA hired unemployed artists, writers, and actors to work on projects for the public's benefit. The Civilian Conservation Corps provided work for unemployed youths. The federal government also gave relief funds to states so they could give money to the needy.

Along with these measures, the New Deal included social programs. Congress passed the Social Security Act to provide old-age benefits and a system of unemployment insurance. (As you have read, some European countries had set up such systems before World War I.) The National Labor Relations Act guaranteed workers' rights to organize unions and bargain collectively. As a result, many workers won better job benefits.

Under the New Deal, the lives of many ordinary people improved. Yet Roosevelt's programs did not restore prosperity to the United States. Unemployment remained high until another world war broke out in Europe in 1939. Whether or not the New Deal was a success is still debated. However, since then, the federal government has played a far larger role in the economy of the nation.

SECTION 3 REVIEW

1. **Identify:** (a) Red Scare, (b) Great Depression, (c) Herbert Hoover, (d) Franklin D. Roosevelt, (e) New Deal.

2. Why did Congress restrict immigration from Europe in the 1920s?

3. What evidence showed the prosperity of the United States in the 1920s?

4. What led to the Great Depression?

5. Describe three measures Roosevelt took to combat the depression.

6. **Critical Thinking** What were the basic differences between President Hoover's attempt to deal with the Great Depression and President Roosevelt's attempt?

---

4 Crises of the 1930s in Europe

READ TO UNDERSTAND

☐ How the British tried to cope with the Great Depression.

☐ How the depression affected France.

☐ Why countries of Eastern Europe turned to dictators in the 1930s.

The stock market crash that began in October 1929 and the Great Depression in the United States had disastrous effects in Europe and elsewhere. As Americans cut back on their investments in Europe, European trade and manufacturing fell. The number of jobless rose. The European Allies still owed large war debts to the United States. But they were unable to pay them, in part because Austria and Germany stopped paying reparations in 1932.

Europeans responded to the Great Depression in different ways, as you will read. In nations still recovering from the impact of the war, the economic collapse increased the sense of desperation. Some people turned to leaders who offered radical solutions to the crises of the 1930s.*

British Response to the Great Depression

In Britain, as elsewhere, the Great Depression brought terrible suffering to the unemployed and their families. The government provided relief payments, popularly called "the dole." But with these, people could buy only the

* You will read about Italy and Germany during the Great Depression in Chapter 30.

barest necessities. Life on the dole meant a diet mostly of white bread, margarine, and tea. Shabby clothes and missing teeth became the unwanted badges of Britons who lived on the dole.

The Labour party was in power when the Great Depression struck. To gain broader support for his policies, Prime Minister Ramsay MacDonald formed a coalition government in which the Labour and Conservative parties shared power. MacDonald headed the coalition until 1935, when the Conservative leader Stanley Baldwin took power.

Conservatives in Britain opposed widespread government intervention, such as President Roosevelt had introduced in the United States. However, the coalition government did try to increase exports. It also passed protective tariffs to help British manufacturing. And it lowered interest rates, which led to a boom in housing construction. The economy gradually recovered after 1932. In fact, by 1937, the British economy was stronger than it had been in the troubled 1920s.

Deep Divisions in France

France was heavily agricultural and less dependent on foreign trade than Britain. As a result, its economy withstood the early shocks of the Great Depression. By 1932, however, the economic slump had affected France, too. Exports fell, and unemployment rose.

Although France escaped some of the worst effects of the depression, the economic slump contributed to political instability. As you have read, there were many political parties in the Third Republic, from socialists on the left to monarchists on the right. None of these parties had enough votes to govern alone. So, for a French government to remain in power, it had to form a coalition of supporters from several parties. If supporters became dissatisfied with government policies, they withdrew from the coalition, causing the government to fall. In 1933 alone, France had five different governments.

Many people on the far right opposed the parliamentary democracy that existed in France. In February 1934, they rioted against the Third Republic when a scandal linked some government officials to a swindler

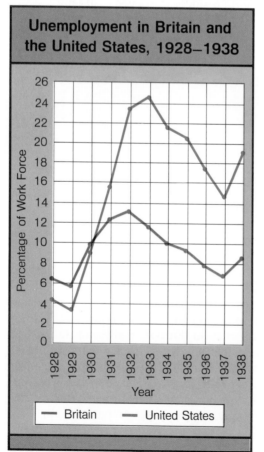

GRAPH STUDY *As the Great Depression spread throughout the world, millions of people lost jobs. According to this graph, was unemployment worse in the United States or in Britain during the 1930s?*

Unemployment in Britain and the United States, 1928–1938

Percentage of Work Force vs. Year (1928–1938)

— Britain   — United States

Source: Angus Maddison, *Economic Growth in the West.*

658

On Halloween night, 1938, millions of Americans clustered anxiously around their radio sets. Announcers grimly reported that invaders from Mars had landed in New Jersey. Although the story was fiction, actor Orson Welles presented *The War of the Worlds* as if it were an actual news broadcast. All over the country, people who had tuned in late and missed the beginning of the show panicked, thinking a real invasion was underway.

The furor set off by Welles's program showed the wide influence of radio. Regular radio programs had started in the United States in 1920. Two years later, there were 550 stations and 1.5 million radios in the United States. In Europe, radio sales also skyrocketed after World War I.

Radio brought the world into people's living rooms. Families that could not afford to go to concerts and had never heard classical music now listened to symphonies in their homes. Sportscasters created a vivid vocabulary to describe prize fights and ball games.

Westerns like *The Lone Ranger* were also very popular. Creative minds found ways to make sound effects that added excitement and realism to the shows. The sound of a storm was created by waving a thin sheet of metal close to the microphone. Crackling tissue paper and breaking matchsticks sounded like fire.

While radio relied on the listener's imagination, movies could actually show fires and storms. During the disruption of World War I, America grabbed the lead in movie making. Directors in Hollywood, a small town in California, made hundreds of silent films. Then, in 1927, filmmakers made a breakthrough. *The Jazz Singer,* the first sound movie, was made in Hollywood that year. Americans flocked to see the latest "talkie."

During the Great Depression, people could escape from their troubles at the movie theaters, watching lavish musicals, gripping gangster movies, and dramas such as *Gone With the Wind*, shown below. Admission to the dream cost only 25 cents.

1. How did radio affect people's lives?

2. **Critical Thinking** (a) Why do you think movies became so popular? (b) Why were they especially important to people during the depression?

named Serge Stavisky. Anti-democratic forces claimed that the Stavisky scandal proved that the Third Republic was hopelessly corrupt.

Supporters of the republic feared that groups on the far right wanted to establish a dictatorship in France. This fear prompted groups on the left to set aside their differences and form a coalition government, the Popular Front.

In 1936, the Popular Front, led by socialist Leon Blum, tried to introduce social reforms such as a 40-hour work week and paid vacations. Although these reforms were popular with workers, business leaders objected to them. As opposition grew, the Popular Front collapsed. Thus, by the late 1930s, France was a deeply divided nation.

A Troubled Era in Eastern Europe

The new nations of Eastern Europe shared many problems in the postwar period. None of these nations was highly industrialized. Only about 10 percent of the people worked in industry. Most people worked on small farms. Land reforms in several countries had given land to the peasants. But their plots were small, and primitive equipment limited their output.

When some of the new nations such as Czechoslovakia, Austria, and Poland gained independence at the end of the war, they adopted democratic constitutions. Yet the peoples in these countries did not have strong traditions of democracy. For centuries, they had been ruled by authoritarian regimes. When economic problems worsened, people often turned to strong leaders who rejected democratic forms of government and created dictatorships.

Austria. A small, landlocked country, Austria suffered from a lack of raw materials and foreign trade. During the 1920s, foreign loans helped Austria to expand its industry, but the onset of the Great Depression ended foreign investment in Austria.

Between 1929 and 1932, industrial production fell by 40 percent, and unemployment soared. Many middle- and upper-class Austrians feared that the economic crisis would help the socialists or communists seize power. In 1933, the Austrian Chancellor, Engelbert Dollfuss, suspended parliament in response to this fear. The next year, he dissolved all opposition political parties, ended the organized labor movement, and had himself officially declared dictator.

Hungary. During the 1920s and 1930s, Hungary had an elected parliament. But the landowning aristocrats dominated the government. Peasants were denied the right to vote, and Hungarian leaders resisted any attempt to pass land reform. During the Great Depression, the extreme right gained power and set up a dictatorship in Hungary. The new government had the support of conservatives and nationalists.

Poland. The Polish constitution of 1921 guaranteed a democratic form of government. It provided for a two-house parliament and universal suffrage. But several political parties jockeyed for power, and first one then another led the government. Because the party in power changed so often, the government could not deal effectively with the nation's problems.

Impatient with democracy, some Poles clamored for a strong leader who would guide their country with a firm hand. They turned to General Joseph Pilsudski (peel SOOT skee), who led a revolt in 1926. After a few days of fighting, the government fell. Pilsudski dissolved the parliament, arrested critics of his regime, and set himself up as dictator.

Czechoslovakia. During the postwar period, Czechoslovakia maintained a democratic government in the face of many difficulties. The government introduced land reform and built up industry. One problem facing the government, however, was the many different ethnic groups living in the country. Czechs made up a majority of the population and controlled much of the nation's wealth and power. This irritated the other ethnic groups, including the Slovaks, Magyars, and Germans.

To reduce tension, the government gave each group some autonomy. For example, Germans were allowed to use German in their schools. Despite such measures, ethnic minorities continued to demand self-rule in the 1930s. Three million Germans lived in the Sudetenland, a region in northern Czechoslovakia. In the late 1930s, the Sudeten Germans would become the focus of an international crisis, as you will read in Chapter 31.

SECTION 4 REVIEW

1. **Identify:** (a) Ramsay MacDonald, (b) Popular Front, (c) Engelbert Dollfuss, (d) Joseph Pilsudski.

2. Describe one way in which the British government responded to the Great Depression.

3. (a) Why was France spared the worst economic effects of the Great Depression? (b) How did the Great Depression affect France politically?

4. List three problems faced by nations of Eastern Europe in the postwar era.

5. Which Eastern European nation or nations remained democratic into the mid-1930s?

6. **Critical Thinking** Choose one Western European nation and one Eastern European country and compare how they responded to the crisis of the Great Depression.

5 Nationalist Struggles Outside Europe

READ TO UNDERSTAND

☐ What changes took places in the Middle East after World War I.

☐ How India gained greater self-government.

☐ What groups battled for power in China.

☐ How nationalism grew in Africa and Latin America.

☐ *Vocabulary:* genocide, nationalize.

Some people saw him as a "half-naked madman." Others thought of him as a misguided idealist. But to tens of millions of Indians, Mohandas Gandhi was the Holy One. In early April 1919, this small, fragile, gentle man called on Indians to observe a day of hartal, abstaining from any economic activity, to protest British rule. To the shock of the British and the surprise of even Gandhi himself, almost everyone in India observed the day. Buses did not move. Ships remained unloaded. Banks could not open.

Gandhi believed that without using violence the Indians could persuade the British to give the people self-rule. He was convinced that they should arouse support for their cause through self-suffering.

World War I had fueled the growing nationalism of the peoples of the Middle East, Asia, Africa, and Latin America. Nationalist leaders, like Gandhi, had hoped that the principle of self-determination, discussed at the peace conference, would apply to European colonies. But their hopes for self-government were disappointed.

Revolution in Turkey

As you have read, the Paris peace settlement broke up the Ottoman Empire. In 1919, Greece seized land still ruled by the Turks in Asia Minor. The sultan did little to resist the Greek attacks. However, Turkish nationalists were outraged. Led by army officer Mustafa Kemal, they resisted the Greeks fiercely. By 1922, Kemal had expelled the Greeks from Asia Minor.

From 1915 to 1922, the Ottoman Empire had expelled or executed almost all of its native Armenian population. The Armenians were Christians, but they had long played a major role in the economy of the Ottoman Empire. During World War I, however, the sultan followed a policy of **genocide**, the systematic killing of a whole people. One and a half million Armenians were exterminated. Many who escaped made their way to the United States.

In 1922, the Ottoman Empire was abolished. A year later, Kemal became the first president of the Republic of Turkey. Kemal made sweeping political and social changes. He wanted to make Turkey a strong modern industrial nation, free from foreign influence. He introduced a constitution and a legal system based on European models. Under the new law code, the power of the Islamic clergy was reduced. Kemal also introduced the western alphabet, a western-style calendar, and the metric system of measurement.

To make Turkey look modern, Kemal banned the wearing of the fez, a brimless felt hat worn by men during the Ottoman Empire.

MAP STUDY   *After World War I, Britain and France received parts of the former Ottoman Empire as mandates. Britain also sought to keep its influence in Egypt and Iran. What mandates did France receive?*

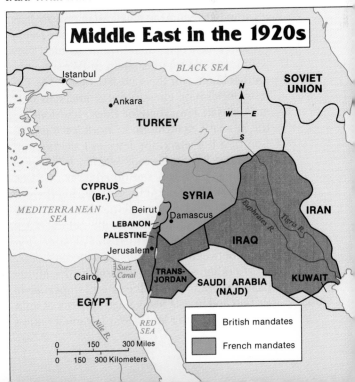

Middle East in the 1920s

British mandates

French mandates

Kemal also introduced the use of surnames. He took the name Atatürk, meaning father of the Turks.

Other changes affected women. Women gained the right to vote and hold office. The government passed laws that discouraged the practice of segregating women in public places. Some Turks welcomed the changes. Many others felt that western ways would destroy their traditional values.

Unrest in the Middle East

As you have read, Ottoman lands in the Middle East were awarded to France and Britain as mandates. (See page 642.) During the postwar period, Arab nationalists there demanded self-government. But the discovery of rich oil fields in the Middle East made western powers unwilling to give up control of this area.

Despite nationalist uprisings, France kept its mandates in Syria and Lebanon. Iraq, a British mandate, gained independence in 1930 and later joined the League of Nations. Egypt, which had been a British protectorate since 1882, was granted independence in 1923. But Britain kept troops in Egypt to protect the Suez Canal. British influence in Iraq remained strong, and Britain also kept complete control over its mandate in Transjordan.

In the 1920s and 1930s, the British mandate of Palestine was the source of growing tension between Arab and Jewish nationalists. In 1917, Britain had issued the Balfour Declaration, which said that Britain would "view with favor the establishment in Palestine of a national home for the Jewish people." The Balfour Declaration encouraged Zionists. In 1897, an Austrian Jew, Theodor Herzl, had founded the Zionist Organization to work for the creation of a homeland for Jews in Palestine.

Many Jews in Europe wanted to settle in Palestine. However, the population of Palestine was 98 percent Arab. Also, during the war, the British had supported the idea of an independent Arab nation that might include Palestine. As more Jews settled in Palestine, tensions between Arabs and Jews increased.

Another source of tension in the Middle East was Iran. During the Age of Imperialism, Britain and Russia had gained spheres of influence in Iran. After World War I, Iranian nationalists found a leader in army officer Reza Khan. In 1925, Reza Khan seized power and took the name Reza Shah Pahlavi. (Shah means king in Persian.) Like Atatürk in Turkey, the shah introduced reforms to modernize and industrialize his nation. But both Britain and Russia competed for influence over Iranian affairs.

India on the Road to Independence

During World War I, Britain had promised to loosen its control over the Indian subcontinent at some time in the future. This vague promise did not satisfy Indian nationalists, who demanded self-government. To deal with growing unrest, Parliament gave British authorities in India the power to imprison nationalist leaders without trial. This move led to even more protests.

In 1919, a British official, Reginald Dyer, banned all public meetings in Amritsar, a town in northern India. When a crowd of unarmed men and women defied his order and assembled in a public area, Dyer ordered his troops to open fire. When the shooting ended, 379 Indians lay dead. More than a thousand others were injured. The Amritsar massacre outraged Indians and even many British, as well as world opinion.

Britain made concessions to Indian nationalists in the Government of India Act of 1919. Under this law, Indians gained control of many local matters. But it left the most important government functions, such as taxation, foreign policy, and justice, in British hands. The nationalist Congress party condemned the act because it did not go far enough.

In the postwar period, the Congress party was led by Mohandas Gandhi. Gandhi was a British-educated lawyer who had first emerged as a spokesman for Indians in South Africa. Gandhi advocated a policy of nonviolent resistance to British rule. He urged Indians to boycott British goods and revive cottage industries such as spinning cotton cloth. These industries had declined when Britain had begun selling its own manufactured goods in India. Gandhi also led a peaceful "march to the sea" so Indians could make salt to protest an unpopular law banning the making of salt from sea water.

Gandhi adopted a simple, austere way of life. He gave up western-style clothing in favor of the dhoti, the homespun garment worn by Hindu men. In time, he became known as Mahatma, meaning "Great Soul," for his dedication to the cause of Indian independence. Gandhi wanted to restore Indians' pride in their traditional culture. Yet he rejected the Hindu caste system, especially the treatment of untouchables as outcastes.

Despite Gandhi's call for nonviolence, there were many riots against British rule. In addition, clashes occurred between Hindu and Muslim nationalists. In 1935, Britain granted Indians an even greater role in government. But Gandhi and the Congress party still demanded complete independence.

Turmoil in China

The Manchu dynasty, you will recall, was overthrown in the Revolution of 1911. However, the revolution did not bring peace. Sun Yat-sen, leader of the revolution, served as president of China for only a month before he was ousted by a general. Gradually, the country fell into

BUILDERS AND SHAPERS Gandhi's Nonviolent Revolution

Mohandas Gandhi lived in South Africa for 20 years. As an Indian, Gandhi was subject to special laws that discriminated against "colored" people. Indians, like blacks, were not allowed to vote or to live in white neighborhoods. It was in South Africa that Gandhi began what he called his "experiments with truth." On one occasion, a train conductor commanded Gandhi to leave a first-class compartment, which was reserved for whites only.

"But I have a first-class ticket."

"That doesn't matter."

"I tell you, I was permitted to travel in this compartment, and I insist on going on in it."

"No, you won't. You must leave this compartment, or I shall have to call a police constable to push you out."

"Yes, you may. I refuse to get out voluntarily."

After the police had ejected Gandhi from the train, he sat in the station and thought about the incident. "I began to think of my duty. Should I fight for my rights or go back to India? It would be cowardice to run back to India without fulfilling my obligation. The hardship to which I was subjected was superficial, only a symptom of the deep disease of color prejudice. I should try, if possible, to root out the disease and suffer hardships in the process."

Gandhi dedicated his life to rooting out the disease of racial prejudice. During his years in South Africa, he developed the policy of satyagraha, or nonviolent resistance, which took its name from the words for "truth" and "firmness." When he returned to India, Gandhi used satyagraha to oppose British rule.

Gandhi taught that satyagraha demanded greater bravery and self-control than did violent struggle. Some Indians thought Gandhi had taken satyagraha too far. After all, they asked, didn't people have a right to defend themselves? But for Gandhi there were no exceptions. "I would welcome even utter failure with nonviolence unimpaired," he said, "rather than depart from it by a hair's breadth."

1. What did satyagraha mean to Gandhi and his followers?

2. **Critical Thinking** Why do you think Gandhi's approach appealed to people with strong religious beliefs?

One of the survivors of the Long March, Huang Zhen, drew this sketch of the Communist army fleeing from Chiang's extermination campaigns. The marchers trekked over rough, mountainous terrain for much of the 6,000-mile journey. This is the only drawing of the march by someone who actually took part in it.

chaos as warlords battled for control of the countryside. They supported their armies by forcing peasants and merchants to pay heavy taxes.

Sun Yat-sen set up a base in Canton and rallied young patriots to the Kuomintang, or Nationalist party. Sun was popular because he held out the hope of building a new China. His ideas were summed up in the "Three Principles of the People." (See page 589.)

Sun realized he would need an army to reunite China and put his principles into practice. Therefore, he organized a Kuomintang army under a young officer, Chiang Kai-shek (CHANG kī SHEHK). In 1927, two years after Sun died, Chiang led his army on a victorious march north from Canton. By 1928, the Kuomintang was powerful enough to proclaim the Republic of China as the nation's government.

At the same time, Chiang had to deal with a rival political organization, the Chinese Communist party. The Chinese Communist party was founded in 1921. Its leaders had encouraged its members to join the Kuomintang.

The Communists hoped that they could eventually control the much larger and more powerful Kuomintang. They were outmaneuvered, however, by Chiang. He struck swiftly in 1927. He expelled Communists from the Kuomintang, killing many of them and forcing the survivors into hiding.

Mao Zedong* (mow dzoo doong) was one of the Communists who escaped. He began to rebuild his party's fortunes in a remote mountain region in southeastern China. He attracted support by helping poor landless peasants. He also spoke out against western imperialism in China. Mao built an army and soon began winning territory.

Chiang launched four "extermination campaigns" against the Communists. Kuomintang forces finally routed Mao's armies in 1934. About 90,000 Communist troops fled from Kiangsi to begin a 6,000-mile (9,600-kilometer) march toward the desolate Shensi Province in northwestern China. Only about 7,000 troops survived this "Long March."

In Shensi, Mao's communist forces were so small and battered that they seemed to have little future. While the Kuomintang and Communists were fighting, another threat to peace in China was developing. As you will read in Chapter 30, in the early 1930s, Japan was expanding onto the Asian mainland.

Nationalism in Africa

During World War I, black African troops had fought in both the British and French armies. African leaders believed that their wartime service would win them more political freedom. They were thus bitterly disappointed when the peace settlement awarded the former German colonies in Africa as mandates to Britain, France, and Belgium.

After the war, Europeans tightened their grip on their African colonies. However, Africans continued to oppose colonial rule. In Morocco and Algeria, nationalists fought

---

*In 1979, the Chinese government adopted a new system of spelling, the Pinyin system. In general, this book uses the traditional Wade-Giles system except for personal names and place names that have become common American usage. Mao Zedong is the Pinyin spelling of Mao Tse-tung.

against French control. Resistance occurred in British colonies, too. In Nigeria, women who sold their goods in markets protested against high taxes. Their protests developed into the Aba Women's Riots. The women's complaints about taxes became a demand that "all white men should return to their country." The British suppressed the riots, in which 50 women were killed.

During the 1920s and 1930s, several future African leaders were studying and working in Europe. In England, Jomo Kenyatta of Kenya wrote a book, *Facing Mount Kenya.* In it, he described how British rule had disrupted the traditional culture of his people. In France, Léopold Senghor gained fame for his poetry and other writings that expressed pride in African culture. Kenyatta and Senghor were part of a growing movement among educated Africans to revive the heritage of Africa. They believed that cultural pride would help unify Africans in the struggle for self-government.

Developments in Latin America

World War I had little political or military impact on Latin America, although the increased wartime demand for raw materials did affect Latin America economies. Between 1910 and 1920, Latin American nations almost tripled their exports. Chile, for example, stepped up its export of nitrate, a mineral used in the making of explosives. These exports fell sharply, however, when the war ended.

After the war, European investments in Latin America also declined. In the 1920s, the United States replaced Britain as the largest investor in the region. The growing economic power of the United States touched off nationalist reactions. In several Latin American nations anti-American protests broke out.

Anti-Americanism increased during the Great Depression, when world market prices for raw materials fell sharply. Latin American nations that depended on the export of one or two raw materials were especially hard hit. Between 1929 and 1932, the value of Latin American exports dropped by 65 percent.

In the early 1920s, the United States continued its policy of military intervention in Latin America. But toward the end of the dec-

ade, that policy began to change. The United States gave up the Roosevelt Corollary, which the United States had used to justify sending troops into several Latin American countries. (See page 614.) Then, in the 1930s President Franklin D. Roosevelt took a more positive, friendlier approach to Latin America by putting into effect a "Good Neighbor Policy." Moreover, to prove its good intentions, the United States canceled the Platt Amendment limiting Cuban sovereignty. It also withdrew troops it had stationed in Haiti.

Still, nationalists in many Latin American nations realized their countries could not become truly independent until they became less dependent on the export of raw materials. Thus, they urged the building of new industries. Nationalist feeling led Mexico to take a bold step in 1938. It seized oilfields owned by Britain, the United States, and the Netherlands in Mexico and **nationalized** them—that is, it brought them under government control. Foreign owners protested strongly, but the Mexicans stood firm. Eventually, the Mexican government paid the foreign companies for the property it had seized.

SECTION 5 REVIEW

1. **Identify:** (a) Mustafa Kemal, (b) Balfour Declaration, (c) Zionists, (d) Chiang Kaishek, (e) Mao Zedong, (f) Jomo Kenyatta, (g) Léopold Senghor.

2. **Define:** (a) genocide, (b) nationalize.

3. List two changes Atatürk introduced in Turkey.

4. What two groups claimed the right to live in Palestine?

5. Why were African nationalists disappointed in the peace settlement?

6. What new policy did the United States follow in Latin America in the 1930s?

7. **Critical Thinking** (a) Describe Gandhi's policy of nonviolent resistance. (b) Why do you think such a policy caused problems for the British in India?

CHAPTER 29 REVIEW

Summary

1. **After World War I, European nations had to rebuild their economies.** Britain suffered from aging industries and foreign competition for world trade. Inflation hurt both France and Germany. Despite economic troubles, diplomats worked to preserve the peace settlement.

2. **The war changed the lives of many Europeans.** Women gained new rights and roles in society. People now enjoyed new technology such as cars and movies. Yet the works of European writers and artists reflected a sense of despair brought on by the terrible slaughter of the war.

3. **After the war, Americans were mainly concerned with developments at home.** Many Americans enjoyed the prosperity of the 1920s. However, the stock market crash of 1929 triggered the Great Depression. In 1933, President Franklin D. Roosevelt introduced the New Deal in the hopes of ending the depression.

4. **The Great Depression spread around the world.** It caused political as well as economic problems. Democracy survived in Britain and France, but dictators came to power in Austria, Poland, and Hungary. Only Czechoslovakia remained democratic.

5. **Nationalists challenged European rule in many parts of the globe.** In India, Gandhi led the Congress party in nonviolent protests against British rule. In China, the Kuomintang and Communist parties competed for power. In Africa, anti-colonial protests took place, while Latin American nationalists pressed for economic independence.

Recalling Facts

Choose the word or phrase that best completes each of the following statements.

1. British workers called the General Strike of 1926 to protest (a) the Versailles Treaty; (b) wage cuts; (c) foreign competition.

2. The Easter Rebellion was an uprising of (a) Irish nationalists; (b) Protestants in Northern Ireland; (c) British troops stationed in Ireland.

3. France built the Maginot Line to (a) limit German economic competition; (b) prevent another German invasion; (c) force Germany to pay reparations.

4. During the New Deal, the United States government tried to (a) reduce unemployment; (b) end federal supervision of banks; (c) reduce welfare benefits.

5. Indian nationalists objected to the Government of India Act because it (a) kept Gandhi out of office; (b) did not grant independence; (c) made Hindus and Muslims equal.

Chapter Checkup

1. (a) What economic difficulties did Britain face after World War I? (b) How did it respond to the crisis in Ireland?

2. (a) Describe the crisis in the Ruhr in 1923. (b) How was it resolved?

3. (a) Why did Americans support isolationism after World War I? (b) Was United States isolationism complete? Explain.

4. Why was the Popular Front formed in France in 1936?

5. Describe what happened to democratic institutions of government in each of the following nations: (a) Austria; (b) Hungary; (c) Poland; (d) Czechoslovakia.

6. (a) What did Arab nationalists in the Middle East want? (b) Why did European nations oppose their demands?

7. (a) How did Sun Yat-sen try to create a new China? (b) What problems did he face in achieving his goals?

8. How did Africans such as Jomo Kenyatta and Léopold Senghor try to strengthen African nationalism?

Critical Thinking

1. **Analyzing** (a) Describe the ways Europeans and Americans tried to prevent another war after 1919. (b) Do you think their efforts were likely to succeed? Explain.

2. **Understanding the Roots of Democracy** During the Great Depression, the United States government became involved in the economy on a large scale. What role do you think the government should play in the economy of a democratic nation?

3. **Relating Past to Present** (a) How did women's horizons expand in the postwar period? (b) How do you think World War I and its aftermath contributed to expanded horizons for women today?

4. **Understanding Economic Ideas** (a) What effects did the Great Depression have on economies around the world? (b) How did the economic crisis test the strength of democracies?

Developing Basic Skills

1. **Graph Reading** Study the graph on page 658. (a) What percentage of Americans was out of work in 1929? In 1933? (b) In which year was unemployment at its worst in Britain? In the United States? (c) Why do you think unemployment was such a difficult problem during the Great Depression?

2. **Researching** Research the background of one of the nationalist leaders you read about in this chapter. (a) Where was the person born and raised? (b) What experiences led him to become a nationalist leader? (c) What goals did he have for his country?

Writing About History

Organizing Note Cards

To organize the information you have gathered for your research paper, look at the subject you have written in the upper right-hand corner of each note card. Correlate the cards with the divisions of your preliminary outline. Choose those cards that support your thesis statement and are related to the outline topics. Decide on the order of supporting information you will use under each topic. Then arrange your cards in that order.

Practice: Imagine that one of the headings for a paper on the depression in Britain is "The Coalition Government." Which of these topics would correlate with that subject? Explain.

1. The Labour party
2. The dole
3. Unemployment in 1930
4. Stanley Baldwin
5. Prime Minister David Lloyd George

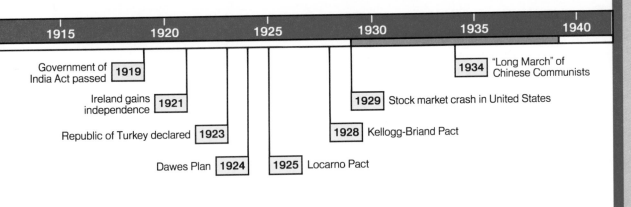

1915   1920   1925   1930   1935   1940

Government of India Act passed | 1919

Ireland gains independence | 1921

Republic of Turkey declared | 1923

Dawes Plan | 1924

1925 | Locarno Pact

1928 | Kellogg-Briand Pact

1929 | Stock market crash in United States

1934 | "Long March" of Chinese Communists

■ The Great Depression

The Rise of Totalitarian States

30

(1922–1936)

Spectators cheer wildly and raise their arms in salute as Nazi troops parade through the Brandenburg Gate in Berlin. Attracted by his promises, millions of Germans enthusiastically supported Adolf Hitler and celebrated his rise to power.

The night was cold, but the 10-year-old girl hardly felt the biting wind. As she clutched her mother's hand, she shared the excitement and joy of the young men and women watching the parade. That January night in 1933, the people were celebrating the election victory of the National Socialist German Workers' party and its leader, Adolf Hitler.

"My parents took us children, my twin brother and myself, into the center of the city," the woman recalled years later. "There we witnessed the torchlight procession with which the National Socialists celebrated their victory. Some of the uncanny [strange] feeling of that night remains with me even today. The crashing tread of the feet, the somber pomp of the red and black flags, the flickering light from the torches on the faces, and the songs with melodies that were at once aggressive and sentimental."

At the time, the girl was thrilled: "I longed to hurl myself into this current, to be submerged and borne along by it." An enormous joy swept over her. "'For the flag we are ready to die,' the torch-bearers had sung. I was overcome with a burning desire to belong to these people for whom it [the flag] was a matter of life and death."

The girl later joined the youth movement organized by the National Socialists, or Nazis, as party members were called. Like millions of other Germans, she believed in the Nazi promise of strength, struggle, and victory.

During the 1920s and 1930s, powerful leaders established authoritarian governments in Russia, Italy, and Japan as well as Germany. With promises of a glorious future, leaders in these countries won the support of millions of people. Often people followed these strong leaders because they offered hope at a time when many were uncertain about the future. The growing power of dictators would put an end to the hopes of a more peaceful world. ■

1 Revolution in Russia

READ TO UNDERSTAND

☐ How Lenin adapted the ideas of Marx to Russian conditions.

☐ What groups fought each other in the Russian civil war.

☐ How Lenin's policies changed economic and social life in Russia.

☐ *Vocabulary:* soviet.

In January 1917, a Russian revolutionary living in exile in Switzerland told an audience of young people, "We of the older generation may not live to see the decisive battles of this coming revolution." Two months later, while the exile was eating his dinner, a friend burst into his room. "There's been a revolution in Russia," he cried.

The exile was Vladimir Ilyich Ulyanov, better known to history as Lenin. Soon after the March revolution, he returned to Russia and prepared for a second revolution that he hoped would bring the collapse of European capitalism.

The threat of revolution had hung over Russia for decades. But the strains of World War I triggered the downfall of the Romanov dynasty and the emergence of a new Russian society.

Prelude to Revolution

The revolution of 1905, you will recall, forced Czar Nicholas II to make some political reforms. (See page 548.) But peasants, factory workers, and many middle-class intellectuals were not satisfied. Moreover, Nicholas II believed it was his sacred duty to preserve the absolute power of the czar. He rejected most efforts at reform and distrusted the advice of the Duma, the Russian legislature.

World War I was a disaster for the Russians. Because they were badly led and poorly armed, Russian armies suffered huge casualties. While Nicholas II tried to rally morale at the front, Czarina Alexandra preserved his absolute power at home. She, in turn, relied almost totally on the advice of Grigori Rasputin, an uneducated and corrupt monk.

Rasputin gained influence over Alexandra because only he seemed able to help Alexis, her only son and the heir to the throne. Alexis suffered from hemophilia, a rare blood disease. A group of nobles, angry at Rasputin's meddling in the government, murdered him in December 1916. The death of Rasputin had little effect on the government. But the czarina was haunted by the monk's prophecy: "If I die or you desert me, in six months you will lose your son and your throne."

The March Revolution

Early in March 1917, as the war dragged on, riots broke out in Petrograd. (See page 633.) Mobs roamed the streets demanding "bread and peace." Hungry rioters looted bakeries. Many of the troops ordered to put down the revolt mutinied and joined the protesters. On March 12, the Duma formed a provisional government and called for the election of an assembly to draw up a constitution for Russia. Three days later the czar abdicated.

Even while Russians celebrated the overthrow of the czar, the Provisional Government faced many problems. Many Russians wanted to continue fighting Germany. Others demanded an immediate peace. Peasants wanted their own land at once, and city workers expected higher wages and more food.

Faced with conflicting demands, the Provisional Government took a moderate course. Its leaders, Prince George Lvov and, later, Alexander Kerensky, were determined to pursue the war and rejected the demand for peace. They introduced some liberal reforms such as freedom of speech and religion and equality of all people before the law. But they resisted pressure for immediate redistribution of land from large estates.

The Provisional Government was not the only political power in Russia. When the revolution began, radical revolutionaries who had been living in exile returned to Russia. In Petrograd and other Russian cities, these radical revolutionaries formed **soviets,** councils of workers, soldiers, and intellectuals. The soviets claimed the right to run factories and issue their own orders to soldiers in the army. Their orders undermined the authority of the Provisional Government, especially at the front.

The soviets were strongest in the cities. But in the countryside, peasants conducted their own revolution, seizing land from nobles. By the summer of 1917, the Provisional Government seemed unable to enforce order in Russia.

Bolshevik Takeover

When the revolution broke out in March, Vladimir Lenin, as you read, was in exile in Zurich, Switzerland. German agents contacted Lenin in Zurich and arranged for a special sealed train to carry him from Switzerland through Germany to Russia. The German government hoped Lenin would contribute to the chaos and disorder in Russia, thereby weakening the Russian war effort.

Lenin returned to Russia in April. As soon as he reached Petrograd, he set to work to gain control of the soviets in order to achieve his own program for revolution.

Leninism. Lenin had been born into a middle-class Russian family. He became a revolutionary after his brother was executed for plotting to kill the czar. As a student, Lenin read the works of Karl Marx and developed a firm belief in revolutionary socialism. (See page 498.) He believed that through revolution, private property would be abolished and a classless society formed.

Marx, you will recall, had predicted that oppressed workers would overthrow industrial capitalism and establish a communist society. Lenin knew that Russia was not an industrial society such as Marx had described. However, even though the industrial working class in Russia was very small, Lenin argued that a socialist revolution could take place there. He thought the masses of Russian peasants would support the revolution. But Lenin believed a socialist revolution would succeed only if it were carried out by a small, well-organized, and highly disciplined group of leaders.

Lenin and his followers made up the more radical wing of the Russian Social Democratic party, which had been founded in the early 1900s. They called themselves Bolsheviks, which means majority in Russian. In April 1917, when Lenin returned to Russia, the Bolsheviks had relatively few members, but Lenin skillfully built up support for his cause. He wrote stinging editorials in Bolshevik newspapers criticizing the Provisional Government and calling for an end to the war. He raised two other demands in the slogans "All land to the peasants" and "All power to the soviets."

During the summer of 1917, the Bolsheviks won control of the key soviets of Petrograd and Moscow. In October, the Petrograd Soviet chose Leon Trotsky, a close associate of Lenin, as its chairman. A brilliant organizer, Trotsky helped plot a Bolshevik takeover of power.

The November Revolution. On the night of November 6, 1917, Bolsheviks moved against the headquarters of the Provisional Government in Petrograd. The Provisional Government had lost most of its popular support because it had failed to restore the morale of the Russia troops, many of whom were deserting and returning home. As a result, the Bolsheviks met only light resistance. They seized government buildings, the railway station, telephone exchanges, and electric lighting plants.

Lenin and Trotsky had timed their move to coincide with a meeting of the All-Russian Congress of Soviets. At this meeting, delegates from soviets all over Russia approved the Bolshevik seizure of power and chose Lenin to lead the new government. Lenin immediately promised to take Russia out of the war and redistribute land to the peasants. As you have read, he quickly negotiated the Treaty of Brest-Litovsk with Germany. His other goals, however, were delayed by the outbreak of civil war.

Civil War in Russia

Even as Lenin negotiated peace with Germany, anti-Bolshevik forces in Russia launched efforts to overthrow the new government. From 1917 to 1921, the Bolsheviks—officially renamed Communists in March 1918—fought a wide range of enemies. Their opponents were unable to unite behind a single leader or accept a single set of goals. Some wanted the czar restored to power. Others supported socialism but opposed Lenin. By 1918, there were 18 rival groups seeking to oust the Communists from power.

By late 1917, the Provisional Government seemed besieged by problems. People demanded food, land, and an end to the war. Lenin, shown here with a group of fellow revolutionaries, believed the time for action had come. "History will not forgive us if we do not assume power now," Lenin declared as he urged the Bolsheviks to take control of the government.

During the civil war, the Communists were called "Reds" because the color red had long been associated with revolutionary socialists. Their chief opponents were the "Whites," various groups that included army officers and nobles as well as peasants and people from the middle class. The Allied powers sent troops to help the Whites. They did not want war supplies they had sent to Russia earlier to fall into German hands, and some in western governments feared a communist victory in Russia.

Although the Communists were almost defeated in 1919, Trotsky organized an efficient Red Army that turned the tide of the civil war. Disunity among the Whites also helped the Communists. Moreover, the Communists persuaded peasants to support their cause. They claimed a White victory would mean an end to land reform. Finally, Allied intervention aroused Russian nationalism so that many non-Communists fought with the Red Army to defend their homeland.

671

Тов. Ленин ОЧИЩАЕТ землю от нечисти.

Lenin envisioned a classless society, free of those who profited from the work of others. In this poster, Lenin vigorously sweeps those he considered exploiters—monarchs and capitalists—off the face of the earth.

Under the czars, few Russians learned to read and write. After the Russian Revolution, many schools were set up for adults. The new schools were open to everyone. Basic courses such as reading, writing, and arithmetic were taught along with courses explaining the benefits of socialism.

During the civil war, Lenin followed a policy called "war communism." The government took control of most industries, railroads, and banks. It ordered peasants to turn over surplus grain to the government, but often it simply seized the grain needed to supply the Red Army. The government also used terror and censorship to silence critics of the revolution. The czar and his family were executed to prevent them from becoming a rallying symbol for opponents to communism. Then, like the czars before them, the Communists created a secret police, the Cheka. Its agents hunted down and executed so-called enemies of the state. In 1921, the efforts of the Communists paid off, and the Whites were defeated.

Lenin's New Economic Policy

The civil war devastated Russia. Peasants cut back on their crops because the government was seizing most of their grain anyway. Then, in 1920 and 1921, crops failed. Millions of Russians died in the resulting famine. Hundreds of thousands of workers fled the cities to search for food in the countryside. Steel production fell far below what it had been in 1914. The economy sputtered to a standstill.

When the civil war ended, Lenin turned his attention to building a new Russian society. His goal was to create a communist state. Communism is a system of government in which the state owns all the means of production, including industry and agriculture. In theory, it calls for a "dictatorship of the people" and promises a classless society. But to achieve his long-term goal, Lenin had to make several compromises with communist theory. His immediate problem was to ease the desperate economic crisis.

In March 1921, Lenin announced the New Economic Policy (NEP), a program designed to rebuild the shattered Russian economy. The NEP eliminated many harsh measures of war communism and permitted the return of some capitalist practices. To encourage farm production, the government stopped seizing grain. Peasants were encouraged to sell their surplus grain on the open market. The government kept control of heavy industry, railroads, and banks, but it allowed small manufacturers to run their own businesses.

Under the NEP, which lasted until 1928, the Russian economy improved. Industry and farm output returned to prewar levels. Workers enjoyed shorter hours and better conditions. For a time, the government relaxed the terror and censorship it had employed during the civil war.

Lenin also introduced political and social changes. Russia was made up of many different nationalities. The Communists recognized this fact by organizing four autonomous, or self-governing, republics. In 1922, Russia was officially renamed the Union of Soviet Socialist Republics (USSR), or Soviet Union. (See the map on page 674.)

During the revolution and afterwards, the old social structure was swept away. Titles of nobility were eliminated, and soldiers stopped addressing officers as "your excellency." The Eastern Orthodox Church, which had been very powerful under the czars, lost its influence. Laws were passed that guaranteed equality for men and women. In the early 1920s, many Russians expected that the revolution would give them greater freedom than they had had under the czars.

SECTION 1 REVIEW

1. **Identify:** (a) Bolsheviks, (b) Leon Trotsky, (c) war communism, (d) Cheka, (e) New Economic Policy, (f) USSR.

2. **Define:** soviet.

3. Describe two reasons for discontent in Russia before the revolution in March 1917.

4. What problems did the Provisional Government face in the spring of 1917?

5. How did Lenin think a revolution in Russia must be carried out in order to succeed?

6. Why did the civil war break out in Russia after the Bolshevik takeover?

7. **Critical Thinking** Some radical communists criticized Lenin for abandoning the principles of communism when he started the New Economic Policy. (a) Do you think this accusation is justified? (b) What other course do you think Lenin might have followed to deal with Russia's crisis?

---

2 The Soviet Union Under Stalin

READ TO UNDERSTAND

☐ What Stalin's goals for the USSR were and how he achieved them.

☐ What a totalitarian state is like.

☐ What the human costs of Stalin's policies were.

☐ *Vocabulary:* collective farm, kulak, totalitarian state.

In 1924, after leading the Soviet Union from revolution to established state, Lenin died. Even before his death, a struggle over who would succeed him had begun. The chief contenders were Leon Trotsky and Joseph Dzhugashvili, better known as Joseph Stalin. Stalin took this name, which means man of steel, as a young revolutionary. Later, he more than lived up to it.

Stalin's Rise to Power

As a young man, Stalin had studied briefly to become a priest, but in 1903 he joined the Bolsheviks. Along with other Bolsheviks, he plotted against the czar. During the Russian Revolution, he rose within the party. By 1922, Stalin had become secretary-general of the Communist party. He used this position to build up support for himself by recruiting and promoting party members loyal to him.

When Lenin died, Stalin set out to outmaneuver Leon Trotsky. Trotsky thought that the Soviet Union should move more quickly toward communism and should increase its efforts to bring about world revolution. Stalin skillfully turned these criticisms of government policies against Trotsky, accusing him of undermining the state.

By 1927, Stalin had won the support of the majority of party members. The party expelled Trotsky and his followers and then exiled Trotsky to Siberia. With Trotsky out of the way, Stalin was able to establish himself as dictator. In 1929, Trotsky left the Soviet Union. He settled in Mexico, where he was murdered in 1940 by political enemies.

673

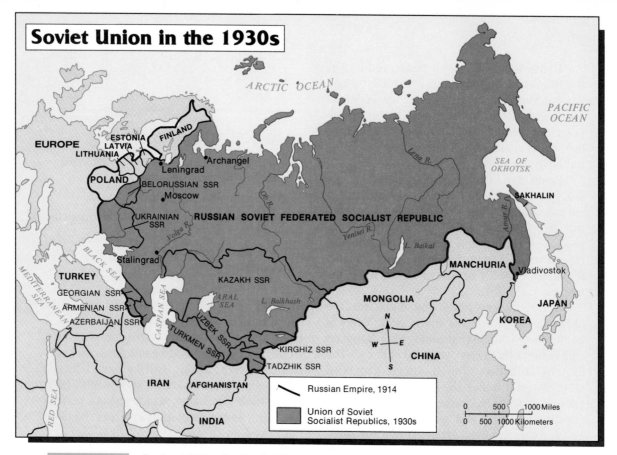

Soviet Union in the 1930s

EUROPE
ESTONIA
LATVIA
LITHUANIA
FINLAND
POLAND
BELORUSSIAN SSR
UKRAINIAN SSR
Leningrad
Archangel
Moscow
RUSSIAN SOVIET FEDERATED SOCIALIST REPUBLIC
Stalingrad
TURKEY
GEORGIAN SSR
ARMENIAN SSR
AZERBAIJAN SSR
KAZAKH SSR
ARAL SEA
L. Balkhash
UZBEK SSR
TURKMEN SSR
KIRGHIZ SSR
TADZHIK SSR
IRAN
AFGHANISTAN
INDIA
MONGOLIA
CHINA
MANCHURIA
Vladivostok
JAPAN
KOREA
SAKHALIN
ARCTIC OCEAN
PACIFIC OCEAN
SEA OF OKHOTSK
L. Baikal
Lena R.
Amur R.
Yenisei R.
Ob R.
Volga R.
BLACK SEA
MEDITERRANEAN SEA
CASPIAN SEA
RED SEA

Russian Empire, 1914
Union of Soviet Socialist Republics, 1930s

0   500   1000 Miles
0   500 1000 Kilometers

MAP STUDY *In the 1930s, the Soviet Union was made up of 11 soviet socialist republics, as this map shows. In theory, each republic was independent. In practice, the Russian Soviet Federated Socialist Republic always dominated the Soviet Union. How does the area ruled by the Soviet Union in the 1930s differ from that ruled by the Russian Empire in 1914?*

The Five-Year Plans

Stalin saw the Soviet Union as surrounded by enemies and economically backward: "We are 50 or 100 years behind the advanced countries. We must make good this distance in 10 years. Either we do it, or we shall go under." Stalin believed the only way the Soviet Union could survive a foreign attack was to develop its industry.

In 1928, Stalin launched his first five-year plan, an economic program that set two specific goals: rapid growth of heavy industry and increased agricultural production through the collectivization of agriculture. In 1933 and 1938, he again made five-year plans to strengthen the Soviet economy.

Plans for industry. Stalin's plans for industry concentrated on building a foundation of basic industries. To accomplish this

goal, he poured the country's resources into building steel mills, electric power stations, chemical plants, cement plants, and oil refineries—all industries that were needed in a strong modern nation.

Between 1928 and 1940, the five-year plans resulted in impressive gains. Steel production more than quadrupled, and oil production tripled. By 1940, the Soviet Union had become the second largest producer of iron and steel in Europe.

The Soviet Union's industrial gains had their dark side, however. Thousands of workers needed for the new industries came from the farms and were jammed into hastily built industrial centers. Money to pay for the industrialization came from heavy hidden sales taxes. And in the interests of heavy industry, basic needs such as food, housing, and clothing were sacrificed.

The government launched a massive propaganda campaign to glorify work and encourage worker productivity. Each factory and each worker had production quotas, or goals. If workers failed to meet their quotas, the government punished them for laziness or sabotage. The greatest cost of industrialization, however, was in the countryside as Stalin moved to collectivize agriculture.

Collectivized agriculture. Stalin realized the Soviet Union needed to make its agriculture more efficient in order to industrialize. He ordered all peasants to give up their land and to form **collective farms,** large, government-run enterprises. On the collective farms, peasants were paid according to the amount of work they did. A portion of a collective's harvest was paid to the government.

Collectivization had many goals. First, it was meant to increase food production by mechanizing agriculture. Second, it was designed to give the government control over farm production. Third, it was intended to free people from farming so they could work in industry. Finally, it was seen as a way to bring socialism to the countryside.

Most peasants opposed collectivization, which began in 1928. The stiffest resistance came from **kulaks,** prosperous peasants who did not want to lose their farms. Protesting kulaks destroyed their livestock and crops. Stalin responded with a brutal crackdown on all opposition. Millions of kulaks were executed or sent to forced-labor camps in Siberia. As a result, farm production fell in the early 1930s, and a terrible famine caused widespread starvation. One of the hardest-hit regions was the Ukraine, home of the earliest civilization in Russia and the country's breadbasket. Millions of Ukrainians starved to death or were killed. Stalin later admitted that 10 million Russians had died as a result of the collectivization drive.

By 1939, most peasants had been forced onto collective farms. But even with the use of farm machinery, production increased slowly. Food shortages continued to occur. Eventually, Stalin compromised. He allowed peasants on collective farms to keep their own small garden plots, which helped feed their families.

A Totalitarian State

Stalin harnessed the skill and energy of the Soviet people to make the Soviet Union a strong communist state. But to achieve this goal, he organized a new kind of government, today called a **totalitarian state.** In a totalitarian state, the government is a single-party dictatorship that controls every aspect of the lives of its citizens. Individual rights count for little or nothing. Citizens are expected to obey the government without question, and critics are quickly silenced. Also, the totalitarian state supports extreme nationalism.

Totalitarian states differ from the absolute monarchies you read about in Chapter 16, although both exercise absolute authority. The totalitarian state has much greater power over the people. In the twentieth century, dictators such as Stalin have used new technology to persuade the masses of people to support their cause. Under Stalin, the government controlled newspapers, the radio, and all other means of communication. He used the press to pour out propaganda praising his policies.

Under Stalin's program of collectivization, the government took over peasants' land, livestock, and farm tools. Party-appointed managers supervised the collective farms. Stalin tried to mechanize agriculture. But in the 1930s, much work was still done by hand, as this photograph of women farm workers shows.

Life Under Stalin

Stalin relied on propaganda and censorship to bolster support for his regime. Soviet writers and artists were expected to glorify the Soviet Union and praise Stalin. In 1932, the government organized writers into the Union of Soviet Writers. The union monitored the work of all writers and rewarded those who praised the state. Those who refused to praise Stalin and the state were expelled from the union and could not get their work published.

Stalin also used terror to silence critics of his rule. As you have read, millions of peasants died during collectivization. In the 1930s, Stalin cracked down on his critics within the Communist party. Thousands of party members were purged, or expelled, from the party. A high party official, Serge Kirov, was assassinated in 1934, probably by Stalin's agents. However, Stalin used Kirov's death as a excuse to launch the Great Purge. In the next four years, millions of men and women were arrested. Many of them were tried and executed. The terror inspired by the purges affected everyone in the Soviet Union. No one was safe from government persecution.

During the 1930s, the standard of living in the Soviet Union remained low. People had to put up with constant food and housing shortages. Stalin's five-year plans continued to emphasize heavy industry at the expense of consumer goods. Thus, many items such as clothing and household appliances were expensive and hard to find. Despite these drawbacks, the Soviet government managed to keep some support among the people. Although wages were low, there was no unemployment. The government also provided old-age pensions and free public education, which had been unknown under the czars.

Many Russians hoped that through education, they could improve their position in society. In theory, communism provides a classless society. In practice, however, under Stalin, a small group of people enjoyed greater privileges than the rest. These included skilled workers such as engineers, artists, and intellectuals who supported Stalin, as well as high party officials.

After the Russian Revolution of 1917, women won equal rights. During the 1920s and 1930s, many women took jobs outside the home, often in factories. Because wages were

This 1935 painting was part of Stalin's propaganda campaign to win support from the Russian people. Smiling, happy men and women representing all ages and ethnic groups march proudly before the Soviet flag. Contrast the festive mood of this painting with that of the photograph on page 675.

"I will not tell lies about myself," Nikolai Bukharin told a supporter of Stalin in 1937. The other man replied, "We'll arrest you, and you'll confess." Bukharin was one of the "Old Bolsheviks" accused of treason and brought to trial in the Soviet Union in the late 1930s. They were called Old Bolsheviks because they were prominent party officials who had been among Lenin's original supporters.

Stalin never appeared in the courtroom during the cleverly staged public trials, but his presence was continually felt. Many defendants made public confessions, admitting their guilt to a variety of crimes against the state. Stalin wanted these confessions so that the defendants would be convicted by their own words and could not be seen as martyrs. While some of the accused were undoubtedly tortured into confessing, others were probably motivated by a lifetime of loyalty and obedience to the Communist party.

Bukharin was arrested and charged with trying to murder Lenin, organizing kulak uprisings, and poisoning livestock. When he refused to confess, his wife and infant son were exiled to a distant city and threatened with death.

Finally, Bukharin made a general confession admitting that he was "politically responsible" for many of the things he was charged with. At his trial, however, Bukharin turned the tables on the prosecutor. He denied each specific charge. Then he cross-examined witnesses and pointed out contradictions in their testimony. Bukharin knew that his actions

would not save his life, but he hoped to reveal the truth.

The prosecutor demanded that Bukharin and the other defendants be "shot like dirty dogs." *Pravda,* the official newspaper of the Communist party, which Bukharin had once edited, declared: "By exterminating them the Soviet land will move even more rapidly along the Stalinist route, the life of the Soviet people will become even more joyous." On March 15, 1938, the Soviet government announced that Bukharin had been executed.

1. Why did some of the Old Bolsheviks confess to crimes they had not committed?

2. **Critical Thinking** In recent years, the Soviet people have been told that the victims of the Great Purge trials were framed. What does this tell you about the Soviet system of justice?

---

so low, their salaries were needed to help their families survive. Women also attended universities and entered professions such as medicine in large numbers.

Quest for Foreign Recognition

When the Bolsheviks seized power in 1917, they expected to lead a world revolution. To coordinate this communist revolution, the Russian Communist party created the Communist International, or Comintern, in 1919.

The Comintern included representatives from communist parties all over the world who were pledged to revolution. In the chaos following World War I, the Comintern supported several communist revolutions that broke out in Germany and in Eastern Europe. These revolutions were quickly suppressed. However, Soviet support for revolutionary activity outside its borders made it an outcast among other nations.

During the 1920s, the Soviet Union downplayed its call for world revolution. Soviet leaders sought diplomatic relations and commercial ties with other nations. In 1924, Britain officially recognized the Soviet government. Other nations soon followed. In 1933, when the Soviet Union promised to end its propaganda activities in the United States, the American government gave it diplomatic recognition. The following year, the Soviet Union joined the League of Nations.

SECTION 2 REVIEW

1. **Identify:** (a) five-year plans, (b) Comintern.

2. **Define:** (a) collective farm, (b) kulak, (c) totalitarian state.

3. How did Stalin become powerful within the Communist party?

4. (a) Why did Stalin launch his five-year plans? (b) Describe two results of the plans.

5. Which group or groups of people had special privileges in Soviet society?

6. **Critical Thinking** Why do you think Stalin was prepared to sacrifice millions of Russian lives to achieve his goals?

---

3 Fascism in Italy

READ TO UNDERSTAND

☐ Why Mussolini was able to come to power in Italy.

☐ What the goals of fascism were.

☐ How the League of Nations responded to Mussolini's aggression.

"A man sent by God," the pope called him. "He made the trains run on time," noted many Italians and foreign admirers. These were the judgments of some who tended to look on Italy's strongman, Benito Mussolini, as a force for order in a chaotic world. But behind the colorful personality who whipped up Italian patriotism was a ruthless dictator.

Mussolini stepped into the limelight after World War I. Italy, you will recall, was one of the "Big Four" powers at the Paris Peace Conference of 1919. But it did not gain all the territory it wanted. As a result, many Italian nationalists denounced the government as weak. Other dissatisfied groups contributed to growing unrest in Italy.

Postwar Unrest

Like most European nations, Italy faced serious political and economic problems in the years after World War I. In the summer of 1920, dissatisfied workers went on strike and occupied factories. In the countryside, landless peasants seized the property of wealthy landlords. Many Italians, especially middle-class property owners, were deeply troubled by these events.

The growing popularity of socialist parties also worried middle-class Italians. In 1919, socialists won more seats in parliament than any other party. When parliament met that year, socialist members shouted "Long live socialism!" instead of offering their greetings to the king, as custom demanded. In 1920, a communist party was formed in Italy, increasing middle-class fears of revolution.

The Italian government was unable to stop worker revolts or preserve order in the countryside. An ambitious politician, Benito Mussolini, used this turmoil to gain power.

Benito Mussolini

As a young man, Mussolini had been a socialist. When World War I broke out, he abandoned socialism and became an enthusiastic nationalist, fighting for Italy. In 1919, Mussolini organized many war veterans into the Fascist party. The word fascist comes from the Latin word "fasces," meaning a bundle of rods tied around an ax handle. During the Roman Empire, the fasces had symbolized unity and authority. Mussolini set out to bind Italians together. He used reminders of the glory of ancient Rome to inspire patriotism and obedience to authority.

Fascism. At first, Mussolini had no clear goals for his Fascist party. Gradually, however, he turned fascism into a political movement. A key idea of fascism was glorification of the state. Mussolini expressed this idea in his slogan: "Everything in the state, nothing outside the state, nothing against the state."

Fascists condemned democracy because they believed rival political parties destroyed the unity of the state. They supported a one-party system guided by a single strong ruler. Fascists despised socialism and communism. They defended private property and private enterprise, which they thought should be regulated by the government.

Another element of fascism was aggressive nationalism. A strong nation, Fascists argued, had every right to take over a weaker one. They believed aggression represented action, while a desire for peace merely indicated weakness. Fascists also glorified military sacrifice.

Appeal of fascism. Fascism appealed to many Italians. Veterans of World War I appreciated the Fascist emphasis on militarism. Italian nationalists applauded the idea of reviving the glories of ancient Rome. Some middle- and upper-class Italians were impatient with Italy's parliamentary government and yearned for a strong leader who would keep order. They also supported Fascist ideas about private property. Mussolini's speeches about "action"

and "struggle" stirred the imaginations of many young Italians.

The "March on Rome." In the early 1920s, bands of Mussolini's followers, uniformed in black shirts, roamed the streets of Italian cities beating up communists, socialists, and union members. These "Black Shirts" ousted communists and socialists from city governments in Bologna and Milan. With each success, the number of Fascists grew.

Sensing a rising tide of support, Mussolini prepared to seize power. In October 1922, he announced he would lead a "March on Rome" to defend the capital from a communist revolution. In fact, there was no threat of a communist revolution, but Mussolini hoped that the approach of his Black Shirts would frighten the government into surrender. And it did. When Fascist bands approached Rome from four directions, King Victor Emmanuel III refused to use the army against them. A few days later, the king named Mussolini prime minister.

Italy as a Fascist State

As prime minister, Mussolini was given emergency powers for one year. Before the year was up, however, he pushed a law through parliament that in effect guaranteed a Fascist

In Italy, political education and military training began at an early age. Here, Mussolini reviews a military parade of Fascist youth during a celebration on the twentieth anniversary of Italy's entry into World War I. Children were taught the virtue of obedience to Il Duce. They chanted such Fascist slogans as "Believe! Obey! Fight!"

majority in parliament. In the next few years, Mussolini steadily increased his power.

Outwardly, the form of government did not change much. Italy remained a monarchy with an elected parliament. But Mussolini had the right to make laws on his own initiative. The Fascist party controlled elections and outlawed all opposition parties.

Like the Communist party in the Soviet Union, the Fascist party controlled Italy. Party members were given important jobs in the government, the army, and the police. Mussolini also used other methods of the totalitarian state. He censored the press and banned any criticism of the government. Fascists bought the leading Italian newspapers and wrote articles full of praise for "Il Duce," meaning the leader, a title Mussolini had adopted.

"Mussolini is always right" was the motto that all Italians were expected to believe in. Police beat up critics of fascism. Many were held in remote prisons. In schools, children were taught Fascist ideas. They wore black uniforms and learned discipline, duty, and obedience—the virtues that Mussolini believed had made ancient Rome strong.

Fascism differed from communism because it supported private enterprise. However, to improve the Italian economy, Mussolini introduced a new type of economic organization, the corporative system. Employers and employees in each industry joined a government-sponsored "corporation." Labor unions were abolished. The corporation controlled such matters as wages and prices in its industry. The corporations were largely dominated by business interests and the government.

In the 1920s, Italy enjoyed a brief economic recovery. However, Mussolini was unable to prevent the Great Depression from having a severe impact on Italy. Mussolini blamed Italy's troubles on world economic conditions and tried to distract the people by embarking on an aggressive foreign policy.

Fascist Foreign Policy

"We have a right to an empire," Mussolini claimed, and he set about building one. In 1924, he negotiated a treaty with Yugoslavia that gave Italy the city of Fiume. Three years later, Mussolini imposed a protectorate over Albania. Then, in the 1930s, he turned to Africa.

As you have read, Italy had acquired colonies in North Africa in the late 1800s. Italians still deeply resented their defeat in 1896 by Ethiopia. (See page 565.) In 1934, a clash on the border between Ethiopia and the Italian colony of Somaliland gave Mussolini an excuse to demand territory from Ethiopia. Ethiopia appealed to the League of Nations for help. But the league delayed action, and Italy invaded Ethiopia in October 1935.

Eventually, the league called for economic sanctions against Italy. That is, league members agreed not to sell arms or lend money to Italy. But they did not cut off oil supplies to Italy, a move that might have slowed the Italian invasion.

The Ethiopians fought bravely, but their cavalry and ancient rifles were no match for Italian planes, tanks, and artillery. In May 1936, Ethiopia fell to the invaders. The next month, Haile Selassie (HĪ lee suh LAS ee), the exiled emperor of Ethiopia, traveled to the League of Nations headquarters in Geneva. Although he made a moving appeal for help, the league took no steps to rescue Ethiopia. In July, the league voted to end the economic sanctions against Italy.

SECTION 3 REVIEW

1. **Identify:** (a) Benito Mussolini, (b) Black Shirts, (c) March on Rome, (d) corporative system, (e) Haile Selassie.

2. Why were many Italians dissatisfied with their government in 1919?

3. (a) What were the main goals of fascism? (b) Who supported fascism in Italy?

4. How did Mussolini increase his power after 1922?

5. **Critical Thinking** Do you think stronger action by the League of Nations would have stopped Mussolini's aggression in Ethiopia? Explain.

4 The Rise of Nazi Germany

READ TO UNDERSTAND

☐ What problems the Weimar Republic faced.

☐ How Hitler gained power in Germany.

☐ How the Nazis created a totalitarian state.

☐ What Hitler's goals for the Third Reich were.

"We could discover no leadership qualities in him," explained an army officer when asked why Adolf Hitler had not risen higher than a corporal in World War I. Yet, in the 1930s, this man without "leadership qualities" would climb to power and set up a brutal totalitarian state in Germany.

The Weimar Republic

Two days before World War I ended in 1918, Germany became a republic. The new government was set up in the town of Weimar. Thus, Germany in the 1920s was often called the Weimar Republic.

The Weimar Republic faced enormous problems from the start. Many Germans despised it because its representatives had signed the hated Versailles Treaty. German generals and other war veterans claimed that Germany had not been defeated but had been "stabbed in the back" by communists, Jews, and liberals in the Weimar government. Although these accusations were untrue, many people looked for someone to blame for the German defeat in the war.

Political extremists caused unrest in postwar Germany. On the far left were communists, who supported the Marxist idea of world revolution. On the far right were fascists and extreme nationalists, who denounced the Versailles Treaty and opposed the democratic goals of the Weimar Republic. Revolts by both communists and fascists rocked the Weimar Republic in its early years.

The inflation of the early 1920s, and later the Great Depression, swelled the ranks of the discontented. Political and economic chaos in Germany created a climate that favored the rise of Adolf Hitler and his Nazi party.

Adolf Hitler

Hitler was born in Austria in 1889, the son of a customs official. He dropped out of high school in 1905 and two years later moved to Vienna. There, he tried unsuccessfully to become an artist. During his stay in Vienna, Hitler listened to Austrian nationalists who talked of the close ties between the German-speaking peoples of Austria and Germany. He also picked up the violent anti-Semitism, or hatred of Jews, that many Austrian and German nationalists preached.

Unemployed German workers were especially vulnerable to emotional messages like the one in this 1932 campaign poster. It proclaimed, "Our last hope—Hitler." Eager to believe that someone could end their suffering, millions of Germans cast their votes for Hitler and the Nazi party.

When World War I broke out, Hitler enlisted in the German army. He emerged from the war an extreme nationalist. He echoed the ideas of those Germans who believed their country had been stabbed in the back. Hitler settled in Munich, Germany, where he became a very effective public speaker who was popular among nationalists. By 1921, Hitler had gained control of the National Socialist German Workers' party, a nationalistic, anti-communist, anti-Semitic organization better known as the Nazi party.

Growth of Nazi Power

Only about 6,000 people belonged to the Nazi party in 1921, but the party grew rapidly. The disastrous inflation of 1922 and 1923 and French occupation of the Ruhr weakened support for the Weimar Republic. In wild, emotional speeches, Hitler attacked the Weimar Republic and denounced the Versailles Treaty. By 1923, Nazi party membership had climbed to 50,000.

Believing that he had enough support to overthrow the Weimar Republic, Hitler led an uprising in Munich on November 8, 1923. But he failed to spark a general revolt, and the army quickly crushed the uprising. Hitler was arrested, tried, and found guilty of treason. He was sentenced to five years in prison but was released within a year.

While in prison, Hitler wrote *Mein Kampf,* or *My Struggle.* In it, he detailed his political ideas for Germany. Hitler claimed that the German people belonged to a superior "Aryan" race that was destined to control inferior races and rule the world. Hitler considered Jews an inferior race. He blamed Jews for Germany's economic troubles and for plotting with communists for world revolution. In addition to Jews and communists, Hitler attacked the Soviet Union as an obstacle to German expansion.

After Hitler was released from prison in 1924, he worked hard to broaden the appeal of the Nazi party. He promised benefits to peasants, workers, and the middle class. He also won support from some wealthy business leaders. The Great Depression greatly helped the Nazis. As unemployment rose, thousands of desperate people flocked to local Nazi party

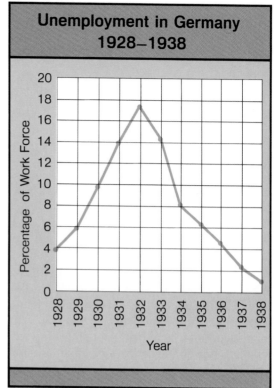

Unemployment in Germany 1928–1938

Source: Angus Maddison, *Economic Growth in the West.*

GRAPH STUDY *In Germany, as elsewhere around the world, unemployment soared during the Great Depression. In what year did unemployment in Germany begin to drop? How did it compare with unemployment in Britain and the United States? (See the graph on page 658.)*

headquarters in search of a free meal and companionship. (See the graph above.) They also found hope in Hitler's ideas about order, unity, and national strength.

By 1932, the Nazis had become the largest single party in the Reichstag, the German legislature. On January 30, 1933, German president Paul von Hindenburg asked Hitler to become chancellor, the head of the German government. Because the Nazis did not have a majority of seats in the Reichstag, Hitler had to form a coalition government. However, he moved swiftly to increase his power.

Hitler called for new elections in March. A week before the elections, a fire, probably set by the Nazis, destroyed the Reichstag building. Hitler accused communists of setting the fire and of planning a revolt. He used the threat of a communist uprising to convince President von Hindenburg to issue emergency orders abolishing freedom of speech and assembly.

The Nazis did not quite win a majority in the March elections, but they forced the Reichstag to give Hitler dictatorial power for four years. In less than a year, however, Hitler had eliminated all opposition parties and established a fascist state in Germany.

Founding the Third Reich

When President von Hindenburg died in August 1934, Hitler combined the offices of president and chancellor. He adopted the title "Führer" (FYOOR uhr), or leader. He also proclaimed the birth of the Third Reich, successor to the Holy Roman Empire and the German Empire, which had lasted from 1871 to 1918. The Third Reich, boasted Hitler, would last a thousand years.

Totalitarian rule. Hitler used many of the methods of Stalin and Mussolini to build a totalitarian state in Germany. In June 1934, he rounded up rivals in the Nazi party as well as hundreds of other political opponents and had many of them murdered. He created a secret police, the Gestapo, to hunt down and arrest anyone suspected of opposing Nazi rule. New laws were passed that made the good of the state more important than individual rights. Hitler also sought and won the loyalty of army officers, who responded eagerly to his plans for German expansion.

The Nazis extended their control to every aspect of life, including the press, schools, and religion. Joseph Goebbels, Hitler's minister of propaganda, made radio stations play military music and speeches glorifying the Nazi state.

Students were encouraged to join the Hitler Youth, an organization that taught military discipline, patriotism, and obedience to the Führer. Many young Germans enthusiastically wore the uniform and badge of the Hitler Youth, which promised excitement and advancement. The Hitler Youth helped Nazis round up "un-German" books, which were burned in huge public bonfires.

The government forced most private Roman Catholic schools to close because Hitler wanted all German children to attend public schools controlled by the Nazis. In 1935, the Nazis reorganized the Protestant churches in Germany and tried to force ministers to deliver pro-Nazi sermons on Sundays.

Campaign against the Jews. As he had promised in *Mein Kampf,* Hitler moved ruthlessly against German Jews. In March 1933, Jews were expelled from all government jobs and from teaching positions in the universities. Soon afterward, Jews were forbidden to practice such professions as law and medicine. The Nuremberg Laws of 1935 deprived German Jews of their citizenship and banned marriages between Jews and non-Jews. Realizing that there was no place for them under Hitler, Jews began leaving Germany for other countries. Many German Jews, including the well-known physicist Albert Einstein, emigrated to the United States.

Nazi policy toward the Jews became harsher in 1938 after a Jewish youth murdered a German diplomat in Paris. On November 10, Nazis organized riots in a number of German cities. Nazi gangs killed many Jews and destroyed hundreds of Jewish shops and synagogues. The government arrested about 20,000

Book burnings were commonplace in Nazi Germany. Here, Nazis collect books to be destroyed. According to one proclamation, any book was to be burned "which acts subversively on our future or strikes at the root of German thought, the German home, and the driving forces of our people." Works of Jewish artists and intellectuals were burned, as well as books by such American authors as Jack London, Helen Keller, and Upton Sinclair.

Jews and sent them to concentration, or prison, camps. It required all Jews to wear a yellow Star of David on their clothing so they could be easily identified. Persecution of Jews would grow worse in the years ahead, as you will read in the next chapter.

Hitler's Programs for Strengthening Germany

Like the Fascists in Italy, the Nazis in Germany preached the need for hard work, sacrifice, and service to the state. Hitler had grand plans

---

BUILDERS AND SHAPERS
Jesse Owens and the Berlin Olympics

In 1936, Adolf Hitler and the Nazi party hosted the Olympics in Berlin, Germany. For months before the games took place, a stormy argument raged in the United States. The Nazis already had a clear program of discrimination against German Jews. Should American athletes travel to Berlin and take part in the "Nazi Olympics"? Or should they stay home to protest German racism?

For Jesse Owens, the question was a personal one. Owens, the tenth child of a poor sharecropper, had moved with his family from Alabama to Ohio, where he had become a track star. Many Americans expected Owens to win more gold medals than any other athlete at the Berlin games. But if black athletes refused to go to the Olympics, they could protest racism in the United States as well as in Germany.

Owens and other black Olympians finally decided that they should go to Germany. "A big part of Hitler's superiority ideas," Owens wrote, "was that his Nazis should rule not just because they were better and smarter, but because they were stronger and healthier." By taking part in the games, black Americans would show racists everywhere how wrong they were.

Jesse Owens lived up to his country's highest hopes. Before the eyes of Hitler and other Nazi leaders, Owens captured four gold medals. Owens returned home a national hero. New York and other cities honored him with parades. Yet in much of the United States, laws still segregated blacks and whites.

Without bitterness, Owens saw the irony of a black American "defeating" Hitler. "In the early 1830s," he later wrote, "My ancestors were brought on a boat across the Atlantic Ocean from Africa to America as slaves for men who felt they had the right to own other men. In August of 1936, I boarded a boat to go back across the Atlantic Ocean to do battle with Adolf Hitler, a man who thought all other men should be slaves to him and his Aryan armies."

Jesse Owens's victories at the 1936 Olympics did little to change the course of German history. But they did help push the United States a step closer toward achieving equality for all Americans.

1. Why was it especially difficult for black athletes to decide whether or not to take part in the 1936 Olympics?

2. **Critical Thinking** Do you think Hitler was displeased by the victories of black Americans in the Olympic games? Explain.

for Germany. He promised economic recovery and "living space" beyond the borders of Germany.

Economic recovery. Hitler's economic goals for Germany were to reduce unemployment and make the country self-sufficient. He launched vast building programs, including housing, highways, and sports arenas. He ignored the Versailles Treaty, which forbade Germany to rearm, and rebuilt the German military. Thousands of workers in munitions factories produced weapons.

To pay for his many programs, Hitler increased taxes and placed strict controls on wages and prices. He banned strikes and outlawed unions. Workers and employers were organized into the National Labor Front. The National Labor Front offered workers inexpensive vacations and supported Nazi propaganda efforts to glorify labor.

In the 1930s, economic recovery became a reality. Unemployment dropped from 6 million in 1933 to 1 million in 1936. Moreover, the standard of living rose for the average worker.

Plans for expansion. In *Mein Kampf,* Hitler had insisted that the "Aryan master race" was destined to rule "inferior peoples." He included the Slavs of Eastern Europe among the "inferior peoples." Thus, he claimed, Germany had the right to expand eastward and win the "living space" he felt Germany needed.

To prepare for German expansion, Hitler increased the German armed forces from the limit of 100,000 imposed in 1919 to more than 500,000. He claimed that the growing size of the Soviet army made German rearmament necessary.

The League of Nations condemned Hitler's actions but took no steps against Germany. (Hitler had already withdrawn Germany from the league in 1933.) However, France was frightened enough by Hitler's ambitions to form an anti-German military alliance with the Soviet Union.

By the mid-1930s, Hitler had made German strength and determination clear to the world. As you will read in Chapter 31, the democratic nations of Western Europe and the United States were not united in their responses to Hitler's aggression.

Although a rearmed Germany posed a very real threat to the nations of Europe, the League of Nations took no action to stop the Nazis' military buildup. This 1935 French cartoon shows a smiling Hitler towering over representatives of the League of Nations. The shadow he casts recalls the military might of Germany in the days before World War I.

SECTION 4 REVIEW

1. **Identify:** (a) *Mein Kampf,* (b) Paul von Hindenburg, (c) Führer, (d) Third Reich, (e) Gestapo.

2. List three problems facing the Weimar Republic in the 1920s.

3. What effect did the Great Depression have on the Nazi party?

4. What steps did Hitler take to ensure his power in the Third Reich?

5. What was Hitler's program for German economic recovery?

6. **Critical Thinking** Explain why Hitler was able to gain the support of many German people.

5 Militarism in Japan

READL TO UNDERSTAND

☐ How Japan was becoming more democratic in the 1920s.

☐ How the military came to power in the 1930s.

☐ What the goals of Japanese expansion were.

The atmosphere was tense as the students lined up outside their school. The school, a Christian one, had been pressured by the government into accepting a portrait of the emperor. Accepting the portrait was a test of the school's loyalty. When the car carrying the portrait reached the school gates, a teacher cried out, "Saikei-rei!" ("Deep bow!")

In the 1920s, the Japanese tradition of unquestioned obedience to the emperor had weakened as democracy had made gains. In the 1930s, however, Japanese military leaders restored the tradition of honoring the emperor. Moreover, people were now expected to report anyone—family, friend, or neighbor—who showed any disrespect for the emperor.

An Era of Democratic Reform

Japan had emerged from World War I with a prosperous economy. In the 1920s, the Japanese moved into many markets once dominated by the British. As a result, Japanese industries grew. The prosperous, well-educated middle class supported democratic institutions. The victory of the democratic Allies in World War I also added to the prestige of democracy in Japan.

Political parties gained greater power in the 1920s. In the past, the emperor's advisors had named the prime minister. During the 1920s, the political party with the most seats in the Diet, or parliament, won this power. Thus, the prime minister needed the support of the Diet to stay in office. This made the government responsible to the Diet and to the voters.

The Japanese also introduced other reforms that made Japan more democratic. In 1925, a law giving the vote to all men over age 25 increased the number of voters by about 9 million. The government created a national health insurance plan and removed some restraints on labor unions.

Impact of the Great Depression

The climate of reform changed in the 1930s. Because it depended so heavily on foreign trade, Japan was hit hard by the Great Depression. From 1929 to 1931, the value of Japanese exports fell by 50 percent. World demand for luxuries such as Japanese silk declined. Many Japanese businesses were ruined. Moreover, industrial nations placed high tariffs on foreign goods to protect their own industries. As a result, Japanese manufacturers lost their foreign markets and unemployment in Japan climbed.

Like governments elsewhere, the government of Japan seemed unable to solve the economic crisis. Critics denounced the government for its weakness. Many people, especially the military, grew impatient with the parliamentary system.

The government's disarmament policy also came under attack. Japan had participated in the naval disarmament conferences of the 1920s. At the London Naval Conference of 1930, Japan agreed to keep the size of its navy below that of either the British or the American fleet. This move was very unpopular with the military and with extreme nationalists who dreamed of creating a Japanese empire in Asia.

The Military in Power

The military had held a respected place in Japanese society since the days of the samurai. (See page 279.) In the climate of crisis of the 1930s, the Japanese military began to take matters into its own hands. In September 1931, the army defied the civilian government and attacked Manchuria, a region of northeastern China. The prime minister resigned to protest the army's disobedience. When his successor asked the emperor to place the army under civilian control, he was assassinated by a group of army officers.

By May 1932, the military had set up a military dictatorship in Japan. Unlike Italy and

Germany, however, Japan did not have a single strong leader or a specific program. Instead, a small group of military leaders dominated the government. They did not abolish the constitution, the Diet, or even political parties. Civilian officials continued in their jobs, but generals dictated policy.

In the 1930s, Japan had many features of a totalitarian state. The government arrested critics, imposed censorship, and dismissed liberal professors from the universities. A secret police force searched out and punished so-called enemies of the state. The press and the schools taught total obedience to the emperor. Extreme nationalist groups glorified war and the empire.

Aggression in Manchuria

A small island nation, Japan lacked important raw materials such as coal and oil. Moreover, the Japanese islands were densely populated, and its population was growing in the 1920s and early 1930s. Japanese exports, as you have read, suffered because of the high tariffs imposed by other nations.

The military leaders of Japan offered a solution to these problems—the acquisition of an overseas empire. Japan had already gained some overseas territory, as you can see from the map above. In 1907, for example, it had established a protectorate over Korea. By adding to these lands, the military promised, Japan could obtain needed raw materials, win new foreign markets, and gain an outlet for its surplus population.

Japan had long been interested in Manchuria, a province of China that bordered on Korea. Manchuria had rich supplies of coal and iron. In 1931, the Japanese invaded Manchuria and quickly crushed resistance by local Chinese forces. They then proclaimed that Manchuria was an independent state, which they called Manchukuo. In reality, Manchukuo was a puppet state controlled by Japan.

China went before the League of Nations to protest Japanese aggression in Manchuria. The league condemned the Japanese invasion. But it took no further action, in part because the major powers were distracted by the Great Depression. Japan withdrew from the league in 1933.

Japanese Expansion to 1934

▮	Japan, 1890
▮	Territory acquired by 1918
▮	Territory acquired by 1934

MAP STUDY The Japanese expanded on the Asian mainland in the early 1900s. In the 1930s, Japanese troops conquered Manchuria and moved into northeastern China. What territory had Japan acquired by 1918?

In the 1930s, Japan took on a new role in Asia. It posed as the leader of people who opposed western imperialism. At the same time, Japan sought support from the fascist powers in Europe. In 1936, it signed a military agreement with Nazi Germany and prepared to launch new adventures in Asia.

SECTION 5 REVIEW

1. **Locate:** (a) Manchuria, (b) Korea.

2. How was Japan becoming more democratic in the 1920s?

3. Why was Japan so severely hurt by the Great Depression?

4. What totalitarian measures were used in Japan in the 1930s?

5. Why did Japan want to expand its empire?

6. **Critical Thinking** Why do you think the military, rather than one individual, created a totalitarian state in Japan?

687

Summary

1. In 1917, the Bolsheviks established a communist regime in Russia. Following a moderate revolution in March 1917, the Bolsheviks, led by Lenin, seized power. After the civil war, Lenin tried to rebuild the devastated Russian economy with his New Economic Policy.

2. After Lenin's death in 1924, Joseph Stalin emerged as dictator of Russia. He crushed all opposition and created a totalitarian state. Stalin made the Soviet Union into a modern industrial state and collectivized agriculture. However, millions of people died or were killed in the process.

3. Political and social unrest in Italy helped Mussolini rise to power. Mussolini made Italy a fascist state. Critics were silenced, and the Fascist party controlled the country. To distract Italians from the economic troubles, Mussolini embarked on a policy of expansion.

4. The Nazi party under Adolf Hitler came to power in Germany in 1933. Hitler replaced the democratic Weimar government. Once in power, Hitler silenced his opponents, attacked Jews, strengthened the economy, and rearmed Germany. By the mid-1930s, he was ready to expand Germany's borders.

5. Japan became a military dictatorship in the 1930s. Military leaders curtailed liberties, glorified war, and restored emperor worship. In 1931, they invaded Manchuria as a means of solving the country's economic and population problems.

Recalling Facts

Identify the country in which each of the following events took place.

1. The New Economic Policy allowed private businesses to operate.

2. The government ignored the Versailles Treaty and began to rearm.

3. The government sent troops to invade Manchuria.

4. Peasants were moved onto collective farms.

5. Jews were forced to wear a yellow Star of David.

6. Newspapers praised Il Duce.

Chapter Checkup

1. (a) How did World War I contribute to the outbreak of the Russian Revolution? (b) How did the Bolsheviks seize power in November 1917?

2. (a) How did Lenin's New Economic Policy differ from war communism? (b) What effect did the NEP have on life in the Soviet Union?

3. (a) What were Stalin's major goals for the Soviet Union? (b) How did he ensure his control over the Soviet Union? (c) How did Stalin's policies affect the Russian people?

4. (a) What conditions in Italy helped Mussolini win power? (b) Why did fascism appeal to many Italians?

5. Explain how the following contributed to Hitler's rise to power: (a) Versailles Treaty; (b) Great Depression; (c) *Mein Kampf.*

6. (a) What accusations did Hitler make against Jews? (b) What policies did he follow toward Jews once he was in power?

7. (a) How did the Great Depression affect the Japanese economy? (b) Why was the Japanese military dissatisfied with the civilian government?

Critical Thinking

1. **Comparing** Compare Lenin's New Economic Policy to Stalin's five-year plans.

2. **Understanding the Roots of Democracy** The Soviet Union had no tradition of democratic rule. Democratic traditions in Italy, Germany, and Japan were fairly recent. (a) How do you think the lack of strong democratic traditions made it easier for totalitarian governments to gain power in these four countries? (b) Can you predict how a dictator would be received in a country that had long been a democracy? Explain.

3. **Relating Past to Present** (a) How does a totalitarian state ensure complete control over the people? (b) Why did totalitarian states of the twentieth century have more power than the absolute monarchs of earlier times? (c) In what ways have modern developments in communications helped totalitarian governments increase their ability to control their people?

Developing Basic Skills

1. **Graph Reading** Study the graph on page 682. (a) What percentage of Germans was out of work in 1928? (b) When did unemployment reach its peak? (c) Why do you think unemployment declined in the mid-1930s?

2. **Map Reading** Study the map on page 687. (a) What territory did Japan control in 1890? (b) What lands did it acquire between 1918 and 1934? (c) What area or areas might have become the object of Japanese expansion in the late 1930s?

3. **Comparing** Make a chart with four rows and three columns. Title the rows Soviet Union, Italy, Germany, and Japan. Title the columns Leader, Economic Program, and Foreign Policy. Complete the chart and answer these questions: (a) Which country or countries had a single strong leader in the 1930s? (b) How were the economic programs of Italy and Germany similar? (c) How did the economic goals of the Soviet Union and Italy differ? (d) How were the foreign policies of the countries similar?

Writing About History

Writing a Topic Outline

Once you have organized your note cards and classified them according to topics, you should prepare a topic outline. A topic outline helps you focus on the main idea and the supporting details. Look at the portion of a topic outline below. The main topics are identified with Roman numerals. Subtopics are labeled with capital letters.

I. Introduction
II. Growth of Nazi Power
   A. Munich uprising
   B. Imprisonment of Hitler
   C. Rebuilding of Nazi party
   D. Hitler named chancellor
   E. Reichstag fire

Practice: Complete the topic outline based on the information in Sections 3 and 4 of this chapter.

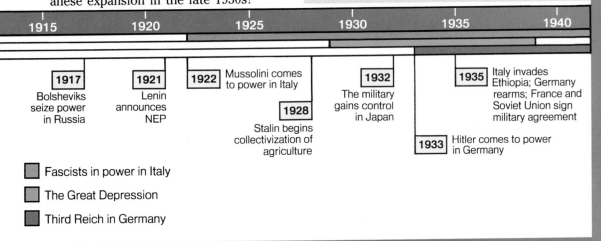

1915   1920   1925   1930   1935   1940

1917 Bolsheviks seize power in Russia

1921 Lenin announces NEP

1922 Mussolini comes to power in Italy

1928 Stalin begins collectivization of agriculture

1932 The military gains control in Japan

1933 Hitler comes to power in Germany

1935 Italy invades Ethiopia; Germany rearms; France and Soviet Union sign military agreement

Fascists in power in Italy

The Great Depression

Third Reich in Germany

689

The World at War

31

(1936–1945)

After France fell, Adolf Hitler turned his energies to the defeat of Britain. In what Winston Churchill called "their finest hour," the British refused to surrender in the Battle of Britain. The Royal Air Force fought valiantly against German air attacks.

The young American newsman peered intently through his binoculars. He stood at the edge of a clearing in the forest of Compiègne, northeast of Paris. Nearby, other reporters spoke in low voices, trying to identify the uniformed figures in the clearing.

A car drove up, its Nazi flags fluttering in the June breeze. Out stepped the well-known mustached figure of Germany's Adolf Hitler. He strode over to a huge granite block inscribed with these words: HERE ON THE 11TH OF NOVEMBER 1918 SUCCUMBED THE CRIMINAL PRIDE OF THE GERMAN PEOPLE. Hitler turned away in scornful anger. His moment of revenge had come. With his keen sense of drama, Hitler had set the stage carefully.

Several weary French generals emerged from another car and walked over to the old railroad car in which the Germans had been forced to sign the armistice 22 years earlier. Today, June 22, 1940, it was France's turn to face the humiliation of defeat. The railroad car had been housed in a French museum, but the Germans pulled down the museum walls and brought it to Compiègne. Draped over the car was a huge swastika, the symbol of Nazi power.

The young reporter noted: "I observed his [Hitler's] face. It was grave, solemn, yet brimming with revenge. There was also in it, as in his springy step, a note of the triumphant conqueror, the defier of the world. There was something else, difficult to describe, in his expression; a sort of scornful, inner joy at being present at this great reversal of fate—a reversal he himself had wrought."

Within the armistice car, Hitler watched as the grim-faced French diplomats, "the picture of tragic dignity," signed the surrender document. In that brief ceremony Hitler avenged the German defeat of 1918.

The defeat of France in 1940 was one of many victories for Nazi Germany. Aggression by Germany, Italy, and Japan in the 1930s eventually led to World War II. The war, which lasted from 1939 to 1945, was the most devastating conflict in human history. ■

1 The Road to War

READ TO UNDERSTAND

☐ How the Spanish Civil War encouraged fascist expansion.

☐ How the policy of appeasement opened the way to World War II.

☐ Why Hitler signed a treaty with the Soviet Union.

☐ *Vocabulary:* Anschluss, appeasement, pacifism.

Monday was market day in the small town of Guernica (GUHR nee kuh) in northern Spain. Farmers gathered in the main square, and families did their shopping. On Monday, April 26, 1937, two nuns looked up at the sky and then ran to sound the alarm. "Aviones! aviones!" ("Planes! planes!") they cried. Suddenly bombs rained death on the men, women, and children in the crowded square. Before the air raid ended, more than 1,600 people had been killed. The dead of Guernica were victims of the Spanish Civil War that had broken out in 1936.

The Spanish Civil War

During the 1930s, Spain had experienced much unrest. In 1931, the king had been forced to step down, and a republican government had been set up. The new government was controlled by liberals and socialists. Under its leadership, the Catholic Church lost its status as the country's official religion, and much of its property was confiscated. The government also reduced the size of the army.

Political unrest continued under the republican government. Socialist unions staged disruptive strikes, and anticlerical forces set fire to Catholic convents. The clergy angrily denounced the policies of the government, and monarchists called for the return of the king.

A more conservative government was elected in 1933, but in the 1936 elections, a coalition of liberals, socialists, and communists won. The government moved against the army by assigning military officers who opposed the republic to remote posts. And it

Pablo Picasso recorded the horrors of the Spanish civil war in his painting Guernica. *Nine waves of German planes bombed the town and strafed defenseless people in the streets. The bombing of Guernica gave the world a view of a terrifying new kind of warfare.*

confiscated some large estates, giving the land to the peasants. Such actions brought a violent response from the right.

In July 1936, a group of generals led by Francisco Franco staged an uprising against the republican government. A civil war had begun. The generals wanted to restore the power of the church and destroy socialism and communism in Spain. Franco's followers, called Nationalists, called for the creation of a fascist state. Defenders of the government were known as Republicans or Loyalists.

The Spanish Civil War soon became an international issue. The League of Nations tried without success to stop arms from reaching either side. Mussolini and Hitler supplied arms and manpower to the Nationalists. The planes over Guernica were German bombers testing the might of German air power.

To both Italy and Germany, Spain offered an excellent battleground in which to try out new weapons and tactics. Cooperation between Italy and Germany in Spain led to the creation in October 1936 of a military alliance known as the Rome-Berlin Axis.

Meanwhile, Stalin sent weapons and advisers to the Republicans, but Soviet aid did not match the assistance provided by the Axis. Britain and France wanted the Spanish republic to survive but did not provide military aid.

Isolationist feelings kept the United States neutral.

The Spanish Civil War ended in 1939 with victory for the Nationalists. Franco then imposed a fascist dictatorship on Spain. The failure of the democratic powers to stop Axis intervention in Spain encouraged Hitler and Mussolini to interfere elsewhere.

Other Challenges to Peace

Even before the Spanish Civil War, Hitler had begun to expand German power. In March 1936, he sent German troops into the Rhineland in violation of the Versailles Treaty. (See the map on page 694.) Britain and France condemned the move but took no action. Many people in Britain thought that the Germans had a right to occupy the Rhineland since it was German territory. The French prime minister favored a strong military response, but he could not act without British support.

Next on Hitler's agenda of expansion was the **Anschluss,** a union between Austria and Germany. Anschluss was forbidden by the Versailles Treaty, but this mattered little to Hitler. In March 1938, the pro-Nazi chancellor of Austria asked Hitler to send troops "to help maintain order." German troops marched into Austria on March 12 to the cheers of many

Austrians. The next day Austria became part of Germany.

The British prime minister, Neville Chamberlain, refused to be alarmed by the Anschluss. He felt that an aggressive stance toward Germany would destroy the possibility of future negotiations. In France, a change of governments prevented effective response to the Anschluss.

The Policy of Appeasement

Chamberlain's attitude toward the Anschluss grew out of a policy of appeasement. **Appeasement** means making concessions to an aggressor in order to preserve the peace. Memories of the slaughter of World War I made British and French leaders reluctant to go to war with Hitler. Further, **pacifism,** or refusal to fight in a war, was strong among the people in both countries.

Other factors also contributed to the policy of appeasement. To many people in Britain, the Rhineland and Austria did not seem important enough to risk a war. Some thought a strong Germany would be a check on Soviet power. A member of the British government told Hitler that "Germany rightly had to be considered as a Western bulwark [barrier] against Communism." In addition, some Britons felt that Germany had been treated too harshly by the Versailles Treaty. The French were not prepared to stand up to Hitler without British backing. At the same time, political problems at home sapped French morale and determination.

The United States followed a policy of isolationism. Both Congress and President Franklin D. Roosevelt were determined to keep the United States out of any European conflicts. In 1935 and 1936, Congress passed neutrality laws that barred the United States from selling arms to any country involved in a war. The laws also prohibited American ships from carrying arms to a warring nation. Roosevelt condemned Hitler's aggressions but refused to join an anti-German alliance.

Crisis Over Czechoslovakia

After the Anschluss, Hitler turned his attention to Czechoslovakia. Three million Germans lived in the Sudetenland, the western border region of Czechoslovakia. In 1938, Hitler encouraged the Sudeten Germans to demand self-government. He promised to come to their aid if the Czech government refused.

A German invasion seemed likely, but Chamberlain and Edouard Daladier (dah luh DYAY), the French premier, tried appeasement to resolve the crisis. They convinced the unhappy Czechs to give self-government to the Sudetenland. Hitler responded with new demands, including the right to send German troops to the Sudetenland.

Chamberlain then asked Hitler to call a four-power conference to settle the Czech crisis. Hitler agreed and invited the leaders of Britain, France, and Italy to meet with him in Munich on September 29, 1938. Neither Czechoslovakia nor its ally, the Soviet Union, was invited to attend the conference.

At the Munich conference, the four powers agreed to allow German troops to occupy the Sudetenland, but they guaranteed the independence of the rest of Czechoslovakia. To Chamberlain's relief, Hitler announced that he had no more territorial claims in Europe. On his return to Britain, Chamberlain declared that the agreement meant there would be "peace for our time."

Hitler's easy victory at Munich encouraged him to move boldly. In March 1939, six months after Munich, German troops occupied the rest of Czechoslovakia. Hitler's violation of the Munich agreement shocked Chamberlain. The policy of appeasement had rested on the false assumption that Hitler could be trusted. The events in Czechoslovakia proved that the policy was bankrupt.

Poland

A week after German troops occupied Czechoslovakia, Hitler turned to Poland. He demanded the return of the city of Danzig and the Polish Corridor. The Versailles Treaty had made the German city of Danzig an independent, international city and had created the Polish Corridor, a small strip of land connecting Poland with the Baltic Sea. (See the map on page 694.)

Hitler's demands alarmed Britain and France. Chamberlain announced to the House

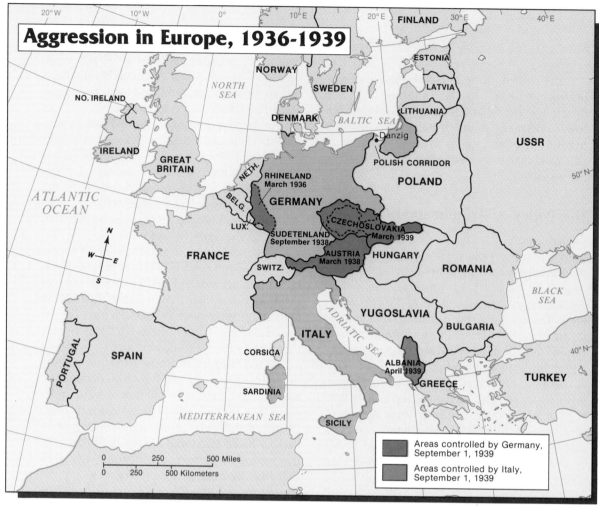

Aggression in Europe, 1936-1939

MAP STUDY *Between 1935 and 1939, Italy and Germany repeatedly threatened the peace in Europe. As you can see on this map, Hitler's aggression against Germany's neighbors increased the size of the Third Reich. In what order did the neighboring lands fall to the Third Reich?*

of Commons that Britain would aid Poland if it was attacked. Britain then set up a military draft and voted more money for defense. France vowed to support Poland and also hurried to rearm.

During the tension-filled spring and summer of 1939, Britain and Germany each negotiated with the Soviet Union. Because of its long border with Poland, the Soviet Union was especially concerned about the Polish crisis. Stalin wanted a military alliance with Britain and France. But the British and French fear of communism and doubts about the effectiveness of the Soviet army caused them to delay making a pact with Stalin. They also rejected

Stalin's demands for Soviet dominance in Eastern Europe.

Meanwhile, Hitler moved with great purpose. Although he detested communism and the Russians, on August 23, he shocked the world by signing a nonaggression treaty with the Soviet Union. In this Nazi-Soviet Pact, Germany and the Soviet Union pledged not to attack each other. In secret clauses, they agreed to divide Poland and other parts of Eastern Europe between them.

The Nazi-Soviet Pact allowed Germany to move against Poland without fear of Soviet interference. At the same time, it provided the Soviet Union at least temporary assurance that Hitler would not attack it. At dawn on September 1, 1939, German troops crossed the Polish border. Two days later, Britain and France declared war on Germany. The second world war of the century had begun.

SECTION 1 REVIEW

1. **Locate:** (a) Rhineland, (b) Sudetenland, (c) Munich, (d) Danzig.

2. **Identify:** (a) Francisco Franco, (b) Rome-Berlin Axis, (c) Neville Chamberlain, (d) Nazi-Soviet Pact.

3. **Define:** (a) Anschluss, (b) appeasement, (c) pacifism.

4. (a) Describe the two sides in the Spanish Civil War. (b) Who aided the Nationalists?

5. (a) How did Britain react to Hitler's occupation of the Rhineland in 1936? (b) How did France react?

6. What policy did the United States take toward European crises of the 1930s?

7. **Critical Thinking** How did the outcome of the Munich conference encourage Hitler?

2 War in Europe

READ TO UNDERSTAND

☐ How Europe fell to the Axis powers.

☐ How the Naxis ruled their empire in Europe.

☐ Why Hitler invaded the Soviet Union.

☐ *Vocabulary:* blitzkrieg.

"Whether nations live in prosperity or starve to death like cattle interests me only insofar as we need them as slaves to our civilization." In those words, one of Hitler's top aides summed up the Nazis' attitude toward the nations they conquered during World War II.

The war pitted the Axis against the Allies. Germany and Italy were the major Axis powers in 1939. Japan joined the Axis in 1940. Several nations in Eastern Europe also supported the Axis. The Allies eventually included Britain, France, the Soviet Union, the United States, China, and 43 other nations.

Early Months

On September 1, 1939, the German army launched a new kind of attack on Poland. It was called **blitzkrieg,** which means lightning war in German. Combined forces of planes, tanks, artillery, and mechanized infantry swiftly pierced Polish defenses.

The Poles fought bravely but were unable to stop the blitzkrieg. The Germans bombed Polish cities and destroyed the Polish air force on the ground. Meantime, in accordance with the Nazi-Soviet Pact, Soviet troops seized the eastern half of Poland. On September 27, 1939, Poland surrendered.

Because Stalin feared that Hitler would eventually attack the Soviet Union, he moved to strengthen his defenses. First, he occupied and then annexed the three small Baltic countries of Estonia, Latvia, and Lithuania. When Finland refused to allow Soviet military bases on its territory, the Soviets invaded. The "winter war" between Finland and the Soviet Union lasted from November 1939 until March 1940. The Soviet Union did not occupy Finland, but Finland was forced to give up some territory.

Collapse in Western Europe

After Germany conquered Poland, little happened for the next seven months. People began talking about the "phony war." Then in April 1940, Hitler unleashed a new blitzkrieg. One by one, Denmark, Norway, Luxembourg, the Netherlands, and Belgium fell to the German onslaught.

France massed troops along the Maginot Line in the northeast, hoping to stop a German invasion. However, the Germans simply bypassed these defenses and attacked France through Belgium. The Germans quickly penetrated deeply into France. By the end of May, they had pushed a combined British and French force to Dunkirk, a French port on the English Channel.

The British rushed every available naval vessel, merchant ship, and pleasure boat across the channel to rescue the troops trapped at Dunkirk. The operation saved over 300,000 troops, but much valuable equipment was left behind. The French soldiers who escaped at Dunkirk formed the Free French, a force that took part in later Allied actions.

France stood on the edge of defeat. Italy invaded southern France while the German army marched into Paris. The French then asked for an armistice. As you read at the beginning of the chapter, the French surrender took place at Compiègne on June 22, 1940.

Germany occupied northern France and governed it directly. In southern France, the Germans oversaw the creation of a puppet state, known as Vichy (VEE shee) France because its capital was at Vichy.

Churchill's leadership inspired the British people throughout the war. In radio speeches, he promised: "We have but one aim and one single, irrevocable [unchangeable] purpose. We are resolved to destroy Hitler and every vestige [trace] of his Nazi regime. From this nothing will turn us—nothing." In this photograph, Churchill is shown inspecting the House of Commons after it was bombed in May 1941.

The Battle of Britain

After the French surrender, Britain stood alone. A German invasion of the British Isles seemed certain. Neville Chamberlain had been forced to resign because of the failure of his appeasement policy. The new prime minister, Winston Churchill, was an inspiring leader. He warned that hard times lay ahead. All that he could offer, he told the British people, was "blood, toil, tears, and sweat." The British rallied behind Churchill's courage and determination. On June 4, after the Dunkirk rescue, Churchill proclaimed:

> We shall defend our island, whatever the cost may be. We shall fight on the beaches, we shall fight on the landing grounds, we shall fight in the fields and in the streets, we shall fight in the hills. We shall never surrender.

Hitler planned to weaken the British will to resist before invading the island nation. Therefore, in July, he ordered German bombers to attack British cities and defense installations. The punishing bombardment, called the Battle of Britain, lasted three months. The city of Coventry was nearly destroyed. London was bombed night after night. Thousands of Londoners slept in subway stations for safety, while firefighters hosed down flaming buildings and rescue teams dug trapped people out of the rubble.

Britain's Royal Air Force (RAF) attacked the German planes with skill and daring. British fighter pilots were aided by radar, a recent British invention. With radar, the British could detect the approach of enemy planes. Churchill expressed the gratitude of the British to the pilots of the RAF when he declared, "Never in the field of human conflict was so much owed by so many to so few."

Instead of destroying British morale, the Battle of Britain strengthened it. By late 1940, Hitler had to cancel plans for an invasion of Britain, although bombing continued off and on for several years.

The Nazi Empire in Europe

Despite Germany's setback in the Battle of Britain, the Axis powers soon controlled all of Western Europe except for neutral Portugal,

Sweden, and Switzerland. Spain, though technically neutral, was pro-Axis and allowed Germany to use its ports. In the east, Germany held Austria, Czechoslovakia, and western Poland. Hungary and Romania joined the Axis late in 1940, and Bulgaria joined early in 1941.

In several occupied countries, such as Poland and the Netherlands, German officials controlled the government directly. Elsewhere, the Germans set up puppet governments run by local people.

The Nazis exploited the economic resources of occupied Europe. They imposed heavy taxes on the French. In Eastern Europe, they sent men and women as slave labor to work in German factories. They also seized manufactured goods and shipped them to Germany. Nazi leaders amassed great art collections by looting the museums of Europe.

As they were doing in Germany, the Nazis persecuted Jews in the areas they occupied. They required Jews to wear yellow identification stars and seized Jewish businesses and other property. The Nazis forced Jews in Poland to move into ghettos, or restricted areas. There, Jews were forbidden contact with the outside world. The Nazis sent millions of Jews to concentration camps, where many starved or were murdered. Only after the war did the Allies discover the extent of Nazi atrocities against Jews and other people the Nazis considered unfit to live. (See page 708.)

Underground movements against Axis rule sprang up throughout Europe. Resistance groups sabotaged Nazi supply depots, derailed trains, and blew up bridges. They supplied the Allies with valuable information about Axis troop movements and hid escaped prisoners and downed pilots.

Further Attacks

In the fall of 1940, the Axis leaders turned their attention to the Balkans and North Africa. Mussolini invaded Greece in October. With the help of German troops, the Axis conquered Greece and Yugoslavia. Meanwhile, the Italians attacked the British in North Africa. They invaded Egypt in September 1940, but the British counterattacked, advancing into Libya and Ethiopia. Fighting in this area seesawed for many months.

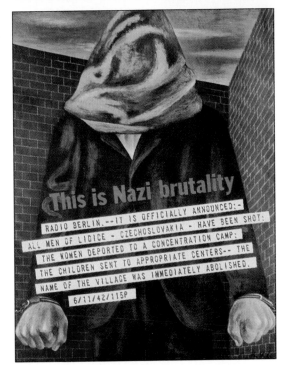

In this 1942 American poster, a hooded, manacled figure awaits execution and a chilling list of atrocities follows the words, "This is Nazi brutality." Hitler encouraged this cruelty and cautioned his soldiers, "Close your eyes to pity!"

Suddenly, news from these fronts was overshadowed by Hitler's surprise attack on the Soviet Union in June 1941. The German leader wanted to seize rich Soviet farmland and oil fields. He was willing to risk a two-front war, something German generals had feared since World War I.

On June 22, about 3 million German soldiers invaded the Soviet Union. The Soviets resisted but were forced to retreat. The effectiveness of Soviet forces was undermined in part by the loss of many top Soviet generals in the purges of the 1930s. As the Soviets withdrew, they destroyed farm equipment and burned crops. This "scorched earth" policy was meant to keep supplies out of enemy hands. Within four months, the Germans had overrun the Ukraine and were approaching Moscow and Leningrad. Then, at the end of 1941, the German advance was halted.

Soviet resistance stiffened, and "General Winter" came to Russia's aid, as it had when Napoleon tried to invade Russia in 1812. (See page 450.) The Germans were unprepared for the bitterly cold winter. They had to rely on long supply lines, which were often disrupted by Soviet soldiers. Both sides dug in for a long campaign. The German siege of Leningrad lasted for over two years. Over one and a half million people died in Leningrad as a result of the fighting, starvation, and disease.

SECTION 2 REVIEW

1. **Locate:** (a) Estonia, (b) Latvia, (c) Lithuania, (d) Dunkirk, (e) Leningrad.

2. **Identify:** (a) "phony war," (b) Winston Churchill.

3. **Define:** blitzkrieg.

4. What was the outcome of the Battle of Britain?

5. (a) How did the Nazis exploit the resources of occupied Europe? (b) What was their policy toward Jews in the areas they occupied?

6. What slowed Hitler's attack on the Soviet Union?

7. **Critical Thinking** Why was the outlook for the Allies so bleak in 1941?

---

3 War in the Pacific

READ TO UNDERSTAND

☐ How the United States responded to the outbreak of World War II.

☐ Why the United States entered the war.

☐ What successes the Japanese achieved early in the war.

☐ How Japan built an empire in the Pacific.

"We are not isolationists," declared President Franklin D. Roosevelt in 1936, "except insofar as we seek to isolate ourselves completely from war." When war broke out in Europe in 1939, the President still hoped to avoid involvement in the conflict. However, as Hitler's armies marched through Europe, Roosevelt declared that he was ready to pursue "all measures short of war" to ensure the survival of the Allies.

American Neutrality

When World War II began, President Roosevelt announced that the United States would remain neutral. While most Americans sympathized with the Allies, they did not want to go to war with Germany.

Isolationist feeling declined, however, with each Nazi success. Americans began to worry about where the Nazis would strike next. In September 1940, the United States transferred 50 destroyers to the British navy. Congress then passed the Lend-Lease Act in March 1941. The act authorized the President to furnish military supplies to nations "vital to the defense of the United States." To the President, the United States had to become "the arsenal of democracy," providing the Allies with what they needed to survive.

Under Lend-Lease, the United States shipped tons of supplies to Britain and later to the Soviet Union. As a result, American merchant vessels soon came under attack by German submarines. Although convoys were organized to protect the ships, many were sunk. It was events in Asia, however, not in Europe, that would plunge the United States into the war.

Japanese Expansion

The United States had watched with growing alarm Japan's aggressive moves in Asia. In 1937, Japan launched a full-scale war against China. Japanese troops poured into northeastern China and fanned out to the south and west. The Chinese resisted, but with little success. By late 1938, Japan controlled northern and central China and restricted the activities of foreign investors there. Japan then announced the creation of a "new order in East Asia." Under it, Japan claimed commercial supremacy in China.

When World War II broke out in Europe, Japan was openly sympathetic to Germany and Italy. In the fall of 1940, it signed an alliance with them, creating the Rome-Berlin-Tokyo Axis. After France and the Netherlands fell to Germany, the Japanese occupied French Indochina and announced that they would assume "protective custody" over the Dutch East Indies.

Attack on Pearl Harbor

The United States took a hard line against Japanese aggression in Asia. When Japan renewed its attack on China, the United States cancelled its commercial treaty with Japan. The United States condemned the seizure of French Indochina in 1940. It then stopped exporting oil and scrap metal to Japan. Early in 1941, it moved the American Pacific fleet from the west coast of the United States to Pearl Harbor in Hawaii to show its military readiness.

Still, the Japanese pushed into Southeast Asia, gaining control of the region's natural resources. The Japanese threat grew more serious after October 1941, when General Hideki Tojo, an outspoken expansionist, became prime minister of Japan. Tojo sent envoys to Washington, D.C., to negotiate with American officials. The Japanese offered to withdraw from southern Indochina if the Americans would resume economic relations. Japan insisted, however, on remaining in China. The United States rejected the proposals.

Even while negotiations were under way in Washington, a decision to attack the United States had been made in Tokyo. The Japanese had already decided that war with the United States was unavoidable. So they planned a surprise attack that would cripple the Americans and guarantee a Japanese victory. American military leaders knew that trouble was brewing. But they expected that the Japanese would attack in the Philippines or in Southeast Asia.

However, early in the morning on Sunday, December 7, 1941, Japanese planes roared out of the sky over the American naval base at Pearl Harbor. During a punishing two-hour raid, the Japanese sank or badly damaged 8 American battleships, crippled 10 other ships, destroyed 188 planes, and killed over 2,500 Americans. The next day a grim-faced President Roosevelt asked Congress to declare war. He called December 7 "a date which will live in infamy." Congress acted at once. Three days later, Japan's allies, Germany and Italy, declared war on the United States.

After bombing Pearl Harbor, Japanese pilots radioed Tokyo with the message, "Tora, tora, tora." Tora, which means tiger, was a code word for: "We have succeeded." Despite the destruction shown here, the Japanese did not destroy the entire American Pacific fleet. Three aircraft carriers were not in the harbor during the attack. In the naval warfare of World War II, these aircraft carriers proved to be valuable weapons.

Japanese Victories

The Japanese followed their successful attack on Pearl Harbor with lightning assaults across the Pacific. Within months, they captured the American islands of Guam and Wake and took the British colony of Hong Kong. Then in rapid order, they seized the Malay Peninsula, Singapore, the Dutch East Indies, and Burma.

Soon after Pearl Harbor, the Japanese attacked the Philippines. United States General Douglas MacArthur led the Allied defense but could not prevent a Japanese victory. In March 1942, when the Japanese had conquered most of the Philippines, MacArthur left with the promise, "I shall return." He set up headquarters in Australia and took command of the Allied forces in the Pacific.

Japan enjoyed several advantages in its drive for an empire. Britain was too involved in Europe to spare resources for fighting in Asia. France and the Netherlands had been defeated so they could not protect their Asian territories. Also, long supply lines between the United States and Asia helped Japan.

The Japanese Empire

Through its conquests, Japan gained rich resources. It controlled about three fourths of the world's rubber and tin, both critical materials in wartime. Oil from the Dutch East Indies fueled Japanese planes and trucks. Rice from Indochina fed Japanese soldiers.

The Japanese played skillfully on the bitterness that many Asians felt toward the British, French, Dutch, and Americans. They stressed the slogan "Asia for the Asians" and claimed to have rescued Asia from European colonial rule. Japan called its empire the "Greater East Asia Co-Prosperity Sphere." In fact, the sphere was totally controlled by Japan.

Although some Asians at first welcomed the Japanese, most soon realized that a new colonial power had merely replaced an old one. Japanese authorities forced local people to work on construction projects, often treating them with great cruelty. Their seizure of local rice crops led to food shortages. They also abused religious leaders and violated religious shrines.

Nationalists in the Asian countries organized resistance to the Japanese. Guerrilla fighters blew up railroad lines and gave information to the Allies. The military skills they developed would help them in their struggles for independence after the war.

SECTION 3 REVIEW

1. **Locate:** (a) Pearl Harbor, (b) Philippines.
2. **Identify:** (a) Lend-Lease Act, (b) Douglas MacArthur, (c) Greater East Asia Co-Prosperity Sphere.
3. What was the initial United States policy toward the war?
4. (a) Why did the Japanese attack Pearl Harbor? (b) What was the American response?
5. What areas did Japan capture in 1942?
6. **Critical Thinking** Why do you think Japan, a small island nation, was able to seize a huge empire in Asia?

---

4 The Tide Turns

READ TO UNDERSTAND

☐ How the Allies mobilized their resources for war.

☐ What the major turning points of the war were.

☐ Why President Truman decided to use the atomic bomb.

Eleven weeks after Hitler's armies invaded the Soviet Union in 1941, the Nazi propaganda machine churned out headlines like this: "The Great Hour Has Struck. The War in the East Is Over." But the Nazis claimed victory too soon. The Soviets hung on.

True, the Axis powers enjoyed nearly unbroken military success between September 1939 and the summer of 1942. But then the tide began to turn in favor of the Allies, both in Europe and in the Pacific.

The Great Mobilization

Although over 40 nations had joined the Allies, it was Britain, the Soviet Union, and the United States that played the decisive roles in defeating the Axis. Their leaders—Churchill, Stalin, and Roosevelt—determined most Allied strategy during the war.

The war effort required a total commitment. In Britain, factories converted to war production. Many consumer goods, from soap to gasoline, were rationed. Women joined the war effort, serving both in industry and in the armed services. Women were largely responsible for staffing the antiaircraft defenses and the radar stations that helped win the Battle of Britain.

The Soviet Union also transformed its economy to fight the war. Even before the German invasion, the Soviets had begun building factories in the remote eastern part of the Soviet Union. After the German attack, the Soviets dismantled some 1,500 factories in western Russia and reassembled them east of the Ural Mountains. Like people in the other Allied nations, Soviet citizens made great personal sacrifices in support of the war effort.

After Pearl Harbor, the United States geared up for war. Production of planes, tanks, and weapons increased dramatically. Through rationing and price controls, the government allocated scarce goods.

A special burden was borne by Japanese Americans, however. The United States government feared that Japanese Americans living on the west coast might support Japan and sabotage the American war effort. As a result, in 1942, the government moved more than 100,000 Japanese Americans—two thirds of them born in the United States—to inland relocation camps. They were detained in the camps for the rest of the war.*

Turning Points in North Africa and Europe

After months of Axis triumphs, two Allied victories offered new hope. The first was in North Africa, when the Allies stopped the brilliant

* In 1988, Congress passed a bill compensating the Japanese Americans who had been held in the relocation camps.

Millions of women joined the war effort. They helped produce badly needed airplanes, ships, and ammunition. In some American factories, women made up 90 percent of the work force. Here, women install cables in a plane.

In occupied France, the Nazis used propaganda to try and win support for their cause. This poster addresses French workers who were required to work in Germany for the war effort. It invokes the memory of those who died in the war. "They gave their blood," it says. "Give your work to save Europe from Bolshevism."

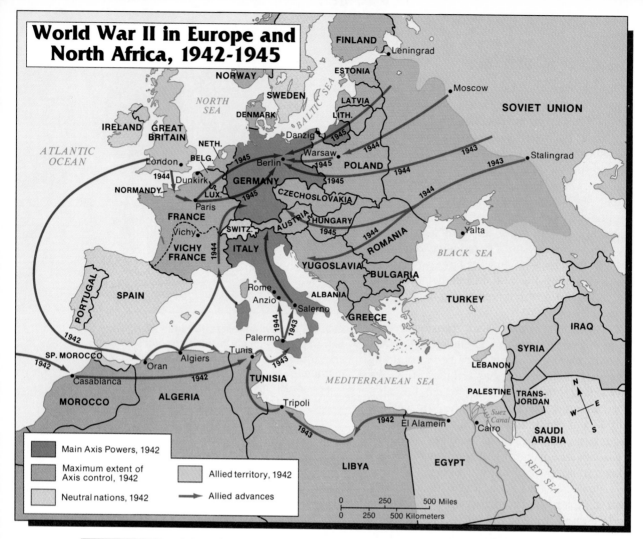

World War II in Europe and North Africa, 1942-1945

MAP STUDY *Axis influence reached its height in Europe and North Africa in early 1942. Soon after, Allied forces began successful offensives in North Africa, indicated by arrows on this map. The Allies invaded Italy in 1943. In June 1944, they landed in Normandy, France, a major step toward their victory in Europe. When did Soviet forces take the offensive to drive Axis armies out of Eastern Europe?*

German tank commander, General Erwin Rommel, known as the "Desert Fox." Rommel had moved against the Allies in the spring of 1942. After forcing the British out of Libya, his tanks threatened the British position at El Alamein in Egypt. If the Germans captured this strategic position, they could seize the Suez Canal and cut the British lifeline to India.

The British, commanded by General Bernard Montgomery, blocked the Nazi thrust at El Alamein and launched a counteroffensive. They drove Rommel back into Tunisia. In the fall of 1942, a combined British-American force under General Dwight Eisenhower landed in Morocco and Algeria. The two Allied

forces converged on Tunisia, trapping Rommel's troops.

In mid-May 1943, the Axis forces in North Africa surrendered. Churchill later called the Battle of El Alamein "the turning point in British military fortunes" during the war. "Up to Alamein, we survived," he said. "After Alamein, we conquered."

The second turning point occurred on the Russian front. In the fall of 1942, Hitler launched a massive offensive against the city of Stalingrad. Fierce house-to-house fighting raged for two months, but the defenders held out. Soviet forces organized a counteroffensive, capturing over 80,000 Germans. Another

200,000 Germans lost their lives in the battle. After their victory at Stalingrad, Soviet armies began to drive the Germans westward out of Soviet territory.

Allied Offensives in Europe

Stalin kept urging Britain and the United States to attack the Axis on a second European front in order to relieve the pressure on the Soviet Union. He wanted them to invade France, but the other Allied leaders decided to strike first in Italy because they considered it "the soft underbelly" of the Axis empire.

The invasion of Italy. On July 10, 1943, a combined British-American force landed in Sicily. They defeated Italian forces there in about a month. Meanwhile, Mussolini was forced out of power. Marshal Pietro Badoglio took control of the government and had Mussolini arrested. But German parachutists rescued Mussolini and took him to northern Italy.

Although Badoglio supported the Allies, thousands of German troops remained in Italy. When the Allies landed on the Italian mainland in September 1943, they encountered stiff resistance. Slowly, they pushed northward. On June 4, 1944, they marched into Rome, the first capital city on the European mainland to be freed from Axis control. However, parts of Italy remained under German control until the spring of 1945.

The invasion of France. While Allied forces were fighting in Italy, their generals were preparing for the invasion of France under the leadership of General Eisenhower. A huge invasion force assembled in Britain. Thousands of ships prepared to ferry the troops—British, Canadian, American, Free French, and others—across the English Channel.

D-Day, the day of the invasion of France, was June 6, 1944. Within 24 hours, 120,000 troops were landed at five beachheads on the Normandy coast. (See the map on page 702.) They were soon joined by over 800,000 more troops. Although the invading force met heavy German artillery fire, it fought its way inland. Meantime, another Allied force had invaded southern France and was pushing northward. The first Allied troops entered Paris on August 25. Cheering crowds lined the boulevards to greet their liberators. Nazi rule of France had ended. The Allies stood poised to invade Germany.

Advance on Berlin

More than a year before the Normandy landing, the Allies had begun heavy bombings of Germany. Air attacks on Germany increased in 1944. Berlin and other major cities were hit repeatedly, as were aircraft factories and oil refineries. In February 1945, Allied planes dropped fire bombs on the city of Dresden, killing over 100,000 civilians. Factories and railroad lines were pounded into rubble.

In December 1944, the Germans, in a surprising show of strength, launched an attack on American positions in Belgium and Luxembourg near the German border. The advancing Germans pushed back the Allies, creating a bulge in the Allied line. In the Battle of the Bulge, the Allies first lost ground but then regained it early in January 1945.

By April 1945, American units were approaching Berlin from the west, while Soviet forces were moving in from the east. Meanwhile, German resistance in Italy was collapsing. Members of the Italian resistance captured Mussolini and killed him.

As Allied troops approached Berlin, Hitler took refuge in an underground bunker. Realizing that defeat was near, he committed suicide on April 30. A week later, on May 7, Germany surrendered. The war in Europe was over. The Allies were now ready to deliver a final blow to Japan.

Turning Points in the Pacific

For six months after Pearl Harbor, the Japanese had won a series of uninterrupted victories. In the summer of 1942, they were poised to attack New Guinea, and from there, invade Australia. However, in May, planes from American carriers attacked a Japanese fleet in the Coral Sea, east of Australia. The planes destroyed several ships and checked the Japanese advance. The Battle of the Coral Sea was Japan's first major defeat.

A second defeat occurred a month later at Midway, about 1,000 miles (1,600 kilometers) northwest of Hawaii. Once again, American planes badly damaged a Japanese fleet. (See the feature at right.) After the Battle of Midway, the United States took the offensive in the Pacific. Its goal was to recapture the Philippines and invade Japan. The Americans devised an "island hopping" campaign, attacking some Japanese-held islands but bypassing others. The captured islands would serve as stepping-stones to their next objectives.

The Americans advanced slowly and with heavy casualties. The Japanese fought with tremendous determination, but they had to give up one strategic outpost after another. In October 1944, General MacArthur fulfilled his promise to return to the Philippines, taking Manila in February 1945.

On the Asian mainland, the Allies supported nationalist forces who resisted the Jap-

MAP STUDY *By 1942, the Japanese empire in Asia had reached its height. Japan controlled much of China, Southeast Asia, the Philippines, and a string of islands across the Pacific. After the Battle of Midway, however, the United States went on the offensive. By island-hopping, Allied forces regained control of strategic bases. When did they retake the Philippines? What major battles were fought as the Allies prepared to invade Japan?*

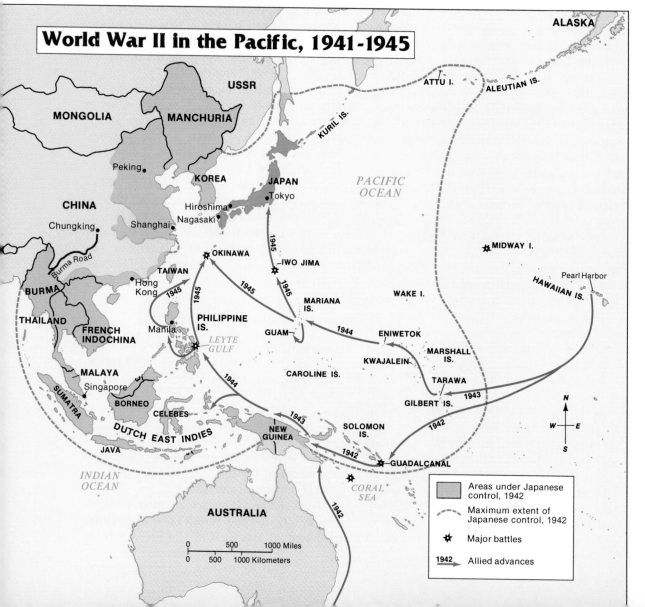

World War II in the Pacific, 1941-1945

Six months after the bombing of Pearl Harbor, American intelligence learned that Japan was massing its navy for a major assault on Midway, two tiny islands lying between Japan and Hawaii. Admiral Chester Nimitz ordered the islands to be fortified. Soldiers laced the beaches with barbed wire and explosive mines. Most important, dozens of airplanes were brought to the islands. Nimitz knew that planes from Japanese aircraft carriers would bomb Midway before troops invaded. American fliers would be Midway's main defense. They would first have to fight off the bombers and then attack the Japanese ships.

The Americans, however, faced an uphill battle. Many ships and airplanes had been lost at Pearl Harbor. As a result, most of the planes at Midway were obsolete. Pilots nicknamed one old model the "Flying Coffin" because it was so slow in combat. In contrast, Japanese aircraft carriers were loaded with fast, agile fighter planes called Zeros, as well as with powerful bombers.

By June 3, 1942, over 180 Japanese ships were steaming toward Midway. The strategy of Japan's Admiral Yamamoto was to lure the weaker American fleet into battle. If he destroyed America's Pacific fleet, Yamamoto could send his ships against Hawaii—and later, perhaps, against California.

"Many planes heading Midway." The curt message from an American spotter came be- fore dawn. Every plane at Midway left the ground to avoid being destroyed. American squadrons flew out to intercept the Japanese fleet. Under fierce attack by Zero fighters, one squadron after another dove toward the ships. Exploding shells made the air so turbu- lent that the pilots could barely hold their course. Outnumbered and outgunned, the American planes fell from the sky in flames. Two-thirds of the planes that flew out from Midway never returned. Of the 82 men on board, 69 died.

Although they failed to sink the Japanese aircraft carriers, the American airmen did not die in vain. America's Pacific fleet, which had avoided meeting the huge Japanese force head on, now sent in its planes. After fierce fighting, American planes sank all four of Ja- pan's aircraft carriers. Dismayed, Admiral Ya- mamoto announced on the morning of June 5: "Occupation of Midway is cancelled."

The United States had won a critical bat- tle. After Midway, it was the Japanese who were on the defensive.

1. Besides taking Midway, what did the Japa- nese hope to accomplish in the battle?

2. **Critical Thinking** Look at the map on page 704. What about the location of Midway made it a crucial base for both the Japa- nese and Americans?

---

anese. In China, the United States aided Chiang Kai-shek. In Indochina, the Allies supplied Ho Chi Minh, leader of a coalition of communists and nationalists known as the Viet Minh. Japan managed to hold on to the mainland, but the fighting there tied up many Japanese troops.

Defeat of Japan

On April 1, 1945, United States forces landed on Okinawa, a small Japanese island about 1,000 miles (1,600 kilometers) from Tokyo. American casualties there were especially heavy. Japanese pilots carried out kamikaze* attacks, suicide missions in which they crashed planes loaded with explosives into American ships. Japanese infantry fought with equal fanaticism. American troops finally cap- tured Okinawa at the end of June. More than 100,000 Japanese soldiers died defending the rocky outpost.

---

* Kamikaze means "divine wind" in Japanese. When the Mongols threatened Japan in the 1200s, the Mongol fleet was destroyed by a typhoon, which the Japanese named kamikaze.

In the Pacific, the war was fought island by island, inch by inch, often against Japanese snipers who were prepared to die rather than surrender. This painting shows American troops landing at Leyte Gulf in the Philippines.

By this time, Allied planes were bombing Japan with ferocity. In a single raid on Tokyo in March 1945, 100,000 people died and over 60 percent of the commercial buildings were wiped out. By mid-1945, most of the Japanese navy and air force had been destroyed. Yet the Japanese still had an army of 2 million men, and their will to fight remained strong. It appeared that the road to final victory for the Allies would be long and costly.

In the United States, President Roosevelt died in April 1945 and Vice President Harry S. Truman succeeded him. In July, the United States successfully tested an atomic bomb in the New Mexico desert. The atomic bomb was much more destructive than conventional bombs. Truman at first hesitated to use the new weapon. But his military advisers warned that an invasion of Japan might cost as many as 1 million Allied lives. Truman decided to use the atomic bomb on Japan if necessary.

From mid-July to early August, Truman, Stalin, and Clement Attlee, the new British prime minister, met at Potsdam in Germany. The Allied leaders warned the Japanese, without being specific, that if they did not surrender they would suffer "complete and utter destruction." The Japanese ignored the warning.

On August 6, 1945, the United States dropped an atomic bomb on Hiroshima. The blast leveled 42 square miles (109 square kilometers) of the city and killed at least 80,000 people at once. Almost 40,000 others were seriously injured. Countless thousands more were stricken with radiation sickness.

Despite the destruction at Hiroshima, Japan still refused to surrender. Three days later a second atomic bomb was dropped on Nagasaki, killing at least 40,000 people. Japan could hold out no longer. On August 14, Japan surrendered, ending World War II.

1. **Locate:** (a) El Alamein, (b) Stalingrad, (c) Normandy, (d) Coral Sea, (e) Midway, (f) Okinawa, (g) Hiroshima, (h) Nagasaki.

2. **Identify:** (a) Erwin Rommel, (b) Bernard Montgomery, (c) Dwight Eisenhower, (d) D-Day.

3. How did the war affect the homefront of the Allies?

4. Describe one turning point in the war in (a) North Africa, (b) Europe, and (c) the Pacific.

5. (a) What was the purpose of the "island hopping" campaign in the Pacific? (b) Was it successful?

6. **Critical Thinking** Put yourself in President Truman's position in July 1945. American military leaders are urging you to drop the atomic bomb on Japan. What factors do you consider as you decide whether or not to use the bomb?

5 Effects of the War

READ TO UNDERSTAND

- ☐ **What the human and economic costs of the war were.**
- ☐ **Why the Allies held war crimes trials.**
- ☐ **What long-term effects World War II had.**
- ☐ *Vocabulary:* **Holocaust.**

Although peace was won at last, it came, as Winston Churchill put it, to "an outraged and quivering world." The war had reached around the globe. Few countries had been untouched by it. People could only guess at the cost in lives. Some estimates put the total number of dead at 75 million worldwide. About 34 million died in Europe alone. The damage to property ran in the billions of dollars.

The Aftermath of the War

With the return of peace, people surveyed the destruction of war. The cost—both human

CHART STUDY

World War II resulted in a staggering number of casualties. Systematic aerial bombing of cities led to many civilian deaths and injuries. The bombings of Hiroshima and Nagasaki resulted in over 150,000 casualties. Which nation bore the greatest burden in both military and civilian dead and wounded?

Casualties in World War II			
	Military Dead	**Military Wounded**	**Civilian Dead**
Britain	398,000	475,000	65,000
France	211,000	400,000	108,000
Soviet Union	7,500,000	14,102,000	15,000,000
United States	292,000	671,000	*
Germany	2,850,000	7,250,000	5,000,000
Italy	77,500	120,000	100,000
Japan	1,576,000	500,000	300,000
All figures are estimates. *Negligible number of civilian dead.			

Source: Henri Michel, *The Second World War.*

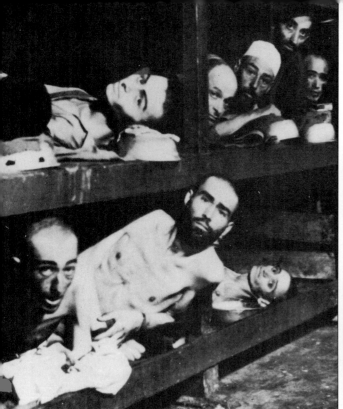

Reports of Hitler's death camps reached the Allies during the war. Nevertheless, Allied soldiers were appalled at what they found when they reached these camps. At Buchenwald, in Germany, deaths by starvation were common. The picture at left shows the emaciated conditions of the prisoners who were freed by Allied troops in 1945. At the right, is the infamous concentration camp at Auschwitz, Poland, where 2.5 million people were executed during the war.

and material—was greater than that of any other war in history.

World War I had been a ground war, fought mainly from trenches. In World War II, planes traveled long distances, spreading destruction everywhere. Both military and civilian deaths reached record numbers. (See the table on page 707.)

Civilians suffered much more in World War II than they had in World War I. In the Soviet Union, for example, 15 million civilians were killed. Throughout much of Europe, millions of "displaced persons" were homeless when the war ended. The war reduced much of Europe and Japan to rubble.

The Holocaust Revealed

During the war, the Allies had received reports about Hitler's attacks on Jews. But in 1945, when Allied troops marched into Germany, they learned the full horror of his campaign of genocide. Hitler had called it the "final solu-

tion of the Jewish question"—the total extermination of Jews in Europe.

In some areas occupied by Nazis, all the Jews of a town had been shot and buried in a mass grave. At Babi Yar in the Ukraine, for example, 33,000 Jews from Kiev were killed in two days. Mass executions by shooting were too slow for the Nazis, so they built huge camps for the express purpose of killing people. The most notorious death camps were Auschwitz, Maidaneck, and Treblinka in Poland and Dachau in Germany. Nazis shipped trainloads of Jews to these camps from all over Europe. There, the Jews were stripped, forced into special chambers, and gassed.

Altogether, some 6 million Jews died in what has come to be called the **Holocaust**—the systematic murder of Jews carried out by the Nazis. Jews were not the only victims of the Nazi death camps. About six million others—Slavs, Gypsies, the physically and mentally disabled, and political prisoners—were also killed.

War Crimes Trials

The horrors of the Holocaust and other crimes committed by the Axis powers shocked the world. The Allies decided that because the enemy had committed atrocities beyond the laws and customs of war, the leaders responsible for these actions should be tried as war criminals. From 1945 to 1947, the Allies held trials for a number of Nazi and Japanese officials. In Germany, the war crimes trials were held at Nuremberg, site of many of Hitler's mass rallies.

Hitler and Goebbels had committed suicide when the Allies closed in on Berlin. But 20 former top Nazis were tried at Nuremberg. Many others were tried elsewhere. The charges included waging aggressive war and "crimes against humanity." Among those crimes were the use of slave labor and the operation of extermination camps. Three Nazi officials were acquitted, seven received life imprisonment, and ten were sentenced to death. The Allies also held war crimes trials in Tokyo. General Tojo, who had approved the attack on Pearl Harbor, was convicted as a war criminal and executed.

The Postwar World

Once the German threat was ended, the old rivalry between East and West* quickly re-emerged in Europe. The future of Eastern Europe became a crucial issue. So, too, did the question of the treatment of Germany. Both issues had been discussed at wartime conferences of the Allies, as you will read in Chapter 32. But after the war, the western allies grew alarmed at Stalin's efforts to impose communist regimes on the nations of Eastern Europe.

The war had other longterm effects. It reduced the influence of Western Europe in world affairs. Enormous casualties, huge expenditures, and physical damage had drained its strength. Leadership passed into the hands of two superpowers, the United States and the Soviet Union.

---

* Since World War II, the United States, the nations of Western Europe, and other nations opposed to Soviet expansion have often been referred to as the "West" or the "western powers." The Soviet Union and its allies are often called the "East" or the "eastern powers."

World War II unleashed the forces of nationalism throughout the world. In colonies ruled by European nations, demands for independence grew stronger. People in some colonies, such as India, had fought with the Allies and had been promised greater freedom as a reward. In other colonies, such as French Indochina, nationalists who had fought against the Japanese were determined to resist a return to European rule.

The war contributed to social changes in many countries. In the United States, for example, black Americans gained job opportunities that had long been denied them. In June 1941, President Roosevelt banned racial discrimination in businesses with government defense contracts. The order raised hopes for further government action against racial discrimination.

The economic role of women also changed. Millions of women had held wartime jobs. Although many returned to their homes with the coming of peace, many others saw a future of wider opportunities.

The war years saw far-reaching developments in science and technology. Scientists invented synthetic materials to replace natural ones that were in short supply. Improvements in airplanes, the invention of radar, and other devices changed the nature of war itself. However, the development of the atomic bomb may have had the most significant impact on the future. Many people have called the years since 1945 the "Atomic Age."

SECTION 5 REVIEW

1. **Define:** Holocaust.

2. What factors contributed to the greater number of civilian deaths in World War II than in World War I?

3. What did Hitler mean by the "final solution of the Jewish question"?

4. Describe one political issue that emerged at the end of the war.

5. **Critical Thinking** Were the Allies justified in holding war crimes trials? Why or why not?

Summary

1. Aggression by Italy and Germany led to the outbreak of World War II. At first, Germany and Italy met little resistance from the democratic nations, who followed a policy of appeasement. But when Germany invaded Poland in September 1939, Britain and France declared war, and World War II began.

2. The German army controlled most of Western Europe by the end of June 1940. However, its efforts to defeat Britain through air attacks failed. In June 1941, the Nazis invaded the Soviet Union, driving deep into Soviet territory.

3. By May 1942, Japan had conquered a large part of East Asia and the Pacific. The United States had entered World War II after the Japanese attacked Pearl Harbor in 1941.

4. Beginning in 1942, the Allies began to advance against the Axis powers. Three years later they inflicted final defeat on the Axis. The Allied invasion of Normandy in June 1944 led to the final defeat of Germany. In the Pacific, the war ended when the United States dropped atomic bombs on two Japanese cities.

5. World War II, the costliest conflict in history, had important aftereffects. Much of Europe and Japan lay in ruins. And the horrors of the Holocaust were revealed. The war left Europe divided between East and West.

Recalling Facts

Review the time line on page 711 and your reading in this chapter. Then choose the letter of the correct time period for each of the following events.

A	B	C	D	E
1936   1938   1940   1942   1944   1946

1. France surrenders to Germany.

2. The British defeat the Germans at El Alamein.

3. German troops invade Poland.

4. The Japanese attack Pearl Harbor.

5. German troops occupy the Rhineland.

6. The Allied invasion of Normandy begins.

Chapter Checkup

1. What lesson did Hitler and Mussolini learn from the Spanish Civil War?

2. Describe how the policy of appeasement worked in: (a) German occupation of the Rhineland; (b) the Anschluss; (c) the Munich conference.

3. Why did Hitler and Stalin sign the Nazi-Soviet Pact?

4. (a) Describe the Nazi conquest of Western Europe. (b) Why was the Battle of Britain important?

5. (a) Why did Hitler invade the Soviet Union? (b) How was the German advance halted at the end of 1941?

6. Why was Japan so successful in the months immediately following Pearl Harbor?

7. Describe the effect of these battles: (a) El Alamein; (b) Stalingrad; (c) Normandy; (d) Coral Sea; (e) Midway.

8. (a) What were the immediate effects of the war on people's lives? (b) What was its long-range impact?

Critical Thinking

1. **Interpreting** Why do you think the Spanish Civil War has been called the "dress rehearsal" for World War II?

2. **Understanding the Roots of Democracy** During World War I, President Woodrow Wilson hesitated to join the Allies because czarist Russia—one of the Allies—was an autocratic state. However, during World War II, Franklin D. Roosevelt sent supplies to the hard-pressed Soviet Union, a totalitarian state. Do you think a democracy such as the United States is ever justified in aiding a state with an oppressive regime? Why or why not?

3. **Relating Past to Present** What development during World War II do you think still has the greatest impact on the world today? Explain.

Developing Basic Skills

1. **Using Visual Evidence** Study the painting on page 690 and photographs on pages 696, 699, and 708. (a) What is the subject of each? (b) What can you learn about the nature of World War II from the painting and photographs?

2. **Map Reading** Study the map on page 702. (a) What were the main Axis nations in Europe in 1942? (b) Which nations were not controlled by the Axis in 1942? (c) Which nation do you think would have control of Eastern Europe by the end of the war in 1945? Why?

Writing About History

Writing and Revising a First Draft

When you are ready to revise your first draft, you should ask yourself these question: Does the introduction lead into the thesis logically? Does each paragraph develop one idea related to the thesis? Are the paragraphs arranged in a logical order? Is all the information logical? Does the conclusion reinforce the thesis? Is the language appropriate and have you explained any unfamiliar technical terms?

Practice: Rewrite the following paragraph to improve the organization and style.

In October 1944 General MacArthur returned to the Philippines. He said, "I shall return." He captured Manila in February 1945. Lots of big battles against the Japanese took place in the Pacific. The Americans did a swell job knocking the Japanese off the islands. Japanese pilots carried out suicide missions. Finally, in August 1945, the United States dropped two atomic bombs on Japan and the Japanese surrendered.

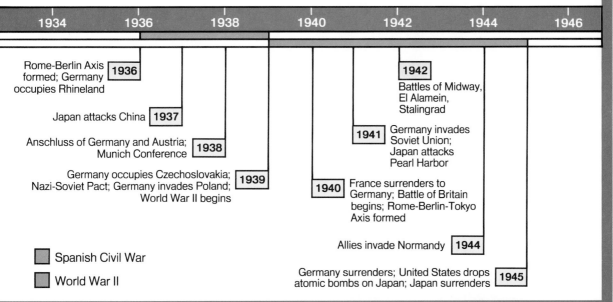

| 1934 | 1936 | 1938 | 1940 | 1942 | 1944 | 1946 |

Rome-Berlin Axis formed; Germany occupies Rhineland **1936**

Japan attacks China **1937**

Anschluss of Germany and Austria; Munich Conference **1938**

Germany occupies Czechoslovakia; Nazi-Soviet Pact; Germany invades Poland; World War II begins **1939**

1942 Battles of Midway, El Alamein, Stalingrad

1941 Germany invades Soviet Union; Japan attacks Pearl Harbor

1940 France surrenders to Germany; Battle of Britain begins; Rome-Berlin-Tokyo Axis formed

Allies invade Normandy **1944**

Germany surrenders; United States drops atomic bombs on Japan; Japan surrenders **1945**

▮ Spanish Civil War
▯ World War II

The Cold War and European Recovery

32

(1945–1968)

Americans showed great compassion for those who had suffered from the ravages of World War II. The actions of individuals, like the soldier in this painting by Ben Shahn, as well as official government policies, like the Marshall Plan, showed American concern about developments in Europe.

Students and townspeople crowded into the small college gymnasium. They shuffled to their seats and then waited for the great man to appear. The place was tiny Westminster College in Fulton, Missouri. Early in 1946, the college president, Franc McCluer, had taken a wild gamble. He invited the former British prime minister, Sir Winston Churchill, to speak on campus. Would the great statesman bother to answer? Indeed he did. He accepted the invitation, noting that he had some things to say.

Churchill spoke bluntly. He reminded his listeners that he had warned of Hitler's tyranny in the 1930s. World War II, he claimed, could have been prevented by timely action. Now he was issuing a new warning. This time the threat came from the Soviet Union.

"From Stettin in the Baltic to Trieste in the Adriatic, an iron curtain has descended across the Continent," Churchill declared. "Warsaw, Berlin, Prague, Vienna, Budapest, Belgrade, Bucharest, and Sofia, all these famous cities and populations around them lie in what I must call the Soviet sphere, and all are subject to a very high and, in many cases, increasing measure of control from Moscow."

The "iron curtain" Churchill referred to put Eastern Europe under Soviet influence and cut it off from the rest of the world. Stalin had clamped strict controls on travel. No "unauthorized" books, newspapers, or magazines were allowed into the Soviet sphere. Foreign radio programs were jammed.

Churchill pleaded for Americans and Britons to take a strong stand against the Soviet Union. "From what I have seen of our Russian friends and allies during the war, I am convinced that there is nothing they admire so much as strength, and there is nothing for which they have less respect than for weakness, especially military weakness."

Churchill, like many Americans and Western Europeans, worried about the gains of communist parties around the world and the expansion of Soviet influence in Eastern Europe. Tension between the Soviet Union and the western powers mounted steadily in the postwar period. The period also witnessed the struggles of European nations to rebuild their devastated economies. ■

1 The Cold War Begins

READ TO UNDERSTAND

☐ What the wartime conferences decided.

☐ How the United States responded to Soviet expansion after World War II.

☐ Why Berlin became a focus of the cold war.

☐ *Vocabulary:* cold war, denazification, containment.

"Uncle Joe" was the way President Roosevelt had referred to Joseph Stalin during the war. Stalin, claimed the American President, was "truly representative of the heart and soul of Russia." Most Americans shared Roosevelt's desire to cooperate with the Russians, who were suffering so severely in the battle against Hitler.

In mid-1945, a public opinion poll showed that 55 percent of Americans thought "we can trust the Russians." But a year later, that number had dropped to 7 percent. What had happened to cause such a drastic change in Americans' attitude to the Russians? When Churchill made his iron curtain speech, some people thought his warnings about Soviet expansion were exaggerated. But by 1946, the warnings of Soviet expansion were coming true, and a cold war had begun. A **cold war** is a state of tension and hostility among nations without armed conflict.

Wartime Conferences

Throughout the war, Allied leaders had met to plan strategy and discuss postwar policy. Even before the United States entered the war, President Roosevelt and Prime Minister Churchill had stated their goals for a postwar settlement. In August 1941, they issued the Atlantic Charter. The document supported "the right of all peoples to choose the form of government under which they will live." It urged economic cooperation and a "permanent system of general security" to protect nations from aggression.

The Big Three—Churchill, Roosevelt, and Stalin—met for the first time in Teheran, Iran, in November 1943. They discussed the upcoming invasion of France and made tentative plans for dealing with Poland and Germany after the war. They met again in February 1945 at Yalta, in southern Russia. There, Churchill and Roosevelt sought Soviet support in the fight against Japan. Stalin agreed to declare war on Japan after Germany surrendered. In return, the Soviet Union would receive some territory in East Asia.

The future of Eastern Europe was also discussed at Yalta. The Allies agreed that free elections would be held in the Eastern European countries. Eastern Poland would become part of the Soviet Union, but Poland would receive part of eastern Germany. Germany was to be divided into American, British, French, and Soviet occupation zones. The three leaders further agreed to take part in the United Nations, an international peacekeeping organization. Although the meeting at Yalta was friendly, the western powers and the Soviet Union would soon disagree about carrying out the decisions reached there.

Conflicts emerged at the last conference, held in Potsdam, Germany, in July 1945. By then, Harry Truman had succeeded Roosevelt as President. Truman was unhappy with the pro-Soviet governments that had been set up in several countries in Eastern Europe. When he demanded free elections in accordance with the Yalta agreement, Stalin refused. "A freely elected government in any of these East European countries would be anti-Soviet," said Stalin, "and that we cannot allow."

The Occupation of Germany

After Germany surrendered, the Soviet Union occupied eastern Germany. The rest of the country was divided among Britain, the United States, and France. Berlin, the former capital, lay within the Soviet zone. It was also divided among the four powers. (See the map on page 715.) The division of Germany into occupation zones was meant to be a temporary measure. However, differences between the Soviet Union and the other Allies made a reunified Germany appear less and less likely.

A crucial wartime conference was held in 1945 at Yalta in the Soviet Union. Every day the Allied leaders posed for the news cameras. In the front row of this photograph, from left to right, are British Prime Minister Churchill, American President Roosevelt, and Soviet Premier Stalin.

Much of Germany had been destroyed by the war. Homes and other buildings lay in rubble, food was scarce, and epidemics were a threat. Millions of refugees displaced by the war added to the chaos. In their zone, the Soviets had little sympathy for the plight of the Germans. They wanted to punish Germany for the terrible losses the Soviet Union had suffered in the war. Soviet troops dismantled factories and shipped heavy machinery, trucks, and locomotives home.

The United States, Britain, and France wanted to rebuild rather than punish Germany. They thought that a German nation with a strong economy and a democratic government was the best guarantee against the rise of another Hitler. Also, a strong Germany would serve as a buffer against the Soviet Union. The Allies set a goal of **denazification,** removing all traces of Nazism in Germany. As you have read, they brought criminal charges against Nazi leaders. Nazi symbols were removed from schools and public places. And Nazi textbooks were replaced with ones that taught respect for democracy.

In 1949, Britain, the United States, and France combined their zones into one nation—the German Federal Republic, or West Germany. Bonn became its capital. The German people elected Konrad Adenauer, leader of the Christian Democratic party, as chancellor.

That same year, the Soviet zone became the German Democratic Republic, or East Germany. As harsh Soviet control continued, thousands of people fled to West Germany.

Expansion of Soviet Influence

Cold war tensions rose not only over the fate of Germany but also over Soviet domination of Eastern Europe. During the war, Soviet troops had moved into Czechoslovakia, Hungary, Romania, and Bulgaria as they forced the Germans westward. Under Soviet occupation, new governments were then set up in these countries. At first, the governments were coalitions of communists and noncommunists. But noncommunists were soon forced out of power.

By 1948, the governments of every Eastern European country were under communist

MAP STUDY *During World War II, the Allies drew up plans for the occupation of Germany. Britain, the United States, France, and the Soviet Union each had its own zone of occupation. Berlin, the capital of Nazi Germany, was divided among the four powers. In which country's zone was Berlin located?*

control. These nations became known as Soviet satellites or Soviet bloc countries.

Stalin had long argued that the Soviet Union needed friendly governments in Eastern Europe as a buffer against any future German attack. However, to many people in Western Europe and the United States, the Soviet Union seemed bent on world domination.

With Soviet backing, communist movements were gaining ground around the world. In Greece, communists were fighting a civil war against the government. Turkey and Iran felt menaced by the Soviet Union. In China, communist revolutionaries were threatening Chiang Kai-shek, as you will read in Chapter 35. In Southeast Asia, communist-led forces battled the French.

The American Response

Weakened by war, Britain and France lacked the resources to stop Soviet expansion. Only the United States had the military and economic strength to counter Soviet ambitions.

Containment and the Truman Doctrine. George Kennan, an American diplomat, urged a policy of **containment.** The United States, he said, should contain, or hold, the Soviets within their current boundaries by political, economic, and, if necessary, military means whenever the Soviets tried to expand.

President Truman applied the policy of containment in Greece and Turkey. When Britain announced that it could no longer afford to send economic aid to the Greek government, Truman feared the communists would win the civil war there. So in March 1947, he proclaimed the Truman Doctrine. It stated that the United States would support free peoples resisting "attempted subjugation [domination] by armed minorities or by outside pressures."

In 1948, the Soviet Union closed all land routes into West Berlin. The United States responded by organizing a massive airlift. Here, Berliners stand on top of a building that was damaged during the war to watch an American cargo plane bringing in food and other vital supplies. In the 11 months of the airlift, more than 2 million tons of goods were flown into Berlin.

Congress approved $400 million in economic aid to Greece and Turkey. With this aid, the Greek government defeated the communists, and the Turks were able to withstand Soviet pressure.

The Marshall Plan. The United States also responded to the threat of communism in war-ravaged Europe with massive economic aid. On a trip to Europe in 1947, Secretary of State George Marshall became aware that millions of people faced a daily battle against "hunger, poverty, desperation, and chaos." He feared that nations that could not deal with these problems were in danger of revolution and collapse.

Marshall then proposed that the United States fund a program of European recovery. The program became known as the Marshall Plan. All European nations, including those in the Soviet bloc, were invited to participate. The Soviet Union attacked the plan as "Yankee imperialism" and kept its satellites from taking part.

Between 1948 and 1952, the United States poured $13 billion of aid into Western Europe. The Marshall Plan bolstered the economies of Western Europe and stimulated industrial growth. By improving economic and political conditions, it reduced the danger of communist revolution.

Focus on Berlin

The cold war came close to becoming a "hot" war over Berlin. In 1948, the United States, Britain, and France were ready to combine their German occupation zones into one country. Stalin was afraid that the combined zone would be the first step toward creating a strong, reunified Germany that would threaten the Soviet Union.

In June 1948, the Soviets stopped all road, rail, and river traffic through East Germany into West Berlin. They hoped to force the western powers to give up Berlin. Truman immediately ordered an American airlift of food and other supplies into West Berlin. When winter came, planes ferried in coal. The Berlin airlift continued until May 1949, when the Soviets lifted their blockade.

Berlin continued to be a focus of the cold war. Between 1949 and 1961, thousands of East

Germans fled into West Berlin. Then, in 1961, the East German government built a wall between East and West Berlin to stop the flow of people. War clouds loomed as President John Kennedy called up United States reserves to reinforce West German garrisons. The crisis passed, but the Berlin Wall remained for 28 years, reminding people of a divided Germany and a divided Europe.

Military Alliances

By 1949, Europe was split into two camps. One, led by the Soviet Union, championed international communism. The other, led by the United States, favored democracy. The split led to the growth of rival military alliances.

In April 1949, representatives of the United States, Canada, and ten Western European nations signed a mutual defense treaty creating the North Atlantic Treaty Organization (NATO). (See the map on page 720.) Members agreed to aid any member nation attacked by an outsider. By joining NATO, the United States committed itself to defend Western Europe against Soviet aggression.

After the war, the Soviet Union was the strongest military power in Europe. This French poster expresses the concern felt by many Western European nations and the United States about the Soviet military threat. Stalin is shown in the center with one foot on a white cross.

THEN AND NOW The Berlin Wall

East Berlin, Nov, 9, 1989 East German leaders meet for hours, debating how to handle the crisis. In recent months, tens of thousands of East Germans have fled to the West through Hungary. Protests have forced Erich Honecker, East Germany's hardline communist leader, to resign. Swiftly, his successor, Egon Krenz, takes a memorable step: He opens the borders between East Germany and West Germany.

Thousands of East Berliners rush to the Berlin Wall—the huge, 12-foot-high concrete barrier that has divided their city, their country, and all of Europe. At Checkpoint Charlie, a gate in the wall, East German border guards have no instructions. Finally, at 11:17 P.M., they open the gates. East Berliners pour across the border. West Berliners welcome them with flowers and champagne.

Until that November night, many Germans thought that the wall would have to go—some day. However, few expected it to crumble so suddenly. Cameras record the joy, laughter, and tears as Berliners celebrate the peaceful victory for freedom.

For almost 30 years, the wall blocked the movement of people between East and West Berlin. It divided families. It separated a church from its graveyard and friends from neighbors. The wall failed, however, to keep out ideas and a desire for freedom. Within days after that November night, cranes and workers began removing the Berlin Wall. As the concrete crumbled, Berliners remembered those who had died trying to escape to freedom.

1. How was the Berlin Wall a symbol of the cold war?

2. **Critical Thinking** Why do you think the Berlin Wall was unable to keep out ideas?

Greece and Turkey joined NATO in 1952. When West Germany joined in 1955, the Soviet Union created its own alliance, the Warsaw Pact. In the Warsaw Pact, the Soviet Union and seven Eastern European nations agreed to provide aid if any of them went to war.

The United Nations

The cold war overshadowed the work of the United Nations (UN), an international organization devoted to world peace. In April 1945, delegates from 50 nations had met in San Francisco and adopted the United Nations Charter. In it, member nations agreed to submit disputes to the United Nations for peaceful settlement. They also agreed to work together to solve the world problems of disease, hunger, and illiteracy.

UN structure. The United Nations has six major bodies. (See the diagram below.) The General Assembly and the Security Coun-

cil are the two most important. The General Assembly has representatives from every member nation. It discusses world problems brought before it and recommends action. The Security Council has five permanent members and ten rotating members. Great Britain, the United States, the Soviet Union, China, and France hold the permanent places.

The Security Council investigates world conflicts and decides on what action the UN should take. For example, it can call for economic sanctions or send peacekeeping forces made up of soldiers from member nations. UN peacekeeping forces have worked in the Middle East, Africa, and Asia.

The Security Council cannot force member nations to agree to its decisions. Furthermore, any one of the five permanent members can veto Security Council decisions. This veto power has often paralyzed the Security Council. Disagreements between the United States and the Soviet Union have weakened the Secu-

CHART STUDY *The Charter of the United Nations created an organization with six major bodies. Which body is responsible for developing UN policies?*

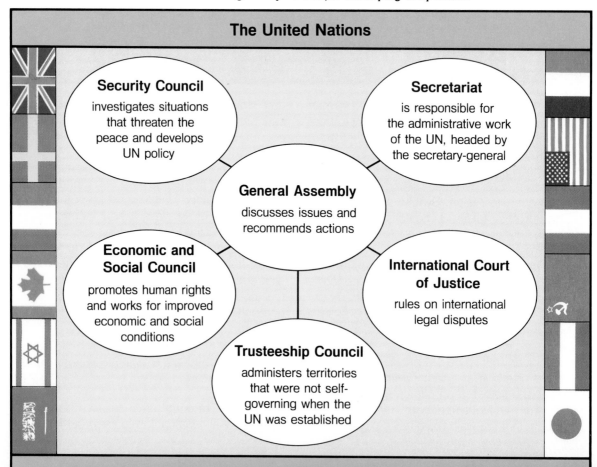

rity Council. It has been powerless to act in many disputes because the two superpowers disagreed on what course to follow.

When disagreements between the Soviet Union and the United States became common, attention shifted to the General Assembly as a forum. The makeup of the General Assembly has changed over the years. As UN membership has increased, the balance of power has swung away from the superpowers to smaller, developing nations. Despite limited success in solving major conflicts, the UN has done much to help developing nations combat disease and improve education.

Peacekeeping efforts in the postwar world. The UN helped bring peace to several unstable areas of the world after the war. In 1947, it proposed that the British mandate of Palestine be divided into an Arab and a Jewish state. In 1948, Jewish residents declared their part of the mandate the state of Israel. Shortly afterwards, war broke out between Arabs and Israelis. UN representatives worked for two years to achieve a cease-fire. A shaky peace was monitored by a UN police force, although fighting erupted again in 1956 and 1967. UN mediation also ended fighting between India and Pakistan in 1949.

SECTION 1 REVIEW

1. **Locate:** Berlin.

2. **Identify:** (a) Truman Doctrine, (b) Marshall Plan, (c) NATO, (d) Warsaw Pact.

3. **Define:** (a) cold war, (b) denazification, (c) containment.

4. How did Stalin justify making the nations of Eastern Europe into Soviet satellites?

5. Was the Marshall Plan successful? Explain.

6. (a) How did President Truman respond to the Soviet blockade of Berlin? (b) Why did Berlin become a focus of the cold war again in 1961?

7. **Critical Thinking** How did the cold war limit the effectiveness of the United Nations?

2 Rebuilding Western Europe

READ TO UNDERSTAND

☐ How Germany, France, and Britain recovered from World War II.

☐ What role individual leaders played in the postwar recovery.

☐ How economic cooperation helped postwar Europe.

☐ *Vocabulary:* welfare state.

After the war, much of Europe, especially Germany, lay in ruins. Over 7.5 million Germans were homeless. All over Western Europe, the most urgent task was economic recovery. With American economic aid under the Marshall Plan and through their own efforts, Western European nations rebuilt their industries, transportation systems, and cities.

The German Economic Miracle

Economic recovery was especially strong in West Germany. Between 1950 and 1958, West Germans doubled their industrial output. The people of West Germany who were facing starvation in 1945 enjoyed one of the highest standards of living by the late 1950s.

There were several reasons for this "economic miracle." The Marshall Plan provided crucial financial aid toward recovery. Under the Marshall Plan, the United States channeled almost $1.4 billion in aid to Germany. Also, since many industrial plants had been destroyed during the war, the Germans rebuilt modern, much more efficient ones.

The leader of the Christian Democrat party, Konrad Adenauer, set the Germans on the road to economic recovery. He served as chancellor from 1949 to 1961. Adenauer brought West Germany into NATO and helped forge alliances with other western nations.

How to reunify Germany was a frequent issue of the 1950s. Adenauer insisted on free elections throughout the divided country before unification. Since the East Germans would not agree to free elections, Germany remained divided.

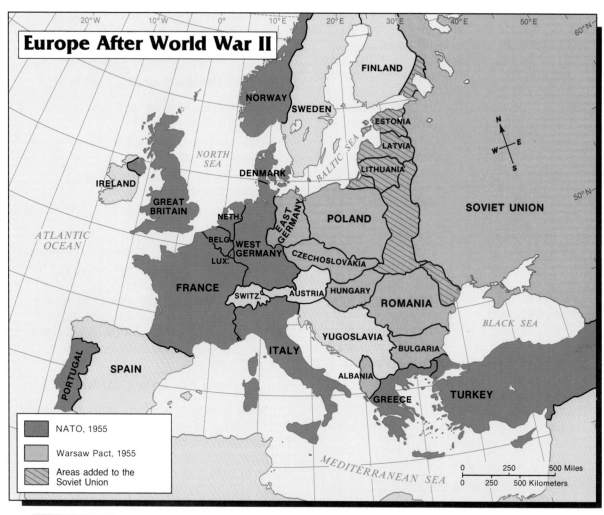

Europe After World War II

NORWAY
SWEDEN
FINLAND
ESTONIA
LATVIA
LITHUANIA
DENMARK
IRELAND
NORTH SEA
BALTIC SEA
SOVIET UNION
GREAT BRITAIN
NETH.
EAST GERMANY
POLAND
ATLANTIC OCEAN
BELG.
WEST GERMANY
LUX.
CZECHOSLOVAKIA
FRANCE
SWITZ.
AUSTRIA
HUNGARY
ROMANIA
BLACK SEA
PORTUGAL
SPAIN
ITALY
YUGOSLAVIA
BULGARIA
ALBANIA
GREECE
TURKEY
MEDITERRANEAN SEA

NATO, 1955

Warsaw Pact, 1955

Areas added to the Soviet Union

0   250   500 Miles
0   250   500 Kilometers

MAP STUDY   *Concern over Soviet domination of Eastern Europe led to the creation of NATO in 1949. The United States, Canada, and ten Western European nations pledged troops and money for mutual defense. In 1955, the Soviet Union created the Warsaw Pact. Which nations belonged to the Warsaw Pact?*

After Adenauer retired, German economic growth leveled off. The slowdown helped the opposition party, the Social Democrats. Under their leader, Willy Brandt, they formed a coalition with the Christian Democrats in 1966. One of Brandt's main goals was to improve relations with East Germany and other Soviet bloc countries.

Postwar France

France worked toward economic recovery during the 1950s and 1960s. Industrial production increased, but political instability slowed the pace of recovery. Under the Fourth French Republic, set up in 1946, the National Assembly was the most powerful body in French government. Its operation depended on coalitions of several political parties. But coalition governments seldom lasted long. In addition, France was burdened with costly colonial wars in Asia and North Africa. As you will read in Chapter 35, the French were forced to withdraw from Indochina in 1954.

Algeria. That same year, civil war erupted in Algeria. Algerian nationalists demanded independence, but French settlers in Algeria opposed it. They wanted France to protect them.

The war in Algeria led to the downfall of the Fourth Republic in May 1958. As civil war threatened, the National Assembly turned to General Charles de Gaulle (duh GAWL) to save France. De Gaulle had led the Free French forces in World War II. The National Assembly gave de Gaulle complete power for six months. It also authorized him to draft a new constitution.

Charles de Gaulle. De Gaulle created the Fifth French Republic. In contrast to the Fourth Republic, it had a strong executive and a weaker National Assembly. Because of the large number of political parties, coalitions were still sometimes necessary, but the breakup of a coalition did not affect the government as much as under the Fourth Republic. In late 1958, French voters overwhelmingly approved the new constitution and elected de Gaulle president.

De Gaulle restored stability in France. In 1962, he formally ended the war in Algeria and recognized Algerian independence. With the end of the colonial wars, the French economy improved.

De Gaulle was determined to restore France to a position of world leadership. He believed that neither the United Nations nor the United States could be relied on to aid Western Europe in time of trouble. Therefore, he insisted on developing French atomic weapons and pursuing an independent course in foreign policy.

In 1966, de Gaulle withdrew French troops from NATO. He also tried to improve relations with the Soviet Union. De Gaulle's independent course caused resentment among his western allies, but it pleased French nationalists.

Postwar Britain

After the war, Britain faced an enormous task of rebuilding and modernizing its factories. It also had to improve its balance of trade. That is, it had to reduce imports and increase exports. To achieve this goal, the British continued wartime rationing. People did without items such as fine British woolens so that they could be sold abroad for foreign currency. The strategy seemed to work. Ten years after the war, the British were more prosperous than they had been in 1938. Farm and industrial output also increased.

A welfare state. After the war, Britons supported the creation of a **welfare state,** one in which the government assumes responsibility for people's social and economic well-being. In the election campaign of 1945, the Labour party promised to increase government services. The voters elected a Labour majority to Parliament, and Clement Attlee became prime minister.

Rebuilding homes and factories that had been reduced to ruins during World War II and modernizing industry were challenging prospects in postwar Europe. This painting by Fernand Léger illustrates the reconstruction that was going on all over Europe.

In 1940, German bombers destroyed most of the city of Coventry, England, including its cathedral, which was built in the 1300s. The city was rebuilt after the war. In 1962, a newly built cathedral was dedicated. However, the ruins of the old cathedral, shown here, were left as a memorial to those who died during World War II.

Once in office, the Labour party carried out its promises. The government nationalized the coal and steel industries. It introduced a national health service and expanded unemployment insurance and old age pensions. When the Conservative party returned to power in 1951, it accepted almost all the Labour party's changes.

In the late 1950s, Britain faced growing competition in international trade. Low productivity, high taxes, and unemployment further hurt the economy. These troubles led to the defeat of the Conservatives in 1964. A Labour government, under Harold Wilson, then tried to revive Britain's sagging economy.

From Empire to Commonwealth. Like France, Britain also saw the breakup of its colonial empire. As you will read in Chapters 33 and 35, most British possessions became independent between 1947 and 1965.

When they gained their independence, most former British colonies chose to join the British Commonwealth of Nations. This association linked countries that had historical and cultural ties with Britain. Commonwealth members were independent, but they met to discuss matters of common interest. They also granted trade advantages to one another.

Changes Elsewhere in Western Europe

In Italy, economic recovery from the war was relatively slow and uneven. The southern part of the country, poor in resources, lagged behind the more prosperous north. With internal reforms and Marshall Plan aid, however, the Italian economy improved.

Throughout the 1950s and 1960s, the Christian Democrats dominated Italian politics. However, they were challenged by a strong Communist party that had the support of part of the Socialist party.

In the postwar period, all the Scandinavian countries introduced some form of moderate socialism and set up welfare states. Most businesses were still privately owned, but the government owned transportation and communication facilities and such vital industries as steel. The people received a wide range of benefits such as free education, medical care, and old-age pensions. These measures helped redistribute income among more people. But they also resulted in very high taxes to pay for the services.

Economic Cooperation

After World War II, European leaders stressed economic cooperation among their countries rather than competition. A first step toward economic cooperation was the Schuman Plan, adopted in 1951. The plan set up the European Coal and Steel Community. France, West Germany, Italy, Belgium, the Netherlands, and Luxembourg pooled their coal and steel resources, eliminating tariffs on these vital materials. Because they had equal access to coal and steel, iron and steel production rose steadily in these nations.

The success of the European Coal and Steel Community led its members in 1957 to create the European Economic Community, usually called the Common Market. Members of the Common Market reduced tariffs and made it easier for people to travel from one member country to another. These measures stimulated the economy of Europe during the 1960s.

Throughout the 1960s, Britain tried unsuccessfully to join the Common Market. France vetoed its applications for membership, partly because of Britain's special economic relationship with members of the British Commonwealth. In 1959, Britain formed a competing trade group, the European Free Trade Association. Its members included Austria, Denmark, Norway, Portugal, Sweden, and Switzerland. Industrial output in these nations increased during the 1960s but at only half the rate of that in the Common Market countries.

SECTION 2 REVIEW

1. **Identify:** (a) Konrad Adenauer, (b) Willy Brandt, (c) Charles de Gaulle, (d) Clement Attlee, (e) European Economic Community.

2. **Define:** welfare state.

3. What was the German economic miracle?

4. How did Charles de Gaulle show France's independence in world affairs?

5. What economic troubles did Britain face in the late 1950s and early 1960s?

6. Describe one action taken by the Common Market to stimulate trade.

7. **Critical Thinking** Why do you think the Fifth Republic in France was more successful than the Fourth Republic?

3 The Soviet Union and Eastern Europe

READ TO UNDERSTAND

☐ **How Khrushchev's policies differed from Stalin's.**

☐ **What the thaw in the cold war meant.**

☐ **How Tito pursued an independent course in Yugoslavia.**

☐ **How the revolts in Poland and Hungary differed.**

Nearly 20 million Russians lost their lives during World War II. After the war, the Soviet Union faced a massive task of reconstruction. Hundreds of thousands of acres of farmland had been laid bare by the Nazi invasion. Entire cities had been destroyed.

Stalin's Last Years

When the war ended, Stalin announced a new five-year plan to rebuild Soviet industry to its prewar level. The plan emphasized heavy industry, construction, and weapons. By 1953, the output of Soviet industry exceeded its prewar level. But farm production lagged far behind, and consumer goods remained in short supply.

Stalin launched a new round of political purges that filled forced-labor camps. Artists, writers, and musicians who did not follow the official party line were viciously attacked. Stalin also kindled anti-Semitism by accusing Jewish doctors of trying to poison him.

When Stalin died in 1953, a power struggle took place among party leaders. The new Communist party boss was Nikita Khrushchev (KROOSH chehf).

The Khrushchev Era

Khrushchev shocked the world in 1956 by denouncing Stalin in a speech to a Communist party congress. He accused Stalin of having been a murderer and a tyrant who committed terrible crimes against the Soviet people. Khrushchev went on to criticize the "cult of personality" that had glorified Stalin.

723

De-Stalinization. The Soviet Union entered a period of reform after Khrushchev's speech. The reforms became known as de-Stalinization. Conditions in some labor camps were eased. Other camps were closed. Writers and artists gained some freedom, and cultural exchange programs with the West were encouraged. The city of Stalingrad was renamed Volgograd. Despite the changes, the Soviet Union remained a totalitarian state. In 1958, for example, it prevented the Russian writer Boris Pasternak from accepting the Nobel prize for his novel *Dr. Zhivago.*

In his economic planning, Khrushchev emphasized farm production. He tried experimenting with less central control of the economy. The government cautiously introduced some incentives to increase production. For example, it gave managers more control over how to meet the production goals of their farms and factories.

As a result of such efforts, the Soviet standard of living improved, but it remained far below that in the United States or Western Europe. One Soviet achievement of this period was the successful launching in 1957 of *Sputnik*, the first artificial satellite to orbit the earth.

A thaw in the cold war. De-Stalinization also led to a thaw in the cold war. Instead of speaking of an inevitable clash between communism and capitalism, Khrushchev talked of the need for "peaceful coexistence" between the superpowers. The new spirit of cooperation favored talks to slow the arms race and ban the testing of nuclear weapons.

Several incidents marred the thaw in the cold war. In May 1960, an American spy plane was shot down over Soviet territory. Khrushchev angrily canceled a summit conference with President Dwight Eisenhower planned for later that month. In the summer of 1961, the Berlin Wall crisis erupted. (See page 717.)

A very serious clash between the Soviet Union and the United States occurred in 1962, when Khrushchev tried to build missile bases in Cuba. You will read more about this incident later in this chapter.

Khrushchev's rule ended in 1964, when party associates forced him to resign from office. His successor, Leonid Brezhnev (BREHZH nehf), backed away from some of Khrushchev's policies, as you will read in Chapter 37.

Yugoslavia's Independent Course

Yugoslavia, led by Marshal Tito, was one Eastern European country that was not a Soviet satellite. Tito, a communist, had organized Yugoslav resistance against the Nazis during World War II. After the Germans were forced

During a visit to the United States in 1959, Soviet Premier Nikita Khrushchev toured a farm in Coon Rapids, Iowa. He told his host, Roswald Garst, that Iowa corn was superior to Soviet corn. Khrushchev was not always as pleased with his visit to the United States as he appears here. He was not allowed to visit Disneyland because police could not guarantee his safety. A disappointed Khrushchev noted: "Just imagine, I, a Premier, a Soviet representative, told that I could not go. Why not? Do you have rocket launching pads there? Or have gangsters taken hold of the place?"

out of Yugoslavia, he assumed power as dictator. He nationalized industry and made plans for economic growth.

Although Tito was a communist, he was also a strong nationalist. He was unwilling to take orders from Stalin and instead followed an independent course. In the communist state that he set up, he granted some measure of economic and individual freedom, but he was quick to crack down on any threats to his dictatorship.

Tito proclaimed Yugoslavia neutral in any East-West conflicts. Yugoslavia did not join the Warsaw Pact or NATO. After Stalin's death, Khrushchev tried to lure Tito into the Soviet bloc. But the Yugoslav leader continued to go his own way.

Unrest in Poland and Hungary

Khrushchev's denunciation of Stalin encouraged Poland and Hungary to try to shake free from Soviet domination. In 1956, Polish workers rioted for higher pay and better working conditions.

The Polish communist leader Wladyslaw Gomulka (VLAH dee slah guh MOOL kuh) took control of the government. Gomulka was an anti-Stalinist who had been imprisoned during Stalin's postwar crackdown. He dissolved the secret police and allowed workers' councils to speak for labor. The Soviets protested Gomulka's actions and threatened to send troops. In the end, however, Khrushchev accepted the new Polish regime. Poland remained a member of the Warsaw Pact, and Gomulka continued to support Soviet foreign policy.

Encouraged by the Polish example, Hungarian students and workers demonstrated in the fall of 1956. Imre Nagy (NAH djuh), like Tito and Gomulka a nationalist communist leader, became premier. Nagy ended one-party rule and called for free elections. He also pledged to withdraw Hungary from the Warsaw Pact, and he appealed to western nations for support.

Nagy's plans for western-style democracy and his withdrawal from the Soviet alliance

In 1956, strong nationalist feelings in Hungary led to demonstrations against Soviet domination. The anti-Soviet movement was spearheaded by students and intellectuals, but it had wide popular support. Here, demonstrators burn pictures of Stalin. The Soviets blamed the Hungarian uprising on foreign intervention. Soviet troops eventually moved in and crushed the uprising.

brought an immediate Soviet response. Khrushchev sent troops into Hungary. Nagy was removed from power and eventually executed. After bitter fighting, Soviet troops crushed the uprising. Western nations took no action, although they welcomed thousands of Hungarians who fled to the West. The Soviet invasion of Hungary showed that the Soviet Union would allow no challenge to its domination of Eastern Europe.

1. **Identify:** (a) Nikita Khrushchev, (b) Marshal Tito, (c) Wladyslaw Gomulka, (d) Imre Nagy.

2. Describe one way in which Stalin imposed totalitarian control of Soviet society.

3. What was one result of the thaw in the cold war after Stalin's death?

4. How did Tito show that he would not be dominated by the Soviet Union?

5. How did Khrushchev react to: (a) Gomulka's policies in Poland; (b) Nagy's policies in Hungary?

6. **Critical Thinking** Why might Khrushchev have decided to criticize Stalin's "cult of personality"?

4 Developments in the United States

READ TO UNDERSTAND

☐ **What postwar domestic problems the United States faced.**

☐ **How the economy changed after the war.**

☐ **How the cold war affected American foreign policy.**

☐ *Vocabulary:* **segregation.**

"I feel as though the moon and all the stars and all the planets have fallen on me." This is what Harry S. Truman told reporters in April 1945 after he had been sworn in as President following the unexpected death of Franklin D. Roosevelt. Within four months, the war was over, but Truman had to lead the nation into peace.

The United States emerged from World War II as the strongest power in a divided world. As a result, most Americans realized that the United States must accept leadership of what was called the "free world."

A Crisis Over Security

The cold war abroad contributed to the fear of communists at home. In the early 1950s, Senator Joseph McCarthy of Wisconsin claimed that many government employees were communists. Although his claim was never proven, it won McCarthy nationwide attention.

For four years, McCarthy's continual charges created an atmosphere of fear and suspicion. The federal government and local governments investigated thousands of employees, looking for "security risks." Businesses, universities, and the entertainment industry carried out similar campaigns. Few communists were found, but many people lost their jobs and their reputations simply because they had been investigated.

In 1954, the Senate televised hearings on McCarthy's charges that there were communists in the army. During the hearings, many Americans saw McCarthy as a bully. Soon after, the Senate censured him for "conduct unbecoming a member." McCarthy lost his popular appeal, and the crisis over security began to fade.

Growing Prosperity

Economic uncertainty plagued the United States after the war. Americans began to demand consumer goods that were in short supply, causing prices to rise rapidly. Labor unions demanded wage increases denied during the war. The result was strikes in many crucial industries. There were more than 5,000 strikes in 1946. The strikes led Congress to pass the Taft-Hartley Act of 1947. The new law allowed the government to delay strikes that threatened health or safety. It also outlawed closed shops, or businesses in which all workers are required to be union members.

Despite economic problems, Truman won the presidential election of 1948. He then proposed a program called the Fair Deal to carry on the traditions of the New Deal. He succeeded with some measures, including one to finance low-income housing and another to extend social security coverage.

In 1952, Americans elected Dwight D. Eisenhower—the general who had led the Allied invasion at Normandy—as President. Eisenhower was reelected in 1956. During Eisenhower's two terms in office, the economy expanded enormously. The nation's output of goods and services increased by 25 percent. The income of the average family went up 15 percent. Most families drove at least one car and owned their own homes.

Demands for Social Change

Many Americans did not share in the prosperity of the 1950s, however. At least 10 percent of Americans lived in poverty. Furthermore, some Americans had little opportunity to improve their lives. Black Americans faced **segregation,** the practice of separating people according to race. In the South, blacks were required by law to attend separate schools and to sit in separate parts of buses and restaurants. In the North, segregation existed by custom though not by law. Black Americans often had to accept inferior housing, jobs, and education.

During the 1950s and 1960s, there was a growing demand for greater civil rights for blacks. In 1954, the Supreme Court ruled in the *Brown* v. *Board of Education of Topeka* case that segregated schools were unconstitutional. It ordered schools to integrate "with all deliberate speed." Many southerners resisted the decision, however.

Black Americans, led by Martin Luther King, Jr., and others, protested segregation through boycotts, "sit-ins," and marches. In 1963, more than 200,000 people took part in a

In 1954, the United States Supreme Court ordered school integration. Three years later, black students tried to enroll in the formerly all-white public schools of Little Rock, Arkansas. The governor of Arkansas called out the National Guard to stop them. President Eisenhower sent federal troops to protect black students traveling to and from school.

Television has made history come alive for millions of Americans. Before their own eyes, they see political candidates face tough questions from reporters and watch weary victims survey damage from fires and floods. Sports events, dramas, and documentaries compete with game shows and family comedies to win new audiences.

Television broadcasting began in the United States in the 1930s, but it did not take off until after World War II. In the 1950s, Americans bought over 40 million television sets. Television boomed in other countries too. By 1980, there were over 400 million sets worldwide.

Television changed the living habits of viewers. People stayed home to watch their favorite programs. When television stations extended their schedules into the night, people stayed up later. Television stars became celebrities. Their fashions and opinions were adopted by many.

The early years of television provided a wide range of entertainment. Milton Berle's popular slapstick comedy earned him the title "Mr. Television" in the 1950s. Ed Sullivan, a former newspaper columnist, hosted a long-running variety show. He introduced Americans to both Elvis Presley and the Beatles, who are shown here. Westerns such as "Gunsmoke" and situation comedies such as "I Love Lucy" attracted loyal audiences.

During the 1950s and 1960s, a growing number of people learned about current events from television rather than from radio or newspapers. Television stations covered the Senate hearings on Senator McCarthy's charges against the army and helped end McCarthy's influence, as you read. In 1963, people clustered around their television sets and watched with horror the events surrounding the assassination of President Kennedy.

With the launching of communications satellites in the 1960s, events such as the Olympics could be broadcast live all over the world. Increasingly people saw programs from other countries. Thus, television helped span the gulf between cultures.

1. How did early television affect people's living habits?

2. **Critical Thinking** Describe the part television plays in your life.

historic "March on Washington," aimed at winning a civil rights law.

President John F. Kennedy, who was elected in 1960, sent Congress a civil rights bill to ban voting and job discrimination. However, before action could be taken on the bill, tragedy struck. On November 22, 1963, President Kennedy was assassinated in Dallas, Texas. Kennedy's vice president, Lyndon B. Johnson, then became President. Johnson won passage of the civil rights bill in 1964.

Under President Johnson, Congress also passed a large number of social welfare bills. These included medical care for the poor and elderly as well as money for education and low-cost housing.

Other groups besides black Americans demanded equality during the 1960s. Hispanics and Native Americans worked to end discrimination. Many women also campaigned for equal rights and equal pay.

Relations with the World

The cold war dominated American foreign policy during the 1950s and 1960s. Preventing the spread of Soviet influence was a main goal of American Presidents. In Korea and Vietnam, this goal led to armed conflict.

The Korean War. Korea tested the American policy of containment. (See page 716.) After World War II, Korea was divided into two zones. The Soviet Union controlled the northern zone. The United States supervised the southern zone. In 1950, Soviet-backed North Korean troops invaded the south. With the approval of the United Nations, the United States came to the aid of the South Koreans. After three years of bitter fighting, a cease-fire was signed in July 1953. The invasion of South Korea had been repelled, and the boundary between North and South Korea was restored. (You will read more about the Korean War in Chapter 35.)

The cold war continues. In 1962, a crisis over Cuba threatened to explode into war between the United States and the Soviet Union. Fidel Castro had led a successful communist revolution in Cuba in the late 1950s. (See page 805.) In October 1962, President Kennedy revealed that the Soviet Union was constructing missile launch pads in Cuba.

The United States demanded that the missile bases be dismantled. It then imposed a naval blockade on Cuba to prevent Soviet ships from bringing missiles to Cuba. As the world watched nervously, Soviet ships approached Cuba. But the ships turned back just as they approached the blockade. Khrushchev ordered the missile bases dismantled, and the Cuban missile crisis ended.

At about the same time, the United States was becoming involved in a war in Southeast Asia. President Kennedy sent military advisers and equipment to help the government of South Vietnam fight communist guerrillas. Under President Johnson, American involvement in Vietnam developed into a full-fledged war, as you will read.

United States territories and neighbors. The status of several United States territories changed after World War II. The Philippines won full independence in 1946. In 1952, Puerto Rico gained commonwealth status. Puerto Ricans wrote their own constitution and elected a governor and legislature but continued to be United States citizens. The question of statehood for Puerto Rico has continued to be a controversial one. Two other territories, Alaska and Hawaii, became states in 1959.

Throughout the 1950s and 1960s, the United States maintained friendly relations with Canada. However, many people in Latin America continued to view the United States as a threatening giant, as you will read in Chapter 36.

SECTION 4 REVIEW

1. **Identify:** (a) Joseph McCarthy, (b) *Brown* v. *The Board of Education of Topeka,* (c) Martin Luther King, Jr.

2. **Define:** segregation.

3. What was one result of the fear of communism at home during the early 1950s?

4. What was the major purpose of the Taft-Hartley Act?

5. (a) List two groups that wanted social change in the 1950s and 1960s. (b) What did each group want?

6. Describe one way in which the United States tried to stop Soviet expansion in the 1950s and 1960s.

7. **Critical Thinking** At the height of the Cuban missile crisis, the American secretary of state commented: "We're eyeball to eyeball, and I think the other fellow just blinked." What did he mean?

Summary

1. A cold war between the Soviet Union and the United States developed after World War II. The Soviet Union kept control of Eastern Europe by setting up communist governments there. The United States acted to prevent further Soviet expansion in Europe and elsewhere.

2. With the help of the Marshall Plan, Western European nations recovered rapidly from the war. Germany's recovery was especially strong. France faced political instability, but under Charles de Gaulle conditions improved. Britain established a welfare state.

3. In the Soviet Union, Stalin rebuilt the economy and restored totalitarian rule. Khrushchev introduced a period of relaxed controls following Stalin's death. Khrushchev's policy of de-Stalinization eased cold war tensions for a time.

4. The United States enjoyed economic prosperity during much of the 1950s and 1960s. In the same period, the civil rights movement grew as black Americans and others demanded justice and equality. The United States fought the Korean War and continued to be involved in the cold war.

Recalling Facts

Decide if the following statements are true or false. If a statement is false, rewrite it to make it true.

1. The Truman Doctrine was issued in response to a civil war in Greece.

2. Members of the Warsaw Pact opposed Soviet aggression in Western Europe.

3. Former British colonies joined the Commonwealth after World War II.

4. Under Marshal Tito, Yugoslavia was a member of the Soviet bloc.

5. The United States aided South Korea when it was invaded by North Korea in 1950.

Chapter Checkup

1. (a) Why did Churchill and Roosevelt want to cooperate with Stalin at Yalta? (b) What agreements were reached at the Yalta Conference? (c) What conflict between the United States and the Soviet Union surfaced at Potsdam?

2. How did the policies of the Allies lead to the division of Germany into East and West Germany?

3. (a) Why did the Soviet Union have control of Eastern Europe after World War II? (b) How did the Truman Doctrine and the Marshall Plan help slow Soviet expansion into other parts of Europe?

4. (a) Why was West Germany able to recover so rapidly from the war? (b) Why was recovery slower in France?

5. (a) What steps did Stalin take to reestablish totalitarian rule after World War II? (b) Describe Khrushchev's attempts to de-Stalinize the Soviet Union.

6. Describe how each of the following affected relations between the Soviet Union and the United States: (a) the Soviet blockade of Berlin in 1948; (b) de-Stalinization; (c) Soviet construction of missile launch pads in Cuba.

7. (a) What economic problems did the United States face after World War II? (b) How was the economic situation different in the late 1950s?

Critical Thinking

1. **Relating Past to Present** Do you think the cold war continues today? Why or why not? Give specific examples to support your answer.

2. **Evaluating** Britain and the Scandinavian countries established welfare states after World War II. (a) Why do you think these countries took this step after the war? (b) Compare the advantages and disadvantages of a welfare state system.

3. **Analyzing** (a) How did Khrushchev's policy of de-Stalinization affect developments in Poland and Hungary? (b) Why do you think Khrushchev accepted Gomulka's regime in Poland but crushed Nagy's government in Hungary?

4. **Understanding the Roots of Democracy** (a) What demands for social change were being made in the United States in the 1950s and 1960s? (b) In what ways were these also demands for greater democracy?

Developing Basic Skills

1. **Map Reading** Compare the maps on pages 642 and 720. (a) What areas did the Soviet Union gain after World War II? (b) How was Germany after World War II different from Germany after World War I? (c) Which war do you think had the greater impact on political borders in Europe?

2. **Using Visual Evidence** Study the poster on page 717. (a) Whom do the figures in the background probably represent? (b) What does the large figure probably represent? (c) How might the poster help explain the creation of NATO?

Writing About History

Proofreading Your Paper

After you have revised your first draft, proofread it for errors. Listed below are the standard proofreading symbols.

Symbol	Meaning of Symbol
b̲	Capitalize a letter.
A̸	Lower-case a letter.
opᴇ̂n	Insert or change a letter or punctuation mark.
ꝛe	Delete a word, letter, or punctuation mark.
w⌢as	Close up space.
andⁱⁿ#	Add a space.
oꝼⱡ	Transpose letters.
¶This	Begin a new paragraph.
⊙	Add a period.
⋀	Add a comma.
Truman˅s	Add an apostrophe.
Step̶n̶e̶v̶e̶r̶	Keep what is crossed out.

Practice: Copy this paragraph and indicate what needs to be changed.

When World war II finaly ended the Allied leders were anxious to aviod the mstakes of the Versailles treaty of World War I They did not nto want the peaace settlements to plant teh seeds of a fu ture war.

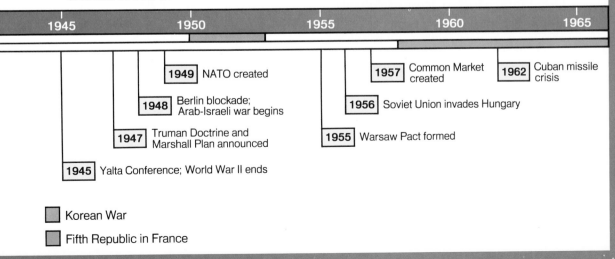

| 1945 | 1950 | 1955 | 1960 | 1965 |

1949 NATO created

1948 Berlin blockade; Arab-Israeli war begins

1947 Truman Doctrine and Marshall Plan announced

1945 Yalta Conference; World War II ends

1957 Common Market created

1956 Soviet Union invades Hungary

1955 Warsaw Pact formed

1962 Cuban missile crisis

☐ Korean War

☐ Fifth Republic in France

Unit Nine   Mini-Atlas

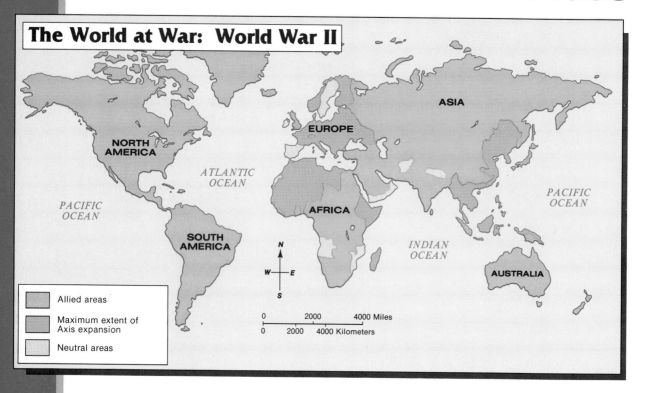

The World at War: World War II

ASIA

EUROPE

NORTH
AMERICA

ATLANTIC
OCEAN

PACIFIC
OCEAN

AFRICA

PACIFIC
OCEAN

SOUTH
AMERICA

N

INDIAN
OCEAN

W — E

S

AUSTRALIA

- Allied areas
- Maximum extent of Axis expansion
- Neutral areas

0   2000   4000 Miles
0   2000   4000 Kilometers

Unit Themes

World War I pitted strong European powers against one another in a worldwide conflict. The fighting took an appalling toll of human lives and had a lasting effect on international affairs. It unleashed forces that produced still more wars and upheavals.

In the 1920s and 1930s, most western nations experienced economic and political crises. Uprisings rocked the nonwestern world as nationalists demanded political freedom from foreign rulers. Ambitious dictators, like Adolf Hitler in Germany, gained power in several countries. Their goal of empire soon launched the world into another global conflict.

The effects of World War II were even more devastating than those of World War I. The two world wars weakened western domination of the world. However, western civilization survived the destructive effects of these wars and continued to influence world developments.

1. **Expressing an Opinion** (a) Compare the causes of World War I and World War II. (b) Which nations, in your opinion, were most responsible for each war? Explain.

2. **Analyzing** (a) Based on the time line, how did the governments of Italy and Germany change between the two world wars? (b) How did Mussolini and Hitler use nationalism to gain their ends?

3. **Synthesizing** (a) According to the world map above, in which areas were Axis nations strongest? (b) Choose one of the main Allied or Axis nations and summarize its history from 1914 to 1945.

4. **Evaluating** (a) Why did the United States refuse to join the League of Nations? (b) Why did it join the United Nations? (c) What are the benefits and the limitations of international peace organizations?

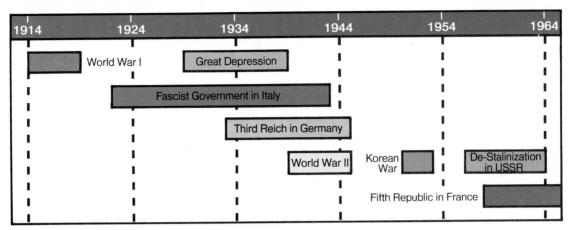

Which economic event occurred between World War I and World War II? When did the Korean War begin? In which decade did de-Stalinization begin? How did France's government change after World War II?

The Allied invasion of northern France in 1944 was code-named Operation Overlord. The code names of the five invading forces were Utah, Omaha, Gold, Juno, and Sword. Which Allied nations participated in the invasion? Which body of water did they have to cross?

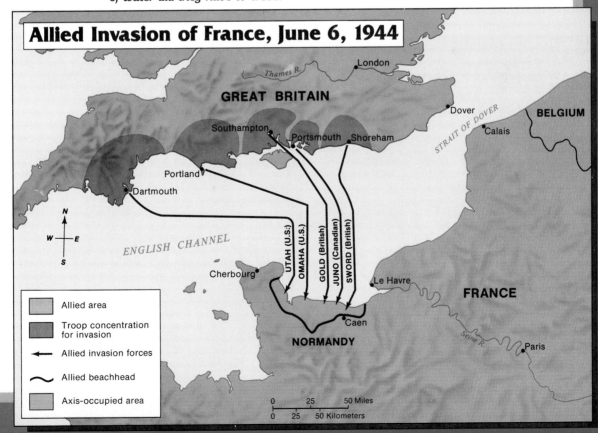

Allied Invasion of France, June 6, 1944

Legend:
- Allied area
- Troop concentration for invasion
- Allied invasion forces
- Allied beachhead
- Axis-occupied area

THE WORLD TODAY

1949 *This Chinese Communist painting glorifies victory over the Nationalists.*

1979 *Margaret Thatcher was the first woman to become prime minister of Britain.*

	1945	1955	1965
POLITICS AND GOVERNMENT	**1947** India divided into India and Pakistan	**1957** Ghana wins independence	**1967** Six-Day War breaks out
ECONOMICS AND TECHNOLOGY	**1947** Invention of transistor opens way for computers	**1958** Great Leap Forward calls on Chinese to increase production	
SOCIETY AND CULTURE	**1948** *Cry, the Beloved Country* describes life under apartheid		**1966** Cultural Revolution disrupts life in China

After independence, African nations maintained their traditions, as seen in this tapestry from Nigeria.

This paper mill, built in Japan, is being towed up the Amazon river in Brazil.

UNIT OUTLINE

Women in Peru create cloth sculptures such as this one to raise money for the families of political prisoners.

Archbishop Desmond Tutu used peaceful means to fight apartheid in South Africa.

1975	1985	PRESENT

1971 General Idi Amin becomes dictator of Uganda

1988 Soviets agree to withdraw from Afghanistan

1970 Aswan Dam in Egypt is completed

1986 Nuclear accident occurs at Chernobyl plant in Soviet Union

1975 Civil War breaks out in Lebanon

1989 China crushes student protesters

Lech Walesa led the trade union Solidarity as it protested economic and political conditions in Poland.

In Japan, as in many nations, traditional culture and high technology coexist.

Africa

(1945–Present)

33

Independence for Ghana was an important "first" because it showed that black Africans were prepared to move out of the shadow of colonial rule and claim their place as citizens of free nations. Here, members of Ghana's police force parade during Independence Day celebrations.

D arkness clings to the midnight sky. Usually at this hour, the city streets are silent. But tonight, they are alive with light and sound. Tens of thousands of people throng the streets of Accra, capital of the Gold Coast, a British colony in West Africa. No one wanted to miss this moment. Tonight, March 6, 1957, at the stroke of midnight, their homeland will become independent.

Their country's new name, taken from an ancient African kingdom, will be Ghana. A solemn ceremony marks the moment of freedom. The flag of Great

Britain—the Union Jack—is lowered from the flagpole. In its place, the red, green, and gold flag of an independent Ghana is raised to the cheers of the people.

"There is a new African in the world," announces Ghana's prime minister, Kwame Nkrumah (KWAH mee en KROO muh). "That new African is ready to fight his own battle. It is the only way in which we can show the world we are masters of our own destiny."

A determined and able leader, Nkrumah had worked for years to liberate his country. He organized strikes and boycotts against British rule and was jailed for these activities. Finally, in the early 1950s, the Gold Coast achieved limited self-government. While still in prison, Nkrumah was elected prime minister of the Gold Coast. However, limited self-government fell short of Nkrumah's goal. As prime minister, he continued to lead the movement for independence, a goal he achieved that day in March 1957.

Ghana was the first black African nation to win independence. But even as the people of Ghana celebrated with parades and dancing, Nkrumah declared: "Our independence is meaningless unless it is linked up with the total liberation of the African continent."

Over the next three decades, more than 50 other African countries won their independence. Even as these new nations proudly raised their own flags, however, they faced many political and economic problems. African leaders wanted to establish stable, unified nations with prosperous economies. In the years since independence, the nations of Africa have experimented with various ways to meet these goals. ■

1 Winning Independence

READ TO UNDERSTAND

☐ **What goals African nationalists worked for.**

☐ **How European nations responded to independence movements in Africa.**

☐ **How the struggle for independence in African nations varied.**

"We are determined to be free. We want education. We want the right to earn a decent living, the right to express our thoughts and emotions. We demand for Black Africa freedom and independence." To the delegates at the Pan-African Congress in 1945, there could be no greater goal than freedom and independence. As African nations broke free from colonial rule, they transformed the map of Africa.

Movements for Independence

The peoples of Africa had long resisted colonial rule. During the Age of Imperialism, independence movements emerged in Egypt, Nigeria, and the Gold Coast. After World War I, demands for self-government increased.

African nationalism. Independence movements grew out of African nationalism. This nationalism was mostly directed against colonial rule. However, it also included a determination to build societies with strong economies based on modern technology and a high level of education.

African leaders, some of whom had been educated in Europe and the United States, admired the democratic institutions of the West. But they deeply resented western colonial rule, which denied Africans the right to self-government and treated them as second-class citizens.

They organized political parties to work for independence. In the Gold Coast, for example, Kwame Nkrumah rallied popular support behind the Convention People's party. Nkrumah and others used the press to spread their ideas. Most of their followers lived in the cities. There, people heard about the independence movement through newspapers and radio broadcasts. Many joined demonstrations and participated in boycotts against colonial rule.

International support. As World War II ended, movements to end colonial rule multiplied around the world. International conditions favored independence movements. Many Europeans questioned the benefits of overseas empires. Administering colonies was expensive, and the economies of European nations had been drained by the war. Also, most Europeans did not want to fight long, costly wars to hold on to overseas colonies.

The two superpowers, the United States and the Soviet Union, called for an end to European imperialism in Africa and elsewhere. Both supported anticolonial movements but for different reasons. The United States hoped independent African nations would become capitalist democracies, while the Soviet Union encouraged socialism in Africa. Both nations wanted access to the vast natural resources of Africa and to its potential markets for consumer goods.

European Responses

At first, European nations were reluctant to give up their African colonies. Under pressure, Britain and France made a few concessions to African demands. Britain, for example, was forced to give the people of the Gold Coast a constitution, allowing them the right to elect a legislature. France introduced reforms that permitted its colonies to elect more representatives to the French National Assembly.

But Africans wanted independence, not limited self-government. When they stepped up the pressure for independence, Britain and France realized that they must give up their colonies. However, other colonial powers, including Belgium and Portugal, were determined to hold on to their African territories by force, if necessary.

As the tide of African nationalism rose, Africans in some areas used violence to win

freedom. Yet most nations achieved independence through peaceful means.

New Nations of Africa

In 1950, there were only four independent countries in Africa: Liberia, Ethiopia,* Egypt, and South Africa. Although South Africa was independent, the white minority controlled the government. During the 1950s and 1960s, a wave of independence swept across the continent. By 1968, 38 new nations had emerged in Africa.

North Africa. Between 1951 and 1956, the North African nations of Libya, Tunisia, and Morocco won their independence peacefully. Algeria, however, became independent only after a bitter eight-year struggle. France considered Algeria part of the French nation and had encouraged large numbers of French to settle there. These settlers fought against independence even after the French government finally agreed to it. In 1962, Algeria became an independent republic.

The peoples of North Africa are largely Muslim and Arabic-speaking. Thus, North African nations have close cultural ties with the Arab nations of the Middle East and often support Arab causes. For example, Libya's Colonel Muammar Qaddafi (guht DAH fee), who became the leader of Libya in 1969, has strongly supported Arab nationalism and opposed Israel's territorial claims in the Middle East.

West and Central Africa. In the late 1950s and 1960s, African nations south of the Sahara Desert won their independence. As you have read, in March 1957 Ghana became the first colony in West Africa to achieve independence. The next year, Guinea declared its independence from France. In the early 1960s, many new nations emerged in West Africa, especially in the region once known as French West Africa.

The British and French had taken some steps that prepared their colonies for independence. They had provided education for Africans and allowed African leaders to gain administrative experience. But the Belgians had done nothing similar in the Congo. Thus, when

---

* Emperor Haile Selassie returned as ruler of Ethiopia after the Italians were defeated in World War II.

the Belgian Congo won independence in 1960, the nation was soon plunged into civil war. Revolts broke out in various parts of the country as rival leaders fought for power. Eventually, the United Nations sent troops to the Congo to help restore order. In 1971, the military leader who had gained control of the Congo renamed the country Zaire. In giving the country an African name, he symbolically rejected its colonial past.

Eastern and southern Africa. Eastern Africa and southern Africa had attracted many white settlers. Like the French in Algeria, British settlers in Kenya, Uganda, Tanganyika, and Rhodesia looked on these countries as their homes. They feared independence because it would give black Africans control of the governments.

Black leaders such as Jomo Kenyatta in Kenya organized opposition to colonial rule. Tanganyika, later renamed Tanzania (TAN zuh NEE uh), won its independence in 1961. In the next three years, other East African nations achieved independence, including Uganda in 1962 and Kenya in 1963.

White settlers in Rhodesia, present-day Zimbabwe (zihm BAH bweh), declared their independence from Britain in 1965 in order to

THEN AND NOW The Ancient Art of Storytelling

The children giggle in small groups while their parents gossip. A log fire sends shadows dancing over the walls of the compound. An elderly man in traditional robes calls for attention. He introduces the storyteller, or griot, who is famed for his lively tales.

"There were once lords and ministers of state," the griot begins. Then he launches into a stirring account of proud rulers and soldiers who died in battle. The storytellers of today, like the griots of the past, are figures of respect in communities throughout West Africa.

But the ancient art of storytelling is facing an uncertain future. Young people in the towns and cities are losing their respect for the old ways. They prefer the world of technology, of radio, television, and movies, to the traditional community gatherings. Yet many educated people in West Africa regret the loss of this ancient art.

The stories have been handed down from generation to generation, shaping people's beliefs and teaching them their people's history. The stories promote values such as honesty, respect, and hospitality. In Ghana, a familiar figure in many stories is Kwaku Anansi. He lives with his large family in a village. In one tale, he gets involved in a scheme to get rich. When he is discovered, he is so embarrassed that he turns into a spider so that he can hide. The story is a fable, teaching a moral about greed and selfishness.

In the glow of firelight, the griot's voice echoes with all the tension and drama of a theatrical performance, and those who have come to listen are spellbound. Sometimes the stories require the listeners to participate. Singers, dancers, and drummers enliven the performances. When the griot and his art have passed, an important part of African life will have disappeared, too.

1. Why is African storytelling disappearing?

2. **Critical Thinking** Do you think storytelling is an effective way of passing on values from generation to generation? Why or why not?

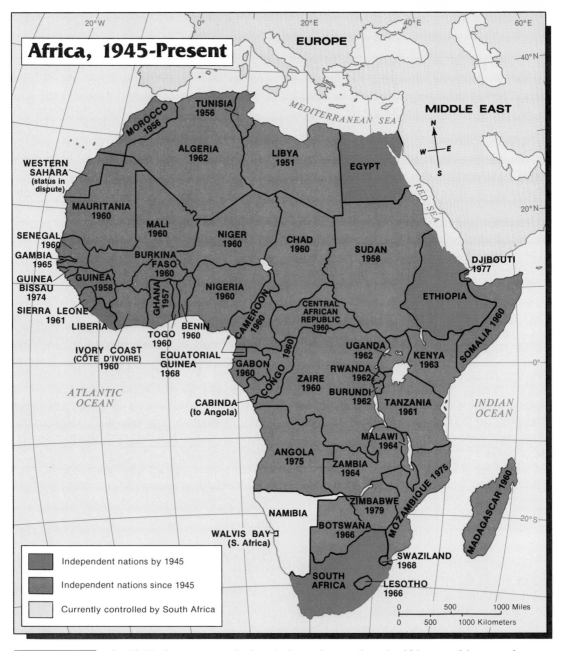

Africa, 1945-Present

EUROPE

MIDDLE EAST

MEDITERRANEAN SEA

MOROCCO 1956

TUNISIA 1956

ALGERIA 1962

LIBYA 1951

EGYPT

WESTERN SAHARA (status in dispute)

MAURITANIA 1960

MALI 1960

NIGER 1960

CHAD 1960

SUDAN 1956

DJIBOUTI 1977

SENEGAL 1960

GAMBIA 1965

GUINEA BISSAU 1974

BURKINA FASO 1960

GUINEA 1958

GHANA 1957

NIGERIA 1960

CENTRAL AFRICAN REPUBLIC 1960

ETHIOPIA

SIERRA LEONE 1961

LIBERIA

TOGO 1960

BENIN 1960

CAMEROON 1960

UGANDA 1962

KENYA 1963

SOMALIA 1960

IVORY COAST (CÔTE D'IVOIRE) 1960

EQUATORIAL GUINEA 1968

GABON 1960

CONGO 1960

ZAIRE 1960

RWANDA 1962

BURUNDI 1962

TANZANIA 1961

ATLANTIC OCEAN

CABINDA (to Angola)

INDIAN OCEAN

MALAWI 1964

ANGOLA 1975

ZAMBIA 1964

MOZAMBIQUE 1975

MADAGASCAR 1960

NAMIBIA

WALVIS BAY (S. Africa)

ZIMBABWE 1979

BOTSWANA 1966

SWAZILAND 1968

SOUTH AFRICA

LESOTHO 1966

RED SEA

Independent nations by 1945

Independent nations since 1945

Currently controlled by South Africa

0   500   1000 Miles

0   500   1000 Kilometers

MAP STUDY *In 1945, there were only four independent nations in Africa, as this map shows. Since then, many new nations have emerged. What nation was the first to gain independence after World War II? What nation gained independence most recently?*

prevent black Africans from gaining a role in government. Britain refused to recognize the new white-ruled nation, and many members of the United Nations boycotted Rhodesia. In a long guerrilla war, blacks struggled to oust the white minority government. Independence finally came in 1980 after a compromise was negotiated. The agreement called for black

majority rule in Zimbabwe and protection of the rights of the white minority.

In southern Africa, Portugal fought to hold on to its colonies, Angola and Mozambique. Nationalist groups fought long and costly guerrilla wars against Portugal. In 1975, Portugal agreed to recognize Angola and Mozambique as independent nations.

1. **Locate:** (a) Algeria, (b) Libya, (c) Ghana, (d) Guinea, (e) Zaire, (f) Tanzania, (g) Zimbabwe, (h) Angola, (i) Mozambique.

2. List three goals of African nationalists.

3. How did World War II affect European attitudes toward overseas colonies?

4. (a) What African nations were independent in 1950? (b) How did this situation change in the late 1950s and 1960s?

5. Why do the peoples of North Africa often support Arab causes in the Middle East?

6. **Critical Thinking** Why was the struggle for independence in Algeria and Rhodesia especially bitter?

2 Challenges Facing African Nations

READ TO UNDERSTAND

☐ **What problems African nations faced after independence.**

☐ **How African leaders tried to solve these problems.**

☐ **What goals African nations set for themselves.**

☐ *Vocabulary:* **modernization, multinational corporation, urbanization, coup d'état.**

"Political independence only serves as a key to the door of economic and social progress. We must open the door for all the people. The big question now is—how do we do this?" In these words, President Kenneth Kuanda of Zambia summed up the challenges facing the newly independent nations of Africa. Some problems were unique to Africa. Others were the same as those faced by developing nations everywhere.

The Colonial Heritage

Some of the problems facing African nations could be traced to their colonial experiences. As you have read, some European nations had done little to prepare their colonies for independence. Even in former British and French areas, where Africans had been allowed to hold some government jobs, the new nations lacked enough experienced leaders during the early years.

During the scramble for Africa, European nations grabbed territories and organized them into colonies. They drew boundaries without regard to geography, religion, language, or the ethnic groups living within an area. Thus, many new African nations had no traditions of unity. Rivalries among peoples with different religions, languages, and cultural traditions have made unity hard to achieve.

The colonial heritage left some positive results, however. Europeans built roads, railroads, schools, and harbors, especially in the last decades before independence. Although these improvements were originally made for the benefit of Europeans, they gave the new nations a framework on which to build.

Economic Development

Today, African leaders support the idea of **modernization**—that is, they want to create stable societies capable of producing a high level of goods and services. They see economic development as the key to modernization. Economic development includes both improving agriculture and developing industry.

Improving agriculture. The majority of Africans depend on farming for a living. There are two main types of agriculture in Africa: subsistence farming and growing cash crops. Subsistence farmers usually live in small villages, producing enough for themselves with some left over to sell. Because they have little to sell, they cannot afford to buy much. Better education, equipment, and transportation are needed to help these farmers produce more.

During the colonial period, Europeans encouraged the growing of cash crops, or

741

Improving agriculture as well as promoting industrial growth are among the chief goals of African nations. African leaders want to strengthen their national economies and reduce dependence on foreign aid and investment. They see education as a basic step toward achieving those goals. At top, students attend graduation ceremonies at the University of Zambia. At bottom, farmers use machines to bag mountains of peanuts, a major cash crop.

crops for export. After independence, African nations continued to grow and sell these crops. Cash crops provide Africans with badly needed capital. However, dependence on a single cash crop can cause problems. World demand for a crop can fall suddenly, reducing prices and upsetting the economy of a nation. Some African nations have tried to diversify their economies to end dependence on a single cash crop.

The climate makes farming in parts of Africa difficult. (See page 243.) The deserts do not get enough rain. Rain forests get too much.

In the savannas, rainfall is unreliable. At the same time, soil in many parts of Africa is less fertile than soil in Europe, Asia, and North America.

From the mid-1970s and into the 1980s, drought caused severe problems in the Sahel. This huge, semi-desert region south of the Sahara stretches from the Atlantic to the Indian Ocean. During the long drought, people living in the Sahel were faced with starvation. Other natural disasters, such as plagues of locusts and cattle diseases, have made agricultural development difficult.

Industrial development. In order to industrialize, African nations need capital, skilled technicians, and raw materials. In the past, the capital to develop certain industries often came from **multinational corporations.** These large enterprises, which have branches in many countries, invested in mining industries and exported cash crops from a number of African nations. Multinationals also exported raw materials from Africa to European factories. They then sold the finished goods at high prices to consumers in Africa.

To prevent powerful foreign corporations from gaining too much influence, some African governments insisted on owning 51 percent of key industries. They used foreign aid and investment to back their efforts to industrialize. Many nations started to process their own food, minerals, and other raw materials.

The debt crisis. By the late 1980s, many African nations had to revise their plans for industrialization. Like other developing nations, they had borrowed heavily to build new industries but then were unable to repay their huge debts. Under pressure from banks, many African nations set up repayment schedules lasting 20, 30, or even 50 years. At the same time, creditors were reluctant to advance more money. This debt crisis grew out of slower-than-expected economic growth, due in part to unsuccessful government programs. It was also the result of an unstable world economy. (You will read more about the foreign debt crisis in the Epilogue.)

Some African governments, recognizing that their policies had played a role in the crisis, turned to new policies. They then chose to put more emphasis on agricultural development and less on industrialization.

Rapid Social Change

After World War II, nations around the world experienced rapid social change. In African nations, these changes included tremendous population growth and **urbanization,** the migration of millions of people from rural villages to cities.

Population growth. Between 1950 and 1990, the population of Africa almost tripled, from 219 million to an estimated 645 million. Improvements in health care, such as new medicines and clinics, contributed to the skyrocketing numbers.

Rapid population growth posed serious problems. In some countries, food output could not keep up with the population explosion. Natural disasters, such as drought, and lack of fertile farmland resulted in food shortages and sometimes famine. Government resources were severely strained to meet even basic needs such as education and housing.

Urbanization. Rapid urban growth is a feature of all industrializing nations. As you read in Chapter 21, European cities mushroomed during the Industrial Revolution. African cities experienced similar growth in the years after independence.

Cities held many attractions, from high-paying jobs and schools to housing with running water and electricity. Cities offered many forms of entertainment, such as movies and sports events. Most important, people were lured to cities by the hope of better jobs and higher incomes.

Unfortunately, many rural people who migrated to the cities found only disappointment. In spite of the crowds, they often felt lonely and isolated in the cities. They missed the close ties that existed in rural villages. At the same time, there were not enough jobs for the millions of newcomers. Also, many did not have the education and skills needed for most jobs.

Shantytowns, or makeshift shelters built of scraps of wood and metal, sprang up around most cities. The jobless lived in these crowded slums, providing for their needs as best they could. Even those with jobs lived in the shantytowns because better housing was not available. Despite the hardships of city life, people did not want to return to villages.

In Africa, more than half the population is under 15 years old. Many young Africans are growing up in shantytowns, like this one, on the outskirts of cities. Since independence, millions of people across the continent have left their villages for the bustle and excitement of cities. Few cities have the resources to house the newcomers, so people manage as best they can. Each day, shantytown residents walk or take buses to jobs or spend their time looking for work.

Emphasis on Education

African leaders have stressed the need for education to meet the challenges of today. A large percentage of each nation's budget goes into education. Governments have built primary and secondary schools as well as universities and technical schools. As populations soar, the number of primary school students increases. So, too, does the cost of providing basic education.

The emphasis on education serves several purposes. Education is a way of encouraging a sense of national unity among the many ethnic and language groups in a country. Education also provides the skilled workers, managers, teachers, and technicians needed for economic development.

Search for Political Stability

When they became independent, African nations wrote their own constitutions. These constitutions generally set up parliamentary democracies and guaranteed individual rights. In the years since independence, many African nations have struggled, with limited success, to preserve stable, democratic governments.

Some nations turned to one-party systems, outlawing opposition parties. They thought this would preserve national unity. They believed that a system with many political parties prevented a nation from working for a common cause. Sekou Touré,* the first president of Guinea, argued that a single party could best represent the interests of the people. He believed that differences of opinion could be worked out within the one-party system.

The military has played a large role in African politics. Some Africans think the military is the only force strong enough to unify their deeply divided nations. Others support military rule in the hope that a strong leader would stop inflation, end government corruption, and provide food for all the people.

In the 1970s and 1980s, military leaders staged **coups d'état** (koo day TAH), or revolts, in many countries. For example, in 1971, General Idi Amin established a brutal military dictatorship in Uganda. To stay in power, Amin murdered opponents and terrorized the population. After eight years, rebels with the aid of neighboring Tanzania overthrew Amin and restored the rule of law.

---

* Touré was a descendant of Samori Touré, who had resisted French rule during the Age of Imperialism. (See page 569.)

GRAPH STUDY *In Africa, as elsewhere, people have left farming villages to live in cities. This graph shows the population growth of Lagos, Nigeria, from 1960 to 1980 and the projected population for 1990 and 2000. What was the population of Lagos in 1960? How much did it grow by 1980?*

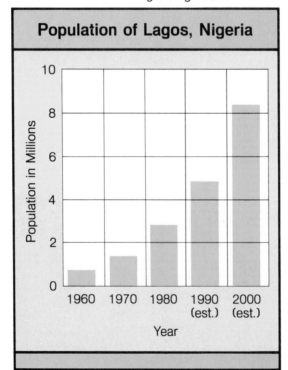

Population of Lagos, Nigeria

(Bar graph: Population in Millions vs. Year)

Year	Population
1960	~0.7
1970	~1.4
1980	~2.8
1990 (est.)	~4.8
2000 (est.)	~8.3

Source: United Nations Department for International Economic and Social Affairs.

SECTION 2 REVIEW

1. **Define:** (a) modernization, (b) multinational corporation, (c) urbanization, (d) coup d'état.

2. How did the boundaries drawn by colonial powers cause problems for independent African nations?

3. (a) List two reasons why improving agriculture in Africa is difficult. (b) What do African nations need to industrialize?

4. Why have millions of Africans moved to the cities?

5. Explain why African leaders think education is an important goal.

6. **Critical Thinking** How does rapid population growth make it difficult for developing African nations to meet their goals?

3 Nigeria and Tanzania: Nations in Transition

READ TO UNDERSTAND

☐ Why Nigerians have sometimes welcomed military rule.

☐ How religious and ethnic divisions affect Nigeria.

☐ How the one-party system operates in Tanzania.

☐ What economic problems Tanzania faces.

The temperature outside soars into the 90s. Car horns blare impatiently in the traffic jams of downtown Lagos, Nigeria. Inside a large modern building, air conditioning cools the offices while young Nigerians work at their computers.

In dusty villages outside Lagos, men and women work the land with hand hoes. Children carry water from wells or water holes. Men fish along the banks of the Niger, while women in flowing gowns sell vegetables and spices to passengers on the riverboats. These scenes—from the city and from the villages— point to the contrasting ways of life in Nigeria and other developing nations of Africa.

Africa is a continent that is experiencing vast changes. In 1960, Nigeria, in West Africa, celebrated its independence. A year later, Tanzania, in East Africa, won its independence. The experiences of these nations since independence illustrate some of the challenges facing all African countries as they work toward modernization.

Nigeria

About 113 million people live in Nigeria, more than in any other African nation. Most Nigerians are farmers living in rural areas. Still, large

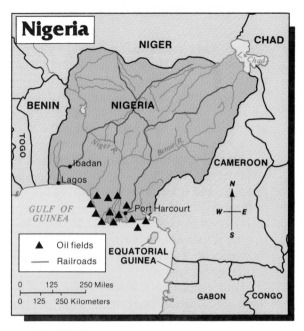

MAP STUDY *The Nigerian government has sought to develop the country economically. The Niger River, the third largest river in Africa, holds great potential for hydroelectric power. How can railroads contribute to the economic development of Nigeria?*

cities such as Lagos and Ibadan are very crowded.

Nigeria exports a number of cash crops, ranging from cacao beans, peanuts, and palm oil to timber and tobacco. The country is rich in natural resources, including oil, columbite (used in making stainless steel), tin, and coal. Oil has helped the nation develop economically, but also brought hard times when the demand for oil dropped sharply.

Shaping a political course. Since independence, Nigeria has charted a rocky course in and out of civilian rule. From 1960 to 1966 and from 1979 to 1983, Nigeria had civilian democratic rule. Each period ended in a military coup that was welcomed by many people. The military did not seek to remain in power permanently. Instead, it responded to critical problems that had emerged. The problems included corruption, government mismanagement, and violence.

During the 1970s, high oil prices helped Nigeria's foreign earnings. But with the world economic recession that began in 1980 came a steep drop in oil prices. For Nigeria, this spelled economic crisis. Corrupt officials seemed more interested in hiding money in foreign bank accounts than in solving the nation's pressing economic problems. As the crisis deepened, General Ibrahim Babangida seized power in 1983. After making reforms, he announced plans to return the country to civilian rule by 1992.

Ethnic divisions. Both military and civilian rulers have had to deal with Nigeria's religious and ethnic rivalries. During the Age of Imperialism, Britain pieced together a colony out of the many diverse peoples who lived in what is today Nigeria. When Nigeria became independent, it included more than 250 ethnic and language groups.

Four major ethnic groups make up about three fifths of the population. They are the Hausa and Fulani in the north, the Yoruba in the southwest, and the Ibo in the southeast. The Hausa and Fulani are largely Muslim. Many Yoruba and Ibo are Christian. Others practice their traditional religions.

In the mid-1960s, ethnic divisions led to a terrible civil war. Charging persecution and seeking to protect their oil wealth, the Ibo set up an independent republic, called Biafra. From 1967 to 1970, the central government of Nigeria fought to reunite the nation. The civil war ended in the defeat of Biafra. Although the nation has remained united, ethnic rivalries remain a fact of political life in Nigeria.

Economic struggles. Like other developing nations in Africa, Nigeria tried to modernize its economy. The civil war disrupted that effort, but with the return of peace came new economic growth. However, the fall in world oil prices in the 1980s pushed Nigeria deeply into debt. In 1987, western creditor nations agreed to reschedule repayment of some of the $19 billion Nigeria owed.

Wealth is unevenly distributed in Nigeria. A tiny percentage of the population controls 75 percent of the wealth. The wealthy few live in luxury in the cities. The vast majority of city dwellers remain in poverty.

A major problem in Nigeria, as in other African nations, is its rapidly expanding population. Food production has not kept pace with

Nigeria's population is expected to top 200 million in the next 20 years. Providing health care, especially to its young people, is a major goal of the nation's leaders. Here, women attend classes at a rural health center, where they learn about food and nutrition. By educating families about sanitation, nutrition, and disease prevention, the government hopes to reduce illnesses that keep people from taking an active role in the nation's development.

the nation's growing numbers. The government must either import food or increase the output of farms. To this end, the government has relocated some city dwellers into the countryside as farmers. In 1985, to force more people to farm, the government banned imports of rice and maize. Food production did increase, but many young people resisted becoming farmers. Even though there are not enough other jobs, they prefer city life.

Tanzania

About 27 million people live in Tanzania. Unlike Nigeria, which has many natural resources, Tanzania has few mineral resources and lacks enough capital to develop its economy. Its chief export is coffee. Tanzania also exports tea, cotton, and sisal, a plant fiber used in making rope.

Most people in Tanzania are farmers. Unlike Nigeria and many other African nations, Tanzania has a common language—Swahili—that helps unify the nation. (Many East Africans speak Swahili as well as their own local languages.)

From colony to nation. In the Age of Imperialism, first Germany and then Britain ruled the area, which was called Tanganyika. In the 1950s, Julius Nyerere (nyuh RAIR ay) led the drive for independence. When the colony won freedom in 1961, Nyerere was chosen president. In 1964, Tanganyika united with Zanzibar and took the name Tanzania.

President Nyerere created a government with a one-party system. Each village and election unit nominates two candidates for public office. The party pays the expenses for all candidates, who campaign together. Thus, when elections are held, voters have a choice. This form of one-party system has gained popular acceptance in Tanzania.

Economic development. President Nyerere set as his goal an improved living standard for the Tanzanian people. He tried to achieve this by improving farming at the local level. He also stressed the need to develop self-reliance instead of seeking foreign aid. At first Tanzania experimented with agricultural cooperatives. Farmers worked together to grow cash crops such as tea and tobacco.

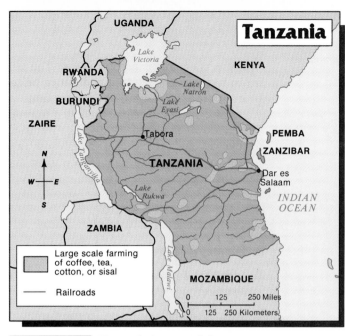

MAP STUDY *Tanzania has much less potential for hydroelectric power than Nigeria. Much of the interior is arid. How is railroad development related to farming areas?*

In the late 1960s, Nyerere announced a program to form "ujamaa" villages. Ujamaa is a Swahili word meaning familyhood. Nyerere's program had three basic ideas: mutual respect, the sharing of production, and the obligation to work. The government provided assistance, including medical care, schools, technical advice, and machinery to the villages. The aim of the program was for each village to become self-reliant.

Nyerere designed a system of education to fit Tanzania's goal of self-reliance. In his book *Education for Self-Reliance,* Nyerere described how schools should be built and run. Schools, he said, should help build national unity and encourage respect for farming.

Unfortunately, poor soil and unreliable rainfall make farming in Tanzania difficult. Severe droughts in 1973–1974 and 1983–1984 further hindered Nyerere's plans for improving agriculture in the villages. In addition, many farmers resisted the advice of government farm experts. Since agricultural exports were needed to pay for new industries, low crop production meant slow industrial growth. The lack of capital forced the government to cut back on medical and educational programs.

747

Tanzania remains a poor nation. The failure to increase farm output and falling prices for cash crops have limited development.

After 24 years in office, the aging Nyerere stepped down as president in 1985. Ali Hassan Mwinyi was elected to replace him. Mwinyi has moved to revitalize Tanzania's economy and stem the decline.

SECTION 3 REVIEW

1. **Locate:** (a) Nigeria, (b) Tanzania.

2. **Identify:** (a) Biafra, (b) Swahili, (c) Julius Nyerere.

3. Why have Nigerians welcomed military rule?

4. Why has national unity been difficult in Nigeria?

5. (a) What goals did Nyerere emphasize for Tanzania? (b) Did he achieve them? Explain.

6. **Critical Thinking** How have economic conditions outside Nigeria and Tanzania affected both nations?

4 Tensions in Southern Africa

READ TO UNDERSTAND

☐ How apartheid affects the people of South Africa.

☐ How people have resisted apartheid.

☐ What problems South Africa's neighbors face.

☐ *Vocabulary:* apartheid.

In recent years, world attention has focused on southern Africa. In the Republic of South Africa, a small white minority has kept tight rein on the country's black majority. The government of South Africa has also become involved in the affairs of its black-ruled neighbors—Mozambique, Namibia, and Angola.

Republic of South Africa

The Republic of South Africa is different from the rest of Africa. Its economy is highly industrialized and diversified. South Africa has much fertile farmland, a favorable climate, and rich mineral resources, including gold, diamonds, platinum, manganese, and uranium.

South Africa has a population of 36 million. About 6 million South Africans, roughly 17 percent of the population, are white. Some whites are Afrikaners, descendants of Dutch farmers who settled in South Africa in the late 1600s and 1700s. Others are descended from British settlers. The majority of South Africans—over 25 million, or 70 percent of the people—are black. The South African government recognizes two other racial groups: Asians, mostly Indians, and "coloreds," people of mixed descent.

As you read in Chapter 25, the Union of South Africa won self-government in 1910. The British granted South Africa full independence in 1931. At that time, the country was dominated by its white population.

Apartheid. In 1948, the white-controlled government set up the system of **apartheid** (uh PAHRT hayt), a policy of rigid separation of races. In theory, apartheid allows for separate development for each racial group. In practice, it severely limits the freedom and rights of nonwhites. For example, blacks and coloreds are not allowed to vote in important national elections and are restricted to living in certain areas.

Apartheid laws affect what jobs blacks hold as well as how much education they receive. Black schools receive less government support than white schools. And there are fewer schools for blacks in proportion to their population than for whites. Education for blacks is not compulsory. As a result, only small numbers of black children complete their education. Most enter the large market of cheap labor that serves white South Africans.

Black homelands. The white-controlled government has established a number of homelands, called bantustans, for blacks. It has stripped blacks of their South African citizenship and forced many of them to move to the homelands. It claims that blacks should

The young man in this picture displays passbooks that South African blacks had to carry in order to travel, work, and live in urban areas. In the mid-1980s, the hated passbook system was replaced by national identity cards. The new cards were issued to all South Africans, but like the passbooks, they were used to keep blacks from moving into urban areas.

develop on their own in the bantustans. However, most of the land set aside as homelands has poor soil, and the homelands are terribly overcrowded.

More than 85 percent of South Africa is reserved for the white minority. Blacks, who make up the majority of the population, are restricted to a tiny fraction of the land. Black men are often forced to get jobs outside their homelands, leaving their families behind.

Opposition to Apartheid

Opposition to apartheid has come from South Africans and from people in other parts of the world. Many black South African leaders in the fight to end apartheid have been imprisoned. When the African National Congress (ANC), the major black anti-apartheid group, was banned in 1960, the government imprisoned its leaders, including Nelson Mandela. Despite world-wide pressure for his release, Mandela was kept in prison for almost 30 years.

Albert Luthuli (luh TOO lee), a Zulu chief, urged passive resistance to apartheid. Like Mahatma Gandhi, Luthuli believed people would win more by peaceful protest than by violence. Another leader, South African Archbishop Desmond Tutu, also supported the use of peaceful means to end apartheid. In 1984, he received the Nobel Peace Prize.

Increased violence. Peaceful protests failed to bring any real change in the apartheid system. Government leaders continued their rigid support of apartheid. Frustration on the part of blacks and their white allies led to an upsurge in protests in the mid-1980s. The police responded with violence against the demonstrators.

In 1985, the South African government declared a state of emergency. It gave the army and police increased powers. Thousands of blacks were killed, beaten, or tortured, and the homes of many more were destroyed.

The government put limits on the news media to keep its citizens from learning about what was happening. Despite the repression, anti-apartheid protests continued. In 1990, the white-controlled government seemed ready to negotiate with the African National Congress. Moderate black leaders expected talks to eventually lead to a system in which blacks would gain political power. These changes might take as long as ten years, however. In

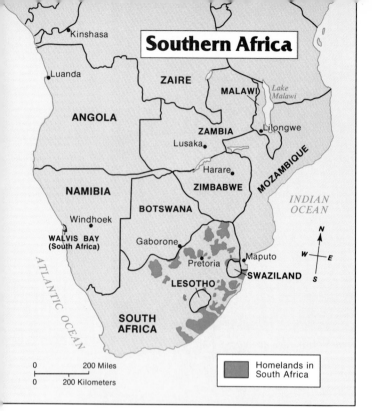

Southern Africa

Kinshasa
Luanda
ZAIRE
MALAWI
Lake Malawi
ANGOLA
ZAMBIA
Lusaka
Lilongwe
Harare
ZIMBABWE
MOZAMBIQUE
NAMIBIA
BOTSWANA
INDIAN OCEAN
Windhoek
WALVIS BAY (South Africa)
Gaborone
Pretoria
Maputo
SWAZILAND
ATLANTIC OCEAN
LESOTHO
SOUTH AFRICA

0   200 Miles
0   200 Kilometers

Homelands in South Africa

MAP STUDY *Under its apartheid system, South Africa has set aside 308 parcels of land to be formed into 11 homelands for black South Africans. Which independent nation is completely surrounded by South Africa?*

For goodness sake, let people not use us as an alibi for not doing the things they know they ought to. We are suffering now, and this kind of suffering seems to be going on and on and on. If additional suffering is going to put a terminus [end] to our suffering then we will accept it.

South Africa's Neighbors

One of South Africa's neighbors to the northeast is Mozambique, which is ruled by a black majority. Mozambique has long had a dispute with South Africa. Mozambique has accused South Africa of supporting rebels fighting to overthrow its government. South Africa, on its part, has accused Mozambique of allowing the outlawed African National Congress to set up bases there. In an effort to reduce tensions, the two nations signed a treaty in 1984. In it, they agreed not to support guerrillas fighting the other's government.

Despite the pact, evidence suggests that South Africa continued to support the guerrillas in Mozambique. In 1988, South Africa again agreed to stop aiding the rebels in Mozambique. Terrorist activities by the guerrillas have caused widespread suffering among the Mozambican people. They have blown up trains, destroyed crops, and massacred villages. The fighting makes economic development nearly impossible as the government struggles to meet the most basic needs of its people.

To the northwest of South Africa is mineral-rich Namibia. Once the German colony of South West Africa, it was put under the temporary control of South Africa after World War I. Instead of preparing the region for independence, South Africa took over Namibia's economy and imposed apartheid.

In 1966, the United Nations voted to end South Africa's mandate. South Africa refused to accept the decision. Since then, black Namibians have fought for independence. In the late 1980s, South Africa finally agreed to withdraw its forces from Namibia, and the UN supervised elections in preparation for independence. However, independence for Namibia was tied to events in neighboring Angola.

Since winning independence in 1975, Angola has suffered from civil war. The Soviet

the meantime, there was hope that the government would negotiate an end to apartheid laws.

World response. Nations around the world condemned South Africa's policies. They tried to put pressure on the white government by banning South African athletes from international competition. Some nations imposed economic sanctions, cutting off trade with South Africa.

In the United States, civil rights groups and other organizations pushed American corporations to divest, or give up, their holdings in South Africa. Congress voted to impose "punitive sanctions" against South Africa in 1987. The sanctions included prohibiting the importation of South African foods and consumer goods.

Some people who do not support economic sanctions argue that black South Africans will suffer the most from the policy. However, Bishop Tutu summed up the response of many blacks when he said:

Union and Cuba have supported the Marxist government of Angola, while the United States and South Africa have backed noncommunist guerrillas there. South Africa has refused to withdraw completely from Namibia until Cuba withdraws the troops it sent to help the Angolan government stay in power. By 1990, both UN and American officials were pressing ahead with peace talks between rebels and the government in the hopes of restoring peace.

SECTION 4 REVIEW

1. **Locate:** (a) South Africa, (b) Mozambique, (c) Namibia, (d) Angola.

2. **Identify:** (a) bantustans, (b) African National Congress, (c) Nelson Mandela, (d) Desmond Tutu.

3. **Define:** apartheid.

4. (a) What racial groups are recognized by apartheid? (b) How have the United States and other nations responded to apartheid?

5. In what way has Angola been a setting for the cold war?

6. **Critical Thinking** What factors have to be considered in deciding whether to support economic sanctions against South Africa?

---

5 Africa in the World Today

READ TO UNDERSTAND

☐ What role African nations play in the United Nations.

☐ How drought and famine have affected parts of Africa.

☐ How African leaders have worked to promote African unity.

☐ *Vocabulary:* Third World.

African nations control valuable mineral resources and export important farm products to many parts of the world. African accom-plishments and problems attract the attention of other nations. In some African nations, the United States and the Soviet Union compete for influence. Other nations, too, are anxious to maintain good political and economic relations with Africa. As a result, African nations play an important role in international affairs today.

Africa and the United Nations

Since gaining independence, African nations have played an active role in the United Nations. Today, they make up the single largest bloc of votes in the UN General Assembly. However, African nations have differing interests and do not necessarily vote as a bloc. On issues concerned with South Africa, they are generally in agreement.

Most African nations are nonaligned. That is, they do not choose to side with either the United States or the Soviet Union. Instead, they join other **Third World,** or developing, nations that share common economic goals. For example, Third World nations want more opportunities to sell their manufactured goods in western markets and greater access to new technology. Because many Third World nations depend on exports, they work through the UN to find ways to keep stable prices for these exports.

Agencies of the UN have helped African nations to develop. The UN has provided farming experts and engineers to train Africans. It has also provided emergency relief when disaster strikes.

Drought and Famine

In the 1970s and 1980s, large areas of Africa were stricken by drought. These included the Sahel, Ethiopia, and Sudan. Hundreds of thousands of people have died as a result of the famine that followed the years of drought. And countless others have been victims of malnutrition and disease.

Complicating the famine in Ethiopia and Sudan have been civil wars. In 1962, Eritrea, a former Italian colony, was annexed by Ethiopia. Since then, rebels in Eritrea and in the adjoin-

A thin goat, its bones visible beneath its hide, lunges at a bit of greenery high up on a tree. The landscape is a graveyard of trees picked bare by goats. Later, people will chop up the skeletal trees for firewood. The grasses that once flourished among the trees have been nibbled down to the ground by cattle. A farmer gazes at the parched land where he used to grow crops. Now the dry soil blows away with each gust of wind. Villages like the one shown here are abandoned to the spreading desert.

Scenes such as these are increasingly common across the Sahel, a region south of the Sahara that includes Mauritania, Mali, Niger, Chad, Senegal, and Burkina Faso. From 1963 to 1973 and again in the 1980s, drought struck the Sahel. As you have read, the drought also struck Ethiopia, as well as Somalia, Sudan, and parts of central and southern Africa.

During the drought, millions of people suffered from malnutrition or starvation when their herds died and crops failed. In the Sahel, even when the rains returned, the problem remained, because the land people once lived on had become desert.

Every year, millions of acres of land on the edges of the Sahara are turned into desert. Experts agree about the causes of desertification, the spread of desert into semi-arid regions nearby. As populations expand in Africa, people need to produce more food. So farmers cultivate semi-arid lands on the edge of the desert. But crop yields soon decline because the thin topsoil is quickly exhausted. Farmers then plow more land to make up the difference. Trees, shrubs, and grasses are eaten by goats and camels or are burned for fuel. The exposed soil, with nothing to hold it down, is blown away, and the desert advances. The same process is taking place in Asia and Latin America as well as in Africa. The spread of deserts is not new. In the 1930s, for example, Americans saw desertification create the Dust Bowl on the Great Plains.

Experts agree that desertification can be reversed. To accomplish this, massive programs are needed to restore the balance between crops, livestock, and trees.

In Ethiopia, the government has supported the planting of trees, which serve as windbreaks to stop erosion. Trees also help to recycle moisture and improve soil fertility. The government has set aside special tree plantations to provide wood for fuel. Programs are also under way to build terraces in hilly regions to hold soil and prevent erosion. In some areas, the size of herds is limited or grazing is forbidden until grasses have reappeared.

1. Why have deserts spread in Africa?

2. **Critical Thinking** Why does the future of land bordering deserts depend on a delicate balance between humans and nature?

ing province of Tigre have been fighting for their independence.

As famine spread in the 1980s, television relayed horrifying pictures of starving men, women, and children. An outpouring of aid from the United States and other countries, the United Nations, and international relief organizations followed.

In both Ethiopia and Sudan, it appeared that government and rebel groups tried to use the relief supplies as a weapon to gain political advantage. In Ethiopia, relief officials told of supplies falling into private hands and then being sold for profit. Rebels charged that the government was refusing to allow aid to be sent to territories they controlled. Because of a shortage of transportation, grain was sometimes left to rot on the docks. International relief efforts did save the lives of many people. However, as long as civil war raged, neither Ethiopia nor Sudan could address the pressing economic and social problems their nations faced.

Efforts to Achieve African Unity

Africa is a continent with more than 50 nations. Each has its own traditions and history. However, African leaders have worked to establish a sense of African unity.

In 1963, representatives from 30 African nations signed a charter founding the Organization of African Unity (OAU). The goals of the OAU are to promote African unity, encourage economic cooperation, settle issues that arise among members, and support the struggle for the independence of black Africans across the continent. Today, the OAU includes all African nations except the Republic of South Africa.

As a unifying force, the OAU has not lived up to its founders' hopes. Most African nations are determined to preserve their independence. Thus, they are not willing to allow outside interference—even by the OAU. As a result, OAU efforts to settle quarrels have had limited success. In addition, the OAU has been unable to prevent civil wars such as those in Nigeria and Ethiopia.

African nations have worked together, however, to promote African culture and to fight diseases such as malaria and river blindness. In recent years, they have faced a new threat. Scientists project that as many as 5 million people in Africa may be infected with the AIDS virus. The cost of stopping the spread of the disease and of treating the sick puts a heavy burden on developing nations. Working with international agencies such as the World Health Organization, African governments have begun to set up programs to combat the epidemic.

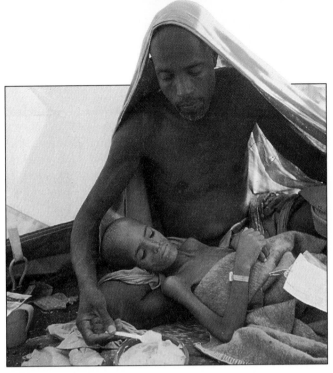

In the early 1980s, two out of every five African countries suffered from drought. More than 150 million people faced starvation. Tens of thousands, like this father and son, flooded into refugee camps. Thanks to international efforts, many lives were saved. However, the problem of hunger remains. Natural disasters, population growth, and the exodus of farmers to cities, have all affected the amount of food grown.

SECTION 5 REVIEW

1. **Locate:** (a) Ethiopia, (b) Sudan.

2. **Identify:** OAU.

3. **Define:** Third World.

4. List three economic goals that Third World nations have in common.

5. Why has the distribution of famine relief in Ethiopia and Sudan been difficult?

6. (a) What efforts have been made toward African unity? (b) How successful have they been?

7. **Critical Thinking** Why might African nations prefer to remain nonaligned rather than side with one of the superpowers?

Summary

1. **By 1963, most African countries had won their independence.** After World War II, Africans stepped up their demands for independence as nationalist movements gained momentum. Many new nations, such as Ghana, achieved independence peacefully. Others, such as Zimbabwe, won independence only after an armed struggle.

2. **After independence, the new African nations faced many problems.** Many lacked traditions of unity and were divided into different ethnic and language groups. All African nations, however, looked for ways to improve agriculture and develop new industries. Rapid population growth and urbanization hampered development.

3. **The experiences of Nigeria and Tanzania show some of the challenges facing African nations.** Nigeria, rich in resources, suffered because of uncertain demand for oil. Ethnic divisions made political unity difficult. Tanzania, with fewer resources than Nigeria, tried to increase farm output to revitalize its economy.

4. **Southern Africa has been an area of conflict.** The white-led government of South Africa has imposed a policy of strict racial segregation known as apartheid. Nations around the world have condemned apartheid. South Africa has involved itself in the affairs of neighboring black nations.

5. **African nations play an important part in world affairs today.** They have taken an active role in international affairs and in the United Nations. Attempts to achieve African unity have met with mixed results.

Recalling Facts

Choose the word or phrase that best completes each of the following statements.

1. The chief aim of African nationalism was (a) freedom from colonial rule; (b) improved education; (c) African unity.

2. Most people in Africa are (a) herders; (b) farmers; (c) factory workers.

3. Nigeria achieved early economic progress largely because of its (a) large population; (b) free education; (c) oil exports.

4. The first president of Tanzania was (a) Julius Nyerere; (b) Kwame Nkrumah; (c) Colonel Qaddafi.

5. The chief goal of apartheid is to (a) preserve black African culture; (b) keep the races separate; (c) improve medical care for nonwhites.

6. One of the countries worst hit by drought in the 1970s and 1980s was (a) Ethiopia; (b) South Africa; (c) Nigeria.

Chapter Checkup

1. (a) How did conditions after World War II favor African independence? (b) What role did educated Africans play in the struggle for independence?

2. Explain how each of the following caused problems for the new nations of Africa: (a) the colonial heritage; (b) subsistence farming; (c) rapid population growth; (d) urbanization.

3. (a) What role did multinational corporations play in Africa? (b) How do some African governments try to limit the influence of these corporations?

4. Describe two problems that have restricted or set back economic progress in (a) Nigeria; (b) Tanzania.

5. Compare Nigeria and Tanzania in each of the following areas: (a) resources; (b) national unity; (c) government.

6. (a) Why did South Africa establish apartheid? (b) How does apartheid affect non-

whites in South Africa? (c) How has the South African government responded to efforts to change its racial policy?

7. (a) What role have African nations played in the UN? (b) How has the UN helped African nations?

Critical Thinking

1. **Relating Past to Present** (a) Describe two ways in which African nations are still affected by their colonial pasts. (b) Do you think these effects are positive or negative? Explain.

2. **Analyzing a Quotation** In the early 1960s, Tanzanian President Nyerere said: "While other nations are trying to reach the moon, we are trying to reach the village." (a) To what "other nations" do you think Nyerere was referring? (b) How did Nyerere try to reach the villages of Tanzania?

3. **Understanding the Roots of Democracy** (a) What circumstances have made the growth of democracy difficult in Nigeria? In South Africa? (b) What changes would be necessary for these countries to become more democratic?

Developing Basic Skills

1. **Researching** Choose one African nation that gained its independence after World War II. Research its history since independence. Then answer these questions:

(a) When did the country win independence? (b) What are its chief economic resources? (c) What problems has it faced in trying to modernize? (d) How successful has it been in solving these problems?

2. **Map Reading** Study the maps on pages 745 and 747. (a) What natural resources are shown on the map of Nigeria? (b) What economic activity is shown on the map of Tanzania? (c) How do you think railroads might affect economic development within each country?

Writing About History

Informal Documentation

You will recall that there are times when you must cite a source of information used in your research paper. (See page 617.) The two most common types of citations are informal citations and footnotes. Informal citations are placed immediately after the facts or quotation you have taken from a source. To write informal citations, include in parentheses the author's name, the title of the source, and the page number where the information can be found. For example: (Steve Biko, *Black Consciousness in South Africa,* 58–63.) Each of the sources you identify must appear in your bibliography.

Practice: Using your textbook as your source, write an example of an informal citation.

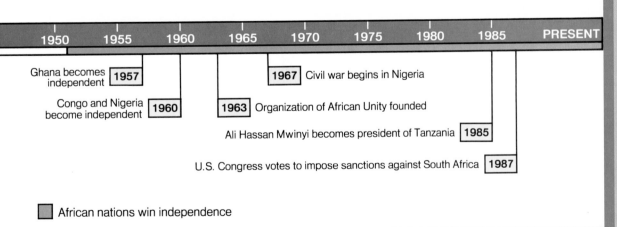

| 1950 | 1955 | 1960 | 1965 | 1970 | 1975 | 1980 | 1985 | PRESENT |

Ghana becomes independent **1957**

Congo and Nigeria become independent **1960**

1967 Civil war begins in Nigeria

1963 Organization of African Unity founded

Ali Hassan Mwinyi becomes president of Tanzania **1985**

U.S. Congress votes to impose sanctions against South Africa **1987**

African nations win independence

755

The Middle East

34

(1945–Present)

"Oh ye men! Listen to my words and take them to heart! Know that every Muslim is a brother to every other Muslim, and that you are now one brotherhood." With these words, Muhammad bound all Muslims together. Today, as in the past, Muslims around the world share a common heritage, including making the pilgrimage to Mecca. The pilgrims shown here came to pray before the Kaaba.

Ibrahim Saeed watched the scene unfold. At first, the vast crowd moved peacefully through the dusty streets. People sang hymns as the midday prayers ended. Then the chanting began. "Death to the Americans! Death to the Soviet Union! Death to Israel!" Knives appeared. Security guards pushed forward. The scene turned into chaos. Screams echoed above the chanting as people were trampled in the confusion. Viewing the scene much later, Saeed saw the shoes, scarves, and slippers left behind by fleeing men and women. The bodies of the dead and injured had been removed.

For Saeed, the day had begun as one of joy. He had realized a lifetime dream. Dressed in the simple white robes of a pilgrim, he had entered the Grand Mosque in Mecca, Saudi Arabia. He could now call himself hajji, a Muslim who has made the pilgrimage to Mecca. For every Muslim, making the pilgrimage to Mecca at least once in a lifetime is a sacred duty.

Mecca is the holiest place of Islam. For more than a thousand years, pilgrims have prayed before the Kaaba, or Black Stone. They follow elaborate rituals, such as circling the Kaaba seven times. Each ritual has symbolic importance.

In 1987, more than 2 million pilgrims had arrived in Mecca by plane, ship, bus, and car. But that year, demonstrations by Iranian Muslims turned into riots. The Saudi Arabian government takes its responsibility as guardian of the Kaaba seriously. And guards moved in to stop the riots.

Although the Middle East is the heartland of Islam and the Kaaba is its most sacred shrine, Muslims are divided by nationality and by sects within the faith. Iranians, for example, are Shiite Muslims. In recent years, they have preached a revolutionary brand of Islam, promoting a return to traditional practices. Iranian nationalists have denounced the superpowers for interfering in the Middle East. Their chants and slogans have found sympathetic listeners among other peoples of the Middle East.

The clash in Mecca symbolizes some of the currents sweeping the Middle East. Its history and traditions are deeply rooted. Today, the Middle East faces a major challenge: how to achieve the benefits of modernization and preserve its heritage. ∎

---

1 Tradition and Change

READ TO UNDERSTAND

- ☐ How differences in geography and religion affect the peoples of the Middle East.
- ☐ What influence Islam has on life in the Middle East.
- ☐ How modernization has caused basic changes in the Middle East.
- ☐ *Vocabulary:* westernization.

The heartland of the Middle East includes the nations of the Arabian peninsula as well as Jordan, Israel, Lebanon, Syria, Iraq, Iran, Turkey, and Egypt. (See the map on page 763.) The nations of North Africa, Pakistan, and Afghanistan are sometimes seen as part of the Middle East because their cultures are influenced by Islam.

GEOGRAPHIC SETTING
A Region of Diversity

The Middle East is a region of diverse climates and geography. One long mountain range stretches from Turkey through Iran to Afghanistan. Another runs along the coast of Lebanon. Vast, high plateaus dominate most of Turkey and large parts of Iran and Afghanistan.

Parts of the Middle East are desert. Some of this desert land can be turned into farmland if it is properly irrigated. Bordering the deserts are the steppes, regions that support some scrubby vegetation. There are also fertile farming regions such as those in the Nile and Tigris-Euphrates valleys. ■

The Middle East is also home to many religious and ethnic groups. The region was the birthplace of three major world religions: Judaism, Christianity, and Islam. These religions share some beliefs. For example, each teaches belief in one God and obedience to God's commandments. The city of Jerusalem, which is sacred to all three religions, symbolizes their common heritage.

In both steppe and desert regions, Middle Eastern farmers have increasingly turned to modern machinery to cultivate the land. These Saudi Arabian farmers use tractors to plow fields that will be planted with wheat. Parts of the desert region of Arabia have winter or spring rains that bring enough moisture to grow crops. Irrigation, storage dams, and underground streams also supply water needed for agriculture.

Today, the vast majority of the peoples of the Middle East are Muslim. Nevertheless, millions of Christians and Jews also live in the region. Different sects, or groups, have developed within each major religion. Islam, for example, split into two major branches— Sunnite and Shiite.* Each group has developed its own traditions.

There are also many ethnic groups in the Middle East. A large number of Muslims are Arabs. But millions of Muslims in the Middle East belong to other ethnic groups. Turks, Kurds, and Persians are non-Arab Muslims. They speak their own languages and are fiercely loyal to their own cultures.

The Impact of History

The Middle East is the crossroads of the world, linking Europe, Africa, and Asia. Ambitious conquerors and migrating peoples have left their mark on the region. Assyrians, Babylonians, Persians, Greeks, and Romans dominated the area in ancient times. Later, Arabs and Mongols controlled large parts of the Middle East. As a result, many cultural traditions flourished side by side.

By 1500, two great empires had emerged in the Middle East: the Ottoman Empire and the Safavid Empire. At its height, the Ottoman Empire reached from the Tigris-Euphrates Valley to Morocco. (See the map on page 389.) The Safavid Empire included most of what is today Iran.

Religious and territorial disputes fueled centuries of bitter fighting between the two empires. The Ottomans were Sunni Muslims, while the Safavid rulers were Shiite. Despite frequent warfare, learning and the arts flourished in both empires. After the 1600s, however, both empires declined.

During the Age of Imperialism, European nations competed for influence in the Middle East. The Ottoman Empire, which joined the Central Powers in World War I, was divided up by the Allies in 1919. (See Chapter 29.) Turkey became a republic, and the Arab lands that

---

* See page 234 for the early history of these groups.

had once been part of the Ottoman Empire became British or French mandates.

In the 1920s and 1930s, Arab nationalists demanded independence. But they did not achieve this goal until after World War II. By the late 1940s, most countries in the Middle East had won formal independence.

Islamic Heritage

Islam is a powerful force that unites Muslims around the world. In the Middle East, Islam influences people's outlooks and beliefs whether they are farmers, city dwellers, or nomadic herders.

Muslims follow the teachings of the Koran. After Muhammad's death, Muslim scholars drew up a complete law code, called the Sharia, based on the Koran. Islamic law governs all aspects of Muslim life from worship and daily conduct to punishments for crimes. In a few Middle Eastern nations, Islamic law still forms the basis for the legal systems. Pious Muslims believe the law of the Koran came directly from God and therefore cannot be altered. However, Islamic law is subject to interpretation. For example, Sunnites and Shiites differ in the way they interpret the law.

Islam supports strong family ties. The Koran gives the father complete authority over the family. Children are taught respect and obedience to their parents. Traditionally, the father arranges the marriages for his children and supervises the activities of the extended family. The Koran protects the property rights of women, but its teachings have been interpreted to support the idea that women are inferior to men.

Patterns of Change

Islamic traditions remain strong in some parts of the Middle East. However, since 1945 sweeping economic and social changes have posed a challenge to some of these traditions and have transformed the nations of this region.

Many Middle Eastern governments have set up programs to improve agriculture and to expand industry. The use of new types of seed and fertilizers, government-sponsored irriga-

For centuries, the coffee house has served as a meeting place for men in the Middle East. They gather to find out what's going on in the community, to gossip, to play cards or backgammon, and to conduct business. In recent years, the coffee house has been "invaded" by modern technology, as television sets have been installed. As a result, the character of the coffee house is changing and its importance in the community is declining.

tion projects, and the introduction of farm machinery have helped increase farm output.

The growth of industry created a need for skilled workers. Many farmers moved to the cities, seeking work in factories. As in Africa, people in rural areas of the Middle East were attracted to the cities by consumer goods, the lure of the good life, and increased opportunities.

In some countries, 50 percent or more of the people live in cities. The population of Cairo, Egypt, numbers more than 6 million, while Teheran, Iran, and Istanbul, Turkey, have each topped 5 million.

Urbanization has created the familiar problems of crowded slums and unemployment. Because of inadequate housing, the families of some workers who have moved to the cities have remained behind in their villages to work the land. This arrangement has sometimes weakened traditional family ties.

759

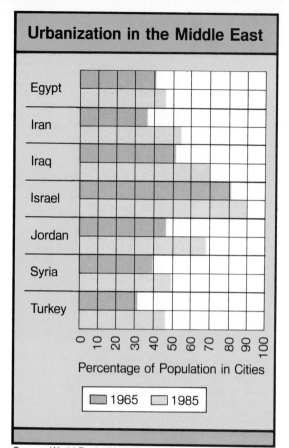

Urbanization in the Middle East

Egypt
Iran
Iraq
Israel
Jordan
Syria
Turkey

0 10 20 30 40 50 60 70 80 90 100

Percentage of Population in Cities

■ 1965 □ 1985

Source: World Bank, *World Development Report* (1987).

GRAPH STUDY *The movement of people to cities has been a challenge to Islamic traditions in the Middle East. Countries are becoming increasingly urban as this graph shows. Which country was most urbanized in 1985? In which country did the percentage of urban population grow the most between 1965 and 1985?*

When entire families moved to the cities, they sometimes found city life lonely and impersonal. However, people from the same village tended to settle in the same part of the city. In that way, they kept the sense of security they had enjoyed in the country.

Many workers leave their homelands to find jobs abroad. About 1 million Turks, for example, live and work in Germany. Thousands of workers from poor Arab lands take jobs in the wealthy Arab nations and send their earnings home to their families.

Changing Roles for Women

Urbanization and better education are affecting the roles of women in Islamic countries. Traditionally, women remained within the home. They followed their parents' wishes until they were married. After marriage, a woman became a member of her husband's family. Women were expected to be modest in behavior and dress. This idea was symbolized by wearing the veil to cover their faces when in public.

Today, women in some Islamic countries have stopped wearing the veil, an outward sign that changes are taking place. In some nations, women are becoming better educated and are taking jobs outside the home. Primary and secondary schools have been opened for girls. Middle Eastern universities now also admit women. In Egypt, Syria, Israel, and Turkey, many careers are open to women.

Many Muslims, however, do not look on the changing roles of women as an advance. Economic development, they feel, should not affect the family. For this reason, most women in the Middle East countries do not work outside the home. They remain in the home and strongly support traditional family ties. As you will read, the Islamic fundamentalist movement rejects western views of women's roles.

The Impact of Oil

Wealth from oil has changed the face of the Middle East even though only six Middle Eastern nations have large amounts of oil. They are the Persian Gulf states of Iran, Iraq, Kuwait, Qatar, Saudi Arabia, and the United Arab Emirates.

These nations belong to the Organization of Petroleum Exporting Countries (OPEC), which was formed in 1960. OPEC includes 13 oil-exporting nations from Africa, Latin America, and the Middle East. They meet regularly to set the price of oil. Between 1969 and 1980, the price of crude, or unrefined, oil jumped from $1.20 to $44.00 a barrel. Oil wealth flooded OPEC nations but caused hardships for countries that had to import oil at the high price. For a decade, high oil prices contributed to inflation.

In the mid-1980s, an oil glut forced prices to drop sharply. Some OPEC nations faced economic recession and political tensions as their incomes fell.

The driver brings the car to a halt outside the guarded gate. A woman steps out, wearing a black cloak reaching to her ankles. Her head and face are covered by a scarf and veil. Carrying a briefcase, she enters the gate. Once inside the building, she removes her cloak and veil and joins dozens of other young women in brightly colored dresses on their way to classes.

The woman, a university student in Saudi Arabia, has joined the growing number of educated Saudi women who will one day take jobs as teachers, lab technicians, bankers, or social workers.

Yet, many restrictions affect women in Saudi Arabia. For example, they are not permitted to drive, and they can attend school only with the permission of their fathers. To travel by airplane, a woman needs the written permission of a male relative. Saudi women and men are strictly segregated, in the workplace and in education. Because women students are not allowed to be seen by male professors, they observe lectures on closed circuit television. If a woman student has a question, she talks to the professor by telephone.

Saudi women in general accept the traditions that they believe are designed to protect them. Some feel the need for change. However, the government has close ties with Islamic religious leaders, who oppose any changes that threaten traditional beliefs.

In other parts of the Middle East, women enjoy many more opportunities. In the 1970s, Jehan Sadat urged her husband, Egypt's president Anwar Sadat, to improve the position of Egyptian women. President Sadat reserved 30 seats in the Egyptian parliament for women and made sure that women were included on local city councils. When a visiting Arab leader told Sadat that he thought it was improper for women engineers to work alongside men, Sadat replied, "Without women, Egypt wouldn't be where she is today."

The revival of Islamic fundamentalism has put pressure on women to resume wearing the black cloak and veil required by tradition. But it has not ended the determination of many women to gain an education and pursue careers outside the home.

1. Give one example of restrictions on women in Saudi Arabia.

2. **Critical Thinking** Why do you think women, in general, lead more traditional lives in Saudi Arabia than in Egypt?

Still, oil wealth has transformed some OPEC nations. Saudi Arabia, for example, is the world's third largest oil producer, after the Soviet Union and the United States. Thanks to its income from oil, the Saudi government has been able to invest billions of dollars in new industries from steel mills to ice-cream factories.

Cities in Saudi Arabia boomed as the government built roads, housing, schools, universities, and hospitals. Free health care and education became available for all citizens. Saudi Arabia and other oil-rich nations of the Middle East used some of their wealth to help poorer Arab lands.

Oil wealth allowed the Saudis and others to buy western technology. However, the Saudi ruling family, led by King Fahd, is determined to preserve Saudi culture and prevent **westernization**—the adoption of western ideas and customs. To the Saudis, western cultural values are destructive of Islamic reli-

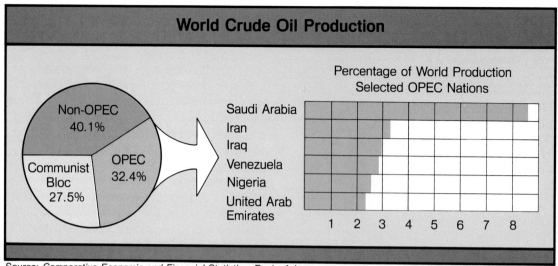

World Crude Oil Production

Source: *Comparative Economic and Financial Statistics,* Bank of Japan.

GRAPH STUDY *In the 1970s, OPEC nations produced more than 50 percent of the world's crude oil. In 1988, that figure was much lower, as the circle graph shows. Which OPEC nation produces the largest share of the world's oil?*

gious and family traditions. The Saudis interpret the Koran strictly and do not allow alcohol, dancing, or movies. Also, few Saudi women work outside the home.

Islamic Fundamentalism

The links between religion and government in Muslim countries have always been strong. However, with modernization, some Muslim countries have adopted western ideas of law and government. For example, some nations have set up secular, or non-religious, schools. And law codes based on western principles have replaced those based on Islamic law. Some Muslims have strongly objected to these changes, which they felt undermined Islam.

In the 1970s and 1980s, the movement known as Islamic fundamentalism gained many followers. Fundamentalists demanded a return to traditional Islamic principles in all areas of life. Militant groups in Egypt, Syria, Iran, and elsewhere put pressure on their governments to replace secular law with Islamic law.

These groups blamed the ills of society on modernization. To cure those ills, they called

for a return to old ways such as relying on Islamic law, keeping the distinction between the roles of men and women, and requiring women to be veiled in public. As you will read, an Islamic revolution in Iran brought Shiite fundamentalists to power in 1979.

SECTION 1 REVIEW

1. **Locate:** (a) Saudi Arabia, (b) Turkey, (c) Iran.

2. **Identify:** (a) Sharia, (b) OPEC.

3. **Define:** westernization.

4. (a) What three religions began in the Middle East? (b) Which religion has the most followers there today?

5. Describe two ways in which Islamic traditions affect daily life in the Middle East.

6. (a) List the six Middle Eastern nations that belong to OPEC. (b) How has oil wealth affected Saudi Arabia?

7. **Critical Thinking** What conflicting pressures do women in the Middle East face?

2 Islamic States of the Middle East

READ TO UNDERSTAND

☐ What changes have taken place in Turkey and Egypt.

☐ What issues have made Lebanon's civil war so complex.

☐ What challenges Iraq has faced in recent years.

☐ How Iran has changed since its revolution.

Like the developing nations of Africa, the nations of the Middle East are seeking ways to advance their economies and offer their people a better life. Despite the common Islamic heritage of most Middle Eastern nations, each country has pursued its goals in its own way.

Critical Choices for Turkey

In the 1920s, Kemal Atatürk introduced reforms aimed at making Turkey a modern, secular state. (See page 661.) Atatürk's policies were accepted mainly in the cities, but devoutly religious Turks and people in rural areas opposed many of the changes. Today, Turkey is still caught between these two forces. Powerful groups press for a return to Islamic principles in education, social life, and law. The government, however, has committed itself to Atatürk's goals of a modern, secular state.

In trying to reach these goals, Turkey has achieved some success. It has built up manufacturing industries such as textiles and automobiles. It has encouraged farm production through the use of better farming methods, fertilization, and improved seeds. Government programs to build roads and railroads have resulted in the best transportation system in

---

MAP STUDY *Oil brought some Middle Eastern nations tremendous wealth. The drop in oil prices in the mid-1980s, however, led to hardship in some OPEC nations. Which Middle Eastern nations belong to OPEC?*

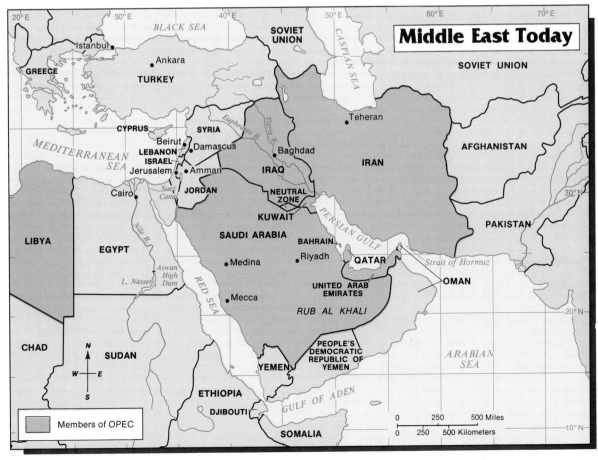

Middle East Today

Members of OPEC

the Middle East. And an emphasis on education has increased literacy.

Improvements in the standard of living have been difficult to achieve in part because of rapid population growth. Turkey has one of the fastest growing populations in the world.

The government of Turkey has changed hands many times. In 1980, the military took over the government to restore order after extremists had staged terrorist acts. The country was returned to civilian rule in 1983.

In foreign relations, Turkey has maintained close ties to the west. In the late 1940s, you will recall, the United States sent aid to Turkey under the Truman Doctrine. (See page 716.) Clashes between Turkey and Greece over the island of Cyprus have caused problems, however. In 1974, Turkey took control of about one third of the island. The government said it did so to protect the rights of the Turkish minority who lived on Cyprus. The United States and other western nations protested this move and reduced their aid to Turkey in an unsuccessful effort to force Turkish troops to withdraw from Cyprus.

Turkey's relations with Arab states have often been strained. In recent years, however, it has strengthened ties with them. Still, the Turkish government looks with suspicion on Islamic fundamentalists both at home and abroad.

Nationalism and Reform in Egypt

Egypt is a nation feeling the full impact of modernization. Its once rural population is increasingly urban. The number of people working in industry grows each year. Despite some progress, however, most Egyptians are extremely poor. The population grows faster than the food supply. Moreover, about 95 percent of the people are crowded into the strip of land along the Nile River. And their homes are rapidly taking over irrigated farmland.

Nasser's goals. In the 1950s, a former army officer, Gamal Abdel Nasser, raised the banner of Egyptian nationalism. Determined to end British influence in Egypt, he helped overthrow the king in 1952 and became president in 1954. He introduced a program of reforms to improve the standard of living of Egyptian peasants. A land reform law required large landowners to sell some land to the peasants. His government built schools and health clinics throughout Egypt.

The Aswan High Dam. Nasser's most ambitious project was the building of a huge dam at Aswan to improve agriculture in Upper Egypt. At first, Britain and the United States agreed to provide loans for the project. However, when Nasser negotiated with the Soviet Union for help, the western powers withdrew their offers of aid.

In 1956, Nasser responded to this action by announcing that Egypt was taking over the Suez Canal from its British and French owners. Britain and France, with the help of Israel, tried unsuccessfully to regain control of the canal by force. (See page 770.)

The Aswan High Dam was completed in 1970 with Soviet aid. The dam provided hydroelectric power and water for irrigation. It has created thousands of acres of farmland. How-

Istanbul, Turkey, controls the waterway between the Black Sea and the Mediterranean Sea. The city was the capital of both the Ottoman Empire and—when it was called Constantinople—the Byzantine Empire. Today, Istanbul is a major port and commercial center. Because it straddles Europe and Asia, Turkey is a crossroads for both railroad and road networks through the Middle East.

Egypt's successes and problems are evident in these two pictures. In 1970, Egyptians proudly opened the Aswan High Dam, left, which supplied the country with much-needed hydroelectric power. At the same time, the country's population was booming. As millions of people crowded into cities, they could find nowhere to live. In Cairo, the homeless, shown at right, moved into cemeteries, creating a City of the Dead among the tombs.

ever, the dam ended the annual flooding of the Nile that had fertilized land along the river. As a result, farmers have had to buy costly artificial fertilizers for their land.

Nasser's successors. When Nasser died suddenly in 1970, Anwar Sadat succeeded him as president. Sadat relaxed many of the harsh measures Nasser had introduced to end dissent and increased freedom of expression. He encouraged foreign investment and restored friendly relations with western nations. As you will read, he also took steps toward achieving better relations with Egypt's longtime enemy, Israel.

In Egypt, as elsewhere, Islamic fundamentalists attacked government policies. In 1981, Egyptian extremists who opposed his agreement with Israel assassinated President Sadat. Vice President Hosni Mubarak then took over. He suppressed the extremists, but at the same time he put renewed emphasis on Egypt's Islamic culture. He also improved ties with Arab countries that had isolated Egypt after Sadat had made peace with Israel.

Crisis in Lebanon

From 1943, when it won independence, until the 1970s, Lebanon was one of the most prosperous nations of the Middle East. Beneath the surface, however, tensions brewed. Its population was about half Christian and half Muslim. Christians were divided among Maronites, Greek Orthodox, and Armenian Christians. Muslims were split between Sunni, Shiite, and Druze sects.

At independence, all political offices were divided among the various groups. At that time, Maronites—and Christians in general—were the single largest element of the population. By the 1970s, however, the situation was reversed. Muslims outnumbered Christians by a large majority. Furthermore, Shiites, who were among the smallest groups in 1945, were now the largest single group. But political offices were still distributed according to the old formula, with Christians holding the most power.

Rivalry among the groups was made worse by the problem of the Palestinians. Hundreds of thousands of Palestinians had fled their homeland when Israel was set up in 1948. Most Palestinians were Muslim, and many settled in Lebanon. During the 1960s and 1970s, the number of Palestinians there increased. Some Palestinian refugees belonged to the Palestine Liberation Organization (PLO), a group that waged guerrilla war against Israel. After

765

1970, the PLO used Lebanon as a base for its activities, and Israelis attacked PLO bases in return.

PLO activities led to increased tension in Lebanon. Most Lebanese Muslims supported the Palestinians and the PLO. Many Lebanese Christians, on the other hand, feared that the growing number of Palestinians was upsetting the balance of political power.

In 1975, civil war broke out. A little later, Syria invaded Lebanon. The result was a power struggle among Syrian, Lebanese Christian, Lebanese Muslim, and PLO forces. In 1982, Israel invaded Lebanon to try to destroy the PLO and weaken the Palestinian cause. Although many PLO leaders were forced to leave Lebanon, the invasion did not accomplish its larger goal. Inside Lebanon, tensions among rival factions remained, with terrorist attacks occurring regularly.

An international peacekeeping force, including Americans, arrived in a futile effort to bring peace. American troops left in 1984, and most Israelis withdrew in 1985. The civil war has cost more than 70,000 lives, and little progress has been made toward peace. Syria still occupies much of Lebanon, while Israel supports Christian forces that rule the southern parts of the country.

Syria: A Regional Leader

Like Lebanon, Syria gained its independence after World War II. During the late 1950s, the Baath party gained power and has retained it since then. It established a socialist economy in which the government controlled industry and foreign trade.

In 1971, a Baath military officer, Hafez al-Assad, became president. Under Assad, the Syrian economy prospered as both agriculture and industry expanded. The government built a railroad network linking cities, ports, and farming areas.

The military remains powerful in Syria. One-sixth of the country's work force serves the military. As you will read, Syria has fought several wars with Israel. Syria is a powerful influence in Middle East affairs. Some western nations have accused Syria of supporting terrorist activity in the Middle East. Yet, Syria has also played a central role in arranging for the release of hostages held by Iranian and Lebanese terrorists.

Iraq and the Gulf War

Iraq, which includes ancient Mesopotamia, became independent in 1933. Iraq has large oil reserves. Income from oil allowed the government to develop agriculture and to improve the standard of living of the largely rural population. But Iraq limited its oil production in order to avoid becoming dependent on oil revenue. To produce other revenues, it pushed to increase food production, hoping to export food to other Middle Eastern nations.

Iraq has also faced the problem of ethnic conflict. Twenty percent of its people are Kurds, non-Arab Muslims with their own culture and language. Kurds have long demanded self-government. The government's failure to satisfy this demand has resulted in battles be-

The scars of civil war are present everywhere in Lebanon, especially in Beirut, once a prosperous, international city. The soldiers here patrol a rubble-strewn street, not sure when or where an attack may occur.

tween Kurdish rebels and Iraqi troops. In the late 1980s, rebels accused the government of using poisonous chemicals against their villages.

In the early 1980s, a border dispute between Iraq and Iran flared into war. During the war, both nations launched missiles at each other's oil fields and cities

The Iran-Iraq war became known as the Gulf War when both nations began planting mines and attacking foreign ships in the Persian Gulf. The mines disrupted oil shipments in this all-important international waterway. In 1987, the United States sent naval forces to the Persian Gulf to protect tankers belonging to its allies in the region. In 1988, Iran and Iraq finally agreed to a UN-sponsored ceasefire. After eight years of war, both nations were exhausted. As many as one million people died in the fighting. Another one million were wounded, and 1.5 million were left homeless.

Revolution in Iran

Modernization, oil wealth, and foreign interference have caused conflict and turmoil in Iran. In the decades after World War II, the shah of Iran pushed for reforms to modernize Iran and to increase his power. He ordered large estates divided up among landless peasants. Schools, highways, and industries were built, and women were given the right to vote. The money to finance these reforms came from oil.

Opposition to the shah. Despite the reforms, Iran's oil wealth did not greatly improve conditions for peasants and poor people in the cities. Instead, the gap between rich and poor widened. Moreover, conservative clergy and other groups opposed the reforms.

As opposition to his reforms grew, the shah exercised power ruthlessly. He used the Savak, his powerful secret police force, to hunt down and arrest critics. Still, he could not silence the protests.

An Islamic republic. Opponents of the shah rallied around the Ayatollah* Ruhollah

---

* Ayatollah (ī uh TOH luh) is a Persian word that means "reflection of Allah." It is the highest title that can be held by a Muslim in the Shiite sect.

Khomeini (roo HOH luh koh MAY nee), a Muslim leader who was living in exile in France. Khomeini wanted Iranians to return to strict Islamic traditions. He called for the overthrow of the shah and the removal of all foreign influence from Iran.

In early 1979, the shah, unable to suppress the growing opposition, fled Iran, and Khomeini returned home in triumph. He and his supporters declared Iran an Islamic republic.

The clergy then led an Islamic revolution and consolidated their power. They restored Islamic law and traditions and banned western music and dancing. Women, who had gone unveiled for years, were required to cover their heads and faces again.

Revolutionaries in Iran were strongly anti-American because the United States had been a strong supporter of the shah. In 1979, a group of young Iranians seized the United States embassy in Teheran and held 59 Ameri-

Iranians young and old supported Khomeini's Islamic revolution in demonstrations like this one. By the late 1980s, however, outside observers noted that the demonstrators seemed less enthusiastic than those who had helped overthrow the shah in 1979. The years of war, hardships, and executions of opponents of the government had taken their toll.

can citizens hostage for more than a year. Iranian terrorists have also been responsible for terrorist attacks on Americans and other westerners in Lebanon and elsewhere.

Khomeini's brand of Muslim fundamentalism won some support from Shiites and other Muslims in the Middle East. But the revolution did not ignite the fires of Islam everywhere as the Iranian leader had hoped. By the late 1980s, Iran faced several problems. Khomeini died in 1989, and rival groups within the country jockeyed for power. The war with Iraq had drained the economy. Iranians faced inflation, rationing, and falling oil revenues.

Even though Iran is richer and has a much larger population than Iraq, it was unable to defeat its neighbor in the Gulf War. Inspired by religious fervor and nationalism, tens of thousands of young Iranians sacrificed their lives in deadly assaults against Iraqi positions. Despite the hardships that resulted from the war, Iran remains a powerful force in the Middle East.

SECTION 2 REVIEW

1. **Locate:** (a) Egypt, (b) Lebanon, (c) Iraq, (d) Persian Gulf.

2. **Identify:** (a) Gamal Abdel Nasser, (b) Anwar Sadat, (c) PLO, (d) Hafez al-Assad, (e) Kurds, (f) Ayatollah Khomeini.

3. (a) Why did Nasser seize the Suez Canal in 1956? (b) How did Britain and France respond to this move?

4. (a) Give one reason why civil war broke out in Lebanon. (b) What four groups fought in Lebanon in the late 1970s and 1980s?

5. What was Iraq's attitude toward oil wealth?

6. (a) How did the shah of Iran seek to modernize his country? (b) What changes did the Ayatollah introduce?

7. **Critical Thinking** Why was the war between Iran and Iraq of concern to other nations?

---

3 Israel and the Arab World

READD TO UNDERSTAND

☐ **How the state of Israel was created.**

☐ **Why conflicts have occurred between Arabs and Israelis.**

☐ **Why efforts to achieve peace have proved difficult.**

☐ *Vocabulary:* **kibbutz.**

> OPEC SETS NEW OIL QUOTAS
> CAR BOMB EXPLODES IN BEIRUT
> TWO MORE KILLED ON WEST BANK
> NEW HOPES FOR MIDEAST PEACE

Headlines like these appear almost daily in the newspapers around the world. Today, as in the past 40 years, events in the Middle East have affected people everywhere. The Middle East has been the scene of an ongoing struggle between Arab countries and the state of Israel. And, because of its strategic location and its oil, the superpowers have competed for influence in this region.

The Creation of Israel

For centuries, Jews around the world dreamed of recreating a Jewish state. In the late 1800s, Zionists called for the establishment of a Jewish homeland in Palestine, the land of the ancient Hebrews. Jews from Eastern Europe began to move there to escape persecution. In the 1920s and 1930s, Jewish immigration to Palestine increased. Many Jews left Germany for Palestine when the Nazis came to power. Yet Palestine was not an empty land. More than 650,000 Arabs lived there, and violence erupted between the Arabs and the newcomers.

After World War II, many Jews who had survived Hitler's death camps sought refuge in Palestine. Once again, the Arabs felt threatened by the new wave of Jewish immigrants. New clashes occurred between Arabs and Jews. The fighting escalated as Arabs and Jews fought to control the towns and villages of Palestine.

Britain had administered Palestine since 1919, but after World War II, it turned the problem of Palestine over to the United Nations. In 1947, a UN commission recommended that Palestine be divided into an Arab state and a Jewish state. The Arabs rejected the plan because they thought it violated their right to self-determination. The Zionists reluctantly accepted it.

When the British withdrew from Palestine in 1948, Jewish residents proclaimed one part of the region the nation of Israel. Israel was at once recognized by the major world powers. However, it faced an immediate threat from Arabs in the rest of Palestine and in neighboring states.

Government and Society in Israel

In 1948, Israelis set up their government as a parliamentary democracy. They worked hard to develop their land economically. They irrigated desert areas, turning them into fertile farms, and built up industry. A few Israelis lived on agricultural and industrial cooperatives called kibbutzim (KEE boo TSEEM). On a **kibbutz,** people live in community housing projects, work together, and share the profits of their labor.

Israel is mainly a nation of Jewish immigrants and the children of immigrants, although 15 percent of its population is Arab.

Settlers arrived in Israel from all over the world. Although these Jewish settlers shared a religious heritage, they brought with them diverse cultures.

The two major Jewish groups in Israel are the Ashkenazic Jews from western countries and the Sephardic Jews from other parts of the Middle East. The Ashkenazim are usually better educated than the Sephardic Jews. As a result, they hold the better jobs and the most political power. However, Sephardic Jews outnumber the Ashkenazim. They are beginning to exert greater influence in government and improve their position in society.

The Arab-Israeli Conflict

Since its creation, Israel has been involved in four wars with its Arab neighbors. In 1948, Arab nations supported the demands of Arabs in Palestine for self-determination. Armies from Egypt, Jordan, Lebanon, Syria, and Iraq invaded Israel. Although the Israelis were outnumbered, they managed to defeat the disunited Arabs.

During the war, Israel annexed a large chunk of Arab territory in Palestine and increased its size by about 30 percent. It also won control of half of Jerusalem. The other portion remained under Arab control. Despite

After World War II, many survivors of the Holocaust sought to build a new life in Palestine. This photograph shows the ship Theodore Herzl *arriving in Palestine in 1947 with refugees from Central Europe. Arabs felt threatened by the arrival of so many Jews. As a result, fighting between Arabs and Jews increased.*

their crushing defeat, Arab nations still refused to recognize Israel.

After the 1948 war, over 700,000 Arabs living in Palestine fled or were expelled from their homes. The United Nations set up refugee camps for these Palestinian Arabs in nearby Arab lands. The issue of the Palestinian refugees has remained a roadblock to peace ever since.

In 1956, a second Arab-Israeli war broke out after Egyptian president Nasser took control of the Suez Canal. Britain, France, and Israel attacked Egypt. Israeli forces swiftly conquered the Sinai Peninsula. The UN then intervened and ordered the attacking forces to withdraw.

MAP STUDY *Since 1948, four wars have broken out between Israel and its Arab neighbors. Tension remains high as Arab residents of the West Bank and Gaza protest against Israeli rule. Which area captured in 1967 did Israel return?*

Arab-Israeli Conflict

Legend:
- Israel in 1949
- Arab territory occupied by Israel after 1967 war
- Area of Israeli withdrawal as of May 1982

0   50   100 Miles
0   50   100 Kilometers

Two more wars. The simmering conflict flared into war again in 1967. Both sides had been building up their armed forces. Fearing an Arab attack, Israel struck first in a surprise move. In six days, the Israelis swept across the Sinai to the Suez Canal. They seized the Golan Heights from Syria as well as the Arab half of Jerusalem and the West Bank from Jordan. The United Nations arranged a cease-fire to end this Six-Day War. The Israelis, however, announced their intention to keep all captured territories until a permanent peace settlement had been negotiated. Attempts to reach such a peace settlement failed.

In October 1973, Egypt and Syria declared war to regain lands lost to Israel. Despite a few early successes, they failed to achieve their goals. Once more the UN arranged a cease-fire, which ended the October War.

The Arab oil embargo. During the October War, the oil-producing Arab countries imposed an oil embargo. That is, they cut off oil shipments to the United States and the Netherlands, two nations that supported Israel. They also cut back on oil production, creating a world oil shortage. Arab governments called on all nations to pressure Israel to withdraw from the occupied territories.

The oil embargo was lifted in 1974. Israel still held the occupied territories, but the Arabs had shown they were prepared to use oil as a weapon against Israel and its supporters. The lifting of the embargo coincided with OPEC's decision to quadruple the price of a barrel of oil. Skyrocketing prices for gasoline and other petroleum products contributed to worldwide inflation in the 1970s.

The Camp David agreement. In 1977, President Anwar Sadat of Egypt visited Israel. This visit eased relations between the two countries. A year later Sadat and Israel's Prime Minister Menachem Begin (mah NAH kem BAY gihn), with President Jimmy Carter's assistance, signed an agreement at Camp David in the United States. The Camp David agreement set a timetable for Israel to withdraw from the Sinai and called for autonomy for Gaza and the West Bank. It also called for a formal peace treaty between Egypt and Israel.

In 1979, Sadat and Begin met in Washington, D.C., and signed the first peace treaty ever reached between an Arab nation and Israel. Other Arab nations condemned Egypt's move. Although President Sadat hoped that other Arab nations would follow his lead, none did.

Obstacles to Peace

In 1988, Israel celebrated its 40th anniversary. Israelis looked with pride on their many achievements. However, as a nation, Israel was still in a state of war with its Arab neighbors. Also, in villages throughout the West Bank and Gaza, Palestinians protested Israeli rule. The Israelis responded to the uprisings with harsh measures.

Three main issues have stood in the way of peace in the Middle East: the Arabs' refusal to recognize Israel, the issue of the Palestinian Arabs, and the future of Israeli-occupied lands. No Arab nation—except Egypt—has agreed to recognize Israel. They refuse to do so until the Palestinian issue is resolved. There are about 3.5 million Palestinian Arabs. Over one third of them live in exile, working in Arab countries, the United States, or Europe. Most Palestinians live in poverty in refugee camps. The vast majority want to live in a Palestinian homeland.

The plight of the Palestinian refugees is closely tied to the Israeli-occupied territories of the West Bank and Gaza. Both areas were occupied by Israeli forces during the Six-Day War. Over 1 million Arabs live there and pay taxes to Israel.

Arabs in the occupied lands feel a strong sense of nationalism. They want to build a Palestinian homeland. Israel has refused to give up the occupied territories because it believes the lands are vital to its defense. Since the late 1970s, Jewish settlers have built homes and set up businesses there. Arabs see the Israeli settlements as part of a long-range plan to drive them out. Their protests have ranged from demonstrations to acts of terrorism.

Israelis are divided over the issue of the occupied lands. Some want to expel all Arabs from the West Bank. Other Israelis favor compromise. Some would accept a Palestinian state west of the Jordan River under certain conditions.

The recent Arab uprisings on the West Bank and in Gaza have led to new calls for peace. As in the past, diplomats from the United Nations, the United States, and other nations have tried to come up with a workable plan. To date, however, no peace plan has succeeded in bringing all sides—Israelis, Palestinians, and neighboring Arab states—to the bargaining table.

Jordan's King Hussein and PLO leader Yasir Arafat (YAH sir AH rah faht) have declared their willingness to agree to peace with Israel under certain conditions. However, Israelis distrust the PLO, which has launched terrorist raids against Israel for years. Palestinians, on the other hand, insist that PLO delegates participate in any peace talks, a condition that Israel has refused to accept.

In November 1988, Palestinian leaders meeting in Algeria issued a formal declaration of independence for the West Bank and Gaza. However, Israel has long opposed the formation of such an independent Palestianian state so the problem of the occupied lands remains unresolved. Thus, while an anxious world watches uneasily, prospects for a peaceful settlement in this strategic sector of the world remain uncertain.

SECTION 3 REVIEW

1. **Locate:** (a) Jerusalem, (b) Suez Canal, (c) Sinai Peninsula, (d) Golan Heights, (e) West Bank, (f) Gaza Strip.

2. **Identify:** (a) Menachem Begin, (b) Yasir Arafat.

3. **Define:** kibbutz.

4. Why did many Jews want to settle in Palestine after World War II?

5. (a) What has been the outcome of the four Arab-Israeli wars? (b) What are the major stumbling blocks to peace?

6. **Critical Thinking** If you were asked to draw up a plan to end the dispute between the Israelis and the Palestinians, what would your recommendations be?

Summary

1. The Middle East is a land of great diversity. Three world religions began in this region, and each has influenced the peoples there. The majority of people are Muslims, and Islamic traditions are deeply rooted. Wealth from oil has sparked changes in some nations. Islamic fundamentalists, however, demand a return to traditional ways.

2. Islamic nations in the Middle East have undergone many changes. Turkey and Egypt have moved toward becoming modern states. In Iran, Islamic revolutionaries overthrew the shah and restored Islamic law and traditions. Warfare has deeply affected life in Lebanon, Iraq, and Iran.

3. Israel has become a highly developed nation. It has been involved in four wars with its Arab neighbors. In 1977, President Sadat of Egypt became the first Arab leader to negotiate with Israel. Among the obstacles to peace has been the issue of the Palestinians who want their own homeland.

Recalling Facts

Match each country at left with the statement at right.

1. Lebanon

2. Iran

3. Syria

4. Turkey

5. Israel

6. Egypt

7. Iraq

a. Kurdish rebels have accused the government of using chemical warfare.

b. The Aswan High Dam was built to irrigate more land.

c. Muslim clergy led a revolution against the shah.

d. The government is committed to Atatürk's goal of a secular state.

e. Settlers organized farming and industrial cooperatives.

f. Civil war broke out between Christians and Muslims.

g. President Assad has tried to expand farming and industry.

Chapter Checkup

1. Explain how each of the following contribute to diversity in the Middle East: (a) geography; (b) religion; (c) history.

2. (a) What two empires flourished in the Middle East during the 1500s? (b) What regions were affected by each empire? (c) Why were these empires often at war with each other?

3. (a) How have Middle Eastern nations tried to improve agriculture? (b) How has the growth of industry affected cities?

4. (a) Who supports modernization in Turkey? (b) Who opposes modernization? (c) Where did Turkey exercise its military strength?

5. (a) How did Nasser express Egyptian nationalism? (b) What economic reforms did he introduce?

6. What effect did oil wealth have on Iran?

7. (a) How was the state of Israel created? (b) Why did the creation of Israel lead to conflict with Arab states?

Critical Thinking

1. **Comparing** (a) How are efforts to modernize similar in the Middle East and Africa? (b) What problems do people in both regions face in developing their economies?

2. **Relating Past to Present** Review pages 231 to 237 in Chapter 11. (a) How does the cultural and religious heritage of Islam unite the peoples in the Middle East? (b) How does modernization threaten traditional ways of life in this region? (c) What has been the reaction of Islamic fundamentalists to modernization?

3. **Expressing an Opinion** (a) Why did the shah lose support for his reforms in Iran? (b) In your opinion, what steps could have been taken to prevent the revolution in Iran?

Developing Basic Skills

1. **Classifying** Make a chart with four rows and two columns. Title the rows Turkey, Egypt, Iran, and Saudi Arabia. Title the columns Programs for Change and Results. Complete the chart and then answer these questions: (a) How are programs for change similar in all four countries? (b) How are the results of these programs similar in all four countries? (c) How are they different?

2. **Map Reading** Study the map on page 770. (a) What Arab lands border Israel? (b) What Arab territory did Israel occupy in the Six-Day War in 1967? (c) What territory has Israel returned to Egypt? (d) Why do you think Israel has returned occupied land to Egypt and not to other Arab nations?

Writing About History

Footnotes for Books

Footnotes are an important means of documentation. Each footnote is numbered. Place the number of a footnote at the end of the information you have borrowed, using a small number raised slightly above the line of type. Then identify the source at the bottom of the page or on a separate numbered list at the end of the paper. Study these examples.

---

[1] Sydney N. Fisher, *The Middle East: A History* (New York: Knopf, 1979), p. 28.

---

[2] Fisher, *The Middle East: A History,* pp. 54–65.

Practice: Write two sample footnotes, using your textbook as the source.

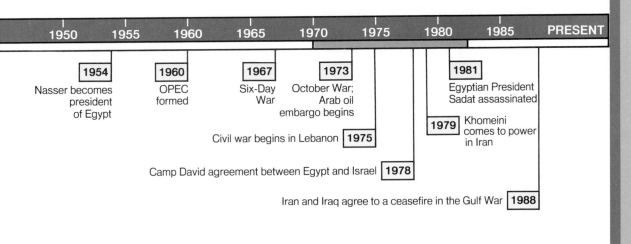

| 1950 | 1955 | 1960 | 1965 | 1970 | 1975 | 1980 | 1985 | PRESENT |

1954 Nasser becomes president of Egypt

1960 OPEC formed

1967 Six-Day War

1973 October War; Arab oil embargo begins

1981 Egyptian President Sadat assassinated

Civil war begins in Lebanon **1975**

1979 Khomeini comes to power in Iran

Camp David agreement between Egypt and Israel **1978**

Iran and Iraq agree to a ceasefire in the Gulf War **1988**

OPEC dominates world oil supply

Asia (1945–Present)

CHAPTER OUTLINE

In Beijing, China, young and old peddle their bicycles along the wide avenues of Tiananmen Square. In the background is the high wall surrounding the palaces of the Forbidden City, where Chinese emperors used to live. The signs on the wall proclaim, "Long Live the People's Republic of China."

Fu Yawen, a quiet 18-year-old, speaks softly in a park near her parents' two-room apartment. Her low voice carries strong feelings. In her last year of high school, Fu Yawen took the college entrance exams but failed. Her parents would not accept the outcome and have made her enroll in a cram course so she can take the exams again.

"I told my mother: Paradise is full, and I'll never pass the entrance exams. I'll get a job, and that's that. But she wasn't having it. There was nothing I could do about it, nothing at all. They've laid down over a dozen rules for me. No novels, no TV, no movies. I told them that was making life impossible, but they just told me, 'Stick out this rough spell because life will be fine once you've got into college.'

"My marks were 52 below the minimum needed to get in, and I can't believe I've got a hope for next year either. But they've told me that even if I fail again next year I'll have to go on trying. 'Don't worry,' they say, 'we can afford to keep you.' They even go on about how taking the exams is for myself, not for them, because they've got pensions to look forward to and won't need me to support them. It all really gets me down."

Fu Yawen resents the pressure her parents put on her to win a coveted place in one of China's universities. However, both she and her parents know that education opens doors to good jobs. The competition for college entrance is intense. Only a small number of students can be accepted each year. Over the years, however, women like Fu Yawen have taken a major role in changing China. China has vast human and natural resources. But it needs modern machinery and technology to develop industry as well as an educated population to achieve the task of modernization.

After World War II, nations throughout Asia struggled for freedom from western control. They then undertook an even longer struggle—transforming their ancient civilizations into modern nations. Japan had built an industrial economy even before the war. Yet it, like other nations of Asia, has made impressive gains since 1945. By the early 1990s, a number of Asian nations had become strong economic competitors, winning a growing share of the world's trade. ■

1 Independent Nations of South Asia

READ TO UNDERSTAND

☐ Why India was partitioned in 1947.

☐ How India moved toward modernization.

☐ What challenges Pakistan and Bangladesh have faced.

South Asia is another name for the subcontinent of India. The region was Great Britain's largest, most prized colonial possession until after World War II. Since 1945, seven nations have emerged in South Asia: India, Pakistan, Bangladesh, Nepal, Bhutan, Sri Lanka, and Maldives. In this section, you will read about the first three.

Partition of India

At the end of World War II, Indians demanded independence from Britain. However, deep divisions existed in India between Hindus and Muslims. (See page 264.) Muslims feared that they would be outnumbered by Hindus in an independent India. So they united behind Muhammad Ali Jinnah, a nationalist leader, who called for a separate Muslim state.

Great Britain realized that civil war would break out unless India was partitioned into a Hindu state and a Muslim state. In 1947, the British Parliament passed the India Independence Act, ending British rule in India. The law set up two independent nations: India, dominated by Hindus; and Pakistan, dominated by Muslims.

The partition of India did not completely separate Hindus and Muslims, however. Millions of Muslims lived in villages scattered throughout the new country of India. About 10 million Hindus lived in Pakistan. Both groups feared persecution when the British withdrew.

As independence approached, Mahatma Gandhi traveled across India preaching religious toleration. But his work failed to prevent violence as millions of Hindus who lived in Pakistan fled to safety in India. At the same time, Muslims abandoned their homes in India to move to Pakistan.

During these mass migrations, bloody riots erupted. About 500,000 people were killed. Millions were left homeless. Gandhi himself became a victim of the violence. He was killed in 1948 by a Hindu fanatic who opposed Gandhi's efforts to keep peace between Hindus and Muslims.

India Since Independence

Leaders of the newly independent nation of India moved quickly to organize a stable democratic government. The first prime minister

GRAPH STUDY *The growth of steel production in India reflects the country's economic development. During which period did steel production make the greatest gains?*

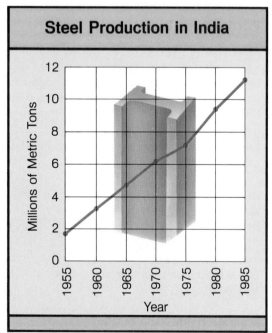

Steel Production in India

Millions of Metric Tons / Year

Sources: United Nations, *Statistical Yearbook* and United Nations, *Statistical Monthly.*

was Jawaharlal Nehru (juh WAH huhr lahl NAY roo).

Nehru had three well-defined goals for India: developing industry, modernizing agriculture, and uniting the Indian people.

Developing industry. India has many of the natural resources it needs to develop industry. Since independence, it has increased the mining of iron ore, coal, and other minerals. By building huge dams, it has increased hydroelectric power for factories and homes. The dams have also prevented floods and supplied water for irrigation.

Indians provided much of the skilled labor and capital to develop their industry. However, the Indian government also asked foreign experts to provide technical assistance. Foreign engineers helped build complex modern plants to boost industrial output.

In the past, India had imported manufactured goods from the West. After independence, it began producing automobiles, bicycles, electrical equipment, radios, and aircraft. Steel production became one of India's leading industries. India also took advantage of high technology, such as computers, and built nuclear power plants. India is now one of the 20 leading industrial nations of the world.

Modernizing agriculture. Besides developing industry, the government of India has pushed to modernize agriculture. About three quarters of the Indian population live in rural villages and work as farmers. Most use traditional methods of cultivating the land. To increase farm production, the government has provided villagers with better seeds and tools. It has also set up agricultural colleges. Graduates of these schools then teach villagers more productive farming methods.

India increased farm output in the 1950s by cultivating more land and using fertilizers. But the rate of growth has slowed. Farming is largely dependent on the monsoon rains. (See page 54.) Too little rainfall results in drought and crop failure. To ensure agricultural progress, India seeks to expand irrigation as well as flood control.

Building national unity. India is home to many religious and cultural groups. Among them are Hindus, Shiite and Sunni Muslims, and Sikhs, whom you will read about later.

Some groups, such as Hindus and Muslims, have been in conflict for centuries. In addition, dozens of languages are spoken in India.

In the face of such diversity, Nehru and his successors sought to build national unity, while at the same time protecting India's many cultural traditions. The Indian constitution of 1950, for example, made all people equal before the law and granted universal suffrage.

The caste system (see page 138), which divided Hindus into separate social and economic groups, is not as strong as it once was, and members of the various castes mingle freely at work and in public places. The Indian constitution outlaws discrimination against untouchables, but these people are still not fully accepted by other Indians.

The government has used education to encourage unity. In schools, students learn the national language, Hindi. At the same time, India's democratic government has defended many local customs and traditions.

Trials of Indian Democracy

Although India has made great progress, it has faced major problems. Between 1950 and 1990, its population soared from 369 million people to over 825 million. Increased food production and new jobs in industry cannot keep pace with the population boom. Millions of Indians live in hunger and poverty despite government efforts to improve their standard of living.

India has also experienced political unrest. In 1966, Nehru's daughter, Indira Gandhi, became prime minister. Although she enjoyed popular support for a time, economic troubles and student protests threatened her government. In 1975, Indira Gandhi proclaimed a state of emergency and assumed dictatorial powers.

Although Gandhi eventually restored democratic rule, violence erupted among some ethnic and religious groups, especially the Sikhs. The Sikhs are a religious minority in India. Their 500-year-old religion is a blend of Hinduism and Islam. In the 1980s, Sikh extremists sought to set up a separate nation and used terrorism to back their demands.

In 1984, Indira Gandhi ordered government troops to storm a temple held by armed Sikhs. Later that year, two of Gandhi's Sikh bodyguards assassinated her. Her son, Rajiv Gandhi, won election as her successor. Rajiv Gandhi held power until 1989. He lost a bid for reelection after failing to solve urgent economic and political problems.

Gandhi's successors faced serious problems of unemployment and clashes among religious and ethnic groups. Like earlier Indian

Education remains one of India's priorities. Since winning independence, India has trained many scientists and engineers. The photograph at left shows botany students at a university in northern India. At right, Indian leader Rajiv Gandhi waves to supporters. The large portraits behind him recall the spirit of three earlier leaders of India—Indira Gandhi, Mohandas Gandhi, and Jawaharlal Nehru.

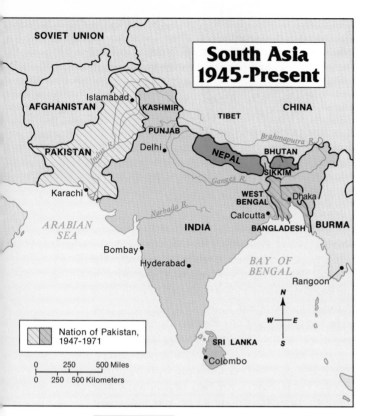

South Asia 1945-Present

Nation of Pakistan, 1947-1971

0   250   500 Miles
0   250   500 Kilometers

MAP STUDY *In 1947, the Indian subcontinent was partitioned between India and Pakistan. Pakistan was made up of two widely separated regions, as you can see on this map. What nation did East Pakistan become in 1971?*

leaders, they had to balance the demands of various groups against the needs of the nation as a whole.

Pakistan and Bangladesh

Like India, Pakistan had to build national unity after independence. Pakistan originally consisted of two areas: East and West Pakistan. The two parts of the country were separated by 1,000 miles of Indian territory. (See the map above.) East Pakistan was more densely populated and poorer than West Pakistan. The two areas had differing economic interests, languages, and cultural traditions. The only real tie between the peoples of East and West Pakistan was their religion, Islam.

Pakistan tried to set up a parliamentary democracy, but since 1958 it has endured long periods of military rule. After independence, leaders from West Pakistan dominated the government. The people of East Pakistan re-

sented this situation. Tension increased in 1970 after terrible floods crippled East Pakistan. Government relief supplies were slow to reach the flooded areas. And people in East Pakistan claimed that the delays were deliberate.

In the 1970 elections, East Pakistan won a majority of seats in the national assembly. But the military dictator in West Pakistan set aside the election results. When riots flared up in East Pakistan, government troops massacred thousands of people. Civil war erupted early in 1971. With help from India, East Pakistan defeated the forces of West Pakistan. Late in 1971, East Pakistan became the independent nation of Bangladesh.

Problems for Bangladesh. Since 1971, Bangladesh has struggled to survive. It remains one of the poorest nations in the world. Foreign aid has helped farmers grow more food, but most gains are offset by the country's population growth. Floods frequently destroy crops, causing famine. As a result, Bangladesh has had to spend money to import food instead of using the funds for development.

Bangladesh has improved food production mostly by using fertilizers. Most farms are too small to take advantage of other advances in technology, such as modern farm machinery.

Bangladesh needs to earn money through exports, but prices for jute, its major export crop, have fallen. Also, Sri Lanka and India have been more successful than Bangladesh in competing for the world tea market. Industrialization, too, remains a distant goal since the country lacks the capital to buy raw materials and build factories.

Prospects for Pakistan. During much of the 1980s, General Mohammad Zia-ul-Haq ruled Pakistan as a military dictator. By the late 1980s, however, he had restored constitutional rule, while keeping a careful watch over his opponents. In 1988, Zia was killed in an airplane crash that most people believe was caused by a bomb. Pakistan, like many nations in the Middle East, has felt the stirrings of Islamic fundamentalism. Zia sympathized to some extent with the movement and set up Islamic courts.

Pakistan's economy has strong potential for growth. In recent years, large numbers of Pakistanis working in Middle Eastern oil fields

Bangladesh is frequently devastated by floods. In 1988, for example, the worst floods in its history left three quarters of the country under water. More than 25 million people were left homeless, like this family being ferried to safety. Thousands were drowned, and many more died from disease and starvation.

spurred development by sending money home. With the collapse of the oil boom, that source of income dried up. However, foreign investments continue to flow into the country.

Relations Between India and Pakistan

Since independence, India and Pakistan have viewed each other with suspicion. Pakistan's claims to Kashmir in northwestern India have long been a source of conflict. Also, India, a secular state, feels threatened by the "sea of Muslims" in the nearby Muslim world.

In the mid-1980s, the leaders of Pakistan and India met to try to improve relations. The effort was short-lived because India's Rajiv Gandhi accused Pakistan of helping Sikh terrorists. In response, Pakistan's President Zia charged India with helping his political opponents.

Both the United States and the Soviet Union have sought the friendship of India and Pakistan. Pakistan has accepted economic and military aid from the United States. India has generally steered a neutral course but has some ties to Moscow.

GRAPH STUDY | *The population of South Asia is growing dramatically. This graph shows population growth in Pakistan. What was the population of Pakistan in 1985? How much is the population expected to grow between 1995 and 2025?*

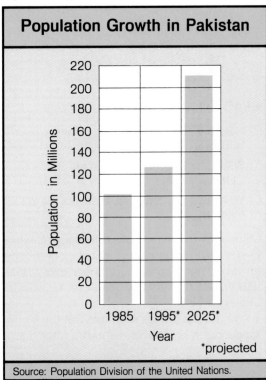

Population Growth in Pakistan

Population in Millions (0–220)

Year: 1985, 1995*, 2025*

*projected

Source: Population Division of the United Nations.

The Soviet invasion of Afghanistan, Pakistan's northern neighbor, in 1979 also affected the subcontinent, especially Pakistan. (See page 829.) During the fighting, more than 3 million Afghanis fled to Pakistan. The United States funneled aid through Pakistan to help the guerrillas.

SECTION 1 REVIEW

1. **Locate:** (a) India, (b) Pakistan, (c) Bangladesh.

2. **Identify:** (a) Muhammad Ali Jinnah, (b) Jawaharlal Nehru, (c) Indira Gandhi, (d) Rajiv Gandhi.

3. Why was India divided into two nations in 1947?

4. What were Nehru's three goals for India?

5. Why has Bangladesh remained such a poor nation?

6. What effect has Islamic fundamentalism had on Pakistan?

7. **Critical Thinking** Why do India's many religious and ethnic groups pose a challenge to democratic government?

2 Revolutionary Changes in China

READ TO UNDERSTAND

☐ How the Communist party gained power in China.

☐ What changes the communists made in Chinese society.

☐ What policies Mao's successors have followed.

China ranks as the world's third largest nation in size. With a population of over one billion, however, the Chinese outnumber every other nation. One of every five people in the world is Chinese.

China has always seen itself as the Middle Kingdom, the center of the earth. After a long and hard struggle, China is making progress toward recapturing its place as one of the leading nations of the world.

Civil War

At the end of World War II, China was plunged anew into civil war. (See page 664.) From 1945 to 1949, Chiang Kai-shek's Nationalist forces battled the Chinese Communists led by Mao Zedong.

During the war against Japan, Mao Zedong had organized a highly disciplined guerrilla army. Traditionally, Chinese armies had plundered villages in their paths. Mao insisted that his soldiers follow three basic rules when they entered peasant villages: "Do not even take a needle or a thread. Consider the people as your family. All that you have borrowed you must return." As a result of this policy, Chinese peasants looked on Mao and his army as their defenders.

The communists defeated Chiang Kai-shek's armies in many battles. Chiang had once enjoyed the support of the Chinese middle class. But spiraling inflation and official corruption destroyed the people's confidence in his leadership. In 1949, the communists won control of mainland China. Chiang Kai-shek and his army retreated to Taiwan, an island about 100 miles (160 kilometers) off the coast of China.

The People's Republic of China

On October 1, 1949, Mao Zedong proclaimed the People's Republic of China. A new constitution provided for a National People's Congress and other democratic institutions. In practice, however, the new government was a dictatorship controlled by the Chinese Communist party. Mao Zedong was the most powerful person in China. He used his power to introduce revolutionary changes.

Land reform. The communist government won the support of the peasants—who had traditionally been exploited by landlords, bandits, and the government—by introducing land reform. At first, farmland was taken from "rich landlords" and was divided among rural families. Then in the early 1950s, the communists ended all private ownership of land and changed traditional ways of farming.

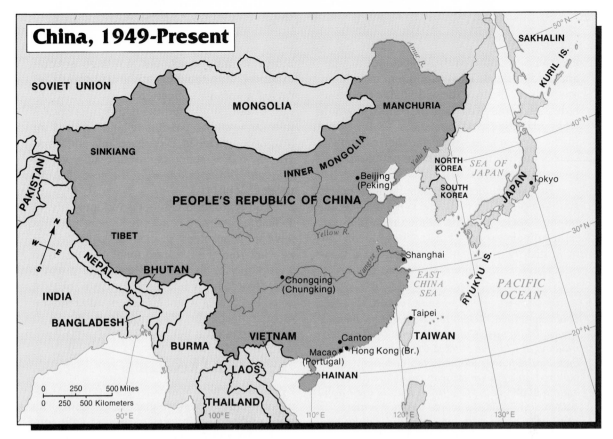

China, 1949-Present

MAP STUDY *In 1949, the victorious Chinese Communists proclaimed the People's Republic of China. The defeated Nationalist forces retreated to the island of Taiwan. Mongolia on China's northern border is closely allied with the Soviet Union. How does the extent of China today compare with the empire of Kublai Khan shown on page 272?*

Under the new system, they converted the tiny plots owned by individual families into large agricultural cooperatives. Peasants contributed their tools and their labor to the cooperative. By working together in large units, farmers raised the level of food production. But food shortages and famine still occurred.

The Great Leap Forward. In 1958, Mao Zedong launched a new program—the Great Leap Forward. It called on the Chinese to greatly increase production. As part of the program, China was divided into communes.

A commune averaged about 10,000 acres and 5,000 family households. In each commune, workers were formed into production brigades. Brigades tended the commune's crops or worked on giant projects such as digging irrigation canals.

The Great Leap Forward was also supposed to expand Chinese industry. The government invested in key industries such as iron and steel manufacturing. Meanwhile, people in the communes set up small factories to manufacture farm tools, clothing, and kitchenware. Some even tried to produce iron in "backyard furnaces."

Although the government used intensive propaganda to support its program, the Great Leap Forward failed. Changes were introduced too quickly and without expert advice. Natural disasters and peasant discontent with the commune system led to famine. As many as 30 million Chinese may have died as a result of this ill-planned policy. In the early 1960s, Mao Zedong abandoned his hope of leading China into the industrial age in a "Great Leap." Instead, the government called for long-range industrial development.

A Revolution in Daily Life

In 1949, the communists set out to revolutionize daily life. Traditionally, scholars had held the highest positions in Chinese society. How-

781

ever, Mao emphasized the importance of peasants and workers. The government used harsh methods to destroy the old social class system. Landlords who had exploited peasants were identified and punished. At the same time, government propaganda campaigns were launched to convince the people to support the new ideas.

The government expanded education to train people in the technical skills needed in a modern society. In the communes, peasants built primary schools. For the first time in Chinese history, most children received a basic education. With limited economic resources,

however, middle schools and high schools expanded less rapidly. Only a few people received a college education.

Schools supported the communist revolution by teaching patriotism and respect for Mao Zedong's ideas. Older peasants and workers, as well as schoolchildren, read from the *Thoughts of Chairman Mao,* the so-called Little Red Book.

The revolution extended to family life. In 1950, the government adopted a new marriage law that guaranteed women full equality. The new law rejected the traditional idea that men were superior to women. No longer could a man divorce his wife if she did not give birth to sons. By freeing women from the domination of their husbands, Mao mobilized women to work outside the home.

The Cultural Revolution

By the mid-1960s, Mao Zedong feared that China's revolution was losing momentum. The once-unified Communist party had split into rival factions. To renew the revolution, Mao launched the "Great Proletarian Cultural Revolution" in 1966. He called on the young to join the struggle and expose "bourgeois power holders." In response, millions of students and young workers formed groups called the Red Guards.

All over China, the Red Guards demonstrated in support of Mao and his ideals. They heaped abuse on government officials, factory managers, and teachers. Schools and universities were closed. Many talented men and women were tortured, beaten, and forced out of their jobs because they were accused of lacking the proper enthusiasm for the Cultural Revolution. City workers were exiled to rural areas, to perform hard work on farms.

The Cultural Revolution ended in 1969, but it disrupted Chinese life into the 1970s. Factory production fell. And there was a severe shortage of trained workers. Even rural farms felt the effects of the chaos of these years.

Changes After Mao

When Mao Zedong died in 1976, a power struggle broke out within the Chinese Communist

This monument honors workers and soldiers in China. During the Cultural Revolution, tens of millions of Chinese studied the Little Red Book, held by the young worker. Mao Zedong, pictured on the banner, was considered the source of all good. "Chairman Mao is the bright golden sun," said the words of one popular song. "Oh how warm, oh how kind, lighting up our peasants' hearts. We are marching on the broad and happy socialist road."

party. Jiang Qing (JYONG JING), Mao's widow, and radicals in the party wanted to renew the Cultural Revolution. However, moderates won power.

By 1980, Deng Xiaoping (DUHNG syow PING) had become the leader of China. Like Mao, Deng was determined to make China a modern nation. However, he chose a different course. Deng reduced the centralized control from Beijing and encouraged initiative by individuals at the local level.

The responsibility system. Eighty percent of China's people are farmers. For them, Deng set up the rural "responsibility system." Land was still owned collectively, but families farmed specific plots. Each family signed a contract stating how much of a crop had to be turned over to the collective. Families kept or sold any surplus they produced. The new system helped to increase farm output as well as the income of peasant farmers.

Deng introduced the responsibility system in industry, too. Factory managers were given more freedom to run their plants but still had to meet basic quotas. Any surplus a factory produced could be sold, and workers shared the profits.

The new system pleased those who improved their incomes. However, some inefficient businesses failed. Business closings came as a shock to the Chinese because in the past the state had protected all industries.

Deng's goal was to quadruple farm and industrial output between 1980 and 2000. To succeed, he turned to younger leaders with technical training. He encouraged foreign investment, allowed students to study abroad, and upgraded the technology used in industry.

Limiting population growth. China's rapidly growing population put severe strains on the economy. To achieve modernization, Chinese leaders pressed forward with a one-child-per-family policy.

Newlyweds were encouraged to pledge to have only one child. In return, they received subsidies and other special treatment. The policy had some success in the cities, where housing was scarce. In rural areas, however, the tradition of a large family remained strong because children were needed to help work the land.

In the cities, where both parents work outside the home, very young children, like the one shown at top, are looked after by grandparents or in day care centers. Since 1949, education has been a priority in both city and countryside. In the classroom, at bottom, students do a language lesson at the chalk board.

Many Chinese worried about who would care for them in old age. In Chinese tradition, children cared for aging parents. The one-child policy would leave the state with the problem of caring for the elderly.

Trends for the future. Deng's economic reforms brought demands for greater democracy. In 1989, students in Beijing and other Chinese cities demonstrated peaceably for political change. The government responded with a brutal military crackdown. Thousands

783

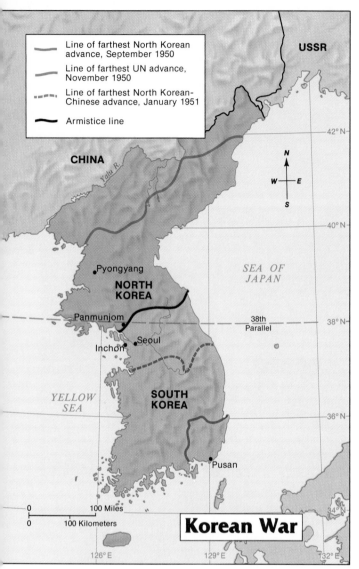

Korean War

—	Line of farthest North Korean advance, September 1950
—	Line of farthest UN advance, November 1950
-■-■-	Line of farthest North Korean–Chinese advance, January 1951
~	Armistice line

CHINA

USSR

Yalu R.

•Pyongyang

NORTH KOREA

SEA OF JAPAN

Panmunjom•

•Seoul

Inchon•

SOUTH KOREA

YELLOW SEA

•Pusan

38th Parallel

42°N
40°N
38°N
36°N
34°N

126°E   129°E   132°E

0 ____ 100 Miles
0 ____ 100 Kilometers

MAP STUDY *In the first months of the Korean War, North Korean troops conquered most of the peninsula, as the solid red line on this map shows. UN forces soon took the offensive and advanced into North Korea. Which nation gained territory as a result of the armistice?*

of people were killed, and many more were arrested. Deng's hardline supporters used the events to slow the economic reforms. China's future course remains uncertain partly because no one knows who will succeed the aging Deng. Reformers hope that Deng's death might bring in leaders who are willing to accept greater democracy.

China's Ties With the World

After the Communists won control of the mainland in 1949, Mao Zedong sought a major world role for China. He preached world revolution, encouraging the peoples of Asia, Africa, and Latin America to follow China's example and overthrow "bourgeois" governments. As a result, many nations, including the United States, refused to recognize the Communist government in China. Instead, they supported Chiang Kai-shek's Nationalist government on Taiwan.

In 1950, China and the Soviet Union formed an alliance. As an ally of the Soviet Union, China soon became involved in the conflict in Korea.

The Korean War. Since ancient times, China had influenced neighboring Korea. When China grew weak in the 1800s, Japan extended its influence into Korea, making Korea a colony in 1911. After the Japanese defeat in World War II, Korea was divided at the 38th Parallel into a northern and southern zone. In the north, Russian troops established a communist government under Kim Il-sung. In the south, American forces supported a noncommunist government under Syngman Rhee (SIHNG muhn REE).

War broke out between North and South Korea in June 1950 when North Korean troops pushed deep into the south. The United States convinced the United Nations to approve a "police action" to stop the North Korean invasion. The United States supplied most of the military forces that fought under the UN banner in Korea.

Early in the war, UN forces launched offensives that forced the North Koreans back almost to the Yalu River, on the border between Korea and China. About 200,000 Chinese "volunteers" then joined the North Koreans.* Thus, Americans and Chinese were soon fighting one another in Korea. During three years of bloody fighting, neither side won a decisive victory. An armistice was finally signed in 1953, restoring the boundary between North and South Korea near the 38th Parallel.

---

* The number of Chinese troops grew to 1 million by the end of the war.

Relations between China and the Soviet Union. During most of the 1950s, China was closely allied to the Soviet Union. With Soviet loans and technological aid, China developed its industry. Yet differences arose between the two allies.

By 1960, the Soviet Union had withdrawn its advisers from China. Soon China and the Soviet Union were competing for influence with developing nations. In the late 1960s, skirmishes took place along the Soviet-Chinese border.

China's new policies after Mao's death brought harsh criticism from the Soviet Union. To the Soviet Union's hardcore leaders, China's moves appeared to be a betrayal of orthodox Marxist principles. However, when the Soviet Union itself began to introduce economic reforms in the mid-1980s, relations between the two countries improved. They then resumed talks to settle their longstanding border dispute.

China reopens its doors. During the Cultural Revolution, China isolated itself from the rest of the world. When that upheaval ended, China developed new ties with the world. In 1971, it gained UN recognition. A year later, President Richard M. Nixon met with Chinese leaders in Beijing. After years of hostility, the United States and China agreed to establish diplomatic relations.

In the 1980s, China increased its contacts with Japan and with western nations. It purchased industrial equipment and sought technical experts to help modernize its economy. Trade with Japan and the West boomed.

SECTION 2 REVIEW

1. **Identify:** (a) People's Republic of China, (b) Great Leap Forward, (c) Cultural Revolution, (d) Deng Xiaoping.

2. How did the marriage law of 1950 affect women in China?

3. Describe the purpose and the result of the Cultural Revolution.

4. What economic changes did Deng Xiaoping introduce?

5. How did Deng Xiaoping's policies affect the Chinese family?

6. How have relations between China and the Soviet Union changed since Mao's death?

7. **Critical Thinking** If Mao Zedong were alive, would he be likely to approve of Deng's reforms? Why or why not?

---

3 Japan: An Economic Giant in Asia

READ TO UNDERSTAND

☐ **What changes the American occupation brought to Japan after World War II.**

☐ **How Japan became a world economic leader.**

☐ **Why trade is so important to Japan.**

☐ *Vocabulary:* **gross national product.**

In 1945, Japan's largest cities lay in ruins. More than 2 million Japanese had been killed. Food was so scarce that thousands of people were near starvation. Yet, by the late 1980s, Japan was a dominant force in the world economy. Other nations looked with envy on its success. They carefully analyzed how a country that had been a defeated nation in 1945 had come so far.

American Occupation of Japan

After World War II, American military forces occupied Japan. President Harry S. Truman set two major goals for the American occupation: to destroy Japanese militarism and to make Japan a strong democratic state.

The Allied powers punished Japan for its part in the war. Japan lost its overseas empire. And following war crimes trials, Japanese military leaders were imprisoned or executed for their wartime activities. To destroy Japan's ability to make war, the Americans disbanded the Japanese armed forces.

The Japanese follow both Buddhist and Shinto traditions during their three-day New Year's celebrations. On New Year's Eve, they go to Buddhist temples, where the temple bells ring 108 times to get rid of the 108 sins of humankind. On New Year's Day, many people dress in traditional kimonos and visit Shinto shrines. Here, families leave the Heian Shrine in Kyoto on the first day of the new year.

A democratic government. President Truman chose General Douglas MacArthur to command the occupation forces in Japan. Under MacArthur's direction, Japan adopted a new constitution in 1947. The constitution made Japan a democracy. The emperor lost his ruling authority and became a figurehead, or national symbol, similar to the monarch of Great Britain.

The constitution set up a Diet, or legislature, with representatives elected by the people. Executive power was held by a prime minister chosen from the majority party in the Diet. The constitution provided for a court system similar to that of the United States. It also gave women full equality, including the right to vote. A strong bill of rights guaranteed freedom of religion, speech, and the press.

New social and economic patterns. Like many other Americans, President Truman believed Japan had been led into war in part because the people had not challenged their military leaders. He hoped that democratic reforms would not only weaken Japanese militarism but would also destroy the authoritarian character of traditional Japanese society.

In traditional Japanese households, for example, men dominated women. The Americans encouraged women to exercise their new rights. They urged women to vote and even to run for public office.

The American occupation forces reformed the Japanese education system as well. The school system was expanded, and laws required all students to complete at least nine years of school. Equally important, textbooks and courses of study were revised. The new books emphasized democratic ideas such as individualism and equality.

Economic reforms also encouraged a democratic spirit. A land reform program allowed peasants to buy land that they had previously rented. This reduced the power of large landowners and gave peasants more control over their own lives. Other reforms limited the power of the zaibatsu, families that owned huge industrial businesses and had great influence over Japan's economy.

Japan had started building democratic traditions in the 1920s. (See page 686.) The reforms of the occupation revived these traditions. Also, democracy was popular because Japan's militarist government had led the nation to defeat and destruction.

Independence restored. By 1948, the Americans began returning responsibility for the government and for the economy over to the Japanese. After China became communist in 1949, the United States saw Japan as a possible ally rather than a former enemy. In 1952, the United States withdrew its remaining forces, and Japan reemerged as an independent nation.

Under their new constitution, the Japanese had given up their right to wage war and maintain armed forces. Therefore, after regaining independence, Japan signed a military agreement with the United States. Under this agreement, the United States pledged to defend Japan against foreign aggression.

The Japanese Economic Miracle

Before World War II, Japan was the most industrialized nation in Asia. Bombing during the war destroyed much Japanese industry. With American aid, Japan rebuilt its factories in the immediate postwar years. However, since the 1950s, the Japanese have forged forward on their own. Their **gross national product** (GNP)—the total value of goods and services produced in a year—has grown at a rapid rate.

The Japanese economy advanced on several fronts. Foreign trade played a large role in

ECONOMICS AND HISTORY The Robot Revolution in Japan

At a plant in Nagoya, Japan, a yellow-steel giant heaved a 16-ton load into place with a slow whine. Then it lumbered back, electronic sensors awake to any interference, to carry another load. Nicknamed "Popeye," this steel giant is one of over 15,000 robots operating day and night in Japan.

A robot revolution is well under way in Japan. Robots are at work everywhere. In hospitals, medical students work on robot "patients" equipped with sensitive monitors that respond to treatment. Restaurant robots beckon customers to come in for a meal. On highways, 10-foot tall police robots direct traffic.

Most robots, however, are found in factories. Robots perform tasks ranging from welding, painting, and lifting to packaging and labeling products. Japanese experts predict that in the future robots will find a place in the home doing the laundry and cooking and serving meals.

Robots have mechanical arms and electronic brains. They are huge, often cumbersome machines. Most are stationary. They perform routine, repetitive jobs without suffering the boredom that human workers do. A Japanese television plant that uses robot workers reports a decline in the number of defective sets produced. On the other hand, robot experts admit these machines will never

be able to do work requiring creativity, judgment, and complicated decision-making.

The United States pioneered in robot technology in the early 1960s. But it was the Japanese who discovered ways to apply this technology in industry. In the 1980s, Japan was enjoying soaring sales of robots. Most of the robots produced in Japan were also used there. A small percentage was exported.

The Japanese government has encouraged robot manufacturing. Factory owners and business leaders were eager to put robots to work. Even Japanese workers accepted robots as coworkers. They often greet robots with a cheerful "Good morning." They name their giant coworkers after baseball stars, movie stars, and popular singers. A Japanese worker who spent years in a factory carrying heavy steel plates now does other work while robots carry the heavy loads. "The robots are really honest and obedient workers," he noted cheerfully.

1. What are Japanese workers' attitudes toward robots?

2. **Critical Thinking** If robots were first developed in the United States, why do you think it was Japan that discovered ways to use this technology?

787

the country's economic success. The Japanese produced quality goods that were sold around the world.

The Japanese also developed a strong home market. With increasing prosperity, Japanese workers in large companies earned better wages. They saved their money and could buy more Japanese products. In the 1950s, the goal of a prosperous Japanese family was a home furnished with a television, refrigerator, and washing machine. In the 1960s, families' expectations were higher, and they bought automobiles, color televisions, and air conditioners.

The government was able to help Japanese industry in part because it spent relatively little on defense. Moreover, the Japanese adopted the latest technological and scientific advances. For example, they carved

out a major market in the electronics industry by improving an American invention—the transistor. By the 1980s, the Japanese were contributing many inventions of their own.

Not all Japanese shared in the general prosperity, however. Workers in small businesses seldom earned as much money as workers in large companies. Nevertheless, Japan entered the 1990s as one of the richest nations in Asia.

A Major World Competitor

Foreigners were fascinated with Japan's success and studied its business methods. Economists pointed out that Japanese strength was due in part to long-range planning by business and government. They also noted the impor-

GRAPH STUDY *Exports have become a major part of Japan's economy. In this graph, you can see the percentage of Japanese exports to different regions of the world in 1985 and what the percentage is projected to be by the year 2000. What region received the largest percentage of imports from Japan in 1985? How is that percentage expected to change by 2000?*

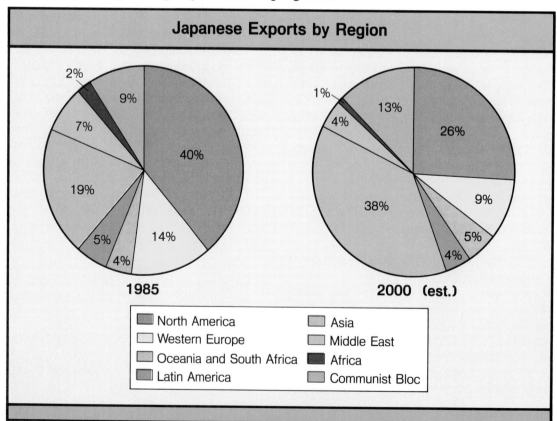

Japanese Exports by Region

1985

2000 (est.)

- North America
- Western Europe
- Oceania and South Africa
- Latin America
- Asia
- Middle East
- Africa
- Communist Bloc

Source: Ministry of Finance, *The Summary Report—Trade of Japan.*

tance of traditional Japanese values—hard work, loyalty to family and employer, and the ability to adapt ideas from other nations.

Foreign trade is essential to Japan's continued economic success. Only about the size of California, Japan has a population half that of the entire United States. It has to import much of its food and lacks many raw materials. More than 90 percent of the oil, iron ore, and coal used by Japanese industry must come from abroad. Thus, the government has tried to maintain friendly relations with the oil-producing nations of the Middle East. It has also helped other nations explore and develop their oil and gas reserves.

By the late 1980s, Japan had huge trade surpluses with nations such as the United States. That is, it exported more to those nations than it imported. Japan's success in selling goods abroad led to anger from frustrated competitors. American businesses called for restrictions on Japanese imports. Leaders from both nations have held discussions about how to improve the trade imbalance.

After years of little contact with its mainland neighbor, Japan has become China's largest trading partner. It provides China with financial and technical assistance. China, in turn, exports light industrial products and raw materials to Japan.

Many Japanese companies begin the day with a "pep talk" to employees, who sing the company song before starting work. Here, sales clerks at a large Tokyo department store receive their morning briefing. When the store opens, the sales clerks line up at each entrance and bow as customers come in. At closing time, music is played to let customers know the store is closing, and sales clerks line up at their counters to bow to the departing customers.

SECTION 3 REVIEW

1. **Define:** gross national product.

2. What were the major aims of the American occupation of Japan?

3. List three ways in which the new constitution guaranteed democracy in Japan.

4. Why did Japan form a military alliance with the United States after it regained independence?

5. Why is trade important to the Japanese economy?

6. **Critical Thinking** Why has Japan's economy created both envy and admiration among other nations?

4 Nations on the Pacific Rim

READ TO UNDERSTAND

☐ **What successes the "four tigers" have achieved.**

☐ **What the causes and results of the Vietnam War were.**

☐ **How democracy was restored in the Philippines.**

☐ *Vocabulary:* martial law.

The sign is printed in large red letters and asks, "Why aren't you a millionaire yet?" It hangs above an office in Taipei, Taiwan, but could just as well be in Seoul, South Korea, in Singapore, or in Hong Kong. The drive to achieve is creating millionaires in many Asian nations. In fact, many westerners and Asians predict that the twenty-first century may be known as the Pacific century.

Taiwan is counted among the NICs (newly industrialized countries) of Asia. In the early 1980s, its exports, including TVs produced at factories like this one, increased by 100 percent. Taiwan's success has been due in part to a low-wage labor force and to the competitive spirit of its major companies. In the future, Taiwan hopes to challenge Japan in high-tech fields such as semiconductors.

The "Four Tigers"

Among the leaders in the Asian drive to success are the "four tigers": Taiwan, Singapore, Hong Kong, and South Korea. All four have chalked up remarkable records of economic growth in recent years.

Taiwan. Taiwan calls itself the Republic of China. In 1949, you will recall, Chiang Kai-shek fled to the small island of Taiwan after losing the Chinese mainland to the communists. Since then, Taiwan has grown from a farming nation into an economic giant, exporting electronics and textiles around the world.

Despite its success, Taiwan faces challenges in the future. It relies heavily on the United States both as a market for its goods and for its defense. However, some Americans who have lost jobs and business because of the large amounts of imports from Taiwan and other Asian nations want to see these imports curtailed, a move that may hurt Taiwan's economy.

Singapore. A former British colony, Singapore became self-governing in 1959. It calls itself a "middle-developed country." It is not poor and undeveloped, but it still has 15 to 20 years of development before it reaches its

goal of modernization. Singapore has a thriving electronics industry and produces quality medical-diagnostic equipment. Although it has many well-trained professionals, much of its population receives little schooling.

Hong Kong. The British gained Hong Kong as a result of the Opium War. (See page 586.) However, Hong Kong is scheduled to be transferred to the People's Republic of China in 1997. Hong Kong has long been a bustling center for international trade and finance. In the 1980s, its trade expanded faster than world trade in general. Uncertainty about what will happen after 1997 has driven some businesses to leave Hong Kong. But residents hope that China will not interfere unduly with the city's thriving capitalist economy.

South Korea. The booming export economy of South Korea is quickly gaining on that of neighboring Japan. South Korea's large companies have competed successfully in semiconductors, consumer electronics such as VCRs and computers, and automobiles. As you have read, South Korea has faced threats

GRAPH STUDY *The gross national product of South Korea has increased dramatically since 1975, as this graph shows. How much did the GNP grow between 1975 and 1980? In which five-year period was the increase the largest?*

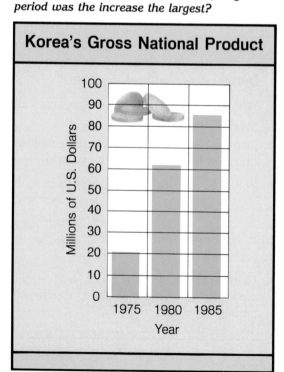

Korea's Gross National Product

Source: The Bank of Japan, *Comparative Economic and Financial Statistics.*

from a hostile North Korea. In addition, it has experienced political unrest as it edges toward more democratic government after years of authoritarian rule. Despite political problems, South Korea gained worldwide attention for successfully hosting the Seoul Summer Olympics in 1988.

Other Asian nations. Thailand, Indonesia, and Malaysia, among other Asian nations, are jockeying for a place in the Pacific century. Thailand was never a European colony. Both Indonesia, a former Dutch colony, and Malaysia, a former British possession, won independence after World War II.

Indonesia was once known as the Dutch East Indies. Achmed Sukarno led Indonesians in a four-year battle for independence. Today, Indonesia is a major oil-exporting nation. Like its fellow members of OPEC, it earned great oil wealth. However, the recent decline in oil prices has hurt its economy.

From the mid-1960s to the mid-1980s, Malaysia enjoyed strong economic growth. But the drop in prices for its export commodities has slowed the economy.

The Philippines, A Fragile Democracy

Another nation on the Pacific rim that has captured world attention is the Philippines. As you have read, the island nation won its independence from Spain in 1898 but was then taken over by the United States. Finally, on July 4, 1946, Filipinos celebrated their independence from the United States. A constitution set up the framework for a democratic government.

In the next decades, conflict grew between the government and peasants who demanded land reform. In addition, communist guerrillas battled the government. In 1972, the Philippine president, Ferdinand Marcos, declared **martial law**—temporary rule by the military. Although Marcos eventually ended martial rule, he kept a tight grip on power.

In 1983, Marcos's chief political rival, Benigno Aquino (beh NEE nyoh ah KEE noh) was gunned down by government agents. Opponents of the Marcos regime rallied around Aquino's widow, Corazon Aquino. Under intense pressure, Marcos held elections in 1986.

After the assassination of her husband Benigno in 1983, Corazon Aquino took up his position as the leading opponent of Ferdinand Marcos. Eventually, she was elected president of the Philippines. Despite the restoration of democratic rule, the Philippines face many economic and social problems. Aquino herself has weathered a number of crises, including several attempted coups.

After a campaign marred by fraud and violence, Marcos declared himself the winner. When the United States refused to recognize his victory and revolt threatened, Marcos went into exile in Hawaii. Corazon Aquino then became president.

Aquino dedicated her government to upholding "truth and justice, morality and decency, freedom and democracy." However, she soon faced severe challenges. Former Marcos supporters as well as communist guerrillas opposed her government. The future of the Philippines remained uncertain as it struggled to preserve its fragile democracy.

War in Vietnam

After World War II, the area known as French Indochina also became the focus of independence movements. French Indochina included the countries that are today called Laos, Cambodia, and Vietnam. Fighting in Indochina lasted for nearly 30 years and had worldwide consequences.

In 1945, two governments emerged in Vietnam. A Vietnamese communist, Ho Chi Minh, gained power in the north. Meanwhile, the French set up a separate, noncommunist government in the southern part of Vietnam. Fighting broke out in 1946 between the two sides.

When the Soviet Union and the People's Republic of China offered aid to Ho Chi Minh's communist forces, the United States backed the French. Despite American aid, France lost the battle for Indochina. In May 1954, communist forces defeated the French army at Dien Bien Phu.

The French withdrew from Indochina after signing the 1954 Geneva Agreement. It divided Indochina into three independent states: Laos, Cambodia, and Vietnam. Vietnam was temporarily divided at the 17th Parallel into North and South Vietnam. Ho Chi Minh's communist forces ruled North Vietnam. Noncommunist Vietnamese controlled the south. Elections were to be held in 1956 to reunite Vietnam, but they never took place.

MAP STUDY *Much of Southeast Asia was a battleground from 1945 to 1975. The 1954 Geneva settlement temporarily divided Vietnam into North Vietnam and South Vietnam. It called for elections to reunite the country, but they never took place. North Vietnam supplied arms to communist guerrillas trying to overthrow the South Vietnamese government. How might the supply routes from North Vietnam have contributed to the widening of the war?*

War in Southeast Asia

American Involvement in Vietnam

In South Vietnam, President Ngo Dinh Diem sought aid from the United States. The United States urged President Diem to adopt programs to win popular support. But he failed to make reforms to help the peasants. As a result, some South Vietnamese joined the Vietcong, communist guerrilla forces supported by North Vietnam.

As the Vietcong grew stronger in the countryside, the United States increased its role in Vietnam. In 1960, there were only 800 American military advisers in South Vietnam. By 1968, more than 500,000 American troops were fighting alongside South Vietnamese government forces.

When the North Vietnamese attacked American warships in the Gulf of Tonkin in 1964, the United States Congress adopted the Gulf of Tonkin resolution. It authorized the President "to take all necessary measures to repel any armed attack and to prevent further aggression." President Lyndon B. Johnson used the resolution to justify American bombing raids on North Vietnam. American planes also bombed the routes used by the North Vietnamese to reach the south. (See the map at left.)

As the war continued, more and more Americans called for an end to American involvement in Vietnam. In 1969, President Richard Nixon ordered a reduction in American forces in Vietnam. But American troops continued to fight in Vietnam. Finally, in January 1973, American and North Vietnamese officials negotiated a cease-fire, and most American troops were withdrawn.

The fighting in Vietnam continued, however, as North Vietnam and South Vietnam battled for control of the south. By April 1975, the communists had won the war. The next year, the communists united North and South Vietnam. Saigon, the capital of South Vietnam, was renamed Ho Chi Minh City.

The Aftermath of War

During the Vietnam War, the fighting spilled over into neighboring Cambodia. Although Cambodia was neutral in the war, the North Vietnamese set up supply bases there. In 1970, American and South Vietnamese forces crossed the Cambodian border to destroy the communist bases. Soon after, Cambodia was plunged into civil war.

The United States helped the noncommunist government combat the Khmer Rouge, as Cambodian communists were called. But in April 1975, Cambodia fell to communist forces. They renamed the country Kampuchea. Neighboring Laos also became communist in 1975.

In Cambodia, the Khmer Rouge imposed a brutal reign of terror. As many as 2 million people were killed. In 1978, Vietnamese communists invaded Cambodia. They overthrew the Khmer Rouge and set up a new communist government in Cambodia. In 1989, Vietnam finally withdrew its troops from Cambodia. The United Nations tried to ensure a peaceful future for the war-torn nation. But the outcome remained uncertain as rival groups, including the Khmer Rouge, competed for power.

Years of fighting in Southeast Asia have resulted in huge numbers of refugees. More than 300,000 refugees from Vietnam and Kampuchea made their way to temporary camps in Thailand, Malaysia, Indonesia, and Hong Kong in the 1970s. Tens of thousands of Vietnamese fled their homeland in whatever boats they could find. A large number of these "boat people" drowned or died of thirst or hunger.

Many nations took in the refugees. The United States has admitted hundreds of thousands of Vietnamese. In addition, the United Nations and voluntary relief organizations distributed supplies and provided medical care to the refugees. Yet many thousands of refugees still live in crowded camps with little hope of returning to their homelands.

The effects of the Vietnam War are still felt across Southeast Asia. Thousands of people continue to flee communist-ruled Vietnam and Cambodia. Many have escaped on boats like this one, surviving for weeks at sea. Crowded into old vessels and exposed night and day to the weather, many boat people have died. Others have been attacked by pirates.

SECTION 4 REVIEW

1. **Locate:** (a) Taiwan, (b) Singapore, (c) Hong Kong, (d) South Korea, (e) Thailand, (f) Laos, (g) Cambodia, (h) Vietnam.

2. **Identify:** (a) "four tigers," (b) Corazon Aquino, (c) Ho Chi Minh, (d) Vietcong, (e) Gulf of Tonkin resolution, (f) Khmer Rouge.

3. **Define:** martial law.

4. In what fields have the "four tigers" achieved economic growth?

5. What threats to democracy exist in the Philippines?

6. **Critical Thinking** How was the United States drawn into the Vietnam War?

Summary

1. **After World War II, the Indian subcontinent was divided into several nations.** India has made significant progress in its drive to modernize. In 1971, a civil war between West and East Pakistan led to the creation of two nations—Pakistan and Bangladesh. As a Muslim country, Pakistan has been affected by Islamic fundamentalism. Bangladesh has remained one of the poorest nations in the world.

2. **The Chinese Communists won control of China in 1949.** They then revolutionized traditional patterns of life. Through campaigns such as the Cultural Revolution, Mao Zedong tried to keep the revolutionary spirit alive. In recent years, Deng Xiaoping has worked to spur economic growth and move China toward modernization.

3. **Japan has become one of the world's leading economic powers.** After World War II, American occupation forces introduced democratic reforms. As a result of an economic miracle in the 1950s and 1960s, Japan has gained a major share of world trade.

4. **Some Asian nations on the Pacific rim made great economic progress, while others were torn by war.** Taiwan, South Korea, Singapore, and Hong Kong have achieved remarkable success. In 1986, democratic government was restored in the Philippines, after years of strongman rule. For decades, war raged in Vietnam, Laos, and Cambodia.

Recalling Facts

Choose the letter of the correct time period for each of the following events.

A	B	C	D	E	F	G

1945 1950 1955 1960 1965 1970 1975 1980

1. President Nixon begins pulling United States troops out of Vietnam.

2. India and Pakistan become separate nations.

3. The Cultural Revolution begins in China.

4. East Pakistan becomes Bangladesh.

5. The Gulf of Tonkin resolution is passed.

6. Mao Zedong announces the Great Leap Forward.

Chapter Checkup

1. Describe the efforts of India in the following areas: (a) industry; (b) agriculture; (c) national unity.

2. (a) Why did civil war break out in Pakistan in 1971? (b) What was the outcome of the civil war?

3. How did the Great Leap Forward affect life in China?

4. Describe the changes Deng Xiaoping introduced in: (a) economics; (b) family life.

5. (a) How did the Americans try to end militarism in Japan? (b) How did they encourage democracy in Japan?

6. (a) Why does Japan try to maintain friendly relations with Arab nations? (b) How have relations between Japan and China changed in recent years?

7. (a) What problems did the Philippine government face after independence? (b) What were the results of the 1986 elections?

8. (a) How did the 1954 Geneva settlement try to restore peace in Vietnam? (b) Why did fighting continue? (c) What was the outcome of the Vietnam War?

Critical Thinking

1. **Relating Past to Present** Review the origins of the Hindu-Muslim conflict in India. (See page 264.) Why do you think hostility between Hindus and Muslims has lasted for so many centuries?

2. **Analyzing a Quotation** In the *Thoughts of Chairman Mao,* Mao states: "We must have faith in the masses and we must have faith in the [Communist] Party." Do you think this statement describes what happened in China after 1949?

3. **Understanding the Roots of Democracy** (a) Which Asian nation do you think had achieved the most democracy by the 1980s? (b) Give reasons to support your answer.

Developing Basic Skills

1. **Comparing** Review what you have read about postwar economic developments in India, China, and Japan. (a) How were economic developments similar in each country? (b) How were they different? (c) Which nation do you think has made the greatest progress? Explain.

2. **Map Reading** Study the map on page 784. (a) What nations border Korea? (b) What part of South Korea did the North Koreans control in September 1950? (c) Why do you think the Chinese joined the North Koreans late in 1950?

3. **Identifying Immediate and Long-Range Causes** (a) What was the immediate cause of the Gulf of Tonkin resolution? (b) What were the long-range causes? (c) How did the resolution increase American involvement in Vietnam?

Writing About History

Footnotes for Articles

Footnotes for different types of sources require different kinds of information. Study the following footnotes and notice the variations.

Magazine and Newspaper Articles:
[1]William R. Doerner, "South Korea: Suddenly a New Day," *Time,* July 13, 1987, p. 34.
[2]"Cambodia Rejects Vietnam Plea," *The New York Times,* October 6, 1988, p. A8.

Encyclopedia Articles:
[1]*The New Columbia Encyclopedia,* 1975 ed., "Chiang Kai-shek."
[2]*The World Book Encyclopedia,* 1988 ed., "Chiang Kai-shek," by Immanuel C. Y. Hsu."

Practice: Rewrite the following as correct footnotes:

1. The New York Times, December 23, 1986: "OPEC Pact Sends Oil Prices Up," p. Dl, by Lee A. Daniels.

2. Mao Zedong, The New Columbia Encyclopedia, 1975 edition.

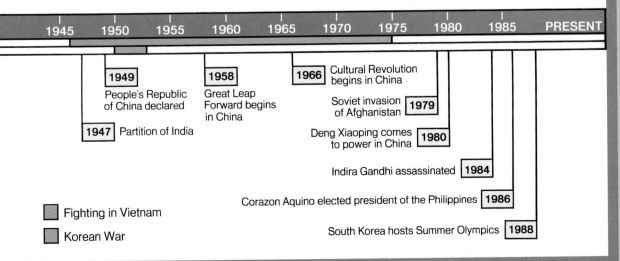

| 1945 | 1950 | 1955 | 1960 | 1965 | 1970 | 1975 | 1980 | 1985 | PRESENT |

1949 People's Republic of China declared

1958 Great Leap Forward begins in China

1966 Cultural Revolution begins in China

Soviet invasion of Afghanistan **1979**

1947 Partition of India

Deng Xiaoping comes to power in China **1980**

Indira Gandhi assassinated **1984**

Corazon Aquino elected president of the Philippines **1986**

Fighting in Vietnam

Korean War

South Korea hosts Summer Olympics **1988**

Latin America

(1945–Present)

36

Throughout Latin America, people have left the poverty of rural towns and villages in search of riches in large cities such as São Paulo, Brazil, above. All too often, their dreams end in the harsh realities of shantytowns that grow up nearby.

The girl flung her few belongings into the cardboard suitcase on the floor. She was only 14 years old, but she was leaving town. She couldn't stand the misery and poverty any longer. She could do better, she was certain. She could even become rich and famous. Buoyed by her dreams, young Eva Duarte headed toward Buenos Aires, the glittering capital of Argentina. The year was 1934.

What she found in the city shocked her. Eva Duarte would say later, "I imagined that great cities were wonderful places where there were only riches. . . . But I found that it was not what I had imagined." Eva eventually became a popular radio actress, who met many politicians. In 1945, she married Juan Perón, an ambitious military officer. A year later, Perón was elected president of Argentina, making Eva "First Lady of Argentina."

During the presidential campaign, Eva helped her husband win the support of the "descamisados," or shirtless ones, as workers were called because they did not wear starched white shirts. The descamisados adored Evita, their name for the president's wife. They believed she was the one who made sure that campaign promises for better wages and working conditions were carried out. Their support for Evita helped Juan Perón against his opponents in the Argentine congress.

Evita defied the all-male tradition in government and took the jobs of Minister of Social Welfare and Secretary of Labor. She used government funds to set up orphanages and homes for young working women. To the women of the descamisados, she promised: "You too will have clothes [as rich as mine]. Some day you will be able to sit next to any rich woman on the basis of complete equality. What we are fighting for is to destroy the inequality between you and the wives of your bosses."

When Evita died in 1952, millions of descamisados mourned for her. Even when it was discovered that Eva Perón had helped herself to much of the wealth she had collected for the descamisados, her image was not tarnished in the eyes of the poor. To many of them, she still symbolized the rise from poverty to wealth.

The gap between rich and poor is one of the most serious problems facing the nations of Latin America. Since 1945, these nations have pursued the goals of modernization and economic development. They have also moved forcefully to take charge of their own destinies and reduce foreign influence. ■

1 Challenges of Modernization

READ TO UNDERSTAND

☐ **What problems have slowed economic progress in Latin America.**

☐ **Why many countries have introduced land reform.**

☐ **How modernization has affected Latin American societies.**

☐ *Vocabulary:* **liberation theology.**

"July 15—The birthday of my daughter Vera Eunice. I wanted to buy a pair of shoes for her, but the price of food keeps us from realizing our desires. Actually we are slaves to the cost of living. I found a pair of shoes in the garbage, washed them, and patched them for her to wear."

Those lines begin the diary of Carolina Maria de Jesus, a poor black woman from the slums of São Paulo, Brazil. Like millions of other people in urban slums, each day was a struggle to find food for herself and her three children. De Jesus, who left school after third grade, kept a record of her life. Almost by accident, she met a reporter who made sure her diary was published as *Child of the Dark*.

Most Latin American nations had won their independence by 1825, as you read in Chapter 27. Since then, they have tried to build stable governments and promote economic growth. Their efforts have met with mixed success, as the lines from the diary show.

The Population Explosion

Efforts to achieve economic growth in Latin America have been hindered by another kind of growth: the population explosion. Since 1940, the population of Latin America has more than doubled. Today, the rate of population growth in Latin America is second only to that of Africa.

The results of the population explosion are devastating. Most Latin American economies cannot expand fast enough to meet the basic needs of their people. Farmers cannot produce enough food, so malnutrition is common. People who lack adequate food are susceptible to diseases that limit their ability to work.

Poverty is a byproduct of the population explosion. It exists both in the countryside and in the cities. Yet many rural people believe that life in the cities is better. Millions of them stream into the cities each year. In Mexico City, for example, officials estimate that over 1,000 newcomers arrive every day.

All too often, the newcomers cannot find jobs or can obtain only temporary, poor-paying work. They crowd into tin shacks and lean-tos, creating vast slums. City governments cannot provide adequate sewage and garbage removal in these areas, and the urban poor often fall victim to disease. In spite of these problems, few people return to the countryside. In cities, they find what their poor villages lacked: the hope of work, schools for their children, medical care, and excitement.

Another byproduct of the population explosion is illiteracy. The illiteracy rate in Latin America is high, although it varies greatly. Countries with more developed economies provide better education than poor countries. Argentina, for example, has an illiteracy rate of only 7 percent. In poorer Guatemala, however, almost half of the people cannot read or write.

Although they may live in the same city, the people in these two pictures live in two different worlds. In the poor sections of the city, families are crowded into flimsy homes, and every day is a struggle. In middle-class areas, people enjoy many comforts, including good food and the chance for a fine education. The gap between rich and poor remains a major challenge for most Latin American nations.

Land and Landowning

Another obstacle to modernization in Latin America has been a shortage of land. Overall, less than 10 percent of the land is good for farming. This problem is made worse by the landowning system. For centuries, a few wealthy landlords controlled most of the land. As late as the 1950s, about 60 percent of all land in Latin America was in the hands of a few landowners, although the amount varied in each country.

The landowning system contributed to rural poverty. About 80 percent of the farm workers in Latin America had no land. They worked on the estates of large landowners, earning miserable wages and longing for plots of their own. Resentment against the uneven distribution of land has caused unrest among the landless poor.

Land reform programs. Before 1950, only Mexico had introduced large-scale land reform. Since then, however, many Latin American countries have done so. Bolivia, for example, took large amounts of land from absentee owners. In a 25-year period beginning in the mid-1950s, it distributed almost 75 million acres (30 million hectares) to some 590,000 peasant families. Venezuela also took over many large estates. Between 1960 and 1980, the government gave 20 million acres (8 million hectares) to 155,000 families that had never owned land before.

One of the most ambitious land reform programs was launched by El Salvador in 1980. The government broke up estates larger than 1,235 acres (500 hectares). It paid the owners and turned the land into cooperatives to be farmed by peasants.

Obstacles to increased farm production. Governments carried out land reform programs not only to meet peasants' needs but also to make the land more productive. Large landowners often left much of their land idle. Supporters of land reform argued that small landowners would farm all their land. And, it was hoped, owners with a personal stake in the products of their labor would work harder and produce more.

In most cases, however, farm production did not increase. Many of the new landowners lacked the money to buy fertilizer, tools, and

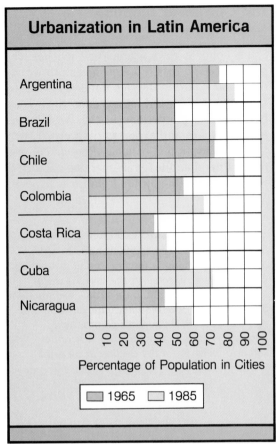

Source: World Bank, *World Development Report* (1987).

GRAPH STUDY *Growing urban populations are common whenever countries industrialize. As you have read, the population of cities in Western Europe and the United States grew rapidly in the 1800s as industry expanded. This graph shows how the urban population of seven Latin American nations grew between 1965 and 1985. In which countries did over 80 percent of the population live in cities in 1985? In which country did the percentage of urban population grow the most between 1965 and 1985?*

other improved technology. As a result, their output remained low.

Food production has not kept pace with the growing population for other reasons as well. In some countries, large landowners successfully opposed land reform efforts. Many of them use inefficient farming methods. For example, they prefer to hire landless workers at low wages rather than to buy modern machinery.

799

The Growth of Economic Nationalism

Since colonial days, Latin America has depended on exports. Foreign investors developed and exported the rich mineral resources of Brazil, Chile, and other countries. They bought large plantations in the West Indies and elsewhere and exported cash crops such as coffee, sugar, and bananas. Foreign companies, rather than the Latin American countries, reaped most of the profits from these exports.

Because of its oil resources, Venezuela enjoys the highest per capita income in Latin America. Oil profits are reflected in the two 50-story towers built in downtown Caracas. Such modern buildings dwarf the old city, with its cathedral and open plazas. Like other oil-producing nations, Venezuela has suffered economic setbacks because of the decline in oil prices.

Because Latin American rulers often benefited from foreign investments, they did little to encourage domestic businesses.

During the Great Depression of the 1930s, the world market for many exports collapsed. The resulting hard times showed how dependent Latin American nations were on strong economies in the industrial nations. World War II reinforced this lesson. During the war, Latin American nations suffered from shortages of the foreign manufactured goods they had always imported.

Since 1945, a spirit of economic nationalism has grown in Latin America. Many nations have tried to free themselves from dependence on Western Europe and North America for both goods and markets. They have developed local industries to produce goods that were once imported. And they have tried growing a variety of cash crops instead of depending on the export of just one or two.

Most nations have reduced their dependence on foreign investment. Venezuela, for example, took control of its highly profitable oil industry, which was previously run by foreign companies. In Brazil, the government has established an equal partnership with a foreign investor to make part of the Amazon jungle into a vast rice-, lumber-, and paper-producing area.

Economic growth has been uneven in Latin America. Mexico, Brazil, and Argentina have expanded faster than many other Latin American nations. The largest cities in Latin America are Buenos Aires, São Paulo, and Mexico City. About 30 percent of all goods manufactured in Latin America are produced in these metropolitan areas.

Movements for Social Change

Modernization has affected the social structure in Latin America. As industry has grown, a new upper class has emerged. Its members are people who have acquired vast wealth through business and industry. The middle class has also grown. It includes business and industry managers, white-collar office workers, and government employees.

In other respects, the social structure is unchanged. The old landowning upper class

Latin America: Economic Activities

Legend:
- ▲ Petroleum
- ● Chemical industries
- ✚ Textile industries
- ■ Mining industries

MAP STUDY *Latin American nations have diversified their economies to avoid relying on a single commodity. This map shows some of the crops and industries of Latin America. Which countries probably depend on oil revenues?*

continues to thrive. The lower classes, made up of farmers and urban workers, remain large and poor. As in colonial times, class divisions are tied to race.

Racial stereotypes help keep blacks, Indians, and dark-skinned mestizos in the lower classes. Whites dominate the upper classes. A black professor from a Brazilian university explained how salespeople who called at her house always assumed she was the maid.

The huge gap between rich and poor has spurred calls for far-reaching change, includ-

ing more land reform as well as programs to increase employment and improve living conditions. Among the leaders pushing for social change are students, middle-class intellectuals, and some clergy of the Roman Catholic Church. A number of priests have adopted a doctrine known as **liberation theology.** It calls for the Church to take an active role in changing conditions that have contributed to poverty.

Ambitious reform programs are expensive. Many Latin American governments lack the resources to pay for them. Further, the wealthy and middle classes have sometimes opposed reforms, such as minimum wages, seeing them as a limit on their freedom.

Failure to bring about social change has contributed to dangerous tensions. The poor want to escape from poverty and win a bigger piece of the economic pie. Especially in the cities, the unemployed and the working poor live in a climate of rising expectations. That is, they see the comforts and luxuries that others enjoy, and they want the same for themselves.

SECTION 1 REVIEW

1. **Define:** liberation theology.

2. Describe two ways in which the population explosion affects Latin American countries.

3. Why have Latin American governments introduced land reform programs?

4. How have Latin American nations reduced their dependence on foreign trade?

5. To what extent has modernization changed the social class structure in Latin America?

6. **Critical Thinking** Why has major social and economic change been difficult in Latin America?

---

2 Politics of Change

READ TO UNDERSTAND

☐ How the goals of the political right and left differ.

☐ Why many countries have moved back and forth between civilian and military rule.

☐ How Castro's communist revolution has affected Cuba.

"I have been in the party for some time now," says a Guatemalan farmer, "and all of the candidates for office pretend. They offer things,

but they never deliver them. They want to win our confidence so that they can win the election."

The farmer's distrust mirrors the attitude of many Latin Americans toward government. The nations of Latin America have witnessed much political unrest and violent change. Bolivia, for example, has had over 60 revolutions since it won independence in 1825. Yet few of the upheavals in Latin America have brought improvement to the majority of citizens.

Deep Political Divisions

Political instability results in part from the deep divisions within many Latin American nations. Groups on the political right and left differ over how much reform is needed and what direction it should take.

On the right are conservative groups, including wealthy industrialists and landowners. They want to preserve the traditional economic system that is the basis of their wealth and power. Conservative groups are often allied with the military. Although military officers generally come from the middle class, they usually oppose reforms that threaten the traditional order.

On the political left are many urban workers and rural poor, as well as students and intellectuals. They favor swift, sweeping reforms. Their goals include more land reform, higher wages, improved working conditions, and better housing. Many leftists support socialism. Thus, they call for nationalization of industries, whether domestic- or foreign-owned.

Many members of the middle class favor some kind of reform. Without it, they fear, the result might be violence and the loss of their comfortable way of life. Some want gradual, moderate reform. Others call for immediate, radical change.

High unemployment, overcrowded slums, and rural poverty have contributed to growing support for leftist groups. But leftists have also emerged in countries such as Argentina and Chile that have relatively high standards of living. Rightist groups, anxious to prevent a social revolution, have urged governments in many Latin American nations to suppress left-wing political parties.

Civilian Versus Military Rule

In many Latin American nations, control has shifted back and forth between civilian and military leaders. In a common pattern, a civilian government tries to improve social and economic conditions, but its efforts lead to turmoil.

The military then seizes power, and a military strongman imposes dictatorial rule. Eventually, the pressure builds to return the government to elected civilian leaders. In recent years, Argentina, Uruguay, and Chile have experienced shifts between civilian and military rule.

Argentina. As you read at the beginning of this chapter, Juan Perón was elected president of Argentina in 1946. He wanted to achieve economic self-sufficiency for Argentina and break the control of foreign interests.

Perón nationalized the railroads, increased workers' wages, and subsidized public works projects. This program was expensive and inflationary. As economic difficulties mul-

Rural poverty has contributed to political unrest in Latin America. Many of the rural poor are Indians whose way of life has changed little in generations. Here, an Indian woman in Bolivia prepares reeds for weaving. Her ancestors were part of the once-powerful Inca Empire.

"Contra La Dictadura" ("Against the Dictatorship") is painted on a wall by young protesters. Many people throughout Latin America hope for the success of democracy. However, democratic governments have often been undone by deep political, social, and economic divisions. Too often, government leaders have pretended to support democracy but in practice have ignored basic human rights.

tiplied, Perón used severe methods to quiet his critics. In 1955, the military overthrew him, and he went into exile in Spain.

The army controlled politics for the next 18 years. Yet Perónistas, or supporters of Perón, remained strong. In 1973, the aging Perón was invited back to Argentina. He ruled less than a year before he died. Power struggles between groups on the left and right led to turmoil and military intervention. The military government arrested thousands of suspected opponents. Most of them were never heard from again.

In 1982, the military government tried to win popular support by seizing the British-ruled Falkland Islands, off Argentina's shores. In the brief war that followed, Britain regained control of the Falklands. The next year, partly in reaction to the defeat, the military gave up power to a democratically elected civilian government.

Uruguay. Uruguay is one of the few Latin American countries that has a long tradition of democratic rule. In the early 1970s, however, the country suffered a grave economic crisis. At the same time, extremists on the left committed terrorist acts such as kidnappings, assassinations, and bombings. In 1973, determined to halt the disorder, the Uruguayan armed forces revolted against the elected government. Military leaders then used severe repression not only to combat terrorist groups but also to silence any kind of dissent.

Accustomed to individual freedoms and democratic processes, Uruguayans hated the military's repression. And they complained bitterly about the country's continuing economic problems. Finally, in 1985 military leaders allowed the election of a civilian government.

Chile. Like Uruguay, Chile had a tradition of democratic rule. Salvador Allende (ah

Until the military overthrew President Salvador Allende in 1973, Chileans had enjoyed a century of democracy. In the next 15 years, a whole generation of Chileans grew up knowing only the repressive dictatorship of General Augusto Pinochet. In 1988, Chileans renewed efforts to restore democracy in their nation. For the first time in years, opposition parties united to urge the people to "Vote No" to Pinochet's bid to remain in power.

YEHN day) was elected president of Chile in 1970. He had campaigned on a platform of socialist reform. Once in office, he began to put his reforms into effect. He nationalized industries and speeded up land reforms already under way.

On the right, industrialists and landowners tried to block Allende's reforms. On the left, some factory and farm workers protested that the new programs were not being pushed through fast enough. The middle class protested the inflation caused by Allende's reforms.

In 1973, as the unrest increased, the Chilean military overthrew the elected government. Allende was killed in the fighting. The military, headed by General Augusto Pinochet (pee noh SHAY), took power. In a brutal crackdown, thousands were arrested and killed. Pinochet's dictatorial regime did not solve Chile's economic and social problems. Pinochet lost a bid to remain in power past 1990. That year, the first freely elected president since 1973 took power, and Chileans welcomed a return to democracy.

In many Latin American countries that have experienced military rule, opponents of the regimes have kept democratic values alive. But protests against dictators are dangerous. In Chile and elsewhere, anti-government demonstrators have been tortured and killed. Military rulers have tried to justify their harsh policies by accusing opponents of seeking to promote communism.

Communist Revolution in Cuba

Although Cuba won its independence from Spain in 1898, Cubans had little control over their own economy. North American and European companies owned many businesses and controlled the major export crop, sugar.

A series of corrupt strongmen ruled Cuba. Unemployment was high, and people in rural areas lived on the edge of starvation. When Fulgencio Batista, an army sergeant, seized power in 1952, he did little to improve conditions.

In the 1950s, Fidel Castro emerged as a leader of revolutionaries opposed to the Batista government. Castro and a handful of rebels established their headquarters in the

On January 8, 1959, Fidel Castro entered Havana in triumph. At first, the new Cuban leader won strong support for his program of land reform and industrialization. A persuasive speaker, Castro used television speeches to explain his communist revolution to the Cuban people.

rugged Sierra Maestra mountains of Cuba. They waged guerrilla warfare against Batista's forces. Thousands of Cubans joined Castro. Finally, the rebels left their mountain stronghold and marched on Havana, the Cuban capital. On New Year's Day, 1959, Batista fled Havana. Five months later, Fidel Castro proclaimed himself premier.

At first, many Cubans welcomed Castro's successful revolution. However, divisions quickly arose between Castro and some of his followers. Soon after he gained power, Castro announced that he was a communist and that he intended to make Cuba a "socialist state." Some people who had allied themselves with Castro disapproved of this goal. Castro forced these opponents into exile.

To achieve his socialist state, Castro launched a massive land reform program. He set up large government-run farms and developed plans to industrialize Cuba. The government also offered free education to all Cubans, provided free health care, and built new public housing.

805

Cuba and the United States

The United States recognized the Castro government in 1959 and offered it aid. But American enthusiasm for Castro soon cooled when the new Cuban leader revealed his belief in communism. Support for Castro waned further after he took over some American-owned properties in Cuba without compensating the owners.

Worsening relations between Cuba and the United States led Castro to seek alliances with the Soviet Union and other communist nations. In 1960, Castro concluded an aid and trade pact with the Soviet Union. Soviet planners soon began arriving in Cuba. The United States grew anxious about Soviet influence in Cuba, which is only 90 miles (145 kilometers) off its southeastern coast.

Castro created further tension in the Western Hemisphere when he encouraged revolutions in other parts of Latin America. He urged poor rural workers and landless peasants to follow his example and organize guerrilla armies to overthrow the governments. He sent aid to rebels in Venezuela, Guatemala, and Bolivia.

The Bay of Pigs invasion. The United States strongly opposed the spread of communism in the Western Hemisphere. In January 1961, it cut off diplomatic relations with Cuba. Many Latin American nations followed suit. Meanwhile, thousands of Cubans had begun seeking refuge in the United States. They were mostly wealthy and middle-class people whose property Castro had seized.

In April 1961, about 2,000 Cuban exiles, trained and armed by the United States, launched an attack on their homeland. They landed at the Bay of Pigs on the southern coast. They hoped that their attack would spark a general uprising against Castro, but the invasion was a disaster. The United States hesitated to give air support, and the expected popular uprising against the government did not take place. About 300 attackers were killed. The rest were captured.

The Cuban missile crisis. After the Bay of Pigs incident, Cuba began building up its defenses. As you read in Chapter 32, in October 1962, the United States discovered that the Soviet Union was building missile bases in Cuba. President John F. Kennedy demanded that the Soviets dismantle the bases, which could be used to launch missiles against the United States.

When Soviet leader Nikita Khrushchev refused, President Kennedy announced a naval blockade of Cuba. American warships were ordered to prevent Soviet ships carrying missiles from reaching Cuba. After a tense showdown as Soviet ships approached the blockade, Khrushchev agreed to stop constructing the bases and to remove the missiles from Cuba.

Relations have improved little between the United States and Cuba since the 1960s. On several occasions, Castro has allowed Cubans opposed to his government to leave. Hundreds of thousands of Cubans have taken these opportunities to flee their homeland. Over 500,000 Cubans live in the Miami region of Florida. Many others have settled in Puerto Rico, Mexico, and Spain.

In 1977, the United States restored limited diplomatic relations with Cuba. But it has maintained a careful watch on Castro's activities inside Cuba as well as on his efforts to export his communist revolution abroad.

SECTION 2 REVIEW

1. **Locate:** (a) Argentina, (b) Uruguay, (c) Chile, (d) Cuba.

2. **Identify:** (a) Juan Perón, (b) Salvador Allende, (c) Augusto Pinochet, (d) Fidel Castro, (e) Bay of Pigs.

3. (a) What goals have groups on the political right supported in Latin America? (b) What goals have groups on the political left supported?

4. (a) Why did the military seize power in Uruguay in 1973? (b) Why did it step down?

5. How did Castro gain power in Cuba?

6. Explain why relations became hostile between Castro and the United States.

7. **Critical Thinking** What conditions have led the military to seize power in countries such as Argentina, Uruguay, and Chile?

3 Different Routes to Modernization

READ TO UNDERSTAND

☐ Why Mexico's economy has faced problems.

☐ Why unrest has disrupted many nations of Central America.

☐ How Venezuela and Brazil have progressed toward modernization.

"We are good people, industrious and capable," wrote the Cuban poet and patriot José Martí, who died fighting for his country's independence from Spain. Martí had a vision for Latin America. He saw it "redeeming itself from its confusion" and "living its own life." Today, people in much of Latin America are still struggling toward those goals.

The many nations of Latin America have taken different routes toward modernization with varied success. In this section, you will look at the progress and problems faced by several nations.

Change in Mexico

Mexico underwent a major political and social revolution in the early 1900s, as you read in Chapter 27. Since then, it has achieved a relatively stable government. The Mexican government has taken a strong hand in directing the nation's economy. It carried out a genuine land reform program in the 1930s. And it nationalized foreign-owned oil companies.

Mexico built up industry to supply many of its own consumer needs. Thus, it reduced its dependence on imports. Government-sponsored programs brought millions of acres of new farmland under cultivation. Schools in rural and urban areas helped increase literacy.

Thanks to its oil exports, Mexico's economy boomed in the 1970s. At the same time, Mexico borrowed heavily to finance further development. Then in 1980 came a drop in oil prices and a rise in interest rates. Those events caused a severe recession in Mexico. By the end of the 1980s, Mexico's economy had recovered somewhat. However, it was still

A devastating earthquake shook Mexico City on September 19, 1985. In a matter of minutes, 100 buildings collapsed, and more than 20,000 people were killed. Many other buildings were so badly damaged that they had to be torn down. In the years since the disaster, residents of Mexico City have rebuilt their shattered lives and homes.

burdened with a huge foreign debt, and unemployment remained high. Mexico's new president, Carlos Salinas, promised to encourage domestic and foreign investment. He also wanted to reduce government control of the economy.

A rapidly expanding population posed another challenge to economic growth. Many rural people cannot find work on farms and have flocked to the cities. As you have read, every week over 1,000 newcomers arrive in Mexico City. The government must find ways to provide basic services such as health care and education as well as jobs for the growing population. Some Mexicans have found work in assembly plants, called maquiladoras, set up by Japanese and American companies to take advantage of the cheap labor. Large num-

807

bers of Mexicans flow across the border into the United States in search of work and a better life.

Unrest in Central America

Mexico's neighbors in Central America have suffered unrest in recent decades. Central America includes the nations of Guatemala, Belize, Honduras, El Salvador, Nicaragua, Costa Rica, and Panama. Although the capital cities of these nations look modern, most people live in poverty-stricken rural areas.

The unrest has been due in part to corrupt military rule and the unequal distribution of wealth. Military rulers are usually supported by a small class of wealthy landowners and businesspeople. Peasants, urban workers, and students have united to demand reform. When their demands are not met, they have often formed rebel guerrilla movements.

Nicaragua. For years, Nicaragua was ruled by a corrupt strongman, Anastasio Somoza. In 1979, a revolution led by the Sandinista National Liberation Front overthrew Somoza and set up a government that included several political parties. Before long, the leftist Sandinistas, led by Daniel Ortega, gained the upper hand. They introduced socialist economic reforms and built ties with

DAILY LIFE Rigoberta Menchú: An Indian Woman Speaks

"My name is Rigoberta Menchú. I am 23 years old. This is my testimony. It is also the testimony of my people." With these words, Menchú begins her story in *I . . . Rigoberta Menchú*. She belongs to the Quiché (kee CHAY) Indian group, one of 22 ethnic groups who live in Guatemala. Until she was 20, Menchú spoke only Quiché. But then she learned Spanish in order to help her people fight for their land.

As a child, Menchú learned the ways of her people. They stressed community and their connections with the earth. "From very small children we receive an education that is very different from white children. We Indians have more contact with nature. That's why they call us polytheistic. But we're not polytheistic. Or if we are, it's good, because it's our culture, our customs. We worship—or rather not worship but respect—a lot of things to do with the natural world, the most important things for us. For instance, water is sacred. Water is pure, clean, and gives life."

When she was 12, Menchú learned about the Catholic religion. "By accepting the Catholic religion," she says, "we didn't abandon our own culture. It was more like another way of expressing ourselves. We accept the forefathers of the Bible as if they were our own ancestors, while still keeping within our own culture and our own customs."

Like many Indians of Latin America, the Quiché are very poor. Menchú and her family worked on the fincas, or large plantations. "I remember going down to the finca when I was just 14, and a friend and I were sent picking cotton. One day, she died of poisoning when they were spraying the cotton."

Menchú's father organized his community to stop landowners from seizing land cleared and farmed by the Indians. Menchú's mother and brother were brutally tortured by government soldiers. Her father, too, died in the struggles.

Menchú turned to the Bible, finding examples in its stories to inspire her people. "There is the story of David, a little shepherd boy who was able to defeat the king of those days, King Goliath."

The government of Guatemala has accused Menchú and other Indian leaders of being revolutionaries. Menchú, however, sees the struggles in other terms. To her, the Indians' struggle began 500 years ago when the Spanish seized the land from her ancestors. The Indians of today are fighting to preserve their heritage and dignity in the face of centuries of rejection and discrimination.

1. What use would Menchú make of her ability to speak Spanish?

2. **Critical Thinking** In what way does Menchú represent Indians of all Latin American countries, not only of Guatemala?

China, Cuba, and the Soviet Union. When moderate and right-wing candidates failed to win in elections, some of them turned to armed attack.

Rightist guerrilla forces opposed the Sandinistas from the outset. By 1985, the largest anti-government group, the Contras, was based in Honduras. The United States aided the Contras with arms and money. Some Americans favored giving aid because they feared that Nicaragua would become a communist stronghold. Others objected to American intervention in Central America. They warned of another Vietnam. After years of civil war, the Contras and Sandinistas agreed to a cease-fire in 1988. Although the fighting lessened, talks between the Sandinistas and Contras produced few results.

El Salvador. In the 1970s, El Salvador was plunged into bloody turmoil. Terrorist groups on the right and left killed thousands and disrupted daily life. "Death squads" from the extreme right assassinated anyone they suspected of leftist sympathies. In the meantime, leftist guerrillas, aided by Cuba and other communist countries, held large parts of the country.

Under pressure from the United States, the government of El Salvador introduced some land reform and held elections. However, long-term stability appeared unlikely because of deep divisions within the country and unsolved economic problems.

Costa Rica. The bright spot in Central America has been Costa Rica. One observer called it "a small democracy with an enlightened citizenry."

Costa Rica has enjoyed political stability and achieved a better standard of living than its neighbors partly because land there was more evenly divided than elsewhere. It was not concentrated in the hands of a few. In addition, the government has set up health and education programs to help the poor. In 1987, Costa Rica's president Oscar Arias won the Nobel Peace Prize for his efforts to negotiate a peace settlement for Central America.

Oil in Venezuela

Like Costa Rica, Venezuela has had a stable democratic government. Largely because of

In recent years, Central America has been the scene of fierce guerrilla fighting. Guerrillas, such as these young men and women in El Salvador, are waging war against governments they claim represent only wealthy landlords and industrialists. The fighting in El Salvador and in other parts of Central America has taken a large toll among civilians.

its vast petroleum deposits, Venezuela has enjoyed economic growth. Oil has given Venezuela the highest average income of any Latin American nation.

The Venezuelan government nationalized the oil industry in 1976. It paid foreign companies—mostly American—for their holdings. The government vowed to "sow the petroleum revenues back into the soil." Thus, it worked to improve agriculture by teaching farmers new planting methods. It introduced land reform to give small farmers their own land. In addition, education and health care were extended into rural areas. Today, more than 80 percent of the people are literate.

Venezuela has suffered from the oil boom and bust. The government also knows that its oil reserves will eventually run out. It is, therefore, developing other industries. However, the effort has had limited success.

As Venezuela heads into the last years of the twentieth century, it faces several challenges. It must battle widespread corruption, high inflation, and a growing gap between rich and poor.

809

A Balancing Act in Brazil

For several decades, Brazil has dreamed of entering the twenty-first century as one of the world's industrial giants. That dream has run into problems, however. Like many other nations of Latin America, Brazil faces the combined problems of economic recession, soaring inflation, a burdensome debt, and political mismanagement. "We are going the wrong way on the avenue of history," commented a Brazilian economist.

As in most Latin American countries, the government in Brazil has played a central role in directing the economy. Government funds and private capital allowed Brazil to develop into the most highly industrialized nation in the region. It developed new industries such

---

GEOGRAPHY IN HISTORY The Vanishing Rain Forests

- A plant whose leaves form a water tank that holds up to 12 gallons of water where mosquitoes and tree frogs breed.
- Ants traveling in packs of 20 million, breaking down lichen, moss, twigs, and other insects into food for their queen.
- An eel that can send an electric charge of 600 volts to stun prey as large as a horse.

These are a few of the more than 5 million species of plants, insects, and animals that inhabit the rain forests of Central and South America. Yet the rain forests of the Americas— and the world—are rapidly vanishing. In 1987, in Brazil alone, 77,000 square miles (199,430 square kilometers) of rain forest were cleared.

Axes, fire, and bulldozers, like those here, are used to strip the land of trees and other plant life. In Central America, ranchers have cleared tens of thousands of acres in order to raise beef cattle for export to the United States. In Brazil, more than 20 percent of the Amazon rain forest has been cleared for plantations, hydroelectric dams, and other development projects.

Dangers to the environment have been ignored. Yet the vanishing rain forests are home to many plants that are used in medicines such as anti-cancer drugs. Scientists believe that certain forest insects might act as natural pesticides, allowing us to reduce our dependence on chemical pesticides.

In Brazil, the clearing of the rain forests has ended a way of life for tens of thousands of Indians. Many have died from diseases introduced by miners, loggers, and road builders. Scientists are rushing to preserve the knowledge of Indians who understand the healing value of many plants.

Scientists point out that rain forests influence climate patterns around the world. The rain forests suck up and hold moisture that is recycled into the atmosphere. Without the forests, floods and mudslides ruin the land. In addition, the rain forests produce oxygen for the atmosphere.

The rain forests pose a dilemma for the nations of Latin America: How to meet the demands of progress without destroying an important balance in nature. Long-term planners are working toward solutions that would allow the commercial development of the rain forests while preserving as much of them as possible.

1. Name two undesirable effects of the disappearance of rain forests in Latin America.

2. **Critical Thinking** Explain how the vanishing rain forests are a local, national, and international problem.

as steel, heavy machinery, and chemicals. At the same time, older industries such as textile manufacturing remained strong. Service industries also grew, accounting for about 60 percent of Brazil's economic output.

Agriculture received less government support than did industry. Yet agricultural exports accounted for much of Brazil's exports. Coffee, cotton, cacao beans, and beef were major exports. The government set up programs to exploit natural resources of inland areas, including the vast Amazon rain forest region. In the late 1980s, however, as people became aware of the dangers of destroying the rain forest, the government had to limit expansion in this area.

During the 1970s, Brazil enjoyed strong economic growth. However, that expansion contributed to social problems. Under the military government that ruled the country from 1964 to 1985, the middle and upper classes prospered. The poor did not. In the crowded favelas, or urban slums, they lived in flimsy shacks and barely survived. Millions of poor children never attended school. Disease and malnutrition were widespread.

The military was unable to solve the problem of a growing population of desperately poor people. In 1985, it stepped aside, allowing a civilian government to be elected. The new government faced a difficult balancing act. The nation had a staggering foreign debt of $110 billion. It needed additional money to finance crucial projects to boost earnings. It also had to ease the crisis facing the poor.

The civilian leaders want to preserve the fragile democracy that is emerging, but the economic hardships threaten stability. The military remains strong, and Brazilians fear that it might move to regain power if future elections put the government into the hands of the left.

SECTION 3 REVIEW

1. **Locate:** (a) Mexico, (b) Nicaragua, (c) El Salvador, (d) Costa Rica, (e) Venezuela, (f) Brazil.

2. **Identify:** (a) Anastasio Somoza, (b) Sandinistas, (c) Daniel Ortega, (d) Contras, (e) Oscar Arias.

3. Why did Mexico suffer from an economic recession after 1980?

4. (a) Give two reasons for unrest in Central America. (b) How is Costa Rica different from most countries in the region?

5. Why were the military rulers in Brazil replaced by civilian leaders?

6. **Critical Thinking** Compare the efforts of Mexico, Venezuela, and Brazil to achieve economic growth.

4 Latin America and the World

READ TO UNDERSTAND

☐ How Latin American nations have cooperated to increase trade and limit conflict.

☐ How the debt crisis has affected Latin American nations.

☐ What role the United States has played in Latin America.

Latin America is made up of over 40 nations. Their political and economic interests vary, and they pursue diverse foreign policies. Despite their difference, Latin American nations have made efforts to cooperate for mutual benefit.

Regional Cooperation

Some efforts at cooperation involve regional trade. For example, Mexico and ten South American nations formed the Latin American Free Trade Area (LAFTA) in the 1960s. Its goals were to break down trade barriers and thereby increase trade among member nations. Increased trade, LAFTA members hoped, would stimulate production and lessen their dependence on the United States and other foreign trading partners.

LAFTA has had limited success, however. Members with relatively little industry found it difficult to trade with more industrialized members. They could not produce enough to afford the goods of their richer partners.

Despite problems, efforts at regional cooperation have continued. Five nations—Colombia, Ecuador, Peru, Bolivia, and Venezuela—belong to the Andean Common Market, which works for regional economic goals. Two similar organizations are the Central American Common Market and a Caribbean trade group called Caricom.

Another example of regional cooperation is the aid offered by Mexico and Venezuela, two oil-producing nations. Despite the recent decline in oil prices, many poor Latin American nations have trouble paying for imported oil. To help them, Mexico and Venezuela have extended credit to Latin American nations, which must import oil.

The largest regional organization is the Organization of American States (OAS). It was founded in 1948 by 21 American republics, including the United States. The chief OAS aims are to uphold the independence of its members and preserve peace in the Western Hemisphere. On several occasions, the OAS has successfully put pressure on member nations to end armed conflict with one another. It has also condemned the intervention of one member nation in the affairs of another.

Another agent of regional cooperation is the Inter-American Development Bank (IADB), founded in 1959. Its members include Latin American countries, the United States, Canada, and several European nations. Members contribute to a common fund. The IADB then makes loans to governments and private companies for specific projects, such as building roads or factories.

The Debt Crisis

By the 1980s, many Latin American nations—like developing nations everywhere—were deeply in debt, and some faced bankruptcy. The problem grew out of the sharp rise in oil prices in the 1970s. Because modern industry is largely fueled by oil, many developing nations had to borrow money to pay for the higher oil costs. They also borrowed to finance programs to improve farming and industry. Even oil-producing countries such as Mexico borrowed in order to increase their production.

Banks encouraged Third World nations to borrow heavily. Many banks had surplus money deposited by the rich OPEC nations. They wanted to put that money to work through investing overseas. Thus, between 1970 and 1980, the foreign debt owed by Latin American nations rose from $15 billion to over $220 billion.

In 1980, interest rates rose sharply. Interest rates are the amounts lenders charge borrowers for the use of their the money. The new rates placed a huge burden on debtor nations. Several announced that they would not be able to meet their interest payments.

GRAPH STUDY *This graph shows the growing foreign debt of Mexico. How would you describe the growth of foreign debt in Mexico between 1975 and 1987?*

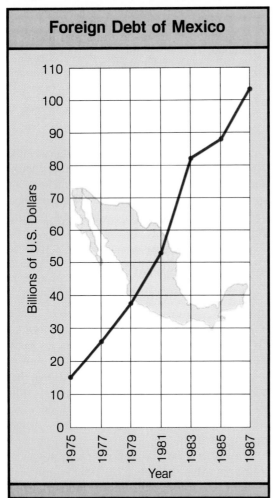

Source: *CIA Handbook of Economic Statistics.*

The nations of Latin America have produced many well-known artists and writers, including such Nobel prize winners as Pablo Neruda and Gabriel Garcia Márquez. One popular art form is the colorful paintings of Haitian artists. In this painting, rural workers harvest corn.

To ease the debt crisis, creditors and debtors worked out various "debt restructuring" arrangements. Interest rates were lowered, the period for repayment was lengthened, or part of the debt was canceled.

The debt crisis had eased somewhat by the late 1980s. Most debtor nations were making interest payments, but their economies had slowed drastically. Also, their already low standards of living slipped even more because money had to be spent on repaying the loans and not on development programs.

The United States and Latin America

Relations between the United States and the nations of Latin America have been marked both by friendship and tension. The United States has extended aid to the people of Latin America. And American movies, fashions, and products are popular there. However, many Latin Americans feel threatened by the United States because of its dominant position in the Western Hemisphere.

Intervention. The United States has a long history of intervention in Latin America. In the early 1900s, you will recall, it sent troops into several Latin American countries to protect American business interests.

In recent decades, the fear of communism has led the United States to use military force against leftist governments. It helped to overthrow a leftist government in Guatemala in 1954 and sent troops into the Dominican Republic in 1965. And as you have read, it trained Cuban exiles for the Bay of Pigs invasion in 1961.

The United States sent aid to anti-Allende groups in Chile in the early 1970s. In 1983, it invaded Grenada, a tiny island nation that had developed close ties with Cuba. It has also supported the Contras in Nicaragua and taken a strong stand against leftist rebels in other Central American countries.

In 1989, President Bush sent troops into Panama with orders to capture Panamanian strongman General Manuel Noriega. Noriega had been indicted in the United States on drug trafficking charges. He had also refused to turn over power to an elected president. In early 1990, Noriega surrendered to United States forces. Many Panamanians welcomed the overthrow of Noriega, but elsewhere in Latin America, people condemned the invasion as yet another example of United States intervention.

Cooperation. Since the "Good Neighbor Policy" of the 1930s, the United States has tried to work with the nations of Latin America in a spirit of partnership. One such attempt was the Alliance for Progress, begun in 1961. It aimed to bring about major social change through a vast aid program. Along with private investors, the United States contributed over $10 billion. But the program was too ambitious, and little change took place.

Another attempt at cooperation involved the Panama Canal. Many Latin American nations, especially Panama, objected to United States control of the Canal Zone. In 1978, the United States signed a treaty with Panama. It set up a timetable to give Panama complete control of the Canal Zone by 2000. Until then, the Canal would be operated by an agency made up of Americans and Panamanians.

Illegal immigration. The huge flow of illegal immigrants from Latin America to the United States has created tensions. Many people from Latin America are attracted by the high standard of living in the north. Others seek safety from repressive governments. Estimates put the number of illegal aliens who slipped into the United States each year in the 1980s at between 500,000 and 1 million. Many people filter across the border from Mexico into Texas, Arizona, New Mexico, and California.

In 1986, the United States passed a law to control illegal immigration. It allowed illegal aliens who had been in the country since 1982 to apply for legal status. But it forbade employers to hire workers who did not have documents proving that they were in the United States legally.

Illegal immigration is a problem for Mexico as well. At least a million illegals have fled to Mexico from Central America. Their needs have strained Mexico's limited resources.

The drug trade. Latin America is the chief source of illegal drugs smuggled into the United States. The drug trade is big business in parts of Latin America. High level officials in some nations are involved in it. Until Colombia declared war on drug lords in 1989, drug dealers virtually controlled the nation's second largest city of Medellin.

The drug trade has brought billions of dollars to drug lords in Latin America. Many Latin American governments have taken steps to curb the growing and smuggling of drugs, as this burning of cocaine in Bolivia proves. However, their efforts have made no dent in the pipeline that supplies drugs to the United States and other nations.

For poor farmers in the Andes, coca is a far more profitable crop than potatoes. Coca grown in Peru and Bolivia is transported to processing centers in Colombia, where it is made into cocaine. From there, it is shipped by boat or plane to the United States.

The United States has put great pressure on Latin American governments to stop the illegal drug trade. The governments have destroyed marijuana crops, raided cocaine factories, and seized drug shipments. But their efforts to stop the powerful drug lords have been undermined by bribery and violence. Drug enforcement agents, prosecutors, and judges have been murdered. Many experts argue that the flood of drugs from Latin America and elsewhere will not stop until the demand for drugs in the United States is curbed.

Human Rights Issues

Turmoil in Latin America has led to violations of human rights. Human rights include freedom of speech, religion, and the press. They also include the right to a fair trial, to earn a living, and to live in safety from attack. Governments that fear revolution clamp down on free expression, close universities, and jail, torture, or murder critics.

Human rights abuses have occurred in many Latin American countries. Dictators in Haiti, Cuba, and, until recently, Paraguay, have committed brutal acts against individuals. Abuses occurred in Brazil, Uruguay, and Chile when those nations were under military rule.

In many parts of Central America, people who work for change risk jail, torture, and murder. In El Salvador and Guatemala, for example, members of labor unions face death threats. Nicaragua has stifled opposition by closing anti-government newspapers.

In the 1970s, the military in Argentina arrested and tortured thousands of citizens. Between 9,000 and 20,000 people became known as the desaparecidos—the disappeared. They were arrested and were never heard from again. Relatives of the disappeared organized protests. Many nations condemned Argentina's military rulers. In 1983, after civilian rule was restored, the government held trials of military officers accused of torturing and executing prisoners.

Families of the "desaparecidos" hold pictures of their loved ones, hoping against hope to learn that they are still alive. In Argentina, Chile, and elsewhere, thousands of people have disappeared without a trace. In many cases, the "disappeared" have been arrested and tortured before being killed. International organizations monitor human rights violations and bring pressure on governments to free people imprisoned because of their beliefs.

SECTION 4 REVIEW

1. **Identify:** (a) LAFTA, (b) Andean Common Market, (c) OAS.

2. (a) What were two goals of LAFTA? (b) What are the chief goals of OAS?

3. Describe two aims of United States policy toward Latin American nations.

4. How has political turmoil contributed to human rights violations in Latin America?

5. **Critical Thinking** How do forces outside the control of Latin America, such as oil prices and interest rates, affect the economies of that region?

Summary

1. The nations of Latin America face many challenges as they try to achieve modernization. The population explosion has put a severe strain on Latin American economies. Moreover, traditional landholding systems have limited economic development. Nevertheless, most Latin American nations have taken steps to industrialize.

2. Divisions between the political left and right have caused turmoil in many nations. To end turmoil, the military has seized power in many Latin American countries. When military governments failed to solve economic problems, some were replaced by democracies. The communist revolution in Cuba brought about changes in the economy and the lives of the people.

3. Latin American countries have followed various routes to modernization. Mexico and Venezuela used oil wealth to modernize and were deeply affected by the oil glut of the 1980s. Political unrest has marked much of Central America. Although Brazil has expanded its industry, it has done so by borrowing heavily.

4. Latin American nations have cooperated with one another for mutual benefit. To further trade, they have formed regional trade organizations. Relations with the United States have sometimes been strained, although the United States has given much aid to the region. Illegal immigration to the United States and the drug trade have created tensions in the hemisphere.

Recalling Facts

Choose the word or phrase that best completes each of the following statements.

1. An obstacle to modernization in Latin America has been (a) land reform; (b) the population explosion; (c) the spread of communism.

2. Leftist political groups in Latin America want to (a) preserve the traditional economic system; (b) introduce moderate changes; (c) bring about wide-ranging reform.

3. Salvador Allende was elected president of (a) Cuba; (b) Uruguay; (c) Chile.

4. Fidel Castro angered the United States when he (a) nationalized foreign-owned companies; (b) led a revolution against Fulgencio Batista; (c) began industrializing Cuba.

5. A major cause of unrest in Central America is (a) overcrowded cities; (b) the gap between rich and poor; (c) industrialization.

6. São Paulo is a major industrial city in (a) Brazil; (b) Argentina; (c) Venezuela.

Chapter Checkup

1. Explain why the following are problems in Latin America: (a) the population explosion; (b) the landowning system; (c) divisions between political right and left.

2. (a) Why do some people in Latin America demand social change? (b) What kinds of change do they think are necessary?

3. (a) How did the military takeovers in Uruguay and Chile affect these countries? (b) Why was military government replaced in some Latin American countries?

4. Describe the progress made toward modernization in: (a) Mexico; (b) Venezuela; (c) Brazil.

5. (a) How did the Sandinistas rise to power in Nicaragua? (b) Why did the United States aid the Contras?

6. How does the illegal drug trade affect both the United States and Latin America?

Critical Thinking

1. **Comparing** Compare the efforts of Latin American nations to modernize to those of

African nations. (a) How are they similar? (b) How are they different?

2. **Relating Past to Present** Review the structure of colonial society in Latin America. (See page 602.) (a) How has this structure remained the same? (b) How has it changed? (c) Why do you think it has not changed more?

3. **Understanding the Roots of Democracy** (a) Explain the cycle of civilian and military rule that has taken place in some Latin American countries. (b) How do social and economic conditions cause problems for democratic governments?

4. **Evaluating** Some Latin American nations have denounced United States policy toward Latin America as "Yankee imperialism." (a) Why do some Latin American nations see the United States as a threat? (b) How has the United States moved toward greater partnership with Latin American nations?

Developing Basic Skills

1. **Graph Reading** Study the graph on page 812. (a) What was Mexico's foreign debt in 1979? In 1985? (b) How much did the debt increase between 1981 and 1983? (c) What development in the early 1980s helps explain that increase?

2. **Researching** Choose one of the nations of Central America. Research its recent history. (a) What is the population of the country? (b) How do most of the people earn a living? (c) What is the per capita income? (d) What economic progress, if any, has the country made in recent years? (e) Have economic conditions affected political developments? Explain.

Writing About History

Creating a Graph
You may find it useful to create a graph to illustrate a topic in your research paper when you have important statistical data. The most common types of graphs are circle graphs, line graphs, and bar graphs. The choice of the type of graph you use depends on the information you want to display and the impact you want to make.

Practice: The following table shows Latin American population from 1950. Decide which is the best type of graph to display this information, then create the graph.

Year	Population (in millions)
1950	165
1955	192
1960	217
1965	249
1970	284
1975	322
1980	362
1985	379
1990 (est.)	417

Source: *Demographic Yearbook,* 1988.

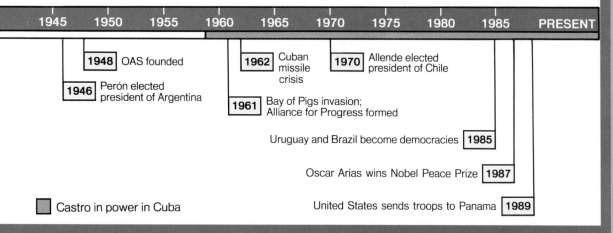

1945   1950   1955   1960   1965   1970   1975   1980   1985   PRESENT

1948 OAS founded

1946 Perón elected president of Argentina

1962 Cuban missile crisis

1961 Bay of Pigs invasion; Alliance for Progress formed

1970 Allende elected president of Chile

Uruguay and Brazil become democracies **1985**

Oscar Arias wins Nobel Peace Prize **1987**

Castro in power in Cuba

United States sends troops to Panama **1989**

Europe and the United States

37

(1968–Present)

Few people expected the rapid political and economic changes that began in 1989 in Eastern Europe and the Soviet Union. Demands for greater democracy were heard throughout the region. Within the Soviet Union, many national groups also demanded independence. This demonstration, in the shadow of Lenin, took place in Baku, Azerbaijan.

Scene 1   Duke William glared at the weather-vane. After two weeks of waiting for a favorable wind, he was impatient to be off. Finally, a wind with a southerly slant blew. William boarded the *Mora* and ordered his fleet to set sail across the English Channel. The next day, William of Normandy landed in England. A few weeks later, his army defeated King Harold's Saxon forces at the Battle of Hastings. The year: 1066. The outcome: England was conquered by the Normans.

Scene 2   The Duke of Medina Sidonia had declined the honor, but it had been forced on him. On that fateful Friday in July, he hoisted the banner blessed by the pope and led a huge invasion fleet into the English Channel. For three weeks, the ships of the Spanish Armada were harried by the English. The year: 1588. The outcome: The Spanish Armada was put to flight.

Scene 3 Napoleon's secretary scribbled rapidly as the emperor dictated. "Memo to be forwarded to Monge to find out if it is worth trying a large-scale experiment." The memo described a plan for an airborne invasion of England using huge hot-air balloons. Each would carry 1,000 men, 25 horses, food, and arms. The year: 1808. The outcome: No airborne landing took place.

Scene 4 A formation of German bombers chased across the English Channel. Along the east coast of England, air raid sirens screamed. Soon the ack-ack of anti-aircraft fire mixed with the noisy explosion of bombs. The year: 1940. The outcome: Hitler's attempt to destroy British morale in the Battle of Britain failed. He did not invade the island nation.

Scene 5 Huge earth scoopers dig deep into the ground at Sangatte, on the French side of the English Channel. Tunneling machines stand ready to undertake the next step in the construction. The year: 1987. The outcome: Excavations begin for "Chunnel," an underground rail tunnel beneath the English Channel and the first fixed link between Britain and France.

Only a few miles separate Britain from the continent of Europe, but some dramatic moments in European history have taken place on the waters of the English Channel. The drama of the past has given way to the technology of today. Work is moving swiftly on Chunnel, Europe's biggest construction project of the century. It is expected to open in 1993.

Chunnel adds to the growing number of links among the nations of Europe. As the world moves toward 2000, many old barriers, such as the English Channel, are receding. The Berlin Wall has crumbled, and the icy blasts of the cold war are fading under the dramatic changes sweeping Eastern Europe. In recent years, the nations of Western Europe have moved toward increased cooperation in economic and political affairs. At the same time, individual countries have maintained a sense of their own national identities. ■

1 Changing Outlooks in Western Europe

READ TO UNDERSTAND

- ☐ What sparked protests in the 1960s and 1970s.
- ☐ What economic challenges Western European nations faced.
- ☐ How Greece, Spain, and Portugal restored democracy.
- ☐ *Vocabulary:* privatization, Ostpolitik.

"To the barricades!" "Down with the government!" The cries of student protesters echoed through the streets of Paris. Burning cars, piles of bricks, and massed ranks of police bore witness to the uprisings. The spring of 1968 saw a wave of protests erupt in universities across Europe.

Emerging Trends

Student protesters demanded reforms in both the universities and society. Students deeply resented government and business leaders, whom they called "the establishment."

The most serious student unrest took place at the Sorbonne, part of the University of Paris. There, students and police fought pitched battles. Many French workers went on strike to show sympathy for the students. Workers demanded changes in work rules and higher wages. For a time, the protests threatened the government of French president Charles de Gaulle.

Student uprisings spread to West Germany, Belgium, Britain, and Italy. In the end, the protests led to more student participation in school administration. Workers, too, gained some say over factory operations.

Anti-nuclear movement. The 1968 student protests drew people's attention to a number of issues and emerging trends. For example, some people showed great concern with what came to be called the "quality of life," meaning a clean, humane environment in which to live and work. The protests also spurred concern about the spread of nuclear weapons.

As you have read, NATO nations prepared to meet any Soviet challenge to Western Europe by maintaining strong military forces. By the late 1960s and the 1970s, those forces were relying more and more on nuclear weapons.

Anti-nuclear activists in Great Britain and West Germany blocked entrances to military bases where nuclear weapons were stored.

They campaigned hard to prevent NATO nations from installing newer, more modern weapon systems. Extremists went beyond civil disobedience, using terrorist attacks on government leaders. The majority of people in Western Europe saw NATO as essential to their security but were concerned about the dangers of nuclear war. The growing debate over nuclear weapons fueled efforts to reach arms control agreements, as you will read later in this chapter.

Concern for human rights. Many groups and individuals in Western Europe have taken up the cause of human rights. A British-based group, Amnesty International, monitored human rights violations around the world. In 1975, at the Helsinki Conference on Security and Cooperation, 35 nations including the United States and the Soviet Union pledged to honor human rights such as freedom of thought and religion. Since then, human rights activists have tried to get governments to abide by the Helsinki Agreement.

Women's new awareness. By the late 1960s, the women's liberation movement had

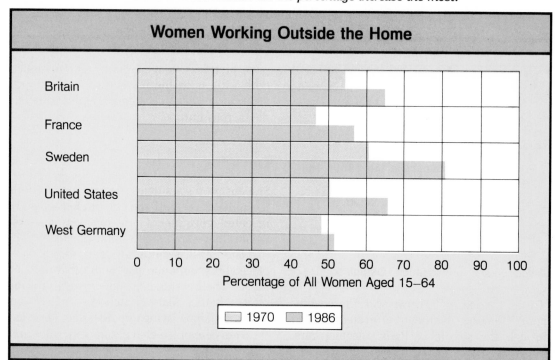

GRAPH STUDY *The number of women who work outside the home rose between 1970 and 1986. This has led to important social changes such as the growing need for day care. How did the percentage of women working outside the home change in France? In which nation did the percentage increase the most?*

Women Working Outside the Home

Britain

France

Sweden

United States

West Germany

0   10   20   30   40   50   60   70   80   90   100

Percentage of All Women Aged 15–64

☐ 1970   ☐ 1986

820

Source: *Statistical Abstract of the United States* (1988).

Unemployment Rates in Four Western Nations

	Percentage of Civilian Labor Force Unemployed				
	1980	1982	1984	1986	1988
Britain	6.5	11.8	11.4	11.6	11.0
France	6.6	8.4	10.0	10.7	11.0
United States	7.2	9.7	7.5	7.0	6.6
West Germany	3.4	6.8	8.1	7.9	7.6

Source: International Monetary Fund, *World Economic Outlook*

CHART STUDY *During the 1980s, unemployment was a stubborn economic problem. In which two countries shown on the graph was unemployment the highest in the late 1980s? Describe the trend in West Germany.*

emerged in Western Europe. As more women took jobs outside the home, they demanded equal pay, a better education, and the same job opportunities as men. By the late 1980s in some countries, more than 70 percent of women were employed outside the home. Many women working outside the home were mothers of young children. They sought affordable day care from employers or the government.

In Western Europe and elsewhere, divorce rates rose, leaving many women as the single heads of households. Women usually earned less than men. Or if they had young children, they could not pursue careers unless low-cost child care was available. As a result, many families headed by women fell close to or below the poverty level.

Economic Affairs

By the late 1960s, the economic growth of the postwar period was slowing down. Serious inflation threatened Western Europe, especially after 1973, when oil prices quadrupled. As you read in Chapter 32, most Western European nations had set up social welfare programs. Inflation pushed up the cost of these programs. As a result, a larger percentage of the national budget went into paying for social services.

Under the pressures of inflation and economic slowdown, many governments had to cut back on spending. By the early 1980s, infla-

tion had been brought under control but at the cost of the highest unemployment since the 1930s.

France and Britain. Both France and Britain experienced economic crises in the 1970s and 1980s. In 1981, François Mitterand, a socialist, was elected president of France. His government was the first leftist government in France since the Popular Front of the 1930s.

Mitterand proceeded slowly with plans to nationalize certain businesses. In 1986, however, the political right won a majority in the French National Assembly. Although Mitterand remained as president, the right-wing leader, Jacques Chirac, became prime minister. He won passage of a law for **privatization,** the selling of state-owned industries to private investors. In France, 65 companies that had been nationalized were returned to private ownership. In 1988, Mitterand won a second seven-year term as president, defeating Chirac's attempt to win the top office.

In Britain, Labour and Conservative governments alternated in the 1960s and 1970s. Neither had much success controlling inflation and reducing unemployment. In 1979, Conservative party leader Margaret Thatcher became Britain's first woman prime minister. She won reelection throughout the 1980s, breaking all modern records for remaining in office.

Known as Britain's "Iron Lady" for her firm policies, Thatcher tried to reduce government spending. Inflation slowed, but unem-

Britain's "Iron Lady," Prime Minister Margaret Thatcher, shows that she can take on any job, even that of bricklayer. Like leaders of other western governments, Thatcher has struggled to reduce her country's budget and trade deficits. By the late 1980s, unemployment was falling in Britain, and Thatcher was promising further tax cuts.

ployment soared. Thatcher saw as her mission to save Britain from socialism. She therefore pushed privatization, selling many industries that had been nationalized by earlier governments. State-owned companies, Thatcher argued, were inefficient and operated at great losses. Once they were returned to private ownership, they would have to be more efficient to survive.

Common Market. The economic problems of recent decades have posed problems for the Common Market. Since the 1970s, the European Economic Community, or Common Market, has grown from 6 to 12 members. In 1973, Britain, Ireland, and Denmark joined. Greece was admitted in 1981. The addition of Spain and Portugal in 1986 meant that the Common Market served over 300 million people.

The Common Market has achieved some successes in lowering trade barriers and establishing a system of exchange rates for member nations. It has given aid to Third World nations and has undertaken programs to compete against Japan and the United States in fields such as telecommunications and biotechnology.

Because the enlarged Common Market has had to balance a wide range of national interests, progress on many issues has been slow. Individual members often vetoed or found ways to get around majority decisions they did not like. Agreeing on a common agricultural policy and solving its budget crisis were two major problems facing the Common Market.

The Spread of Democracy in Western Europe

During the mid-1970s, three European nations ruled by dictators—Greece, Portugal, and Spain—became democracies. Since 1967, Greece had been ruled by right-wing military officers known as "the colonels." They had suspended the constitution and imposed a harsh authoritarian regime. In 1974, however, the colonels were forced out of power, and constitutional government was restored.

In Portugal, Antonio Salazar had ruled as dictator since the 1930s. After his death, Portugal moved gradually toward democracy. In 1976, it held its first free elections in more than 50 years.

Spain had been ruled by dictator Francisco Franco since the Spanish Civil War. (See page 692.) Toward the end of his life, Franco declared that the Spanish monarchy under Juan Carlos would be restored. After Franco died in 1975, King Juan Carlos moved Spain from a dictatorship to democracy by sponsoring parliamentary elections. Even when a socialist prime minister won office in 1983, Spain's emerging democracy survived.

Ongoing Challenges

As the nations of Western Europe entered the 1990s, they had many achievements to applaud. In general, their people enjoyed a high standard of living, and they had stable democratic governments. Inflation was under control, and unemployment had fallen somewhat. Scientists and engineers were pushing ahead in research and technology. Yet, at the same time, they faced many challenges.

Controlling terrorism. Many nations in Europe and elsewhere felt the tragic effects of terrorism. Extremists used terrorism as a form of blackmail. They hoped to force nations into releasing their imprisoned colleagues in return for kidnapped hostages. Terrorists also used bombing, arson, and hijacking to publicize their causes.

In Spain, for example, Basque separatists set off car bombs, killing and injuring many people. Italy's prime minister Aldo Moro was kidnapped and murdered in 1978. In 1981, Pope John Paul II was wounded in an assassination attempt.

In France, terrorists bombed trains and stores in an effort to gain the release of imprisoned Arab extremists. The French government took stern measures against some aliens in an effort to combat terrorists. However, some nations criticized the French government when it negotiated the release of French citizens held hostage by terrorist groups in Lebanon.

Violence smoldered between Catholics and Protestants in Northern Ireland. Since 1921, Northern Ireland had been self-governing, but it was still part of Great Britain. The Protestant majority of Northern Ireland controlled the government and economy. Discrimination against the large Catholic minority was widespread. Catholic discontent erupted into violence in 1969. Britain sent troops to restore order, but unrest continued. Catholic and Protestant extremists carried out bombings and murders. After 20 years of violence, peace seemed as far off as ever.

The future of Germany. Since World War II, Germany has been a divided nation. The two Germanies reflected the cold war division of Europe between the democratic nations of the West and the Soviet-led communist bloc.

In 1969, West Germany's prime minister, Willy Brandt, set out to improve relations with the Soviet Union and other communist countries of Eastern Europe. His policy was called **Ostpolitik,** which is German for "eastern policy." Ostpolitik led to better relations between the two Germanies.

Fanatical supporters of a variety of causes have used death and destruction to win publicity and to blackmail governments. Here, rescue workers in Paris help the victim of a terrorist attack on a local department store.

In 1989, events in East Germany raised the issue of the future of Germany. That year, East Germans ousted their hardline communist rulers, replacing them with reformers who promised democratic changes. East Germany opened its borders, and all Germans celebrated the dismantling of the Berlin Wall. (See the feature on page 717.) Tens of thousands of East Germans demonstrated in favor of reuniting the two Germanies. Many West Germans also supported reunification.

Germany's neighbors watched events with unease. The Soviet Union as well as nations in Western Europe feared a united Germany because they had suffered at the hands of German militarism in the past. Some experts warned that a united Germany could become a military superpower. Others argued that since 1945 Germans have showed that they are "responsible citizens of the world."

Cutbacks in social programs. By the late 1980s, many western nations faced the problem of budget deficits. That is, they spent more than they took in from taxes and other sources. To balance budgets, they cut back spending on health care, education, housing, and other social programs.

Making cutbacks involved difficult decisions. In western societies, people were living longer than ever before. In Great Britain and elsewhere, the elderly relied on free or subsidized health care. However, sharply rising medical costs forced governments to spend more on health care. Britain's Prime Minister Thatcher tried to curb spending on health care. But her government had to weigh the need to cut spending on social programs against its responsibility toward senior citizens.

Reduced government spending contributed to the growing number of homeless in the cities of Western Europe as well as in the United States. Some governments reduced their commitment to building low-income housing. As a result, the poor could not find affordable housing. Job training programs were also cut back, leaving thousands of people without the skills to find work. Finding ways to meet urgent social needs without increasing budget deficits remain as a challenge for the 1990s.

The opening of the Berlin Wall in late 1989 was greeted with jubilant celebrations, such as the one shown here. For the first time since the wall was built in 1961, Germans could travel freely between East and West Germany.

SECTION 1 REVIEW

1. **Identify:** (a) Helsinki Agreement, (b) François Mitterand, (c) Margaret Thatcher, (d) Willy Brandt.

2. **Define:** (a) privatization, (b) Ostpolitik.

3. Describe two issues that political activists have worked for since 1968.

4. What were Western Europe's major economic problems in the 1970s and 1980s?

5. Which Western European nations became democracies in the 1970s?

6. **Critical Thinking** Does history support French and Soviet fears of a united Germany? Explain.

2 Whirlwind of Change in Eastern Europe

READD TO UNDERSTAND

- ☐ How central economic planning caused problems in the Soviet Union.
- ☐ What domestic and foreign policy changes Gorbachev has introduced.
- ☐ What changes have taken place in Eastern Europe.
- ☐ *Vocabulary:* dissident, perestroika, glasnost, détente.

"History has begun to develop very quickly in this country," noted Vaclav Havel (VAHTS lahv HAH vel), a Czechoslovakian playwright, in November 1989. In seven weeks, a stunning drama unfolded in Czechoslovakia. It began in Prague, the Czech capital, as students and others demanded democratic reforms.

As the demonstrations grew, the Czech Communist party was forced to give up its 41-year monopoly on power. Havel, who had worked for human rights in his homeland, was elected president. He then moved to restore democratic government.

Dramatic changes transformed other Eastern European nations as well as the Soviet Union. In fact, the Soviet leader, Mikhail Gorbachev, had paved the way for the changes when he opened the door to reform in his own country.

Soviet Society

Soviet leaders have long struggled with the problems of an unproductive economy in which inefficiency and corruption were widespread. The problems were due in part to central economic planning. A huge bureaucracy draws up and carries out economic plans. All too often, bottlenecks occur. A factory might have to shut down because needed materials have not arrived.

Until recently, workers kept their jobs because the system assured them lifetime job security. The quality of products was often poor because workers and managers had little incentive to produce better goods.

Shortages of fresh fruit and vegetables often occur in Soviet cities. However, families on collective farms grow food on small private plots. They sell these products in marketplaces such as this one in Moscow. Although prices at these "free" markets are higher than at state-run stores, the quality of the produce is often much better.

Economic failures. Shortages of food and consumer goods are common. The Soviets have to buy grain from other countries, including the United States. Consumers stand in line for hours to buy food, clothing, and household goods. People have to wait for up to three years for delivery of an automobile. The scarcity of goods has produced an active black market, in which people illegally bargain for goods, services, and privileges.

In the Soviet Union, all citizens are supposed to be equal. But the system has favored Communist party officials and some professional people. These privileged few have access to luxury housing, automobiles, and vacations abroad.

Voices of dissent. For decades, most Soviet citizens did not question government policies, at least not publicly. Among the intellectuals, however, there were **dissidents,** men and women who spoke out against the regime. Some dissidents criticized political abuses, especially the use of secret police and censorship. Some wanted more autonomy for non-Russians, such as Armenians. Many Soviet

825

Jews were dissidents because Jews suffered from discrimination. Some Jews were allowed to emigrate, but many others were not.

Dissidents circulated writings through an underground press network. Many were convicted of distributing "anti-Soviet" literature and were sent to forced labor camps. Some were labeled mentally ill and were sent to mental hospitals.

Gorbachev's Reforms

In 1985, a new Soviet leader, Mikhail Gorbachev, rose to power. Gorbachev was better educated and younger than his predecessors. Like Deng Xiaoping in China, he made economic reform a major goal. But Gorbachev saw the need to go further.

Restructuring Soviet society. Gorbachev realized that he must take bold steps to improve productivity in industry and agriculture. He called for **perestroika** (pehr uh STROI kuh), or the restructuring of the economy and society.

Soviet fashion designers are making a bid for international recognition, holding fashion shows like this one. In recent years, Soviet consumers have demanded better-made and better-designed clothing. Raisa Gorbachev, wife of Mikhail Gorbachev, has blazed a fashion trail not seen among wives of Soviet officials in the past.

He blasted corruption and inefficiency. Factories, he said, would be judged on their output, sales, quality of goods, and fulfillment of contracts on time. He called for less centralized control of the economy. Gorbachev fired hundreds of bureaucrats. Many Soviets applauded his moves and hoped for more radical reform. Others resisted changes that threatened their security.

To ensure change, Gorbachev supported **glasnost,** a policy of openness and speaking out honestly. Glasnost was meant to end the silence surrounding failures in Soviet society. Newspapers began to publish articles about poor harvests, alcoholism, crime, and corruption in order to expose problems and find solutions.

Under glasnost, Soviets enjoyed greater cultural and intellectual freedom. Soviet writers began to challenge official views of history. Newspapers reported on controversial issues that would not have been mentioned in the past. Some dissidents were released from prison.

Rising nationalism. Glasnost released the forces of nationalism, creating severe tensions. The Soviet Union includes 15 republics and more than 120 ethnic groups. By 1990, the Baltic republics of Lithuania, Latvia, and Estonia, along with other national groups, were demanding independence. Many of these groups had a history as independent peoples before they were swallowed up by the Soviet Union.

Historic conflicts between ethnic groups flared into violence in some regions. For example, Christian Armenians and Muslim Azerbaijanis fought pitched battles. Gorbachev sent troops in 1990 to restore order. Such conflicts posed threats to Gorbachev's efforts to reform Soviet society.

Soviet Foreign Policy

During the early 1970s, Soviet relations with the West centered on **détente** (day TAHNT). Diplomats used that French term, meaning relaxation, to describe the easing of tension between the Soviet Union and the United States. In 1972, President Richard Nixon visited Moscow. He was the first American President to

"Karabakh was and will be Armenian" is the slogan painted on the red banner held high by Armenian protesters in Moscow. Armenians, one of the Soviet Union's many ethnic groups, are demanding that Karabakh, an Armenian-dominated area within the Azerbaijan Soviet Socialist Republic, be united with the Armenian SSR. With glasnost has come an easing of restrictions on the press and protests. As a result, many ethnic groups inside the USSR are voicing demands for their rights.

visit the Soviet Union since World War II. That year, the superpowers signed the SALT I agreement, limiting the number of nuclear warheads and missiles that each country would keep. (SALT stands for Strategic Arms Limitation Talks.)

Détente ended in 1979 after the Soviets sent troops into Afghanistan to back a communist government against Muslim rebels. The Soviets feared that Muslims who opposed the Afghan government would encourage Soviet Muslims to rebel. For more than eight years, Soviet troops suffered heavy losses as they battled Afghan guerrillas. Finally, Gorbachev realized that the war was too costly and withdrew Soviet troops.

To achieve his economic reforms, Gorbachev had to increase domestic spending and limit the military budget. As you will read, the Soviet Union and the United States agreed to new arms control packages. In addition, Gorbachev cut back on support for communist movements around the world. As cold war tensions eased and Eastern European nations moved away from Soviet domination, Gorbachev agreed to withdraw Soviet troops from Warsaw Pact nations.

March to Freedom

By 1990, Soviet relations with Eastern Europe were undergoing great changes. For decades, the Soviet Union had kept a tight rein on its Eastern European satellites. Efforts at reform were quickly crushed.

Crackdowns on reform. In 1968, Alexander Dubček (DOOB chechk), the communist leader of Czechoslovakia, introduced liberal reforms. The government eased restriction on the press and allowed freedom of expression. The Soviet leader at the time, Leonid Brezhnev, feared that liberal Czech policies might spread to other Eastern European nations and weaken the Soviet bloc. He sent Soviet and other Warsaw Pact troops into Czechoslovakia to crush the reforms.

Brezhnev then declared that if socialism was threatened in one country it was a concern of all socialist countries. The Brezhnev Doctrine, as it was called, served as a warning to Eastern European nations not to become too independent of Moscow.

In 1980, Polish workers demanded reforms. Solidarity, a trade union, led by Lech Walesa (lehk vah WEHN sah), tried to force the government to accept worker demands for reforms, including free elections. The government responded with a harsh crackdown. It imposed martial law and arrested members of Solidarity. But it could not end the severe economic crisis in Poland, which highlighted the desperate need for reforms.

Lifting the Iron Curtain. The work of Solidarity in Poland and Gorbachev's reforms in the Soviet Union set off a chain reaction in

BUILDERS AND SHAPERS Lech Walesa's Way of Hope

"You never know when you start something how things will turn out," observed Lech Walesa, leader of Poland's Solidarity movement in his autobiography, *A Way of Hope.* Walesa, a young worker, started something when he became involved in the politics of the huge Lenin shipyard in Gdansk, Poland.

Before long, Walesa was protesting safety conditions, especially after 22 workers were burned alive in an accident that could have been avoided. Then, he joined other workers to protest increases in food prices. After the military fired on the striking workers, killing 50, Walesa vowed to make Poland's communist government hear the voice of workers.

During the 1970s and 1980s, Walesa suffered arrest and harassment as he struggled to win rights for Polish workers. He helped organize the national Solidarity movement by supporting the efforts of workers in other industries to win better conditions. In the picture at right, Walesa—in the center—walks through the Gdansk shipyard with other Solidarity leaders.

In 1980, Solidarity won a partial victory, forcing Poland's communist leaders to agree to broad economic and social reform. News reports about Solidarity's struggle helped to make Walesa an international figure. Soon, the shipyard worker was meeting with Pope John Paul II, himself a Pole. The Polish people, strong in their Catholic faith after more than 40 years of communism, appreciated the support of church leaders.

The hopes of Walesa and Solidarity suffered a crushing blow in December 1981 when the government imposed martial law. Walesa and other Solidarity leaders were arrested. Walesa was eventually released. Despite constant police surveillance, Walesa continued his work for reform.

As Poland's economic crisis worsened, Solidarity won increasing popular support. In 1983, Walesa was awarded the Nobel Peace Prize. His greatest reward, however, came in 1989, when a Solidarity-led government gained power in Poland. Although Walesa took no official position in the new government, his way of hope had opened the minds of the people to the possibility of change.

Today, the founder of the Solidarity movement is seeking international help for Poland as it rebuilds its economy. Walesa has asked the United States for aid on the scale of the Marshall Plan. Such aid, he says, is "an investment in freedom, democracy, and peace."

1. What was the goal of the Solidarity movement?

2. Critical Thinking Why do you think Walesa calls American aid "an investment in freedom, democracy, and peace"?

Eastern Europe. At the end of the 1980s, the people of Eastern Europe moved swiftly to free themselves from communist domination and to sample the fruits of democracy.

In Poland, Hungary, East Germany, Czechoslovakia, Bulgaria, and Romania, popular demands for reform led to the ouster of communist rulers, who had monopolized power for more than 40 years. Most of the changes were peaceful. Romanians, however, had to fight a brief but bloody revolution to overthrow the dictator Nicolae Ceausescu.

The reformers who gained power in each country had similar goals. They supported a multi-party system, free elections, an end to censorship, and new constitutions that would guarantee democratic rule. Their hopes were high, but achieving their goals would not be easy. The people were inexperienced in democracy. In Bulgaria and elsewhere, ethnic unrest with historical roots threatened stability.

The greatest challenge facing these nations was economic. Each nation chose its own course as it moved away from centralized planning toward a market-driven system. Most experimented with some form of mixed economy, combining capitalist and socialist ideas.

SECTION 2 REVIEW

1. **Identify:** (a) Mikhail Gorbachev, (b) Alexander Dubček, (c) Brezhnev Doctrine, (d) Solidarity, (e) Lech Walesa.

2. **Define:** (a) dissident, (b) perestroika, (c) glasnost, (d) détente.

3. What effect has central planning had on the Soviet economy?

4. Describe two problems Gorbachev hopes to solve in the Soviet Union.

5. (a) What was the result of reforms in Czechoslovakia in 1968? (b) How did the outcome of reforms in Eastern Europe in 1989 and 1990 differ from earlier experiences?

6. **Critical Thinking** Why might perestroika and glasnost be considered radical ideas in the Soviet Union?

3 Challenges in the United States

READ TO UNDERSTAND

☐ Why many Americans joined protest movements in the 1960s and 1970s.

☐ What economic and social problems the United States has faced.

☐ How relations between the United States and the Soviet Union have changed.

Chanting slogans, thousands of American students took to the streets in the late 1960s and early 1970s. Like their counterparts in Western Europe, they demanded justice and social change. By the 1980s, however, many Americans had rejected the turmoil. They sought stability and a return to traditional values.

An Era of Protests

From 1968 to 1974, student unrest and protests from many groups swept the nation. The most explosive issue of this era was the Vietnam War.

Antiwar protests. As you have read, the United States became deeply involved in Vietnam in the 1960s. By 1968, more than 500,000 American troops were fighting there. As the number of casualties rose, opposition to the Vietnam War grew. Many Americans demanded that the United States withdraw its troops from Vietnam. Others argued that the United States should try to win the war.

When Richard Nixon became President in 1969, he introduced the policy of Vietnamization. South Vietnamese forces were supposed to take greater responsibility for the fighting so that American troops could be withdrawn. However, to support South Vietnam during the American pull-out, Nixon resumed the bombing of North Vietnam and authorized the invasion of neighboring Cambodia. Those actions intensified the antiwar protests.

In May 1970, four students from Kent State University in Ohio and two from Jackson State University in Mississippi were killed during antiwar demonstrations. Their deaths underscored the bitterness the war was causing.

Tens of thousands of Americans fought and died in the Vietnam War, while many people at home protested the nation's involvement in the fighting. The debate over the war left the nation deeply divided. Only in 1982, almost ten years after most American troops were withdrawn, was the Vietnam Memorial, shown here, completed. The stark black marble wall lists the names of more than 50,000 American dead.

Nixon's secretary of state, Henry Kissinger, began secret negotiations with the North Vietnamese in 1972. Finally, in January 1973, a peace agreement was signed. The last American combat troops were withdrawn by March. The war had taken more than 58,000 American lives and cost the United States over $100 billion.

The Watergate crisis. By late 1972, public attention had switched from protests against the Vietnam War to the Watergate crisis. During the 1972 presidential campaign, burglars tried to break into Democratic party headquarters in Washington's Watergate Hotel. The burglars were traced to President Nixon's reelection committee, and they had been in touch with top Nixon aides.

At first, Nixon denied all knowledge of the Watergate break-in. At congressional hearings, however, it became clear that the President had known about the burglary and had tried to cover up information about it. Faced with possible impeachment for obstructing justice, Nixon resigned in August 1974. He was the first President of the United States to resign from office. The Watergate affair shocked the nation, but it proved that the American system of government could survive such a crisis.

Continuing Struggles for Equality

Protests of the 1960s and 1970s also focused on the demands by women and minorities for equality. Many women supported a proposed Equal Rights Amendment to the Constitution. However, it failed to win the necessary approval of three-fourths of the states. The women's rights movement shifted its focus to bringing lawsuits against businesses and governments accused of discriminating against women.

Women did make gains. Their enrollment in law schools and medical schools rose. Women moved into many professions and took on important roles in government. In 1981, for example, Sandra Day O'Connor became the first woman to be appointed to the United States Supreme Court. Three years later, Congresswoman Geraldine Ferraro became the Democratic party's vice-presidential candidate, the first woman to be nominated for that office by a major political party.

By the late 1980s, more than 55 percent of American women worked outside the home. While some held high-paying jobs, most women still worked at such traditional jobs as secretaries, clerks, and nurses. These jobs generally were low paying, so on the average women earned about 64 percent of what men earned. Many women were single parents, trying to raise children on low incomes. As a result, the number of women and children living in poverty was on the rise.

In the late 1960s and 1970s, black Americans also enrolled in higher education and entered white collar positions in increasing numbers. Outside the professional fields, however, some blacks faced setbacks. As jobs grew scarce in industries such as steel and automobile manufacturing, more blacks were laid off first and had trouble finding new work. In general, the wages of black Americans lagged behind those of whites, and unemployment among blacks was much higher than among whites. This was particularly true of young blacks.

The number of other minorities, especially Hispanics, grew in the 1970s and 1980s. Many immigrants came from Cuba, Mexico, and other Latin American countries. About two million newcomers also came from Asian nations such as Vietnam, Korea, and India. Skilled immigrants made major contributions in fields such as medicine, engineering, and university teaching. But others, less skilled, found no work or only low-paying jobs.

To remedy the effects of past job discrimination, the federal government and many state and local governments required businesses and other organizations to adopt affirmative-action programs. Under these programs, members of minority groups and women are given preference in hiring and promotion. Some people, however, challenged these programs in court.

Economic and Social Challenges

The economy of the United States, like that of Europe, suffered from inflation and slow economic growth in the 1970s. Low productivity and foreign competition weakened some industries. After OPEC forced up the cost of oil in 1973, the government tried to reduce dependence on foreign oil. It encouraged conser-

American families have kept their standard of living in part because many women have taken jobs outside the home. A union worker, such as this woman at an automobile plant in Michigan, earns the same pay as a man. However, despite making advances in education and job opportunities, women are concentrated in low-paying traditionally "female" jobs.

Today, as in the past, hundreds of thousands of immigrants reach the United States each year. They come from all parts of the globe, and many apply for citizenship. At a vast ceremony held in the Orange Bowl in Miami in 1984, almost 10,000 immigrants became citizens at one time. Some showed their feelings about their new country by waving huge flags.

vation and looked for alternative sources of energy. The oil glut of the 1980s slowed the search for alternative energy sources.

Inflation was brought under control in the 1980s. However, the country faced two other serious challenges. First, the federal budget deficit skyrocketed. Second, the trade deficit grew. By the late 1980s, the United States had become a debtor nation because it imported far more than it exported.

Fears about the growing deficits led to a plunge in stock market prices in October 1987. The government continued to struggle to achieve a balanced budget, but that goal was difficult to achieve, in part because it required cutbacks in social programs that many Americans felt were necessary.

Despite the budget and trade gap, American voters in the 1988 election chose to stay with the Republican policies of Ronald Reagan. They chose his Vice President, George Bush, to be the 41st President of the United States. As Americans look toward the 1990s, they face several challenges. For example, American manufacturers look for ways to produce goods that could compete against foreign imports. And to improve social conditions, Americans have to find ways to curb the use of illegal drugs, help the homeless, and stop the spread of AIDS. (See page 841.)

Foreign Affairs

As you have read, détente led to the signing of the SALT I treaty in 1972. However, SALT II, signed by President Jimmy Carter and Soviet General Secretary Leonid Brezhnev in 1979, was never approved by the United States Senate. By then Americans were suspicious of Soviet actions in various parts of the world, including the Soviet invasion of Afghanistan.

In the 1980s, President Ronald Reagan increased military spending to bolster American defense. At the same time, he met with Soviet leader Mikhail Gorbachev on several occasions to discuss arms control. In 1987, the two leaders signed an INF treaty. (INF means intermediate-range nuclear forces.) The treaty banned all medium-range nuclear missiles from Europe.

By the early 1990s, cold war tensions were easing in Europe. In meetings, both President George Bush and Gorbachev agreed to further arms control talks. Bush welcomed the move toward democracy in the nations of Eastern Europe and applauded the Soviet promise to withdraw its troops from Warsaw Pact nations. Many Americans hoped that the easing of tensions would lead to a "peace dividend" of lower military spending.

Global issues. The United States adjusted its policies to meet changing conditions around the world. In the 1970s, the United States and China increased business and cultural exchanges. Finally, in 1979, the United States extended formal diplomatic recognition to China. Although the United States condemned the Beijing massacre in 1989, it maintained ties with Chinese leaders.

In the late 1980s, the United States was faced with rising imports from many Asian

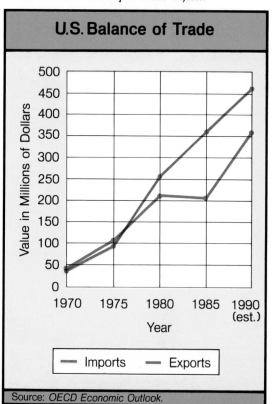

GRAPH STUDY *In the United States, as in many industrialized countries, budget deficits and trade deficits will continue to be economic challenges into the 1990s. A trade deficit exists if a nation imports more than it exports. This graph shows American imports and exports between 1970 and 1990. During which 5-year period did the United States develop a trade deficit?*

U.S. Balance of Trade

Value in Millions of Dollars

Year

— Imports   — Exports

Source: *OECD Economic Outlook.*

The INF treaty between the United States and Soviet Union called for the dismantling of medium-range nuclear missiles in Europe. The agreement allowed each side to send inspectors to witness the process. Here, Soviet officials begin the job of taking apart a missile in the province of Kazakhstan.

nations, especially Japan, South Korea, and Taiwan. While some Americans called for more limits on imports, others warned that such controls might lead to trade wars.

Terrorism. A pressing problem facing the United States was how to deal with terrorism. In Lebanon, Muslim extremists with ties to Iran held a number of Americans hostage. President Reagan refused publicly to negotiate with terrorists. Secretly, however, American officials sought Iran's aid to win the release of the hostages. Although selling arms to Iran was illegal under United States law, they negotiated a secret arms deal. When the deal became public, it caused a scandal. First, the United States appeared to be negotiating with terrorists. Second, profits from the arms deal were secretly used to help the Contras in Nicaragua. (See page 809.)

The United States tried to reduce Middle East tensions by seeking a peace plan to bring Israel and its Arab neighbors to the negotiating table. At the same time, it used a show of force—the United States navy—to keep the Persian Gulf open to shipping during the Iran-Iraq war.

(See page 809.)

SECTION 3 REVIEW

1. **Identify:** (a) Vietnamization, (b) Sandra Day O'Connor, (c) Geraldine Ferraro, (d) INF treaty.

2. How did growing American involvement in Vietnam lead to public protests?

3. (a) What economic gains have black Americans made? (b) In what ways have they continued to lag behind whites?

4. What economic problems did the United States face (a) in the 1970s; (b) in the 1980s?

5. How did the Reagan administration attempt to free American hostages held by terrorists in Lebanon?

6. How did Presidents Reagan and Bush work to ease cold war tension?

7. **Critical Thinking** Evaluate the progress toward equality made by women since the late 1960s.

833

Summary

1. Student protests in the late 1960s began a period of reexamination in Western Europe. As economic growth slowed in the early 1980s, some countries introduced a policy of privatization of industry. Greece, Portugal, and Spain became democracies. And many Germans called for reunification of their divided country.

2. Winds of change swept over Eastern Europe and Soviet Union in the late 1980s. In the 1980s, Mikhail Gorbachev introduced reforms designed to restructure the Soviet economy. The new openness encouraged the nations of Eastern Europe to free themselves from communist domination and to experiment with democracy and market economies.

3. In the United States, the late 1960s and early 1970s were a time of protest. Minorities and women demanded equality and justice. As in Europe, inflation and slow rates of growth marred the economy. Although these problems faded in the 1980s, the nation still faced a huge budget deficit and a large trade imbalance.

Recalling Facts

Decide if the following statements are true or false. If a statement is false, rewrite it to make it true.

1. Conservative politicians supported a program of privatization in France.

2. Britain joined the Common Market in 1973.

3. Willy Brandt opposed the policy of Ostpolitik.

4. Mikhail Gorbachev favored a drastic overhaul of the Soviet economic system.

5. American involvement in Vietnam increased during the 1960s.

6. The Equal Rights Amendment was ratified in the 1970s.

7. The federal budget deficit declined under President Reagan.

Chapter Checkup

1. (a) How did inflation during the 1970s affect France and Britain? (b) How did the British government try to improve the British economy? (c) Was it successful? Explain.

2. Describe how two Western European countries returned to democratic rule during the 1970s.

3. (a) What were the goals of Deng Xiaoping in China and Gorbachev in the Soviet Union? (b) How were conditions in these nations similar? (c) How were conditions different?

4. (a) Explain what détente meant in the 1970s. (b) Why did détente end? (c) How is the easing of the cold war today different from détente in the 1970s?

5. (a) What are three goals of reformers in Eastern Europe? (b) What problems do Eastern European nations face?

6. (a) Why did Watergate shock the American people? (b) How did the outcome of the Watergate events show the strength of the American system of government?

Critical Thinking

1. **Interpreting** "Gorbachev is with us," read a sign in an Eastern European store window. How did Gorbachev's policies in the Soviet Union influence events in Eastern Europe?

2. **Understanding the Roots of Democracy** (a) Give three examples of how public opinion has influenced government policy in a democratic country since the late 1960s. (b) How is public opinion becoming more important in the Soviet Union? (c) What effect might that have on the government of the Soviet Union?

3. **Relating Past to Present** The origin of the conflict in Northern Ireland is deeply rooted. Review discussions of the relationship between Britain and Ireland on pages 422, 514, 648, and 823. (a) How did bitterness between Catholics and Protestants develop? (b) Do you think a solution to the conflict is possible? Why or why not?

Developing Basic Skills

1. **Preparing an Oral Report** Choose one Eastern European nation that moved toward democracy in 1989 and 1990. Research the following questions and prepare an oral report on your findings. (a) How did the country end communist rule? (b) What problems does the country face? (c) Is democracy likely to work there? Why or why not?

2. **Placing Events in Time** Review what you have read about events in Europe since World War II. (See also Chapter 32, pp. 712–731.) Then create a time line showing what you consider to be the five most important events in Europe between 1945 and today. Below the time line, explain why you chose each of the five events.

3. **Chart Reading** Study the chart on page 821. (a) Which nation had the highest unemployment in 1980? In 1984? (b) How did the unemployment rate in France change between 1980 and 1988? (c) Why do you think conservatives in France and Britain believe that privatization will help lower the rate of unemployment?

Writing About History

Preparing a Final Draft

The appearance of a research paper is important. It reflects the care with which you prepared it. The following are general guidelines to follow when preparing the final draft.

HANDWRITTEN
Paper: Lined, white 8-1/2″ x 11″
Ruled left margin
Text: Written or printed neatly in ink
One side only
Indent all paragraphs
Single spaced
Light corrections allowed

TYPEWRITTEN
Paper: Unlined, white 8-1/2″ x 11″
Text: One side only
Indent all paragraphs
Double spaced
Single spaced
Light corrections allowed

WORD-PROCESSED
Paper: Tractor guides removed
Text: Double-strike mode, if possible

You should have a title page that includes the title of your report, your name and class, the date, and your teacher's name. Number and write your last name on all the pages. Staple, bind, or paper-clip the pages together.

Practice: Compare one of your written assignments with the guidelines above. Write a brief paragraph explaining the reasons for these guidelines.

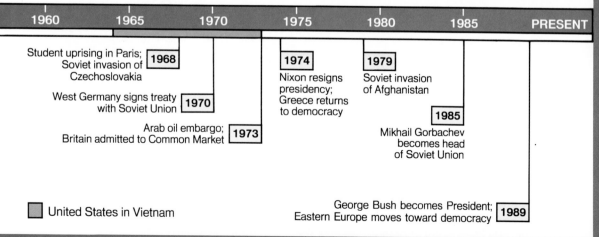

| 1960 | 1965 | 1970 | 1975 | 1980 | 1985 | PRESENT |

Student uprising in Paris; Soviet invasion of Czechoslovakia **1968**

West Germany signs treaty with Soviet Union **1970**

Arab oil embargo; Britain admitted to Common Market **1973**

1974 Nixon resigns presidency; Greece returns to democracy

1979 Soviet invasion of Afghanistan

1985 Mikhail Gorbachev becomes head of Soviet Union

■ United States in Vietnam

George Bush becomes President; Eastern Europe moves toward democracy **1989**

A New Age of Exploration (1945–Present)

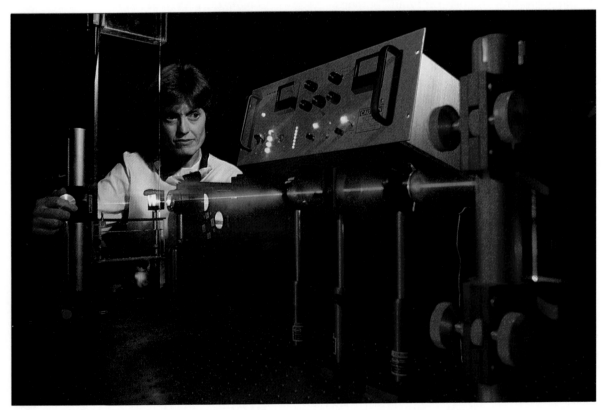

Laser beams have changed the worlds of science, medicine, industry, and art. Here, a researcher uses lasers to analyze the chemical makeup of DNA, the building blocks of life.

The surgeon carefully examined the large purplish birthmark on the patient's forehead. She then injected a local anesthetic to numb the man's face. After testing to see that the anesthesic had taken effect, she picked up a penlight-size instrument. She moved it to the edge of the purple stain and pressed a firing mechanism. A light flashed, and a faint popping sound was heard. The doctor repeated the process all across the stain.

The doctor, a plastic surgeon, was treating her patient with one of medicine's newest technologies—the laser. Each time the laser—a thin, extremely powerful beam of light—was fired, it closed one of the blood vessels that made up the purple birthmark. The procedure would make the birthmark lighter and remove the danger that it would bubble and bleed as the patient grew older.

Today, lasers are a common tool in many forms of surgery. Lasers are used for many other purposes as well, from boring holes in diamonds, to welding metals, to guiding space satellites. The machines that read product codes at supermarket checkout counters use lasers. Lasers are used in video discs and in creating spectacular three-dimensional images called holograms. Lasers carry voices on long-distance telephone lines, help transmit live television shows, and measure microscopic changes in the earth's crust.

"In the future, lasers may serve us in ways science fiction never dared imagine," says a pioneer in laser technology, Arthur Schawlow. "Entirely new and radically different kinds of lasers will probably appear—and as our knowledge of light and matter grows, lasers will make practical what can barely be done today, and make possible what is not yet even dreamed of."

In the second half of the twentieth century, scientists and other researchers have gone far beyond the worlds invented by science-fiction writers of earlier ages. New technologies have revolutionized daily life. In space, medicine, agriculture, and every other field, age-old questions have been answered and solutions to puzzling problems have been found. Often, however, the answers have raised new questions and opened other worlds for further exploration. ■

---

1 The New Scientific Revolution

READ TO UNDERSTAND

☐ How space exploration has added to our knowledge.

☐ How computers revolutionized daily life.

☐ How advances in medicine have affected our lives.

☐ *Vocabulary:* superconductor, transistor, genetic engineering.

Since the 1900s, researchers have made major advances in chemistry, physics, biochemistry, and medicine. Their achievements have revolutionized our lives. Many advances came about as a result of World War II. During the war, governments poured resources—both human and financial—into scientific research. They wanted to develop weapons, medicines, and other technologies needed to win the war. British scientists developed radar, a device that uses radio waves to detect objects. And in the United States, scientists found a way to harness the energy released when atoms are split and put it to use in the atom bomb.

Since 1945, both industries and governments have invested billions of dollars in scientific research. Their efforts have resulted in thousands of new products and inventions.

Space Exploration

Some of the most spectacular advances in science and technology have occurred in the exploration of space. After World War II, the United States and the Soviet Union competed fiercely to develop space programs. Their goal was to build rockets powerful enough to send satellites beyond the earth's atmosphere.

Beginning of the Space Age. The age of space exploration began in 1957, when the Soviet Union launched the first satellite, *Sputnik I,* into orbit around the earth. The first American spacecraft, *Explorer I,* was sent into

After making design and safety changes, the United States resumed its space shuttle program in 1988, two years after the Challenger disaster. Once again, a reusable spacecraft, Discovery, lifted off from the Kennedy Space Center to deploy commercial and military satellites.

orbit in 1958. In 1961, Soviet cosmonaut Yuri Gagarin was the first person sent into orbit. His flight was soon matched by that of John Glenn, the first American to orbit the earth.

Scientists then aimed at more distant goals. On July 20, 1969, American astronauts Neil Armstrong and Buzz Aldrin stepped out of their *Apollo 11* spacecraft onto the surface of the moon. "That's one small step for a man," noted Armstrong, "one giant leap for mankind." In later moon shots, other American astronauts gathered much useful data. In the 1970s and 1980s, the Soviet Union launched orbiting laboratories. Soviet scientists conducted experiments to determine the effects of prolonged space travel on humans.

The United States and the Soviet Union launched dozens of unpiloted spacecraft to explore the planets. Soon, scientists were getting photographs and information about Venus, Mars, and even the more distant planets of Jupiter and Saturn. The American *Voyager 2* photographed Saturn and Uranus before heading out of our solar system. It carries information about life on earth, including recordings of crickets and Beethoven's Fifth Symphony, in case it encounters intelligent life in space.

Putting satellites to work. By the 1980s, other nations, including India, China, and Japan as well as nations of Western Europe, had put satellites into orbit. Satellites provided useful information about weather, crop yields, volcanoes, and even the movement of swarms of locusts that threatened farmers in North Africa and Europe. Other satellites transmitted signals for radio, television, and telephone communications.

In the 1980s, the United States launched several space shuttles. These reusable spacecraft released and repaired communications satellites and served as space laboratories for experiments in biology, medicine, and manufacturing. The space shuttle program suffered a tragic setback in 1986. With seven astronauts aboard—one a social studies teacher—the shuttle *Challenger* exploded seconds after liftoff. Despite the setback, the American space program continued but under stricter controls.

Computers have changed our world both at home and in the workplace. In the United States and other industrial nations, students learn to use computers at an early age, although traditional means of study are still important.

New Technologies

Scientific journals are full of reports on the latest research in chemistry, physics, biology, and other fields. Even before the reports appear, researchers are looking for practical applications.

Superconductors. In 1986, two scientists from Switzerland announced a sensational breakthrough when they discovered a new class of substances called high-temperature superconductors. A **superconductor** is a material that conducts electricity without resistance and thereby saves energy.

Superconductors offer the possibility of bullet trains that travel at speeds of 300 miles (480 kilometers) per hour or more. They can be used to make smaller, faster computers, safer nuclear reactors, and cheaper electricity. The recent breakthroughs have led to a frantic race to find industrial and military uses for superconductors. Before the end of the cen-

tury, superconductors may revolutionize our lives the way computers transformed them in the 1970s and 1980s.

Computers. The search for machines that process information at great speed has been going on for hundreds of years. The first of today's high speed, mass-produced computers were developed in the 1950s. These early computers were enormous machines that filled an entire room.

Two inventions, the transistor in 1947 and the integrated circuit, or chip, in the 1960s, revolutionized computers. **Transistors** are devices used to control electric currents. With them, scientists were able to make computers smaller and faster. Chips are units that contain many transistors. Tiny microchips made computers still smaller and faster, which led to a large drop in prices. As a result, computers came into widespread use.

Today, computers handle telephone communications, route airplanes, and store vast

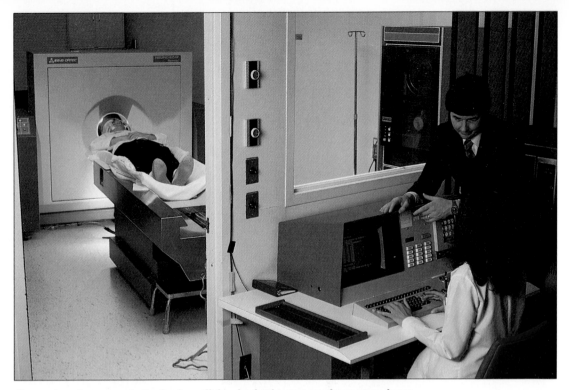

Computers have revolutionized medicine by letting researchers store large amounts of information as well as by providing data for highly accurate diagnoses. Here, the technician in the foreground sits at a terminal while a patient undergoes a CAT-scan. (CAT stands for Computerized Axial Tomography.) The CAT-scanner provides detailed pictures of body tissues.

amounts of information needed by businesses and governments. Engineers, scientists, and mathematicians use computers to solve complex problems. Personal computers have become common in homes and schools. And computerized video games are a popular form of entertainment.

Advances in Medicine

Computers and other advanced technology have ushered in a "machine age" in medicine. Hospitals and doctors now rely on a wide variety of new devices to help them diagnose and treat illness.

Medical technology. Modern hospitals use a variety of monitoring devices. In intensive care units, for example, information from sensors attached to patients is fed into a computer. At a central nursing station, warning bells ring if a patient's pulse falters or breathing stops.

New medical technology has led to organ transplants to save lives. In 1952, the first kidney transplant took place. A year later, surgeons performed the first open-heart operation. In the 1960s, the development of the pacemaker improved heart care. A pacemaker is a tiny electronic device that is implanted in the body to regulate a patient's heartbeat.

In 1967, Dr. Christiaan Barnard of South Africa performed the first successful human heart transplant. Since then, doctors have greatly improved transplant procedures, and the survival rate of transplant patients has risen. By the 1990s, surgeons expect to be able to perform transplants of human limbs such as fingers and toes.

The field of microsurgery is a recent development. Using microscopes and tiny instruments, surgeons operate on small areas such as the inner ear. As you have read, lasers are widely used in surgery. The concentrated light in a laser beam can burn away unwanted tissue in a fraction of a second without harming nearby tissue. In eye surgery, surgeons can correct a detached, or loose, retina in the eye by "welding" it in place with a laser beam.

Antibiotics and vaccines. Today's medical technology has grown out of the work of earlier scientists. In 1928, for example, British bacteriologist Sir Arthur Fleming discovered that a mold called penicillin killed bacteria. During World War II, penicillin was widely used as an antibiotic to prevent infection of battlefield wounds. The discovery of sulfa drugs, which also kill bacteria, was followed by their widespread use as antibiotics. Today, antibiotics are used in the treatment of many diseases caused by bacteria and other microorganisms. The use of antibiotics has cut down drastically the number of deaths caused by such diseases as tuberculosis, pneumonia, and scarlet fever.

Vaccines that combat viruses were first developed in the late 1700s. In the 1800s, Louis Pasteur developed vaccines against rabies and anthrax. But it was not until this century that scientists were able to develop vaccines against many viral diseases, including measles, mumps, diphtheria, typhoid, and cholera. In the 1950s, Jonas Salk and Albert Sabin developed vaccines to fight a frightening disease, polio. Like antibiotics, vaccines have revolutionized health care.

Since 1945, international efforts have helped to wipe out or control epidemic diseases that once killed millions. Smallpox, for example, has virtually disappeared. But other problems remain. An epidemic of a new, deadly disease known as AIDS threatens the world. AIDS is a disorder that destroys the body's ability to resist disease and usually results in death. By 1991, experts estimate that over one million cases of AIDS will have been diagnosed.

Researchers are scrambling to develop an effective treatment and cure for AIDS. Meanwhile, governments and health groups are educating the public about how AIDS is spread and how to avoid it. They are warning that AIDS can be contracted through sexual contact with an infected partner or by using contaminated needles while taking drugs.

Genetic engineering. One growing field of research is genetic engineering. **Genetic engineering** refers to laboratory techniques that alter the hereditary material—the genes— of an organism. Scientists have used genetic engineering to produce disease-resistant crops and to raise cows that produce more milk. They hope to be able to produce microorganisms that will break down garbage and other wastes into alcohol or natural gas. Researchers have also found ways to create proteins that will aid in fighting some diseases that are now incurable.

GRAPH STUDY *Because of advances in medicine, people are living longer than ever before. Compare this graph with the graph on page 503. In what period did life expectancy make the greatest advance?*

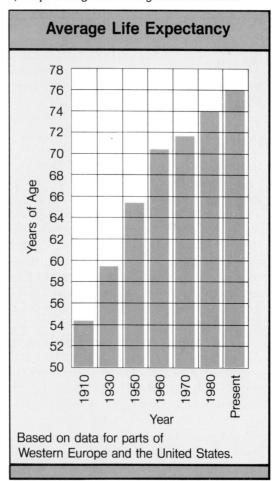

Average Life Expectancy

Years of Age vs. Year (1910, 1930, 1950, 1960, 1970, 1980, Present)

Based on data for parts of Western Europe and the United States.

Sources: *Historical Statistics of the United States;* OECD, *Child and Family;* and United Nations, *Demographic Yearbook.*

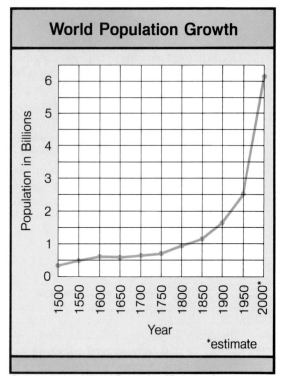

World Population Growth

Population in Billions (y-axis: 0 to 6)
Year (x-axis): 1500, 1550, 1600, 1650, 1700, 1750, 1800, 1850, 1900, 1950, 2000*

*estimate

Source: *Atlas of World Population History* and Population Division of the United Nations.

GRAPH STUDY *The population of the world grew slowly for hundreds of years. When did it begin to grow more rapidly? When did it begin its greatest rise?*

Ethical Issues

Technological advances in medicine have raised many ethical questions. Many people are awaiting organ transplants. When organs become available, the question arises of who should be given them first. Most life-saving operations are expensive, and some people have criticized health care systems that discriminate against poor people. Another question that has stirred debate concerns whether dying patients should be allowed to refuse life-sustaining treatment.

Genetic engineering has also aroused much discussion. Despite the successes of genetic engineering, some people question the morality of changing genetic material, the basic stuff of life. They fear that harmful bacteria may be accidentally released. They also warn against the danger of tinkering with human genetic materials. Medical professionals and governments in many nations have begun to set safety guidelines for laboratories that work with genes.

842

2 Challenges for the Future

READ TO UNDERSTAND

☐ Why the gap between rich and poor nations is difficult to close.

☐ Why the earth's resources have been endangered.

☐ How mass communication has affected daily life.

☐ *Vocabulary:* ecology, revolution of rising expectations.

Advances in science and technology have improved the lives of millions of people around the globe. Today, fewer babies die of disease, and people live much longer than in the past. In the last 40 years, the world's population has more than doubled, from 2.5 billion in 1950 to an estimated 5.2 billion in 1990.

The use of computers and space satellites, along with faster transportation systems, has put people into instant communication with one another. Once, fearless explorers took months or years to cross the world's oceans and deserts. Today, a ship's captain rounding Tierra del Fuego, at the tip of South America, can talk by phone with the ship's owners in Japan or Turkey. The achievements of recent decades are impressive. They also have changed the lives of individuals and nations in both positive and negative ways.

Economic Links

Every month, Liu Wen, a stockbroker in Hong Kong, rushes to his computer terminal to read the latest trade data released by the United States government. At the same time, financial people in Tokyo, Paris, London, and New York read the same news. Within hours, the news—good or bad—has begun to have an impact not only on stock prices but also on business decisions ranging from building a new factory to hiring more workers.

In today's shrinking world, nations are increasingly tied together economically. As you have read, when OPEC raised oil prices in the 1970s, the result was inflation around the globe. A decade later, many Third World nations were unable to pay their debts when a recession struck the world. The resulting debt crisis affected not only the debtor nations but also banks in developed nations that had loaned the money. And the October 1987 stock market crash on Wall Street shook financial markets from Western Europe to Asia.

Experts agree that the global economic links are growing. Individual nations will continue to pursue their own economic policies. However, more and more, those decisions will be affected by events and pressures beyond their borders.

Rich Lands, Poor Lands

The global world economy has affected relations between rich nations and poor nations around the world. Rich lands include developed nations such as West Germany, France, Japan, and the United States. These nations have the advantages of well-developed agriculture and industry, advanced technology,

and strong education systems. Poor lands include many developing nations in Africa, the Middle East, Asia, and Latin America.

Problems. Closing the gap between rich and poor lands poses many difficult challenges. Developed nations have provided aid such as food and technical assistance to Third World nations. Western investors have also made loans of billions of dollars. But developing nations face serious obstacles in their drive to develop modern industrial economies. As you have read, the population explosion, inflation, and natural disasters have upset the development plans of many Third World nations.

In addition, governments of newly independent nations have sometimes overemphasized industrial growth and neglected farming. Thus, food production lagged even as the population boomed. Even with financial help, most Third World nations have had trouble juggling their meager resources between developing industry and agriculture and providing basic services to their people.

People in many less-developed nations are crowded into urban slums, such as this one in Peru, or live in rural poverty. Because of limited resources, governments have been unable to improve the standard of living.

In the 1980s, you will recall, interest rates rose, further hurting developing economies. Nations were then faced with paying off even greater debts. At the same time, many nations suffered from reduced demand for their products. The result was a slowdown in economic growth. By the end of the decade, many poor countries seemed to have slipped even further behind the developed nations.

Hunger and famine have plagued many poor nations. Food aid from the governments of developed countries, the United Nations, and private relief organizations has provided a short-term answer. But long-range plans are needed to increase food production and improve distribution.

GRAPH STUDY *Foreign debt grew steadily during the 1980s, as this graph shows. What was the foreign debt of nations in Africa in 1984? Of nations in Europe? Which region had the largest debt in 1988?*

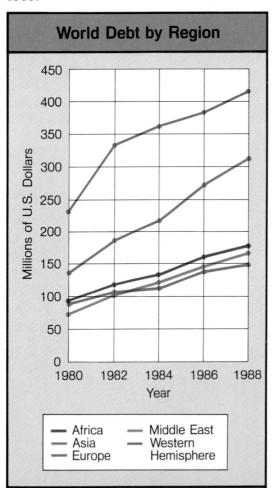

World Debt by Region

Source: International Monetary Fund, World Economic Outlook.

Progress. Progress has been made in the area of food production. In the 1960s, efforts to increase food production led to the "Green Revolution." Researchers found ways to double and even triple the amount of food produced on the same amount of land. "Yields which had been almost unchanged for centuries," a UN report noted, "leapt forward."

Experts developed new varieties of high-yield crops and taught farmers better soil management methods. Increased use of pesticides, fertilizer, and farm machinery helped boost harvests in India, Mexico, the Philippines, Southeast Asia, and elsewhere. In the 1980s, researchers used genetic engineering to develop disease-resistant and drought-resistant crops.

The Green Revolution has had some unexpected consequences, however. Many farmers were forced out of business because their small plots of land could not support the cost of the machinery and chemical fertilizers needed for high yields. And it was found that some of the new varieties of plants were particularly subject to plant diseases and insect pests.

The Earth's Resources

Modern, high-tech agriculture relies on using large amounts of chemical pesticides and fertilizers. In many places of the world, including those where the Green Revolution has taken hold, these practices pollute the soil and water supplies. In 1962, an American writer, Rachel Carson, published a book called *Silent Spring*. In it, she described the devastating effects that pesticides were having on the land and water, as well as on other wildlife.

Carson's book pointed to the dangers of abusing the earth's resources. As a result, scientists began paying more attention to **ecology,** the relationship between living things and their environments. Studies revealed that delicate balances exist in nature. Over-development and pollution are threatening these balances around the globe.

Limits to growth. In recent years, air pollution, acid rain, and damage to the earth's ozone layer have aroused concern. The earth's temperature appears to be climbing, which

Population of the World's Largest Urban Areas
(in thousands)

1350 B.C.		1000 A.D.		1600 A.D.	
Thebes, Egypt	100	Cordova, Spain	450	Peking, China	706
Memphis, Egypt	74	Constantinople, Turkey	450	Constantinople, Turkey	700
Babylon, Iraq	54	Kaifeng, China	400	Agra, India	500
Chengchow, China	40	Sian, China	300	Cairo, Egypt	400
Khattushas, Turkey	40	Kyoto, Japan	200	Osaka, Japan	400

1925 A.D.		1985 A.D.		2000 A.D. (projected)	
New York, US	7,774	Tokyo, Japan	18,800	Mexico City, Mexico	25,800
London, England	7,742	Mexico City, Mexico	17,300	São Paulo, Brazil	24,000
Tokyo, Japan	5,300	São Paulo, Brazil	15,900	Tokyo, Japan	20,200
Paris, France	4,800	New York, US	15,600	Calcutta, India	16,500
Berlin, Germany	4,013	Shanghai, China	12,000	Bombay, India	16,000

All figures are estimates.

CHART STUDY *The centers of population have changed in the past 3,000 years. This table shows the five largest urban areas at five points in history. It also shows the urban areas projected to be the largest in 2000. Which country appears on the chart most often?*

could cause the polar ice caps to melt and flood low-lying lands. Efforts to protect the environment require international cooperation and may involve limiting the use of certain fuels and chemicals. Because they are rich, industrial nations have been able to buy and use whatever resources they needed. Today, some of them are taking steps to curb waste and stop pollution.

Third World nations are anxious to industrialize quickly and cannot afford expensive programs to prevent pollution. Many developing nations are willing to risk some pollution from pesticides in order to increase desperately needed food supplies.

Changing landscapes. Industrial development has threatened food sources such as fish and has endangered wilderness areas. Population pressures have led to the clearing of forests and the destruction of natural habitats. The destruction of forests and the use of trees for pulp and fuel has caused untold damage to soil and water resources. Some nations have tried to stop developing certain areas and thereby save the wildlife they contain. Nations in Africa, Asia, North America and

Scientists in their laboratories are seeking ways to repair the damage done to our environment. They have begun to unravel the delicate balance in nature and have warned that the destruction of the world's forests threatens the planet's atmosphere. Today, biologists have found ways to clone, or reproduce, fast-growing pine trees that can be planted to prevent flooding and soil erosion.

elsewhere have sponsored reforesting programs to prevent floods and soil loss as well as to meet the needs for timber.

In the past 50 years, people have contributed to the spread of deserts over land that was once productive. (See page 752.) In some areas, overgrazing by sheep and goats has destroyed plants that held dry soil in place. Wind has blown the soil away, making land unsuitable for growing plants. In other areas, poor irrigation methods have caused a build-up of salt in the soil, creating "salt deserts."

In places such as Israel, farmers have developed ways of pushing back the desert. They have planted trees to hold the soil. They have also installed pipes to carry water directly to plant roots, preventing evaporation.

Other environmental concerns. In the mid-1980s, industrial accidents caused damage in many parts of the world. In 1984, a leak from a giant chemical factory in Bhopal, India, released deadly fumes into the air. It was the world's worst industrial accident, in which more than 2,000 people died, and at least 150,000 were injured. In Switzerland, a warehouse fire sent tons of toxic chemicals into the Rhine River. The Rhine, Western Europe's most important inland waterway, flows through heavily populated areas of several nations.

In 1986, an explosion and fire at the Soviet nuclear power plant at Chernobyl (chern NOH bul) released large amounts of radioactive material into the air that were detected in distant parts of Europe. The Chernobyl incident raised questions in the minds of many people about the safety of nuclear energy plants in general.

When industrial accidents occur, experts often disagree about the extent of the environmental damage. Some companies have taken steps to prevent industrial leaks and spills. And they are developing ways to limit the damage if mishaps occur.

The Energy Puzzle

Many problems of the environment are linked to the world's energy needs. Both industrialized and developing nations require energy to fuel their economies. Fossil fuels—oil and coal—are the chief sources of energy. In poor rural areas, people depend on wood from trees to cook their meals and heat their homes.

DAILY LIFE The Giant Panda: An International "Treasure"

For years, people have flocked to zoos around the world to watch the antics of giant pandas. The Chinese have the most pandas in captivity. China is also the only place where giant pandas live in the wild. They inhabit the bamboo forests in a mountainous region in south central China. Good-natured but shy, giant pandas have no natural enemies. They weigh between 200 and 300 pounds. Chinese experts estimate that today fewer than 1,000 giant pandas live in the wild. Only about 50 giant pandas live in zoos.

Nearly every country has made efforts to save its wildlife from extinction. The Chinese government has declared pandas "national treasures" and has sent zoologists to study them in the wild.

While some zoologists study giant pandas in the wild, others are trying to raise pandas in captivity. At birth, pandas weigh about four ounces and look like hairless white mice. However, they soon gain weight and their distinctive coat of white and black fur.

The birth of a panda cub in a zoo is a cause for international celebration because so few pandas in captivity have produced offspring. In August 1981, a panda at the Mexico City Zoo gave birth to a cub named Cancun. Cancun is the first giant panda to be born and survive outside China. He is one indication that the international effort to save the giant panda might succeed.

1. Why has China declared pandas a "national treasure"?

2. Critical Thinking Why do you think people want to save endangered species?

846

Industrial accidents along with emissions from factories have caused enormous damage to the environment. In 1986, a fire at a warehouse near Basel, Switzerland, resulted in the dumping of 1,000 tons of toxic chemicals into the Rhine River. Four countries, France, the Netherlands, West Germany, and Switzerland, had to close all plants that processed Rhine water for household use. The protesters are fishermen from Alsace. Their sign "Danke, Merci" says a sarcastic "thank you" in German and French to the company whose chemicals poisoned all fish in the area.

Fossil fuels are nonrenewable sources of energy. As they are used, they cannot be replaced. Experts differ on how long they estimate fossil fuels can meet the world's energy needs. Moreover, the use of such fuels contributes to environmental damage. Therefore, scientists and others have called for new approaches to the uses of energy.

The energy crisis, brought on by OPEC price increases in the 1970s, revealed how much industrialized nations depended on imported oil. It also made people aware that world oil reserves would someday be exhausted. And it raised difficult questions about how to produce enough energy for the world and how to pay for it.

Alternative energy sources. Part of the answer to the energy problem has been to conserve energy. Another part has been to harness energy from alternative sources, such as the sun, the wind, and the ocean tides. Some researchers have explored water power, a major energy source in the early Industrial Revolution. Others have worked with geothermal energy from deep in the earth. Industries in some countries are using solid wastes, or garbage, to provide energy.

Experiments are under way to produce inexpensive fuels from a variety of substances. For example, in Brazil, researchers have found that a mixture of gasoline and alcohol made from sugar cane can be used to power cars and trucks.

Nuclear power. Much research has gone into exploring nuclear power. Nuclear power plants have been built in 26 countries. But breakdowns and accidents, such as the one at Chernobyl, have raised fears about the

847

World Atomic Power, 1987
(Selected Countries)

	Number of Nuclear Reactors	Percentage of Electricity Generated by Nuclear Energy
United States	101	17%
Brazil	1	2%
Argentina	2	13%
Britain	37	18%
France	44	65%
Belgium	8	60%
Netherlands	1	5%
West Germany	20	31%
Switzerland	5	40%
Czechoslovakia	5	15%
Bulgaria	4	32%
U.S.S.R.	51	11%
Sweden	12	50%
India	6	4%
Pakistan	1	2%
Japan	32	26%
South Korea	4	18%
Taiwan	6	52%

CHART STUDY *Worldwide use of nuclear power is increasing. Despite objections from environmental groups, many nations with limited natural resources have turned to nuclear power. Based on this chart, which nation appears to be the most dependent on nuclear power?*

safety of nuclear power and the future of nuclear plants.

Today's nuclear plants use nuclear fission, a process that produces not only energy but also radioactive wastes. Safe disposal of these wastes is a problem. For years, researchers have been trying to master nuclear fusion. Fusion produces enormous amounts of power but much less radioactive waste than nuclear fission. Although some progress has been made, no one expects a working nuclear fusion plant before 2000. Nevertheless, the work of these scientists represents a step toward the development of a safe and unlimited source of energy into the future.

New Patterns of Culture

The Seoul Summer Olympics in 1988 were beamed via satellite to more than 70 countries. An estimated 750 million people watched the games on television. The huge audience underscored the impact of mass communication on the world.

Mass communication. Radio, television, and other forms of mass communication allow people to receive information and entertainment from around the world. In the 1980s, the world saw the leaders of the superpowers, Ronald Reagan and Mikhail Gorbachev, shake hands over a new arms-control agreement. People watched in horror as television cameras recorded the brutal acts of terrorists. They witnessed the protests of Palestinians on the West Bank to win a homeland and of black South Africans to gain freedom in their own land. The governments of Israel and South Africa eventually stopped camera crews from recording these events because they believed such coverage further inflamed people.

Broadcasts enable people from many countries to share a common bond. Television pictures of famine in Africa moved people to action. In 1985, rock stars and others organized the Live Aid Concerts. More than 1.6 billion people saw the concerts via satellite hookups and helped raise $70 million for African relief efforts.

In developed nations, especially, television has become an important part of daily life. One survey showed that the average American adult watches nearly 30 hours a week of television.

Like television, movies have a worldwide audience. Since the 1950s, filmmakers in other countries have challenged American dominance in this field. Britain, France, Japan, Italy, India, and Sweden are among the nations that have produced film classics. Some films have given moviegoers vivid insights into life in other lands.

Television and movies have also contributed to the **revolution of rising expectations**, the desire of people in developing nations to enjoy the high standards of living of people in the industrialized world. American-made programs, such as "Dallas," have created images of the "good life." The wide distri-

848

bution of American movies and television series has also spread American fads and fashions around the world. In some parts of the world, people have criticized such western influences and have tried to preserve their local cultures.

The performing arts. Even though movies, television, and radio have captured large audiences, live performances in theaters have continued to flourish. New musical sounds forged vast audiences in the postwar period. Fusing traditions of American country and western music and rhythm and blues, American musicians created rock 'n' roll in the 1950s. With its pounding beat, youth-oriented lyrics, and amplified sound, rock became a shared experience among young people around the globe. Today, rock groups throughout the world attract tens of thousands to a single concert.

Audiences have also grown for other performing arts from ballet and drama to opera and classical music. Since the 1950s, dancers and other artists have performed around the globe. Through cultural exchanges, for example, leading Soviet ballet companies—such as the Bolshoi and Kirov—have toured the West.

American orchestras, choirs, and groups such as the Dance Theatre of Harlem have performed in cities from Moscow to Tokyo. Mexico has sent its Ballet Folklorico on world tours, while Chinese acrobatic groups have impressed global audiences with amazing balancing feats developed a thousand years ago.

Finding a Balance

The postwar period has brought tremendous changes. New nations in Africa, the Middle East, and Asia have taken prominent roles in world affairs. Improved communications and transportation have put people around the world in close touch with each other. In addition, nations have been tied more closely together by economic needs.

An information explosion has occurred. Both developed and developing nations emphasize education. Schools and universities have expanded their courses of study to include new knowledge. And college attendance has soared.

Important changes have taken place in the workplace. Working conditions and fringe benefits have improved. New inventions spurred

Through satellite telecommunications, news and entertainment are flashed instantly around the world. An estimated 12 billion total viewers watched the games of the 1986 World Cup soccer matches on television, with about 500 million seeing the final match alone. The picture at left shows sophisticated equipment at a telecommunications station in Riyadh, Saudi Arabia. The picture at right shows children in Beijing, China, watching a popular cartoon program.

the growth of new industries, and computers have revolutionized industry. On farms, new crops and machinery have changed the way food is produced.

As you have read, millions of rural people have moved to cities. In cities and suburbs, people have greater access to education, jobs, and popular entertainment.

Changes in technology, education, and attitudes have affected the lives of women. In developed countries, women have entered the workforce in ever increasing numbers. Women in many countries have expanded their roles in public life.

The patterns of growth and change pose challenges to all nations. New technologies and attitudes have forced people to give up traditional ways of life. In crowded urban slums, for example, people lack the traditional supports that existed in small rural communities. Even among the affluent, family patterns have changed. Often both parents work outside the home. Parents and children may live far from grandparents and other relatives. So children have less contact than in the past with older generations.

In many countries, people have become alarmed at the breakdown of traditional values

THEN AND NOW   The Find of the Century

The story of the greatest archaeological find in the Americas begins like an episode of a police drama. In Peru, art dealers were puzzled when beautiful and unusual ancient jewelry turned up in local shops. Where did the pieces come from? Peruvian police began an investigation. In February 1987, they raided a home and found many fine artifacts, apparently stolen from an ancient burial site. A second raid ended in a gun battle. The police, with the help of archaeologists, finally traced the priceless relics to their source. What they found, in the words of one scientist, "is the richest tomb ever excavated . . . in the Western Hemisphere."

The tomb, not far from the town of Sipán, Peru, belonged to a Moche warrior priest who died 1,500 years ago. The Moche people lived along the Pacific Coast from about 250 A.D. to 700 A.D. Long before the Incas built their empire, the Moche created a complex civilization, as the tomb revealed.

The warrior priest, who was about 30 when he died, had been buried in a many-layered funeral garment. Around him were placed hundreds of ceramic pots with food for his journey to the afterlife. Several servants, guards, and a favorite dog were buried alongside him.

What had attracted the grave robbers, however, were the gold and silver works in the tomb. The corpse was draped with gold objects, including a massive crown and shield. Among the other items found in the

tomb were a gold mask, a sceptre, and gold and turquoise earrings.

The treasure trove told only a little about the Moche people. There was no evidence to explain why the Moche disappeared suddenly around 700 A.D. However, the discovery of the tomb showed how much more there is to learn about the history of people in the world.

1. What alerted authorities to the possibility of a new ancient burial site in Peru?

2. **Critical Thinking** Why do you think government authorities want to stop people who loot ancient burial sites?

Throughout this text, you have read, analyzed, and interpreted various kinds of historical evidence. In order to make the best use of evidence, however, you must be able to synthesize it—that is, pull several pieces together to form a whole pattern of a historical event or development.

You will use four pieces of evidence to practice the skill of synthesizing: the graph of world population growth on page 842, the table of large urban areas on page 845, the map of world population density on pages 858–859 in the Reference Section, and the picture on page 843.

1 **Analyze each piece of evidence.** (a) According to the graph on page 842, what was the approximate population of the world in 1800? In 1900? In 2000? (b) According to the table on page 845, what was the largest urban area in 1350 B.C.? In 1925? In 1985? (c) According to the map on pages 858–859, what is the population density in most of Europe? In most of North Africa? In most of Morocco? (d) What is the subject of the picture on page 843?

2 **Find relationships among the pieces of evidence.** (a) How does the information in the table support the information in the graph? (b) How does the picture illustrate the information in the table? (c) Find the place on the map where you think each of the largest urban areas in 1985 is located. Check your answers on maps in the Reference Section.

3 **Synthesize the evidence in order to draw conclusions.** (a) What conclusion can you draw about the change in the total world population since the early 1900s? Cite specific evidence to support your conclusion. (b) Does the evidence support the conclusion that world population is not very evenly distributed over the land surface? Explain.

and the increase in social problems, such as crime and the use of illegal drugs. Some people have called for a return to the fundamentalist faiths of the past. In the Middle East, as you have read, the Iranian revolution ignited a revival in Islamic traditions. In the West, especially in the United States, religious fundamentalists pressed for renewed commitment to Christian moral and religious teachings.

Even as we move ahead into the space age, people are taking a new interest in the past. Museums, the storehouses of many cultures, have opened their doors to millions of people. In museums of art and archaeology, people learn about societies of the past. In science museums, people explore the complicated technology of today.

Yet the past is alive in more than well-planned museum exhibits. It survives in the cultures it has shaped on every continent and in every nation. Today, people are responding to a basic challenge—how to find a balance between the ways of life that worked in the past and the needs of today's world. And they look to the past to find answers for tomorrow's world.

SECTION 2 REVIEW

1. **Identify:** (a) Green Revolution, (b) Rachel Carson.

2. **Define:** (a) ecology, (b) revolution of rising expectations.

3. What are three problems that poor nations face in their efforts to modernize?

4. Explain two ways in which the environment is threatened by today's technology.

5. What alternative sources of energy to fossil fuels are scientists exploring?

6. How have mass communications affected people around the world?

7. **Critical Thinking** Why do some people refer to the world as a "global village"?

Summary

1. Since 1945, science has brought great changes. The computer revolution has been felt in almost every part of our lives. Advances in medicine have eliminated many diseases and improved the treatment and prevention of others. Genetic engineering is a growing field of research, but it has raised important ethical questions.

2. The nations of the world are increasingly tied together. Although new sources of food have been developed, world hunger remains a major challenge. Also, the gap between rich and poor nations continues to grow. Satellite communications bring world events to every home and help create connections among the world's people.

Recalling Facts

Decide if the following statements are true or false. If a statement is false, rewrite it to make it true.

1. Radar was developed during World War I.

2. John Glenn was the first American to orbit the earth.

3. The development of transistors and lasers permitted small, fast, inexpensive computers to be built.

4. The use of vaccines has helped wipe out smallpox.

5. Populations are growing fastest in Western Europe.

6. The Green Revolution helped increase food production mainly in the United States.

7. American television and movies have played a part in the revolution of rising expectations in Third World countries.

Chapter Checkup

1. (a) What were the major Soviet achievements in space exploration? (b) What were the major American achievements?

2. (a) How were computers developed and improved? (b) How are they used today?

3. (a) Why was the discovery of penicillin important? (b) What has been the result of the development of vaccines? (c) How are lasers used in medicine?

4. (a) What steps have been taken to increase food production? (b) What have been some of the unexpected results of the Green Revolution?

5. (a) Why are people looking beyond fossil fuel for energy? (b) Why do many people worry about nuclear power?

Critical Thinking

1. **Relating Past to Present** You have probably seen on television pictures of people people gathered at Cape Canaveral to watch the liftoff of a spacecraft. Review the description of dawn at Stonehenge on pages 2 and 3. (a) What similarities do you find between the people at Stonehenge and those at Cape Canaveral? (b) What are the differences? (c) How might the builders of Stonehenge have reacted to the liftoff at Cape Canaveral?

2. **Analyzing** (a) Why do rich nations use more of the earth's resources than poor ones? (b) Why do many poor nations ignore the dangers of pollution? (c) Imagine you were a member of a commission created to write a plan protecting the environment. What would you recommend?

3. **Understanding Economic Ideas** Developed nations have poured aid and advice into developing nations. However, some Third World nations continue to exist on the edge of poverty. (a) Based on your reading in Unit Ten, what are some of the causes of the economic problems of the Third World? (b) How have international

developments such as the rise in interest rates in the 1980s slowed economic progress in the Third World? (c) Why is food aid only a temporary solution to world hunger?

Developing Basic Skills

1. **Researching** Choose one of the advances in technology since World War II. Research how this advance was achieved. (a) What earlier developments contributed to this advance? (b) Was it the work of a single individual or of a number of people? Explain. (c) What has been the major result of the advance?

2. **Graph Reading** Study the graphs on page 503 and page 841. (a) How did the average life expectancy in Western Europe and the United States change between 1910 and 1930? Between 1950 and 1960? (b) During which period between 1910 and the present did life expectancy increase the most? (c) How does average life expectancy in Western Europe and the United States today compare to the average life expectancy in these areas in 1850?

3. **Forecasting Future Trends** No one can say exactly what will happen in the future. But people can make forecasts based on trends, or changes taking place in the present. Make a list of five major trends since World War II. Note what aspect of people's lives each has affected. Then answer these questions: (a) Describe a political trend.

(b) Is it likely to continue? Explain. (c) What economic trends have affected people's lives? (d) Which trend do you think will have the greatest impact on future developments?

Writing About History

Putting Your Research Paper in Historical Context

Now that you have completed and handed in your research paper, you have one more task to perform to get the most out of the research you did. You need to put the theme and content of your paper into its historical context.

Assume, for example, that your paper has dealt with an important individual. To get the most out of your experience in writing about him or her, you should now try to answer questions such as: What was the impact of your subject on the period in which he or she lived? Were there other individuals who made similar contributions? What might have happened if your subject had never lived?

You can develop similar questions on any topic that will move that topic back into the mainstream of the history of the period or country you have covered.

Practice: Assume you have written a paper on a topic related to the content of this chapter. Write several questions that would help you understand how your specific topic is important to the broader themes of the chapter.

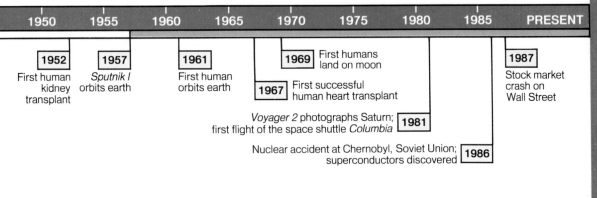

| 1950 | 1955 | 1960 | 1965 | 1970 | 1975 | 1980 | 1985 | PRESENT |

1952 First human kidney transplant

1957 *Sputnik I* orbits earth

1961 First human orbits earth

1969 First humans land on moon

1967 First successful human heart transplant

Voyager 2 photographs Saturn; first flight of the space shuttle *Columbia* **1981**

Nuclear accident at Chernobyl, Soviet Union; superconductors discovered **1986**

1987 Stock market crash on Wall Street

☐ Space Age

Unit Ten　　　　Mini-Atlas

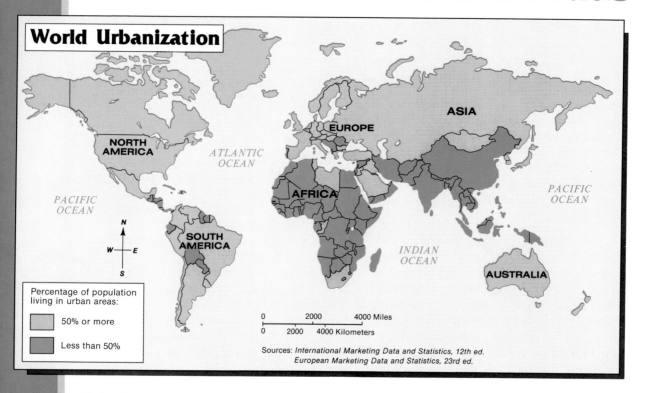

World Urbanization

ASIA

EUROPE

NORTH AMERICA

ATLANTIC OCEAN

PACIFIC OCEAN

AFRICA

PACIFIC OCEAN

SOUTH AMERICA

N
W — E
S

INDIAN OCEAN

AUSTRALIA

Percentage of population living in urban areas:

50% or more

Less than 50%

0　　2000　　4000 Miles
0　2000　4000 Kilometers

Sources: *International Marketing Data and Statistics, 12th ed.*
European Marketing Data and Statistics, 23rd ed.

Unit Themes

The years since World War II have been a time of tremendous change around the world. Western powers gave up their colonies. Their influence has remained strong. But, other centers of power also emerged.

Since 1945, many new nations have gained independence in Africa, the Middle East, and Asia. These nations, as well as the developing nations of Latin America, have experienced rapid growth and change. They have undergone scientific, political, and industrial revolutions similar to those that had occurred earlier in Europe.

Science and technology, especially, have helped to knit the world together in many ways. And international cooperation has become increasingly important. Economic, social, and political changes create challenges for every nation. As in the past, however, individual nations have developed their own distinctive patterns to meet the challenges of a constantly changing world.

1. **Applying Information** (a) Based on the map above, which continents are dominated by nations that are over 50 percent urbanized? (b) How does industrialization affect urbanization? (c) What effect has rapid urbanization had on developing nations?

2. **Understanding Economic Ideas** (a) According to the map at right, which nations had over 51 percent growth in export trade from 1980 to 1986? (b) What is the danger of relying on one main product for export?

3. **Synthesizing** (a) How have countries cooperated with each other since World War II? (b) What benefits and problems have resulted from cooperative efforts?

4. **Analyzing** (a) According to the time line, in which decade did the Space Age begin? (b) Which event began the Space Age? (c) How has space age technology brought the world closer together?

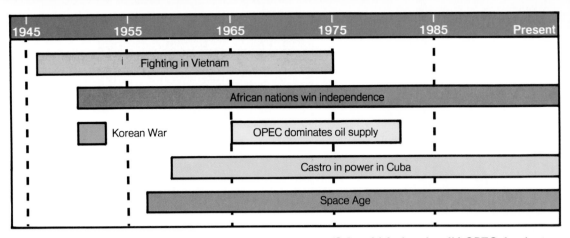

In what year did fighting in Vietnam end? In which decades did OPEC dominate oil supplies?

Most of the countries on the Pacific rim have experienced an increase in export trade from 1980 to 1986. In which nations did export trade decline during this period? Why might this be so?

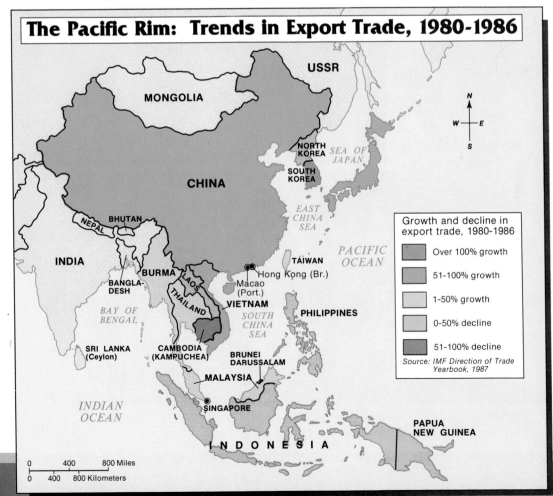

The Pacific Rim: Trends in Export Trade, 1980-1986

Growth and decline in export trade, 1980–1986

- Over 100% growth
- 51-100% growth
- 1-50% growth
- 0-50% decline
- 51-100% decline

Source: IMF Direction of Trade Yearbook, 1987

REFERENCE SECTION

World Population

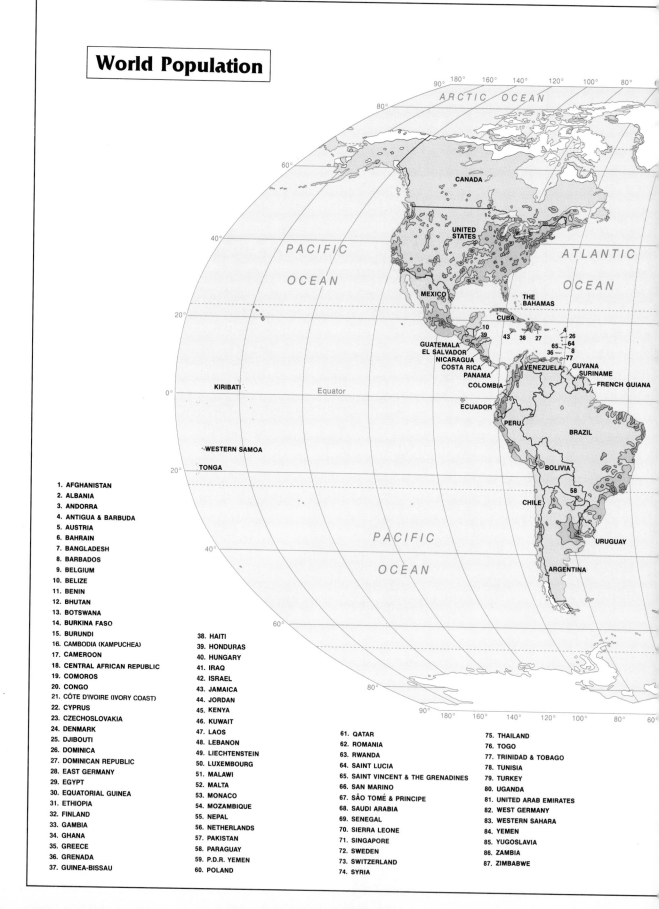

ARCTIC OCEAN

80°

60°

CANADA

40°

PACIFIC

OCEAN

20°

ATLANTIC

OCEAN

MEXICO

THE BAHAMAS

CUBA

10

39

43 38 27

4

26

64

8

65

36

77

GUATEMALA

EL SALVADOR

NICARAGUA

COSTA RICA

PANAMA

COLOMBIA

VENEZUELA

GUYANA

SURINAME

FRENCH GUIANA

0°

KIRIBATI

Equator

ECUADOR

PERU

BRAZIL

WESTERN SAMOA

TONGA

20°

BOLIVIA

58

CHILE

40°

PACIFIC

OCEAN

URUGUAY

ARGENTINA

60°

80°

90° 180° 160° 140° 120° 100° 80° 60°

1. AFGHANISTAN
2. ALBANIA
3. ANDORRA
4. ANTIGUA & BARBUDA
5. AUSTRIA
6. BAHRAIN
7. BANGLADESH
8. BARBADOS
9. BELGIUM
10. BELIZE
11. BENIN
12. BHUTAN
13. BOTSWANA
14. BURKINA FASO
15. BURUNDI
16. CAMBODIA (KAMPUCHEA)
17. CAMEROON
18. CENTRAL AFRICAN REPUBLIC
19. COMOROS
20. CONGO
21. CÔTE D'IVOIRE (IVORY COAST)
22. CYPRUS
23. CZECHOSLOVAKIA
24. DENMARK
25. DJIBOUTI
26. DOMINICA
27. DOMINICAN REPUBLIC
28. EAST GERMANY
29. EGYPT
30. EQUATORIAL GUINEA
31. ETHIOPIA
32. FINLAND
33. GAMBIA
34. GHANA
35. GREECE
36. GRENADA
37. GUINEA-BISSAU

38. HAITI
39. HONDURAS
40. HUNGARY
41. IRAQ
42. ISRAEL
43. JAMAICA
44. JORDAN
45. KENYA
46. KUWAIT
47. LAOS
48. LEBANON
49. LIECHTENSTEIN
50. LUXEMBOURG
51. MALAWI
52. MALTA
53. MONACO
54. MOZAMBIQUE
55. NEPAL
56. NETHERLANDS
57. PAKISTAN
58. PARAGUAY
59. P.D.R. YEMEN
60. POLAND

61. QATAR
62. ROMANIA
63. RWANDA
64. SAINT LUCIA
65. SAINT VINCENT & THE GRENADINES
66. SAN MARINO
67. SÃO TOMÉ & PRINCIPE
68. SAUDI ARABIA
69. SENEGAL
70. SIERRA LEONE
71. SINGAPORE
72. SWEDEN
73. SWITZERLAND
74. SYRIA

75. THAILAND
76. TOGO
77. TRINIDAD & TOBAGO
78. TUNISIA
79. TURKEY
80. UGANDA
81. UNITED ARAB EMIRATES
82. WEST GERMANY
83. WESTERN SAHARA
84. YEMEN
85. YUGOSLAVIA
86. ZAMBIA
87. ZIMBABWE

Persons per square mile	Persons per square kilometer
over 512	over 200
256–512	100–200
128–256	50–100
26–128	10–50
0–26	0–10
uninhabited	uninhabited

World Climate Zones

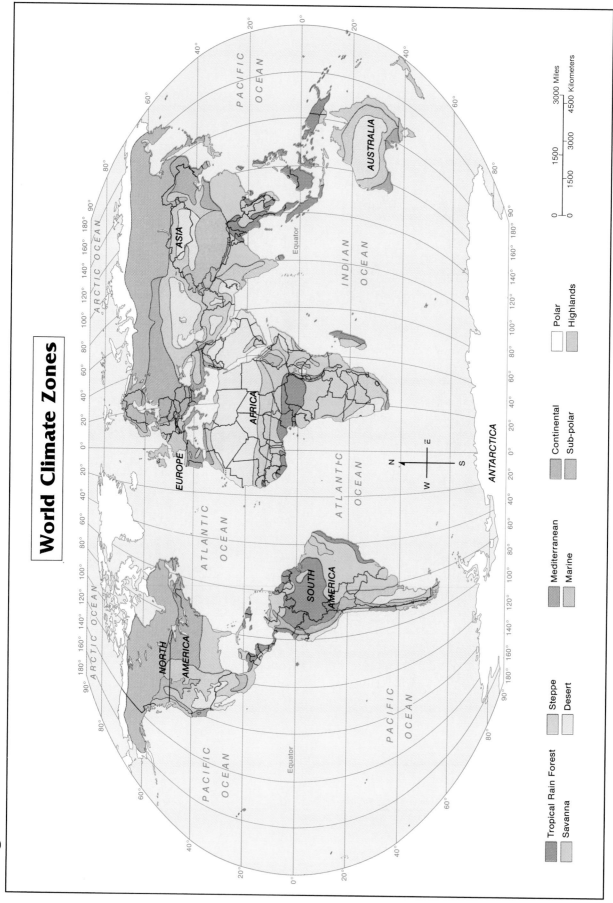

Legend:

Tropical Rain Forest
Savanna
Steppe
Desert
Mediterranean
Marine
Continental
Sub-polar
Polar
Highlands

Mineral Resources of the World

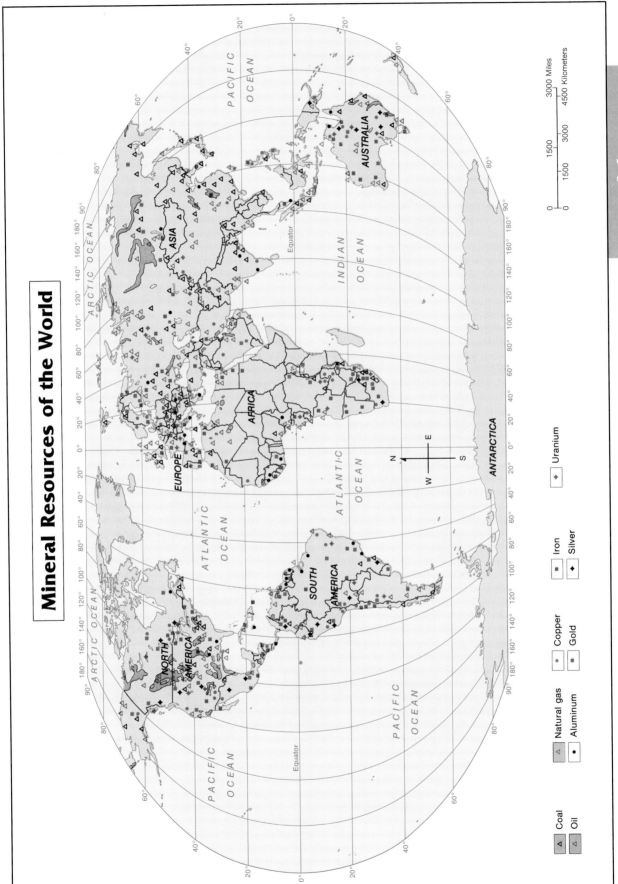

Coal ◁

Oil ◁

Natural gas ◁

Aluminum ●

Copper ●

Gold ■

Iron ■

Silver ◆

Uranium ◆

ARCTIC OCEAN

PACIFIC OCEAN

ASIA

EUROPE

AFRICA

AUSTRALIA

INDIAN OCEAN

ATLANTIC OCEAN

NORTH AMERICA

SOUTH AMERICA

ANTARCTICA

Equator

N E W S

0 1500 3000 Miles
0 1500 3000 4500 Kilometers

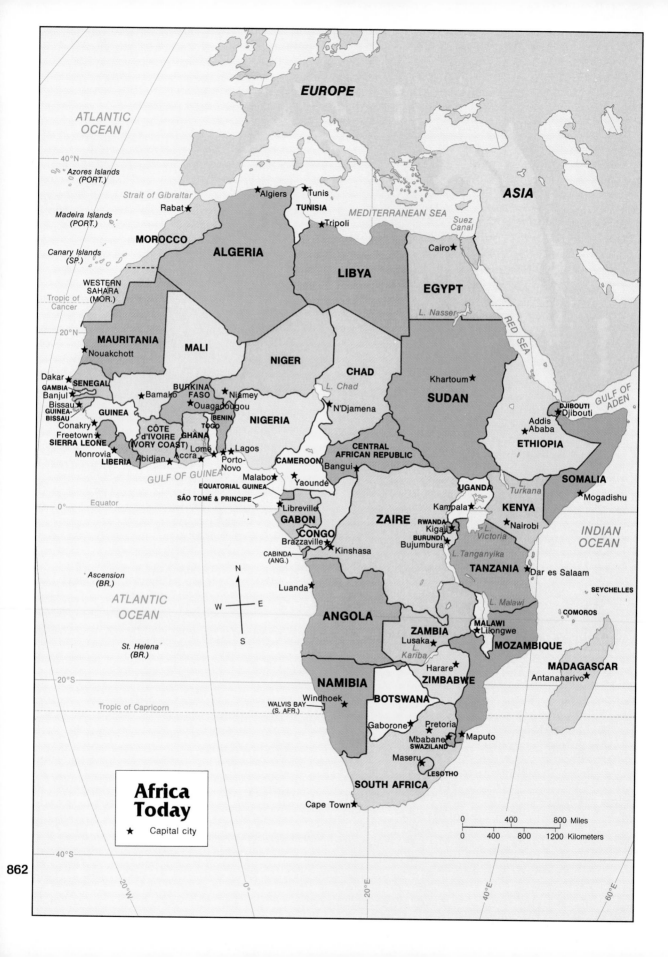

ATLANTIC
OCEAN

EUROPE

ASIA

MEDITERRANEAN SEA

Suez
Canal

★ Algiers   ★ Tunis
Rabat ★   TUNISIA

Strait of Gibraltar

40°N

Azores Islands
(PORT.)

Madeira Islands
(PORT.)

Canary Islands
(SP.)

Tropic of
Cancer

MOROCCO

WESTERN
SAHARA
(MOR.)

ALGERIA

LIBYA

★ Tripoli

Cairo ★

EGYPT

L. Nasser

RED SEA

GULF OF
ADEN

20°N

MAURITANIA

★ Nouakchott

MALI

NIGER

CHAD

L. Chad

Khartoum ★

SUDAN

DJIBOUTI
Djibouti ★

Addis
Ababa ★

Dakar ★
GAMBIA
Banjul ★
Bissau ★
GUINEA-
BISSAU
Conakry ★
Freetown ★
SIERRA LEONE
Monrovia ★
LIBERIA

SENEGAL

Bamako ★

BURKINA
FASO
★ Niamey
Ouagadougou ★

GUINEA

CÔTE
d'IVOIRE
(IVORY COAST)
Abidjan ★

BENIN
TOGO
GHANA
Lomé ★
Accra ★

NIGERIA

N'Djamena ★

Lagos ★
Porto-
Novo ★

CENTRAL
AFRICAN REPUBLIC

ETHIOPIA

CAMEROON

Bangui ★

SOMALIA

GULF OF GUINEA

Malabo ★

EQUATORIAL GUINEA

SÃO TOMÉ & PRINCIPE

Yaoundé ★

UGANDA

L.
Turkana

Mogadishu ★

Kampala ★

KENYA

Equator

0°

Libreville ★

GABON

CONGO

Brazzaville ★

CABINDA
(ANG.)

★ Kinshasa

ZAIRE

RWANDA
Kigali ★
BURUNDI
Bujumbura ★

Nairobi ★

L.
Victoria

L. Tanganyika

INDIAN
OCEAN

Ascension
(BR.)

ATLANTIC
OCEAN

N

W   E

S

Luanda ★

TANZANIA

Dar es Salaam ★

SEYCHELLES

L. Malawi

COMOROS

St. Helena
(BR.)

ANGOLA

ZAMBIA

Lusaka ★

Kariba

MALAWI
Lilongwe ★

MOZAMBIQUE

MADAGASCAR

Antananarivo ★

20°S

Harare ★

ZIMBABWE

NAMIBIA

Windhoek ★

WALVIS BAY
(S. AFR.)

BOTSWANA

Tropic of Capricorn

Gaborone ★

Pretoria ★

Mbabane ★ ★ Maputo
SWAZILAND

Maseru ★

LESOTHO

SOUTH AFRICA

Cape Town ★

Africa
Today

★ Capital city

0   400   800 Miles

0   400   800   1200 Kilometers

862

20°W

0°

20°E

40°E

60°E

40°S

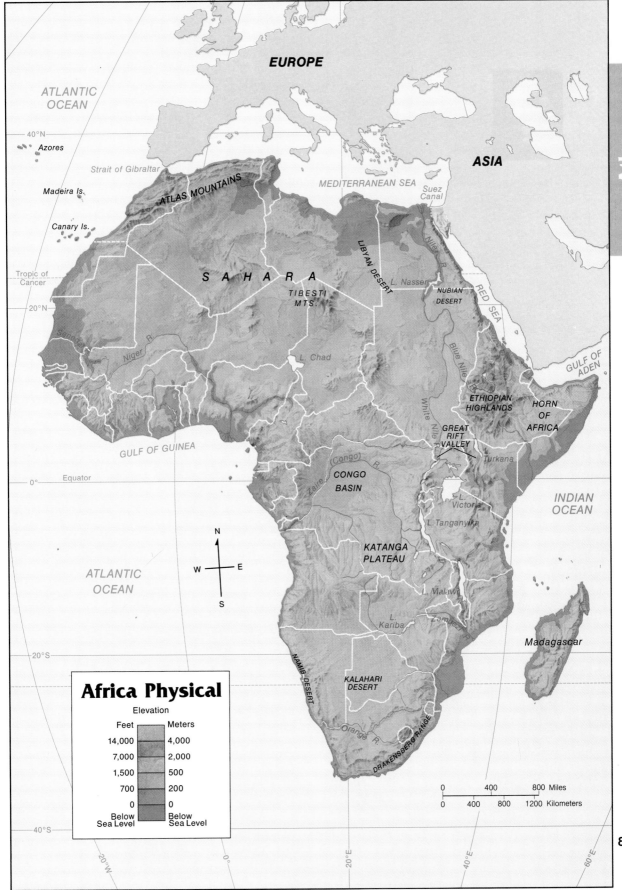

Africa Physical

Elevation

Feet		Meters
14,000		4,000
7,000		2,000
1,500		500
700		200
0		0
Below Sea Level		Below Sea Level

ATLANTIC OCEAN

EUROPE

ASIA

Azores

Strait of Gibraltar

Madeira Is.

ATLAS MOUNTAINS

MEDITERRANEAN SEA

Suez Canal

Canary Is.

Tropic of Cancer

S A H A R A

LIBYAN DESERT

L. Nasser

NUBIAN DESERT

RED SEA

TIBESTI MTS.

Senegal R.

Niger R.

L. Chad

Blue Nile

GULF OF ADEN

ETHIOPIAN HIGHLANDS

HORN OF AFRICA

White Nile

GREAT RIFT VALLEY

GULF OF GUINEA

(Congo) R.

Zaire

CONGO BASIN

Turkana

Equator

L. Victoria

INDIAN OCEAN

L. Tanganyika

N

W   E

S

ATLANTIC OCEAN

KATANGA PLATEAU

L. Malawi

Madagascar

L. Kariba

Zambezi

NAMIB DESERT

KALAHARI DESERT

Orange R.

DRAKENSBERG RANGE

0		400		800 Miles
0	400	800	1200	Kilometers

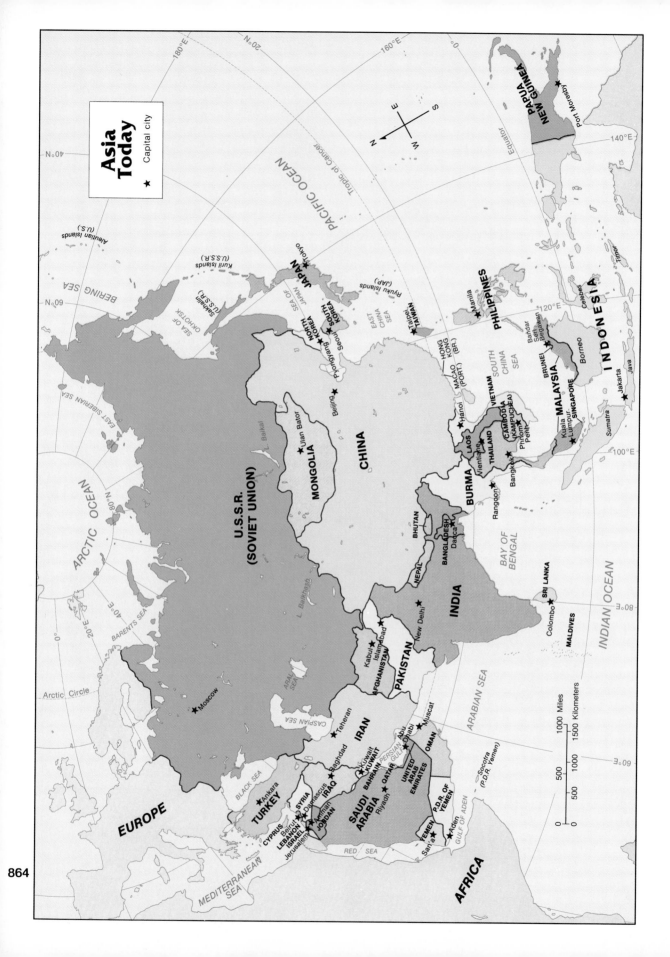

Asia Today

★ Capital city

ARCTIC OCEAN

PACIFIC OCEAN

Tropic of Cancer

Equator

140°E

160°E

180°E

PAPUA NEW GUINEA

Port Moresby ★

Aleutian Islands (U.S.)

Kuril Islands (U.S.S.R.)

BERING SEA

SEA OF OKHOTSK

Sakhalin (U.S.S.R.)

Ryūkyū Islands (JAP.)

SEA OF JAPAN

JAPAN

Tokyo ★

NORTH KOREA

Pyongyang ★

SOUTH KOREA

Seoul ★

EAST CHINA SEA

Taipei ★

TAIWAN

HONG KONG (BR.)

MACAO (PORT.)

PHILIPPINES

Manila ★

120°E

Bandar Seri Begawan ★

BRUNEI

Borneo

Celebes

INDONESIA

Timor

EAST SIBERIAN SEA

U.S.S.R. (SOVIET UNION)

L. Baikal

MONGOLIA

Ulan Bator ★

CHINA

Beijing ★

VIETNAM

Hanoi ★

LAOS

Vientiane ★

SOUTH CHINA SEA

MALAYSIA

Kuala Lumpur ★

SINGAPORE

Sumatra

Jakarta ★

Java

100°E

BARENTS SEA

ARCTIC OCEAN

80°N

60°N

40°N

20°E

0°

BURMA

Rangoon ★

THAILAND

Bangkok ★

CAMBODIA (KAMPUCHEA)

Phnom Penh ★

L. Balkhash

ARAL SEA

CASPIAN SEA

Moscow ★

Arctic Circle

40°E

BHUTAN

BANGLADESH

Dacca ★

NEPAL

INDIA

BAY OF BENGAL

SRI LANKA

Colombo ★

MALDIVES

8°N

INDIAN OCEAN

Kabul ★

AFGHANISTAN

Islamabad ★

PAKISTAN

New Delhi ★

BLACK SEA

Ankara ★

TURKEY

Teheran ★

IRAN

Baghdad ★

IRAQ

ARABIAN SEA

Muscat ★

OMAN

Abu Dhabi ★

UNITED ARAB EMIRATES

PERSIAN GULF

Kuwait ★

KUWAIT

BAHRAIN

QATAR

60°E

CYPRUS

Beirut ★

LEBANON

Damascus ★

SYRIA

Amman ★

ISRAEL

JORDAN

Jerusalem ★

SAUDI ARABIA

Riyadh ★

P.D.R. OF YEMEN

Aden ★

YEMEN

San'a ★

Socotra (P.D.R. Yemen)

GULF OF ADEN

RED SEA

MEDITERRANEAN SEA

EUROPE

AFRICA

1000 Miles

1500 Kilometers

1000

500

500

0

864

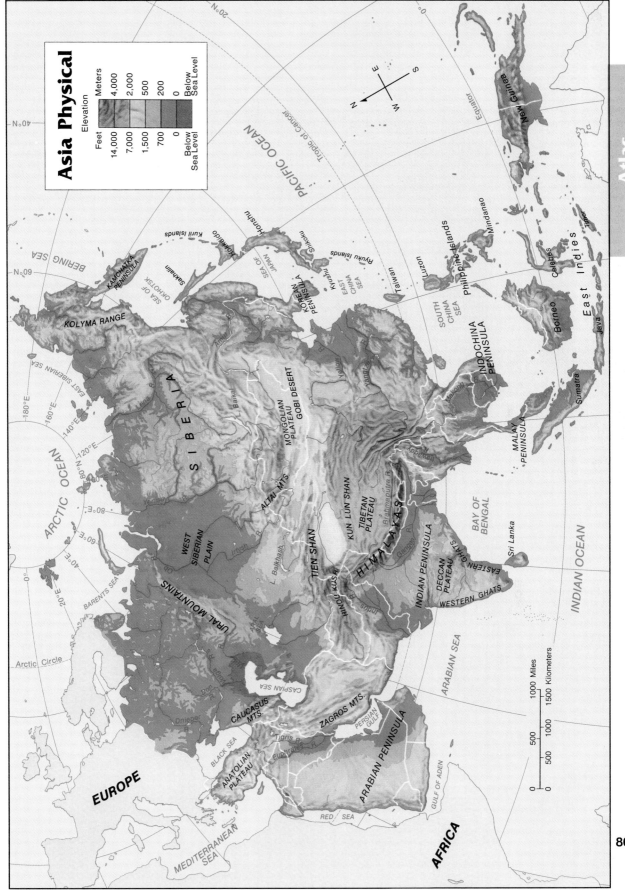

Asia Physical

Elevation

Feet	Meters
14,000	4,000
7,000	2,000
1,500	500
700	200
0	0
Below Sea Level	Below Sea Level

E — S — N — W

PACIFIC OCEAN

Tropic of Cancer

Equator

New Guinea

Mindanao

Philippine Islands

Celebes

East Indies

Luzon

Timor

Borneo

Taiwan

Java

SOUTH CHINA SEA

EAST CHINA SEA

Ryukyu Islands

Kyushu

Shikoku

Honshu

Hokkaido

Kuril Islands

Sakhalin

SEA OF JAPAN

SEA OF OKHOTSK

KOREAN PENINSULA

KAMCHATKA PENINSULA

BERING SEA

KOLYMA RANGE

SIBERIA

ARCTIC OCEAN

EAST SIBERIAN SEA

Lena

Baikal

Amur

MONGOLIAN PLATEAU

GOBI DESERT

ALTAI MTS.

TIEN SHAN

KUN LUN SHAN

TIBETAN PLATEAU

HIMALAYAS

HINDU KUSH

Brahmaputra R.

Ganges

Indus

Mekong

Yangtze

INDOCHINA PENINSULA

MALAY PENINSULA

Sumatra

BAY OF BENGAL

Sri Lanka

INDIAN PENINSULA

DECCAN PLATEAU

EASTERN GHATS

WESTERN GHATS

INDIAN OCEAN

ARABIAN SEA

ARABIAN PENINSULA

PERSIAN GULF

ZAGROS MTS.

CASPIAN SEA

Tigris R.

Euphrates

CAUCASUS MTS.

BLACK SEA

ANATOLIAN PLATEAU

URAL MOUNTAINS

WEST SIBERIAN PLAIN

Ob

Irtysh

L. Balkhash

Yenisey

BARENTS SEA

Arctic Circle

Aral Sea

Volga

Don

Dnieper

EUROPE

AFRICA

MEDITERRANEAN SEA

RED SEA

GULF OF ADEN

Atlas

Arctic Circle

20° N.

40° N.

60° N.

80° E.

60° E.

40° E.

20° E.

0°

180° E.

160° E.

140° E.

120° E.

100° E.

1000 Miles				
0	500	1000	1500 Kilometers
0	500	1000	

865

Europe Today

★ Capital city
● Other city

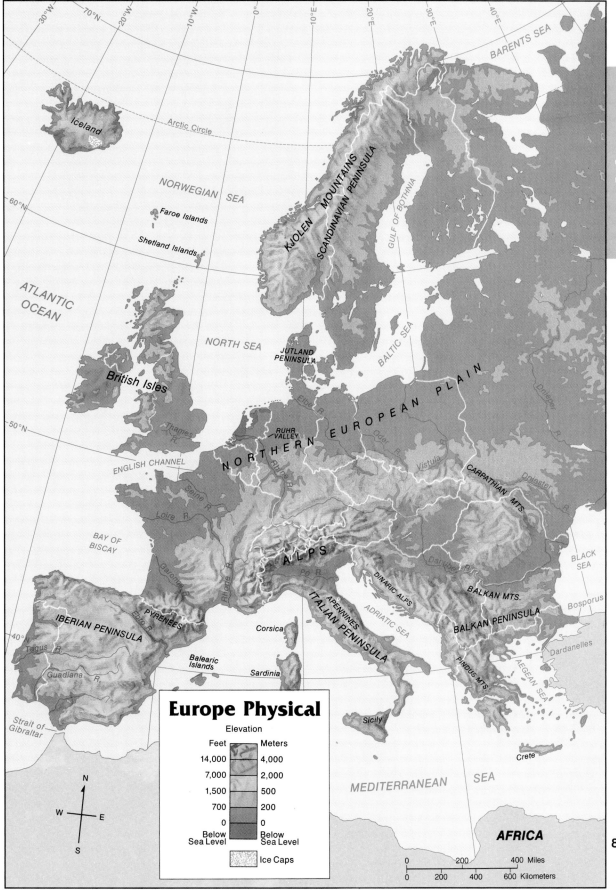

Iceland

Arctic Circle

BARENTS SEA

NORWEGIAN SEA

Faroe Islands

Shetland Islands

KJÖLEN MOUNTAINS

SCANDINAVIAN PENINSULA

GULF OF BOTHNIA

ATLANTIC
OCEAN

NORTH SEA

BALTIC SEA

JUTLAND
PENINSULA

British Isles

Dnieper R.

NORTHERN   EUROPEAN   PLAIN

Elbe R.

RUHR
VALLEY

Oder R.

Vistula

CARPATHIAN   MTS.

Dniester R.

Thames R.

ENGLISH CHANNEL

Rhine R.

Seine R.

Loire R.

BAY OF
BISCAY

Garonne R.

Rhône R.

A L P S

Po R.

DINARIC ALPS

ADRIATIC SEA

Danube R.

BLACK
SEA

Bosporus

BALKAN MTS.

BALKAN PENINSULA

APENNINES

ITALIAN PENINSULA

IBERIAN PENINSULA

PYRENEES

Ebro R.

Corsica

Tagus R.

Balearic
Islands

Sardinia

Guadiana R.

Strait of
Gibraltar

Sicily

PINDUS MTS.

AEGEAN
SEA

Dardanelles

Crete

Europe Physical

Elevation

Feet		Meters
14,000		4,000
7,000		2,000
1,500		500
700		200
0		0
Below Sea Level		Below Sea Level

Ice Caps

N
W E
S

MEDITERRANEAN   SEA

AFRICA

0   200   400 Miles

0   200   400   600 Kilometers

867

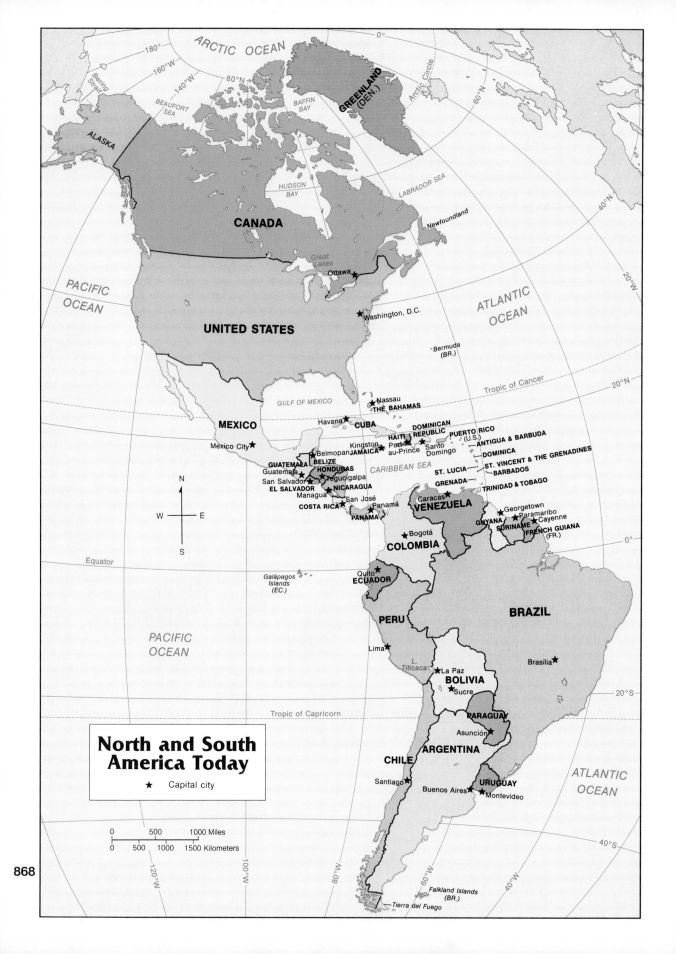

North and South America Today

★ Capital city

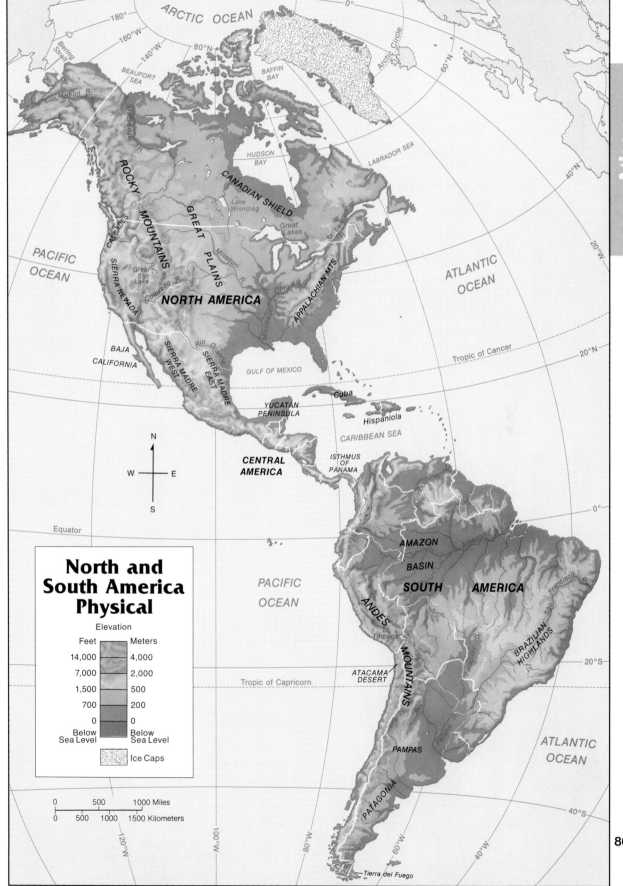

ARCTIC OCEAN

180°

160° W

140° W

BEAUFORT SEA

Yukon R.

BERING STRAIT

80°N

BAFFIN BAY

Arctic Circle

60°N

40°N

Atlas

HUDSON BAY

Mackenzie R.

ROCKY MOUNTAINS

CANADIAN SHIELD

LABRADOR SEA

20°W

GREAT PLAINS

Lake Winnipeg

Great Lakes

St. Lawrence R.

PACIFIC OCEAN

CASCADES

SIERRA NEVADA

Great Salt Lake

Colorado R.

Missouri R.

Mississippi R.

Ohio R.

APPALACHIAN MTS.

ATLANTIC OCEAN

NORTH AMERICA

BAJA CALIFORNIA

SIERRA MADRE WEST

SIERRA MADRE EAST

Rio Grande

GULF OF MEXICO

Tropic of Cancer

20°N

YUCATAN PENINSULA

Cuba

Hispaniola

CARIBBEAN SEA

N

W ← → E

S

CENTRAL AMERICA

ISTHMUS OF PANAMA

Orinoco R.

60°W

Equator

AMAZON

Amazon R.

0°

North and South America Physical

Elevation

Feet	Meters
14,000	4,000
7,000	2,000
1,500	500
700	200
0	0
Below Sea Level	Below Sea Level

Ice Caps

PACIFIC OCEAN

BASIN

SOUTH AMERICA

ANDES

Titicaca

São Francisco R.

BRAZILIAN HIGHLANDS

MOUNTAINS

ATACAMA DESERT

20°S

Tropic of Capricorn

Paraguay R.

Paraná R.

0 500 1000 Miles

0 500 1000 1500 Kilometers

PAMPAS

ATLANTIC OCEAN

PATAGONIA

120°W

100°W

80°W

60°W

40°W

40°S

Tierra del Fuego

869

A Chronology of World History

This chronology includes some of the most important events and developments in world history. It can be used to trace developments in different parts of the world in the areas of government and society, science and technology, the arts and literature, and religion and philosophy. The number next to each entry refers to the chapter in which the event or development is discussed in the text.

	Government and Society	Science and Technology
3000 B.C.– **2501 B.C.**	Civilizations develop in river valleys **Introduction** Old Kingdom in Egypt 1 Sumerian city-states 2	Great Pyramid of Khufu in Egypt 1 Egyptian calendar 1 Sumerian arithmetic 2
2500 B.C.– **2001 B.C.**	Middle Kingdom in Egypt 1 Sargon in Mesopotamia 2 Indus Valley civilization 3	Chinese calendar 3 Irrigation of Nile Delta 1
2000 B.C.– **1501 B.C.**	Minoan civilization 4 Hammurabi's law code 2 Shang dynasty in China 3 New Kingdom in Egypt 1	Indus cities planned 3 Shang mathematics and astronomy 3
1500 B.C.– **1001 B.C.**	Aryans in India 3 Trojan War 4 Tutankhamon in Egypt 1 Dorians invade Peloponnesus 4 Chou dynasty in China 3	Beginning of Iron Age 2
1000 B.C.– **501 B.C.**	Efficient government in Assyria 2 Solomon's rule in Israel 2 Persian Empire 2 Caste system emerges in India 3	Chaldean mathematics and astronomy 2 Great Royal Road in Persian Empire 2 Hippocrates 4
500 B.C.– **1 B.C.**	Persian Wars 4 Athenian democracy 4 Alexander the Great 4 Asoka in India 7 Roman Republic 5	Alexandria in Egypt center of Hellenistic science 4 Colosseum built in Rome 6 Roman aqueducts and roads 6

1 A.D.–
500 A.D.
	Han dynasty in China 7
	Roman Empire 5, 6
	Maya civilization in Central
	  America 12
	Fall of Rome 6
	Gupta Empire in India 7
		Natural History by Pliny the Elder 6
		Medical encyclopedia of Galen 6
		Decimal system and concept of zero
		  in India 7
		Paper invented in China 7
		Maya develop calendar and zero 12

The Arts and Literature	Religion and Philosophy	
Gilgamesh Epic 2	Pharaohs as god-kings in Egypt 1 Dumuzi and Inanna in Sumer 2	**3000** B.C.– **2501** B.C.
Temples at Luxor and Karnak 1 Egyptian literature 1	Osiris worshipped in Egypt 1 Mother goddess worshipped in Indus Valley 3	**2500** B.C.– **2001** B.C.
Chinese bronzes and silk 3 Chinese writing 3 Minoan frescoes 4	Ancestor worship and use of oracle bones in China 3	**2000** B.C.– **1501** B.C.
Temple of Hatshepsut in Egypt 1 Obelisks built in Egypt 1	Vedas and Upanishads in India 3 Hinduism develops 3, 7 Akenaton in Egypt 1 Herbrew belief in one God 2	**1500** B.C.– **1001** B.C.
Library at Nineveh 2 Phoenician alphabet 2 *Ramayana* in India 3 *Book of Odes* in China 3 *Iliad* by Homer 4	Olympian gods in Greece 4 Buddhism founded 7 Zoroaster in Persian Empire 2 Confucius in China 7	**1000** B.C.– **501** B.C.
Parthenon in Greece 4 *Antigone* by Sophocles 4 *Aeneid* by Virgil 5 Stupas built in India 7	Socrates, Plato, and Aristotle in Athens 4 Stoics and Epicureans in Greece 4 Legalism in China 7	**500** B.C.– **1** B.C.

The Annals by Tacitus 6
Roman mosaics 6
Kalidasa in India 7
First Chinese dictionary 7
Ajanta cave paintings 7
	Christianity founded 6
	Christianity becomes official religion
	  of Roman Empire 6
	Confucianism influences Chinese
	  government 7
		1 A.D.–
		500 A.D.

	Government and Society	Science and Technology

501–1000	Charlemagne in Europe 8
	Emergence of feudalism in Europe 8
	Expansion of Islamic Empire 11
	Golden Age of T'ang in China 13
	Kingdom of Ghana in West Africa 12
		Stirrup, heavy plow, three-field
		  system in Europe 8
		Arab advances in science and
		  mathematics 11
		Printing in China 13

1001–1499	Crusades 9 Decline of feudalism in Europe 10 Kublai Khan in China 13 Fall of Constantinople to Turks 11	Flying buttress, clocks, glass in Europe 9 Inca roads and terraces 12 Printing press in Europe 14

1500–1599	Aztec and Inca empires conquered
	  in New World 15
	Magellan rounds Cape Horn 15
	Height of Ottoman Empire 16
	Akbar in India 13
		Scientific Revolution begins in
		  Europe 17
		Copernicus studies planets 17
		Vesalius studies anatomy 17

1600–1699	Emergence of absolute monarchs
	  in Europe 16
	Thirty Years' War 16
	Louis XIV in France 16
	Tokugawa shoguns isolate Japan 13
	English Bill of Rights 18
		Galileo challenges traditional
		  thinking 17
		Invention of microscope 17
		Newton develops mathematical
		  laws 17
		Steam-driven engine developed 21

1700–1799	Enlightened monarchs in Europe 17 American Revolution 18 French Revolution 19	Agricultural Revolution in Europe 21 Industrial Revolution begins in Britain 21 Inventions in textile industry 21

1800–1899	Congress of Vienna 20
	Independent nations in Latin
	  America 27
	Unification of Italy 24
	Unification of Germany 24
	American Civil War 23
	Age of Imperialism 25, 26, 27
		Spread of Industrial Revolution 21
		Fulton develops steamship 21
		Telephone and electric light
		  invented 21
		Advances in physics and chemistry 22
		Improvements in medicine 22

1900–Present	World War I 28 Great Depression 29 Rise of totalitarian states 30 World War II 31 Nations of Africa, Middle East, and Asia win independence 33, 34, 35	Assembly-line production 21 Flight at Kitty Hawk 21 Airplanes used in war 28, 31 Space Age begins Epilogue Invention of computers Epilogue

Chronology

Glossary

This glossary defines many important historical terms and phrases. Many of the terms are phonetically respelled to aid in pronunciation. See the Pronunciation Key below for an explanation of the respellings. The page number following each definition is the page on which the term or phrase is first discussed in the text. Most of the entries appear in boldface the first time they are used in the text.

Pronunciation Key

When difficult terms or names first appear in the text, they are respelled to aid pronunciation. A syllable in LARGE CAPITAL LETTERS receives the most stress. Syllables with a secondary stress appear in SMALL CAPITAL LETTERS. The key below lists the letters used for respelling. It includes examples of words using each sound and shows how they would be respelled.

Symbol	Example	Respelling
a	hat	(hat)
ay	pay, late	(pay), (layt)
ah	star, hot	(stahr), (haht)
ai	air, dare	(air), (dair)
aw	law, all	(law), (awl)
eh	met	(meht)
ee	bee, eat	(bee), (eet)
er	learn, sir, fur	(lern), (ser), (fer)
ih	fit	(fiht)
ī	mile	(mīl)
ir	ear	(ir)
oh	no	(noh)
oi	soil, boy	(soil), (boi)
oo	root, rule	(root), (rool)
or	born, door	(born), (dor)
ow	plow, out	(plow), (owt)

Symbol	Example	Respelling
u	put, book	(put), (buk)
uh	fun	(fuhn)
yoo	few, use	(fyoo), (yooz)
ch	chill, reach	(chihl), (reech)
g	go, dig	(goh), (dihg)
j	jet, gently, bridge	(jeht), (JEHNT-lee), (brihj)
k	kite, cup	(kīt), (kuhp)
ks	mix	(mihks)
kw	quick	(kwihk)
ng	bring	(brihng)
s	say, cent	(say), (sehnt)
sh	she, crash	(shee), (krash)
th	three	(three)
th	then, breathe	(thehn), (breeth)
y	yet, onion	(yeht), (UHN-yuhn)
z	zip, always	(zihp), (AWL-wayz)
zh	treasure	(TREH-zher)

A

absolute monarch ruler who has complete authority over the government and the lives of the people (page 374)

acropolis (uh KRAPH uhl ihs) hilltop fortress in a city-state of ancient Greece (page 78)

adobe sun-dried brick used for house building by early peoples in the American southwest (page 253)

age grade in African family organization, all the boys and girls born in the same year (page 250)

alchemist medieval scientist who attempted to change worthless metals into gold (page 190)

Anschluss (AHN shlus) union between Germany and Austria (page 692)

anthropologist (AN thruh PAHL uh jihst) scientist who studies the ways people organize societies (page 7)

apartheid (uh PAHRT hayt) policy of rigid separation of races; practiced in South Africa (page 748)

appeasement (uh PEEZ mehnt) making concessions to an aggressor in order to preserve peace (page 693)

apprentice (uh PREHN tihs) young person who learns a trade from a master craftsman (page 184)

aqueduct (AK wuh DUKHT) in ancient Rome, canal-like stone structure that carried water to the cities from reservoirs in the country (page 121)

archaeologist (AHR kee AHL uh jihst) scientist who studies the lives of early peoples by analyzing objects they left behind (page 7)

archipelago (AHR kuh PEHL uh GOH) chain of islands (page 275)

archons (AHR kahns) in ancient Greece, three officials heading the governing council of the aristocracy (page 80)

aristocracy (AR uh STAH kruh see) government headed by a privileged minority or upper class (page 78)

armistice (AHR muh stihs) end to fighting in a war (page 638)

artifact (AHR tuh FAKT) object made by human beings (page 7)

artisan (AHR tuh zuhn) skilled craftsperson (page 14)

assembly line production method that breaks down a complex job into a series of smaller tasks (page 483)

assimilation (uh SIHM uh LAY shuhn) policy whereby an imperial power tries to absorb a colony politically and culturally (page 575)

astrolabe (AS truh LAYB) instrument used to calculate a ship's latitude by measuring the positions of the stars (page 350)

atman (AHT muhn) in Hinduism, the universal soul (page 137)

autocracy (aw TAH kruh see) government in which the ruler has unlimited power (page 545)

autonomy (aw TAHN uh mee) self-government (page 549)

B

bailiff (BAY lihf) during the Middle Ages, the agent of a lord who managed the lord's smaller estates (page 172)

barter economy system in which one set of goods is exchanged for another (page 14)

Bessemer process procedure developed in the 1850s that made steel production cheaper and easier (page 476)

bill of exchange in the Middle Ages, bank paper allowing merchants to exchange coins for paper in one city, redeem paper for coins in a distant city (page 195)

blitzkrieg (BLIHTS kreeg) German for lightning war; swift, massive attack, practiced by the armies of Nazi Germany (page 695)

boyar powerful Russian noble under the czars (page 230)

brahma (BRAH muh) in Hinduism, the single, supreme force uniting everything in the universe (page 137)

bronze hard metal composed of copper combined with tin, developed in the late Neolithic Age (page 12)

bureaucracy (byoo RAH kruh see) system of organizing government by departments or bureaus (page 66)

bushido (BOO shee DOH) the way of the warrior; during the feudal period in Japan, a code of conduct for samurai stressing obedience to one's lord (page 279)

C

cabildo (cah BEEL doh) in sixteenth century Spanish America, city council appointed by the king of Spain (page 359)

caliph (KAY lihf) successor to the prophet Muhammad who acted as both religious and political leader (page 234)

capital money that can be invested in business (page 367)

capitalist person who invests in business in order to make a profit (page 369)

cash crop crop that can be sold on the world market for money (page 563)

caste social group based on birth; in India, caste determined the jobs people could hold (page 59)

cataract waterfall and rapids posing obstacles to navigation (page 21)

caudillo (kow DEE yoh) during the 1800s in Latin America, a military dictator (page 608)

censor official in ancient Rome who registered the population for tax and voting purposes and enforced the moral code (page 103)

charter in the Middle Ages, written document guaranteeing the rights of townspeople (page 184)

chivalry (SHIHV 'l ree) code of conduct during the Middle Ages that combined Christian values with the values of a warrior (page 169)

city-state independent town or city and the surrounding countryside (page 37)

clan family group that traces its origin to a common ancestor (page 275)

coalition temporary alliance between parties in government (page 520)

cold war state of tension and hostility among nations without armed conflict (page 713)

collective farm large government-run farm; created in the Soviet Union in the 1930s (page 675)

collective security group of nations acting together to preserve peace (page 650)

coloni in Ancient Rome farmers who worked land they had given to nobles in return for protection (page 128)

colony territory that an outside power controls directly (page 560)

comedy in Ancient Greece, play which ridiculed people, ideas, and social customs (page 89)

commercial colonialism practice by which the English East India Company controlled India's foreign trade and kept friendly local rulers in power (page 582)

common law system of law in England based on decisions of royal courts that became accepted legal principles (page 201)

communism form of complete socialism in which there is public ownership of all land and all the means of production (page 498)

conquistador (kohn KEES tah DOHR) conqueror; person given the right by rulers of Spain to establish outposts in the Americas (page 358)

conservatism during the 1800s, philosophy that supported the traditional political and social order and resisted change (page 455)

consul official from the patrician class who administered the laws of ancient Rome (page 102)

containment policy whereby the United States tried to prevent the Soviet Union from expanding beyond its borders; first applied in the late 1940s (page 716)

corporation business owned by many investors who buy shares of stock and risk only the amount of their investment (page 484)

coup d'état (koo day TAH) revolt by military leaders against a government (page 744)

covenant binding agreement (page 47)

creole (KREE ohl) descendant of Spanish settlers born in the Americas (page 603)

crusade a military expedition by Christians against Muslims who controlled the Holy Land (page 192)

cultural bias the way a person's culture shapes his or her attitude toward an event (page 574)

culture customs, ideas, and way of life of a group of people (page 15)

cuneiform (kyoo NEE uh FORM) term used to describe the wedge-shaped writing of the ancient Sumerians (page 38)

Cyrillic alphabet (suh RIHL ihk) alphabet devised in the ninth century by Greek monks Cyril and Methodius (page 228)

czar (zahr) Russian word for Caesar; title of the ruler of the Russian Empire (page 230)

D

daimyo (DĪ myoh) powerful warrior knights, directly below the shogun, in Japan during the feudal period (page 278)

delta triangular area of marshy flatlands formed by deposits of silt at the mouths of some rivers (page 20)

demesne (dih MAYN) during the Middle Ages, a portion of manor land a lord reserved for his own use (page 171)

democracy government in which citizens have ruling power; first developed in ancient Athens (page 79)

denazification removal of all traces of Nazism in Germany after World War II (page 715)

détente (day TAHNT) French word meaning relaxation; easing of international tension, especially between the Soviet Union and the United States (page 828)

devalue to lower the value of items such as coins (page 115)

dictator ruler with absolute power; in ancient Rome, a dictator could hold power for only six months (page 103)

direct democracy system of government in which citizens participate directly rather than through representatives (page 86)

direct primary election in which voters select candidates for office (page 527)

dissident (DIHS uh duhnt) person who speaks out against a government (page 825)

domestic system system in which a merchant paid peasants in the countryside to do work such as spinning and weaving, thus bypassing guild regulations (page 369)

donatario in sixteenth century Brazil, landowner of territory granted by the king of Portugal (page 362)

dynastic cycle rise and fall of Chinese dynasties according to the Mandate of Heaven (page 66)

dynasty (DI nuhs tee) ruling family that passes the right to rule from one member to another (page 23)

E

ecology (ee KAHL uh jee) relationship between living things and their environment (page 844)

émigré (EHM uh gray) person who flees his or her country for political reasons (page 439)

empire group of territories or peoples controlled by one ruler (page 25)

enclosure movement during the 1700s in Britain, the practice of fencing off common lands by individual landowners (page 474)

encomienda (ehn koh mee EHN dah) right the Spanish government granted settlers in the Americas to demand taxes or labor services from Indians living on land (page 359)

Enlightenment name applied to the 1700s, when philosophers emphasized the use of reason, which they believed would free people from ignorance and perfect society (page 401)

entrepreneur (AHN truh pruh NER) merchant willing to take financial risks in the hope of making large profits (page 366)

ephor in Sparta, overseer elected by the assembly to direct state affairs and supervise helots (page 82)

exchequer central treasury of England (page 201)

excommunication (EHKS kuh MYOO nuh KAY shun) exclusion from the sacraments of the Roman Catholic Church (page 176)

extended family large family group usually made up of a husband and wife, their unmarried children, their married sons, and the sons' wives and children (page 59)

extraterritoriality (EHKS truh TEHR uh TAWR ee AL uh tee) the right of foreigners to be protected by the laws of their own nations (page 586)

F

factory system system in which workers and machines are brought together in one place to manufacture goods (page 476)

feudal contract in the Middle Ages, rules governing the relationship between lord and vassals, based on traditional practices (page 167)

feudalism (FYOOD 'l ihzm) system of rule by local lords who were bound to a king by ties of loyalty; developed in Western Europe during the Middle Ages (page 166)

fief (feef) during the Middle Ages, an estate that a lord provided a vassal (page 167)

flying buttress in Gothic cathedrals, stone arm leaning against outside wall to help support weight of roof (page 186)

fossil evidence of plant or animal life preserved in rock (page 7)

frame of reference the way a historian's environment shapes how he or she interprets a historical event (page 631)

free market market in which goods are bought and sold without restrictions (page 406)

fresco (FREHS koh) wall painting (page 76)

G

general strike mass walkout by unionized workers in all industries (page 648)

genetic engineering laboratory techniques that alter the genes of an organism (page 841)

genocide (JEH noh sīd) the systematic killing of a whole people or nation (page 661)

geography study of people, their environments, and their resources (page 3)

glacier thick sheet of ice that spread down from polar regions during the ice ages (page 10)

glasnost policy of "openness" toward the West, instituted by Soviet leader Mikhail Gorbachev (page 826)

grand jury jury deciding whether enough evidence exists to bring a case to trial (page 201)

gross national product total value of goods and services produced by a nation in a year; abbreviated GNP (page 787)

guerrilla warfare (guh RIHL uh WAHR fahr) Spanish word for little war; fighting comprised of hit-and-run attacks (page 449)

guild association of merchants or artisans that governed a town or craft in the Middle Ages (page 184)

H

haiku (HĪ koo) short Japanese poem with 17 syllables that creates a mood or describes a scene (page 280)

hejira (hih JĪ ruh) Muhammad's journey from Mecca to Medina in 622 (page 231)

Hellenistic civilization culture blending eastern and western influences that emerged in Greece and other lands conquered by Alexander the Great (page 96)

helot in Sparta, slave who worked the land (page 82)

heretic according to the early Roman Catholic Church, anyone not belonging to the Church (page 162)

hierarchy (HĪ uh RAHR kee) organization in which officials are arranged according to rank (page 127)

hieroglyphics (HĪ er oh GLIHF ihks) system of writing developed by Egyptian priests in which pictures were used to represent words and sounds (page 22)

Holocaust (HAHL uh KAWST) the systematic murder of over 6 million Jews by the Nazis before and during World War II (page 708)

humanities subjects taught in ancient Greek and Roman schools, including grammar, rhetoric, poetry, and history; stressed by Renaissance scholars (page 326)

I

ideogram (IHD ee uh gram) picture that symbolizes an idea or action (page 22)

illumination decoration in the margins and on the first letter of paragraphs of Bibles made by monks in the Middle Ages (page 164)

imperator in Ancient Rome, commander-in-chief of the Roman armies (page 111)

imperialism (ihm PIHR ee uhl ihzm) domination by one country of the political, economic, or cultural life of another country or region (page 560)

indulgence reduction of the punishment a sinner would suffer in purgatory; often granted by medieval and Renaissance popes (page 338)

inflation economic cycle in which an increase in the money supply results in an increase in prices (page 115)

intendant royal agent appointed by French monarchs to govern the provinces (page 380)

interchangeable parts identical components that can be used in place of one another in manufacturing (page 482)

J

joint-stock company private trading company in which shares are sold to investors to finance business ventures (page 367)

journeyman person who completed an apprenticeship and then worked for a master craftsman to perfect his or her skills (page 184)

just price in the Middle Ages, price established by craft guilds, allowing for cost of materials and reasonable profit (page 184)

K

kami (KAH mee) spirits that early Japanese believed controlled the forces of nature (page 275)

karma (KAHR muh) in Hinduism, all the actions in a person's life that affect his or her fate in the next life (page 138)

kibbutz (kih BOOTS) Israeli settlement in which people live in community housing projects, work together, and share the profits of their labor (page 769)

knight in the Middle Ages, lesser noble who served as a mounted warrior for a lord (page 167)

kulak (koo LAHK) prosperous peasant in the Soviet Union who opposed collectivization during the 1930s (page 675)

L

laissez faire (LEHS ay FEHR) French phrase meaning let people do as they choose; used to describe an economic system in which the government does not interfere with the economy (page 495)

latifundia (LAT uh FUHN dee uh) vast estate in ancient Rome (page 108)

latitude (LAT uh TOOD) distance north or south of the Equator; measured in degrees (page 4)

law of gravity mathematical formula devised by Isaac Newton explaining the attraction of objects (page 403)

lay investiture (lay ihn VEHS tuh chuhr) practice during the Middle Ages whereby political rulers appointed many high Church officials (page 205)

legion military formation of ancient Rome made up of about 6,000 soldiers (page 103)

legitimacy (luh JIHT uh muh see) Metternich's principle of restoring to power the royal families that had lost their thrones when Napoleon conquered Europe (page 457)

liberalism during the 1800s, philosophy that supported guarantees of individual freedom, political change, and social reform (page 455)

liberation theology doctrine supported by many Catholic priests, calling for the Church to take an active role in changing the conditions that contribute to poverty (page 801)

limited monarchy government in which a monarch's powers are limited, usually by a constitution and a legislative body (page 202)

loess fine soil distributed by wind and flood waters (page 61)

longitude (LAHN juh TOOD) distance east or west of the Prime Meridian (page 4)

lord in the Middle Ages, powerful noble who maintained his own land but owed allegiance to the king (page 167)

lycée government-run school set up by Napoleon to develop knowledge and patriotism in children of the wealthy (page 447)

lyric poem in Ancient Greece, poem in which the poet's emotions or thoughts are sung by a musician playing a lyre (page 90)

M

mandate after World War I, a territory that was administered but not owned by members of the League of Nations (page 641)

manor during the Middle Ages, the lands, including a village and surrounding lands, administered by a lord (page 171)

martial law (MAHR shul) temporary rule by the military under which individual rights are limited (page 791)

martyr (MAHR ter) person who dies or suffers for his or her beliefs (page 125)

mass production method of manufacturing large quantities of identical goods (page 483)

matrilineal (MAT ruh LIHN ee uhl) describes a family in which children trace their family line through their mother (page 250)

mercantilism (MER kuhn tihl ihzm) economic philosophy maintaining that a nation's economic strength depends on exporting more goods than it imports (page 368)

messiah savior chosen by God (page 123)

mestizo (mehs TEE zoh) person in Spain's colonies in the Americas who was of mixed European and Indian heritage (page 603)

Middle Ages period of history in Europe following the fall of the Roman Empire and lasting from about 500 to 1350 (page 161)

militarism glorification of the military and readiness for war (page 537)

minaret slender tower from which Muslims are called to prayer (page 237)

mir in Czarist Russia, village community where peasants were given land to farm, which they paid for over a period of 49 years (page 546)

missi dominici (MIH see DOHM in NEE kee) during Charlemagne's reign, royal officials who checked on the administrations of local nobles (page 163)

mobilization process of calling troops into active service (page 628)

modernization creation of a stable society capable of producing a high level of goods and services (page 741)

monarchy (MAHN uhr kee) government headed by a king or queen (page 78)

money economy economic system based on the exchange of money rather than on barter (page 47)

monopoly (muh NAHP uh lee) total control of the market for a particular product by one corporation (page 484)

monotheism (MAHN uh thee ihzm) worship of a single god (page 26)

monsoon (mahn SOON) seasonal wind; in India, the summer monsoon brings rain and the winter monsoon brings hot, dry weather (page 54)

mosaic picture formed of chips of colored stone (page 119)

mosque meeting place where Muslims assemble to pray (page 232)

multinational corporation large enterprise that operates in many countries (page 742)

N

nationalism feeling of pride for and devotion to one's country (page 449)

nationalize (NASH uh nuh LĪZ) to bring a part of the economy under government control (page 665)

nirvana (nihr VAH nuh) in Hinduism and Buddhism, the ultimate goal of life; the condition of wanting nothing (page 139)

nomad person who travels in search of food (page 10)

nuclear family family made up of parents, children, and occasionally grandparents (page 249)

O

oracle bones according to religious beliefs of the Shang dynasty in China, bones that could be used to predict the future (page 63)

ostracism (AHS trah sihzm) in ancient Greece, the temporary exile of a citizen from a city-state (page 81)

Ostpolitik policy of improving relations with communist nations of Eastern Europe, instituted in West Germany by Willy Brandt (page 823)

P

pacifism refusal to fight in a war (page 693)

papyrus (puh PĪ ruhs) reed that grows along marshy shores; used for making paper in ancient Egypt (page 20)

parable short story with a simple moral lesson (page 125)

parish rural district first organized by the Roman Catholic Church during Charlemagne's reign (page 163)

passive resistance nonviolent opposition and refusal to cooperate (page 649)

paternalism (puh TER n'l ihzm) system in which an imperial power governs its colonies closely because it believes that the people are not able to govern themselves (page 574)

patriarch in the Byzantine empire, bishop of a major city appointed by the emperor (page 226)

patrician (puh TRIHSH uhn) member of the class of wealthy landowners in ancient Rome (page 102)

patrilineal (PAT ruh LIHN ee uhl) describes a family in which children trace their family line through their father (page 250)

patroon wealthy landowner in New Netherland, who had much power in governing the estate (page 363)

peninsular (peh NIHN suh LAHR) official sent by Spain to rule Spanish colonies in the Americas (page 602)

perestroika (pehr uh STROI kuh) restructuring of the Soviet economy and society, instituted by Mikhail Gorbachev (page 826)

phalanx (FAY langks) in ancient Greece, a massive formation of heavily armed foot soldiers (page 79)

pharaoh (FAIR oh) title of the rulers of ancient Egypt who had absolute control over people's lives (page 23)

philosophe (fee loh ZOHF) French word meaning philosopher; person during the Enlightenment who believed that the use of science and reason would lead to human progress (page 406)

philosopher in ancient greece, person seeking wisdom and knowledge through systematic study and logic (page 90)

physiocrat (FIHZ ee uh KRAT) philosophe who searched for natural laws to explain economics (page 406)

pictogram (PIHK tuh gram) picture used to represent an object (page 22)

plantation large estate operated by the owner or overseer and farmed by workers living on it (page 361)

plebeian (plih BEE uhn) member of the class of common people in ancient Rome, including farmers, artisans, small merchants, and traders (page 102)

pogrom (poh GRAHM) violent raid on a Jewish community, often conducted by government troops (page 547)

polis in ancient Greece, a city-state consisting of a fortified hilltop and its surrounding fields (page 78)

polytheism (PAHL ih thee ihzm) belief in many gods (page 13)

pope title meaning "father of the Church," taken by Christian bishops of Rome (page 127)

potlatch (PAHT latch) feast given by wealthy families among Native Americans who lived on the Pacific coast to prove their high social position (page 253)

predestination (pree DEHS tuh NAY shun) idea that God has chosen who will be saved (page 342)

prehistory period of time before writing was invented (page 7)

primary source first-hand account written by the person who experienced the event (page 132)

prime minister head of the cabinet in parliamentary governments, usually the leader of the largest party in the legislature (page 423)

privatization selling of state-owned industries to private investors (page 821)

productivity the amount of goods a worker can produce in a specific time (page 482)

projection way mapmakers show the curved earth on a flat surface (page 7)

proletariat (PROH luh TAIR ee uht) the working class (page 498)

propaganda (PRAHP uh GAN duh) spread of ideas to further a cause or damage an opposing cause (page 635)

proprietary colony (pruh PRĪ uh TAIR ee) English colony in North America owned by an individual, usually a friend of the king (page 364)

protectorate (pruh TEHK tuhr iht) country with its own government, but whose policies are directed by an outside power (page 560)

psychology the study of individual behavior (page 503)

pueblo in the early Southwest, small town with its own elected officials and council of elders (page 253)

purdah (PER duh) practice of secluding women; probably originated in northern India and spread to Islamic lands (page 265)

Q

quipu (KEE poo) cord with many knotted strings that was used by the Inca to record census data, the size of a harvest, and historical events (page 258)

R

rajah (RAH juh) elected chief of an Aryan tribe in ancient India (page 57)

recall vote that allows voters to remove elected officials from office if the officials are considered incompetent (page 527)

reconquista (REE kahn KEES tah) crusade launched by Christian knights to expel Muslims from Spain (page 208)

regionalism loyalty to a small geographic area (page 608)

reincarnation (REE ihn kahr NAY shuhn) rebirth of the soul in another bodily form; a belief of Hinduism and Buddhism (page 58)

Renaissance (REHN uh SAHNS) period from about 1350 to 1600 in which European scholars revived the learning of ancient Greece and Rome (page 325)

reparation (REHP uh RAY shuhn) payment for war damages (page 640)

republic system of government in which citizens who have the right to vote choose their leaders (page 102)

revolution of rising expectations desire of people in developing nations to enjoy the high standard of living of people in the industrialized world (page 848)

S

sachem Iroquois chief who belonged to a council, which settled disputes among members of tribes belonging to the Iroquois league (page 254)

sacrament (SAK ruh mehnt) one of the seven sacred rites administered by the Roman Catholic Church (page 176)

salon (suh LAHN) informal gathering at which writers, musicians, painters, and philosophes exchanged ideas (page 409)

samurai (SAM uh rī) warrior knights of Japan during the feudal period (page 277)

satrapy province in the Persian Empire ruled by a governor responsible to the king (page 44)

savanna (suh VAN uh) grasslands dotted with scattered trees in which rainfall is often unreliable (page 243)

scholasticism (skuh LAS tuh sihzm) school of thought in which reason and logic were used to support Christian belief (page 190)

scientific method an approach to the study of the natural world in which experiments, observation, and mathematics are used to prove scientific theories (page 402)

scribe in ancient times, a person who knew how to read and write (page 15)

secondary source second-hand account based on writings or evidence not directly experienced (page 132)

segregation (SEHG ruh GAY shuhn) practice of separating people according to race (page 727)

sepoy (SEE poi) Indian soldier who served in a European army (page 582)

seppuku ritual suicide performed by disgraced samurai in feudal Japan (page 279)

serf peasant who was tied to the lord's land (page 171)

shogun (SHOH guhn) after 1192, the chief general in Japan, who held more political power than the emperor (page 278)

silt a soil rich in minerals deposited by flooding rivers (page 12)

simony in the Middle Ages, buying and selling of religious offices (page 177)

socialism economic and political system in which society as a whole rather than private individuals own all property and operate all businesses (page 461)

sociology the study of society (page 503)

Socratic method in ancient Greece, question-and-answer technique, developed by Socrates, that used reasoning in the search for truth (page 91)

soviet (SOH vee iht) council of workers, soldiers, and intellectuals formed by Russian revolutionaries in 1917 (page 670)

sphere of influence region in which an outside power claims exclusive investment or trading privileges (page 560)

status quo (STAYT uhs KWOH) existing state of affairs (page 458)

stupa (STOOP uh) large dome-like Buddhist structure containing the remains of a saintly monk (page 142)

suffrage the right to vote (page 512)

sultan (SUHL t'n) Muslim ruler (page 264)

superconductor material that conducts electricity without resistance, thereby saving energy (page 839)

survival of the fittest Darwin's theory of natural selection, which states that the best-adapted individuals survive (page 499)

T

tao (DOW) in Taoism, a universal force that can only be felt; also the way a person achieves harmony with that force (page 148)

technology (tehk NAHL uh jee) tools and skills people use (page 11)

theocracy (thee AHK ruh see) form of government in which priests serve as kings (page 14)

Third World in the late twentieth century, developing nations that share common economic goals and problems (page 751)

tithe (tīth) payment to the Church of 10 percent of a person's income (page 163)

totalitarian state (toh TAL uh TAIR ee uhn) country in which the government is a single-party dictatorship that controls every aspect of citizens' lives (page 675)

tragedy in Ancient Greece, drama focusing on the causes of suffering, usually ending in disaster (page 88)

transistor small device controlling electrical currents, which contributed to the mass production of computers (page 839)

trial jury jury giving verdicts on cases brought to trial (page 201)

tribe group of related families who recognize a common ancestor, speak the same language, and share traditions and beliefs (page 57)

tribune (TRIHB yoon) official in ancient Rome who was elected by plebeians to speak for their interests (page 103)

tribute (TRIHB yoot) payment conquered areas were forced to make to the conquering state (page 108)

troubadour (TROO buh DOR) wandering poet who entertained at feudal castles (page 170)

tyranny (TIR uh nee) government headed by a single individual who seizes power by force (page 79)

U

ultimatum (UHL tuh MAYT uhm) final set of demands (page 628)

universal male suffrage right of all adult men to vote (page 462)

urbanization movement of millions of people from rural villages to cities (page 743)

usury (YOO zhoo ree) during the Middle Ages, practice of lending money for interest (page 194)

V

vassal in the Middle Ages, a lesser noble who served a powerful lord (page 167)

vernacular (ver NAK yuh ler) everyday language of people (page 187)

veto power to block the action of another person or government body (page 103)

W

welfare state state in which the government assumes responsibility for people's social and economic well-being (page 721)

westernization adoption of western ideas and customs by nonwestern nations (page 761)

Z

zaibatsu (ZĪ baht soo) wealthy Japanese families who bought the chief industries of the country in the 1880s and came to dominate the Japanese economy (page 591)

zemstvo (ZEHMST voh) local elected assembly created by the Russian government under Alexander II (page 547)

ziggurat (ZIHG u rat) temple of a god of a city-state in ancient Sumer (page 37)

Index

Italicized page numbers refer to illustrations. The *m*, *p*, or *c* preceding the number refers to a map (*m*), picture (*p*) or chart (*c*) on that page. An *n* following a page number refers to a footnote.

887

Index

891

895

Index

ernment, 102–03, 133; army, 103; art, *p103, p104, p118,* 119–20, *p133;* civil war, 88 B.C., 109; education, 104, *p104;* family, *p104,* 104–05; religion, 105, *p105, p118,* 118–19, 123–27, 301–02, *p302;* women, 105, *p121,* 123, *p301;* roads, 106, 120; rivalry with Carthage, 106–07; expansion of, 106–08, *m107,* 299–300, *m300;* empire, 108, 111–15, *m114,* 127–33, *m131, m156,* 300–02; decline of republic, 108–11, 300; fire, 64 A.D., 112; revolts and upheavals, 109; and American Revolution, 110; chariot races, 113; as international city, 114; trade and commerce, *m114,* 114–15; social conditions, 115, 133; early Christianity in, 127, 301–02; economy, 115, 133, 300–01; architecture, 119–20; Greco-Roman civilization, 119–23, 301; technology and science, 120–21; literature, 121; law, 122–23; rule in Palestine, 123–24; and Germanic kingdoms, 161–62; in Renaissance, 325, 329; 1849 nationalist revolt, 464; annexed to Italy, 535–36; Fascist march on, 679; World War II and, 703. *See also* Roman Empire; Roman Republic.
Rommel, Erwin, 702
Romulus and Remus, 100–01
Roosevelt, Franklin D.: New Deal, 657; Good Neighbor Policy, 665; neutrality in World War II, 693, 698; declaration of war, 699; death, 706; Atlantic Charter, 713; Yalta Conference, 714, *p714*
Roosevelt, Theodore, 528, 593, 611, 614, *p615*
Roosevelt Corollary, 614, 665
Rosetta Stone, 22, *446n*
Roundhead, *p418,* 419
Rousseau, Jean Jacques, 406, 408
Rubicon River, *m107,* 109
Ruhr Valley, 537, 541; French occupation of, 649, 682
Russia, *m230, m284;* Kiev, 228–29; Mongols, 229; Moscow princes, 229–30; religion, 316; and European balance of power, 387–88; Romanovs, 389–90; Peter the Great, *p390,* 390–91, *p391;* Catherine the Great, 391–92; peasant rebellion, 392; growth of, *m393;* and Napoleon, 450, 451, *m469;*

serfdom, 544–45, *p546;* in early 1800s, 544–46; autocracy, 545–46; reform period, 546–47; repression, 547; 1905 revolution, 547–48, *p548,* 669; nationalities, *m550;* Balkan states, 550–51, 626–27; World War I, 625, 628, 632, *p633;* 1917 revolution, 632–33, 669–71; civil war, 671–72; Lenin's economic policy, *p672,* 672–73. *See also* Soviet Union.
Russian Orthodox Church, 547. *See also* Eastern Orthodox Church.
Russian Revolution of 1905, 547–48, *p548,* 669
Russian Revolution of 1917, 632–33, 640, 654, 670–72
Russo-Japanese War, 592–93
Rwanda, *m740*

Saar Basin, *m642*
Sabin, Albert, 841
Sachems, 254
Sacraments, 176, 308
Sadat, Anwar, 761, 765, 770–71
Sadat, Jehan, 761
Safavid Empire, 758
Sahara Desert, *m242,* 243
Sahel, 742, 752
St. Bartholomew's Day Massacre, 378
St. Lawrence River, 363, 364
St. Petersburg, 391, 392. *See also* Leningrad; Petrograd.
Sakharov, Andrei, 826
Sakkara, 24
Saladin, 193
Salamis, Battle of, 85, *m86*
Salazar, Antonio, 822
Salk, Jonas, 841
Salons, 409–10, *p410*
Salt, 245, 247
SALT (Strategic Arms Limitation Talks), 829, 832
Salt trade, in Africa, 245–46, 247
Samurai, 277–79, *p279,* 280, 320–21, 591
Sandinistas, 808–09
San Martín, José de, 604–05
Sanskrit, 58, 294
San Stefano, Treaty of, 551
Santa Anna, Antonio, 609
Santa Sophia, Church of, 226, *p227*
São Paulo, *p796,* 797, 800
Sappho, 90
Sarajevo, 627, *m637*
Saratoga, Battle of, 428
Sardinia, *m107, m457,* 464, 534, 535

Sargon, Akkadian emperor, 40
Satellites, 838
Satrapies, 44
Saudi Arabia, *p758,* 761–62, *m763*
Savannas, 243
Savery, Thomas, 476
Savonarola, Girolamo, 339
Savoy, *m327, 533n,* 534, *m534,* 536
Saxons, *m131,* 162, 163, 175, 199
Saxony, 388, *m457,* 458
Scandinavia, 130, 164; Viking period, 164–65, 175, 200, 203, 209; missionaries to, 209; medieval kingdoms, 209–10; Protestantism in, 341, *m344;* socialism in, 722. *See also* Denmark; Norway; Sweden.
Schleswig-Holstein, 538, *m539*
Schlieffen Plan, 628
Schliemann, Heinrich, 77–78
Scholasticism, 190, 309
School. *See* Education.
Schuman Plan, 722–23
Schurz, Carl, 465
Science: Chinese, 64, 148, 152; Greek, 90–91; Egyptian, 31; Hellenistic, 96–97; Roman, 120–21; Indian, 145; medieval, 190; Islamic, 237; Renaissance, 401–05, 407; Industrial Revolution, 481–82, 495; in 1800s, 499–503; World War II and, 709; postwar advances, 837–43
Scientific method, 401–02
Scientific Revolution, 401
Scotland, *387n,* 416, 418, 420; united with England, 423, *m424*
Scribes: ancient, 15, 289; Egyptian, 30–31, *p31;* Sumerian, 35, 38–39; Chinese, 62
Sculpture: Greek, 90; Roman, 119; Indian, 144–45; Renaissance, 329, 331, *p331*
Sea of Japan, *m254*
Secret ballot, 512
Security Council, UN, 718–19
Segregation, 727
Selassie, Haile, 680, *738n*
Seljuk Turks, 234
Senate, Roman, 102–04, 108–11
Senate, U.S., 429
Senegal, 566, 569, *m740*
Senghor, Leopold, 665
Separation of powers, 406–07, 429
Sephardic Jews, 769
Sepoy Rebellion, 582
Sepoys, 582
Seppuku, 279
Serbia, 551, *m551,* 626–28, 632
Serfs, 171, 195, 308, 390, 544–45, 546, *p546*
Seven Weeks' War, 538

Seven Years' War, 387–88, 515
Seville, 210
Shah Jahan, 263, *p267*
Shah of Iran, 662
Shaka, Zulu king, 569, 570
Shakespeare, William, 333, 335
Shang dynasty, *m13,* 61–64, *p64,* 65, 294
Shelley, Percy Bysshe, 504
Shih Huang Ti, 149–50, 304–05
Shiite Muslims, 234, 758, 765
Shikoku, 275, *m275*
Shinto religion, 275, 276, 280, 320, 321
Ships: Minoan, 76; medieval, 194, *p194;* in China, 273, *p274;* for exploration, 350; navigation, 350; steam, 477; submarines, 632, 636–37
Shiva, 137, *p138*
Shogun, 278, 279–80, 281, 321
Shotoku, Japanese prince, 276
Siam. *See* Thailand.
Siberia, 545
Sicily, 101, *m102, m107,* 115, *m534, m702,* 703; Roman conquest, 106; Austrian control of, 382; revolution of 1848, 464; Garibaldi's liberation, 535, *p535*
Sikhs, 777, 779
Silent Spring (Carson), 844
Silesia, *m385,* 386, 387
Silk industry: in China, 64, 153, 268, 270, *p271;* in Byzantine Empire, 225
Silt, 12
Silver, 359, 367–68, 377, *c377, m861*
Simony, 177
Sinai Peninsula, 21, 23, 25, *m36,* 770
Singapore, *m596,* 790
Sinkiang, 60, *m61*
Si River, 64
Sistine Chapel, 331
Six-Day War, 770, *m770*
Skyscrapers, 507
Slavery: in early civilizations, 14; in Egypt, 29; in Greece, 79, 80, 81, 82, 87; in Rome, 102, 104, 105, 107, 108, 109, 115, 123; Maya, 256; Indian, 360, 361; slave trade, *p361,* 361–62, 566–67; Enlightenment and, 406, 407; abolition of, 444, 513, 524, 567–68, *567n,* 570, 608; in U.S., 523–24; in Africa, 566–68; in Haiti, 603; in World War II, 697
Slavs: invasions in Europe, 164; conversion to Christianity, 175, 228, *p229;* in Byzantine Empire, *m225,* 316; organized states in Eastern Europe, 228; in Balkans, 626

Slovaks, 549, *m550,* 660
Smallpox, 267, 841
Smith, Adam, 495
Social classes. *See* Society; specific societies.
Social contract, 405–06, 408
Social Darwinism, 500, 560
Social Democratic party: German, 542–43, 720; Russian, 670
Socialism, 461, 497, 821; utopian, 497; scientific, 498–99; Marxist, 498, 543, 670–71; in Scandinavia, 722; in Africa, 738; in Latin America, 802, 805
Social Security, 657
Society: of early civilizations, 14; ancient Egyptian, 27–31, 291; Aryan, 58–59; Chinese, 63, 66–67, 270–71, 781–82; African, 249–51; Japanese, 275–76, 786; Renaissance, 336–37; Enlightenment views, 406, 408; Industrial Revolution, 487; Latin American, 608, 800–02; Middle Eastern, *p759,* 759–60; cutbacks in European social programs, 824
Society of Jesus, 344–45. *See also* Jesuits.
Sociology, 503
Socrates, 91–92, 296–97
Socratic method, 91, 299
Solar system, 121, 402–03
Solferino, Battle of, 534, *m534*
Solidarity, 827, 828
Solomon, king of Israel, 47–48
Solon, 80–81
Solzhenitsyn, Alexander, 826
Somme, Battle of the, *m629*
Somoza, Anastasio, 808
Songhai, 247–48, *m248, m284*
Song of Roland, 187
Sonni Ali, king of Songhai, 247
Sophists, 91
Sophocles, 88, 89
Sorbonne, 819
South Africa, *m740;* geography, 241–43; early kingdoms, 243–49; early settlers, 569–70; about 1850, *m570;* Boer War, 570–71; mineral resources, 570, 571, *p571,* 748; independence, 570–71, 738; forming of, 571; Gandhi, 663; apartheid, 748–50, *p749, m750;* homelands, *m750;* neighbors, 750–51; today, *m862*
South America: early civilizations, *m13,* 258–59, 319; geography, 252, *m253,* 607, 608; early exploration, 353, 354; Spanish and Portuguese empires, 358–62; colonies, 600–01, *m602;* wars of independence, 603, 604–05;

today, *m868. See also* Latin America; specific nations.
South Asia, 775–80. *See also* India; Pakistan; Bangladesh.
Southeast Asia: geography, 594; history, 594; peoples of, 594; spice trade, 594; European colonies, 594, 596, *m596;* colonial rule, 597; World War II, *m704. See also* specific nations.
South Korea, *m784,* 790–91
South Vietnam, 729, 792–93
Southwest (U.S.), 253
Southwest Africa. *See* Namibia.
Soviets, 670
Soviet Union: under Stalin, 673–78, *m674, p676,* 723; five-year plans, 674–75, 676, 723; collective farms, 675, *p675;* Nazi-Soviet Pact, 694; World War II, 695, 697–98, 701, 702–03; expansion of influence, 715, *p717,* 725; under Khrushchev, 723–24; de-Stalinization, 724; economy, 724; and China, 785; consumer shortages, 825, *p825;* dissent, 825–26; fashion, *p826;* under Gorbachev, 826; and Eastern Europe, 826–27; foreign policy, 828–29; today, *m866. See also* Cold War; Russia.
Space exploration, 837–38, *p838*
Space shuttle, 838
Spain: Greek colonies, 79; under Carthage, 106–07; during Roman Empire, 108, 109, 110, *m114;* Muslims in, 162, 189, 194, 208–09, 233, *m233;* Islam, *p207, m208,* 208–09; Christian reconquest, *m208,* 208–09, 312, 351; Jews in, 209; religion, 209, 312, 375–76, 377; during Byzantine Empire, 224, *m225;* Renaissance in, 328, 333; exploration, 351–53, *m352–53,* 354, *m356,* 357, 358; New World conquests, 358–59, *p359;* and Native Americans, 359–60; settlements, 362–63, 365; Golden Age, 373–78; culture, 376–77; economy, 377–78; revolt in Netherlands, 375–76; warfare against English, 376; warfare against French, 375, *m441,* 448–49; War of the Spanish Succession, 381–82; in Africa, 560, *m561,* 568; in Philippines, 594; in South America, 600–05, 611; in Mexico, 601, 605; in Central America, 605; civil war, 691–92, *p692;* in World War

II, 697; today, 822, *m866*
Spanish-American War, 596, 597, 613
Spanish Armada, 376, 819
Spanish Civil War, 691–92
Spanish Netherlands, 376, *m385*
Sparta, 75, 82–84, *m86,* 87, 298
Spencer, Herbert, 500
Sphere of influence, 560, 586–87
Spice Islands, 355, *m356*
Spice trade, 594
Spinning jenny, 475
Spinning mule, 475
Spirit of Laws, The (Montesquieu), 406, 429
Sputnik I, 838
Sri Lanka, 778, *m864*
Stalin, Joseph, 673–76; rise to power, 673; five-year plans, 674; collective farms, 675; totalitarianism, 675; life under, 676; World War II, 694, 695, 703, 713; Yalta Conference, 714, *p714;* expansion of Soviet influence, 715–16, *p717;* Berlin blockade, 716; last years, 723
Stalingrad, *m702,* 702–03, 724
Stamp Act, 425–26
Stanley, Henry, 568
Statistics, 212
Status quo, 458–59
Stavisky, Serge, 659
Steam engine, 476, *p476, p477*
Steel: industry, 480; architecture, 506–07; Krupp Works, 541; in Soviet Union, 674
Stephenson, George, 477
Stirrup, 167
Stock market, *p655,* 655–56, 843
Stoics, 97
Stolypin, Peter, 548
Stone Age: Old, 10; tools, 10; geographic setting, 10–11; art, *p11, p289;* New, 11–12; technology of, 11–12; in Africa, 243, *p244;* people, 289
Stonehenge, *p2,* 2–3
Strait of Malacca, 355, *m356*
Strategic Defense Initiative (SDI), 832
Strikes, 648, 726
Student unrest, 819–20
Stupas, 142, 144
Suárez, Francisco, 377
Submarines, 632, 636–37
Sudan, *m561,* 751, 752–53
Sudras, 59
Suez Canal: opening of, 562, *p563;* British interest in, 564; Israeli-Arab conflict, 770, *m770*
Suffrage: universal male, 462; in Great Britain, 512; women's, 513, 651; in 13 colonies, 523; black, 528

Sukarno, Achmed, 791
Suleiman, 374, 388–89
Sulla, Lucius Cornelius, 109
Sullivan, Louis, 507
Sultans, 264, 265, 319
Sumerian civilization, *m13, p34,* 34–40, 292; writing, 35, 38; geography, 36, *m36;* city-states, 37; religion, 37–38; written language, 38–39; inventions, 38–39; legacy, 39–40; architecture, 40; mathematics, 40
Summa Theologica (Aquinas), 190
Sundiata Keita, 246
Sung dynasty, 268–70, *p270,* 320
Sunnite Muslims, 234, 758
Sun Yat-sen, *p588,* 589, 663–64
Superconductors, 839
Survival of the fittest, 499
Swahili, 248
Sweden, *m175,* medieval period, 209–10; North American settlements, 363; Thirty Years' War, 384; war with Russia, 391; in World War II, 696–97, *m866*
Switzerland: Reformation in, 341–42; Peace of Westphalia and, 384, *m385;* in World War II, 696–97; *m866*
Syria: Roman province, 109, *m114;* in Crusades, 193, 195; Islamic state, 234; French mandate, 642, *m661,* 662; government, 766; Lebanese civil war and, 766; wars against Israel, 769, 770; *m864*

Tacitus, 121–22, 130
Taft, William Howard, 614
Taft-Hartley Act, 726
Taghaza, 245, *m248*
Tahiti, *p597*
Taiping Rebellion, 587
Taiwan, *m781,* 789–90
Taj Mahal, 263, 266, *p314*
Tale of Genji, The, (Murasaki), 276, 278
Tale of Sinuhe, 25
Talleyrand, Maurice de, *p456,* 457, 458
Tamerlane, 264
Tamil kingdoms, 143, *m143,* 145
Tanganyika. *See* Tanzania.
T'ang dynasty, 268–70, *p269,* 320
Tanks, 630
Tannenburg, Battle of, 632, *m637*
Tanzania, 739, *m740, m747,* 747–48

Index

Illustration Credits

(continued from p. iv)

Worcester Art Museum; 150 Woodfin Camp/Bob Davis; 152 TBM; 153 Bibliothèque Nationale.

UNIT THREE Page 158 tl Collection of Laurie Platt Winfrey; tr Giraudon/Art Resource; bl The Granger Collection; br Collection of Laurie Platt Winfrey; 159 tl The Granger Collection; tr Giraudon/Art Resource; bl, br Collection of Laurie Platt Winfrey; 160 Scala/Art Resource; 164 Giraudon/Art Resource; 168 TBM; 169 The British Library; 170 TBM; 173 The British Library; 177 Bodliean Library;

180 Explorer; 183 Bibliothèque Nationale; 185 Bodliean Library; 186 Bibliothèque Nationale; 187 Giraudon/Art Resource; 188 Michael Holford; 189 Staatlich Museum Preussischer Kulturbesitz, Berlin (West); 191 G. Dagli Orti; 193 EPA/Scala; 194 Bibliothèque Nationale; 198 Scala/Art Resource; 200 Explorer/FUPMIA; 201 Municipal Museum of Bayeux; 202 The British Library; 205 EPA/Scala; 207 Rose Fujimoto; 210 Michael Holford; 214 EPA/Scala; 215 Explorer.

(continued on p. 904)   **903**

(*continued from p. 903*)

UNIT FOUR   Page 220 *tl* Lee Boltin; *tr* The Granger Collection; *bl* Collection of Laurie Platt Winfrey; *br* Giraudon/Art Resource; **221** *tl* Art Resource; *tr* Scala/Art Resource; *bl* Lee Boltin; *br* Giraudon/Art Resource; **222** Scala/Art Resource; **227** Lius Villota/The Stock Market; **229** The Bettmann Archive, Inc.; **234** The Metropolitan Museum of Art; **236** The Metropolitan Museum of Art, The Cora Timken Burnett Collection of Persian Miniatures and Other Persian Art Objects, Bequest of Cora Timken Burnett; **237** The Granger Collection; **240** Michael Holford; **244** Erich Lessing/Magnum; **245** *l, r* TBM; **246** Bibliothèque Nationale; **249** Bridgeman Art Library/Art Resource; **251** TBM; **255** The Peabody Museum, Harvard University; **256** Dallas Museum of Art; **258** LC; **262** The Metropolitan Museum of Art; **267, 269** Michael Holford; **270** The Metropolitan Museum of Art; **271** Museum of Fine Arts, Boston; **277** Scala/Art Resource; **280** Art Resource; **281** Musée Guimet.

A BRIEF SURVEY   Page 287 EPA; **289** Explorer; **291** TBM; **294** Museum of Fine Arts, Boston; **296** EPA/Scala; **298** Nelson-Atkins Museum of Art; **301** The Louvre; **302** Art Resource; **306** EPA; **308** TBM; **312** Explorer; **314** EPA/Scala; **319** LC; **320** Art Resource.

UNIT FIVE   Page 322 *tl, tr, bl, br* Scala/Art Resource; **323** *tl* National Maritime Museum, Greenwich, England; *tr* The Granger Collection; *bl* Versailles; *br* Giraudon/Art Resource; **324, 326, 328** Scala/Art Resource; **330** Art Resource; **331** *t* Art Resource; *b* Scala/Art Resource; **332** The Fotomas Index; **333** Walters Art Gallery; **335** The Fotomas Index; **336** Nelson-Atkins Museum of Art; **337** Art Resource; **339, 340** Scala/Art Resource; **343** Art Resource; **345** Michael Holford; **348** G. Dagli Orti; **354** The National Gallery, London; **357** Werner Forman Archives; **359** The Fotomas Index; **361** National Maritime Museum, London; **363** The National Gallery of Art; **367** EPA/Scala; **369** The Fotomas Index; **372** Giraudon/Art Resource; **374, 375** Michael Holford; **376** Scala/Art Resource; **379** The National Gallery, London; **381** Giraudon/Art Resource; **387** The Granger Collection; **390** Michael Holford; **391** The Granger Collection.

UNIT SIX   Page 398 *tl* The Granger Collection; *tr* Giraudon/Art Resource; *bl* Collection of Laurie Platt Winfrey; *br* The Granger Collection; **399** *tl* Giraudon/Art Resource; *tr* Scala/Art Resource; *bl* The Granger Collection; *br* © Yale University Art Gallery; **400** Scala/Art Resource; **402** The Granger Collection; **404** The Granger Collection; **407** Wedgwood; **408** The Granger Collection; **410** EPA/Giraudon; **411** The Granger Collection; **414** Historical Society of Pennsylvania; **416** The Granger Collection; **417** EPA/Scala; **422** The Granger Collection; **426** American Antiquarian Society; **427** Yale University Art Gallery; **432** Versailles; **436, 437, 439** Giraudon/Art Resource; **443** The Granger Collection; **446, 451** Giraudon/Art Resource; **454** Jean-Loup Charmet; **456** The Granger Collection; **458** Copyright reserved to HM, the Queen; **460** Jean-Loup Charmet; **461** The Granger Collection; **463** The Granger Collection.

UNIT SEVEN   Page 470 *tl* JOSSE/Art Resource; *tr, bl* The Granger Collection; *br* TBM; **471** *tl* Chicago Historical Society; *tr, bl* The Granger Collection; *br* Collection of Laurie Platt Winfrey; **472, 475** Tallandier; **476** Art Resource; **477** Tallandier; **481** Culver Pictures, Inc.; **482** U.S. Department of the Interior, National Park Service, Edison National Historic Site; **483** UPI; **485** Art Resource; **488** The Granger Collection; **489** The Bettmann Archive; **491** Insurance Company of North America; **494** The Tate Gallery (detail); **496** Collection of the Nelson-Atkins Museum of Art, Kansas City, Missouri; **497** The Granger Collection; **498** Tallandier; **500** The Granger Collection; **501** Giraudon/Art Resource; **502** The Granger Collection; **505** The Museum of Fine Arts, Boston; **506** The Denver Art Museum; **507** The Granger Collection; **510** The Museum of London; **513** The Bettmann Archive, Inc.; **515** The Granger Collection; **516** The Museum of London; **519** Art Resource; **520** The Phillips Collection; **521** EPA/Scala; **526** LC; **528** Los Angeles Museum of Art; **529** LC; **532** Art Resource; **535, 536** The Granger Collection; **540** The Bettmann Archive, Inc.; **541** The Krupp Foundation; **543** The Granger Collection; **545** The Granger Collection; **546** New York Public Library; **548** EPA.

UNIT EIGHT   Page 556 *tl* New Haven Colony Historical Society; *tr* ORION/Art Resource; *bl* Casa Pardo, Buenos Aires; *br* The Granger Collection; **557** *tl* Collection of Laurie Platt Winfrey; *tr* The Bettmann Archive; *b* Scala/Art Resource; **558** Art Resource; **563** Tallandier; **565** American Museum of Natural History; **569** Explorer; **571** EPA/Snark; **572** The Granger Collection; **576** Royal Geographic Society, London; **577** The Mansell Collection; **580** The Granger Collection; **582** Michael Holford; **584** The Granger Collection; **586** EPA/Scala; **588** UPI; **590** The Granger Collection; **593** Museum of Fine Arts, Boston; **595** The Granger Collection; **597** EPA/Scala; **600** The Museum of Modern Art; **604** The Granger Collection; **605** Caribbean Tourism Association; **606** Laurie Platt Winfrey; **609** Michael Holford; **610** EPA; **612** Tallandier; **615** LC.

UNIT NINE   Page 620 *tl* Indiana University of Art; *tr* Scala/Art Resource; *bl, br* The Granger Collection; **621** *tl* Giraudon/Art Resource; *tr* LC; *bl,* The Granger Collection; *br* LC; **622, 625** Art Resource; **627** UPI; **630** Imperial War Museum; **632** The Bettmann Archive; **633, 635** Art Resource; **636** *l, r* Scala/Art Resource; **639** National Archives; **641** Imperial War Museum; **646** Giraudon/Art Resource; **648** Michael Holford; **649** Culver Pictures, Inc.; **650** Mary Evans Picture Library/Photo Researchers, Inc.; **651** The Bettmann Archive; **653** Giraudon/Art Resource; **655, 656** LC; **659** © Turner Entertainments; **663** Henri Cartier-Bresson; **664** Rene Burri/Magnum; **668** Photo Researchers, Inc.; **671, 672** *t* The Granger Collection; *b* Sovfoto; **675** Culver Pictures, Inc.; **676** Scala/Art Resource; **677** The Granger Collection; **679** Brown Brothers; **681** Photo Researchers, Inc.; **683** Culver Pictures, Inc.; **684** The Bettmann Archive; **685** The Granger Collection; **690** The Granger Collection; **692** EPA; **696** UPI; **697** Scala/Art Resource; **699** National Archives; **701** *tl* LC; *b* Giraudon/Art Resource; **706** The Granger Collection; **708** *l* Culver Pictures; *r* Art Resource; **712** Art Resource; **714** Newsweek Books Picture Collection; **716** Black Star; **717** LC; **721** Art Resource; **722** Fred Mayer, Woodfin Camp & Assoc.; **724** Hank Walker/ Life Magazine © 1959, Time Inc.; **725** Erich Lessing, Magnum Photos, Inc.; **727** Ed Clark/ Life Magazine © 1957, Time Inc.; **728** Art Resource.

UNIT TEN   Page 734 *tl* Rene Burri/ Magnum; *tr* Steve Benbow/ Woodfin Camp & Assoc.; *bl* Marc & Evelyne Bernheim/Woodfin Camp & Assoc.; *br* Ludwig/ Pictorial Parade; **735** *tl* M. Heron; *tr* Tannenbaum/Sygma; *bl* Peter Marlow/Magnum; *br* Rene Burri/ Magnum; **736** Victor Englebert, Black Star; **739, 742** *t* Marc & Evelyne Bernheim/Woodfin Camp & Assoc.; *b* Campbell/Sygma; **743** P. Jordan/Gamma Liaison; **746** Marc & Evelyne Bernheim/Woodfin Camp & Assoc.; **749** Selwyn Tait/Black Star; **752** Steel Perkins/ Magnum Photos; **753** Campbell/Sygma; **756, 758** Sygma; **759** Fabian/Sygma; **761** P. Robert/Sygma; **764** Nik Wheeler/Black Star; **765** *l* EPA/Scala; *r* Tom Zimberoff/Sygma; **766** M. Attar/Sygma; **767** Michael Coyne/Black Star; **769** Keren Hayesod, United Israel Appeal; **774** J.P. Laffont/Sygma; **777** *l* Marc & Evelyne Bernheim/ Woodfin Camp & Assoc.; *r* Baldev/Sygma; **779** Anthony Suau/Black Star; **782** Bob Davis/Woodfin Camp & Assoc.; **783** *t, b* J.P. Laffont/ Sygma; **786** Nik Wheeler/Black Star; **789** Allen Green/Photo Researchers, Inc.; **790** Michael K. Nichols/Magnum Photos, Inc.; **791** P. Durand/Sygma; **793** J.P. Laffont/Sygma; **796** Pascal Maitre/Gamma; **798** *l* Claus C. Meyer/Black Star; *r* Steve Northup/Black Star; **800** Hugh Rogers/Monkmeyer; **803** *t* Loren McIntyre/Woodfin Camp & Assoc.; *b* C. Carrion/Sygma; **804** C. Carrion/Sygma; **805** UPI; **807** Joseph Rodriguez/Black Star; **809** Cindy Karp/Black Star; **810** Bruno Barbey/Magnum Photos, Inc.; **813** EPA; **814** S. Rickey Rogers/Black Star; **815** C. Carrion/Sygma; **818** Robert White/ Sygma; **822** D. Hudson/Sygma; **823** J. Pavlovsky/Sygma; **824** D. Aubert/Sygma; **825** The Society of Geographical Photography, EPA; **826** Peter Turnley/Black Star; **827** F. Hibon/Sygma; **828** AP/ Wideworld Photos; **830** Christopher Morris/Black Star; **831** *l* Andrew Sacks/Black Star; *r* Greenwood/Gamma Liaison; **833** Sygma; **836** Roger Ressmeyer; **838** Gamma Liaison; **839** Michal Heron; **840** Roger Ressmeyer; **843** Claus Meyer/Black Star; **845** Brownie Harris/ The Stock Market; **847** Jacques Gardin/Sygma; **849** *l* Sygma; *r* Forrest Anderson/Gamma Liaison; **850** National Geographic Society.

REFERENCE SECTION   Page 856 *tl* The Fotomas Index; *tr* Giraudon/Art Resource; *m* EPA/Scala; *b* TBM; **857** *tl* Ronald Sheridan; *bl, r* The Granger Collection; **870** *l, r* EPA; **871** *l* The Cleveland Museum of Art, Gift of George P. Bickford, *r* EPA/Scala; **872** *l* TBM; *r* EPA; **873** *l* EPA/Scala; *r* EPA.

904